International Human Rig

Human rights law is a complex but   ⌐udents
but also confuses them. This innovi   ⌐ores human rights law
from a theoretical and practical pers⌐   ⌐ve. Case studies and interviews with
specialist practitioners, NGO activists and policy-makers show how theory is
applied in real life. The up-to-date coverage includes introductions to important fields such as globalisation, poverty and advocacy. Student learning is
supported by questions to stimulate seminar discussion and further reading
sections that encourage independent study. The authors' combined expertise,
engaging writing style and ability to clarify not simplify ensures that this
important new book will become required reading for all students of human
rights law.

Ilias Bantekas is Professor of International Law and Human Rights at Brunel
University and a senior fellow at the Institute of Advanced Legal Studies,
University of London. He has advised governments, international organisa-
tions and NGOs in most fields of human rights and international law.

Lutz Oette is lecturer at SOAS, University of London, and Counsel at REDRESS,
an international human rights organisation seeking justice and reparation
for torture survivors. He has been involved in human rights cases before
regional and international bodies, and has engaged with a range of actors in
comparative research, advocacy and reform projects aimed at developing and
implementing international human rights standards.

International Human Rights Law and Practice

Ilias Bantekas and Lutz Oette

CAMBRIDGE
UNIVERSITY PRESS

CAMBRIDGE UNIVERSITY PRESS
Cambridge, New York, Melbourne, Madrid, Cape Town,
Singapore, São Paulo, Delhi, Mexico City

Cambridge University Press
The Edinburgh Building, Cambridge CB2 8RU, UK

Published in the United States of America by Cambridge University Press, New York

www.cambridge.org
Information on this title: www.cambridge.org/9780521196420

First published 2013

Printed and bound in the United Kingdom by the MPG Books Group

A catalogue record for this publication is available from the British Library

Library of Congress Cataloguing in Publication data
Bantekas, Ilias.
International human rights law and practice / Ilias Bantekas and Lutz Oette.
    p. cm.
Includes index.
ISBN 978-0-521-19642-0 (hardback)
1. Human rights.   2. Practice of law.   I. Oette, Lutz.   II. Title.
K3240.B36 2013
341.4′8 – dc23   2012039914

ISBN 978-0-521-19642-0 Hardback
ISBN 978-0-521-15236-5 Paperback

CONTENTS

ABBREVIATIONS

AA	*American Anthropologist*
AC	Appeal cases law reports (England)
ACHPR	African Charter on Human and Peoples' Rights
ACHR	American Convention on Human Rights
ACJ	African Court of Justice
ACP	African, Caribbean and Pacific
ACtHPR	African Court on Human and Peoples' Rights
AD	Annual Digest
ADB	African Development Bank
Afr. Hum. Rts. L. J.	*African Human Rights Law Journal*
AHRLR	African Human Rights Law Reports
AI	Amnesty International
AICHR	ASEAN Intergovernmental Commission on Human Rights
AIR	All India Reports
AJICL	*African Journal of International and Comparative Law*
AJIL	*American Journal of International Law*
All ER	All England Reports
ALR	Australian Law Reports
Am. J. Comp. L.	*American Journal of Comparative Law*
Am. U. Int'l L. Rev.	*American University International Law Review*
Anon	Anonymous
APJHRL	*Asia Pacific Journal on Human Rights and the Law*
AQ	*Americas Quarterly*
ASEAN	Association of South East Asian Nations
ASQ	*African Studies Quarterly*
AU	African Union
AYIL	*Australian Yearbook of International Law*
BCLR	Butterworth's Constitutional Law Reports (RSA)
BDT	Bangladeshi taka
Berkeley J. Int'l L.	*Berkeley Journal of International Law*
BGH	*Bundesgerichtshof* (German Federal Court of Justice)
BHRC	Butterworth's Human Rights Cases
BiH	Bosnia and Herzegovina

BIT	bilateral investment treaty
BLD	Bangladesh Legal Decision (reports)
BLR	Botswana Law Reports
BOP	balance of payments
Brook. J. Int'l L.	*Brooklyn Journal of International Law*
B.U. Int'l L. J.	*Boston University International Law Journal*
BVerfGE	*Bundesverfassungsgericht* (German Constitutional Court)
BVerwGE	*Bundesverwaltungsgericht* (Federal Administrative Court of Germany)
BYIL	*British Yearbook of International Law*
CA	*Cultural Anthropology*
Cal. W. Int'l L. J.	*California Western International Law Journal*
CAT	Convention against Torture and other Cruel, Inhuman or Degrading Treatment or Punishment
CED	Committee on Enforced Disappearances
CEDAW	Convention on the Elimination of All Forms of Discrimination against Women
CEJIL	Centre for Justice and International Law
CERD	Committee on the Elimination of Racial Discrimination
CESCR	Committee on Economic, Social and Cultural Rights
CETS	Council of Europe Treaty Series
Chi. J. Int'l L.	*Chinese Journal of International Law*
CIA	Central Intelligence Agency
CIF	commodity investment fund
CIL	customary international law
CJE	*Cambridge Journal of Education*
CJQ	*Civil Justice Quarterly*
CLP	*Current Legal Problems*
CLR	Commonwealth Law Reports
Cm	Command Paper (UK)
CMW	Committee on Migrant Workers
CoE	Council of Europe
COHRE	Centre on Housing Rights and Evictions
Colum. Hum. Rts. L. Rev.	*Columbia Human Rights Law Review*
Colum. J. Transnat'l L.	*Columbia Journal of Transnational Law*
CoM	Committee of Ministers (Europe)
CommHR	Commission on Human Rights (UN)
Conn. J. Int'l L.	*Connecticut Journal of International Law*
CPA	comprehensive peace agreement
CPED	International Convention for the Protection of All Persons from Enforced Disappearance

CPP-NPA	Communist Party of the Philippines – New People's Army
CPT	European Committee for the Prevention of Torture and Inhuman or Degrading Treatment or Punishment
CRC	Convention on the Rights of the Child
CRPD	Convention on the Rights of Persons with Disabilities
CSCE	Conference on Security and Cooperation in Europe
CSOs	civil society organisations
CtAT	Committee against Torture
CtEDAW	Committee on the Elimination of Discrimination against Women
CtRC	Committee on the Rights of the Child
CtRPD	Committee on the Rights of Persons with Disabilities
DaC	*Development and Change*
DAC	Development Assistance Committee (OECD)
DEVAW	Declaration on the Elimination of Violence Against Women
DLR	Dominion Law Reports
DPP	Director of Public Prosecutions (England)
D & R	Decisions and Reports of the European Committee on Human Rights
DTA	Detainee Treatment Act (USA)
EAC	East African Community
EBA	everything but arms
EC	European Communities
ECHR	European Convention on Human Rights
ECJ	European Court of Justice
ECOSOC	Economic and Social Council
ECOWAS	Economic Community of West African States
ECR	European Court Reports (ECJ)
ECSR	European Committee of Social Rights
ECtHR	European Court of Human Rights
EHRLR	*European Human Rights Law Review*
EHRR	European Human Rights Reports
EJIL	*European Journal of International Law*
Emory Int'l L. Rev.	*Emory International Law Review*
ESC	European Social Charter
ESC[R]	economic, social and cultural rights
EU	European Union
EWHC	High Court of England and Wales
F.	Federal reporter (USA)
FAO	Food and Agriculture Organisation
FCO	Foreign and Commonwealth Office (UK)

FDI	foreign direct investment
FGC	female genital cutting
FGM	female genital mutilation
FILJ	*Fordham International Law Journal*
FPIC	free, prior and informed consent
FRY	Federal Republic of Yugoslavia
G-77	Group of 77 (nations)
Ga. J. Int'l & Comp. L.	*Georgia Journal of International and Comparative Law*
GATT	General Agreement on Tariffs and Trade
GDP	gross domestic product
GDR	German Democratic Republic (East Germany)
GEF	Global Environmental Facility
Geo. Int'l Envtl. L. Rev.	*Georgia International Environmental Law Review*
Geo Wash Int'l L. Rev	*George Washington International Law Review*
GJIL	*Göttingen Journal of International Law*
GPQ	*The Geneva Post Quarterly*
GRI	Global Reporting Initiative
GSP	Generalised System of Preferences
GYBIL	*German Yearbook of International Law*
Harv. Hum. Rts. J.	*Harvard Human Rights Journal*
Harv. Int'l L. J.	*Harvard International Law Journal*
Harv. L. Rev.	*Harvard Law Review*
Hastings Int'l & Comp. L. Rev.	*Hastings International and Comparative Law Review*
Hastings L. J.	*Hastings Law Journal*
HCJ	High Court of Justice (Israel)
HDI	Human Development Index
HIPC	highly indebted poor countries
HKLJ	*Hong Kong Law Journal*
HPG	Humanitarian Policy Group
HRBA	human rights-based approach
HRC	Human Rights Council
HRCtee	Human Rights Committee
HRLJ	*Human Rights Law Journal*
HRLR	*Human Rights Law Review*
HRQ	*Human Rights Quarterly*
HRW	Human Rights Watch
IACHR	Inter-American Commission on Human Rights
IACtHR	Inter-American Court of Human Rights
IBP	international budget partnerships

IBRD	International Bank for Reconstruction and Development
ICC	International Criminal Court
ICCPR	International Covenant on Civil and Political Rights
ICERD	International Convention on the Elimination of All Forms of Racial Discrimination
ICESCR	International Covenant on Economic, Social and Cultural Rights
ICHRP	International Council on Human Rights Policy
ICJ	International Court of Justice
ICL	international criminal law
ICLQ	*International and Comparative Law Quarterly*
ICRC	International Committee of the Red Cross
ICRMW	International Convention on the Protection of the Rights of All Migrant Workers and Members of Their Families
ICSPA	International Convention on the Suppression and Punishment of the Crime of Apartheid
ICTR	International Criminal Tribunal for Rwanda
ICTY	International Criminal Tribunal for the former Yugoslavia
IDPs	internally displaced persons
IFHR	International Federation for Human Rights
IGO	inter governmental organisation
IHL	international humanitarian law
IJCL	*International Journal of Constitutional Law*
IJHR	*International Journal of Human Rights*
IJNfPL	*International Journal of Not-for-Profit Law*
IJTJ	*International Journal of Transitional Justice*
ILA	International Law Association
ILC	International Law Commission
ILM	International Legal Materials
ILO	International Labour Organisation
ILR	International Law Reports
IMF	International Monetary Fund
IMT	International Military Tribunal at Nuremberg
Int'l Crim. L. Rev.	*International Criminal Law Review*
Int'l Hum. Rts. L. Rev.	*International Human Rights Law Review*
Int'l Law.	*International Lawyer*
IOLR	*International Organisations Law Review*
IP	intellectual property
IPC	Immovable Property Commission (TRNC)
IPCC	Independent Police Complaints Commission (England and Wales)

IPP	indigenous peoples plan
IPPF	indigenous peoples planning framework
IRA	Irish Republican Army
IRRC	*International Review Red Cross*
ISC	Intelligence and Security Committee (UK)
Israel L. Rev.	*Israel Law Review*
JAL	*Journal of African Law*
JCL	*Journal of Comparative Law*
JHRP	*Journal of Human Rights Practice*
JICJ	*Journal of International Criminal Justice*
JIDS	*Journal of International Dispute Settlement*
J. Int'l Econ. L.	*Journal of International Economic Law*
JMEWS	*Journal of Middle East Women's Studies*
JRAI	*Journal of the Royal Anthropological Institute*
JWIP	*Journal of World Intellectual Property*
KB	King's Bench
KFOR	Kosovo Force
LDCs	least developed countries
LGBT	lesbian, gay, bisexual and transgender
LJIL	*Leiden Journal of International Law*
LNTS	League of Nations Treaty Series
LOPJ	*Ley Orgánica del Poder Judicial*
LSI	*Law and Social Inquiry*
LTTE	Liberation Tigers of Tamil Eelam
MDER	minimum dietary energy requirements
MDGs	Millennium Development Goals
Melb. J. Int'l L.	*Melbourne Journal of International Law*
MER	*Middle East Report*
MFI	micro-financing institution
MI5	military intelligence, section 5 (UK)
MIGA	Multilateral Investment Guarantee Agency
Mil L. Rev.	*Military Law Review*
MLJ	Malaysian Law Journal
MLR	*Modern Law Review*
MMDA	Model Mine Development Agreement
MNC	multinational corporation
MoU	memorandum of understanding
MPA	Metropolitan Police Authority (England)
MPYBUNL	*Max Planck Yearbook of United Nations Law*
NATO	North Atlantic Treaty Organisation
NBC	nuclear, biological and chemical first aid kit
NgHC	Nigerian High Court
NGO	non governmental organisation
NHRI	national human rights institution

NJIL	*Nordic Journal of International Law*
NLM	national liberation movement
Notre Dame L. Rev.	*Notre Dame Law Review*
NQHR	*Netherlands Quarterly of Human Rights*
NSAs	non-state actors
NTC	National Transitional Council (Libya)
N.Y.U.J. Int'l L. & Pol.	*New York University Journal of International Law and Politics*
OAS	Organisation of American States
OAU	Organisation of African Unity
ODA	overseas development assistance
OECD	Organisation for Economic Cooperation and Development
OHCHR	Office of the High Commissioner for Human Rights
OIC	Organisation of Islamic Cooperation
OJ	Official Journal (EC)
OLC	Office of the Legal Counsel (US Dept. of Justice)
OP	Operational Policy (World Bank)
OPCAT	Optional Protocol to the Convention against Torture
OPML	Oplam Missing Link
OSCE	Organisation for Security and Co-operation in Europe
PAT	poverty assessment tool
PATH	Peace Advocates for Truth, Healing and Justice
PB	participatory budgeting
PCIJ	Permanent Court of International Justice
PII	public interest immunity
PKK	Kurdistan Workers' Party
PLD	All Pakistan Legal Decisions
PLO	Palestine Liberation Organisation
PNS	parasympathetic nervous system
POW	prisoner of war
PRGF	poverty reduction growth facility
PRSP	poverty reduction strategy paper
PSBS	*Procedia Social and Behavioral Sciences*
QB	Queen's Bench
R 61	Rule 61 decision (ICTY)
RdC	*Recueil des Cours/Académie de Droit International de La Haye*
RHM	*Reproductive Health Matters*
ROE	rules of engagement
RSA	Republic of South Africa
RSLR	River State Law Reports (Nigeria)
RTD	right to development
RTHE	right to a healthy environment

SA	South African (law reports)
SADC	South African Development Community
SADCLJ	*SADC Law Journal*
SALR	South African Law Reports
SAP	structural adjustment programme
SCC	Supreme Court Cases (India)
SCR	Supreme Court Reports (India)
SCR	Supreme Court Reports (Canada)
S. Ct.	Supreme Court Reports (USA)
SERAC	Social and Economic Rights Action Centre
SIA	social impact assessment
SIA	Sovereign Immunities Act (UK)
SME	small and medium enterprises
SNS	sympathetic nervous system
SPISGSS	*Social Politics: International Studies in Gender, State and Society*
SPLM	Sudan People's Liberation Movement
SPT	Subcommittee on the Prevention of Torture
SSM	*Social Science & Medicine*
SSN	South–South Network
Stan. J. Int'l L.	*Stanford Journal of International Law*
Stan. L. Rev.	*Stanford Law Review*
Stat.	US Statutes at-large
SUR-IJHR	*SUR–International Journal on Human Rights*
Tex. L. Rev.	*Texas Law Review*
TI	*Transparency International*
Transnat'l L. & Comp. Probs.	*Transnational Law and Contemporary Problems*
TRIPS	Trade-Related aspects of Intellectual Property Rights
TRNC	Turkish Republic of Northern Cyprus
UCLA L. Rev.	*University of California Los Angeles Law Review*
UDHR	Universal Declaration of Human Rights
UHRC	Uganda Human Rights Commission
UK	United Kingdom
UKHL	UK House of Lords
UKSC	UK Supreme Court
UN	United Nations
UNAMID	AU/UN Hybrid operation in Darfur
UNCAC	UN Convention against Corruption
UNCTAD	UN Commission for Trade and Development
UNDP	UN Development Programme
UNDRIP	UN Declaration on the Rights of Indigenous Peoples
UNEP	United Nations Environment Programme
UNESCO	United Nations Educational, Scientific and Cultural Organisation

UNGA	UN General Assembly
UNHCR	UN High Commissioner for Refugees
UNICEF	UN International Children's Emergency Fund
UNMIK	UN Mission in Kosovo
UNMIS	UN Mission in Sudan
UNOSAT	UN Operational Satellite Applications Program
UNOSOM	UN Operation in Somalia
UNRIAA	UN Reports of International Arbitral Awards
UNSC	UN Security Council
UNTS	UN Treaty Series
U. Pa. J. Bus. L.	*University of Pennsylvania Journal of Business Law*
U. Pa. J. Int'l L.	*University of Pennsylvania Journal of International Law*
UPR	universal periodic review
U. Rich. L. Rev.	*University of Richmond Law Review*
US	US Supreme Court [reporter]
USA	United States of America
USC	United States Codes
Vand. J. *Transnat'l L.*	*Vanderbilt Journal of Transnational Law*
Vand L. Rev.	*Vanderbilt Law Review*
VAT	value added tax
VCLT	Vienna Convention on the Law of Treaties
VIJVNO	*Voluntas: International Journal of Voluntary and Nonprofit Organizations*
Virginia JIL	*Virginia Journal of International Law*
WAF	Women's Action Forum (Pakistan)
WFS	world food summits
WG	working group
WGEID	working group on enforced or involuntary disappearances
WHO	World Health Organisation
WLR	Weekly Law Reports
WMA	World Medical Association
WTO	World Trade Organisation
WW	World War
Yale Hum. Rts. *& Dev. L. J.*	*Yale Human Rights and Development Law Journal*
Yale J. Int'l L.	*Yale Journal of International Law*
Yale L. J.	*Yale Law Journal*
ZACC	Constitutional Court of South Africa [reports]
ZaöRV	*Zeitschrift für ausländisches und öffentliches Recht*

TABLE OF CASES

ARBITRATION TRIBUNALS

INTERNATIONAL CASES

African Commission on Human and Peoples' Rights

African Committee of Experts on the Rights and Welfare of the Child

African Court on Human and Peoples' Rights

Committee against Torture

Committee on the Elimination of Discrimination against Women

Committee on the Elimination of Racial Discrimination

European Committee of Social Rights

European Court of Justice

Human Rights Chamber for Bosnia and Herzegovina

Human Rights Committee

Inter-American Commission on Human Rights

Inter-American Court of Human Rights

International Court of Justice

International Criminal Court

International Criminal Tribunal for Rwanda

International Criminal Tribunal for the former Yugoslavia

Permanent Court of International Justice

South African Development Community Tribunal

India

Ireland

Israel

Kenya

Sudan

Switzerland

United Kingdom

United States

Venezuela

INTRODUCTION

The gap between the promise embodied in international human rights law and actual practice is frustrating, as those working in the field know only too well. A critical observer may well turn round saying 'I told you so, your belief in the power of law was mistaken in the first place'. Yet a believer in the system may counter, 'yes, we are facing some problems, but we're still just at the beginning, we need more law and things will improve'. These opposing strands point to broader questions, namely whether human rights provide the best language to safeguard core values and, if so, whether law is a suitable vehicle to promote, protect and vindicate them. Posing the very question suggests that human rights law has somehow lost its innocence – or naivety – in the sense that it is no longer self-evidently good or considered able to provide solutions to the myriad contemporary challenges. This is not a bad thing: on the contrary. Human rights are born out of intense struggles and develop in constant contestation with power and power relations. The law on human rights is therefore at any given time a temporary reflection of an understanding that is already pregnant with future developments and challenges. Being aware of the contentious nature of human rights protects from developing self-congratulatory attitudes and guards against their misappropriation by elites. Ultimately, human rights are not something fragile out there that need protection. Instead, they are constantly claimed and developed if not made anew by multiple actors, all of us, who engage with them in one way or another, as rights-holders, advocates or otherwise, if only by reading this book.

The book is based on this premise, which it seeks to mainstream into the format of a textbook. As this is primarily an international human rights *law* textbook, it seeks to do justice to both the law and the struggle for human rights, and how they interact in practice. With these considerations in mind, the book aims to offer both a sound exposition of the law and a contextual perspective of the realities in which the law is set and how various actors use it. Our intention is to go beyond theory, including human rights jurisprudence, and to bring out and reflect on the thinking, challenges and dilemmas faced by the various actors making up the system. To this end each chapter includes a substantial part on practical application, including a series of case studies that seek to capture the complex realities of international human rights law in action. This approach provides unique insights into the global endeavour for human rights protection and how human rights and international human rights law are constructed in the process. We hope that this will encourage critical contextual thinking and provide a good sense of what international human rights law means in practice. Given the inherent limitations of a textbook, each chapter provides a list of further reading, comprising literature and key websites, for the reader wishing to engage in depth with the issues raised and to undertake further research.

Being true to the importance of discourse in human rights, the book is enriched by a plurality of voices. Twenty-two practitioners speak to us through a series of interviews. These practitioners are directly concerned with human rights and many of them have been at the forefront of critical developments. Indeed, several interviewees have suffered violations of human rights and/or faced repercussions on account of their work. The interviewees have been selected so as to share a range of different perspectives. They include grass-roots activists using multiple strategies to advocate human rights protection and changes to the system; representatives of non-governmental organisations (NGOs) known for innovative approaches; lawyers who have litigated human rights cases at the national, regional and international level; doctors who have been at the heart of documenting violations; academics combining theory and practice; those working for and with human rights bodies at the national, regional and international level; and military legal advisors reflecting on the issue of battlefield compliance.

The book covers the foundations of human rights and international human rights law, institutional protection, a number of individual and collective rights, and a series of cross-cutting issues posing particular challenges for the effective protection of human rights in various contexts. It comprises seventeen chapters. Chapters 1–3, 5–8 and 13 were written by Lutz Oette, Chapters 4, 9, 10, 12, 14–17 by Ilias Bantekas, and Chapter 11 by Rupa Reddy.

In the first three chapters, we address foundational questions of international human rights, including its law and practice. In Chapter 1 we chart the development of international human rights law and introduce theories of human rights and their critiques. The chapter revisits the 'universality and relativism' debate and explores its resonance in the context of the uprisings in the Arab world. Moataz El Fegiery, a scholar and human rights activist in Egypt, provides a regional perspective on these developments, identifying critical challenges ahead. The controversy surrounding the practice of female genital cutting mutilation is used as a case study to illustrate the challenges faced when confronting embedded practices.

In Chapter 2 we set out the international law framework governing human rights law. The chapter explains and analyses its key components, namely sources, the nature of rights and obligations, the implementation of human rights law and its enforcement. In his interview, Med S. K. Kaggwa, the chairperson of Uganda's Human Rights Commission, reflects on the achievements and difficulties faced by national human rights institutions seeking to promote and protect human rights. The general part is complemented by a detailed case study on the experiences of challenging Pakistan's *Hudood* legislation under which women in particular faced the punishment of stoning for adultery. Sohail A. Warraich, a women's rights campaigner who used street theatre as an integral part of awareness raising, recalls pivotal aspects of the campaign and identifies lessons learnt.

In Chapter 3 we focus on key human rights actors and their strategies. The chapter explores the meaning, commonalities and differences of categories such as civil society, social movements, NGOs and human rights defenders. It assesses their distinctive contributions to the promotion and protection of human rights while equally exploring the tensions that their roles and practices have engendered. The story of the Khartoum Centre for Human Rights and Environmental Development in Sudan serves as an example to demonstrate the multiple challenges faced by NGOs working in repressive environments. Following a brief consideration of the role of legal and medical professionals as well as human rights field officers, the chapter shifts to the strategies employed by human rights actors, analysing the nature, effectiveness and – potential – problems of documentation, reporting, monitoring advocacy as well as awareness raising and education. Elham Saudi, Director of Lawyers for Justice in Libya, provides insights into how her organisation and lawyers in Libya tackled the difficulties of documenting violations during conflict in a highly volatile environment where most local actors had limited capacity. Huma Shakeb Khan, a UN human rights officer in Iraq, shares her experiences of life and work at her duty station and the challenges facing UN human rights field officers operating in situations requiring diplomatic skills as well as awareness of and commitment to the protection of human rights. The chapter also briefly refers to the role of litigation, which is covered in depth in Chapters 7 and 13.

In Chapters 4 to 6 we set out the institutional framework of human rights protection; these are complemented by Chapter 7, which focuses specifically on individual complaint procedures.

Chapter 4 examines the evolution and entrenchment of human rights within the framework of the United Nations (UN). The reader will not fail to appreciate the struggle between effective protection and politics, which has culminated in the creation of mechanisms such as the Human Rights Council, which is less politicised and more transparent than its predecessors. The chapter additionally examines the human rights dimension of the Security Council, the General Assembly and human rights-specific institutions and looks at the challenges faced by the Commission of Inquiry for Gaza. The UN Special Rapporteur on the effects of debt on human rights, Cephas Lumina, provides a candid account of the realities of his post.

In Chapter 5 we turn to the practice of UN human rights treaty bodies. The chapter critically examines their main functions, namely reporting, general comments and, by way of an overview of jurisprudence to date, complaints procedures. It assesses their contribution to the development of international human rights law and protection, while equally discussing the critical challenges that the system faces in terms of legitimacy and effectiveness. Lesley Ann Foster, who coordinated a South African women's rights network that submitted a shadow report to the Committee on the Elimination of Discrimination against Women (CtEDAW) sheds light on the making and impact of alternative reports to UN treaty bodies. Professor Eibe Riedel, a member of the Committee on Economic, Social and Cultural Rights (CESCR), reflects on his work, the potential of the Optional Protocol to the International Covenant on Economic, Social and Cultural Rights (ICESCR), and the challenges facing the UN treaty body system.

In Chapter 6 we canvass the development of regional human rights systems, focusing primarily on the European, Inter-American and African systems. The chapter analyses their founding principles, their applicable legal frameworks, and their contribution to international human rights law in general and to regional human rights protection in particular. It also highlights the political and capacity challenges faced, particularly by the European system. A series of interviews with long-term participants in, and observers of, the respective systems provide critical insider perspectives. Professor Bill Bowring, who has litigated a series of cases before the European Court of Human Rights (ECtHR) against Turkey, Russia and other states, reflects on litigation experiences, implementation of the Convention and the shortcomings of the European system. Dr Başak Çali, who has led a major project on the legitimacy of the ECtHR, reflects on its role in addressing legacies of serious violations and impunity, particularly its failure to act as catalyst for domestic acknowledgement in Turkey. Oswaldo Ruiz-Chiriboga, who has worked with the Centre for Justice and International Law (CEJIL), a highly influential regional NGO, and as Senior Staff Attorney at the Inter-American Court of Human Rights (IACtHR), recalls his time at the Court and identifies the strengths and weaknesses of the Inter-American system. Ibrahima Kane, a prominent regional human rights advocate, provides a nuanced assessment of the achievements of, and challenges facing, the African human rights system, identifying a number of critical factors affecting rights protection in the region. The examination of the three major regional systems is complemented by a brief account of developments in Asia and the Middle East. This includes a note on lessons that can be gleaned from existing arrangements for the development of new regional human rights treaty systems.

In Chapter 7 we provide a detailed account of complaint procedures from a litigant's perspective. The chapter examines the various stages of proceedings, namely admissibility requirements, merits, the nature of decisions and judgments, and their implementation. It identifies key issues, controversies and developments, which are illustrated by a series of case studies. Mandira Sharma, former executive director of Advocacy Forum, Nepal, shares insights on her organisation's approach to litigation before the UN Human Rights Committee (HRCtee) and the challenges experienced in the course of her work. The chapter concludes with a study of the *Hissène Habré* case, which demonstrates the multiple fora in which human rights cases can be litigated, and the complex legal and political issues that litigation efforts in the case have encountered over the last decade.

Chapter 8 examines civil and political rights, addressing the right to life; the prohibition of torture; the right to liberty and security; the right to a fair trial; the prohibition of enforced disappearance; and qualified rights, particularly freedom of expression. The chapter identifies the nature of violations at stake and discusses the challenges of giving effect to the rights. It highlights major debates, particularly in relation to competing rights. Defamation of religion is used as an example to examine the relationship between freedom of expression, and freedom of religion. The discussion surrounding the wearing of the veil illustrates the tensions between freedom of religion and the rights of others. Önder Özkalipçi, one of the coordinators of the Istanbul Protocol, reflects on its practical value as a tool to document torture and highlights some of the broader difficulties faced by the anti-torture movement. M. C. Iqbal, former secretary of two of Sri Lanka's Commissions of Inquiry into Disappearances, looks back on his work, the nature of enforced disappearances, and how the failure to bring about accountability has undermined the rule of law in Sri Lanka.

Chapter 9 looks at ESC rights and tries to dispel the myth that they are vague or unenforceable. In fact, an abundance of evidence is furnished from courts in South America, South Africa, Asia and Europe to demonstrate how states should incorporate ESC rights effectively. The practical focus of the chapter analyses the relevance of implementation indicators, justiciability, the concept of resource implications and concludes by examining four particular entitlements: the rights to food, water, health and education. An interview is provided by Tzanetos Antypas, director of the NGO Praksis, who gives an account of the health implications of poverty in post-debt Greece. An analysis linking redundancy and ill health aims to show that the right to work is fundamental to developing one's psyche and personality.

Chapter 10 discusses those entitlements that belong to groups, as opposed to individuals, namely minorities, self-determination and the rights of indigenous peoples. The practical dimension of the chapter seeks to understand how the World Bank sees the needs of indigenous peoples when funding projects that have an impact on them. The Chad–Cameroon pipeline project provides a clear indication that indigenous peoples entertain ambitions much the same as everybody else.

Chapter 11 focuses on the rights of women and notions of vulnerability. It explores key issues of vital importance in the debates and practice surrounding women's rights, including the meaning and scope of non-discrimination, the public/private divide and due diligence. The chapter examines feminist legal theory in depth, as theoretical debates have had a profound impact on practice, for example by raising awareness of the need to differentiate and respond adequately to multiple violations, such as intersectional discrimination. A case study on the prosecution of honour crimes in England and Wales, which uses extracts from interviews with police officers and NGOs on the issue, demonstrates both the practical challenges of translating international law in the domestic sphere and the advantages of developing a contextual approach informed by an understanding of gender-based violence.

Chapter 12 looks at the right to development from the point of view of what it means to live a dignified life. To do so, we examine the jurisprudence of courts around the world demonstrating that well-being – the essence of development – is inextricably linked to all other entitlements. We go on to demonstrate that this right is impeded by artificial financial limitations and that development aid should not resemble charity. In this regard, the role of international financial institutions is vital as is international cooperation in the form of the Millennium Development Goals (MDGs). Some radical ideas, such as odious debt, are also introduced. The chapter aims to identify various ideas that have been applied to reduce poverty, the most prominent of which is micro-credit. An extensive analysis of how this has worked is followed by an interview with Ramanou Nassirou, general manager of the Togolese NGO WAGES, who tells us about the success story of micro-credit in her country.

In Chapter 13 we discuss the rights of victims. The chapter explores the notion of reparation and examines the development of the right to an effective remedy and reparation in international law, a development that reflects a shift in emphasis on the actual vindication of rights. The exposition of the law and jurisprudential practice is complemented by several studies on the practical dimension of victims' rights, including victims' politics, Holocaust reparations, and litigation. Basil Fernando, a senior lawyer who has played an instrumental role at the Asian Human Rights Commission, discusses the innovative approaches the organisation has taken to working with, and representing victims, combining litigation and advocacy 'from below'.

In Chapters 14–17 we examine human rights in the broader context, discussing both promises and challenges that have become apparent in addressing pressing issues. This includes protection during times of armed conflict, individual criminal accountability, counter-terrorism and human rights, the difficulties posed by non-state actors (NSAs) for the system of human rights protection, and the detrimental impact of the process of globalisation.

Chapter 14 traces the links between human rights and international humanitarian law (or laws of war) and examines the role of international criminal law in the pursuit of human rights objectives. Two senior legal advisors, with significant experience in field operations, explain what it feels like to take part in combat operations and apply the laws of war in practice. This is followed by a brief physiological analysis which brings together various studies demonstrating how the body and the mind cope under extreme stress, such as that experienced on the battlefield. Real-life examples of battlefield compliance and rules of engagement are presented in order to demonstrate best practices.

Chapter 15 discusses the application of human rights to anti-terrorism operations, both in terms of the treatment of suspected terrorists as well as the obligation of the state to take positive measures to prevent terrorism. The analysis necessarily traces the post-9/11 jurisprudence and examines the efforts to expose abuse and restore fair trial guarantees. The practical section focuses on advocacy efforts to expose Guantánamo Bay and other illegal detention sites and the legal strategies to secure the rights of detainees. A prominent barrister behind these efforts, Clive Stafford Smith, provides an incisive interview explaining, among other things, his motivation for undertaking such cases.

Chapter 16 looks at the growing role of non-state actors as contributors to human rights violations and as implementers. Specifically, we examine multinational corporations (MNCs), international organisations and rebel movements and consider the ongoing debate about the human rights dimension of these actors. Readers will hear how Bobby Garcia turned from young rebel fighter to victim of serious abuses at the hands of his comrades, and later became an author and human rights activist. His account is complemented by an interview with Philippine judge and human rights advocate Soliman Santos, who discusses violations by non-state actors in the national and regional context, providing a Southern perspective.

Chapter 17 sheds some light on the dark sides of the processes of globalisation. It demonstrates the detrimental effect of trade liberalisation on agriculture and global food security, the effects of the international intellectual property regime on drug availability, and the impact of poverty on global patterns of migration. These policy dimensions often escape human rights lawyers though a clear understanding is imperative to effectively address their – all too frequently – devastating impact. Eric Holt-Giménez, executive director of Food First, aptly conceptualises these issues in his interview and the chapter concludes with an exposition of the *McLibel* case which demonstrates how the Davids of this world can overcome their Goliaths if they are committed and believe in their cause.

The text was completed in July 2012, and we have endeavoured to include developments up to that date as much as possible. Every effort has been made to ensure that all website links were live as of that date.

While writing a book can be a rather solitary endeavour, it is also always a collective process and achievement. This collective nature is evident in the book itself and we greatly appreciate the contribution of those interviewed for the book, namely Tzanetos Antypas, Bill Bowring, Başak Çali, Moataz El Fegiery, Basil Fernando, Lesley Ann Foster, Charles Garraway, Eric Holt-Giménez, M. C. Iqbal, Med S. Kaggwa, Ibrahima Kane, Huma Shakeb Khan, Cephas Lumina, Ramanou Nassirou, Önder Özkalipçi, Eibe Riedel, Oswaldo Ruiz-Chiriboga, Soliman M. Santos, Elham Saudi, Mandira Sharma, Clive Stafford Smith and Sohail A. Warraich as well as Robert Francis Garcia for his contribution. We are also grateful for the valuable research assistance and other contributions by a good number of people, particularly Menna Seged Abraha, Laila Alodaat, Julie Bardeche, Madeeha Dani, Mariam Fazal Faruqi, Yusuke Hara, Melanie Horn, Laura Imogen Mcleish, Julie Marie Olesen, Jose Sebastiao Manuel, Guillermo Otalora, Kharunya Paramaguru, Veronica Ranza, Virginie Rouas, Fahad Siddiqui, Salma Yusuf and Parisa Zangeneh.

We also thank Sinéad Moloney at Cambridge University Press, for her encouragement and support throughout.

Our greatest debt belongs to those whose attitude inspired the book, that is all those who cannot stand injustice and have, by word or by deed, given substance to what a life in dignity, freedom and equal rights means.

1 International human rights law and notions of human rights: foundations, achievements and challenges

CONTENTS

1.1 INTRODUCTION

The term human rights is frequently used as if it were self-explanatory. It is tempting and not uncommon to view 'human rights' as something intrinsically good. Human rights are often labelled (somewhat mockingly) as the new religion, a label which illustrates the elevated status they appear to enjoy. On closer inspection, it becomes evident that the term human rights is used freely and sometimes loosely by members of different disciplines and the public at large, meaning different things – both positive and negative – to different people depending on the context and the purpose for which it is used. It is therefore important to clarify the meaning(s) of the term by tracing its genealogy and examining its use in various contexts.

This undertaking cannot be confined to charting the development of international human rights law. Equating human rights with rights recognised in international treaties and/or other legal sources may in practice suffice when addressing particular human rights issues. Beyond this, it amounts to taking a purely positivist position that provides little guidance in response to a crucial question. Can a claim that something be recognised as a human right, for example the right to same-sex marriage, be justified, even if it is currently not explicitly recognised in law?

Human rights have an important dual function: they are claims based on particular values or principles and often also legal rights that entail entitlements and freedoms. Philosophical and political conceptions of human rights are broader than international human rights law, which is essentially a normative term referring to rights validated in recognised sources. While the two spheres are closely intertwined, they do not necessarily share a causal or automatic relationship, i.e. that every claim must turn into a legally recognised right. Nor is the relationship always harmonious. A legally recognised right may be defined too narrowly and may therefore exclude certain categories: for example age may not explicitly fall within the purview of the right to non-discrimination, or conversely a recognised right may be wider than thin theories of human rights.

To take the meaning of human rights for granted, or simply to refer to formulas denoting rights that we have by virtue of being human, would ignore the controversy surrounding their foundations and validity. Theories of human rights abound, including substantive (based on moral values or foundational postulates), formal (constructive, pragmatic, discourse), subaltern (human rights as distinctive practices born out of struggle) and postmodern (empathy for the other) approaches, as well as political theories, such as liberal or socialist notions of human rights. It is in particular the purported universality of human rights that has given rise to enduring debates. Those often, somewhat misleadingly, labelled 'cultural relativists' have raised important challenges regarding the supposed origins, validity, scope of application and politics of human rights. The question of political use and/or abuse of the language of human rights reaches beyond the universality debate but is an integral part of what can be seen as an increased probing of the 'innocence' of human rights. These overlapping debates may be seen as bewildering if not downright counterproductive, potentially undermining support for human rights at a time when much needs to be done to ensure their effective protection. However, downplaying or dismissing the importance of these debates may lead to a failure to answer satisfactorily the question of what we mean when we refer to human rights, which is critical in situations where the very idea is being challenged. It is perhaps inevitable that the notion of human rights is and will remain charged and will be used for differing if not contradictory ends. This does not mean that the notion is entirely open ended, but it counsels against using it lightly without having considered its multiple dimensions. For human rights advocates, developing an understanding that is critically aware of these aspects is arguably the best way forward to being convincing in the recurring public debates about human rights.

1.2 THE DEVELOPMENT OF HUMAN RIGHTS AND INTERNATIONAL HUMAN RIGHTS LAW

The founding document of international human rights law, i.e. the Universal Declaration of Human Rights (UDHR), refers in its preamble and article 1 to claims and freedoms that human beings enjoy by virtue of their humanity: that is, inherent rights. These rights are based on the principles of dignity, equality and liberty, and are underpinned by notions of solidarity. While the notion of human rights is arguably of more recent origin, it is part of a broader development that can be traced back to the early stages of human history.

At the core of human rights lie fundamental questions about the nature of human beings and their relationship with each other as members of societies, including 'international society'. In this context human rights address the relationship of individuals to others, in particular to those in a position of power (especially civil and political rights, equality and non-discrimination) and the relationships of groups and its members to others (minority rights, right to self-determination, rights of indigenous peoples); the settlement of disputes and administration of justice (fair trial in modern parlance); rights to participate in the polis (particularly freedom of expression and related rights, including the right to vote); and the material (in the broadest sense) conditions for a life of dignity and freedom (social, economic and cultural rights, the right to development).

This section traces the historical development of human rights and its most prominent manifestation, international human rights law. It examines the antecedents and formation of human right with a view both to locating them in a broader socio-political history and to identifying their specific nature. This undertaking is important at a time when the validity of human rights, though seemingly triumphant, is being called into question on account of their association with particular historical and political developments and ideas that are associated with Western secular liberal democracies. Reflecting on shared concerns throughout history and identifying strands of thought and practices that have contributed to their development can in this context open up perspectives that provide human rights with broad-based legitimacy.

1.2.1 Foundations

International human rights law is a rather late addition to the body of international law whose modern origins are commonly located in the seventeenth and eighteenth centuries.[1] International law governed the relationship between states, which were recognised as its sole subjects. States were considered

[1] See for a thorough account, W. G. Grewe, *The Epochs of International Law* (Berlin, New York: Walter de Gruyter, 2000), and for a concise summary, S. C. Neiff, 'A Short History of International Law', in M. D. Evans (ed.), *International Law*, 3rd edn (Oxford University Press, 2010), 3–31.

sovereign, which meant that the treatment of citizens and other individuals on their territories fell within their exclusive prerogative. While certain human rights concerns, such as about religious persecution, were at times raised between states, individual or collective rights as understood today did not form part of the corpus of international law. This explains why international human rights law, when it emerged with considerable force following World War II, drew heavily on ethical imperatives, concepts of rights and historical sources, as well as national declarations and constitutions. This was evident in the preparatory work to the UDHR, which was informed by the views of a number of philosophers and intellectuals about the nature and content of human rights and borrowed substantially from national rights declarations.[2]

Ancient and traditional cultures and societies, and the world's major religions, share a deep concern about human nature, ethics and justice. The major religions were faced with the task of constructing an ethical framework for the conduct of their members. This often took the form of commandments and the definition of desirable if not obligatory conduct, adherence to which would bring the reward the respective religion offered. This ranged from the principle of ahimsa, non-violence, shared by Hindus, Jains and Buddhists, to the ten commandments of the Old Testament, including 'thou shalt not kill', and the vision of a just society based on respect for the sanctity of life in Islam, complemented by exhortations to limit wealth and distribute material goods fairly.[3] Indian rulers such as Kautilya (350–283 BC) extolled the virtue of the rule of law in the treatise *Arthashastra*, or, as in the case of Asoka (304–232 BC), declared religious tolerance.[4] African societies also developed intricate principles and rules that governed the rights and duties of their members.[5] While notions of individual autonomy and rights were known in some societies, the question of how human beings treat each other and how best to exercise power in a polis was frequently framed as a matter of virtuous conduct and justice in conformity with reason or religious or customary commands. The principal concern was therefore the creation of a harmonious and just society rather than the protection of the rights of individuals. Nevertheless it is clear that the principles, commandments and practices sketched out above have contributed to the development of modern human rights law.[6]

---

[2] See below at 1.2.6.

[3] See for a good account of 'early ethical contributions to human rights', M. R. Ishay, *The History of Human Rights: From Ancient Times to the Globalization Era* (Berkeley, Los Angeles, London: University of California Press, 2008), 16–61.

[4] Ibid., 29–30.

[5] See M. Mutua, *Human Rights: A Political and Cultural Critique* (Philadelphia: University of Pennsylvania Press, 2002), 71–93, and the work of F. M. Deng on the Dinka, a good overview of which, together with further references, can be found in W. Twining, *General Jurisprudence: Understanding Law from a Global Perspective* (Cambridge University Press, 2009), 378–93.

[6] As evident in the UN Educational, Scientific and Cultural Organisation (UNESCO) inquiry informing the UDHR. See below at 1.2.6.

1.2.2   The American and French declarations of rights

The US Declaration of Independence (1776) (and later the Bill of Rights (1791)) and the French Declaration of the Rights of Man and of the Citizen (1789) were the outcome of political struggles that drew on natural law and liberal theories of rights.[7] The American Declaration emphasised the right to life, liberty and the pursuit of happiness while the French Declaration stressed the right to liberty, property, security and resistance to oppression. Both declarations had a considerable influence on international human rights law, particularly the UDHR. However, a critical analysis shows that the declarations foreshadowed a number of problems that have continued to haunt international human rights law and are at the heart of many of today's debates. Their shortcomings are readily apparent: the declarations speak of the rights of 'man'; the rights granted are predominantly civil and political, reflecting and privileging certain class interests; and the documents failed to address a number of practices that violate fundamental rights. It is indeed a (telling) paradox that it was not seen as contradictory that these rights were declared while the American settlers were invading indigenous peoples' land, destroying their cultures and practising slavery. At the same time, the French (and others) pursued a policy of imperialism and colonialism and large groups of individuals in their own societies, such as women, were effectively excluded and barred from the enjoyment of rights.[8]

From their inception, the language of rights found in the declarations faced a virulent backlash and attacks from various schools of thought. Those opposed to the liberal bourgeois ideas reflected in the French Declaration, such as Edmund Burke (1729–1797), criticised the abstract and individualistic nature of rights.[9] Burke defended traditional rights, claiming that these reflected long-standing developments and inhered organically in the community. Rights were complemented by duties and did not allow the overthrow of the government. This 'conservative' perspective has proved highly influential in informing communitarian critiques of the concept of human rights[10] and finds its echoes in contemporary debates on a British Bill of Rights.[11]

[7] See in particular the works of Thomas Hobbes, John Locke, Thomas Paine, Jean-Jacques Rousseau and Montesquieu. On the historical context and particularly the French Declaration, see J. Waldron (ed.), *Nonsense upon Stilts: Bentham, Burke and Marx on the Rights of Man* (London, New York: Methuen, 1987), 7–28.

[8] See in this context U. Baxi, *The Future of Human Rights*, 3rd edn (Oxford University Press, 2008), 59–95.

[9] See account in Waldron, above note 7, 77–95.

[10] See on communitarianism, W. Kymlicka, *Contemporary Political Philosophy*, 2nd edn (Oxford University Press, 2002), 212–21.

[11] L. Maer and A. Horne, 'Background to proposals for a British Bill of Rights and Duties', SN/PC/04559 (3 February 2009), online, at www.parliament.uk/documents/commons/lib/research/briefings/snpc-04559.pdf. See also www.publications.parliament.uk/pa/jt200708/jtselect/jtrights/165/165i.pdf.

The French Declaration was derided as 'nonsense upon stilts' by writers such as Jeremy Bentham (1748–1832), who launched a scathing attack on the notion of natural rights.[12] Bentham argued that rights were only rights if they had been recognised by law, i.e. they must be posited and do not have an independent existence. As the foremost utilitarian thinker, Bentham viewed the primary purpose of rights as maximising aggregate happiness (based on security, subsistence, abundance and equality). The utilitarian attack was characterised by a strong adherence to positivism as a means to escape the metaphysical uncertainty, if not fiction, of natural law. However, legal positivism's faith in a formal law-making process as self-validating bears the inherent risk that the very existence of a law is seen as sufficient justification for its commands irrespective of its substance. The risk posed by extreme positivism was cruelly exposed in the twentieth century during the Nazi period and after the fall of communist states, such as the German Democratic Republic (GDR), when officials justified violations by referring to existing national laws. Germany's judiciary responded to this challenge by invoking the Radbruch formula. Gustav Radbruch (1878–1949) argued that statutory law should be set aside if it is entirely incompatible with the idea of justice, in particular where the law deliberately denies equality and does not seek to advance the ultimate goal of any law, i.e. to serve justice.[13] Radbruch's formula marked a partial return to natural law which was also propagated by other legal philosophers such as Ernst Bloch (1885–1977), who had become disenchanted with the decoupling of law and justice inherent in positive law.[14]

The industrial revolution in Europe was characterised by stark inequalities and the inhuman conditions in which a large number of children and adults had to work and live.[15] Unsurprisingly, the nineteenth-century working-class and labour movements had mixed views of the conceptions of rights embodied in the American and French declarations. Karl Marx (1818–1883) argued in his work 'On the Jewish Question' that human rights as defined in the declarations, in particular the right to property, were used to secure

---

[12] Reproduced, with commentary, in Waldron, above note 7, 34–45.

[13] See on the practice of German courts in respect of crimes committed by officials of the GDR, *Streletz, Kessler and Krenz* v. *Germany*, (2001) 33 EHRR 31, para. 22, at (cc), and the findings of the ECtHR, ibid., para. 87: 'that a State practice such as the GDR's border policing policy, which flagrantly infringes human rights and above all the right to life, the supreme value in the international hierarchy of human rights, cannot be covered by the protection of Article 7 § 1 of the Convention [prohibition of retroactive application of criminal law]'.

[14] See for a discussion of Bloch's ideas C. Douzinas and A. Greary, *Critical Jurisprudence: The Political Philosophy of Justice* (Oxford: Hart, 2005), 99–103.

[15] See, for example, F. Engels, *The Condition of the Working Class in England* (London: Penguin Classics, 2006 (first published in 1844)).

the interests of the capitalist class.[16] He saw human rights as antithetical to a communist society that would overcome the antagonism between the individual and the state by providing for everyone according to their needs. Workers, trade unions, socialist movements and leftist political parties have against this background often been critical of the notion of human rights and the very apparatus of the state and the law meant to protect these rights. Nevertheless it is clear that these actors have made important contributions to the development of human rights law, particularly in respect of the right to non-discrimination, political rights, economic, social and cultural rights, as well as collective rights.[17]

Notwithstanding these criticisms, the American and French declarations exerted symbolic significance and became important reference points as the language of rights and liberties was increasingly invoked to buttress demands for equality, freedom and self-determination.

1.2.3   The struggle for rights in the nineteenth century

The nineteenth century witnessed a growing struggle for rights which was often inspired by the language of the declarations. Feminists, for example, advocated a Declaration of the Rights of Women (Olympe de Gouges (1748–1793) in 1790) and non-discrimination (Mary Wollstonecraft, 1759–1797).[18] Although these endeavours were unsuccessful at the time, they laid the foundation for later women's rights movements.[19] Another major movement evolved to call for the abolition of slavery, an ancient practice that had been transformed into a globalised commercial enterprise negating liberty and dignity and inflicting extreme suffering. The abolitionist movement had been active since the late eighteenth century[20] and in France the Jacobins abolished slavery in 1794. However, the practice continued elsewhere and it was only ended after a series of struggles, such as those by François-Dominique Toussaint-L'Ouverture (1743–1803), who led a successful anti-colonial uprising in Haiti,[21] and the American civil war.[22] The transnational

---

[16] See discussion in Waldron, above note 7, 122–4.

[17] Ishay, above note 3, 118–72.

[18] M. Wollstonecraft, *A Vindication of the Rights of Women* (London: Penguin Classics, 2004 (first published 1792)). Olympe de Gouges' Declaration of the Rights of Women can be found in M. R. Ishay, *The Human Rights Reader*, 2nd edn (London, New York: Routledge, 2007), 175–80.

[19] See Chapter 11.

[20] J. R. Oldfield, *Popular Politics and British Anti-slavery: The Mobilisation of Public Opinion against the Slave Trade, 1787–1807* (London: Frank Cass, 1998).

[21] J. D. Popkin, *You are All Free: The Haitian Revolution and the Abolition of Slavery* (Cambridge University Press, 2010).

[22] D. Waldstreicher, *The Struggle against Slavery: A History in Documents* (Oxford University Press, 2002).

movement advocating the abolition of the slave trade played a pivotal role in universally outlawing slavery, as reflected in a series of international treaties.[23] These developments set important international precedents for the recognition of dignity, equality and freedom as fundamental principles applying to the whole of humanity. Equally, nationalist movements throughout the nineteenth and the twentieth centuries invoked the principles of the declarations to demand self-determination and independence for colonised countries.[24] However, power relations and international law edifices developed in the nineteenth and early twentieth centuries combined to delay the end of colonialism,[25] a practice that was marked by large-scale rights violations. The legacy of colonialism continues to exert a profound and largely adverse influence on the protection of human rights.

In the realm of international law the American and French declarations, for all their influence on national constitutions, did not translate into a state practice that recognised human rights and pierced the veil of sovereignty. The nineteenth century witnessed nascent developments in the field of international humanitarian law, which grew out of a desire to limit excesses on the battlefields.[26] However, international humanitarian law was primarily conceived as a system that imposed an obligation of restraint on the warring parties rather than one that conferred any subjecthood on individuals. One seeming exception to the lack of protection of individuals under international law at the time was the diplomatic protection relating to the minimum standard of treatment of 'aliens'.[27] According to this rule, injury to an alien, including what would be considered human rights violations by today's standards, constituted an injury to the state of which the alien was a national. The state could in turn exercise its right to diplomatic protection on behalf of the individual (as a right of the state, not the individual) and demand appropriate forms of reparation under the rules of state responsibility. This rule became prominent in the nineteenth century when it was often used as a device of imperial powers to protect the economic interests of their nationals, in particular against expropriation. This reflected the

---

[23] J. S. Martinez, *The Slave Trade and the Origins of International Human Rights Law* (Oxford University Press, 2012).

[24] F. Cooper, *Africa since 1940: The Past of the Present* (Cambridge University Press, 2002), pp. 66–84. See also B. Anderson, *Imagined Communities: Reflections on the Origin and Spread of Nationalism*, rev. edn (London: Verso, 2006), and for radical forms of the anti-colonial struggle, F. Fanon, *The Wretched of the Earth* (London: Penguin Classics, 2001 (first published in 1961)).

[25] See in particular A. Anghie, *Imperialism, Sovereignty and the Making of International Law* (Cambridge University Press, 2004).

[26] See section 14.2.

[27] See on diplomatic protection in particular the work of the International Law Commission (ILC), including the 2006 Draft Articles on Diplomatic Protection, online, at http://untreaty.un.org/ilc/guide/9_8.htm.

inequalities between states and generated considerable opposition.[28] The use of diplomatic protection at the time can hardly be seen as a precedent for the recognition of individual rights but the notion has since undergone considerable changes, assuming a potentially stronger role in the field of international human rights law.[29]

1.2.4   World War I, the League of Nations and human rights

World War I marked the culmination of a prolonged power struggle between European states and came at a time of growing calls for independence and the overthrow of old orders such as that of Russia. Nationalism, imperialism and the availability of industrially produced weapons in combination with a wanton disregard for human life resulted in a disastrous war that shattered the existing order. This was to have a profound influence on the development of international human rights which was, however, initially not reflected in the international legal order. It strengthened the position of women who had become more publicly engaged as a result of the war and now demanded equal rights, with the suffragettes in England calling for women's right to vote;[30] it buttressed calls by socialist movements for the realisation of social and economic rights;[31] and it laid the foundation for the recognition of the right to self-determination and minority rights.

The crisis also gave birth to international institutions, marking a significant shift in the system of international relations and international law. Besides the International Labour Organisation (ILO) established in 1919, the most important institution was the League of Nations, established 'to promote international co-operation and to achieve international peace and security'.[32] It did not have an explicit human rights mandate and the language of its preamble speaks to the traditional paradigm of international law: 'maintenance of justice and a scrupulous respect for all treaty obligations in the dealings of organised peoples with one another'. However, the League of Nations established a system of minority protection mainly for Eastern Europe, Turkey and Iraq which was seen as integral to maintaining peace following the break up of the Habsburg and Ottoman empires in the region.[33] Treaties under the

---

[28] Anghie, above note 25, 209.

[29] See *Ahmadou Sadio Diallo* (*Republic of Guinea* v. *Democratic Republic of the Congo*), Preliminary objections, ICJ Report 2007, 582, at 599, para. 39. See also section 2.3.1.

[30] See H. Smith, *The British Women's Suffrage Campaign: 1866–1928*, 2nd edn (London: Longman, 2009).

[31] Ishay, above note 3, 176–8.

[32] See R. Henig and A. Sharp, *Makers of Modern World Subscription: The League of Nations* (London: Haus Publishing, 2010).

[33] See L. Thio, *Managing Babel: The International Legal Protection of Minorities in the Twentieth Century* (Leiden, Boston: Martinus Nijhoff, 2005), 27–98, and P. Thornberry, *International Law and the Rights of Minorities* (Oxford: Clarendon Press, 1991), 38–52.

system, as well as declarations made by states, which were to be supervised by the League Council, provided for the protection of the right to life and liberty, freedom of religion and non-discrimination. They also guaranteed minority rights such as the use of a particular language or education. While the League's minority system was incomplete and inadequately supervised, it established important principles for the protection of members of minorities and provided the basis for the subsequent development of minority rights under international human rights law.

World War I also bolstered demands for self-determination following the rise of nationalist movements and declarations by the then US president, Woodrow Wilson, which resulted in reconfigurations in Eastern Europe in line with the Versailles Treaty.[34] However, in other regions, the colonial powers largely succeeded in containing such demands by delaying transfer of sovereignty through the mandate system established by the League of Nations. Article 22 of the Covenant of the League of Nations set out the general framework of the mandate system and article 23 stipulated minimum standards of treatment of the 'native inhabitants', besides entrusting the League with 'secur[ing] and maintain[ing] fair and humane conditions of labour' and supervising both the implementation of agreements relating to trafficking and drugs, as well as the arms trade. However, instead of paving the way for genuine self-determination and protection of rights, the mandate system introduced the development paradigm into international relations, which largely perpetuated colonial power relationships.[35] In addition, the monitoring exercised by the League was generally seen as weak and ineffective.[36]

1.2.5   World War II, the Holocaust and the foundations of the international human rights system

The measures taken following World War I proved inadequate and failed to build a stable international order. Instead, the global economic crisis in the late 1920s contributed to the rise of extremist political movements and aggressive nationalist states, particularly in Nazi Germany, Italy and Japan, and ultimately resulted in World War II. The war was characterised by its brutality and enormous death toll. Its significance for the development of international human rights is largely due to the parallel Holocaust, the systematic destruction of the Jewish people based on a racist ideology, as well as murderous campaigns targeting Sinti and Roma, homosexuals, persons with disabilities, political opponents and others, planned with the use of modern

---

[34] See section 10.2.1.

[35] B. Rajagopal, *International Law from Below: Development, Social Movements and Third World Resistance* (Cambridge University Press, 2003), 50–72.

[36] Ibid., 70–1, and Anghie, above note 25, 149–56.

bureaucracy and executed in an industrial manner by Nazi Germany.[37] The shock to the international system caused by these developments triggered a reordering of the international system. The years 1945–50 were a truly foundational period for the development of international human rights law and related fields, providing a window in which states were willing to create institutions and a legal framework to address a series of concerns.

The objective of the UN, which was established in 1945, was to put in place an effective international organisation built on a system of collective security with strong enforcement powers. Owing to the impetus from states, such as the USA following Franklin Delano Roosevelt's declaration of the four freedoms (freedom of speech and expression, freedom of worship, freedom from want and from fear) and public figures and groups, the question of human rights had been on the agenda since the very beginning of the UN. The USA, as a result of the advocacy and lobbying of civil society, and Latin American countries were behind efforts to enshrine human rights provisions in the UN Charter.[38] The Charter's preamble proclaims that the UN members are determined 'to reaffirm faith in fundamental human rights, in the dignity and worth of the human person, in the equal rights of men and women and of nations large and small'. Article 1(3) lists human rights as one of the purposes of the UN, and articles 55 and 56 make human rights an integral part of the UN's international economic and social cooperation obligations. Human rights are also part of the mandate of the Economic and Social Council (ECOSOC) (articles 62, 68) and of the international trusteeship system (article 76(c)). As the text of articles 1(3) and 55 demonstrates, the Charter's drafters perceived human rights protection as imperative to a new international order conducive to peace, thus emphasising its instrumental value in international relations. The creation of the UN Human Rights Commission pursuant to article 68 also signalled the importance of the UN as an institutional setting for the development of the international human rights regime.

Parallel developments witnessed the UN War Crimes Commission (1943–8), the Nuremberg and the Tokyo war crimes trials (1945–9 and 1946–8 respectively), which laid the foundation for international criminal law, and the adoption of the Genocide Convention (Convention on the Prevention and Punishment of the Crime of Genocide) in 1948. The substantial expansion of the scope of application and protection of international humanitarian law through the four Geneva Conventions adopted in 1949, and the recognition of refugee rights in the Convention Relating to the Status of Refugees (the Refugee Convention) in 1951, are further milestones.

---

[37] See Z. Bauman, *Modernity and the Holocaust* (Cambridge: Polity Press, 2000).
[38] See G. T. Mitoma, 'Civil Society and International Human Rights: The Commission to Study the Organization of Peace and the Origins of the UN Human Rights Regime', *HRQ* 30(3) (2008), 607–30.

1.2.6   The Universal Declaration of Human Rights: origins, content, significance

The work on establishing a universal human rights system began in the early 1940s and culminated in the UDHR in 1948, which was seen as an integral part of the International Bill of Human Rights then envisaged by the UN. The UDHR is the UN's foundational human rights document and the cornerstone for the international human rights system, setting a framework for the understanding and content of rights that has stood the test of time.[39] States differed on whether to make a Bill of Rights an integral part of the Charter, and once it was decided that it should be separate whether to have a nonbinding declaration followed by a legally binding covenant or to agree on such a covenant from the outset. The majority in the UN Human Rights Commission, which had been established by ECOSOC in 1946 and had eighteen members at the time, opted for a declaration as a first step to agreeing on basic principles and as an educational tool. It was envisaged that the declaration would be followed by a covenant and measures of implementation to form an International Bill of Human Rights. The Commission tasked a committee of eight members from Australia, Chile, China, France, Lebanon, the USSR, the UK and the USA with drafting the UDHR under the leadership of Eleanor Roosevelt. The process took two years during which the drafting committee consulted leading thinkers for their views on human rights. The draft articles were subject to intense scrutiny and sustained debates in the UN Human Rights Commission, ECOSOC and the UN General Assembly (UNGA).[40] Most states were in support of a universally shared set of principles. However, several objections were raised to the draft articles at the time. Communist countries in particular criticised the draft for not paying due regard to sovereignty, different stages of economic development and economic, social, cultural and collective rights. South Africa objected to racial equality because of its apartheid system and Saudi Arabia to the freedom to change one's religion.[41]

The UNGA adopted the UDHR on 10 December 1948 (that date was later declared International Human Rights Day). Forty-eight of the

---

[39] See on the UDHR, A. Eide *et al.* (eds.), *The Universal Declaration of Human Rights: A Commentary* (Oxford University Press, 1992); G. Johnson and J. Symonides, *The Universal Declaration of Human Rights: A History of its Creation and Implementation, 1948–1998* (Paris: UNESCO Publishing, 1998); J. Morsink, *The Universal Declaration of Human Rights: Origins, Drafting, and Intent* (Philadelphia: University of Pennsylvania Press, 1999); M. A. Glendon, *A World Made Anew: Eleanor Roosevelt and the Universal Declaration of Human Rights* (New York: Random House, 2002).

[40] Documents can be found at UN, The Universal Declaration of Human Rights: An Historical Record of the Drafting Process, online, at www.un.org/Depts/dhl/udhr.

[41] See in particular UN Doc. A/PV.183, Verbatim Record of the Hundred and Eighty-third Plenary Meeting, Palais de Chaillot, Paris, Friday (10 December 1948), online, at www. un.org/Depts/dhl/landmark/pdf/a-pv183.pdf.

then fifty-eight member states of the UNGA voted in favour and eight states abstained (Byelorussia, Czechoslovakia, Poland, Saudi Arabia, the Ukrainian Soviet Socialist Republic, the Union of South Africa, the Union of Soviet Socialist Republics and Yugoslavia), with two members being absent. The individual provisions were also put to a vote. There was a remarkable degree of agreement with unanimous votes for most rights, the only exceptions being the first recital of the preamble and articles 1, 2(2) (principle of non-distinction), 14 (right to asylum), 19 (freedom of expression), 20 (freedom of assembly and association), 27 (cultural life) and 29 (duties and limitations).[42]

The UDHR endorses the universality of human rights according to which all human beings have the same inherent rights, which should be recognised and observed universally 'in a spirit of brotherhood'. This is reflected in the first recital of the preamble – 'Whereas recognition of the inherent dignity and of the equal and inalienable rights of all members of the human family is the foundation of freedom, justice and peace in the world' – and in article 1 – 'All human beings are born free and equal in dignity and rights.' The UDHR sets out the rights referred to as a 'common standard of achievement for all peoples and all nations'. It formulates these rights in plain language in line with its mission to be an educational tool for the promotion of human rights. Article 2 stipulates the right to non-discrimination, articles 3–20 civil rights and liberties, article 21 political rights, articles 22–27 economic, social and cultural rights, article 28 the right to an international order in which the declaration's rights can be realised, article 29 duties and limitations of rights, and article 30 the principle that the rights granted in the UDHR do not confer a right to destroy the same. With the exception of minority rights and collective rights, the UDHR encompasses most rights later recognised in the main international human rights treaties, though the rights are formulated in a broad rather than a detailed manner (compare, for example, article 10 UDHR with article 14 of the International Covenant on Civil and Political Rights (ICCPR)).

The UDHR's status was subject to some debate during the drafting stage, with some representatives arguing that it constituted an authoritative interpretation of the UN Charter. Most representatives and commentators held the view that it was essentially a non-binding declaration of principles.[43] This reading appears to be in line with the UDHR's purpose of serving as a document that is accessible and of general validity, and acts as a springboard for the development of international human rights law. It also reflects the fact that the UDHR declares rights of universal application without specifying the obligations of duty-holders such as states or providing enforcement

---

[42] Ibid.
[43] See discussion in Morsink, above note 39, 8.

mechanisms. While the UDHR was not binding at the time, many if not most of its provisions have by now been recognised as customary international law through their recognition in other treaties and declarations as well as in national laws and jurisprudence.[44]

The UDHR was hailed as a major achievement at the time and since.[45] However, it has also been subject to scathing criticism for its supposed ethnocentrism. This is based on the argument that the UN was not representative of all peoples at the time and that the UDHR reflects strong Western influences.[46] It is certainly correct that the UDHR is liberal in spirit with an emphasis on individual rights, owing a lot to continental European and Latin American notions of rights. However, it would be misleading to portray the UDHR as a straightforward 'Western' imposition. The very universality of the declaration is in considerable part a compromise forged in lengthy sessions and debates which included a discussion of ideological and cultural differences. The UDHR reflects women's concerns, emphasises economic, social and cultural rights and recognises duties, in particular as limitations of rights. It was formulated against the background of decolonisation, with some newly-independent states such as India contributing to debates. This is not to deny that the UDHR is also a political document that reflects prevailing power relationships at the time – forming part of broader ideological battles on the eve of the Cold War – but it is equally clear that there was a strong, shared desire to formulate a set of generally valid rights in response to the atrocities of World War II. It is indeed its clarity of vision, language and structure that has proved to be enduring.

For all its apparent shortcomings, such as the lack of recognition of collective rights, the UDHR has provided standards that have enabled actors to debate and develop the nature and content of international human rights and demand their recognition and protection.[47] Notably, a number of newly independent states have endorsed the UDHR, not out of any apparent compulsion but as a symbolic statement of sharing the ideals and principles contained therein. The idea of the universality of human rights may have suffered since then but it is clear that the UDHR still constitutes its most impressive articulation.

---

[44] See section 2.2.2.

[45] See for example the UN website on sixty years UDHR, www.un.org/events/humanrights/2008/declaration.shtml.

[46] See A. Schwab and P. Pollis, *Toward a Human Rights Framework* (New York: Praeger, 1982), 4 and, in contrast, Å. Samnoy, *Human Rights as International Consensus: The Making of the Universal Declaration of Human Rights, 1945–1948* (Fantoft-Bergen, Norway: Chr. Michelsen Institute, 1993), 105.

[47] M. Mutua, 'Standard Setting in Human Rights: Critique and Prognosis', *HRQ* 29(3) (2007), 547–630, at 556, captures this point by saying that 'the UDHR should be seen more as a credible promise than a holy text'.

1.2.7 Cold War and decolonisation

The Cold War and decolonisation are arguably the two most important factors that shaped the development of international human rights from the 1950s to the 1980s.

The divide into political camps – in particular the USA and other 'Western' states versus 'socialist' states and later several newly established states – slowed down the realisation of the International Bill of Rights. Differences over the nature of rights and suitable modes of protection resulted in the adoption of two treaties in 1966, the ICCPR and the ICESCR. The Cold War also witnessed the increasing politicisation of human rights, which were mainly used by Western states, foremost among them the USA, to evaluate the conduct of other states critically, to demand that certain action be taken and, in so doing, to demonstrate their own superior legitimacy.[48] One outcome of the intensified human rights diplomacy was the Final Act of the Conference on Security and Co-operation in Europe in 1975 signed by thirty-five 'capitalist' and 'communist' states, which – while emphasising sovereignty and non-intervention – included provisions for the protection of human rights. The process resulted in the establishment of the Organisation for Security and Co-operation in Europe (OSCE) under Chapter VIII of the UN Charter and contributed significantly to greater human rights diplomacy and more weight being accorded to human rights in communist states.[49] However, it did little to change the political economy of human rights which were still selectively invoked or ignored to serve political ends.[50]

Decolonisation was a complex and uneven struggle and political process. The UN Charter recognised the obligation to 'promote … the well-being of the inhabitants' (of non-self governing territories) and to 'ensure, with due

---

[48] According to its website, 'The US Department of State submits [human rights] reports on all countries receiving assistance and all United Nations member states to the US Congress in accordance with the Foreign Assistance Act of 1961 and the Trade Act of 1974.' The influential reports can be found, at www.state.gov/j/drl/rls/hrrpt. See also R. Müllerson, *Human Rights Diplomacy* (London, New York: Routledge, 1997), 102–17, and D. P. Forsythe, *Human Rights in International Relations* (Cambridge University Press, 2006), 152–87, with further references.

[49] D. J. Galbreath, *The Organization for Security and Co-operation in Europe* (London, New York: Routledge, 2007).

[50] Baxi, above note 8, 30–2.

respect for the culture of the peoples concerned, their political, economic, social, and educational advancement, their just treatment, their protection against abuses, and to promote self-government'.[51] It also created a trusteeship system towards this end. However, colonising states frequently resisted domestic uprisings and decolonisation efforts through force and violations. Notorious examples are the suppression of the Mau Mau by the British forces in Kenya[52] and of the Algerian independence movement by France.[53] Political movements and leaders from emerging and newly independent states were targeted, such as Lumumba (1925–1961) in what is now the Democratic Republic of Congo and Ho Chi Min (1890–1969) in Vietnam, which contributed to precipitating political instability and war. White settler regimes resisted decolonisation in the country formerly known as Rhodesia (1965–79), now Zimbabwe, and reinforced the system of apartheid in South Africa (1948–94). These developments provided the impetus to anti-racism initiatives in the UNGA and led to the adoption of the International Convention on the Elimination of All Forms of Racial Discrimination (ICERD) in 1965 and the International Convention on the Suppression and Punishment of the Crime of Apartheid (ICSPCA) in 1973.[54]

Newly independent states were often politically vulnerable internally because of their artificial nature, particularly in Africa, and externally because of great power interests and their economic fragility and dependency. 'Third World' states sought to meet this challenge by stressing their political sovereignty and calling for development and a reform of the international economic system. Attempts to institute a New International Economic Order based on greater economic equality and share of resources between states failed in the 1970s.[55] Subsequently, similar political efforts were channelled into calls for the recognition of the right to development.[56] The surrounding debates have brought to the fore different conceptions of rights, in particular the collective nature of human rights.[57] While the legacy of colonialism and the challenges inherent in the decolonisation process still loom large in international law, it is already

---

[51] Article 73 UN Charter.

[52] See D. Anderson, *Histories of the Hanged: Britain's Dirty War in Kenya and the End of Empire* (London: Weidenfeld and Nicolson, 2005), and C. Elkins, *Imperial Reckoning: The Untold Story of Britain's Gulag in Kenya* (New York: Henry Holt, 2005). See on the case brought by four Kenyan survivors of torture against the United Kingdom before the High Court of England and Wales, www.leighday.co.uk/Our-expertise/international-claims/Kenya.

[53] See M. Evans, *Algeria: France's Undeclared War* (Oxford University Press, 2012).

[54] Baxi, above note 8, 53–5.

[55] Declaration for the Establishment of a New International Economic Order, UNGA resolution 3201 (S-VI) (1 May 1974). See M. Bedjaoui, *Towards a New International Economic Order* (New York: Holmes Meier, 1979).

[56] See in particular the Declaration on the Right to Development, UNGA resolution 411128 (4 December 1986).

[57] See sections 2.3.1 and 10.2.

clear that this process has added important dimensions to the understanding of human rights and the development of international human rights law.

1.2.8   The growth of international human rights law

A series of struggles, advocacy by the international human rights movement, the increasing importance of human rights in international relations, a determination to tackle (at least some) persistent problems, and a concerted effort to develop a more coherent system have contributed to the rapid growth of standard setting since the 1970s, in particular at the UN level. These standards further elaborate specific individual rights already recognised in the UDHR and ICCPR, such as the Convention against Torture and other Cruel, Inhuman or Degrading Treatment or Punishment (CAT) (1984), or govern specific violations not expressly recognised in the International Bill of Rights, such as the Protocol to Prevent, Suppress and Punish Trafficking in Persons, especially Women and Children (1990), and the International Convention for the Protection of All Persons from Enforced Disappearance (CPED) (2006). The increasing awareness of the need to recognise – and provide better protection for – the rights of members of particular groups is reflected in the Convention on the Elimination of All Forms of Discrimination against Women (CEDAW) (1979) and the seminal Convention on the Rights of the Child (CRC) (1989), the treaty with the most states parties in the field of human rights. It became increasingly clear that generic sets of rights such as those contained in the ICCPR do not adequately capture the situation of members of groups who face systematic discrimination and disadvantages on account of their status. This has led to the adoption of treaties such as the International Convention on the Protection of the Rights of All Migrant Workers and Members of Their Families (ICRMW) (1990) and the Convention on the Rights of Persons with Disabilities (CRPD) (2006). After a prolonged struggle, collective group rights have recently been recognised in the UN Declaration on the Rights of Indigenous Peoples (2007), which may over time result in a treaty protecting the rights of indigenous peoples.[58] Human rights conferences[59] and initiatives to address global economic and environmental problems, as well as related emerging concerns such as the role of business in the violation of human rights, have spurred the growth of soft law in the field of human rights.[60]

In a parallel development, a series of treaties and resolutions have been adopted at the regional level, particularly in the European, American and

---

[58] See section 10.4.

[59] In particular the World Conference on Human Rights, which resulted in the Vienna Declaration and Programme of Action on 25 June 1993. See also M. Nowak (ed.), *World Conference on Human Rights, Vienna, June 1993: The Contributions of NGOs: Reports and Documents* (Vienna: Manz, 1994).

[60] See sections 2.2.4 and 16.3.

African systems, often as a result of specific historical experiences and advocacy thereby adding important regional dimensions to the understanding of human rights.[61] The process of standard-setting and institution building has been complemented by a growth in human rights jurisprudence at the national, regional and international levels, which has contributed to clarifying the normative content of rights and to generating the impetus for the adoption of treaties, such as in relation to enforced disappearance (CPED).

Traditional international human rights law, with its focus on the state both as protector and (potential) violator, lacks an important dimension, namely individual criminal liability and mechanisms to ensure accountability, to respond to serious human rights violations. This was seen as an evident weakness of the system that had remained unaddressed since the Nuremberg and Tokyo trials. However, a change in political constellations following the end of the Cold War, the establishment of *ad hoc* tribunals by the UN Security Council (UNSC) in the 1990s in response to the conflict in former Yugoslavia and the genocide in Rwanda, strong NGO movements, and the leadership of several states resulted in the re-emergence of international criminal justice efforts. This culminated in the establishment of the International Criminal Court (ICC) in 1998 and led to the setting up of several mixed/hybrid courts, such as those in East Timor, Cambodia and Sierra Leone.[62] In an important broadening of the scope of international criminal law, the statutes of international tribunals recognise that war crimes can also be committed in internal armed conflicts.[63] In parallel, several human rights treaty bodies, the International Court of Justice (ICJ) and others have recognised the applicability of human rights in the course of armed conflicts.[64] These developments have resulted in the growing convergence of international human rights law, international humanitarian law and international criminal law, in particular when addressing violations in internal armed conflicts. At the national level, meanwhile, the end of conflicts and/or authoritarian systems has triggered complex processes often referred to as transitional justice.[65] These processes are

---

[61] See Chapter 6.

[62] See on international criminal law generally, A. Cassese, *International Criminal Law*, 3rd edn (Oxford University Press, 2012); R. Cryer *et al.*, *Introduction to International Criminal Law and Procedure*, 2nd edn (Cambridge University Press, 2010); I. Bantekas, *International Criminal Law* (Oxford: Hart, 2010); and for resources on tribunals and hybrid courts, www.law.monash.edu.au/research/projects/icjp/compilation-project/general/tribunals-hybrid-courts.html.

[63] See articles 5–8 ICC Rome Statute 1998.

[64] See sections 14.4 and 14.5.

[65] The field has generated a vast body of documents and literature. See in particular UN Secretary General, The Rule of Law and Transitional Justice in Conflict and Post-Conflict Societies, UN Doc. S/2004/616 (23 August 2004); R. Teitel, *Transitional Justice* (Oxford University Press, 2000); N. Roht-Arriaza and J. Mariezcurrena (eds.), *Transitional Justice in the Twenty-First Century: Beyond Truth versus Justice* (Cambridge University Press, 2006); K. McEvoy and L. McGregor, *Transitional Justice from Below: Grassroots Activism and the Struggle for Change* (Oxford: Hart, 2008); and the *International Journal of Transitional Justice (IJTJ)*.

characterised by the need to address legacies of violations. This includes having to determine what should be done in respect of truth, accountability and justice, how the legal system and institutions should be reformed and how to promote reconciliation, particularly with a view to preventing future violence and violations. The principles and rules of international human rights and international criminal law form an important if not integral part of such processes, which have in turn affected and enriched international human rights law.[66]

1.3 CURRENT CHALLENGES

The proliferation of international human rights standards, the increasing recognition of the indivisible, interdependent and interrelated nature of human rights and the growing number of institutions tasked with protecting human rights constitute important progress in the field. International human rights have developed into an impressive body of law and an increasingly mature regime characterised by specific rights, obligations and supervisory mechanisms. However, serious violations persist and a number of challenges oblige the system to address them in order to become truly effective and credible.

1.3.1   International/cross-border dimension of violations

The process of economic globalisation coupled with persisting if not growing inequalities and conflicts has heightened the cross-border, international dimension of violations. Environmental crimes, such as the dumping of toxic waste, the arms trade, and economic policies and projects resulting in impoverishment, exploitation, corruption, displacement, trafficking and forced migration are some key issues of concern. The prevalence of increased human insecurity and poverty has brought about a greater awareness of the interconnectedness of violations and the need to develop effective responses.[67] The latter poses a number of challenges: (1) qualifying an act such as corruption as a violation, and developing an adequate framework of protection; (2) determining the causality between certain acts and their consequences, such as neo-liberal policies and poverty; (3) identifying responsibility where a multitude of actors are involved, including international institutions, MNCs or transnational criminal networks; (4) providing a forum in which victims of these acts are able to obtain effective access to justice and perpetrators are held to account.[68]

---

[66] See on how Inter-American human rights bodies have dealt with questions of transitional justice in sections 6.3.2 and 6.3.3.

[67] See in particular the reports regularly published by the UN Special Rapporteur on extreme poverty and human rights, online, at www.ohchr.org/EN/Issues/Poverty/Pages/SRExtremePovertyIndex.aspx.

[68] See in particular Chapter 16.

These features are particularly challenging because they are in marked contrast to the traditional conception of human rights, which focuses on the state as a territorial unit. In response, local and international movements and coalitions have increasingly called for new standards and systems of accountability, such as corporate criminal liability, if not fundamental changes to the international economic system altogether.[69] They have also led efforts using transnational litigation, particularly to hold MNCs to account.[70] These emerging areas of international human rights law are in a state of flux but are likely to grow in importance. The present system cannot ignore the consequences of a range of damaging activities if it wants to be taken seriously in its role of protecting human dignity, equality and well-being.

1.3.2   Responsibility of multiple actors

International human rights law is based on the responsibility of states, which has given human rights a distinctively state-centric prism. This is for good reason, as it has been mainly states that have committed the most serious violations in the twentieth century. Claims that the power of states is waning in times of globalisation may to some degree be correct in terms of the state's economic decision-making power. However, as a cursory reading of annual human rights reports shows, states still retain considerable powers in policy-making and immense powers in the sphere of law enforcement. The exercise of such powers is often at its most intense where economic and political stakes are particularly high, as in many oil-rich countries and/or where the state's power is challenged, as recent developments in the Middle East demonstrate. However, the increasing role of international institutions in the flow of finances and projects, their involvement in conflict and post-conflict situations, the growing number of *de facto* states and rebel groups using force, the expanding scope of MNC operations, as well as violence and discrimination committed by other private actors have equally raised the question of their respective responsibility and accountability. While the responsibility of non-state actors has traditionally been located outside the international human rights framework, there is a discernible trend to bring them into the fold. This includes the violation of the rights of women, which

---

[69]   Rajagopal, above note 35, 219–22; W. Kaleck and M. Saage-Maβ, 'Corporate Accountability for Human Rights Violations Amounting to International Crimes: The Status Quo and its Challenges', *JICJ* 8(2) (2010), 699–724.

[70]   D. Stoichkova, *Towards Corporate Liability in International Criminal Law* (Antwerp: Intersentia, 2010); P. Muchlinski, 'The Provision of Private Law Remedies against Multinational Enterprises: a Comparative Law Perspective', *JCL* 4(2), (2009), 148–70; S. Joseph, *Corporations and Transnational Human Rights Litigation* (Oxford: Hart, 2004). See for cases raising the liability of corporations for human rights abuses before US courts under the Alien Torts Claim Act, particularly *Kiobel* v. *Royal Dutch Petroleum Co.*, http://ccrjustice.org/ourcases/current-cases/kiobel.

was for a long time downplayed if not altogether ignored as a result of the public–private divide according to which the private sphere was not the domain of state interest. These developments have been complemented by a broadening of the positive obligations assumed by states to protect individuals from threats and harm inflicted by NSAs, which points to a widening of the field of application of international human rights law, albeit one that poses considerable challenges to the system.[71]

1.3.3   Effective monitoring and implementation

The growth of the international human rights regime has not been matched by an equally effective enforcement system. Human rights treaty bodies have adopted new procedures, and additional protocols have been agreed upon to enhance protection and compliance. Recent additions of note are the Protocols to the ICESCR and CRC that provide a complaints procedure for the violation of economic, social and cultural rights and children's rights respectively and the Optional Protocol to CAT, which put in place an international preventive mechanism. However, it is clear that the system essentially relies on the goodwill of states, which may be based on a political calculus according to which it is more beneficial to be seen to respect their human rights. In practice, a considerable number of states still fail to adequately implement their human rights obligations due to systemic and institutional shortcomings and/or deliberate disregard. Worryingly, it is in particular non-cooperating states that have succeeded in isolating themselves that may seemingly violate human rights with impunity.[72] The limits of the promotion and protection approach of the international human rights treaty and Charter body system raises the question of resort to force in the case of serious violations.

The so-called right to humanitarian intervention has recently been effectively superseded by the Responsibility to Protect doctrine, which emphasises the primary obligation of states to protect their populations and the subsidiary duty of the 'international community', particularly acting through the UNSC, where the state concerned fails to do so.[73] While this doctrine is often either hailed as major progress or criticised as simply another form of interventionism,[74] the problem remains. Is a political body such as the UNSC, or, in lieu of it, states and other entities, able to formulate and implement effective practices of human rights protection? The political (and grossly unrepresentative) nature of the UNSC seems to suggest the contrary, as selective responses to human

---

[71] See sections 2.3.2 and 16.2.

[72] See for example P. Goedde, 'Legal Mobilization for Human Rights Protection in North Korea: Furthering Discourse or Discord?', *HRQ* 32(3) (2010), 530–74.

[73] See 2005 World Summit Outcome, UNGA resolution 60/1 (24 October 2005), paras. 138–9.

[74] C. Gray, *International Law and the Use of Force*, 3rd edn (Oxford University Press, 2008), 51–3.

rights violations illustrate.[75] States may also invoke humanitarian considerations for what appear to be unilateral foreign policy goals. This is problematic because it is often not clear to what degree such policies are underpinned by a genuine desire to promote human rights or whether they are driven by ulterior motives such as hegemony or human rights imperialism. Even where there is some willingness to act out of genuine concern, situations such as Darfur highlight the complexity of interventions falling short of armed force, which is likely to remain the exception.[76] It is clear that human rights diplomacy is of utmost importance in such circumstances but may equally not escape politicisation. While such extreme situations do not indicate an abysmal failure of the international human rights regime, they painfully illustrate the limitations of a system that ultimately depends on the readiness of states and international institutions to take timely action.

1.3.4   Human rights imperialism and exceptionalism

The international human rights system is an integral part of international relations and as such subject to political considerations on the part of its actors.[77] This is a truism and the resulting constraints and opportunities for the promotion and protection of human rights are widely recognised. However, the integrity of the system risks being seriously undermined where human rights language is used, or appears to be used, to further the interests of major powers and/or where states seek to rewrite the rules or to exempt themselves from the system with reference to overriding considerations, in particular national security.[78]

The often vague use of human rights language by major powers to justify interventions and conditionality, and the invocation of human rights to protect the commercial interests of powerful economic actors, has generated considerable unease.[79] Human rights are in this context often seen as instruments through which Western states in particular seek to dictate what policies other states ought to pursue, thereby cementing unequal power

---

[75] See in particular M. Koskenniemi, 'The Police in the Temple. Order, Justice and the UN: a Dialectical View', *EJIL* 6(3) (1995), 325–48.

[76] See case study 3.2.

[77] See on human rights in international relations, R. J. Vincent, *Human Rights and International Relations* (Cambridge University Press, 1986); Forsythe, above note 48.

[78] See in particular International Commission of Jurists. *Assessing Damage, Urging Action: Report of the Eminent Jurist Panel on Terrorism, Counter-Terrorism and Human Rights* (Geneva: International Commission of Jurists, 2009); M. Goodhart and A. Mihr (eds.), *Human Rights in the 21st Century: Continuity and Change since 9/11* (New York: Palgrave Macmillan, 2011); reports by the Special Rapporteur on the promotion and protection of human rights and fundamental freedoms while countering terrorism, online, at www.ohchr.org/EN/Issues/Terrorism/Pages/SRTerrorismIndex.aspx.

[79] Baxi, above note 8, 294–302.

relationships (as Western states are frequently not subject to the same level of scrutiny by other states) and at times providing the pretext for economic or military interventions that may serve geo-strategic rather than genuine human rights interests. The role of the USA, international organisations such as the North Atlantic Treaty Organisation (NATO), international financial institutions such as the World Bank and the International Monetary Fund (IMF), and the European Union (EU) are pivotal and highly ambiguous in this context.[80] While these entities also contribute to the promotion and protection of human rights, the conflation of the pursuit of foreign policy interests with human rights language carries the risk of discrediting the latter.

The USA in particular has sought to reinterpret international human rights norms, such as the definition of torture, and international humanitarian law through the introduction of the term 'unlawful enemy combatants' in order to justify measures it has taken in response to terrorist threats.[81] This has privileged security paradigms that seemingly override human rights considerations, the most extreme being the tightly regulated 'legal black hole' of Guantánamo Bay.[82] These developments have caused considerable damage to the fabric of the international human rights system as they may serve as a blueprint for the justification of measures that are on the face of them clear violations. The national and international struggle against the US 'war on terror' policy has been impressive and successful in upholding and reinforcing international human rights law but has demonstrated how fragile the system is when one of its supposed champions embarks on a policy that is contrary to its own basic tenets.[83]

QUESTIONS

1 What is the link between social, political, and philosophical developments in the eighteenth and nineteenth centuries and the contemporary system of international human rights law?

2 What role has decolonisation played in the development of international human rights law?

3 Has international human rights law shown that it is capable of effectively addressing contemporary challenges?

[80] Ibid., 234–75. See also Chapter 17.
[81] See P. Sands, *Torture Team: Rumsfeld's Memo and the Betrayal of American Values* (New York: Palgrave Macmillan, 2008), and K. J. Greenberg and J. L. Dratel (eds.), *The Torture Papers: The Road to Abu Ghraib* (Cambridge University Press, 2005).
[82] See J. Steyn, 'Guantanamo Bay: The Legal Black Hole', *ICLQ* 53(1) (2004), 1–15. The US detention regime has generated a considerable body of literature and reports by UN Special Rapporteurs since its establishment in 2002.
[83] See J. Fitzpatrick, 'Speaking Law to Power: the War Against Terrorism and Human Rights', *EJIL* 14(2) (2003), 241–64 and, more broadly, M. Byers and G. Nolte (eds.), *United States Hegemony and the Foundations of International Law* (Cambridge University Press, 2003).

1.4   THE IDEA OF HUMAN RIGHTS: THEORIES AND CRITIQUES

Human rights face a paradox. At a time when they seem to have attained the status of the dominant discourse, their potential shortcomings are also becoming apparent, leading some authors to raise the spectre of the 'end of human rights'.[84] These are fundamental challenges. Satisfactorily addressing questions about the nature and validity of human rights is increasingly important for their effective protection in a rapidly changing world characterised by persistent and newly emerging patterns of threats, such as large-scale poverty and the impact of new technologies.[85] While the universal aspiration of human rights remains one of its main attractions as a cross-cultural, worldwide goal and yardstick, it is clear that in order to be true to its claim it must be accompanied by increasing sensitivity to context and to those excluded from both debates and access to protection and legal remedies. The human rights discourse faces a difficult task in these circumstances, that of engaging with broader notions of justice and avoiding undue reliance on overly legalistic approaches to what are often complex political and societal problems without losing its distinctive focus on rights.

Human rights theories can be categorised into several schools.[86] A useful way of doing so is to group theorists into natural scholars (human rights as given), deliberative scholars (as agreed upon), protest scholars (as fought for) and discourse scholars (as talked about).[87] This section provides a brief account of the moral and liberal theories of human rights which have formulated universal postulates with a considerable influence on the development of human rights law. These theories have equally attracted a number of critiques; these will be examined, together with other notions of human rights, not least with a view to understanding whether and how they can live up to their inherent promise.

1.4.1   Moral and liberal human rights theories

The UDHR is silent and ostensibly agnostic on the foundation of human rights. Several thinkers consulted during the drafting stage offered their own understanding of the nature of human rights but the drafters of the

---

[84] C. Douzinas, *The End of Human Rights: Critical Legal Thought at the Turn of the Century* (Oxford: Hart, 2000).

[85] T. Pogge, *World Poverty and Human Rights: Cosmopolitan Responsibilities and Reforms*, 2nd edn (Cambridge: Polity Press, 2008); T. Murphy (ed.), *New Technologies and Human Rights* (Oxford University Press, 2009).

[86] See for good overviews, J. W. Nickel and D. A. Reidy, 'Philosophy', in D. Moeckli, S. Shah and S. Sivakumaran (eds.), *International Human Rights Law* (Oxford University Press, 2010), 39–63; Twining, above note 5, 173–201; C. R. Beitz, *The Idea of Human Rights* (Oxford University Press, 2009).

[87] M.-B. Dembour, 'What Are Human Rights? Four Schools of Thought', *HRQ* 32(1) (2010), 1–20.

UDHR took a pragmatic view, fearing that any disagreement about the underlying philosophy of human rights might jeopardise agreement about the contents of the declaration.[88] However, the UDHR's drafting history and language suggest that moral and liberal theories exerted a strong influence on the development and understanding of human rights following World War II.[89] Moral theories of human rights draw on the language of inherent (natural) rights found in the American and French declarations and restated in the UDHR.[90] Human rights are seen as universally applicable standards that transcend time, location and culture. This position provides a strong metaphysical grounding for the universal nature of human rights.[91] However, ideas based on 'epistemic universality'[92] can be challenged on the ground that they do not have any objective validity. The very 'universality' may be the expression of a subjective viewpoint, if not the outcome of a political project that reflects Western bias, as critics of the UDHR have argued.[93] The postulate of an anterior moral theory that informs the development of human rights law may also fail to reflect the complex political processes that result in the recognition of particular rights.[94] Authors have responded to the objections raised against substantive (moral) accounts by grounding theories of human rights in personal autonomy as agency.[95] However, the list of core rights flowing from this is rather narrow and fails to provide a satisfactory basis for addressing global concerns.[96] Others have located human rights in human capabilities,[97] a notion that provides a useful combination of agency and an instrumental approach to the protection of human rights.

---

[88] Morsink, above note 39, 125; M. Ignatieff, 'Human Rights as Politics, Human Rights as Idolatry', *The Tanner Lectures on Human Values* (2000), 327–47, at 328, online, at www.tannerlectures.utah.edu/lectures/documents/Ignatieff_01.pdf.

[89] See for example L. Henkin, *The Age of Rights* (New York: Columbia University Press, 1990), pp. 6–10, and J. Donnelly, *Universal Human Rights in Theory and Practice*, 2nd edn (Ithaca, London: Cornell University Press, 2003), 1, 13–4.

[90] Moral theories may ground human rights in religious or moral principles, notions of personal agency (Gerwith), autonomy (Griffins) or a plurality of values (Tasioulas). See for a concise overview of moral theories, Twining, above note 5, 202–17.

[91] See J. Morsink, *Inherent Human Rights: Philosophical Roots of the Universal Declaration* (Philadelphia: University of Pennsylvania Press, 2009).

[92] Ibid., 50.

[93] Mutua, above note 5, 39–70, particularly 46–7.

[94] This is the main critique of deliberative or constructivist scholars, see for example Ignatieff, above note 88, 337. In an interesting observation, Twining, above note 5, pp. 180–1, notes that human rights law may include rights not provided for in moral theories, thus reversing the oft-assumed causality of anterior moral rights.

[95] J. Griffin, *On Human Rights* (Oxford University Press, 2008).

[96] Twining, above note 5, 122–32. See also Twining's discussion of J. Tasioulas's theory of a 'pluralist conception of human interests' that seeks to meet this challenge.

[97] A. Sen, *Development as Freedom* (Oxford University Press, 1999).

Liberal theories played a significant role in shaping the understanding of human rights, both as a concept and as a feature of political and international relations. Liberalism views the individual as an autonomous subject who may exercise his or her rights as long as they do not conflict with the rights of others.[98] The role of the state is to provide for order, security (and basic welfare) without unjustified interference with the rights of individuals. This view resulted in an emphasis on civil and political rights in the early human rights discourse, dubbed the first generation of rights, which at the national level may act as trumping other considerations.[99] It was based on the divide between the public and private sphere, a conception that has been identified as reflecting and entrenching a male bias in international human rights law.[100]

Rawls, who became well known for his work on justice as fairness, developed a theory of political liberalism at the global level in his work *The Law of Peoples*.[101] He constructed an international system composed of what he termed well-ordered liberal and hierarchical societies, outlaw states, societies burdened by unfavourable conditions and benevolent absolutisms. Further, he stipulated principles that 'well-ordered societies' would embrace and identified situations in which humanitarian intervention would be justified, namely where a state fails to respect basic human rights. In this world, effectively, human rights serve as benchmark for the acceptability of a state, which is primarily to be judged by 'reasonable liberal peoples'. While constituting an interesting attempt at explaining the role of human rights in international relations, Rawls's theory is widely seen as parochial, outdated and unsuitable in addressing the challenges facing the global system.[102] Even though attempts to construct grand liberal theories have failed, liberal thinking continues to be influential in the invocation of human rights in international relations and prominent in the text and interpretation of treaties, with human rights being celebrated or criticised as a liberal political project.[103] Some of the rhetoric used in the Arab uprisings beginning in 2010 has demonstrated the revolutionary potential of liberal language couched in universal standards, which critiques both national regimes and ('liberal') foreign states that compromise if not betray human rights for the sake of *realpolitik*.[104]

[98] See in particular J. Rawls, *Political Liberalism* (New York: Columbia University Press, 1996).

[99] R. Dworkin, 'Rights as Trumps', in Waldron, above note 7, 153–67.

[100] See H. Charlesworth and C. Chinkin, *The Boundaries of International Law: A Feminist Analysis* (Manchester University Press, 2000), 28–32.

[101] J. Rawls, *The Law of Peoples* (Cambridge, MA, London: Harvard University Press, 2001).

[102] See discussion and reference to critics in Twining, above note 5, 159–62, as well as an account of T. Pogge's attempt to reinterpret Rawls's work, 163–72.

[103] See T. Dunne and M. Hanson, 'Human Rights in International Relations', in M. Goodhart (ed.), *Human Rights: Politics and Practice* (Oxford University Press, 2009), 59–74, with further references.

[104] See M. El-Ghobashy, 'The Praxis of the Egyptian Revolution', *MER* 258(41) (2011), online, at, www.merip.org/mer/mer258/praxis-egyptian-revolution; R. Khalidi, 'Preliminary Historical Observations on the Arab Revolutions of 2011', *Jadaliyya* (21 March 2011), www.jadaliyya.com/pages/index/970/preliminary-historical-observations-on-the-arab-re.

1.4.2 Meeting the challenge: reconstructing human rights

A number of interlinked processes, beginning with the Cold War divide and decolonisation, largely destroyed any seemingly existing consensus and resulted in growing scrutiny and criticism of the unspoken assumptions under-pinning human rights. With their increasing use as part of foreign policy, in particular by the USA in the 1970s, human rights became widely seen as a political instrument used selectively to create or maintain hegemony.[105] The perceived individualistic, and for many societies supposedly culturally alien, nature of human rights was viewed as an integral part of the process of glo-balisation and increasingly objected to.[106] At the national level, civil liberties movements, student and feminist actors and a number of thinkers engaged in alternative practices and critical discourses that questioned both moral and political (liberal) assumptions and biases, in particular male bias, which were seen as inherent in the prevailing doctrine of rights and the reliance on law to protect human rights.[107] This was complemented by post-modern critiques of reason and foundational theories.[108] These challenges seemingly subsided in the wake of the liberal triumphalism following the break up of the Soviet Union and the concomitant revolutions in Eastern Europe. However, unease has since resurfaced and arguably intensified,[109] as human rights have come to dominate political discourse and have again assumed a prominent place in foreign policy. Their elevated status has attracted many followers but has also resulted in closer inspection and interrogation of their nature and role in national and international politics. This has opened up the human rights discourse and generated what appears at first sight a bewildering number of theories that seek to address some, if not all, of the challenges faced.

One of the main challenges to human rights is that they can hardly be called universal if they only reflect the preferences of a particular culture or group of like-minded states, as critics of the 'Western' nature of human rights have claimed. Indeed, any substantive theory risks being accused of positing an understanding of human rights that does not reflect global diversity. Agreement or discourse theories, many of which have been influ-enced by Habermas's communication theory, seek to address this challenge by placing emphasis on open-ended arguments in situations of level playing

---

[105] Mutua, above note 5, 39–70.

[106] Ibid. See on the Asian values debate brief overview with further references in Twining, above note 5, 198–9.

[107] See for a discussion of the relationship between law and politics, C. Gearty, *Principles of Human Rights Adjudication* (Oxford University Press, 2004), 8–30.

[108] See C. Gearty, *Can Human Rights Survive?* (Cambridge University Press, 2006), 17–21, and R. Rorty, 'Human Rights, Rationality and Sentimentality', in S. Shute and S. Hurley (eds.), *On Human Rights* (New York: Basic Books, 1993), 111, 115.

[109] As evident in titles such as *The End of Human Rights* (Douzinas) and *Can Human Rights Survive?* (Gearty). See also Baxi, above note 8, 82–5.

fields.[110] The advantage of this approach is that its democratic nature is seemingly conducive to reaching an understanding if not consensus that strengthens the acceptability of human rights as defined by the participants. This is of particular importance in cross-cultural situations[111] and the UDHR process itself can at least partly be seen as a successful manifestation of this approach.[112] However, it is of limited value in situations of power asymmetry and/or where there is no willingness to engage in dialogue, be it generally or on specific issues seen as non-negotiable.[113]

The difficulty if not apparent futility of agreeing on a foundational theory of human rights has led some authors to turn to pragmatism, arguing that human rights are seen as inherently political and that they should be promoted through education.[114] In a similar vein, constructivist theories seek to draw on areas of overlapping consensus and/or other principles, such as common interests,[115] with a view to identifying common ground if not convincing others to accept the human rights standards in question. The advantage of these theories is their flexible and realistic stance that is cognisant of the political nature of human rights discourses and practices. However, the theories provide limited guidance as to why human rights should be valid and may fail to convince others, especially if they are associated with particular political projects, such as the promotion of liberal democracy.

Critical legal scholars and movements have articulated one of the most concerted critiques of contemporary conceptions and practices of human rights. They argue that human rights as a language of political discourse is too narrow and crowds out other equally valid if not preferable modes, such as social justice.[116] Further, it is seen as negating policy choices by framing decision-making as a question of rights to be adjudicated upon[117] rather than being subject to political debate.[118] As such, human rights language may

---

[110] See overview by Twining, above note 5, 217–24.

[111] A. A. An Na'im, Introduction, in An Na'im (ed.), *Human Rights in Cross-Cultural Perspectives: A Quest for Consensus* (Philadelphia: University of Pennsylvania Press, 1992), 1–15, at 1–8.

[112] In particular the consultation of philosophers and the approach of drawing on various notions of human rights.

[113] See Gearty, above note 108, 40: 'There is nothing that allows us to say "You have got to do this" in the endless deliberation that now seems the best we can hope for.'

[114] Rorty, above note 108.

[115] Donnelly, above note 89, 15–16, and 40–53.

[116] See M. Koskenniemi, 'The Effect of Rights on Political Culture', in P. Alston (ed.), *The EU and Human Rights* (Oxford University Press, 1999), 99–116; D. Kennedy, 'The International Human Rights Movement: Part of the Problem', *Harv. Hum. Rts. J.* 15 (2002), 101–26.

[117] See for a critical legal theory approach on the nature of adjudication, particularly in the American context, D. Kennedy, *A Critique of Adjudication* (Cambridge, MA, London: Harvard University Press, 1998).

[118] Koskenniemi, above note 116, 99–100. See also Gearty, above note 108, 60–98, on this point.

not constitute the discourse of emancipation it promises to be. It may overly focus on endless, often individualistic identity politics that are increasingly couched in terms of rights instead of addressing underlying structural problems and inequalities or fostering solidarity.[119] There is also a risk that rights which have served as challenges to dominant orders are being harnessed and used to serve class, economic or political interests, a concern that is in line with Marxist criticism of human rights.[120] A case in point is the invocation of property rights that have been used to stifle land reforms.[121]

The multitude of discourses has added an important critical dimension to the understanding of human rights. Even though these critical voices have had limited visible impact on the prevailing growth of international human rights law and the role of human rights in international relations, they are vital in ensuring that human rights do not lose what may be considered their defining features: their interrogation of power and violence; their focus on unnecessary and unacceptable suffering; their utopian potential to imagine and demand a different world based on shared core values; and their capacity to give voice to and empower those who have been excluded from legal recognition and attendant rights (such as stateless persons, refugees and indigenous peoples) or who are otherwise marginalised.[122]

QUESTIONS

1 Do theories of human rights matter? If so, why?

2 Why is the strong appeal of moral theories of human rights at the same time their biggest weakness?

3 Do the critiques of human rights theories point to a fatal flaw in their conception or are they healthy reminders of the importance of a plurality of political practices?

1.5 UNIVERSAL HUMAN RIGHTS: CONTESTATIONS AND PRACTICES

1.5.1 The debate

The question of universality is one of the recurring debates at the heart of human rights. Universality is invoked as the cornerstone of human rights by some and derided as the embodiment of ethnocentric, politically biased

---

[119] Ibid. and Douzinas, above note 84.

[120] Baxi calls this the politics of human rights as opposed to the politics for human rights. See Baxi, above note 8, 57–8, 252–3.

[121] See Mutua, above note 5, 142–4, in the South African context.

[122] See in particular Baxi, above note 8. See also Pogge, above note 85; Douzinas, above note 84; Gearty, above note 108 (arguing for compassion); and feminist theories based on the ethics of care – see C. Gilligan, *In a Different Voice: Psychological Theory and Women's Development* (Cambridge, MA, London: Harvard University Press, 1982).

and narrow conceptions thereof by others. It is one of the paradigms of the international human rights system, as evident in the name of the UDHR and expressed in its self-description as 'common standard of achievement for all peoples and all nations'. The term universality is used to denote the nature and validity of rights that are common to all human beings by virtue of their humanity.[123] This 'abstract universality'[124] is reflected in the use of language in the UDHR, such as 'everyone' and 'all human beings'. However, the notion of universality is subject to multiple understandings (e.g. as natural right or political aspiration, as a ground for validity of rights or scope of their application) and the UDHR itself provides a series of essentialist and instrumentalist justifications of human rights.[125] The moral and political dimension of the notion of universality as a founding principle has provided a strong impetus for the development of international human rights law. However, it has also been subjected to close scrutiny over the years, resulting in several strands of critique, if not outright rejection.

At the core of debates about universality is the tension between a set of rights that supposedly apply to everyone at all times and the lack of, or limited recognition, understanding and practical application of these rights around the world. This tension is closely tied up with the political struggle for decolonisation, self-determination and development policies, which includes attempts to define rights and values deemed appropriate in their particular contexts. It has gained further impetus in the clash between global homogenisation and local and regional identity politics.

Critics of universality argue that cultures and societies have developed different understandings of the nature of human beings and of 'rights', which may include a rejection of the notion that rights provide a suitable means of governing social relationships. The idea of universal rights is deemed illusory because rights are informed by and applied in specific societal and cultural contexts.[126] It is also seen as culturally inappropriate, effectively imposing an alien concept (individual rights with a focus on civil and political rights) that is the outcome of a particular historical development and is specific to particular political systems (liberal democracies) on cultures that have different value systems (religious, communitarian rather than liberal and individualistic). While

---

[123]   Donnelly, above note 89, 1.

[124]   Baxi, above note 8, 167–9.

[125]   Ibid., 164–5.

[126]   See 'Statement on Human Rights, The Executive Board, American Anthropological Association', in *American Anthropologist* (*AA*), new series 49(4)1 (Oct–Dec 1947), 539–43. See in contrast, 'Declaration on Anthropology and Human Rights Committee for Human Rights; American Anthropological Association, Adopted by the AAA membership June 1999', online, at www.aaanet.org/stmts/humanrts.htm, and for a discussion of the role played by these documents in the history of anthropology and human rights, M. Goodale, *Surrendering to Utopia: An Anthropology of Human Rights* (Palo Alto, CA: Stanford University Press, 2009), 18–39, which also reprints both documents as appendices.

some reject the notion of universality altogether, others argue that culture provides the context in which universal notions of rights have to be interpreted and appropriated in order to be meaningful and effective.[127] Indeed, there is ample evidence that this process is already taking place in the regional human rights systems and in respect of certain rights, such as the rights of indigenous peoples.

The universality debate is of particular practical importance where consensus over certain practices is lacking, be it ostensibly on religious grounds, as a justification for corporal punishment, or for traditional or cultural reasons, for example female genital cutting/mutilation (see below at 1.5.2). Rather than simply insisting on absolute standards in these situations, a number of authors call for a dialogue, both between and within cultures,[128] to arrive at a solution that is acceptable for those concerned. As has been rightly highlighted, genuine dialogue about human rights must engage in addressing the content of the subject of disagreement where 'we' must be able to adequately answer challenges, for example why pornography should be tolerated, before postulating a right as a standard for others.[129] The outcome of such dialogue may be the acceptance of universal standards, possibly subject to the phasing out of traditional practices, e.g. polygamy,[130] the context specific interpretation of rights – similar to the concept of margin of appreciation applied by the ECtHR[131] – or their rejection, for example where one side rejects the right of the other to discuss certain practices, for example because they are seen as commanded by God. The latter position shows the limits of dialogue where differences cannot be bridged. However, the very act of seeking an open dialogue can be helpful in fostering a human rights culture if it is grounded in a 'cosmopolitan' spirit that takes the arguments of others seriously and brings different points of view to the table. The recognition of the need to be context specific must not necessarily equate with an abandonment of universality, which can still provide a valuable framework of culturally transcendent and genuinely universal aspirations.[132]

The universality debate has important political dimensions for international human rights. The charges of ethnocentrism highlight the bias apparent in the mainstream human rights discourse that has for a long time been dominated by authors with a broadly shared cultural background and value

[127] See S. E. Merry, 'Transnational Human Rights and Local Activism: Mapping the Middle', *AA* 108(1) (2006), 38–51, and Rajagopal, above note 35, 210.

[128] An Na'im, above note 111, and M. Baderin, *International Human Rights and Islamic Law* (Oxford University Press, 2005), 5.

[129] J. Waldron, 'How to Argue for a Universal Claim', *Colum. Hum. Rts. L. Rev.* 30(2) (1999), 305–14.

[130] See article 5 African Protocol on the Rights of Women on the elimination of harmful practices.

[131] See in this context, Baderin, above note 128, 231–5.

[132] See Baxi, above note 8, 185.

system.[133] This practice has been criticised as neo-colonial and patronising, focusing the West's gaze on 'the other' and generating a narrative of savages ('the perpetrators' who are bad), victims (the poor and faceless masses who are good and in need of protection) and saviours (Western human rights organisations and their counterparts).[134] This criticism highlights the reproduction of simplistic views that are prone to reinforce stereotypes and prejudices and ignore agency. Such an outcome is clearly antithetical to human rights based on notions of respect for dignity, freedom and equality. The interrogation of authorship and power dynamics underlying the development of human rights law, including in the field of human rights work, is therefore an important corrective and ongoing task that is needed to ensure the continuing legitimacy of human rights and their advocates.

A further charge is that notions of universality can be used for ideological purposes in order to mask the intent behind what is essentially a political project. According to this argument, the tenets of universality are derived from liberal democracy and aimed at its promotion as a political ideology. This narrow focus frequently fails to provide adequate solutions to pressing governance issues, such as social justice and land reform in many African countries, or worse, may protect the interest of certain individuals or classes at the expense of the public good.[135] Some of the opposition to universal human rights is ostensibly directed against the export of the political ideology that they seem to imply. Indeed, the language of universal rights may be appropriated to pursue hegemonic objectives and to promote modes of globalisation serving certain power interests.[136] This is a challenge that human rights defenders invoking universal standards must and can address – while there is a political dimension to universal human rights that may be used to justify power relationships, human rights reach beyond this to protect core human freedoms and to limit the exercise of power, which may include that of the very entities invoking the universality of human rights.

The politics of universality is evident within the international human rights system in debates over the recognition of rights, in particular collective ones such as the right to development, the validity of reservations to human rights treaties, for example in relation to Shari'a (Islamic law), and the inclusion and interpretation of rights in regional treaties.[137] The universal language of human rights primarily employed by Western actors in international relations has also triggered a number of confrontations and largely defensive reactions. This includes the Asian value debate in the 1990s where

---

[133] Mutua, above note 5, 39–70.
[134] M. Mutua, 'Savages, Victims and Saviors: the Metaphor of Human Rights', *Harv. Int'l L. J.* 4 (2001), 201–45.
[135] Mutua, above note 5, 142–4.
[136] Baxi, above note 8, 170–5; Anghie, above note 25, 279–91.
[137] See Chapter 6, particularly section 6.2.5.

states such as Singapore and Malaysia claimed that Asian communitarian values differed from Western individualistic values reflected in international human rights.[138] This debate was closely related to differences over models of development and may have reflected the political interest of Asian states in fending off the use of human rights discourse to attack their economic policies;[139] while it has largely subsided, different approaches to human rights within Asia are still apparent.[140] Another example is the opposition of states with Muslim majorities to what is seen as the imposition of secular notions that violate religious beliefs, such as liberal interpretations of freedom of expression, which have led to concerted efforts at the Human Rights Council (HRC) to redefine the relationship between these rights.[141] The 'universality v. relativism' schism has also resurfaced in debates surrounding the exercise of international criminal justice in Africa where the ICC and other bodies have been portrayed as pursuing Western notions of retributive justice that are contrary to African modes of reconciliation.[142]

These debates, while seemingly focusing on different conceptions of rights, are at their heart also about ownership of human rights discourses and practices. While objections to universality raise valid concerns, it is often questionable how representative and genuine they are. The notion of culture as something immutable is essentialist and its use is prone to presenting one strand within a culture as 'the culture'. This may ignore, if not suppress, other voices and thereby replicate the very mode of discourse that universality is accused of. Cultural specificity may also be invoked to deflect criticism over certain practices that are increasingly seen as incompatible with basic rights, such as discrimination against women, and serve as a variant of arguments used to demand non-interference.

However, it is equally clear that arguments surrounding human rights may open up valuable debates, which reflect the fact that they are developed in a continuous process of contestation and contextual adjustment. It is not necessarily the idea of universal human rights but the power relationships and modes of invoking and seeking to enforce them that appear problematic. Building strong and credible national and regional systems that protect and promote fundamental values and rights while being sensitive to local contexts would appear to be the most important step in changing this equation. Indeed, there is a growing realisation of the need to develop a 'decentered

---

[138] See for nuanced and critical discussions of the points raised, Y. Ghai, 'Asian Perspectives on Human Rights', *HKLJ* 23 (1993), 342–57; A. Sen, 'Human Rights and Asian Values' (New York: Carnegie Council on Ethics and International Affairs, 1997).

[139] Rajagopal, above note 35, 202–16.

[140] See for the fledgling sub-regional ASEAN system of human rights, section 6.5.

[141] See section 8.7.3.

[142] O. Oko, 'The Challenges of International Criminal Prosecutions in Africa', 31 *FILJ* (2007–2008), 343–414, and generally, V. O. Nmehielle (ed.), *Africa and the Future of International Criminal Justice* (The Hague: Eleven International, 2012).

understanding of [human rights as] normative construct'[143] and a 'global perspective'[144] that reflects the plurality of voices. 'Relativist' critiques themselves may at times overstate the Western dominance by ignoring the multitude of authors and movements that have contributed, and continue to contribute, to the development of human rights and human rights law. This is particularly evident in the African context, where regional human rights treaties reflect distinctive approaches to human rights, such as an emphasis on duties and collective rights, and novel approaches in areas such as women's rights and the rights of internally displaced persons.

Ultimately, universality is a global concern that cuts across cultures and 'symbolise[s] *universality of collective human aspiration to make power more accountable, governance progressively more just and states incrementally more ethical*.'[145] If seen as a framework to address myriad local, national and international injustices, universality can serve both as an important yardstick and a means to foster global solidarity.

INTERVIEW 1.1

Human rights and the uprisings in the Arab world

(Moataz El Fegiery)

Moataz El Fegiery is the former executive director of the Cairo Institute for Human Rights Studies and a member of its board of directors. He is presently working on a research project on 'Islamic Activism and International Human Rights Law: the Muslim Brotherhood in Egypt as a Case Study'.

What role has the language of and reference to human rights played in triggering the uprisings in the Arab world?

One reason behind the popular revolt in Arab states has been the lack of respect for human rights. For decades, people in Tunisia, Egypt and Libya have been subjected to repressive regimes with poor human rights records. The quest for social justice, human dignity and freedom has been manifested in the key slogans chanted by demonstrators in different Arab states. In Egypt, for example, the systematic practice of torture and ill treatment by the security forces under Mubarak's regime prompted activists and youth movements to revolt on 25 January 2011, which is an official holiday, 'the police day', in order to send a clear message to Mubarak and

---

[143] J. Habermas, *Time of Transitions* (Cambridge, Malden, MA: Polity, 2006), 155.
[144] Twining, above note 5.
[145] Baxi, above note 8, 185 (emphasis in original).

the Ministry of Interior that the misuse of power by the security forces would no longer be acceptable. In the following days, massive popular demonstrations swept across Egypt demanding drastic political changes. The important role that respect for human rights played in chants, blogs and debates during the uprising can in no small part be attributed to the work of local human rights organisations over the last decade that raised public awareness about the patterns of human rights violations through advocacy and litigation. In Egypt, the rise of private media from 2003 onwards has enabled human rights NGOs to reach a wide popular audience across the country.

Were there any objections to the invocation of universal human rights?

Political and social forces that have taken to the streets in Arab states are diverse and have different political visions for the future of their countries. These forces agree on the necessity of political change and of addressing the severe injustice created by the policies of the outgoing regimes. While political forces have not necessarily mentioned international human rights law explicitly, the underlying norms have become part of the day-to-day political interactions during the revolutionary and transitional period. Most political forces agree that the new regimes should comply with the prohibition of torture, the right to effective remedies, the right to a fair trial, political rights and economic and social rights.

However, positions diverge when it comes to the interpretation of human rights. For instance, Islamist political parties such as the Freedom of Justice party established by the Muslim Brotherhood in Egypt clearly state in their platforms that international human rights should be implemented as long as they are in line with Islamic Shari'a. Other non-Islamist parties also oppose some aspects of international human rights law as inappropriate for their society's religion and culture. Human rights issues that tend to give rise to controversy in the context of Arab societies are those related to gender equality, freedom of religion, the rights of religious minorities, and some aspects of the rights of children, such as the prohibition of child marriage and female genital mutilation.

For all the diversity of views on human rights, it is important to recognise the increasing role played in the region by human rights defenders who tirelessly struggle to embed international human rights in local cultural traditions. In the transitional period in Egypt, for example, human rights NGOs proposed a road map for constitutional, legal and institutional reform based on international human rights law. However, these NGOs have been marginalised and attacked by the transitional authority in Egypt.

Islamist movements are often seen as antithetical to human rights, particularly international human rights standards. Is this view borne out by your research and experience?

Islamist movements are not monolithic. The discourse on Islamic law and international human rights is highly contingent upon the political and social contexts in different Muslim states and even at different times. There has certainly been considerable progress in the thought and practice of many Islamist parties, which have chosen to engage in peaceful democratic political processes. Following the eruption of the revolutions, Islamists in Tunisia and Egypt have been eager to explain to the public and to the international community that they adopt a moderate and liberal understanding of Islam and that they are committed to human rights. Islamists are now the leading political force in Egypt and Tunisia. They have also achieved a significant victory in Morocco's parliamentary elections.

The practices of the Muslim Brotherhood in Egypt and the *al-nahda* ('awakening') movement in Tunisia concerning legislative reforms and broader policies will be a real test of their commitment to human rights in the years to come. However, available sources, such as official documents, pamphlets, writings of ideologues and scholars, and their record in parliamentary politics to date, can already help us better understand the attitudes of these parties towards human rights. The *al-nahda* movement in Tunisia, particularly according to the writings of its leader Rashid al-Ghanoushi, has sought to reconcile Islamic law and human rights. While it has interpreted the methods, principles and rules of Islamic law to affirm the rights of women and religious freedom, Tunisian human rights defenders and feminists are worried that the movement may reverse the existing family law that gives significant rights such as the abolition of polygamy to Tunisian women.

In Egypt, the Muslim Brotherhood has been eager to portray its position as being in conformity with international human rights law. However, the group interprets many international human rights restrictively. For instance, its members and leaders have usually been critical of the conception of gender equality in CEDAW. They argue that international women's rights corrupt Islamic social values and morals. Instead, they advocate the concept of complementary roles between men and women. This means that not all rights enjoyed by men are provided for women. This understanding influences the discriminatory positions that have been developed by the Muslim Brotherhood towards marriage, divorce and the political rights of women.

How do you view the role of international human rights in the current situation. To what degree will they form part of the politics of transition?

This differs from one country to another based on the forms of transitional authority and transitional arrangements that are in place. In Egypt the Military Council has managed the transitional period poorly, failing to institute tangible human rights reforms. The situation has led to tensions in the relationship between the transitional authority and the human rights community in Egypt, as the latter has been vocal in denouncing the deteriorating status of human rights and the reluctance of the Military Council to implement much needed reforms. During the transitional period, human rights defenders in Egypt have been subject to an unprecedented campaign of surveillance and persecution. Although Mubarak and other senior members of the former regime have been subject to trial on charges related to violence against demonstrators during the revolution and corruption, the prosecution and trial of Mubarak has been handled in a rushed manner to placate public outrage and was marred by bias given that the security apparatus and the prosecution were still dominated by pro-Mubarak figures. In Tunisia, however, there has been a more inclusive transitional process where civil society and all political forces have taken part in the transitional arrangements, with human rights defenders playing a leading role.

What is the future of human rights in the Arab region, including in terms of the development of an effective regional human rights system?

The future of human rights in Egypt, Tunisia, Libya and Yemen is contingent first upon the success of transitional political arrangements. These countries face immense challenges to restructure their political institutions, constitutions and laws. Secondly, the performance of Islamist forces will be critical for whether the relationship between Islamic law and human rights in this region becomes more harmonious or adversarial.

The future of the regional human rights system in the Arab region will be influenced by the direction of political changes. Transitions in Egypt, Libya, Tunisia, Yemen and Syria are crucial in this respect. The modernisation of the Arab Charter of Human Rights, which falls short of international human rights standards and has in any case only been ratified by few states, is among the tasks that need to be handled by the new political regimes in the region. However, at present this is not seen as a priority due to the prevailing political instability. Finally, the emergence of Islamist political forces in Arab states is likely to strengthen the role of the Organisation of Islamic Cooperation. The recent developments might encourage the members of the Organisation to act on the proposal to establish a human rights commission and develop an Islamic human rights system.

1.5.2   Experiences in combating female genital cutting/mutilation

Female genital cutting (FGC), which will be referred to as female genital mutilation (FGM)[146] consists of the total or partial removal of the female genital, or other harmful procedures to the female genitalia. FGM is practised in twenty-eight African and Middle Eastern countries and immigrant communities and affects over a hundred million girls and women. It is a traditional socio-cultural practice and initiation rite based on beliefs surrounding female sexuality and purity, maintained through significant pressure by family members, communities and peers. The cutting is commonly carried out by traditional female practitioners. It frequently results in pain, harm and lasting health damage to girls and women. Regional and international human rights treaties, treaty bodies and special procedures have classified FGM as a form of gender-based violence that violates a series of rights of the girl-child and women (freedom from torture and ill treatment, right to health, right to non-discrimination).[147] States have a positive obligation to protect these rights and to eliminate harmful practices as set out in particular in article 5(a) CEDAW and article 5(b) of the protocol to the African Charter on Human and Peoples' Rights (ACHPR) on the Rights of Women in Africa, the latter of which explicitly refers to the prohibition of all forms of FGM.

Beyond its legal qualification and obligations arising under international human rights law, FGM has become a focal point for intense debates about cultural relativism and feminism. What makes FGM particularly challenging is that it is a deep-rooted practice that is often seemingly endorsed by women themselves. If it is only communities or 'cultures' themselves that can define the validity of rights and practices, FGM may be justified on the grounds of the legitimacy it commands.[148] In contrast, universalists, including Western feminists, have called it a violation that is based on discrimination and coercion.[149] The girls and women supporting this practice, so the argument

---

[146] The term itself is contested as female genital cutting is seen as neutral in contrast to female genital mutilation. There is a considerable body of literature on the law and practice of FGM. See in particular A. Rahman and N. Toubia, *Female Genital Mutilation: A Guide to Laws and Policies Worldwide* (London: Zed Books, 2000); F. Banda, *Women, Law and Human Rights: An African Perspective* (Oxford: Hart), pp. 207–46; World Health Organisation, *Eliminating Female Genital Mutilation: An Interagency Statement, OHCHR, UNAIDS, UNDP, UNECA, UNESCO, UNFPA, UNHCR, UNICEF, UNIFEM, WHO* (New York: WHO, 2008).

[147] See for a brief overview, WHO, above note 146, 8–10. See also Report of the Special Rapporteur on torture and other cruel, inhuman or degrading treatment or punishment, Manfred Nowak, UN Doc. A/HRC/7/3 (15 January 2008), paras. 50–5.

[148] See in this context contributions in J. K. Cowan, M.-B. Dembour and R. A. Wilson (eds.) *Culture and Rights: Anthropological Perspectives* (Cambridge University Press, 2001).

[149] F. P. Hosken, *Stop Female Genital Mutilation*. Women Speak: Facts and Actions (Lexington, MA: Women's International Network News, 1995). See also C. J. Walley, 'Searching for Voices: Feminism, Anthropology, and the Global Debate over Female Genital Operations', *CA* 12(3) (1997), 405–38.

goes, have internalised the dominant discourse that legitimises FGM. Such reasoning, however, denies any agency, particularly if applied to women over the age of eighteen. It has been called 'imperialist' feminism, and advocacy based on the argument that FGM is violent, despicable and wrong has proved ambivalent if not counterproductive.[150] This constellation has pitted those advocating the application of universal human rights standards against others calling for respect for cultural diversity. It has also led to criticism of feminists who supposedly turn a blind eye to forms of 'voluntary' genital mutilation in the West, such as cosmetic surgery.[151] While the controversy surrounding FGM has been intense, the debate has been healthy in as much as it has stressed the need for a cross-cultural understanding and a sharpening of strategies on how best to respond to harmful cultural practices.

Several states have adopted legislation that outlaws FGM, which has in many instances been complemented by awareness campaigns. The prohibition and criminalisation of FGM as a means of protecting women's rights is an important step, both as a public rejection of the practice and as deterrent. However, experiences show that these measures alone often have limited effectiveness. In the African context this practical challenge has been addressed at two levels. Women's rights groups have formed networks to develop regional awareness and binding regional standards, such as in the African Protocol on the Rights of Women. Civil society groups have also increasingly pursued a community-based approach, which has enjoyed the support of the UN International Children's Fund (UNICEF), other UN agencies and several governments, such as in Senegal. This approach is based on the insight that legislative measures and campaigns based on women's rights may not bring about a change in practice unless they are complemented by programmes that directly engage affected communities.

The international NGO Tostan has developed what it calls a community empowerment programme. The programme is run by local Tostan facilitators who take a participatory and 'respectful approach that allows villagers to make their own conclusions about FGC and to lead their own movements for change'.[152] The educational programme uses interactive methods to share information and raise awareness, *inter alia*, of human rights and the harmful impact of FGM. The programme seeks to facilitate dialogue and claims to be non-judgemental, seeking to enable participants to make informed choices. It also takes a community based, rather than individualistic, approach to changing social convention. According to independent evaluations, the programme has raised villagers' awareness of human rights, reproductive health

---

[150] See H. Lewis, 'Between Irua and "Female Genital Mutilation": Feminist Human Rights Discourse and Cultural Divide', *Harv. Hum. Rts. J.* 8(1) (1995), 1–55.

[151] See in this context, 'Cosmetic Surgery, Body Image and Sexuality', *RHM* 18(35) (2010).

[152] See the Tostan website, www.tostan.org.

and the adverse impact of FGM.[153] Tostan's programmes have achieved notable successes; over 4,500 communities have publicly declared that they have abandoned FGM. Other programmes have initiated alternative rites of passage and sought to provide employment opportunities for cutters to change the cultural and economic factors that sustain the practice.

A UNICEF study on FGM identified several key elements of change, namely non-coercive and non-judgemental approaches with focus on empowerment; awareness on the part of the community of the harm caused by FGM; the decision to abandon FGM as a collective choice; public affirmation; organised diffusion from one community to another; and an environment that enables and supports change.[154] These elements, based on practical experiences, demonstrate that discussions which frame the issue of FGM and women's rights as a clash between universal human rights and culture may miss the point. Instead of a stark dichotomy of abstract principles versus immutable culture, experiences show that FGM is often an embedded practice that those concerned may be willing to change under the right circumstances. In this context the language of human rights becomes part of a broader package of persuasion that will only succeed if translated and related to local practices and concerns. The agency of local actors is crucial, as is the sensitivity of local, regional and international NGOs and other actors to socio-cultural factors as well as the needs of local communities. This is critical because failure to create an environment conducive to abandoning FGM will inevitably test if not expose the limits of states' ability to fulfil their positive obligations to protect the rights of those concerned. The debate and practices surrounding FGM demonstrate starkly that it is not sufficient to condemn a certain harmful practice by invoking universal human rights; it needs to be tackled through creative and often painstaking engagement before it can be changed for good.

QUESTIONS

1   Should the notion of universality be replaced with that of plurality?

2   Are the debates surrounding universality mainly concerned with the substance of universal human rights, the process by which they are formulated, or the underlying assumptions evident in the mainstream discourse?

3   What lessons do grassroots initiatives to combat FGM hold for the language and application of universal human rights?

---

[153]   See UNICEF Innocenti Digest, *Changing a Harmful Social Convention: Female Genital Mutilation/Cutting* (Florence: UNICEF Innocenti Research Centre, 2005, reprinted 2008), 24, and UNICEF, *Long-term evaluation of the Tostan Programme in Senegal: Kolda, Thies and Fatick Regions* (New York: UNICEF, 2008).

[154]   UNICEF Innocenti Digest, above note 153, 13–14.

FURTHER READING

Anghie, A., *Imperialism, Sovereignty and the Making of International Law* (Cambridge University Press, 2004).

An Na'im, A. A. (ed.), *Human Rights in Cross-Cultural Perspectives: A Quest for Consensus* (Philadelphia: University of Pennsylvania Press, 1990).

Arendt, H., *The Origins of Totalitarianism* (New York: Schocken Books, 1951).

Baxi, U., *The Future of Human Rights*, 3rd edn (Oxford University Press, 2008).

Cook, R. J. (ed.), *Human Rights of Women: National and International Perspectives* (Philadelphia: University of Pennsylvania Press, 1994).

Donnelly, J., *Universal Human Rights in Theory and Practice*, 2nd edn (Ithaca and London: Cornell University Press, 2003).

Douzinas, C., *The End of Human Rights: Critical Legal Thought at the Turn of the Century* (Oxford: Hart, 2000).

Eide, A. *et al.* (eds.), *The Universal Declaration of Human Rights: A Commentary* (Oxford University Press, 1992).

Evans, T. (ed.), *Human Rights Fifty Years on: A Reappraisal* (Manchester University Press, 1998).

Freeman, M., *Human Rights: An Interdisciplinary Approach*, 2nd edn (Cambridge Malden, MA: Polity Press, 2011).

Gearty, C. and Douzinas, C., *The Cambridge Companion to Human Rights Law* (Cambridge University Press, 2012).

Goodale, M., *Surrendering to Utopia: An Anthropology of Human Rights* (Palo Alto, CA: Stanford University Press, 2009).

Ishay, M. R., *The History of Human Rights: From Ancient Times to the Globalization Era* (Berkeley, Los Angeles, London: University of California Press, 2008).

Morsink, J., *Inherent Human Rights: Philosophical Roots of the Universal Declaration* (Philadelphia: University of Pennsylvania Press, 2009).

Mutua, M., *Human Rights: A Political and Cultural Critique* (Philadelphia: University of Pennsylvania Press, 2002).

Pogge, T., *World Poverty and Human Rights: Cosmopolitan Responsibilities and Reforms*, 2nd edn (Cambridge: Polity Press, 2008).

Rajagopal, B., *International Law from Below: Development, Social Movements and Third World Resistance* (Cambridge University Press, 2003).

Twining, W., *General Jurisprudence: Understanding Law from a Global Perspective* (Cambridge University Press, 2009).

Waldron, J., *Nonsense upon Stilts: Bentham, Marx and Burke on the Rights of Man* (London, New York: Methuen, 1987).

2 International human rights law: the normative framework

CONTENTS

2.1 INTRODUCTION

The multiple voices making up the field of international human rights are one of its defining characteristics. Diplomats, officials, politicians, social movements, NGOs, academics from various disciplines, commentators and the public at large contribute to debate and practice. They add to, and often complement, the work of (international) lawyers. The interaction of this multitude of actors has stimulated the development of international human rights law. However, it has also increased the scope for misunderstandings and misrepresentations of the law that may be misleading, if not damaging. International human rights law is a normative legal system that has its own rules and methods, which, even if contested, frame the consideration of arising questions. For example, claims that the death penalty is unlawful under international law, while welcome from an advocacy perspective, may be seen as turning what ought to be the law (*de lege ferenda*) into a statement about what the law is (*de lege lata*). If such a claim were to be framed as a legal argument, it would have to be developed very carefully with adequate references so as not to risk undermining the (legal) credibility of the person or organisation making it. Such a risk is particularly evident when assertions made – such as that a successor government may not be responsible for the violations committed by the government preceding it (in an NGO report on Iraq) – reveal fundamental misconceptions of international law, in this case the difference between the succession of governments and states.[1]

The need for a sound understanding of the normative legal framework and for conceptual clarity applies particularly to those working in the field of international law. The sociology of international law has been aptly described as one of practice ('commentators' such as legal advisors and judges seeking to determine the law), propaganda (states using legal arguments) and principle (academics reflecting on foundational questions).[2] In other words, the standpoint(s) of the various actors are informed by their positions and how they approach the law. This plurality of actors may give rise to prolonged debates, especially where no judicial (or quasi-judicial) body is called upon to adjudicate the legal questions raised, which broadens the scope for legal indeterminacy. This indeterminacy opens space for the progressive development of international human rights law but may equally create tension, particularly where states disagree with certain interpretations. Conflicts also arise because of the ever widening reach of adjudication of questions of human rights law, such as its application to the extraterritorial conduct of states. This process may result in what has been referred to as the fragmentation of international law, which raises the spectre that different bodies, such as the ICJ, international criminal tribunals and human rights treaty bodies, develop diverging interpretations of the law.[3] An informed discourse is in these contexts important for the coherence and legitimacy of the system.

International human rights law is part of the broader normative legal framework of public international law[4] and shares a number of its features, including sources, obligations (primary rules) and state responsibility (secondary rules).[5] While international human rights law has formed within the broader setting of international law, it has developed distinctive features. Traditional international law was an order based on the sovereign interests of states as its sole subjects. In contrast, international human rights law is

---

[1] Succession of governments is generally considered not to affect state responsibility whereas state succession may. See P. Dumberry, *State Succession to International Responsibility* (Leiden, Boston: Martinus Nijhoff, 2007).

[2] M. Mendelson, 'Practice, Propaganda and Principle in International Law (Inaugural Lecture)', *CLP* 42 (1989), 1–19.

[3] See Report of the Study Group of the ILC, Fragmentation of International Law: Difficulties Arising from the Diversification and Expansion of International Law, UN Doc. A/CN.4/L.682 (13 April 2006) and UN Doc. A/CN.4/L.682/Add.1 (2 May 2006).

[4] See in this context, M. T. Kamminga and M. Scheinin (eds.), *The Impact of Human Rights Law on General International Law* (Oxford University Press, 2009).

[5] See on the applicability of the ILC Draft Articles on State Responsibility their article 33(2).

characterised by its emphasis on common interests that reflect the fundamental values of the international legal order. This value-based approach is
evident in the concept of *jus cogens*, or peremptory norm, and the notion of
erga omnes, obligations owed to the international community as a whole.
The substantive emphasis on common interests is mirrored in the preference for multilateral instruments. The making of treaties and declarations,
such as the CRC or the UN Declaration on the Rights of Indigenous Peoples,
frequently involves a large number of actors, including international civil
society. Human rights treaties agreed upon in these processes are 'objective
regimes' that are meant to benefit individual and collective rights-holders
rather than serving reciprocal state interests. They also typically encompass
monitoring bodies that have sought to develop the distinctive features of
human rights treaties in their practice. The HRCtee, for example, has limited
the scope for reservations and declared successor states bound by human
rights, these being interpretations that diverge from positions considered to
reflect general international law.[6] The supervisory features of human rights
treaties have raised the question of whether they are self-contained or special
regimes, i.e. systems that exclude recourse to other measures of enforcement,
a question that goes to the core of the relationship between international
human rights law and general international law.

Undoubtedly, international human rights can form an important component of a new international order[7] or international constitutionalism. However, unilateralism, selectivity and fragmentation, in addition to challenges
of effective implementation, are restraining factors that may slow down if not
undermine the development at the international level.[8] This chapter examines these dynamics and discusses the key building blocks of international
(human rights) law: its sources;[9] its rights and obligations and the scope of
their application; and its implementation as well as state responsibility and
enforcement.

---

[6] See HRCtee, General Comment 24: Issues relating to reservations made upon ratification or
accession to the Covenant or the Optional Protocols thereto, or in relation to declarations
under article 41 of the Covenant, UN Doc. CCPR/C/21/Rev.1/Add.6 (4 November 1994) and
general comment 26: Continuity of obligations, UN Doc. CCPR/C/21/Rev.1/Add.8/Rev.1
(8 December 1997).

[7] See P. Allott, *Eunomia: New Order for a New World*, 2nd edn (Oxford University Press,
2001).

[8] See for a thorough debate and for an approach based on social constructivism,
O. Diggelmann and T. Altwicker, 'Is there Something like a Constitution of International
Law: Critical Analysis of the Debate on World Constitutionalism', *ZaöRV* 68 (2008),
623–50.

[9] General principles as one of the sources referred to in article 38(1) of the ICJ Statute are not
dealt with separately in this chapter. See for a brief discussion of general principles, O. De
Schutter, *International Human Rights Law* (Cambridge University Press, 2010), 53–5.

2.2   SOURCES

2.2.1   Treaties

Treaties are referred to in article 38 of the ICJ Statute as one of the recognised sources of international law. They are bilateral or multilateral agreements between states[10] governed by the Vienna Convention on the Law of Treaties (VCLT) of 1969, which is widely seen as reflecting customary international law.[11] In the human rights sphere treaties take several names, such as 'covenant', 'convention', 'charter' or 'protocol' where they relate to another treaty. The name of a treaty reflects the symbolic significance attached to it by its drafters but does not entail separate legal consequences. As an agreement, a treaty requires consent, which can be expressed by way of 'signature, exchange of instruments constituting a treaty, ratification, acceptance, approval or accession, or by any other means if so agreed'.[12] The surest way to find out about the actual status of a treaty, i.e. date of adoption, coming into force, states parties, reservations, etc., is to access the databases available online, in particular the UN Treaty Collection.[13]

Treaty-making

Multilateral human rights treaties are frequently the outcome of a long and often complex deliberative process involving a number of actors. Nevertheless, once agreed upon, their existence and content are often taken for granted and do indeed have a self-validating quality, not least as a matter of positive law. However, there are several reasons why an understanding of the treaty-making process is important. It can shed light on the various interpretations put forward by states, experts and others, which, in the form of the so-called *travaux préparatoires* (preparatory work), can help in interpreting the treaty.[14] In addition, it can reveal the historical context and the political motives, role and positions of states and others, such as international organisations and civil society. It may also explain why certain states have (not)

---

[10] See on the nature of agreements between states and non-state actors, particularly peace agreements, C. Bell, *On the Law of Peace, Peace Agreements and the Lex Pacificatoria* (Oxford University Press, 2008), 127–43.

[11] See A. Aust, *Modern Treaty Law and Practice*, 2nd edn (Cambridge University Press, 2007), 6–31.

[12] See article 11 VCLT.

[13] The UN Treaty Collection is accessible at http://treaties.un.org. The status of regional treaties can be found on the websites of the respective organisations, namely the Council of Europe (CoE), Organisation of American States (OAS) and African Union (AU).

[14] Article 32 VCLT. See for example the selected preparatory works for the ICCPR, available at http://untreaty.un.org/cod/avl/ha/iccpr/iccpr.html.

become parties, and why a treaty has been a success or a failure. The position of states in these processes is also important in evaluating whether a specific norm contained in a treaty has the status of customary international law (see below at 2.2.2).

Multilateral treaties go through a series of stages before adoption and coming into force. There is no fixed process or formula for the making of treaties. The idea, initiative or impetus for a treaty can emerge from different sources, which have included individuals (Raphael Lemkin in respect of the Convention against Genocide);[15] NGOs (Amnesty International (AI) and others on the CAT);[16] states (Caribbean states on the ICC);[17] intergovernmental organisations (IGOs) (the UN on the International Bill of Rights);[18] expert commissions (such as the ILC);[19] or a combination of these.[20] The power of actors, the ability to participate effectively and the capacity to own both the process and the product have been identified as key factors in these processes.[21]

The process of '[h]uman rights treaty negotiations may involve the UNGA, the Committee,[22] the Economic and Social Council, the Human Rights Council and an intergovernmental conference'.[23] Depending on the procedures and practice of the body concerned or the conference convened, civil society will have varying degrees of influence.[24] NGOs may be able to observe and lobby delegates but also to make submissions, which may be taken into consideration during the drafting.[25] The ICC Rome Statute is a recent example of the important role played by NGOs in the development of international treaties. At the Rome conference NGOs were well represented, gave public statements, lobbied and succeeded in strengthening several

---

[15] See R. Lemkin, *Axis Rule in Occupied Europe: Laws of Occupation, Analysis of Government, Proposals for Redress* (Washington, DC: Carnegie Endowment for International Peace, 1944), 79–98 and W. Schabas, *Genocide in International Law: The Crime of Crimes*, 2nd edn (Cambridge University Press, 2009), 17–90.

[16] J. H. Burgers and H. Danelius, *The United Nations Convention against Torture: A Handbook on the Convention against Torture and Other Cruel, Inhuman or Degrading Treatment or Punishment* (Dordrecht: Martinus Nijhoff, 1988), 13–29.

[17] See UNGA resolution 44/39 (1989).

[18] See section 1.2.5.

[19] See for the ILC's work, www.un.org/law/ilc/index.htm.

[20] See for further examples, M. Mutua, 'Standard Setting in Human Rights: Critique and Prognosis', *HRQ* 29(3) (2007), 547–630.

[21] Ibid., 557.

[22] See for the work of the UNGA's third committee, www.un.org/en/ga/third.

[23] See A. Boyle and C. Chinkin, *The Making of International Law*, (Oxford University Press, 2007), 166–83.

[24] See on a duty to consult NGOs, S. Charnovitz, 'Nongovernmental Organizations and International Law', *AJIL* 100(2) (2006), 348–72, at 368–72.

[25] For further examples of the role of NGOs in treaty-making, see Boyle and Chinkin, above note 23, 41–97, and Mutua, above note 20, 593–604.

areas of the treaty, such as by the inclusion of gender crimes and victims' rights.[26]

Draft texts often undergo a series of changes, with articles added or omitted and the text being amended, as a result of deliberations that reflect the positions of states and their willingness to compromise. Political stakes, leverage, force of personality and argument, as well as the dynamics of the moment, will often dictate the outcome of treaty negotiations. A major factor is the acceptability of the final draft, which poses a perennial dilemma: to what degree should the text of a document be compromised in order to persuade other states to join? This is a delicate balance that needs to be struck at the drafting stage, which is closely related to the procedure for adopting the text. Consensus may enhance acceptability but may come at the price of compromising the text. Conversely, where a text is adopted by majority, opposition and subsequent non-ratification may undermine the universality and effectiveness of the treaty concerned. Following adoption, the treaty will be open for signature. Multilateral treaties need to have a sufficient number of states parties to command legitimacy. The number of ratifications[27] needed for a treaty to come into force varies but most instruments set the bar at twenty ratifications. An initially low number of parties may help in creating momentum by making the treaty a reality, which may attract other states to follow. There is, however, an equal risk that a treaty limps along and carries limited weight if the number remains low.[28] This explains why fundamental treaties setting up institutions with universal scope, such as the ICC Rome Statute, require a larger number of states parties (sixty);[29] the high threshold is justified by the universal ambition and the commitments that states parties have to undertake in order to make such a treaty work.

The number of states parties a treaty attracts depends on several factors: degree of consensus; acceptability; strength of ratification campaigns; international and institutional support for a treaty; and the record of the body established to monitor the treaty's implementation. Examples of treaties with a high number of states parties are both covenants (ICCPR and ICESCR) and the CRC,[30] which are widely seen as treaties to which a state must be party to show a degree of 'human rights acceptability'. Other treaties have been

---

[26] See in particular the work of the Coalition for the ICC, www.iccnow.org. See also M. J. Struett, *The Politics of Constructing the International Criminal Court: NGOs, Discourse and Agency* (New York, Basingstoke: Palgrave Macmillan, 2008).

[27] Or other means expressing consent to be bound.

[28] See for example the 1986 Convention on the Non-applicability of Statutory Limitations to War Crimes and Crimes against Humanity, which has only attracted fifty-four parties as of 14 May 2012.

[29] Article 126(1) ICC Rome Statute.

[30] As of 14 July 2012, CPED as the latest treaty to come into force had 34 parties, CRPD 117 parties, CAT 150, ICESCR 160, ICCPR 167, ICERD 175, CEDAW 187 and the CRC 193.

less successful because they are perceived to carry less weight or are politically more controversial. An example is the ICRMW which has been ratified and acceded to by most migrant sending states but has received virtually no endorsement by receiving states, which has undermined the object of the treaty.[31]

As instruments, treaties are the hallmark of positive law, i.e. the law posited and explicitly agreed upon by states in a formal procedure. It is mainly for this reason that they are a prized tool in advocacy efforts aimed at standard-setting and strengthening the legal recognition and implementation of human rights. While important, adoption and ratification of treaties are not ends in themselves. The number of treaties and treaty parties does not automatically translate into better protection, as there frequently remains a considerable gap between the treaty rhetoric and motives for accession thereto, on the one hand, and the reality of implementation on the other.[32]

Reservations

Unless a treaty provides otherwise, states can enter reservations, defined as 'a unilateral statement, however phrased or named, made by a State, when signing, ratifying, accepting, approving or acceding to a treaty, whereby it purports to exclude or to modify the legal effect of certain provisions of the treaty in their application to that state'.[33] In other words, reservations allow states to limit the scope of their obligations; in practice, states often do.[34]

Reservations to human rights treaties essentially constitute a compromise that seeks to address the fundamental dilemma between sovereignty and the pursuit of collective goals. A categorical position, i.e. prohibiting states from making reservations, risks having fewer states parties while placing no limits on entering reservations may defeat the object and purpose of a treaty. Reservations are in this light a pragmatic device that allows states to overcome potential stumbling blocks to becoming a party, namely obligations that are not agreeable. However, this pragmatism comes at the price of fragmentation because the fact that not all states have the same obligations may undermine the integrity of a treaty and frustrate its objectives. Reservations therefore raise a series of questions. What are the acceptable limits to making reservations? What should be the consequence of invalid reservations? And who should decide on the validity of reservations and their consequences?

---

[31] Forty-six states parties as of 14 July 2012.

[32] See in particular the much discussed study by O. A. Hathaway, 'Do Human Rights Treaties Make a Difference?', *Yale L.J.* 118(8) (2002), 1935–2042.

[33] Article 2(1)(d) VCLT.

[34] The text of reservations can be found on the UN Treaty Collection website, http://treaties.un.org, under 'Status of Treaties' following the chart for signatures and ratifications.

Some treaties prohibit the making of reservations, whereas others apply the general rule, whether explicitly stated or not, that reservations must not run counter to the object and purpose of the treaty. This rule was developed by the ICJ and incorporated in the VCLT, replacing the previous purely consent-based system under which states could make reservations that other parties were free to accept or reject.[35]

There is no general rule that says when a reservation runs counter to a treaty's object and purpose. However, the practice of states and treaty bodies provides ample illustration and guidance. To begin with, states parties cannot derogate from *jus cogens* norms and non-derogable rights that are fundamental to a treaty.[36] Reservations in relation to other rights may be incompatible with general principles, such as equality, or may undermine the very rationale of the treaty concerned. An example of this kind is the reservation entered by the government of Kuwait to CEDAW according to which it 'reserves its right not to implement the provision contained in article 9, paragraph 2, of the Convention,[37] inasmuch as it runs counter to the Kuwaiti Nationality Act, which stipulates that a child's nationality shall be determined by that of his father'.[38] Beyond this, human rights treaty bodies and states have frequently raised concerns about general and vague statements that do not provide a sufficiently clear indication of how they affect a state's obligations and may effectively nullify them.[39] This applies in particular to declarations that a treaty or a specific article is to be interpreted in conformity with national legislation.[40] For example, Saudi Arabia entered the following reservation to CEDAW: 'In case of contradiction between any term of the Convention and the norms of Islamic law, the Kingdom is not under obligation to observe the contradictory terms of the Convention'. Finland objected to the reservation, stating that:

A reservation which consists of a general reference to religious law and national law without specifying its contents...does not clearly define to other Parties to the

---

[35] Article 19 VCLT. See also *Reservations to the Convention on the Prevention and Punishment of the Crime of Genocide*, Advisory opinion, ICJ Reports 1951, 15.

[36] HRCtee, General Comment 24, paras. 8–10, in which the HRCtee applies this rule equally to rights having the status of customary international law.

[37] 'States Parties shall grant women equal rights with men with respect to the nationality of their children.'

[38] See reference to text and objections by other states parties, Finland, the Netherlands, Sweden, online, at http://treaties.un.org/Pages/ViewDetails.aspx?src=TREATY&mtdsg_no=IV-8&chapter=4&lang=en#31.

[39] See article 57(1) ECHR: 'Reservations of a general character shall not be permitted under this Article', and HRCtee, General Comment 24, para. 19.

[40] See for example Bangladesh's reservation to article 14 CAT and Spain's response thereto, online, at http://treaties.un.org/Pages/ViewDetails.aspx?src=TREATY&mtdsg_no=IV-9&chapter=4&lang=en#14.

Convention the extent to which the reserving State commits itself to the Convention and therefore creates serious doubts as to the commitment of the reserving State to fulfil its obligations under the Convention. Furthermore, reservations are subject to the general principle of treaty interpretation according to which a party may not invoke the provisions of its domestic law as justification for a failure to perform its treaty obligations.[41]

As a matter of general practice, human rights treaty bodies regularly recommend, albeit with limited success, that states parties withdraw reservations made.[42]

General international law, as developed by the ICJ and codified in the VCLT, principally leaves it to other states parties to object to what they consider invalid reservations. In principle, the relevant treaty provisions apply between the states parties concerned unless the objecting state expressly states its intention that they should not do so.[43] This approach, which is effectively based on reciprocity, is unsatisfactory when applied to international human rights treaties whose primary objective is to create an objective regime binding all parties. The HRCtee strongly made this point in its general comment 24, in which it reserved the right to decide whether a particular reservation was compatible with the ICCPR's object and purpose.[44] In its jurisprudence, it held that a reservation by Trinidad and Tobago according to which the HRCtee was not competent to consider death penalty cases was incompatible with the ICCPR's object and purpose because it 'singles out a certain group of individuals for lesser procedural protection than that which is enjoyed by the rest of the population'.[45] The ECtHR found in *Belilos* v. *Switzerland* that Switzerland's declaration on the right to a fair trial was too general and was incompatible with (the then) article 64 ECHR.[46] Similarly, a declaration made by Turkey that limited the ECtHR's jurisdiction in relation to Northern Cyprus was held to violate (the then) articles 25 and 46 ECHR.[47]

Importantly, as a result of their findings, the ECtHR and the HRCtee have simply excluded invalid reservations with the effect that a state party is bound by the treaty (provision) in question. This is problematic because treaty bodies assume the right effectively to overrule the lack of state consent. As a result, a state that makes a reservation to a human rights treaty

---

[41] See http://treaties.un.org/Pages/ViewDetails.aspx?src=TREATY&mtdsg_no=IV-8&chapter=4&lang=en.

[42] See HRCtee, General Comment 24, para. 20, and, generally, the concluding observations of UN human rights treaty bodies.

[43] Articles 20(4)(b) and 21 VCLT.

[44] HRCtee, General Comment 24, para. 18.

[45] *Kennedy* v. *Trinidad and Tobago*, UN Doc. CCPR/C/67/D/845/1999 (2 November 1999), para. 6.7.

[46] *Belilos* v. *Switzerland*, (1988) 10 EHRR 466, paras. 50–60.

[47] *Loizidou* v. *Turkey*, Preliminary objections, (1995) 20 EHRR 99, paras. 15, 27, 90–98.

faces the risk of being fully bound even if this outcome runs counter to its declared intention. From the perspective of an effective multilateral regime, severing reservations is preferable to the exclusion of a state party or the *de facto* acceptance of an incompatible reservation. However, it carries the risk that a state may choose not to become a party where it expects that its reservation may be invalidated. A state that is already a party may oppose the interpretation and question the right of the treaty body to impose an obligation it has not consented to, which may potentially result in a stand-off or even the denunciation of a treaty.[48] The repercussions of the approach taken by human rights treaty bodies became highly visible when France, the USA and the UK objected strongly to General Comment 24, accusing the HRCtee of effectively usurping the rights of states parties and acting *ultra vires* (beyond its competence).[49] Further instances of disagreements over reservations can be expected. However, it is difficult to see how human rights treaty bodies can resolve the dilemma of invalid reservations other than by severing them without compromising the integrity of the treaty in question.

2.2.2   Customary international law

Customary international law, namely 'international custom, as evidence of a general practice accepted as law'[50] – in other words state practice accompanied by *opinio juris*, i.e. belief in the binding nature of a rule – is the other main source of international law.[51] Establishing the recognition and content of a rule under customary international law will often be crucial to determine what, if any, legal obligations a state has. The subject matter of several areas of international human rights law may not (yet) be (fully) governed by a treaty. This applies to most human rights at some stage in their development; current examples are the law governing the rights of indigenous peoples[52] and

---

[48] Trinidad and Tobago denounced the Optional Protocol after the HRCtee had ruled in *Kennedy v. Trinidad and Tobago* that the reservation entered was invalid. See *Kennedy v. Trinidad and Tobago*, UN Doc. CCPR/C/74/D/845/1998 (26 March 2002), para. 10.

[49] The observations by the UK, the USA and France on General Comment 24 can be found in Report of the HRCtee, UN Doc. A/50/40 (3 October 1995), Annex IV (USA and UK), and UN Doc. A/51/40 (13 April 1997), Annex VI (France).

[50] Article 38(1)(b) of the ICJ Statute.

[51] See on customary international law generally, H. Thirlway, 'Sources of International Law', in M. Evans (ed.), *International Law*, 3rd edn (Oxford University Press, 2010), 95–121, and ILA, *Final Report of the Committee, Statement of Principles Applicable to the Formation of General Customary International Law*, London Conference, 2000, available on the Association's website, www.ila-hq.org.

[52] The rights of indigenous peoples have been recognised in UNGA resolution 61/295 (2007) but have not been explicitly recognised in treaty law though human rights treaty bodies have provided some recognition and protection in their jurisprudence. See section 10.4.

internally displaced persons.[53] Alternatively, a treaty may govern a particular area of the law but a state may not be a party. Random examples are the US non-ratification of the CRC and Thailand's non-ratification of the Refugee Convention. In addition, alleged violations may date back a long time, for example, torture during colonial times, and it may not be clear whether the prohibition was already recognised at the time. Customary international law is in these circumstances critical to establishing a state's obligation and responsibility and to monitor compliance with international standards.

Customary international law is by its nature rather indeterminate. Beyond some well-established categories, such as the prohibition of torture, there is considerable uncertainty about which rights have customary status. This relative flexibility and openness can become an important tool for advocates to make claims that a rule or a right has attained or is in the process of attaining such status under international law. Where such claims gain traction, they can be highly effective. An example would be the long-standing campaign to outlaw the death penalty, which has contributed to its regional abolition in Europe.[54] On the political plane, states can use multilateral channels to develop and garner support for a rule of customary international law or, conversely, to put forward positions that thwart the recognition of rights viewed as contrary to a state's interest. Attempts aimed at achieving the recognition of the right to development illustrate this struggle. While the UNGA issued a landmark resolution on this right in 1986, its customary law status has remained the subject of controversy.[55]

The process of establishing custom, i.e. determining what constitutes evidence, poses a number of methodological challenges.[56] This is particularly pronounced in the field of human rights where evidence of custom is often largely based on declaratory sources, such as the UDHR, rather than on other forms of state practice.[57] The privileging of statements and values expressed in such instruments is problematic as it may open a gap between aspirations

---

[53] With the exception of the 2009 Kampala Convention on Internally displaced persons (IDPs).

[54] See section 8.2.5.

[55] See S. P. Marks, 'The Human Right to Development: between Rhetoric and Reality', *Harv. Hum. Rts. J.* 17 (2004), 137–68, and Arjun Sengupta, 'On the Theory and Practice of the Right to Development', *HRQ* (24)4 (2002), 837–89. See also section 12.3.

[56] For a critical assessment of the ICJ's approach see Boyle and Chinkin, above note 23, 278–85.

[57] See on evidence of state practice in the field of human rights, American Law Institute, *Restatement (Third) of the Foreign Relations Law of the United States*, §701 (2). See for a recent example of practical application in a related field the International Committee of the Red Cross (ICRC) landmark study, J.-M. Henckaerts and L. Doswald-Beck (eds.), *Customary International Humanitarian Law*. Vol. I: *Rules* and vol. II: *Practice* (ICRC and Cambridge University Press, 2005), and ICRC Customary International Humanitarian Law Database, www.icrc.org/customary-ihl/eng/docs/home.

and reality, i.e. 'words are cheap'.[58] A further challenge consists in establishing the evidentiary value of conflicting state practice, torture being a well-known and vexing example. While states regularly vote for declarations affirming the absolute prohibition of torture with national laws stipulating such prohibition, torture is still practised all too frequently. However, the actual practice is widely considered irrelevant where states do not seek to justify it as lawful. This is effectively what the ICJ held in a well-known passage in *Nicaragua* v. *USA*.[59] The rationale for the position is sound because customary international law concerns the normative status of a rule. The discrepancy between normative requirements and realities on the ground is an unfortunate feature of international human rights law, and upholding and reinforcing the normative status of a rule has been one of the key means of limiting existing discrepancies. However, it is equally clear that persistent breaches of a norm, even if publicly denied by the alleged offenders, may undermine the normative force of custom if it is seen as something that states pay lip service to but do not adhere to in actual practice.

A different question arises where the right or rule is already governed by a treaty, namely whether treaties count as state practice. For example, when seeking to specify the USA's obligations in respect of the rights of the child (the USA is not a party to the CRC), is it possible to use CRC-related practice as evidence that its standards are of a customary nature? Treaties are a separate source and by becoming a party states incur rights and obligations according to treaty law. However, it would be paradoxical if the very fact of overwhelming treaty membership were to preclude resort to a treaty as evidence of custom.[60] It is therefore generally accepted that treaties count as state practice. This is particularly important for multilateral – so-called lawmaking – treaties aimed at codifying or 'crystallising' customary international law, which includes major human rights treaties. While treaty practice carries some weight, its evidentiary value for determining the customary status of a particular article or right needs to be assessed with reference to supporting state practice. The question of treaties as state practice needs to be distinguished from the relationship between treaties and customary international

---

[58] In International Criminal Tribunal for the Former Yugoslavia (ICTY), *Prosecutor* v. *Tadić*, Appeals Chamber Decision on the defense motion for interlocutory appeal on jurisdiction (2 October 1995), para. 99, the Tribunal emphasised that since in the field of international humanitarian law it would be impracticable to discern state practice with reference to the conduct of troops on the battlefield, 'reliance must primarily be placed on such elements as official pronouncements of States, military manuals and judicial decisions'.

[59] *Military and Paramilitary Activities in and against Nicaragua* (*Nicaragua* v. *United States of America*), Merits, Judgment, ICJ Reports 1986, 14, paras. 206–9 (regarding the principle of non-intervention).

[60] See R. R. Baxter, 'Multilateral Treaties as Evidence of Customary International Law', *BYIL* 41 (1965–6), 275–300.

law. Treaties governing the same subject matter will be *lex specialis* but customary international law may still apply where there is a gap or a conflict on jurisdictional grounds.[61] In addition, subsequent practice of states parties may affect the interpretation of a treaty.[62]

The legal consequence of a rule of customary international law is that a state is bound to respect the right in question. This applies irrespective of whether a state has consented to the rule, unless it has persistently objected to it. The exception of a persistent objector is recognised in order to allow states to opt out of permissive custom (with the exception of peremptory norms having *jus cogens* status, see below) but plays a limited role in the practice of international human rights law.[63] New states are widely considered to be bound by customary international law although this argument can be contested on the grounds that it violates consent, which some consider to be a basis of any obligation under international law.[64]

The UDHR and customary international law

The UDHR is still paradigmatic for the role of custom in the field of international human rights law. As a UNGA declaration, it constitutes neither a treaty nor a formal source of international law. However, it is often assumed or claimed that the UDHR has the status of customary international law. Such an assertion needs careful consideration. (1) Did the UDHR constitute state practice? Yes, voting for UNGA declarations is recognised as state practice. (2) Was this practice accompanied by *opinio juris*? This question is more difficult to answer in the affirmative because the UDHR was primarily seen as an agreement on, and declaration of, fundamental principles serving as a first step towards a binding International Bill of Rights rather than referring to binding rights and obligations or constituting an authoritative interpretation of the UN Charter (a treaty). (3) Has the UDHR been recognised in state practice since its adoption? Answering this question requires evaluating the weight given to the declaration or its provisions at the time and an analysis of its subsequent application in state practice. Relevant evidence comprises in particular recognition of UDHR articles in treaties; reference to the UDHR or its articles in declarations, resolutions or similar statements; reference to the UDHR or its articles in the practice of international and regional bodies; incorporation of the UDHR or its articles in national constitutions and legislation as well as application by national courts and other bodies.

---

[61] *Nicaragua* v. *USA*, paras. 175–9.

[62] See in particular article 31(3)(b) VCLT.

[63] See ILA, above note 51, 27–9, and P. Dumberry, 'Incoherent and Ineffective: the Concept of Persistent Objector Revisited', *ICLQ* 59(3) (2010), 779–802.

[64] See for a critical analysis, M. Craven, 'The Problem of State Succession and the Identity of States under International Law', *EJIL* 9(1) (1998), 142–63, particularly at 157.

Note that the list refers both to the declaration and its articles as a lot of relevant state practice concerns particular UDHR provisions rather than the UDHR as a whole. This is important because some UDHR articles have undoubtedly become customary international law, such as the principle of non-discrimination or the prohibition of slavery, while others may not have, such as the right to rest and leisure.[65] Determining the customary status of any given UDHR article requires rigorous scrutiny of available state practice (reference in treaties, declarations, number of national laws or judgments, etc.) and weight attached to it (number of states parties, voting for declarations, prevalence of laws or judgments). This can be a painstaking methodological exercise. However, bypassing its rigours risks undermining the credibility of any assertion made regarding the customary status of a particular right.[66]

2.2.3   Jurisprudence as source of law

Article 38 of the ICJ statute recognises 'judicial decisions…as subsidiary means for the determination of rules of law'. This provision states the obvious: jurisprudence can provide valuable evidence of the status and content of norms through their interpretation in a given case. It also makes clear that judicial bodies are not considered to have a law-making function.[67] This theoretical premise must not, however, be overstated as such bodies play an increasingly important role in the development of international law.

A number of international treaty bodies apply and interpret international human rights law, drawing on recognised methods of treaty interpretation.[68] By definition, this includes bodies specifically tasked with monitoring a particular human rights treaty and interpreting its provisions. Prominent examples at the international level are the HRCtee and the ECtHR, IACtHR and the African Commission on Human and Peoples' Rights at the regional level.[69] Other international judicial bodies are also increasingly called upon to adjudicate human rights questions. The ICJ, in particular, has made important rulings in a series of contentious cases and advisory opinions that have

---

[65] See for example H. Hannum, 'The Status of the Universal Declaration of Human Rights in National and International Law', *Ga. J. Int'l & Comp. L.* 25 (1/2) (1995–6), 287–397, and critical discussion in B. Simma and P. Alston, 'The Sources of Human Rights Law: Custom, *Jus Cogens* and General Principles', *AYIL* 12 (1988–9), 82–108.

[66] See Simma and Alston, ibid., particularly 83–100.

[67] See Boyle and Chinkin, above note 23, 263–311, on the role of courts in law-making.

[68] Article 31 VCLT. See for an assessment of the practice of UN treaty bodies in this regard, K. Mechlem, 'Treaty Bodies and the Interpretation of Human Rights', *Vand. J. Transnat'l L.* 42(3) (2009), 905–48.

[69] See Chapters 5 and 6.

a direct bearing on international human rights law.[70] Recently established international criminal tribunals also refer to, or apply human rights law in their jurisprudence, for example when interpreting the elements of crimes or when defining the rights of the defence.[71] Regionally, the European Court of Justice (ECJ) and African regional community courts have issued landmark judgments in the field of human rights, such as the ECJ in *Carpenter*[72] and the Economic Community of West African States (ECOWAS) Court in *Mani* v. *Niger*.[73] In addition, domestic courts are frequently seized with cases in which they have to interpret international human rights law. Courts have become particularly prominent in adjudicating a series of highly charged cases in the context of counter-terrorism measures and human rights, such as the UK House of Lords in *A and others* v. *Secretary of State*, which effectively ended the system of indefinite detention of foreign nationals suspected of terrorism.[74]

These developments have led to an intensification of the adjudication of international human rights law, largely prompted by victims, human rights lawyers and NGOs, as well as states and others in cases before the ICJ.[75] The increased application, along with the scrutiny and cross-referencing that it entails, has resulted in a more sophisticated understanding and maturing of international human rights law. However, it has also increased the risk of fragmentation, diverging interpretations of rules depending on which body is seized with a particular question.[76] As there is no formal hierarchy

---

[70] See G. Zyberi, *The Humanitarian Face of the International Court of Justice: Its Contribution to Interpreting and Developing International Human Rights and Humanitarian Law Rules and Principles* (Antwerp: Intersentia, 2008), and S. R. S. Bedi, *The Development of Human Rights Law by the Judges of the International Court of Justice* (Oxford: Hart, 2007).

[71] See multiple contributions in C. Eboe-Osuji (ed.), *Protecting Human Rights: Essays in International Law and Policy in Honour of Navanethem Pillay* (Leiden, Boston: Martinus Nijhoff, 2010).

[72] Case C-60/00, *Mary Carpenter* v. *Secretary of State for the Home Department* [2002] ECR I-6279 (right of spouse not to be deported).

[73] *Mme Hadijatou Mani Koraou* v. *The Republic of Niger* (Judgment of 27 October 2008), ECW/CCJ/JUD/06/08 (prohibition of slavery).

[74] *A and Others* v. *Secretary of State for the Home Department*, [2004] UK House of Lords (UKHL) 56.

[75] For example, NGO advocacy has been credited with leading to the UNGA resolution referring the *Nuclear Weapons* case before the ICJ for an advisory opinion. See R. Falk, 'The Nuclear Weapons Advisory Opinion and the New Jurisprudence of Global Civil Society', *Transnat'l L. & Contemp. Probs.* (1997), 333–52, at 340–2.

[76] See ILC, Fragmentation, above note 3, which discusses several cases, including the difference between the jurisprudence of the ICTY and ICJ on the question of 'overall control' v. 'effective control'. See *Application of the Convention on the Prevention and Punishment of the Crime of Genocide* (*Bosnia and Herzegovina* v. *Serbia and Montenegro*), Judgment, ICJ Reports 2007, 43, paras. 402–6, rejecting the ICTY's approach as 'unpersuasive'.

between courts, diverging judgments can lead to uncertainty over the state of the law, which in turn may undermine its integrity. However, this risk must not be overstated. It can also be seen as a sign of healthy pluralism where differences in judicial opinion are not resolved through predetermined hierarchies but where contextual 'translation' at the national level[77] and acceptance by other actors will determine legitimacy. Observing the increased adjudication and potential fragmentation of international human rights law, one should not lose sight of the fact that the development of this body of law is far from linear or comprehensive in coverage. Much will depend on what type of cases come before the bodies concerned. This will in turn depend on a range of factors, with the work of human rights lawyers and NGOs being particularly influential in determining the human rights questions that these bodies will address. Given the limited resources of human rights treaty bodies they often rely heavily on pleadings and cases brought by NGOs and other interested groups. Compare, for example, the submissions by complainants and the decision of the African Commission in a recent case against Egypt, in which the Commission found that the imposition of the death penalty following allegations of torture and an unfair trial before the Supreme State Security Emergency Court violated several rights under the ACHPR.[78]

2.2.4   Soft law

What is the status of declarations, resolutions, conference statements and other such documents? These instruments, which are not binding as such, are often referred to as 'soft law'. 'Soft law' is not a formal source of law in its own right. Rather, the term is mainly used to describe non-binding instruments that set standards and/or form part of the law-making process. It may also refer to vague provisions in treaties that do not create discernible obligations.[79] Soft law can therefore be understood as a broad category that captures the increasing plurality and complexity of standard setting and law-making processes. Though strongly contested at times,[80] the term continues to be used as a convenient shorthand.

Soft-law instruments can be part of the formative stages of customary international law or treaty-making. States and international organisations

---

[77] See in particular K. Knop, 'Here and There: International Law in Domestic Courts', *N.Y.U.J. Int'l L. & Pol.* 32 (1999–2000), 501–35.

[78] *Egyptian Initiative for Personal Rights and Interights* v. *Arab Republic of Egypt*, 334/06 (2011).

[79] See for a good overview, A. Boyle, 'Soft Law in International Law Making', in Evans, above note 51, 122–40.

[80] P. Weil, 'Towards Relative Normativity in International Law', *AJIL* 77 (1983), 413–42.

frequently adopt resolutions and such instruments with a view to developing the law. These instruments constitute international law in an embryonic state, which may in time become recognised through one of the formal sources. The UDHR is the best-known example of its kind but there are several other instances in which a treaty has been preceded by a series of resolutions or other soft-law instruments.

In the field of human rights there is a range of documents used for standard-setting aimed at developing best practices and interpreting binding obligations of states. Examples are the UN standards on detention, such as the Standard Minimum Rules for the Treatment of Prisoners, which have been used in the jurisprudence of human rights treaty bodies to determine acceptable conditions of detention.[81] A further example is the Maastricht Guidelines on economic, social and cultural rights developed by a group of experts that has greatly contributed to the normative recognition and justiciability of these rights.[82] Such documents demonstrate the important role that various actors can play in developing and advancing international standards.

Soft-law instruments are also increasingly used by international organisations and states when addressing the role of NSAs. Prominent examples are a number of standard-setting instruments and codes of conducts providing that MNCs adhere to international human rights standards in their operations.[83] Politically, these instruments are based on the premise that MNCs should be directly engaged and that it is in their best interest to adhere to standards. However, limited evidence of compliance and the lack of adequate monitoring and enforcement mechanisms have resulted in criticism that the essentially voluntary arrangements are not effective.[84]

2.2.5   The UNGA Declaration on the Rights of Indigenous Peoples: a soft law success story?

The 2007 UNGA Declaration on the Rights of Indigenous Peoples (UNDRIP) was the outcome of a long process of deliberation, in which the actors achieved a high degree of consensus (143 member states voted in favour

---

[81] See for example HRCtee, General Comment 21: Replaces general comment 9 concerning humane treatment of persons deprived of liberty (Art. 10) (1992), para. 5, referring to relevant UN standards, which have been consistently applied in the Committee's jurisprudence, such as in *Akwanga* v. *Cameroon*, UN Doc. CCPR/C/101/D/1813/2008 (22 March 2011), para. 7.3.

[82] Maastricht Guidelines on Violations of Economic, Social and Cultural Rights 1997, which followed the earlier Limburg Principles on the Implementation of the International Covenant on Economic, Social and Cultural Rights 1987.

[83] See section 16.3.

[84] Ibid.

and 11 states abstained) on a series of controversial matters, such as the individual and collective dimension of indigenous peoples' rights, self-determination and land rights. The four states that voted against the declaration – Australia, Canada, New Zealand and the USA – subsequently endorsed it. This development demonstrates the value that soft-law instruments can have in generating a pull factor and enhancing prospects of compliance.[85]

UNDRIP shows that soft law can have distinct practical advantages. Actors may prefer using soft-law instruments because the very fact that these instruments are non-binding may facilitate reaching consensus. This gives states flexibility to tailor instruments to their needs without having to adhere to the formal requirements involved in treaty-making and amendment, both at the international and national level. However, doubts continue to be expressed over soft law serving as a convenient means for states to escape binding obligations and create mere appearances only.[86] Yet in a system whose enforcement mechanisms are relatively weak and where compliance depends on numerous factors the binding nature of an instrument may not be decisive. This applies especially where states and international organisations have a sufficiently strong interest in adherence. The success of UNDRIP will in this light need to be judged by the extent to which its promise is realised. In practice, while actors have often focused on developing formally binding standards, i.e. treaties, in the field of international human rights law, strategic considerations may weigh in favour of soft-law instruments that promise greater acceptance and may act as a stepping stone for a treaty where needed.

POINTS TO CONSIDER

1 Does UNDRIP demonstrate that giving priority to treaty obligations is misplaced?

2 To what extent can the factors contributing to UNDRIP's success be utilised in other areas of international human rights law? Consider, for example, developments in respect of the rights of internally displaced persons.[87]

---

[85] M. Barelli, 'The Role of Soft Law in the International Legal System: the Case of the United Nations Declaration on the Rights of Indigenous Peoples', *ICLQ* 58(4) (2009), 957–83.

[86] See for an overview of positivist critiques of soft law, J. d'Aspremont, 'Softness in International Law: a Self-serving Quest for New Legal Materials', *EJIL* 19(5) (2008), 1075–93.

[87] See documents relating to relevant international standards on the website of the UN Special Rapporteur on the human rights of internally displaced persons, www.ohchr.org/EN/Issues/IDPersons/Pages/IDPersonsIndex.aspx.

2.2.6   *Jus cogens* and *erga omnes*

The notions of *jus cogens* and *erga omnes* are at the heart of claims that international law is being transformed from a system based on state consent to a constitutional order based on higher values.[88] *Jus cogens* was initially conceived as a principle governing the invalidity of treaties, i.e. delineating the limits of what states could agree on as a matter of treaty law. This rule is laid down in articles 53 and 64 of the VCLT. Article 53 provides that:

> A treaty is void if, at the time of its conclusion, it conflicts with a peremptory norm of general international law. For the purposes of the present Convention, a peremptory norm of general international law is a norm accepted and recognized by the international community of states as a whole as a norm from which no derogation is permitted and which can be modified only by a subsequent norm of general international law having the same character.

An obvious example would be an agreement between two states to torture a person, which would on the face of it be invalid (the example is not as outlandish as it seems given reports about complicity of states in interrogating suspected terrorists).[89] Beyond this narrow scope, *jus cogens* is widely understood to denote a hierarchy of fundamental norms.[90] The resulting, somewhat mythical, status given to *jus cogens* has been mocked and criticised;[91] not surprisingly, the use of the notion opens up the long-standing debate between positive law and natural law, with *jus cogens* seen as a Trojan horse for the revival of the latter.[92]

While the notion of *jus cogens* is often used to elevate certain claims, its source, contents and legal consequences are not fully settled and its practical significance is frequently misunderstood. As a general rule, *jus cogens* norms are formed in the same way as customary international law. Their peremptory status can only be changed if the *opinio juris* that vested the norm with its fundamental nature changes in line with state practice, although this is slightly paradoxical, allowing state practice to change a norm that is deemed absolute and of superior value.[93] In practice, courts either have been reluctant

---

[88] A. Orakhelashvili, 'Peremptory Norms as an Aspect of Constitutionalisation in the International Legal System', in S. Muller and M. Frishman (eds.), *The Dynamics of Constitutionalism in the Age of Globalization* (The Hague: TMC Asser Press, 2009), pp. 153–80. See for a concise overview, D. Shelton, 'International Law and "Relative Normality"', in Evans, above note 51, 141–71, particularly at 146–57.

[89] See section 15.8.1.

[90] See for a feminist critique of *jus cogens* as prioritising male perspectives, H. Charlesworth and C. Chinkin, 'The Gender of *Jus Cogens*', *HRQ* 15(1) (1993), 63–76.

[91] A. D'Amato, 'It's a Bird, it's a Plane, it's *jus cogens*', *Conn. J. Int'l L.* 6(1) (1990), 1–6.

[92] See D. Dobois, 'The Authority of Peremptory Norms in International Law: State Consent or Natural Law?', *NJIL* 78(2) (2009), 133–75.

[93] See critical remarks on this point by D'Amato, above note 91.

to use the term *jus cogens* or have often not elaborated on how they have derived a finding that a norm has attained such status.[94]

The starting point is often the ICJ's famous dictum in the *Barcelona Traction* case, which mentioned genocide, slavery and racial discrimination as obligations *erga omnes* (which may imply their *jus cogens* status, see below).[95] The prohibition of torture has also been referred to as a *jus cogens* norm by courts and human rights treaty bodies.[96] The fact that a right is non-derogable may be indicative, but not all such rights are understood to constitute *jus cogens*.[97] As there is no clear-cut methodology or list of *jus cogens* rights, their acceptance will essentially remain a matter of state practice and judicial interpretation. This opens space for indeterminacy and for the making of broad claims that seek to elevate the status of the norms invoked.[98] A pertinent example that illustrates the possible range of positions is the right to development; while some contest that this has been recognised as a binding right, others have accorded it *jus cogens* status.[99]

Many human rights appear to be natural candidates for *jus cogens* classification and have indeed been referred to, if not recognised, as such.[100] However, claims that a rule has attained *jus cogens* status are at times not only misconceived, they are also often not necessary if the principal aim is to demonstrate that a norm has binding force. This raises the question of the additional legal value of *jus cogens* status beyond its symbolic weight. Beyond the invalidity of treaties, judicial decisions and state practice suggest that states have a duty not to recognise (or contribute to the perpetuation of) situations resulting from violations of *jus cogens* norms and to take measures to bring such situations to an end. In its advisory opinion in the *Wall* case, the ICJ found that states had a duty 'not to recognise the illegal situation resulting from the construction of the wall' arising from the breach of the right to self-determination and fundamental principles of human rights (found to apply *erga omnes*).[101]

---

[94] See Shelton, above note 88.

[95] *Barcelona Traction, Light and Power Company, Limited (Spain* v. *Belgium)*, Judgment, ICJ Reports 1970, 3, para. 33.

[96] Section 8.3.

[97] See for example article 11 ICCPR: 'No one shall be imprisoned merely on the ground of inability to fulfil a contractual obligation', which is non-derogable pursuant to article 4(2) ICCPR.

[98] See U. Linderfalk, 'Normative Conflict and the Fuzziness of the International *ius cogens* Regime', *ZaöRV* 69 (2009), 961–77.

[99] See e.g. M. Bedjaoui, 'The Right to Development', in Bedjaoui (ed.), *International Law: Achievements and Prospects* (Paris, Dordrecht: UNESCO and Martinus Nijhoff, 1991), 1177–1204, at 1183, and S. Chowdhury *et al.*, 'Significance of the Right to Development: an Introductory View', in Chowdhury *et al.* (eds.), *The Right to Development in International Law* (Dordrecht: Nijhoff, 1992), 7–23, at 21.

[100] See Shelton, above note 88, 146–57.

[101] *Legal Consequences of the Construction of a Wall in the Occupied Palestinian Territory*, Advisory opinion, ICJ Reports 2004, 136, para. 159.

Further, it has been recognised that international crimes may not be subject to amnesties[102] and that the international community, through the UN, has a responsibility to protect those at risk of such crimes.[103] However, beyond this the legal consequences of *jus cogens* are less clear.[104]

For example, in the case of *Al Adsani* v. *United Kingdom*, the ECtHR recognised that the prohibition of torture is a *jus cogens* norm but declined to find that it trumped state immunity where a torture victim brought a suit in a third state.[105] The fact that the judgment was based on the narrowest of margins (nine to eight votes) shows that the notion of *jus cogens* can pose considerable challenges, both of a legal and policy nature, for courts and others seized with interpreting the law, where cases pit fundamental values against deeply entrenched rules of international law based on sovereign equality. The call to focus on the values underlying *jus cogens* as a means of a flexible and contextual interpretation of the law rather than the 'mechanical paradigm of non-derogability' is merited.[106] Yet, *jus cogens* is bound to remain a notion that galvanises international lawyers, perhaps for the very reason of its great but elusive, even mystical, promise.[107]

Erga omnes is closely related to but conceptually different from *jus cogens*. It denotes obligations that a state has towards all other states because of the fundamental nature of a particular norm. The scope of the obligation means that all states, as an exception to general rules of international law, have an interest and standing. As stipulated in article 48(1)(b) of the ILC Draft Articles on State Responsibility, states may 'invoke the responsibility of another state ... if the obligation breached is owed to the international community as a whole'. This shift beyond bilateral and reciprocal forms of responsibility applies in particular in the field of human rights characterised by multilateral, shared concerns.[108] Since the ICJ dictum in the *Barcelona Traction* case, the notion of *erga omnes* has been recognised in the ILC Draft Articles

---

[102] *Prosecutor* v. *Furundzjia*, IT-95-17/1-T, ICTY Trial Chamber Judgment of 10 December 1998, para. 155.

[103] See 2005 World Summit Outcome, UNGA 60/1 (24 October 2005), paras. 138–9. See also S. Zifcak, 'The Responsibility to Protect' in Evans, above note 51, resolution 504–29.

[104] See for an engaging discussion of some of the issues raised, A. Bianchi, 'Human Rights and the Magic of *jus cogens*', *EJIL* 19(3) (2008), 491–508.

[105] *Al-Adsani* v. *United Kingdom*, (2001) 273, para. 61. See also *Jurisdictional Immunities of the State* (*Germany* v. *Italy*: Greece intervening), ICJ Judgment of 3 February 2012, paras. 92–7.

[106] Bianchi, above note 104, 505.

[107] Ibid.

[108] See further M. Koskenniemi, 'Solidarity Measures: State Responsibility as a New International Order?', *BYIL* 72 (2001), 337–56, and I. Scobbie, 'The Invocation of Responsibility for the Breach of "Obligations under Peremptory Norms of General International Law"', *EJIL* 13(5) (2002), 1201–20.

on State Responsibility and referred to in jurisprudence.[109] While it has been suggested that all human rights norms apply *erga omnes*,[110] the scope of the obligation is subject to further development in state practice and through judicial determination. It would seem logical that *jus cogens* norms apply *erga omnes*. However, the opposite is not taken for granted[111] and many doctrinal questions remain concerning the relationship of the two concepts and the scope of *erga omnes*.[112]

In practical terms, states can invoke the responsibility of another state (or states) that is in breach of its *erga omnes* obligation to demand that it ceases the wrongful act, guarantees non-repetition and provides reparation to the injured party or beneficiaries.[113] However, the utility of *erga omnes* is somewhat limited because it does not in and of itself confer jurisdiction that does not otherwise exist, as held by the ICJ when Portugal invoked the principle of self-determination in the *East Timor* case to this effect.[114] Where the court or body concerned has jurisdiction, the *erga omnes* nature of the norm at issue may replace the need for a state, as an admissibility criterion, to demonstrate that one of its interests has been affected. Incidentally, this is already standard procedure for inter-state applications under human rights treaty body complaints procedures, where states are assumed to have an interest in compliance by other states parties with the treaty obligations irrespective of whether their own interests are at stake.[115]

QUESTIONS

1   Is the distinction between binding sources of law and soft law artificial, and is it time to abandon it?

2   Why has the notion of *jus cogens* played such an important role in the context of international human rights law?

---

[109] See overview in C. J. Tams, *Enforcing erga omnes Obligations in International Law* (Cambridge University Press, 2005), and ILC Draft Articles on Responsibility of States for Internationally Wrongful Acts with commentaries, 2001, in *Yearbook of the International Law Commission* Vol. II, Part II (United Nations, 2001), 110–16, and 126–7.

[110] See HRCtee, General Comment 31: The nature of the general legal obligation imposed on states parties to the Covenant, UN Doc. CCPR/C/21/Rev.1/Add.13 (26 May 2004), para. 2.

[111] T. Meron, 'On a Hierarchy of International Human Rights', *AJIL* 80 (1986), 1–23 at 11; M. Byers, 'Conceptualising the Relationship between *jus cogens* and *erga omnes* Rules', *NJIL* 66 (1997), 211–39 at 237.

[112] Ibid.

[113] Article 48 ILC Draft Articles on State Responsibility.

[114] *East Timor* (*Portugal* v. *Australia*), Judgment, ICJ Reports 1995, 90, para. 29.

[115] See on this point particular HRCtee, General Comment 31, para. 2.

2.3 RIGHTS, OBLIGATIONS AND SCOPE OF APPLICATION

2.3.1 Rights

A right requires a right-holder. Traditionally, states were considered the only subjects of international law, i.e. as having rights because of their statehood and being able to bring claims against each other. This included the exercise of diplomatic protection where states could raise a claim on behalf of their nationals concerning the violation of minimum standards (many of which would fall within today's human rights guarantees) by a third state.[116] However, importantly, this was seen as the right of a state 'to ensure, in the persons of its subjects, respect for the rules of international law'.[117] While minimum standards for the treatment of aliens and protection for minorities may have provided the nucleus, it was only after 1945 that the individual (in the broadest sense) became recognised as a subject of international law.[118] This means that individuals can hold rights and bring claims, where avenues are available. It also means that individuals are liable for certain breaches of international law, in particular international crimes. The question of whether the individual or the state is, or should be, the true subject of international law, and to what degree the subject status of individuals is dependent on the state, has been widely debated.[119] What matters for practical purposes is that treaties and customary international law recognise individuals as rights-holders, and hence as subjects. Significantly, the recognition of rights is independent of the existence of available remedies, i.e. the fact that an individual may not be able to claim his or her right before any body neither deprives the right of its quality nor the individual of his or her status as a subject.[120]

Rights can be divided into several categories with respect to their: (1) origin and source of validity (natural and positive rights – see Chapter 1); (2) subject or right-holder (individual and group rights); (3) subject matter (civil and

---

[116] *Mavrommatis Palestine Concessions*, Judgment no. 2, 1924; Permanent Court of International Justice (PCIJ), Ser. A, no. 2, 2; ICJ, *Barcelona Traction*, paras. 78–9. See further I. Brownlie, *Principles of Public International Law* (Oxford University Press, 2008), 57–67, and P. Okowa, 'Issues of Admissibility and the Law on International Responsibility', in Evans, above note 51, 472–503, at 476–89.

[117] *Mavrommatis Palestine Concessions*, 2.

[118] See A. A. Cançado Trindade, *The Access of Individuals to International Justice* (Oxford University Press, 2011), 1–16; R. McCorquodale, 'The Individual and the International Legal System', in Evans, above note 51, 284–310; A. Orakhelashvili, 'The Protection of the Individual in International Law', *Cal. W. Int'L L. J.* 31 (2001), 241–76.

[119] See literature in preceding footnote with further references.

[120] *Appeal from a Judgment of the Hungaro/Czechoslovak Mixed Arbitral Tribunal*, Judgment (1933) PCIJ Ser. A/B, no. 61, 208, 231.

political rights; economic, social and cultural rights; collective rights); (4) type (negative or positive rights); and (5) nature (absolute and other, particularly qualified rights).

Most of the rights recognised in international human rights treaties are conceptualised as individual rights. This harks back to the notion that human beings have rights by virtue of their humanity, which was traditionally understood to apply to individuals only. While some of the most prominent human rights in the early twentieth century had a collective dimension, i.e. minority rights, these rights were understood to belong to the individual members of minorities, not to any collective entity.[121] Several objections have been raised against the recognition of collective rights, ranging from the position that human rights can by definition only be vested in the individual, to a number of pragmatic concerns. These include questions of delineation: how to identify groups that should qualify as the right-holder; the nature of rights granted, such as the right to development; the exercise of such rights (representation); conflict between group rights and individual rights; and utility, namely whether group rights are necessary and best suited to protecting the interests and values in question.[122] Politically, Western states and scholars have often been suspicious of collective rights because they were seen as a vehicle for what were considered political demands by socialist and 'Third World' states, in particular in relation to the right to development.[123] This intransigence over the recognition of collective rights has fuelled the debate about the (lack of true) universality of human rights.[124] However, collective rights have now been recognised in treaties, particularly the ACHPR, UN declarations, especially in relation to indigenous peoples, and in the jurisprudence of human rights treaty bodies.[125] While several challenges remain, such as who is entitled to exercise collective rights, how to identify corresponding duty-holders and obligations, such as in respect of the right to development, and how to resolve conflicts between individual and collective rights, the recognition of collective rights has become a fact of international human rights law. Given the collective nature of many human rights violations, it can be expected that collective rights will be of increasing importance in years to come.

---

[121] HRCtee, General Comment 23: The rights of minorities (Art. 27), UN Doc. CCPR/C/21/Rev.1/Add.5 (8 April 1994), paras. 1, 3; P. Thornberry, *International Law and the Rights of Minorities* (Oxford: Clarendon Press, 1991), 113–37.

[122] J. Donnelly, *Universal Human Rights in Theory and Practice*, 2nd edn (Ithaca, NY: Cornell University, 2003), 208–11. See also section 10.2.

[123] See for the political background, B. Rajagopal, *International Law from Below: Development, Social Movements and Third World Resistance* (Cambridge University Press, 2007), 216–22.

[124] Section 1.5.1.

[125] Chapter 10.

Civil and political rights, ESC rights as well as collective rights have been referred to as the three generations of rights, reflecting a narrative according to which these rights have been recognised in that order, which may also be taken to indicate a shift in emphasis.[126] The metaphor of generations has served as a convenient shorthand but constitutes a rather crude and at least partly inaccurate way of describing the development of international human rights law. For practical purposes, each of the three categories has some features which distinguish it from the other categories. However, the main traditional distinction, i.e. that ESC rights have resource implications and are therefore not justiciable, and that collective rights are not genuine rights, has increasingly been called into question.[127] The move towards a more nuanced and holistic understanding of rights is reflected in the oft-repeated mantra that human rights are 'indivisible, interdependent and interrelated', which also serves the political goal of strengthening all sets of rights.[128]

Before systematising the types and nature of rights, it is important to be aware of the role played by fundamental principles that permeate international human rights law, namely equality, freedom and dignity prominently referred to in article 1 UDHR. As stated by the HRCtee '[n]on-discrimination, together with equality before the law and equal protection of the law without any discrimination, constitute a basic and general principle relating to the protection of human rights'.[129] Tellingly, measures taken in derogation from human rights in times of emergency must themselves conform to the principle of non-discrimination, as article 4(1) ICCPR makes clear. While there is no generic right to freedom, its fundamental role is underscored by its mention in respect of several rights and the general principle that the onus is on the state to justify an interference. As respect for the notion of human dignity provides a crucial *raison d'être* for rights if not a right itself, for example article 10(1) ICCPR. Dignity is important both for the recognition of new rights and for measures to protect rights against emerging threats. It is also of increasing relevance in giving substance to rights in adjudication.[130]

Rights can be negative, i.e. freedom from something, such as the right not to be enslaved, or positive, i.e. the right to something, such as the right to be protected against trafficking, or the right to education. By their nature rights can either be absolute or subject to limitations or qualifications. Absolute

---

[126] See K. Vasak, 'Le droit international des droits de l'homme', *RdC* 140 (1974), 333–415, at 343–5.

[127] See on justiciability, section 9.6.

[128] See Vienna Declaration and Programme of Action, UN Doc. A/Conf.157/23 (12 July 1993), paras. 5 and 18.

[129] HRCtee, General Comment 18: Non-discrimination (Thirty-Seventh Session, 1989), para. 1.

[130] See C. McCrudden, 'Human Dignity and Judicial Interpretation of Human Rights', *EJIL* 19(4) (2008), 655–724.

rights, such as freedom from slavery, allow for no exceptions and cannot be derogated from. Even in highly exceptional situations, such as states of emergency, states are not permitted to interfere with such rights.[131] However, not all non-derogable rights are absolute rights. For example, the right to life, though fundamental and non-derogable, is not absolute as the use of lethal force may be lawful under international human rights law (and international humanitarian law) in particular circumstances.[132] Several rights, such as the right to liberty and security, are limited; they can be interfered with, e.g. by way of detention, where the legal grounds for such interference are adhered to, and may be subject to derogations.[133]

Qualified rights, such as the right to privacy and freedom of expression, may be, and frequently are restricted on specific grounds relating to the rights of others, national security, public order or public morals.[134] These grounds, which are set out in so-called clawback clauses, must be based on law, be proportionate and not allow states to deprive the rights of their essence.[135] Qualified rights provide states with considerable scope to restrict the exercise of rights and are therefore frequently subject to complex interpretation, which needs to balance the rights of individuals with the rights of others and societal concerns as put forward by the state.[136] While qualified rights can be derogated from, the need and scope for derogation is limited as states may invoke security considerations when restricting such rights; special circumstances, such as an emergency, may, however, influence the proportionality of measures taken.[137] This distinction between types of rights was first developed in the field of civil and political rights. The CESCR has now interpreted ESC rights to contain a non-derogable core obligation of 'minimum essential levels of each of the rights'.[138] This was an important step in strengthening the status of these rights because the ICESCR's formula that they were to be realised progressively depending on available resources provided no clearly identifiable minimum standards,

---

[131] See HRCtee, General Comment 29: States of Emergency (article 4), UN Doc. CCPR/C/21/Rev.1/ Add.11 (31 August 2001), paras. 7–16. See generally O. Gross and F. Ní Aoláin, *Law in Times of Crisis: Emergency Powers in Theory and Practice* (Cambridge University Press, 2006).

[132] See e.g. article 2(2) ECHR.   [133] See section 8.4.4.

[134] See e.g. articles 8 ECHR and 19(3) ICCPR.

[135] See for a concise summary of applicable standards in the ICCPR context, HRCtee, General Comment 34: Freedoms of opinion and expression, UN Doc. CCPR/C/GC/34 (12 September 2011), paras. 21–36.

[136] See in particular section 8.7.

[137] See on the derogability of these rights, HRCtee, General Comment 29, para. 5, and, generally, L. Doswald-Beck, *Human Rights in Times of Conflict and Terrorism* (Oxford University Press, 2011).

[138] CESCR, General Comment 3: The nature of States parties obligations (Art. 2, par.1) (14 December 1990), para. 10.

while seemingly giving states parties considerable leeway in fulfilling their obligations.[139]

2.3.2   Obligations

By becoming a party to a treaty, or as a matter of customary international law, a state incurs obligations. The basic binary distinction is between negative and positive obligations. Traditionally, liberties and civil and political rights were conceived as essentially imposing 'negative' duties on the state, i.e. to refrain from interfering with a right, e.g. 'do not arbitrarily detain a person'. However, it is evident that states must also take certain measures to ensure rights. For example, states must not only not arbitrarily take life but must also take measures to protect the life of those within their jurisdiction against apparent risks.[140] This dual obligation is articulated well in article 2(1) ICCPR, according to which each state party 'undertakes to *respect* and to *ensure* to all individuals within its territory and subject to its jurisdiction the rights recognized in the present Covenant' (emphasis added). This encompasses 'legislative, judicial, administrative, educative and other appropriate measures [taken] in order to fulfil [a state's] legal obligations'.[141] The general obligation to protect and fulfil rights means that a state has to take measures to prevent and repress violations, irrespective of whether they are committed by state or non-state actors, and provide adequate remedies in case of breach.[142] This duty is one of means, not result, as it may be impossible to prevent certain violations.[143] States have to exercise 'due diligence', i.e. take all measures that can reasonably be taken in the circumstances in order to ensure the rights granted. This may consist of a series of measures, for example criminalising certain forms of rape, overhauling ineffective systems of investigations in rape cases and changing judicial interpretations that address obstacles to effective protection.[144] Treaties may also specify measures, such as the enactment of legislation, reviews, provision of training and other similar steps which states have to take in order to fulfil their obligations.[145] In the field of ESCR rights, states have a duty to protect, promote

---

[139] Report of the UN High Commissioner for Human Rights (focusing on the progressive realisation of ESC rights under international human rights law), UN Doc. E/2007/82 (25 June 2007).

[140] Section 8.2.6.

[141] HRCtee, General Comment 31, para. 7.

[142] Ibid., para. 8.

[143] As articulated succinctly in the landmark case of *Velásquez-Rodríguez* v. *Honduras*, Merits, Judgment of 29 July 1988, Ser. C no. 4, paras. 172–7.

[144] See for example *M. C.* v. *Bulgaria*, (2005) 40 EHRR 20, paras. 109–87, and *Vertido* v. *The Philippines*, UN Doc. CEDAW/C/46/D/18/2008 (16 July 2010), paras. 8.1–8.10.

[145] See for example articles 4(1), 5, 10, 11, 13 and 14 CAT.

and fulfil rights. This entails taking measures so that rights are not infringed by others; it also means being proactive, to the point of implementing direct measures to provide certain goods and services if these are needed to fulfil minimum standards, such as food to prevent starvation.[146]

The broadening of positive obligations in international human rights law is significant and potentially far reaching. It signals that states have duties beyond simple non-interference as conceived in traditional liberal theories, and have to actively consider the impact of policies and measures, or lack thereof, on human rights protection. This duty has resulted in a streamlining of human rights, the extent of which is still being developed in the ever-growing jurisprudence of human rights bodies on positive obligations.[147]

2.3.3   Scope of application

The scope of application of human rights is confined to a state's jurisdiction. It is understood to be primarily territorial, which means that states have to respect and ensure the rights of all individuals within their territory.[148] In principle, this applies to 'everyone' within the state territory without distinction,[149] with the exception of rights which by their nature are confined to individuals belonging to certain groups or specific groups, such as certain political 'citizen' rights and the rights of minorities.[150] There are also a growing number of situations where the conduct of states outside their territory has a bearing on human rights.[151] These include clandestine operations, such as renditions, as well as military or other operations, such as targeted killings, custodial torture in an occupied country or cooperation with states violating certain rights. At first sight, international human rights treaties do not apply because these acts take place outside the state's territory. However, treaty bodies and courts have widened the scope of application, largely using the test of 'effective control' to determine whether the existing degree of control justifies bringing certain conduct within the jurisdiction of the state

---

[146] See for example CESCR, *The Right to Adequate Food* (Art. 11), UN Doc. E/C.12/1999/5 (12 May 1999), para. 15.

[147] Positive obligations have been discussed particularly in the context of ECtHR jurisprudence; see A. R. Mowbray, *The Development of Positive Obligations under the European Convention of Human Rights by the European Court of Human Rights* (Oxford: Hart, 2004), and D. Xenos, *The Positive Obligations of the State under the European Convention on Human Rights* (London, New York: Routledge, 2012).

[148] See e.g. article 2(1) ICCPR.

[149] HRCtee, General Comment 31, para. 10.

[150] See for example articles 25 and 27 ICCPR respectively. See on the status of 'non-citizens' in particular, D. Weissbrodt, *The Human Rights of Non-Citizens* (Oxford University Press, 2008).

[151] See section 7.2.1.

concerned.[152] Military engagements abroad and the internationalised nature of anti-terrorism measures, such as the use of drones, are bound to lead to further litigation and challenges both to delineate the territorial scope of human rights law and to apply human rights standards extraterritorially.[153]

2.4   IMPLEMENTATION

Upon becoming party to a treaty a state commits itself to give effect to a series of obligations in the domestic sphere (and extraterritorially in so far as applicable).[154] Treaties, or customary international law for that matter, are built on the assumption that states will comply with their obligations. Compliance denotes the degree to which a state succeeds in respecting and ensuring human rights. It also refers to a phenomenon of international relations and politics that describes complex processes affecting a state's ability and willingness to meet its obligations under international law. Theories abound in this respect, ranging from the convergence of interests that motivates states to comply, the legitimacy of international law, to the importance of the interplay between international institutions and domestic political processes.[155]

Implementation serves as the measure of a state's compliance with its obligations. As a general rule, states have discretion as to how they implement a treaty in their domestic order unless a treaty specifies implementing modalities.[156] An example of the latter is article 4 CPED according to which 'Each State Party shall take the necessary measures to ensure that enforced disappearance constitutes an offence under its criminal law.' Beyond these prescriptions, states may choose how best to give effect to the obligations incurred. Article 26 VCLT provides that states must do so in good faith.

The obligation to give effect to treaty rights binds all branches of the state, requiring the state to take legislative, administrative, judicial and other measures,[157] which includes adopting human rights-based approaches in

---

[152] See in particular M. Milanović, *Extraterritorial Application of Human Rights Treaties: Law, Principles, and Policy* (Oxford University Press, 2011).

[153] See case study 8.1.   [154] See for example article 2(2) ICCPR.

[155] See in particular H. H. Koh, 'Why do Nations Obey International Law?'. *Yale L.J.* 106(8) (1997), 2599–659; R. Goodman and D. Jinks, 'Incomplete Internalization and Compliance with Human Rights Law', *EJIL* 19(4) (2008), 725–48; T. M. Franck, *The Power of Legitimacy Among Nations* (Oxford University Press, 1990); O. C. Okafor, *The African Human Rights System, Activist Forces and International Institutions* (Cambridge University Press, 2007), 12–62 (focusing primarily on relationship between institutions and domestic forces).

[156] HRCtee, General Comment 31, paras. 4, 13.

[157] Ibid., para. 7.

policy-making. States must bring their laws into conformity with the requisite treaty standards because they cannot rely on national laws that are at variance with their international obligations,[158] for example legislation providing for judicially sanctioned corporal punishment. This is logical as any other result would effectively nullify obligations meant to serve as general overriding standards.[159] Yet, international law does not prescribe a particular mode of incorporation; what matters is that states fulfil their obligations. Modes of incorporation are traditionally distinguished as monism, where international law and domestic law are part of the same legal order and the former takes precedence over the latter, mainly applicable in civil law countries, and dualism, where international law is separate and not directly applicable in the domestic order unless incorporated, a mode mainly followed in common law countries.[160]

The practice of states does not necessarily fall neatly into either category, as national practices often combine both elements and interpret international law in the local context.[161] There is therefore a need to establish for each country: (1) the constitutional recognition of international human rights treaties and customary international law; (2) the rank of these sources within the national legal order; and (3) the judicial interpretation concerning the relationship between the international and the national legal system. International human rights treaty bodies regularly exhort states to adopt specific implementing legislation that would give the treaty concerned a clear status in domestic law.[162] Several constitutions expressly recognise ICCPR and ICESCR rights[163] and several states have adopted statutory laws implementing supranational, particularly regional, treaties.[164] However, even

---

[158] Article 27 VCLT.

[159] It is for this reason that reservations to the effect that human rights treaty provisions are to be interpreted in line with national legislation are generally considered invalid. See above at 2.2.1.

[160] See for a good overview E. Denza, 'The Relationship between International and National Law', in Evans, above note 51, 411–38.

[161] See ibid., and Knop, above note 77.

[162] See in particular general comments/recommendations on the implementation of treaty obligations and concluding observations on states parties' reports by various treaty bodies, which regularly exhort parties to implement the respective treaty in domestic law where they have not done so already.

[163] C. Heyns and F. Viljoen, *The Impact of the United Nations Treaties on the Domestic Level* (The Hague, London, New York: Kluwer Law International, 2002), 7–46; C. Harland, 'The Status of the International Covenant on Civil and Political Rights (ICCPR) in the Domestic Law of States Parties: an Initial Global Survey Through UN Human Rights Committee Documents', *HRQ* 22(1) (2002), 187–260.

[164] See both Heyns/Viljoen and Harland, ibid. See also for example Ireland's European Convention on Human Rights Act, 2003, and Nigeria's African Charter on Human and Peoples Rights (Ratification and Enforcement) Act 1990, Chapter 10.

where international treaties have constitutional status, statutory law is often not in conformity with relevant international standards. This anomaly is particularly prevalent in states that become parties to treaties but do not have the legislative will to carry out the requisite reforms, and/or a judiciary empowered and willing to strike down laws incompatible with international standards.[165]

The judiciary plays a particularly important role in the protection of all sets of rights and in ensuring that states and their organs adhere to international obligations. Traditionally, courts are often seen to show a preference for relying primarily on national law in their jurisprudence. However, national courts have developed a growing awareness of their role in applying relevant international standards, though practice differs considerably.[166] Some courts have flatly rejected the binding nature of international treaty standards. For example, the Sri Lankan Supreme Court held in the *Singarasa* case that the ICCPR had no binding force under domestic law and refused a retrial even though the HRCtee had found that Singarasa had been convicted and sentenced to thirty-five years' imprisonment under anti-terrorism laws in violation of the right to a fair trial.[167] In another case, Sudan's Constitutional Court effectively held that immunity from prosecution granted to officials under national law was compatible with human rights standards without adequately considering international jurisprudence, which holds otherwise.[168]

In contrast, other courts have upheld international standards even in the face of pressing security concerns, such as the UK House of Lords in several cases, leading to fundamental changes in the UK anti-terrorism scheme,[169] or have taken a lead role in progressively interpreting constitutional rights, thus advancing the development of international human rights law. An example is the South African Constitutional Court in the *Grootboom* case, a major precedent on the right to housing and protection against forced

---

[165] See for example on Sudan's Bill of Rights, L. Oette, 'Law Reform in Times of Peace Processes and Transitional Justice: the Sudanese Dimension', in Oette (ed.), *Criminal Law Reform and Transitional Justice: Human Rights Perspectives for Sudan* (Farnham: Ashgate, 2011), 11–31, at 22–9.

[166] See generally M. Kirby, 'Domestic Courts and International Human Rights Law: the Ongoing Judicial Conversation (The Hondis Lecture 2008)', *NQHR* 27(2) (2009), 291–307; N. Jayawickrama, *The Judicial Application of Human Rights Law: National, Regional and International Jurisprudence* (Cambridge University Press, 2002); B. Conforti (ed.), *Enforcing International Human Rights in Domestic Courts* (The Hague: Kluwer Law International, 1997); A. Nollkaemper, *National Courts and the International Rule of Law* (Oxford University Press, 2011).

[167] *Singarasa* v. *Attorney General*, S.C. SPL (LA) no. 182/99 (2006).

[168] *Farouq Mohamed Ibrahim Al Nour* v. *(1) Government of Sudan; (2) Legislative Body*; Final order by Justice Abdallah Aalmin Albashir President of the Constitutional Court (6 November 2008).

[169] See T. Bingham, *The Rule of Law* (London: Allen Lane, 2010), 133–59.

evictions.[170] Ultimately, it is not the reference to international standards but the recognition and protection of rights that courts are able to provide which matters. Examples are Germany's Constitutional Court, Colombia's Constitutional Court and the Indian apex courts, which have significantly enhanced our understanding of rights, and, in the Indian case, the availability of remedies.[171] The jurisprudence of domestic courts constitutes important state practice and can be expected to play an even more important role with the increasing awareness of international standards. However, it is equally clear that decisions in individual cases, including their implementation, will depend on a number of domestic factors characterising the delicate relationship between the legislature and the executive on the one hand and the judiciary on the other. The importance of an independent judiciary in this context could have not been better put by the late Lord Bingham in his landmark book on the rule of law: 'There are countries in the world where all judicial decisions find favour with the powers that be, but they are probably not places where any of us would wish to live.'[172]

2.4.1   The role of national human rights institutions

A number of states have established national human rights institutions (NHRIs). According to the Paris Principles, NHRIs should be independent bodies tasked with promoting and protecting human rights, using a range of measures in respect of all spheres of human rights.[173] The high hopes initially placed in NHRIs have given way to a more nuanced assessment.[174] It has become increasingly clear that many NHRIs lack one or more of the key features of independence, powers and/or capacity. In addition, the faith

---

[170] See *Government of the Republic of South Africa and Others* v. *Grootboom and Others* (CCT11/00) [2000] ZACC 19; 2001 (1) SA 46; 2000 (11) BCLR 1169 (4 October 2000); article 39(1) of the South African Constitution mandates South African courts to consider international law when interpreting the Bill of Rights.

[171] See on India the various contributions in C. Raj Kumar and K. Chockalingam (eds.), *Human Rights, Justice and Constitutional Empowerment* (Oxford University Press, 2007).

[172] Bingham, above note 169, 65.

[173] Principles relating to the Status of National Institutions (The Paris Principles), UNGA resolution 48/134 of 20 December 1993. See on NHRIs, Office of the High Commissioner for Human Rights (OHCHR), *National Human Rights Institutions: History, Principles, Roles and Responsibilities*, Professional Training Series no. 4 (rev. 1) (Geneva and New York: United Nations, 2010), and R. Murray, *The Role of National Human Rights Institutions at the International and Regional Levels: The Experience of Africa* (Oxford: Hart, 2007).

[174] See B. Lindsnaes, L. Lindholt and K. Yigen (eds.), *National Human Rights Institutions: Articles and Working Papers* (Copenhagen: Danish Centre for Human Rights, 2000); International Council on Human Rights Policy (ICHRP), *Assessing the Effectiveness of National Human Rights Institutions* (Geneva: ICHRP, 2005).

in the ability of NHRIs to provide protection may be misplaced where they
act as poor substitutes for courts in a system where the rule of law is weak.
Nevertheless, some NHRIs have played useful or even leading roles, particularly where they have enhanced awareness of human rights and have been
able to identify a country's human rights problems and articulate a domestic
human rights vision in equal measure.[175] Such NHRIs can form a critical part
of broader civil society efforts to demand respect for human rights, which are
often at the heart of enhanced implementation.

INTERVIEW 2.1

Reflections on the work of Uganda's Human Rights Commission

(Med S. K. Kaggwa)

Med S. K. Kaggwa is a distinguished Ugandan lawyer who is the
Chairperson of Uganda's Human Rights Commission (UHRC)[1] and
Commissioner of the African Commission on Human and Peoples' Rights.

What are the mandate and powers of Uganda's Human Rights Commission?

The UHRC is an 'A' status independent NHRI established under article 51(1)
of the Constitution of the Republic of Uganda and the UHRC Act of 1997
that is mandated to:

Receive and investigate, at its own initiative or on a complaint made by any person
or group of persons against the violation of any human right; to visit places of
detention or related facilities with a view to assessing and inspecting conditions of
the inmates and make recommendations; to establish a continuing programme of
research, education and information to enhance respect of human rights; and to
recommend to Parliament effective measures to promote human rights including
provision of compensation to victims of violations of human rights, or their
families.

It is also mandated to create and sustain within society the awareness
of the provisions of this Constitution as the fundamental law; to create
awareness about human rights and civic obligations; to monitor the
government's compliance with international treaty and convention
obligations on human rights; and to perform such other functions as may
be provided by law.

[1] www.uhrc.ug.

[175] See for example Afghanistan's Independent Human Rights Commission, www.aihrc.
org.af/en, and Kenya's National Commission on Human Rights, www.knchr.org. See for
further information on the work of NHRIs and OHCHR, www.ohchr.org/en/countries/nhri/
pages/nhrimain.aspx.

Under article 52(2), the UHRC is required to publish periodical reports and submit annual reports to Parliament on the state of human rights and freedoms in the country. Importantly, the UHRC also has a quasi-judicial function as stipulated under article 53(1) of the Ugandan Constitution which empowers it to provide redress to victims of human rights violations through tribunals.

Article 54 of the Constitution guarantees the independence of the UHRC. The UHRC is expected to be independent and should not, in the performance of its duties, be subject to the direction or control of any person or authority. However, article 52(3)(b) of the Constitution permits the Commission to request the assistance of any department, bureau, office, agency or person in the performance of its functions.

What would you say has been its most valuable achievement?

The UHRC's establishment, powers and functions comply with the UN Paris Principles and it is accredited with 'A' status by the International Coordinating Committee of National Human Rights Institutions. It has regularly reported on the state of human rights in the country up to this day; fourteen annual reports have been produced and submitted to Parliament with recommendations for improvement. These reports provide some measure of accountability to the public.

In 2009 Parliament discussed findings and recommendations contained in UHRC reports that had been submitted from 1997 to 2007.[2] Recommendations on human rights and freedoms in the country were analysed and recommended for further action by various government institutions. Parliament also approved the creation of a human rights committee to discuss recommendations made by the UHRC and monitor government compliance with human rights among other responsibilities. For instance, the UHRC had always recommended to Parliament the enactment of a law that prevents torture. In 2006 the UHRC together with NGOs under the Coalition Against Torture drafted the Prevention and Prohibition of Torture Bill 2010 which was passed by Parliament on 26 April 2012. The Bill awaits presidential assent to become an enforceable law.

The UHRC has established nine regional offices. In addition to the regional offices, with support from the UNDP it has established sub-regional offices in the north and north-eastern parts of Uganda to take services closer to the local population that were majorly affected by the Lord's Resistance Army insurgency. These offices are well coordinated by the Directorate of Regional Services. The UHRC has established a Right to Health Unit, Vulnerable Persons Unit and a Human Rights Defenders' Desk under the Directorate of Monitoring and Inspections. The two units and the Human

---

[2] www.parliament.go.ug/index.php.

Rights Defenders' Desk are responsible for monitoring the implementation of the right to health, the rights of vulnerable groups and the rights of human rights defenders.

The UHRC has also helped to establish district human rights desks and committees in seventy-six districts of the country in order to ensure protection and promotion of human rights at that level. These have been able to support the UHRC in mediating some cases of human rights violations at the district level such as Tororo and Kiruhura. However, some of the human rights desks and Committees are not functional due to lack of funding.

The UHRC has a good working relationship with security agencies which never used to be the case in the past. It is allowed to freely inspect places of detention (police cells, prisons and military detention facilities). It also receives prompt responses to investigation inquiries especially from the Uganda People's Defence Forces and prisons. This progress is attributed to the numerous human rights training programmes carried out by the UHRC for security agents.

The institution is considered credible both at national and international level. On several occasions the UHRC has been a point of reference and has been called upon to carry out capacity-building for other NHRIs in the region. UHRC commissioners and staff have been called upon as experts/resource persons to share experiences and best practices on the establishment, powers and functions of an NHRI with NHRIs of Kenya, Sierra Leone, Sudan, Tanzania, Somaliland, Ethiopia, Malawi and Swaziland. As a result of its credibility the UHRC has previously chaired the African Network of National Institutions and Commonwealth Forum for National Human Rights Institutions.

What are the main challenges it faces?

Government takes a long time to honour UHRC tribunal awards or compensate victims of human rights violations.[3] The failure to have a single entity coordinating civic education programmes in the country often leads to duplication of results and imbalances in the coverage of interventions. In addition, inadequate financial resources make it difficult for the UHRC to fully implement its broad mandate.

With only nine regional offices in the country, the UHRC still faces a challenge in ensuring that human rights services are accessed by people in geographically distant and hard to reach areas. The limited funding for the institution's activities has been exacerbated by a decline in donor funding. The institution relies significantly on government funding in addition to

---

[3] UHRC, *14th Annual Report*, 2011, 14.

funding received from its donors.[4] Funds received from donors on the other hand are usually earmarked for particular programmes. Therefore it becomes difficult to ensure that the Commission's mandate is met within the different budget allocations.

What steps have you taken to address these challenges?

The UHRC uses a mobile complaints handling system. In this system, staff in regional offices travel to distant places within their areas of jurisdiction to receive complaints and also to sensitise people to their rights. Through its annual reports on the state of human rights in the country, the UHRC urges the government to put in place a mechanism where the victims of human rights violations are compensated urgently. As already mentioned, with effect from 1 July 2011 the UHRC established sub-regional field offices in the northern and north-eastern parts of Uganda in order to take services closer to the rural population.[5]

What contributions can NHRIs make, and what are their limitations?

NHRIs have a responsibility to monitor government's compliance with international treaties. This often includes analysis of government policies and laws to ensure that they are consistent with human rights principles. By this means, NHRIs can ensure that national laws protect the rights of all categories of people including human rights defenders.

NHRIs are also an appropriate source of information on the human rights situation in the country. Such information can be used to publicise national human rights concerns at the international level in search for an appropriate remedy.

The hope that NHRIs effectively guarantee human rights has not been fulfilled in many countries. What do you see as the main reason for the apparent weakness of some NHRIs, and how do you think it can be overcome at the regional and international level?

Most NHRIs have limited funding to fully implement all the activities they should be carrying out as per their mandates and the Paris Principles. NHRIs have very limited capacity to investigate human rights violations and also monitor the human rights situation in conflict areas. In addition, the procedure for appointing chairpersons and commissioners varies from one NHRI to another. It therefore becomes hard to ensure protection and promotion of human rights at a uniform level in various countries, particularly where the NHRI lacks the necessary independence and does not conform to the UN Paris Principles.

---

[4] UHRC, *13th Annual Report*, 2010, 134.
[5] UHRC, *14th Annual Report*, 2011, 50.

Recommendations: NHRIs: ought to lobby their respective governments for an increase in funding to be able to implement their mandates. They could also rely on funding from donors or any other source to support implementation of their mandates as long as they do not compromise the independence of the institution. NHRIs can coordinate efforts to promote dialogue between conflicting parties and mediate through or with networks and coalitions. They could also coordinate efforts to ensure that victims of the conflict, such as those in Northern Uganda, have access to remedy and reparation, which can constitute a challenge in transitional contexts. Finally, NHRIs can work through networks and coalitions at the national, regional and international level for technical and financial support in the protection and promotion of human rights within their areas of jurisdiction.

2.5   HUMAN RIGHTS TREATIES AS SELF-CONTAINED REGIMES

The ILC Draft Articles on State Responsibility are regularly referred to by international courts and in state practice and are largely seen as codifying customary international law on the attribution of state responsibility and its consequences.[176] The articles govern the responsibility owed by states to other states.[177] Their rules of attribution and legal consequences are important in the human rights context, particularly where states invoke human rights violations as being of an *erga omnes* character or as a violation of their rights, and inform the jurisprudence in human rights cases.[178] As far as the practice under human rights treaties is concerned, it is human rights treaty bodies and courts that monitor state compliance through reporting and individual and inter-state complaints procedures.[179] Their decisions determine whether a state has breached its treaty obligations and spell out the legal consequences under the treaty, i.e. cessation and the various forms of repa-

---

[176] See for a concise overview, C. Crawford and S. Olleson, 'The Nature and Forms of International Responsibility' in Evans, above note 51, 441–71, and for a detailed study, S. Ollesen, *The Impact of the ILC's Articles on Responsibility of States for Internationally Wrongful Acts*, Preliminary Draft (London: British Institute of International and Comparative Law, 2007).

[177] See article 33(1). However, article 33(2) clarifies that this is 'without prejudice to any right, arising from the international responsibility of a State, which may accrue directly to any person or entity other than a State'.

[178] See ICJ judgment on the *Application of the Convention on the Prevention and Punishment of the Crime of Genocide (Bosnia and Herzegovina v. Serbia and Montenegro)* and ICJ Reports 2007, 43; *Legal Consequences of the Construction of a Wall in the Occupied Palestinian Territory*, Advisory opinion, discussed further in Ollesen, above note 176.

[179] See in particular Chapter 4.

ration that such a finding entails. This set up has raised the question of whether human rights constitute a so-called self-contained or special regime that excludes recourse to other mechanisms and countermeasures,[180] such as sanctions.[181] For example, where a human rights treaty provides for an inter-state complaints procedure, it seems reasonable to suggest that states should have recourse to this procedure as the most specialised available instead of taking other steps, such as countermeasures. The rationale is clear; the system has been set up for a particular purpose and has developed its own procedures and jurisprudence. It is therefore in the interest of functional integrity and efficiency that states use the specialised system. In practice, states are expected to, and often act with reference to a treaty and use available procedures.

Following extensive debates within the ILC, and in light of judicial practice, there are no cogent policy reasons or support to make international human rights treaties closed systems and bar states from having recourse to general countermeasures.[182] It is nevertheless reasonable for states parties to use a special regime unless the remedies it provides 'would be manifestly unavailable or ineffective or where it would be otherwise unreasonable to expect recourse to it'.[183] In such circumstances, states may either have recourse to other international bodies, including the ICJ, which has been increasingly seized with questions of international human rights law, or use proportionate countermeasures. The problems posed by countermeasures are often more of a political rather than legal nature. The international human rights system is multilateral and embedded in the UN, particularly its specialised bodies, i.e. the HRC, and regional political bodies, such as the CoE, EU, AU and OAS. Proponents may claim that unilateral sanctions or even the use of force in the form of 'humanitarian intervention' are necessary where these institutional structures are ineffective. However, such unilateral moves are frequently seen as politically motivated and aimed at establishing regional or international hegemonies. This has prompted developments to formulate doctrines, such as the Responsibility to Protect, according to which the UN has primary responsibility to take effective action where a state (and, implicitly, institutional systems of protection) failed in its duty to protect those within its territory from serious human rights violations, namely international crimes.[184]

---

[180] See articles 49–55 ILC Draft Articles on State Responsibility.

[181] See discussion in ILC, Fragmentation, above note 3, paras. 123–94, with further references.

[182] The HRCtee seems to imply this in its General Comment 31, para. 2.

[183] ILC, Fragmentation, above note 3, para. 152.

[184] 2005 World Summit Outcome, paras. 138–9, and Zifcak, above note 103.

QUESTIONS

1 The role of NHRIs is frequently overrated. Rather than providing an effective means for the promotion and protection of human rights, they have more often than not become a façade that embodies the weakness rather than the strength of a national system. Discuss.

2 The system for the enforcement of international human rights obligations is underdeveloped and ineffective. Discuss.

2.6 PRACTICAL APPLICATION: THE ROLE OF LAW REFORM

The mismatch between ratification and effective implementation of treaties is one of the most glaring shortcomings of the international human rights system. It calls into question its basic premise of setting out standards that states parties will seek to adhere to if not realise immediately. In practice, it is often a combination of factors and complex dynamics, including the interplay between national and international actors, that determine the nature of implementation, if any, as an examination of legislative reforms aptly demonstrates.

Best practice in the area of legislative reform is relatively easy to identify. States should actively seek to incorporate relevant human rights standards in their domestic legislation. This can be done by conducting compatibility studies and identifying those laws or provisions that need to be repealed, amended or adopted in order to bring domestic law into conformity with international standards.[185] Such studies should ideally be undertaken before ratification but may for practical purposes follow it. They should be complemented by legislation that recognises the rights concerned and provides for effective protection. Such legislation should, where applicable, form part of broader policies, and be accompanied by institutional reforms and the training of officials to whom it is addressed. The rights reflected in such legislation should also be an integral element of broader human rights education and awareness-raising programmes so that those whose rights are concerned know what their rights are and how best to exercise them. In turn, this requires that the rights are justiciable and that effective remedies are available in case of breach.

Reality frequently fails to live up to these best practices. This applies in particular to the reform of statutory laws. A common refrain is to say that a state lacks political will to bring its laws into conformity with international standards. While this may well be true, as a general statement it often obscures more than it reveals unless it is clear what is meant by 'political will'. This is

---

[185] Heyns and Viljoen, above note 163, 7–46.

obvious where a government flatly refuses to undertake specific reforms or, worse, pursues or even adopts legislation that runs counter to its obligations, such as draconian emergency laws following a *coup d'état* or in times of crisis,[186] or laws that impose severe punishment for consensual homosexual acts.[187] However, actual practice is frequently less clear cut, with reforms failing to materialise because they are caught in a web of multiple political, institutional and practical obstacles. International institutions and/or domestic civil society for their part may lack the awareness or may not give priority to a particular issue and therefore fail to generate the momentum needed to make the government concerned act. Even where such actors exercise some influence, a government may refrain from passing legislation if the political (or financial) cost is deemed too high. For example, in South Africa, trauma crisis and counselling support, the morning-after pill and legal representation for victims were excluded from legislation governing sexual violence on the grounds of resource constraints.[188]

Resistance to legislative reforms can take numerous forms. Law-enforcement agencies are often strongly opposed to legislation that results in restrictions to their power and/or greater oversight and accountability. For example, in India the armed forces have opposed calls for the repeal of the Armed Forces Special Powers Act in force in Kashmir and the north-east of India, which grants them extraordinary powers in contravention of international human rights standards.[189] Religious groups may decisively influence the debate on reforms, for example in respect of abortion or blasphemy laws affecting reproductive rights and the freedom of expression.[190] Nationalist groups may be opposed to

---

[186] See for some pertinent examples the Queen's University Belfast Emergency Law Database, online, at www.qub.ac.uk/schools/SchoolofLaw/Research/HumanRightsCentre/Resources/StatesofEmergencyDatabase/EmergencyLawDatabase-Introduction.

[187] See Report of the UN High Commissioner for Human Rights, Discriminatory Laws and Practices and Acts of Violence Against Individuals Based on their Sexual Orientation and Gender Identity, UN Doc. A/HR/C/19/41 (17 November 2011), which was published against a background of a series of anti-homosexuality bills or laws contemplated or adopted in countries such as Uganda and Nigeria.

[188] See R. Manjoo, G. Kweka and S. O. Ofuani, 'Sexual Violence and the Law: Comparative Legislative Experiences in Selected Southern African Countries', in Oette, above note 165, 269–295, at 287–8.

[189] See AI, *India: Security Forces Cannot Claim Immunity under AFSPA, Must Face Trial for Violations* (7 February 2012), online, at www.amnesty.org/en/news/india-security-forces-cannot-claim-immunity-under-afspa-must-face-trial-violations-2012-02-07.

[190] See on the criminalisation of abortion, Interim report of the Special Rapporteur on the right of everyone to the enjoyment of the highest attainable standard of physical and mental health, UN Doc. A/66/254 (3 August 2011), and on blasphemy laws in Pakistan, UN Special Rapporteur on the independence of judges and lawyers, Ms Gabriela Knaul, Preliminary observations on the official visit to the Islamic Republic of Pakistan, Islamabad, 29 May 2012, online, at www.ohchr.org/EN/NewsEvents/Pages/DisplayNews.aspx?NewsID=12194&LangID=E.

granting rights to minorities and public sentiment may result in restricting the rights of certain categories of persons, such as stateless persons, immigrants and refugees.[191] External political pressure, such as structural adjustment programmes advocated by international agencies, may contribute to a political climate detrimental to reforms protecting basic rights.[192] In addition to these political factors, the institutional set up may not be conducive. Several states seemingly lack the capacity to draft good implementing legislation. Law reform commissions, where in place, can help in identifying areas for reform and ensuring that technical expertise benefits from consultation.[193] However, even here political priorities or approaches taken may undermine reforms. A telling example concerns attempts to legislate on polygamy in Uganda, which did not end in a ban, which was also the result of a consultation with rural communities that found some support for the practice.[194] The law-making process itself is contingent on political majorities, often also at the federal level, which may compromise reforms. The time within which legislation has to be adopted is another factor that frequently derails or substantially delays reform proposals.[195]

How can international standards be used to bring about legislative reforms where domestic law fails to guarantee and protect rights? This is one of the key strategic questions facing domestic actors. International human rights treaty bodies, UN Special Rapporteurs or other bodies may have identified laws in need of reform. This may help in raising awareness but does not by itself guarantee that the requisite steps will be taken. Indeed, such recommendations are routinely ignored. Worse, international 'pressure' and reference to international standards may even create a backlash. National actors therefore often have to develop their own strategies and activities to challenge laws incompatible with international standards.

---

[191] The treatment of refugees and their 'rightlessness' had already been highlighted by Hannah Arendt in her seminal work, *The Origins of Totalitarianism* (New York: Schocken Books, 1951). See on the political context also M. A. Schain, 'The State Strikes Back: Immigration Policy in Europe', *EJIL* 20(1) (2009), 93–109.

[192] See Report of the Independent Expert on the Effect of Economic Reform Policies and Foreign Debt on the Full Enjoyment of all Human Rights, Bernards Mudho, UN Doc. A/HRC/4/10 (3 January 2007), paras. 26–69, and M. R. Abouharb and D. Cingranelli, *Human Rights and Structural Adjustment* (Cambridge University Press, 2007).

[193] See for example the substantive work undertaken by South Africa's Law Reform Commission, http://salawreform.justice.gov.za.

[194] Uganda's polygamy laws have thereafter been challenged by human rights groups before Uganda's Constitutional Court. See J. Shore, 'Human Rights Group Challenges Uganda's Polygamy Laws', Centre for Human Rights and Humanitarian Law, *The Human Rights Brief* (6 April 2010).

[195] It took twenty-two years and countless lapsed bills to turn the constitutional prohibition of torture in the Philippines into an anti-torture law in 2009.

The campaign to change the *Hudood* laws in Pakistan is an instructive example of the multifaceted challenges.[196] The *Hudood* laws were adopted in 1979 by the then military ruler Zia ul-Haq as part of a policy of Islamisation. The law rendered *zina* (extramarital sexual intercourse) subject to harsh, fixed punishments, including flogging and stoning. Significantly, it also turned rape into a form of *zina* to which Islamic laws of evidence applied. This meant that four male eyewitnesses had to testify to the rape; if insufficient evidence was available to sustain an allegation, especially in case of pregnancy, a woman faced prosecution for *zina*. The law resulted in a moral witchhunt and confused application by specially constituted Shari'a councils, which often turned rape victims into suspects. Pakistani women's rights groups found it difficult to campaign against the laws given the repressive political climate and the prevalence of conservative morals supporting the law in rural areas. Religious factions accused these groups of pursuing a Western agenda as a means of discrediting them, especially following criticism from Western countries, such as in cases that upheld the punishment of stoning.

In these circumstances, women's rights activists adopted a two-track approach, which aimed at exposing the discriminatory and harmful impact of the law. They used local meetings, theatre performances and a variety of publications to undermine the laws in the public eye, in particular in rural areas. In parallel, human rights lawyers defended those accused of *zina* before the courts, seeking to demonstrate the flawed and inconsistent application of the law. These measures, accompanied by sustained international criticism of the laws, served to erode support for the laws in Pakistan, which were increasingly seen as an ill-conceived embarrassment even by several Islamic scholars. In the wake of this change in public mood, several civil society groups, supported by some political parties, campaigned and lobbied for a repeal of the laws. This campaign faced hostile reactions from religiously motivated parties. However, ten years after Pakistan had ratified the CEDAW in 1996, the efforts resulted in some significant changes, albeit in the form of a compromise package that, while repealing the rape law, retained a number of discriminatory pieces of legislation.

The Pakistani experience holds important lessons. It is difficult to repeal laws that find their way on to the statute book even where they are seemingly discredited. This is especially the case where they can claim some legitimacy, which can be religious but may equally derive from security considerations or similar rationales. Opponents of such legislation have to embark on sustained engagement, combining awareness-raising, litigation, advocacy and

---

[196] The following account draws on S. A. Warraich, 'Through the Looking Glass: the Emergence, Confused Application and Demise of Pakistan's *Hudood* Rape Laws', in Oette, above note 165, 243–67.

lobbying in order to bring about at least some limited changes. This engagement also illustrates the nature of the struggle over legislative reforms, which are often about symbolic legitimacy. In times of severe political repression, the legal system can become a site for exposing apparent flaws, which has the advantage that one can refer to texts (and international commitments of states) rather than to (often contested) information about facts. This painstaking work may in time result in a change of attitudes and/or may prepare the ground for genuine reforms once the opportunity arises. A change of government or the end of a conflict constitutes an important opening for legislative reforms. However, by its very nature, law reform is a complicated process whose outcome is a reflection of a number of political factors and legal considerations.

INTERVIEW 2.2

The campaign to repeal Pakistan's *Hudood* laws

(Sohail A. Warraich)

Sohail Warraich is a women's rights activist who actively campaigned for the repeal of the *Hudood* laws, working on behalf of the Shirkat Gah women's resource centre and performing street plays with his theatre group that exposed how the law victimised women.

How did you get involved in the campaign to repeal the *Hudood* laws?

I had just joined university when I read the news of punishment of flogging pronounced under the *Zina* Ordinance to Safia Bibi, a blind girl, for being pregnant outside of marriage. Her plea was one of rape. The international press also publicised this case and the Women's Action Forum (WAF) strongly protested against it. This case introduced me to the *Zina* Ordinance and its problems. Though Safia was acquitted upon appeal the injustices of this law continued in case after case. In 1987 Shahida Parveen from Karachi was given a sentence of stoning to death by the trial court. She had remarried after being divorced by her first husband but following her remarriage her former husband claimed that she was still married to him. He claimed that had he divorced her he would have followed the procedure given in law. Shahida and her second husband were tried under the *zina* law and convicted. She was sentenced to stoning to death while her second husband was sentenced to a hundred lashes. This verdict shocked everyone. Amnesty International issued an action alert against Shahida's sentence. That was my first active participation for the repeal of the *Zina* Ordinance. After that, I learnt more about the problems of this law and joined protest meetings and demonstrations organised by WAF and other rights groups. The theatre group I worked for (Ajoka Theatre) performed street plays on the injustices suffered by rape victims under this law. In the early 1990s, I joined the Shirkat Gah women's resource centre, a leading women's rights organisation, which was at the forefront in the campaign for the repeal of *Hudood* ordinances. In 2006 the enactment of the Women's Protection Act, which repealed many provisions of the *Zina* and *Qazaf* Ordinances, was a first major success of the campaign against these laws but the struggle has to continue until their total repeal.

What was the key to the successful campaign?

A firm clear position and consistency in demanding repeal of *Hudood* laws over the years was key to the campaign which was ultimately met with success to the extent that major amendments to these laws were introduced to prevent abuse. Women's rights activists for years demanded repeal of these laws without mincing words. The relevant positions were based on the rights of people rather than shifting stances.

Case after case also provided opportunities to protest against the verdicts and further campaign against these laws. The old argument that any law can be misused was successfully countered from a number of cases demonstrating that the potential for abuse and misuse was from within the law rather than being its mere misapplication. Explaining to people in very simple words with examples from actual cases in which contradictory verdicts had been pronounced proved helpful in removing misperceptions about the widely propagated 'Islamic' nature of these laws. To this end, I wrote handbills in simple Urdu and, together with my colleagues, wrote campaign materials including a small booklet titled *Why Hudood Ordinances Should be Repealed*, in Urdu and English. It was widely distributed at public meetings and also sent to members of Parliament.

What were some memorable moments in the campaign?

In fact for me the memorable moment was the case of Zafran Bibi, who was sentenced to stoning to death by a trial court in March 2002. This case again exposed the absurdity and unjust nature of this law, as happened in some of the previous cases. Zafran was a married pregnant woman and her husband was serving a sentence in a jail. She went to the police station with her father-in-law to register a complaint of rape against another man. She was sent for a medical examination and being found pregnant was held under the offence of *zina*. Before the conclusion of the trial she gave birth to a female child. During trial her statement that she gave birth to a child was taken as her confession of having committed *zina*. She was sentenced under *hadd* (maximum fixed punishment which was stoning to death for a married Muslim man or a woman). This case helped the campaign a lot. It exposed the ambiguities and injustices of this law to everyone. It became a lot easier to talk about repeal of these laws with the help of this case. A momentum built and there were public meetings on the injustices of these laws and demands for repeal were strengthened. In the public meetings and handbills extracts were used from the verdicts of higher courts including the Federal Shariat Court where the application of the law was criticised and injustices were exposed. In many verdicts of the 1990s, the courts referred extensively to the *zina* law, short of asking for amendments or repeal. The courts' observations and remarks provided first hand material for the campaign against *Hudood* laws.

Zafran Bibi's case occurred at a very critical and decisive time. It exposed the inherent contradictions, inequalities and extreme potential for misuse in the provisions of *zina* and rape in the *Hudood* law and the judgment of the Federal Shariat Court demonstrated that the defenders and proponents of *Hudood* laws were left with only very weak arguments. The longest paragraph of the judgment was not on the merits of the case itself but rather on the admonition of organisations and individuals who protested against the verdict of stoning to death.

From the *Zafran* case onwards the campaign gained a different momentum. During month-long debates over the Bill, inside and outside Parliament there were many memorable moments. Some of the debates on TV exposed the hollow defence of these laws by traditional clerics and their anti-women mindset. In most of these debates clerics were invited and some of the TV channels and other factions of the media portrayed the issue as religious alone, on which these clerics were the sole authority. These debates showed that the battle on these laws was an issue of political power, spearheaded by certain conservative forces, rather than a purely legal question. It gave a real opportunity to discover the obstructions and difficulties faced by legislative reform brought in the name of religion and how religion was used as an instrument to prevent reform. Reports about government committees constituted to bargain with leaders of religious political parties and their allied clerics and the bargains being negotiated were hilarious as well as embarrassing. Finally, when the amendments happened, the so called 'divineness' attached to the *Hudood* laws was dented. Though the result achieved was short of what we desired, in political terms it was a landmark. That will never be forgotten.

What are the lessons for other countries?

The first and foremost is that criminal laws (especially those related to sexual acts and offences) introduced in the name of Islam in some Muslim majority states are a political tool to gain some 'legitimacy' and support for the rulers and also to keep control through harsher punishments. Experience tells us that these laws are enacted in haste, carry inherent inequalities and are aimed at disadvantaged sections of the society. They are divisive in nature and divide society on the basis of sex and religion.

The cover of Islam is used to silence any opposition to these laws. The suggestion from Pakistan's experience is to contest these laws from your own positions of strength. Public support can be gained by taking the problems of law to the public and linking them to their lives. Emblematic cases can be used to agitate against these laws. There is no monolithic Shari'a and in each Muslim majority state each sect has its own interpretations. So attempts to fight on arguments from within religion may not be of much help. In certain circumstances that can be a tactic but not a real long-term strategy. There can be arguments from within the religious discourse against a particular text of laws enforced in a jurisdiction but that may mean replacing one text with another which on the face of it may seem better than before but may ultimately bring similar problems.

FURTHER READING

Boisson de Chazournes, L. and Kohen, M. G. (eds.), *International Law and the Quest for its Implementation. Liber amicorum Vera Gowlland-Debbas* (Leiden: Brill, 2010).

Boyle, A. and Chinkin, C., *The Making of International Law* (Oxford University Press, 2007).

Goodman, R., 'Human Rights Treaties, Invalid Reservations and State Consent', *AJIL* 96(3) (2002), 531–60.

Heyns, C. and Viljoen, F., *The Impact of the United Nations Treaties on the Domestic Level* (The Hague, London, New York: Kluwer Law International, 2002).

Kamminga, M. T. and Scheinin, M. (eds.), *The Impact of Human Rights Law on General International Law* (Oxford University Press, 2009).

Meron, T., *Human Rights and Humanitarian Norms as Customary Law* (Oxford: Clarendon Press, 1989).

Mutua, M., 'Standard Setting in Human Rights: Critique and Prognosis', *HRQ* 29(3) (2007), 547–630.

Nollkaemper, A., *National Courts and the International Rule of Law* (Oxford University Press, 2011).

Orakhelashvili, A., *Peremptory Norms in International Law* (Oxford University Press, 2006).

Symposium: Assessing the Work of the International Law Commission on State Responsibility, *EJIL* 13(5) (2002), 1053–1257.

Tams, C. J., *Enforcing Obligations Erga Omnes in International Law* (Cambridge University Press, 2005).

3 Human rights in practice

CONTENTS

3.1 INTRODUCTION

Human rights are constructed by multiple actors acting simultaneously within the given political and legal structures, and challenging and changing them in the process. While the political struggle for human rights is universal and potentially engages all human beings, our focus is on key agents, both the 'true authors' of human rights[1] and others who play an influential role. The 'human rights movement' includes individuals and communities fighting for their rights, NGOs, the somewhat amorphous 'civil society', social movements and transnational networks that engage in local and global power struggles. More recently, the term 'human rights defenders' has increasingly become a catch-all category to embrace the range of actors concerned.

The human rights movement is by no means uniform and a series of challenges, both within the movement and in respect of its role as a political actor, have become more pronounced with the increasing power of human rights and its advocates. This development has cast the light on human rights advocates, such as NGOs, and has raised questions both of legitimacy – who are you to

---

[1] See on the authorship and ownership of human rights, U. Baxi, *The Future of Human Rights*, 3rd edn (Oxford University Press, 2008), 32–58.

make claims in the name of human rights or on behalf of certain people? Are you living up to human rights principles in your own practice? – and effectiveness – are you really making the positive difference in people's lives you claim to make? Responses to these challenges testify to a growing self-awareness and critical assessment of the nature of human rights work, which includes an evaluation of the efficacy of strategies used to promote and protect human rights. Inevitably, human rights advocates are increasingly drawn into the political domain and are faced with the difficult task of marrying principle with pragmatism. This chapter explores the tensions arising in these contexts and assesses the strategies used by human rights actors, namely documentation, human rights reporting, advocacy, awareness-raising, training and education and, where relevant, litigation (which is considered in more detail in chapters 7 and 13).

3.2   CIVIL SOCIETY

The last decades have witnessed a growing emphasis on civil society, both as a collective group of actors that promote human rights and as a societal structure or forum that enables the exercise of rights.[2] This development has to a considerable degree been due to the waning of political ideologies and traditional parties at the national level and the process of globalisation at the international level.[3] In the process, non-state actors, including NGOs, social movements and transnational networks have grown in size and importance.[4] While the notion of 'civil society' is often invoked, if not celebrated, its meaning remains subject to diverging interpretations and its role contested.

National civil society has been described '[as] the intermediary layer between the public sphere of the state and the private sphere of households and organizations within it that are voluntary and autonomous'.[5] Its international

[2] T. Risse, 'The Power of Norms vs. the Norms of Power: Transnational Civil Society and Human Rights', in A. M. Florini (ed.), *The Third Force: The Rise of Transnational Civil Society* (Carnegie Endowment for International Peace, Washington, DC, 2000), 177–210; S. Batliwala, 'Grassroots Movements as Transnational Actors: Implications for Global Civil Society', *VIJVNO* 13(4) (2002), 393–410; J. Keane, *Global Civil Society?* (Cambridge University Press, 2003); B. de Sousa Santos and C. A. Rodriguez-Garavito, *Law and Globalization from Below: Towards a Cosmopolitan Legality* (Cambridge University Press, 2005); M. Edwards (ed.), *The Oxford Handbook of Civil Society* (Oxford University Press, 2011). See on the UN and Civil Society, online, at www.un.org/en/civilsociety/index.shtml.

[3] J. Keane, 'Global Civil Society', in H. Anheier, M. Glasius and M. Kaldor (eds.), *Global Civil Society 2001* (Oxford University Press, 2001), 23–47.

[4] M. E. Keck and K. Sikkink, *Activists beyond Borders: Advocacy Networks in International Politics* (Ithaca, London: Cornell University Press, 1998).

[5] H. M. Zafarullah and Md. H. M. H. Rahman, 'Human Rights, Civil Society and Nongovernmental Organizations: the Nexus in Bangladesh', *HRQ* 24(4) (2002), 1011–34, at 1016–17.

counterpart, 'global' civil society, has been defined as 'the sphere of ideas, values, institutions, organisations, networks, and individuals located between the family, the state and the market and operating beyond the confines of national societies, polities, and economies'.[6] This broad definition makes it clear that civil society cannot be simply equated with NGOs. Nevertheless, it is equally clear that NGOs form an important organised element of civil society. This is evident in definitions such as those of the World Bank, which understands

the term civil society to refer to the wide array of non-governmental and not-for-profit organizations that have a presence in public life, expressing the interests and values of their members or others, based on ethical, cultural, political, scientific, religious or philanthropic considerations. Civil Society Organizations (CSOs) there-fore refer to a wide array of organizations: community groups, non-governmental organizations (NGOs), labor unions, indigenous groups, charitable organizations, faith-based organizations, professional associations, and foundations.[7]

These definitions suggest that civil society is clearly separate from both the state and political actors as well as the economic sphere.[8] This is seem-ingly reflected in the stance of civil society actors who decide to keep a marked distance from political parties and even formal political processes, focusing instead on using their moral credibility to influence public opinion in order to achieve their objectives. This makes for a clear and important demarcation. However, locating civil society entirely outside the political sphere creates a questionable dichotomy favouring liberal political models leading to an 'NGOization',[9] and may come at the expense of remoteness from democratic processes and a broader public appeal. Yet, in the prac-tice of many countries, particularly in repressive regimes and transitional periods, actors may engage simultaneously in human rights work and polit-ical activities that blur the boundaries between the two spheres.[10] Moreover, the interaction between various voluntary groups and political and economic

---

[6] *Global Civil Society Yearbook*, 2001, quoted in M. Glasius, 'Dissecting Global Civil Society: Values, Actors, Organisational Forms', *openDemocracy* (2 November 2010).

[7] The World Bank, *Defining Civil Society*, online, at http://web.worldbank.org/WBSITE/EXTERNAL/TOPICS/CSO/0,contentMDK:20101499~menuPK:244752~pagePK:220503~piPK:220476~theSitePK:228717,00.html.

[8] This notion of civil society is traced back to A. Gramsci; see M. Shaw, 'Civil Society', in L. Kurtz (ed.), *Encyclopaedia of Violence, Peace and Conflict* (San Diego: Academic Press, 1999), 269–78.

[9] B. Rajagopal, *International Law from Below: Development, Social Movements and Third World Resistance* (Cambridge University Press, 2003), 260–1.

[10] See e.g. L. Laakso, 'Opposition Politics in Zimbabwe', *ASQ* 7(2&3) (2003), online, at http://web.africa.ufl.edu/asq/v7/v7i2a6.htm, and C. Tilly and L. J. Wood, *Social Movements, 1768–2008*, 2nd edn (Boulder, CO, London: Paradigm Publishers, 2009), 1–2.

actors is often fluid. NGOs, for example, are frequently funded by states or by regional or international institutions and enter into strategic partnerships with them.[11]

'Civil society' is commonly associated with the idea of people doing something good. While this may often be true, it is important to recognise that civil society is a multifaceted sphere that forms part of political processes. This means that civil society groups may adopt diametrically opposed positions, some of which may be highly questionable from a human rights perspective. The struggle over the right to abortion between proponents, particularly women's rights groups, and opponents, such as the Catholic Church and others, is an illustration of such dynamics in the field of reproductive rights.[12] What makes civil society valuable, therefore, is not that it provides a particular ('human-rights friendly') view of the world but that it allows the political space in which rights, and competing versions thereof, can be advocated and exercised.

3.3   SOCIAL MOVEMENTS

Human rights advocacy may be founded on 'self-interest', such as the rights of workers, indigenous peoples or lesbian, gay, bisexual or transgender persons (LGBT), or flow from an ethical belief, such as in the case of human rights NGOs or faith-based organisations. Such groups and others often come together to form social movements that are characterised by 'collective challenges ... by people with common purposes and solidarity in sustained interactions with elites, opponents and authorities'.[13] These movements constitute important forms of mobilisation by a cross-section of actors who frequently focus, either directly or indirectly, on human rights issues. The anti-slavery movement, suffragettes advocating women's rights, the struggle for decolonisation, and anti-apartheid and anti-racism campaigns are particularly prominent instances of successful (and often internationalised) campaigns.[14] A key feature of such social movements is the fight against injustice, both at the national and international level. This may target local or single-issue

---

[11] J. Keane, *Cosmocracy* (Centre for the Study of Democracy, 2002), 27, online, at http:// johnkeane.net/wp-content/uploads/2011/01/cosmocracy.pdf.

[12] See J. M. Joachim, *Agenda Setting, the UN, and NGOs: Gender Violence and Reproductive Rights* (Washington, DC: Georgetown University Press, 2007), 133–62; R. Fleishman, 'The Battle against Reproductive Rights: the Impact of the Catholic Church on Abortion Law in Both International and Domestic Areas', *Emory Int'l L. Rev.* 14(1) (2000), 277–314.

[13] S. Tarrow, *Power in Movement: Social Movements and Contentious Politics*, 3rd edn (Cambridge University Press, 2011), 9. See also Tilly and Wood, above note 10, 1–11.

[14] See Keck and Sikkink, above note 4.

violations, such as the fight against development projects, caste-based discrimination or corruption in India, or global concerns, such as campaigns against the adverse impact of globalisation.[15] However, it is important to recognise that some of the methods of social movements may be used by other forces for different causes, such as campaigns against immigration and immigrants that can be seen as antithetical to human rights. In other words, the form of mobilisation does not inherently determine its content.

Social movements do not necessarily frame their cause in human rights terms. Even where a movement deals with an issue that clearly raises human rights concerns, such as poverty or racism, its members may decide not to use human rights language if they believe that it will not resonate and be effective in mobilising others and influencing opinion and behaviour. In the USA, for example, campaigners have frequently preferred to use the language of civil rights because the term 'human rights' is associated with foreign policy and other countries.[16] In the field of ESC rights, social movements may find the language of social justice more potent, such as in the European context with its roots in social democracy and green politics in particular, as well as Christian ideals. How best to frame a campaign that clearly has a human rights dimension can for these reasons constitute a considerable challenge for social movements. This is, however, not merely an instrumental question. Movements may have ambivalent if not deeply hostile attitudes towards the state, which may affect their views on human rights law and its utility as a means of addressing their grievances. Rather than operating within existing legal frameworks, the very thrust of social movements may be to transform systems that are based on non-recognition, exclusion and ultimately violence.[17]

Social movements have increasingly articulated forms of resistance that address injustices with a view to challenging elite agendas and institutionalised decision-making processes. This development has been hailed as an alternative human rights discourse that redefines civil society and democracy 'based on cultural politics of identity, autonomy and territory'[18] and 'offers a local and indigenous ... way of questioning the violence of the postcolonial development state'.[19] This rejection of the state and the search for autonomous political space is, however, open to criticism in so far as it may undermine broader democratic forces and processes, which may in turn weaken the protection of human rights. Nevertheless, social movements must

---

[15] M. Mohanty, P. N. Mukherji with O. Tornquist (eds.), *People's Rights Social Movements and the State in the Third World* (New Delhi: Sage, 1998).

[16] A. C. Finnegan, A. P. Saltsman and S. K. White, 'Negotiating Politics and Culture: the Utility of Human Rights for Activist Organizing in the United States', *JHRP* 2(3) (2010), 307–33.

[17] Rajagopal, above note 9, 262.   [18] Ibid., 236.   [19] Ibid., 254.

be credited with having addressed a number of blind spots in the existing system, including too much faith in institutional forms of protection that may effectively maintain the status quo and reinforce exclusion. This has brought about a reconfiguration of the human rights paradigm, particularly an increased recognition of collective rights and of the need for systems to be more responsive to the demands and particular circumstances of those who are different from the 'mainstream'.

3.4   NGOs

3.4.1   General considerations

NGOs have taken on an ever more important role in the national, regional and international promotion and protection of human rights. The precursors of NGOs date back to the nineteenth century with the emergence of organisations such as Anti-Slavery International.[20] NGOs became recognised as international actors in the formative stages of the UN, as reflected in article 71 of the UN Charter and in ECOSOC resolution 288(X) (1950) which referred to NGOs and gave them consultative status.[21] Today, there are thousands of NGOs working in the field of human rights and related areas, as a glimpse at the – by no means exhaustive – list of NGOs with consultative status at the UN demonstrates.[22]

The ECOSOC eligibility criteria for consultative status in particular provide some useful guidance on the constitutive elements of NGOs. ECOSOC resolution 1996/31[23] considers as NGOs '[a]ny such organization that is not established by a governmental entity or intergovernmental agreement' (organisations set up by governments to appear like NGOs are often, slightly ironically, referred to as GONGOs). In addition to qualitative criteria, such as conformity 'with the spirit, purposes and principles' of the UN Charter and possession of recognised standing within its field, the resolution sets out key organisational elements. NGOs must have established premises, a democratically adopted constitution, as well as democratic and transparent decision-making processes. They should also have authority to speak for their members, a representative structure and appropriate accountability mechanisms.

---

[20] See www.antislavery.org/english. M. Kaye, *1807–2007: Over 200 Years of Campaigning Against Slavery* (London: Anti-Slavery International, 2005), online, at www.antislavery.org/includes/documents/cm_docs/2009/1/18072007.pdf.

[21] Consultative status enables NGOs to attend meetings (e.g. at the UN HRC), make written submissions and oral presentations during meetings.

[22] See http://csonet.org/index.php?menu=17.

[23] ECOSOC resolution 1996/31: Consultative Relationship between the United Nations and Non-governmental Organizations.

Other criteria, such as those relating to profit-making, political nature and registration, are potentially problematic. The assumption that NGOs are not for profit, which is largely based on the ideal that they undertake valuable (and charitable) work for the public good, is increasingly called into question.[24] NGOs need to generate money to sustain themselves and carry out their activities. As a result, they secure funds from individuals, institutions (trusts, foundations or other such donors) or (inter)governmental bodies. However, such funds may be difficult to obtain for particular types of activities and moreover generate dependency on – often shifting – donor agendas. In addition, in several countries, national laws restrict NGO access to funds.[25] Furthermore, some NGOs may wish to provide employment for their beneficiaries, such as displaced persons, a purpose that is typically not covered by funding. Making a profit that relates to aims, such as the sale of publications, or profit intended solely to further the objectives of the organisation, such as rehabilitation for victims of human rights violations, may therefore be seen as compatible with the notion of NGOs outlined above.[26] The European Convention on the Recognition of Legal Personality of International Non-Governmental Organisations appears to recognise as much, given its emphasis on the 'non-profit-making *aim*' (emphasis added) of NGOs. However, engaging in profit making activities raises critical issues for NGOs, such as becoming more market oriented, and may encourage abuse, such as using their mandate as a cover for business activities. It will therefore often constitute good practice to limit such activities, if not refrain from them altogether.

NGOs may carry considerable political weight and many of their members may, and often do, share certain political affiliations. However, they should be distinguished from political parties whose ultimate purpose is to participate in the political system and seek to govern. This is recognised in a useful definition that views NGOs as 'independent voluntary association[s] of people acting together on a continuous basis, for some common purpose, other than achieving government office, making money [see above] or illegal activities'.[27]

---

[24] Judge L. Fernando and A. W. Heston, 'Introduction: NGOs between States, Markets, and Civil Society', in Fernando and Heston, *The Role of NGOs: Charity and Empowerment*, The Annals of the American Academy of Political and Social Science (London, Thousand Oaks, CA: Sage, 1997), 8–20, at 11: 'The distinction between for-profit and nonprofit continues to become blurred. In their drive toward financial self-sufficiency, NGOs function as for-profit organizations.'

[25] See for example NGO laws in Sub-Saharan Africa, *Global Trends in NGO Law*, 3(3) (2011), and *Survey of Arab NGO Laws* 1(4) (2010), online, at the International Centre for Not-for-Profit Law, www.icnl.org.

[26] J. Bennett *et al.*, *NGO Funding Strategies: An Introduction for Southern and Eastern NGOs* (Oxford: INTRAC,1996), 1.

[27] P. Willets, *What is a Non-Governmental Organisation?* (undated), online, at www.staff.city.ac.uk/p.willetts/CS-NTWKS/NGO-ART.HTM.

NGOs are commonly registered as charities or voluntary organisations or similar structures in their home country or, in the case of international NGOs, in the place of their headquarters.[28] However, restrictive national legislation or repression may prevent organisations from registering, or lead to revocation of their registration, in violation of their freedom of association.[29] International resolutions governing consultative status or questions of legal personality require that NGOs are registered and limit the grounds on which such registration may be denied. For example, registration within a member state of the European Convention on the Recognition of Legal Personality of International Non-Governmental Organisations is constitutive of legal personality in all member states.[30] However, registration remains a problem if not a paradox where NGOs are expected to operate formally within a system that may be deeply hostile to their very existence.

3.4.2   Human rights NGOs

Broadly speaking, human rights organisations include any NGO that commits itself to promoting and/or protecting human rights. The ultimately rights-oriented nature of their mandate distinguishes human rights NGOs from related NGOs, such as those working in the humanitarian, development or environmental field. However, such distinctions can be somewhat artificial as some of these NGOs may equally engage in human rights activities, either directly or indirectly. An example is the organisation Médecins sans frontières which provides humanitarian services but also documents human rights violations (*témoignage* = bearing witness), an approach that has brought it into conflict with governments when operating in conflict zones, such as in Darfur.[31]

Many human rights NGOs initially replicated the separation found in the International Bill of Rights between civil and political rights on the one hand and ESC rights on the other.[32] AI, for example, began in the 1960s

---

[28] See for example the UK 2011 Charities Act.

[29] See for detailed studies in the European context the three annual reports of the Expert Council on NGO Law, *Conditions of Establishment of Non-Governmental Organisations*, OING Conf/Exp (2009); *The Internal Governance of Non-Governmental Organisations*, OING Conf/Exp (2010); *Sanctions and Liability in Respect of NGOs*, OING Conf/Exp (2011).

[30] Article 2 of the European Convention on the Recognition of Legal Personality of International Non-Governmental Organisations, CoE, European Treaty Series no. 124. See also Guidelines for Participation by Civil Society Organizations in OAS, CP/RES. 759 (1217/99), para. 2.

[31] Médecins sans frontières, *The Crushing Burden of Rape: Sexual Violence in Darfur* (2005), online, at www.artsenzondergrenzen.nl/docs/Final%20Report%20Sexual%20Violence%20Darfur%20Mar%2005.doc; 'Second Arrest in Sudan; Dutch Coordinator For MSF in Darfur Held This Morning' (31 May 2005), online, at www.doctorswithoutborders.org/press/release_print.cfm?id=1501.

[32] See M. Mutua, 'Standard Setting in Human Rights: Critique and Prognosis', *HRQ* 29(3) (2007), 547–630, at 592–3.

with a mandate to protect peaceful political prisoners.[33] Following sustained demands for a change in focus so that it was better able to respond to the multifaceted nature of human rights violations worldwide, the organisation decided in 2001 to broaden its mandate to include ESC rights. This reflects a strong pull towards a broader mandate as constituencies expect the weight of an organisation to be used to address a range of problems, which may, however, come at the expense of heightened efficacy. At AI this change was characterised by at times heated debates between its members, many of whom were concerned that it would jeopardise what they viewed as the core function of the organisation.[34]

These debates illustrate the difficulties related to mandates, which are at the core of an NGO's identity. The mandate circumscribes what an NGO should be doing and thereby defines its profile. It may be broad or very specific, and may cover all types of human rights, a certain category of rights,[35] or specific rights, such as freedom from torture;[36] or certain groups, such as children's rights[37] or minority rights.[38] NGOs may be associated with a particular area of expertise, or even specific projects at times, such as the Association for the Prevention of Torture with the campaign for the adoption of the Optional Protocol to the Convention against Torture (OPCAT).[39] A shift in the nature of violations, political realities or funding opportunities may tempt NGOs to broaden their mandate, either explicitly or *de facto*. However, such a move frequently creates tensions within (between the 'old guard' and reformers) and may even weaken an NGO where it compromises what are seen as its core strengths.

Human rights NGOs are also sometimes characterised by their organisational set-up, particularly whether or not they function as membership organisations, or described according to their *modus operandi*, i.e. advocacy, policy-making, capacity-building, legal, etc.[40] This may be useful for a better understanding of the approach taken by the NGO in question; however, what matters for NGOs in practice is that they are able to identify and use the strategies that are most effective to achieve their objectives. In terms of their

---

[33] See P. Benenson, 'The Forgotten Prisoners', *The Guardian* (28 May 1961), www.guardian.co.uk/uk/1961/may/28/fromthearchive.theguardian?INTCMP=ILCNETTXT3487.

[34] S. Hopgood, *Keepers of the Flame: Understanding Amnesty International* (Ithaca, London: Cornell University Press, 2006), 92–6 and 181–8.

[35] See for example the Center for Economic and Social Rights, www.cesr.org.

[36] See member organisations of the Coalition of International NGOs against Torture, www.apt.ch/cinat/CINAT.pdf.

[37] See for regional examples the Africawide Movement for Children, www.africawidemovement.org.

[38] See Minority Rights Group International, www.minorityrights.org.

[39] www.apt.ch.

[40] See for a good overview of the nature of NGOs and their activities, ICHRP, *Human Rights Organisations: Rights and Responsibilities*, Final Draft Report (Geneva: ICHRP, 2009), paras. 12–28.

territorial reach, national NGOs frequently link with external actors and use the international arena to bring about domestic change,[41] while international NGOs for their part often work at the national level to strengthen domestic protection efforts and achieve thematic objectives, such as campaigning for the abolition of the death penalty where it still exists.

3.4.3   Assessing the role of human rights NGOs

NGOs have become major players at various levels. Nationally, they have often been at the forefront of campaigns that resulted in reforms, such as in respect of sexual violence in Southern African countries,[42] and as strategic litigators, as was the case with the right to food in India.[43] Regionally and internationally, NGOs have been pivotal in using available treaty and charter bodies and in developing standards, such as women's rights coalitions campaigning for the adoption of the African Protocol on the Rights of Women, as well as the coalitions for an anti-landmine treaty and the ICC Rome Statute.[44] Meanwhile, the increasing power and influence wielded by NGOs has raised a number of questions about their nature and work, as well as their role as political actors, which centre on legitimacy, accountability and effectiveness.[45]

---

[41] Keck and Sikking, above note 4. See also Case Study 3.1 below.

[42] See R. Manjoo, G. Kweka and S. O. Ofuani, 'Sexual Violence and the Law: Comparative Legislative Experiences in Selected South African Countries', in L. Oette (ed.), *Criminal Law Reform and Transitional Justice: Human Rights Perspectives for Sudan* (Farnham: Ashgate, 2011), 269–95.

[43] In 2001, the People's Union for Civil Liberties launched ground-breaking public interest litigation on behalf of starving people before India's Supreme Court on the right to food. The Supreme Court held that the Indian government had a direct responsibility to prevent starvation. It ordered that the country's food stocks be used without delay to prevent hunger and starvation and that all the food-based schemes across India be fully implemented. See *People's Union for Civil Liberties* v. *Union of India & Ors*, in the Supreme Court of India, Civil Original Jurisdiction, Writ Petition (Civil) no. 196 of 2001 (2 May 2003).

[44] See Mutua, above note 32, 589–604; F. Banda, *Women, Law and Human Rights: An African Perspective* (Oxford: Hart, 2005), 66–78; International Campaign to Ban Landmines, www.icbl.org; F. Faulkner, *Moral Entrepreneurs and the Campaign to Ban Landmines* (Amsterdam, New York: Rodopi, 2007); for a critical perspective, K. Anderson, 'The Ottawa Convention Banning Landmines, the Role of International Non-governmental Organizations and the Idea of International Civil Society', *EJIL* 11(1) (2000), 91–120. See also M. Glasius, *The International Criminal Court: A Global Civil Society Achievement* (London, New York: Routledge, 2006).

[45] P. J. Spiro, 'NGOs and Human Rights: Channels of Power', in S. Joseph and A. McBeth (eds.), *Research Handbook on International Human Rights Law* (Cheltenham, UK, Northampton, MA: Edward Elgar, 2010), 115–38; M. T. Kamminga, 'The Evolving Status of NGOs under International Law: a Threat to the Inter-State System?', in P. Alston (ed.), *Non-State Actors and Human Rights* (Oxford University Press, 2005), 93–112; H. Slim, *By What Authority? The Legitimacy and Accountability of Non-governmental Organisations* (Geneva: ICHRP, 2002); Mutua, above note 32, 604–19.

Legitimacy refers to the supposed democracy deficit of NGOs. While NGOs themselves draw legitimacy from their cause, others have questioned whether 'self-appointed groups [are] an adequate substitute for mass movements'.[46] The answer may be 'no' but it must be equally recognised that the growth of NGOs corresponds with the demise of political ideologies and mass movements and is an effect rather than the cause of that demise. Indeed, it is notable that many of those who were active in party politics in a number of countries later became actively engaged in NGOs as an alternative form of politics. NGOs therefore represent a specific form of public engagement. They may be, and often are, a part of social or mass movements. Moreover, an NGO may derive legitimacy from the nature of its engagement and representation, which applies particularly to membership organisations. In the field of human rights NGOs are presumed to act in the broader public interest. This is particularly the case where they seek the protection of rights that have been widely recognised. However, even where an NGO acts as a pressure group for rights not (yet) recognised its work can be considered as an integral part of a pluralistic society.

A further critique of NGOs concerns their composition and mode of operation. NGOs are often seen as professional elites who interact with other elites and, while claiming to represent marginalised persons or groups, 'are very different from the people they seek to save'.[47] This criticism, which is seemingly directed at certain types of NGOs, draws on notions of voluntarism and grassroots self-organisation where people take action either as a matter of principle or to pursue a common cause. While this type of commitment constitutes an ideal, interventions such as complex litigation are time consuming and require considerable professional skills. Nevertheless, the critique highlights the risk that NGOs may become too self-referential and concerned with project cycles and the careers of their members rather than the well-being of those they claim to represent or whose cause they purport to advance.

At the international level, NGOs may develop a self-righteousness that is divorced from the realities on the ground, an accusation that has been repeatedly levelled against major international human rights NGOs.[48] This is seemingly illustrated by the fact that it is often highly educated Western elites who travel and speak on behalf of persons or groups with whom they have little in common or only limited contact.[49] These actors are viewed as

---

[46] R. Pinkney, *NGOs, Africa and the Global Order* (Basingstoke: Palgrave Macmillan, 2009), back cover and introduction, 1–10.

[47] See M. Mutua, *Human Rights: A Political and Cultural Critique* (Philadelphia: University of Pennsylvania Press, 2002), 36–7.

[48] See on the role of international NGOs as 'Missionaries or Imperialists?', Pinkney, above note 46, 157–83. See on the problem of 'human rights messenger' from the 'West' (state functionaries, development planners and programmers) and their 'evangelical claim', Baxi, above note 1, 34–6.

[49] D. Kennedy, 'The International Human Rights Movement: Part of the Problem', *Harv. Hum. Rts. J.* 15 (2002), 101–26, at 121.

carriers of Western bias who, even with the best of intentions, advance liberal notions and objectives that may set false priorities,[50] such as focusing on civil and political rights violations instead of the adverse impact of globalisation. National NGOs collaborating with international NGOs are in this scheme of things frequently elite beneficiaries who are not genuinely representative of the people and may not be interested in addressing deep-seated structural problems.[51] These problems are compounded by the way NGOs are funded because they rely on external donor funding that often comes from Western governments or intergovernmental bodies. This means that funds may be used to advance certain foreign policy goals, create dependency and open the door to corruption.

The issue of corruption leads on to the question of accountability.[52] It is increasingly seen as contradictory and ironic that NGOs frequently call for transparency and accountability but may seemingly be unable or unwilling to follow such standards themselves.[53] This has become particularly acute given the potential for abuse inherent in the power of NGOs in relation to the framing of critical issues and resources as well as individuals and groups of persons who they claim to represent or interact with. Many NGOs have recognised that accountability is imperative to maintaining their credibility, which is their major asset, both in terms of garnering public support for their positions and of obtaining funds. Transparency is also critical to counter attacks by governments and others that may wrongly accuse NGOs of misconduct, often as a pretext for banning national NGOs or expelling/preventing entry of international NGOs or undermining their work more generally. NGOs have therefore taken a number of initiatives to affirm their responsibility and take appropriate action, for example in the form of codes of conduct and the international NGO Accountability Charter,[54] with a view to ensuring respect for human rights in their own work and to striving for best practices in relation to governance, effectiveness, independence, truthfulness and transparency *vis-à-vis* their various constituencies.[55] These are important first steps that signal a shift from NGOs as 'moral' forces to political actors who must not only say that they do good but also demonstrate that this is actually the case.

Effectiveness essentially concerns the question of whether NGOs are doing what they are supposed to be doing, whether they are doing it well and

---

[50] Ibid., 114–16. See also Mutua, above note 47, 39–70.

[51] Banda, above note 44, 289–91; Mutua, above note 32, 593.

[52] The ICHRP prefers the term responsibility. See ICHRP, above note 40, para. 83.

[53] See for a brief overview, ibid., paras. 79–82. See also J. McGann and M. Johnstone, 'The Power Shift and the NGO Credibility Crisis', *IJNfP* 8(2) (2006), 65–77; M. Marschall, 'Legitimacy and Effectiveness: Civil Society Organizations Role in Good Governance', *Transparency International* (*TI*) (1 November 2002).

[54] See www.ingoaccountabilitycharter.org.   [55] ICHRP, above note 40, paras. 132–206.

whether they have the intended impact. This is critical for NGOs' legitimacy. In other words, are their claims in respect of any of these points justified? Unlike companies or political parties who (ideally) face the judgement of the market or the electorate respectively, NGOs report back to their donors or their members, where applicable. Beyond this, it is often difficult to tell to what degree an NGO has been effective. Many NGOs undertake evaluations, which can be a useful tool, especially where they are carried out throughout project cycles and with the active participation of beneficiaries.[56] However, while some NGOs' may be able to point to successes, such as the adoption of the Rome Statute in the case of the Coalition for the ICC, the long-term nature of their work, for example advocating reforms in repressive regimes, frequently makes it difficult if not impossible to identify tangible impacts. These realities call for a nuanced assessment of what constitutes effectiveness, including such broad notions as creating rights awareness, which is ideally based on considerable empirical work where researchers chart the impact of NGOs' human rights work over a substantial period of time.[57]

The criticism levelled against NGOs can act as a healthy mirror to counteract complacency or self-congratulatory attitudes. Questions of legitimacy deficit, limited accountability, concern over effectiveness and unequal power relationships between national and international NGOs are all too real. However, it is important not to lose sight of the fact that a large number of NGOs respond to genuine problems and needs and frequently play a critical role in opening political space. The uprisings in the Arab world in 2010 and 2011, for example, showed that NGOs had forged close links with bloggers, youth movements and other political actors, and were often part and parcel of developments rather than constituting aloof elites.[58] While unequal power relationships between international and national NGOs remain, which reflect global relationships more generally, national and regional NGOs in the Americas, Africa and Asia have made considerable progress in developing their capacity, which is slowly changing the international dynamics. Western-based international NGOs are often still dominant because they are close to the centres of powers and are frequently better resourced. However, there is an increased realisation that the legitimacy of NGOs demands more substantial equality, which is also reflected in the debates and decisions made by international NGOs.[59] Nevertheless, the risk that international NGOs

---

[56] See for example C. Thomas, 'Evaluation at Minority Rights Group', *JHRP* 1(3) (2009), 488–98.

[57] Ibid.

[58] See Interview 1.1 with Moataz El Fegiery, Chapter 1.5.2., and L. Al-Zubaidi, 'Digital Activism: Arabs Can Do It Themselves: Interview with Sami Ben Gharbia', in *People's Power: The Arab World in Revolt, Perspectives: Political Analysis and Commentary from the Middle East*, 2, special issue, (2011): 86–9.

[59] Hopgood, above note 34, 161–75.

unduly dictate what is best and how things are done should not be taken lightly. What is needed, therefore, is a self-reflective practice of how best to join forces based on a spirit of mutual respect and solidarity.

3.5   HUMAN RIGHTS DEFENDERS

'Human rights defenders' is a broad, catch-all term that is not confined to NGOs with an explicit human rights mandate or 'human rights activists' but includes 'individuals, groups and associations ... contributing to ... the effective elimination of all violations of human rights and fundamental freedoms of peoples and individuals'.[60] The category therefore reflects realities in which anyone can defend human rights irrespective of his/her/their profession, which captures the multiple efforts by individuals and groups around the world. The notion of human rights defenders derives its importance from the fact that it has been endorsed by the UN and entails a set of rights and obligations, as well as protection mechanisms. NGO advocacy and UN concern resulted in the 1998 UN Declaration on Human Rights Defenders adopted by consensus by the UNGA.[61] Significantly, this resolution, which was motivated by the desire to give legitimacy to the work of human rights defenders and to enhance protection, recognises that '[e]veryone has the right, individually and in association with others, to promote and to strive for the protection and realization of human rights and fundamental freedoms at the national and international levels'. It constitutes an important recognition of the valuable work done by human rights defenders and identifies a number of existing rights and corresponding duties of states, which have undoubtedly been formulated with a view to countering practices that states have used to restrict the work of human rights defenders. The declaration's rights are largely based on the freedom of expression, assembly and association, including the right to 'form, join and participate in non-governmental organizations, associations or groups'. The declaration also addresses prerequisites for human rights work, such as the right to receive funds, including from abroad, and to engage in activities such as advocacy, trial observation and complaints, as well as the right to an effective remedy and protection.

The protection of human rights defenders has become a major concern. Defenders have been increasingly subjected to harassment, threats, arbitrary arrest, detention and unfair trials, various forms of ill treatment and

---

[60] Declaration on the Right and Responsibility of Individuals, Groups and Organs of Society to Promote and Protect Universally Recognized Human Rights and Fundamental Freedoms, UNGA resolution 53/144 (8 March 1999).

[61] Ibid. See also Mutua, above note 32, 564–5.

extrajudicial killings. There are numerous examples where those who bear witness to human rights violations and/or seek to counter them have themselves been targeted.[62] This applies in particular to sensitive cases where individuals or organisations collect evidence that may expose corrupt practices, jeopardise business interests (of both government and non-state actors) and contribute to criminal prosecutions. Cases in point are the suspicious death in custody, allegedly as a result of ill treatment, of the Russian lawyer Sergei Magnitzky who had investigated a major tax fraud implicating several officials, the killing in Sri Lanka of Lasantha Wickrematunge, a well-known investigative journalist whose newspaper had run a series of articles about human rights violations,[63] and the murder of human rights defender Jesús María Valle Jaramillo in Colombia after having 'actively denounced the crimes perpetrated by paramilitary elements, as well as the collaboration and acquiescence between the latter and members of the National Army'.[64] The arbitrary arrest and unfair trials resulting in the execution of Ken Saro Wiwa and other Ogoni people who had fought against the ills of oil exploration during Nigeria's dictatorship in the 1990s is another infamous example of an egregious violation.[65] Those who protest on behalf of indigenous peoples, ethnic minorities or other marginalised groups, such as women's rights or LGBT groups, have also been under attack, as illustrated by the killing of the Ugandan gay rights activist David Kato in 2011.[66] Foreign nationals may equally be targeted and states have resorted to questioning, threatening and expelling international NGO members, human rights activists and UN staff members whose presence has attracted unwelcome attention to their human rights record.[67]

---

[62] Report of the Special Rapporteur on the situation of human rights defenders, Addendum: Summary of Cases Transmitted to Governments and Replies Received, UN Doc. A/HRC/16/44/Add.1 (28 February 2011); IACHR, Report on the Situation of Human Rights Defenders in the Americas, OEA/Ser.L/V/II.124 (7 March 2006).

[63] See on the *Magnitzky* case, REDRESS, 'Allegation letter regarding Mr Sergei Magnitzky (Russian Federation)', (21 December 2010), online, at www.redress.org/case-docket/ allegation-letter-to-un-special-rapporteurs-on-torture-and-on-the-independence-of-the-judiciary.pdf; L. Wickrematunge, 'And Then They Came for Me', *Sunday Leader* (11 January 2009) (editorial published after his killing), at www.thesundayleader.lk/20090111/ editorial-.htm.

[64] *Valle-Jaramillo* v. *Colombia*, Merits, reparations and costs, Judgment of 27 November 2008, Ser. C, no. 192, para. 73.

[65] See *International Pen and Others* v. *Nigeria*, 137/94, 139/94, 154/96 and 161/97 (1998).

[66] N. Pillay, UN High Commissioner for Human Rights, 'What David Kato's Death can Teach the World' (1 February 2011), online, at www.ohchr.org/en/NewsEvents/Pages/ DisplayNews.aspx?NewsID=10750&LangID=E.

[67] See for example the measures taken against NGOs in Sudan, Report of the Special Rapporteur on the situation of human rights defenders, Addendum: Summary of Cases Transmitted to Governments and Replies Received, UN Doc. A/HRC/13/22/Add.1 (24 February 2010), paras. 2114–18.

The UN has responded to these developments by establishing the position of Special Representative of the UN Secretary-General on Human Rights Defenders in 2000, which was later replaced by the UN Special Rapporteur on human rights defenders in 2008.[68] The Special Rapporteur has identified a number of developments of concern and exercises an important protective function where human rights defenders are at risk. Dialogue with governments and others is critical to prevent violations but may often not be sufficient, in which case it becomes crucial to react promptly to serious threats. The UN and others have advocated putting in place mechanisms to help in a quick and informal way where human rights defenders face adverse repercussions, such as by granting visa exemptions. These efforts have been complemented by EU/CoE initiatives to support human rights defenders in the region and beyond.[69] However, there are limits to the level of protection various official actors can provide in practice and human rights defenders themselves are increasingly taking precautionary measures to minimise the risk. There are now an increasing number of NGOs and networks, such as Protection International,[70] whose principal mandate is to provide protection for human rights defenders.[71]

Beyond the issue of protection, human rights defenders, particularly NGOs, continue to be subjected to a barrage of restrictive practices aimed at controlling their work. In early 2010, several NGOs expressed their concerns at attempts made by several states in the HRC to narrow the definition of human rights defenders and 'better' regulate their work so as to avoid the 'political abuse' of NGO status and 'evasion of national laws'.[72] These attempts, which were ultimately unsuccessful, illustrate the atmosphere of distrust and hostility in which many human rights defenders have to operate. While some human rights defenders are reported to have engaged in questionable practices, including corruption, the thrust of the latest debate is clearly directed against the right to challenge state practices recognised in the UN Declaration on Human Rights Defenders, which is still anathema to many governments.

---

[68] www.ohchr.org/EN/Issues/SRHRDefenders/Pages/SRHRDefendersIndex.aspx.

[69] Declaration of the Committee of Ministers on Council of Europe Action to Improve the Protection of Human Rights Defenders and Promote their Activities (6 February 2008).

[70] www.protectioninternational.org.

[71] See on the issue of protection more broadly, REDRESS, *Ending Threats and Reprisals against Victims of Torture and Related International Crimes: A Call to Action* (London: REDRESS, 2009).

[72] On 23 March 2010, a joint NGO statement expressed alarm at attempts during the negotiations to selectively quote from, rewrite, or restrict the clear provisions of the Declaration on Human Rights Defenders in order to regulate the work of NGOs and restrict protection only to those working on issues that governments had accepted or agreed with. See www.ishr.ch/council-news/730-human-rights-council-hears-calls-for-protection-of-human-rights-defenders.

CASE STUDY 3.1
NGOs and human rights protection in Sudan

After its military coup in 1989, the Sudanese regime embarked on a crackdown against civil society activists and political opposition characterised by serious human rights violations, including a wave of bans, arbitrary arrests and detention, unfair trials, torture and extrajudicial killings.[1] Throughout the 1990s any work related to human rights inside Sudan was extremely difficult due to the prevailing repressive atmosphere. Later, in 2001 and 2002, lawyers, doctors and journalists were able to establish two human rights organisations in Sudan, the Khartoum Centre for Human Rights and Environmental Development and the Amal (Hope) Centre for the Rehabilitation of Victims of Torture, which operated closely with a London-based organisation of Sudanese victims in exile. While the Khartoum Centre engaged in legal aid litigation and advocacy, the Amal Centre provided – for the first time in Sudan – regular specialised treatment for victims of violations, including for victims of rape in Darfur after 2004.

The centres quickly gained in reputation, due to a combination of the capacity of their staff and their ability to monitor human rights violations and to reach out to a broad network inside Sudan and internationally. This development, taking place against the backdrop of the conflict in Darfur characterised by massive violations and political changes following the North–South peace agreement in 2005, brought with it a series of opportunities and challenges. There were only few human rights organisations in Sudan with some capacity, which meant that international organisations were keen to work with the centres and donors were eager to fund a broad range of activities. As a result, the Khartoum Centre and the Amal Centre, particularly in Darfur, had to cope with increasing demand that stretched their own capacities.

These developments also left the centres vulnerable to corruption and security interference, with one leading staff member accused of having misused considerable sums of money and of reporting back to the Sudanese security services about internal affairs. The staff and the centres' network came under increasing pressure in the form of repeated arrests, interrogation, raids of meetings and other measures, some of which had been sanctioned by a newly enacted law, the Organisation of Humanitarian and Voluntary Work Act 2006, which allowed the authorities greater control over the growing number of human rights NGOs. This situation deteriorated following the application for an arrest warrant for Sudan's President Al-Bashir by the ICC Prosecutor in July 2008. According to a complaint brought before the African Commission on

---

[1] See *Amnesty International and Others* v. *Sudan*, 48/90, 50/91, 52/91, 89/93 (1999).

Human and Peoples' Rights, two human rights defenders associated with the Khartoum Centre were tortured in November 2008 and its then director was threatened with torture.[2] Amid further threats the key staff members decided to leave the country and the Centre was closed down by the authorities, who froze its accounts and confiscated the Centre's belongings, including its extensive human rights library, notwithstanding the presence of UNMIS, the UN Mission in Sudan, in Khartoum. Other organisations suffered a similar fate while some NGOs and individuals were able to continue their human rights work in an extremely repressive environment. The story of the Khartoum Centre and the Amal Centre, which played a critical role in documenting and monitoring violations and providing legal and medical support to victims in the period 2001–2009, demonstrates the often fragile position of national NGOs and their members. They must frequently work in situations where there is a need to respond to serious human rights violations and to interact with a range of national, regional and international actors while at the same time building their own capacity, ensuring the effective functioning of the organisation and navigating a repressive political environment. National NGOs may in such situations overreach themselves and their members or associates may risk losing touch with local realities where they have easy access to money and are fêted internationally; international actors, such as other NGOs and donors, for their part need to be careful not to inadvertently encourage corruption or exposure of national human rights defenders to security threats because their ability to protect individuals or organisations from harm or closure may be limited.

POINTS TO CONSIDER

- To what extent does the story of the Khartoum Centre and the Amal Centre bear out concerns that have been raised about the relationship between national NGOs and international actors?

- What violations of the UN Declaration on Human Rights Defenders are evident?

- Are developments in Sudan exceptional or do they raise generic concerns that illustrate the need to make the international system pertaining to the work of human rights defenders, particularly NGOs, more effective?

---

[2] *Monim Elgak, Osman Hummeida and Amir Suliman* v. Sudan, 379/2009 (pending as of July 2012).

3.6   LEGAL PROFESSIONALS AND HUMAN RIGHTS

The broad definition of human rights defenders rightly suggests that the promotion and protection of human rights is not the domain of any particular type of actor or profession. Nevertheless, it is clear that the legal profession plays an important role, both in the development of standards and their practical application. The dominance of lawyers and the supposedly increasingly legalistic approach to human rights has been lamented but constitutes a reality that is perhaps inevitable, at least as far as the growth of and recourse to international human rights law is concerned.

The legal profession comprises lawyers, judges, prosecutors, legal advisors, academics and others who may pursue rather different objectives and approaches in respect of human rights. Indeed, they are often pitted against each other. What unites them is that they frequently use the law to argue for or against the recognition, or particular interpretation, of human rights, or responsibility for a breach in a given instance. Unsurprisingly, legal professionals have been both at the forefront of the human rights movement, for example the International Commission of Jurists,[73] and at the heart of repressive regimes that ignore the rule of law and violate human rights. There is a long list of legal officials, attorney generals and judges who have effectively served as handmaidens of regimes. This has included drafting infamous laws that are blatantly discriminatory or providing for broad powers and/or punishments that serve as a recipe for human rights violations.[74] It has also consisted in politically motivated prosecutions, staging of show trials and/or handing down clearly disproportionate punishments. The role of legal professionals was particularly notorious in the Soviet Union under Stalin and in Nazi Germany, with the Prosecutor-General Andrey Vyshinsky and the judge of the Nazi Peoples' Court Roland Freisler representing two particularly infamous prototypes.[75] In a number of countries, judges have failed to uphold human rights, for example by imposing the death penalty after blatantly unfair trials.[76] Legal professionals, such as US legal advisors in the context of the so-called war on terror, have tried to reinterpret the law, here the prohibition of torture, so as to justify practices that amounted to violations, in this instance through the prohibition of torture.[77]

---

[73] www.icj.org.

[74] This observation applies virtually to any regime that enacts such legislation. See for a particularly pertinent example the role of lawyers in Nazi Germany, I. Müller, *Hitler's Justice: The Courts of the Third Reich* (Cambridge, MA: Harvard University Press, 1992).

[75] Ibid., and A. Vaksberg, *Stalin's Prosecutor: The Life of Andrei Vyshinsky* (New York: Grove, Weidenfeld, 1991).

[76] See for an excellent study of how the legal system and the judiciary were employed in Sudan to prop up the then Nimeri regime, which resulted in the execution of the 'Sudanese Muslim reformer', Mahmoud Muhammad Taha in 1983, A. A. An-Na'im, 'The Islamic Law of Apostasy and its Modern Applicability: a Case Study from Sudan', *Religion* 16 (1986), 197–224.

[77] See in particular P. Sands, *Torture Team: Rumsfeld's Memo and the Betrayal of American Values* (New York: Palgrave Macmillan, 2008).

Notably, academics have at times sought to lend a degree of credibility to such endeavours.[78]

While law is a contested sphere, i.e. actors have different views on how to interpret rights and obligations depending on their standpoint, the realm of acceptability is arguably left behind where an overwhelming body of opinion strongly rejects the arguments put forward. This is particularly the case where the legal professionals concerned are aware that their arguments legitimise violence for political ends, although such intent will be difficult to prove in practice. In noteworthy contrast, many legal professionals have taken a stance to defend human rights. Examples include lawyers who provide legal assistance, often pro bono (free of charge), in politically sensitive cases, legally oriented NGOs using advocacy and legal avenues to bring about broader changes or hold perpetrators of violations accountable, or a combination of actors, for example when pursuing Pinochet in Spain and the UK.[79] Legal professionals are increasingly using the media or journalistic methods to reach a broad audience when contesting particular practices, such as in respect of violations alleged to have been committed in the war against terror and in the course of armed conflicts in Afghanistan and Iraq.[80] Professional bodies, such as bar associations, can also play an important role though they often work in repressive environments where they either lack independence or find it difficult to engage effectively in human rights work. Nevertheless, some associations, such as in Pakistan, have taken prominent action in defence of the independence of the judiciary, protesting and successfully calling for the reinstatement of Chief Justice Muhammad Chaudhry who had in their view been unfairly dismissed by the then President Musharraf in 2007.[81]

Legal officials are often pivotal to human rights protection, particularly during transitional periods or where a government with a strong commitment to human rights, or at least certain rights, is in power. Their role is particularly important where they stand up to human rights violations.

---

[78] See for example J. Addicott, 'No Torture, No Prosecution', *Opinio Juris* (8 May 2009). See also the account of a writer who, after his positions on interrogation methods were challenged, voluntarily underwent waterboarding; C. Hitchens, 'Believe Me, It's Torture', *Vanity Fair* (August 2008).

[79] See in particular A. Dorfman, *Exorcising Terror: The Incredible Unending Trial of General Augusto Pinochet* (New York: Seven Stories Press, 2002), 32, and N. Roht-Arriaza, *The Pinochet Effect: Transnational Justice in the Age of Human Rights* (Philadelphia: University of Pennsylvania Press, 2006), 208.

[80] See for example Phil Shiner of Public Interest Lawyers, at www.publicinterestlawyers.co.uk/aboutus.php.

[81] See Notes, 'The Pakistani Lawyers' Movement and the Popular Currency of Judicial Power', *Harv. L. Rev.* 123 (2010), 1705–26; International Bar Association, *The Struggle to Maintain an Independent Judiciary: A Report on the Attempt to Remove the Chief Justice of Pakistan* (London: IBA, 2007).

However, as the targeting of magistrates and ombudsmen in countries such as Colombia demonstrates,[82] it is clear that their room for manoeuvre is limited where there is a lack of protection, particularly where high-ranking officials or influential individuals are implicated in human rights violations.

The role of judges in human rights protection has been widely acknowledged. Indeed, judges themselves have repeatedly affirmed their responsibility in this regard.[83] There are numerous examples of judges at the national, regional and international level who have applied and consciously developed the scope of international human rights law, including in politically tense contexts such as counter-terrorism policies in the UK.[84] One of the most remarkable examples of judicial activism in this regard is public interest litigation in South Asia, particularly India, where Indian judges relaxed the rules of standing and interpreted fundamental rights broadly so as to protect human rights more effectively.[85] This has resulted in an impressive body of jurisprudence but limited changes on the ground for lack of enforcement, which highlights the limits of the law as a tool for social change where judicial and political forces are not in agreement.

Many academics working in the field of human rights have close links with NGOs and litigate human rights cases.[86] Several universities run human rights centres and clinics that often provide valuable research and have carried out important work to support advocacy and litigation efforts.[87] Universities also provide a forum for discourse and nurture new generations of human rights scholars and activists. However, due to repressive environments and resource constraints, it is mainly universities in Western countries

---

[82] See Report of the Special Rapporteur on the situation of human rights defenders, Mission to Colombia, UN Doc. A/HRC/13/22/Add.3 (4 March 2010).

[83] See for example the Bangalore Principles of Judicial Conduct, 2002, adopted by the Judicial Group on Strengthening Judicial Integrity, at the Round Table Meeting of Chief Justices held at the Peace Palace (The Hague, 25–6 November 2002).

[84] See in this regard, T. Bingham, *The Rule of Law* (London: Allen Lane, 2010), 133–59.

[85] See S. Deva, 'Public Interest Litigation in India: a Critical Review', *Civil Justice Quarterly* (*CJQ*) 28 (2009), 19–40.

[86] See interview 6.2 with Bill Bowring in Chapter 6.

[87] See for example the Centre for Human Rights of the Faculty of Law, University of Pretoria, which was established 'as part of domestic efforts against the apartheid system of the time' and has now 'positioned itself in an unmatched network of practising and academic lawyers, national and international civil servants and human rights practitioners across the entire continent, with a specific focus on human rights law in Africa, and international development law in general'. See www.chr.up.ac.za. See for a further example from Iran, M. M. Meghdadi and A. Erfani-Nasab, 'The Role of Legal Clinics of Law Schools in Human Rights Education: Mofid University Legal Clinic Experience', *PSBS* 15 (2011), 3014–17, and, on the US experience, D. R. Hurwitz, 'Lawyering for Justice and the Inevitability of International Human Rights Clinics', *Yale J. Int'l L.* 28 (2003), 505–50.

that can provide such opportunities, including for overseas students, thereby reinforcing existing divides. Nevertheless, efforts are being made around the world to establish centres that provide local spaces and respond to regional if not wider concerns, and it will be important to support initiatives that are of lasting value in building a global community of human rights lawyers.

3.7   HEALTH PROFESSIONALS AND HUMAN RIGHTS

Health professionals occupy a particularly sensitive position in respect of human rights. Their knowledge and skills can be used either to commit or facilitate violations or, alternatively, to document and respond to breaches, mitigate their consequences or, ideally, prevent them. Doctors and health professionals have been implicated in notorious violations, such as experiments and killings during the Holocaust,[88] and have assisted in the execution of the death penalty and torture.[89] It was not least in protest against the conduct of their professional colleagues that health professionals started engaging in efforts aimed at the protection of human rights. This has included providing treatment and rehabilitation to victims of serious violations,[90] and entailed developing tools, such as the Istanbul Protocol and the Minnesota Protocol, to document torture and extrajudicial killings respectively.[91] These are important instruments as medical reports and forensic findings frequently constitute crucial evidence both in human rights cases and in criminal trials relating to human rights violations. Psychologists and psychiatrists also assess the consequences of violations for victims, families and communities at large,[92] and these can be highly valuable in legal proceedings, such as when determining adequate reparation measures.[93]

[88] H. H. Fryhofer, *The Nuremberg Medical Trial: The Holocaust and the Origin of the Nuremberg Medical Code* (New York: Peter Lang, 2004); R. J. Lifton, *The Nazi Doctors: Medical Killing and the Psychology of Genocide* (New York: Basic Books, 2000).

[89] See for example British Medical Association, *Medicine Betrayed: The Participation of Doctors in Human Rights Abuses* (London: Zed Books, 1992).

[90] See in particular the website of the International Rehabilitation Council for Torture Victims, www.irct.org, and the Rehabilitation and Research Centre for Torture Victims www.rct.org.

[91] 'Manual on the Effective Investigation and Documentation of Torture and Other Cruel, Inhuman or Degrading Treatment or Punishment (Istanbul Protocol)', submitted to the UN High Commissioner for Human Rights, 9 August 1999, and Manual on the Effective Prevention and Investigation of Extra-legal, Arbitrary and Summary Executions, UN Doc. E/ST/CSDHA/12 (1991).

[92] See for example D. Somasundaram, *Scarred Minds: The Psychological Impact of War on Sri Lankan Tamils* (New Delhi: Sage, 1998), and S. Priebe *et al.*, 'Experience of Human Rights Violations and Subsequent Mental Disorders: a Study Following the War in the Balkans', *SSM* xxx (2010), 1–8.

[93] See for example *Gutiérrez-Soler* v. *Colombia*, Merits, reparations and Costs, Judgment of 12 September 2005, Ser. C, no. 132, para. 127(5).

Significantly, initiatives have not been confined to individuals. Health professionals have established and run important NGOs, such as Physicians for Human Rights[94] and professional bodies have committed themselves to human rights standards. The World Medical Association, for example, has issued a number of resolutions on the role and duties of health professionals in relation to particular situations and violations, including the duty to speak out against violations.[95]

3.8 HUMAN RIGHTS FIELD OFFICERS

Human rights field operations have become an important component of many UN, OHCHR, OAS, AU or OSCE missions or programmes, which are typically mandated by resolutions or agreements with the host country.[96] While this practice is taken for granted today, it is actually a fairly recent development that began in the early 1990s, with the first deployment of human rights field workers to El Salvador (1991) and then to Cambodia, Haiti and former Yugoslavia.[97] The mandate of missions differs depending on the situation but several core areas of human rights field work have been identified on the basis of surveys carried out in 2004 and 2008, namely 'monitoring, reporting, advocacy/intervention, capacity-building, engaging with humanitarian and development partners, support to peace processes and transitional justice, in-mission sensitisation and participation in UN governance of transitional territories'.[98] In the beginning, human rights field workers operated with limited guidance and often in an *ad hoc* fashion. This was soon considered inadequate, if not outright irresponsible, because it could put both people in country and human rights field officers themselves at risk. For example, handing out questionnaires to detainees in Rwanda to report about their treatment is said to have resulted in acts of retaliation

---

[94] www.physiciansforhumanrights.org.

[95] See for example Resolution on the Responsibility of Physicians in the Documentation and Denunciation of Acts of Torture or Cruel or Inhuman or Degrading Treatment (54th World Medical Association (WMA) General Assembly, September 2003 as amended by the 58th WMA General Assembly, October 2007); Resolution on Health and Human Rights Abuses in Zimbabwe (58th WMA General Assembly, October 2007); Council Resolution on Genocide in Darfur (176th WMA Council Session, May 2006); all available at www.wma.net.

[96] See B. G. Ramcharan (ed.), *Human Rights Protection in the Field* (Leiden: Brill, 2006), and M. O'Flaherty (ed.), *The Human Rights Field Operation: Law, Theory and Practice* (Farnham: Ashgate, 2007).

[97] See M. O'Flaherty and G. Ulrich, 'The Professional Identity and Development of Human Rights Field Workers', in O'Flaherty and Ulrich (eds.), *The Professional Identity of the Human Rights Field Worker* (Farnham: Ashgate, 2010), 9–10.

[98] Ibid., 23.

against them because no precautions or protective measures had been taken by the human rights field officers at the time.[99]

The situation in mission countries is frequently characterised by a series of complex political, legal and practical challenges and the need to provide effective protection against ongoing violations. Operating in such environments requires a range of skills, necessitating increasing professionalism on the part of international and national officers. The Human Rights Law Centre of the University of Nottingham, together with several partners, took the initiative of drawing up two major documents that provide guidance on critical issues, namely the 2008 *Guiding Principles for Human Rights Officers Working in Conflict and Post-Conflict Environments* and the *Statement of Ethical Commitments of Human Rights Professionals.*[100] Both documents set out relevant principles in some detail and have proved useful tools. However, there are still concerns about the limited practical training and guidance that human rights field officers receive prior to deployment.[101] They often have to develop the relevant knowledge and skills on the job and make a number of difficult choices in what is typically a highly politicised and fluctuating environment, both within organisations and in the host country itself. This includes questions on how to respond to violations (effective protection without putting anyone at risk), engaging with authorities (having to rely on cooperation while being critical at the same time), and relating to civil society (which may not be responsive enough or too close – human rights operations may also weaken civil society by recruiting talented personnel). It also concerns ethical questions as to how human rights field officers relate to others, particularly vulnerable people and victims of violations, and how they conduct themselves in the host country generally.[102] Beyond allegations of misconduct of individual officers forming part of broader concerns about abuses by UN personnel,[103] in-country missions can have other unintended impacts, such as inflating prices, and human rights officers frequently operate in and share a space of power imbalance *vis-à-vis* the majority of the population.

---

[99] W. G. O'Neill, 'The Guiding Principles for Human Rights Field Officers Working in Conflict and Post-Conflict Environments: a Commentary', ibid., 33–48, at 39.

[100] Text can be found ibid.

[101] J. Horowitz, 'OHCHR Pre-deployment Human Rights Training: Adapting to the Evolving Roles, Responsibilities, and Influence of UN Human Rights Officers', *JHRP* 2(1) (2010), 49–70.

[102] See Principle no. 10: 'Do No Harm', 2008 Guiding Principles.

[103] See UN Secretary General, A Comprehensive Strategy to Eliminate Future Sexual Exploitation and Abuse in United Nations Peacekeeping Operations, UN Doc. A/59/710 (24 March 2005), and E. P. Flaherty and S. Hunt, 'Rule without Law: Injustice at the United Nations?', *GPQ* (April 2006), 21–54.

INTERVIEW 3.1
Experiences of a UN human rights officer
(Huma Shakeb Khan)

Huma Shakeb Khan works as a UN human rights officer in Iraq. She joined the mission in 2009 and has served in various places across Iraq, with Erbil, the capital of the autonomous Kurdish region, being her duty station in 2012.

What training and guidance did you receive prior to deployment to Iraq?

I received a four-day security training which was geared towards military questions and was fairly racist in its approach towards Iraq and Iraqis. It was extremely gender insensitive and I have never used a single thing from that training in my three years of work in Iraq. The training was mandatory and the contractor charged large amounts of money from the mission. In truth, it felt more like a scam. The UN's only concern seemed to be about security before deploying their staff. There was a brief session on cultural sensitivity and we were not given any reading material about Iraq, so we were basically left to our own devices in finding out more about the country.

What have been the main human rights problems in Iraq during your time there?

The problems in Iraq and the autonomous Kurdish region differ from each other considerably. In the Kurdish region weak institutions are one of the key problems. Security institutions do not abide by the rule of law, the anti-terror law is misused, and weak democratic institutions allow freedom of expression to be compromised. Violence against women and ill treatment of migrant workers are further problems, as well as ensuring that the work of oil companies does not result in harm to the local people and environment. One of the main issues is the disputed territories between the autonomous Kurdish region and the federal government of Iraq. These areas have a significant Kurdish population and the demography has changed a lot due to the policies of the former regime that had expelled a large number of Kurds, though many of them returned after 2003. In these areas both Kurdish and Iraqi military arrest people without following proper legal procedure and enforced disappearances are still common. In addition, there are several insurgent groups and attacks on civilians are common.

What is your typical day like working in Erbil?

We live in a compound which has an office and accommodation. I am in the office by 8.30 am. In Erbil it is easy to move outside. So on a regular day I have a few meetings outside, and sometimes within the compound either with victims, NGO or UN agencies. I usually work until 6–7 pm. In the evenings, I either stay in my room after dinner or go out somewhere with colleagues. Previously we could only leave the compound in the presence of security officers but the situation has improved a lot, particularly compared to places like Kirkuk and Baghdad. Some colleagues have lived there for two years and may not have seen a single regular Iraqi shop or market.

How do you monitor the human rights situation, and how effective is this monitoring?

We conduct visits to places of detention, meet with detainees in private, visit government and NGO-run shelters, meet with civil society and follow up cases in court. We also go to the various districts and sub-districts and meet witnesses and victims. In other parts of Iraq one has to rely a lot on local staff, phone calls and civil society to obtain information, which changes the nature of monitoring. The mandate in the Kurdish region focuses more on technical assistance and supporting the government.

It is hard to measure the impact of monitoring. In the Kurdish region it has had some impact as the government is keen to collaborate with international organisations and is receptive, and the UN is generally well liked for the role it played during the Kurdish uprising. In other parts of Iraq the UN is mainly associated with the occupation forces and thus does not really command a lot of respect from local actors. In addition to dealing with the government concerned, there are a lot of internal struggles within the UN system as we are part of a political mission run by the Department of Political Affairs, which can lead to a clash between the political aspects of the mission and human rights, usually ending in favour of the former.

What are the biggest challenges you experienced in fulfilling your tasks?

As a human rights activist I used to struggle a lot with the diplomatic nature of the organisation. It is a constant balancing act, which can be valuable in so far as it means that we gain more attention from the government than activists do. Moreover, working in an extremely insecure environment makes work really challenging. There are also several blind spots, such as the role played by NATO in Iraq which affected human rights, but that is not within our mandate. The UN's weakness in respect of the occupation of Iraq also makes it difficult to 'preach' to Iraqis. I try to work around this by keeping issues at a very local level, offering assistance in improving and acknowledging the limitations of the organisation.

What lessons can be learned from your experience for individual human rights officers and for field operations more generally?

Human rights work takes place in a particular political and social context, which defines international human rights law. Human rights officers need to be very aware and keen to understand that context and work with local team members and interlocutors to define the issues accordingly. It is important to not come across as being on a civilising mission where the world is divided between 'uncivilised' and 'civilised'. Having examples from different countries to show how things can be done is helpful in this respect. Keeping polite and humble always helps. Drawing upon civil society organisations from within the country always strengthens the work of human rights officers and one should invest in developing meaningful partnerships. Finally, it is important to understand the difference in the work of the UN compared to Human Rights Watch (HRW) or AI. Each one has its own value although they are very different. The UN has to work in close collaboration with the government concerned as per our respective mandates in field missions. Maintaining that constant dialogue and offering assistance is very important for UN human rights officers. In some sense working in the UN's human rights component means being part diplomat, part activist. It is a difficult balance to keep but that is the key to understanding the role of the UN human rights field officer.

QUESTIONS

- Is civil society a liberal vision that has little relevance where marginalised groups and communities face systemic discrimination and denial of justice?
- Has the increasing professionalisation of human rights NGOs suffocated the human rights movement?
- What is the practical utility of using the term human rights defenders?
- Why is the role of the medical profession so important in the protection of human rights?

3.9   HUMAN RIGHTS STRATEGIES

All human rights defenders essentially share the same goal, i.e. how best to promote and protect human rights. Over time, the various non-governmental, autonomous (national human rights institutions), regional and international actors (such as field officers and special procedures mandate holders) have developed an array of strategies to achieve this objective, This section examines the nature, use and effectiveness of several key strategies, namely documentation, fact-finding and human rights reporting; monitoring; advocacy; and awareness-raising and capacity-building.

3.9.1   Documentation and fact-finding

Documentation refers to any measures taken with a view to establishing an accurate record of an incident or patterns of human rights violations; in other words, to find out the 'truth' of what happened. This practice serves multiple purposes. Documenting violations may be part of monitoring by individuals, NGOs and specifically mandated bodies, including *ad hoc* commissions of inquiry. The materials and information obtained may be used for awareness-raising, advocacy, for example, reporting violations and calling for action, litigation – as evidence – and to inform political and policy responses, such as the UNSC mandating peacekeeping troops or setting up a criminal tribunal. Documentation also serves to establish an alternative record to official versions of events; such a record may become particularly important during subsequent transitional periods where there may be greater political will to act on findings.[104]

There is no uniform standard for documenting human rights violations whose main aim is to obtain as much information as possible about the 'what', 'who', 'where', 'when', and 'how' of an incident or patterns of violations, as well as the 'why', i.e. the context and factors that help explain them. Doctors, lawyers and others have produced a number of important manuals on how best to document particular types of violations, such as the Istanbul Protocol on torture and the Minnesota Protocol on extrajudicial killings, which set out in detail what information to obtain from victims (torture) or witnesses (both) in relation to alleged violations.[105] Systematic documentation of violations, which is often the function of commissions of inquiry or fact-finding missions such as those in Darfur, Gaza or Libya, primarily consists of interviewing and taking statements of victims and witnesses, reviewing documents (for example legislation, instructions, custody records, policy papers), on-site observations, assessment of available audio-visual materials (for example photographs or satellite images of locations) and forensic evidence, including medical reports, exhumations and autopsies.[106] The documentation of long-term violations of ESC rights may require

---

[104] See on the methods used and challenges faced in this regard by various truth commissions, P. Ball, H. F. Spirer and L. Spirer (eds.), *Making the Case: Investigating Large Scale Human Rights Violations Using Information Systems and Data Analysis* (Washington, DC: American Association for the Advancement of Science, 2000).

[105] Istanbul Protocol (1999) and Minnesota Protocol (1991).

[106] Report of the International Commission of Inquiry on Darfur to the United Nations Secretary-General (25 January 2005), paras. 12–25; Report of the United Nations Fact-Finding Mission on the Gaza Conflict, UN Doc. A/HRC/12/48 (25 September 2009),

using additional methods, such as compiling statistics to demonstrate the impact of policies and measures on issues such as food, health and education over a period of time.[107]

Documentation increasingly relies on video materials, satellite images and mapping, which have been used in a number of instances to expose the consequences of conflict, such as in Darfur,[108] or the consequences of large-scale violations, for example the environmental impact of oil exploration in Ogoni land adversely affecting ESC rights.[109] The availability and prevalence of audiovisual evidence is perhaps the most important development in respect of documentation. Taken by witnesses, victims and often the perpetrators themselves, these images have been widely distributed with considerable impact, particularly in the case of photographs of abuse taken by US wardens in the Iraqi prison of Abu Ghraib.[110] The photos of the body of Khaled Said, who had been beaten to death by police, played an important role in triggering public protests in Egypt in 2010. Another recent example of footage that exposed serious violations is the graphic evidence broadcast by Channel 4, UK, of international crimes committed in the last phase of the Sri Lankan war in 2009 that was used by the UN Panel of Experts on Accountability for War Crimes in Sri Lanka.[111] NGOs such as Witness[112] systematically use video advocacy to document and highlight a range of violations.[113]

The broadening of documentation through new technologies has resulted in a considerable shift in the ongoing struggle between truth-seeking and denial, making it increasingly difficult to conceal violations. However, several challenges remain. The nature of documentation often depends on what should be documented, as defined, for example, by the mandate of a mission or of an organisation. As a result, breaches of certain rights or violations

paras. 159–64, and Report of the International Commission of Inquiry to Investigate all Alleged Violations of International Human Rights Law in the Libyan Arab Jamahiriya, UN Doc. A/HRC/17/44 (1 June 2011), paras. 1–10. For an overview of the practical issues affecting the Gaza mission's documentation work, see section 17.6.

[107] See on statistical indicators below at section 3.9.3.

[108] See AI's 'Eyes on Darfur' project, online, at www.eyesondarfur.org. See on the use of geomapping as a new tactic, www.newtactics.org/en/blog/new-tactics/geo-mapping-human-rights.

[109] See UN Environment Programme (UNEP), *Environmental Assessment of Ogoniland* (2011), online, at www.unep.org/nigeria, which is not a human rights report but whose findings are important for an assessment of Nigeria's compliance with its obligations.

[110] See 'Torture Scandal: the Images that Shocked America', *Guardian* (undated), online, at www.guardian.co.uk/gall/0,8542,1211872,00.html.

[111] 'Egypt: "We are all Khaled Said"', *BBC* (17 February 2011), online, at www.bbc.co.uk/worldservice/programmes/2011/02/110217_outlook_egypt_protests_khaled_said.shtml and 'Sri Lanka's Killing Fields', Channel 4 (14 June 2011), online, at www.channel4.com/programmes/sri-lankas-killing-fields/4od.

[112] www.witness.org.

[113] S. Gregory, 'Cameras Everywhere: Ubiquitous Video Documentation of Human Rights, New Forms of Video Advocacy, and Considerations of Safety, Security, Dignity and Consent', *JHRP* 2(2) (2010), 191–207.

by perpetrators such as non-state actors may be overlooked or underrepresented. The documentation itself may be *ad hoc* or limited, particularly where there is lack of timely access to crucial information or where capacity and resources are not available, especially to undertake the long-term documentation of patterns of violations. Documenting violations often requires ingenuity and insistence in the face of denial and obfuscation. A commission of inquiry into disappearances in Sri Lanka, for example, was only able to find out the number of detained persons in custody when it compared the custody records (which had a falsified entry) with the records for food allocation (which showed the real number of inmates).[114] Members of fact-finding missions and monitoring bodies have repeatedly reported how they grappled with the authorities to gain access to crucial locations or to individuals that allowed them to obtain a more accurate record.[115] However, even where they gain access and documentation is carried out according to accepted standards, the material often requires an element of interpretation where facts are not unambiguous.[116]

Where documentation is not in line with best practice, vital proof may be lost. For example, it may be impossible to verify the remains of individuals who have been 'disappeared', which may be a problem where local populations have access to mass graves. Interviews with victims of human rights violations may only be possible once and crucial information may be lost if it is not elicited at the right time. It is therefore important that they adhere to particular standards of criminal procedure, in case they are rejected as hearsay, especially if the original victim or witness cannot be present at the trial. Beyond their evidentiary value, interviews also raise broader questions of confidentiality and security. Those taking interviews have a particular responsibility towards victims and witnesses to avoid further traumatisation and prevent harm.[117] In addition, the protection of those documenting violations and of witnesses is a major concern, which reinforces the need to adhere to best practices. This concern is particularly acute where states are reluctant to cooperate and actively thwart documentation, putting victims, witnesses and human rights defenders at risk.[118] Human rights defenders therefore increasingly use special databases, such as Martus, 'to document human rights violations systematically and securely'.[119]

[114] See interview 8.2 with M. C. Iqbal in Chapter 8.

[115] See, for example, A. Cassese, *Inhuman States, Imprisonment, Detention and Torture Today* (Cambridge: Polity, 1996); M. Nowak, 'Fact-Finding on Torture and Ill-Treatment and Conditions of Detention', *JHRP* 1(1) (2009), 101–19.

[116] P. Alston, 'The Challenges of Responding to Extrajudicial Executions: Interview with Philip Alston', *JHRP* 2(3) (2010), 355–73, at 356.

[117] Istanbul Protocol (1999), paras. 119–59.

[118] See in the context of proceedings of international criminal tribunals, REDRESS, above note 71, 52–5.

[119] www.martus.org.

INTERVIEW 3.2

Documenting human rights violations in volatile environments: the Libyan experience

(Elham Saudi)

Elham Saudi is Director of Lawyers for Justice in Libya (LFJL) (www. libyanjustice.org), an NGO working closely with a network of Libyan lawyers and human rights defenders to 'defend and promote justice through the promotion of human rights, the rule of law and democracy'.

How did your organisation seek to document violations during the conflict in Libya?

As an organisation started in the diaspora, LFJL had to find innovative and collaborative ways to document violations occurring on the ground.

1 Capacity building of legal professionals: the need to document violations became apparent very early in the Libyan revolution, as the Gaddafi regime attacked civilians from the first moment. LFJL began its training of lawyers on the ground as early as April 2011, less than two months from the start of the revolution. At this early stage, only the eastern part of Libya was liberated. We therefore arranged for two young lawyers to come to Egypt where we, with international investigative experts, trained them on the documentation of violations. On their return, they trained the remaining members of the fact-finding committee set up by the legal department of the National Transitional Council.

   We conducted further training by Skype for those in places which had not yet been liberated. In addition to these 'guerrilla' style trainings, we held a workshop in Tunisia in September, after the liberation of Tripoli, for over thirty people from more than ten cities in Libya, which benefited from the expertise of a number of international NGOs. Training lawyers in Libya was challenging during the conflict because of the obvious security concerns and so we had to use measures such as Skype instead of telephone lines and external training. It was difficult to work with people for substantial periods of time in order properly to engage with the detailed process of documenting violations. This was one of the reasons why the events were held outside Libya to ensure enough 'space' and clarity of focus to absorb the information in a setting that is distant from the conflict.

2 Standardisation of documentation: in order to simplify both the training and documentation processes, we decided to produce a pro forma witness statement. In cooperation with various organisations, we produced this document and used it as the basis for all our training. This provided a pro forma that ensured that many of the key questions were asked and was intended to minimise the scope for leading questions or

for testimonies based on 'collective' memory and not a recollection of actual facts. The form also encouraged corroborative evidence by cross-referring to such evidence. Finally, the forms ensured that identification data (e.g. name, address, etc.) were retained by LFJL and not shared with international bodies. This was to ensure security: first, by not having documented the identification data in the same place as the testimony so that if Gaddafi forces found the files – remember this was still during the conflict – they could not easily trace the witnesses and, second, to ensure that the details of those providing were not divulged, intentionally or inadvertently, without informed consent at the time of the use of the testimony by any international bodies. The form was used by those lawyers we trained, but also by others trained by them and, most importantly, the official fact-finding committees set up by the NTC and outlined in (3) below.

3 Network of fact-finding committees: following the initial training in Egypt, we discussed the need for documentation on a nation-wide scale with the then still nascent NTC. In cooperation with the NTC's legal department, we developed the concept of fact-finding committees tasked with investigating all alleged violations committed since 15 February 2011 across the country. Each committee would be appointed by the NTC, thus providing a form of legitimacy for their work and, we hoped, easier access to victims and witnesses. We also hoped that this process would enlist a sense of responsibility and accountability with the NTC itself. LFJL assisted the NTC, at that time the publicly known members consisting mainly of people from the east of Libya, with identifying suitable lawyers and investigators in key cities. The committees did some excellent work, some of which was crucial to both the ICC file and that of the Commission of Inquiry.

4 A link to international advocacy and accountability: during the conflict, LFJL was in the privileged position of having direct access to international bodies both for advocacy and accountability. Key among these were the HRC in Geneva, the Foreign and Commonwealth Office in London, the African Commission in Banjul and the ICC in The Hague. We were able to serve as a link between the networks we had helped establish in Libya and these bodies. For example, we were able to allow all those participating in the Tunisia workshop time with ICC investigators to share their findings, learn on developing their work and be recognised for their crucial role in the ICC process.

What were the main challenges to establishing an accurate record of violations?

There were several. The speed with which events were uncovering meant that those working on the ground had to be creative and resourceful in documenting violations and securing evidence. On our side, it meant we also had to be resourceful about how we ensured that the documentation would stand up to scrutiny and be useful in the future. Further, the small population in Libya means that on a community by community basis people know each other personally. This made it difficult for knowledge not to be presumed by those conducting interviews and also for 'collective' memory not to play a part in the documentation of the violations. Also, the regional nature of some of the subsequent fighting meant that there was a degree of 'selective' documentation taking place. Finally, the sense of victor's justice, which emerged with the powerful militias, means that there is the risk of an unbalanced account of violations emerging. Although reinforced by the NTC in its Law 38 granting an amnesty for acts done in the name of the 17 February Revolution, this sense of skewed justice is not being tolerated by civil society, which is active in demanding accountability for all acts. This gives some hope that with time a more thorough record of what has happened in the Libyan conflict, including in the rape file, will be established.

Did you find any evidence of rape?

Yes, our network of lawyers found evidence in two regions. Through the testimony of medical doctors who had treated women with injuries and symptoms consistent with rape and limited victim testimony, as well as some video footage confiscated from the mobile telephones of some regime soldiers, we were able to establish that rape had occurred. We were not, however, able to get a full picture of the extent to which it happened and may be regarded as systematic. The publicity that the question of rape received almost instantly halted the flow of information on these crimes to us. The shame factor of being named a victim of rape in a conservative culture appeared to be a dissuading factor, with a handful of those from whom we had secured witness testimonies withdrawing their consent to our using those testimonies in any international or local case.

What were the consequences of reports that claims about rape had been unfounded or exaggerated?[1]

The primary consequence of such reports was not dissimilar to the consequence of when the reports of rape received significant attention – disengagement by those affected. The reporting of rape, in whatever guise, resulted in a withdrawal of cooperation by victims and witnesses. The fear of being 'exposed' once more by becoming a public subject meant that

---

[1] P. Coburn, 'Amnesty Questions Claim that Gaddafi Ordered Rape as Weapon of War', *Independent* (24 June 2011), online, at www.independent.co.uk/news/world/africa/amnesty-questions-claim-that-gaddafi-ordered-rape-as-weapon-of-war-2302037.html.

some victims with whom we started conversations decided to stop speaking. We saw this with female and male victims of rape.

A further consequence, which I believe is the result of the fear created by the stories of rape – exaggerated or not – is the use of an accusation of rape as a threat to secure confessions for other violations. We have had at least two testimonies by persons detained by militias who were threatened with a charge of rape in this manner. This not only brings into question all confessions of rape but also highlights how far we are as a community from dealing with the true repercussions of this part of the conflict.

How do you view the work done by others, such as the ICC or the Commission of Inquiry, in documenting violations in Libya?

The primary flaw with the work of both the ICC and the Commission of Inquiry was the limited time spent on the ground, building rapport and investing in their counterparts within Libya. They did not take their mandate as active and so did little to help improve the local system, building rapport and seeing their mandate as helping to improve the local system. The perception that they were, to varying degrees, 'in bed with' the transitional authorities was not very helpful either. In my view the ICC lost an opportunity to establish its credentials in Libya. It had the perfect storm of a wide mandate, a population willing to speak and share its information and a legal community willing to assist; yet its tangible involvement stagnated after the issue of the initial arrest warrants and it was often hampered by its own red tape.

What are the lessons from the Libyan experience for documenting violations in similar contexts?

The key lesson is adaptability. In a fast moving conflict, in a country with a vast landscape, and where culture and custom play a strong role, it was vital not to adapt a 'cut and paste' approach to the documentation of violations. This was most clearly demonstrated in the rape cases. There was a presumption on the part of some of the media and advocacy and investigative authorities that highlighting rape cases would create a 'safe' environment for victims to come forward. This approach is familiar to those in the West and often bears fruit. However, in Libya, a conservative country where 'honour', in its most proscribed definitions, is paramount, the attention that rape cases received served as a deterrent for victims. We often heard the phrase 'I don't want my name to be known like Iman El Obeidi's'[2] when attempting to persuade victims to provide testimonies. 'It is personal', we were told, and 'I would prefer for the world not to be involved.'

[2] Iman Obeidi publicly complained about being raped by Gaddafi forces during the war and her case became instantly known across Libya and worldwide. She later fled the country.

3.9.2   Human rights reporting

States, national human rights institutions, regional and international bodies, NGOs, think tanks, journalists and individuals publish reports relating to human rights, which may focus on law, policy and/or practice. Human rights reports, particularly by the UN or UN-appointed bodies and NGOs can be highly influential. They are one of the most important means of establishing a record of human rights situations, including violations, and often explicitly counter official versions of events. Reports frequently identify the underlying factors, nature and consequences of violations in a wide range of contexts. They are also an integral part of monitoring and their findings can play a critical role in advocacy efforts. Reports contribute to debates about the development of standards, legislative or institutional reforms, changes in policy, for example an end to military cooperation or, in urgent situations, serve as one of the factors resulting in preventive action. Human rights reports are also frequently relied upon in legal proceedings to corroborate certain methods and patterns of violations,[120] which may also help to investigate international crimes and establish individual liability.[121] More generally, human rights reports help to generate awareness, both in a particular context and more broadly, for example by casting the spotlight on un-/underreported types of violations.[122]

---

[120] For example, a 2000 UN Expert Report and 2003 Global Witness report were used in the case against Guus van Kouwenhoven, a Dutch businessman, who was accused of supplying arms to Charles Taylor, the former President of Liberia, in exchange for logging rights. See, *Kouwenhoven* case, Court of First Instance, The Hague (7 June 2006), Case no. AX7098, and Court of Appeal, The Hague (10 March 2008), Case no. BC6068. See also Global Witness, *The Usual Suspects. Liberia's Weapons and Mercenaries in Cote d'Ivoire and Sierra Leone: Why it's Still Possible, How it Works and How to Break the Trends* (2003), online, at www.globalwitness.org/library/usual-suspects; Report of the Panel of Experts appointed pursuant to Security Council Resolution 1306 (2000) in relation to Sierra Leone, UN Doc. S/2000/1195 (20 December 2000).

[121] See generally, M. Bergsmo and W. H. Wiley, 'Human Rights Professionals and the Criminal Investigation and Prosecution of Core International Crimes', in S. Skåre, I. Burkey and H. Mørk (eds.), *Manual on Human Rights Monitoring: An Introduction for Human Rights Field Officers*, 3rd rev. edn (University of Oslo: Norwegian Center for Human Rights, 2008), 1–30, and further, L. S. Sunga, 'How can UN human rights special procedures sharpen ICC fact-finding?', *IJHR* (2011) 15(2): 187–205, at 198. See for a practical example references to reports in Office of the Prosecutor, The Prosecutor of the ICC opens investigation in Darfur, (6 June 2005), online, at www.icc-cpi.int/menus/icc/press+and+media/press+releases/2005/the+prosecutor+of+the+icc+opens+investigation+in+darfur.

[122] See for example ICHRP and TI, *Corruption and Human Rights: Making the Connection* (Geneva: ICHRP and TI, 2009), and Discriminatory Laws and Practices and Acts of Violence against Individuals Based on their Sexual Orientation and Gender Identity, Report of the UN High Commissioner for Human Rights, UN Doc. A/HRC/19/41 (17 November 2011).

AI and later HRW in particular have developed a widely recognised model for human rights reports to ensure an accurate record of violations and/or analysis of an issue that is informed by an understanding of the given context. Researchers undertake background research about the thematic right or country-specific situation, examine available documentation, consult with a wide range of experts, activists and others on the situation relating to the particular issue, for example migrant workers in Middle Eastern countries,[123] and ideally visit locations and those concerned to collect and verify available information. Any factual allegation and information should be corroborated by another source so as to ensure reliability. The style of writing is as objective as possible, combining factual information and case stories with legal and policy analysis, as well as recommendations. A report is then vetted internally (some NGOs share drafts with governments concerned for their comments) and published.[124]

A report is a tool and should therefore form part of a broader strategy that considers both thematic priorities and its use, including media strategy, advocacy and follow up. However, it is not always clear what impact particular reports will have (which forms part of the prior strategic assessment) or have had (evaluation), which raises the broader question of effectiveness. In 2005, for example, HRW produced a report on violations committed during the presidency of Alberto Fujimori in Peru.[125] Following the publication of the report, Fujimori was extradited from Chile to Peru, and convicted by the Peruvian Supreme Court on charges of serious human rights violations. HRW argued that its report was crucial in providing evidence for the extradition of Fujimori and in changing the perception that there was no evidence against him.[126] However, the report was not mentioned explicitly in the judgment of the Chilean Supreme Court in which it decided to extradite Fujimori. Moreover, Peruvian and other international actors had also worked to counter perceptions of Fujimori's innocence.[127] These considerations show the difficulty of attributing and assessing impact, an assessment that may also be influenced by an organisation's interest in advancing its reputation. In practice, reports of this nature are frequently one among several factors that contribute to, and influence, complex processes that may eventually result in accountability.

[123] HRW, *Slow Reform: Protection of Migrant Domestic Workers in Asia and the Middle East* (New York: HRW, 2010); International Federation of Human Rights (FIDH) and Egyptian Organisation for Human Rights, *Migrant Workers in Saudi Arabia* (Paris and Cairo: FIDH and EOHR, 2003).

[124] Hopgood, above note 34, 74–92.

[125] HRW, *Probable Cause: Evidence Implicating Fujimori* (New York: HRW, 2005), online, at www.hrw.org/en/reports/2005/12/21/probable-cause.

[126] HRW, 'Peruvian Court Convicts Fujimori for Human Rights Violations' (5 May 2009), online, at www.hrw.org/en/news/2009/05/05/peruvian-court-convicts-fujimori-human-rights-violations.

[127] L. Mallinder, 'Law, Politics and Fact-Finding: Assessing the Impact of Human Rights Reports', *JHRP* 2(1) (2010), 166–76, at 173.

Reports may also have unintended adverse consequences. For example, a human rights report documenting abuses committed by serving officials in Afghanistan[128] was said to have inadvertently contributed to, if not prompted, the latter's decision to approve an amnesty for all combatants involved in the 1992 and 1993 conflict covering crimes perpetrated during that period.[129] This example shows that the impact of reports can be unpredictable and that a nuanced assessment is needed about what type of report and demands may best support effective strategies at a particular point in time. While reports by NGOs and/or official bodies may be effective and lead to identifiable results their long-term impacts are often less apparent. As pointed out by Manfred Nowak, the former UN Special Rapporteur on torture,

I have not been able to objectively assess, either on the basis of follow-up missions or on other methods of fact-finding, whether my missions and reports had any sustainable impact on the goal of eradicating torture and of improving the general conditions of detention in the countries visited.[130]

This rather sobering assessment shows the need for further empirical research to evaluate impact, which would require studies using social science methods to better understand what role the various types of human rights reports play, particularly in influencing the perceptions and decision-making of relevant actors.

3.9.3   Monitoring

According to an OHCHR training manual, human rights monitoring is

a broad term describing the active collection, verification and immediate use of information to address human rights problems. Human rights monitoring includes gathering information about incidents, observing events (elections, trials, demonstrations, etc.), visiting sites such as places of detention and refugee camps, discussions with government authorities to obtain information and to pursue remedies and other immediate follow-up...[131]

Monitoring can be situation specific, such as during elections, but is often of a long-term nature to observe and analyse a human rights situation at the local, national, regional or international level.

The UN definition demonstrates that monitoring refers to a range of interventions whose main purpose is to identify what problems, if any, exist in a

---

[128] HRW, *Blood-Stained Hands: Past Atrocities in Kabul and Afghanistan's Legacy of Impunity* (New York: HRW, 2005), online, at www.hrw.org/en/reports/2005/07/06/blood-stained-hands.

[129] Mallinder, above note 127, 174.   [130] Nowak, above note 115, 118.

[131] OHCHR, *Training Manual on Human Rights Monitoring* (New York and Geneva: United Nations, 2001), p. 9.

particular context and, in so far as needed and possible, to take action with a view to ensuring respect for human rights. Monitoring may be conducted by state authorities, national human rights institutions, NGOs, UN human rights field officers, regional and international special rapporteurs, the media and others, and combines documentation and observation with remedial action.[132] In recognition of past failures, mechanisms have been put in place to act where monitoring evidences a risk of conflict and violations, including threats and harassment of individuals. This applies in particular to early warning mechanisms in situations that may result in serious violations, such as the UN Office of the Special Advisor on the Prevention of Genocide.[133]

Long-term monitoring focuses on structural factors and developments over time. It principally applies to all sets of rights, particularly in relation to the positive obligations of states. In practice, it has been used especially in respect of ESCR and the right to development. The duty to 'progressively realise' these rights is one of their distinctive features, which implies that a process is set in train towards better fulfilment of the right concerned. The monitoring of relevant rights, such as the right to health or the right to food, poses considerable methodological and practical challenges. Methods and statistics relating to health or food were primarily formulated in the development context, as reflected in sources such as the WHO Statistical Information System and the Human Development Index prepared annually by the Development Programme (UNDP).[134] UN human rights bodies and others have stressed the need for human rights-based monitoring but have grappled with developing an adequate framework, including how to use data generated by UN agencies, regional institutions and others that has an apparent bearing on human rights but is primarily used for other purposes.[135] In practice, prior mapping and indicators have been widely used to establish whether states have met certain targets (benchmarks) within a given timeframe.[136]

Monitoring can be internal or external evaluation. Ideally, external monitoring is based on constructive engagement informed by a series of principles.[137] In practice, however, states are frequently hostile to being

[132] See strong emphasis on interviewing and collecting testimonies ibid.

[133] www.un.org/en/preventgenocide/adviser/index.shtml.

[134] See http://hdr.undp.org/en/statistics.

[135] See for an overview, 'Databases: Statistics and Indicators for Monitoring ESC Rights', online, at www.cesr.org/article.php?id=317.

[136] See on use of indicators and benchmarks in relation to various rights, Report on Indicators for Promoting and Monitoring the Implementation of Human Rights, UN Doc. HRI/MC/2008/3 (6 June 2008), para. 7. For an extensive discussion, see section 9.7.

[137] The OHCHR *Training Manual*, above note 131, 87–94, lists the following: do no harm; respect the mandate; know the standards; exercise good judgement; seek consultation; respect the authorities; credibility; confidentiality; security; understand the country; need for consistency, persistence and patience; accuracy and precision; impartiality; objectivity; sensitivity; integrity; professionalism; and visibility.

monitored. They may reject the presence of international monitors altogether, for example in the case of Sri Lanka,[138] or may obstruct the work of national and international human rights monitors in myriad ways, for example by revoking licences, threatening personnel with expulsion or denying access to certain facilities, persons or documentation.[139] Monitors are in this context frequently confronted with the dilemma of how to respond to apparent human rights violations; if they speak out, they may not be able to continue their monitoring function; if they do not raise the issue (or raise the issue with the government but to no avail) their monitoring risks failing to fulfil its basic objective, namely to ensure enhanced protection.

3.9.4   Advocacy

Advocacy, i.e. the act of arguing for something to be done, denotes the various strategies used to strengthen the promotion and protection of human rights, either in respect of a specific case/situation or more broadly. The breadth of this definition means that there are numerous human rights advocates, beyond well-known advocacy organisations or prominent individual human rights activists. This includes popular movements, UN officials requesting respect for particular rights, such as the UN High Commissioner for Human Rights[140] and may include states and their representatives who seek to influence other states and international organisations to take a certain course of action that results in greater recognition of, or respect for, human rights.[141]

Human rights advocacy can pursue specific short-term goals, for example prompting UNSC action in response to reports about violations in the context of conflicts, such as in Syria in 2011 and 2012, or broader, long-term objectives, such as the creation of a strong international human rights system. The latter advocacy entails campaigning for the recognition of particular rights, the setting of standards and the establishment of effective institutions.[142] Several campaigns have had a considerable degree of success to this end. For example, the women's rights movement succeeded in having a number of specific rights recognised, such as reproductive rights in the African Protocol

---

[138] This is one of the recommendations made by several states during the universal periodic review that Sri Lanka objected to. Report of the Working Group on the Universal Periodic Review Sri Lanka, UN Doc. A/HRC/8/46 (5 June 2008), para. 84.

[139] Nowak, above note 115, 105.

[140] 'Pillay Presents Groundbreaking UN Study on Violence, Discrimination against People because of their Sexual Orientation' (7 March 2012), www.ohchr.org/EN/NewsEvents/Pages/DisplayNews.aspx?NewsID=11917&LangID=E.

[141] See R. Müllerson, *Human Rights Diplomacy* (London, New York: Routledge, 1997), in particular pp. 118–47, and D. P. Forsythe, *Human Rights in International Relations*, 2nd edn (Cambridge University Press, 2006), 152–87.

[142] See for a good overview, Mutua, above note 32.

on the Rights of Women, establishing institutions, such as CEDAW's complaints procedure and UN special procedures[143] and seeking accountability for violations, such as those before the ICC.[144] Other examples are ratification campaigns, such as in relation to the CRC,[145] the ban on landmines[146] and efforts resulting in developing standards, such as on the rights of indigenous peoples[147] and IDPs.[148]

These campaigns show how networks of actors have been able to influence and shape the international system. This is a continuous process as new demands emerge, such as for the recognition and effective protection of LGBT rights, whose proponents often face a considerable struggle to gain acceptance, even by liberal 'gatekeepers'.[149] Similar mechanisms are at play in national systems where (networks of) actors seek to influence policy-making and practices to bring about legislative, judicial or institutional reforms. However, it is often not possible to neatly separate national, regional and international advocacy efforts. On the contrary, networks of national and international actors, particularly NGOs, together with like-minded states, frequently use international fora as arenas of legitimacy to exert pressure on repressive states with a view to bringing about gradual changes from denial to engagement and compliance.[150] In practice, the outcome of such efforts depends largely on the receptiveness of states. When faced with alleged violations, states have developed sophisticated arsenals of denial[151] and have often successfully built alliances in crucial fora that allow them to escape censure and the need for change. The model of transnational networks sketched out above was developed in the 1990s and was based on a world where 'liberal' states wielded considerable influence, including in international fora, such as the UN human rights bodies. However, power relationships have shifted

---

[143] See UN Working Group on the issue of discrimination against women in law and in practice, www.ohchr.org/EN/Issues/Women/WGWomen/Pages/WGWomenIndex.aspx; UN Special Rapporteur on violence against women, its causes and consequences, www.ohchr.org/EN/Issues/Women/SRWomen/Pages/SRWomenIndex.aspx.

[144] See on Crimes of Sexual Violence, 'Case Study: The Women's Caucus for Gender Justice in the ICC', online, at www.endvawnow.org/en/articles/1193-campaigns-for-institutional-change.html.

[145] For further examples, see U. Oberdörster, 'Why Ratify? Lessons from Treaty Ratification Campaigns', *Vand. L. Rev.* 61(2) (2008), 681–712, at 697.

[146] See above at section 3.4.3.

[147] C. Charters, L. Malezer and V. Tauli-Corpuz (eds.), *Indigenous Voices: The UN Declaration on the Rights of Indigenous Peoples* (Oxford: Hart, 2013).

[148] African Union Convention for the Protection and Assistance of Internally Displaced Persons in Africa (Kampala Convention), 2009.

[149] B. Clifford (ed.), *The International Struggle for New Human Rights* (Philadelphia: University of Pennsylvania Press, 2009).

[150] Keck and Sikkink, above note 4.

[151] S. Cohen, *States of Denial: Knowing about Atrocities and Suffering* (Cambridge: Polity Press, 2001); Mutua, above note 32, 602–4.

significantly over the last decade, which has changed political dynamics, as evident, for example, in attempts to reduce if not abolish altogether the country mandates forming part of the special procedures of the HRC.[152]

Advocacy consists of several methods that can be used to influence the targeted actors, be they governments, regional or international institutions or non-state actors. Advocates may use public campaigns (reports, letter writing, collecting signatures, demonstrations, media appearances), lobbying (speaking directly with influential persons) and complementary means such as litigation to achieve the desired result, often combining these methods as needed.[153] In the sustained and ultimately successful efforts to change Pakistan's *Hudood* rape laws, actors reached out to local communities and used litigation, street theatre, the media, reporting and lobbying.[154] Developing effective advocacy therefore requires a range of skills, including strategic vision, thematic understanding, political acumen, network building talents and public relations knowhow.

One major challenge for those engaging in advocacy is to assess its efficacy. This is important for several reasons. Advocacy is resource and time intensive. Actors therefore need to decide what advocacy efforts are worthwhile; members of organisations or funders, for their part, may request some evidence that the advocacy effort made has achieved its objective or is making progress towards this end. Ultimately, not being able to show that advocacy works, or believing that it does not make a difference, may lead some actors to question its very *raison d'être* and undermine the morale of those engaged in it. In practice, evaluating the impact of advocacy is fraught with difficulties, 'First, one must establish criteria for success. What degree of change qualifies a network campaign as effective?'[155] Second, if such change has been identified, to what degree can it be attributed to the particular advocacy, given that this is frequently one among several factors and that decision-makers may not acknowledge that changes were made in response? While this impact may often prove difficult to establish, there are evident success stories, particularly where a campaign had a clear goal which was eventually achieved, such as the adoption of a treaty protecting specific rights, for example the CRPD.

The outcome of advocacy is particularly difficult to measure where the goals are long term and where immediate changes are unlikely in the present circumstances, such as advocating legislative and institutional reforms in repressive regimes. However, as the campaigns in apartheid South Africa showed, these efforts created an important alternative discourse that both

---

[152] See section 4.3.   [153] See ICHRP, above note 40, para. 22.

[154] See interview 2.2 with Sohail A. Warraich in Chapter 2.

[155] S. D. Burgerman, 'Mobilizing Principles: the Role of Transnational Activists in Promoting Human Rights Principles', *HRQ* 20(4) (1998), 905–23, at 912.

undermined the legitimacy of the regime(s) at the time and prepared the ground for changes following the end of apartheid.[156] The multiple efforts undertaken to close Guantanámo Bay, including campaigns, NGO and UN reports in addition to litigation, provide a similarly instructive example of long-term impact even though developments following a change in the US administration showed that considerable practical difficulties may remain – such as which countries will receive Guantanamo Bay detainees tainted by suspicion of terrorism – which may militate against immediate solutions.[157]

3.9.5   Awareness-raising, capacity-building and human rights education

Awareness-raising refers to the process of engaging – by means of information sharing, educational activities or other communication – with particular groups or the public at large. Its aim is to foster a better understanding of human rights in general and/or alerting the target group to a specific human rights issue and ways of how best to address it. Ideally, awareness-raising positively influences those targeted and helps in promoting the goal pursued, such as 'to foster respect for the rights and dignity of persons with disabilities' and 'to combat stereotypes, prejudices and harmful practices relating to persons with disabilities'.[158] Raising human rights awareness serves multiple objectives. It is a cornerstone of promotion: rights-holders, authorities, judges and others need to know what human rights are and what they entail in order to assert, implement or adjudicate them. Accordingly, it is recognised that states 'have the primary responsibility to promote and ensure human rights education and training', including adequate human rights training for 'state officials, civil servants, judges, law enforcement officials and military personnel'.[159] The UDHR goes further, stating that 'every individual and every organ of society ... shall strive by teaching and education to promote respect for these rights and freedoms ... to secure their universal and effective recognition and observance'. It therefore sees teaching and education as the building blocks for a human rights culture that spans the national and the international sphere. Raising awareness of human rights also serves an instrumental purpose as part of advocacy campaigns. Imparting knowledge

---

[156] P. J. Schwikkard, 'Reflections on Law Reform Pertaining to Arrested, Detained and Accused Persons in South Africa', in Oette, above note 42, 139–53, at 153.

[157] See in this context, AI, *USA – Guantanamo: A Decade of Damage to Human Rights and 10 Anti-Human Rights Messages Guantanamo Still Sends* (London: AI, 2011).

[158] See article 8(1)(a), (b) CRPD.

[159] See article 7(4), UN Declaration on Human Rights Education and Training, UNGA. resolution 66/137 (19 December 2011). See also articles 10 CAT and 23 CPED for treaty-based obligations to train law-enforcement officials and others in relation to the prohibition of torture and enforced disappearance respectively.

about the nature and importance of human rights, or framing an issue as a question of human rights, is often an essential component of such campaigns. This is particularly the case when mobilising grassroots constituencies or seeking the recognition of new rights.

Awareness-raising is also closely related to capacity-building in the field of human rights, which refers to 'the process by which individuals, organizations, institutions and societies develop abilities to perform functions, solve problems and set and achieve objectives'.[160] For example, marginalised communities, such as the Dalits in India, may frame and articulate their grievances as human rights issues and may be able to use legal and other channels to seek prevention and claim accountability and justice.[161] Such an approach may not necessarily result in enhanced protection or the desired outcome and a shift to internationalised advocacy and the concomitant need to mainstream discourses may depoliticise efforts and limit the impact of such strategies.[162] Nevertheless, it can signify an important step towards empowerment of individuals and groups demanding respect for their rights rather than being beneficiaries who are at the mercy of local authorities and others.[163] Awareness of the international human rights regime can also be critical for national human rights activists and others who want to use available avenues to highlight human rights concerns, request urgent intervention and seek accountability and justice.

Human rights education is an integral component of awareness-raising, which the UN in particular has promoted since the very beginning of its human rights-related work.[164] In the most recent development, the HRC set up an open-ended working group, which in 2011 led to the adoption of the UN Declaration on Human Rights Education and Training.[165] The Declaration evidences a broad understanding of human rights education and training, which

---

[160] Note by the UN Secretariat, Definition of Basic Concepts and Terminologies in Governance and Public Administration, UN Doc. E/C.16/2006/4 (5 January 2006), para. 33.

[161] P. Kumar Shinde, *Dalits and Human Rights* (Delhi: Isha Books, 2005); B. Clifford, '"Dalit Rights Are Human Rights": Caste Discrimination, International Activism, and the Construction of a New Human Rights Issue', *HRQ* 29(1) (2007), 167–93.

[162] J. Lerche, 'Transnational Advocacy Networks and Affirmative Action for Dalits in India', *DaC* 39(2) (2008), 239–61.

[163] See also article 2(2)(c) UN Declaration on Human Rights Education and Training: 'Education for human rights, which includes empowering persons to enjoy and exercise their rights and to respect and uphold the rights of others.'

[164] See preamble and article 26(2) UDHR; UNESCO recommendation concerning education for international understanding, cooperation and peace and education relating to human rights and fundamental freedoms adopted by the Geneva Conference at its eighteenth session (Paris, 19 November 1974); the UN Decade for Human Rights Education (1995–2004).

[165] UNGA resolution 66/137 (16 February 2011).

comprises all educational, training, information, awareness-raising and learning activities aimed at promoting universal respect for and observance of all human rights and fundamental freedoms and thus contributing to, inter alia, the prevention of human rights violations and abuses by providing persons with knowledge, skills and understanding and developing their attitudes and behaviours, to empower them to contribute to the building and promotion of a universal culture of human rights.[166]

It adds that '[h]uman rights education and training is a lifelong process that concerns all ages'.[167] This outlook is reflected in the work of many NGOs and human rights educators who have developed multiple approaches to the teaching of human rights, and have produced a wealth of educational materials.[168]

While the advantages of human rights education are widely recognised, it is equally clear that there are fundamental challenges. The very subject of human rights itself is open to various interpretations and often contested; while this can be positive if taught in a manner that encourages a contextual understanding, respect for tolerance and diversity informed by fundamental rights, it may easily result in skewed visions and distortions. Governments may interpret human rights education in a selective fashion that differs significantly from the UN Declaration and the approaches of NGOs or human rights teachers. This may include taking rather a narrow view of human rights education. For example, Australia's Second/Third Reports to the Committee on the Rights of the Child, when reporting on the aims of education under article 29 CRC,[169] only focused on anti-racism programmes and policies, protecting children from sexual abuse and improving school discipline.[170] In the UK, human rights education has been criticised for neglecting ESC rights and collective rights, as well as failing to acknowledge problematic aspects of the UK's own record and the fact that human rights are born out of social struggles.[171] The purpose of human rights teaching may also be very different, for example either forming part of general, formal education or being a cornerstone of targeted efforts aimed at bringing about broader

---

[166] Ibid., article 2(1).   [167] Ibid., article 3(1).

[168] See P. Gerber, 'Human Rights Education: a Slogan in Search of a Definition', in Joseph and McBeth, note above 45, 541–66.

[169] Article 29(1) CRC provides: 'States Parties agree that the education of the child shall be directed to ... (b): The development of respect for human rights and fundamental freedoms, and for the principles enshrined in the Charter of the United Nations.'

[170] Second and Third Periodic Reports of States Parties due in 1998 and 2003: Australia, UN Doc. CRC/C/129/Add.4 (29 December 2004), paras. 372–84, discussed by Gerber, above note 168, 550–4. See on an initiative in the Australian state of Victoria, E. Branigan and P. Ramcharan, 'Human Rights Education in Australia: Reflections on the Meaningful Application of Rights and Values in Practice', *JHRP* 4(2) (2012), 233–52.

[171] B. Bowring, 'Human rights and public education', *CJE* 42(1) (2012), 53–65.

transformation,[172] which may result in conflicting approaches and widely diverging outcomes depending on the approach taken which may not produce 'true citizens of the world'.[173]

In legal education, human rights law may form part of constitutional/ public law, regional systems, for example European law, or public international law. However, the subject is often optional or confined to postgraduate studies. Many law students still leave university without having developed a clear understanding of human rights and human rights law. This is a particularly acute problem in countries where lawyers and activists are faced with human rights violations, or their legacy, but may lack the knowledge and requisite skills that would help them deal with the issues arising in such contexts. The staple response of international actors has been to provide human rights training for officials, judges and lawyers, such as in the case of Iraq following the end of the Saddam Hussein regime. Carefully designed training programmes that meet actual needs, address gaps in knowledge and enhance the skills of participants can be useful measures in such circumstances.[174] However, training has often been used as a poorly designed short-cut measure where external actors with limited understanding of the situation and needs of participants share largely theoretical knowledge. Such training is often attractive for organisers, trainers and funders who can claim successful project implementation; meanwhile, participants enjoy the opportunity to travel and frequently receive handsome per diems. For these reasons, there is a risk that training lacks a sense of focus, i.e. that it is not an integral part and means of a broader, organically developed long-term strategy but becomes an end in its own right. The larger impact of such training beyond evaluation by its participants is often not clear, particularly where officials receive training but the structural conditions facilitating violations remain in place.[175] To be effective, developing and implementing human rights training should therefore be an integral element of a carefully

---

[172] Gerber, above note 168. See for an analysis of, and case study (India), on various models of human rights education ('global citizenship', 'coexistence' and 'transformative action'), M. Bajaj, 'Human Rights Education: Ideology, Location, and Approaches', *HRQ* 33 (2011), 481–508.

[173] See on the potential of such education, U. Baxi, 'Human Rights Education: the Promise of the Third Millennium?' in G. J. Andreopoulos and R. P. Claude (eds.), *Human Rights Education for the Twenty-first Century* (Philadelphia: University of Pennsylvania Press, 1997), 142–54.

[174] See www.humanrightseducation.info, and www.ohchr.org/en/publicationsresources/ pages/trainingeducation.aspx for the main UN websites. See also International Human Rights Network, 'What is effective training?', online, at www.ihrnetwork.org/files/7.%20 What%20is%20Effective%20Training.PDF.

[175] See for an interesting case study on the political question of whether to conduct human rights training in repressive systems, D. Kinley and T. Wilson, 'Engaging a Pariah: Human Rights Training in Burma/Myanmar', *HRQ* 29(2) (2007), 368–402.

designed strategy that identifies realistic objectives, including follow up and sustainability.

The focus on training also risks masking deeper structural problems. Legal education in countries marked by years of dictatorship or conflict often declines markedly, resulting in a noticeable gap in knowledge and skills between the older and younger generation. Training is a means to narrow this gap but cannot by itself replace good university education. Donors may be reluctant to fund public institutions such as universities and university human rights work. However, support, either from funders or from other universities, adds an important financial and moral dimension that can act as a welcome boost for universities and lecturers who often work in extremely difficult circumstances. Rethinking approaches in this regard should form part of broader reflections on how capacity can be generated from within countries on a sustainable basis.

CASE STUDY 3.2
Responding to serious human rights violations in Darfur, Sudan – strategies, critiques, impact

The conflict in Darfur, Sudan (2003 and ongoing as of 2012) has been characterised by massive human rights violations that have been attributed primarily to the government of Sudan and the Janjaweed (militias) but also to rebel groups.[1] The UN and the AU responded by undertaking a number of fact-finding missions and inquiries, issuing resolutions and, in the case of the UNSC, referring the situation to the Prosecutor of the ICC in 2005.[2] The UN and AU also worked together to provide protection on the ground through the AU UN Hybrid Mission in Darfur (UNAMID) whose presence the government of Sudan agreed to in 2007.[3] In 2008 the ICC applied for an arrest warrant against Sudan's President Al-Bashir (which was issued in 2009), which triggered considerable debate and opposition by the Arab League, the AU and others.[4] The AU made a renewed effort to resolve the crisis in 2009 through the AU High-Level Panel on Darfur, which was mandated to 'examine the situation in depth and submit recommendations to the Council on how best the issues of accountability and combating impunity, on the one hand, and reconciliation and healing, on the other, could be effectively addressed'.[5]

[1] See in particular Report of the International Commission of Inquiry on Darfur, 2005, and J. Flint and A. de Waal, *A New History of a Long War*, 2nd edn (London: Zed Books, 2008).
[2] UNSC resolution 1593 (2005). See for an overview, L. Oette, 'Peace and Justice, or Neither? The Repercussions of the al-Bashir Case for International Criminal Justice in Africa and Beyond', *JICJ* 8(2) (2010), 345–64, at 347–50.
[3] UNSC resolution 1769 (2007).   [4] See Oette, above note 2, 357–64.
[5] Darfur: The Quest for Peace, Justice and Reconciliation, Report of the African Union High-Level Panel on Darfur (AUPD), PSC/AHG/2 (CCVII) (29 October 2009).

The situation constituted a major challenge for national and international NGOs and other human rights actors who worked in an environment characterised by constant flashpoints. This included the crisis in Darfur, major milestones in the implementation of the Comprehensive Peace Agreement (2005–2011),[6] such as elections and the referendum concerning the independence of the South, conflicts in other parts of Sudan and 'routine' human rights violations. This often meant that actors seemingly had to follow events rather than being able to pursue coherent strategies. There were also a number of practical challenges. National NGOs simultaneously had to respond to complex factual and political developments, to operate in a repressive environment and to build their capacity. Meanwhile, regional and international actors, particularly the AU and the UN, struggled to fulfil their mandate to monitor and protect human rights, frequently facing obstruction and adverse reactions ranging from a lack of cooperation to expulsion of their staff members.

The Darfur crisis has been characterised by the creative, and at times controversial, use of human rights strategies. Documenting violations was difficult because of inaccessibility, security concerns and the limited capacity of local actors. However, actors have been able, by employing a range of methods, to obtain valuable information about violations. This included clandestine expert missions to the area, interviews, particularly with refugees in neighbouring Chad but also with militia leaders and others, leaks, satellite images, videos and photography, as well as medical evidence.[7] Much of this documentation was undertaken by NGOs and concerned individuals, including international humanitarian NGOs in Darfur and local groups. The UN and the AU undertook fact-finding missions that provided detailed accounts[8] and the ICC carried out its own investigations although it did not officially visit Darfur. These sources yielded a considerable body of evidence, and some reports, such as those by the UN Commission of Inquiry have been highly influential, resulting in the ICC referral. The government of Sudan, meanwhile, has persistently downplayed the scale of violations and attributed casualties and incidents to both sides and banditry.[9] While this clearly constitutes a tactic

---

[6] The Comprehensive Peace Agreement settled the conflict between the Government of Sudan and the southern Sudan People's Liberation Movement/Army.

[7] See the evidence provided by the ICC Prosecutor, reports by major international human rights organisations and the documentary film by A. Sundberg and R. Stern, *The Devil Came on Horseback* (2007). See also A. C. Tsai *et al.*, 'Medical Evidence of Human Rights Violations against Non-Arabic Speaking Civilians in Darfur: a Cross-Sectional Study', *PLOS Medicine* 9(4) (2012), 1–10.

[8] Report of the International Commission of Inquiry on Darfur, 2005, and Report of the African Commission on Human and Peoples' Rights' Fact-Finding Mission to the Republic of Sudan in the Darfur Region, 8–18 July 2004, EX.CL/364 (XI) (20 September 2004).

[9] See Interview with President Omar al-Bashir, *BBC* (14 May 2009), online, at http://news.bbc.co.uk/1/hi/programmes/hardtalk/8050309.stm.

of denial, there are certain areas, such as the scale of rape, which remain contested, largely because of the difficulty of reliably documenting violations.

The Darfur crisis caught the attention of a broad cross-section of actors and resulted in major advocacy campaigns. The highly vocal Save Darfur campaign came under stringent criticism for its allegedly simplistic portrayal of the conflict and exaggeration of the scale of violations.[10] It was accused of having mobilised the public in states such as the USA, while failing to engage politically with Sudan and within Africa. Accordingly, it was considered to be part of the problem of external interference rather than the solution.[11] This criticism highlights potentially problematic aspects of advocacy used to influence policies, such as calling for troops to be deployed to Darfur, which may further aggravate the situation. However, the criticism ignores the plurality of advocacy efforts, including by regional networks such as the Darfur consortium, which pursued more nuanced strategies.[12] In practice, one of the main problems has been the lack of concerted domestic advocacy and mobilisation, not least due to the repressive environment (though considerable efforts have been made to build the capacity of local actors), which shielded Khartoum (the capital of Sudan, often used synonymously with the government) from more serious domestic repercussions.

Human rights violations in Darfur also became the subject of litigation before human rights treaty bodies, such as the African Commission on Human and Peoples' Rights in 2009,[13] while several cases are pending before the ICC.[14] These efforts have contributed to building up a body of evidence concerning human rights violations in Darfur but have largely failed to make a difference in practice because of the limited enforcement powers of the bodies involved. While the threat of ICC prosecutions is considerable and has resulted in a number of legal and political responses on the part of the government of Sudan, the evidence after almost ten years of conflict illustrates the limits of international human rights law, international humanitarian law and international criminal law in providing protection and justice. Nevertheless, the multiple initiatives comprising documentation, reporting, advocacy, awareness-raising and litigation have resulted in an important record that may yet prove decisive for greater human rights protection and justice.

---

[10] M. Mamdani, *Saviors and Survivors: Darfur, Politics, and the War on Terror* (London, New York: Verso, 2009), 48–71. See for a contrasting account, R. Hamilton, *Fighting for Darfur: Public Action and the Struggle to Stop Genocide* (New York: Palgrave Macmillan, 2011).

[11] Mamdani, above note 10, 297.

[12] L. Oette, 'Book Review: Mahmood Mamdani, Saviors and Survivors, Darfur, Politics and the War on Terror', *Journal of African Law* (*JAL*) 54(2) (2010), 313–18.

[13] *Sudan Human Rights Organisation & Centre on Housing Rights and Evictions (COHRE)* v. *Sudan*, 279/03-296/05 (2009).

[14] See for current status, www.icc-cpi.int/Menus/ICC/Situations+and+Cases/Situations/Situation+ICC+0205.

POINTS TO CONSIDER

- What factors explain the innovative approaches to documentation in response to violations in Darfur?
- Do efforts in respect of Darfur show that advocacy is frequently at risk of being self-serving if not irrelevant altogether?
- What lessons do developments in Sudan hold for the international human rights movement?

QUESTIONS

1 What makes documentation so fundamental in the promotion and protection of human rights?

2 What methodological and practical difficulties does monitoring pose?

3 Is there any evidence that advocacy enhances human rights promotion and/or protection?

4 Should there be a change in approaches taken toward human rights training?

FURTHER READING

Baehr, P., *Non-governmental Human Rights Organizations in International Relations* (New York: Palgrave Macmillan, 2009).

Baxi, U., *The Future of Human Rights*, 3rd edn (Oxford University Press, 2008).

Charnovitz, S., 'Nongovernmental Organizations and International Law', *AJIL* 100(2) (2006), 348–72.

Clifford, B. (ed.), *The International Struggle for New Human Rights* (Philadelphia: University of Pennsylvania Press, 2009).

Dupuy, P.-M. and Vierucci, L. (eds.), *NGOs in International Law: Efficiency in Flexibility?* (Cheltenham, Northampton, MA: Edward Elgar, 2008).

Goodhart, M. (ed.), *Human Rights: Politics and Practice* (Oxford University Press, 2009).

Keck, M. E. and Sikkink, K., *Activists beyond Borders: Advocacy Networks in International Politics* (New York: Cornell University Press, 1998).

Kennedy, D., *The Dark Side of Virtue: Reassessing International Humanitarianism* (Princeton University Press, 2004).

Landman, T. and Carvalho, E., *Measuring Human Rights* (London, New York: Routledge, 2010).

Nelson, P. J. and Dorsey, E., *New Rights Advocacy: Changing Strategies of Development and Human Rights NGOs* (Washington, DC: Georgetown University Press, 2008).

O'Flaherty, M. and Ulrich, G. (eds.), *The Professional Identity of the Human Rights Field Worker* (Farnham: Ashgate, 2010).

OHCHR, *Training Manual on Human Rights Monitoring* (New York and Geneva: United Nations, 2001).

Pinkney, R., *NGOs, Africa and the Global Order* (Basingstoke: Palgrave Macmillan, 2009).

Rajagopal, B., *International Law from Below: Development, Social Movements and Third World Resistance* (Cambridge University Press, 2007).

Stammers, N., *Human Rights and Social Movements* (London: Pluto Press, 2009).

4 The United Nations Charter system

CONTENTS

4.1 INTRODUCTION

The UN Charter was not designed to address human rights, at least directly, but was instead a mechanism primarily intended to maintain and secure international peace and security. None the less, some scant references to human rights are visible therein, but as will be discussed in this chapter these were not originally meant to confer strict obligations on states or otherwise to establish a global order of rights-holders. Despite these shortcomings the human rights framework of the Charter remains crucially important because in the sixty or so years since its adoption many of the Charter's principal organs and their subsidiary institutions have been instrumental in the promotion and protection of human rights worldwide. Given that the Charter is a living instrument it is only natural that organs originally devoted to human rights have fallen into desuetude and others have surfaced to take their place. Thus, the Charter represents a constantly changing battleground of ideas, institutions, actors and activities within which politics and human rights are at odds. In the midst of this battleground, however, one finds a plethora of actors, both states and NGOs, that seek to close this gap between politics and rights.

Although initially this seemed like a vain uphill struggle on account of the fact that the UN is quintessentially a political organisation, since the end of the Cold War in the early 1990s there has been a shift towards a more visible human rights-centred approach. This is evidenced from the increased depoliticisation of human rights institutions, the adoption of a human rights agenda by the Security Council and the mainstreaming of human rights within the Organisation as a whole. Thus, as will become evident in the next section the UN Charter can no longer be construed in accordance with the political climate and notions of state sovereignty prevailing in 1945. In equal manner, article 2(7) of the Charter, which forbids the Organisation to intervene in the domestic affairs of states, necessarily now excludes human rights violations from its ambit.

A comprehensive discussion of the UN's human rights work and institutions is an infinite task given that every atom of the organization is engaged in one way or another in the promotion or protection of rights. As a result, this chapter is confined to the examination of the principal human rights institution, the HRC, and the various mechanisms operating under its wing. This includes a discussion of the universal periodic review (UPR), the Council's complaint procedure, as well as its so-called special procedures. The chapter then goes on to analyse the important human rights dimension of the General Assembly and the Security Council since both possess authority to take direct action against violations, in addition to their standard-setting capacity. Institutions that have produced important human rights work, but whose mandate is otherwise peripheral to human rights, such as the ICJ, are referred to in this chapter but are not extensively analysed. Equally, space precludes us from examining specialised agencies such as UNICEF and the UN High Commissioner for Refugees (UNCHR).

It should be pointed out that Charter-based institutions are distinguished from treaty organs engaged in human rights work, such as the HRC of the ICCPR.[1] Although all of these treaty organs reside within the UN they are in fact independent from the organisation itself, unless treaty members have entered into a collaboration agreement to the contrary with the UN. As a result, treaty organs are not susceptible to the authority of the Security Council, as is the case with Charter-based organs.

4.2 THE HUMAN RIGHTS DIMENSION OF THE CHARTER

The Charter is rightly viewed as having a *constitutional* force over and above other international treaties and obligations assumed by states because article 103 thereof expressly says so. This necessarily implies that the human rights provisions of the Charter prevail over any conflicting provisions contained in other treaties and are derogable solely in accordance with the Charter. This observation is of practical significance only if the Charter's human rights

---

[1] The CESCR, on the other hand, is not a treaty organ, but was founded by ECOSOC resolution 1985/17 (28 May 1985). For reasons of coherency its work is explored in the chapters dealing with international treaty systems and ESC rights.

provisions are couched in the form of concrete obligations for member states. If not, and particularly if the language employed is hortatory, then the risk is that human rights may be marginal to the Charter framework and outside the strict purview of the mandate assigned to its organs and institutions. A literal reading of the Charter demonstrates that human rights were not a priority among delegates to the San Francisco conference that preceded its adoption and in fact the majority of members were averse to any reference to them. It is well known that even the meagre human rights provisions in the Charter were the result of the determined efforts by human rights lobbyists and Eleanor Roosevelt, the wife of the then US president.

Be this as it may, the *travaux préparatoires* (preparatory work) of the San Francisco conference are of little use in analysing the human dimension of this constitutional instrument, as are its human rights provisions. The preamble and article 1(3) of the Charter prescribe the purposes of the organization, which includes among others the reaffirmation of fundamental human rights, equal rights for men and women and self-determination of peoples. This is followed by article 55 which provides that the UN shall 'promote ... universal respect for, and the observance of, human rights and fundamental freedoms for all without distinction as to race, sex, language or religion'. The purposes of article 55 are to be achieved by 'all members pledg[ing] to take joint and separate action in cooperation with the Organisation', in accordance with article 56. If one considers that pledges within the UN are not viewed as binding promises and that the 'promotion' and 'observance' of human rights constitute weak, and rather ineffective, obligations, it is evident that from a strict textual reading the Charter is not a legal basis for the assumption of serious human rights obligations.

Like most contemporary treaties, the UN Charter is a living instrument which by necessity must be construed in accordance with the evolutionary method of interpretation.[2] This method rejects literal interpretation or interpretation based on the original intent of the drafters, but instead adopts meanings derived from current state practice and particular understandings shared between nations, which are themselves derived from practice.[3] An illustration is poignant. The cornerstone of the Charter in 1945 and in subsequent years was the containment of armed conflict across international frontiers with a view to averting yet another world war. As a result UN member states were willing to turn a blind eye to authoritarian regimes that

---

[2] Express acceptance of this method was made, for example, by the IACtHR in *The Right to Information on Consular Assistance in the Framework of the Guarantees of Due Process of Law*, Advisory Opinion OC-16/99, of 1 October 1999, Ser. A, no. 16, para. 193.

[3] See S. Fish, *Is There a Text in the Class? The Authority of Interpretative Communities* (Cambridge, MA: Harvard University Press, 1980), who coined the theory of interpretative communities and according to which sovereign actors have formed an interpretative community in which they share common understandings about certain notions, including human rights, and interpret these notions in a relatively uniform manner.

committed genocide or blatantly abused fundamental human rights. Thus, human rights on many occasions lost out to the Charter's strict reading of international peace and security as the organisation's paramount priority.

Such an interpretation is no longer viable for several practical reasons. For one thing, it is now universally acknowledged that international peace and security may be threatened by domestic conflicts, either because they tend to spill over into neighbouring nations, or because they cause large migration and refugee flows, or destabilise entire regions. The disintegration of the former Yugoslavia is a poignant reminder. Moreover, it is now well understood that the absence of rule of law and human rights leads sooner or later to weak, fragile or indeed failed states. The Fund for Peace maintains an annual 'failed states index' which is premised on twelve indicators, a number of which are pertinent to this discussion: massive refugee or internally displaced person movements, uneven economic development, criminalisation/delegitimatisation of the state, widespread violation of human rights, lack of the rule of law, and the security apparatus operating as a state within a state.[4] Finally, the entrenchment of human rights has become so fundamental to the activities and *raison d'être* of the international community that even the very notion of peace and security cannot be divorced or read separately from human rights.[5] As a result, the rather hortatory or weak language of the Charter should not mislead us into thinking that fundamental rights are not an integral part of the UN's principal external aims and priorities. It is correct therefore to construe the provisions of the Charter in conformity with fundamental human rights.

The dynamic nature of the UN Charter is especially evident in respect of the institutions originally destined to promote and observe human rights. The chief protagonist was one of the five principal organs of the organization, namely ECOSOC. ECOSOC in turn set up the CommHR, the predecessor to what is now the HRC.[6] As will be discussed in the next section, although the Commission largely failed to take effective measures to protect and enforce human rights[7] it did none the less succeed in pushing forward

---

[4] See the Fund for Peace, 'Failed states index 2009', available at: www.fundforpeace.org/web/index.php?option=com_content&task=view&id=99&Itemid=140.

[5] UNGA resolution 65/281 (20 July 2011), preamble, which stresses that 'peace and security, development and human rights are the pillars of the UN system and the foundations for collective security and well-being'. Equally, the Security Council has underlined the perils of HIV/AIDS for regional security and post-conflict reconstruction; UNSC resolution 1983 (7 June 2011).

[6] At the same time, ECOSOC set up another Commission, that on the Status of Women.

[7] In fact, the Commission adopted a statement in 1947 whereby it argued that it had no power to take any action with respect to complaints alleging violations of human rights. (CommHR report of first session E/259 (1947), paras. 21–22). For a background analysis, see T. Gonzales, 'The Political Sources of Procedural Debates in the United Nations: Structural Impediments to Implementation of Human Rights', *New York University Journal of International Law and Politics* (*NYUJ Int'l L. & Pol.*) 13 (1981), 427, at 450.

a standard-setting agenda, followed by the drafting of substantive human rights treaties. The Commission is credited with the Bill of Rights, which consists of the Universal Declaration of Human Rights, in addition to the ICCPR and the ICESCR. It was also responsible for the drafting of other important treaties, such as the International Convention on the Elimination of All Forms of Racial Discrimination. Yet ECOSOC has remained largely peripheral to the human rights developments stemming from within the organization and did not live up to the expectations of the Charter's drafters. On the other hand, the General Assembly, and particularly its third committee, the Security Council and their respective subsidiary organs, have adopted a mix of significant political decisions and legal initiatives in the field of human entitlements. Equally, the ICJ, although by no means designed to address individual complaints or human rights disputes, has on many occasions addressed violations through the prism of state responsibility, while at the same time taking the opportunity to elaborate upon relevant human rights rules.[8]

The slow realisation of rights within the organization is explained by the fact that its principal organs are political in nature – save for the ICJ – and this is also true in respect of many of their subsidiary organs. Political, as opposed to independent, appointees are not impartial and owe allegiance to the governments that appointed them. This has inhibited bodies such as ECOSOC and the CommHR to respond even to the most flagrant violations that came to their attention. During the Cold War the UN institutions largely declined to collaborate with, or make use of, information provided by external stakeholders, particularly human rights NGOs. Although it is true that most European nations generally welcome the participation of civil society, countries with poor human rights records fiercely resisted private intrusions into their domestic affairs. The organization has now become responsive to external stakeholders and this is evident, for example, in the mandate of the HRC, its complaints procedures and the UPR, all of which will be analysed shortly.

Finally, some mention should be made of the OHCHR. This was established in 1993 by the General Assembly, its purpose being to mainstream[9] and coordinate the organisation's human rights activities as well as to promote and ensure realisation of rights – particularly by making recommendations to other UN bodies – within the framework of the Charter and the Bill of Rights.[10] Although a large portion of the OHCHR's work is clerical, especially given that it is not staffed to undertake more substantive roles or missions, ever since Mary Robinson's tenure it has become much more activist. This

---

[8] See R. Higgins, 'Human Rights in the International Court of Justice', *Leiden Journal of International Law* (*LJIL*) 20 (2007), 745.

[9] Although this task seems to have now been shouldered by the HRC, on the basis of UNGA resolution 65/281 (20 July 2011), Annex, para. 42.

[10] UNGA resolution 48/141 (20 December 1993), para. 4.

has been achieved through vibrant human rights diplomacy and the maintenance of a vocal and public profile. By way of illustration the OHCHR did not hesitate to criticise the USA for its handling of the Guantánamo detainees, demanding that they be entitled to fundamental rights under human rights and humanitarian law.[11]

The following section and subsections will focus on the mandate and work of the HRC.

4.3   THE HUMAN RIGHTS COUNCIL

The HRC, although among the newest human rights bodies in the UN system, is certainly among the most important. Its establishment is the result of the acute politicisation and lack of credibility of its predecessor,[12] the CommHR and ECOSOC. While it is true that the Commission achieved significant landmarks in both standard-setting and rule-making through the promulgation of declarations and treaties, it also struggled with the political agendas of many of its member states, many of which were anti-human rights oriented. A number of nations were driven to hold seats in the Commission with the sole purpose of obfuscating and preventing condemnation of their human rights records, as well as those of their allies.[13] It is true to say that with the exception of Israel and South Africa – both of which were, however, politically isolated – the Commission never really managed to condemn or seriously investigate the gross human rights abuses committed by any country against its own people. This state of affairs was tolerated because of the lack of an alternative option, particularly during the Cold War, the futility of attempting to amend the relevant part of the UN Charter and also because the liberal democracies in the Commission were satisfied that this body was at least contributing to the promulgation of positive human rights law. By the early 2000s it had become apparent that the Commission could no longer fulfil a serious role in the protection and monitoring of human rights worldwide and that it would have to be replaced by a new institution that was not prone to political manipulation and which would enjoy the confidence of public and private actors alike.

A number of events prompted the need for the creation of the HRC, besides the overpoliticisation and loss of credibility of its predecessor. For one thing, the USA and its European allies had long lost the requisite majority to thwart

---

[11] See CommHR, Situation of Detainees at Guantánamo Bay, UN Doc. E/CN.4/2006/120 (15 February 2006).

[12] Report of the High-level Panel of Threats, Challenges and Change, A More Secure World: Our Shared Responsibility, UN Doc. A/59/565 (1 December 2004), para. 283.

[13] UN Secretary-General Report, In Larger Freedom: Towards Development, Security and Human Rights for All, UN Doc. A/59/2005/Add.3 (26 May 2005), paras. 140–7.

Third World politics within the Commission. Secondly, the monitoring and complaint mechanisms of the Commission had become merely ceremonial and had been replaced in practice by the various UN treaty mechanisms and the work of treaty bodies. Thirdly, much of the work which would otherwise have been the domain of the Commission had been assumed by the Third Committee of the General Assembly and to a much lesser degree by the Security Council. Fourthly, the political 'aberration' previously associated with the notion that the UN could collaborate with civil society organisations in the field of human rights had long been replaced by a global climate where such collaboration was welcome at all levels. Lastly, following the end of the Cold War era, which was plagued by the complete inability of the UN to tackle human rights catastrophes such as that of Cambodia, industrialised nations and their populations were now inclined to be vocal against human rights abuses and the political cost no longer seemed acceptable to politicians and the masses.

By and large, the UN's human rights agenda could certainly have survived without bodies such as the Commission or the Council, given that all its organs, bodies and entities are already actively engaged with human rights issues. Moreover, human rights are incorporated and streamlined in all UN activities and operations.[14] So why the need for yet another dedicated, yet still political, human rights body? As the global guarantor of peace and security, including human rights, the UN no doubt needs a permanent standing body dedicated solely to advancing, protecting and monitoring human rights, lest the otherwise welcome diffusion and overlap of human rights agendas within the organization risks becoming random, uncoordinated and perhaps also conflicting. The ideal permanent body must moreover enjoy significant political clout, otherwise it will be ignored, sidelined or made irrelevant. Such clout can only be derived from the active participation of sovereign states at the helm, as opposed to a self-standing court, quasi-court or civil society organisations. The latter, as important as they are, can only play a complementary role to that of states in the protection and promotion of rights, particularly with respect to countries that openly and blatantly flout most human entitlements. Finally, apart from condemnatory resolutions by the Security Council and the General Assembly, there exists no other mechanism within the UN system where states can discuss their human rights

---

[14] By way of illustration, all entities within the UN system involved in development projects adopted in 2003 a Statement on a Common Understanding of a Human Rights-based Approach (HRBA) to Development Cooperation. Therein it is stated that all projects must be guided by the Bill of Rights and that development cooperation 'contributes to the development of the capacities of "duty-bearers" to meet their obligations and of "rights-holders" to claim their rights'. Equally, mainstreaming gender perspectives into all policies and programmes of the UN was formally institutionalised in 1997. See UN Doc. E/1997/66 (12 June 1997).

issues in an open and non-confrontational manner with a view to exposing such problems and potentially – although certainly not always – finding solutions. Despite their precedential value, human rights tribunals and treaty mechanisms are only useful for resolving individualised violations and do not allow the international community to address the culprit state, with the aid of NGOs, in a detailed discussion of *all* its human rights problems. The HRC aspires to assume this unique role.

Unlike the Commission, which was set up by ECOSOC, the HRC was set up by the General Assembly and is a subsidiary organ thereof.[15] Its task is to carry on the work of the Commission, as well as assume its responsibilities[16] and as a result its creation was not meant to sever all ties with the past. Its legal status allows it to bring all matters relating to human rights, whether urgent or long term, for discussion before the General Assembly, which certainly enjoys far more exposure and political power than ECOSOC. The HRC was entrusted with three major responsibilities: (1) a thorough and ongoing review of the human rights record of all UN members, known as UPR; (2) examination and investigation of situations concerning gross and systematic violations of human rights; and (3) optimisation of the UN's institutional capacity to deal with human rights.

The first two will be examined in discrete sections in this chapter, so it is prudent briefly to discuss institutional optimisation at this stage. Since 1945 every entity within the UN has assumed some kind of human rights function and over time this has given rise to unnecessary duplication and overlap. This is not only costly, but risks generating friction and inefficiency. The HRC is responsible for rationalising and coordinating the various human rights mandates and functions, save for the standing work of the General Assembly and the Security Council. Moreover, despite the fact that the UN is automatically associated with human rights, it is not self-evident that all its departments and institutions are guided by a specific human rights agenda and policy. By way of example, a strategy of sanctions designed to prevent a regime from amassing nuclear weapons but which causes malnutrition, child mortality and deaths as a result of the lack of health care is devoid of a human rights orientation. Equally, policies that promote rights but which do not take into consideration the particular needs of women and girls are devoid of a gender perspective. It was therefore crucial that the HRC was entrusted with mainstreaming gender and human rights considerations into all UN policies and actions.[17]

If all of these laudable aspirations which the new Council is poised to fulfil are to be achieved, it needs to be impartial, objective, transparent and results oriented. This is a tall order given the politicised nature of its predecessor

---

[15] UNGA resolution 60/251 (3 April 2006), para. 1.   [16] Ibid., para. 5(g).

[17] Ibid., paras. 3 and 6.

and certainly cannot be achieved by mere rhetoric. That is why the Assembly decided on the imposition of certain, seemingly stringent, conditions for the election of states to the forty-seven members comprising the HRC. Although membership of the Council is open to all UN members, the Assembly 'shall take into account the contribution of candidates to the promotion and protection of human rights and their voluntary pledges and commitments made thereto'.[18] Although this falls rather short of requiring a solid human rights record of potential members it does represent a significant departure from past practices and no doubt states with poor records may find themselves dissuaded or simply discouraged. Moreover, in extreme cases, the Assembly, by a two-thirds majority of present and voting members, may suspend a particular member engaged in gross and systematic violation of human rights.[19] In practice, because membership to the Council is highly valued from a strategic perspective, states have vied for election to it and in their pledges to the Assembly made a serious effort to demonstrate their commitment to human rights both domestically and internationally. Of course, this usually does not amount to much when it comes from countries with a history of repression and abuse.[20] Certain groups of states went as far as publicly declaring their voting criteria, as was the case with EU members which committed themselves not to vote for candidates that were subject to UN sanctions for human rights violations.[21] The USA, although a member of the Council since 2009, initially voted against resolution 60/251 because it only required a simple majority, for the election of members, as opposed to a more stringent two-thirds majority, and also because it did not automatically exclude candidates subject to UN sanctions.[22]

Yet the system is far from perfect and has faced legitimacy concerns from the outset. Membership to the Council is based on equitable geographical distribution among the various regional groups.[23] Ideally, states will compete for available seats and will thus be elected by their regional peers on the basis of their human rights record. In practice, many regional groupings

---

[18] Ibid., para. 8.   [19] Ibid.

[20] For example, see Egyptian Pledge, UN Doc. A/61/878 (23 April 2007), 5, where the then Mubarak regime pledged, *inter alia*, to preserve the freedom of the press and of the judiciary and to strengthen civil society and political dialogue! The texts of all 2007 election pledges are available at: www.un.org/ga/61/elect/hrc/.

[21] H. Upton, 'The Human Rights Council: First Impressions and Future Challenges', *HRLR* 7 (2007), 29, at 33.

[22] In fact, in April 2008 the Bush administration announced that it would be withholding a portion of its contribution to the 2008 UN regular budget, equivalent to the country's share of the HRC budget. In June of the same year it further announced that the USA would engage with the HRC 'only in matters of deep national interest'. The Obama administration reversed this hostile climate and in 2009 the USA was elected to the Council, submitting its first UPR in 2010.

[23] UNGA resolution 60/251, para. 7.

operate manufactured (or closed) slates, meaning that competition within the group is discouraged because seats are allocated under the table by mutual agreement between group members. Astonishingly, Syria's candidacy for the Council was unopposed within the Asian group in the run up to the 2011 elections, despite global reports that its security forces had killed more than 800 demonstrators at the time. Following widespread condemnation the Asian group finally urged Syria to withdraw its candidacy and nominated Kuwait in its place.[24] Despite these shortcomings the Council is a far cry from its predecessor where the withdrawal of a candidacy for persistent human rights violations would have seemed laughable. This conclusion is reinforced by the suspension of Libya from the Council by the General Assembly on 1 March 2011,[25] only nine months after it was elected on a closed African slate. The practice of closed slates that encompass autocratic and brutal regimes has somewhat alarmed the western European group, which although itself put forward a closed slate for the 2011 elections, promised competitive rounds in the future. These developments certainly indicate an evolving dynamic permeating the operation and membership of this new institution. The UPR mechanism, examined in the following subsection, justifies a reserved excitement about this dynamic.

4.3.1   The universal periodic review

The UPR is a creature born out of Assembly resolution 60/251.[26] It assumes that an HRC composed as far as possible of countries that promote and implement human rights can serve as a forum for a holistic, honest, yet non-confrontational, discussion of each nation's persistent human rights issues. The Assembly made it clear that this reporting mechanism should not duplicate existing reporting obligations, must avoid becoming burdensome to the UN and its member states and should moreover add value to the promotion of human rights. Before going any further it is important to examine in what way the UPR is different from similar reporting mechanisms within the UN system, particularly the seven treaty-based mechanisms and any Charter-based periodic reports. Charter-based reporting is no longer available, its last manifestation, a periodic self-reporting mechanism,[27] having been formally terminated in 1980 as obsolete and far too marginal to be of any relevance.[28] The reporting dimension of the treaty bodies, on the other hand, has fared much better and has enhanced the effectiveness of individual communications, general comments, inter-state complaints and on-site inquiries, where available. None the less, despite the extensive comments and

---

[24] HRW, 'UN: Limited Choice Marks Rights Body Election' (20 May 2011).
[25] UNGA resolution 65/265 (1 March 2011).   [26] Para. 5(e).
[27] ECOSOC resolution 624B (XXII) (1 August 1956).
[28] UNGA resolution 35/209 (17 December 1980).

recommendations of the various treaty bodies in their responses to national reports, these are necessarily confined to the limited number of rights contained in the treaties. Moreover, this process is confined only to those states that have ratified the treaties.

By contrast, under the UPR states are reviewed on the basis of obligations arising from the UN Charter, the UDHR, instruments to which they are parties and any unilaterally assumed voluntary pledges and commitments.[29] These may in fact turn out to be more extensive than most treaty obligations. Even further, although the treaty bodies are not supported by an enforcement mechanism, their comments and recommendations on the parties' periodic reports are not meant to serve as mere points of discussion. On the contrary, because the obligations arising out of human rights treaties are binding, the recommendations of the treaty bodies aim, among other things, to demonstrate where and how compliance is poor or ineffective. In this sense the treaty bodies' periodic reporting mechanisms are not necessarily free from friction and compulsion. Finally, treaty bodies employ for their reporting processes independent experts, whereas the UPR is premised on peer review, which is conducted by the representatives of states elected to the HRC.

The reader may well ponder what makes a country that is not a party to any, or a few, treaty-based mechanisms decide to take part in a UPR where the entirety of its human rights record risks being scrutinised before the rest of the world. The simple answer to this question lies in the fact that even the most brutal regimes, with the exception perhaps of North Korea, is weary of a perpetual political and financial isolation and is cognisant that its human rights record will eventually surface, thanks to the pace of modern media and the speed of information exchange. As a result, even countries such as Myanmar have submitted themselves to the scrutiny of the UPR.

The process is relatively straightforward. To start with, states are under an obligation to submit a national report which should discuss the state of human rights in their country and which ideally should be prepared on the basis of a broad consultation with all relevant stakeholders.[30] This national report should not exceed twenty pages, unlike the extensive reports submitted before human rights treaty bodies. No doubt these national reports will attempt to paint a favourable picture and in many cases deflect attention from serious abuses or hide behind laws that were never meant to be respected or implemented by the authorities. In order for the Council to assess the national report the UPR provides for the compilation of two distinct sources of information that are made publicly available: (1) information contained in the reports of treaty bodies, special procedures, including observations

---

[29] HRC resolution 5/1 (18 June 2007), Annex, para. 1.
[30] HRC resolution 5/1, Annex, para. 15(a).

and comments by the state concerned, and other relevant UN documents which shall not exceed ten pages;[31] (2) a summary of credible information provided by other relevant stakeholders, namely NGOs, which again must not exceed ten pages.[32] In practice, given the vibrancy and organisation of the international human rights NGO movement, the information provided in national reports is quite literally picked apart in the NGO summaries. By way of illustration, NGOs have consistently emphasised that torture is not only widespread but publicly sanctioned in Uzbekistan and that the country has wholly failed to implement the right to fair trial, having resorted to exaction of forced confessions, denial of defence rights and government appointment of judges.[33] In respect of Myanmar, the contributing NGOs contested the suggestion of the government that the new constitution was transparent and democratic, noting *inter alia* that article 445 of this instrument effectively granted a blanket amnesty to government officials for past and future serious crimes.[34]

The national report along with the compiled information is then processed and reviewed by a working group consisting of three rapporteurs, selected by the drawing of lots among the members of the Council and from different regional groupings (also known as the troika).[35] The conduct of the review is conducted through an interactive dialogue, which may involve the participation of observer states and other stakeholders.[36] The purpose of this format is to pose meaningful and pressing questions to the reviewed state by any interested party sharing particular human rights concerns, thus also avoiding giving the impression that the troika operates in a quasi-judicial manner. A list of questions or issues may be prepared in advance by observer nations and submitted to the state under review with a view to facilitating its preparation and providing some focus for the interactive dialogue.[37] In practice, this list of issues and questions has become a significant part of the process, particularly since many of the issues raised have evoked strong responses on account of their sensitive nature.

The Uzbek delegation, for example, reacted forcefully to allegations that it had covered up its military repression of government dissent in Andijan province which resulted in the loss of hundreds of lives, noting that this was a national security issue which it was not willing to discuss further.[38] In other instances, the list of questions against liberal democracies has addressed a

---

[31] Ibid., para. 15(b).   [32] Ibid., para. 15(c).

[33] NGO summary on Uzbekistan, UN Doc. A/HRC/WG.6/3/UZB/3 (16 September 2008), paras. 8, 9, 14.

[34] NGO summary on Myanmar, UN Doc. A/HRC/WG.6/10//MMR/3 (18 October 2010), paras. 5, 12.

[35] HRC resolution 5/1, Annex, para. 18(d).   [36] Ibid., para. 18(b) and (c).

[37] Ibid., para. 21.

[38] Report of the WG on the Uzbek UPR, UN Doc. A/HRC/10/83 (11 March 2009), para. 97.

variety of non-mainstream human rights issues. The USA, for example, was criticised, among other things, for its poverty discrepancy between blacks and whites, for rapes in prison and discrimination against indigenous peoples.[39] No doubt, states are compelled to respond to the questions posed, even if to dismiss them. The interactive dialogue itself, with the presence of observers and stakeholders, is scheduled to last no more than three hours.[40] This is followed by the deliberation of the troika and the adoption of a so-called outcome. Prior to its adoption, the country under review will have a chance to respond to the issues raised.[41] The outcome is equivalent to the report adopted by treaty bodies and consists of a summary of the proceedings, a conclusion and/or recommendations and a list of the voluntary commitments of the state concerned.[42]

Because the UPR is founded on the principle of cooperation, country involvement and non-confrontation, the conclusion/recommendation section of the outcomes does not criticise countries under review. Instead, it offers suggestions for improvement, shares best practices, and offers the possibility of cooperation, technical assistance and capacity-building, among other things.[43] The idea underlying the UPR is to identify problems, discuss them with the state concerned and offer assistance to overcome them, and in practice most countries tend to adopt at least some of the recommendations offered in the course of their UPR.[44] At the same time it has to be acknowledged that the HRC, special procedures and treaty bodies have identified a plethora of instances where states have paid mere lip service even to pledges made by themselves. The HRC may decide if and when any specific follow up is necessary, and in situations where a state fails to take any remedial action the HRC may address as it deems appropriate all instances of persistent non-cooperation.[45]

Overall, the UPR, despite its drawbacks, has managed to make deliberation transparent and open to external actors, particularly NGOs, and has forced governments to respond to questions they would otherwise prefer not to engage with. It is still too early to assess whether it is effective, but it is a reality that a number of nations have taken steps to remedy problematic situations mainly through the introduction of new legislation.

---

[39] Report of the WG on the United States, UPR, UN Doc. A/HRC/16/11 (4 January 2011), paras. 76, 78–9.

[40] HRC resolution 5/1, Annex, para. 22.   [41] Ibid., paras. 28–32.

[42] Ibid., para. 26.   [43] Ibid., para. 27.

[44] Chad, for example, agreed to ratify the OPCAT and to establish a national prevention mechanism, something applauded by the Committee against Torture (CtAT). See Concluding Observations on Chad, UN Doc. CAT/C/TCD/CO/1 (4 June 2009), para. 36.

[45] HRC resolution 5/1, paras. 37–8. In practice, special procedures also warn recalcitrant countries of failing to implement both their pledges as well as the most pertinent recommendations addressed to them in their UPR. See Special Rapporteur on North Korea, UN Doc. A/HRC/16/58 (21 February 2011), para. 74.

4.3.2   The Council's complaints procedure

Given the myriad individual complaint mechanisms available through the UN's treaty bodies and regional human rights tribunals, an additional procedure seems rather superfluous. This is all the more true considering that the so-called 1503 procedure,[46] the predecessor to the Council's current complaints mechanism, is confidential, time consuming and oriented towards achieving a friendly settlement with the culprit state, rather than addressing the plight of the victims. As a result, it is not self-evident why the Assembly thought it wise to renew the life cycle of the 1503 procedure.[47] There are some cogent reasons. For one thing, whereas individual complaint mechanisms require the consent of states for the submission of communications by their nationals, the 1503 procedure does not. Moreover, the procedure is triggered only with respect to gross and systematic violations of human rights,[48] not mere individual and isolated infractions. In terms of effectiveness the 1503 procedure was largely discredited because it failed to seriously investigate many of the widespread violations of its era, including the glaring crimes of the Argentine junta in the 1980s and those of the Fujimori regime. The case of the Rwandan genocide is also illustrative. Although the Commission had ample information a year before the genocide that it was in fact impending, it none the less decided to keep the situation confidential under the 1503 procedure. What is more alarming is that Rwanda at the time held a seat on the Commission.

Other criticisms against the Commission is that it addressed only a limited number of civil and political rights, thus excluding altogether ESC rights, and demonstrated a deep political bias which rendered it unable to act against particular governments.[49] Between 1974 and 2005 a total of eighty-four countries were examined with violations ranging from mass killings and disappearances to forced labour and religious persecution.[50] Although little information has become publicly available, it is known at least that the CommHR adopted condemnatory resolutions only in respect of seven countries, while three were referred directly to the public (as opposed to the confidential nature of the 1503 mechanism) 1235 procedure.[51]

---

[46] It is known as such because it was enunciated in ECOSOC resolution 1503 (XLVIII) (27 May 1970), as amended by ECOSOC resolution 2000/3 (19 June 2000). CommHR resolution 2000/109 (16 April 2000) further reduced the procedural steps for the filing of communications from five to four.

[47] See para. 3 of UNGA resolution 60/251, wherein the Assembly decided to retain this mechanism.

[48] ECOSOC resolution 1503, para. 1.

[49] P. Alston, 'The Commission on Human Rights', in P. Alston (ed.), *The United Nations and Human Rights: A Critical Appraisal* (Oxford: Clarendon Press, 1995), 151.

[50] H. Tolley, 'The Concealed Crack in the Citadel: The UN Commission on Human Rights' Response to Confidential Communications', *HRQ* 6 (1984), 420.

[51] ECOSOC resolution 1235 (XLII) (6 June 1967). This followed the 1503 procedure and was originally intended to allow the Commission to consider the situations in South Africa,

The revamped 1503 complaints procedure[52] has remedied many of the defects of its predecessor and as a result of the proliferation of treaty-based and regional communications mechanisms its role is practically limited to being an early warning system and a complementary political pressure mechanism. Quite significantly it is expressly applicable to all rights and not only to those considered fundamental, as long of course as their violation is gross.[53] It is also hailed as victim oriented on account of the fact that it requires the Council to reach an outcome within a maximum of two years from the submission of the complaint to the state and also because it provides for the involvement of the complainant.[54] Given that the procedure is directed towards gross, and therefore ongoing, human rights violations it is evident that a two-year process involving deliberations with the culprit state is inadequate for addressing urgent situations. It is also unlikely that the Security Council will be in the dark in relation to gross and widespread human rights violations likely to endanger peace and security, and no doubt other early warning mechanisms, both intergovernmental and private, will be more alert to the first signals of crimes and violations. Much like the use of the ICJ to impose interim measures in the *Bosnian Genocide* case,[55] which although unable to yield any immediate relief for the victims was none the less able to put pressure on Serbia, the revamped 1503 procedure will ultimately serve as a complementary forum for political pressure.

From a procedural point of view it is no different from other complaint mechanisms. In order to be considered admissible an application must not be politically motivated, should adequately describe alleged violations and be submitted by the victim or any person or group with direct and reliable information, even second-hand, as long as the information is not based exclusively on media reports. Moreover, local remedies need to have been exhausted, assuming they are effective, and the case should not have been

---

Rhodesia and Portuguese colonies. However, the Sub-Commission on Human Rights, now disbanded, hijacked the process and allowed NGOs to make oral interventions or circulate statements, which in turn allowed it to recommend to the Commission that it establish a committee of experts to consider situations in Greece and Haiti during 1967. A shocked Commission then adopted the 1503 confidential procedure to avoid further political embarrassment. The rationale of the 1235 procedure has none the less been retained in the revamped procedure under HRC resolution 5/1, Annex, para. 109(d).

[52] Its modalities are elaborated in HRC resolution 5/1, Annex, Part IV.

[53] Ibid., para. 85.

[54] Ibid., paras. 85 and 105–8. Minimal is an understatement, given that the complainant has no access to what is being discussed in the relevant proceedings administered by the working groups.

[55] Case Concerning *Application of the Genocide Convention* (*Bosnia* v. *FRY*), Provisional Measures Order of 8 April 1993 ICJ Reports 1993, 3.

referred to another human rights procedure.[56] Communications are filtered for the purposes of admissibility, including an assessment of whether the alleged violations are indeed gross and persistent, by a working group on communications that is staffed by members of the Council's advisory committee.[57] Once considered admissible the complaints filtered are passed to a working group on situations, whose task is to investigate the allegations. This is composed of Council members serving, however, in their personal capacity.[58] As already noted, the procedure is confidential, albeit the plenary of the Council is notified of all proceedings.[59] The state under investigation must cooperate and make every effort to provide a response no later than three months after receiving the request. Five potential outcomes are available from this process: (1) full discontinuation; (2) retention of the situation under review followed by a request to the state to provide further information; (3) retention under review and appointment of a country rapporteur; (4) discontinuation of the confidential procedure and reverting to a public consideration of the situation; and (5) recommendation of technical assistance, capacity-building or advisory services through the OHCHR to the state under consideration.[60]

4.4   SPECIAL PROCEDURES

It was in 1980 that the then Sub-Commission on the Promotion and Protection of Human Rights recommended to the CommHR the establishment of a working group (WG) on enforced or involuntary disappearances (WGEID) which were at the time common place among South America's dictatorial regimes.[61] The WG was immensely successful because it proved flexible and was able to visit numerous countries for on-site investigations, something which neither the Commission nor the Sub-Commission were able to do.[62] Moreover, the WG was able to respond quickly to urgent situations and as a result it became a useful paradigm for human rights reporting and investigation.

The function and nature of special procedures is quite different from that of other Charter-based and human rights treaty bodies. Special procedures are set up to scrutinise and/or investigate specific countries where acute human rights violations are alleged to have taken place, or investigate

---

[56] HRC resolution 5/1, Annex, para. 87.   [57] Ibid., paras. 91–5.   [58] Ibid., paras. 96–7.
[59] Exceptionally, the Council may decide to conduct a public meeting in those situations of 'manifest and unequivocal lack of cooperation', in accordance with para. 104, ibid.
[60] Ibid., para. 109.   [61] CommHR resolution 20(XXXVI) (29 February 1980).
[62] The Sub-Commission had prior to 1980 set up intersessional and sessional working groups, such as those on slavery (1975) and the administration of justice (1974).

and report on the trends, developments and implementation of particular entitlements around the world. The former are known as country-specific mandates, whereas the latter are known as thematic mandates. Thematic mandates may be established in the form of a WG or by means of an independent expert or special rapporteur (which is a standing institution unlike the expert). Although their establishment has never been driven by particular methodological imperatives, for instructive purposes thematic mandates can be distinguished in three ways: (1) by reference to their pursuits those that seek to investigate and analyse the state and implementation of rights clearly established in the Bill of Rights (e.g. enforced or involuntary disappearances, torture, freedom of religion or belief, racism and racial discrimination); (2) those who seek to demonstrate the impact of contemporary situations on the enjoyment of rights (e.g. those of people of African descent, the effects of foreign debt and other related international financial obligations of states on the full enjoyment of human rights, mercenaries, countering terrorism, extreme poverty); and (3) those that investigate the status and viability of new and emerging rights (e.g. international solidarity, transnational corporations and their impact on rights, contemporary forms of slavery, migrants).[63]

What distinguishes the UN's special procedures from other Charter-based mechanisms is that all mandate-holders are independent from any government. In fact, although a certain degree of lobbying is necessarily involved, interested candidates are urged to apply independently. In practice, such posts have largely been assumed by human rights academics, who are able to combine their academic activities with the exigencies of their mandates. This is by no means a trivial issue because other than their expenses mandate-holders are not entitled to a salary and it is natural, given the time-consuming nature of these posts, that they only attract the wealthy or academics (equipped with human rights expertise) able to rearrange their schedules. Since most thematic mandates demand a team of full-time staff to deal with the increasing load of communications and research, it is evident that mandate-holders from developing nations have little, or no, access to the level of resources and funding of their wealthier counterparts. This in turn has been counterproductive for the work of some mandates and the Assembly recently addressed this critical issue by requesting the OHCHR to make available requisite funding from the UN budget as well as from extrabudgetary sources.[64]

Special procedures are not meant to process individual complaints in the manner practised by Charter-based mechanisms (e.g. the 1503

---

[63] By August 2011 there were thirty-three thematic mandates and eight country mandates.
[64] UNGA resolution 65/281 (20 July 2011), Annex, paras. 31–4.

procedure) or treaty bodies, which exercise a judicial or quasi-judicial function. Equally, they have no authority to demand that culprit states undertake any particular action.[65] Finally, UN member states have no general reporting obligations towards any of the special procedures, as well as no obligation to respond to particular allegations. None the less, special procedures have played an immensely significant role in shaping human rights policies in areas insufficiently understood by policy-makers,[66] as well as in addressing urgent human rights crises in a manner that other bodies with judicial authority could not. By way of illustration, it has aptly been demonstrated that the right of access to food is affected by domestic agricultural policies, gender discrimination and global market fluctuations, among other things. Equally, special rapporteurs have adduced concrete evidence that government debt affects all fundamental rights.[67] The following subsections aim to show how mandate-holders have employed the three tools in their armoury to make their mandates flexible, responsive and relevant. It is precisely because of their flexibility and immediate response to violations that special procedures mandate-holders are a constant nuisance for many countries. More often than not they have been made the object of political attack and have been asked to resign.[68] In one case the special rapporteur on the independence of judges and lawyers was convicted and incarcerated by his native Malaysian courts because it was considered that he defamed certain firms which he accused of being involved in corruption. The ICJ emphatically pointed out that things said or done in the course of a special rapporteur's mandate are immune from prosecution.[69]

---

[65] Of course, this has not stopped special procedures, in cases of recalcitrant governments, of notifying the Security Council recommending that it take appropriate action to ensure that the culprit government respect its human rights obligations. See Report of the Special Rapporteur on Belarus, UN Doc. E/CN.4/2006/36 (16 January 2006), para. 80.

[66] Some special procedures have even proceeded to issue general comments in the same manner as treaty bodies. See the WGEID, General Comments on enforced disappearance as a continuous crime, and the right to the truth in relation to enforced disappearances. Available on the WG's website, at: www.ohchr.org/EN/Issues/Disappearances/Pages/DisappearancesIndex.aspx.

[67] See Draft Guiding Principles on Foreign Debt and Human Rights, adopted by the UN Special Rapporteur on the effects of debt on the enjoyment of human rights.

[68] See 'Statement by US Ambassador to the HRC for the Resignation of Special Rapporteur Richard Falk' (7 July 2011), available at http://geneva.usmission.gov/2011/07/07/donahoe-statement/. The Special Rapporteur is alleged to have posted a cartoon on his blog depicting a dog labelled 'USA' wearing a Jewish head cover urinating upon a female who was meant to depict justice.

[69] *Difference Relating to Immunity from Legal Process of a Special Rapporteur of the Commission on Human Rights* (1999), ICJ Reports 62, paras. 39ff.

INTERVIEW 4.1

With UN Special Rapporteur

(Cephas Lumina)

Cephas Lumina, a Zambian national, is UN Special Rapporteur on the effects of debt on the enjoyment of human rights, having been appointed in 2008.

How are you able to combine your position as SR with your busy academic and professional schedule? Do you receive any secretarial or other assistance from the UN or other bodies?

It is very difficult to combine academic and professional responsibilities with work as a UN special procedures mandate-holder. A number of colleagues either have low teaching loads or have been granted leave of absence by their institutions in order to devote more time to UN work. Unfortunately, this has not been the case with me and I was constrained to leave my academic position because the workload did not leave me sufficient time for my academic work and my home institution was not very supportive in this regard.

Although the OHCHR is enjoined to provide administrative assistance, this is quite limited due to budgetary constraints, which means that fewer human and financial resources are available to support the work of the special procedures. I personally receive no support from other sources (I think due to the contentious nature of my mandate), but some of my colleagues get extra funding from some countries which allow them to engage additional support staff or undertake thematic studies. There are also problems flowing from a high staff turnover in the OHCHR which is attributable to staff career movements and cumbersome UN recruitment procedures. Some of the support staff work on short-term contracts and therefore are forced to seek longer-term, and more secure, job opportunities elsewhere. To illustrate the gravity of the problem, I have had a total of seven OHCHR staff supporting my mandate since I assumed it in May 2008 until early 2012 (some lasting only a couple of months)!

Do you think that affected individuals and communities are aware of your mandate and that by communicating with you they feel they can make a difference?

No. Many individuals and communities do not seem to be aware of my mandate and in particular the connection between foreign debt and human rights. I do not know the reasons for this but I suspect that generally there is little public awareness of the UN special procedures and how they can assist affected individuals and communities. Personally, I have endeavoured to increase the visibility of my mandate by participating in public events such as conferences and by drawing global attention to the human rights implications of foreign debt through media statements focusing on a range of issues, including climate change and commercial creditor litigation against impoverished countries.

In practice, how receptive have governments and international finance institutions been to your reports and recommendations?

Developing countries have generally been very receptive to my reports and recommendations while developed countries and international financial institutions have not. That said, there are occasions when I have engaged constructively with the World Bank and the African Development Bank, both of which have been involved in the consultations that have been held concerning the Draft Guiding Principles on foreign debt and human rights which I am developing in the context of my mandate. Norway and Australia have also engaged with the mandate and commented positively on aspects of my country mission reports. I have engaged with the IMF and the Asian Development Bank during missions but their response has generally not been encouraging.

What are your primary sources of information?

I draw my information from a broad range of sources but this depends on the type of report I have to produce. For thematic reports, I rely principally on academic research, official (UN and government) documents and studies by NGOs. For country mission reports, I rely on official documents (including national legislation and policy documents), UN documents, academic research and information from discussions with government officials and other stakeholders (such as development partners and NGOs).

4.4.1   Communications

A good number of special procedures are entitled to receive information concerning human rights violations from governments, NGOs, intergovernmental organisations, victims and witnesses. When credible information is furnished, showing that a violation within the scope of the mandate has occurred or is about to occur, the mandate-holder possesses the discretion to intervene with the government concerned and communicate its findings. The Code of Conduct for special procedures sets out the relevant admissibility criteria,[70] which are the same as those required for the complaints procedure of the HRC, described above. Two types of communication are available. The first concerns situations that are ongoing, life threatening or in respect of which harm is imminent and thus require urgent action.

[70] HRC resolution 5/2 (18 June 2007), Annex.

Such communications are known as urgent appeals and their motivation is to inform the state of the situation with a view to making an immediate intervention that will terminate or prevent the violation. The second type concerns violations that have already occurred and in respect of which the relevant communications are known as letters of allegation. In neither case does the mandate-holder have authority to make the case public or condemn the target government – a case is publicised when the special rapporteur submits his/her report to the Council or the Assembly – but rather urges it to take all appropriate action to investigate and address the allegations. In practice, the press releases issued by mandate-holders can be sharp and rather accusatory,[71] which is a sign of the confidence and respect they enjoy.

In 2010, 604 communications were sent to 110 states, covering 1,407 individuals of whom 19 per cent were women. Of the total number of communications, 66 per cent were issued jointly by more than one mandate. Governments responded to 35 per cent of communications, 18 per cent of which were subsequently followed up.[72]

4.4.2   Country visits

Country visits are an integral part of the work of the special procedures because they allow mandate-holders to perform on-site investigations in respect of urgent situations and draft accurate and detailed reports. Yet, no state is obliged to provide access to special rapporteurs, or any other mechanism for that matter, to conduct on-site investigations. Country visits are only possible following a standing invitation or an *ad hoc* invitation issued by the requesting nation. Standing invitations allow all mandate-holders to visit the country concerned for work related to their mandate without the need to make a formal request. Even so, special rapporteurs must notify the authorities in advance of each visit and the institutions or persons they intend to converse with. As of 31 December 2010 a total of seventy-eight countries had extended standing invitations to special procedures, including all EU member states and some countries with poor human rights records, such as Kuwait, but excluding Russia, China and the USA. During the 1980s and 1990s at a time when states zealously guarded their domestic jurisdiction from external scrutiny over their human rights practices and thus refused all country visits, mandate-holders stationed themselves in neighbouring countries that provided them access and interviewed refugees and those in flight. This was particularly true in respect of the Israeli and Chilean country mandates.

---

71 See press release by Special Rapporteur on the right to food, 'Madagascar's Hungry Population is Taken Hostage Denounces UN Special Rapporteur' (22 July 2011).

72 OHCHR, UN Special Procedures: Facts and Figures 2010 (April 2011), 8–10. The WGEID is not included in this report. According to its own 2010 annual report it transmitted 105 cases of enforced disappearance to twenty-two states.

Once an invitation is issued the government should not stifle the mission with administrative or other hurdles, or by imposing conditions. In fact, a coherent body seems to have emerged of customary principles pertinent to fact-finding missions,[73] which are wholly applicable to country visits. This includes full freedom of movement and inquiry, access to all requested facilities, contact with all requested persons and organisations (confidential and unsupervised where relevant), including prisoners and NGOs, and full access to documentary material pertinent to the mandate. It is also crucial that the government provide assurance that no person interviewed or in contact with the special rapporteurs will suffer threats, harassment or punishment.[74] In practice, reprisals are common, as will be analysed shortly. In 2010 sixty-seven country visits to forty-eight countries were undertaken, 48 per cent of which were to countries that had not issued a standing invitation.[75]

Besides facilitating the investigative work of special procedures, country visits have given rise to an additional dimension that is of great significance. Any visit is always an event much-talked about in the media of the visited nation and the public perception is that a UN human rights body would not undertake an official visit unless a serious issue was at stake. This tension obviously trickles down to the country's political institutions which are keen, in most cases, to appease public sentiment and the nation's image abroad. A visit therefore may act as a pressure point for a number of changes.[76]

4.4.3   Annual reports

The reporting function of special procedures may seem trivial compared to the dispatch of communications and country visits. None the less, both annual and *ad hoc* reports are extremely important. Reports provide a unique insight into particular human rights situations for the benefit of public institutions as well as other private stakeholders. Given the independence of special rapporteurs their reports are both critical and revealing and as a result the information contained in them is often attacked by target states. This evidently renders them all the more valuable and in practice they are employed as authoritative secondary sources of law and fact by scholars and UN institutions. We have already explained that the UPR relies to a great extent on the reports issued by special procedures. Moreover, in situations

---

[73] See F. Viljoen, 'Fact-finding by UN Human Rights Complaints Bodies: Analysis and Suggested Reforms', *MPYBUNL* 8 (2004), 49; see also Declaration on Fact-finding by the UN in the Field of Maintenance of International Peace and Security, UNGA resolution 46/59 (9 December 1991), Annex.

[74] Terms of Reference for Fact-finding Missions by Special Rapporteurs/Representatives of the Commission on Human Rights, UN Doc. E/CN.4/1998/45 (20 November 1997), Appendix V.

[75] Facts and Figures 2010, above note 72, 11.   [76] Ibid.

where the law is yet to crystallise, is unregulated by treaty or lacks concrete state practice, as in the case of transnational corporations, human rights defenders, the right to development, the impact of sovereign debt on human rights and other matters, the reports of special rapporteurs usually mould and shape legal developments.

CASE STUDY 4.1
Reprisals against those collaborating with UN human rights procedures

A little-exposed facet of the work of the various procedures of the HRC concerns the fate of the individuals providing information, making complaints or simply collaborating with the Council and its institutions. Although, as explained, most of the procedures involve a large degree of confidentiality, it is inevitable that during country visits the identity of those conversing with special rapporteurs is made known, as is also the case *mutatis mutandis* when urgent communications are issued in respect of particular violations. Reprisals against such persons take the form of harassment, intimidation, arbitrary arrests, physical aggression, refusal to issue travel documents, death threats and killings. The HRC has identified the seriousness of the problem, which greatly undermines the entirety of its human rights work, and has called for governments to take urgent and remedial action.[1] It should be stressed that reprisals are committed not only by government agents, but also by non-state actors, as the following case aptly illustrates.

On February 2005 Sister Dorothy Stang was shot several times as she walked to attend a meeting in the town of Anapu, in Brazil. The victim was an environmentalist, human rights defender and member of the Pastoral Land Commission, whose aim is to defend the rights of rural land workers and bring about land reform. On October 2004 Sister Dorothy had met the UN Special Rapporteur on the Independence of Judges and Lawyers, during the latter's visit to Belem, Brazil and a week prior to her murder she had met the Brazilian Human Rights Minister to report that four local farmers had received death threats from loggers and landowners. Following immediate communications from several UN special procedures the government of Brazil initiated prosecutions and soon after made several arrests.[2]

In other cases where the culprits were government-sanctioned agents, the authorities generally took no remedial action. While on the one hand the issue highlights the vulnerability of victims, defenders and collaborators, on the other hand it demonstrates that UN procedures are perceived as a powerful tool against violations by those who commit them.

[1] HRC resolution 12/2 (12 October 2009).
[2] CommHR Report, Cooperation with Representatives of United Nations Human Rights Bodies, UN Doc. E/CN.4/2006/30 (6 February 2006), paras. 6ff.

QUESTIONS

- What are the benefits and disadvantages of independent and government-appointed human rights posts within the United Nation's machinery?
- Is there any institution, principal organ or body – other than the Security Council – which presides and oversees the work of other human rights entities within the UN Charter framework?
- Is the United Nations legally bound by international human rights law? Your response should consider whether the UN is bound institutionally (e.g. in respect of its employees' labour rights), as well as with regard to its external operations.
- The human rights procedures and mechanisms operated by UN institutions – other than the Security Council – do not carry the element of compulsion which one finds in most international courts and tribunals. How effective do you consider they are and what recommendations would you make to render them more effective?
- What is the additional value generated by the UPR, given that most states already face extensive reporting obligations on account of their membership to multilateral universal human rights treaties?

4.5   THE GENERAL ASSEMBLY AND HUMAN RIGHTS

The Assembly is a principal organ of the organization under article 7 of the UN Charter. It is political in nature but unlike other organs its membership is universal and each state is entitled to a single vote of equal value. With very few exceptions, its resolutions are not binding on member states, but at the very least all its unanimous, or near-unanimous, resolutions are highly persuasive. The Assembly's influence and law-making capacity is also manifest in the fact that states are careful in their statements and endorsements of resolutions adopted therein because of possible estoppel implications (i.e. they cannot renege on statements made before the Assembly). Moreover, it is strongly argued that unanimous resolutions that are subsequently re-endorsed are concrete evidence of consistent state practice (whether in the form of *usus* or *opinio juris*) and thus may well crystallise into custom.[77] As a result, the standard-setting work of the Assembly in the field of human rights assumes increased significance.

The Assembly possesses a rather broad power to deal with human rights, given that articles 10 and 11 of the UN Charter authorise it to discuss any

---

[77] G. Sloan, 'General Assembly Resolutions Revisited: (Forty Years Later)', *BYIL* 58 (1987), 39.

questions or matters within the scope of the Charter and make appropriate recommendations to the states concerned, as well as the Security Council. Exceptionally, the Assembly is not competent to deal with an issue that is under examination by the Security Council. The Assembly's vast workload is diffused through six committees and despite the many linkages between their respective thematic mandates for the purpose of this section the third committee deals with human rights. Unlike the Security Council, the Assembly has from the outset maintained that human rights are not encompassed under article 2(7) of the UN Charter and are thus susceptible to discussion and investigation. It supported this view on the basis that articles 1, 2 and 55 of the Charter render the enforcement of human rights a matter of international concern. As a result, the Assembly recommended in 1946 the suspension of Spain (under Franco) from UN membership[78] and later rejected the applicability of article 2(7) to the Soviet invasion of Hungary, arguing that this was in violation of article 2(4) and moreover constituted genocide.[79]

From a practical perspective the Assembly's human rights work has three dimensions: (1) promotion of human rights and humanitarian law through standard-setting resolutions (e.g. UDHR), discussion of emerging issues, such as HIV/AIDS and poverty, as well as acting as a forum for the adoption of treaties; (2) condemnation of specific human rights violations and where competent taking measures against culprit states, culminating in the expulsion of certain UN entities, such as that of Libya from the HRC;[80] and (3) establishment and funding of peacekeeping, peace enforcement, observer and other missions with a view to dispatching them to troubled areas. The Assembly's authority in setting up peacekeeping missions is crucial because of its exclusive authority under article 17 of the Charter to decide on budgetary issues, with money being the most necessary prerequisite for such missions to materialise.[81] Transitional, or post-conflict, justice and management are now a significant aspect of the Assembly's human rights agenda although in practice their implementation is undertaken by the HRC and the OHCHR.[82]

---

[78] UNGA resolution 39(I) (12 December 1946).

[79] UNGA resolution 1132(XI) (10 January 1957); UNGA resolution 1133(XI) (14 September 1957), and especially UNGA resolution 1127(XI) (21 November 1956).

[80] UNGA resolution 65/265 (1 March 2011).

[81] For the period 1 July 2011 to 30 June 2012 the Assembly authorised a budget for its peacekeeping operations at a cost of $7 billion. UNGA resolution 65/303 (1 July 2011).

[82] The Assembly may even leave the initiative to the Council. For example, the HRC dispatched an independent commission of inquiry in respect of the 2010 post-electoral violence in Côte d'Ivoire without a prior resolution from the Assembly relying on the basis of its founding mandate in UNGA resolution 60/251. See HRC resolution 16/25 (25 March 2011).

4.6   THE SECURITY COUNCIL

Although it is not readily obvious, the Security Council has the potential to be the most effective institution in the protection of human rights. This is reinforced by the stipulation in articles 24 and 25 of the Charter which confer upon it primary responsibility for the maintenance of international peace and security through the adoption of decisions that are binding on all UN member states. We have already alluded to the fact that the contemporary construction of peace and security encompasses human rights and humanitarian law, and given that the Council is designed to be a quick-response mechanism to crises and unfolding international situations, its vested authority necessarily renders it an ideal forum for immediate action. This is unlike any other human rights organ or institution within the UN or otherwise, all of which are unable to respond immediately and/or with force if necessary, against culprit states or non-state actors. While it is well known that during the Cold War the Security Council was effectively precluded from taking any action with respect to situations of gross human rights violations, since the early 1990s this has no longer been the case. Of course, when reading Council resolutions one must not forget that these are primarily intended as political decisions, and as a result significant political considerations underlie them.[83] At the same time, and while the Council is not bound to any institutional precedent, it cannot lightly disregard its own resolutions on the same or similar matters.[84] This is true irrespective of the veto power held by the Council's permanent members and it is now common practice for persistent rights violators to be identified. Thus it may be said that the Council's political and humanitarian considerations since the early 1990s have tended to merge more and more, although they are no doubt still distinguishable.

The human rights work of the Council is not susceptible to neat categorisations for the simple reason that on many occasions human rights considerations are only obvious as secondary effects; moreover, the Council deals with crises as and when they arise and only rarely maintains an annual agenda of particular issues, as does the General Assembly, for example. Thus, the Council's human rights 'jurisprudence' may be derived principally from resolutions concerning specific country situations and secondarily from general thematic resolutions. The latter type is employed typically in order to reinforce and bolster existing rules and in a handful of cases also for the purpose of standard-setting. By way of illustration, resolution 1261 and its successors

[83] E. Papastavridis, 'Interpretation of Security Council Resolutions under Chapter VII in the Aftermath of the Iraqi Crisis', *ICLQ* 56 (2007), 53.

[84] This of course does not mean that the Council must establish the same mechanisms in respect of similar situations, as is the case with criminal tribunals. Logistical, financial and political considerations may certainly preclude their establishment in particular cases.

concerned the recruitment and use of children in armed conflict, stressing that this was an international crime and a violation of children's rights.[85] These resolutions effectively quashed any appeal to cultural sensitivities that may have been entertained by various warlords under the guise of tribal custom, thus reinforcing the relevant rules in the CRC and paving the way for the optional protocol to the CRC on the Involvement on Children in Armed Conflict, adopted a year later. Of equal standard-setting value is resolution 1325 and its successors, which urged states to ensure increased participation of women at all decision-making levels and called on all actors negotiating peace agreements to adopt a gender perspective.[86]

The Council's authority as a potent protector of rights is reflected in its practices for determining country situations. For one thing, unlike other organs that meet periodically, the Council can, and does, meet at any time. Moreover, it need not receive an official request or communication in order to deliberate on a crisis and in practice it is only a matter of hours – unfortunately not always – from the start of a crisis before a meeting is convened, albeit it does not always adopt a resolution straight away. Given that an important facet of any armed conflict, humanitarian disaster or brutal repression is human plight and the violation of rights – the other being the spill over into neighbouring nations – the Council has employed its general powers under Chapter VII in various forms. Depending on the cooperation of the target state, the escalation of violence and the threat to human safety and well-being, the Council may well decide to dispatch an observer mission, a peacekeeping or a peace-enforcement contingent. Whereas the objective of the first of these is to monitor and report on the prevailing situation, the latter two play a substantive role in the protection of civilian populations from the calamities of conflict and may assist in containing the conflict itself. What is more, if these missions are authorised to use armed force (under the Council's standard terminology of 'all necessary means') in order to fulfil their mandate, they are no longer idle bystanders to violations but can effectively protect the victims. In the case of Somalia where armed factions were indiscriminately killing civilians and looting food supplies, thus raising the risk of widespread famine, the Council authorised the UN operation in Somalia (UNOSOM) to use all necessary means to establish a secure environment for humanitarian relief operations.[87]

Exceptionally, Council resolutions condemning particular acts of repression against civilians are used as a platform by certain nations, with or without opposition by others, as justification for subsequent forceful measures. By way of illustration, although resolution 688 against Iraqi repression

---

[85] UNSC resolution 1261 (30 August 1999). See also UNSC resolution 1612 (26 July 2005).
[86] UNSC resolution 1325 (31 October 2000), paras. 1 and 8.
[87] UNSC resolution 794 (3 December 1992), para. 10.

of the country's Kurdish population was merely condemnatory,[88] it was none the less relied upon by western European nations to set up a safe haven and a no-fly zone in northern Iraq. This type of implied authorisation is not widely accepted as legitimate under international law, irrespective of the nature or the objective upon which the relevant action relies; yet, it has been routinely invoked by three of the Council's permanent members, namely France, USA and UK, to the chagrin of Russia and China.[89]

Besides urgent action through the deployment of military contingents, the Council has been concerned with post-conflict justice, victims and national reconciliation. Chief among its political objectives has been the eradication of impunity and to this end the Council has not hesitated to establish international criminal tribunals for the prosecution of those most responsible for serious violations of human rights and humanitarian law. The tribunals for the former Yugoslavia (ICTY)[90] and Rwanda (ICTR)[91] are paradigmatic of this objective and despite the Council's lesser involvement in the establishment of subsequent tribunals (e.g. Sierra Leone, Cambodia, Iraq) it is no less determined to fight impunity. Although the authority of the Council to set up international tribunals was initially challenged in the mid-1990s,[92] it is now an uncontested feature of international relations.

The endorsement and spread of criminal justice mechanisms necessarily means that the Council is not only addressing states as violators of rights, but also non-state actors, something which is alien to inter-state human rights courts. Indeed, the Council has not only directly condemned non-state actors[93] but has ordered measures involving the use of force or the enforcement of criminal jurisdiction against them. This is true, for example, in respect of Somali pirates.[94]

Yet although it is now unquestionable that the Council is a capable and willing defender of rights, there is still considerable debate as to whether the Council's choice of enforcement, particularly the use of sanctions, is compatible with fundamental human rights. The Council may infringe human rights and, here are three pertinent examples. (1) The Council imposes an import embargo on the brutal and dictatorial regime of country A, which significantly impedes the availability of basic medicines, food and water to its

---

[88] UNSC resolution 688 (5 April 1991), with paragraph 3 insisting that Iraq allow access to humanitarian organisations to all those in need of assistance.

[89] See C. Gray, 'From Unity to Polarisation: International Law and the Use of Force against Iraq', *EJIL* 13 (2002), 1, at 8ff.

[90] UNSC resolution 827 (25 May 1993).   [91] UNSC resolution 955 (8 November 1994).

[92] See *ICTY Prosecutor* v. *Tadić*, Decision on the defence motion for interlocutory appeal on jurisdiction (2 October 1995), paras. 32–40, where the idea that the Council did not enjoy the power to set up international tribunals was dismissed by the ICTY appeals chamber.

[93] UNSC resolution 814 (26 March 1993), para. 13, calling on Somali factions to desist from breaching humanitarian law and reaffirming their criminal liability for any violations.

[94] UNSC resolution 1950 (23 November 2010), para. 12.

civilian population and as a result a large number of children and vulnerable people die. (2) The Council imposes targeted sanctions on specific individuals suspected of terrorist-related offences, encompassing asset freezing and arrest. The sanctions are final and binding on member states and the suspects have no recourse to any appeal or review mechanism. (3) The Council orders the use of armed force against country A, which is ruled by a brutal dictator. The Council is aware that the regime will strenuously resist its downfall and is fully prepared to sacrifice the lives of many of its people in the process in order to defend itself against a multinational force.

In all of these cases the Council has to take difficult decisions that directly affect the fundamental rights of a large number of people, despite other possible benefits, such as democracy-building, rule of law and cessation of human rights violations. Although it is generally acknowledged that the Council's practice in scenario (2) would be disproportionate and lacking legal support,[95] the other two find an equal amount of support and opprobrium.[96] Yet the Council should not lightly infringe fundamental rights under the guise of collateral damage and should explore other alternatives before deciding to employ sanctions that are likely to affect the rights of entire populations.[97] The Iraq sanctions regime provides an instructive lesson in this respect, not least because it eventually resulted in major changes to the Council's practice towards smarter sanctions.[98] While the comprehensive sanctions imposed against Iraq in the aftermath of the 1990 Gulf War excluded foodstuff and medicine used for humanitarian purposes, it soon became apparent that these limited exceptions were insufficient to provide for the needs of the population. After much wrangling, resolution 986 was adopted in 1995, allowing Iraq to export oil in exchange for foodstuff, medicine and humanitarian goods.[99] The Oil for Food programme thus introduced was referred to as 'a temporary measure to provide for the humanitarian needs of the Iraqi people'.[100] However, the programme's design and implementation undermined its effectiveness, as a result of a combination of factors, particularly the lack of

---

[95] In *Kadi and Al Barakaat International Foundation* v. *Council of the European Union* [2008] ECR I-6351, paras. 335–7, 349, the ECJ held that the imposition of targeted sanctions (freezing orders in the case at hand) against a suspected terrorist by the EU without any remedy whatsoever in the form of judicial review or a hearing violated the right of effective judicial protection. In similar fashion in *R* (*on the application of Al Jedda*) v. *Secretary of State for Defence* [2007] UKHL 58, Lord Bingham argued that Council resolutions authorising extensive powers of detention 'must ensure that the detainee's rights under article 5 [of the ECHR] are not infringed to any greater extent than is inherent in such detention'.

[96] See S. D. Bailey, *The UN Security Council and Human Rights* (New York: St Martin's Press, 1994).

[97] CESCR, General Comment 8, UN Doc. E/C.12/1997/8 (12 December 1997), para. 3.

[98] C. C. Joyner, 'United Nations Sanctions after Iraq: Looking Back to See Ahead', *Chinese Journal of International Law* (*Chi. J. Intl L.*) 4 (2003), 329–53.

[99] UNSC resolution 986 (14 April 1995), para. 8.   [100] Ibid., preamble.

availability of adequate funds for infrastructure, blocking of dual-purpose goods by the Sanctions Committee, as well as corruption and maladministration. The resulting persistent humanitarian crisis led to repeated adjustments of the programme which, ultimately, failed adequately to offset the adverse impact of sanctions imposed against Iraq at the time.[101] It is for this reason that there is widespread disinclination against all types of broad sanctions because they are deemed incompatible with the enjoyment of human rights.[102]

CASE STUDY 4.2
The Security Council and human rights in North Korea

The secretive and autocratic North Korean regime has been one of the most brutal human rights violators for the last six decades. Although little information is made available, particularly because foreign journalists are not allowed in the country and the local press is tightly controlled by the state, NGOs have been able to paint a picture on the basis of interviews taken from escapees. It is reported that anyone suspected of having religious beliefs or an anti-government ideology is arrested, along with all family members and close friends, and taken without trial to concentration camps for indefinite periods – usually never to be released. These camps are the size of cities and many thousands are held there and subjected to all types of ill treatment.[1]

Despite the corroboration of these allegations through other reports, the Security Council has never discussed North Korea's human rights issues for two reasons. First, it is known that China denies refugee status to all North Korean escapees entering its territory and sends them back although its authorities are fully aware of the consequences for returnees. China is also worried that a disintegration of North Korea will send waves of refugees across its land frontier. The second reason is that the Council's agenda with North Korea is primarily, if not exclusively, concerned with the country's nuclear build up and its military relations with South Korea. Thus, the Council seems to believe that

---

[1] See in particular, Christian Solidarity Worldwide, 'North Korea: a Case to Answer, a Call to Act' (London: 2007).

---

[101] UNSC, Report of the Second Panel Established pursuant to the Note by the President of the Security Council (S/1999/100) of 30 January 1999, concerning the Current Humanitarian Situation in Iraq (30 March 1999) UN Doc. S/1999/356 Annex II. H. von Sponeck, *A Different Kind of War: The UN Sanctions Regime in Iraq* (New York, Oxford: Berghahn Books, 2006).

[102] Sub-Commission on the Promotion and Protection of Human Rights, The adverse consequences of economic sanctions on the enjoyment of human rights, UN Doc. E/CN.4/Sub.2/2000/33 (2000), para. 71.

giving a forum to North Korea's gross human rights violations would deflect from the other issues on the agenda and would in fact undermine them. Moreover, its members probably feel that raising the issue of human rights would make no practical difference whatsoever and so other organs and bodies are best suited to take up this matter.

This is a characteristic case in which international peace and security concerns are not necessarily absorbed or intertwined with human rights considerations.

QUESTIONS

- Is the United Nations bound by the three instruments encompassed within the Bill of Rights? More generally, is the United Nations bound by customary human rights law?

- You are the legal advisor to a small human rights NGO. Through your investigations it transpires that the government of country A is engaged in the enforced disappearance of its political dissidents. The abductees number in the hundreds and their family members are too scared to confront the local authorities or approach any international bodies. Under the circumstances, which institution or organ within the United Nations would you inform and what would you expect to achieve? Justify your response.

- What is the function of standard-setting within the United Nations?

- Does the practice of the HRC include the 'name and shame' technique?

- If the Security Council authorises the use of armed force in order to oust a brutal regime it risks setting in motion a war that may cost thousands of lives. Should it instead rely on sanctions or should it support a popular uprising by financial, technological and political assistance? Discuss with reference to the invasion of Iraq in 2003 and the Egyptian uprising in 2011.

- Following the adoption of resolution 1373 (2001) by the Security Council in the aftermath of 9/11 a number of countries justified violation of fundamental rights in order to ensure compliance with the terms of the resolution which demanded that states take all necessary measures to prevent and punish terrorist attacks.[2] Should the Council's resolutions expressly stipulate conformity with fundamental human rights, or is this already implicitly understood?

---

[2] The Human Rights Committee, among other treaty bodies, emphasised in its examination of state reports that all measures adopted for the implementation of resolution 1373 should be in full compliance with the Bill of Rights. See UN Concluding Observations on Moldova, UN Doc. CCPR/CO/75/MDA (5 August 2002), para. 8.

4.6.1   Fact-finding in practice: the UN mission on the Gaza conflict

Following the Israeli army's incursion into the Gaza strip in late December 2008 (known as operation Cast Led) a significant number of civilian casualties were reported, in addition to a pattern demonstrating the destruction of

Gaza's economic and social infrastructure. The HRC decided to set up a fact-finding mission to:

investigate all violations of international human rights law and international humanitarian law by the occupying power, Israel, against the Palestinian people throughout the occupied Palestinian territory, particularly in the occupied Gaza strip, due to the current aggression, and calls upon Israel not to obstruct the process of investigation and to fully cooperate with the mission.[103]

The terms of the mandate are important in this case because although it demands that *all* violations be investigated, thus implying any committed also by Palestinians, the remainder of the mandate, and the inclusion of words such as [Israeli] aggression, clearly preempt the investigation by suggesting that only Israeli military actions be scrutinised. The ambassador of Israel to the country's permanent mission to the UN in Geneva, in a letter to the head of the UN fact-finding mission, Richard Goldstone, refused to extend his country's cooperation to the mission on the following grounds:

This grossly politicised resolution prejudges the issue at hand, determining at the outset that Israel has perpetrated grave violations of human rights and implying that Israel has deliberately targeted civilians and medical facilities and systematically destroyed the cultural heritage of the Palestinian people. It calls for urgent international action directed only against Israel and, as regards the proposed fact-finding mission, makes clear that it regards its mandate as exclusively focused on Israeli violations of human rights and humanitarian law. The fact that several distinguished individuals approached to head the Mission declined reflects the problematic nature of the mission and its mandate.[104]

The four-person mission, composed of three legal experts and a military analyst, received personal attacks during the course of its work and one member, Professor Chinkin, was accused of conflicting interests. In an interview following the completion of the report, Goldstone made the point that:

Obviously nobody enjoys being attacked. A lot of the attacks have been in intemperate terms not so much in the media but in emails and private messages and that's unpleasant but let me immediately say that it hasn't affected our work. We've gone ahead and did what we had undertaken to do and what our mandate required us to do and the fact we were attacked I don't think came as a surprise to any of us. The vehemence of some of it may have surprised me speaking for myself but if one does this sort of work one's going to be attacked. It's not the first time and probably not the last.[105]

[103] HRC resolution A/HRC/S-9/L.1 (12 January 2009), para. 14.
[104] Letter dated 7 April 2009, in Report of the Fact-finding Mission: Human Rights in Palestine and Other Occupied Arab Territories (Fact-Finding Report), UN Doc. A/HRC/12/48 (25 September 2009), Annex II, 436.
[105] Unofficial transcript of the press conference of 29 September 2009, available at: www2. ohchr.org/english/bodies/hrcouncil/specialsession/9/factfindingmission.htm.

Chinkin's alleged bias was based on a letter she signed along with other leading academics, which was published in *The Times*, where she and her colleagues argued against the legality of operation Cast Led. In fact, the letter made no reference to human rights or international humanitarian law (IHL) violations; it simply examined operation Cast Led from a *jus ad bellum* perspective.

Goldstone rightly dismissed all claims of bias as 'clutching at straws'.[106] The USA complained, among other things, that during the mission's on-site visits to Gaza there was a visible presence of Hamas security in the vicinity, thus exacerbating the mission's bias. Goldstone retorted that none of the mission's members noticed any inappropriate presence of Hamas police during the investigation of witnesses and that even if they were in the vicinity they could not 'in any way [have] overheard or in any way exercised any direct influence on any of the witnesses we saw'.[107] The narration of these incidents is intended to highlight the political intricacies behind the appointment and mandate of a human rights investigative mission and the variety of pressures on individual members.

Based on these criticisms, and despite the terms of the Council's resolution, Goldstone wisely expanded the HRC resolution's mandate by deciding to investigate alleged violations by both sides to the conflict. This clearly provided an additional degree of legitimacy to the final report and the overall work of the mission. It is not unusual for fact-finding missions or other UN subsidiary organs to construe their mandates expansively, whether in temporal or substantive terms. Such a construction is generally dictated by the material exigencies of each particular mission, albeit in respect of the Gaza mission it was prescribed by a desire to rectify the perception of bias without impairing in any way its original mandate.

Fact-finding missions are not meant to ascertain the criminal liability of perpetrators but generally to provide a clear picture of events to their appointing body. As a result, the missions are free to employ any type of evidence and mechanism of inquiry, although ultimately the quality of the evidentiary material will determine the quality of the report and recommendations. In the present instance, the Gaza mission placed particular emphasis on the plight of the victims and resorted to some degree to narrative storytelling. The readers will be able to judge for themselves whether this was an appropriate mechanism under the circumstances. The mission had intended to conduct on-site investigations in Gaza and Israel and interview victims and participants on both sides. However, as a result of Israel's refusal to cooperate the mission was not only precluded from visiting Israel and the West Bank but was unable to enter Gaza, save through Egyptian territory. It was thus forced to ascertain the Israeli side of events from material evidence

[106] Ibid.   [107] Ibid.

and witness statements in Gaza and affected neighbouring countries. Besides interviews it employed reports from international organisations, NGOs, medical records, video and satellite images provided by the UN Operational Satellite Applications Program (UNOSAT), forensic analysis of weapons and ammunition remnants collected at incident sites, publicly available material[108] and public hearings in Gaza and Geneva.[109] In numerous cases the mission held that NGO data was more reliable than official government data. By way of illustration, in considering the number of Palestinians who lost their lives during the operation, it relied on NGO reports because the data presented was generally more consistent than that in official Palestinian and Israeli data.[110]

The storytelling dimension of the report, setting out the historical context of the conflict and the basis of operation Cast Led, was apparent from the use of so-called public hearings. These were broadcast live and their purpose was:

to enable victims, witnesses and experts from all sides to the conflict to speak directly to as many people as possible in the region as well as in the international community. The mission is of the view that no written word can replace the voice of victims. While not all issues and incidents under investigation by the Mission were addressed during the hearings, the thirty-eight public testimonies covered a wide range of relevant facts as well as legal and military matters. The mission had initially intended to hold hearings in Gaza, Israel and the West Bank. However, denial of access to Israel and the West Bank resulted in the decision to hold hearings of participants from Israel and the West Bank in Geneva ... Participants in the hearings were identified in the course of the mission's investigations, and had either first-hand experience or information or specialized knowledge of the issues under investigation and analysis. In keeping with the objectives of the hearings, the mission gave priority to the participation of victims and people from the affected communities.[111]

This mechanism resembles public confessions free of criminal liability accepted in the course of truth and reconciliation commissions,[112] as well as the rationale for the participation of victims in international criminal proceedings. It is innovative for the purposes of a fact-finding mission whose role is generally to ascertain facts, not to give a voice to the victims. Yet it does not wholly seem out of place given that fact-finding missions have in the past tended to focus excessively on the type and scale of violations, in this manner dehumanising somewhat the victims of the crimes. It is not far

---

[108] A number of Israeli soldiers involved in the operation had by that time narrated personal stories to the Israeli press, which in turn made them public.

[109] Fact-Finding Report, above note 104, para. 159.   [110] Ibid., para. 30.

[111] Ibid., para. 166.

[112] P. Parker, 'The Politics of Indemnities: Truth Telling and Reconciliation in South Africa', *HRLJ* 17 (1996), 1.

fetched to claim that the aim of fact-finders has typically been to recount the scale and intensity of violations, rather than the victims' suffering, with a view to offering political space and legitimacy to their mandators to undertake further action, whether through sanctions or the establishment of criminal tribunals. Offering a personalised voice to the victims, on the other hand, assists in giving a voice to the facts and restoring the victims' faith in the relevant process.[113] It is a welcome follow-up to the practice of UN special procedures to narrate in their reports the specific crimes committed by governments and non-state actors against their victims, most of which are spelt out by name.[114] The Israeli opposition to these public hearings is instructive:

This procedure is unprecedented as part of fact-finding operations. The very point of a fact-finding mission is that a team of experts bring their experience and judgment to bear in assessing the available evidence and drawing responsible conclusions – not that raw evidence, perhaps of questionable authenticity, is directly broadcast into the public arena. Such a trial by public opinion, which of necessity cannot give any weight to confidential or sensitive information, can serve little purpose in ascertaining the truth, and is only likely to prejudice public opinion in advance of any other conclusion.[115]

No doubt, UN investigations and fact-finding are not straightforward exercises. There will always be states with opposing interests that will stifle country visits or prevent its agents and nationals from providing testimony of any kind. Such states and their allies will attack the integrity of the mission, and members will be subject to attacks, not necessarily physical, against their persons. Heads of missions need to be creative and not be afraid to explore new methodologies while fulfilling their mandate. Most importantly, they must ensure that their very mandate is even handed, objective and fair and if it is not, to employ their discretionary or implied powers to mould it as such. Ultimately, a mission is not legitimised by its hard work, but largely by its fairness and impartiality.

---

[113] One should not, of course, be oblivious to the risk that listening to victims alone creates a one-sided truth and prevents a clear understanding of the roots of the conflict. In a study encompassing 120 interviews of ordinary people among Bosnia's three ethnic communities, each vehemently denied the crimes committed by his or her own ethnic group, emphasising that they were perpetrated by members of the other groups. J. N. Clark, 'Transitional Justice, Truth and Reconciliation: an Under-explored Relationship', *Int'l Crim. L. Rev.* 11 (2011), 241, at 256–7.

[114] See e.g. Report by the Special Rapporteur on torture, Mission to Nepal, UN Doc. E/CN.4/2006/6/Add.5 (9 January 2006), 16ff.

[115] Letter dated 2 July 2009, Fact-Finding Report, 448.

FURTHER READING

Alston, P., 'Reconceiving the UN Human Rights Regime: Challenges Confronting the new UN Human Rights Council', *Melbourne Journal of International Law* (*Melb. J. Int'l L.*) 7 (2006), 185.

Alston, P. and Crawford, J. (eds.), *The Future of UN Human Rights Treaty Monitoring* (Cambridge University Press, 2000).

Andrassy, J., 'Uniting for Peace', *AJIL* 50 (1956), 563.

Bantekas, I., 'United Nations Employment Law and the Causes for its Failed Senior Female Appointments Record', *International Organisations Law Review* (*IOLR*) 6 (2009), 225.

Flood, P. J., *The Effectiveness of UN Human Rights Institutions* (Westport: Praeger, 1998).

Franck, T. M. and Fairley, H. S., 'Procedural Due Process in Human Rights Fact-finding by International Agencies', *AJIL* 74 (1980), 308.

Gaer, F. D., 'A Voice not an Echo: Universal Periodic Review and the UN Treaty Body System', *Human Rights Law Review* (*HRLR*) 7 (2007), 109.

Ghanea, N., 'From the UN Commission on Human Rights to UN Human Rights Council: One Step Forwards or Two Steps Sideways?', *ICLQ* 55 (2006), 695.

Katayanagi, M., *Human Rights Functions of United Nations Peacekeeping* (Leiden, Boston: Martinus Nijhoff, 2002).

Lauren, P. G., 'First Principles of Racial Equality: History and the Politics of Diplomacy of Human Rights Provisions in the United Nations Charter', *HRQ* 5 (1983), 1.

Meron, T., *Human Rights Law-Making in the United Nations: A Critique of Instruments and Processes* (Oxford University Press, 1987).

Mertus, J., *The United Nations and Human Rights: A Guide for a New Era* (London, New York: Routledge, 2009).

Ramcharan, B. G., *The United Nations High Commissioner for Human Rights: The Challenges of International Protection* (Leiden, Boston: Martinus Nijhoff, 2002).

The UN Human Rights Council (London, New York: Routledge, 2011).

Rudolf, B., 'The Thematic Rapporteurs and Working Groups of the United Nations Commission on Human Rights', *Max Planck Yearbook of United Nations Law* (*MPYBUNL*) 4 (2000), 289.

Schwelb, E., 'The International Court of Justice and the Human Rights Clauses of the Charter', *AJIL* 66 (1972), 337.

Sen, P., *Universal Periodic Review of Human Rights: Towards Best Practice* (London: Commonwealth Secretariat, 2009).

5 The UN human rights treaty system

CONTENTS

5.1 INTRODUCTION

UN treaty bodies constitute the main institutional vehicle for the application of international human rights law. Bodies such as the UN HRCtee are by no means the only international mechanisms that address issues of human rights protection. Indeed, bodies as diverse as the ILO[1] and the World Bank[2] employ special procedures dealing with human rights questions. International tribunals and courts, particularly the ICJ, are increasingly adjudicating cases that have a bearing on international human rights law.[3] Yet, human rights treaty

---

[1] www.ilo.org. See for a good overview and nuanced assessment of the ILO's contribution to the promotion of social justice and human rights, particularly labour rights, and its supervisory system, G. Oberleitner, *Global Human Rights Institutions: Between Remedy and Ritual* (Cambridge: Polity, 2007, reprinted 2008), 106–12.

[2] See on the World Bank 1993 Inspection Panels, ibid., 129–35; S. Skogly, *Human Rights Obligations of the World Bank and the International Monetary Fund* (London: Cavendish, 2001), 35–6 and 180–5; and, more generally, M. Darrow, *Between Light and Shadow: The World Bank, the International Monetary Fund and International Human Rights Law* (Oxford: Hart, 2003).

[3] The ICJ has increasingly addressed human rights questions, both in its contentious and advisory jurisdiction. See S. Sivakumaran, 'The International Court of Justice and Human Rights', in S. Joseph and A. McBeth, *Research Handbook on International Human Rights Law* (Cheltenham, Northampton, MA: Edward Elgar, 2010), 299–325; B. Simma, 'Mainstreaming Human Rights: the Contribution of the International Court of Justice', *JIDS* 3(1) (2012), 7–29.

bodies fulfil a special role in that they are the only entities within the UN system that states have explicitly mandated to monitor compliance with their human rights treaty obligations.

Treaty bodies fulfil a range of functions, from promotional activities to monitoring and adjudicating complaints. These tasks, which are taken for granted today, are the result of states' willingness to vest treaty bodies with the mandate of monitoring compliance. This constituted a remarkable shift away from earlier notions of sovereignty in a system where states were, essentially, the sole authors, interpreters and enforcers of rights and obligations. What accounts for this change and why do states agree to be part of such regimes? This question, which has attracted considerable attention in recent years, poses a particular challenge because it does not seem to conform to the realist views that used to hold considerable sway in international relations, according to which states use institutions as a means to exercise power. Alternative theories emphasise states' interests (enhancing reputation and avoiding sanctions) or point to 'acculturation'.[4] This denotes a process of interaction of various actors which generates a pull to build and join credible human rights mechanisms as part of an international order. Indeed, these mechanisms form part of broader international institution-building, particularly at the UN level. The development of UN treaty bodies has witnessed a steady growth after a slow beginning in which it took over twenty years and numerous debates to set up the first two, the Committee on the Elimination of Racial Discrimination (CERD) and the HRCtee.

The proliferation of treaties, treaty bodies and increased ratification does not automatically equate to a coherent and effective international system that is well placed to achieve its objectives, particularly strengthening protection at the international and national level. On the contrary, this development may strain the capacity of the parties and institutions involved and lead to duplication as well as system fatigue. The discussions surrounding states' reporting obligations before UN treaty bodies illustrates these capacity challenges. Treaty bodies have struggled with state compliance, both procedurally (reporting) and substantively (implementing human rights obligations), and this continues to be an area of major concern. These factors have contributed to the perceived weakness of UN treaty bodies and triggered a series of reform proposals. Paradoxically, this process is taking place at the same time as a growing number of national and international actors seek to use these very bodies to advance human rights promotion and protection, which inadvertently deepens existing institutional and systemic challenges.

This development raises serious questions about the ability of these bodies to respond adequately to human rights concerns. Beyond these operational

---

[4] See for a good overview of the various theories O. C. Okafor, *The African Human Rights System, Activist Forces and International Institutions* (Cambridge University Press, 2007), 12–62; Oberleitner, above note 1, 6–22.

difficulties lurk more fundamental issues concerning the very nature of a system that depends on states and in which treaty bodies 'oscillate between the desire to supervise and the need to cooperate'.[5] The search for gradual improvement takes place in an institutional framework whose dynamics may make it incapable of addressing 'larger issues of power, domination, and legitimacy'.[6] Mandate constraints, bureaucracy and the still largely state-centric nature of the process, all contribute to a situation where the bodies may not respond effectively to serious violations and/or fashion effective remedies. Nevertheless, their work provides an important forum for developing international human rights law and engaging with states; this very engagement allows domestic actors, NGOs, other states and international institutions to seek changes that may over time result in an improved human rights situation. However, the task of strengthening the role of treaty bodies in the protection of human rights will continue to pose a considerable challenge in a system that is ultimately based on the 'goodwill' of states, which it constantly has to test in order to be effective.

5.2 COMMON FEATURES OF INTERNATIONAL HUMAN RIGHTS TREATY BODIES

Debates surrounding the drafting of international human rights treaties centred not only on the substance of the instruments but also on what, if any, type of body should be mandated to exercise particular functions. The idea of setting up bodies composed of independent experts to monitor state conduct in the domestic sphere constituted a departure from the then prevailing notion of state sovereignty; it was not entirely unprecedented, though, as the Permanent Mandates Commission established under article 22 of the Covenant of the League of Nations had earlier operated a petitions procedure against the mandatory that also dealt with human rights-related matters.[7] Subsequently, proposals made by states in the formative years of the UN human rights system show the breadth of options pondered, ranging from calls for an International Court of Human Rights (Australia)[8] to a rejection of special monitoring bodies on the ground that they would represent an unwarranted interference with state sovereignty (Romania).[9] The model of treaty bodies

---

[5] B. Rajagopal, *International Law from Below: Development, Social Movements and Third World Resistance* (Cambridge University Press, 2003), 66–7.

[6] Ibid., 67.

[7] Ibid., 67–71, and A. Anghie, 'Colonialism and the Birth of International Institutions: Sovereignty, Economy, and the Mandate System of the League of Nations', *N.Y.U.J. Int'l L. & Pol.* 34 (2002), 513–633, at 523–8.

[8] A. Devereux, 'Australia and the International Scrutiny of Civil and Political Rights: an Analysis of Australia's Negotiating Policies, 1946–1966', *AYIL* 22 (2003), 47–75, at 54–60.

[9] See for references to debates in the General Assembly in 1952, Y. Tyagi, *The UN Human Rights Committee: Practice and Procedure* (Cambridge University Press, 2011), 58–60.

that eventually emerged inevitably reflects a compromise that has resulted in the dynamics and challenges evident today.

Beginning with CERD[10] in 1969, followed in 1976 by the most prominent body, the HRCtee,[11] the total number had risen to ten treaty bodies in 2012. This includes the CEDAW (hereinafter CtEDAW) (1982),[12] the CAT (hereinafter CtAT) (1987),[13] the CRC (hereinafter CtRC) (1991),[14] the Committee on the Protection of the Rights of All Migrant Workers and Members of their Families (CMW) (2003),[15] the CRPD (hereinafter CtRPD) (2008),[16] and the Committee on Enforced Disappearances (CED) (2011).[17] In addition, the Subcommittee on Prevention of Torture (SPT) was set up under the OPCAT in 2006.[18] With the exception of the CESCR, all international human rights treaty bodies are established by states parties and based on the founding treaty that sets out their respective mandate and functions.[19] Their close institutional links, including reporting to the UNGA and being serviced by the OHCHR and financed out of the UN budget, means that human rights treaty bodies effectively form part of the UN human rights architecture.[20]

Human rights treaty bodies fulfil their monitoring function primarily by means of considering states parties' reports and adjudicating on complaints. In addition, several treaty bodies, such as the CtAT,[21] the CtEDAW,[22] the CED,[23]

---

[10] Articles 8–16 ICERD, www2.ohchr.org/english/bodies/cerd/index.htm.

[11] Articles 28–45 ICCPR; www2.ohchr.org/english/bodies/hrc/index.htm.

[12] Articles 17–22 CEDAW; www2.ohchr.org/english/bodies/cedaw/index.htm.

[13] Articles 17–24 CAT; www2.ohchr.org/english/bodies/cat/index.htm.

[14] Articles 43–5 CRC; www2.ohchr.org/english/bodies/crc/index.htm.

[15] Articles 72–8 ICRMW; www2.ohchr.org/english/bodies/cmw/index.htm.

[16] Articles 34–9 CRPD; www.ohchr.org/EN/HRBodies/CRPD/Pages/CRPDIndex.aspx.

[17] Articles 26–36 CPED; www.ohchr.org/EN/HRBodies/CED/Pages/CEDIndex.aspx.

[18] Articles 5–16 OPCAT; www2.ohchr.org/english/bodies/cat/opcat/index.htm.

[19] ECOSOC resolution 1985/17 (28 May 1985). See on steps taken to correct this anomaly, HRC resolution 4/7 (30 March 2007): Rectification of the legal status of the Committee on Economic, Social and Cultural Rights. For an analysis of the CESCR's work, see also Chapter 9.

[20] See for a brief overview, including facts and figures, *Strengthening the United Nations Human Rights Treaty Body System*, A report by the United Nations High Commissioner for Human Rights, N. Pillay (United Nations, June 2012), 16–19, online, at www2.ohchr.org/english/bodies/HRTD/docs/HCReportTBStrengthening.pdf.

[21] Article 20 CAT. The Committee has to date made eight confidential inquiries: Turkey, Egypt, Peru, Sri Lanka, Mexico, Serbia and Montenegro (Former Yugoslavia), Brazil, and Nepal. See www2.ohchr.org/english/bodies/cat/confidential_art20.htm.

[22] Articles 8, 9 Optional Protocol CEDAW. The Committee has to date made one inquiry relating to Mexico, see Report on Mexico produced by the Committee on the Elimination of Discrimination against Women under Article 8 of the Optional Protocol to the Convention, and Reply from the Government of Mexico, UN Doc. CEDAW/C/2005/OP.8/MEXICO (27 January 2005).

[23] Article 33 CPED. See also article 34 ibid.

the CtRPD,[24] the CtRC[25] and the CESCR[26] are, or will be, mandated to conduct confidential inquiries upon receipt of reliable information of systematic or serious violations or, in the case of the CERD, through early warning and urgent action procedures.[27] The SPT differs from other bodies; it neither considers states parties reports nor complaints. Instead, in line with its preventive function it focuses on visiting mechanisms, providing advice to national preventative mechanisms and offering cooperation.[28]

It is tempting to measure the strength of a treaty body by reference to its power to adjudicate complaints because this is still frequently seen as the function that really matters, drawing on analogies with national law. Complaints procedures are undoubtedly important, especially those providing individuals with access to international justice.[29] However, these procedures do not automatically result in enhanced respect for rights and implementation of states parties' obligations. What must therefore be considered crucial is the ability of treaty bodies to utilise all means at their disposal to contribute to the development of an international 'culture' in which human rights are recognised and translated into actual promotion and protection at the national level.

Human rights treaty bodies are composed of between ten to twenty-five members who are elected by states parties and commonly serve for four years and up to eight years if re-elected.[30] The 'ideal' body has a group of individuals of high repute, outstanding expertise, dedication and independence who represent various regions of the world. This ideal has been met to varying degrees by the various bodies; the HRCtee, in particular, has been credited for the capacity of its members, which reflects its prominent role and status. However, the lack of equitable geographical representation and gender balance in human rights treaty bodies has been a cause for concern and steps have been taken to address these shortcomings.[31]

---

[24] Articles 6, 7 Optional Protocol CRPD.

[25] Articles 13, 14 Optional Protocol CRC on a Communications Procedure.

[26] Articles 11, 12 Optional Protocol ICESCR.

[27] See Guidelines for the Early Warning and Urgent Action Procedures, Annual Report, UN Doc. A/62/18, Annexes, Chapter III, adopted at the CERD's 71st session in August 2007. See for the practice of using these procedures, www2.ohchr.org/english/bodies/cerd/early-warning.htm

[28] Article 11 OPCAT.

[29] See in particular A. A. Cançado Trindade, *The Access of Individuals to International Justice* (Oxford University Press, 2011), and Chapter 7 on complaints procedures.

[30] Articles 8 ICERD; 28–34 ICCPR; 17 CEDAW; 17 CAT; 43 CRC; 72 ICRMW; 34 CRPD; 26 CPED; 5–10 OPCAT.

[31] See Promotion of equitable geographical distribution in the membership of the human rights treaty bodies, UNGA resolution 64/173 (18 December 2009), and Composition of the staff of the Office of the United Nations High Commissioner for Human Rights, UNGA resolution 16/10 (26 March 2011); Pillay, above note 20, 74–7, and, on gender representation, H. Charlesworth, 'Not Waving but Drowning: Gender Mainstreaming and Human Rights in the United Nations', *Harv. Hum. Rts. J.* 18 (2005), 1–18.

The committees work on a part-time basis and meet at least twice a year in Geneva or New York for brief sessions to review state party reports and, depending on the body, to consider individual communications and/ or adopt general comments. The working methods of the committees are set out in their respective rules of procedure, which detail the role of committee members, decision-making, publicity of meetings and so on.[32] The periodic sessions become an intense focus of committee work and an important forum for interaction with states parties, UN agencies, NGOs and others. However, the geographic focus of the committee work in Geneva and New York, while having logistical advantages, can contribute to a sense of remoteness, especially for actors from Asia and Africa. Webcasting of Committee sessions and having more regional meetings are some of the initiatives taken to make the committee work more accessible.[33]

The growing number of states parties' reports and communications, together with the need for enhanced coordination between the various bodies, increasingly strains the capacity of the committees. They are served throughout the year by their respective secretariats through the OHCHR, but there are consistent complaints that the time allocated and the resources available are inadequate to undertake the work effectively without overstretching the personal capacity of those involved.[34] In practice a lot depends on the initiative of individual committee members and the dynamics of the bodies concerned, and their level of engagement and output can differ markedly. The lack of remuneration (expenses only) may underscore the integrity of the committee members but is prone to limit the additional time such individual experts are able to spend on committee work.

Problems of capacity, coordination and limited visibility in the broader public have contributed to calls for the strengthening, if not the wholesale reform, of the treaty body system. This includes revived calls for a human rights World Court, which will be considered in more detail following an examination of how the committees fulfil their functions in practice.

---

[32] The text of the rules of procedures can be found on the websites of the treaty bodies, see www.ohchr.org/EN/HRBodies/Pages/HumanRightsBodies.aspx.

[33] See Inter-Committee Meeting of the human rights treaty bodies, The structure of the dialogue between treaty bodies and States parties, the structure and length of concluding observations, and the mode of interaction of treaty bodies with stakeholders, in particular national human rights institutions and civil society actors, UN Doc. HRI/ICM/2011/2 (18 May 2011), para. 66, and Report of the Chairs of the human rights treaty bodies on their twenty-third meeting, Implementation of Human Rights Instruments, UN Doc. A/66/175 (22 July 2011), para. 8.

[34] See Pillay, above note 20, 27–8, 32–4.

5.3   REPORTING PROCEDURE

5.3.1   Overview

Periodic reporting, the only generally accepted procedural obligation of states, has a special place in the work of human rights treaty bodies.[35] The reporting procedure serves multiple goals. Its overall objective is to ensure that states parties comply with their treaty obligations or, as article 2(2) of the ICCPR puts it, 'to give effect to the rights recognised'. It provides an opportunity for states to review their law and practice, to develop a better understanding of the nature of problems identified, including by developing adequate policies, and to evaluate progress made in respect of implementation. The reporting procedure also offers an occasion for civil society and other national and international actors, including UN agencies, to provide input and scrutinise state conduct. Viewed from this perspective, reporting is essentially an enabling process engaging a number of actors, with the committees concerned acting as focal points that guide, helping them to evaluate and assist states on how best to implement their obligations.[36] This understanding is based on the implicit instrumental assumption that states are more likely to comply if engaged in a 'constructive dialogue (also called constructive discussion)', which is the approach pursued by the treaty bodies.[37]

Reporting procedures were first mooted in 1956[38] and later incorporated as a general obligation of states parties in subsequent treaties.[39] However, treaty bodies grappled with framing this obligation and developing a suitable format for reports. This was largely due to the vague wording of relevant provisions and resistance by some committee members to subjecting states' records to a critical examination, including the adoption of concluding observations. This prompted treaty bodies to adopt a series of general comments to clarify states parties' reporting obligations.[40] Since then, the reporting practice has

---

[35] See generally OHCHR, *Manual on Human Rights Reporting under six major international human rights instruments* (Geneva: United Nations, 1997); A. Bayefsky (ed.), *The UN Human Rights Treaty System in the 21st century* (The Hague: Kluwer Law International, 2000).

[36] See for example article 40 ICCPR and OHCHR, *The United Nations Human Rights Treaty System: An Introduction to the Core Human Rights Treaties and the Treaty Bodies*, Fact Sheet no. 30 (Geneva: UN, 2005), 27; P. Alston, 'The Purposes of Reporting', in OHCHR *Manual*, above note 35, 19–24.

[37] See Harmonized Guidelines on Reporting under the International Human Rights Treaties, including Guidelines on a Common Core Document and Treaty-specific Documents, UN Doc. HRI/MC/2006/3 (10 May 2006), para. 11.

[38] ECOSOC resolution, E/Res/624 B (XXII) (1 August 1956).

[39] See Alston, above note 36, 19–20.

[40] See for example HRCtee General Comments 1, 2 (both 1981) and 30 (2002), online, at www2.ohchr.org/english/bodies/hrc/comments.htm.

developed, resulting in the adoption of harmonised guidelines on reporting.[41] Treaty bodies generally follow a similar format. An initial report is to be submitted within one or two years of a state becoming a party, depending on the treaty in question.[42] It is expected to set out the legislative, institutional and administrative framework in relation to the rights concerned and the report effectively serves as a baseline for later reports. The committee concerned considers the report based on information received from a variety of sources, including other UN agencies, national human rights institutions and NGOs. A list of issues, which is put to the state party before the session and allows NGOs and others to submit further information, subsequently forms the basis of discussions with the state delegates.

At the end of this process the committee deliberates and adopts concluding observations that set out positive developments, areas of concern and recommendations.[43] This includes requesting the state party to inform the committee concerned of measures taken to implement its recommendations within a certain time period. For example, the HRCtee identifies a number of important recommendations that states should implement within one year and which are supervised by a follow up rapporteur who draws up follow-up reports.[44] The state party may respond to the concluding observations, an option that is often used by states, primarily to object to some findings or recommendations made.[45] Next, the state party is obliged to submit further (periodic) reports (the period varies under the various rules of procedures, from two years (CERD) to five years (most treaty bodies)).[46] Periodic reports are more targeted in nature. States are expected to report on relevant developments in the reporting period and to set out what measures they

[41] See UN Doc. HRI/MC/2006/3. See also Consolidated Guidelines for State Reports under the International Covenant on Civil and Political Rights, UN Doc. CCPR/C/66/GUI/Rev.2 (26 February 2001).

[42] Articles 9 ICERD, 40 ICCPR, 18 CEDAW, 19 CAT, 44 CRC, 73 ICRMW, 35 CRPD, 29 CPED. See for an overview, Pillay, above note 20, 20.

[43] The concluding observations are available on the OHCHR website, www.ohchr.org, both by treaty body (see sessions), and by country (see name of the country). The Universal Human Rights Index, http://uhri.ohchr.org, provides a search function according to treaty body, state and specific rights.

[44] See, for example, Concluding Observations on Colombia, UN Doc. CCPR/C/COL/CO/6 (4 August 2010), para. 27: 'In accordance with rule 71, paragraph 5, of the Committee's rules of procedure, the state party should provide, within one year, relevant information on its implementation of the recommendations made by the Committee in paragraphs 9, 14 and 16' (relating to impunity, extrajudicial killings and forced disappearances).

[45] See, for example, Comments by the Government of the People's Democratic Republic of Algeria, UN Doc. CCPR/C/DZA/CO/3/Add.1 (19 November 2007), contesting the accuracy of the Committee's findings and several of the concerns it raised, such as in relation to amnesties, secret detention, enforced disappearances, torture and pre-trial detention in the counter-terrorism context, freedom of expression, assembly and association and the status of women.

[46] Pillay, above note 20, 20.

have taken to comply with the recommendations made in the preceding concluding observations of the treaty body concerned. Following the initiative of the CtAT in 2007, the HRCtee and the CMW introduced a new optional reporting procedure 'whereby [the HRCtee] would send States parties a list of issues ... and consider their written replies in lieu of a periodic report'.[47] This measure was introduced to make reporting more targeted and efficient, and initial responses by states parties were favourable, resulting in an increase of reports submitted.[48] Upon receipt of the report the reporting cycle continues as set out above.

The increased participation of civil society actors has considerably changed the nature of the reporting procedure. NGOs and others can play an important role in the review of law and practice during the preparation of reports. Ideally, this already constitutes part of a broader domestic dialogue about a state's human rights performance.[49] Indeed, some states involve NGOs, national human rights institutions and others at the drafting stage, but the practice is far from uniform. Where it is based on a genuine dialogue rather than consultation for the sake of it this practice has the potential to result in a contextualised report reflecting existing challenges and shortcomings. This stands in contrast to reports that simply restate the law or use selective and often irrelevant information, or otherwise do not present an accurate picture of affairs. The treaty bodies have responded to such shortcomings through the adoption of detailed guidelines and by pursuing dialogue with state delegates, as well as, on occasion, by requesting supplementary reports. However, states frequently appear either unable or unwilling to provide a sufficiently detailed and/or accurate report.[50] The information provided by UN agencies, NGOs and others provides an important counterweight and alternative source of information.[51] Drawing on a rich pool of information enables treaty bodies to identify a list of issues that are relevant in light of the actual practice and to ask probing questions

---

[47] See HRCtee, Focused Reports Based on Replies to Lists of Issues prior to Reporting (LOIPR): Implementation of the New Optional Reporting Procedure (LOIPR procedure), UN Doc. CCPR/C/99/4 (29 September 2010), para. 1.

[48] Pillay, above note 20, 48.   [49] UN Doc. HRI/MC/2006/3, para. 10.

[50] This may take the form of a clearly inadequate report, such as the one-page initial report submitted by Nepal to the CAT, UN Doc. CAT/C/16/Add.3 (16 December 1993), or rather sophisticated but highly 'selective' reports, such as Uzbekistan's report to the CAT, UN Doc. CAT/C/UZB/3 (28 July 2006).

[51] 'Alternative' or 'shadow' reports can be found on the respective treaty bodies websites under 'The Committee and its Work', 'Sessions', 'Information provided to the Committee (or NGO Information/Information provided by other sources). See A. Clapham, 'The UN Human Rights Reporting Procedures: an NGO Perspective', in J. Crawford and P. Alston (eds.), *The Future of UN Human Rights Treaty Monitoring* (Cambridge University Press, 2000), 175–98, and OHCHR, *Working with the United Nations Human Rights Programme: A Handbook for Civil Society* (New York and Geneva: United Nations, 2008), Chapter IV, at www.ohchr.org/Documents/Publications/NgoHandbook/ngohandbook4.pdf.

during the constructive dialogue.[52] This includes highlighting specific cases or incidents that have been taken up by treaty bodies to illustrate systemic problems, enhance engagement and make follow-up more targeted.[53]

The increased level of engagement is frequently reflected in the concluding observations of treaty bodies. Concluding observations, that is the 'verdict' of the treaty body, are often the most contentious part of the reporting process. Inevitably, such observations raise issues and include recommendations that are objected to by states. Irrespective of what one considers to be the legal nature of concluding observations – positions range from an 'authoritative pronouncement on whether a state has or has not complied with its obligations'[54] to mere opinions or recommendations[55] – they will have to be sufficiently specific, practical and persuasive to command the authority needed to enhance the prospect for implementation.[56] This includes the soundness of the legal arguments made, which have at times been the subject of controversy. A prominent example is the USA's disagreement over the interpretation of the law by the HRCtee. The latter's concluding observation had challenged several of the states parties' interpretations of its obligations in the context of counter-terrorism operations, including the definition of torture and the applicability of the Covenant on Civil and Political Rights to the Guantánamo Bay detention regime.[57] This was a highly politicised and exceptional incident that directly challenged the foundations of the extraordinary legal regime that the then US government had sought to erect. More generally, however, it is clear that concluding observations can be highly authoritative and are increasingly referred to in legal arguments made and in jurisprudence on human rights issues, such as by the ICJ in the *Wall* case.[58]

---

[52] However, see the critical account of the frustrating reality of treaty body proceedings, T. Kelly, 'The Cause of Human Rights: Doubts about Torture, Law, and Ethics at the United Nations', *JRAI* 17 (2011), 728–44.

[53] See for example List of Issues, Sri Lanka, UN Doc. CAT/C/LKA/3-4 (24 June 2011); and South Africa, UN Doc. CEDAW/C/ZAF/Q/4 (2 September 2010).

[54] T. Buergenthal, 'The UN Human Rights Committee', *MPYBUNL* 5 (2001), 341–98, at 351.

[55] See e.g. *Jones* v. *Ministry of Interior Al-Mamlaka Al-Arabiya AS Saudiya (the Kingdom of Saudi Arabia)* [2006] UKHL 26, on the CtAT's comments on article 14 CAT in relation to Canada's state party report; Lord Bingham of Cornhill, para. 23, 'no more than a recommendation'; Lord Hoffmann, para. 57, 'no value'.

[56] See C. Heyns and F. Viljoen, *The Impact of the United Nations Human Rights Treaties on the Domestic Level* (The Hague: Kluwer Law International, 2002), 26–7, and Tyagi, above note 9, 252–9, on the nature of concluding observations.

[57] Comments by the Government of the United States of America on the concluding observations of the Human Rights Committee, UN Doc. CCPR/C/USA/CO/3/Rev.1/Add.1 (12 February 2008).

[58] The ICJ referred to the HRCtee's concluding observations on Israel's second period report when discussing the applicability of the ICCPR to the occupied territories in *Legal Consequences of the Construction of the Wall in the Occupied Palestinian Territory*, Advisory opinion, ICJ Reports 2004, 136, para. 110.

INTERVIEW 5.1
Using shadow reports to promote gender equality and combat sexual violence: South Africa

(Lesley Ann Foster)

Gender discrimination, sexual violence and other *de jure* or *de facto* violations of women's rights constitute major problems in South Africa. In 2011 South Africa was due for review before CtEDAW. Several NGOs used the opportunity to submit alternative reports, including a joint shadow report submitted by over twenty NGOs.[1] CtEDAW issued its concluding observations on the report on 5 April 2011.[2] The following is an interview with Lesley Ann Foster, executive director of the Masimanyane Women's Support Centre,[3] which took the lead in preparing the joint shadow report.

What did you hope to achieve by submitting the shadow report?

The then UN Special Rapporteur on Violence against Women, Radhika Coomaraswamy, had visited South Africa saying that it had the highest levels of violence against women in the world for a country not at war. This remark, together with the group's own knowledge and experience, provided sufficient motivation for us to focus on this issue. Another thing that counted in the group's favour was that violence against women had been raised high on the political agenda and it had been acknowledged as one of the most critical issues facing the country. We adopted a broad understanding of violence against women. It encompassed many other facets of women's rights, such as education, employment, literacy, health, welfare and similar issues, all with links to violence against women. Our main objective was to see a strengthening of the state's response to violence against women. We had identified various challenges in the implementation of state policies and called for a better legislative framework as well as improved institutional arrangements.

How did you succeed in having so many NGOs join the endeavour?

We started off with a strong network of partner organisations. Next we purposefully identified the groups we knew should be included. Anyone else could join so when groups expressed an interest we let them be a part of it. We asked various organisations to conduct the focus group discussions or participate in the field work. This included marginalised

---

[1] *South African Shadow Report on the Implementation of the Convention on the Elimination of All Forms of Discrimination against Women*, submitted to the CEDAW Committee's 48th Session (17 January–4 February 2011), online, at: www2.ohchr.org/english/bodies/cedaw/docs/ngos/Joint_NGO_Report_for_the_session_SouthAfrica.pdf.

[2] UN Doc. CEDAW/C/ZAF/CO/4.   [3] www.masimanyane.org.za.

groups, including people working on LGBT issues, a transgender group and a sex workers group. We did not contact the group of disabled women whom we work with and this was a gap in our recent report. We made sure that everyone was given the opportunity to input into the process. We went into communities and trained women's groups on the principles of the CEDAW and then invited them to participate in the process. All of this made it possible to draw people into developing the shadow report and participating in different ways in the process.

What was the division of labour between NGOs in preparing the report?

The approach of how to write a report on violence against women generated much discussion. An audit of the available skills was done. The group had medical expertise, legal expertise, media, education, financial and advocacy and lobbying skills. Most of the group had strong links to various networks. It was also helpful that they came from different provinces within the country so were able to provide information on violence against women in different geographical, social, cultural and political settings.

How did you ensure the accuracy of information used?

We recorded the focus group discussions using electronic tools (video and recording devices). We also used published research and official state documents. All those involved in the process were briefed on the CEDAW and provided training on research, which helped in selecting and verifying relevant information.

How was the report received and used by the committee?

The final report was distributed to all the participating organisations throughout the country and every government minister and department was sent a copy. This was done after the report was sent to the CEDAW committee members. There were very audible grumblings in government circles about the report and some attempts were made to discredit the information contained in it. A harsh attack by the head of the government delegation was made to one of our representatives whom she knew well. The attack centred on her view that we were out of order in providing alternative information and that we should have been supportive of the government as it was a government of the people for the people. She did not accept our view that we had an important monitoring role to play.

The report was read by the CEDAW committee members. We then had a lunch briefing with the committee prior to our state reporting. They asked for clarifications on issues raised in the report and asked us to elaborate our concerns. They asked us what questions should be put to our state. This was very useful and extremely powerful. Eighteen out of the final twenty-six recommendations made by the CtEDAW focused on aspects of violence against women as highlighted in the NGO shadow report. Perhaps one of the most significant concluding comments was the suggestion that the South African government develop specific equality legislation. All of the concluding comments were sound suggestions which the group welcomed.

Some members of the group travelled back to South Africa with the government delegation. During the trip some discussion took place and the delegation acknowledged that the presence of the NGO delegation was a good thing. The representatives said that the concluding comments gave the delegation bargaining tools for greater political commitment and resource allocation for addressing women's rights in the country. They realised that if the report had been accepted without an honest critique and recommendations it would have led to complacency within government. This was an important shift.

Are you using the concluding observation in domestic advocacy, if so, how and with what impact?

We are currently disseminating the concluding observations. We have a national advocacy strategy in place to take up some of the issues on an ongoing basis. We are exploring further use of the convention, such as by applying the optional protocol to the CEDAW. We are also considering requesting an inquiry into some forms of discrimination in the country. The government has taken some action. It used the report to develop a strategy for addressing violence against women in the country, including research on lived realities of women. Extensive legislative reform took place and more than 4,000 laws were reviewed to ensure non discrimination against women and girls. Equality legislation was developed but has not as yet been passed. Extensive programmes have been established in the country to support women and girls who are victims of gender-based violence. Research has been commissioned by the national government to develop the data systems related to violence against women.

What are the lessons you learned from the process?

Shadow reporting is a vital strategy for getting international attention on the plight of women in your country. We learned that you have to be prepared and you need to understand how the system works. We also learned that the work after the reporting session is as important as the development of the shadow report. One needs to use every opportunity to teach women about discrimination and inequality. Finally, we have learned that the state and women themselves do not have a strong enough understanding on discrimination.

5.3.2   Strengthening the reporting procedure

Non-compliance with treaty reporting is one of the notorious, systemic challenges confronting the UN human rights treaty system. Many states have failed to submit any reports or submitted them several years after they were due.[59] The reasons for this are both state specific and systemic. States may lack the political incentive or have limited capacity, including lack of adequate data, to submit reports in time. The treaty bodies have limited 'enforcement' powers and there is no apparent political cost for late submissions, unlike with the UPR which is a much more state-driven political process.[60] One major problem facing the system is the growing number of reporting obligations that states find it increasingly difficult to meet.[61] The treaty bodies and the OHCHR have taken a series of measures to address non-reporting and delays.[62] This includes supporting states in building their capacity to prepare and submit reports, encouraging states to submit core documents[63] and offering states the possibility to report on a list of issues rather than submitting a full periodic report.[64] Treaty bodies may name and shame late or non-reporting states; they also increasingly decide to consider the situation in a state even in the absence of a report on the basis of other information received.[65] In practice, the threat of doing so has often been sufficient to prompt a state to engage and ultimately submit a report.[66] This demonstrates a degree of effectiveness which ironically may generate the reverse problem. The treaty bodies themselves may not have the capacity to

---

[59] According to Pillay, above note 20, 21, only 16 per cent of reports 'were submitted in strict accordance with the due dates established in the treaties or by the treaty bodies'. As of April 2012, a total of 626 reports – 315 initial reports and 311 periodic reports – were overdue; see ibid., 23.

[60] See section 4.3.1 for a discussion of the UPR.

[61] See Report by the Secretariat, Concept Paper on the High Commissioner's Proposal for a Unified Standing Treaty Body, UN Doc. HRI/MC/2006/2 (22 March 2006), para. 16; Pillay, above note 20, 25.

[62] See W. Kälin, 'Examination of State Reports', in H. Keller and G. Ulfstein (eds.), *UN Human Rights Treaty Bodies* (Cambridge University Press, 2012), 16–72, at 32, and Tyagi, above note 9, 188–210, for the HRCtee.

[63] The core document should contain general information about the state, the general framework for the promotion and protection of human rights, information on non-discrimination and equality and effective remedies; see UN Doc. HRI/MC/2006/3, paras. 31–59.

[64] See UN Doc. CCPR/C/99/4.

[65] For example, in relation to Gambia, in 2008 the HRCtee considered the situation in the absence of a report in 2002, 'declared the state party to be in breach of its obligation to cooperate with the Committee in the performance of its functions under Part IV of the Covenant', and, in 2009, 'referred [the matter] to the High Commissioner for Human Rights, Report of the Special Rapporteur for follow-up on concluding observations', UN Doc. CCPR/C/95/2/rev.1 (26 May 2009), 2, 3.

[66] See for example Concluding Observations of the Human Rights Committee: Rwanda, UN Doc. CCPR/C/RWA/CO/3 (7 May 2009), para. 2.

hear reports within a reasonable time if reporting were to increase, which would in all likelihood considerably add to the already existing backlog.[67]

This challenge, together with concerns about adequate coordination and lack of impact of treaty bodies, led to a concerted review process in the 2000s.[68] In the course of this process the OHCHR proposed the establishment of a unified standing treaty body. It argued that the creation of such a body would

> provide…a framework for a comprehensive, cross-cutting and holistic approach to implementation…a consistent approach to interpretation of provisions in the treaties…extend…the period of the dialogue…members…be available on a permanent basis…be more visible…[provide a] unified monitoring structure.[69]
>
> In addition, a comprehensive, overall assessment of the implementation of international legal obligations under human rights treaties for countries in one single document…would be more likely to attract heightened attention from political bodies such as…[the] Human Rights Council or the Security Council.[70]

In spite of these apparent advantages the proposal did not garner much support. This was due to concerns that it might undermine protection for specific rights and that the attempt to integrate all treaties would be fraught with difficulties. In 2009 the High Commissioner for Human Rights initiated a treaty body strengthening process involving a range of relevant stakeholders, with a major focus on measures aimed at harmonising the working methods of treaty bodies, as expressed in the Dublin Statement on the Process of Strengthening of the United Nations Human Rights Treaty Body System.[71] NGOs welcomed this process and submitted a number of proposals to make the system more visible and accessible for NGOs to contribute.[72] The process

---

[67] See UN Doc. A/66/344, para.11: 'As of May 2011, 263 reports were pending consideration under the nine treaty bodies with a reporting procedure.' See ibid., p. 12, Table 2 for an overview of the backlog, and para. 21: 'The observation, made by an independent expert reporting on the same issue to the United Nations in 1997, that the treaty system "can function only because of the large-scale delinquency of states" remains true today (see UN Doc. E/CN.4/1997/74, para. 48).'

[68] Reform efforts date back to the 1980s, see UNGA resolution 43/115 (8 December 1988), para. 15. See for the important role played by the UN Secretary-General, Strengthening of the United Nations: An Agenda for Further Change, UN Doc. A/57/387 (9 September 2002), paras. 52–4, and In Larger Freedom: Towards Development, Security and Human Rights for All, UN Doc. A/59/2005 (21 March 2005), para. 147.

[69] UN Doc. HRI/MC/2006/2, paras. 27–35.   [70] Ibid., para. 36.

[71] See www2.ohchr.org/english/bodies/HRTD/docs/DublinStatement.pdf. See for further documents generated as part of the review process, OHCHR, 'The Treaty Body Strengthening Process', online, at www2.ohchr.org/english/bodies/HRTD/index.htm.

[72] Dublin Statement on the Process of Strengthening the United Nations Human Rights Treaty Body System: Response by non-governmental organizations, November 2010 (recommendations include holding occasional meeting outside of Geneva, advance notice for NGOs, communications, protection against reprisals for NGOs, enhanced membership of treaty bodies, better coordination), online, at www.apt.ch/region/unlegal/DublinStatementNGO_JointResponse1110en.pdf.

culminated in a major report by the UN High Commissioner for Human Rights in 2012, which compiled a series of recommendations. These included:

> establishing a comprehensive reporting calendar…enhancing independence and impartiality of members and strengthening the election process; establishing a structured and sustained approach to capacity-building for States parties for their reporting duties…increasing accessibility and visibility of the treaty body system, through webcasting of public meetings and use of other new technologies; a simplified focused reporting procedure…alignment of other working methods to the maximum extent without contradicting the normative specificities of the treaties; limitation of the length of documentation.[73]

There is a clear understanding of the problems and needs as reflected in the measures suggested. This includes availability of greater resources to respond to the increased workload resulting from the expansion of treaty bodies and states parties, improved communications, more targeted reporting and follow up and better coordination between the treaty bodies.[74] These measures, if implemented, would contribute to enhanced efficiency. However, it is questionable whether they will be sufficient to satisfactorily address the underlying factors, particularly fragmented mandates, limited powers and the low visibility of UN treaty bodies. This raises the more fundamental question of whether the current system is based on structures and processes that can be successfully strengthened or whether it suffers from systemic shortcomings that require a radical rethink and reforms. The risks to the human rights treaty body architecture inherent in such drastic changes have acted as a bulwark that has kept the current system in place. However, ongoing concerns, if not frustration, with a system seen as dysfunctional may give renewed impetus to the idea of a unified standing treaty body, or even a World Court of Human Rights,[75] which several observers believe would be the authority needed to give human rights the standing it warrants at UN level.

It would seem tempting to dismiss the reporting procedure as an onerous and futile 'soft' mechanism that generates the illusion of progress but in reality produces a dialogue that allows states and other actors in the system to be seen as doing something while largely maintaining the status quo. However, for all its apparent and supposed weaknesses the reporting procedure has become an integral part of the system that has contributed, at least to some degree, to the promotion and protection of human rights. It has within its confines: (1) produced an impressive source of information

[73] Pillay, above note 20, 10–11.

[74] Ibid., and Measures to Improve Further the Effectiveness, Harmonization and Reform of the Treaty Body System, UN Doc. A/66/344 (7 September 2011).

[75] See M. Nowak and J. Kozma, *A World Court of Human Rights* (June 2009), online, at www.udhr60.ch/report/hrCourt-Nowak0609.pdf, and T. Buergenthal, 'A Court and Two Consolidated Treaty Bodies', in Bayefsky, above note 35, 299–302.

and record in respect of states' implementation of their human rights obligations; (2) advanced to varying degrees the interpretation and understanding of rights and obligations under the various treaties; (3) provided a forum and instrument for human rights advocacy; and (4) contributed to some changes in law and practice, although the state record of implementing recommendations is patchy.[76] In addition to strengthening the technical aspects of reporting in order to increase efficiency the main task for treaty bodies is to enhance implementation. This includes better visibility and most importantly fostering practices that enable domestic actors, particularly civil society, to use the process as an advocacy tool to improve the human rights situation in the country concerned.

QUESTIONS

1 Is the reporting system fundamentally flawed or simply in the process of becoming an effective means of monitoring of and engagement on states' human rights record?

2 What is the evidence that the model of 'constructive dialogue' adopted by the treaty bodies has really been constructive?

3 Would the establishment of a unified standing body proposed by the OHCHR or a World Human Rights Court constitute the breakthrough needed to substantially strengthen the reporting procedure or would it weaken the more targeted protection existing human rights treaty bodies are mandated to provide?

4 What are the strategic openings and challenges for NGOs in the reporting process?

5.4 GENERAL COMMENTS/RECOMMENDATIONS

General comments (also referred to as general recommendations by the CtEDAW and CERD) are written instruments that treaty bodies adopt, with varying frequency, to set out their views as to the rights and obligations under the treaty concerned.[77] These comments are an integral aspect of the treaty body practice and a vital tool for the interpretation of the respective treaties. The practice of adopting general comments was pioneered by the CERD in 1972, based on the power of treaty bodies to make general

---

[76] The most thorough study on implementation is that of Heyns and Viljoen, above note 56. See also UN Doc. HRI/MC/2006/2, paras. 11–14.

[77] The General Comments can be found in UN Doc. HRI/GEN/1/Rev.9 (vols. I and II) (27 May 2008), and on the websites of the respective treaty bodies.

recommendations in relation to their function of examining states parties' reports.[78] This direct link was particularly evident in the first generation of general comments that specified states parties' reporting obligations. Subsequently, general comments have become instruments that enable treaty bodies to interpret treaty provisions with a view to promoting effective rights protection and the implementation of treaties. They can serve a number of purposes, combining legal analysis with important policy and practice direction functions.[79]

The adoption of a general comment typically involves a number of stages that are followed with some variation by all treaty bodies. A member or members of a treaty body propose(s) the drafting of a general comment. If this proposal is supported a member or a group composed of several members is tasked with preparing a draft or drafts for consideration by the committee. The draft is then further revised and formally adopted after a detailed discussion of its contents.[80] In this process the committee consults with a range of actors from within the UN system, such as specialised agencies, and from without, such as NGOs. In practice, general comments are the outcome of particular dynamics within the treaty body. Is there a readiness to use general comments generally or in relation to a particular issue? Who is taking the lead? How well informed and capable are the drafters? And how successfully does the body overcome internal and external differences to produce an authoritative draft?

The practice of adopting general comments differs markedly between committees. Whereas many bodies adopt one general comment every two years on average, others, notably CtAT, have only adopted two in over twenty years. The HRCtee had adopted an impressive number of thirty-four general comments by 2011, and these constitute an important guide to its understanding of the ICCPR.[81] These comments broach the obligation of states parties under the Covenant and the Optional Protocol, reporting obligations, general questions such as reservations and the majority of substantive rights (including revised comments in relation to several important articles). Compared to the initial, rather cursory general comments of treaty bodies, the more recent ones are greatly substantive. They include at times detailed analysis of the treaty bodies' jurisprudence and relevant international law as well as consideration of topical themes, such as

---

[78] See Report on the Working Methods of the Human Rights Treaty Bodies Relating to the State Party Reporting Process, UN Doc. HRI/ICM/2010/2 (10 May 2010), para. 120, based on article 9(2) ICERD.

[79] See the study by H. Keller and L. Grover, 'General Comments of the Human Rights Committee and their Legitimacy', in Keller and Ulfstein, above note 62, 116–98, at 143.

[80] See Buergenthal, above note 54, 388, and UN Doc. HRI/ICM/2010/2, paras. 122–4.

[81] Available at www2.ohchr.org/english/bodies/hrc/comments.htm. See on the role of General Comments in the Committee's practice, Keller and Grover, above note 79, 116–98, and Tyagi, above note 9, 277–307.

sanctions,[82] non-citizens,[83] children and HIV/AIDS.[84] General comments have served to clarify the fundamental norms of a treaty, such as the application of non-discrimination to violence against women,[85] and the relationship between torture and other forms of cruel, inhuman or degrading treatment or punishment.[86] They can also act as key reference points for states parties, such as on the nature of their obligations, and others where they articulate important principles of international law.[87] General comments have been particularly valuable for bodies that do not have the competence to hear complaints. The CESCR in particular has used its general comments to develop a sophisticated understanding of states parties' obligations necessitated by the controversies surrounding the nature of ESC rights and of corresponding obligations,[88] which in turn has been referred to in national jurisprudence.[89]

General comments are not binding or vested with any formal legal status. Instead, they are widely seen as interpretations of the respective treaties by an authoritative body, which may also serve to restate and clarify its jurisprudence.[90] As such, general comments have become influential not only for the practice of treaty bodies but also because they are cited as authoritative in the jurisprudence of other national and international bodies.[91] It is therefore apt to refer to general comments as 'important instruments in the lawmaking process of the [Human Rights] Committee'[92] and compare them to advisory opinions.[93] Indeed, the ICJ believes that 'it should ascribe great

---

[82] CESCR, General Comment 8: The Relationship between Economic Sanctions and Respect for Economic, Social and Cultural Rights, UN Doc. E/C.12/1997/8 (12 December 1997).

[83] CERD, General Comment 30: Discrimination against Non-Citizens, UN Doc. HRI/GEN/1/Rev.7/Add.1 (4 May 2005).

[84] CtRC, General Comment 3: HIV/AIDs and the Rights of the Children, UN Doc. CRC/GC/2003/3 (17 March 2003).

[85] CtEDAW, Violence against Women, General Recommendation 12 (1989) and General Recommendation 19 (1992).

[86] CtAT, General Comment 2: Implementation of Article 2 by States Parties, UN Doc. CAT/C/GC/2 (24 January 2008).

[87] HRCtee, General Comment 31: The Nature of the General Legal Obligation imposed on States Parties to the Covenant, UN Doc. CCPR/C/21/Rev.1/Add.13 (26 May 2004).

[88] This practice started with its General Comment 3 on general obligations, which was followed by comments concerning the states parties obligations in relation to substantive rights.

[89] See for example *Government of the Republic of South Africa and Others* v. *Grootboom and Others*, 2000 (11) BCLR 1169 (CC), (4 October 2000), paras. 29–31, 45.

[90] See Tyagi, above note 9, 301–7, with further references. However, see Keller and Grover, above note 79, 133, who refer to the US and UK position rejecting 'the idea that the Committee is "the" authoritative interpreter of the Covenant'.

[91] See for example the ICJ in the *Wall* Advisory opinion, para. 136 (reference to General Comment 27); *Ahmadou Sadio Diallo* (*Republic of Guinea* v. *Democratic Republic of the Congo*), Judgment of 30 November 2010, para. 66 (General Comment 15); para. 77 (General Comment 8).

[92] Buergenthal, above note 54, 387.   [93] Ibid., 386.

weight to the interpretation adopted by this independent body [the HRCtee] that was established specifically to supervise the application of that treaty'.[94]

The legitimacy of General Comments has been attributed to a number of factors, which a recent study based on a series of interviews with committee members identified as determinacy, symbolic validation, coherence, adherence and democratic decision-making.[95] While many General Comments have been favourably received their authority has been challenged in some notable instances. The HRCtee's General Comment 24 is an example that elicited considerable controversy. Several states, namely the UK, USA and France, took exception to the HRCtee's position that it rather than the states parties themselves has the competence to decide on the validity of reservations, as has been the traditional understanding in international law.[96] The General Comment was the subject of close scrutiny and questions were raised about the Committee's reasoning and limited legal analysis.[97] Such reactions generate moments of tension that can damage the relationship between states and treaty bodies and serve to undermine the latter's authority. However, the committees, being the guardians of the treaty in question, also have a responsibility to strengthen the effectiveness of human rights treaties. Using general comments to break new ground to this effect can be a risky undertaking but may over time be vindicated if a sufficient number of relevant actors subscribe to the treaty bodies' position, which in turn generates momentum for others to follow.

5.5   COMPLAINTS PROCEDURES AND JURISPRUDENCE OF TREATY BODIES

5.5.1   Overview

Treaty-based complaints procedures (individual and inter-state communications) are an important means to monitor compliance of states parties with their obligations and to develop the law under the respective treaty. Importantly, and exceptionally as compared to other areas of international law, individual complaints procedures provide victims of human rights violations with a remedy at the international level.[98] This is in contrast to related areas, such as international refugee law and international humanitarian law, where no

---

[94] *Ahmadou Sadio Diallo*, para. 66.   [95] Keller and Grover, above note 79.

[96] See observations by the USA, the UK and France on General Comment 24, in *Report of the HRCtee*, UN Doc. A/50/40 (3 October 1995), Annex IV (USA and UK), and UN Doc. A/51/40 (13 April 1997), Annex VI (France).

[97] See K. Korkelia, 'New Challenges to the Regime of Reservations under the International Covenant on Civil and Political Rights', *EJIL* 13(2) (2002), 437–77, at 446–68; E. A. Baylis, 'General Comment 24: Confronting the Problem of Reservations to Human Rights Treaties', *Berkeley J. Int'l L.* 17 (1999), 277–329.

[98] See Chapter 7.

comparable treaty bodies and procedures exist. However, human rights treaty bodies are, with few exceptions, not vested with the automatic competence to consider communications. They can only deal with individual cases where states parties make a declaration to this effect or become parties to an optional protocol.[99] The lack of a compulsory complaints procedure historically reflected the reluctance of states to expose themselves to any scrutiny other than the reporting procedure. This has slowly changed as many states (with some significant exceptions, see below) have now recognised the competence of treaty bodies to consider complaints of alleged human rights violations.[100]

Procedures for inter-state cases before the various treaty bodies differ. Communications may be heard by the committee concerned (CAT, ICRMW and CPED)[101] or dealt with by *ad hoc* conciliation commissions (ICERD and ICCPR).[102] Disputes regarding the interpretation and application of the respective treaty may be settled through negotiation, arbitration, or, ultimately referral to the ICJ (ICERD, CEDAW, CAT, ICRMW and CPED).[103] The rather elaborate UN treaty system for inter-state complaints has not been used. This may appear odd at first sight because states included the relevant provisions in the first place and a number of states parties have made declarations accepting the complaints procedures concerned. States' reluctance to use formal inter-state procedures before treaty bodies to resolve disputes may be attributed to a preference for political bodies, such as the UN HRC, to address human rights concerns and a desire to avoid adverse diplomatic repercussions. However, there have been a growing number of inter-state cases over the breach of human rights obligations before other courts, namely the ECtHR and the ICJ.[104] Notably, in several judgments, the ICJ adjudicated cases with reference to the ICCPR, among other applicable sources.[105] This suggests that states prepared to use formal proceedings prefer to resort to courts, where possible. The reason for this may be the prospect of obtaining a binding judgment that

---

[99] Optional protocols become necessary where the primary treaty, as is the case with the ICCPR, does not provide for a complaints procedure. See, more recently, the OPICESCR and OPCRC (Complaints Procedures).

[100] See http://treaties.un.org/Pages/Treaties.aspx?id=4&subid=A&lang=en.

[101] Articles 21 CAT, 74 ICRMW and 32 CPED.

[102] Articles 11–13 ICERD (automatic/compulsory) and 41–43 ICCPR (upon declaration).

[103] Articles 22 ICERD, 29 CEDAW, 30 CAT, 92 ICRMW and 42 CPED. See for an interpretation of article 22 ICERD (dispute settlement between ICERD states parties and referral to the ICJ), case concerning *Application of the International Convention on the Elimination of All Forms of Racial Discrimination* (*Georgia* v. *Russian Federation*), Preliminary Objections, Judgment of 1 April 2011, paras. 115–84; on article 29 CEDAW, *Armed Activities on the Territory of the Congo* (*New Application:2002*) (*Democratic Republic of the Congo* v. *Rwanda*), Jurisdiction and admissibility, Judgment, ICJ Reports 2006, p. 6, paras. 87–93; and, on article 30 CAT, *Questions relating to the Obligation to Prosecute or Extradite* (*Belgium* v. *Senegal*), ICJ Judgment of 20 July 2012, paras. 42–55.

[104] See section 6.2.4 on the ECtHR.

[105] See in particular the *Wall* advisory opinion and *Ahmadou Sadio Diallo* case.

carries greater weight than quasi-judicial or other dispute settlement procedures for inter-state cases provided for in the UN human rights treaty system.

By July 2012 six treaty bodies had the competence to receive individual communications. Individual complaints mechanisms are either provided for in the respective treaty, such as the ICERD, the CAT, the ICRMW (procedure not in force as of July 2012) and the CPED,[106] or in an optional protocol, as is the case with the ICCPR, the CEDAW and the CRPD. The optional protocol to the CEDAW (1999), the ICESCR (2008, not in force as of July 2012) and the CRC (on complaints procedure) (2011, not in force as of July 2012) were adopted twenty years, forty-two years and thirty-two years respectively after the adoption of the treaty setting out the substantive rights. This time lag shows that the acceptance of individual complaints procedures is often the outcome of protracted processes. These processes are usually driven by a range of actors comprising civil society organisations, like-minded states parties, UN bodies and individual experts who frequently encounter considerable obstacles when advocating changes to the system. This includes objections based on the supposed lack of justiciability of rights (ICESCR)[107] and the reluctance to vest bodies such as the CtEDAW with the power to consider complaints in what are seen as sensitive areas. The challenges surrounding the recognition of an individual complaints procedure were also evident in recent debates in the HRC concerning an optional protocol to the CRC.[108]

The level of state acceptance as regards the competence of the various treaty bodies to consider communications varies considerably.[109] There is a significant regional imbalance which undermines the universal reach of procedures. The USA, India, China and Middle Eastern states in particular have not accepted the competence of treaty bodies to receive complaints against them. Even where states have recognised such competence, there are sizeable differences in the number of communications that reach the various committees. The HRCtee has dealt with by far the most complaints, followed by the CtAT, the CERD, the CtEDAW and the CtRPD.[110]

---

[106] Articles 14 ICERD, 22 CAT, 77 ICRMW and 31 CPED.   [107] See section 9.6.

[108] See Optional Protocol CRC on a communications procedure, A/HRC/RES/17/18 (14 July 2011), and documents of the Open-ended Working Group on an Optional Protocol to the CRC to provide a communications procedure, online, at www2.ohchr.org/english/bodies/hrcouncil/OEWG/index.htm.

[109] The status of ratifications and acceptance of treaty bodies' competence to consider complaints is available online at www2.ohchr.org/english/bodies/petitions/index.htm.

[110] The relevant statistics are provided in the overview for each treaty body following in this chapter, with the exception of CtRPD due to its limited jurisprudence to date. CtRPD decided its first case on 19 April 2012, *H. M. v. Sweden*, UN Doc. CRPD/C/7/D/3. The case concerned the 'refusal to grant building permission for the construction of a hydrotherapy pool for the rehabilitation of a person with a physical disability on grounds of incompatibility of the extension in question with the city development plan', with the Committee finding a violation of articles 5(1), 5(3), 19(b), 25 and 26, read alone and in conjunction with articles 3(b), (d) and (e), and 4(1) (d) CRPD.

The respective committee(s) often plays a valuable role for some countries or in some regions while it may be of marginal interest in others. In this context, it is important not to see the number of communications brought against a particular state as a reliable indicator of the seriousness of the human rights situation in a country, though this may constitute one factor influencing whether or not cases are brought. Other factors include awareness, the presence of activist lawyers and NGOs taking up cases, the availability of effective domestic remedies that make recourse to the treaty bodies unnecessary, a preference for regional procedures where available and the degree of belief in the utility of the procedure.[111] Finally, state acceptance of complaints procedures has not automatically translated into compliance with decisions made.[112]

5.5.2   Human Rights Committee

The optional protocol had been accepted by 114 of the 167 states parties to the ICCPR as of 27 July 2012. The HRCtee had found 764 violations in the 1,815 concluded cases out of a total of 2,034 communications with respect to eighty-four countries as of 23 April 2012.[113] It has developed an impressive body of jurisprudence that has been marked by its response to systemic and/or serious violations in several countries and regions and by the development of its case law on particular rights. The 1970s and 1980s were characterised by a large number of decisions against Uruguay in cases involving torture and disappearances.[114] Colombia and Zaire featured prominently in the 1980s in respect of serious violations committed in the course of conflict and dictatorship.[115] Jamaica in the late 1980s and throughout the 1990s and Trinidad and Tobago in the 1990s and 2000s were the subject of dozens of decisions, particularly in respect of the death penalty regime in place in both countries. This included findings that the mandatory death penalty was incompatible with the right to life, an emphasis on compliance with the right to a fair trial as prerequisite for the imposition of the death penalty and

---

[111] Heyns and Viljoen, above note 56, 28–30.   [112] See section 7.5.

[113] See statistical survey of complaints considered, www2.ohchr.org/english/bodies/hrc/procedure.htm.

[114] Beginning with the case of *Massera* v. *Uruguay*, Communication no. R.1/5 (15 August 1979), the first HRC decision on the merits that found violations of articles 7, 9(1–4), 10(1), 14(1, 2, 3), 25. All of the Committee's first twelve views concerned Uruguay, with a total of forty-seven views as of 7 March 2012.

[115] See for example *Herrera* v. *Colombia*, Communication no. 161/1983 (2 November 1987), paras. 10.1–11 (violation of articles 6, 7, 10(1)); *Muteba* v. *Zaire*, Communication no. 124/1982 (24 July 1984), paras. 10.1–12 (violation of articles 7, 9 (3, 4), 10(1), 14(3 (b),(c),(d)), 19); *Mpandanjila et al.* v. *Zaire*, Communication no. 138/1983 (26 March 1986), paras. 8.1–9 (violation of articles (9(1), 10(1), 12(1), 14(1), 19 and 25).

holding that the so-called death row phenomenon may constitute inhuman and degrading treatment.[116]

In the 2000s the geographic focus broadened. It included Algeria and Libya (particularly enforced disappearances);[117] Belarus (denial of various rights resulting from political repression);[118] Central Asian states, particularly Tajikistan, Kyrgyzstan and Uzbekistan (mainly torture and imposition of the death penalty following an unfair trial);[119] Russia (multiple violations);[120] and several Asian states, particularly the Philippines and Sri Lanka (mainly in relation to the death penalty before its abolition in the Philippines, as well as torture, arbitrary arrests and detention and unfair trials).[121] The HRCtee has over the years also heard a number of complaints in relation to particular states for which it constitutes the only available international complaints procedure. This included Spain in respect of the right to an appeal as part of the right to a fair trial, primarily because Spain had until recently not been a party to protocol no. 7 to the ECHR which recognises such a right.[122]

---

[116] See *Kennedy* v. *Trinidad and Tobago*, UN Doc. CCPR/C/67/D/845/1999 (2 November 1999), para. 7.3 (mandatory death penalty); *Price* v. *Jamaica*, UN Doc. CCPR/C/58/D/572/1994 (6 November 1996), paras. 9.2–9.3 (death penalty following an unfair trial); *Pratt and Morgan* v. *Jamaica*, Communication nos. 210/1986 and 225/1987 (6 April 1989), para. 15 (commutation as appropriate remedy); *Johnson* v. *Jamaica*, UN Doc. CCPR/C/56/D/592/1994 (25 November 1998), para. 10.4 (death row).

[117] See *Benaziza* v. *Algeria*, UN Doc. CCPR/C/99/D/1588/2007 (26 July 2010), paras. 9.1–10 (violation of articles 6(1), 7, 9, and 2(3)); *El-Abani* v. *Libyan Arab Jamahiriya*, UN Doc. CCPR/C/99/D/1640/2007 (26 July 2010), paras. 7.1–8 (violation of articles 6(1), 7, 9, 10(1), 14(1, 3 (a–d)), 16 and 2(3)).

[118] See *Korneenko and Milinkevich* v. *Belarus*, UN Doc. CCPR/C/95/D/1553/2007 (20 March 2009), paras. 8.1–9 (violation of articles 19(2), 25, 26); *Lukyanchik* v. *Belarus*, UN Doc. CCPR/C/97/D/1392/2005 (21 October 2009), paras. 8.1–9 (violation of article 25(b) in conjunction with article 2); *Tulzhenkova* v. *Belarus*, UN Doc. CCPR/C/103/D/1838/2008 (26 October 2011), paras. 9.1–10 (violation of article 19(2)).

[119] See *Iskandarov* v. *Tajikistan*, UN Doc. CCPR/C/101/D/1499/2006 (30 March 2011), paras. 6.1–7 (violation of articles 7, 9(1, 3), 14(1), 3(b),(d),(e),(g)); *Akhadov* v. *Kyrgyzstan*, UN Doc. CCPR/C/101/D/1503/2006 (25 March 2011), paras. 7.1–8 (violation of articles 6, 7, 9, 14(1), (3)(g)); *Kasimov* v. *Uzbekistan*, UN Doc. CCPR/C/96/D/1378/2005 (30 July 2009), paras. 9.1–10 (violation of articles 7, 14(3)(b), (g)).

[120] See *Lantsova* v. *Russia*, UN Doc. CCPR/C/74/D/763/1997 (26 March 2002), paras. 8.1–10 (violation of articles 6, 10(1)), and *Andrei Khoroshenko* v. *Russia*, UN Doc. CCPR/C/101/D/1304/2004 (29 March 2011), paras. 9.1–10 (violation of articles 6, 7, 9(1–4), 14(1), (3)(a), (b), (d), (g)).

[121] See *Wilson* v. *Philippines*, UN CCPR/C/79/D/868/1999 (30 October 2003), paras. 7.1–8 (violation of articles 7, 9(1–3), 10(1, 2)); *Singarasa* v. *Sri Lanka*, UN Doc. CCPR/C/81/D/1033/2001 (21 July 2004), paras. 7.1–7.5 (violation of articles 14(1), (2), (3)(c), (f), (g), 5, 2(3) and 7); *Rajapakse* v. *Sri Lanka*, UN Doc. CCPR/C/83/D/1250/2004 (14 July 2006), paras. 9.1–10 (violation of articles 7, 9(1–3), 10 as well as 2(3)).

[122] See *Gayoso Martínez* v. *Spain*, UN Doc. CCPR/C/97/D/1363/2005 (19 October 2009), paras. 9.1–10 (violation of article 14(5)).

A large number of cases before the HRCtee concern articles 2, 6, 7, 9, 10 and 14, which reflects the prevalence and close nexus of arbitrary detention, torture, ill-treatment and enforced disappearance, or unfair trials and the death penalty, as well as the lack of effective remedies. The HRCtee has made an important contribution to the international jurisprudence in this respect.[123] It has also adopted a number of influential views in respect of other articles, including on freedom of expression,[124] discrimination[125] and minority rights.[126]

The HRCtee's jurisprudence constitutes an authoritative record of violations in the cases brought before it. While the value of its views as a remedy for individuals has been undermined by limited state compliance,[127] it has vindicated claims, set precedents and served as an advocacy tool for tackling systemic violations.[128] In conjunction with the reporting system its jurisprudence has eroded the acceptability of certain practices. This has contributed to changes in the practice of states parties, such as the suspension or abolition of the death penalty.[129]

The views of the HRCtee have been referred to by other courts, including the ICJ, human rights treaty bodies, other UN bodies, national courts and

---

[123] *Bleier* v. *Uruguay*, Communication no. 30/1978 (R.7/30) (29 March 1982), paras. 13.1–14 (violation of articles 6, 7, 9, 10(1)); *Sharma* v. *Nepal*, UN Doc. CCPR/C/94/D/1469/2006 (28 October 2008), paras. 7.1–10 (violation of articles 6, 7, 9, 10 and 2(3)); *Alzery* v. *Sweden*, UN Doc. CCPR/C/88/D/1416/2005 (25 October 2006), paras. 11.1–12 (violation of article 7, 2 and article 1 of the optional protocol). See also HRCtee, General Comment 32: Article 14: Right to Equality before Courts and Tribunals and to a Fair Trial, UN Doc. CCPR/C/GC/32 (23 August 2007).

[124] See HRCtee, General Comment 34: Article 19: Freedoms of Opinion and Expression, UN Doc. CCPR/C/GC/34 (12 September 2011) and, for example, *Yong-Joo Kang* v. *Republic of Korea*, UN Doc. CCPR/C/78/D/878/1999 (15 July 2003), paras. 7.1–8 (political opinion), (violation of articles 10 (1, 3), 18, 19, 26).

[125] See on article 26 *Zwaan-de Vries* v. *The Netherlands*, Communication no. 182/1984, (9 April 1987), paras. 10–16, and *Albareda et al.* v. *Uruguay*, UN Doc. CCPR/C/103/D/1637/2007, 1757 and 1765/2008 (24 October 2011), paras. 9.1–10.

[126] On article 27, see *Lovelace* v. *Canada*, Communication no. R.6/24 (30 July 1981), paras. 13.2–19 (violation); *Lubicon Lake Band* v. *Canada*, UN Doc. CCPR/C38/D/167/1984 (26 March 1990), paras. 32.1–33 (violation); *Länsman et al.* v. *Finland*, UN Doc. CCPR/C/52/D/511/1992 (26 October 1994), paras. 9.1–10 (no breach); *Diergaardt et al.* v. *Namibia*, UN Doc. CCPR/C/69/D/760/1996 (25 July 2000), paras. 10.1–11 (violation of article 26, not 27); *Mahuika et al.* v. *New Zealand*, UN Doc. CCPR/C/70/D/547/1993 (27 October 2000), paras. 9.1–9.9 (no breach); *Mavlonov and Sa'di* v. *Uzbekistan*, UN Doc. CCPR/C/95/D/1334/2004 (19 March 2009), paras. 8.6–9 (violation); *Poma* v. *Peru*, UN Doc. CCPR/C/95/D/1457/2006 (27 March 2009), paras. 7.1–8 (violation); *Georgopoulos et al.* v. *Greece*, UN Doc. CCPR/C/99/D/1799/2008 (29 July 2010), paras. 7.1–8 (violation).

[127] See section 7.5.

[128] See for an assessment of its impact, Heyns and Viljoen, above note 56, 15–19.

[129] Reference to this development is made in *Lumanog and Santos* v. *Philippines*, UN Doc. CCPR/C/92/D/1466/2006 (20 March 2008), para. 8.2.

others.[130] The importance of the ICCPR as part of the International Bill of Rights, the nature of issues raised before the Committee and the standing of individual committee members have all contributed to the authority that the HRCtee's jurisprudence generally commands. However, there are several grounds on which the HRCtee's jurisprudence can be, and has been criticised, including by its own members. These include its handling of facts and evidentiary problems – the HRCtee has no fact-finding capacity and relies on written submissions rather than hearings – and the paucity of its reasoning, generally attributed to the limited time and resources available and the search for consensus. Critics also mention taking positions that have far-reaching consequences with limited explanation and reference to the jurisprudence of other bodies.[131]

5.5.3   Breadwinners, social security and discrimination: *Zwaan-de Vries* v. *The Netherlands*

The author, Mrs F. H. Zwaan-de Vries, was denied benefits under the Dutch Unemployment Benefits Act in 1979/1980, which excluded married women 'who were neither breadwinners nor permanently separated from their husbands', but not married men.[132] The legislation had been based on the view that 'all married men who had jobs could be regarded as their family's breadwinner'. In 1985, in implementing an EC Council directive, the Netherlands amended its legislation in order to provide for equal treatment. The author argued that she had been a victim of discrimination (article 26 ICCPR) in relation to social benefits. In response, the state party posed the question of whether the way it had fulfilled its obligations under article 9 (right to social security) in conjunction with articles 2 and 3 ICESCR could become, by way of article 26 ICCPR, the object of an examination by the HRCtee. It further argued that if the Committee were to find article 26 ICCPR applicable, the article would need to be interpreted so as to impose simply an obligation of periodic review to ensure that a state took measures to progressively eliminate discrimination in its national legislation. In addition, the state party claimed that the notion of breadwinner was not discriminatory as the provisions of the Act were 'based on reasonable social and economic considerations which are not discriminatory in origin'.

On the merits, the Committee held that:

---

[130]   A. Nollkaemper and R. van Alebeek, *The Legal Status of Decisions by Human Rights Treaty Bodies in National Law*, ACIL Research Paper no. 2011-02 (11 April 2011), 18–19.

[131]   See for example controversy surrounding the case of *Kennedy* v. *Trinidad and Tobago*, in which the HRCtee denied the validity of Trinidad and Tobago's reservation to the Optional Protocol, including individual, dissenting, opinions of Committee members Nisuke Ando, Prafulachandra N. Bhagwati, Eckart Klein and David Kretzmer, ibid.

[132]   *Zwaan-de Vries* v. *the Netherlands*, paras. 10–16.

article 26 does not merely duplicate the guarantees already provided for in article 2. It derives from the principle of equal protection of the law without discrimination, as contained in article 7 [UDHR], which prohibits discrimination in law or in practice in any field regulated and protected by public authorities. Article 26 is thus concerned with the obligations imposed on States in regard to their legislation and the application thereof…what is at issue is not whether or not social security should be progressively established in the Netherlands but whether the legislation providing for social security violates the prohibition against discrimination contained in article 26 [ICCPR] and the guarantee given therein to all persons regarding equal and effective protection against discrimination. The right to equality before the law and to equal protection of the law without any discrimination does not make all differences of treatment discriminatory. A differentiation based on reasonable and objective criteria does not amount to prohibited discrimination within the meaning of article 26…Under [the Act] a married woman, in order to receive WWV benefits, had to prove that she was a 'breadwinner' – a condition that did not apply to married men. Thus a differentiation which appears on one level to be one of status is in fact one of sex, placing married women at a disadvantage compared with married men. Such a differentiation is not reasonable…

The case sets an important precedent for the interpretation of article 26 ICCPR, giving it a broad scope of application in relation to any legislation, even where the latter purports to regulate social rights. The finding of discrimination was the inevitable consequence of this interpretation given the outdated terms of the law. It was facilitated by the fact that the Netherlands had already changed the very legislation to provide for equal treatment, which constituted an implicit acknowledgement. The Netherlands reacted strongly to the decision and even threatened to withdraw from the Optional Protocol.[133]

While the Netherlands ultimately refrained from denouncing the Optional Protocol, other states such as Jamaica, Guyana and Trinidad and Tobago have done so. It is clear that the HRCtee has to tread a fine balance. The acceptance of its views in a given case, and of the legitimacy of the HRCtee as a quasi-judicial body, depends to a considerable degree on the persuasiveness of its views, which require careful reasoning where they seemingly depart from widely held understandings. *Zwaan-de Vries* v. *The Netherlands* broke important ground in this regard.

5.5.4   Committee on the Elimination of Racial Discrimination

Fifty-four of the 174 states parties had made a declaration under article 14 of the ICERD (recognising CERD's competence to hear individual complaints) as of 2 September 2011.[134] The CERD has considered a much lower number

---

[133] See C. Tomuschat, *Human Rights: Between Idealism and Realism*, 2nd edn (Oxford University Press, 2008), 51–2.

[134] Report of the Committee on the Elimination of Racial Discrimination, UN Doc. A/66/18 (2011), para. 2 and Annex I.

of complaints than the HRCtee (forty-eight as of 2011), which shows that its complaints procedure remains underutilised.[135] The majority of communications have concerned a few states parties only (Australia, Denmark, the Netherlands, Norway, Sweden, Slovakia). As a result, its jurisprudence has to date not fully captured the manifold forms of violations and problems arising in the context of racial discrimination, which has limited its overall impact. Nevertheless, the CERD's decisions have highlighted inadequate responses to racial discrimination and racial hatred, such as the lack of effective investigations of racist incidents in Denmark[136] and the tolerance of hate speech in Norway.[137] The CERD also dealt with cases such as the removal of the word 'Nigger' from a sign put up in an Australian town in 'honour of a well-known sporting and civic personality' (the word 'Nigger' had been the latter's nickname), which reflected that changed perceptions can make the public display of certain words racially offensive.[138] Within the given limitations the CERD's jurisprudence has contributed to the clarification of the notion of racial discrimination, the difference between direct and indirect discrimination and the positive obligations of states in response to (allegations of) racial discrimination, particularly the nature of effective remedies.

5.5.5   Still facing discrimination: *Durmic* v. *Serbia and Montenegro*

In *Koptova* v. *The Slovak Republic* the Committee found that two municipal resolutions banning Romani families from entering the towns concerned constituted a violation of article 5(d)(i) of the Convention (prohibition of discrimination in the enjoyment of civil rights, in particular 'the right to freedom of movement and residence within the border of the State'). In *Ms L. R. et al.* v. *Slovak Republic* (*Dobsina*), the cancellation of a low-cost housing project for Romas following a hostile local petition was found to constitute discrimination in relation to housing in violation of article 5(d)(iii). In both cases there was a lack of effective remedy.[139]

---

[135] Ibid., para. 74.

[136] *Ahmad* v. *Denmark*, UN Doc. CERD/C/56/D/16/1999 (13 March 2000), paras. 6.1–8 (violation of article 6); *Gelle* v. *Denmark*, UN Doc. CERD/C/68/D/34/2004 (6 March 2006) and *Adan* v. *Denmark*, UN Doc. CERD/C/77/D/43/2008 (14 August 2010), both paras. 7.1–8 (both violations of articles 2(1)(d), 4, 6); *Dawas and Yousef Shava* v. *Denmark*, UN Doc. CERD/C/80/D/46/2009 (6 March 2012), paras. 7.1–8 (violation of articles 6 and 2(1)(d)). See also *L. K.* v. *Netherlands*, Communication no. 4/1991 (16 March 1993), paras. 6–6.8 (lack of diligent investigation into threats of racial violence – violation of articles 6, 4).

[137] *The Jewish Community of Oslo* v. *Norway*, UN Doc. CERD/C/67/D/30/2003 (15 August 2005), paras. 10.1–11 (violation of articles 4, 6).

[138] *Hagan* v. *Australia*, UN Doc. CERD/C/62/D/26/2002 (20 March 2003), paras. 7.1–7.4 (articles 2(1)(c), 5, 6, 7 – violation).

[139] *Koptova* v. *Slovak Republic*, UN Doc. CERD/C/57/D/13/1998 (8 August 2000), and *Ms L. R. et al.* v. *Slovak Republic (Dobsina)*, UN Doc. CERD/C/66/D/31/2003 (7 March 2005).

In *Durmic* v. *Serbia and Montenegro*

in 2000 the Humanitarian Law Center (HLC) carried out a series of 'tests' across Serbia, to establish whether members of the Roma minority were being discriminated against while attempting to access public places. It was prompted to such action by numerous complaints alleging that the Roma were denied access to clubs, discotheques, restaurants, cafes and/or swimming pools, on the basis of their ethnic origin ... two Roma individuals ... and three non-Roma individuals, attempted to gain access to a discotheque in Belgrade. All were neatly dressed, well behaved and were not under the influence of alcohol. Thus, the only apparent difference between them was the colour of their skin. There was no notice displayed to the effect that a private party was being held and that they could not enter without showing an invitation. The two individuals of Roma origin were denied entry to the club on the basis that it was a private party and they did not have invitations. When the petitioner asked the security guard how he could obtain an invitation there and then, he was told that it was not possible and that the invitations were not for sale ... The three non-Roma individuals were all allowed to enter, despite having no invitations for the so called private party and making this clear to the security personnel at the time.

A criminal complaint submitted to the Public Prosecutor to investigate a case of racial discrimination did not result in any prosecution and a case brought before the Constitutional Court remained pending for over fifteen months without any response. Following a detailed discussion of challenges to admissibility the Committee found a violation of articles 5(f) and 6 of the Convention, holding, *inter alia*, that:

The State party has ... failed to establish whether the petitioner had been refused access to a public place, on grounds of his national or ethnic origin in violation of article 5(f) of the Convention. Owing to the police's failure to carry out any thorough investigation into the matter, the failure of the public prosecutor to reach any conclusion and the failure of the Court of Serbia and Montenegro even to set a date for the consideration of the case some six years after the incident, the petitioner has been denied any opportunity to establish whether his rights under the Convention had been violated.

The decisions cast an important spotlight on racial discrimination against the Roma, demonstrating a pattern in which discriminatory acts are followed by wholly inadequate responses of the authorities and judicial systems, effectively denying legal protection. They added to the growing evidence of the systemic nature of this group-specific discrimination in the region and form an important part of broader efforts to combat discrimination and the 'rightlessness' of the Roma.[140]

---

[140] See in this regard in particular the work of the European Roma Rights Centre, www.errc.org.

5.5.6 Committee against Torture

The competence of the CtAT to hear individual complaints pursuant to article 22 CAT has been recognised by 64 of the 147 states parties as of 3 June 2011.[141] The CtAT had dealt with 462 individual communications as of 6 June 2011, finding 60 violations in the 324 concluded cases concerning twenty-nine states.[142] The majority of complaints have concerned alleged violations of article 3 (*refoulement*) brought mainly against Australia, Canada, France, the Netherlands, Sweden and Switzerland. The CtAT's jurisprudence on article 3 includes several important decisions, including in the context of renditions[143] and in relation to situations where the risk of torture or ill treatment emanates from non-state actors (Somalia).[144] The Committee has also specified states parties' obligation to investigate allegations of torture effectively and to provide reparation, including in several cases against Serbia and Montenegro, Spain and Tunisia, which highlighted systemic shortcomings.[145] It also considered the issue of acquiescence in respect of a state's failure to protect individuals against violence by non-state actors, namely mob violence against a Roma settlement in Montenegro.[146] In addition the CtAT has ruled on the scope of universal jurisdiction as part of the ramifications of the *Habré* case, the former Chadian president, accused of being responsible for international crimes, who had fled to Senegal, which has engaged several treaty bodies and courts.[147] These cases show the potential of CtAT to contribute to the jurisprudence on the prohibition of torture, particularly if

---

[141] Report of the CtAT, UN Doc. A/66/44 (2011), paras. 1, 2 and Annexes I and III.

[142] Statistical survey of individual complaints considered, www2.ohchr.org/english/bodies/cat/procedure.htm.

[143] Return to Egypt was considered a violation of article 3 in *Agiza* v. *Sweden*, UN Doc. CAT/C/34/D/233/2003 (20 May 2005), paras. 13.1–14 (see case study below), but not in *Attia* v. *Sweden*, UN Doc. CAT/C/31/D/199/2002 (17 November 2003), para 12.1–13.

[144] *Elmi* v. *Australia*, UN Doc. CAT/C/22/D/120/1998 (14 May 1999), paras. 6.4–7 (violation of article 3).

[145] *Nikolic* v. *Serbia and Montenegro*, UN Doc. CAT/C/35/D/174/2000 (24 November 2005), paras. 6.2–7 (violation of articles 12, 13); *Dimitrijevic* v. *Serbia and Montenegro*, UN Doc. CAT/C/33/D/207/2002 (24 November 2004), paras. 5.3–6 (violations of articles 2(1), 1, 12, 13, 14); *Guridi* v. *Spain*, UN Doc. CAT/C/34/D/212/2002 (17 May 2005), paras. 6.4–7 (violation of articles 2, 4, 14); *Bouabdallah Latief* v. *Tunisia*, UN Doc. CAT/C/31/D/189/2001 (14 November 2003), paras. 10.3–11 (violation of articles 12, 13); *Keremedchiev* v. *Bulgaria*, UN Doc. CAT/C/41/D/257/2004 (11 November 2008), paras. 9.2–10 (violation of articles 12, 16); *Hanafi* v. *Algeria*, UN Doc. CAT/C/46/D/341/2008 (3 June 2011), paras. 9.1–10 (violation of articles 1, 2(1), 11, 12, 13, 14); *Sonko* v. *Spain*, UN Doc. CAT/C/47/D/368/2008 (25 November 2011), paras. 10.1–10.8 (violation of articles 12 and 16).

[146] *Hajrizi Dzemajil et al.* v. *Serbia and Montenegro*, UN Doc. CAT/C/29/D/161/2000 (21 November 2002), paras. 9.1–10 (violation of articles 16, 12, 13). See also *Osmani* v. *Serbia*, UN Doc. CAT/C/42/D/261/2005 (8 May 2009), paras. 10.3–11 (violation of articles 16, 12, 13).

[147] *Guengueng* v. *Senegal*, UN Doc. CAT/C/36/D/181/2001 (17 May 2006), paras. 9.1–9.12 (violation of article 7 and 5(2)). See also section 7.7.

it engages in more in-depth considerations of the normative questions posed in a given case rather than their cursory treatment that is characteristic of some of its decisions.

5.5.7   Rendered defenceless: *Agiza* v. *Sweden*

In 1998 Ahmed Hussein Mustafa Kamil Agiza, an Egyptian national, was tried *in absentia*, convicted and sentenced to twenty-five years' imprisonment for belonging to a terrorist group. In 2000 he claimed asylum in Sweden. Following the views of the Swedish security police the government denied him asylum. According to an investigation by the Parliamentary Ombudsman he was deported to Egypt in 2001 on an aircraft provided by the American Central Intelligence Agency. The complainant alleged that he was tortured by the Egyptian state security officers upon his return. After finding the complaint admissible, on the merits, the Committee considered in detail whether there was a substantial risk of torture upon the complainant's return, finding that:

> it was known, or should have been known, to the State party's authorities at the time of the complainant's removal that Egypt resorted to consistent and widespread use of torture against detainees, and that the risk of such treatment was particularly high in the case of detainees held for political and security reasons ... It follows that the state party's expulsion of the complainant was in breach of article 3 of the Convention. The procurement of diplomatic assurances, which, moreover, provided no mechanism for their enforcement, did not suffice to protect against this manifest risk.

Importantly, in its assessment of the procedural dimension of article 3, the Committee found that

> in order to reinforce the protection of the norm in question and understanding the Convention consistently, the prohibition on refoulement contained in article 3 should be interpreted the same way to encompass a remedy for its breach, even though it may not contain on its face such a right to remedy for a breach thereof ... The nature of refoulement is such, however, that an allegation of breach of that article relates to a future expulsion or removal; accordingly, the right to an effective remedy contained in article 3 requires, in this context, an opportunity for effective, independent and impartial review of the decision to expel or remove, once that decision is made, when there is a plausible allegation that article 3 issues arise.

On the facts, the Committee found that the lack of judicial or independent administrative review of the government's decision to expel the complainant constituted a breach of article 3 CAT and that the state party had also violated its duty under article 22 CAT to cooperate with the Committee.

Agiza v. *Sweden* set an important precedent in the jurisprudence on renditions, showing how states' security cooperation undermines the prohibition of *refoulement* and exposes individuals to the risk of torture.[148] It proved to be influential in cases before other human rights treaty bodies, particularly the largely similar *Alzery* case decided by the HRCtee.[149] Most importantly for the interpretation of CAT, the Committee read a general procedural obligation to provide an effective remedy into article 3 and the Convention as a whole, thereby strengthening legal protection, particularly against future violations.

5.5.8   The Committee on the Elimination of Discrimination against Women

A hundred of 186 states parties had recognised the competence of the CtEDAW to hear complaints under the optional protocol as of 4 February 2011.[150] The CtEDAW assumed its function of considering individual complaints in 2001. It had decided relatively few cases (twenty-three) by March 2012 and these concerned a limited number of states parties, with Hungary, Austria, the Philippines, Bulgaria, Belarus, Brazil, Peru, Canada and Turkey found to have violated their obligations under the treaty. The CtEDAW's jurisprudence has primarily addressed positive obligations, particularly the duty to take effective action to provide protection against domestic violence.[151] The Committee dealt with a case on involuntary sterilisation of a Roma woman, which highlighted the intersection between racial and gender-based discrimination.[152] It has also recognised intersectional discrimination in access to health care as a violation,[153] and in the case of an aboriginal woman who did not have effective legal protection when seeking to regain her property.[154] The CtEDAW has strengthened reproductive rights in a case where a girl who had become pregnant as a result of sexual abuse was denied surgery.[155] In addition, it has addressed stereotyping in employment matters and criminal proceedings (*Vertido* v. *Philippines*, see below).[156]

---

[148] See section 15.8.   [149] *Alzery* v. *Sweden.*

[150] Report of the Committee on the Elimination of Discrimination against Women, UN Doc. A/66/38 (2011), 145, paras. 1–2.

[151] *Yildrim* v. *Austria*, UN Doc. CEDAW/C/39/D/6/2005 (6 August 2007) and *Goekce* v. *Austria*, UN Doc. CEDAW/C/39/D/5/2005 (6 August 2007), both paras. 12.1–12.2 (violation of article 2(a), (c)–(f), 3, 1); *V. K.* v. *Bulgaria*, UN Doc. CEDAW/C/49/D/20/2008 (25 July 2011), paras. 9.1–9.15 (violation of article 2(c), (d), (e) and (f), article 1, and article 5(a), 16(1)).

[152] *A. T.* v. *Hungary*, UN Doc. CEDAW/C/32/D/2/2003 (26 January 2005), paras. 9.1–9.6 (violation of articles 2(a), (b), (e), 5(a), 16).

[153] *Teixeira* v. *Brazil*, UN Doc. CEDAW/C/49/D/17/2008 (25 July 2011), paras. 7.1–8 (violation of articles 12, 2(c), (e), 1).

[154] *Kell* v. *Canada*, UN Doc. CEDAW/C/51/D/19/2008 (28 February 2012), paras. 10.1–11 (violation of articles 2(d) and (e), 16(1) and 1).

[155] *L. C.* v. *Peru*, UN Doc. CEDAW/C/50/D/22/2009 (17 October 2011), paras. 8.6–9 (violation of articles 2(c), (f), 3, 5, 12, 1).

[156] *R. K. B.* v. *Turkey*, UN Doc. CEDAW/C/51/D/28/2010 (24 February 2012), paras. 8.1–8.10 (violation of articles 2(a), (c) and 1, 5(a), 11(1)(a) and (d)).

The importance of the Convention in the custodial context was underscored in a case concerning humiliating treatment of women and conditions in detention facilities.[157] The nature of these cases and the approach taken by the Committee hint at the important role that it can play in strengthening the rights of women in international human rights law.

5.5.9 'We don't believe you': *Vertido* v. *The Philippines*

Karen Tayag Vertido alleged that she had been raped by the former president of the Davao City Chamber of Commerce and Industry in March 1996. She underwent a medical examination and complained to the police. The case eventually reached a trial court where it remained pending from 1997 to 2005.[158] Two experts testified that the author suffered from post-traumatic stress disorder due to the rape. There were no further witnesses and the accused claimed 'that the sexual intercourse was consensual'. In April 2005 the Regional Court of Davao City acquitted the accused, relying on several criteria established in a previous Supreme Court ruling.

After finding the case admissible the CtEDAW considered

the author's allegations that gender-based myths and misconceptions about rape and rape victims were relied on by Judge Hofileña-Europa in the Regional Court of Davao City in its decision ... leading to the acquittal of the alleged perpetrator, and will determine whether this amounted to a violation of the rights of the author and a breach of the corresponding state party's obligations to end discrimination in the legal process under articles 2(c), 2(f) and 5(a) of the Convention.

It found that the length of the trial breached the author's right to a remedy in relation to article 2(c), stating 'while acknowledging that the text of the Convention does not expressly provide for a right to a remedy, [it] considers that such a right is implied in the Convention'. Further, '[t]he Committee finds that one of [the guiding principles applied in the case], in particular, according to which "an accusation for rape can be made with facility", reveals in itself a gender bias...' Moreover,

[i]t is clear from the judgement that the assessment of the credibility of the author's version of events was influenced by a number of stereotypes, the author in this situation not having followed what was expected from a rational and 'ideal victim' or what the judge considered to be the rational and ideal response of a woman in a rape situation ... [the author had reacted 'both with resistance at one time and submission at another time', which the judge saw as contradictory]. Further misconceptions are to be found in the decision of the Court, which contains several references to stereotypes about male and

---

[157] *Abramova* v. *Belarus*, UN Doc. CEDAW/C/49/23/2009 (25 July 2011), paras. 7.1–8 (violation of articles 2, 5(a)).

[158] *Vertido* v. *The Philippines*, UN Doc. CEDAW/C/46/D/18/2008 (16 July 2010), paras. 8.1–8.9 (violation of article 2(c), (f), 5(a),1).

female sexuality being more supportive for the credibility of the alleged perpetrator than for the credibility of the victim.

Moreover, '[w]ith regard to the definition of rape, the Committee notes that the lack of consent is not an essential element of the definition of rape in the Philippines Revised Penal Code ... [emphasising] that rape constitutes a violation of women's right to personal security and bodily integrity and that its essential element was lack of consent'. The Committee then recommended that the state party pay compensation to the author and undertake far-reaching reforms in its legislation on rape and procedures in rape cases, including

training for judges, lawyers, law enforcement officers and medical personnel in understanding crimes of rape and other sexual offences in a gender-sensitive manner so as to avoid revictimization of women having reported rape cases and to ensure that personal mores and values do not affect decision-making.

The views of the Committee provide an anatomy of how a legal system fails rape victims. Given the prevalence of gender stereotypes worldwide the decision reaffirms the Committee's understanding of rape and clarifies states parties' obligation to treat rape cases in an expeditious and non-discriminatory manner. While not explicitly referring to it, the case can be viewed in light of judgments by other bodies, such as the ECtHR in *M. C.* v. *Bulgaria*, in which states failed in their positive obligation to adequately respond to rape allegations. It therefore forms part of a growing jurisprudence that both exposes domestic failings in rape cases and helps in developing best practices.

5.5.10   Achievements and challenges

The individual complaints procedure before international treaty bodies has contributed to the development of international human rights law. It has also provided some form of remedy for individuals and brought about changes as a result of subsequent implementation.[159] However, several treaty bodies, such as the CERD, the CtAT and the CtEDAW, remain underutilised. Ironically, this development also shields them to some degree from the opposite problem, namely an increasing caseload that would adversely affect the effectiveness of complaints procedures.

Several crucial areas remain unaddressed in the current system of complaints procedures. This applies in particular to ECSR, which is bound to change with the (eventual) coming into force of the Optional Protocol to the ICESCR.[160] An individual complaints procedure for children's rights will also constitute an important contribution to the system, not least because it

---

[159] See section 7.5.

[160] As of May 2012, eight states had become parties to the Optional Protocol. For a discussion of this procedure, see section 9.6.1.

has the potential to let children themselves more clearly articulate their best interests.[161] However, an increase in existing complaints procedures will pose a challenge in its own right, particularly for the coherence and capacity of the system to ensure effective rights protection.

The recourse to individual complaints procedures has increased to 478 communications pending examination as of 1 February 2012 compared to 214 in 2000. In response, the OHCHR proposed a series of measures, particularly aligning working approaches by means of common practices to strengthen the system of individual complaints procedures, inquiries and country visits.[162] The challenges facing the system run deeper than operational matters. Their function as expert bodies that examine complaints on a part-time basis without having public hearings or undertaking fact-finding, and which issue decisions that often do not attract great visibility and are repeatedly not complied with, limits their effectiveness. This is particularly evident in the lack of implementation. Treaty bodies have sought to address this problem by strengthening follow-up procedures, including by means of follow-up rapporteurs, though with limited success to date.[163] While important, these top-down measures may on their own be insufficient to enhance implementation. As highlighted by observers, making the complaints procedure an effective and meaningful remedy for victims and an advocacy tool will require broader changes to the system, focusing particularly on its relevance in the domestic context.[164]

INTERVIEW 5.2
Working for the CESCR
(Eibe Riedel)

Dr Eibe Riedel is Professor Emeritus and Visiting Professor at the Geneva Academy of International Humanitarian Law and Human Rights, previously having taught public law and international law at several universities in Germany, Britain, Switzerland and Australia. Among a number of other positions held, he has been a member of the UN Committee on Economic,

---

[161] 'On 19 December 2011, the UN General Assembly approved a third optional protocol on a Communications Procedure which will allow individual children to submit complaints regarding specific violations of their rights under the Convention and its first two optional protocols. The Protocol opens for signature in 2012 and will enter into force upon ratification by 10 UN Member States.' See www2.ohchr.org/english/bodies/crc.

[162] Pillay, above note 20, 68–74.

[163] See Open Society Justice Initiative, *From Judgment to Justice, Implementing International and Regional Human Rights Decisions* (New York: Open Society Foundations, 2010), 117–36.

[164] See section 7.5.

Social and Cultural Rights since 1997, with his term due to expire on 31 December 2012.

How would you describe your experience as a member of the Committee on Economic, Social and Cultural Rights – rewarding, frustrating, or a bit of both?

A bit of both, but mainly rewarding. And a lot of work.

The reporting procedure has been much maligned; how do you assess its effectiveness and prospects for its strengthening or more fundamental reforms?

This is a very broad question that cannot be answered easily. With permanent cuts in financial resources for all the treaty bodies, any method of strengthening the system seems flawed. What is needed in the medium term is a proper reform of the entire system towards a unified treaty body monitoring. After initial failure in 2004, this real reform drive has to start soon – with ten treaty bodies making the whole process cumbersome, unwieldy, and at times repetitive and unfocused – both in the state reporting and during the committee questionings. If work started on reforms now, I reckon it would take about ten years to achieve it.

Do General Comments sometimes play the role of a Trojan horse for fundamental reinterpretations of treaty provisions or general rules of international law. If so, where are the limits?

Sometimes they may indeed give the appearance of Trojan horses – but the process is really quite transparent. The issue remains how far interpretation can go. Views differ considerably as to how far interpretation (legitimate) and acting like a legislator (illegitimate) can go. My own view is that General Comments should only interpret the Committee's approach in dialogues with states parties, explaining the meaning of terms used in the ICESCR. But sometimes, newer developments have to be taken on board, like the issue of the right to water, deduced from articles 11 and 12 ICESCR. By way of example, maybe have a look at the CESCR statement on resource allocation and the standard of reasonableness and proportionality in the Committee's work, adopted a little while ago when the Optional Protocol was discussed[1] to explain how far the Committee can go and what the 'margin of appreciation/discretion' of states parties really entails.

Considering the procedure under the Optional Protocol to the ICESCR, the question of justiciability, and the experience of other UN treaty bodies with individual complaints procedures, what do you see as the

---

[1] See www2.ohchr.org/english/bodies/cescr/docs/statements/Obligationtotakesteps-2007.pdf.

main challenges and prospects for the Committee once the optional protocol comes into force?

Again a very big question.[2] In a nutshell: the Committee should take great care not to overstep its role once the Optional Protocol is in force (we need two more ratifications) with forty signatures at the moment. It would be wise to choose micro-level issues first and to keep away from macro-issues like the extraterritorial application of ICESCR rights, or poverty generally, or environment protection issues on a large scale. This would definitely frighten off many states from ratifying. The fact that a reference to article 1 of both Covenants – which never played a role in the practice of the HRCtee – was kept in the Optional Protocol, despite no treaty body practice on it, will frighten off many countries that have large minorities and self-determination problems. In 2008 about fifty states voiced clear objections to that issue in an individual communications procedure. Those macro-questions should be left to the HRC, the General Assembly, ECOSOC or even to the Security Council. In fact, the CESCR only refers to self-determination occasionally in the state reporting procedure and then usually in conjunction with a particular Part III article.

Once the Optional Protocol is in force and in operation (first cases to come about two years after the exhaustion of local remedies, optimistically in 2014, if the Optional Protocol enters into force in 2012) I expect that interpretation of the broadly and vaguely formulated Covenant provisions will be easier and help to focus discussions, as happened with the Optional Protocol to the ICCPR. To be successful the cases dealt with have to be really convincing individual – or groups of individuals – cases, showing clear violations in order to attract proper worldwide attention. I would warn against overambitiousness, at least at the beginning, because that would scare off many potential ratifiers.

What role do NGOs play as users of the system and as critical supporters of the Committee on Economic, Social and Cultural Rights?

NGOs continue to play a crucial role in the whole procedure(s). But sometimes, they overdo it; for example, by raising budget issues in a very broad manner or by negating discretionary powers of states in making policy choices. When NGOs provide carefully drafted alternative or parallel reports Committee members find them really helpful. Sometimes, though, they are one-issue overstatements, or even alternative government positions, of the opposition that may just have lost a general election. But the information is crucial, anyway, for the Committee to do its work

---

[2] See E. Riedel, 'New Bearings to Social Rights: the Communications Procedure under the ICESCR', in U. Fastenrath *et al.*, *From Bilateralism to Community Interest, Essays in Honour of Bruno Simma* (Oxford University Press, 2011), 574–89.

properly. Civil society has been excellent in propagating Henry Shue's triple obligations, as popularised by Asbjoern Eide, 'respect, protect, fulfil', which by now most states know of and accept almost without opposition, even though the Covenant is silent on that issue.

POINTS TO CONSIDER

- Have UN treaty bodies played a leading role in the development of international human rights law?
- Is the proliferation of individual complaints procedures the way forward or is it time for a radical rethink? What are the issues that a more effective system should address?
- How do the practical challenges facing treaty bodies affect their legitimacy?

FURTHER READING

Alen, A. *et al.* (eds.), *A Commentary on the United Nations Convention on the Rights of the Child* (Leiden, Boston: Martinus Nijhoff, 2005).

Baderin, M. and McCorquodale, R., 'The International Covenant on Economic, Social and Cultural Rights: Forty Years of Development', in Baderin and McCorquodale (eds.), *Economic, Social and Cultural Rights in Action* (Oxford University Press, 2007), pp. 3–24.

Keller, H. and Ulfstein, G., *UN Human Rights Treaty Bodies: Law and Legitimacy* (Cambridge University Press, 2012).

Langford, M. (ed.), *Social Rights Jurisprudence: Emerging Trends in International and Comparative Law* (Cambridge University Press, 2008) (various contributions on the role of several committees).

McGoldrick, D., *The Human Rights Committee: Its Role in the Development of the International Covenant on Civil and Political Rights*, 2nd edn. (Oxford: Clarendon Press, 1994).

Nowak, M., *UN Covenant on Civil and Political Rights: CCPR Commentary*, 2nd edn (Kehl am Rhein: Engels, 2005).

Nowak, M. and McArthur, E., *The United Nations Convention against Torture: A Commentary* (Oxford University Press, 2008).

Schöpp-Schilling, H. B. and Flinterman, C. (eds.), *The Circle of Empowerment: Twenty-Five Years of the UN Committee on the Elimination of Discrimination Against Women* (New York: The Feminist Press, 2007).

Sohn, L. B. and Buergenthal, T., *International Protection of Human Rights* (Indianapolis: Bobbs-Merrill, 1973).

Wolfrum, R., 'The Committee on the Elimination of Racial Discrimination', *MPYBUNL* 3 (1999), 489–519.

Websites

UN: www.un.org (main UN organs).

OHCHR: www.ohchr.org (providing links to all human rights treaty and charter bodies, i.e. HRC and Special Procedures, country specific documents; text of international treaties and status of ratification).

Universal Human Rights Index Database: www.ohchr.org/EN/HRBodies/Pages/ UniversalHumanRightsIndexDatabase.aspx (provides easy access to country-specific human rights information emanating from international human rights mechanisms in the United Nations system: the treaty bodies, the special procedures and the UPR).

6 Regional human rights treaty systems

CONTENTS

6.1 INTRODUCTION

Initial concerns that regional human rights systems may undermine the universality of rights have largely given way to a more positive appreciation of their beneficial role.[1] Regional human rights systems provide a crucial layer of protection. They are closely connected with regional political developments and integration which potentially gives them more traction than the UN system. Moreover, increasing references to their jurisprudence and practice evince how they contribute to, and enrich, international human rights law.

An examination of regional human rights systems suggests the following typical process. States agree on the need for closer regional cooperation if not integration. Human rights are accepted as one element of, and a yardstick for, the regional political order. A foundational human rights instrument is adopted. Further, a human rights body with a mandate to promote human rights and monitor states parties' compliance with their treaty obligations is set up. Over time, responding to demands and with a view to strengthening the effectiveness and credibility of the system, substantive rights are broadened and the role of victims (and others, particularly NGOs) in raising the

---

[1] See Vienna Declaration and Programme of Action, UN Doc. A/CONF.157/23 (12 July 1993), para. 37.

issue of, or complaining about, human rights violations is enhanced. As the system matures this momentum eventually results in the establishment of a judicial body. Parallel efforts to foster regional political integration reinforce the importance of human rights at all levels as a marker of the system's ability to provide a stable order based on the rule of law and the protection of fundamental rights.

The European, Inter-American and African human rights systems share a number of these idealised features, which indicates that there is a pull to develop a stronger normative framework and monitoring mechanisms. However, a look at their development demonstrates that these goals are not always shared across a region (see for example the ambiguous role of the USA in the Inter-American system). Regional political support for human rights systems can vary considerably, which may in turn affect the latter's effectiveness. Moreover, a focus on institutional features where the availability of a judicial body is often equated with a strong system may obscure what is one of its fundamental tasks, namely contributing to the development of a regional human rights culture and enhanced domestic protection. Lawyers, NGOs, human rights defenders, the media, like-minded politicians and states all play a crucial role in this context in using and developing regional instruments to transform them into living systems that make a positive impact, particularly at the national level.

Regional human rights systems, being simultaneously creatures and 'masters' of states, and frequently forming part of broader political dynamics, face a number of common challenges. These include: (1) the existence of an adequate legal and institutional framework; (2) the capacity of bodies to fulfil their mandate effectively; (3) their responsiveness to human rights violations, particularly systematic and massive violations; (4) effectiveness in ensuring compliance; and (5) their ability to contribute to regional acceptance of and respect for human rights. The effectiveness of a system depends to a large degree on its legitimacy, that is the authority it commands, which in turn requires that a sufficient number of states are supportive. The persuasiveness of responses by the relevant bodies, both in relation to individual cases and systemic problems, their awareness of political realities and their ability to fashion a human rights culture that reflects regional features and offers space for national actors are all critical in this regard.

Assessments of the record of regional human rights systems vary considerably. They range from being a driving force for the advancement of human rights to being essentially conservative and ineffective because of their limited ability to respond to gross and systematic violations, accommodating the position of states and the lack of strong enforcement powers.[2] In practice,

---

[2] See O. C. Okafor, *The African Human Rights System, Activist Forces and International Institutions* (Cambridge University Press, 2007), 67–90, for a critical review and analysis of positions, particularly in the African context.

normative and institutional developments testify to the continuing relevance of regional human rights systems, as is evident in the growing recourse to them. Indeed, one of the major challenges for regional human rights bodies is that they are at risk of becoming a victim of their own success; it is in particular the capacity problems encountered that raise serious questions about their effectiveness. It is against this background that this chapter examines the historical development, legal framework, institutional set-up and practice, as well as the impact and challenges facing the major regional human rights system today. It also examines the prospects for their development in various parts of Asia, which to date have no, or only extremely weak, systems in place.

6.2   THE EUROPEAN HUMAN RIGHTS SYSTEM

6.2.1   Overview

The ECHR and the ECtHR[3] are the cornerstones of the larger European human rights architecture that has been developed largely under the aegis of the CoE.[4] Forming part of regional responses to World War II, the CoE was established in 1949 in a process driven by France, Italy, the UK, Ireland and the Benelux and Scandinavian countries.[5] It constitutes the main European intergovernmental political body, with the Committee of Ministers (CoM) and the Parliamentary Assembly as its main organs. The CoE's aim 'to achieve a greater unity between its members for the purpose of safeguarding and realising the ideals and principles which are their common heritage and facilitating their economic and social progress' is to be pursued 'by agreements and common action ... in the maintenance and further realisation of human rights and fundamental freedoms'.[6] Crucially, CoE membership is made conditional upon acceptance of the rule of law and human rights.[7] This was part of an essentially political project of liberal Western European states to create a stable political order which was also developed as a contrasting model to Communist countries at the time.[8] Today, the CoE is the primary body in the field of human rights, both in terms of standard-setting and monitoring. It has developed into an impressive system with forty-seven member states,

---

[3] www.echr.coe.int.   [4] www.coe.int.

[5] See in particular E. Bates, *The Evolution of the European Convention on Human Rights: From its Inception to the Creation of a Permanent Court of Human Rights* (Oxford University Press, 2010). See on the CoE, J. Petaux, *Democracy and Human Rights for Europe: The Council of Europe's Contribution* (Strasbourg: Council of Europe, 2009), and R. Kicker (ed.), *Pioneer and Guarantor for Human Rights* (Strasbourg: Council of Europe, 2010).

[6] Article 1 Statute of the Council of Europe 1949.   [7] Article 3, ibid.

[8] See Bates, above note 5, 5–8.

having witnessed a substantial expansion following the disintegration of the Soviet Union, and now includes states in Eastern Europe, the Caucasus, Turkey, Ukraine and Russia, with Belarus and Kazakhstan being the only non-member states in the region.

A number of human rights treaties were developed within the CoE setting and adopted by its CoM. The ECHR, which was adopted in 1950 and entered into force in 1953, largely focused on civil and political rights and was influenced by the UDHR, which is referred to in its preamble. Significantly, in the light of recurring opposition to the ECHR and the ECtHR in the UK, it was a conservative British lawyer, Sir David Maxwell-Fyfe, who played a leading role in the drafting.[9]

The almost exclusive focus on civil and political rights in the ECHR reflects its political outlook, and bias, at the time. Partly responding to this lacuna, the CoE adopted the European Social Charter on 18 October 1961, with the European Committee of Social Rights becoming its main supervisory body. The charter's aim was to secure 'the enjoyment of social rights ... without discrimination' (preamble), with a strong focus on the right to work. However, this aim was compromised by its selective approach which allows states to opt for a certain number of articles that they agree to be bound by.[10] The adoption and acceptance of the charter therefore came at the expense of a unified normative framework. This fact, together with limited visibility, undermined its potential to strengthen ESC rights, which still play a secondary role in the European system.[11] Other treaties followed, particularly the European Convention for the Prevention of Torture (1987), which developed into an important preventive mechanism supervised by the European Committee for the Prevention of Torture and Inhuman or Degrading Treatment or Punishment (CPT) [12] which provided the impetus for the UN OPCAT. The European Charter for Regional and Minorities Languages (1992) and the Framework Convention for the Protection of National Minorities (1995),

---

[9] See A. Donald, J. Gordon and P. Leach, *The UK and the European Court of Human Rights*, UK Equality and Human Rights Commission Research report 83 (London: Metropolitan University, Human Rights and Social Justice Research Institute, 2011), 8–9.

[10] Article 20(1) European Social Charter, 1961, and Part III, article A(1) of the European Social Charter (Revised), 1996. See section 9.6.2.

[11] See D. Harris and J. D. Arcy, *The European Social Charter: The Protection of Economic and Social Rights in Europe*, 2nd edn (New York: Transnational Publishers, 2001), and G. de Búrca, B. de Witte and L. Ogertschnig (eds.), *Social Rights in Europe* (Oxford University Press, 2005), particularly Part II. See for a critical account, T. Novitz, 'Remedies for Violations of Social Rights within the Council of Europe: the Significant Absence of a Court', in C. Kilpatrick, T. Novitz and P. Skidmore (eds.), *The Future of Remedies in Europe* (Oxford: Hart, 2000), 231–52, at 232–5.

[12] www.cpt.coe.int. See for reflections combined with a practical account of its work, A. Cassese, *Inhuman States: Imprisonment, Detention and Torture in Europe Today* (Cambridge: Polity Press, 1996).

whose implementation is monitored by the CoM, represent further important instruments. In the wake of the dramatic political changes on the continent in the late 1980s and the early 1990s, the Framework Convention recognises the importance of the rights of minorities and provided a framework for their regional protection.[13] Beyond the CoE, the EU (see below at 6.2.8) and the OSCE have played important roles in addressing questions of human rights protection in Europe within their respective mandates.[14]

6.2.2 European Convention on Human Rights

The ECHR recognises key political and civil rights, including: (1) rights of an absolute nature, i.e. the prohibition of torture, slavery and forced labour and the prohibition of retroactive punishment which cannot be derogated from in times of emergency (article 15); (2) non-derogable rights that are subject to limited exceptions, namely the right to life (article 2); (3) rights that may be derogated from within limits, such as the right to liberty and security (article 5), and the right to a fair trial (article 6); and (4) qualified rights, that is the right to privacy, freedom to manifest one's religion or beliefs,[15] freedom of expression as well as the right to peaceful assembly and to association guaranteed in articles 8–11 respectively. The Convention obliges all states parties (called High Contracting Parties) to secure these rights within their jurisdictions (article 1). This entails both negative (for example to refrain from torture) and positive obligations, as stipulated, for example, in article 2(1) on the right to life ('protected by law'), and, more broadly, as inherent in the right to a fair trial in article 6. Significantly, the ECHR requires states to provide an effective remedy in case of breach of any of the Convention rights (article 13).

However, there were several notable omissions in the scope of rights initially recognised in the Convention, which necessitated the adoption of a number of subsequent protocols. The first of these (1952) recognised – in a rather curious mixture – the right to property, the right to education and the right to free elections. Further protocols mainly concerned criminal justice matters and the scope of the right to a fair trial, including the prohibition of imprisonment for debt, the right of appeal in criminal matters, compensation for wrongful conviction and the right not to be punished twice, thereby closing some of the existing gaps compared to other treaties, such as the

---

[13] M. Weller (ed.), *The Rights of Minorities: A Commentary on the European Framework Convention for the Protection of National Minorities* (Oxford University Press, 2005); A. Verstichel *et al.* (eds.), *The Framework Convention for the Protection of National Minorities: A Useful Pan-European Instrument?* (Antwerp: Intersentia, 2008).

[14] www.osce.org. See for the nature of its work, OSCE, *Annual Report 2011*, and D. J. Gaelbreath, *The Organisation for Security and Cooperation in Europe* (London, New York: Routledge, 2007).

[15] Note that article 9(1) ECHR does not allow interference with the internal aspect of the freedom to hold thoughts and beliefs.

ICCPR.[16] Freedom of movement, the prohibition of expulsion of nationals and of collective expulsion of aliens, as well as procedural safeguards relating to the expulsion of aliens, were also recognised.[17] Significantly, the CoE also took steps to abolish the death penalty, which was implicitly recognised in article 2(1) ECHR. Protocol no. 6 (1983) abolished the death penalty save in time of war and Protocol no. 13 (2002) brought the process to a conclusion with the complete abolition of the death penalty. A further notable addition is Protocol no. 12, which recognises the general prohibition of discrimination, thereby going beyond article 14 ECHR, which only applies to non-discrimination in relation to the rights granted in the Convention.[18] While the adoption of these protocols has largely addressed the normative gaps evident in the ECHR it has contributed to a fragmentation of the system; as treaties, the protocols are subject to separate ratification, which has been uneven in practice and has resulted in different levels of protection.[19]

6.2.3 Key institutions

The European supervisory mechanism is effectively a complaints procedure, providing for both individual and inter-state complaints. The original system consisted of (1) a European Commission of Human Rights, which was created in 1954 and was competent to receive individual complaints and to bring them before the Court where states had recognised its competence to do so; (2) the ECtHR, which became operational in 1959 and could hear inter-state cases and individual complaints brought before it by the Commission provided the state concerned had accepted its jurisdiction; and (3) the CoM responsible for the enforcement of judgments. In this model, the Commission effectively acted as a quasi-judicial filter for cases to be brought before the ECtHR as a judicial body.[20] The Commission played a leading role in the development of the system and issued some landmark decisions, notably its report on the *Greek* case in 1969 in response to a series of violations committed by the then Greek dictatorship (1967–74).[21] However, a growing caseload that had resulted from a greater awareness and a significant increase in member states following political changes in eastern and south-eastern

---

[16] See articles 1 of Protocol no. 4, and 2, 3 and 4 of Protocol no. 7.

[17] See articles 2, 3 and 4 of Protocol no. 4, and 1 of Protocol no. 7.

[18] See for a concise account of the ECtHR's jurisprudence on article 14 ECHR, O. de Schutter, *International Human Rights Law* (Cambridge University Press, 2010), 571–4.

[19] See http://conventions.coe.int/Treaty/Commun/ListeTraites.asp?MA=3&CM=7&CL=ENG for a link to the status of ratification for each protocol.

[20] See articles 20–37 of the 1950 ECHR.

[21] The *Greek* case, application nos. 3321/67, *Denmark* v. *Greece*; 3322/67, *Norway* v. *Greece*; 3323/67, *Sweden* v. *Greece*; 3324/67, *Netherlands* v. *Greece* (1969). See on the role of the European Commission, e.g. D. Harris, M. O'Boyle and C. Warbrick, *Law of the European Convention on Human Rights* (Oxford University Press, 1995), 571–603.

Europe prompted a fundamental reform of the system in the 1990s. Protocol no. 11 (1998) abolished the Commission and created a Court with two chambers. In what was a revolutionary step for international human rights bodies whose competences are often curtailed by states jealously guarding their sovereignty, the Protocol provided mandatory direct individual access to the Court. The CoM retained its role of supervising the execution of judgments in what is the present two-tier system.

6.2.4   European Court of Human Rights: structure and functions

The ECtHR has forty-seven judges (one per member state), which are elected by the CoE's Parliamentary Assembly 'from a list of three candidates nominated by the High Contracting Party'[22] and sit in their personal capacity.[23] Following the changes made in Protocol no. 14, the Court sits in 'single-judge formations' (admissibility), committees of three judges and a Chamber of seven judges deciding on admissibility and merits, as well as a Grand Chamber of seventeen judges.[24] The Grand Chamber is strictly speaking not an appeal body. Rather, its main function is to develop and ensure the consistency of the Court's jurisprudence in the interpretation or application of the Convention, including its protocols.[25] The Grand Chamber may decide to hear a case where the Chamber relinquishes jurisdiction or where a party requests referral following a Chamber judgment.[26]

Individual complaints form the bulk of the Court's work. By 2011 it had issued over 15,000 judgments, 14,000 of them since Protocol no. 11 (1999).[27] In contrast, there have only been sixteen inter-state cases, most of which, unsurprisingly, have been of a high profile nature.[28] The Court has to date issued three judgments on the merits in inter-state cases.[29] It can also issue advisory opinions but has used this power on only three occasions because of the narrow remit provided for in article 47 ECHR.[30]

---

[22] Article 22 ECHR.   [23] Article 21 ECHR.
[24] Article 26 ECHR.   [25] Article 30 ECHR.
[26] Article 31 ECHR. As of 19 April 2012, the Grand Chamber had issued 285 judgments, advisory opinions and decisions.
[27] ECtHR, *Annual Report 2011* (Strasbourg: European Court of Human Rights, 2012), 14.
[28] See overview at www.echr.coe.int/NR/rdonlyres/5D5BA416-1FE0-4414-95A1-AD6C1D77CB90/0/Requêtes_interétatiques_EN.pdf.
[29] *Ireland* v. *United Kingdom* (1978) 2 EHRR 25; *Cyprus* v. *Turkey*, (2002) 35 EHRR 30; *Denmark* v. *Turkey*, (2000) 29 EHRR 36. Two cases of *Georgia* v. *Russia* were pending in 2012.
[30] Decision on the *Competence of the Court to give an advisory opinion*, Grand Chamber (2 June 2004); Advisory opinion on *certain legal questions concerning the lists of candidates submitted with a view to the election of judges to the European Court of Human Rights*, Grand Chamber (12 February 2008); Advisory opinion on *certain legal questions concerning the lists of candidates submitted with a view to the election of judges to the European Court of Human Rights* (*no. 2*), Grand Chamber (21 January 2010).

6.2.5   Jurisprudence of the European Court of Human Rights

A brief review of the Court's history shows that it adjudicated few cases in its early years – issuing seven judgments on the merits in its first decade – beginning with *Lawless* v. *Ireland* in 1960.[31] It was only in the early 1990s (205 in total by 1990) that the number of decisions and judgments began to grow steadily, with the Court handing down over a hundred annually since 1996, a figure that has risen to over a thousand annually since 2005. Initially, the majority of cases concerned the right to liberty and security, and the right to a fair trial, with the case of *Ireland* v. *the United Kingdom*, which concerned in particular violations of article 3, constituting a notable exception. The 1990s brought about a significant shift that led the Court increasingly to consider both systemic and serious, large-scale violations in different contexts. Largely as a result of NGO-driven litigation the Court was seized with a number of cases concerning serious violations in the north-east of Turkey.[32] It was also faced with a series of deep-seated structural problems in post-communist countries that had become parties to the ECHR, particularly Romania, Bulgaria and Poland, in relation to ill-treatment, administration of justice and property rights.[33] In addition, Ukraine's and Russia's acceptance of the Court's jurisdiction in 1997 and 1998 respectively resulted in a steady rise of cases against them, many of which have been characterised by serious violations.[34] In recent years, the Court has also ruled on several high-profile cases concerning the extraterritorial conduct (i.e. outside the territory of ECHR contracting parties) of armed forces and counter-terrorist measures.[35] These developments were complemented by a large number of repeat cases concerning systemic violations, particularly in respect of the length of proceedings in Italy[36] and the regulation of property rights in Poland.[37] The significant increase in the number and nature of cases led to unprecedented challenges to the system, which will be considered in more detail below.

---

[31] *Lawless* v. *Ireland (No. 1)* [1960] ECHR 1.

[32] By 2011, there had been a total of 2,747 judgments in cases against Turkey, which is the highest number of judgments for any contracting state. See *Overview 1959–2011* (Strasbourg: European Court of Human Rights, 2012), 7.

[33] Ibid., 6–7.

[34] A total of 822 judgments against the Ukraine and 1,212 judgments against Russia by 2011. See ibid., 7.

[35] See *Al-Jedda* v. *United Kingdom*, (2011) 53 EHRR 23; *Al-Skeini and Others* v. *United Kingdom*, (2011) 53 EHRR 18; *Al-Saadoon and Mufdhi* v. *United Kingdom*, (2010) 51 EHRR 9; *Saadi* v. *Italy*, (2009) 49 EHRR 30; *Othman (Abu Qatada)* v. *United Kingdom*, [2012] ECHR 56; *Babar Ahmed and Others* v. *United Kingdom*, [2007] ECHR 603.

[36] In 1,155 out of 2,166 judgments against Italy. See ECtHR, *Overview 2011*, 6. See in particular *Bottazzi* v. *Italy*, [1999] ECHR 62, and *Scordino* v. *Italy*, (2007) 45 EHRR 7.

[37] See in particular *Broniowski* v. *Poland*, (2005) 40 EHRR 21 and (2006) 43 EHRR 1.

The ECtHR has made a major and influential contribution to the development of international human rights law. This applies in particular to its jurisprudence on the right to life, especially in respect of positive obligations,[38] the prohibition of torture and ill-treatment,[39] including sexual violence,[40] and the right to liberty, security and a fair trial, including the right of access to justice.[41] It also comprises leading judgments that gave a broad reading to aspects of the right to privacy,[42] including in relation to environmental concerns[43] and an extensive (and in parts controversial) jurisprudence on qualified rights such as freedom of expression[44] and the freedom of assembly and association, including in relation to trade unions.[45] It has broadened the scope of the right to property[46] and affirmed the right to vote, particularly for prisoners.[47] In its more recent jurisprudence the Court – though not always entirely consistently – has strengthened the rights of minorities[48] and individuals facing discrimination, including on the basis of sexual orientation and sexual identity.[49]

The Court has developed a number of important doctrines in its interpretation of the ECHR. As a general principle, it has sought to interpret the Convention authoritatively and in the most effective fashion while at the same time respecting the principle of subsidiarity (according to this principle, which is grounded in sovereignty, it is foremost states themselves that are responsible

[38] See *Anguelova* v. *Bulgaria*, (2002) 38 EHRR 659; *Osman* v. *United Kingdom*, (1998) 29 EHRR 245; *Öneryildiz* v. *Turkey*, (2005) 41 EHRR 20; *Kelly and Others* v. *United Kingdom*, [2001] ECHR 328.

[39] *Aksoy* v. *Turkey*, (1997) 23 EHRR 553; *Selmouni* v. *France*, (2000) 29 EHRR 403; and *Soering* v. *United Kingdom*, (1989) 11 EHRR 439; *Chahal* v. *United Kingdom*, (1996) 23 EHRR 413; *Saadi* v. *Italy*, in relation to *non-refoulement*.

[40] *M. C.* v. *Bulgaria*, (2005) 40 EHRR 20; *Opuz* v. *Turkey*, (2010) 50 EHRR 28; *V. C.* v. *Slovakia*, [2011] ECHR 1888; *M. and C.* v. *Romania*, 29032/04, Judgment of 27 September 2011; and *Rantsev* v. *Cyprus and Russia*, (2010) 51 EHRR 1 (trafficking, which the Court located in article 4 rather than article 3 ECHR).

[41] *Golder* v. *United Kingdom*, (1975) 1 EHRR 524.

[42] The right to respect for private and family life, home and correspondence in article 8 has spawned a rich jurisprudence that has been particularly important in such diverse areas as personal identity, data protection, reproductive rights, family life, housing, correspondence, stop and search, and immigration. See for a selection of key cases, A. Mowbray, *Cases and Materials on the European Convention of Human Rights* (Oxford University Press, 2012), 488–597.

[43] See *López Ostra* v. *Spain*, (1994) 20 EHRR 277; *Guerra and Others* v. *Italy* (1998) 26 EHRR 357; *Hatton* v. *United Kingdom*, (2003) 37 EHRR 28; *Dubetska and Others* v. *Ukraine*, [2011] ECHR 256; *Deés* v. *Hungary*, [2010] ECHR 1772.

[44] See section 8.7.

[45] See *Young, James and Webster* v. *United Kingdom*, (1981) 4 EHRR 38, and *Sørensen and Rasmussen* v. *Denmark*, (2006) 46 EHRR 572.

[46] See *Öneryildiz* v. *Turkey* and *Broniowski* v. *Poland*.

[47] See *Hirst* v. *United Kingdom*, (2006) 42 EHRR 41.

[48] See *D. H. and Others* v. *The Czech Republic*, (2008) 47 EHRR 3.

[49] See *Goodwin* v. *United Kingdom*, (2002) 35 EHRR 18.

for guaranteeing the rights granted).[50] When faced with how to construe terms such as 'law' or 'civil rights' in articles 5 and 6 ECHR respectively the Court gave them an 'autonomous meaning' under the Convention.[51] This was an important step in establishing its authority *vis-à-vis* national systems and developing a coherent understanding of the Convention. The Court has stressed that the Convention is part of a constitutional order, which, in combination with considerations of effectiveness, underpins the purposive interpretation of its provisions.[52] It views the Convention as a living instrument whose provisions need to be 'interpreted in light of present-day conditions',[53] which may also include changing its own interpretation of the ECHR over time.[54] On several occasions it has refused to recognise and accommodate 'traditional' views when considering the compatibility of laws or practices with the Convention, including for example discrimination against children born outside marriage[55] and the criminalisation of homosexual conduct.[56] However, it has been less willing to overturn practices such as in respect of the right to privacy where it has identified a lack of European consensus.[57]

On the whole, the Court has been mindful of diverging national approaches and largely respectful of the jurisprudence of national courts, as it is clear that in order to maintain its legitimacy it must strike a delicate balance between its supervisory role and respect for contracting states' decisions.[58] Observers and actors from different political backgrounds have repeatedly criticised (or commended) the ECtHR both for its broad interpretation of the Convention and for being too deferential when key national interests or sensitivities are at stake, criticisms that will be explored further below.

The doctrine of proportionality

The Court has relied heavily on the principle of proportionality, stating that 'inherent in the whole of the Convention is a search for a fair balance between

---

[50] See G. Letsas, *A Theory of Interpretation of the European Convention of Human Rights* (Oxford University Press, 2007).

[51] See for example *König v. Federal Republic of Germany*, (1978) 2 EHRR, paras. 88–9.

[52] See *Loizidou v. Turkey*, (1995) 20 EHRR 99, para. 75.

[53] *Tyrer v. United Kingdom*, (1978) 2 EHRR 1, para. 31.   [54] *Selmouni v. France*, para. 101.

[55] *Marckx v. Belgium*, (1979) 2 EHRR 330, and *Vermeire v. Belgium*, (1993) 15 EHRR 488 (violation of article 8 and 14).

[56] *Dudgeon v. United Kingdom*, (1982) 4 EHRR 149 (violation of article 8). See also P. Johnson, *Homosexuality and the European Court of Human Rights* (London, New York: Routledge, 2012).

[57] See for a critical assessment of the Court's approach in this regard, M.-B. Dembour, *Who Believes in Human Rights? Reflections on the European Convention* (Cambridge University Press, 2006), particularly at 197–201, 206–10 and 238–41.

[58] See on the Court's legitimacy in particular the research output of the project on the 'Legitimacy and Authority of Supranational Human Rights Courts', online, at http://ecthrproject.wordpress.com.

the demands of the general interest of the community and the requirements of the protection of the individual's fundamental rights'.[59] This principle has been particularly important when considering whether states could justifiably restrict the exercise of qualified rights. The margin of appreciation developed in this context is perhaps the most prominent of the ECtHR's doctrines.[60] First articulated in *Handyside* v. *UK* (1976), the Court has used it as a device that gives states some discretion in applying Convention guarantees, particularly when determining what measures are necessary to restrict rights on grounds such as public morals, which involve certain value judgments.[61] The Court has also given states some flexibility in determining whether a factual situation exists that threatens the life of the nation (application of article 15)[62] and in respect of positive obligations.[63] The margin of appreciation is based on the principle of subsidiarity and is a pragmatic device for the Court to defer to states' assessment where it considers it inappropriate to make an assessment itself. The discretion inherent in this margin is not unlimited as the Court has repeatedly stressed that its application 'goes hand in hand with European supervision'.[64] In addition, the scope of the margin differs considerably. States have been given a fairly broad margin where there is a lack of European consensus, where they make value judgments and where conflicting rights or interests need to be balanced, for example restricting freedom of expression on grounds of public morals.[65] However, in areas where interference may encroach on the core of a right, such as political freedom of expression, the Court has been much less generous in trusting the assessment of contracting states. This is evident in a series of Austrian cases where journalists faced prosecutions and fines for 'defamation' of politicians.[66]

Responses to the ECtHR's jurisprudence

The Court has been the subject of at times scathing criticism for its supposed deference to contracting states.[67] Indeed, in a number of cases the

---

[59] *Soering* v. *United Kingdom*, para. 89.

[60] See in particular Y. Arai-Takahashi, *The Margin of Appreciation Doctrine and the Principle of Proportionality in the Jurisprudence of the ECHR* (Antwerp: Intersentia, 2002); and Letsas, above note 50, 80–98.

[61] *Handyside* v. *United Kingdom*, (1976) 1 EHRR 737, paras. 48–50.

[62] *Demir and Others* v. *Turkey*, (1998) 33 EHRR 43, para. 43; *A and Others* v. *United Kingdom*, (2009) 49 EHRR 29, paras. 173–4.

[63] *M. C.* v. *Bulgaria*, paras. 154–5.

[64] *Handyside* v. *United Kingdom*, para. 49.

[65] *Müller and Others* v. *Switzerland*, (1988) 13 EHRR 212, paras. 32, 36, and *Wingrove* v. *United Kingdom*, (1997) 24 EHRR 1, paras. 58, 61, 64.

[66] See for example *Lingens* v. *Austria*, (1986) 8 EHRR 103, paras. 39–47.

[67] Dissenting opinion of Judge Spielmann in *Müller* v. *Switzerland*; Dembour, above note 57, 162–6.

Court has seemingly accepted state reliance on moral values or local sentiments at the expense of a robust affirmation of rights, especially in the field of artistic work.[68] This comes perilously close to accepting majoritarian views, an approach that runs counter to the very essence of liberal models of defending individual rights. This applies in particular to those who claim a right to be different. In *Refah Partisi and Others* v. *Turkey* and *Leyla Sahi* v. *Turkey*, the Court gave preference to the protection of Turkey's secular state when pitted against freedom of religion, freedom of association and women's rights.[69] *Lautsi* v. *Italy*, where the Grand Chamber reversed a Chamber judgment on freedom of religion following a public outcry in Italy over the ban of crucifixes in the classroom, is another case in point.[70]

Such cases raise broader questions of the political stance taken by the Court, which has been accused of being too accommodating and 'conservative'.[71] However, the jurisprudence of the Court is rather mixed in this regard. In several instances it has given a broad interpretation to rights, for example by identifying positive obligations to provide protection against environmental pollution pursuant to articles 2 and 8.[72] It has also issued a number of judgments against states that were highly politically charged. This includes *McCann* v. *UK* where the Court held that the killing of three IRA operatives by British security forces violated their right to life because there were ample opportunities of apprehending them; *Hirst* v. *UK* concerning prisoners' right to vote and several cases relating to serious violations in the conflicts in Turkey and Russia discussed below.

Conversely, some of the Court's jurisprudence may be viewed as reassuring states that it will not rule against them in highly sensitive cases of national interest. *Banković* v. *Belgium*, *Lautsi* v. *Italy*, *Refah Partisi* v. *Turkey* and *Gäfgen* v. *Germany* are examples pointing to such practice.[73] While this approach is prudent in so far as the Court is more likely to enjoy the acceptance of states if it respects certain 'red lines', it potentially undermines itself

---

[68] See for example *Müller and Others* v. *Switzerland*, paras. 32, 36, 43. See section 8.7.2.

[69] *Refah Partisi (The Welfare Party) and Others* v. *Turkey*, (2002) 35 EHRR 3, paras. 49–136; *Leyla Şahin* v. *Turkey*, (2005) 44 EHRR 5, paras. 30–123 and 163–6. See sections 8.7.2 and 8.7.4 for further discussion.

[70] *Lautsi and Others* v. *Italy*, [2011] ECHR 2412. See for a prompt, critical response, L. Zucca, 'A comment on Lautsi', *EJIL Talk* (19 March 2011), online, at www.ejiltalk.org/a-comment-on-lautsi.

[71] See S. Meckled-Garcia and B. Çali, 'Lost in Translation: the Human Rights Ideal and International Human Rights Law', in Meckled-Garcia and Çali, *The Legalization of Human Rights: Multidisciplinary Perspectives on Human Rights and Human Rights Law* (London, New York: Routledge, 2006), 10–29.

[72] See for example *Öneryildiz* v. *Turkey* and *Hatton* v. *United Kingdom*.

[73] *Banković and Others* v. *Belgium and Others*, (2011) 11 BHRC 435 (discussed briefly in section 7.2.1); *Lautsi* v. *Italy*; *Refah Partisi* v. *Turkey*; *Gäfgen* v. *Germany*, (2010) 52 EHRR 1 (discussed in section 8.3.4).

as a guardian of rights, especially in difficult circumstances. This is particularly the case where the Court's reasoning is seen as too cursory (or categorical) and lacking in critical engagement with fundamental underlying questions.[74] The strong dissenting opinions in cases such as *Lautsi* v. *Italy*, *Gäfgen* v. *Germany* and *Refah Partisi* v. *Turkey* provide glimpses of the dissatisfaction that such reasoning is bound to cause, both within and outside the Court.[75] The Court's reasoning has also been criticised in other cases, such as in *Behrami and Saramati* v. *France, Germany and Norway*, a case concerning the responsibility of national troops acting in Kosovo under UN authorisation.[76] In *Kononov* v. *Latvia*, the Grand Chamber appeared to realise that the Chamber's application of international law had been highly questionable when it reached a judgment diametrically opposed to that of the Chamber. It held that article 7 ECHR (prohibition of retrospective application) did not prevent Latvia from prosecuting Mr Kononov for war crimes committed in 1994 even though applicable domestic law at the time did not recognise war crimes.[77]

6.2.6   Impact

The ECHR and ECtHR have had a profound impact on the development of international and national human rights law. The ECHR is, somewhat ironically, one of the colonial legacies that left its imprint in national systems of human rights protection[78] and the ECtHR's jurisprudence has been referred to by national, regional and international bodies. The system is at the heart of the regional human rights culture in Europe, with the ECHR as the main reference point for human rights that underpins the CoE's work. As interpreted by the ECtHR and national courts the ECHR has also become increasingly influential for the EU. Respect for human rights is one of the accession criteria for EU membership, and it has been used as a yardstick for countries such as Bulgaria, Romania and Turkey.[79] The Charter for

---

[74] See in this regard critique by Judge Loucaides, 'Reflections of a Former European Court of Human Rights Judge on his Experiences as a Judge' (26 July 2010), online, at www.errc.org/cikk.php?page=8&cikk=3613.

[75] See dissenting opinions by Judge Malinverni joined by Judge Kalaydjieva in *Lautsi* v. *Italy*; joint partly dissenting opinion of judges Rozakis, Tulkens, Jebens, Ziemele, Bianku and Power in *Gäfgen* v. *Germany*; and of Judge Tulkens in *Leyla Şahin* v. *Turkey*.

[76] See on the *Behrami* and *Saramati* case, section 7.2.1.

[77] *Kononov* v. *Latvia*, [2010] ECHR 667.

[78] K. Vasak, 'The European Convention of Human Rights beyond the frontiers of Europe', *ICLQ* 12(4) (1963), 1206–31.

[79] According to the Copenhagen membership criteria, a 'candidate country must have achieved stability of institutions guaranteeing democracy, the rule of law, human rights and respect for and protection of minorities'.

Fundamental Rights, now incorporated in the Lisbon Treaty, draws on the ECHR.[80] Plans for the EU to become a party to the ECHR further underscore the Convention's status as the central European human rights instrument with the ECtHR as the final arbiter.

At the national level the ECHR has been directly incorporated in its member states[81] and consistently applied, or referred to, by national courts.[82] The ECtHR's jurisprudence has affected a number of rights and compelled states to undertake a series of legislative and institutional changes. This includes granting particular rights, such as equal rights for children born out of wedlock in Belgium,[83] and strengthening the rights of mentally disabled persons in Russia.[84] It also comprises reforms in the administration of justice, particularly providing adequate remedies, such as in several post-communist countries,[85] or in policing practices, such as in the UK.[86] The potential application of the ECHR to acts committed abroad, particularly where forces are engaging in operations extraterritorially, such as the UK's forces in Iraq,[87] significantly extends its reach and has profound consequences for member states engaged in armed conflict beyond their borders. However, the Court has faced opposition when addressing sensitive or deeply engrained practices. This includes issues where national sentiments run strongly, such as the right of prisoners to vote in the UK or the use of religious symbols in Italy. Systemic shortcomings, such as chronic delays in legal proceedings in Italy, or deep-seated discrimination, such as faced by migrants across the continent or the Roma in several Eastern European countries, have been particularly taxing, often generating a large number of cases without resulting in the changes needed to ensure effective protection. Even though it has repeatedly emphasised states' positive duty to investigate violations, the ECtHR has found it difficult to break cultures of impunity, particularly in the Turkish and Russian context, as the following interviews demonstrate.

---

[80] See below at section 6.2.8.

[81] See R. Blackburn and J. Polakiewicz (eds.), *The European Convention on Human Rights and its Member States, 1950–2000* (Oxford University Press, 2001).

[82] See M. Andenas and E. Bjorge, *National Implementation of ECHR Rights: Kant's Categorical Imperative and the Convention*, University of Oslo Faculty of Law Legal Studies Research Paper Series (2011) no. 2011–15.

[83] *Marckx* v. *Belgium* and *Vermeire* v. *Belgium*.

[84] *Shtukaturov* v. *Russia*, [2008] ECHR 223. See also Mental Disability Advocacy Centre, 'Russia: Strategic litigation leads to law reform', online, at http://mdac.info/node/708.

[85] See in particular *Broniowski* v. *Poland*; *Kudla* v. *Poland*, (2000) 35 EHRR 198; and *Burdov* v. *Russia*, (2009) 49 EHRR 2.

[86] See A. Donald *et al.*, *Evaluating the Impact of Selected Cases under the Human Rights Act on Public Services Provision* (Manchester: Equality and Human Rights Commission, 2009), 28–39.

[87] See *al-Jedda* v. *United Kingdom*, and *al-Skeini* v. *United Kingdom*.

INTERVIEW 6.1

The nature and impact of litigation concerning Turkey

(Dr Başak Çali)

Turkey – a party to the ECHR since 1954, having accepted the right of individual petition in 1987 – has experienced military dictatorships and conflict in the Kurdish-populated south-east of the country. Its reliance on a secular nation state built on a strong military led to systemic problems that were frequently characterised by serious human rights violations. In the 1990s Turkish lawyers, academics and NGOs such as the Essex European Court of Human Rights Litigation Project,[1] the Human Rights Association, Diyarbakir[2] and the Kurdish Human Rights Project[3] identified litigation before the ECtHR as one of the strategies to seek justice and bring about systemic changes. The goal of this endeavour was to establish a public record of violations and to compel Turkey to hold perpetrators accountable, provide reparation and undertake substantial reforms. The litigation resulted in a large number of cases that provided an anatomy of violations, especially in the south-east of the country, and shortcomings in the Turkish legal system. Turkey had a strong incentive to comply because of its wish to accede to the EU. It has paid considerable amounts of compensation and carried out a series of legislative reforms, such as removing immunity for officials or abolishing the death penalty at the time of the *Öcalan* case. However, the ECtHR's overall impact has been limited by the fact that Turkey has been less willing to investigate and prosecute serious human rights violations and impunity remains a problem.

Dr Başak Çali is a legal academic and practitioner. She is a senior lecturer in human rights at the University College of London and has litigated cases before the ECtHR. She recently completed a major study on the legitimacy and authority of supranational human rights courts and has examined the impact of cases brought before the ECtHR from south-east Turkey between 1996 and 2006 on the acknowledgement of state violence in Turkey.[4]

You write that '[s]upranational human rights courts are institutional sites that provide specialized vocabulary, structure, and opportunities for participation in addressing state violence and the process of acknowledgement'. What is the ECtHR's record in relation to Turkey in this regard?

[1] See the Essex Human Rights Centre, www.essex.ac.uk/human_rights_centre/default.aspx.
[2] www.ihd.org.tr/english.   [3] www.khrp.org.
[4] B. Çali, 'The Logics of Supranational Human Rights Litigation, Official Acknowledgement and Human Rights Reform: the Southeast Turkey cases before the European Court of Human Rights between 1996–2006', *LS*, 35(2) (2010), 311–37.

The south-east Turkey cases discuss exactly that. While the cases themselves offer this crucial vocabulary and enabled victims of human rights violations to access justice, the judgments are not the final say on acknowledgement of state violence, in particular in the context of counter-terrorism operations. That is, human rights judgments can act as tools of acknowledgement only if state authorities are willing to accept them as such. In Turkey we have seen resistance to that.

NGOs and others have pursued a number of cases and the ECtHR has established a considerable record of violations. However, you still suggest that litigation failed to act as catalyst for domestic acknowledgement. What are the factors that explain the failed 'transmission' of these cases?

In my study I argue that such factors are mostly discursive and political (some also call them ideological or ideational). In other words Turkey is not a country that faces shortcomings in its material or institutional capacity to implement human rights judgments. I argue that Turkish ruling elites have not seen the counter-terrorism operations from a human rights perspective and have, therefore, regarded judgments against themselves as taking sides, i.e. supporting the terrorists against the Turkish state. This has been a major obstacle for recognising the human rights violations for what they are.

You take issue with a reading that views Europe's (ECtHR, CoE and EU) reform efforts *vis-à-vis* Turkey as exemplary in bringing about major domestic changes. What approach other than the 'technical-bureaucratic' one you criticised could the European bodies have taken in engaging with Turkey in what are surely long-term processes?

One of the ECtHR's weaknesses has been its lack of attention to truth and acknowledgement in its approach to remedies. On the one hand this is understandable. The ECHR as well as a large proportion of the Court's case law has not been about adjudicating gross and systemic human rights violations. The CoM also has not taken a bold stance. For example, it has never asked Turkey to publicly apologise to the victims or institute other processes of public acknowledgement or healing. It has limited itself to asking for statistics of prosecutions of security forces involved in human rights violations. In contrast, such apologies are an everyday practice in the Inter-American Human Rights System. This leaves the EU – an institution pretty much free to make demands from Turkey under its Copenhagen accession criterion of human rights. However, the EU has sidelined truth and acknowledgement in favour of an approach demanding that Turkey grant more rights to its Kurdish citizens. This has meant that – albeit for different reasons – no international pressure was there to help push the acknowledgement of violations other than the voices of the judgments themselves. The approach I advocate is clear: international organisations should have insisted on public acknowledgement of state violence.

What are the broader lessons that can be learned from the impact of ECtHR litigation in Turkey?

The ECtHR litigation in Turkey has addressed very diverse issues, ranging from state-sponsored violence to freedom of expression, from property rights to administration of justice and arbitrary detention. The impact of such litigation has also varied depending on the issue – this is not surprising and is to be expected in other countries, too. The south-east Turkey cases are special in one sense as official bodies challenged the very basis of these judgments, the evidence provided by the witnesses and the authenticity of victims. While Turkey has paid monetary compensation and carried out a number of legislative reforms, the prosecution rates of state officials have remained low and the violations have never been officially acknowledged. It is, of course, not reasonable to expect too much from the ECtHR judgments. I think that full implementation is generally more puzzling than no implementation when we analyse judgments from supranational human rights courts with no final authority over states. Lessons we learn from the south-east Turkey litigation are that (1) each issue in each country brings with it a complex constellation of factors that explain why human rights judgments are implemented, contested or ignored, and these should be addressed even when litigating a case; (2) different remedies face different levels of resistance in terms of implementation. The remedies that require a change in mindset are those that are hardest to implement.

In Russia, developments show some parallels. Domestic NGOs, such as the Nizhny Novgorod Regional Committee against Torture[88] and Memorial,[89] as well as external actors, such as the European Human Rights Advocacy Centre,[90] seized on the opportunity offered and brought a number of applications before the ECtHR. These cases concerned both systemic problems of law enforcement and the administration of justice, as well as serious violations committed in the conflict in Chechnya.[91] Russia introduced some changes as a result but systemic challenges regarding the rule of law remain. This includes in particular impunity for serious human rights violations committed in counter-terrorism operations and in the conflict in Chechnya. An

---

[88] www.pytkam.net.   [89] www.memo.ru/eng.
[90] www.londonmet.ac.uk/research-units/hrsj/affiliated-centres/ehrac.
[91] See for a good overview, www.londonmet.ac.uk/research-units/hrsj/affiliated-centres/ ehrac/ehrac-litigation/chechnya – echr-litigation-and-enforcement/chechnya – echr-litigation-and-enforcement_home.cfm.

important feature of developments in Russia is the readiness of numerous individuals and lawyers in Russia independently to take cases to Strasbourg. While this has resulted in a large number of inadmissibility decisions it has given Russian cases before the ECtHR a pluralistic complexion. It also means that the ECHR and recourse to the ECtHR are increasingly seen as an integral extension of Russia's legal system and that domestic actors are much more aware of the ECHR's role and value, both as an additional remedy and as a means to advocate change.

INTERVIEW 6.2
Nature and impact of litigation concerning Turkey and Russia
(Bill Bowring)

Bill Bowring is a Professor at Birkbeck College and a Barrister at Field Court Chambers, Gray's Inn, who has litigated over a hundred cases against Azerbaijan, Estonia, Georgia, Latvia, Russia and Turkey before the ECtHR. He has published widely on international law, human rights and Soviet and Russian law.[1]

How would you describe the nature of cases that you brought against Turkey and Russia before the ECtHR?

First, with the Kurdish Human Rights Project, I litigated a number of cases against Turkey in the 1990s. Significant examples concerned freedom of expression, murder of journalists, positive duty of the state,[2] death in custody, death by torture,[3] and disappearance of an applicant's two sons at the hands of the army.[4]

In 2003 I founded the European Human Rights Advocacy Centre, in partnership with the Memorial Human Rights Centre in Moscow and the Bar Human Rights Committee, with a €1 million grant from the European Commission. We litigated the first six Chechen cases against Russia.[5] We also brought the first environmental case against Russia – *Fadeeva* v. *Russia*[6] – as well as many Chechen, environmental, discrimination and

[1] See in particular B. Bowring, *The Degradation of the International Legal Order? The Rehabilitation of Law, and the Possibility of Politics* (London, New York: Routledge, 2008).
[2] *Özgür Gündem* v. *Turkey*, App. no. 00023144/93, 16 March 2000. References provided by Bill Bowring.
[3] *Aktaş* v. *Turkey*, App. no. 00024351/94, 24 April 2003.
[4] *Ipek* v. *Turkey*, App. no. 25760/94, 17 February 2004.
[5] *Khashiyev* v. *Russia*, App. no. 57942/00, *Akayeva* v. *Russia*, App. no. 57945/00, *Isayeva* v. *Russia*, (2005) 41 EHRR 38, *Yusupova* v. *Russia*, App. no. 57948/00, *Bazayeva* v. *Russia*, App. no. 57949/00 and *Isayeva* v. *Russia*, App. no. 57950/00 all decided on 24 February 2005.
[6] *Fadeeva* v. *Russia*, App. no. 55723/00, 9 June 2005.

other cases since then. I am now representing the applicant in *Carter* v. *Russia* (murder of Aleksandr Litvinenko).

The Turkish judgments are important in the Russian context as they are constantly referred to in the pleading and judgments especially in the Chechen cases which still continue.

What has been the main goal of bringing cases before the ECtHR?

We take a case to complain about specific violations suffered by specific victims. The objective, in cases which take at least five to six years is to vindicate the individual applicants' complaints. Therefore, the main goal is to win a judgment against the state in question. Cases vary. In most cases what the applicants want is certainly not money but affirmation by the highest judicial organ in Europe of the truth of what has happened to them and their relatives. Furthermore, in the many disappearance cases against Turkey and Russia, what the applicants really want from enforcement is a thorough and effective investigation into the disappearance of their children and close relatives and the identification and prosecution of those responsible.

What would you say are the main achievements of litigation in relation to Russia before the ECtHR?

Russia has in every case paid the just satisfaction ordered by the Court, providing some measure of justice for individual victims. As a result of *Kalashnikov* v. *Russia* and eighty more cases up to *Ananyev* v. *Russia* there have been real reforms in the penitentiary system. Russia is now subject to pilot judgments in *Ananyev* v. *Russia* (conditions in pre-trial detention), in addition to *Burdov* v. *Russia No. 2* (non-enforcement of judgments). The Chechen cases have given the applicants and the whole Chechen people unassailable accounts of what happened from 1999 onwards. Russian law textbooks and commentaries are now full of Strasbourg judgments, which shows that the ECHR and the ECtHR jurisprudence have become part and parcel of the Russian legal system.

What are the challenges for the ECtHR to fulfil its role effectively in relation to countries such as Russia?

The main challenge is for states to implement the Convention properly in their domestic systems as they have bound themselves to do. In every CoE member state this is a long and complex process. Russia has done not at all badly in complying with the twenty-nine obligations it undertook in 1996 on joining the CoE. The UK is presently the only member state defying the Court (*Hirst* v. *UK*).

The European system also has its own limitations, particularly: (1) the ECHR is effectively an eighteenth-century document, very antiquated compared to the ICCPR, ACHR and the ACHPR; (2) the Court is excessively deferential to states; (3) cases take from six to twelve years after exhaustion of domestic remedies; enforcement is very slow, opaque and weak.

POINTS TO CONSIDER

- How effective has litigation been in securing individual justice and addressing systemic human rights problems in Turkey and Russia?
- What are the lessons from the Turkish and Russian experience for human rights lawyers dealing with countries confronted with systematic and systemic violations?

6.2.7   The struggle for efficiency, effectiveness and institutional reforms

The ECtHR is facing two critical challenges: how to cope with its caseload and how to enhance implementation of its judgments. The problems caused by forever rising numbers of applications, particularly increasing delay in the resolution of cases and the need for more resources, has been apparent since the 1990s. Protocol no. 11, which effectively abolished the European Commission for Human Rights, was meant to streamline procedures. However, a growing number of member states and the greater awareness and willingness of those within their jurisdictions to resort to the Court has since resulted in an exponential rise in applications. In 2011 there was a monthly deficit of over a thousand in respect of 'cases allocated and cases disposed of', which resulted in a 9 per cent increase of pending applications, totalling 151,600 by the end of the year.[92] It is readily apparent that this situation is unsustainable. The Court and CoE have pursued two parallel responses to this crisis, in the form of pilot judgments and by means of procedural reforms.

The pilot-judgment procedure was developed in response to systemic problems resulting in a series of applications that essentially address the same issue and clog the system. Instead of dealing with each application individually the Court started using a new procedure in the case of *Broniowski* v. *Poland*, which concerned over 80,000 claims for compensation relating to expropriation of property.[93] The purpose of the procedure is to settle a large number of pending cases and prevent repeat applications by inducing the state effectively to resolve systemic problems. The procedure may be initiated by the Court 'on its own motion or at the request of one or both parties'.[94] If the Court identifies a systemic problem giving rise to violations it adjourns all pending cases and grants states a limited period of time to address the matter, including by providing effective national remedies, or face the prospect of a series of adverse judgments. In its practice, the ECtHR has issued several

---

[92] See ECtHR, *Analysis of Statistics 2011* (Strasbourg: ECHR, 2012), 4–6.
[93] *Broniowski* v. *Poland*.   [94] Rule 61(2) Rules of Court.

high profile pilot judgments that concerned a range of systemic issues, such as excessive length of domestic proceedings, non-enforcement of domestic judgments, prison conditions and investigation of violations.[95]

The pilot-judgment procedure constitutes an innovative approach that has had some success, particularly where domestic bodies, such as constitutional courts, have been supportive and states have had an interest in resolving the underlying issues.[96] It therefore holds some promise for the Court having a 'constitutional' impact and contributing to the strengthening of domestic procedures and remedies. However, a number of practical questions concerning selection, application and impact of the procedure on individual claimants remain.[97] Moreover, it has already become apparent that the procedure on its own is unlikely to reduce the number of cases reaching the Court sufficiently.

A number of individuals, states and bodies within the CoE framework have been working to identify what other steps can be taken to increase the effectiveness of the system. One major outcome was Protocol no. 14, which was opened for signature in 2004 and came into force in 2010 after substantial delays caused by Russia's initial non-ratification.[98] The Protocol introduces a number of changes aimed at streamlining procedures.[99] Significantly, a single judge can rule on the admissibility of applications (instead of three judges previously). Cases can be dismissed where they are manifestly inadmissible or 'where the applicant has not suffered a significant disadvantage'.[100] The latter formula is problematic because it curtails the right to individual access for violations.[101] It is therefore subject to certain safeguards[102] and the Court's dealing with cases on this ground can be expected to be the

---

[95] P. Leach *et al.*, *Responding to Systemic Human Rights Violations: An Analysis of Pilot Judgments of the European Court of Human Rights and their Impact at National Level* (Antwerp: Intersentia, 2010), pp. 15–23, refer to *Broniowski* v. *Poland* (2004); *Hutten-Czapska* v. *Poland* (2006); *Burdov* v. *Russia (No. 2)* (2009); *Olaru and Others* v. *Moldova* (2009); *Yuriy Nikolayevich Ivanov* v. *Ukraine* (2009); *Suljagić* v. *Bosnia and Herzegovina* (2009). See also ECtHR, *Factsheet-Pilot Judgments* (June 2012), online, at www.echr.coe.int/NR/rdonlyres/61CA1D79-DB68-4EF3-A8F8-FF6F5D3B3BB0/0/FICHES_Arrets_pilotes_EN.pdf, which additionally refers to *Ananyev and Others* v. *Russia* (2012); *Rumpf* v. *Germany* (2010); *Athanasiou and Others* v. *Greece* (2010); *Dimitrov and Hamanov* v. *Bulgaria* and *Finger* v. *Bulgaria* (2011); *Ümmühan Kaplan* v. *Turkey* (2012); *Michelioudakis* v. *Greece* (2012); *Kurić and Others* v. *Slovenia* (2012); and *Atanasiu and Poenaru* v. *Romania and Solon* v. *Romania* (2010).

[96] Leach, above note 95, 177–8.   [97] Ibid., particularly 171–85.

[98] This delay necessitated the adoption of Protocol no. 14bis in 2009.

[99] See P. Lemmens and W. Vandenhole (eds.), *Protocol No. 14 and the Reform of the European Court of Human Rights* (Antwerp: Intersentia, 2005).

[100] Article 35(3)(b) ECHR.

[101] See X. B. Ruedin, 'De minimis non curat the European Court of Human Rights: the Introduction of a New Admissibility Criterion Article 12 of Protocol No. 14', *EHRLR* 1 (2008), 80–105.

[102] Article 35(3)(b) ECHR provides in particular that 'no case may be rejected on this ground which has not been duly considered by a domestic tribunal'.

subject of close scrutiny. Conversely, a committee of three judges can rule on the admissibility and merits where 'the underlying question in the case ... is already the subject of well-established case-law of the Court'.[103] Protocol No. 14 also seeks to facilitate friendly settlements and strengthens the role of the Court in the enforcement of judgments upon referral by the CoM.[104]

The measures envisaged in Protocol no. 14 are bound to make the Court more efficient. However, there is general consensus that more needs to be done to resolve the current crisis.[105] Enhancing domestic implementation through legislative and institutional reforms as well as judicial protection is key, because it would make recourse to the Court unnecessary.[106] It is clear that domestic actors, including NGOs, the media, parliamentarians, courts and others, such as national human rights institutions,[107] play a vital role in bringing about the requisite changes in what is an ongoing, long-term task.

Is the only solution to the current problems facing the Court for it effectively to become a constitutional Court of Europe? In response to this question, it has been suggested that the Court should focus only on fundamental questions, which would shift the emphasis on national implementation.[108] The pilot-judgment procedure and the admissibility requirements in Protocol No. 14 ('no significant disadvantage') already point to a more constitutional role for the Court. It is also true that the suggested shift would have a positive impact on the Court's resources and would allow it to further develop its jurisprudence on fundamental questions of wider importance. However, these proposals have triggered serious concerns that they would, if adopted, undermine the individual relief that is by many seen as being at the heart

---

[103] Article 28(1)(b) ECHR.   [104] Articles 39 and 46(3) and (4) ECHR.

[105] See Report of the Group of Wise Persons to the Committee of Ministers, CM(2006)203 (2006), and website for updates, online, at www.echr.coe.int/ECHR/EN/Header/The+Court/ Reform+of+the+Court/Conferences.

[106] See Brighton Declaration, adopted by the High Level Conference on the Future of the European Court of Human Rights in April 2012, online, at www.coe.int/en/20120419-brighton-declaration.

[107] Such as, for example, the Joint Committee on Human Rights in the UK, www.parliament. uk/business/committees/committees-a-z/joint-select/human-rights-committee/human-rights-judgments.

[108] See S. Greer, 'What's Wrong with the European Convention on Human Rights?', *HRQ* 30(3) (2008), 680–92, and J. Christofferson, 'Individual and Constitutional Justice: Can the Power Balance of Adjudication be reversed?', in J. Christofferson and M. R. Madsen (eds.), *The European Court of Human Rights between Law and Politics* (Oxford University Press, 2011), 181–203. The move towards a more constitutional role is to some extent reflected in paras. 30–4 of the 2012 Brighton Declaration. However, para. 31 of the Declaration equally stresses that 'The right of individual application remains a cornerstone of the Convention system.'

of the system.[109] There is indeed a risk that individual complaints may be curtailed and that the Court may become selective in responding to European human rights problems. The debate surrounding the nature of the Court demonstrates current faultlines; it also shows that there are no easy solutions to the problems facing it. As developments over the last two decades show, the system cannot escape continuous adjustments. How to effectively function and move beyond crisis management is vital for an institution which, despite all its achievements to date, faces recurring political challenges and is at risk of frustrating those whose rights it is meant to protect.

6.2.9   The European Union

The precursor to the EU, the European Community (EC), was meant to be an organisation aimed at European integration principally through the movement of goods, persons, services and capital. Hence, it was not concerned with human rights *per se*. However, it is clear that the EU, an international organisation based on a 'unique economic and social partnership between 27 countries',[110] has a special role in the promotion and protection of human rights in Europe and beyond in the course of its external human rights policy.[111] While early, ambitious attempts to include human rights protection in the system failed, the ECJ subsequently developed a notable jurisprudence on human rights through its interpretation of Community law.[112] However, it was not until the 1992 Maastricht Treaty that human rights were formally recognised in EU law. At present, article 6(3) of the Treaty of Europe, as revised by the Lisbon Treaty,[113] stipulates that '[f]undamental rights, as guaranteed by the European Convention for the Protection of Human Rights and Fundamental Freedoms and as they result from the constitutional traditions common to the Member States, shall constitute general principles of the Union's law.'[114] The Charter of Fundamental Rights of the European Union of 2000, which became binding as an integral part

---

[109] See for the position taken by many NGOs, 'Joint Statement for the High Level Conference on the Future of the European Court of Human Rights', Izmir, Turkey (26–27 April 2011), online, at www.coe.int/t/dghl/standardsetting/conferenceizmir/Amnesty%20International%20-%20Joint%20NGO%20Statement.pdf.

[110] http://europa.eu/about-eu/basic-information/index_en.htm.

[111] See P. Alston (ed.), *The EU and Human Rights* (Oxford University Press, 1999), and D. Ehlers (ed.), *European Fundamental Rights and Freedoms* (Berlin: De Gruyter, 2007).

[112] See A. T. Williams, *Human Rights and the European Court of Justice: Past and Present Tendencies*, Warwick Research Papers (2011) no. 2011/06.

[113] Treaty of Lisbon amending the Treaty on European Union and the Treaty Establishing the European Community, EN 17 December 2007 Official Journal of the European Union C306/1.

[114] Consolidated Version of the Treaty on European Union, EN 30 March 2010 Official Journal of the European Union C83/13.

of the Lisbon Treaty,[115] presently constitutes the EU's major human rights instrument. It encompasses a range of civil, political, social, cultural and economic rights that are contained in its six chapters (dignity, freedoms, equality, solidarity, citizens' rights and justice).[116] However, EU policies and practices in respect of human rights have been contradictory. In contrast to its leading role in developing anti-discrimination instruments, the EU's policies and conduct in other fields have been the subject of considerable criticism. This applies particularly in respect of asylum and immigration, the EU's limited progress in effectively protecting rights of minorities, such as the Roma, and its focus on, and inconsistencies in, its external human rights policies.[117]

The relationship between the EU and the ECtHR constitutes a critical and complex question for human rights protection in Europe. The role of the EU *vis-à-vis* its member states, particularly its ability to mandate action that may result in a breach of states' obligations under the ECHR, inevitably raised the question whether the EU itself should be bound by European human rights law. National courts, such as the German Constitutional Court, as well as the ECtHR, have shown considerable reluctance to find that the EU may provide lesser protection than that granted in national constitutions or the ECHR respectively.[118] Nevertheless, this unresolved situation was considered unsatisfactory and contributed to the drafting of the Charter of Fundamental Rights. The Charter, which essentially contains ECHR rights, is binding on the EU and on member states 'only when they are implementing [European] Union law'.[119] The Lisbon Treaty also resolved another fundamental question, namely providing that the EU 'shall accede' to the ECHR[120] and thus become subject to the jurisdiction of the ECtHR (interestingly, the EU had already become a party to the CRPD, which allows supranational organisations to do so).[121] Discussions about the modalities of becoming a party were ongoing in 2012 but it is already clear that such a step would have significant ramifications. It places the ECtHR firmly at the apex of the European human rights architecture. The Court can be expected to be seized with cases that may have potentially far-reaching repercussions for EU policies. Such a development would pose a challenge regarding the scope of review, namely whether the EU would still benefit from a presumption of compliance.[122] At the same

---

[115] Article 6(1) Treaty on European Union.

[116] See W. B. T. Mock (ed.), *Human Rights in Europe, Commentary on the Charter of Fundamental Rights of the European Union* (Durham, NC: Carolina Academic Press, 2010).

[117] G. de Búrca, 'The Road not Taken: the European Union as a Global Human Rights Actor', *AJIL* 105(4) (2011), 649–93.

[118] See in particular *Bosphorus* v. *Ireland*, (2006) 42 EHRR 1, paras. 150–8.

[119] Article 51(1) of the Charter.   [120] Article 6(2).   [121] Article 42 CRPD.

[122] As applied in *Bosphorus* v. *Ireland*, para. 156. The presumption is rebuttable if the 'protection of Convention rights was manifestly deficient'.

time, the broadened scope of the ECJ's jurisdiction, which is now mandated to apply the Fundamental Charter, has raised the possibility of divergence arising from the parallel jurisdiction of both courts (as well as the ECSR).[123] Judging by the ECJ's jurisprudence to date, it is reasonable to expect that it will take a pragmatic line that seeks to reflect the ECtHR's jurisprudence as much as possible.[124] Nevertheless, the scope for legal uncertainty inherent in these developments cannot be denied.

QUESTIONS

1 For all its supposed progressiveness, the ECtHR has been rather conservative in its overall approach and has frequently refrained from demanding fundamental changes that appeared merited with a view to securing stronger rights protection. Would this statement constitute a fair assessment of the Court's record to date?

2 Should the ECtHR become more akin to a constitutional court and only hear cases of fundamental importance?

3 Are the Fundamental Rights Charter in the Lisbon Treaty and EU accession to the ECHR the final steps towards a coherent European human rights system?

6.3   THE INTER-AMERICAN HUMAN RIGHTS SYSTEM

6.3.1   Overview

The origins of the Inter-American system date back to regional efforts in the nineteenth century to strengthen cooperation based on mutual respect and non-intervention, which resulted in the establishment of the Pan American Union in 1889–90.[125] Following World War II, in a process aimed at establishing a peaceful, democratic and liberal regional order, the OAS was established in 1948 by virtue of the OAS Charter with twenty-one member states

---

[123] Importantly, article 52(3) of the Charter provides that '[i]n so far as this Charter contains rights which correspond to rights guaranteed by the Convention for the Protection of Human Rights and Fundamental Freedoms, the meaning and scope of those rights shall be the same as those laid down by the said Convention. This provision shall not prevent Union law providing more extensive protection.'

[124] See for example Case C-112/00, *Schmidberger* v. *Republik Österreich*, [2003] ECR I-5659, paras. 71–3.

[125] See generally D. Harris and S. Livingstone (eds.), *The Inter-American System of Human Rights* (Oxford: Clarendon Press, 1998); J. M. Pasqualucci, *The Practice and Procedure of the Inter-American Court of Human Rights* (Cambridge University Press, 2003); R. K. Goldman, 'History and action: The Inter-American Human Rights System and the Role of the Inter-American Commission on Human Rights', *HRQ* 31(4) (2009), 856–87.

at the time (thirty-five as of April 2012). One of its first steps was the adoption of the American Declaration on the Rights and Duties of Man, 1948, which predated the UDHR. The American Declaration had a strong emphasis on civil and political rights. Notably, it also acknowledged a number of ESC rights and a list of duties, drawing inspiration, among other sources, from the four freedoms formulated by Roosevelt in 1943.[126] The OAS Charter and the American Declaration constituted the initial normative framework for human rights protection. However, in the first decade it was not complemented by any institutional mechanisms and it took until 1959 to set up the Inter-American Commission on Human Rights (IACHR). The difficulty in reaching agreement on and developing effective procedures was evident as it was only in 1965 that the Commission was given the power to examine individual complaints based on a violation of the OAS Charter and/or the American Declaration.[127]

In a parallel process, the American Convention on Human Rights (ACHR) was adopted in 1969 after a ten-year drafting period. The Convention focuses mainly on civil and political rights. Notably, it recognises the right to a juridical personality, the right to a name and the right to a nationality,[128] reflecting regional concerns over deprivations of these rights. The Convention also stipulates rights of the child, democratic rights (the right to participate in government) and the progressive development of economic, social and cultural rights.[129] This range of rights gives the Convention a fairly broad scope, which comes, however, at the expense of specific guarantees in relation to the rights of the child and ESC rights.[130]

The resulting gap was in part rectified through the adoption of an additional protocol on ESC Rights in 1988.[131] Further treaties were adopted as part of responses to certain types of serious violations experienced in the region. This comprises the Inter-American Convention to Prevent and Punish Torture in 1985, the Inter-American Convention on Forced Disappearance of Persons in 1994 and the Inter-American Convention on the Prevention, Punishment and Eradication of Violence against Women, 1994, which added important normative layers of protection and international precedents in their respective fields of application.

The adoption of the ACHR and the establishment of the IACtHR in 1979 resulted in a two-track system of human rights protection:

---

[126] Section 1.2.5.   [127] Goldman, above note 125, 868.

[128] Articles 3, 18 and 20 ACHR.   [129] Articles 19, 23 and 26 ACHR.

[130] See on the political dynamics resulting in the weak status of economic, social and cultural rights, Goldman, above note 125, 860–3, 879, 885.

[131] The other such protocol adopted is the Additional Protocol to the American Convention on Human Rights to Abolish the Death Penalty (1990).

1   The majority of states in the region, twenty-four at present, have become
    parties to the American Convention, twenty-one of which have accepted
    the jurisdiction of the Court.[132] Individual petitions are first brought
    before the Commission. The Commission is empowered to consider cases
    brought by 'any person or group of persons, or any nongovernmental
    entity legally recognized in one or more member states'[133] and may
    submit a case to the Court where it finds a violation and a friendly settle-
    ment cannot be reached.[134]

2   Cases against other states (that have either not become a party to the
    ACHR or do not recognise the jurisdiction of the IACtHR) can only be
    considered by the Commission. Where the state concerned, such as the
    USA or Canada,[135] is not a party to the ACHR, the Commission applies the
    OAS Charter and the American Declaration.

6.3.2   The Inter-American Commission on Human Rights

The Commission, which is composed of seven independent members elected
by the OAS General Assembly and based in Washington DC, has a broad
promotional and protective mandate.[136] This includes:

- awareness-raising, including by means of thematic reports. Several
  of these reports have been highly influential in identifying and addressing
  human rights problems in specific situations and in the region at
  large;[137]
- observation of the human rights situation in member states, including by
  way of conducting country visits. The Commission had conducted over
  ninety on-site visits by the end of 2011.[138] It has published over fifty
  country reports, which often provide a detailed account of human rights

---

[132] Article 62 ACHR.   [133] Article 44 ACHR.   [134] Article 51 ACHR.

[135] The USA and Canada have not become parties by virtue of a combination of concerns,
    particularly regarding the impact of the ACHR on federal law-making and competences,
    and on individual rights, such as the right to life on abortion policies. See *Enhancing
    Canada's role in the OAS: Canadian Adherence to the American Convention on Human
    Rights: Report of the Standing Senate Committee on Human Rights* (Ottawa: Senate of
    Canada, 2003), and C. Cerna, 'The United States and the American Convention on Human
    Rights: Prospects and Problems of Ratification', in D. Forsythe (ed.), *The United States
    and Human Rights: Looking Inward and Outward* (Lincoln: University of Nebraska Press,
    2000), 94–109.

[136] See articles 106 OAS Charter and 41 ACHR. Information about the work of the
    Commission is available on its website at www.cidh.oas.org.

[137] See for example Report on Terrorism and Human Rights, OEA/Ser. L/V/II.116 Doc.5 rev.1
    corr. (22 October 2002), and Report on Citizen Security and Human Rights, OEA/Ser. L/V/
    II Doc. 57 (31 December 2009).

[138] Ninety-two as of January 2012, see www.oas.org/en/iachr/activities/countries_all.asp for
    updated status on in loco visits.

problems encountered, thereby producing an important record of the human rights situation in the continent;[139]

- making recommendations to OAS member states regarding the regional protection of human rights. The Commission has issued several resolutions, including on transnational challenges such as the human rights of migrants and on specific situations, such as granting precautionary measures in respect of detainees in Guantanamo Bay;[140]
- considering petitions by individuals and NGOs. The Commission has to date considered over 12,000 cases. Its caseload has grown steadily and it received over 1,600 petitions in 2011, with the majority relating to Colombia, Mexico, Peru, Argentina and Chile;[141] and
- submitting cases to the IACtHR. The Commission has referred an average of around twelve cases per year to the Court since 2003 (with an average of fewer than five cases previously).[142]

The Commission has also created a system of rapporteurships, which monitor and promote respect for specific thematic rights.[143]

The Commission has been credited for its role in responding to serious human rights violations in the 1970s and 1980s. Notwithstanding the adoption of the ACHR in 1969 the Inter-American system was confronted with serious human rights violations and apparent non-compliance by military dictatorships such as those in Argentina, Chile, Paraguay and Uruguay. Steps taken by the Commission in response, such as an on-site visit to Argentina in 1979 and subsequent exposure of human rights violations, have been viewed as an important factor in reducing violations and undermining the legitimacy of the then regime.[144] Similarly, the Commission played a critical part in responding to conflict, repression and impunity in countries such

---

[139] The country reports are available on the Commission's website. See for a recent example, Honduras: Human Rights and the Coup d'Etat, OEA/Ser. L/V/II Doc.55 (30 December 2009).

[140] See resolution 3/08, Human Rights of Migrants, International Standards and the Return Directive of the EU, and resolution 2/11, Regarding the Situation of the Detainees at Guantanamo Bay, United States, MC 259-02, and Guantanamo Bay Precautionary Measures (2002).

[141] Statistical data are included in the Commission's annual reports.   [142] Ibid.

[143] Freedom of expression, rights of women, rights of migrant workers and their families, rights of the child, rights of human rights defenders, rights of indigenous peoples, rights of persons deprived of liberty, rights of Afro-descendants and against racial discrimination. See www.oas.org/en/iachr/mandate/rapporteurships.asp.

[144] Report on the Situation of Human Rights in Argentina, OEA/Ser. L/V/II.49, Doc. 19 corr.1 (11 April 1980). See also Goldman, above note 125, 873, and S. Canton, 'The Inter-American Commission on Human Rights: 50 Years of Advances and the New Challenges', *Americas Quarterly* (*AQ*) (Summer 2009), online, at www.americasquarterly.org/Inter-American-Commission-Human-Rights.

as Colombia, Guatemala and Peru in the 1980s and 1990s.[145] The Commission has equally developed a strong focus on assistance in transitional processes, such as in Colombia.[146] It has also paid special attention to the promotion and protection of rights in respect of specific groups, such as the rights of women and indigenous peoples, or in particular contexts, such as counter-terrorism.[147] Over the years the Commission has contributed to the development of American human rights law through its thematic reports and petitions. Several cases before it concerned critical issues, such as the protection of unborn life in the *Baby Boy* case.[148] Considering the breadth of its mandate it comes as no surprise that the Commission, like other bodies of its kind, suffers from limited resources and a lack of capacity that threaten to undermine the efficiency and effectiveness of its work.[149]

6.3.3   The Inter-American Court of Human Rights

The Court was established in 1979. It is composed of seven judges elected by the states parties to the Convention at the OAS General Assembly[150] and is based in Costa Rica. The Court has contentious jurisdiction over cases in relation to alleged violations of the ACHR and any other protocols to which a state is a party.[151] It can also issue advisory opinions regarding the interpretation of the ACHR or other OAS treaties.[152] The exercise of its contentious jurisdiction is circumscribed by two important factors: (1) the state(s) concerned has/have to recognise the Court's competence to hear contentious cases;[153] (2) only the Commission or states parties can submit cases.[154] This means that the Commission acts as gatekeeper in the individual

---

[145] Goldman, above note 125, 875–8; V. Abramovich, 'From massive violations to structural patterns: new approaches and classic tensions in the Inter-American human rights system', *SUR – International Journal on Human Rights* (*SUR-IJHR*), 11, (2009), 7–37, at 23.

[146] See in this regard, Statement by the Inter-American Commission on Human Rights on the Application and Scope of the Justice and Peace Law in Colombia, OEA/Ser. L/V/II125, Doc. 15 (1 August 2006); Violence and Discrimination against Women in the Armed Conflict in Colombia, OEA/Ser. L/V/II Doc.67 (18 October 2006); Principal Guidelines for a Comprehensive Reparation Policy, OEA/Ser. L/V/II.131, Doc.1 (19 February 2008).

[147] See for the Commission's reports, www.cidh.oas.org/publi.eng.htm.

[148] *White and Potter* v. *The United States* (*The Baby Boy* case), HRLJ 2 (1981) 110.

[149] See Report of the Special Working Group to Reflect on the Workings of the Inter-American Commission on Human Rights with a view to Strengthening the Inter-American Human Rights System for consideration by the Permanent Council, OEA/Ser. G, GT/SIDH-13/11 rev. 2 (13 December 2011), 7–16.

[150] Articles 52–4 ACHR.

[151] Articles 62 and 19(6) Additional Protocol on Economic, Social and Cultural Rights. See generally on the scope of the Court's jurisdiction (with a particular focus on the Convention of Belém do Pará), *González et al. (Cotton Field)* v. *Mexico*, Preliminary objection, merits, reparations and costs, Judgment of 16 November 2009, Ser. C, no. 205, paras. 31–81.

[152] Article 64 ACHR.   [153] Article 62 ACHR.   [154] Article 61 ACHR.

complaints procedure. Unlike in the ECHR system, individuals cannot bring cases directly before the Court. Initially, applicants did not have any independent role in proceedings. This was problematic where their views diverged from that of the Commission, which was increasingly seen as an anomaly that over time prompted the Court to develop changes in its practice.[155] Under the 2001 and 2009 Rules of Procedures the victims and their representatives have been given a prominent role and effectively function as parties following the referral of a case; they 'may submit their brief containing pleadings, motions and evidence autonomously and shall continue to act autonomously throughout the proceedings',[156] which signals a decisive shift towards the recognition of victims as parties. In addition, the role of Inter-American defender has been established to represent victims who do not have the benefit of legal assistance.[157]

By June 2012 the Court's Series C on contentious cases had reached 244, many of which had been initiated by national and regional NGOs, such as the CEJIL.[158] The inter-state procedure, in contrast, has effectively remained dormant, with not a single judgment on the merits.[159] In the 1980s and 1990s the Court was seized with a limited number of cases of serious violations, including massacres, enforced disappearances, torture and lack of judicial protection, as well as unfair trials.[160] In the 2000s the Court adjudicated a series of cases characterised by large-scale and systematic violations, many of which had been committed in the course of conflict and counter-insurgency (such as in Colombia, Guatemala and Peru), and had taken place in a climate of impunity.[161] The Court was also increasingly called upon to

---

[155] See *Five Pensioners* v. *Peru*, Merits, reparations and costs, Judgment of 28 February 2003, Ser. C, no. 98, paras. 152–7; L. Burgorgue-Larsen and A. Ú. de Torres, *The Inter-American Court of Human Rights, Case Law and Commentary* (Oxford University Press, 2011), 40–7.

[156] Article 25(1) Rules of Procedure (2009), at www.corteidh.or.cr/reglamento/regla_ing.pdf.

[157] Article 37 ibid.

[158] www.cejil.org. See more generally on strategic litigation in the Inter-American system, Abramovich, above note 145, 14–16.

[159] One case was declared inadmissible by the Inter-American Commission for failure to exhaust domestic remedies. See *Nicaragua* v. *Costa Rica*, *Annual Report 2007*, Report no. 11/07, Interstate Case 01/06, OEA/Ser. L/V/II.130, Doc.22 rev. 1 (29 December 2007). Another inter-state case between Ecuador and Colombia brought in 2009 was pending in early 2012, see Report no. 112/10, Inter-State Petition IP-02, Admissibility, *Franklin Guillermo Aisalla Molina, Ecuador* v. *Guatemala*, OEA/Ser. L/V/II.140, Doc. 10 (21 October 2010).

[160] The Court issued judgments on the merits in a total of twenty-two cases between 1987 and 2000, including its first, *Velásquez Rodríguez* v. *Honduras* (enforced disappearance), Merits, Judgment of 29 July 1988, Ser. C, no. 4; *Aloeboetoe et al.* v. *Suriname* (attack by soldiers on community), Preliminary objections and merits, Judgment of 4 December 1991, Ser. C, no. 11; *(Street Children) Villagrán Morales et al.* v. *Guatemala* (abduction, torture, and murder of minors), Merits, Judgment of 19 November 1999, Ser. C, no. 63.

[161] See in particular the 'massacre' cases, *Mapiripán Massacre* v. *Colombia*, Merits, reparations and costs, Judgment of 15 September 2005, Ser. C, no. 134; *Pueblo Bello*

rule on inadequate responses to violations in countries such as Bolivia, Brazil and Mexico, reflecting the influence of transitional justice processes.[162] In addition, it focused on collective rights, notably in respect of the rights of indigenous peoples, which have served as international precedents.[163] The Court's jurisprudence on children's rights has also been noteworthy.[164] Moreover, the Court issued landmark rulings in cases of sexual violence, such as *Castro-Castro Prison* v. *Peru*, where its interpretation of rape and forced nakedness have proved influential, and the *Cotton Field* case on due diligence obligations in respect of gender-based violence.[165] Overall, the Court's recent jurisprudence has been viewed as signalling a shift in focus 'to structural violence by police on marginal communities, collapsed prison systems and deeply problematic judiciaries'.[166] This jurisprudence in contentious cases has been complemented by a series of important advisory opinions, such as on the derogability of judicial protection during states of emergencies and the rights of migrants.[167]

Massacre v. *Colombia*, Merits, reparations and costs, Judgment of 31 January 2006, Ser. C, no. 140; *Ituango Massacres* v. *Colombia*, Merits, reparations and costs, Judgment of 1 July 2006, Ser. C, no. 148; *La Rochela Massacre* v. *Colombia*, Merits, reparations and costs, Judgment of 11 May 2007, Ser. C, no. 163; *Plan de Sánchez Massacre* v. *Guatemala*, Merits, Judgment of 29 April 2004, Ser. C, no. 105; *Las Dos Erres Massacre* v. *Guatemala*, Preliminary objections, merits, reparations and costs, Judgment of 24 November 2009, Ser. C, no. 211; *Miguel Castro-Castro Prison* v. *Peru*, Merits, reparations and costs, Judgment of 25 November 2006, Ser. C, no. 160.

[162] *Gomes Lund et al.* v. *Brazil*, Preliminary objections, merits, reparations and costs, Judgment of 24 November 2010, Ser. C, no. 219; *Renato Ticona-Estrada et al.* v. *Bolivia*, Merits, reparations and costs, Judgment of 27 November 2008, Ser. C, no. 191; *Radilla-Pacheco* v. *Mexico*, Preliminary objections, merits, reparations and costs, Judgment of 23 November 2009, Ser. C, no. 209. See also Abramovich, above note 145, 8.

[163] See *Yakye Axa Indigenous Community* v. *Paraguay*, Merits, reparations and costs, Judgment of 17 June 2005, Ser. C, no. 125; *Sawhoyamaxa Indigenous Community* v. *Paraguay*, Merits, reparations and costs, Judgment of 29 March 2006, Ser. C, no. 146; *Saramaka People* v. *Suriname*, Preliminary objections, merits, reparations and costs, Judgment of 28 November 2007, Ser. C, no. 172; *Xákmok Kásek Indigenous Community* v. *Paraguay*, Merits, reparation and costs, Judgment of 24 August 2010, Ser. C, no. 214. See also Abramovich, above note 145, 20-2.

[164] See in particular the *Street Children* case and *Juridical Condition and Human Rights of the Child*, Advisory opinion of 28 August 2002, Ser. A, no. 17. See for an analysis of the Court's jurisprudence, M. Feria Tinta, *The Landmark Rulings of the Inter American Court of Human Rights on the Rights of the Child: Protecting the Most Vulnerable at the Edge* (Leiden, Boston: Martinus Nijhoff, 2008).

[165] *Castro-Castro Prison* v. *Peru*, paras. 304–13, and *Gonzalez* v. *Mexico*, paras. 222–411.

[166] P. Engstrom and A. Hurrell, 'Why the Human Rights Regime in the Americas matters', in M. Serrano and V. Popovski (eds.), *Human Rights Regimes in the Americas* (Tokyo, New York, Paris: United Nations University Press, 2010), 29–55, at 42.

[167] *Habeas Corpus in Emergency Situations* (Arts. 27(2), 25(1) and 7(6) American Convention on Human Rights), Advisory opinion OC-87 of 30 January 1987, Ser. A, no. 8; *Judicial Guarantees in States of Emergency* (Arts. 27(2), 25 and 8 American Convention on

Faced with patterns of systematic violations the Court has been cognisant of their political context and dimension, particularly marginalisation, discrimination, institutional rule of law weaknesses and impunity.[168] It has articulated a number of principles and fashioned approaches that have broken new ground in the international understanding of human rights. One prominent example is its jurisprudence on forced disappearances. The Court found that this practice entails multiple (and ongoing) violations, recognised family members as victims in their own right and identified positive obligations of the state to investigate alleged violations where the perpetrators cannot be identified.[169] It has also been at the forefront of the development of the right to truth, which includes access to state-held information.[170] This comes within the context of its strong emphasis on states' duty to combat impunity, holding in particular that amnesties are incompatible with the duty to investigate and offer effective access to justice for violations such as the right to life and freedom from torture.[171]

The Court's approach is characterised by its sensitivity towards the human rights problems facing the region. It has developed a practice of hearing detailed evidence, which makes its judgments important records of violations in their own right. The Court's interpretation of the Convention demonstrates a strong focus on effectiveness, particularly effective remedies. Its jurisprudence on reparation in particular is considered to constitute a major contribution to human rights law.[172] However, the Court has at times been criticised for articulating positions that may find limited support in international human rights law, such as locating the question of labour protection of undocumented workers as a question of non-discrimination having attained the status of *jus cogens*[173] and for introducing notions, such as the *proyecto*

Human Rights), Advisory opinion of OC-9, 6 October 1987, Ser. A, no. 9; *Juridical Conditions and Rights of the Undocumented Migrants*, Advisory opinion OC-18 of 17 September 2003, Ser. A, no. 18.

[168] See on the point of structural inequality in particular Abramovich, above note 145.

[169] See in particular the landmark case of *Velásquez Rodríguez* v. *Honduras*, as well as *Goiburú* v. *Paraguay*, Merits, reparations and costs, Judgment of 22 September 2006, Ser. C, no. 153, and *La Cantuta* v. *Peru*, Merits, reparations and costs, Judgment of 29 November 2006, Ser. C, no. 162.

[170] See *Bámaca Velásquez* v. *Guatemala*, Merits, Judgment of 25 November 2000, Ser. C, no. 70, paras. 197–202; *La Cantuta* v. *Peru*, para. 128; *Gomes Lund* v. *Brazil*, paras. 138–9, 151, 173, 200, 201, 211, 217, 219, 240, 297.

[171] See in particular *Barrios Altos* v. *Peru*, Merits, Judgment of 14 March 2001, Ser. C, no. 75, paras. 41–44, and *Gomes Lund* v. *Brazil*, paras. 149–80.

[172] See section 13.10.

[173] See *Juridical Condition and Rights of the Undocumented Migrants*, para. 101. See critical comments on this approach, J. Cavallaro and S. E. Brewer, 'Reevaluating Regional Human Rights Litigation in the Twenty-First Century: the Case of the Inter-American Court', *AJIL* 102 (2008), 768–827, at 822–4.

da vida (life plan) as a component of reparation,[174] without applying them consistently in its jurisprudence.

6.3.4   Impact

The IACHR and IACtHR have played an important role in responding to systematic and widespread violations in the region. This includes their emphasis on victims' rights, access to justice and accountability, which has contributed to a significant shift in the regional human rights culture. At the domestic level, states have taken a number of legislative and institutional measures to bring their systems into conformity with the Convention, either in response to specific judgments or independently, even though compliance has been uneven.[175] This forms part of the growing normative influence of the Inter-American system and its impact on political and judicial actors in the region.[176] However, several problems remain. At the regional level, the non-ratification of the ACHR by the USA and Canada, in combination with the lack of recognition of the Court's jurisdiction by several Central American states, has given the system a decidedly Latin American orientation. This signals embedded faultlines that still hinder the development of a truly American system. At the national level, marginalisation and impunity remain deeply engrained and the Inter-American system has struggled to make an impact on underlying structural political and economic factors that foster violations.[177]

The Inter-American system also faces familiar institutional challenges.[178] While the caseload of the Commission and the Court – the latter because of the limited number of referrals – is still light in comparison to that of the ECtHR, a growing awareness and willingness to resort to these regional mechanisms is putting an increasing strain on the system.[179] The inadequate resources made available have already forced the Court to reduce the number of hearings, which undermines one of its important functions as a public forum to expose human rights violations.[180] These developments may in time

---

[174] T. M. Antkowiak, 'Remedial Approaches to Human Rights Violations: the Inter-American Court of Human Rights and Beyond', *Colum. J. Transnat'l L.* 46 (2008), 351–419, at 371, fn. 101. See also section 13.10.8.

[175] See F. Basch *et al.*, 'The Effectiveness of the Inter-American System of Human Rights Protection: a Quantitative Approach to its Functioning and Compliance With its Decisions', *SUR-IJHR* 12 (2010), 9–36, and Open Society Justice Initiative, *From Judgment to Justice, Implementing International and Regional Human Rights Decisions* (New York: Open Society Foundations, 2010), 63–92. See also section 7.5.

[176] See for a detailed study, Cavallaro and Brewer, above note 173, and Engstrom and Hurrell, above note 166.

[177] See in particular Abramovich, above note 145.

[178] See IACHR, Position Document on the Process of Strengthening of the Inter-American System for the Protection of Human Rights, OEA/Ser. L/V/II, Doc. 68 (8 April 2012).

[179] Ibid.   [180] Cavallaro and Brewer, above note 173, 797–808.

result in further reforms, considering experiences in the European system and provide victims with direct access to the Court.

INTERVIEW 6.3

An intimate experience of the Court as litigant and Senior Staff Attorney

(Oswaldo Ruiz-Chiriboga)

Oswaldo Ruiz-Chiriboga worked as lawyer for CEJIL before serving for six years as Senior Staff Attorney at the IACtHR. At the time of writing, he was undertaking research at Ghent University (Belgium) on indigenous customary law in Ecuador and its compatibility with international human rights standards.[1]

What has been your experience as a litigant before the Inter-American human rights system?

My first exposure came from November 2001 to October 2002 when I coordinated the work of the students of the Human Rights Clinic at the Pontifical Catholic University of Ecuador. We represented victims in several cases before the IACHR and in one case before the IACtHR (*Tibi* v. *Ecuador*). From 2003 to 2005, I worked for CEJIL, which is a major NGO that engages with the Inter-American system at several levels. In my work on the Legal Defence Programme, I led cases on human rights from Honduras and Nicaragua before the Commission and Court. This included researching the case background and precedents, drafting and editing briefs, attending hearings, developing legal arguments, communicating with client NGOs and victims and negotiating with state agents, among other functions. Since I was the only Ecuadorian at CEJIL I also worked closely with its Washington DC office on all the Ecuadorian cases. In addition, as part of my work on the training and dissemination programme, and the Campaign to Strengthen the Inter-American System, I travelled around Central America conducting meetings, seminars and courses with NGOs, public servants, victims of human rights violations and indigenous peoples, among others.

You later on became Senior Staff Attorney at the Court. What did this role entail and how has it changed your views of the Court?

I served in the Court from February 2005 until September 2010. As Senior Staff Attorney I coordinated one of the then six working groups of the Court's permanent Registry (nowadays there are seven groups). Under

---

[1] Oswaldo Ruiz-Chiriboga maintains a blog on the Inter-American system (in Spanish), at http://corteidhblog.blogspot.co.uk.

the general supervision of the Court's Registrar I was in charge of 20 per cent of the cases pending before the Court, exercising executive and operational authority over the unit. This consisted of judicial support, coordination and supervision of the work of interns and junior attorneys. The work entailed a range of tasks. In particular, I drafted legal documents and opinions and provided the necessary legal direction on substantive and procedural issues. This included complex or novel questions on a wide range of international law and human rights issues, including violent conflicts and democratic transitions. My most important task was to assist the Court's judges in drafting the Court's decisions, judgments and advisory opinions.

Serving as a staff attorney was a wonderful experience. It showed me how the Court is able to deal with all its duties and functions even though it does not have sufficient financial and human resources. As is well known, the Court's budget is not enough to cover all its needs, which has forced it to look for external funding. The lack of resources has many implications, the most important being the work overload of all the attorneys. We had to deal with all the contentious cases, advisory opinions and provisional measures. Moreover, since the Court is also in charge of monitoring the compliance of its judgments we had to analyse all the compliance reports submitted by the states and the observations sent by the Commission and the victims' representatives. In short, a case is not over when the Court delivers its judgment. It is only closed when the state has complied with the judgment and this can take years. This fact increases the workload of the Court because it has to deal with pending but also already decided cases. Finally, another consequence of the inadequate funding of the Court is the poor quality of the translations of its decisions.

What impact has the Inter-American Commission and the Court's jurisprudence had in your country?

In *Chaparro-Álvarez and Lapo-Íniguez* v. *Ecuador*, the Court ordered the state to modify its Constitution and its national law, because: (1) the *habeas corpus* remedy was decided by majors and not by judges, and (2) the national law posed arbitrary burdens on persons accused of drug-dealing (the individual had to pay a fee for the administration of his/hers seized goods, even if he or she was acquitted). Ecuador complied with these orders. However, it is hard to say that the Court's judgment played a significant role in the relevant constitutional amendment, because during that time the country was already in the process of adopting a new Constitution and local stakeholders had a considerable voice. In general terms, I think that one of the major impacts of the Court's judgments in

Ecuador and the region is its doctrine of 'Conventionality Control', i.e. the duty of national judges to interpret and apply domestic law in accordance with the Convention.

Overall, what do you see as the strengths and weaknesses of the Inter-American system?

Some of the main points of concern are the insufficient budget for both the Commission and Court; delays in the procedure before the Commission; and lack of transparency in the process of appointing and electing judges and commissioners that may affect the impartiality of the Court and the Commission. OAS states have raised several points of concern regarding the work of the Commission, pointing out weaknesses in the procedure of precautionary measures, friendly settlements, preparation of annual reports and the work of the rapporteurships though I am not sure how justified they are, except in respect of the system of rapporteurships. In addition, the Court has at times not been clear in its interpretation of the Convention and other regional treaties, for instance in *Acevedo-Buendía et al.* v. *Peru* it declared it has contentious jurisdiction over article 26 ACHR (ESC rights), but in doing so it ignored the Protocol of San Salvador. On other occasions the Court has imported decisions of other tribunals, particularly the ECHR, without considering that such decisions were based on the European regional consensus, which may not be similarly present in the Americas.

As to its strengths, the Court is very open to interpreting the Convention in such a way that groups traditionally excluded, for instance indigenous peoples, could find international protection for their cultural particularities. It is also the leading tribunal on reparation issues. In addition, the Court has modified its Rules of Procedure to expedite the process before it, to facilitate the participation of victims, to allow the participation of new actors (the Inter-American Defender, for instance) and to minimise the expenses of victims (e.g. the Fund for Victims).

In light of this, what do you see as the main challenges facing the Inter-American system today?

The main challenges include achieving universality of the Inter-American system by encouraging ratification of its treaties by all the OAS Member States; ensuring full compliance with the recommendations and decisions made; improving procedures and ensuring strict observance of the regulatory frameworks in the individual petitions system; increasing efficiency and expediency in the processing of petitions and cases and moving toward greater transparency in the management of the system, particularly the Commission.

QUESTIONS

- What are the defining regional characteristics of the Inter-American system?

- Is it possible to speak of a truly American human rights system?

- Have the Inter-American bodies successfully responded to human rights problems prevailing in the continent?

- What role did the Inter-American system play in the context of national transitions from dictatorships, such as those in Argentina and Peru?

6.4   THE AFRICAN HUMAN RIGHTS SYSTEM

6.4.1   Overview

Human rights formed part of the broader agenda of the Pan-African Congresses in the anti-colonial struggle prior to independence.[181] However, the Organisation of African Unity (OAU) established in 1963 largely omitted any mention of human rights, emphasising decolonisation, state sovereignty and development instead. It was only in the late 1960s that proposals for an African human rights instrument began to be put forward that ultimately resulted in the adoption of the ACHPR in 1981 and the establishment of the African Commission on Human and Peoples' Rights (African Commission). The ACHPR is remarkable as it covers a wide spectrum of civil and political rights, though not always drafted with sufficient precision, such as the right to a fair trial,[182] as well as ESC rights. It is the only major human rights treaty that recognises a set of collective rights, including the right to development, the right to peace and security and the right to a satisfactory environment.[183] The ACHPR also lists a number of individual duties 'towards his [and her] family and society, the state and other legally recognized communities and the international community'.[184] The emphasis on duties, together with the recognition of collective rights, has been viewed as a genuine African feature

---

[181] See on the development of the African human rights system, K. O. Kufuor, *The African Human Rights System: Origin and Evolution* (New York: Palgrave Macmillan, 2010); F. Ouguergouz, *The African Charter on Human and Peoples' Rights: A Comprehensive Agenda for Human Rights* (The Hague: Martinus Nijhoff, 2003), 19–48; F. Viljoen, *International Human Rights Law in Africa*, 2nd edn (Oxford University Press, 2012), 151–69; M. Killander, 'African Human Rights Law in Theory and Practice', in S. Joseph and A. McBeth (eds.), *Research Handbook on International Human Rights Law* (Cheltenham, Northampton, MA: Edward Elgar, 2010), 388–413.

[182] Compare article 7 ACHPR to articles 6 ECHR, 8 ACHR and 14 ICCPR. The shortcoming has been largely rectified by means of the Principles and Guidelines on the Right to Fair Trial and Legal Assistance in Africa, DOC/OS(XXX)247 (2001).

[183] See articles 19–24 ACHPR.   [184] Article 27 ACHPR.

of the treaty.[185] Yet the impact is limited because there are no procedures to enforce these duties and hold individuals liable for a breach; in practice, the relevant provisions (articles 27–9) serve to qualify rights, that is they provide the grounds on which states may restrict the exercise of rights such as freedom of expression.[186]

After a hesitant beginning the African human rights system has gained considerable momentum since the 1990s. Political changes and democratisation processes in several states, institutional reforms at the regional level and increasing NGO engagement have contributed to a stronger focus on human rights and several instruments were adopted that addressed various apparent lacunae in the regional system of protection. These include the African Charter on the Rights and Welfare of the Child (1990), the Protocol on the Rights of Women in Africa (2003) and the AU Convention for the Protection and Assistance of Internally Displaced Persons in Africa (Kampala Convention) 2009, the latter being the first treaty on the subject in international human rights law.[187]

Important institutional developments include in particular the establishment of the AU in 2002 (including all African states with the exception of Morocco because of the disputed status of Western Sahara).[188] In notable contrast to its predecessor, one of the AU's objectives as set out in its Constitutive Act of 2000 is to 'promote and protect human and peoples' rights in accordance with the [ACHPR] and other relevant human rights instruments'.[189] The Act explicitly mentions '[R]espect for democratic principles, human rights, the rule of law and good governance; humanity' as one of the AU's principles.[190] As an exception to the principle of non-interference the Act also recognises 'the right of the Union to intervene in a member State pursuant to a decision of the Assembly in respect of grave circumstances, namely: war crimes, genocide and crimes against humanity'.[191] Significantly, the AU established a number of bodies and procedures with a

---

[185] See in particular M. Mutua, *Human Rights: A Political and Cultural Critique* (Philadelphia: University of Pennsylvania Press, 2002), 82–92.

[186] See *Media Rights Agenda and Others* v. *Nigeria*, 105/93, 128/94, 130/94, 152/96 (1998), paras. 68–71, and, for a discussion of the African Commission's jurisprudence in this regard, K. Olaniyan, 'Civil and Political Rights in the African Charter: Articles 8–14', in M. Evans and R. Murray (eds.), *The African Charter on Human and Peoples' Rights: The System in Practice 1986–2006*, 2nd edn (Cambridge University Press, 2008), 213–43, at 220–3.

[187] For current status, see OAU/AU treaties, conventions, protocols and charters, online, at http://au.int/en/treaties.

[188] See http://au.int/en/about/nutshell; and on the AU's historical development, R. Murray, *Human Rights in Africa: From the OAU to the African Union* (Cambridge University Press, 2004), 1–48, and Viljoen, above note 181, 151–69.

[189] Article 3(h) Constitutive Act of the AU.   [190] Article 4(m) ibid.

[191] Article 4(h) ibid.

bearing on human rights and has generally assumed a more proactive role in this field, albeit with a rather mixed record to date.[192] In addition, a Protocol to establish an African Court on Human and Peoples' Rights (ACtHPR) (to become part of the African Court of Justice and Human Rights) was adopted in 1998 to provide stronger judicial human rights protection in the region.[193]

Sub-regional developments complement the African human rights architecture. States in the crisis-ridden Great Lakes region have agreed on the Great Lakes Pact, an impressive instrument that seeks to strengthen human rights, accountability and justice in the area.[194] However, its impact has been limited due to the lack of adequate institutional mechanisms.[195] Human rights have also become an important component of sub-regional economic integration. Significantly, the courts of regional economic communities, particularly the East African Community (EAC), the Economic Community of West African States (ECOWAS) and the Southern African Development Community (SADC), have increasingly interpreted their jurisdiction as enabling them to adjudicate human rights cases.[196] Some of these developments have met with resistance or non-compliance and the proliferation of mechanisms does not necessarily equate with increased effectiveness. Nevertheless, they testify to the growing regional efforts to address human rights at the normative and institutional level. The recognition of the close link between respect for human rights, a stable and democratic order and economic development must count as an important factor behind these changes, which have received added impetus thanks to creative litigation by NGOs and the largely human rights-friendly jurisprudence of the courts.

6.4.2   The African Commission on Human and Peoples' Rights

The African Commission is based in the Gambia and composed of eleven members who are elected by the AU Assembly of Heads of State and

---

[192] See for a good overview, Viljoen, above note 181, 169–212.

[193] Protocol to the ACHPR on the Establishment of an ACtHPR (adopted 10 June 1998, in force since 25 January 2004), (1998 Protocol).

[194] See for further information and the text of the Pact the website of the International Conference on the Great Lakes Region, online, at, www.icglr.org/spip.php?article2.

[195] See for an in-depth assessment, D. Clancy, 'Lessons from a State of Flux: the International Justice Laboratory of the Great Lakes Pact', in L. Oette (ed.), *Criminal Law Reform and Transitional Justice: Human rights perspectives for Sudan* (Farnham: Ashgate, 2011), 197–226.

[196] See in particular L. N. Murungi and J. Gallinetti, 'The Role of Sub-Regional Courts in the African Human Rights System', *SUR-IJHR* 7(13) (2010), 119–44. For latest developments, see the websites of the respective courts, www.eacj.org/judgments.php; www.courtecowas.org; www.sadc-tribunal.org.

Government and serve in their personal capacity.[197] It has a broad mandate to promote and protect human rights as laid down in article 45 ACHPR. Its promotional mandate includes the consideration of states parties' reports, the study of human rights issues and country-specific situations, including by means of fact-finding missions and a system of special rapporteurs and working groups.[198] The Commission's protection mandate comprises the consideration of individual and inter-state complaints, a competence that it derived from articles 55 and 56 ACHPR. The Commission meets biannually for its general sessions to fulfil its mandate and may convene special (extraordinary) sessions where called for.[199]

In what was effectively its first decade the Commission adopted a number of important decisions in the 1990s. These concerned a series of cases, mainly brought by NGOs making use of the broad standing provided for in the Charter, which predominantly addressed mass violations (including violations of the right to life, prohibition of torture, right to liberty, right to a fair trial and mass expulsions).[200] However, the Commission's decisions were largely confined to short findings of violations, lacked broader visibility and were frequently not complied with. The execution of Ken Saro Wiwa by Nigeria's dictatorship, in blatant disregard of an interim measure by the Commission calling for the very suspension of the punishment, is one of the most glaring examples in this respect.[201] Following a series of impor-

---

[197] Article 13 ACHPR. See on the Commission more generally, articles 30–44 ACHPR, and its website www.achpr.org.

[198] See, Viljoen, above note 181, 289–390.

[199] The session reports are available on the Commission's website, at www.achpr.org.

[200] See in particular, *Krishna Achuthan (on behalf of Aleke Banda), Amnesty International (on behalf of Orton and Vera Chirwa), Amnesty International (on behalf of Orton and Vera Chirwa)* v. *Malawi*, 64/92-68/92-78/92 (1994); *Organisation mondiale contre la torture, Association Internationale des juristes démocrates, Commission internationale des juristes, Union interafricaine des droits de l'Homme* v. *Rwanda*, 27/89-46/91-49/91-99/93 (1996); *Free Legal Assistance Group, Lawyers' Committee for Human Rights, Union Interafricaine des Droits de l'Homme, Les Témoins de Jehovah* v. *Democratic Republic of Congo*, 25/89-47/90-56/91-100/93 (1996); *Union interafricaine des droits de l'Homme, Fédération internationale des ligues des droits de l'Homme, RADDHO, Organisation nationale des droits de l'Homme au Sénégal and Association malienne des droits de l'Homme* v. *Angola*, 159/96 (1997); *Amnesty International, Comité Loosli Bachelard, Lawyers' Committee for Human Rights, Association of Members of the Episcopal Conference of East Africa* v. *Sudan*, 48/90-50/91-52/91-89/93 (1999); and in the early 2000s, *Malawi African Association, Amnesty International, Ms Sarr Diop, Union interafricaine des droits de l'Homme and RADDHO, Collectif des veuves et ayants-Droit, Association mauritanienne des droits de l'Homme* v. *Mauritania*, 54/91-61/91-96/93-98/93-164/97-196/97-210/98 (2000); and *Movement burkinabé des droits de l'Homme et des peuples* v. *Burkina Faso*, 204/97 (2001).

[201] *International PEN, Constitutional Rights Project, Civil Liberties Organisation and Interights (on behalf of Ken Saro Wiwa Jnr)* v. *Nigeria*, 137/94-139/94-154/96-161/97 (1998), para. 115: 'This is a blot on the legal system of Nigeria that will not be easy

tant cases against Nigeria in the 1990s,[202] the Commission developed its jurisprudence throughout the 2000s. The violations and countries concerned have become more varied, with several high-profile cases against Guinea, Zimbabwe, Eritrea, Angola, Cote D'Ivoire, Sudan and Cameroon.[203] Its first inter-state decision, *Democratic Republic of Congo v. Burundi, Rwanda and Uganda*, which concerned the responsibility of the defendant states for a series of violations committed in the course of the conflict in the Democratic Republic of Congo, is remarkable for its parallel application of international human rights and international humanitarian law by virtue of article 60 ACHPR.[204] *Social and Economic Rights Action Center (SERAC) and Center for Economic and Social Rights (CESR) v. Nigeria*, which concerned multiple violations committed in the context of oil extraction in Ogoniland, is a leading case, setting a major precedent for its broad application of ESC rights.[205] It contains important considerations on collective rights, a jurisprudence that was later complemented in cases of indigenous peoples[206] and groups targeted in the course of conflict, such as in Darfur, Sudan.[207] The Commission has in its recent jurisprudence also increasingly emphasised the positive obligations of states to secure rights, such as to take measures to protect individuals from post-election violence in Cameroon.[208]

---

to erase. To have carried out the execution in the face of pleas to the contrary by the Commission and world opinion is something that we pray will never happen again. That it is a violation of the Charter is an understatement.'

[202] By July 2012, Nigeria was the country with the highest number of cases (thirty-two) in the African system. See www.achpr.org/communications. See for an account of the impact of the African system on Nigeria, Okafor, above note 2, 91–154.

[203] See *Institute for Human Rights and Development in Africa (on behalf of Sierra Leonean refugees in Guinea) v. Guinea*, 249/02 (2004); *Zimbabwe Human Rights NGO Forum v. Zimbabwe*, 245/02 (2006); *Article 19 v. Eritrea*, 275/03 (2007); *Institute for Human Rights and Development in Africa (on behalf of Esmaila Connateh & 13 others) v. Angola*, 292/04 (2008); *Mouvement ivoirien des droits humains (MIDH) v. Cote d'Ivoire*, 246/02 (2008); *Sudan Human Rights Organisation & Centre on Housing Rights and Evictions (COHRE) v. Sudan*, 279/03–296/05 (2009); *Association of Victims of Post Electoral Violence & Interights v. Cameroon*, 272/03 (2009). See also *Statistics on the Implementation of the African Charter on Human and Peoples' Rights, 30 years later* (Banjul: African Commission on Human and Peoples' Rights, September 2011).

[204] *Democratic Republic of Congo v. Burundi, Rwanda, Uganda*, 227/99 (2003).

[205] *Social and Economic Rights Action Center (SERAC) and Center for Economic and Social Rights (CESR) v. Nigeria (Ogoniland case)*, 155/96 (2001).

[206] *Centre for Minority Rights Development (Kenya) and Minority Rights Group (on behalf of Endorois Welfare Council) v. Kenya (Endorois case)*, 276/03 (2009).

[207] *Sudan Human Rights Organisation and Centre on Housing Rights and Evictions (COHRE) v. Sudan*.

[208] See *Association of Victims of Post Electoral Violence & Interights v. Cameroon*, paras. 83–112, and *Zimbabwe Human Rights NGO Forum v. Zimbabwe*, paras. 142–64.

The Commission's interpretation of the ACHPR has by and large not been underscored by clearly articulated doctrines.[209] Instead, it has been rather pragmatic, drawing freely on a range of sources (on the basis of article 60 ACHPR) to support its reasoning.[210] It has emphasised the lack of derogability of rights and has interpreted clawback clauses ('according to the law', 'before the law') broadly to include international law standards, thereby preventing states from narrowing the scope of applicability of rights.[211] The Commission has endorsed the principles of subsidiarity and the margin of appreciation in a recent case but has otherwise not applied these doctrines in its jurisprudence.[212]

The Commission's approach, while seemingly progressive in some instances, appears at times to lack coherence and consistency. It has construed obligations broadly, holding that due diligence is an obligation of results not means.[213] It has also read rights into the ACHPR, such as the right to housing and food in *Social and Economic Rights Action Center (SERAC) and Center for Economic and Social Rights (CESR)* v. *Nigeria*, which can be viewed either as progressive interpretation or a dangerously loose construction of the treaty that was not necessary to achieve the desired level of protection.[214] Conversely, it has adopted a rather narrow interpretation of state responsibility and obligations where a more purposive one could have been expected to advance the effective protection of human rights, such as in its interpretation of Zimbabwe's fulfilment of its positive obligations in relation to serious violations attributed to the ruling party ZANU-PF.[215] Its fashioning of remedies for violations has been rather general, notably not specifying amounts of compensation, although some, particularly more recent decisions have identified a series of specific remedies.[216] The jurisprudence of the Commission therefore provides a rather mixed picture characterised by an element of unpredictability that leaves considerable scope for further development.

---

[209] However, see for the Commission's jurisprudence on aspects of admissibility, particularly exhaustion of domestic remedies, F. Viljoen, 'Communications under the African Charter: Procedure and Admissibility', in Evans and Murray, above note 186, 76–138.

[210] According to article 60, '[t]he Commission shall draw inspiration from international law on human and peoples' rights'.

[211] See in particular *Media Rights Agenda and Constitutional Rights Project* v. *Nigeria*, paras. 65–70.

[212] *Garreth Anver Prince* v. *South Africa*, 255/02 (2004), paras. 50–4.

[213] *Association of Victims of Post Electoral Violence and Interights* v. *Cameroon*, para. 111.

[214] See for critical comments on this point, Viljoen, above note 181, 327–8.

[215] *Zimbabwe Human Rights NGO Forum* v. *Zimbabwe*, paras. 135–87.

[216] See in particular *Social and Economic Rights Action Center (SERAC) and Center for Economic and Social Rights (CESR)* v. *Nigeria*; *Sudan Human Rights Organisation and Centre on Housing Rights and Evictions (COHRE)* v. *Sudan*; and *Endorois* case. See on this point also OSJI, above note 175, 100–4.

CASE STUDY 6.1
Modise v. *Botswana* and the question of nationality rights

John K. Modise v. *Botswana* is a landmark case on the right to a nationality.[1] Modise, who was born in South Africa but grew up in Botswana, was deported to South Africa because of his political activities. With neither Botswana nor South Africa recognising his citizenship status Modise ended up spending seven years in a South African homeland and, after being deported from there, had to spend five weeks in no-man's land before being admitted back to Botswana on humanitarian grounds. The case revolved around Botswana's refusal to grant Modise nationality, which was found to violate his right to equal protection of the law and to the recognition of his legal status. His deportation and subjection to a miserable state of uncertainty was also held to violate the prohibition of torture and inhuman treatment, the right to family life, freedom of movement, the right to property and the right to participate freely in the government of his country. The case highlighted a number of the many problems surrounding nationality which have beset the continent, and led to the first case before the African Committee of Experts on the Rights and Welfare of the Child[2] and initiatives to draft a separate instrument on citizenship rights.[3]

POINT TO CONSIDER

• Why is the *Modise* case so emblematic of the challenges facing human rights protection in the African context?

---

[1] *John K. Modise* v. *Botswana*, 97/93 (2000).
[2] *IHRDA and Open Society Justice Initiative (OSJI) (on behalf of children of Nubian descent in Kenya)* v. *Kenya*, 002/09 (2011).
[3] See Recommendations of the Civil Society Meeting on African Union mechanisms and the Protection of Refugee, IDP and Citizenship Rights (2009), para. 18, online, at www.trustafrica.org/documents/CRAI_communique.pdf.

6.4.3 Impact

The Commission's sessions have become an important forum for the deliberation of human rights in Africa. In its jurisprudence it has begun to develop the contours of a regional human rights culture. Further cross-fertilisation can be expected with subregional courts and the ACtHPR, which is examined below. However, the Commission's impact has been hampered by a chronic lack of resources, which has undermined the visibility, efficiency and quality of its work and has resulted in ever increasing delays.[217] In addition, pressure exerted by states through the AU appears to have adversely influenced decision-making, such as in relation to the situation in Zimbabwe.[218] The Commission's impact has also been undermined by insufficient state compliance.[219] This is due to the weak enforcement mechanisms and the limited incorporation and application of the ACHPR, which suggests inadequate domestic awareness and take-up. Yet, the situation varies considerably between countries such as Nigeria, where the ACHPR was made part of national laws and has been applied by the judiciary,[220] and others where its impact is seemingly negligible, such as in Sudan. However, owing to the increasing mobilisation of regional and domestic human rights lawyers and NGOs, greater bottom-up impetus can be expected to enhance the role of the ACHPR at the domestic level and across the continent.[221] This will also lead to increased pressure on the system to respond more urgently to a series of regional human rights challenges, including women's rights, LGBT, HIV/AIDS, marginalisation and entrenched poverty, which have to date been insufficiently addressed in the Commission's jurisprudence.

6.4.4   The African Court on Human and Peoples' Rights

The desire to create a judicial body that addresses some of the Commission's weaknesses was the driving force behind NGO advocacy and regional diplomacy to set up a regional human rights court.[222] This movement resulted in the 1998 Protocol which set up the ACtHPR and came into force in 2004. The ACtHPR took up its work in 2006 with its seat in Tanzania. However, a controversial decision made in 2004 to merge the African Court of Justice (ACJ)[223] and the ACtHPR complicated matters during the interim period.[224] In 2008 the AU adopted a protocol to merge the two courts (which replaces the 1998 and 2003 Protocols for each of the respective courts) with a view to the creation of the African Court of Justice and Human Rights one year after

---

[217] See concerns set out in Joint Letter of Litigants to the Working Group on Communications of the African Commission on Human and Peoples' Rights, 4 December 2011, online, at www.cihrs.org/?p=353&lang=en.

[218] Viljoen, above note 181, pp. 188–9.

[219] See F. Viljoen and L. Louw, 'State Compliance with the Recommendations of the African Commission on Human and Peoples' Rights, 1994–2004', *AJIL* 101 (2007), 1–34; OSJI, above note 175, 93–115.

[220] Okafor, above note 2, 148–54.   [221] Ibid., in particular 300–1.

[222] www.africancourtcoalition.org.

[223] The ACJ was set up by a protocol in 2003 (which came into force in 2009).

[224] See for an account of these developments, I. Kane and A. C. Motala, 'The Creation of a New African Court of Justice and Human Rights', in Evans and Murray, above note 186, 406–40.

the deposit of the fifteenth ratification.[225] The merged Court is envisaged to consist of a general affairs and a human rights section. The present ACtHPR and future merged Court has advisory and contentious jurisdiction, can make provisional orders, issue binding judgments and has an explicit mandate to award reparation and refer binding judgments to the AU Assembly for enforcement.[226] In short, the Court has the potential to substantially strengthen protection and visibility of human rights in Africa.

The protocols establish a two-tier system. Individuals or NGOs can bring cases directly before the Court only following prior acceptance of the Court's competence by member states; otherwise they have to rely on the Commission for doing so.[227] The fact that only five states had recognised the competence of the Court to receive individual and NGO communications directly as of July 2012 demonstrates the initial reluctance of states to broaden access in a way that would put the Court in a position to fulfil what is arguably its core function.

While only five states had ratified the merger Protocol as of July 2012, the new merged court will in all likelihood be established in the near future. In the meantime, the ACtHPR will be tasked with developing its case law. Its first case was a non-starter and declared inadmissible because it had been brought by an individual against Senegal, a state that had not recognised the Court's competence to receive such complaints.[228] In a more significant development the Court adopted provisional measures against Libya in the early stages of the conflict in 2011 to 'immediately refrain from any action that would result in loss of life or violation of physical integrity of persons' following an application by the Commission.[229] While there were no indications that Libya complied with the order/request, the decision provided a glimpse of the types of interventions the Court can make. It was also the first time that the Commission referred a matter to the Court. This is of particular interest as there are a number of questions concerning the relationship between the Commission and the Court (including the future merged Court) that will need to be addressed in practice.

---

[225] See Protocol on the Statute of the African Court of Justice and Human Rights (adopted on 1 July 2008), (2008 Protocol).

[226] Articles 27–31, 1998 Protocol: 35, 45, 46, 2008 Protocol. The provisions applying to the human rights section are broadly similar to the ones contained in the 1998 Protocol, with the exception of the enforcement procedure which envisages an enhanced role for the AU Assembly in the execution of judgments.

[227] Articles 34(6), 1998 Protocol; 30(f), 2008 Protocol.

[228] *Michelot Yogogombaye* v. *The Republic of Senegal*, Application no. 01/2008, Judgment of 15 December 2009.

[229] In the matter of *African Commission on Human and Peoples' Rights* v. *Great Socialist People's Libyan Arab Jamahiriya*, App. no. 004/2011, Order of provisional measures (25 March 2011).

6.4.5   Regional economic courts

A review of judicial developments in Africa would be incomplete without a brief reference to its regional economic courts.[230] These courts are principally mandated to adjudicate matters falling within the scope of the treaties governing regional economic unions. Upon application by individuals and NGOs, several regional economic courts have interpreted their broad jurisdiction to include the competence to hear human rights cases. The ECOWAS court, which has an explicit human rights mandate, issued a landmark judgment in which it found that Niger had violated the prohibition of slavery and ordered a series of remedial measures.[231] In another case it found that Gambia, the respondent state, was responsible for prolonged arbitrary detention in breach of the right to liberty and security and the right to a fair trial. It ordered the respondent state to pay $100,000 compensation, which is in noteworthy contrast to the African Commission's practice of not specifying amounts of compensation.[232] The East African Court of Justice, in a case concerning violations of fair trial rights in Uganda, considered itself competent to consider human rights matters notwithstanding article 27(2) of the EAC treaty, according to which such jurisdiction is subject to a separate protocol.[233] It acknowledged that it is precluded from adjudicating 'on disputes concerning human rights violations *per se*' (emphasis in original), but stressed that it 'will not abdicate from exercising its jurisdiction of interpretation under Article 27 (1) merely because the reference includes allegation of human rights violation'.[234]

The growing number of judgments by regional economic courts is evidence of the creative use made by individuals and NGOs of existing opportunities to litigate human rights cases. It also demonstrates the willingness of African regional courts to effectively exercise their jurisdiction to address human rights concerns, which is often seen as integral to the legitimacy of economic and political unions. However, the practice raises difficult questions, particularly whether regional economic courts have jurisdiction to adjudicate human rights cases, and if so, what law to apply. The proliferation of courts with jurisdiction over human rights carries the risk of fragmentation or inconsistencies, and of forum shopping (there is no need to exhaust

---

[230] S. T. Ebobrah, 'Litigating Human Rights before Sub-regional Courts in Africa: Prospects and Challenges', *African Journal of International and Comparative Law* (*AJICL*) 17(1) (2009), 79–101; Murungi and Gallinetti, above note 196.

[231] *Mme Hadijatou Mani Koraou* v. *The Republic of Niger*, ECW/CCJ/JUD/06/08, Judgment of 27 October 2008. See H. Duffy, 'Hadijatou Mani Koraou v. Niger: Slavery Unveiled by the ECOWAS Court', *HRLR* 9(1) (2009), 151–70.

[232] See *Manneh* v. *Gambia*, ECW/CCJ/APP/04/07, Judgment of 5 June 2008.

[233] *Katabazi and 21 Others* v. *Secretary General of the East African Community and Another* (Ref. no. 1 of 2007) [2007] EACJ 3, Judgment of 1 November 2007.

[234] Ibid., 16.

domestic remedies), thus potentially sidelining the Commission.[235] It is also politically controversial as states have objected to the regional economic courts' exercise of jurisdiction over human rights matters. This applies particularly to a highly politically charged case against Zimbabwe where the SADC tribunal ruled in 2008 that the expropriation of the land of the applicant (a white farmer) had been discriminatory and that the respondent state should pay fair compensation.[236] The government of Zimbabwe refused to comply with the order, claiming that it was not binding. The High Court of Zimbabwe ruled that the judgment could not be enforced and SADC itself, apparently yielding to pressure from Zimbabwe, suspended the tribunal in 2011.[237] This is a salutary lesson on how judicial activism can backfire, at least temporarily, with the SADC developments seemingly constituting a victory for state sovereignty. However, in a region where activist forces are becoming increasingly vocal and effective in creating political space for contestation, satisfactorily addressing human rights concerns is a challenge that regional institutions cannot ignore lest they compromise their legitimacy. This task, as well as the one of building a coherent system based on the consistent application of the Charter combined with effective remedies, constitutes the main challenge facing the African human rights system.

INTERVIEW 6.4

Making the system work

(Ibrahima Kane)

Ibrahima Kane, presently Director of African Union Advocacy, East African Initiative, Open Society Initiative for Eastern Africa, has been working to promote and protect human rights in Africa for over two decades, engaging at the grassroots level as well as in strategic litigation and helping to strengthen regional human rights systems. In the course of his work, he has become one of the major civil society voices on human rights in Africa.

The African human rights system has repeatedly been described as weak and ineffectual. What is your response to such assessments?

If a human rights system is an 'order' of human rights institutions and political bodies, which are connected to each other and cannot perform

---

[235] See for an assessment, Murungi and Gallinetti, above note 196, 130–1.

[236] *Mike Campbell (PVT) and Others* v. *Republic of Zimbabwe*, SADC(T) Case no. 2/2007, Judgment of 28 November 2008. See also *Luke Munyandu Tembani* v. *Republic of Zimbabwe*, SADC(T) Case no. 07/2008, Judgment of 14 August 2009.

[237] See P. N. Ndlovu, 'Campbell v. Republic of Zimbabwe: A moment of truth for the SADC Tribunal', *SADCLJ* 1 (2011), 63–79; D. Matyszak, *The Dissolution of the SADC Tribunal* (19 August 2011), online, at www.researchandadvocacyunit.org.

efficiently individually, I doubt whether it can really be called a system. We have at the continental level, under the control and supervision of the Assembly of Heads of State and Government and the Peace and Security Council of the AU, the African Commission of Human and People's Rights, the Committee of African Experts on the Rights and Welfare of the Child, the ACtHPR, and to some extent, the African Board on Corruption. We will even have very soon a new mechanism for the implementation of the African Charter on Democracy, Elections and Governance, which has a lot of provisions related to human rights. At the sub-regional level the courts of justice of many regional economic communities are vested with a human rights mandate and three of them (ECOWAS, SADC, EAC) play an increasingly important role in that regard. This is complemented by national human rights institutions and other human rights mechanisms in member states. The problem is that these developments are not really joined up. However, the institutions themselves are making real efforts to fill the gaps and coordinate better, even though ultimately implementation needs to be facilitated by the political bodies. So it is wise to suggest that the system is still under construction.

Secondly, the African human rights 'system' needs to be seen in perspective. The Commission is only twenty years old (only one generation!). A lot of progress has been made in turning it from a toothless entity into a respected body whose reports are taken seriously by states at the AU level. It is important to recognise that a body is not what it says on paper but what people, and here one needs to recognise the work of the current generation of Commissioners, make of it. Recent developments where Bolivia and Venezuela have called into question the Inter-American human rights system, and British attacks on the ECtHR, are a reminder that these systems are not set in stone; if we look at the question from that angle, human rights protection on our continent has come a long way.

You have engaged closely with the African Commission and other human rights bodies in the region. How has this worked in practice and how effective have you been in your work?

In my work I seek to contribute both to developing institutions and to advancing normative standards and their effective implementation. The fact that the Commission has put in place a system that better ensures the independence of Commissioners, also in response to demands by civil society, has greatly facilitated our work. Indeed, the Commissioners themselves have repeatedly taken steps to make the system more effective, such as referring the *Endorois* (Kenya) case to the Court, asking it to take measures to ensure implementation.

It is important to have a good working relationship for advocacy to work. I have worked closely with the Commission in the drafting of many standards, including the guidelines on fair trials, on economic, social and cultural rights and the resolution on the protection of human rights in the fight against terrorism in Africa. We are currently advocating the adoption of a protocol on citizenship in Africa. These standards have been important in informing the Commission's jurisprudence and when advocating specific rights across the continent or in particular situations.

There have been several important developments in the region, particularly an increasing number of normative texts, institutions and judicial bodies adjudicating human rights cases. What are the promises and challenges that this development entails for the African human rights system?

We only have fourteen African human rights treaties to date, which is clearly insufficient. There are a number of gaps where important issues are not addressed, such as minority rights and people with disabilities. The biggest shortcoming, however, is the inability of our continental human rights 'system' to deal with all the massacres (the African Charter calls them gross and massive human rights violations) that are taking place in the continent. According to the UN, more than 5 million people lost their lives in the Democratic Republic of Congo but there has been an almost complete failure to act, to prevent the violations and bring the perpetrators to justice. There are currently plans to broaden the jurisdiction of the African Court to cover international crimes. These moves are geared towards dealing with the most serious perpetrators; but it is just as important to deal with perpetrators at the local level where the victims want to see justice done for those who committed these crimes hands on.

I do not see the proliferation of bodies adjudicating human rights questions as a problem. The bodies have drawn on, and supported each other. Rather than seeing conflicting decisions, we are witnessing a genuine attempt to develop minimum standards. Ultimately, it is best to be practical about these developments. Sub-regional courts, for example, are often more flexible and all in all a greater choice of forum is good for the protection of human rights. All the various actors are part of the system we are building. In other words, let the 'legal market' of the liberal political system we are experiencing these days determine those who can effectively protect the rights and liberties of individuals in our continent.

What are the lessons that the African system may hold for the development of regional human rights systems elsewhere?

Regional human rights systems tend to go through stages. At the beginning, they are controlled by politicians who consider human rights issues as sensitive problems that require political solutions. As the systems evolve and institutions become stronger and more independent, there is greater scope for dialogue and progress. In addition, as the European system shows, a critical mass of cases is needed to put effective pressure on states, such as Turkey and Italy. If we look at new systems such as in the ASEAN context it is important to support the work of the institutional actors and, from a civil society perspective, to take an approach that is both strategic and constructive.

An important lesson is the need for more dialogue based on objective criticism. African activists and NGOs have had more influence than big Western NGOs in this respect; using the flexibility inherent in the system has been more useful than teaching it lessons. Having said that, it is critical that regional institutions learn from other systems; the African system has certainly benefited from the European and the Inter-American systems in this regard.

What areas do you see as current or emerging frontiers for human rights protection in Africa?

There are several pressing issues, in addition to how best to respond to massacres that I already mentioned. Citizenship and nationality is a major concern. Well over 60 per cent of children born in Africa do not have a birth certificate, which has greatly contributed to discrimination based on nationality. Discrimination more generally, including sexual discrimination, is still a key problem across the continent. Other issues concern freedom of movement in Africa and the rights of victims of terrorism, which has become a major scourge. Another challenge is how to advance economic, social and cultural rights, which is extremely difficult given the realities on the ground. However, initiatives such as the Charter for the Public Service in Africa (2001) are a first step to put the framework in place that is needed to implement these rights more effectively. We should not forget that human rights are rights for the normal citizen when he/she can use the law to effectively 'force' the state to comply with its treaty obligations and to change his/her own daily life.

QUESTIONS

- Has the African Commission developed a jurisprudence that adequately responds to, and reflects the multiple human rights challenges in the continent?
- Does the fact that states need to recognise the standing of individuals and NGO before the African Court inspire confidence that it will be able to become an effective judicial body?
- Can the regional economic courts act as catalysts for a stronger African human rights system or is their human rights jurisprudence a passing phenomenon?
- Is the African human rights system at risk of fragmentation?

6.5   TOWARDS AN ASIAN HUMAN RIGHTS SYSTEM?

Asia has not witnessed the impetus that led to the establishment of a human rights system as an important part of a regional or sub-regional political body. However, the call by the 1993 Vienna Conference on Human Rights to establish 'regional and sub-regional arrangements for the promotion and protection of human rights' was taken up by the Association of South East Asian Nations (ASEAN), which, fourteen years later, adopted the ASEAN Charter in 2007. The Charter envisages the establishment of an ASEAN human rights body, which was inaugurated as the ASEAN Intergovernmental Commission on Human Rights (AICHR) on 23 October 2009.[238] The AICHR is mandated to promote and protect human rights and fundamental rights. This is to be done primarily through awareness-raising, capacity building, provision of advisory services and technical assistance, the development of common approaches and positions on human rights matters, as well as the preparation of studies on thematic issues. It has also been tasked with elaborating an ASEAN Declaration on Human Rights. The AICHR is composed of ten members, meets biannually, and adopts a model of decision-making 'based on consultation and consensus'. Its promotional mandate and consultative functions reflect ASEAN member states' reluctance to establish a body with quasi-judicial, let alone judicial, functions.

The AICHR model does not follow the typology of human rights bodies in other regions and its apparent weakness has raised concerns about its ability to develop a regional human rights culture and contribute to the effective protection of rights.[239] However, the evolutionary process envisaged does provide a point of reference for engagement and contestation for civil society actors and others to advocate stronger human rights protection. Judging by the experiences of other institutions, the AICHR may be receptive to calls for a progressive interpretation and a broadening of its mandate. Indeed, this would provide it with an opportunity to gain and maintain credibility as a human rights body. In 2012, the work of the AICHR progressed slowly but its very establishment constitutes an important development for Asia as a whole. Its further development and relationship with member states is bound to hold critical lessons for regional human rights protection in Asia.

---

[238] Cha-Am Hua Hin Declaration on the Inauguration of the ASEAN Intergovernmental Commission on Human Rights (23 October 2009), online, at www.aseansec.org/documents/Declaration-AICHR.pdf. See H. D. Phan, 'The evolution towards an ASEAN human rights body', *APJHRL* 9(1) (2008), 1–12; J. Munro, 'The Relationship between the Origins and Regime Design of the ASEAN Intergovernmental Commission on Human Rights', *IJHR* 15(8) (2011), 1185–1214.

[239] D. A. Desierto, 'Universalizing Core Human Rights in the "New" ASEAN: A Reassessment of Culture and Development Justifications against the Global Rejection of Impunity', *GJIL* 1(1) (2009), 77–114.

6.6   COMPARISON OF REGIONAL SYSTEMS

The review of regional human rights systems yielded important findings for each of the systems but also for other regions where systems are weak and/or deficient, such as in respect of ASEAN to date and the Arab League,[240] or non-existent, such as in South Asia. The situation in these regions may change following political developments, particularly in the Middle East, which would in turn pose anew the question of an effective regional human rights system. The general case for such a system has been widely recognised. Indeed, regional systems can make a significant contribution to 'regional universality', bridging international standards and domestic implementation and developing a distinctive regional human rights culture.

Experience to date suggests that the desire for greater regional political unity is a critical factor and can serve to generate the impetus for the establishment of regional human rights systems. In their initial phase, such systems tend to reflect considerable compromises between the member states' intention to create a credible system and to retain control over the institutions mandated to monitor its effective application and implementation. Regional human rights bodies frequently seek to use and expand their powers, not least to attain a degree of legitimacy. This has resulted in frictions and member states may undermine the effectiveness of bodies by not providing adequate resources. Nevertheless, most systems have largely succeeded in developing stronger institutional human rights cultures over time, although their political and popular acceptance can be precarious. The strength of systems and their impact depends to a large degree on their embeddedness in the overall political culture and their contribution to the resolution of conflict and political transitions. The growth of regional networks of actors that claim and thereby reinforce respect for the principles and goals for which the system had been set up is another important element. These interrelated factors and the degree to which they contribute to domestic implementation processes, including by empowering local actors, are critical for the effectiveness of regional human rights systems.

As a general rule, it is important that the type of human rights system chosen is suitable in the particular circumstances. For example, there may be some merit in creating bodies with a strong promotional mandate first rather than focusing predominantly or exclusively on judicial bodies. However, it is equally clear that complaints procedures that provide access for individuals (and NGOs) play a pivotal role. They compel states to respond to specific allegations and to demonstrate their respect for human rights through taking concrete measures, in contrast to other procedures largely based on a rather broad constructive dialogue. Against this background it is the public in the

---

[240] R. Mervat, 'The Revised Arab Charter on Human Rights', *HRLR* 5(2) (2005), 361–76.

region, particularly individuals, NGOs and the media, that plays a crucial role in articulating legitimate expectations that reflect local and regional priorities based on experiences of suffering and notions of justice.

QUESTIONS

1 Is there a natural progression from bodies with a largely promotional mandate to fully fledged judicial bodies in the development of regional human rights systems?

2 Are there common lessons that can be gleaned from the existing regional systems for other regional bodies contemplating the setting up of a new human rights system?

FURTHER READING

European human rights system

Bates, E., *The Evolution of the European Convention on Human Rights: From its Inception to the Creation of a Permanent Court of Human Rights* (Oxford University Press, 2010).

Christofferson, J. and Madsen, M. R. (eds.), *The European Court of Human Rights between Law and Politics* (Oxford University Press, 2011).

Greer, S., *The European Convention on Human Rights: Achievements, Problems and Prospects* (Cambridge University Press, 2006).

Hodson, L., *NGOs and the Struggle for Human Rights in Europe* (Oxford: Hart, 2011).

Leach, P., *Taking a Case to the European Court of Human Rights*, 3rd edn (Oxford University Press, 2011).

Websites

ECHR: www.echr.coe.int.
CoE: www.coe.int.
EU: http://europa.eu.

Inter-American human rights system

Burgorgue-Larsen, L. and Ubeda de Torres, A., *The Inter-American Court of Human Rights: Case Law and Commentary* (Oxford University Press, 2011).

Harris, D. and Livingstone, S. (eds.), *The Inter-American Convention on Human Rights* (Oxford University Press, 1998).

Pasqualucci, J. M., *The Practice and Procedure of the Inter-American Court of Human Rights* (Cambridge University Press, 2003).

Serrano, M. and Popovski, V. (eds.), *Human Rights Regimes in the Americas* (Tokyo, New York, Paris: United Nations University Press, 2010).

Websites

IACHR: www.oas.org/en/iachr.
IACtHR: www.corteidh.or.cr.
Organisation of American States: www.oas.org.

African human rights system

Evans, M. and Murray, R. (eds.), *The African Charter on Human and Peoples' Rights: The System in Practice 1986–2006*, 2nd edn (Cambridge University Press, 2008).

Kufuor, K. O., *The African Human Rights System: Origin and Evolution* (New York: Palgrave Macmillan, 2010).

Okafor, O. C., *The African Human Rights System, Activist Forces and International Institutions* (Cambridge University Press, 2007).

Viljoen, V., *International Human Rights Law in Africa*, 2nd edn (Oxford University Press, 2012).

Websites

African Commission: www.achpr.org.
ACtHPR: www.african-court.org.
African Committee of Experts on the Rights and
    Welfare of the Child: www.acerwc.org.
See on the jurisprudence of all three of the above
    also African Human Rights Law Case Analyser:
    http://caselaw.ihrda.org.
AU: www.african-union.org.
Community Court of Justice – ECOWAS:
    www.courtecowas.org./
East African Court of Justice: www.eacj.org
SADC Tribunal: www.sadc-tribunal.org

ASEAN human rights system

Nasu, H. and Saul, B. (eds.), *Human Rights in
    the Asia-Pacific Region: Towards Institution
    Building* (London, New York: Routledge, 2011).
Tan, H.-L., *The ASEAN Intergovernmental
    Commission on Human Rights: Institutionalising
    Human Rights in South East Asia* (Cambridge
    University Press, 2011).

Websites

ASEAN Intergovernmental Commission on Human
    Rights: www.aseansec.org/22769.htm.

7 Individual complaints procedures

CONTENTS

7.1 INTRODUCTION

Individual complaints procedures offer a unique opportunity for individuals and groups to have claims of human rights violations considered and their rights vindicated in a judicial or quasi-judicial procedure. For NGOs and human rights lawyers, complaints procedures are an important avenue to pursue strategic objectives, in addition to supporting victims in individual cases. States, on the other hand, may find themselves having to defend allegations of specific or systemic violations. Ideally, complaints procedures act as a mirror that provides an opportunity for states to bring their practices into conformity with the respective treaty. In practice, however, states often view unfavourable decisions as unwarranted criticism, which may create difficulties at the implementation stage. The treaty bodies themselves are in theory neutral arbiters that apply the treaty provisions and rules of procedures. However, inevitably, their position as bodies created by states, and relying on states' cooperation on the one hand and seeking the effective protection of human rights on the other, raises a host of challenges in actual practice.

This chapter is written generically from the perspective of litigants (which will mainly be referred to as applicants throughout the chapter), examining the common stages of admissibility, merits, decision, remedies and implementation that are characteristic of complaint procedures before treaty bodies (the term is used in this chapter to refer to both UN treaty bodies and regional human rights commissions and courts). Questions considered include in particular, (1) jurisdiction. Who can bring a case against whom in relation to what types of violation alleged to have been committed, when and where? (2) Exhaustion of domestic remedies: what are the reasons for requiring that a litigant take legal steps (pursue remedies) first in the state where the alleged violation occurred? Is it always clear what steps need to be taken? Are there any exceptions? Who carries the burden of proof? (3) Others: are there any time limits for submitting applications? Can a case be brought before more than one treaty body? Does it need to be written in a particular language, etc.? As for the merits, what does it take to prove a complaint? And finally, what is the nature of the decisions treaty bodies can make and the types of remedies awarded? For the post-decision phase, the chapter examines the challenge of implementation. In particular, what steps can treaty bodies and litigants take, and have they taken, to enhance the prospect of a state complying with a decision? In addition, we briefly consider specific procedures which play an important role in practice, though they are only relevant where resorted to, or agreed upon, by the parties: interim (provisional) measures and friendly settlements. Questions to be considered include: when can interim measures be used, are they binding, how effective are they in practice? What are the conditions for friendly settlements, and are they necessarily a good outcome if this is what parties agree on?

The stages and features of regional and international complaints procedures are broadly similar and the following is a generic overview rather than a detailed examination of all available procedures; where applicable, notable differences or different approaches taken by the respective treaty bodies are indicated. Inter-state complaints share most features of individual complaints procedures and are not dealt with separately given their limited relevance to date.[1]

7.2   ADMISSIBILITY

Admissibility refers to the procedural requirements that need to be fulfilled for a judicial or quasi-judicial body to consider the substance of a case, i.e. its merits, though bodies sometimes rule on admissibility and merits simultaneously. The admissibility criteria are laid down in the applicable

---

[1] Inter-state complaints have primarily featured in the European system. See S. C. Prebensen, 'Inter-State Complaints under Treaty Provisions: the Experience under the European Convention on Human Rights', in G. Alfredsson *et al.* (eds.), *International Human Rights Monitoring Mechanisms: Essays in Honour of Jakob Th. Möller*, 2nd rev. edn (Leiden, Boston: Martinus Nijhoff, 2009), 439–64.

treaty – including optional protocols where the main treaty does not envisage a complaints procedure – that sets out the mandate and functions of the treaty body concerned.[2] These criteria determine who may bring a case against which state about what kind of violation. They also reflect, through the requirement to exhaust domestic remedies, the principle that supranational bodies are not meant to replace domestic courts. Rather, their role is to monitor whether states have complied with their obligation to respect and protect rights 'within their jurisdiction'.

In practice, many if not most cases fail at the admissibility hurdle, particularly on the grounds of a failure to exhaust domestic remedies. An inadmissibility decision does not necessarily preclude an applicant from lodging another case concerning the same matter if circumstances have changed, particularly where domestic remedies have been exhausted subsequently.[3] However, given the length of proceedings before supranational bodies, applicants whose case is declared inadmissible may face added evidentiary challenges domestically and may have missed time limits to pursue domestic remedies. Equally important, an applicant may lose the belief that the supranational bodies will remedy the alleged violation. Inadmissibility decisions by supranational bodies can therefore effectively spell the end of any efforts to remedy violations even where the underlying claim of a violation is justified. Applicants and anyone advising individuals or groups who contemplate bringing a case before a supranational body must therefore be careful to ensure that the admissibility requirements have been fulfilled so that a case will be heard on its merits.

7.2.1   Jurisdiction

Rationae personae: who?

As a general rule, anyone claiming to be a victim of a violation can submit an application, which is also referred to as communication or complaint. The rationale behind this rule is that those who claim that their rights have been violated have an interest and are entitled to a remedy. A person claiming to be a victim of a violation of the ICCPR or ECHR, for example, must show that he or she is directly affected, i.e. that the acts or omissions in question must have

---

[2] Articles 14 ICERD; 22 CAT; 77 ICRMW; 31 CPED; Optional Protocols to ICCPR, CEDAW, CRPD, ICESCR (not in force as of July 2012), CRC (Communication Procedure, not in force as of July 2012); 34, 35 ECHR; 44–7 ACHR; 55, 56 ACHPR.

[3] See, for example, *Rules of Procedure of the HRCtee*, UN Doc. CCPR/C/3/Rev.10 (11 January 2012), Rule 98(2): 'If the Committee has declared a communication inadmissible under article 5, paragraph 2, of the Optional Protocol, this decision may be reviewed at a later date by the Committee upon a written request by or on behalf of the individual concerned containing information to the effect that the reasons for inadmissibility referred to in article 5, paragraph 2, no longer apply.'

a direct bearing on his or her right(s).[4] The same applies to a group of persons whose members have suffered violations or a group that suffered a violation of its collective right (where the complaints procedure in question provides standing for such claims).[5] The position of legal persons differs; whereas the Optional Protocol to the ICCPR only allows individuals to claim violations,[6] the ECtHR grants standing to such applicants where their rights have been affected, such as a newspaper outlet in relation to freedom of expression.[7]

The criterion of being 'directly affected' is problematic where an actual violation has not yet taken place. For example, it would be unreasonable to wait for a violation of the right to privacy to materialise to materialise and face criminal sanctions for homosexual conduct. It may also be unclear whether a violation is already taking place or about to occur, such as where a person is subjected to telephone tapping in violation of his or her right to privacy without knowing it. Treaty bodies and courts have therefore recognised that applications can be brought in these circumstances but only if a violation is reasonably foreseeable or imminent.[8]

Applicants before the HRCtee or the ECtHR may authorise someone else, including NGOs, to act on their behalf.[9] In exceptional circumstances, 'when

[4] See for the notion of victim in the HRCtee's jurisprudence, *Aumeeruddy-Cziffra et al.* v. *Mauritius*, UN Doc. CCPR/C/12/D/35/1978 (9 April 1981), para. 9.1.; *B. d. B. et al.* v. *Netherlands*, UN Doc. CCPR/C/35/D/273/1988 (30 March 1989), para. 6.6.; and the ECtHR, *Klass and Others* v. *Germany*, (1978) 2 EHRR 214, para. 33 and *Amuur* v. *France*, (1996) 22 EHRR 533, para. 36. The African and the Inter-American systems distinguish between petitioner and victim. See in this regard the distinction made between 'original claimants' and 'parties to the case' (victims or alleged victims) in article 2 of the IACtHR's Rules of Procedure (2009).

[5] The HRCtee does not recognise standing of persons or groups alleging a violation of the right to self-determination; see *Diergaardt et al.* v. *Namibia*, UN Doc. CCPR/C/69/D/760/1996 (25 July 2000), para. 10.3, and *Lubicon Lake Band* v. *Canada*, UN Doc. CCPR/C/38/D/167/1984 (26 March 1990), para. 13.3.

[6] See ibid. and *Länsman III* v. *Finland*, UN Doc. CCPR/C/83/D/1023/2001 (17 March 2005), para. 6.1. See also Y. Tyagi, *The UN Human Rights Committee: Practice and Procedure* (Cambridge University Press, 2011), 401, with further references.

[7] E.g. *The Sunday Times* v. *UK*, (1980) 2 EHRR 245. See in the African system, *Zimbabwe Lawyers for Human Rights and Associated Newspapers of Zimbabwe* v. *Zimbabwe*, 284/03 (2009), particularly para. 178. Legal persons cannot claim to be victims in the Inter-American system. However, the IACtHR recognised that individuals, such as shareholders, may in specific circumstances be able to vindicate their rights 'even when they are encompassed in a legal figure or fiction created by the same system of law'. See *Cantos* v. *Argentina*, Preliminary objections, Judgment of 7 September 2001, Ser. C, no. 85, para. 29.

[8] *Norris* v. *Ireland*, (1988) 13 EHRR 186, paras. 28–34, and *Toonen* v. *Australia*, UN Doc. CCPR/C/50/D/488/1992 (31 March 1994), para. 5.1 (homosexuality); *Klass and Others* v. *Germany*, (1978) 2 EHRR 214, para. 34 (telephone tapping). See for the Inter-American system, *International Responsibility for the Promulgation and Enforcement of Laws in Violation of the Convention* (articles 1 and 2 of the American Convention on Human Rights), Advisory opinion OC-14/94 (9 December 1994), Ser. A, no. 14 (1994), paras. 40–50, and *Suárez Rosero* v. *Ecuador*, Merits, Judgment of 12 November 1997, Ser. C, no. 35, para. 98.

[9] Rule 36 of the ECtHR's 2011 Rules of Court.

it appears that the individual in question is unable to submit the communication personally', such as in the case of enforced disappearance, 'a communication submitted on behalf of an alleged victim may, however, be accepted if submitted by next of kin close to the case'.[10] As a general rule, applicants must show a 'sufficient link' (HRCtee)[11] or a personal and specific link to the direct victim, such as family members of someone who died as a result of an alleged violation (ECtHR).[12] Next of kin may also have standing as victims of a violation in their own right, such as the right not to be subjected to inhuman treatment where a (close) relative has been forcibly disappeared.[13]

States are often reluctant to give standing to individuals, groups or organisations other than the direct victims out of concern that this would open the 'floodgates' for public interest litigation. The question of how broadly or narrowly standing is defined is therefore a measure of the control states seek to retain over those involved in procedures. In contrast to the Optional Protocol to the ICCPR and the ECHR, article 44 ACHR and article 55 ACHPR considerably broaden standing for cases brought before the Inter-American Commission and the African Commission respectively.[14] The African Commission has emphasised the rationale for this relaxation in cases where the victims themselves may be unable to bring cases: '[it] has adopted an *actio popularis* approach where the author of a communication need not know or have any relationship with the victim. This is to enable poor victims of human rights violations on the continent to receive assistance from NGOs and individuals far removed from their locality'.[15] The broad standing also enables NGOs to bring strategic cases in response to mass violations or systemic breaches.[16] It therefore facilitates access to international justice and opens avenues for public interest litigation.[17]

---

[10] Rule 96(b) of the HRCtee's 2012 Rules of Procedure.

[11] See *Massera et al.* v. *Uruguay*, Communication no. R.1/5 (15 August 1979), para. 5.

[12] See *Yaşa* v. *Turkey*, (1999) 28 EHRR 408, paras. 61–6.

[13] *Kurt* v. *Turkey*, (1999) 27 EHRR 373, para. 134; *Sharma* v. *Nepal*, UN Doc. CCPR/ C/94/D/1469/2006 (28 October 2008), para. 7.9. See in the context of the Inter-American system, *Ituango Massacres* v. *Colombia*, Preliminary objections, merits, reparations and costs, Judgment of 1 July 2006, Ser. C, no. 148, Separate Concurring Opinion of Judge S. Garcia Ramirez, paras. 10–12.

[14] Notably, the broad standing has been retained for the ACtHPR. See article 5(3) of the 1998 Protocol to the ACHPR and article 30 of the 2008 Protocol on the Statute of the African Court of Justice and Human Rights.

[15] *Article 19* v. *Eritrea*, 275/03 (2007), para. 65.

[16] See in particular *Centre for Minority Rights Development (Kenya) and Minority Rights Group (on behalf of Endorois Welfare Council)* v. *Kenya*, 276/03 (2009); *Interights, Institute for Human Rights and Development in Africa, and Association mauritanienne des droits de l'Homme* v. *Mauritania*, 242/01 (2004); *Social and Economic Rights Action Center (SERAC) and Center for Economic and Social Rights (CESR)* v. *Nigeria*, 155/96 (2001).

[17] See more broadly on the 'exercise of the right of access to international justice', A. A. Cançado Trindade, *The Access of Individuals to International Justice* (Oxford University Press, 2011), 17–49.

Against whom can a complaint be brought?

Applicants can only bring cases against a state that is party to the treaty concerned and has recognised the competence of the treaty body to consider complaints (unless they have denounced such competence, for example Trinidad
and Tobago).[18] This is automatically the case before the IACHR and African
Commission, which have compulsory jurisdiction relating to the relevant OAS
instruments and the ACHPR respectively,[19] as well as before the ECtHR following changes in 1998 (Protocol no. 11) that revolutionised the European
system. Other treaty bodies and courts only consider applications where the
state concerned has accepted their jurisdiction. The ACtHPR, for example,
found the first case brought before it inadmissible because the respondent
state had not recognised its competence to hear cases lodged by individuals.[20]

Applicants cannot bring cases against NSAs because individuals, armed
rebel groups, businesses or others falling within this category are not recognised as parties to human rights treaties. The same applies in principle to
international organisations though this may change should the EU become
a party to the ECHR.[21] Yet the involvement of international organisations
raises complex questions of attribution. Can a state be held responsible for
acts or omissions in contexts where it acted as part of multinational forces
and/or purported to act pursuant to binding resolutions by international
organisations? The jurisprudence of human rights treaty bodies is not settled in this regard. In the *Behrami* case, the applicants argued that French
KFOR (international forces in Kosovo) troops' failure to clear clusterbombs
dropped by NATO, which resulted in the killing of one boy and serious injuries to another, constituted a violation of the right to life. The ECtHR refused
to entertain the application *rationae personae* on the grounds that the acts
in question were attributable to the international organisation, here the UN
Mission in Kosovo (UNMIK) acting pursuant to UNSC authorisation. In *Saramati*, the detention authorised by a Norwegian and later a French KFOR commander in a station located in a sector led by Germany – which the applicant
alleged to constitute a violation of articles 5, 6 and 13 ECHR – was equally
found not to be attributable to the states concerned because the UN Security
Council retained 'ultimate authority and control'.[22] The decision was heavily

---

[18] The treaty body will also not have jurisdiction for acts occurring after a state party has
effectively denounced the treaty in question. See for example Trinidad and Tobago's
declarations in relation to the ICCPR Optional Protocol and the ACHR with effect from 26
August 1998 and 29 May 1999 respectively.

[19] See sections 6.3.1 and 6.4.2.

[20] *Michelot Yogogombaye* v. *The Republic of Senegal*, Appl. no. 01/2008, Judgment of
ACtHPR (15 December 2009).

[21] See section 6.2.8. Note, however, that the EU ratified the CRPD in 2010 pursuant to article
42 (though not its Optional Protocol to date).

[22] *Behrami* v. *France* and *Saramati* v. *France, Germany and Norway*, Appl. nos. 71412/01 and
78166/01, Grand Chamber decision of 2 May 2007, paras. 121–52, particularly at 144–52.

criticised, particularly for its interpretation of the rules of attribution and its policy implications of depriving the ECHR of any application.[23]

In contrast, in the later case of *Al-Jedda*, the ECtHR rejected the argument that the UK was not responsible for the internment of civilians in Iraq because it was carried out pursuant to UNSC resolutions, holding that the 'Security Council had neither effective control nor ultimate authority and control over the acts and omissions of troops within the multi-national force'.[24] This case demonstrates the centrality of the criterion of 'ultimate authority and control' used by the ECtHR to attribute responsibility. In addition, the ECtHR has made clear that the collective veil will not always be available where states transfer part of their sovereignty to an international organisation, namely the EU, and the international organisation does not provide for equivalent protection,[25] particularly where 'the protection of Convention rights was manifestly deficient'.[26]

CASE STUDY 7.1
Protection against the implementation of UN Security Council sanctions: *Sayadi and Vinck* v. *Belgium*

The UNSC has increasingly imposed sanctions against individuals believed to be involved in terrorism. These individuals are placed on lists and may face serious restrictions, including the freezing of all financial assets. In *Sayadi and Vinck* v. *Belgium*, the authors had been placed on such a list by the Belgian authorities. They brought a case against Belgium before the HRCtee, alleging a series of violations. Belgium argued that the case was inadmissible because the implementation of UNSC resolutions was a matter for the European Community and that the authors were precluded 'from disputing United Nations rules concerning the fight against terrorism before the Committee'.[1] The HRCtee held that:

While [it] could not consider alleged violations of other instruments such as the Charter of the United Nations, or allegations that challenged United Nations rules concerning the fight against terrorism, the Committee was competent to admit a communication alleging that a State party had violated rights set forth in the Covenant, regardless of the source of the obligations implemented by the State party.[2]

[1] *Sayadi and Vinck* v. *Belgium*, UN Doc. CCPR/C/94/D/1472/2006 (22 October 2008), para. 4.11.
[2] Ibid., para. 7.2.

---

[23] M. Milanovic and T. Papic, 'As Bad as it Gets: the European Court of Human Rights' Behrami and Saramati Decision and International Law', *ICLQ* 58(2) (2009), 267–96.
[24] *Al-Jedda* v. *United Kingdom*, (2011) 53 EHRR 23, para. 84.
[25] See in particular *Bosphorus Hava Yollari Turizm Ve Ticaret Anonim Şirketi* v. *Ireland*, (2006) 42 EHRR 1 440, paras. 143–56.
[26] Ibid., para. 156.

In a nuanced decision, it then found that Belgium was responsible for the violations resulting from placing the individuals on the sanctions list even though Belgium was later unable to have the names removed from it.[3] Some of the Committee members dissented, arguing that the communication was unsubstantiated because article 103 UN Charter[4] takes priority over competing obligations under the Covenant.[5] This decision is an important piece in a series of cases that revolved around the question as to what extent human rights treaty bodies may review UNSC resolutions and European implementing regulations and provide adequate human rights protection.[6]

POINTS TO CONSIDER

- Why do cases such as *Sayadi and Vinck* v. *Belgium* raise complex questions of law?

- What is the significance of *Sayadi and Vinck* v. *Belgium* for the question at issue, i.e. protection of human rights in respect of sanctions imposed by the UNSC, and beyond?

---

[3] Ibid., paras. 10.1–11.
[4] Article 103 UN Charter: 'In the event of a conflict between the obligations of the Members of the United Nations under the present Charter and their obligations under any other international agreement, their obligations under the present Charter shall prevail.'
[5] See dissenting opinions of Ms Ruth Wedgwood and Mr Ivan Shearer.
[6] See *Bosphorus* v. *Ireland*, and *Kadi* v. *Commission* [2010] EUECJ T-85/09.

Rationae materiae: *what rights?*

An applicant must allege the violation of a right that falls within the scope of the treaty concerned and binds the state party concerned, which excludes rights in respect of which a valid reservation has been entered.[27] An applicant cannot, for example, claim a violation of the right to property before the HRCtee or the right to self-determination before the ECtHR because the respective treaties do not guarantee these rights as such. Nor can an applicant claim a violation of rules of international humanitarian law *per se* because human rights treaties do not confer jurisdiction to rule on such violations.[28]

---

[27] *Kozlova and Smirnova* v. *Latvia*, Appl. no. 57381/00, Decision of 23 October 2001.
[28] However, see case of *Bámaca-Velásquez* v. *Guatemala*, Merits, Judgment of 25 November 2000, Ser. C, no. 70, paras. 208–9; the court 'can observe that certain acts or omissions that violate human rights, pursuant to the treaties that they do have competence to apply, also violate other international instruments for the protection of the individual, such as the 1949 Geneva Conventions and, in particular, common Article 3'. See also *Democratic Republic of Congo* v. *Burundi, Rwanda, Uganda*, 227/99 (2003), where the African Commission made extensive reference to international humanitarian law pursuant to article 60 ACHPR. See also section 14.5.

Instead, an applicant would need to demonstrate that the alleged violation, such as the bombing of a village, fell within the scope of the treaty concerned, such as constituting a violation of the right to life, as in the case of *Isayeva* v. *Russia*.[29] Beyond these rather clear-cut cases applications may give rise to difficult legal questions, for example whether tax proceedings concern 'civil rights and obligations' and therefore fall within the scope of article 6 ECHR.[30]

Jurisdiction and violations committed outside a state's territory

Applications are increasingly brought in relation to violations alleged to have taken place outside a state's territory. Such applications may be simply considered inadmissible *rationae loci* for lack of territorial link. However, these cases frequently raise complex questions of jurisdiction that are closely related to the material applicability of a treaty. A state's obligation to respect human rights under the respective treaties is in principle confined to its territorial jurisdiction. For example, article 2(1) ICCPR stipulates that a state party 'undertakes to respect and to ensure to all individuals within its territory and subject to its jurisdiction the rights recognized in the present Covenant'. This is in line with the general rule of international law according to which jurisdiction refers primarily to state territory, including air space as well as aircraft and vessels that are registered in the state or fly its flag.[31] In most cases the act or omission complained of will have taken place on the territory of a state and the jurisdiction of the treaty body will be apparent. This includes cases that have a link to other countries, such as sending someone to a country where he or she is at risk of torture, because the state action, such as a deportation, takes place on its territory.[32]

Jurisprudence is less clear on the circumstances under which treaties apply to conduct abroad (extraterritorial application) beyond the recognised exceptions of 'acts of diplomatic and consular agents ... present on foreign territory'[33] and 'the exercise of extra-territorial jurisdiction by a Contracting State when, through the consent, invitation or acquiescence of the Government of that territory, it exercises all or some of the public powers normally to be exercised by that Government'.[34] A look at the potential scope of cases shows the importance of this issue: does the kidnapping or arrest of a person

---

[29] See e.g. *Isayeva* v. *Russian Federation*, (2005) 41 EHRR 38, paras. 162–201.

[30] *Ferrazzini* v. *Italy*, (2002) 34 EHRR 45, paras. 14–31.

[31] See on jurisdiction, I. Brownlie, *Principles of Public International Law*, 7th edn (Oxford University Press, 2008), pp. 299–300; V. Lowe and C. Stalker, 'Jurisdiction', in M. Evans, *International Law*, 3rd edn. (Oxford University Press, 2010), 313–39.

[32] As explicitly recognised in article 3 CAT and the jurisprudence of international treaty bodies. See section 8.3.6.

[33] *Al-Skeini and Others* v. *United Kingdom*, (2011) 53 EHRR 18, para. 134.

[34] Ibid., para. 135.

by agents of a state party in a third country bring the case within the purview of the treaty concerned?[35] Does the detention of a person in a war conducted abroad, for example by UK troops in Iraq and Afghanistan, and subsequent transfer to the local authority, fall within the UK's jurisdiction?[36] What about the conduct of Turkey in Northern Cyprus, that of the USA in Guantánamo Bay and of Israel in the occupied territories?[37] And what about the use of firepower in a combat situation in a third country[38] or the bombing of a television station in a non-member state?[39] Human rights treaty bodies, including national courts, have largely used the criterion of 'effective control' to establish whether such acts fall within the jurisdiction of a state. Determining whether a state exercises 'effective control' is a question of fact that depends on physical control over a person or military presence and other factors evidencing the state's influence in the territory concerned.[40] However, the application of this criterion which has parallels with the rules of attribution in the law on state responsibility[41] has been far from consistent and has caused a considerable deal of controversy and legal uncertainty.[42]

Extending the application of treaties to conduct abroad may from a teleological perspective strengthen the effective protection of human rights. However, it frequently encounters considerable resistance on the parts of states that oppose such interpretation.[43] The European experience is instructive in this regard because it has generated most of the existing case law. In one of its most controversial cases, concerning the NATO bombing of a television station in Belgrade, *Banković and Others* v. *Belgium and Sixteen Other Contracting States*, the ECtHR found the ECHR inapplicable, holding that there was no effective control of the territory and its inhabitants.[44] In a potentially far-reaching paragraph, it stressed that the protection of the Convention was

---

[35] *Burgos* v. *Uruguay*, Communication no. R.12/52 (29 July 1981), paras. 12.1–12.3.

[36] *Al-Skeini and Others* v. *United Kingdom; Al-Saadoon and Mufdhi* v. *United Kingdom*, (2010) 51 EHRR 9; *ER (on the application of Evans)* v. *Secretary of State for Defence*, [2011] ACD 11, [2010] EWHC 1445 (Admin).

[37] *Loizidou* v. *Turkey* (Preliminary objections), (1995) 20 EHRR 99; Concluding observations of the HRCtee on the USA, UN Doc. CCPR/C/USA/CO/3/2006 (15 September 2006), para. 10; and Israel, UN Doc. CCPR/C/ISR/CO/3/2010 (3 September 2010), para. 5.

[38] Compare *Issa and Others* v. *Turkey*, (2005) 41 EHRR 27, paras. 65–81, with *Al-Skeini* v. *United Kingdom*, paras. 149–50 (during occupation).

[39] *Bankovic and Others* v. *Belgium and Others*, (2001) 11 BHRC 435.

[40] *Al-Skeini* v. *United Kingdom*, para. 139.

[41] See in particular *Military and Paramilitary Activities in and against Nicaragua (Nicaragua v. United States of America)*, Merits, Judgment, ICJ Reports 1986, 14, paras. 109 and 115.

[42] See section 14.6.1.

[43] Such as the UK in the *Al-Skeini* v. *United Kingdom*, Turkey in *Loizidou* v. *Turkey*, and the USA in relation to extraterritorial counter-terrorism operations, UN Doc. CCPR/C/USA/CO/3/2006, para. 10 and *Djamel Ameziane* v. *United States*, Report no. 17/12, Petition P 900-08, Admissibility, OEA/Ser. L/V/II. 144, Doc. 21 (20 March 2012).

[44] *Banković and Others* v. *Belgium and Others*, paras. 54–82.

meant to guarantee a public European order and did not extend 'beyond the legal space (*espace juridique*) of the Contracting States'.[45] Equally, the UK House of Lords adopted a narrow reading, finding that UK troops operating in Iraq exercised 'effective control' where an individual was in custody but not in a combat situation,[46] a distinction that seems rather artificial, particularly where the troops concerned are in control of an area.

7.2.2   The long reach of the ECHR: *Al-Skeini* v. *UK*

The *Al-Skeini* v. *UK* judgment substantially clarified the ECtHR's jurisprudence. The case concerned the killing of six civilians at the hands of UK troops, both in custody and on the streets of Basra, Iraq, and the UK's failure to comply with its procedural duty under article 2 ECHR to effectively investigate the killings. The outcome of the case hinged on the question of jurisdiction. Once the ECtHR found that the UK's 'authority and responsibility for the maintenance of security in South East Iraq' provided the jurisdictional link under article 1 ECHR,[47] a finding of a violation of article 2 ECHR became almost inevitable due to the apparent lack of independence of investigations.[48] The judgment effectively abandoned the Court's reservation that the ECHR does not apply extraterritorially (see *Banković*). However, it retains a case-by-case approach that focuses on the element of direct control over a person and effective control over an area to establish a jurisdictional link. In a persuasive concurring opinion Judge Bonello criticised the Court for having missed an opportunity to develop a more coherent approach to the question of extraterritorial application based on functional considerations according to which 'a State has jurisdiction for the purposes of Article 1 whenever the observance or the breach of any of these functions [negative and positive obligations in respect of human rights] is within its authority and control'.[49]

One important follow-up question is what rights should apply, for example whether occupying forces, such as in Iraq, should ensure the right to privacy under the ECHR, which has given rise to debates about the risk of 'human rights imperialism' by applying regional standards beyond the territory of member states.[50] While there are still grey areas in this respect, a state effectively

---

[45] Ibid., para. 80. See for a detailed discussion of the *Banković* case, M. Milanovic, 'From Compromise to Principle: Clarifying the Concept of State Jurisdiction in Human Rights Treaties', *HRLR* 8(3) (2008), 411–48.

[46] *Al-Skeini & Ors* v. *Secretary of State for Defence*, [2007] UKHL 26 (13 June 2007), summarised in *Al-Skeini* v. *United Kingdom*, paras. 83–8.

[47] Ibid., para. 149.   [48] Ibid., paras. 151–77.

[49] See the Concurring Opinion of Judge Bonello, ibid., para. 11.

[50] R. Wilde, 'Compliance with human rights norms extraterritorially: 'human rights imperialism?', in B. de Chazournes and M. G. Kohen (eds.), *Human Rights and the Quest for its Implementation* (Leiden: Brill, 2010), 319–48.

exercising public authority extraterritorially should be responsible for ensuring the rights it is able to protect, particularly in relation to its own conduct.[51] The rules on occupation under international humanitarian law can provide guidance in this respect.[52] Given the multiple instances in which states act abroad it can be expected that the jurisdictional question will continue to vex human rights treaty bodies, although a teleological approach focusing on effective protection appears best suited to these situations, not least so as to avoid a situation described by Judge Bonello of states acting as 'gentlemen at home, hoodlums elsewhere'.[53]

POINTS TO CONSIDER

1 Do you agree with Judge Bonello's functional approach, or would this be 'tantamount to arguing that anyone adversely affected by an act imputable to a Contracting State, wherever in the world that act may have been committed or its consequences felt, is thereby brought within the jurisdiction of that State for the purpose of Article 1 of the Convention'?[54]

2 The UK argued (see Judge Bonello's concurring opinion) that exporting the ECHR to Iraq would amount to 'human rights imperialism'. Discuss.

In an interesting reverse scenario, Moldova argued in 2004 in the *Ilaşcu* case that it did not exercise jurisdiction over Transdniestra, a breakaway region that had effectively been under Russian control since 1991. The ECtHR rejected this argument, finding that a state retains jurisdiction over its territory 'even where the exercise of the State's authority is limited in part of its territory'.[55] This was an important ruling because it strengthened the protection of persons, such as Ilaşcu, who find themselves in the power of a *de facto* authority. However, it is debatable whether a state's nominal authority over its territory should necessarily be equated with effective control, which is a factual question. The ECtHR tempered the legal consequences, though, by finding that the limited control did affect the nature of Moldova's positive obligation to prevent and remedy violations.[56]

---

[51] Concurring Opinion of Judge Bonello in *Al-Skeini* v. *United Kingdom*, para. 32.
[52] See R. Wilde, 'Triggering State Obligations Extraterritorially: the Spatial Test in Certain Human Rights Treaties', *Israel L. Rev.* 40(2), (2007), 503–26, and Milanovic, above note 45, at 424.
[53] Concurring Opinion of Judge Bonello in *Al-Skeini* v. *United Kingdom*, para. 18.
[54] *Banković and Others* v. *Belgium and Others*, para. 75.
[55] *Ilaşcu and Others* v. *Moldova and Russia*, (2005) 40 EHRR 46, paras. 300–31, 313; also *Assanidze* v. *Georgia*, (2004) 39 EHRR 32, paras. 132–50, which the ECHR contrasted to its rulings in *Loizidou* v. *Turkey* and *Cyprus* v. *Turkey* (lack of effective control).
[56] *Ilaşcu and others* v. *Moldova and Russia*, paras. 332–5.

Rationae temporis: when?

Applicants can only bring a case that falls within the period after which a state has recognised the competence of a treaty body to consider applications against it, for example following entry into force of the Optional Protocol to the ICCPR for the state concerned. This is based on the general rule of non-retroactivity of obligations (because of a lack of state consent for the preceding period).[57] However, applicants may exceptionally bring cases in circumstances that qualify this general rule. The most important situations are ongoing violations, such as enforced disappearances,[58] or violations of property rights,[59] which commenced before the state concerned became bound by the complaints procedure but continued to generate effects thereafter.[60] The consideration of other violations, such as the inordinate length of proceedings, is in principle confined to the period after a state is subject to the complaints procedure. However, treaty bodies have qualified this principle and have considered relevant factors prior to that date.[61] In the case of trials, for example, the HRCtee has held that the upholding of convictions by higher courts allows it to consider proceedings as a whole where a judgment constitutes an affirmation of the original violation, which it was precluded from considering because of non-retroactivity.[62] Importantly, a state may also be held responsible for its failure to comply with its positive obligation to investigate violations even where they occurred prior to it being bound. The HRCtee initially held that the duty to investigate was not an independent obligation that could be detached from the violation of a substantive ICCPR right. However, it later found that it has jurisdiction where proceedings had already been pending at the time the ICCPR and the Optional Protocol came into force for the state party.[63]

---

[57] *Blečić* v. *Croatia*, (2006) 43 EHRR 48, paras. 51–93 (court termination of tenancy before entry into force); *E. J. and C. M. Drake* v. *New Zealand*, UN Doc. CCPR/C/59/D/601/1994 (3 April 1997), para. 8.2. (1951 peace treaty with Japan that was alleged not to provide adequate compensation for New Zealand nationals and residents); *R. A. V. N. et al.* v. *Argentina*, UN Doc. CCPR/C/38/D/343/1988 (26 March 1990), para. 5.2 (amnesty laws).

[58] See for an overview of jurisprudence of international bodies, *Varnava and Others* v. *Turkey*, [2009] ECHR 1313, paras. 93–106, and of the ECtHR, ibid., paras. 130–50. See also *J. E. Zitha and P. J. L. Zitha* v. *Mozambique*, 361/08 (2011), paras. 73–94.

[59] See e.g. *Loizidou* v. *Turkey*, (1996) 23 EHRR 513, paras. 46–7, and *Hutten-Czapska* v. *Poland*, (2007) 45 EHRR 4, paras. 152–3.

[60] But state may limit jurisdiction to acts that had begun after a certain date, see e.g. *Serrano-Cruz Sisters* v. *El Salvador*, Preliminary objections, Judgment of 23 November 2004, Ser. C, no. 118, paras. 57–79.

[61] See for an overview of ECtHR jurisprudence, *Šilih* v. *Slovenia*, [2009] ECHR 571, paras. 140–7.

[62] Here conviction under Sri Lanka's Prevention of Terrorism Act based on evidence allegedly extracted under torture, see *Singarasa* v. *Sri Lanka*, UN Doc. CCPR/C/81/D/1033/2001 (21 July 2004), para. 6.3.

[63] Compare *R. A. V. N. et al.* v. *Argentina*, para. 5.3, with *Mariama Sankara et al.* v. *Burkina Faso*, UN Doc. CCPR/C/86/D/1159/2003 (28 March 2006), para. 6.3.

The ECtHR, in holding that the procedural obligation to investigate alleged violations under articles 2 and 3 ECHR had developed into a separate and autonomous duty, found that procedural acts or omissions might constitute an interference that brings a case within the Court's jurisdiction.[64] However, it qualified this general rule by requiring a 'genuine connection' between the substantive violation and the procedural steps, 'a significant proportion [of which] will have been or ought to have been carried out after the critical date [entry into force]'.[65] This connection could 'in certain circumstances ... also be based on the need to ensure that the guarantees and the underlying values of the Convention are protected in a real and effective manner'.[66] A case concerning the lack of investigations by Russian authorities into the war crimes committed in Katyn, Poland, during World War II illustrated the difficulties of determining such a link in cases dating back a long time. After setting out relevant principles, the Court concluded 'that there were no elements capable of providing a bridge from the distant past into the recent post-ratification period [after 1998] and that the special circumstances justifying a connection between the death and the ratification [such as newly discovered evidence] have not been shown to exist'.[67] Nevertheless, the jurisprudence shows that applicants may under certain circumstances be able to bring cases alleging a violation of the duty to investigate even where they are barred from raising the violation giving rise to such duty, such as in the case of extrajudicial killings.

7.2.3   Exhaustion of domestic remedies

The requirement to exhaust domestic remedies frequently constitutes one of the most formidable challenges for applicants. The exhaustion rule recognises that victims have a right of access to justice and that states have the primary duty, and should be given the opportunity, to remedy violations at the domestic level. The rule reflects the subsidiarity of supranational human rights treaty bodies which are not meant to replace national courts or act as appeal courts.[68] From a pragmatic perspective the rule also prevents a supranational

---

[64] IACtHR, see also *Serrano-Cruz Sisters*, paras. 77–96, particularly at para. 77 ('independent facts' even though court barred from examining actual violations alleged because of limitation pursuant to El Salvador's declaration); *Moiwana Community* v. *Suriname*, Preliminary objections, merits, reparations and costs, Judgment of 15 June 2005, Ser. C, no. 124, paras. 37–44.

[65] *Šilih* v. *Slovenia*, paras. 159–67, particularly para. 163.

[66] Ibid., para. 163.

[67] *Janowiec and Others* v. *Russia*, Appl. nos. 55508/07 and 29520/09, Judgment (16 April 2012), para. 140.

[68] E.g. *Selmouni* v. *France*, (2000) 29 EHRR 403, para. 74; *Kudla* v. *Poland*, (2002) 35 EHRR 198, para. 152; *Velasquez Rodríguez* v. *Honduras*, Merits, Judgment of 29 July 1988, Ser. C, no. 4, para. 61; *Dawda Jawara* v. *The Gambia*, 147/95-149/96 (2000), para. 31;

body from being seized with a large number of cases (although the floodgate argument has not stopped a large stream of applications reaching the ECtHR). The jurisprudence on the exhaustion of effective remedies varies considerably between treaty bodies and even in the practice of individual bodies over time. This is unsurprising given the difficulty of determining whether domestic remedies are available and effective. The determination also has a political dimension because it implies a verdict on the capacity of the domestic legal system in question to respond adequately to an alleged violation.

What remedies must be exhausted?

An applicant needs to exhaust remedies that are available and effective. A remedy is considered available if it is accessible in theory and practice[69] and can be 'pursued without impediment'.[70] It is effective where it offers a prospect of success, that is redress for the violation complained about.[71] In principle, applicants must pursue all available remedies, including appeals to the highest courts and fundamental rights petitions. However, there are several recognised exceptions. There is no need to exhaust purely discretionary procedures such as pardons because they are not based on the determination of rights.[72] In cases of serious violations, such as alleged violations of the right to life or the prohibition of torture, purely administrative or disciplinary proceedings are not considered sufficient or effective.[73] In these instances remedies must be of a judicial nature; they must also be capable of establishing the facts and the criminal responsibility of those responsible. This means, for example, that a respondent state cannot refer to the possibility of pursuing a case before a national human rights commission that lacks binding powers where an applicant shows that effective judicial remedies are not available.[74]

T. K. v. *France*, UN Doc. CCPR/C/37/D/220/1987 (8 November 1989), para. 8.3. See on the application of the principle in public international law, P. Okowa, 'Issues of Admissibility and the Law on State Responsibility', in Evans, above note 31, 472–503, at 494–500.

[69] *Akdivar and Others* v. *Turkey*, (1997) 23 EHRR 143, para. 66.

[70] *Dawda Jawara* v. *The Gambia*, para. 32.

[71] Ibid., *Sejdovic* v. *Italy* [2006] ECHR 181, para. 46; *Godínez-Cruz* v. *Honduras*, Reparations and costs, Judgment of 21 July 1989, Ser. C, no. 8, paras. 67–9; *Patino* v. *Panama*, UN Doc. CCPR/C/52/D/437/1990 (21 October 1994), para. 5.2.

[72] *Singarasa* v. *Sri Lanka*, para. 6.4; *Prince* v. *Jamaica*, UN Doc. CCPR/C/44/D/269/1987 (30 March 1992), para. 5.1; *A. H.* v. *Sweden*, UN Doc. CAT/C/37/D/265/2005 (16 November 2006), para. 4.10; *Tüm Haber Sen and Çinar* v. *Turkey*, (2008) 46 EHRR 19; *Constitutional Rights Project* v. *Nigeria*, 60/91 (1995), para. 10.

[73] See in particular HRCtee decisions in *Vicente et al.* v. *Colombia*, UN Doc. CCPR/C/60/D/612/1995 (29 July 1997), para. 5.2, and *Coronel et al.* v. *Colombia*, UN Doc. CCPR/C/76/D/778/1997 (24 October 2002), para. 6.2.

[74] *Ilesanmi* v. *Nigeria*, 268/03 (2005), para. 42. Conversely, it is not sufficient for an applicant to submit a case before a national human rights institution without also seeking recourse to courts, see *Alfred B. Cudjoe* v. *Ghana*, 221/98 (1999), para. 13; *Brough* v. *Australia*, UN Doc. CCPR/C/86/D/1184/2003 (17 March 2006), para. 8.7.

This jurisprudence demonstrates the link between the nature of violations and the types of remedies that are considered effective in the circumstances.

Remedies also need not be exhausted if they are futile, for example where there is already settled case law by the highest courts on the point raised.[75] Equally, there is no need to exhaust unduly prolonged remedies, which are by their very nature considered ineffective as recognised in several treaties and the jurisprudence of treaty bodies.[76] There are no hard and fast rules on when a remedy is unduly prolonged – treaty bodies generally consider the conduct of the parties and the complexity of the case to determine whether the length of time is reasonable.[77] Applicants are for example able to rely on this rule where investigations into alleged violations have been pending for years without any evidence of progress or where judicial proceedings have dragged on for several years, particularly where remedies have been turned into 'delaying instruments'.[78]

Other exceptions to the general rule of exhaustion are based on structural policy considerations. The African Commission, in particular, has repeatedly held that it would be impracticable to require applicants to exhaust domestic remedies in cases of serious or massive violations where – even though the violations must have been known to the state – it failed to take adequate action.[79] The ECtHR also held for some time that applicants need not exhaust domestic remedies in the south-east of Turkey 'where an administrative practice consisting of a repetition of acts incompatible with the Convention and official tolerance by the State authorities has been shown to exist, and is of such a nature as to make proceedings futile or ineffective'[80] – a practice that resulted in a large number of cases before the Court. Such jurisprudence makes it easier for applicants to pursue cases but may result in difficulties at the enforcement stage if a state opposes the interpretation of the treaty body concerned.

Applicants need not exhaust domestic remedies that are not accessible. This rule has been applied where someone cannot return to a country to pursue a case out of fear for his or her life, particularly following a violation.[81]

---

[75] *Länsman et al.* v. *Finland*, UN Doc. CCPR/C/52/D/511/1992 (26 October 1994), para. 6.2; *Pressos Compania Naviera S. A. and others* v. *Belgium*, (1996) 21 EHRR 301, para. 27.

[76] Articles 5(2)(b) Optional Protocol ICCPR; 56(5) ACHPR; 46(1)(c) ACHR.

[77] See e.g. *Todorov* v. *Bulgaria* [2005] ECHR 30, para. 45. See for a detailed review of the HRCtee's jurisprudence on this point, Tyagi, above note 6, 487–92.

[78] *Las Dos Erres Massacre* v. *Guatemala*, Preliminary objection, merits, reparations, and costs, Judgment of 24 November 2009, Ser. C, no. 11, paras. 119 and 121; *Rajapakse* v. *Sri Lanka*, UN Doc. CCPR/C/87/D/1250/2004 (14 July 2006), para. 9.4.

[79] See e.g. *Sudan Human Rights Organisation and Centre on Housing Rights and Evictions (COHRE)* v. *Sudan*, 279/03 and 296/05 (2009), para. 102.

[80] *Akdivar* v. *Turkey*, (1997) 23 EHRR 143, para. 67.

[81] However, see on the contradictory aspects of the ACHPR's jurisprudence in this regard, F. Viljoen, 'Communication under the African Charter: Procedure and Admissibility', in M. Evans and R. Murray (eds.), *The African Charter on Human and Peoples' Rights: The*

Remedies are also not accessible where someone has been subjected to threats preventing him or her from accessing legal remedies, either personally or through lawyers. This includes situations where a 'general fear in the legal community to represent [a person] prevents a complainant ... from invoking domestic remedies' as found by the IACtHR in its advisory opinion on *Exceptions to the Exhaustion of Domestic Remedies.*[82]

The IACtHR also held that a lack of means to afford legal assistance does not absolve a person from having to exhaust domestic remedies unless 'it can be shown that an indigent needs legal counsel to effectively protect a right which the Convention guarantees and his indigency prevents him from obtaining such counsel'.[83] This finding entails that states have to offer legal aid where needed to secure effective access to remedies. Other courts, such as the ECtHR, have been reluctant to consider lack of resources as a ground on which applicants can forgo the requirement of exhaustion of domestic remedies.[84] Applicants relying on this argument therefore run a considerable risk of their case being declared inadmissible.

7.2.4 'An affront to common sense and logic': *Dawda Jawara* v. *The Gambia*

Dawda Jawara, the complainant, was 'the former Head of State of the Republic of The Gambia. He allege[d] that after the Military coup of July 1994, that overthrew his government there has been "blatant abuse of power by ... the military junta". The military government is alleged to have initiated a reign of terror, intimidation and arbitrary detention.' The respondent state party claimed that the complainant had not exhausted domestic remedies, arguing that 'he should have sent his complaint to the police who would in turn have investigated the allegations and prosecuted the offenders "in a court of law"'. The Commission held that 'in a situation where the jurisdiction of the courts have been ousted by decrees whose validity cannot be challenged or questioned, as is the position with the case under consideration, local remedies are deemed not only to be unavailable but also non-existent'. Moreover,

System in Practice 1986–2006, 2nd edn (Cambridge University Press, 2008), 76–138, at 121–3, contrasting *John D. Ouko* v. *Kenya*, 232/99 (2000) with *Institute for Human Rights and Development in Africa (on behalf of Simbarakiye)* v. *Democratic Republic of Congo*, 247/2002 (2003).

[82] *Exceptions to the Exhaustion of Domestic Remedies* (Arts. 46(1), 46(2)(a) and 46(2)(b) of the American Convention on Human Rights), Advisory opinion OC-11/90, 10 August 1990, Ser. A, no. 11, para. 32.

[83] Ibid., para. 31; *Hilaire, Constantine and Benjamin et al.* v. *Trinidad and Tobago*, Merits, reparations and costs, Judgment of 21 June 2002, Ser. C, no. 94, para.152(b). See also *Purohit and Moore* v. *The Gambia*, 241/2001(2003), paras. 36–8; *Henry* v. *Jamaica*, UN Doc. CCPR/C/43/D/230/1987 (1 November 1991), para. 7.3: 'it is not the author's indigence which absolves him from pursuing constitutional remedies, but the State party's unwillingness or inability to provide legal aid for this purpose'.

[84] *Van Oosterwijck* v. *Belgium*, (1981) 3 EHRR 557, para. 38.

[t]he complainant in this case had been overthrown by the military, he was tried in absentia, former Ministers and Members of Parliament of his government have been detained and there was terror and fear for lives in the country. It would be an affront to common sense and logic to require the complainant to return to his country to exhaust local remedies.

Consequently, the Commission found the case admissible and in so doing established an important precedent for the understanding of what constitutes an effective remedy.

QUESTION

1   A human rights defender who has credible evidence that he has been tortured because of his work and who left the country concerned out of fear for his safety considers that he would face further risk of torture if he were to return to pursue the case. Would he still need to pursue domestic remedies, possibly through a lawyer?

Who carries the burden of proof concerning the exhaustion of domestic remedies?

Applicants bear the initial burden of proof of showing that they have exhausted domestic remedies or that effective remedies are not available. Where the applicant makes out a prima facie case to this effect the state must demonstrate that effective remedies were available, i.e. 'sufficiently certain in theory and practice', but have not been exhausted.[85] If the state succeeds in doing so the applicant has to exhaust any remaining remedies.[86] Arguments to this effect are frequently at the heart of admissibility decisions and constitute one of the major hurdles that applicants need to overcome.

7.2.5   Other procedural requirements

Time limits

There is no uniform practice concerning the time within which an application has to be submitted. Before both the ECtHR and the IACHR applications need to be brought within six months after the final decision or six months from the time either of the act constituting the alleged violations or after

---

[85] *Dalia* v. *France*, (2001) 33 EHRR 26, para. 38.
[86] *S. H. B.* v. *Canada*, Communication no. 192/1985 (24 March 1987), para. 7.2; *Epözdemir* v. *Turkey*, Appl. no. 57039/00, Admissibility decision of 31 January 2002, mere doubt not sufficient.

it becomes clear that no effective remedies are available.[87] As held in *Varnava* v. *Turkey*, the 'object of the six-month time-limit under Article 35 §1 is to promote legal certainty'.[88] The rule can pose significant challenges for applicants who have to make sure that they submit applications in time. This includes situations where an applicant mistakenly pursues remedies that may be considered ineffective, and, in so doing, fails to adhere to the six-month limit.[89] The only UN treaties that include an express time limit (of one year) are the recently adopted Optional Protocols to the ICESCR and CRC.[90] Other complaints procedures may reject applications that are submitted after an unduly long time on the ground that they constitute an abuse of the right. The HRCtee has clarified its understanding of what constitutes an abuse of right by stipulating a general, comparatively generous, five-year period from the exhaustion of domestic remedies or three years after the 'conclusion of another procedure of international investigation or settlement'.[91] The ACHPR provides that applications should be submitted 'within a reasonable time from the time domestic remedies are exhausted'.[92] The African Commission has for a long time applied this rule generously but has since the late 2000s begun to declare cases inadmissible for having been submitted out of time where the applicant(s) cannot show why the application was not made earlier.[93] This jurisprudence, which is far from consistent, shows that an indeterminate limit, such as 'within a reasonable time', introduces an element of uncertainty and possibly of arbitrariness.

Duplication

Complaints procedures provide that applications are inadmissible if the same matter is being examined (Optional Protocol to the ICCPR; ACHR; CPED) or has been examined (ECHR–ACHPR) by the same body or 'another procedure of international investigation or settlement' (both under CAT; ICPMW; Optional Protocols CEDAW, ICESCR, CRPD, CRC). The rationale behind this rule is to prevent forum shopping, to contribute to the settlement of disputes and to

---

[87] *Hamail Bayram and Şekir Yildrim* v. *Turkey*, Appl. no. 38587/97, Admissibility decision of 29 January 2002.

[88] *Varnava* v. *Turkey*, [2009] ECHR 1313, para. 156.

[89] See for an overview of relevant jurisprudence, P. Leach, *Taking a Case to the European Court of Human Rights* (Oxford University Press, 2011), 4.101; D. J. Harris *et al.*, *Law of the European Convention on Human Rights*, 3rd edn (Oxford University Press, 2009), 776–81.

[90] Articles 3(2)(a) OP ICESCR and 7(h) OP CRC on a communications procedure.

[91] Rule 96(c) of the HRCtee's Rules of Procedures.   [92] Article 56(6) ACHPR.

[93] See for example *Michael Majuru* v. *Zimbabwe*, 308/05 (2008), para. 110 (twenty-two months considered too long in the circumstances); *Article 19 and Others* v. *Zimbabwe* 305/05 (2010) (two years); *Darfur Relief and Documentation Centre* v. *Sudan*, 310/05 (2009), paras. 78–9 (twenty-nine months).

reduce the scope for diverging decisions. The requirement is less restrictive for applicants than it may appear at first sight because it effectively requires that the application is identical in relation to the facts, the parties concerned and the allegations raised in another case, and does not rely on new information.[94] It also only applies to other binding complaints procedures. Procedures that cannot consider complaints, determine responsibility and afford remedies, such as the UN special procedures (with the possible exception of the Working Group on Arbitrary Detention),[95] confidential UN charter body proceedings, such as the 1503 procedure, or preventive bodies, such as the CPT, fall outside of its scope.[96] These factors considerably limit the importance of this admissibility criterion in practice.

Well-foundedness

Applicants must demonstrate that their case is not manifestly ill-founded or unsubstantiated (HRCtee), a notion that allows treaty bodies to dismiss claims that are deemed without merit.[97] This requirement involves a preliminary examination of the substance of the case. Applications have been found to be manifestly ill-founded where they effectively asked the treaty body to act as court of appeal, where there is no apparent violation or where the allegations are not sufficiently substantiated.[98] Effectively, this means that an applicant has to make out a prima facie case and adduce at least some evidence that supports any claims made. Protocol no. 14 to the ECHR has added a related, and controversial, criterion of 'no significant disadvantage', which means that the Court may declare applications inadmissible even where they may be well-founded but are not considered sufficiently serious to merit its attention.[99]

Abuse of rights

'Abuse of rights' is a general and flexible device in the hands of treaty bodies to dismiss applications that are designed to cause annoyance, use offensive

---

[94] See e.g. *Fanali v. Italy*, Communication no. 75/1980 (31 March 1983), para. 7.2; *Smirnova and Smirnova v. Russia*, Appls. nos. 46133/99 and 48183/99, Decision of 3 October 2002; *Varnava v. Turkey*, para. 118.

[95] *Peraldi v. France*, Appl. no. 2096/05, Decision of 7 April 2009, and *Iliu and Others v. Belgium*, Appl. no. 14301/08, Decision of 19 May 2009.

[96] See for a review of relevant jurisprudence Tyagi, above note 6, 466–71, and *Nikolai, Ljubov and Oleg Mikolenko v. Estonia*, Appl. no. 16944/03, Decision of 5 January 2006.

[97] See e.g. articles 3(2)(e) Optional Protocol ICESCR; 35(3)(a) ECHR; 47(b) and (c) ACHR.

[98] See e.g. *Hussain and Singh v. Guyana*, UN Doc. CCPR/C/85/D/862/1999 (25 October 2005), para. 5.4.

[99] Article 53(3)(b) ECHR.

language or are otherwise considered inappropriate.[100] The criterion of offensive language can be problematic where the body concerned applies value judgements to applications of victims who may have a strong sense of injustice and thereby deprive them of the opportunity to hear a case on the merits.[101] In practice, the criterion of abuse of rights does not play a major role but it is still one that applicants need to be mindful of.

Anonymity

Most complaints procedures require that applications are not lodged anonymously.[102] The reason for this is that the treaty body needs to know who it is dealing with; it also enables the respondent state to better respond to the facts. However, the requirement can be problematic where an applicant fears that the disclosure may put him or her at risk of reprisals. This is a genuine risk in many cases as the relevant jurisprudence and UN reports demonstrate. For example, in *Aksoy*, the first torture case against Turkey, the applicant was killed before the ECtHR could hear the case on the merits.[103] Some courts have therefore accepted exceptions, such as the use of pseudonyms, as long as it is clear who is behind the application.[104] In practice, applicants will often find it difficult to hide their identity, particularly given the factual evidence they need to provide to substantiate their claims.

7.3 MERITS

Once a case has been found admissible (and sometimes simultaneously) a human rights treaty body considers the merits to determine whether the rights of the applicant(s) have been violated, in other words whether the allegations made are well founded and reveal a breach of the state party's obligations. This determination is not confined to the violations claimed by the applicant; rather, treaty bodies can determine on their own motion what violations the proven facts disclose.[105] The evidentiary rules in proceedings before human rights treaty

---

[100] See in particular articles 3 Optional Protocol-ICCPR, 35(3)(a) ECHR; 56 ACHPR.

[101] Article 56(3) ACHPR. See critical comments by F. Viljoen, *International Human Rights Law in Africa*, 2nd edn (Oxford University Press, 2012), 314–15.

[102] Articles 3 Optional Protocol to ICCPR; 35(2)(a) ECHR; 46(d) ACHR; 56(1) ACHPR.

[103] *Aksoy* v. *Turkey*, (1997) 23 EHRR 553, para. 22.

[104] *Shamayev and Others* v. *Georgia and Russia*, Decision and judgment, [2005] ECHR 233, para. 275.

[105] See in particular F. Viljoen, 'Fact-finding by UN Human Rights Complaints Bodies – Analysis and Suggested Reforms', *MPYBUNL* 8 (2004), 49–100. See for an example of a case where the complainants did not invoke any particular provision of the CAT, but the CtAT found that the case raised an issue under article 3 and possibly article 16 of the convention, *Njamba and Balikosa* v. *Sweden*, UN Doc. CAT/C/44/D/322/2007 (14 May 2010), para. 1.1.

bodies, particularly quasi-judicial bodies, are characterised by less rigidity than those before national courts. As a general rule, the applicant carries the burden of proof in the sense that he or she has to make out a prima facie case.[106] This means having to adduce sufficient evidence to disclose a violation of his, her, their rights by the respondent state party, otherwise the application is (partly or fully) unfounded. In practice, this burden is eased in a series of circumstances. Where a state party does not respond to an application or fails to contest the allegations, the facts are considered proven where the applicant makes out a prima facie case.[107] In addition, the burden of proof is effectively reversed where the state party's lack of cooperation prevents the establishment of the facts, such as where it withholds crucial documents.[108] This rule also applies where it can be shown that a person was taken into custody in good health but sustains injuries or even dies while in detention without the state giving a satisfactory explanation.[109] The rationale behind this exception is that the circumstances lie exclusively in the sphere of the state and it is frequently virtually impossible for applicants to prove state responsibility. Moreover, where the facts disclose state interference with a qualified right, such as the right to privacy, the state party needs to show that such interference was necessary and proportionate.[110]

The standard of proof, that is the level of proof required for a treaty body to uphold a complaint, differs between treaty bodies and is not clearly defined. Most bodies appear to apply a standard akin to that known from civil proceedings, namely preponderance of probabilities (more likely than not).[111] The ECtHR has applied a higher standard of proof 'beyond reasonable doubt', which it has defined as 'the coexistence of sufficiently strong, clear and concordant inferences or of similar unrebutted presumptions of fact'.[112] While it has been emphasised that this standard is not identical to that applied in national criminal proceedings, it seems to be inappropriately high for human rights cases and its application has been repeatedly criticised.[113]

[106] See in particular J. Kokott, *The Burden of Proof in Comparative and International Human Rights* (The Hague: Kluwer Law International, 1998).

[107] See e.g. *Michael Bailey* v. *Jamaica*, UN Doc. CCPR/C/47/D/334/1988 (31 March 1993), paras. 9.2–11.1.

[108] *Akkum and Others* v. *Turkey*, (2006) 43 EHRR 26, para. 211. See for an early example of the HRCtee's jurisprudence, *Bleier* v. *Uruguay*, Communication no. 30/1978 (29 March 1982), para. 13.3.

[109] *Tomasi* v. *France*, (1993) 15 EHRR 1, para.108; *Selmouni* v. *France*, (2000) 29 EHRR 403, para. 87; *Kurt and Others* v. *Turkey*, (2007) 44 EHRR 36, para. 124. See also *Velásquez Rodríguez* v. *Honduras*, paras. 135–8.

[110] See e.g. *Van der Velden* v. *the Netherlands*, (2006) ECHR 1174; *Coster* v. *United Kingdom*, (2001) 33 EHRR 479; *Leander* v. *Sweden*, (1987) 9 EHRR 433.

[111] See for a brief overview, R. Murray, 'Evidence and Fact Finding by the African Commission', in Evans and Murray, above note 81, pp. 139–70, at. pp. 159–62.

[112] *Salman* v. *Turkey*, (2000) 34 EHRR 425, para. 100.

[113] Partly Dissenting Opinion of Judge Bonello, *Veznedaroğlu* v. *Turkey*, (2001) 33 EHRR 59, particularly para. 12.

Evidence is freely admissible and courts have shown flexibility in its assessment, often stressing that this is required by the nature of human rights cases.[114] Proceedings before UN treaty bodies are in writing only, relying mainly on affidavits and documentary evidence.[115] The IACtHR, in contradistinction, has developed an elaborate practice of hearing witnesses and expert testimony in oral proceedings. This is important for applicants because it enables them to put a comprehensive account of alleged violations on the record and before the Court for consideration.[116] The regional human rights courts and bodies can also undertake fact-finding missions to establish the evidence.[117] However, practice is rather *ad hoc* and hampered by the lack of power to compel witnesses.

Applicants in human rights proceedings are well advised to draw on as many credible sources of evidence as possible to substantiate any allegations made. Types of evidence may include witness statements (affidavits), official documents (including judgments, documentation by national human rights institutions, custody records, policy papers) and expert testimony (particularly medical reports). Reports by both national and international organisations and human rights bodies frequently play an important role in recording cases and establishing patterns of violations that can be relied on to enhance the credibility of claims made.[118] Courts may also consider audiovisual materials (satellite images, photographs and videos) as evidence.[119]

Human rights courts may admit third parties to submit *amici* on particular points of law as 'friends of the court' where this is considered to be in the 'interests of the proper administration of justice'.[120] Although interveners

---

[114] *Ireland* v. *the United Kingdom*, (1978) 2 EHRR 25, para. 209; *Velasquez Rodriguez* v. *Honduras*, paras. 122–38.

[115] See e.g. article 5(1) Optional Protocol and rule 100(1) of the HRCtee's Rules of Procedure.

[116] J. Cavallaro and S. E. Brewer, 'Reevaluating Regional Human Rights Litigation in the Twenty-First Century: the Case of the Inter-American Court', *AJIL* 102 (2008), 768–827.

[117] See ibid., 780, 793–6, 803–8, 814–16; P. Leach, C. Paraskeva and G. Uzelac, *International Human Rights and Fact-Finding: An Analysis of the Fact-finding Missions Conducted by the European Commission and Court of Human Rights* (London: Human Rights and Social Justice Research Institute, Metropolitan University, 2009); Murray, above note 111, 146–8.

[118] *Sudan Human Rights Organisation and Centre on Housing Rights and Evictions (COHRE)* v. *Sudan*, paras. 151–3; *Baboeram et al.* v. *Suriname*, Communications nos. 146/1983 and 148–54/1983 (4 April 1985), para. 12.2.

[119] See the Center for Research Libraries, *Human Rights Electronic Evidence Study: Final Report* (Chicago: The Center for Research Libraries, 2012), particularly 146–8. See also for an example of a video admitted as evidence in front of the IACtHR, case of *Gangaram Panday* v. *Suriname*, Merits, reparations and costs, Judgment of 21 January 1994, Ser. C, no. 16, paras. 2 (e), 8, 52–6. According to the OHCHR, 'Procedure for complaints by individuals under the human rights treaties', 'it has not been the practice to receive oral submissions from the parties or audio or audio-visual evidence (such as audio cassettes or videotapes)'. See www2.ohchr.org/english/bodies/petitions/individual.htm#merits.

[120] See e.g. article 36(2) ECHR and rule 44(3) (a) ECtHR Rules of Procedure.

are supposedly neutral, *amicus curiae* submissions can provide an excellent opportunity for NGOs to advocate a particular interpretation of rights and broaden the scope of analysis and thereby possibly advance jurisprudence in the field of human rights.[121] In practice, *amici* have played an important role in providing information and setting out questions of law that have been referred to by parties and formed part of the deliberations of the respective court.[122]

7.4   DECISIONS BY HUMAN RIGHTS TREATY BODIES

A glimpse at the decisions of human rights treaty bodies shows that decision-making is on the basis of the majority which sets out its reasoning in the decision.[123] Separate opinions (to elaborate on a point of law or principle) and dissenting opinions (to set out the grounds on which the judge(s) member(s) disagree with the majority) are an integral and instructive part of many decisions. Such opinions can provide an invaluable insight into the different positions within a treaty body; they are frequently relied upon by those who criticise particular reasoning and/or decisions and may be so persuasive as to lead to changes in jurisprudence.

The types of decision differ between treaty bodies and courts. Proceedings before UN treaty bodies and regional human rights commissions are quasi-judicial and such bodies adopt decisions. There is a continuing debate about the legal nature of these decisions, which some bodies refer to as 'views' or 'opinions'. Some observers, and frequently states parties or domestic courts, such as the Sri Lankan Supreme Court, claim that they are purely recommendatory.[124] The formal arguments put forward in support of this position are not very convincing. While there is general agreement that they are not

---

[121] M. Schachter, 'The Utility of Pro Bono Representation of US-Based Amicus Curiae in Non-US and Multi-National Courts as a Means of Advancing the Public Interest', *FILJ* 28 (2004), 88–144; A. Wilkowska-Landowska, '"Friends of the Court": The Role of Human Rights Non-governmental Organisations in the Litigation Proceedings', (undated), online, at www.nottingham.ac.uk/hrlc/documents/publications/hrlcommentary2006/friendsofthecourt.pdf.

[122] See for example the joint NGO amicus in the case of *Al-Saadoon and Mufhdi* v. *the United Kingdom* (Application no. 61498/08), *Written Comments by the Bar Human Rights Committee of England and Wales, British Irish Rights Watch, the European Human Rights Advocacy Centre, Human Rights Watch, the International Commission of Jurists, the International Federation for Human Rights, Justice, Liberty and Redress* (9 April 2009), available at www.liberty-human-rights.org.uk/about/legal/interventions/al-saaadoonfinal.pdf.

[123] However, see Tyagi, above note 6, 552–6, on the HRCtee's practice to rely on consensus as much as possible.

[124] *Singarasa* v. *Attorney General*, S. C. SPL (LA) no. 182/99 (2006).

binding as such, it is appropriate to see these decisions as 'authoritative interpretations' of the respective treaties that determine to what extent, if any, a state has failed to comply with its obligations.[125] As a consequence, states parties are required to take the necessary measures to remedy any violations found and bring their conduct in conformity with their obligation to give effect to treaties, such as required under article 2 ICCPR.[126]

In practice, there are considerable differences concerning the types of remedy identified by treaty bodies and awarded by courts. Remedies in the decisions of treaty bodies (other than courts) are often of a general and standardised nature. Treaty bodies tend to refrain from specifying amounts of compensation, stipulating that the state party should provide adequate compensation or reparation in line with national or international standards.[127] They also frequently request states parties to take measures against the perpetrators of violations, particularly to undertake investigations and ensure the prevention of 'similar violations in the future'. Yet practice has been far from consistent and UN treaty bodies have not developed an elaborate jurisprudence on reparation. In the regional systems, the Inter-American Commission has tended to be more specific and elaborate than the African Commission in respect of the reparations recommended. However, the African Commission has recently issued decisions that demonstrate greater emphasis on the nature of remedies.[128]

Human rights courts issue binding judgments on the merits that the parties undertake to comply with.[129] These judgments are final. The only exceptions are ECtHR Chamber judgments that may be brought before the Grand Chamber where they raise fundamental matters and the Grand Chamber accepts a request made.[130] The ECtHR has repeatedly stated that its judgments are declaratory. It has largely confined itself to stating that a judgment constitutes satisfaction but, especially in cases of violations of articles 2, 3 and 5 ECHR, where requested by the applicant, the ECtHR awards specific amounts of compensation for pecuniary and non-pecuniary harm.[131] This practice is based on the Court's interpretation of its competence to award 'just satisfaction' according to which it is primarily for the respondent state to take the measures necessary to comply with its obligations, under the supervision of the CoM. The ECtHR's approach has been repeatedly criticised for its 'conservative' nature but the Court has in some recent judgments ordered states to take specific measures, such as retrial

[125] HRCtee, General Comment 33: The Obligations of States Parties under the Optional Protocol to the International Covenant on Civil and Political Rights, UN Doc. CCPR/C/GC/33/CRP.3 (25 August 2008), para. 13.

[126] Ibid., particularly paras. 14, 15.   [127] Section 13.10.7.   [128] Ibid.

[129] Articles 44, 46(1) ECHR; 67, 68 ACHR; 28(2), 30 of the 1998 Protocol to the ACHPR and 46 of the 2008 Protocol on the Statute of the African Court of Justice and Human Rights.

[130] Article 43 ECHR.   [131] Section 13.10.7.

or release, which may indicate a willingness to develop its own reparation regime.[132] However, these cases are still exceptional and the ECtHR's jurisprudence on reparation remains underdeveloped. Protocol no. 14 adopted in 2010 has given the Court a greater role in the enforcement of judgments and it remains to be seen whether it will result in changes in the ECtHR's approach.

The IACtHR's jurisprudence, based on article 63 ACHR, provides a stark contrast, standing out for its deliberately progressive, detailed and victim-oriented approach towards awarding reparation that both reflects the nature of harm and seeks to bring about systemic changes to ensure compliance.[133] The ACtHPR has not had the opportunity to develop its jurisprudence on reparation. Notably, the Court has the mandate to award appropriate remedies, a power that many hope it will use with a view to strengthening the effectiveness of the African human rights system.[134]

7.5   IMPLEMENTATION OF DECISIONS AND JUDGMENTS

Implementation, also referred to as compliance or enforcement, represents one of the main challenges for litigants because non-compliance is a systemic problem in the international human rights system. The fact that most human rights treaties provide for no or only rudimentary enforcement procedures suggests that their significance was not well appreciated at a time when the primary focus was on standard-setting. The assumption that states parties that voluntarily subject themselves to a complaints procedure could be expected to comply with any decisions made has proven highly questionable. Indeed, implementation has become one of the Achilles heels of complaints procedures given the prevalence of partial or complete non-compliance. This is due to a range of factors, particularly the lack of adequate legal and institutional frameworks that would facilitate implementation.[135] The available data show that compliance with the decision of UN treaty bodies is

---

[132] See P. Leach, 'Beyond the Bug River: a New Dawn for Redress before the European Court of Human Rights?', *EHRLR* 2 (2005), 148–64, referring to cases such as *Ilaşcu* v. *Moldova and Russia*, and *Assanidze* v. *Georgia*. However, the Court has failed to use opportunities to widen the scope of reparation awarded. See in particular arguments put forward in *Varnava* v. *Turkey*, Intervention Submission by the Redress Trust (2 October 2008), which were ignored by the Court; see *Varnava* v. *Turkey*, paras. 215–25.

[133] See for a recent example of the breadth and detailed nature of reparation measures awarded, *Cabrera Garcia and Montiel Flores* v. *Mexico*, Preliminary objections, merits, reparations and legal costs, Judgment of 26 November 2010, Ser. C, no. 220, paras. 208–61.

[134] Articles 27 of the 1998 Protocol to the ACHPR and 45 of the 2008 Protocol on the Statute of the African Court of Justice and Human Rights.

[135] See Tyagi, above note 6, 579–80, for the HRCtee.

inconsistent;[136] the same applies to decisions by the African Commission.[137] Most states comply with orders by the IACtHR or the ECtHR to pay compensation. In both systems, states have also undertaken a series of general measures, particularly legislative reforms, to give effect to judgments.[138] However, respondent states have largely failed to undertake investigations and hold the perpetrators accountable where ordered or obliged to do so; this is a serious challenge as impunity constitutes one of the main factors that perpetuate a climate that facilitates human rights violations.[139]

The UN treaty bodies have responded to unsatisfactory implementation by taking various measures, such as setting timelines for reporting back on steps taken, the appointment of special rapporteurs for follow-up on views[140] and the inclusion of references to the lack of implementation in concluding observations on states parties' reports.[141] However, these measures ultimately rely on persuasion or naming and shaming because there are no effective sanctions. This means that they have been of limited use where needed most, that is when dealing with recalcitrant states. The development of more effective enforcement procedures remains a major challenge for the credibility of the UN human rights treaty system and has been one of the arguments for a unified human rights body or even a world court on human rights.

In the regional systems, the IACHR operates a flexible but rather *ad hoc* system in which it may request parties for information and hold hearings and reports on the state of compliance.[142] The African Commission has committed itself to establishing follow-up mechanisms but limited progress has been made beyond reporting on the status of implementation.[143] Successful cases of implementation have been attributed to the efforts of litigants and other bodies rather than the African Commission's follow-up activities.[144]

---

[136]   Several states have a persistent record of partial or complete non-compliance. See e.g. the 2011 *Annual Report of the HRCtee*, UN Doc. A/66/40 (vol. I), paras. 247–51. However, in several cases, compensation was paid and some legislative reforms and change were made, see Tyagi, above note 6, pp. 626–9, for a brief overview.

[137]   F. Viljoen and L. Louw, 'State Compliance with the Recommendations of the African Commission on Human and Peoples' Rights, 1994–2004', *AJIL* 101 (2007), 1–34.

[138]   Peru abolished its amnesty laws following the case of Barrios Altos and several European states changed their legislation, particularly with a view to complying with pilot judgments. See further sections 6.2.6 and 6.3.4.

[139]   Open Society Justice Initiative, *From Judgment to Justice, Implementing International and Regional Human Rights Decisions* (New York: Open Society Foundations, 2010), 33–92.

[140]   See 'Follow-up Progress Reports on Individual Communications'.

[141]   See Tyagi, above note 6, 584–6, for an overview of the action that the HRCtee can take.

[142]   Article 48(1) of the 2009 Rules of Procedure.

[143]   Resolution on the Importance of the Recommendations of the African Commission on Human and Peoples' Rights and rule 112 of the 2010 Rules of Procedure.

[144]   OSJI, above note 139, 104–8.

'Enforcement' procedures differ in the Inter-American and European system (the system before the ACtHPR is not considered further because of lack of sufficient practice at the time of writing). The IACtHR strengthened the system when it found that it had implied powers to follow up on judgments.[145] It has changed its rules of procedures and developed a practice of convening regular meetings with the parties involved, which appears to be conducive to enhanced compliance.[146] However, this practice requires intense engagement and may by itself prove insufficient to overcome entrenched systemic problems hindering implementation. The European system is unique in so far as a political body, the CoE's CoM, is tasked with supervising the execution of judgments. This includes individual and general measures and the CoM regularly monitors steps taken by the respondent states.[147] However, it has had limited success in challenging systemic non-compliance, such as by Russia and Turkey in relation to conflict-related violations.[148] In practice, NGOs increasingly provide information about the status of implementation to enable the CoM to exercise its mandate more effectively[149] but limited political will and institutional resistance still remain major obstacles. Protocol no. 14 responded to criticisms concerning the division of tasks between the ECtHR and the CoM by giving the Court a greater role in the execution of judgments.

It is clear that any institutional supranational 'enforcement' procedures have inherent limits. There is no authority in international law with binding enforcement powers comparable to national systems; the ultimate sanction for non-compliance may be exclusion from the political body in question but this is a momentous step that requires a considerable degree of political support.[150]

---

[145] *Baena-Ricardo* v. *Panama*, Competence, Judgment of 28 November 2003, Ser. C, no. 104.

[146] Article 69 of the IACtHR's 2010 Rules of Procedure.

[147] Article 46(2) ECHR; Reports on the execution of judgments can be found online, at www.coe.int/t/cm/humanrights_en.asp.

[148] See interviews 6.1 and 6.2. See also interim resolution CM/ResDH(2011)292: Execution of the judgments of the European Court of Human Rights in 154 cases against the Russian Federation concerning actions of the security forces in the Chechen Republic of the Russian Federation.

[149] See for example 'Communication from a group of the NGOs in the Mikheyev group of cases against the Russian Federation: Information made available under Rule 9.2 of the Rules of the Committee of Ministers for the supervision of the execution of judgments and of the terms of friendly settlements', DH-DD(2010)385E /1 September 2010.

[150] See Protocol No. 14, to the Convention for the Protection of Human Rights and Fundamental Freedoms, amending the control system of the Convention, Explanatory report (CETS no. 194) Agreement of Madrid (12.5.2009), para. 100: 'None the less, it appeared necessary to give the Committee of Ministers, as the competent organ for supervising execution of the Court's judgments, a wider range of means of pressure to secure execution of judgments. Currently the ultimate measure available to the Committee of Ministers is recourse to Article 8 of the Council of Europe's Statute (suspension of voting rights in the Committee of Ministers, or even expulsion from the Organisation).'

From a functional perspective, it may work as an effective threat for a state that wants to be part of a system but fails where this is not the case and it is most needed. Human rights treaty bodies and courts therefore have to rely largely on their legitimacy, which includes persuasiveness of decisions made and a collective interest in making the system work, including by means of compliance with decisions made.[151]

Participants and observers increasingly recognise that a top-down institutional perspective must be complemented with bottom-up approaches to enhance compliance. This turns the focus firmly on the domestic sphere and the ability of domestic actors to have decisions made implemented. Human rights treaty bodies have affirmed that states are expected to comply with their decisions.[152] Accordingly, it should be sufficient to simply request payment of adequate compensation (which is often subject to negotiations) as well as asking the state to take the additional measures needed to provide the remedies granted or recommended. In practice, states repeatedly fail to do so. The strength of the position of an applicant then depends on whether domestic law recognises the binding force of decisions by human rights treaty bodies – which is often the case for human rights courts but not UN treaty bodies[153] – so that they are enforceable. In the absence of such legislation, domestic courts have repeatedly declined to give effect to decisions by UN treaty bodies. One glaring example is the decision of Sri Lanka's Supreme Court in the *Singarasa* case. The HRCtee had found that Singarasa's conviction and sentence to thirty-five years' imprisonment under the Prevention of Terrorism Act had been in violation of his right to a fair trial under article 14 ICCPR. When lawyers sought a retrial in Sri Lanka in line with the Committee's views, Sri Lanka's Supreme Court found that there was no obligation on the Sri Lankan government under domestic law to enforce the views, which the Court considered non-binding.[154]

The legal status of decisions by treaty bodies and the availability of national implementation mechanisms are important. However, it is clear that implementation also depends on other factors, such as the degree of legitimacy of the body concerned and the extent to which the domestic legal community contributes to it. The strength of civil society, including NGOs and the media, to advocate implementation is often equally critical. This applies particularly where implementation is part of domestic political processes, such as reforms during transitional periods, or takes place within a broader

---

[151] See research project, 'Judicial Legitimacy and Authority of Supranational Human Rights Courts: a Comparative Analysis of the Perception of the European Court of Human Rights', online, at www.esrc.ac.uk/my-esrc/grants/RES-061-25-0029/read.

[152] HRCtee, General Comment 33, paras. 14–15.

[153] ILA, *Final Report on the Impact of Findings of the United Nations Human Rights Treaty Bodies* (Berlin Conference, 2004).

[154] *Singarasa* v. *Sri Lanka*.

political context, for example where it is used as a yardstick for membership in a regional organisation, such as in respect of EU accession.

CASE STUDY 7.2
Restoring ancestral lands to indigenous peoples – *Mayagna (Sumo) Awas Tingni Community* v. *Nicaragua*

In 2001 the IACtHR found that Nicaragua, through its failure to demarcate the communal lands of the Awas Tingni Community and other measures, had breached the applicants' right to judicial protection (article 25 ACHR) and the private right to property (article 21 ACHR) in relation to articles 1(1) and 2 ACHR.[1] It held that the

State must adopt the legislative, administrative, and any other measures required to create an effective mechanism for delimitation, demarcation, and titling of the property of indigenous communities, in accordance with their customary law, values, customs and mores... [which was to be carried out] within a maximum term of 15 months, with full participation by the Community and taking into account its customary law, values, customs and mores.

The Court also decided that '[t]he State must invest, as reparation for the immaterial damages, in the course of 12 months, the total sum of US$50,000 ... in works or services of collective interest for the benefit of the Awas Tingni Community, by common agreement with the Community and under the supervision of the Inter-American Commission.' The approach taken by the Court reflects what may be called a participatory approach when awarding reparation for a breach of the collective rights of indigenous peoples. While Nicaragua enacted legislation in 2003 to give effect to the judgment, it took until 2008 when a change in government finally resulted in over 70,000 hectares of land being given to the community. This is an important example of compliance through legislative reforms which has been attributed to the role played by President Ortega, a factor that demonstrates the importance of political support in implementing judgments.[2]

POINTS TO CONSIDER

- What is innovative about the IACtHR's approach in respect of reparation for the violation of collective rights?
- Can 'political will' said to be *the* factor when it comes to the implementation of decisions and judgments?

---

[1] *Mayagna (Sumo) Awas Tingni Community* v. *Nicaragua*, Merits, reparations and costs, Judgment of 31 August 2001, Ser. C, no. 79.
[2] See further OSJI, above note 139, 72–4.

7.6   ADDITIONAL PROCEDURAL OPTIONS

7.6.1   Interim measures

Applicants can request interim measures (also referred to as provisional measures) at any stage of proceedings before the final decision, and often do so at the very beginning of the procedure. These measures are important where an applicant is at risk of an imminent violation of his or her rights; their main purpose is to prevent a deterioration of a situation that adversely affects rights and leads to harm that cannot be made undone. Treaty bodies have either explicit or implied powers to order (request) interim measures, either upon application or ex officio (on their own motion).[155] Interim measures may be ordered where the treaty body has jurisdiction and there is prima facie evidence of a serious risk that action taken or threatened by a state, including a failure to act, may result in irreparable harm to the rights of a party. Interim measures have been ordered primarily to stay the imminent deportation, expulsion or extradition or other transfer of detainees that may result in a violation of rights[156] and to suspend the execution of the death penalty.[157] Treaty bodies have also ordered such measures to protect the health of detainees[158] and to protect complainants, including communities,[159] from threats.[160] The decision to order interim measures in the form of a stay of deportation or stay of execution is provisional. Its main objective is to preserve rights; interim measures should therefore not be prejudicial and impact on the determination of merits, not least because the decision to order such measures is not based on a full consideration of the available evidence.

Most treaty bodies have recognised that interim measures have binding force. This interpretation is not as obvious as it seems. Indeed, the question

---

[155] Article 63(2) ACHR; rule 39 ECtHR 2009 Rules of Court; rule 98 of the African Commission's 2010 Rules of Procedure; E. Rieter, *Preventing Irreparable Harm: Provisional Measures in International Human Rights Adjudication* (Antwerp: Intersentia, 2010); C. B. H. Herrera, *Provisional Measures in the Case Law of the Inter-American Court of Human Rights* (Antwerp: Intersentia, 2010). See also Order of the IACtHR of 9 July 2009, *Provisional Measures regarding Venezuela, Matter of Liliana Ortega et al.*, paras. 3–4, even independent of any pending case.

[156] *Cruz Varas and Others* v. *Sweden*, (1992) 14 EHRR 1; *Weiss* v. *Austria*, UN Doc. CCPR/C/77/D/1086/2002 (3 April 2003), para. 8.3.

[157] *Öcalan* v. *Turkey*, (2005) 41 EHRR 45; *International Pen and Others* v. *Nigeria*, nos. 137/94, 139/94, 154/96 and 161/97 (1998); *Pratt and Morgan* v. *Jamaica*, Communication no. 210/1986 and 225/1987 (6 April 1989); Tyagi, above note 6, 516, fn. 619: over two hundred requests; *LaGrand* case (*Germany* v. *United States*), Judgment, ICJ Reports 2001, 466.

[158] *Altesor* v. *Uruguay*, Communication no. 10/1977 (29 March 1982), para. 4.

[159] Order of the IACtHR of 26 November 2007, *Provisional Measures regarding Nicaragua Case of the Mayagna (Sumo) Awas Tingni Community*.

[160] *Fernando* v. *Sri Lanka*, UN Doc. CCPR/C/83/D/1189/2003 (31 March 2005), para. 5.5.

of the binding nature of interim measures had been problematic because of
the lack of explicit provisions to that effect. In the earlier judgment of *Cruz
Varas* v. *Sweden*, the ECtHR held that the binding force of interim measures,
which were only envisaged in the rules of procedures of the Court, cannot
be derived from the right to an individual petition.[161] This jurisprudence was
reversed[162] in light of several leading judgments, such as by the IACtHR in
the *Constitutional Court* case and the ICJ in the *LaGrand* case, which held
that interim measures were binding.[163] Indeed, it would run counter to a
purposive interpretation of human rights treaties to deny the binding power
of interim measures. This would effectively leave it within states parties' discretion whether or not to comply and undermine the very protection of the
treaty rights in question that interim measures seek to preserve.[164]

In practice, one of the main challenges for applicants is to act in time so
that the treaty body concerned can order interim measures before irreparable harm has occurred. However, even where interim measures have been
ordered, states have repeatedly failed to comply. The execution of Ken Saro
Wiwa in Nigeria, of Joey Ramiah in Trinidad and Tobago and of the LaGrand
brothers in the USA are cases in point.[165] In another example, UK troops
handed over two applicants to Iraqi authorities in breach of an interim
order not to do so because they were at risk of facing the death penalty.[166]
Acting contrary to interim measures would normally constitute a violation
of the respective treaty, such as the right to bring individual petitions before
the ECtHR or the Optional Protocol to the ICCPR.[167] Yet, these legal consequences, and the affirmation of the binding force of interim measures, do not
appear to constitute sufficient safeguards in all cases. This is highly problematic, particularly where it results in a violation of substantive rights and is
damaging for the human rights treaty system as it undermines the authority
of treaty bodies. Given the limited capacity of treaty bodies to impose sanctions for non-compliance, finding the means that deter states from violating
interim measures will continue to be a major challenge for the effectiveness
of complaints procedures.

---

[161] *Cruz Varas and Others* v. *Sweden*, para. 99.

[162] *Mamatkulov and Askarov* v. *Turkey*, (2005) 41 EHRR 25.

[163] Order of the IACtHR of 14 August 2000, *Provisional Measures regarding the Case of the
Constitutional Court* v. *Peru*, para. 14 (operative part), and *LaGrand*, paras. 100–9.

[164] *LaGrand*, paras. 102–3.

[165] *International Pen and Others* v. *Nigeria*; *Hilaire, Constantine and Benjamin et al.* v.
Trinidad and Tobago, paras. 196–200; *LaGrand* respectively.

[166] *Al-Saadoon and Mufdhi* v. *United Kingdom*, Appl. no. 61498/08, 30 June 2009,
paras. 162–6.

[167] See ECtHR in *Mamatkulov and Askarov* v. *Turkey*, paras. 99–129; ignoring an interim
order constituted a breach of the right to individual petition (article 34); *Ruzmetov* v.
Uzbekistan, UN Doc. CCPR/C/86/D/915/2000 (30 March 2006), para. 5.3, finding a breach
of the Optional Protocol.

7.6.2   Friendly settlements

Friendly settlements are a means at the disposal of the parties, i.e. the applicant(s) and respondent state(s), to settle a case amicably, which is explicitly provided for in the procedures for the European, Inter-American and African courts, as well as in the Optional Protocols to the ICESCR and CRC.[168] A settlement can typically be reached at all stages of proceedings before the decision on the merits, is confidential in nature and concludes the case where a respective treaty body is satisfied that it is compatible with respect for human rights.[169] In the European system, this takes the form of a decision that sets out the facts and the solution reached, after which the case is struck off the list.[170]

Friendly settlements have been agreed upon in a number of cases. Respondent states have paid compensation (normally *ex gratia*), have issued apologies and have agreed to undertake legislative changes, including in the course of pilot-judgment procedures.[171] These settlements play an important role in the system of complaints procedures. Indeed, they have many advantages. They save time, reduce the caseload of treaty bodies and allow the parties to negotiate terms that are agreeable and that states may be more likely to comply with. It is for these reasons that treaty bodies encourage friendly settlements. For states, avoiding an adverse judgment and a public finding of state responsibility provides an additional incentive. Litigants, on the other hand, often face a dilemma over whether to agree to friendly settlements because it deprives them of the opportunity to obtain a finding on the merits that may include a public vindication by holding the state responsible for the violations alleged. The dilemma can be particularly acute where the case is of strategic importance and NGOs and others have a strong interest in it being pursued further, although ultimately it is for the applicant(s) to decide. In addition, a case may involve a large number of victims who may be divided over whether to agree to a friendly settlement.

QUESTIONS

1 A UNSC resolution authorises the use of force against Somali pirates. A European state deploys an armed contingent to the region, which kills several pirates in the course of its operations. Their relatives claim that the pirates were captured, ill treated and executed. A lawyer who has been approached by the relatives lodges a case before the ECtHR following the exhaustion of domestic remedies, alleging

---

[168] Articles 39 ECHR; 49 ACHR; 9 Protocol to the ACHPR; 7 Optional Protocol ICESCR; 9 Optional Protocol CRC Communication Procedure.

[169] H. Keller, M. Forowicz and L. Engi, *Friendly Settlements Before the European Court of Human Rights* (Oxford University Press, 2010).

[170] See e.g. article 39 ECHR.   [171] *Broniowski* v. *Poland*, (2006) 43 EHRR 43.

a violation of articles 2 and 3 ECHR. What objections is the state likely to raise concerning admissibility, considering in particular the location of the alleged violation and the international context in which the operation had taken place?

2   A woman brings a case before the HRCtee, alleging that her husband has been abducted by state agents. She has eye-witness accounts to show that he was taken into custody by the armed forces. Would this be sufficient to make out a prima facie case and obtain a decision on the merits that her husband has been the victim of an enforced disappearance and the violation of several rights that this may entail?

3   In the same case consider that the alleged abduction had taken place in 2005. The applicant had complained several times to local authorities but no action had been taken. The state ratified the ICCPR and its Optional Protocol with effect from 2010. Can the applicant bring a case before the HRCtee alleging a substantive violation, such as that the enforced disappearance amounts to torture, or a procedural violation, i.e. failing to investigate her complaint, or both?

4   Is the need to exhaust domestic remedies still the rule given the many exceptions recognised by treaty bodies?

5   Do supranational individual complaints procedures constitute effective remedies for victims of human rights violations?

6   Under what circumstances should applicants consider requesting interim measures?

7   Why are friendly settlements a double-edged sword for applicants?

INTERVIEW 7.1

Nepal before the Human Rights Committee

(Mandira Sharma)

The Advocacy Forum is the first Nepalese NGO that started using the individual complaints procedure before the HRCtee (Nepal acceded to the Optional Protocol to the ICCPR in 1991). It has brought a series of cases that address the legacy of serious human rights violations and the culture of impunity in Nepal. The following is an interview with Mandira Sharma, Advocacy Forum's former director (until May 2010), who was instrumental in developing their litigation strategy.

How many cases have you brought in relation to what violations, and what has been the outcome?

We have brought six cases on behalf of fourteen victims to date. Those six cases concern torture, extrajudicial executions and enforced disappearance. Two cases have been decided. In both cases the committee has found violations of multiple articles of ICCPR. Following the decisions the government has provided interim relief in the form of monetary compensation to victims. We are continuously working to secure implementation of other recommendations. This process has helped to raise the awareness of the government officials on this subject.

How do victims of alleged violations contact you and how do you select cases (including type of violations)?

We have been working with the victims for the last twelve years. Initially, we ourselves used to go to the villages as many victims did not know us and how to contact us. Now we have offices in many districts and we are known to the victims, so they come to us. As we have been providing legal aid to the victims and their families, we are following up those cases carefully. While we exhaust local remedies and victims would not get justice, we explain to them and their family the possibility of going to the HRCtee. If victims want us to help them with this we start working on the case. Even if we are asked to do so we might not be able to help every victim to go to the Committee, and as a result we select emblematic cases. So, we explain to victims how the jurisprudence established in other cases can be helpful for them locally.

What are your case-specific and strategic considerations in your litigation, in other words, what are your main goals?

The goal is to establish jurisprudence and to have the HRCtee's views on issues which are difficult to address before local courts. For example, we took a case of enforced disappearance to the Committee as the Nepalese government refused to investigate, stating that this would be done by the forthcoming truth and reconciliation commission and the commission of inquiry on enforced disappearance. We wanted the Committee to hold that the government had an obligation to undertake a criminal investigation in the case and that the commission of inquiry was not suitable for this purpose. So, the Committee's view on this is helping us to shape our discourse on this issue. Similarly, we are working on a case of sexual violence where the victim's request to initiate an investigation was denied because of statutes of limitation in Nepalese law – thirty-five days – to file a complaint in cases of rape.

How difficult is it to substantiate cases some of which date back to the mid 1990s?

So far we have taken cases where we have been confident that the available evidence is sound and sufficient. What is advantageous about taking cases to the HRCtee is that as it does not determine individual guilt and that the threshold of evidence is not that high. In contrast, difficulties in obtaining evidence can be a major obstacle when initiating criminal investigations back home.

What challenges have you faced in relation to the admissibility of cases?

We are in a peculiar situation in Nepal. One of the difficulties that we face is that Nepal has maintained that all the crimes committed in the past will be dealt with by the Truth and Reconciliation Commission and the Commission of Inquiries on Disappearance once set up. However, it is clear that as long as these mechanisms are not in place there is nothing to be exhausted. In addition, the government's arguments are based on the lofty plans it has developed, including the National Human Rights Commission. So, while it can at times be difficult to overcome admissibility hurdles, we have been able to demonstrate convincingly how these plans and institutions have not been able to provide effective remedies for victims of violations.

How successful have you been in implementing decisions?

The record has been mixed. We have been successful in obtaining interim relief in the form of compensation for victims but the authorities have largely failed to undertake investigations in line with the HRCtee's views. The decisions also had a broader impact, raising awareness of government officials about the government's obligations under the ICCPR. Civil society and the legal community are also increasingly taking an interest in the subject.

How can the HRCtee's impact in Nepal be maximised and what are the main challenges in this regard?

Using the HRCtee's views in emblematic cases to expand the jurisprudence at local level is critical with a view to facilitating implementation of human rights standards as we cannot take each and every case to the Committee. In addition to this the Committee's jurisprudence plays an important role for wider policy reform initiatives and trainings. However, the main challenge that we face is that perpetrators still enjoy *de facto* immunity. Even the decisions of the Nepalese Supreme Court have been ignored. The weak rule of law is therefore at the heart of human rights violations and the lack of accountability and justice. One way of addressing this is to create a link between the implementation of the Committee's views and the UPR and international support to Nepal. Once we are able to make this link, the state would be under pressure to observe the HRCtee's views to bring about change at the local level.

7.7 THE *HISSÈNE HABRÉ* CASE: THE INTERPLAY BETWEEN DOMESTIC, REGIONAL AND INTERNATIONAL PROCEEDINGS

Attempts to bring Hissène Habré to trial have given rise to a remarkable history of legal proceedings that have occupied national, regional and sub-regional courts (ECOWAS), the CtAT and the ICJ. The case also resulted in initiatives at the AU level to establish a mixed court. Situated at the interface of international criminal law and the human rights obligation to extradite or prosecute, the case is an extraordinary example of the quest for justice before a multitude of judicial, quasi-judicial and political bodies. This endeavour has been well documented, largely thanks to the efforts of several protago-nists, including Souleymane Guengueng of the Association of Victims of Crimes and Political Repression and Reed Brody, HRW, who also feature in the film *The Dictator Hunter*.

Hissène Habré came to power in Chad in 1982. He is alleged to have been responsible for serious human rights violations, including large-scale torture and extrajudicial killings amounting to international crimes. After being forced from power in 1990, Habré eventually fled to Senegal where he has stayed since. After several years Chadian victims and human rights defenders, particularly the Association of Victims, together with HRW, began using various avenues to bring Habré to trial. First attempts in Senegal failed because the Dakar Court of Appeal in 2000, in a judgment upheld by the Court of Cassation in 2001, ruled that the Senegalese criminal procedure code did not provide for universal jurisdiction[172] over crimes against humanity committed in third countries. In parallel, 'a Belgian national of Chadian origin and Chadian nationals'[173] and others lodged complaints against Habré in Belgium in 2000 and 2001 using Belgian universal jurisdiction laws. Meanwhile, Souleymane Guengueng and others submitted a communication against Senegal before CtAT. In May 2006 the Committee found that the lack of implementing legislation establishing jurisdiction over acts of torture in Senegal violated article 5(2) CAT.[174] Equally, the failure to prosecute Habré (in the absence of an extradition) was considered a violation of article 7 CAT. Senegal finally changed its legislation in 2007, making international crimes subject to universal jurisdiction. A further constitutional reform of 2008 ensured that proceedings for international crimes would not fall foul of the principle of non-retroactivity. However, Senegal still did not prosecute Habré, invoking financial and logistical challenges.

Meanwhile, in a legal counter-attack, Habré challenged these legislative amendments before the ECOWAS court, arguing among other points that

---

[172] See on universal jurisdiction section 14.9.1.

[173] ICJ, 'Belgium institutes proceedings against Senegal and requests the Court to indicate provisional measures', Press Release, no. 2009/13 (19 February 2009).

[174] *Guengueng* v. *Senegal*, UN Doc. CAT/C/36/D/181/2001 (17 May 2006).

they violated the principle of non-retroactivity (prosecuting someone for an offence that was not on the statute books at the time when it was committed). The ECOWAS court, in its far from convincing judgment of 18 November 2010, found that the retroactive nature of the law may violate international law.[175] It also considered the exception that this rule did not apply to international crimes, and fashioned a 'compromise' solution, stating that Habré should be tried before an *ad hoc* court. This reflected parallel developments at the AU level, suggesting that the Court was influenced by considerations relating to regional 'politics of justice', which is explained below. Another challenge against Senegal's legislation, which similarly argued that it violated the principle of non-retroactivity and ran counter to the search for an African solution, constituted the first case before the ACtHPR.[176] The application was given short shrift and declared inadmissible because Senegal had not accepted the Court's jurisdiction.

Meanwhile, Belgian authorities had investigated the complaints lodged in 2000/2001 and in September 2005 issued an international arrest warrant against Habré for genocide, crimes against humanity, war crimes, torture and other violations. An extradition request made by Belgium was turned down by the *Chambre d'accusation* of the Dakar Court of Appeal. By now, the *Habré* case had become a dilemma for Senegal, which asked the AU to find an African solution. In January 2006 the AU established a committee of eminent African jurists which proposed that a mixed tribunal should be set up to try Habré in Africa. In July 2006, the AU 'mandate[d] the Chairperson of the [African] Union, in consultation with the Chairperson of the Commission [of the Union], to provide Senegal with the necessary assistance for the effective conduct of the trial'. However, over six years and countless meetings later, efforts to bring Habré to trial in Africa still have not come to fruition because of continuing discussions over who should finance it. Belgium, for its part, significantly increased the pressure on Senegal and the AU. In February 2009 it instituted proceedings against Senegal before the ICJ, arguing that 'Senegal's failure to prosecute Mr H. Habré, if he is not extradited to Belgium to answer for the acts of torture that are alleged against him, violates the Convention against Torture'.[177] The ICJ, in a judgment dated 20 July 2012 whose admissibility was based on article 30 CAT, found that Senegal had breached its obligations under article 6(2) CAT 'by failing to make immediately a preliminary inquiry into the facts relating to the crimes allegedly committed by Mr Hissène Habré' and under article 7(1) CAT 'by failing to submit the case of Mr Hissène Habré to its competent authorities for the purpose of prosecution'. Consequently, it found that the Republic of Senegal 'must, without further

---

[175] *Hissène Habré* v. *Republic of Senegal*, ECW/CCJ/APP/07/08 (18 November 2010).
[176] *Yogogombaye* v. *Senegal*.   [177] ICJ, above note 173.

delay, submit the case of Mr Hissène Habré to its competent authorities for the purpose of prosecution, if it does not extradite him'.[178]

The account of multiple proceedings shows that various actors have used legal avenues at the national, regional and international level. Victims and NGOs brought cases (criminal prosecutions in Senegal, CtAT case) which complemented their ongoing advocacy campaigns to have Habré prosecuted. Chad tried Habré *in absentia* (and sentenced him to death for international crimes).[179] Habré himself, and those acting in his support, used the ECOWAS Court and the ACtHPR to challenge Senegal's legislation. Belgium, meanwhile, has emerged as the major state player. It has used proceedings before the ICJ, ostensibly for Senegal to extradite or prosecute Habré; indirectly, it also put pressure on the AU and others involved to expedite initiatives to try Habré.

The *Habré* case represents a momentous struggle to hold a former head of state accountable that is being fought out at the legal and political level. The fact that there are still no prosecutions more than ten years after the first legal challenges illustrate the difficulty of implementation where the political will is not clear, and legal and financial obstacles stall progress. Nevertheless, the persistence of key protagonists has kept up the imperative for accountability in the case, clarified Senegal's obligations and prompted the AU into action, which may ultimately result in an outcome that strengthens international human rights and provides a measure of justice for the victims of the Habré regime.

POINT TO CONSIDER

1 After more than ten years of litigation efforts before national, regional and international bodies and courts without Habré being tried, the case demonstrates the limit of complaints procedures to ensure justice. Discuss.

FURTHER READING

Burgorgue-Larsen, L. and Ubeda de Torres, A., *The Inter-American Court of Human Rights: Case Law and Commentary* (Oxford University Press, 2011).

Evans, M. and Murray, R. (eds.), *The African Charter on Human and Peoples' Rights: The System in Practice 1986–2006*, 2nd edn (Cambridge University Press, 2008).

Joseph, S., Schultz, J. and Castan, M., *The International Comment on Civil and Political Rights: Cases, Materials and Commentary*, 2nd edn (Oxford University Press, 2004).

---

[178] *Questions relating to the Obligation to Prosecute or Extradite* (*Belgium* v. *Senegal*), ICJ Judgment of 20 July 2012, para. 122.

[179] S. Czajkowski, 'Chad Court Sentences Ex-dictator Habre to Death in absentia', *Jurist* (16 August 2008).

Keller, H., Forowicz, M. and Engi, L., *Friendly Settlements before the European Court of Human Rights* (Oxford University Press, 2010).

Leach, P., *Taking a Case to the European Court of Human Rights*, 3rd edn (Oxford University Press, 2011).

Open Society Justice Initiative, *From Judgment to Justice, Implementing International and Regional Human Rights Decisions* (New York: Open Society Foundations, 2010).

Rieter, E., *Preventing Irreparable Harm: Provisional Measures in International Human Rights Adjudication* (Antwerp: Intersentia, 2010).

Websites

ACtHPR: www.african-court.org

African Commission: www.achpr.org

ECtHR: www.echr.coe.int

IACtHR: www.corteidh.or.cr

IACHR: www.oas.org/en/iachr

ICJ: www.icj-cij.org

OHCHR: www.ohchr.org (providing links to all human rights treaty bodies).

Compilations and databases providing access to documents and judgments

American Society of International Law: Electronic Resource Guide www.asil.org/resource/humrts1.htm.

Project Diana Online Human Rights Archive: http://avalon.law.yale.edu/subject_menus/diana.asp.

University of Minnesota- Human Rights Library: www1.umn.edu/humanrts.

World Courts: www.worldcourts.com.

Bayefsky: UN Human Rights Treaty System: www.bayefsky.com.

Commonwealth and International Human Rights Law Database: www.interights.org/commonwealth-and-international-law-database/index.html.

8 Civil and political rights

CONTENTS

8.1 INTRODUCTION

Civil and political rights emerged out of fundamental rights conceptions protecting life, integrity and liberty of a person against an overbearing state. The twentieth century demonstrated that these rights were at risk in multiple contexts, ranging from genocidal campaigns, dictatorships and arbitrary law enforcement to conflict and a breakdown of law and order. Rights such as freedom from ill treatment may also be at risk from other sources, namely non-state actors in the domestic and other spheres, which have taken on a growing importance in the wake of states' withdrawal from public functions. While international human rights standards have been developed to provide adequate protection in these circumstances, their implementation requires certain structures without which it is unlikely that core civil and political rights can be effectively protected. The rule of law (although a rather ambiguous term), the administration of justice and democratic structures are key components in this regard. While international human rights law does not mandate that a particular political system be in place, it is difficult to see how rights can be effectively protected without having at least a minimum of checks and balances.

Equally, however, a democratic system as such is not a panacea for rights protection. Indeed, there are deep-seated structural factors that can, and have, undermined the effective protection of rights in all systems. Social exclusion, inequality and discrimination in particular are prone to significantly increase vulnerability, as evident in the higher likelihood of persons from certain ethnic or class or national backgrounds being subject to arbitrary arrest, detention, ill treatment and other violations.[1] As a yardstick of power relations in a society, social exclusion, inequality and discrimination are also closely related to lack of access to justice, which both reflects and compounds vulnerabilities and impunity. The lack of effective remedies and accountability of those responsible has been identified as a central factor contributing to the perpetuation of violations. The resulting impunity constitutes both a cause and manifestation of a malfunctioning system that fails to protect. Against that background this chapter identifies the normative content of the right to life, the prohibition of torture, the right to liberty and security, the right to a fair trial and qualified rights, particularly freedom of expression, and examines the challenge of ensuring their effective protection. It also considers the issue of enforced disappearance, one of the most serious violations that has spawned a rich jurisprudence but has only recently become the explicit object of an international treaty.

8.2   THE RIGHT TO LIFE

8.2.1   Practice

Life is at risk both through a state's use of force and its failure to provide adequate protection.[2] The use of lethal force comprises the deliberate killing of individuals or groups, including targeted extrajudicial executions, torturing to death in custody, enforced disappearances (where they take the form of illegal kidnapping and murder), killings in armed conflicts, massacres or even genocides. Members of marginalised groups and opposition movements, as well as journalists, have been particularly vulnerable to extrajudicial killings. In addition, while there is a growing trend towards the abolition of judicially sanctioned killing, i.e. capital punishment, sixty-seven countries imposed over 2,000 death sentences in 2010, and twenty-three countries carried out at least 527 executions by means of beheading, electrocution, hanging, lethal injection and shooting.[3]

[1] See for example Interim Report of the Special Rapporteur of the Commission on Human Rights on the question of torture and other cruel, inhuman or degrading treatment or punishment, UN Doc. A/55/290 (11 August 2000), paras. 34–7.

[2] See for a good overview, *UN Special Rapporteur on Extrajudicial Executions Handbook*, which is part of the Project on Extrajudicial Executions of the Centre for Human Rights and Global Justice, New York University School of Law, online, at www.extrajudicialexecutions.org.

[3] Amnesty International, *Death Sentences and Executions 2010* (London: AI, 2011), 5–6.

Lethal force may also be used without the direct intention to kill but in the knowledge that this may be the outcome. An example is the use of live ammunition to quell a protest, as was the official response to public uprisings in countries such as Egypt, Libya and Syria in 2011 and 2012.[4] The state may also accidentally cause the death of persons through its personnel, for example soldiers mistakenly shooting a passerby during an exercise, or through potentially lethal operations, such as accidents at state-run nuclear power stations.

Individuals and groups face numerous threats to their life from sources other than the state. This is often most pronounced during conflict where rebel groups may be responsible for more killings than governmental forces.[5] It also applies during peace-time, both in relation to acts of violence, such as deadly 'domestic' abuse[6] and sexual violence,[7] as well as health hazards emanating from private actors, such as the operation of dangerous plants.[8] As discussed in more detail below the state has a duty to protect life in these circumstances.

8.2.2   Sources

The right to life is recognised in all major international and regional human rights instruments.[9] Its mention as the first substantive right in most of these treaties reflects its fundamental importance. The recognition in treaty law is complemented by international standards, such as the Principles on the Effective Prevention and Investigation of Extra-legal, Arbitrary and Summary Executions[10] and the Basic Principles on the Use of Force and Firearms by Law Enforcement Officials.[11] The right not to be arbitrarily deprived of one's life is considered to have attained the status of customary

---

[4] See on the protection of the right to life in the context of policing assemblies, Report of the Special Rapporteur on extrajudicial, summary or arbitrary executions, UN Doc. A/HRC/17/28 (23 May 2011), paras. 12–133.

[5] See, for example, Report of the Special Rapporteur on extrajudicial, summary or arbitrary executions, Addendum Follow-up to country recommendations: Afghanistan, UN Doc. A/HRC/17/28/Add.6 (27 May 2011), paras. 17–33.

[6] See in particular *Opuz* v. *Turkey*, (2010) 50 EHRR 28, and CtEDAW jurisprudence. It is estimated that 'approximately 5,000 women are murdered each year by family members in honour-related violence'. See Report of the Special Rapporteur on violence against women, its causes and consequences, UN Doc. A/66/215 (1 August 2011), para. 32.

[7] See in particular *González et al.* (*Cotton Field*) v. *Mexico*, Judgment on preliminary objection, merits, reparations and costs, 16 November 2009, Ser. C, no. 206.

[8] See for example *Öneryildiz* v. *Turkey*, (2005) 41 EHRR 20.

[9] See articles 3 UDHR, 6 ICCPR, 6(1) CRC, 9 ICRMW, 10 CRPD, and at the regional level articles 2 ECHR, 4 ACHR and 4 ACHPR.

[10] Recommended by UN ECOSOC resolution 1989/65 (24 May 1989).

[11] Adopted by the Eighth UN Congress on the Prevention of Crime and the Treatment of Offenders, Havana, Cuba (27 August to 7 September 1990).

international law[12] and to be non-derogable.[13] The taking of life may also constitute an international crime, namely genocide (particularly killing members of a group), crimes against humanity (murder, extermination, persecution and other inhumane acts) or a war crime (particularly willful killing or murder).[14]

8.2.3   The prohibition of arbitrary deprivation of life

Even though the right to life has repeatedly been referred to as a 'fundamental right',[15] it is not absolute in so far as international treaties such as the ICCPR, ACHR and ACHPR permit the use of lethal force that is not 'arbitrary'. Under article 2(2) ECHR, the use of such force may be justified (a) 'in defence of any person from unlawful violence'; (b) 'in order to effect a lawful arrest or to prevent the escape of a person lawfully detained';[16] (c) 'in action lawfully taken for the purpose of quelling a riot or insurrection'.[17] Killings that are lawful under international humanitarian are recognised as a further exception.[18]

As a general rule the use of force must be regulated by law and must be exceptional.[19] Where its use may be justifiable it must be absolutely necessary and proportionate to the legitimate aim sought.[20] 'Necessary' means that there are no less serious alternatives available to achieve the aim, for example using baton rounds instead of live ammunition to disperse a crowd. 'Proportionate' requires that the means used, i.e. lethal force, is not out of proportion to the aim pursued, for example shooting to arrest an unarmed man who has committed a petty theft. Determining proportionality in the particular circumstances can pose considerable difficulties as international jurisprudence demonstrates.

---

[12] Restatement (Third) of the Foreign Relations Law of the United States, §702; Rule 89 of the ICRC Customary International Humanitarian Law Database (ICRC, CIHL Database), online, at www.icrc.org/customary-ihl/eng/docs/home.

[13] HRCtee, General Comment 6: The right to life (30 April 1982), para. 1, and General Comment 24: Issues relating to reservations made upon ratification or accession to the Covenant or the Optional Protocols thereto, or in relation to declarations under article 41 of the Covenant, UN Doc. CCPR/C/21/Rev.1/Add.6 (4 November 1994), para. 10.

[14] See articles 6–8 of the ICC Rome Statute respectively.

[15] See e.g. *Baldéon Garcîa* v. *Peru*, Merits, reparations and costs, Judgment of 6 April 2006, Ser. C, no. 147, para. 82, and *McCann and Others* v. *United Kingdom*, (1996) 21 EHRR 97, para. 147.

[16] *Nachova and Others* v. *Bulgaria*, (2006) 42 EHRR 43, para. 95.

[17] *Güleç* v. *Turkey* [1999] 28 ECHR 121, para. 71.   [18] See section 14.4.

[19] See *Nachova and Others* v. *Bulgaria*, para. 96. See also articles 1 and 11 of the Basic Principles on the Use of Force and Firearms by Law Enforcement Officials (August/ September 1990), and 3 of the Code of Conduct for Law Enforcement Officials, UNGA resolution 34/169 (17 December 1979).

[20] See *McCann* v. *UK*, para. 149, and on the limited application of the principle in cases of deliberate, state-sanctioned killings, *Pueblo Bello Massacre* v. *Colombia*, Merits, reparations and costs, Judgment of 31 January 2006, Ser. C, no. 140, para. 133.

8.2.4   *McCann* v. *UK*: necessity and proportionality in the ECtHR's jurisprudence

McCann v. *UK* is a leading case in which the ECtHR interpreted the circumstances under which the use of lethal force 'in defence of any person from unlawful violence' under article 2(2)(a) ECHR is necessary and proportionate. In that case the applicants alleged that the killing of their relatives by UK soldiers in Gibraltar as part of a 'shoot-to-kill' policy constituted a violation of the right to life. The Court agreed that the soldiers honestly believed for good reason that the three known IRA operatives were about to launch an attack, which in principle justified the use of force in the particular circumstances even where the belief turned out to be wrong. However, in a significant expansion of the scope of a state's obligation, the Court broadened its consideration of proportionality to include the planning and conduct of the operation. It found that the planning did not take the necessary precautionary measures and that consequently the use of force had not been absolutely necessary.[21] Several judges in *McCann* v. *UK* expressed their concern over reasoning that is based on the benefit of hindsight in operational questions. While the Court needs to be careful not to lightly substitute its own views for that of the state in this regard, the test developed by the ECtHR in *McCann* has an important legal policy dimension. It takes a holistic view of what is 'absolutely necessary' and compels law enforcement officials to plan and control actions in such a way that the use of force is minimised or truly becomes a measure of last resort. Such an approach takes into consideration that operations are the result of a series of decisions for which the state remains responsible. This is appropriate as responsibility should be seen in the overall context and not be artificially limited to focusing solely on the actual belief of the law enforcement official(s) using force at the end of a chain of events, which may be genuine but mistaken because of earlier erroneous judgments.

QUESTIONS

1   What is the importance of the *McCann* v. *UK* ruling from a legal policy perspective aimed at ensuring that the right to life is effectively protected in all circumstances?

2   In 2005 Charles de Menezes, a Brazilian living in London where he was working as an electrician, was mistakenly identified as a terrorist who it was believed was about to attack the London underground. After a series of operational errors de Menezes was allowed to board a train where police officers killed him with multiple shots at point-blank range without warning, in line with the police policy at the time. The case is pending before the ECtHR.[22] What bearing is the standard developed in *McCann* v. *UK* likely to have on the case?

---

[21] *McCann* v. *UK*, paras. 202–14.
[22] See *Armani da Silva* v. *United Kingdom*, App. no. 5878/08, 28 September 2010.

CASE STUDY 8.1
The killing of Bin Laden and the right to life

On 2 May 2011 Osama Bin Laden, the head of Al-Qaeda, was killed in a raid conducted by a US military unit in Abbottabad, Pakistan, apparently without the prior express consent or knowledge of the Pakistani authorities.[1] Accounts of the circumstances of the killing have been conflicting. In particular, it is not clear whether Bin Laden tried to defend himself when confronted by US forces.[2] The killing of Bin Laden raised a series of complex questions concerning its lawfulness under international law, including international humanitarian law and international human rights law,[3] which forms part of the broader debate about 'targeted killings'.[4] US government officials asserted that international humanitarian law applied and that the killing was lawful because Bin Laden had been a legitimate target and had not given himself up.[5] This position would be correct if the 'conflict' between the USA and Al-Qaeda at the time could be characterised as a situation of armed conflict. This is questionable and contested, not least because it is difficult to determine whether asymmetrical warfare of this kind reaches the requisite threshold and whether a situation of armed conflict continues to apply even if there has been no resort to force or violence for quite some time.[6] If the circumstances qualify as an armed conflict at the time, the lawfulness of the killing would depend on the rules of international humanitarian law, particularly the question of whether Bin Laden was a legitimate target and, if so, had surrendered at the time of his killing (which would have rendered his killing unlawful).

---

[1] See A. S. Deeks, 'Pakistan's Sovereignty and the Killing of Osama Bin Laden', *ASIL Insights* (5 May 2011) 15(11).

[2] See for an immediate request for a clarification of the facts to assess the lawfulness of the use of lethal force, Osama bin Laden: statement by the UN Special Rapporteurs on summary executions and on human rights and counter-terrorism (6 May 2011). See for an official US account, 'Press Briefing by Press Secretary Jay Carney' (5 March 2011), online, at www.whitehouse.gov/the-press-office/2011/05/03/press-briefing-press-secretary-jay-carney-532011.

[3] See B. van Schaack, *The Killing of Osama Bin Laden & Anwar Al-Aulaqi: Uncharted Legal Territory*, Santa Clara University Legal Studies Research Paper No. 02-12 (2012), 7–10; A. P. V. Rogers and D. McGoldrick, 'Assassination and Targeted Killing: the Killing of Osama Bin Laden', *ICLQ* 60(3)(2011), 778–88.

[4] See sections 14.4 and 15.6.2.

[5] See for an overview, Van Schaack, above note 3, 7–10.

[6] Ibid., 24–31.

POINTS TO CONSIDER

- What questions would need to be considered when examining the compatibility of the killing with international human rights law, in relation to both where it was done and how it was carried out?
- What grounds may justify the use of lethal force?
- Would a shoot to kill policy be lawful?[7]

[7] See also section 15.6.2.

8.2.5   The death penalty under international law

The ICCPR, the ECHR and the ACHR explicitly acknowledge the death penalty as an exception to the right to life,[23] and the death penalty has been interpreted as not constituting an 'arbitrary' deprivation of life under the ACHPR.[24] However, the language of article 6 ICCPR already acknowledges the desirability of the abolition of the death penalty.[25] This objective has found expression at the international level in the Second Optional Protocol to the ICCPR, aiming at the abolition of the death penalty, which had seventy-five parties as of 14 July 2012. At the regional level, developments are most advanced in the Americas and Europe, as reflected in the Protocol to the ACHR to Abolish the Death Penalty and Protocols no. 6 and no. 13 to the ECHR. The latter two protocols successively and effectively abolished the death penalty in the European system.[26] Despite this trend the death penalty as such is arguably not yet unlawful under present international human rights law. Where it is still imposed and applied, however, the death penalty is subject to a series of conditions, particularly procedural safeguards that must be complied with strictly for it to be lawful. It may only be imposed for the most serious crimes[27] and must not be mandatory because a court has

[23] Articles 6(2) ICCPR, 2(1) ECHR, 4(2) ACHR.

[24] *Interights et al. (on behalf of Mariette Sonjaleen Bosch)* v. *Botswana*, 240/2001 (2003), para. 43.

[25] See P. Hodgkinson and W. A. Schabas (eds.), *Capital Punishment: Strategies for Abolition* (Cambridge University Press, 2004); R. Hood and C. Hoyle, *The Death Penalty: A Worldwide Perspective*, 4th edn (Oxford University Press, 2008).

[26] See *Öcalan* v. *Turkey*, (2005) 41 EHRR 45, paras. 150–75, and *Al-Saadoon and Mufdhi* v. *United Kingdom*, (2009) 49 EHRR SE11, paras. 115–22, where it considered (para. 120) 'that Article 2 has been amended so as to prohibit the death penalty in all circumstances. Against this background, the Court does not consider that the wording of the second sentence of Article 2 §1 continues to act as a bar to its interpreting the words "inhuman or degrading treatment or punishment" in Article 3 as including the death penalty.'

[27] See HRCtee, General Comment 6, para. 6; *Restrictions to the Death Penalty (Arts. 4(2) and 4(4) American Convention on Human Rights)*, Advisory opinion OC-3/83 of 8 September

to be able to consider mitigating or special circumstances when imposing it as a punishment.[28] Certain categories of persons should be exempt from the death penalty, namely children who were under eighteen years of age at the time when the crime was committed[29] and mentally ill persons.[30] A person may only be sentenced to death following a fair trial (which will in death penalty cases invariably be subject to particularly close scrutiny),[31] including the right to an appeal.[32] Where foreign nationals face the death penalty they need to be granted consular assistance.[33] These conditions, which reflect the serious, irreversible nature of the death penalty, raise the threshold in terms of crimes, categories of persons and nature of trials, which, taken together, considerably limit the scope for the punishment to be lawfully imposed.

The death penalty has a close relationship with the prohibition of torture and cruel, inhuman or degrading treatment or punishment. Its imposition following an unfair trial has been considered inhuman treatment.[34] Separately, the conditions of waiting for one's execution (death row phenomenon) may in certain circumstances amount to inhuman treatment.[35] Further, the method of execution itself may constitute cruel punishment.[36] In addition, the failure to inform relatives of the execution and the burial place has also been found to violate the prohibition of ill-treatment.[37]

It is cogent to argue that the death penalty itself is inherently and invariably inhuman.[38] If followed, this reasoning would make the death penalty

1993, Ser. A, no. 3, para. 54; *Hilaire, Constantine and Benjamin et al.* v. *Trinidad and Tobago*, Merits, reparations and costs, Judgment of 21 June 2002, Ser. C, no. 94, para. 102.

[28] *Hilaire et al.*, ibid., paras. 98–109; *Weerawansa* v. *Sri Lanka*, UN Doc. CCPR/C/95/D/1406/2005 (17 March 2009), para. 7.2.

[29] Articles 37(a) CRC and 6(5) ICCPR.

[30] *Sahadath* v. *Trinidad and Tobago*, UN Doc. CCPR/C/74/D/684/1996 (2 April 2002), para. 7.2.

[31] See e.g. *Khoroshenko* v. *Russian Federation*, UN Doc. CCPR/C/101/D/1304/2004 (29 March 2011), para. 9.11; *Öcalan* v. *Turkey*, para. 166; *International Pen and Others* v. *Nigeria*, 137/94, 139/94, 154/96 and 161/97 (1998), para. 103.

[32] See article 4(6) ACHR; HRCtee General Comment 6, para. 7, and *Khalilov* v. *Tajikistan*, UN Doc. CCPR/C/83/D/973/2001 (30 March 2005), paras. 7.5–7.6.

[33] Advisory opinion OC-16/99 of 1 October 1999, *The Right to Information on Consular Assistance in the Framework of the Guarantees of the Due Process of Law*, para. 137, and *LaGrand* case *(Germany* v. *United States of America)*, ICJ Reports 2001, p. 466, para. 77.

[34] *Öcalan* v. *Turkey*, paras. 167–75; *Al-Saadoon and Mufdhi* v. *UK*, paras. 120–2, and *Mwamba* v. *Zambia*, UN Doc. CCPR/C/98/D/1520/2006 (10 March 2010), para. 6.8.

[35] *Soering* v. *United Kingdom*, (1989) 11 EHRR 439, paras. 92–111; *Hilaire et al.* v. *Trinidad and Tobago*, paras. 168–9. But see *Ashby* v. *Trinidad and Tobago*, UN Doc. CCPR/C/74/D/580/1994 (21 March 2002), para. 10.6, according to which 'detention on death row for a specific period does not violate, as such, article 7 of the Covenant in the absence of further compelling circumstances'.

[36] *Ng* v. *Canada*, UN Doc. CCPR/C/49/D/469/1991 (5 November 1993), paras. 16.2–16.4 (gas asphyxiation).

[37] See e.g. *Schedko* v. *Belarus*, UN Doc. CCPR/C/77/D/886/1999 (3 April 2003), para. 10.2.

[38] Report of the Special Rapporteur on torture and other cruel, inhuman or degrading treatment or punishment, UN Doc. A/HRC/10/44 (14 January 2009), paras. 29–48.

unlawful under international law by shifting the focus from the right to life to the prohibition of inhuman treatment or punishment if not torture. This is problematic in so far as it would run counter to the death penalty constituting an explicit exception to the right to life. However, it may be justifiable as a subsequent interpretation of the treaty by its parties, with the effect that the exception to the right to life becomes obsolete.[39] An argument can also be made *a fortiori* that if corporal punishment is unlawful (see below at section 8.3.5) then this must apply even more so to the death penalty.[40] There has been insufficient practice by treaty bodies and others to support such an interpretation to date. However, current debates show that the death penalty is increasingly seen as an anomaly in the international human rights system.

8.2.6   Positive obligations to protect the right to life

Several treaties expressly stipulate that the right to life shall be protected by law.[41] This obligation has been interpreted as requiring states to: (1) regulate the protection of life[42] and prohibit the arbitrary deprivation of life; (2) take measures to protect an individual at risk; (3) minimise the risk of potentially lethal hazards;[43] (4) and criminalise, investigate, prosecute and punish unjustified killings; and (5) provide effective remedies in case of breach.

Protection against killing by unknown or private perpetrators

Irrespective of the source of the risk to life, be it state or non-state actors, it is recognised that states have a 'primary duty ... to put in place a legislative and administrative framework designed to provide effective deterrence against threats to the right to life'.[44] This includes making unjustified killings subject to proportionate criminal sanctions and disciplinary sanctions as appropriate.[45] States must also ensure that their laws, such as abortion laws,

---

[39] *Al-Saadoon and Mufdhi* v. *UK*, para. 120.

[40] This point was raised by the Special Rapporteur on torture, above note 38, para. 38.

[41] Article 6(1) ICCPR, 6 CRC, 9 ICRMW, 19 CPRD, 2(1) ECHR, and 4(1) ACHR.

[42] See on the beginning of life, left open in the *Baby Boy* case, Resolution no. 23/81, Case 2141, US, OAS/Ser. L/V/II.54, Doc. 9 Rev. 1 (6 March 1981), paras. 18–31, and *Vo* v. *France*, (2004) 40 EHRR 259 GC, paras. 74–95, and conversely, on the end of life (right to die), rejected in *Pretty* v. *UK*, (2002), 35 EHHR 1, para. 39.

[43] See e.g. *Öneryildiz* v. *Turkey*, para. 90, and *Albekov and others* v. *Russia*, [2008] ECHR 1029, para. 88.

[44] *Öneryildiz* v. *Turkey*, para. 89. See also *Pueblo Bello Massacre* v. *Colombia*, Merits, reparations and costs, Judgment of 31 January 2006, Series C no. 140, para. 120, and *Camargo* v. *Colombia*, UN Doc. CCPR/C/15/D/45/1979 (31 March 1982), paras. 13.1–13.3.

[45] See for example *Mapiripán Massacre* v. *Colombia*, Merits, reparations and costs, Judgment of 15 September 2005, Ser. C no. 134, para. 232. The ECtHR held that in certain cases, namely where the killing was not intentional, civil sanctions may be sufficient, see *Vo*

do not result in a situation that effectively puts persons at risk, here women forced to undergo life-threatening illegal abortions.[46]

8.2.7   *Osman* v. *UK*: protecting life at risk

In the leading ECtHR case of *Osman* v. *UK*, [47] Mr Osman was killed by his son's teacher who had developed an obsession with his son. The school received a series of complaints about the teacher's conduct, graffiti of a sexual nature appeared around the school and a brick was thrown through the window of Mr Osman's property. Later, the teacher was seen near Mr Osman's house but though the police were informed they did not take any measures at the time. The teacher 'on being arrested ... stated "why didn't you stop me before I did it, I gave you all the warning signs?"'. The Court found that

it must be established to its satisfaction that the authorities knew or ought to have known at the time of the existence of a real and immediate risk to the life of an identified individual or individuals from the criminal acts of a third party and that they failed to take measures within the scope of their powers which, judged reasonably, might have been expected to avoid that risk.[48]

On the facts, it held that 'the applicants have failed to point to any decisive stage in the sequence of the events leading up to the tragic shooting when it could be said that the police knew or ought to have known that the lives of the Osman family were at real and immediate risk from Paget-Lewis [the teacher]'.[49] The *Osman* test has served as a foundation for subsequent cases and has been used to guide policing in the UK.[50] While the ECtHR's approach is pragmatic and seemingly offers the authorities considerable leeway,[51] it may come at the expense of more precise guidance.

v. *France*, para. 90, and *Calvelli and Ciglio* v. *Italy*, [2002] ECHR 3, paras. 51–7. This reasoning was subject to strong criticism in the Partly Dissenting Opinion of Judge Rozakis joined by Judges Bonello and Strážnická.

[46] See Concluding Observations by the Human Rights Committee: Venezuela, UN Doc. CCPR/CO/71/VEN (26 April 2001), para. 19.

[47] *Osman* v. *United Kingdom*, (1998) EHRR 245, paras. 115–22. See for a discussion of the positive obligation in the jurisprudence of the ECtHR and the IACtHR, Concurring Opinion of Judge Diego Garcia-Sayan in Relation to the Judgment of the Inter-American Court of Human Rights in *González et al. (Cotton Field)* v. *Mexico*, Preliminary objection, merits, reparations and costs, Judgment of 16 November 2009, Ser. C, no. 205, paras. 3–15.

[48] *Osman* v. *United Kingdom*, para. 116.   [49] Ibid., para. 121.

[50] A. Donald *et al.*, *Evaluating the impact of selected cases under the Human Rights Act on public services provision* (Manchester: Equality and Human Rights Commission, 2009), 28–39.

[51] *Osman* v. *United Kingdom*, para. 116: 'bearing in mind the difficulties involved in policing modern societies, the unpredictability of human conduct and the operational choices which must be made in terms of priorities and resources, such an obligation must be interpreted in a way which does not impose an impossible or disproportionate burden on the authorities'.

POINT TO CONSIDER

1 Are the standards developed in *Osman* sufficient to ensure that the authorities prioritise the protection of the right to life?

The nature of the authorities' duty to protect life depends on the circumstances. A heightened duty applies particularly where there is a known risk, for example a series of attacks on human rights defenders and/or journalists. Where a person at risk complains about being followed and targeted, the authorities need to investigate promptly, prosecute the perpetrators where applicable and offer special protection.[52] This is also the case where it is clear that persons belonging to a certain group that is vulnerable have previously been targeted, such as young, marginalised women who had been victims of a spate of murders in Mexico.[53] A heightened duty to exercise due diligence is also recognised in the custodial context where the state needs to protect the life of those under its physical control.[54] This obligation entails putting in place custodial safeguards against violence by officials and providing adequate medical assistance.[55] The state also needs to protect prisoners against self-harm and violence from other prisoners.[56] Such violence may engage the responsibility of the state both under the right to life and the prohibition of ill-treatment.[57] The general principle has broad application. It requires the authorities to consider the vulnerability of certain prisoners to violence at the hands of others – including because of the nature of the crime they have committed – and the risk that some – particularly violent or mentally ill – prisoners may pose to others and to take adequate precautionary measures. A tragic example is the case of *Edwards* v. *UK* where the authorities ignored these risks and a young detainee was killed by his violent cell mate who had a history of mental illness.[58]

---

[52] *Gongadze* v. *Ukraine*, (2005) 43 EHRR 967, paras. 164–71 and 175–180; *Valle Jaramillo et al.* v. *Colombia*, Merits, reparations and costs, Judgment of 27 November 2008, Ser. C, no. 192, paras. 73–106; *Zimbabwe Human Rights NGO Forum* v. *Zimbabwe*, 245/2002 (2006), para. 160. Where there is evidence linking the police to prior threats and the authorities subsequently fail to respond to complaints, the state may be held directly responsible for a violation (of article 6 ICCPR). See *Pathmini Peiris* v. *Sri Lanka*, UN Doc. CCPR/C/103/D/1862/2009 (26 October 2011), para. 7.2.

[53] *González* v. *Mexico*, paras. 249–402.

[54] *Salman* v. *Turkey*, (2000) 34 EHRR 425 GC, para. 99; *Anguelova* v. *Bulgaria*, (2002) 38 EHRR 659, para. 110.

[55] As stipulated in the UN standards for the treatment of detainees and developed in jurisprudence. See on the rights of mentally ill persons in mental health institutions, *Ximenes-Lopes* v. *Brazil*, Merits, reparations and costs, Judgment of 4 July 2006, Ser. C, no. 149, paras. 101–11 and 120–50.

[56] European Committee for the Prevention of Torture and Inhuman or Degrading Treatment or Punishment, CPT Standards, CPT/Inf/E (2002) 1 – Rev. 2010, 21, para. 27.

[57] See *Paula and Audrey Edwards* v. *United Kingdom*, (2002) 35 EHRR 19, para. 57.

[58] Ibid.

Duty to investigate, prosecute and punish and to provide redress

The violation of the right to life is both facilitated and compounded by impunity. Responses to allegations have frequently been characterised by inaction, delays, lack of victim and witness protection, the taking of inadequate measures particularly of a forensic nature and limited if non-existent independence of the investigating authorities.[59] Legal obstacles such as amnesty or immunity laws or unduly short statutes of limitation, which bar prosecutions, or making cases against suspected (army) perpetrators subject to the jurisdiction of military courts, have also constituted major obstacles.[60]

The IACtHR has developed a particularly rich jurisprudence in which it has taken a contextual approach to identify the factors contributing to impunity and its impact on victims and society at large.[61] In the seminal case of *Velásquez Rodríguez* it held that states have a duty to investigate alleged violations of the right to life, irrespective of the identity of the perpetrators.[62] This is important because a state may still be held responsible for a procedural failure even where its responsibility for the substantive violation cannot be established. The due diligence obligation requires that adequate criminal laws are in place and that state authorities undertake an investigation, either following a complaint or *ex officio* (on their own motion) upon receiving credible information about a violation of the right to life, which needs to be prompt, impartial and effective.[63] Effectiveness requires the authorities to take all necessary investigative steps capable of establishing the facts and the identity of the perpetrators.[64]

---

[59] See in this regard Independent Study on Best Practices, including Recommendations, to assist States in strengthening their domestic capacity to combat all aspects of impunity, by Professor D. Orentlicher, UN Doc. E/CN4/2004/88 (27 February 2004).

[60] *Barrios Altos* v. *Peru*, Merits, Judgment of 14 March 2001, Ser. C, no. 75, para. 41; HRCtee, General Comment 31, Nature of the General Legal Obligation Imposed on States Parties to the Covenant, UN Doc. CCPR/C/21/Rev.1/Add.13 (26 May 2004), para. 18.

[61] See in particular *La Cantuta* v. *Peru*, Merits, reparations and costs, Judgment of 29 November 2006, Ser. C, no. 162, paras. 110, 115, 157, 160, 222, 226, 227, 239, including Separate Opinion of Judge S. Garcia Ramirez.

[62] *Velásquez Rodríguez* v. *Honduras*, Merits, Judgment of 29 July 1988, Ser. C, no. 4, paras. 172–7.

[63] See e.g. *Mapiripan* v. *Colombia*, para. 219; *Hugh Jordan* v. *United Kingdom*, (2001) 37 EHRR 52, paras. 105–8.

[64] *Nachova and Others* v. *Bulgaria*, para. 113; *Cepeda Manuel Vargas* v. *Colombia*, Preliminary objections, merits, reparations, costs, Judgment of 26 May 2010, Ser. C, no. 213, paras. 116–22, at para. 118: 'In complex cases, the obligation to investigate includes the duty to direct the efforts of the apparatus of the State to clarify the structures that allowed these violations, the reasons for them, the causes, the beneficiaries and the consequences, and not merely to discover, prosecute and, if applicable, punish the direct perpetrators.'

Where investigations establish sufficient evidence the authorities must prosecute the perpetrators who must, if convicted, be subject to adequate punishments.[65] In addition, victims of violations, particularly relatives, need to be informed of the outcome of investigations and must have access to effective remedies.[66]

A right to survival?

Traditionally, the right to life has been understood as a civil right that protects against extrajudicial killings and other unjustified use of lethal force. Recognising a duty of the state to provide the basics necessary for survival would potentially transform the right, or elements of it, into an economic, social and cultural right. A nexus between the right to life and 'survival and development' is explicitly made in article 6 CRC.[67] Beyond this, there is limited jurisprudence evidencing a broader understanding. The HRCtee has emphasised that it 'would *be desirable* for State parties to take all possible measures to reduce infant mortality and to increase life expectancy, especially in adopting measures to eliminate malnutrition and epidemics' (emphasis added).[68] In *Mapiripán Massacre* v. *Colombia*, the IACtHR referred to the dismal living conditions of displaced persons following a massacre in the context of finding a violation of the right to life.[69] In *Cyprus* v. *Turkey*, the ECtHR left open whether article 2 ECHR entails a minimum level of general health care.[70] While there is a measure of reluctance to extend the scope of the right to life, it is equally clear that states must be considered to have an obligation to take steps that can reasonably be expected to ensure the survival of their populations. The jurisprudence of national courts, notably India's apex courts, point the way to a broader and more comprehensive understanding of the right to life as governing all aspects of life.[71]

---

[65] *Öneryildiz* v. *Turkey*, paras. 91–118; *Mapiripan* v. *Colombia*, paras. 296–9; *Pathmini Peiris* v. *Sri Lanka*, para. 7.4.

[66] *Jordan* v. *UK*, para. 109; *Gonzales* v. *Mexico*, para. 424 (lack of information about investigations one of the factors constituting degrading treatment of relatives).

[67] Article 6(2) CRC: '2. States Parties shall ensure to the maximum extent possible the survival and development of the child.' See M. Nowak, *A Commentary on the United Nations Convention on the Rights of the Child, Article 6: The Right to Life, Survival and Development* (Leiden, Boston: Martinus Nijhoff, 2005).

[68] HRCtee, General Comment 6, para. 5. See also Concluding observations of the Human Rights Committee: Democratic People's Republic of Korea, UN Doc. CCPR/CO/72/PRK (27 August 2001), para. 12.

[69] *Mapiripán* v. *Colombia*, para. 186.

[70] *Cyprus* v. *Turkey*, (2002) 35 EHRR 30, paras. 216–22, in particular at 219.

[71] See section 9.11.

1 What is problematic about the proposition that the death penalty itself constitutes a violation of the prohibition of torture and ill-treatment, considering the current status of the right to life under international law?

2 Have treaty bodies interpreted the duty to protect life in such a way that it is sufficiently clear what measures states need to take to counter existing threats?

8.3   THE RIGHT TO BE FREE FROM TORTURE

8.3.1   Practice

The practice of torture persists in many countries despite its absolute pro-hibition under international law.[72] Authoritarian and dictatorial states have a history of deliberately using torture as a means to control and repress the population and destroy their 'enemies'.[73] Torture is also a weapon of war used to instil terror and to gather intelligence in order to weaken the enemy. Democratic and other countries alike have resorted to torture for counter-insurgency purposes, often facilitated by emergency laws.[74] The response to the 9/11 attacks in the USA has given rise to the practice of (extraordi-nary) rendition – transferring someone outside the protection of the law to a country for interrogation where he or she is at risk of torture – and allega-tions of complicity in the torture of terrorism suspects.[75] Torture also fre-quently constitutes part of routine law enforcement.[76] This practice is often tolerated if not encouraged in order to 'combat crime' but is simultaneously self-serving as a tool of power for corrupt and brutal law-enforcement offi-cials. Non-state actors have also used torture methods, although it is often difficult to establish the nature and extent of practices in these contexts.[77] Gender-based violence, particularly sexual violence, is widespread and has been recognised as a form of torture.[78]

---

[72] See in particular reports by the UN Special Rapporteur on torture, www.ohchr.org/EN/ Issues/Torture/SRTorture/Pages/SRTortureIndex.aspx. See also N. Rodley and M. Pollard, *The Treatment of Prisoners under International Law*, 3rd edn (Oxford University Press, 2011).

[73] See K. Millet, *The Politics of Cruelty: An Essay on the Literature of Political Imprisonment* (London: Norton, 1995).

[74] D. Rejali, *Torture and Democracy* (Princeton University Press, 2007).

[75] See Joint Study on Global Practices in Relation to Secret Detention in the Context of Countering Terrorism, UN Doc. A/HRC/13/42 (19 February 2010), particularly paras. 132–58. See section 15.8.

[76] See for example *Mikheyev* v. *Russia*, [2006] ECHR 78.

[77] REDRESS, *Not only the State: Torture by Non-State Actors, Towards Enhanced Protection, Accountability and Effective Remedies* (London: REDRESS, 2006). See also section 16.5.1.

[78] See Report of the Special Rapporteur on torture and other cruel, inhuman or degrading treatment or punishment, UN Doc. A/HRC/7/3 (15 January 2008), paras. 44–58.

There is a large arsenal of torture methods, i.e. torture is anything capable of inflicting severe physical or mental pain or suffering. Where there is a risk of accountability, methods of torture tend to be of a nature that does not leave physical traces, whereas torture is often crude and extremely brutal in countries where the forces act with little or no restraint.[79] The multiple consequences of torture, particularly post-traumatic stress disorder, have been well documented over the years.[80] The impact of torture is not confined to the individual subjected to it; it also often has a detrimental effect on the families who bear the brunt of the suffering of the survivor/victim. Beyond this, torture can paralyse communities and instil fear in entire societies, which is often part and parcel of its perverse rationale.[81]

8.3.2   Sources

The prohibition of torture and ill-treatment is enshrined in a series of international and regional instruments.[82] The most detailed treaty is the CAT and at the regional level, the Inter-American Convention to Prevent and Punish Torture. There are also separate treaties focusing on the prevention of torture, namely the European Convention for the Prevention of Torture and Inhuman or Degrading Treatment or Punishment and the OPCAT.

Torture and other ill-treatment are prohibited under international humanitarian law.[83] Moreover, torture is considered an international crime subject to universal jurisdiction and constitutes an element of genocide, war crimes and crimes against humanity.[84]

8.3.3   The absolute prohibition of torture

The prohibition of torture is absolute and non-derogable,[85] having attained the status of *jus cogens*.[86] This absolute prohibition is the outcome of long political struggles and the recognition that torture is so egregious that it

---

[79] Rejali, above note 74.

[80] See Manual on the Effective Investigation and Documentation of Torture and Other Cruel, Inhuman or Degrading Treatment or Punishment (Istanbul Protocol), submitted to the UN High Commissioner for Human Rights, 9 August 1999.

[81] For a detailed case study, see A. Doney, 'The Psychological After-Effects of Torture: A Survey of Sri Lankan Ex-Detainees', in D. Somasundaram, *Scarred Minds: The Psychological Impact of War on Sri Lankan Tamils* (New Delhi: Sage, 1998), 256–87.

[82] Articles 5 UDHR, 7 and 10 ICCPR, 37 ICRC, 10 ICRMW, 15 CRPD, 3 ECHR, 5 ACHR and 5 ACHPR.

[83] See ICRC, CIHL Database, Rule 90.

[84] See in particular articles 6(b) (genocide), 7(1)(f) (crimes against humanity), 8(2)(a)(ii) and 8(2)(c)(i) (war crimes) ICC Rome Statute.

[85] Articles 1 and 2(2) CAT; 4(2) and 7 ICCPR; 3 and 15(2) ECHR; 5 and 27(2) ACHR; and 5 ACHPR.

[86] See e.g. *Prosecutor* v. *Furundzija* (IT-95-17/1-T), ICTY Trial Chamber Judgment of 10 December 1998, paras. 153–7; CtAT, General Comment 2: Implementation of article 2 by States parties,

cannot be justified under any circumstances. Nevertheless, there are recurring demands to permit exceptions which have become particularly prominent in the 'torture debate' largely, but not exclusively, triggered by the 'war on terror'.[87] The debate has revolved around the 'ticking bomb scenario': should it be lawful to torture an individual if this would possibly result in the lives of (a large number of) people being saved?

While the state has a duty to protect the life and security of anyone within its jurisdiction there are good reasons why torture should not be an acceptable way of doing so. From a rule of law perspective, torture is incompatible with the presumption of innocence and due process; information extracted under torture must therefore not be used in judicial proceedings. As an interrogation method it is apparent that information extracted under torture is frequently not reliable. Crucially, allowing torture in specific circumstances risks turning the exceptional into the rule. Indeed, the Israeli experience where interrogators routinely relied on the ticking bomb exception appears to support this slippery slope argument.[88] Vesting judges with the power to issue 'torture warrants' in ticking bomb situations, as has been suggested,[89] and thereby judicially sanction 'state violence', appears both unrealistic and highly inappropriate. Ultimately, the torture debate concerns the limits of the exercise of state power and the core of human dignity. Even if there are utilitarian grounds international law is based on the premise that a person should not be turned into a mere object and that the state should not be allowed to destroy someone's personality.

8.3.4   The case of *Gäfgen* and the German torture debate

The German case of *Gäfgen* illustrates the difficult legal and moral questions raised by the absolute prohibition of torture. Magnus Gäfgen, a young law student, kidnapped and murdered an eleven-year-old boy, Jacob Metzler, in order to extort money from the family to lead a lavish lifestyle and impress his girlfriend. The police apprehended him following the hand-over of the ransom. Thinking that Jacob was still alive, the head of the Frankfurt police and one of his officers threatened Gäfgen that he would be subjected to severe pain if he did not reveal the boy's whereabouts. Gäfgen – terrified by the threat – admitted that he had already killed Jacob and led the police to

---

UN Doc. CAT/C/GC/2 (24 January 2008), para. 1; *Questions relating to the Obligation to Prosecute or Extradite* (*Belgium* v. *Senegal*), ICJ Judgment of 20 July 2012, para. 99.

[87] See in particular Y. Ginbar, *Moral, Practical and Legal Aspects of the Ticking Bomb Justification for Torture* (Oxford University Press, 2008) and J. Waldron, *Torture, Terror and Trade-Offs: Philosophy for the White House* (Oxford University Press, 2010).

[88] See *Public Committee Against Torture* v. *The State of Israel* HCJ 5100/94 (1999).

[89] A. Dershowitz, 'Is There a Torturous Road to Justice?', *Los Angeles Times* (8 November 2001).

the place where he had hidden the child's body. Gäfgen was later tried, convicted and sentenced to life imprisonment for murder.

The case triggered a major debate in Germany, both within the legal profession and the broader public, with many supporting the acts of the police director because he had acted to save a child's life. The German courts affirmed the absolute prohibition of torture but did not rule that Gäfgen's conviction had been unlawful. Gäfgen then took his case to the ECtHR. Eventually, the Grand Chamber held that: (1) the threat of torture fell within article 3 (though not constituting torture); (2) the punishment of the police director and the police officer (they received a suspended fine, the lowest possible punishment) had not satisfied the procedural requirement to adequately punish violations of article 3; and (3) the substantial delay of ruling on Gäfgen's compensation claim (more than three years at the time) had breached his right to an effective remedy for torture.[90] However, the Grand Chamber found no violation in relation to the most controversial aspect of the case, namely the admission of evidence, i.e. Jacob Metzler's body, obtained as a result of the threat (which it considered under article 6).[91] The majority of the Grand Chamber agreed with Germany's argument that the evidence had not been material because Gäfgen had confessed voluntarily at the end of the trial. Gäfgen's lawyer had rejected this argument, saying that Gäfgen had been left with no genuine choice, knowing that he would have been convicted on the basis of the available evidence irrespective of the confession. This position found support in a scathing dissenting opinion that criticised the Court's artificial construct of a 'break in the causal chain' on account of Gäfgen's confession and emphasised that the absolute nature of the prohibition requires that all evidence obtained in breach should be excluded.[92] Such a finding, however, would have necessitated a retrial. It is clear that the majority must have been keenly aware that this would have prompted an outcry in Germany, which may have been a factor influencing its judgment, although this remains a matter of conjecture. Ultimately, the judgment shows that affirming the absolute prohibition of torture is often only the first step, with the crucial question being what legal consequences should flow from its absolute nature in a given case.

POINTS TO CONSIDER

1   Does the judgment of the ECtHR Grand Chamber do justice to the facts?

2   What is the legal significance of the *Gäfgen* case?

---

[90]   *Gäfgen* v. *Germany*, (2011) 52 EHRR 1, paras. 75–132.
[91]   Ibid., paras. 133–88.
[92]   Ibid., Joint Partly Dissenting Opinion of Judges Rozakis, Tulkens, Jebens, Ziemele, Bianku and Power.

8.3.5   The role of the definition of torture and other forms of ill-treatment and punishment

The prohibition under international law encompasses both torture and other forms of ill-treatment. While there is a noticeable trend not to differentiate sharply between the two,[93] torture still carries a special stigma. In addition, the nature of the remedies may be influenced by a finding of torture, including the amount of compensation. A clear understanding of the legal meaning of torture can therefore be of considerable importance in a given case.

The definition in article 1 CAT is widely seen as the most authoritative and has been referred to by most international and regional human rights treaty bodies in their jurisprudence. Broken down into its constitutive elements the definition sets out the following elements of torture:[94]

- Infliction of severe mental or physical pain or suffering: an act of torture can be objectively severe, i.e. applying electroshocks or rape, or may be severe because of the circumstances, including the duration, impact and personal characteristics, i.e. subjective elements, such as 'sex, age and state of health'.[95] Importantly, the definition comprises not only physical pain but also mental pain or suffering, such as mock executions which the laws of many countries still do not recognise as 'torture'.
- Intent: the intentional infliction is one of the factors distinguishing torture from other forms of ill-treatment. For example, poor conditions of detention as such do not amount to torture unless they are used, either solely or in combination, to deliberately inflict severe pain or suffering for a particular purpose.
- Purpose: the purpose element makes it clear that torture is a means to an end. The 'classical' purpose is to extract information or a confession but article 1 CAT is broader in scope. It also includes several other purposes, notably discrimination of any kind, which can be particularly important in cases of sexual violence. The list of purposes is illustrative rather than exhaustive, i.e. 'such purposes as', and it is difficult to envisage circumstances where an official inflicts severe pain or suffering, even for ostensibly purely selfish purposes, where no link could be made to any of the purposes mentioned.[96]

---

[93] CtAT, General Comment 2. However, see also M. Nowak, 'What Practices Constitute Torture? US and UN Standards', *HRQ* 28(4) (2008), 809–41.

[94] See for a thorough discussion and attempt at redefining torture, S. Dewulf, *The Signature of Evil: (Re)Defining Torture in International Law* (Cambridge: Intersentia, 2011).

[95] *Ireland* v. *the United Kingdom*, (1978) 2 EHRR 25, para. 162; *Selmouni* v. *France*, (2000) 29 EHRR 403, paras. 100–5; *Loayza-Tamayo* v. *Peru*, Merits, Judgment of 17 September 1997, Ser. C, no. 33, para. 57; *Hajrizi Dzemajl et al.* v. *Yugoslavia*, UN Doc. CAT/C/29/D/161/2000 (21 November 2002), paras. 8.6 and 9.2.

[96] See Dewulf, above note 94, particularly 338–55.

- Official involvement: the formula used in article 1 CAT 'inflicted by or at the instigation of or with the consent or acquiescence of a public official or other person acting in an official capacity' serves to attribute responsibility. The CAT definition therefore excludes 'torture' by non-state actors, such as rebel groups (unless they exercise state-like functions).[97] However, an act such as domestic violence, prisoner-on-prisoner violence or a pogrom by a mob, committed by (a) private individual(s) may come within the ambit of torture if the officials concerned acquiesce, such as by encouraging the commission or continuation of relevant acts, including through inaction.[98] In these situations, the lack of due diligence to prevent and respond to relevant acts constitutes the crucial nexus that potentially broadens the scope of torture to a wider range of actors.[99] Beyond the confines of article 1 CAT, there is an increasing debate as to whether the public official requirement is intrinsic to the notion of torture, which is of immense relevance for the scope of acts and actors that may fall within the definition.[100] Notably, international criminal law does not require a public official to be involved for an act to constitute torture.[101]

The definition of torture contained in article 3 of the Inter-American Convention to Prevent and Punish Torture is similar to that in article 1 CAT, but is broader in that it refers to 'any purpose', and to 'methods upon a person intended to obliterate the personality of the victim or to diminish his physical or mental capacities, even if they do not cause physical pain or mental anguish'.

Article 3 ECHR is structured differently, simply prohibiting torture, inhuman or degrading treatment or punishment. The ECtHR has developed a sophisticated, though at times controversial, jurisprudence on the definition of torture in which it distinguishes between ill-treatment (reaching the required threshold of a 'minimum level of severity'), inhuman treatment (premeditated, applied for hours, causing either actual bodily injury or intense physical and mental suffering) and torture (deliberate inhuman treatment causing very serious and cruel suffering).[102] The Court has therefore applied a seemingly high threshold for an act to be considered torture. It seemed to acknowledge as much when it stated in *Selmouni* v. *France* that it

---

[97] See in particular *Sadiq Shek Elmi* v. *Australia*, UN Doc. CAT/C/22/D/120/1998 (14 May 1999), para. 6.5.

[98] *Opuz* v. *Turkey*, paras. 158–76; *Wilson* v. *Philippines*, UN Doc. CCPR/C/79/D/868/1999 (30 October 2003), para. 7.3; *Dzemajil* v. *Serbia and Montenegro*, para. 9.2.

[99] CtAT, General Comment 2, para. 18.

[100] See Separate Opinion of Judge Cecilia Medina Quiroga in *Gonzalez* v. *Mexico*, paras. 7 and 16, and Dewulf, above note 94, 363–99.

[101] See for a concise overview, ibid., 376–81.

[102] See for example *Jalloh* v. *Germany*, (2007) 44 EHRR 32, paras. 67–8, and *Selmouni* v. *France*, para. 96.

considers that certain acts which were classified in the past as 'inhuman and degrading treatment' as opposed to 'torture' could be classified differently in future. It takes the view that the increasingly high standard being required in the area of the protection of human rights and fundamental liberties correspondingly and inevitably requires greater firmness in assessing breaches of the fundamental values of democratic societies.[103]

This was widely seen as a barely veiled reference to its earlier, heavily criticised finding in *Ireland* v. *UK* that the five techniques (wall standing, hooding, subjection to noise, sleep deprivation and deprivation of food and drink) constituted inhuman treatment, but did not amount to torture.[104]

The difference between article 1 CAT and the definition developed by the ECtHR has given rise to a debate between those who view purpose as the central element in distinguishing between torture and ill-treatment – with a high entry threshold for ill-treatment – and those who consider severity as a more suitable device to recognise the scale of different forms of ill-treatment.[105] This debate, though highly relevant for a clear understanding of the nature of torture, has had limited resonance in the jurisprudence of treaty bodies; even the ECtHR seems to invoke both article 1 CAT and its own definition which may be seen as part of an attempt to show that a certain act constitutes torture under all possible definitions.[106]

A further element of torture introduced by the then Special Rapporteur on torture Manfred Nowak is that of 'powerlessness'.[107] While this notion has potentially negative connotations for victims, the element of powerlessness can play a useful role in respect of the degree of factual control and in capturing the crucial (and terrifying) power imbalance inherent in torture situations. It can therefore be important when distinguishing between custodial ill-treatment and other situations, such as the use of excessive force during demonstrations.

Beyond the rather flexible formula developed by the ECtHR, other forms of inhuman, cruel or degrading treatment not amounting to torture are not defined in international law. By its nature ill-treatment is a broad category with a wide field of application as evidenced by the often casuistic jurisprudence. Examples include inhuman conditions of detention, denial of medical care, destruction of homes and excessive use of force.[108] Treatment has been defined as degrading if it arouses 'feelings of fear, anguish and inferiority

---

[103] *Selmouni* v. *France*, para. 121.

[104] *Ireland* v. *UK*, para. 167; *Selmouni* v. *France*, para. 101.

[105] See M. Evans, 'Getting to Grips with Torture', *ICLQ* 51(2) (2002), 365–83.

[106] See for example *Jalloh* v. *Germany*, para. 48.

[107] See Special Rapporteur on torture, above note 78, paras. 28–30, 45, 52, 57.

[108] See e.g. *Ananyev and Others* v. *Russia*, [2012] ECHR 21 (pilot judgment on inhuman and degrading conditions in pre-trial detention); *Todorov* v. *Ukraine*, [2012] ECHR 30, paras. 51–5 (denial of adequate medical care); *Dulaş* v. *Turkey*, [2001] ECHR 60, paras. 49–56 (destruction of homes); *Güler and Öngel* v. *Turkey*, [2011] ECHR 1513, paras. 23–31 (excessive use of force during protests).

capable of humiliating and debasing the victim',[109] such as unnecessary strip searches.[110]

The category of cruel, inhuman or degrading punishment has been applied in particular to corporal punishments. Treaty bodies have been uniform in their jurisprudence according to which officially sanctioned corporal punishment is a degrading attack on a 'person's dignity and physical integrity',[111] for example in cases of birching on the Isle of Man (UK), the use of tamarind switch in Jamaica, the cat-o-nine tails in Trinidad and Tobago or flogging in Sudan.[112]

The second sentence of article 1(1) CAT excludes from the definition of torture 'pain or suffering arising only from, inherent in or incidental to lawful sanctions'. This provision may be read as justifying any sanctions prescribed under national law, including corporal punishments. However, such an interpretation would give states unfettered discretion to define the scope of application of article 1, even to the point of passing laws that stipulate punishments clearly falling within the definition of torture. It is for this reason that most observers consider that 'lawful' refers to both national and international law, a reading that effectively makes the provision redundant. If the sanction constitutes torture according to the second sentence of article 1(1) CAT it can no longer be a valid exception; if it does not constitute torture there is no need for an exception.[113] Nevertheless, several states retain judicial corporal punishment which raises the question of whether there can be regional or religiously-based exceptions. However, the absolute nature of the prohibition of torture under customary international law leaves no room for any contravening practice.[114] The issue of cruel, inhuman or degrading punishment has also been considered in the context of certain detention regimes. This includes being kept in isolation, being locked up in a small room for twenty-three hours a day[115] and life imprisonment without the possibility of release,[116] the nature and consequences of which may reach

---

[109] *Ireland* v. *UK*, para. 167.

[110] See for example *Wieser* v. *Austria*, [2007] ECHR 170, paras. 39–41.

[111] *Tyrer* v. *the United Kingdom*, (1978) 2 EHRR 1, para. 33.

[112] Ibid., paras. 28–35; *Osbourne* v. *Jamaica*, UN Doc. CCPR/C/68/D/759/1997 (15 March 2000), para. 9.1; *Caesar* v. *Trinidad and Tobago*, Merits, reparations and costs, Judgment of 11 March 2005, Ser. C, no. 123, paras. 56–89; *Curtis Francis Doebbler* v. *Sudan*, 236/2000 (2003), paras. 29–44.

[113] M. Nowak, 'Challenges to the Absolute Nature of the Prohibition of Torture and Ill-treatment', *NQHR* 23(4) (2005), 674–88.

[114] See REDRESS and SHRM, *No More Cracking of the Whip: Time to End Corporal Punishment in Sudan* (London: REDRESS, 2012), pp. 28–31. See also CtRC, The right of the child to protection from corporal punishment and other cruel or degrading forms of punishment (arts. 19; 28, para.2; and 37, inter alia), UN Doc. CRC/C/GC/8 (2 March 2007).

[115] *G.B.* v. *Bulgaria*, [2004] ECHR 112, paras. 82–8.

[116] See *Kafkaris* v. *Cyprus*, (2009) 49 EHRR 35, paras. 95–108; *Vinter and others* v. *the United Kingdom*, [2012] ECHR 61, paras. 87–96; also *Babar Ahmed and Others* v. *United Kingdom*, App. nos. 24027/07, 11949/08, 36742/08, 66911/09 and 67354/09, Judgment (10 April 2012), paras. 205–44.

beyond what detainees can be expected to suffer in the course of lawful deprivation of their liberty.[117]

8.3.6   Obligations

Under the prohibition, states have a negative obligation to refrain from engaging in any torture or ill-treatment and a positive obligation to prevent, investigate, prosecute and punish, and redress such acts. As is clear from article 2 CAT, the overarching duty and primary objective of the prohibition is to prevent acts of torture through 'effective legislative, administrative, judicial or other measures'. The effective implementation of the prohibition requires state actors to take a series of measures in law and practice that are designed to significantly reduce the risk of torture.[118] This includes incorporating the prohibition of torture in national law,[119] stipulating that evidence and confessions extracted under torture are inadmissible[120] and providing custodial safeguards. Safeguards such as access to a lawyer of one's choice, the right to inform family members of the arrest, regular health checks and the right to challenge the lawfulness of detention before a judge are all meant to minimise the risk of torture, particularly during the initial phase of detention.[121] Visiting mechanisms, particularly in the form of regular independent external monitoring, can serve as an important deterrent and as a form of engagement that may result in gradual changes leading towards enhanced compliance. Such mechanisms are in place at the national, regional and international level.[122] According to international treaties and best practices, visiting mechanisms should be independent, composed of a group of mixed professionals with the required expertise and adequately resourced.[123] The mechanisms need to have unrestricted access to all detention facilities at short notice and the opportunity to interview detainees in private. Some

---

[117] See Interim report of the Special Rapporteur of the Human Rights Council on torture and other cruel, inhuman or degrading treatment or punishment, UN Doc. A/66/268 (5 August 2011) (on solitary confinement and isolation).

[118] General Recommendations of the Special Rapporteur on the question of torture, UN Doc. E/CN4/2003/68 (17 December 2002), para. 26.

[119] L. Oette, 'Implementing the Prohibition of Torture: the Contribution and Limits of National Legislation and Jurisprudence', *IJHR* 16(5) (2012), 717–36.

[120] Article 15 CAT, see Report of the Special Rapporteur on torture and other cruel, inhuman or degrading treatment or punishment, UN Doc. A/61/259 (14 August 2006), paras. 44–62; *Singarasa* v. *Sri Lanka*, UN Doc. CCPR/C/81/D/1033/2001 (21 July 2004), paras. 7.1–7.5.

[121] CtAT, General Comment 2, para. 13.

[122] In particular the CPT in Europe, the SPT under the OPCAT, and the ICRC. See also Association for the Prevention of Torture, www.apt.ch.

[123] Second Annual Report on the Subcommittee on Prevention of Torture and Other Cruel, Inhuman or Degrading Treatment or Punishment, UN Doc. CAT/C/42/2 (7 April 2009), paras. 33–42.

countries have responded positively to recommendations by visiting bodies such as the CPT in Europe and there were considerable hopes that the preventive mechanisms under the OPCAT will have an equally positive impact worldwide. Finally, states must not expose individuals to the risk of torture or ill-treatment, a principle known as *non-refoulement* explicitly stipulated in article 3 CAT and generally recognised in international jurisprudence.[124]

Impunity is a major factor perpetuating torture and the approach underpinning the CAT is that of combating crime. Accordingly, states must make torture a crime in their national laws and must extradite or prosecute anyone present on their territory who is suspected of having committed an act of torture, which effectively requires states to establish universal jurisdiction over acts of torture.[125] Individuals alleging torture must have an effective right to complain and states have a corresponding duty to investigate allegations of torture promptly, impartially and effectively.[126] Where substantial evidence is found, perpetrators of torture must be subject to adequate punishments.[127] Similarly to the right to life, anyone suspected of torture should not benefit from immunities, amnesties or pardons, and torture should not be subject to statutes of limitation.[128] Accountability is also an important element of the right of torture victims to an effective remedy and reparation, which is recognised as a separate right in article 14 CAT and in the jurisprudence of human rights treaty bodies and courts as being inherent in the relevant treaties.[129]

INTERVIEW 8.1

The role of medical documentation in combating torture: Istanbul Protocol

(Dr. Önder Özkalipçi)

The Istanbul Protocol was developed in the 1990s by a coalition of human rights organisations, doctors and lawyers and has since become an important, internationally recognised manual and guide on how to document and investigate torture cases. The following is an interview with Dr Önder Özkalipçi, one of the three project coordinators at the time, who has also conducted a series of trainings on the Istanbul Protocol around the world.

---

[124] See in particular article 3 CAT. See also section 15.8.

[125] Articles 4–8 CAT. See its role in the *Habré* case, see section 7.7.

[126] See in particular articles 12, 13 CAT.

[127] *Gäfgen* v. *Germany*, paras. 121–5; *Zontul* v. *Greece*, Appl. no. 12294/07, ECtHR Judgment (17 January 2012), paras. 95–109.

[128] See for example *Guridi* v. *Spain*, UN Doc. CAT/C/34/D/212/2002 (17 May 2005), para. 6.7; *Barrios Altos* v. *Peru*, Merits, Judgment of 14 May 2001, Ser. C, no. 75, paras. 41–4 and HRCtee, General Comment 31, para. 18.

[129] See sections 13.9 and 13.10.

Why 'Istanbul Protocol'?

The idea of calling the guidelines 'Istanbul Protocol' emerged during the first meeting of the authors and contributing organisations in 1996 – the name reflects the fact that the main meetings were held in the Forensic Medicine Department of the Medical Faculty, Istanbul University.

What explains the prominent role played by Turkish activists and organisations in drafting the Istanbul Protocol?

First of all, the Istanbul Protocol is a joint product of seventy-five experts from forty different organisations. A number of NGOs, such as Physicians for Human Rights-USA and Action for Torture Survivors (HRFT)-Geneva, and individuals made important contributions which was facilitated by three coordinators (Vincent Iacopino, Caroline Schlar and myself). At the time, torture was an important public health problem in Turkey (unfortunately it still is today). Several key organisations, namely Human Rights Foundation of Turkey, Turkish Medical Association and Forensic Physicians Society of Turkey, teamed up to respond to this challenge. Our thinking was that if we could succeed in making a strong contribution to an international document that could be accepted by the UN, then this might help our struggle against torture and ill-treatment in our own country. The Istanbul Protocol is clearly the outcome of international collaboration and an international document, but it is equally true that the Turkish experience and expertise was an important element that inspired and invigorated the work of colleagues from other countries.

What are the main challenges relating to the documentation and investigation of torture?

Besides attempts to justify torture that are at times evident in public opinion, impunity is the biggest challenge in practice. By definition, the crime of torture is committed by state officials or 'at the instigation of or with the consent or acquiescence of state officials or other persons acting in official capacities'. This means that perpetrators already operate within a state network that allows them to cover the traces of their crime and rely on 'friends' within the system. One of the key tools of protecting perpetrators is to delay investigations. Investigations last so long that the case is dismissed because of the expiry of time limits for prosecutions, the perpetrator may become an important state official or retires or dies because of old age, or the evidence is lost.

Given these challenges the independence of the experts taking part in the investigation is critical. In several countries, forensic doctors work under the authority of the Ministry of Justice or Ministry of Interior. How can you prevent doctors from being subject to pressure by high state officials if they are working in the same ministry as the alleged perpetrator(s)? In practice, this has been a real problem for medical experts when preparing medical reports documenting torture. Threats are another major concern. There is always the risk of threats to the victim, his or her family, lawyers and the experts playing a role in the investigation, such as medical experts and even prosecutors and judges. Sadly, one of our colleagues, Dr German Antonio Ramirez Herrera, who took part in trainings on the Istanbul Protocol and submitted a detailed report that included several medico-legal reports on serious human rights violations, was assassinated in Ecuador in 2010. We know of several other cases of threats to forensic experts and there is still a long way to go worldwide. Lack of standards and knowledge of how best to investigate allegations of torture is another issue. In many cases the 'doctors' help the perpetrators, deliberately or inadvertently, because of the poor quality of their medical reports. Where a doctor concludes 'no evidence', a prosecutor or judge finds it easier not to prosecute or convict the perpetrator(s).

How does the Istanbul Protocol assist in addressing these challenges?

Essentially, the Istanbul Protocol highlights the responsibility of states to investigate allegations of torture promptly and effectively and provides the tools on how to do this in practice. States must work towards improving the quality of investigations. Training medical doctors how to document and prepare a report on the physical and psychological findings of torture and making judges and prosecutors aware of the value of high quality medico-legal reports remains a priority task.

Has the Istanbul Protocol been used in practice, and has it made a difference?

Yes, there are dozens of examples of decisions from national or international courts that cite the Istanbul Protocol when ruling on allegations of torture. High quality medical reports prepared in line with the Protocol's standards are challenging the forensic systems of countries. After years of training and engagement countries such as Georgia, Serbia, Turkey, Mexico and Egypt have begun introducing positive changes such as using medical report templates consistent with relevant standards and making significant investments to forensic medicine. The CtAT has also started recommending training on the Istanbul Protocol in its concluding observations on states parties' reports. If states implement these trainings effectively there is some hope that the prevalence of torture decreases although we all know that the global picture of torture is not very satisfactory today.

What is the broader significance of the Istanbul Protocol in the struggle against torture?

The Istanbul Protocol is an important tool for legal and health professionals who should work together to combat torture more effectively – such cooperation has considerable potential to bring about changes. Ultimately, a manual or protocol cannot protect individuals from torture if there is no rule of law. However, guidelines that represent best practices agreed upon by professionals worldwide can contribute to societies based on the rule of law where, we would hope, torture is the exception and – should it happen – its perpetrators will be punished.

QUESTIONS

- **Does the absolute prohibition of torture need to be revisited in light of the threat of terrorist attacks?**
- **Is the distinction between torture and other forms of ill-treatment still relevant?**
- **Is it time to revisit the international approach to combating torture given that the practice continues to be prevalent around the world?**

8.4   THE RIGHT TO LIBERTY AND SECURITY

8.4.1   Practice

The modern system of imprisonment grants states considerable power to deprive persons of their liberty and control their freedom.[130] This power inevitably gives rise to concerns that are particularly pronounced in respect of special detention regimes, including prison camps, preventive detention (based on the alleged threat of a person or the need to protect public safety irrespective of any suspicion of having committed a crime), detention under emergency laws (curtailing detainee's rights) and secret detention (lack of acknowledgement), such as in the 'war on terror'.[131] Many of these detention regimes are characterised by their lack of due process and safeguards, which has often facilitated other violations, notably torture and enforced disappearance and resulted in the denial of fair trials that require effective defence from the outset.[132] In addition, detention regimes tend to

---

[130] See M. Foucault, *Discipline and Punish: The Birth of the Prison* (London: Penguin, 1991).
[131] Reports of the Working Group on Arbitrary Detention, UN Docs. A/HRC/7/4 (10 January 2008), paras. 59–68; and A/HRC/13/30 (18 January 2010), paras. 72–80; Joint Study, above note 75, paras. 57–86.
[132] Ibid.

be far from 'neutral'. Individuals who belong to marginalised communities or groups are more likely to be targeted by the authorities, such as members of ethnic or other minorities, foreign nationals, Afro-Americans in the USA or Muslims in the UK following the terrorist attacks and are therefore particularly vulnerable to the state's power to arrest and detain.[133] Arrest and detention can entail devastating and potentially irreversible consequences such as stigmatisation, loss of employment, the breakdown of a relationship, psychological damage, illnesses contracted in prison. This makes it imperative that the public's interest in punishment and/or safety is counterbalanced by adequate due process guarantees against arbitrariness applying to all forms of detention, including confinement in psychiatric hospitals.

8.4.2   Sources

The right to liberty and security is recognised in several international and regional instruments,[134] which are complemented by UN 'soft law' standards[135] that can be used to specify states' obligations. International humanitarian law includes numerous provisions on arrest and detention, particularly regarding the internment of prisoners of war.[136] Systematic or widespread 'imprisonment or other severe deprivation of physical liberty in violation of fundamental rules of international law' constitutes a crime against humanity[137] and unlawful confinement (as a grave breach) a war crime.[138] The prohibition of arbitrary arrest and detention is considered to constitute customary international law.[139] Moreover, certain aspects of the right to liberty and security, such as the right to *habeas corpus*, are considered to be

---

[133] See in particular reports of the UN Working Group on Arbitrary Detention, online, at www.ohchr.org/EN/Issues/Detention/Pages/WGADIndex.aspx.

[134] Articles 9 UDHR, 9 ICCPR, 37 (b) CRC, 14 CRPD, 16 ICRMW, 17 CPED, 5 ECHR, 7 ACHR and 7 ACHPR.

[135] Standard Minimum Rules for the Treatment of Prisoners, adopted by the First UN Congress on the Prevention of Crime and the Treatment of Offenders, held at Geneva in 30 August 1955, and approved by ECOSOC in its resolutions 663 C (XXIV) (31 July 1957) and 2076 (LXII) (13 May 1977); UN Body of Principles for the Protection of All Persons under Any Form of Detention or Imprisonment, adopted by General Assembly resolution 43/173 (9 December 1988).

[136] See for a concise overview, ICRC, CIHL, Database Rule 99.

[137] Article 7(1)(e) ICC Rome Statute.

[138] Article 8(2)(a)(vii) ibid.

[139] HRCtee, General Comment 24: Issues relating to reservations made upon ratification or accession to the Covenant or the Optional Protocols thereto, or in relation to declarations under article 41 of the Covenant, UN Doc. CCPR/C/21/Rev.1/Add.6 (4 November 1994), para. 8. According to §702 (e) of the US Restatement (Third) on Foreign Relations 'prolonged arbitrary detention' violates customary international law.

non-derogable at any time and permissible derogations are subject to a strict proportionality test.[140]

8.4.3 Scope of the right to liberty and security

The right prohibits arbitrary deprivation of liberty. The term liberty refers to 'physical liberty' as opposed to 'mere restriction of freedom of movement'.[141] Deprivation of liberty differs from restriction upon liberty – which may constitute an interference with the right to freedom of movement – in terms of its degree or intensity rather than its nature or substance.[142] It has an objective and subjective element, i.e. confinement to a certain limited place for a not negligible length of time without valid consent.[143] The subjective element is particularly important in cases of psychiatric confinement, in which it acts as a safeguard where the individual concerned is in a position to express his or her consent.[144]

8.4.4 Justification of arrest and detention

International human rights law prohibits the 'arbitrary' deprivation of liberty. Importantly, it is not sufficient that arrest or detention are permitted by national law; this would give states carte blanche to allow deprivation on the flimsiest of grounds, as is indeed often the case, particularly under emergency laws.[145] As stated by the HRCtee in the defining case of *Mukong* v. *Cameroon*, 'arbitrariness' is:

not to be equated with 'against the law' but must be interpreted more broadly to include elements of inappropriateness, injustice, lack of predictability and due process of law ... remand in custody pursuant to lawful arrest must not only be lawful but reasonable in the circumstances ... [146]

---

[140] HRCtee, General Comment 29: States of Emergency (article 4), UN Doc. CCPR/C/21/Rev.1/Add.11 (31 August 2001), para. 4. See also Habeas Corpus in Emergency Situations (Arts. 27(2), 25(1) and 7(6) American Convention on Human Rights), OC-8/87 (30 January 1987), paras. 11–13; Judicial Guarantees in States of Emergency (Arts. 27(2), 25 and 8 American Convention on Human Rights), C-9/87 (6 October 1987), paras. 20–30 and 36–40.

[141] *Guzzardi* v. *Italy*, (1980) 3 EHRR 333, para. 92. See for a broader conception of liberty and security in the context of article 7(1) ACHR, *Chaparro-Álvarez and Lapo-Íñiguez* v. *Ecuador*, Preliminary objections, merits, reparations and costs, Judgment of 21 November 2007, Ser. C, no.170, para. 53.

[142] *Guzzardi* v. *Italy*, para. 93.

[143] *Storck* v. *Germany*, (2005) 43 EHRR 96, paras. 74–8.

[144] Ibid.

[145] *Amnesty International, Comité Loosli Bachelard, Lawyers' Committee for Human Rights, Association of Members of the Episcopal Conference of East Africa* v. *Sudan*, 48/90-50/91-52/91-89/93 (1999), para. 59.

[146] *Mukong* v. *Cameroon*, UN Doc. CCPR/C/51/D/458/1991 (21 July 1994), para. 9.8.

As a general rule, a state must comply with the (substantive) law that may justify deprivation of liberty and the (procedural) law stipulating arrest and detention procedures, which themselves must be reasonable, foreseeable and proportionate.[147] The authorities must demonstrate the existence of grounds that justify arrest, such as reasonable suspicion of a crime having been committed, or continued detention, for example to prevent flight, interference with evidence or the recurrence of crime.[148] Notably, some grounds, such as imprisonment for debt or disability, are explicitly prohibited under international human rights law as a justification for arrest or detention.[149] The ECHR differs from other treaties as it sets out a list of exhaustive grounds on which the deprivation of liberty is permitted. These include the arrest and detention of persons suspected of having committed criminal offences,[150] of persons of 'unsound mind, alcoholics or drug addicts or vagrants'[151] and in the immigration and deportation/extradition context.[152]

International human rights treaties stipulate a number of procedural safeguards against arbitrary arrest and detention. As a first step, anyone arrested must be promptly informed of his or her rights.[153] This right is meant to enable the arrested or detained person to effectively exercise his or her rights, with a view to challenging the lawfulness of the deprivation of liberty and defending any criminal charges where applicable.[154] Judicial control constitutes the most important safeguard against arbitrary deprivation of liberty. In criminal cases states have to ensure that any suspect is brought promptly before a judge or judicial authority,[155] that is normally within the first forty-eight hours.[156] This rule recognises that anyone facing criminal charges is

---

[147] See *Tibi* v. *Ecuador*, Preliminary objections, merits, reparations and costs, Judgment of 7 September 2004, Series C, no. 114, para. 98; *Gusinskiy* v. *Russia*, (2005) 41 EHRR 1, para. 52–5; 62–9; *Steel* v. *United Kingdom*, (1998) 28 EHRR 603, para. 54.

[148] *A* v. *Australia*, UN Doc. CCPR/C/59/D/560/1993 (3 April 1997), para. 9.4.

[149] Articles 11 ICCPR and 1 of Protocol no. 4 to the ECHR, and 14(1)(b) ICRPD.

[150] See e.g. *Lawless* v. *Ireland (No. 3)*, (1961) 1 EHRR 15, and *Fox, Campbell and Hartley* v. *UK*, (1990), 13 EHRR 157, para. 32.

[151] See e.g. *Winterwerp* v. *Netherlands*, (1979) 2 EHRR 387, paras. 38–42 ('unsound mind'); *Enhorn* v. *Sweden*, (2005) 41 EHRR 1267, paras. 40–56 (HIV); *De Wilde, Ooms and Versyp* v. *Belgium* (1971), 1 EHRR 373, paras. 66–70 ('vagrants'); *Witold Litwa* v. *Poland*, (2000) 33 EHRR 1267, paras. 72–80 ('alcoholic').

[152] *Saadi* v. *United Kingdom*, (2008) 47 EHRR 17, paras. 61–80.

[153] Articles 9(2) ICCPR, 5(2) ECHR, 7(4) ACHR and principle M.2(a) of the Principles and Guidelines on the Right to a Fair Trial and Legal Assistance in Africa, 2001.

[154] *Juan Humberto Sánchez* v. *Honduras*, Preliminary objections, merits, reparations and costs, Judgment of 7 June 2003, Ser. C, no. 99, para. 82; *Fox, Campbell and Hartley* v. *UK*, para. 40.

[155] A public prosecutor is not a 'judicial authority', see *Kulomin* v. *Hungary*, UN Doc. CCPR/C/50/D/521/1992 (22 March 1996), para. 11.3 and *Tibi* v. *Ecuador*, para. 117.

[156] In *Brogan and others* v. *United Kingdom*, (1988) 11 EHRR 117, the Court found that 'even the shortest of the four periods of detention, namely the four days and six hours spent in police custody ... falls outside the strict constraints as to time permitted by the

particularly vulnerable and that there is a heightened interest in ensuring judicial control of executive action at the earliest opportunity.[157] States have repeatedly sought to extend the period between arrest and appearance before a judicial authority, particularly in emergency situations. However, human rights treaty bodies have allowed limited extensions only where they are shown to be necessary and where adequate safeguards are in place, knowing well that detainees are most at risk of torture and other ill-treatment in the initial days of detention.[158] A detainee on remand also has a right to be tried within a reasonable time (taking into consideration the complexity of the case and conduct of the parties) or to be released pending trial.[159] This right flows from the presumption of innocence and continued detention can only be justified on specific, narrow grounds, such as to prevent escape. It reaches its absolute limit where the time spent on remand exceeds the maximum length of imprisonment a detainee would face in the case of conviction.[160]

Beyond the specific rules applying to criminal cases anyone deprived of his or her liberty has the right to challenge the lawfulness of detention, which entails the (non-derogable) right to have his or her case heard by a court, also referred to as *habeas corpus*.[161] This right provides an important safeguard, particularly against 'institutionalised' deprivation of liberty, such as in psychiatric hospitals, or excessive detention regimes, such as in the immigration context.[162] *Habeas corpus* proceedings must examine the factual and legal grounds for detention. This has proved difficult where authorities have relied on confidential information on national security grounds. Importantly, an applicant must be able 'effectively to challenge the allegations' and the state concerned must provide procedures, so that the right of the defence can be exercised.[163]

first part of Article 5 para. 3 (art. 5-3)'. See also *Borisenko* v. *Hungary*, UN Doc. CCPR/C/75/D/852/1999 (14 October 2002), para. 7.4 (three days too long).

[157] *Tibi* v. *Ecuador*, para. 114, and principle M.3(b) of the 2001 African Fair Trial Principles.

[158] Contrast *Brannigan and McBride* v. *United Kingdom*, (1993) 17 EHRR 539, paras. 32 and 56, with *Aksoy* v. *Turkey* (1996), 23 EHRR 553, para. 78. See also *Castillo-Petruzzi et al.* v. *Peru*, Merits, reparations and costs, Judgment of 30 May 1999, Ser. C, no. 52, paras. 109–12. The ACHPR does not provide for derogability as reaffirmed in principle R. 2(a) of the 2001 African Fair Trial Principles.

[159] *Wemhoff* v. *Federal Republic of Germany*, (1968) 1 EHRR 55, paras.4–17; *Suárez-Rosero* v. *Ecuador*, Merits, Judgment of 12 November 1997, Ser. C, no. 35, paras. 38–66; principle M.1(e) of the 2001 African Fair Trial Principles; HRCtee, General Comment 8: Right to liberty and security of persons (article 9), 30 June 1982, para. 3.

[160] See for an in-depth discussion, *W.* v. *Switzerland*, (1994) 17 EHRR 60, para. 43, and Dissenting Opinion of Judge Pettiti.

[161] Articles 9(4) ICCPR, 5(4) ECHR, 7(6) ACHR, principle M.5 of the 2001 African Fair Trial Principles.

[162] *Shtukaturov* v. *Russia* [2008] ECHR 223, paras. 121–35 ('applicant with mental disorder'), and *Chahal* v. *United Kingdom*, (1996) 23 EHRR 413, paras. 124–33.

[163] *A and Others* v. *United Kingdom*, (2009) 49 EHRR 29, paras. 217–24.

Custodial safeguards, in addition to preventing unlawful arrest or detention, are meant to minimise the risk of torture and ill-treatment and guarantee the rights of the defence. Incommunicado detention (also referred to as 'secret detention'), i.e. holding someone without access to the outside world, is the very antithesis of these safeguards. It violates the right to liberty and also constitutes a form of ill-treatment, if not torture, in its own right.[164] The right of access to a lawyer of one's choice is another crucial safeguard that applies from the earliest stage of proceedings.[165] For foreign nationals, access to a consular official – referred to in article 36(1) Vienna Convention on Consular Relations – has been recognised as a human right, which is particularly important given the vulnerable position of foreign nationals.[166] In practice, its effectiveness depends on the ability and willingness of consular officials to take action to protect the rights of their nationals. In addition to due process rights during arrest and detention, international human rights law also recognises a right to compensation for 'arbitrary' arrest and/or detention.[167] This right serves as vindication for the violation suffered and, ideally, acts as a deterrent for the state.

8.4.5   Preventive detention: Israeli law, power and control

Preventive detention, also referred to as administrative detention, is based on an administrative decision and is ostensibly aimed at preventing a danger to the public. It is not explicitly prohibited in international human rights law[168] but is considered problematic because it essentially constitutes detention without trial. This form of detention is therefore subject to strict requirements; it must be defined by law, necessary (to achieve the legitimate object pursued) and subject to continuous judicial review.[169]

---

[164] See above at section 8.3.5.

[165] *Öcalan* v. *Turkey*, paras. 131–7; *Bulacio* v. *Argentina*, Merits, reparations and costs, Judgment of 18 September 2003, Ser. C, no. 100, paras. 130 and 132.

[166] *LaGrand* case (*Germany* v. *United States*), Judgment, ICJ Reports 2001, 466. para. 77. See also *Avena and other Mexican nationals* (*Mexico* v. *United States of America*), Judgment, ICJ Reports 2004, 12, paras. 58–106; *The Right to Information on Consular Assistance in the Framework of the Guarantees of the Due Process of Law*; *Chaparro-Alvarez and Lapo-iniguez* v. *Ecuador*, Preliminary objections, merits, reparation and costs, Judgment of 21 November 2007, Ser. C, no. 170, para. 164; principle M. 2 (e) of the 2001 African Fair Trial Principles.

[167] Articles 9(5) ICCPR, 5(5) ECHR, principle M. 1(h) of the 2001 African Fair Trial Principles.

[168] Article 5 of the ECHR is an exception as it does not list preventive detention as one of the grounds of legitimate arrest and detention (other than in the immigration context, see article 5(1)(f) ECHR). See *Lawless* v. *Ireland (No. 3)*, (1961) I EHRR 15, paras. 10–15.

[169] HRCtee, General Comment 8, para. 4. See for a good analysis of the risk of preventive detention and the approach of the IACtHR, Concurring Opinion of Judge Sergio García Ramírez to the Judgment in the case of *Bayarri* v. *Argentina*, of 30 October 2008, Ser. C, no. 187.

In practice, preventive detention has been an integral part of states' arsenal to control and stifle opposition. It has been revived in the context of counter-terrorism operations, including in the detention regimes of Guantánamo Bay (USA) and Belmarsh prison in the UK, which have raised serious concerns about their compatibility with the right to liberty and security.[170] Indeed, it has been argued that prolonged detention without trial constitutes a form of ill-treatment in its own right.[171]

The Israeli administrative detention regime illustrates the risks inherent in this form of detention. Thousands of Palestinians from the occupied territories have been held in administrative detention by Israeli authorities over the years, particularly during the various uprisings.[172] Several pieces of military laws provide Israeli authorities with wide-ranging powers, namely the Emergency Powers (Detention) Law, the Order Regarding Security Provisions and the Incarceration of Unlawful Combatants Act.[173] Under the 2002 Incarceration of Unlawful Combatants Act,[174] the military may detain individuals suspected of having participated in 'hostile acts against the State of Israel' or being a member of a force perpetrating such acts for up to fourteen days without judicial review. It may also restrict access to a lawyer for up to seven days on security grounds. Detention may be renewed for up to six months at a time under judicial supervision as long as the person concerned is considered to constitute a risk for public security. Besides this Act, which is used to detain persons from the Gaza strip, administrative detention in the West Bank is governed by the Order Regarding Security Provisions, Military Order 1651.[175] This Order authorises the Israeli Defence Forces to detain a person for an initial ninety-six hours without judicial supervision. Detention may be ordered for up to six months, where the commander 'has reasonable cause to believe that reasons of regional security or public security require that a certain person be held in detention', a period which may be extended for a further six months. The terms 'regional security or public security' are not defined. Combined with the fact that the regular judicial review takes place

---

[170] Situation of detainees at Guantánamo Bay Report of the Chairperson of the Working Group on Arbitrary Detention, Ms. L. Zerrougui et al., UN Doc. E/CN.4/2006/120 (15 February 2006), paras. 17–29; and *A and Others* v. *United Kingdom*, paras. 162–72.

[171] This argument was rejected by the ECtHR in *A and Others* v. *United Kingdom*, paras. 126–36, on the ground that the detainees were not without prospects of release because effective remedies were available.

[172] The most recent B'Tselem statistics show that as of 29 February 2012, Israeli prison services held 503 residents of the occupied territories in administrative detention, 183 of whom were minors. See online, at www.btselem.org/administrative_detention/statistics.

[173] See Hamoked and B'Tselem, *Without Trial, Administrative Detention of Palestinians by Israel* (Hamoked and B'Tselem, 2009), 4.

[174] Law no. 5762/2002.

[175] See Order Regarding Security Provisions [Consolidated Version] (Judea and Samaria) (No. 1651), 5770–2009, articles 271–94.

in routine procedures, which may be based on classified information and conducted in the absence of the detainee, detainees are effectively hardly able to challenge the legality of detention.

Israel has justified this practice with reference to 'the provisions of international humanitarian law'.[176] However, even under IHL, such detention should be exceptional. Moreover, the regime has been criticised for its lack of due process, its use as alternative to criminal proceedings, its frequent and extensive application, including for the detention of political opponents and Palestinians more generally and its incompatibility with international standards.[177] The example demonstrates the difficulty of ensuring that adequate safeguards are in place in a system designed to maximise executive control based on security paradigms. Inherently, such detention regimes render detainees vulnerable to other violations, particularly torture. Given the legacy of abuse of systems of preventive detention worldwide, there are good reasons to minimise if not prohibit it altogether.

QUESTIONS

1 Is preventive detention a suitable response to security threats; what alternatives exist under international law?

2 What is the difference between the prohibition of 'arbitrary' arrest and detention in the ICCPR and the system provided for in the ECHR?

3 Why is the adherence to the various obligations arising from the right to liberty and security so central for the protection of multiple rights?

8.5   THE RIGHT TO A FAIR TRIAL

8.5.1   Practice

The administration of justice is at the heart of human rights protection and the rule of law. It denotes a system based on the fundamental tenets of an independent judiciary, effective access to justice and equality of arms. Conversely, its absence has facilitated and contributed to perpetuating myriad violations. Authoritarian and dictatorial states have frequently used criminal trials as an extension of state power, applied by a pliant judiciary in

---

[176] See with reference to discussion of the jurisprudence of Israeli courts, T. Stahlberg and H. Lahmann, 'A Paradigm of Prevention: Humpty Dumpty, the War on Terror and the Power of Preventive Detention in the United States, Israel and Europe', *Am. J. Comp. L.* 59(4) (2011), 1051–87, at 1066–73.

[177] See concerns expressed in Report of the Special Rapporteur on the promotion and protection of human rights and fundamental freedoms while countering terrorism – Mission to Israel, including visit to Occupied Palestinian Territory, UN Doc. A/HRC/6/17/ Add.4 (16 November 2007), paras. 22–9.

proceedings stripped of due process. This is particularly apparent in proceedings that subject civilians, often members of the opposition, to the jurisdiction of special or military courts.[178] The systemic failure to ensure the independence of the judiciary and due process is still a common feature in many countries.[179] Beyond deliberate maladministration, many systems face major structural problems that may result in a denial of justice, ranging from lack of basic infrastructure and personnel, corruption and delays to inadequate guarantees of defence rights, to name just some recurring problems. The lack of access to justice in particular is a fundamental problem. Systemic inequalities frequently impact adversely on the ability of members of particular groups, such as foreign nationals, minorities, women and the poorer strata of society more generally, to access justice, creating a vicious cycle that enhances their vulnerability to other human rights violations.[180]

8.5.2 Sources

The right to a fair trial is recognised in a series of international and regional instruments.[181] Most treaties provide that the right applies in proceedings relating to criminal charges and civil rights and obligations, with article 8 ACHR going further by rendering it applicable to all proceedings. Notwithstanding some variations, the core of the right to a fair trial is guaranteed in all of these instruments. This treaty-based recognition is complemented by a number of international and regional standards.[182] The right to a fair trial also forms part of international humanitarian law[183] and its violation may constitute a war crime.[184] These sources are testimony to the importance of the right to a fair trial, whose essential components are widely seen to represent customary international law.[185]

---

[178] See in particular F. Andreu-Guzmán, *Military Jurisdiction and International Law: Military Courts and Gross Human Rights Violations* (Geneva: International Commission of Jurists, 2004).

[179] See regular reports of the Special Rapporteur on the independence of judges and lawyers, Summary of information, including individual cases, transmitted to Governments and replies received, for example, UN Doc. A/HRC/17/30/Add.1 (19 May 2011).

[180] See for example OHCHR Nepal, *Opening the Door to Equality: Access to Justice for Dalits in Nepal* (Kathmandu: OHCHR, 2011).

[181] Articles 10 UDHR, 14 ICCPR, 40(2)(iii) CRC, 18 ICRMW, 11(3) CPED, 6 ECHR, 8 and 25 ACHR and 7 ACHPR. See also article 13 CRPD.

[182] See in particular Basic Principles on the Independence of the Judiciary, adopted by the Seventh UN Congress on the Prevention of Crime and the Treatment of Offenders (UNCPCTO) (Milan, 26 August to 6 September 1985), and endorsed by UNGA resolutions 40/32 (29 November 1985) and 40/146 (13 December 1985); Basic Principles on the Role of Lawyers and Guidelines on the Role of Prosecutors, both adopted by the Eighth UNCPCTO (Havana, 27 August to 7 September 1990); 2001 African Fair Trial Principles.

[183] See ICRC, CIHL, Database, rule 100.   [184] See article 8(2)(a)(vi) ICC Rome Statute.

[185] See references in ICRC, CIHL, Database, rule 100.

Essential judicial guarantees are not subject to derogations. Where permitted, derogations to the right to a fair trial during times of emergency must be strictly necessary.[186] As emphasised by the HRCtee, '[t]he guarantees of fair trial may never be made subject to measures of derogation that would circumvent the protection of non-derogable rights',[187] particularly in relation to article 6 ICCPR (trials resulting in the death penalty) and article 7 ICCPR (evidence extracted under torture admitted at trial).

8.5.3   Main features of the right to a fair trial

General principles

The independence and impartiality of the judiciary is an absolute guarantee and a crucial component of the right to a fair trial, referring both to the position of judges (appointment; security of tenure; safeguards against interferences and appearance of independence)[188] and the institutional independence of the judiciary from the executive and legislature.[189] Tribunals must also be impartial, that is free from undue bias (fair and seen to be fair).[190] A judicial system has to be accessible to all whose rights are affected so that it can fulfil its elementary function, i.e. the dispensation of justice. The right of access to justice has been recognised as an integral part of the right to a fair trial by the HRCtee and in the Inter-American system through the combination of articles 8 and 25 of the ACHR.[191] The ECtHR has read it into the right to a fair trial in the seminal case of *Golder* v. *UK*.[192] Golder, a prisoner, was refused permission by the UK Home Secretary to write to his lawyer in order to bring a libel case against a prison officer. The majority of the Court found that the right to a fair trial applied to both court proceedings and the opportunity to bring a case, which has become an integral part of the Court's subsequent jurisprudence on article 6 ECHR. However, it is important

---

[186] See in particular Judicial Guarantees in States of Emergency.

[187] HRCtee, General Comment 32: Article 14: Right to equality before courts and tribunals and to a fair trial, UN Doc. CCPR/C/GC/32 (23 August 2007), para. 6.

[188] S. Trechsel, *Human Rights in Criminal Proceedings* (Oxford University Press, 2005), 53-61, with further references.

[189] See HRCtee, General Comment 32, para. 19, and Report of the Special Rapporteur on the independence of judges and lawyers, UN Doc. A/HRC/11/41 (24 March 2009), paras. 14–84 and 95–104.

[190] Trechsel, note 188, 61–79.

[191] HRCtee, General Comment 32, paras. 9-11; Judicial Guarantees in States of Emergency; A. A. Cançado Trindade, *The Access of Individuals to International Justice* (Oxford University Press, 2011), 63–75; 2001 African Fair Trial Principles C (b)(i) and K; F. Francioni (ed.), *Access to Justice as a Human Right* (Oxford University Press, 2007); Report of the Special Rapporteur on the independence of judges and lawyers, UN Doc. A/HRC/8/4 (13 May 2008), paras. 15–54.

[192] *Golder* v. *United Kingdom*, (1975) 1 EHRR 524.

to recall that a state is not required to create a substantive right where none exists.[193] Where such a right is in principle available, restrictions must have a legitimate aim and be proportionate.[194]

'Fairness' is the hallmark of justice. This central component of proceedings is reflected in the right to equality before courts and tribunals, a far-reaching right that imposes a positive obligation on states to provide equal access to courts and procedural rights in their legal systems. Equality of arms is a fundamental principle according to which the parties to proceedings must have equal procedural rights (unless distinctions can be objectively justified) and be able to present their case – in principle in a public hearing – without being at a substantive disadvantage *vis-à-vis* the other party or parties.[195] It differs from non-discrimination, which concerns the administration of justice rather than the adversarial relationship of the parties.[196] However, discrimination may also violate equality of arms, for example where an indignant foreign national is not provided with legal aid or language assistance to argue his or her case.[197]

Criminal proceedings

Criminal proceedings are of a particularly sensitive nature because of what is at stake for the parties, particularly the defendant. Several principles and specific rights apply to criminal proceedings only. Their main purpose is to ensure equality of arms and protect defendants against the potential abuse of state power in the administration of criminal justice. The principle of legality governing criminal proceedings includes in particular the prohibition of retroactive substantive laws that flows from the maxim *nulla poena sine lege* (no punishment without a crime). It is based on the notion that individuals should know what conduct is liable to punishment at any given time so as to have the choice of acting in compliance with the law or face punishment.[198] Importantly, the principle does not apply to crimes recognised in international law, thus enabling national systems to disregard objections to the retroactive prosecution of international crimes,[199] such as in the case of

---

[193] *Al-Adsani* v. *United Kingdom*, paras. 46–7.

[194] See for examples, L. Doswald-Beck, *Human Rights in Times of Conflict and Terrorism* (Oxford University Press, 2011), 319–30.

[195] HRCtee, General Comment 32, para. 13.

[196] See on the relationship between the principle of equality and the prohibition of discrimination, Trechsel, above note 188, 94–5.

[197] HRCtee, General Comment 32, para. 13.

[198] See articles 15 ICCPR, 7 ECHR, 9 ACHR and 7(2) ACHPR.

[199] Article 15(2) ICCPR. See in this respect particularly *Streletz, Kessler and Krenz* v. *Germany*, (2001) 33 EHRR 751 GC. See for discussion of these and further cases, Doswald-Beck, above note 194, 300–17.

Kononov v. *Latvia*.[200] The presumption of innocence is another important principle which is reflected in rules on the right to remain silent and the burden of proof being on the state. It is meant to protect against unjust convictions and safeguard the reputation of persons accused of having committed crimes.[201] The principle of *ne bis in idem* or double jeopardy (no one should be prosecuted twice for the same crime) protects the individual from repeated prosecutions, thereby compelling the authorities to prepare their case carefully, and promotes legal certainty.[202]

The right of the defence in criminal proceedings comprises both equality of arms and a set of specific rights for the defendant.[203] This includes the right of the defendant to be present at trial (as international human rights law is generally hostile to trials *in absentia*),[204] to be defended by a lawyer of his or her choice[205] and to free legal aid 'when the interests of justice so require'.[206] The rights of the defence can conflict with other principles of the administration of justice, such as protecting the anonymity of witnesses. This presents a challenge as a successful prosecution often depends on evidence given by informants, persons at risk of reprisals and vulnerable witnesses such as children or victims of sexual violence. Where the defence is not able to cross-examine a witness at trial the judicial authorities must adopt procedures that 'sufficiently counterbalance ... the handicaps under which the defence labour[s]', such as arrangements made to question witnesses in special hearings where the defence counsel is present.[207] Finally, states have to provide for compensation in cases of miscarriages of justice, which serves as an important right of those who have been wronged and as deterrent against the abuse of the criminal justice system.[208]

---

[200] See section 6.2.5.

[201] HRCtee, General Comment 32, para. 30. See in particular *John Murray* v. *UK*, (1996) 22 EHRR 29, para. 54, where the ECtHR held that the right to remain silent was not violated where an accused was found at the scene of a crime and, at his later trial, a court drew inferences from his lack of explanation and refusal to provide evidence.

[202] HRCtee, General Comment 32, paras. 54–7.

[203] See articles 14(3) ICCPR; 6(3) ECHR; 8(2) ACHR, 67 ICC Rome Statute. See General Comment 32, paras. 31–41. See for victim's right and fair trial, Trechsel, above note 188, 36–41.

[204] Article 14(3)(d) ICCPR.

[205] Articles 14(3)(d) ICCPR; 6(3)(c) ECHR; 8(2)(d) ACHR; 7(1)(c) ACHPR.

[206] Articles 14(3)(d) ICCPR; 6(3)(c) ECHR; 8(2)(e) ACHR.

[207] *Doorson* v. *the Netherlands*, (1996) 22 EHRR 330, para. 72; *Van Mechelen and Others* v. *Netherlands*, (1997) 25 EHRR 647, para. 54.

[208] Articles 9(5) ICCPR, 3 Protocol no.7 to ECHR and 10 ACHR. See also HRCtee, General Comment 32, paras. 52–3.

CASE STUDY 8.2
The problem with military and special courts

Military justice is governed by principles of military discipline and expeditiousness. It is generally accepted that military personnel may be subject to the jurisdiction of military courts, in relation to service-related offences. However, there have been recurring concerns over subjecting civilians to the jurisdiction of military courts, primarily because the presence of members of the forces on the bench does not guarantee independence.[1] Politically, military courts, also known as courts-martial, have been repeatedly (ab)used to try rebels and political opposition members without the benefit of a fair trial (and conversely of shielding military personnel from full accountability for human rights violations).[2] One such example is *Akwanga* v. *Cameroon*, where Mr Akwanga, a political opponent, had been targeted, tortured and unjustly convicted to twenty years' imprisonment by a military court.[3] In a highly critical individual opinion in that case, the HRCtee member Fabián Omar Salvioli reiterated his position that the Committee's line of reasoning, which still permits military courts to have jurisdiction over civilians in exceptional cases, is out of step with the development of international human rights law. Salvioli argues that the Committee fails to make the clear distinction between military and civilian trials needed in light of the negative experiences throughout history. In his opinion, only the absolute prohibition of civilians being tried by military courts would be compatible with the right to a fair trial guaranteed in article 14.[4]

The practice of security courts in Egypt illustrates how the use of emergency legislation and extraordinary measures becomes routine and facilitates a range of violations.[5] Three men were sentenced to death by the Supreme State Emergency Security Court in November 2006 for their alleged participation in a series of attacks on Egyptian tourist resorts in 2004 and 2005. The men were subjected to torture while in detention and were only given access to legal presentation at the trial stage. The Court convicted them relying on confessions extracted under torture; the verdict was subject to ratification by the President and could not be appealed. The African Commission on Human and Peoples' Rights found Egypt to be in breach of the prohibition of torture, the right to a fair trial and the independence of the judiciary (articles 5, 7 (1)(a),(d) and

---

[1] Andreu-Guzmán, above note 178.

[2] See Opinion of Fabián Omar Salvioli in *Akwanga* v. *Cameroon*, UN Doc. CCPR/C/101/D/1813/2008 (22 March 2011), para. 7.

[3] Ibid., para. 2.6.

[4] Ibid., Individual Opinion of Committee Member Mr Fabián Omar Salvioli.

[5] *Egyptian Initiative for Personal Rights and Interights* v. *Arab Republic of Egypt*, 334/06 (2011).

26 ACHPR), emphasising in particular that '[t]ribunals that do not use the duly established procedures of the legal process shall not be created to displace the jurisdiction belonging to the ordinary courts or judicial tribunals'.[6]

POINT TO CONSIDER

- Is jurisprudence too accommodating when considering that proceedings seemingly antithetical to the right to a fair trial, such as the trial of civilians before military courts, may be justifiable in certain circumstances?

[6] Ibid., para. 204.

8.6   ENFORCED DISAPPEARANCE AS MULTIPLE HUMAN RIGHTS VIOLATION

Enforced disappearance is a method that has been used by states to establish complete control over a person by rendering him or her invisible. It has often been used systematically, mostly through covert plain-clothes operations, as a means to facilitate the torture and/or killing of its targets. By its nature it constitutes a form of state terror, aimed at spreading uncertainty and fear of an all-powerful state.[209] The practice greatly enhances the vulnerability of anyone subjected to it and frequently has profound psychological – and, depending on the circumstances, physical – consequences, in addition to any other violations suffered, particularly torture. It also leads to anxiety and uncertainty for relatives and friends of the disappeared who may therefore be victims of ill-treatment in their own right.[210]

The practice of enforced disappearances was a modus of political murder used by regimes such as Nazi Germany and later became a particularly notorious practice of Latin American dictatorships to combat (and kill) opponents, including members of ethnic communities.[211] In Argentina, for example, many victims were drugged and then thrown naked from an aircraft or helicopter into the sea, where they would drown. The UN Working Group on Enforced Disappearances had, in 2010, received 53,778 complaints

[209] See for example, *Goiburú et al.* v. *Paraguay*, Merits, reparations and costs, Judgment of 22 September 2006, Ser. C, no. 153, para. 65, which refers to a decision by the National Court of Spain that characterised 'Operation Condor' as 'a sort of "international terror mechanism"'.

[210] M. Blaauw and V. Lähteenmäki, '"Denial and silence" or "acknowledgement and disclosure"', *IRRC* 84(848) (2002), 767–82.

[211] See in particular the findings of truth commissions, for example, in Argentina, Bolivia, Chile, Guatemala and Uruguay.

of enforced disappearances since 1980.[212] This number, while indicating the prevalence of the practice, does not reflect its true extent. By its very nature it is difficult to verify how many persons have been forcibly disappeared and estimates of the number of persons disappeared in some countries alone, such as Iraq, are significantly higher than the overall number of complaints received by the Working Group.[213] The practice has, over the last thirty years, not been confined to a few countries or a particular region, as the UN Working Group has received more than one hundred complaints each in respect of over twenty countries.[214] Iraq (16,548) and Sri Lanka (12,460) stand out as having the highest number of complaints submitted.[215]

Legal developments relating to enforced disappearance owe a lot to the concerted efforts by relatives of the disappeared, lawyers and human rights defenders, particularly in Latin America, who have persistently raised the issue. This has spawned multiple responses both at the domestic level, particularly following political transitions and at the regional human rights level. The IACHR and IACtHR were seized with a number of cases, with the Court's judgment in the *Velásquez Rodríguez* setting a leading precedent. The Court noted that 'the forced disappearance of human beings is a multiple and continuous violation of many rights under the Convention that the States Parties are obliged to respect and guarantee',[216] which entails a positive obligation to prevent, and effectively respond to allegations of such violations.[217]

In 1994 the Inter-American Convention on Forced Disappearance of Persons was adopted. At the international level, concerns over the practice resulted in the 1992 Declaration on the Protection of All Persons from

---

[212] Report of the Working Group on Enforced or Involuntary Disappearances, UN Doc. A/HRC/19/58/Rev.1 (2 March 2012), para. 7.

[213] The UN Working Group on Enforced or Involuntary Disappearances reported that there were 16,410 outstanding cases in Iraq as of November 2011 (Working Group, ibid., para. 265). Other estimates put the number of disappeared between 250,000 and 1 million (International Commission on Missing Persons, *Iraq*, online, at, www.ic-mp.org/icmp-worldwide/middle-east/iraq).

[214] Working Group, above note 212, Annex V. Over a hundred cases were transmitted between 1980 and 2011 from Algeria, Argentina, Chile, China, Colombia, Republic of Congo, El Salvador, Ethiopia, Guatemala, Honduras, India, Indonesia, Iran, Iraq, Lebanon, Mexico, Morocco, Nepal, Nicaragua, Pakistan, Peru, Philippines, Russia, Sri Lanka, Sudan, Timor-Leste, Turkey and Yemen.

[215] Ibid., Annex IV.

[216] *Velásquez Rodríguez* v. *Honduras*, para. 155. On enforced disappearance as a continuous crime, see also Working Group on Enforced or Involuntary Disappearances, General Comment on Enforced Disappearance as a Continuous Crime, UN Doc. A/HRC/16/48 (26 January 2011), 10–12; General Comment on the Right to the Truth in Relation to Enforced Disappearances, ibid., 12–17.

[217] *Velásquez Rodríguez* v. *Honduras*, paras. 166, 176–7; *Juan Humberto Sánchez* v. *Honduras*, Merits, Judgment of 7 June 2003, Ser. C, no. 99, para. 184; *Quinteros et al.* v. *Uruguay*, Communication no. 107/1981 (21 July 1983), para. 15; *Kurt* v. *Turkey*, (1999) 27 EHRR 373, para. 124.

Enforced Disappearance[218] but were at the time not translated into any binding international treaty. Rather, it was left to human rights treaty bodies and regional courts to grapple with a number of complex legal questions raised by the multiple violations characteristic of enforced disappearance. It was generally accepted that enforced disappearance constitutes a violation of the right to liberty and security of the person (where the link to the state could be made), which is the thrust of the legal definition of enforced disappearance (see below).[219] It was also recognised that victims have a right to a remedy and states a corresponding duty to investigate, prosecute and punish the perpetrators.[220] However, it was less clear what other rights enforced disappearances violated in a given case. Do they constitute torture and ill-treatment in their own right (i.e. even in the absence of evidence that the disappeared person was ill treated)?[221] Where a person remains disappeared, what are the factors that allow a finding of a violation of the right to life?[222] Under what circumstances do enforced disappearances constitute a violation of the rights of others, particularly the right of family members not to be subjected to inhuman treatment?[223] What are the rights of victims in relation

[218] UNGA resolution 47/133 (18 December 1992).

[219] *Velásquez Rodríguez* v. *Honduras*, paras. 155 and 187; *Bleier Lewenhoff* v. *Uruguay*, Communication no. 30/1978 (29 March 1982), para. 14; *Kurt* v. *Turkey*, paras. 123–4; *Mouvement Burkinabé des Droits de l'Homme et des Peuples* v. *Burkina Faso*, 204/97 (2001), para. 44.

[220] *Bautista de Arellana* v. *Colombia*, UN Doc. CCPR/C/55/D/563/1993 (27 October 1995), para. 8.6; *Aboussedra* v. *Libyan Arab Jamahiriya*, UN Doc. CCPR/C/100/D/1751/2008 (25 October 2010), para. 9; *Aouabdia* v. *Algeria*, UN Doc. CCPR/C/101/D/1780/2008 (22 March 2011), para. 9; *Varnava* v. *Turkey*, [2009] ECHR 1313, para. 149; *Mouvement Burkinabé des Droits de l'Homme et des Peuples* v. *Burkina Faso*, para. 42; *Goiburú et al.* v. *Paraguay*, para. 84.

[221] *Kurt* v. *Turkey*, para. 116 (needed specific evidence); *Çakıcı* v. *Turkey*, [1999] ECHR 43, para. 92 (testimony given by witness who shared a room with the victim was sufficient to prove torture); *Velásquez Rodríguez* v. *Honduras*, para. 187 (mere subjection of an individual to prolonged isolation and deprivation of communication is in itself cruel and inhuman treatment); *Aouabdia* v. *Algeria*, paras. 7.4–7.5 (incommunicado detention amounted to a violation of article 7 ICCPR); *Article 19* v. *Eritrea*, 275/03 (2007), para. 102; *Amnesty International, Comité Loosli Bachelard, Lawyers' Committee for Human Rights, Association of Members of the Episcopal Conference of East Africa* v. *Sudan*, 48/90-50/91-52/91-89/93 (2000), para. 54 (incommunicado detention amounted to a violation of article 5 ACHPR).

[222] *Bámaca-Velásquez* v. *Guatemala*, Merits, Judgment of 25 November 2000, Series C no. 70, paras. 130 and 173 (presumption of execution after passage of eight years without any news given the state practice of forced disappearances and extrajudicial killings); *Mojica* v. *Dominican Republic*, UN Doc. CCPR/C/51/D/449/1991 (15 July 1994), para. 5.6 (since state party did not deny that Rafael Mojica had disappeared and that his disappearance had been caused by state agents, the right to life had not been effectively protected); *Baysayeva* v. *Russia*, (2007) 48 EHRR 33, paras. 115–20 (detention by unidentified servicemen without any subsequent acknowledgement can be regarded as life-threatening).

[223] *Varnava* v. *Turkey*, [2009] ECHR 1313, para. 200 (depends on circumstances, particularly nature of the 'failure by the authorities to respond to the quest for information by the

to the right to truth (which was largely developed in the context of enforced disappearances)?[224] Treaty bodies and courts developed their own, and at times diverging jurisprudence, with the IACtHR taking a broader and the ECtHR a more restrictive approach to recognising violations of rights other than the right to liberty and security. In addition, the enforced disappearance of persons has been explicitly recognised as a crime against humanity.[225]

The adoption of the international Convention on Enforced Disappearance in 2006 was seen as an important addition to the international legal framework and a step towards enhanced protection. Article 2 CPED reflects what is now commonly considered to constitute 'enforced disappearance', namely

> the arrest, detention, abduction or any other form of deprivation of liberty by agents of the State or by persons or groups of persons acting with the authorization, support or acquiescence of the State, followed by a refusal to acknowledge the deprivation of liberty or by concealment of the fate or whereabouts of the disappeared person, which place such a person outside the protection of the law.

The Convention is modelled in large part after CAT, requiring states to make enforced disappearance a crime effectively subject to universal jurisdiction that they are duty bound to investigate, prosecute and punish as well as provide reparation for.[226] Unsurprisingly, another strong emphasis is on effective safeguards, which are stipulated in some detail and the non-observance of which should be subject to sanctions.[227] Notably, the Convention reflects the jurisprudence of treaty bodies and regional courts according to which relatives who suffered harm are to be considered victims and have the right to truth and reparation.[228] Nevertheless, questions such as whether enforced disappearance constitutes a violation of the prohibition of torture and the right to life would still need to be considered separately. The Convention entered into force on 23 December 2010, having mainly been ratified or acceded to by Latin American and European states but also some African states and, significantly, Iraq. It is premature to assess the Convention's impact but the existence of a UN treaty regime on enforced disappearance constitutes an important development.

relatives'); *Valle Jaramillo et al.* v. *Colombia*, Merits, reparations and costs, Judgment of 27 November 2008, Ser. C, no. 192, para. 119 (presumption that close family members suffered). See also *Amnesty International and Others* v. *Sudan*, para. 54; *Sharma* v. *Nepal*, UN Doc. CCPR/C/94/D/1469/2006 (28 October 2008), para. 7.9; *Aouabdia* v. *Algeria*, para. 7.6 (finding that the suffering caused to the relative as by the enforced disappearance constituted a violation of article 5 ACHPR and article 7 ICCPR respectively).

224   *Bámaca-Velásquez* v. *Guatemala*, para. 201; Working Group, General Comment on the Right to the Truth in Relation to Enforced Disappearances, above note 216, 12–17.

225   Article 7(1)(i) ICC Rome Statute.

226   Articles 3 (duty to investigate), 6 (duty to prosecute), 7 (duty to punish), and 24 (right to reparation) CPED.

227   Ibid., articles 17 and 18 (safeguards); 22 (sanctions).

228   Ibid., article 24.

INTERVIEW 8.2

Inquiries into enforced disappearances in Sri Lanka

(M. C. Iqbal)

Sri Lanka is one of the countries with the highest number of recorded disappearances in the world, committed both in campaigns against uprisings in the south of the country (1971 and 1987–90) and in the context of the conflict in the north-east of the country (which lasted, with some interruptions, from 1983 to 2009). In 1995, the then President Chandrika Bandaranayke established three zonal commissions to inquire into disappearances since 1988, and another all-island commission was appointed in 1998. The commissions received around 30,000 complaints (including multiple complaints). In addition to those, approximately 16,000 complaints which did not come within the mandates of these commissions had been received and were eventually passed on to the National Human Rights Commission of Sri Lanka for further action. The commissions were able to meticulously document the practice of enforced disappearances and recommended prosecution of the perpetrators and reparation for the victims. However, more than a decade later, with the exception of a few isolated prosecutions and limited amounts of compensation paid to victims, these recommendations have not been implemented. The following is an interview with M. C. Iqbal, former Secretary of two zonal commissions of inquiry and Secretary of the Committee of Inquiry into Disappearances of the Human Rights Commission of Sri Lanka, who has published several articles on the subject.[1]

What were some of the most striking findings of the Commissions of Inquiry about the nature and extent of violations?

Many innocent young men who happened to be either children of those who were not supporters of the government of the time, or young men who had been actively involved in criticising the government, had been taken away on suspicion that they were insurgents and had disappeared. A graphical analysis of the dates and places revealed that the peaks of disappearances had been a few days before and after the presidential and parliamentary elections that took place in 1989 and the 1990s, which is indicative of their political nature.

There was evidence that most persons abducted, arrested or detained had been tortured in places specially maintained for this purpose in order to extract information before they were caused to be disappeared. At a particular period, bodies or parts of the bodies of persons who had been killed had been allowed to remain on roadsides and culverts for long

---

[1] See in particular at http://groundviews.org.

periods, purportedly to instil fear among the people who were against the then government. There had been evidence that interested persons had provided the police and security forces lists with names of persons who had been taken away after calling for them by name at the houses of the respective persons. In some instances this had resulted in persons who had the same name as the person they had been looking for being taken away and disappearing.

You have interviewed victims and studied thousands of files. Can you describe a case that has left a particularly lasting impression?

A young man who had been a victim of an abduction and had been released after rehabilitation spoke about a torture chamber that existed then at the St Sylvester's College, Kandy. He said that he was detained in this chamber and was tortured. From time to time detainees were taken away in the night, supposedly to be transferred to other detention centres. He was among those taken away on a particular date to be transferred to another centre. A few of them were taken with their hands tied in a truck through a dark stretch of road with two other vehicles following. From time to time one by one a military officer would push a detainee down from the moving vehicle and ask him to run. While he was running someone from the second vehicle would shoot down the detainee. He said an officer from the third vehicle would stop near the fallen detainee, pour petrol on his face and set fire to it. When it was his turn to be pushed down, someone from the third vehicle shouted, 'enough for the day, petrol is over'. Thereafter he was taken back to the camp where the other detainees who heard what happened nicknamed him the *chance karaya* (the lucky one). Sometime later he was sent along with a few others for rehabilitation and released after a few years.

By its very nature enforced disappearances are secretive and tend not to be recorded. How were the commissions able to verify that persons had disappeared?

The commissions used a range of steps such as checking lists of detainees obtained from all detention centres, employment records, corroborative evidence, such as a copy of a complaint to the ICRC, police or other persons in authority and observing the demeanour of complainants. It also interviewed witnesses, including those who had been released in some way or had escaped. The commissions also had to be creative, in particular by looking for supplementary evidence of being in police custody subsequent to removal or abduction. For example, there were discrepancies between the information books (IB) in the police stations which did not mention persons taken in to be disappeared and the diet registers for food provided, which did. Similarly, in some cases there were no official records of the officer-in-charge or any other police officer having travelled to the area from which the disappearance had taken place. The commission then found that the driver of the vehicle used by the police had entries in his running chart, which demonstrated he had travelled to that particular place with other police officers on the relevant dates.

The Commissions made a number of specific recommendations which have by and large not been implemented. Why did successive governments not act on the recommendations?

The interim reports of the commissions identified several perpetrators. The then president issued a directive to the army commander and the Inspector General of Police asking them to take prompt action against the perpetrators identified and report within one month of the steps that had been taken. This directive was the headline in some of the newspapers of the day. A couple of days later another headline appeared in the newspapers stating that no such order had been issued. Discrete inquiries revealed that the then Deputy Minister of Defence who was in the midst of a military operation against the Liberation Tigers of Tamil Eelam (LTTE) had asked the President whether she wanted him to fight the terrorists now or instead start a fight against the security forces and the police based on the findings of the Commissions. That was the end of that directive.

The cases in which perpetrators had been identified were handed over by the President to the Missing Persons Unit of the Attorney-General's Department for them to initiate prosecutions. The Attorney-General's Department needed further evidence to be recorded by the Criminal Investigation Department (CID). That was because the inquiries by the commissions were confined only to the point where 'credible material indicative of the perpetrator' is elicited. It was not for the commissions to look for 'evidence beyond reasonable doubt'. But the Attorney-General needed that evidence to initiate legal action. The CID's Disappearances Investigation Unit dealt with these cases. The brotherly feeling among the members of the Disappearances Investigation Unit who were themselves police officers led to these cases being handled at a snail's pace, if at all, and often with half a mind. Consequently most of the cases, which had been filed very much later, eventually failed, partly because of the way in which the Unit and the Missing Persons Unit handled these cases and partly because by the time the cases came for trial it was almost twenty years after the incident and many material witnesses were no more or not with their memory in a good state.

Have you faced any repercussions for speaking out publicly on the need to act on the recommendations?

Yes. I had to face consequences for speaking out about them at different levels. I was a lecturer on human rights at the Institute of Human Rights in

Sri Lanka where many police and military officers were following a course to obtain their diploma in human rights which was a must then, for their promotions. One of the topics I had to lecture on was the manner in which disappearances of persons took place in Sri Lanka and how the rights of individuals had been violated in the process. At discussion stages many of the students from the police and the security forces had argued with me on the human rights issues concerned. Subsequently, a petition had been sent to the Institute asking them not to allow me to lecture as my lectures were derogatory about the conduct of the security forces and the police in the past. The Institute ignored this petition and I was asked to continue to lecture for several years, much to the chagrin of my students from the forces.

The organisations of parents and guardians of the disappeared used to invite me for their annual meetings. Some of its members continued to ask me from time to time why no action was being taken against the perpetrators whom they had identified and referred to while giving evidence. I had to appease them by reassuring them that action would be taken in due course. As a follow up to this, wherever possible I had been putting pressure on the authorities through my writings and other disclosures reminding the authorities on the need to deal with the perpetrators identified by the commissions. Perhaps, it was some of them who repeatedly threatened me over the telephone that if I did not stop working for the international organisation for which I was working while I was in Sri Lanka during 2007, that I would be killed. I left the country thereafter.

What are the consequences of the failure to act for the victims and society at large?

The commissions on disappearances conducted their inquiries and investigations in all earnest and the people in general and the complainants in particular were anxiously waiting to see identified perpetrators punished and abducted or disappeared persons to be found. The failure of successive governments to diligently implement most of the recommendations of the commissions led to the people losing faith in such institutions and the perpetrators becoming emboldened. Eventually it was found the successive governments continued to use abductions and disappearances of persons as a convenient method of dealing with dissent or with those who became a thorn in their sides. One could say without hesitation that the non-implementation of the recommendations of the commission on specific provisions in the terms of reference of these commissions, viz. to deal with perpetrators according to the law, to consider the measures recommended to prevent such incidents in the future, and to make appropriate changes to the existing laws which facilitated abductions and disappearances, eventually led to the proliferation of impunity and the breakdown of law and order in the country.

QUESTIONS

- Has the adoption of CPED closed an important normative gap in international human rights law?
- What is the broader relevance for international human rights law of the rights and duties identified in the jurisprudence on enforced disappearance?
- What lessons does the experience of Sri Lanka's commissions of inquiry hold for the effective protection of rights?

8.7 QUALIFIED RIGHTS, WITH A PARTICULAR FOCUS ON FREEDOM OF EXPRESSION

8.7.1 Practice

The exercise of freedom of expression, assembly and association serves as a critical measure of a pluralistic and tolerant society and as a key to participatory rights in its political life. Taken together with the freedom of thought, conscience and religion as well as the right to privacy, i.e. rights that largely protect the space of an individual against unwarranted interference, they constitute core civil and political rights. However, with the exception of the internal dimension of freedom of thought, conscience and religion, these rights are not absolute. The degree to which, and the grounds upon which they may be restricted, are therefore frequently the subject of intense debates. There can be marked 'cultural' differences, particularly in respect of freedom of expression. Some countries favour an almost unlimited liberty, such as the USA, whereas others ban speech seen as offensive or glorifying totalitarian regimes, such as Nazi Germany, or as unacceptable attacks on religion. The curtailment of these rights is often the hallmark of repression and defining feature of totalitarian regimes and authoritarian states. However, even some nominally democratic states have a poor record of protecting these fundamental freedoms. Political and community activists, human rights defenders and journalists are particularly vulnerable to intimidation, harassment, ill-treatment and murder. Dozens of journalists and media workers are killed every year; in many cases the authorities are either seemingly implicated or palpably fail to protect those at risk. The murder of Anna Politkovskaya in

Russia[229] and of Lasantha Wickrematunge, who wrote an editorial predicting his murder shortly before he was shot dead in Sri Lanka,[230] are two particularly chilling examples of attacks on investigative journalists that form part of broader attempts to hide the truth, stifle dissent and silence critical voices. The importance of critical voices became strikingly clear during the uprisings in the Arab world where the exposure, debate and sharing of information by bloggers and others provided the impetus for the exercise of the freedom of expression and assembly in the form of mass demonstrations across the region.[231]

8.7.2   Sources

Freedom of expression, association and assembly are recognised in the ICCPR and all regional human rights treaties, as well as in ILO treaties in the case of freedom of association.[232] Freedom of expression has a broad scope of application encompassing political and artistic expression, the media as well as commercial advertising.[233] It also includes the right of access to information, which is particularly important in relation to personal data and information. Whereas the ECtHR has interpreted article 10 ECHR to protect against state interference in receiving information, the IACtHR has interpreted it more broadly as a right of substantive access to information.[234]

The main differences between the relevant treaty provisions are the grounds on which the rights can be restricted. These grounds include protecting the rights or reputation of others, national security, public order, or public health or morals. Article 10 ECHR goes further by recognising 'preventing the disclosure of information received in confidence' and 'maintaining the authority and impartiality of the judiciary' as legitimate grounds. These grounds appear to give states considerable leeway, particularly in relation to such vague notions as national security or public morals. However, as is clear from the jurisprudence of human rights treaty bodies, restricting freedom of

---

[229] See 'In praise of … Anna Politkovskaya', *The Guardian* (9 October 2006), online, at www.guardian.co.uk/commentisfree/2006/oct/09/russia.media?INTCMP=SRCH.

[230] L. Wickrematunge, 'I Hope my Murder will be Seen not as a Defeat of Freedom but an Inspiration', *The Guardian* (13 January 2009), online, at www.guardian.co.uk/commentisfree/2009/jan/13/wickrematunga-final-editorial-final-editorial.

[231] See Al Jazeera, 'Blogging on the Nile: We Look at the Role of Social Media in Egypt and at the Bloggers who Sowed the Seeds of a Multi-media Uprising', online, at www.aljazeera.com/programmes/witness/2011/02/20112181938841767.html.

[232] Articles 19, 21, 22 ICCPR; 10, 11 ECHR; 13, 15, 16 ACHR; 9–11 ACHPR; ILO Conventions 87 (1948) (Freedom of Association and Protection of the Right to Organise) and 98 (1949) (Right to Organise and Collective Bargaining).

[233] HRCtee, General Comment 34: Article 19: Freedoms of opinion and expression, UN Doc. CCPR/C/GC/34 (21 July 2011), paras. 11–12.

[234] *Claudio-Reyes et al.* v. *Chile*, Merits, reparations and costs, Judgment of 19 September 2006, Ser. C, no. 151, paras. 61–103.

expression on any of these grounds can only be justified if it is prescribed by law, necessary and proportionate in the circumstances and providing it does not impair the essence of the right.[235] Courts such as the ECtHR have provided states with a margin of appreciation to assess the proportionality of restrictions, particularly in the sphere of public morals on the ground that they are in a better position to judge what is in the public interest.[236] While acknowledging local and national differences such a margin carries the risk of privileging majoritarian or state-centric interpretations of rights. It is also for this reason that other bodies, such as the HRCtee, recently affirmed that it does not assess the scope of freedom of expression 'by reference to a "margin of appreciation".[237]

While freedom of expression, assembly and association are not explicitly non-derogable, the HRCtee suggested that the grounds provided to restrict these freedoms already vest states with sufficient powers during emergencies.[238] This means that emergency situations can be considered when assessing the proportionality of measures to restrict rights, such as the freedom of assembly on national security grounds, but may not have to be invoked to derogate from the right.[239]

8.7.3   Freedom of religion v. freedom of expression

Salman Rushdie's *Satanic Verses* and the Jyllands-Posten Danish cartoons of Prophet Mohammed are two instances in which the exercise of freedom of expression met with protests and violent responses on the ground that they were insulting to religion. While this clash has been particularly pronounced in relation to Islam, it is by no means confined to this faith. Indeed, it raises fundamental questions about the relationship between freedom of expression and freedom of religion, including the protection of individuals and minorities against discrimination and attacks on religion. Attempts made by the Organisation of the Islamic Conference in the then Human Rights Commission and later in the HRC to prohibit the 'defamation of religions'[240] have

---

[235] HRCtee, General Comment 34, paras. 21–36, and Doswald-Beck, above note 194, 414–43.

[236] See section 6.2.5.

[237] HRCtee, General Comment 34, para. 36. However, see *Hertzberg et al.* v. *Finland*, Communication no. R. 14/61 (2 April 1982), where the Committee appears to grant national authorities a 'margin of discretion'.

[238] HRCtee, General Comment 29, paras. 5–6.

[239] See in the Inter-American system, *Zambrano-Vélez* v. *Ecuador*, Merits, reparations and costs, Judgment of 4 July 2007, Ser. C, no. 166, paras. 51–2.

[240] Compare for a recent shift in emphasis, 'Combating defamation of religions', UN Doc. A/HRC/RES/13/16 (15 April 2010), and 'Combating intolerance, negative stereotyping and stigmatization of, and discrimination, incitement to violence, and violence against persons based on religion or belief', UN Doc. A/HRC/RES/16/18 (12 April 2011).

met with considerable resistance because they are seen as overly restricting freedom of expression.[241] There is also an apparent risk of political manipulation and of making freedom of expression contingent on the sentiments of the majority.

In the ICCPR, freedom of expression is subject to restrictions under article 19(3) and the absolute limitations provided for in article 20, which prohibits propaganda for war and advocacy of national, racial or religious hatred. However, such hatred is only prohibited where it 'constitutes incitement to discrimination, hostility or violence'. Most commentators agree that the broad nature of these terms give rise to a degree of legal uncertainty and that there is a need to demonstrate both 'hatred' and its causal link to the prohibited incitement.[242] Article 20 ICCPR was intended to counter vicious propaganda targeting vulnerable individuals and communities rather than protecting belief systems as such, as is evident from its high threshold. Article 18 ICCPR (freedom of religion) for its part arguably provides protection against attacks on religion only in so far as they interfere with the freedom to hold a belief and exercise one's religion.[243] Prohibiting 'defamation of religion' would therefore need to be justifiable under the grounds stipulated in article 19(3) ICCPR, namely respect for the rights or reputation of others; protection of national security or of public order (*ordre public*), or of public health or morals. As is clear from jurisprudence, this requires a careful assessment of the circumstances, i.e. whether it would be proportionate to restrict freedom of expression, even if it was considered 'offensive'.[244] The question of religious hatred has also been discussed in the context of article 4 ICERD which prohibits racial discrimination, with the CERD holding that 'discrimination based exclusively on religious grounds was not intended to fall within the purview of the Convention'.[245]

The exercise of the individual right to manifest one's religion or express one's opinion is seen as a normal state of affairs unless it infringes on the rights of other persons or clearly runs counter to legitimate public concerns. As qualified rights are by their nature indeterminate, the balancing of rights is bound to result in differences of opinion on where the appropriate line should be drawn and who should decide in this respect.

---

[241] S. Parmar, 'The challenge of "defamation of religions" to freedom of expression and the international human rights', *EHRLR* 3 (2009), 353–75.

[242] See Expert seminar on the links between articles 19 and 20 of the ICCPR: *Freedom of expression and advocacy of religious hatred that constitutes incitement to discrimination, hostility or violence* (Geneva: United Nations, 2-3 October 2008), online, at www2.ohchr.org/english/issues/opinion/articles1920_iccpr/index.htm.

[243] See on the scope of the right, HRCtee, General Comment 22: The right to freedom of thought, conscience and religion (article 18), UN Doc. CCPR/C/21/Rev.1/Add.4 (30 July 1993).

[244] HRCtee, General Comment 34, para. 11.

[245] See *P. S. N. v. Denmark*, UN Doc. CERD/C/71/D/36/2006 (8 August 2007), para. 6.3.

Observers have called for a duty of self-restraint and a need to use freedoms responsibly.[246] While this sounds eminently reasonable, different actors will have different understandings and perceptions of what acceptable limits are, and a duty of self-restraint may be seen as stifling freedom of expression. Ultimately, authorities, courts and human rights treaty bodies need to make the difficult decision of where the limits of tolerance are while being mindful that the liberty underlying this very tolerance forms the essence of the right.

8.7.4 To wear or not to wear: freedom of conscience and religion, the rights of women and the veil

The veil has become a highly symbolic feature which has triggered intense debates about freedom of religion and women's rights. While women are in some countries virtually given no choice but to cover their heads, others, such as France, have banned the wearing of full-face veils in public, or, in the case of Turkey, prohibit wearing the veil in public buildings.[247] Unsurprisingly, these laws and regulations have been challenged before courts and human rights treaty bodies have grappled with the issues raised. In *Hudoyberganova* v. *Uzbekistan*, the HRCtee found that regulations banning the wearing of religious symbols at a public university violated the applicant's right to freedom of thought, conscience and religion.[248] While this constituted a recognition of the right to wear a veil in principle, which is also echoed in its General Comment 22,[249] the Committee equally recognised that this freedom was subject to restrictions. In the particular case, since the state party provided no justification, the Committee found a violation.[250] The ECtHR, in contrast, held in *Sahin* v. *Turkey* that a ban on the wearing of headscarves at Turkish universities did not violate article 9 ECHR. It found that the grounds provided by Turkey to justify the ban, namely protecting the secular order of the state and the rights of others, were legitimate and proportionate in the circumstances. This judgment has

---

[246] V. Muntarbhorn, '"Religion" and "Expression" in the Human Rights Framework: Walking the Middle Path', Conference Paper no. 7, 2008 Expert Seminar, above note 242.

[247] See Z. Ashraf, 'Contested Meaning of the Veil and Political Ideologies of Iranian Regimes', *JMEWS* 3(3) (2007), 75–98; W. G. Leane, 'Rights of Ethnic Minorities in Liberal Democracies: Has France Gone Too Far in Banning Muslim Women from Wearing the Burka?', *HRQ* 33(4) (2011), 1032–61; Z. A. Saktanber and G. Çorbacioğlum, 'Veiling and Headscarf-Skepticism in Turkey', *SPISGSS* 15(5) (2008), 514–38.

[248] *Hudoyberganova* v. *Uzbekistan*, UN Doc. CCPR/C/82/D/931/2000 (5 November 2004), para. 6.2.

[249] HRCtee, General Comment 22, para. 4.

[250] *Hudoyberganova* v. *Uzbekistan*, para. 6.2.

been the subject of considerable criticism, particularly from a feminist perspective.[251] The Court failed to consider the impact of the right to privacy under article 8, which, according to its own jurisprudence, provides for a considerable sphere of 'personal autonomy'.[252] Doing so would have enabled the court to better appreciate the agency of Leyla Sahin – the woman affected by the ban – that is to what extent her personal choice should be respected and take priority. Instead, the Court accepted Turkey's views that the veil, being an expression of Islamic fundamentalism, negated gender equality.[253]

Granting a state a wide margin of appreciation in this field raises serious concerns as it affects a series of rights, including the right to education. More generally, the case raised broader questions about the limits of tolerance, particularly the degree to which a state may enforce its vision of society. The Court, by yielding to Turkey's strong version of secularism, ultimately endorsed a system based on uniform notions that may pay scant regard to the rights of the individual. Irrespective of the outcome, the ECHR's handling of the case therefore constituted a missed opportunity to engage in more depth with this fundamental question. Considering its topicality, particularly following France's ban of wearing a full veil in public,[254] the issue is bound to be the subject of further contentious proceedings.

QUESTIONS

1 Do you agree with the legal reasoning and policy considerations evident in the ECtHR's judgment in *Sahin* v. *Turkey*?

2 What approach may it have chosen to strike a different balance between the competing versions?

3 Do the grounds permitting restrictions of the freedom of expression provide states with too much latitude, especially considering the fundamental importance of the right for the promotion and protection of human rights more generally?

4 Has the tension between freedom of expression and freedom of religion been satisfactorily resolved in jurisprudence and UN practice?

---

[251] J. Marshall, 'Conditions for Freedom? European Human Rights Law and the Islamic Headscarf Debate', *HRQ* 30(3) (2008), 631–54.

[252] M.-B. Dembour, *Who Believes in Human Rights? Reflections on the European Convention* (Cambridge University Press, 2006), 213.

[253] *Leyla Şahin* v. *Turkey*, (2005) 44 EHRR 5, paras. 104–23.

[254] *Dogru* v. *France*, (2009) 49 EHRR 8, paras. 47–78 (sanction for refusal to remove headscarf for physical education class, no violation).

FURTHER READING

Doswald-Beck, L., *Human Rights in Times of Conflict and Terrorism* (Oxford University Press, 2011).

Franck, T. M., 'The Emerging Right to Democratic Governance', *AJIL* 86(1) (1992), 46–91.

McGoldrick, D., *Human Rights and Religion: The Islamic Headscarf Debate in Europe* (Oxford: Hart, 2006).

Macken, C., *Counter-Terrorism and the Detention of Suspected Terrorists: Preventive Detention and International Human Rights Law* (London, New York: Routledge, 2011).

Murray, R. *et al.*, *The Optional Protocol to the UN Convention against Torture* (Oxford University Press, 2011).

Nowak, M., *UN Covenant on Civil and Political Rights: CCPR Commentary*, 2nd edn (Kehl am Rhein: Engels, 2005).

Nowak, M. and McArthur, E., *The United Nations Convention against Torture: A Commentary* (Oxford University Press, 2008).

Office of the High Commissioner for Human Rights in Cooperation with the International Bar Association, *Human Rights in the Administration of Justice: A Manual on Human Rights for Judges, Prosecutors and Lawyers*, Professional Training Series no. 9 (New York and Geneva: United Nations, 2003).

Rodley, N. and Pollard, M., *The Treatment of Prisoners under International Law*, 3rd edn (Oxford University Press, 2009).

Schabas, W. A., *The Abolition of the Death Penalty in International Law*, 3rd edn (Cambridge University Press, 2002).

Scovazzi, T. and Citroni, G., *The Struggle against Enforced Disappearance and the 2007 United Nations Convention* (Leiden, Boston: Martinus Nijhoff, 2007).

Tomuschat, C., Lagrange, E. and Oeter, S. (eds.), *Right to Life* (Leiden, Boston: Martinus Nijhoff, 2010).

Trechsel, S., *Human Rights in Criminal Proceedings* (Oxford University Press, 2005).

9 Economic, social and cultural rights

CONTENTS

9.1 INTRODUCTION

Economic, social and cultural (ESC) rights include a number of entitlements, such as the right to work and the enjoyment of just and favourable conditions of work; the right to form and join trade unions; the right to social security; the protection of the family, mothers and children; the right to an adequate standard of living, which includes adequate food, clothing and housing and continuous improvement of living conditions; the right to the highest attainable standard of mental health; the right to education; and the right to participate in cultural life and enjoy the benefits of scientific progress. All these are protected under ICESCR.

Several differences are traditionally cited to distinguish the disparate legal nature of ESC and civil and political rights. Whereas states are obliged to implement the latter immediately, most ESC rights are subject to progressive realisation under the terms of the ICESCR. Moreover, because civil and political rights are considered negative obligations and thus generally only require entrenchment in the legal order of states, they are justiciable and enforceable before the courts. On the other hand, a number of states suggest that ESC rights are not justiciable, not only because they are not immediately realisable but also because their implementation requires funds and resources which parties may not possess. Thus, resource scarcity is a significant impediment to the fulfilment of ESC rights, but is also a justification for those states that are unwilling to invest money in social welfare services, especially towards the vulnerable, marginalised and the indigent. These issues will be explored in detail in this chapter.

It will also be demonstrated that ESC rights are by no means the poor relative of civil and political rights. In fact, many of the latter are meaningless without ESC rights. By way of illustration, the right to life is to some degree dependent on adequate food and water, decent housing and healthcare. Equally, a decent education is a good platform for an informed exercise of the freedom of expression. It will be shown that ESC rights are not vague obligations but to a large degree are now susceptible to qualitative and quantitative measurement. One of the sections in this chapter analyses in detail the advancement of indicators and benchmarks that have developed since the mid-1990s in order to set out realistic targets for states with a view to assessing their performance.

The final sections of the chapter concentrate on four distinct ESC rights: the right to education, the right to health and the rights to food and water. These should be read together with the right to development where it is explained that most developmental objectives generally overlap with ESC rights. There it will be demonstrated that several ESC rights that are not perceived as justiciable in certain nations were brought before the courts as necessary extensions of other justiciable civil and political rights (indirect justiciability).

9.2   BRIEF HISTORICAL CONTEXT OF ECONOMIC, SOCIAL AND CULTURAL RIGHTS

ESC rights are clearly recognised in articles 22–7 of the UDHR as well as article 55(a) and (b) of the UN Charter and were later elaborated in more detail in the ICESCR. Yet, even to this day scholars argue about the intention of the drafters of the ICESCR, which were at the time divided into two political camps, socialist or Soviet-bloc nations, on the one hand and Western liberal states on the other. For the socialist bloc the provision of a comprehensive and free social welfare system encompassing all ESC rights was a natural extension of its political ideology and state organisation. Most liberal democracies conditioned ESC rights, such as that of work and adequate living standards, on the forces of free market economics, which rested on private initiative, non-state interference and the promotion of entrepreneurship. The idea was that a well-functioning market economy would generate enough jobs and wealth for all members of society to enjoy high quality ESC benefits. Some liberal democracies, but certainly not all, put in place a social safety net for those unable to take advantage of the bounties of the free market system.

As a result, most liberal states objected to the assimilation of ESC rights with civil and political rights, at least in terms of their implementation.[1] The USSR at the time argued that ESC rights should be immediately enforceable and justiciable, which was vehemently opposed by the USA, its Western allies and most developing nations. Thus, the USA and its allies pressed the Commission on Human Rights to remove ESC rights from the text of the impending covenant that it was in the process of drafting. When the matter came to the General Assembly it swiftly overturned the Commission's decision[2] and subsequently the Commission prepared a single draft covenant containing seventy-three articles governing both ESC and civil and political rights. It was at this point that the heated debates between the two political camps intensified, leading to a compromise solution whereby ESC rights were to be incorporated in a covenant that was distinct from civil and political rights.[3] Scholars such as Whelan and Donnelly attribute this Western persistence to technical questions of legal implementation (namely objections to justiciability and immediate implementation), rather than substantive ideological concerns.[4] The truth lies somewhere in the middle. Whereas it is true that ESC rights were not central to certain liberal states[5] – a prime example being the lack of welfare for the multitude of victims of the Great Depression in the USA[6] – they none the less accepted and protected most ESC rights in their legal systems; yet, their conception of fulfilment was fundamentally different from that of the USSR. Standing out among

---

[1] A. Kirkup and T. Evans, 'The Myth of Western Opposition to Economic, Social and Cultural Rights? A Reply to Whelan and Donnelly', *HRQ* 31 (2009), 221, 228–9.

[2] UNGA resolution 421(V) (4 December 1950).

[3] UNGA resolution 543(VI) (5 February 1952), noting however that ESC and civil and political rights are interconnected and interdependent.

[4] D. J. Whelan and J. Donnelly, 'The West, Economic and Social Rights and the Global Human Rights Regime: Setting the Record Straight', *HRQ* 29 (2007), 908.

[5] S. L. Kang, 'The Unsettled Relationship of Economic and Social Rights in the West: a Response to Whelan and Donnelly', *HRQ* 31 (2009), 1006, at 1007–8. Other liberal democracies, such as Germany, have elevated universal social welfare to a constitutional principle. Article 20(1) of Germany's Basic Law (the *Grundgesetz*) establishes the so-called *Sozialstaatsklausel*, or social state principle which obliges the government to provide the minimum core ESC rights so that people can live with dignity. The Federal Constitutional Court (the *Bundesverfassungsgericht*) has interpreted this minimum core to include essential foodstuff, housing, clothing and healthcare (BVerfGE 82, 60 (80), 1990). This has given rise, among other things, to a constitutional entitlement to a minimum of benefits, as decided by the Federal Administrative Court (BVerwGE 1, 159 (1954)).

[6] It should be noted, however, that in direct response to the Great Depression the Roosevelt administration implemented a set of economic programmes between 1933 and 1936 whose aim included, among other things, the provision of relief to the poor and the unemployed.

its other liberal counterparts, particularly the set of countries that now form the EU, the USA has been nothing less than vociferous in proclaiming that ESC rights are not rights at all but goals which states aspire to achieve. By way of illustration, in response to an OHCHR questionnaire in 2007 on the domestic implementation of the right to water, the US position paper bluntly conceded that its government 'does not share the view that a right to water [broadly understood] exists under international human rights law'.[7] Such a position expressed by the world's superpower certainly hampers efforts to give prominence to ESC rights worldwide but has not halted the tide of laws, constitutional amendments and judicial pronouncements in many parts of the globe to bring about the justiciability of ESC rights.

As will be explained in following sections, the perceived legal differences between civil and political and ESC rights was ultimately reflected in their respective monitoring in the two covenants. Whereas the implementation of civil and political rights is monitored by the HRCtee, whose mandate is derived from the ICCPR itself, the drafters of the ICESCR decided against a monitoring mechanism and naturally objected to the possibility of an optional protocol giving rise to individual complaints. When the ICESCR came into force in 1976, ECOSOC set up working groups composed of government experts to assist with the review of country reports. Their operation was generally considered unsatisfactory, leading one group in 1985 to propose transforming the existing system into a committee of independent experts. This suggestion was endorsed by ECOSOC which went ahead and set up the CESCR.[8] Although it was only provided with the power to review the parties' periodic reports and offer non-binding recommendations, it has gone ahead and issued general comments, in the mould of the Human Rights Committee, and in more recent years these comments have slowly began to use the language of 'violations' attributable to actions and omissions of states parties.[9]

9.3   PROGRESSIVE REALISATION AND THE NATURE OF STATE OBLIGATIONS

The nature of obligations addressed to states in their implementation of ESC rights is predicated in article 2(1) of the ICESCR, which reads as follows:

---

[7] 'Views of the USA on human rights and access to water, submitted to OHCHR' (June 2007), para. 4. It did, however, go on to say that water rights are an important part of water governance in the USA and a complex array of entitlements exist primarily at the state level.

[8] ECOSOC resolution 1985/17 (28 May 1985).

[9] See e.g. CESCR Concluding Observations on Israel, UN Doc. E/C12/1/Add 27 (4 December 1998), para. 11, in respect of Israel's alleged discriminatory practices between Jewish and Palestinian property rights.

Each state party to the present Covenant *undertakes to take steps*, individually and through international assistance and co-operation, especially economic and technical, to the *maximum of its available resources*, with a view to achieving *progressively* the full realisation of the rights recognised in the present Covenant by all appropriate means, including particularly the adoption of legislative measures [emphasis added].[10]

This language is in stark contrast to the obligations contained in article 2(1) of the ICCPR, which stipulates that each party undertakes to 'respect *and ensure* to all individuals ... the rights recognised in the present Covenant', as well as article 2(3) according to which parties undertake to 'ensure that any person whose rights or freedoms ... are violated shall have an effective remedy'. Therefore, it would seem that the rights in the ICESCR are framed as goals that are to be achieved progressively, contingent on the maximum use of a nation's available resources. In addition, whereas the ICCPR directly addresses its intended rights-holders (i.e. 'everyone shall have the right'), the ICESCR does so through the medium of the state (i.e. 'state parties to the present Covenant recognise the right of everyone'). As a result, it has been questioned whether an obligation that is not immediately enforceable, not overtly justiciable and which is contingent on available resources can ever give rise to an entitlement at all.

It is beyond doubt that ESC rights are binding on states. This is true not only in respect of those obligations that are subject to immediate implementation but in respect of all rights.[11] This is so because every right in the ICESCR entails obligations of conduct and obligations of result. These may further be broken down to three further levels of obligation, namely to respect, protect and fulfil. The obligation to respect requires states to refrain from interfering directly or indirectly with the enjoyment of the right, such as by denying or impeding access or enforcing discriminatory practices. The obligation to protect requires states to take measures that prevent third parties from interfering with the right. In relation to the right to health, for example, this includes the adoption of legislation or other measures ensuring equal access to healthcare and health-related services provided by third parties; ensuring that the privatization of the health sector does not constitute a threat to the availability, accessibility, acceptability and quality of health facilities, goods and services; and controlling the marketing of medical equipment and medicines by third

---

[10] This definition is essentially reproduced with minor variations in article 26 of the ACHR, 36 UNTS 1144, as well as article 1 of the 1988 Additional Protocol to the American Convention on Human Rights in the Area of Economic, Social and Cultural Rights (San Salvador Protocol) (1989) 28 *ILM* 156.

[11] ESC rights that have been recognised by the CESCR as being of immediate application include articles 3, 7(a)(i), 8, 10(3), 13(2)(a), (3) and (4) and 15(3). CESCR General Comment 3: nature of ICESCR obligations, UN Doc. E/1991/23 (14 December 1990), paras. 5, 7; CESCR General Comment 9: domestic application of ICESCR, UN Doc. E/C12/1998/24 (3 December 1998), para. 10.

parties. Finally, the obligation to fulfil requires the adoption of appropriate legislative, administrative, budgetary, judicial, promotional and other measures.[12]

As far as the duty to fulfil is concerned, the CESCR has iterated that it involves an obligation to facilitate and a duty to provide. Facilitation requires the creation of appropriate conditions that lead to the enjoyment of the right in question, such as the establishment of a national health policy in respect of the right to health. The duty to provide requires states to provide the commodity that is the essence of a particular right (e.g. water, food, health services) 'whenever an individual or group is unable, for reasons beyond their control' to enjoy the right by the means at their disposal.[13] This is no doubt a controversial point of view because it is said to ignore the fundamental premise of the ICESCR, i.e. progressive realisation. None the less, the CESCR's view is in full conformity with the accepted position that water and food, among other things, should not be treated as commodities but as means necessary for survival and welfare.

In respect of those ESC rights that require the state to provide a resource (e.g. water) or a service (e.g. healthcare) the CESCR has formulated a set of criteria against which the obligation to fulfil should be assessed. The first concerns availability of the resource in question. Water, for example, must be sufficient and continuous for consumption, sanitation, cooking and other purposes. The second is quality, meaning that it should be safe. The third is accessibility, without discrimination, which consists of physical, economic and information accessibility.[14]

The concept of progressive realisation of the rights guaranteed in the Covenant derives from the reality that most, if not all, states are unable to provide the entire range of ESC rights, at least with immediate effect, because of resource constraints. Unlike civil and political rights, which are generally viewed as requiring negative obligations of non-interference (e.g. right to life, freedom of expression, freedom of assembly) and are thus (erroneously) seen as devoid of implementation costs,[15] ESC rights are positive in nature and are not susceptible to implementation without significant resources.[16] As a result, states have been unwilling to assume the onerous obligations associated with

---

[12] CESCR General Comment 14: right to health, UN Doc. E/C12/2004 (11 August 2000), paras. 33–6.

[13] CESCR General Comment 12: right to food, UN Doc. E/C12/1999/5 (12 May 1999), para. 15; CESCR General Comment 14, para. 37; CESCR General Comment 15: right to water), UN Doc. E/C12/2002/11 (20 January 2003), para. 25.

[14] CESCR General Comment 15, para. 12.

[15] This is not however true. States are under an obligation to take positive measures to protect civil and political rights. For example, there exists an obligation to protect the right to life and other personal freedoms by maintaining an effective police force or by averting deadly terrorist attacks. See section 15.4.

[16] In a subsequent section we shall, however, explore the CESCR's 'violations' approach in identifying the negative components of ESC rights.

ESC rights if not accompanied by the condition that their realisation would be progressive, as opposed to immediate. No doubt this saving clause has been abused and has served as a basis for justifying inaction, principally through claims of state indigence.[17] In most cases where such claims have been made, the state in question has been responsible for widespread corruption, clan favouritism and large-scale human rights abuses.

In *Bermúdez Urrego* v. *Transmilenio* a disabled person argued that the public transport system of Bogota provided no accessibility for wheelchair users. In discussing possible remedies for the violation of the petitioner's freedom of movement, the Colombian Constitutional Court held that freedom of movement in this context was a progressive right, subject to two important observations. First, a right is not considered progressive simply because it entails a positive action on behalf of the state. The protection of some rights may, in some circumstances, be so urgent as to warrant an immediate response. Secondly, that a right is to be ensured progressively does not mean that it cannot be enforced. The Court emphasised that 'taking rights seriously equally demands taking their progressive nature seriously'. It held that: (1) the progressive definition of the level of enjoyment of a right cannot continuously exclude certain groups of the population (such as disabled persons); (2) the state must gradually make advances as to the fulfilment of the right; and (3) the state may define the level of fulfilment that it is prepared to ensure, albeit rationally, and this must be made public by legislation and the right itself must be made justiciable.[18]

Article 2(1) of the ICESCR envisages progressive realisation of rights through the 'taking of steps' 'by all appropriate means'. The Committee has rightly commented that:

While the full realisation of the relevant rights may be achieved progressively, steps towards that goal must be taken within a reasonably short time after the Covenant's entry into force for the States concerned. Such steps should be deliberate, concrete and targeted as clearly as possible towards meeting the obligations recognised in the Covenant.

The fact that realisation over time, or in other words progressively, is foreseen under the Covenant should not be misinterpreted as depriving the obligation of all meaningful content. It is on the one hand a necessary flexibility device, reflecting the realities of the real world and the difficulties involved for any country in ensuring full realisation of ESC rights. On the other hand, the phrase must be read in the light of the overall objective, indeed the *raison d'être*, of the Covenant which is to establish clear obligations for States parties in respect of the full realisation of the rights in question. *It thus imposes an obligation to move as expeditiously as possible towards that goal* [emphasis added].[19]

[17] See S. Leckie, 'Another Step towards Indivisibility: Identifying the Key Features of Violations of Economic, Social and Cultural Rights', *HRQ* 20 (1998), 81, at 94.
[18] *Bermúdez Urrego* v. *Transmilenio*, T-595/2002.
[19] CESCR, General Comment 3, paras. 2, 9.

That states are under an obligation to implement ESC rights, even if these have not been rendered justiciable, follows from their indivisibility from civil and political rights. People are living organisms, composed of myriad functions that are inseparable from the whole. In this sense, the right to life is not meaningful only when the state refrains from killing or protects individuals from crime, as this is simply one of the many dimensions of life. Others include access to food and water for immediate survival. When bare survival has been achieved living a decent life that amounts to well-being[20] (which includes adequate access to housing, healthcare, education and other things) is important because without well-being political rights seem luxurious and theoretical pursuits to those who cannot afford to provide the bare essentials for their families. It is for this reason that most, if not all, ESC rights have been rendered justiciable by domestic and international judicial bodies as necessary correlations of civil and political freedoms and entitlements. In subsequent chapters this indirect justiciability will be demonstrated in respect of the right to development,[21] the right to a healthy environment[22] and the right to be free from corruption.[23] The IACtHR is among those international tribunals that have provided a broad interpretation to civil and political rights so as to encompass by extension ESC rights. In the *Street Children* case state agents of Guatemala were found to have practised abhorent systematic violence against abandoned street children, including executions and torture. The Court employed articles 4 (right to life) and 19 (rights of the child) of the American Convention in order to construct the right to a dignified existence which it stipulated should be guaranteed by the state. It found that in the case at hand Guatemala had deprived street children of the minimum conditions for a dignified life and prevented them from the full and harmonious development of their personality.[24]

Finally, brief mention should be made to the link between the right to development and the implementation of ESC rights. The former refers to the constant improvement of the well-being of peoples through an enabling environment that is respectful of all human rights, which include ESC rights. The realisation of the right to development requires domestic as well as international action, in the same manner that ESC rights in article 2(1) of the

---

[20] Well-being is a central notion in the pursuit of the right to development, which is explained in section 12.2.

[21] Section 12.3.1.   [22] Section 12.8.   [23] Section 12.7.

[24] *Villagrán Morales et al.* v. *Guatemala*, IACtHR Ser. C, no. 63 (19 November 1999, paras. 144, 191; in its Advisory opinion on *Juridical Condition and Human Rights of the Child*, OC-17/02, IACtHR Ser. A, no. 17 (28 August 2002), para. 84, it was held that a dignified life for children separated from their families encompassed the right to education and the right to health. See J. L. Cavallaro and E. Schaffer, 'Less as More: Rethinking Supranational Litigation of Economic and Social Rights in the Americas', *Hastings Law Journal* (*Hastings L. J.*) 56 (2004), 217, at 272, who argue in favour of an expansive construction of the right to life and property in order to encompass a large number of ESC rights.

ICESCR and 56 of the UN Charter are dependent also on international assistance and cooperation. International assistance is typically provided through a range of multilateral partnerships for the financing of development, discussed elsewhere in this book,[25] as well as through technical cooperation and the delivery of capacity-building expertise.

9.4   RESOURCE IMPLICATIONS: THE OBLIGATION TO UTILISE 'MAXIMUM AVAILABLE RESOURCES'

Article 2(1) of the ICESCR, as do other instruments related to the fulfilment of economic and social rights,[26] stresses that states are obliged to realise ESC rights by making the maximum use of their available resources. No doubt, although the resources of one nation will vary, and sometimes staggeringly so, from those of another, the assessment of a nation's available resources and its maximum utilisation of these resources towards implementing a particular right may be measured by reference to objective criteria. First of all, it is crucial to define and ascertain a state's available resources. The question is by no means simple, since one could argue that human capital, intellectual property rights, uncollected taxes and government loans, among other matters, may fall within the purview of public resources. Economists generally contend that a country's available resources should not be measured only by the ratio of governmental expenditure to gross domestic product (GDP), which represents the market value of a country's products and services in any one year. Available resources should also include development assistance, borrowing and running a deficit, as well as the monetary space made possible by central banks by, for example, currency devaluations, fluctuation of interest rates and others. This is referred to as the fiscal space diamond.[27]

The maximum utilisation of these resources raises a number of compelling arguments. For example, is a country justified for failing to allocate funds to implement basic ESC rights on the ground that it is obliged to service its

---

[25] See section 12.4.

[26] Article 4, CRC; article 4(2), CRPD. See also CtRC, General Comment 5: general measures of implementation, UN Doc. CRC/GC/2003/5 (27 November 2003), paras. 6–8, 51. The CtRC has criticised most countries for their failure in this regard. See Concluding Observations on Slovenia, UN Doc. C/CRC/15/ADD.230 (26 February 2004), para. 15, which called for the development of a 'systematic and detailed allocation of resources in order to provide a clear picture of trends in budget allocations and [which] ensures that resources are made available … to the maximum extent of available resources in order to meet the needs of all children and correct poverty-related disparities'.

[27] See UNDP, 'The fiscal space challenge and financing for MDG achievement', available at: http://content.undp.org/go/cms-service/stream/asset/;jsessionid=axMCGVWNrEb4? asset_id=2223965, at 7.

foreign debt which accounts for 90 per cent of its annual resources? If rights are truly indivisible and interdependent then the right to life is of equal value with the right to a free education, adequate housing, health and food, which cannot be denied on account of debt servicing.[28] The CESCR has pointed out the minimum requirements for the implementation of ESC rights, irrespective of a country's financial situation. These consist of the so-called minimum core obligations, which will be discussed in the next section, consisting of the minimum essential levels pertinent to each right.[29] Resource constraints can under no circumstances be claimed as a justification to deny implementing the minimum core. Moreover:

> even in times of severe resource constraints whether caused by a process of adjustment, of economic recession, or by other factors the vulnerable members of society can and indeed must be protected by the adoption of relatively low-cost targeted programmes.[30]

No doubt, states have often claimed that although they are utilising the maximum of their resources these are none the less insufficient.[31] In most cases, however, they do not make the best use of their resources and this is something that is often pointed out by judicial institutions and intergovernmental entities. One poignant example concerns the distributive failures of so-called regressive tax regimes. These generally rely on the assumption that the rich will invest money in the economy if their personal and property taxes are reduced, taking into account that they already pay corporate tax and provide jobs to the masses. As a result, regressive regimes balance their shortfall by imposing higher taxes on goods and services, which are, however, consumed by low- and middle-income households. Thus, they generate inequitable outcomes and fail to distribute wealth across the population because the poor end up paying more of their income on taxes than the rich.[32] Countries adhering to regressive regimes are clearly not making maximum use of their resources and should consider reverting to progressive taxation where the wealthy are taxed according to their real income.

There is some debate about whether the assessment of resource availability and its appropriate utilisation should be a justiciable matter, in addition to encompassing unavoidable political considerations. The CESCR, although admitting that determinations of this nature are not ordinarily justiciable,

---

[28] See section 12.6 for a discussion of debt relief and human rights.

[29] CESCR, General Comment 3, para. 10.

[30] CESCR, General Comment 3, para. 12.

[31] See R. Robertson, 'Measuring State Compliance with the Obligation to Devote the Maximum Available Resources to Realising Economic, Social and Cultural Rights', *HRQ* 16 (1994), 693.

[32] The German Federal Constitutional Court has held that the state's power of direct taxation – as opposed to indirect taxation – cannot be used to deprive people of the means for their 'existential minimum' (BVerfGE 82, 60(85), BVerfGE 87, 153(69)).

has gone on to say that courts are already involved in a considerable range of matters encompassing resource implications and possess the authority to do so 'within the limits of the appropriate exercise of their functions of judicial review'.[33] None the less, there exists a significant thread of jurisprudence in constitutional democracies whereby domestic courts have questioned the authority of the state to divert resources for the implementation of particular ESC and ordered their redirection or suggested the need for reforms.[34] By way of illustration the South African Constitutional Court in the *Treatment Action Campaign* case decided that the non-public availability of a drug that was found to prevent the transmission of HIV from mothers to babies was unreasonable and breached the right of poor mothers and their newborns to effective healthcare.[35]

Similarly, the Argentine Supreme Court has issued orders in a long list of cases to public authorities and hospitals demanding that they provide HIV and other life-saving medication and treatment to the indigent.[36] In the same fashion the Colombian Constitutional Court has issued *amparo* and *tutela* injunctions, which are intended to protect people from unlawful and arbitrary governmental acts through urgent judicial review.[37] The right of *amparo* is stipulated in article 25(1) of the American Convention on Human Rights. In the *Rivera* case the Constitutional Court ordered a lower court to determine whether the petitioner was in a situation of 'absolute indigence' for the purpose of providing him with free medical treatment. The test for indigence was found to be premised on (1) absolute incapacity to sustain oneself by one's own means; (2) the existence of a vital need which,

---

[33] CESCR, General Comment 9, paras. 10 and 14.

[34] In *Campaign for Fiscal Equality* v. *State of New York* 100 N.Y. 2d 893 (2003) the New York Court of Appeals suggested that New York state reformed its school finance system so that it could provide a sound basic education to all of its districts. Upon the state's failure to implement any reforms, the court ordered that US$5.6 billion be allocated to annual school-operating expenses and another US$9.2 billion for a five-year capital projects programme. The state's appeal against the order was rejected. *Campaign for Fiscal Equity* v. *State of New York* 861 N.E. 2d 50 (N.Y., 2006). This led the New York governor in early 2007 to adopt the State Education Budget and Reform Act which envisaged significant state-wide increases in education aid.

[35] *South African Minister of Health* v. *Treatment Action Campaign*, 2002 (5) SA 721.

[36] *Campodónico de Beviacqua, Ana Carina* v. *Ministerio de Salud y Banco Drogas Neoplásicas*, Judgment (24 October 2000). A year earlier, the Venezuelan Supreme Court in *Cruz Bermúdez and Others* v. *Ministerio de Sanidad y Asistencia Social*, Judgment no. 916 (15 July 1999), ordered the distribution of HIV drugs to 170 indigent sufferers.

[37] In *Restrepo and López* v. *Salud Colmena*, T-849/2001 two HIV sufferers were denied testing since they were not included in the mandatory state-financed health plan. Neither could afford to pay for the tests. On the basis of the right to life the Constitutional Court held that diagnostic tests were essential to protect the right to health of HIV patients, being necessary to monitor the progress and effectiveness of HIV treatments. Thus, it ordered the private hospital (Salud Colmena) to carry out these tests free of charge, further authorising it to charge this additional cost to a government fund.

left unsatisfied, would seriously injure human dignity; and (3) the material absence of family support. If all three conditions were found to have been satisfied the lower court could order the state to contribute to that person's sustenance.[38]

As a result, it is wrong to suggest that courts are ill placed, or that they do not possess the authority, to question and annul budgetary decisions that affect the implementation of ESC rights. In fact, an important function of judicial review is to prevent the implementation of government acts that carry a financial impact on rights.

CASE STUDY 9.1
United States budget allocated to primary and secondary education

In 2004 the USA ranked eighth in its commitment to public education spending. In 2003–4 it spent US$472.3 billion, which represented almost 6 per cent of the country's GDP. This appears to demonstrate a significant commitment to government-funded education, although the numbers are deceptive. The level of public funding for education is dependent on local property taxes, not on a system of wealth redistribution that promotes equal quality of education for all children irrespective of income. As a result, wealthier neighbourhoods generate more money for public schools than low-income and deprived neighbourhoods. It is estimated that affluent public schools spend US$15,000 for each student, whereas poorer schools can only afford an amount close to US$4,000. It is evident that school districts with the largest percentage of minority students receive the least amount of general education revenues.[1]

Under the terms of the ICESCR the USA would have failed to utilise its maximum available resources to fulfil the right to education because of the discrimination inherent in the current system of public education funding.

[1] Center for Women's Global Leadership, 'Maximum Available Resources and Human Rights: Analytical Report' (2011), 7.

9.5   MINIMUM CORE OBLIGATIONS

In one of its first general comments the CESCR made it clear that, at the very least, states are under an obligation to ensure the satisfaction of the minimum essential levels of each ESC right. It has referred to these as minimum core obligations.[39] By way of illustration, in cases of severe food

---

[38] *Rivera* case, T-533/1992. This is in conformity with case T-426/1992 which reproduces the German doctrine of 'minimum level of existence' (*Existenzminimum*).

[39] CESCR, General Comment 3, para. 10.

shortages or serious epidemics threatening the very existence of a population, or a group thereof, the state is obliged to provide essential foodstuffs
and vaccine or other healthcare. Although minimum core obligations are
not derogable,[40] in extremes cases where 'every effort has been made to use
all the resources [at the disposal of a state] in an effort to satisfy, as a matter
of priority, minimum core obligations' the state in question is not considered
at fault.[41]

It has been suggested that minimum core obligations anticipate three
accomplishments: (1) provision of a specific direction in the implementation
of ESC rights by disassembling the inherent relativism of their otherwise
'progressive realisation'; (2) advancement of a baseline level of protection
irrespective of socio-economic policies and disparate levels of available
resources; and (3) signalling an acceptable global redistributive debate.[42]
At the same time, however, what remains unanswered is whether the mini-
malist approach associated with minimum core obligations presupposes differentiated standards between developed and developing countries. Some
critics have further argued that the continued insistence on the performance
of developing states, in respect of assessing minimum core obligations has
steered focus away from low- and middle-income classes in the developed
world.[43] To respond to the question of whether differentiated standards are
justified – which necessarily poses a relativist dimension – one must first
assess the values pertinent to human existence recognised under general
international law. The majority of the globe's population still live in abject
poverty, suffering unnecessary deaths from diseases, infections and malnour-
ishment. The Human Development Index (HDI) has consistently emphasised
that human development and well-being should be measured on the basis
of longevity, knowledge and decent living standards.[44] Under this light, a
needs-based core minimum set of obligations premised on the preservation
of bare survival would not meet the HDI threshold and is in any event antithetical to the notion that the right to life is not exhausted by biological survival alone but is instead multidimensional. As a result, several scholars have
rejected the needs-based approach, arguing in favour of value-based core
minimum obligations by putting emphasis on what it means to be human,
encompassing within their methodology the notions of dignity, equality and
freedom.[45]

---

[40] CESCR, General Comment 14, para. 18.   [41] CESCR, General Comment 3, para. 10.
[42] K. Y. Young, 'The Minimum Core of Economic and Social Rights: A Concept in Search of
Content', *Yale J. Int'l L.* 33 (2008), 113, 121–2.
[43] M. Craven, *The International Covenant on Economic, Social and Cultural Rights: A
Perspective on its Development* (Oxford University Press, 1995), 143–4.
[44] UNDP, *Human Development Report* (Oxford University Press, 1990), 11.
[45] See Young, above note 42, 128–38.

This line of thinking seems to conform more closely to the CESCR's approach, given that its formulation of core minimum obligations in respect of rights such as that of water require much more than the formulation of needs-based policies by states parties.[46] The Committee is not alone in its value-based conception of the minimum core. In fact, the German Constitutional Court has long developed the doctrine of 'minimum level of existence' (*Existenzminimum*), whereby the state is constitutionally obliged to establish a social welfare system that enables people to live with dignity.[47] Equally, in the USA the courts have employed their power of judicial review in order to suggest budgetary reforms that overturn existing economic and social policies, as is the case with the discrepancy in quality of public secondary education offered to underprivileged classes.[48] The courts were not merely content that children attended school but emphasised that the level of secondary education should be such as to prepare students for higher education and render them capable of competing in the employment market.[49] This by no means suggests a bare minimum.

The implementation of minimum core obligations does not always require the infusion of tangible resources but may instead simply need on a change of policies. By way of illustration, food and employment security in poor nations could be significantly boosted by the protection of small-scale farming, access to subsidies or micro-financing and insistence on local consumption with a view to minimising cost. In this manner valuable foodstuffs would not be exported cheaply out of countries reliant on them for their well-being and farmers could continue to grow their produce without fear of being outpriced or taken over by large collectives.[50]

Despite the fact that core minimum obligations must be construed as value based rather than needs based, in emergency situations it is not expected that the state should implement the higher thresholds of ESC rights. In the *Grootboom* case, which concerned the eviction of homeless people from their informal settlements, the South African Constitutional Court held that even though the government was working towards a housing policy to provide adequate, low-cost housing for the poor, it was under a legal duty to accommodate as a matter of priority the 'absolutely homeless'.[51]

---

[46] CESCR, General Comment 15, para. 37.   [47] BVerfGE 1, 97 (104); BVerfGE 45, 187 (229).

[48] *Campaign for Fiscal Equality* v. *State of New York* 100 N.Y. 2d 893 (2003).

[49] The House of Lords in *R* v. *East Sussex Council ex parte Tandy* [1998] 2 All ER 769 adopted a similar stance in a case where a disabled child who was unable to physically attend school had his home tuition hours slashed from five to three by his local council on financial grounds. The Lords argued that although the Council was entitled to choose how to best spend its resources, it was none the less obliged to offer all children a 'suitable education', as per section 298 of the Education Act 1993.

[50] See section 17.3.1, dealing with globalisation.

[51] *Government of South Africa and Others* v. *Grootboom and Others*, 2001 (1) SA 46 (CC).

9.6   JUSTICIABILITY OF ECONOMIC, SOCIAL AND CULTURAL RIGHTS

The concept of justiciability refers to the capacity of a particular claim to receive judicial scrutiny or determination on the basis of mandatory rather than discretionary rules.[52] The capacity or not of an applicant to entertain the claim (legal standing) is irrelevant to the justiciability of the claim itself. The right to water, as indeed all ESC rights, constitutes a legitimate claim and, as already pointed out, confers both rights and obligations. For some time, especially during the deliberations on the drafting of the ICESCR, it was contended that ESC rights did not possess a justiciable character. In order to justify this line of thinking it was argued that these were not in fact rights entailing legal entitlements but rather policy directives, or that their progressive realisation rendered them non-susceptible to judicial determination,[53] or finally that the courts could not possibly have a say on how governments determined their fiscal priorities. In the *Nigerian Education* case, for example, the government claimed that education was not a legal entitlement for its citizens and that as a result of widespread corruption it lacked the funds necessary to cover the shortfall of its educational budget, effectively denying large numbers of children the right to education. The ECOWAS court confirmed that the right to primary education was both justiciable and binding on Nigeria irrespective of the resources available to it.[54]

These types of anti-justiciability claims led a number of countries to avoid adopting legislation that would have made ESC claims justiciable before local courts. The Swiss Federal Supreme Court, for example, determined that the rights enshrined in the ICESCR were not justiciable because they did not manifest the characteristics of directly applicable norms.[55] Such arguments focusing on the alleged absence of direct applicability tend to bypass the fact that the rights in question are in one way or another enshrined in the national constitution, and in any event it is not all that hard to conceptualise the right to health in respect of a sufferer requiring specific treatment or of

[52] See M. J. Dennis and D. P. Stewart, 'Justiciability of Economic, Social and Cultural Rights: Should There be an International Complaints Mechanism to Adjudicate the Rights to Food, Water, Housing and Health?', *AJIL* 98 (2004), 462, at 474–5, who take a narrow view, arguing that a claim should be considered justiciable only where its adjudication contributes to a practical result that is susceptible to implementation. For a comprehensive analysis of many of the cases cited in this section, see ICJ, 'Courts and the Legal Enforcement of Economic, Social and Cultural Rights: Comparative Experiences of Justiciability' (2008).

[53] This argument was rejected by the Colombian Constitutional Court, especially in situations where the government has not taken the requisite steps to fulfil the right in question: *Bermúdez Urrego* v. *Transmilenio*, T-595/2002.

[54] *Social and Economic Rights Action Center (SERAC)* v. *Federal Republic of Nigeria and Universal Basic Education Commission*, ECW/CCJ/APP/07/10, Judgment, 6 December 2010.

[55] *T* v. *Neuchâtel County Compensation Bank*, Judgment, 20 July 1995.

a destitute child in need of food and shelter. Even so, through a process of strategic litigation initiated mainly by human rights NGOs, local courts have been urged to entertain claims based on the violation of economic and social rights, whether directly or by reference to civil and political rights. We have explained elsewhere in what manner the Indian Supreme Court subsumed the right to a healthy environment, adequate housing and other matters under the right to life. The Inter-American Court and Commission of Human Rights have adopted a similar methodology in respect of ESC rights that are not written into the American Convention. In *Bosico* v. *Dominican Republic*, for example, two Haitian children born in the Dominican Republic were denied birth certificates and nationality by the authorities of that country and as a result were not allowed to attend school and were deprived of a juridical personality. The Court found a violation of article 3 (right to juridical personality), article 19 (children's rights) and article 20 (right to nationality), among others, in order to affirm the obligation of states to provide without discrimination an education that is free and which fosters children's intellectual development.[56]

In countries where ESC rights have found their way into national constitutions[57] the courts have developed a significant string of jurisprudence which confirms their justiciable character, as we have already demonstrated earlier in this chapter. Of course, it should be pointed out that the courts are not necessarily the best forum for implementing ESC rights, as this is a job best suited to the executive power of central and regional governments by means of action plans and practical measures, such as the supply of drugs and housing. None the less, a free and independent judiciary plays an important role in clarifying the exact content of obligations, monitoring their implementation against possible discrimination, and determining the validity of omissions to fulfil based on reasonableness and proportionality. The last two principles, whether directly or indirectly, have been invoked by a number of courts in order to assess the propriety of governmental restrictions upon ESC rights and have been further incorporated in article 8(4) of the 2008 Optional Protocol to the ICESCR.[58] The South African Supreme Court has been instrumental in this regard, particularly through its much celebrated *Grootboom* judgment, but similar decisions have been reached elsewhere. In the *Multiple*

---

[56] *Girly Yean and Bosico* v. *Dominican Republic*, Judgment, 8 September 2005, Ser. C, no. 130, para. 185. See M. F. Tinta, 'Justiciability of Economic, Social and Cultural Rights in the Inter-American System of Protection of Human Rights: Beyond Traditional Paradigms and Notions', *HRQ* 29 (2007), 431, at 445–51.

[57] For example, Colombian Constitution, chapter II, articles 42–77.

[58] This stipulates that in the examination of individual communications for violations of ESC rights, the CESCR shall 'consider the reasonableness of the steps taken by the state party … bearing in mind that the state party may adopt a range of possible policy measures for the implementation of the rights set forth in the Covenant'.

Sclerosis case, the Argentine Supreme Court was called upon to decide the validity of a regulation issued by the Ministry of Health which excluded multiple sclerosis treatment from the country's mandatory minimum health insurance plan. This regulation affected sufferers who were already encompassed under the plan and the Court deemed it unreasonable and contrary to the right to health.[59]

A poignant facet of ESC rights is the obligation incumbent on states to refrain from deliberately imposing retrogressive measures, such as would reverse any achievements made in the realisation of a particular right.[60] Retrogressive measures essentially deny existing rights-holders their legitimate entitlements, and many states during the post-2008 global financial crisis justified cuts to pensions, education and health by reference to spiralling public debt. By 2011 the Greek government, in order to secure international funds and avoid bankruptcy, slashed civil service pensions by more than 30 per cent and increased property and fuel taxes and began to charge for otherwise subsidised medicines. These measures adversely affected the living conditions of the infirm, the elderly and low-income households. Retrogressive measures have been successfully challenged before national courts, particularly in the areas of pensions, healthcare and education.[61]

Finally, it should be remembered that because justiciability does not only encompass claims against public authorities, the actions and omissions of private actors may also equally be challenged before the courts. Although non-state actors are not charged with specific ESC obligations under the ICESCR or general international law, to the extent that they effectively discharge economic and social rights in substitution for the state they have been viewed by some courts as legitimate duty-holders and have thus accepted the justiciability of claims brought against them. In *Etcheverry* v. *Omint* the applicant, who was an HIV sufferer, was provided membership to a private health plan by his employer. When he later became redundant he sought to continue his membership through private funds but the insurance company refused. The Argentine Supreme Court held that private health providers were under a duty to protect the right to health of their customers and that their special relationship was not simply of a contractual nature.[62] International bodies dealing with ESC rights claims but with no jurisdiction against non-state actors, such as the European Committee of Social Rights, will typically find that the state concerned has violated its obligations under the European

---

[59] *Asosiación de Esclerosis Múltiple de Salta* v. *Ministerio de Salud-Estato Nacional* (*Multiple Sclerosis* case) judgment (18 December 2003).

[60] CESCR, General Comment 3, para. 9.

[61] The Latvian Constitutional Court, Judgment no. 2009/4301 (21 December 2009) and the Romanian Constitutional Court, Judgment no. 872 (25 June 2010) held that pension cuts implemented on the basis of loan agreements with the IMF were unconstitutional.

[62] *Etcheverry* v. *Omint Sociedad Anónima y Servicios*, Judgment (13 March 2001).

Social Charter by failing to take action against recalcitrant private actors.[63] This alternative is also open to national courts through the function of judicial review.

The following sections discuss the two available international quasi-judicial mechanisms that deal with individual and collective complaints associated with violations of ESC rights; the Optional Protocol to the ICESCR and the European Social Charter. In addition to these, the San Salvador Protocol on Economic Social and Cultural Rights establishes a weak periodic reporting mechanism, as well as an outlet for individual communications but only in respect of two specific rights (article 19(6)): the right to form and participate in trade unions under article 8(a) and the right to education in accordance with article 13. Finally, the ACHPR incorporates ESC rights and does not distinguish their justiciable character from that of other rights. As a result, individual communications are available in respect of any violations.

9.6.1   Individual communications and the ICESCR Optional Protocol

As has already been explained, on account of the unique legal nature of ESC rights (i.e. their progressive realisation, resource constraints and other matters), it was inconceivable to the majority of states during the drafting of the Covenant that a body equivalent to the UN HRCtee could receive individual communications. This was further reinforced by the fact that it was doubted whether the rights in the Covenant were justiciable in the first place before the parties' domestic courts. With the issue of non-justiciability having long been disposed of the idea of a complaints procedure began to be discussed within the UN in 1991 and in 2001 the Commission on Human Rights appointed an independent expert on the Question of an Optional Protocol to the ICESCR.[64] The baton was later passed to a working group[65] and following a series of high-level discussions the text of the Protocol was adopted by the UN General Assembly in late 2008.[66] This was by no means a smooth ride and despite the strong consensus from many quarters there was also significant dissent, with some commentators claiming that empowering a committee with powers over the implementation of ESC rights risks

---

[63] The CESCR in its General Comment 19 (right to social security), UN Doc. E/C12/GC/19 (4 February 2008), para. 65, noted that a state violates its duty to provide social security where it fails to adequately regulate the activities of private companies that deny this entitlement to rights-holders.

[64] Comm HR resolution 2001/30 (20 April 2001).

[65] Comm HR resolution 2003/18 (22 April 2003).

[66] For a background to events and discussions leading to its adoption, see C. de Albuquerque, 'Chronicle of an Announced Birth: the Coming into Life of the Optional Protocol to the International Covenant on Economic, Social and Cultural Rights: the Missing Piece of the International Bill of Human Rights', *HRQ* 32 (2010), 144.

establishing a judicially controlled command economy through a counter-democratic process (i.e. a quasi-judicial or other adjudicatory institution).[67]

The Protocol envisages three particular types of communication: individual or group complaints, inter-state communications and an inquiry procedure. The idea behind all three is for the target state to reach a settlement with the complainant or consider reforming those laws and institutions that are found to infringe a particular right. This non-confrontational character of the procedures is reinforced by the fact that the CESCR's recommendations are not meant to be binding. Under article 2, communications may be received by, or on behalf, of individuals or groups of individuals, implying that the procedure is open to minority groups, indigenous persons, trade unions and even NGOs. Significantly, and in line with the jurisprudence of other international tribunals, the violation need not have taken place on the territory of the state party but may occur in any place where the party exercises effective control.[68] A communication is admissible if it does not reveal that the author has suffered a clear disadvantage; even so the Committee may still consider the communication if it raises a serious issue of general importance.[69] Following the admissibility stage the Committee will examine the communication and at the same time it will transmit it to the target state for further statements and explanations.[70] Upon examination the Committee transmits its views, along with its recommendations, to the parties. The target state must give due consideration to the views and recommendations of the Committee and come back within six months with a response on any subsequent action taken.[71]

Given the sparse use made of inter-state complaints before other human rights mechanisms, it would be unlikely that this one would constitute a shining exception. Finally, the inquiry procedure is triggered by the receipt of reliable information indicating grave or systematic violations of ECS rights, upon which the CESCR will invite the target state to cooperate in the examination of available information and submit its observations. Like the other two procedures, this one is also confidential and upon reaching its findings the CESCR will transmit its views to the state concerned, to which it has six months to respond.[72]

9.6.2   The European Committee of Social Rights

Within the context of the Council of Europe a relatively vibrant and successful mechanism came into existence following the adoption of the European Social Charter in 1961. Unlike the ICESCR, which addresses a broad

---

[67] Dennis and Stewart, above note 52, 466.

[68] M. Ssenyonjo, *Economic, Social and Cultural Rights in International Law* (Oxford: Hart, 2009), 34.

[69] Article 4, Optional Protocol.   [70] Article 6, ibid.   [71] Article 9(1) and (2), ibid.

[72] Article 11, ibid.

range of economic and social rights, the Charter largely protects labour and workplace-related rights, though it also encompasses the right to protection of health and to social security,[73] among others. The Charter is monitored by the ESCR which is composed of independent experts. Member states are under an obligation to submit a report every two years discussing the measures they have taken to protect and fulfil the rights stipulated in the Charter, which the Committee duly evaluates. The other function of the Committee is to receive collective complaints alleging unsatisfactory application of the Charter. Such complaints can only be submitted by international organisations of employers and trade unions, NGOs listed under the CoE and representative national organisations of employers and trade unions within the jurisdiction of the targeted state party.[74] Individual communications are not available under the Charter.[75]

QUESTIONS

1   Some liberal democracies take the view that persons who do not contribute to the economy by working and paying taxes and other contributions are not entitled to public goods such as healthcare, water and housing. Discuss by reference to the role of the state.

2   By setting out minimum core obligations the citizens of developed nations risk being disadvantaged because the focus of minimum core obligations is on what poor nations can provide for their people. Discuss.

3   Country A has limited resources and is poor. In designing its national educational plan it reckons its people would benefit if it were to educate more scientists, particularly doctors, nutritionists, agricultural experts and others so that it can offer a better life for its people. In doing so the government is forced to cut educational funding from all remote villages. It justifies this decision by claiming that 95 per cent of rural children ultimately end up as farmers and that therefore providing them with six years of education is a waste of money that could be better spent on training much needed scientists. In any event, this will help rural populations because they will have access to much improved healthcare, housing, water and crop management. Is this exclusion justified under human rights law?

4   It is not the place of the courts to decide on budget allocation because this involves executive considerations. Discuss whether the courts' ordinary judicial review powers cover, or should cover, budgetary matters that affect the

---

[73] Articles 11 and 12, European Social Charter, CETS no. 35.
[74] Article 1, 1995 Additional Protocol to the European Social Charter, CETS no. 158.
[75] See generally, G. de Búrca and B. de Witte, *Social Rights in Europe* (Oxford University Press, 2005).

enjoyment of civil and political and ESC rights. Would the denial of elections be a plausible justification to a claim that a government does not have enough money to hold them? Why should a similar argument refusing to uphold fundamental ESC rights be any different?

5   The new mantra in the post-2008 financial crisis era is that governments should reduce their deficits by drastically curbing public spending. This entails loss of work for many, the charging of end-user fees for services that would otherwise be free, such as healthcare, and the reduction of social welfare services to the vulnerable. Is economic recovery and growth under these terms compatible with fundamental ESC rights? If not, design a brief policy that conforms to social justice, respects ESC rights and yet is financially viable.

9.7   INDICATORS AND BENCHMARKS FOR MEASURING COMPLIANCE

One of the shortcomings associated with the monitoring of states' obligations to respect, protect and fulfil human rights is the lack of verifiable quantitative criteria through which to measure with some degree of accuracy success and failure. This shortcoming is even more visible in the field of ESC rights which encompasses mostly positive obligations required to realise the various entitlements. The idea of introducing practical indicators as a tool for measuring the implementation of rights has been discussed since the early 1990s[76] but it was not until the specific recommendations of Paul Hunt, a UN special rapporteur, that the move to indicators started to become more methodical, informed and streamlined. Human rights indicators are specific information on the state of an event, activity or outcome related to human rights norms and standards which are used to assess and monitor the promotion and protection of rights.[77] In large part this information is of a quantitative character in the form of numbers and percentages. Examples include the percentage of persons covered by social security, access to healthcare, education enrolment rates and the number of women with a fixed income.

The formulation of indicators is subject to several considerations. First, indicators must be anchored in the normative content of particular rights, as opposed to simply reflecting the socio-economic or developmental content of the right. By way of illustration, health indicators compiled by the WHO serve largely different objectives from indicators assessing implementation of the right to health. The latter are not intended to determine the general levels

---

[76] See, for example, the Vienna Declaration and Program of Action, world conference on human rights, UN Doc. A/CONF 157/24 (1993), para. 98.

[77] Report on Indicators for Monitoring Compliance with International Human Rights Instruments, UN Doc. HRI/MC/2006/7 (11 May 2006), para. 7.

of health in a particular nation, but rather to assess to what degree adequate healthcare is available, accessible and known to the population.[78] As a result, human rights indicators require ascertaining the various attributes of rights, which are generally found in the definitions of international treaties and their elaboration by their respective treaty bodies. The attributes of the right to food, for example, are found in article 11 of ICESCR and General Comment 12 of the CESCR on the right to adequate food. They consist of nutrition, food safety and consumer protection, food availability and food safety.[79] These, in turn, are derived from the CESCR's recognition that economic and social rights must be available, accessible (physically and economically, non-discriminatory and people must be well informed) and of a decent quality.[80]

The second consideration is to avoid divorcing cross-cutting human rights norms in the choice of indicators, as would be the case if one were to distinguish non-discrimination, equality, participation, indivisibility and empowerment instead of considering them as elements of a single unit.[81] Without these all other rights are rendered meaningless. In fact, the OHCHR conceded that many of the assessments made by development agencies with regard to North Africa and Arab regions prior to the uprisings of 2011 failed to take adequate account of the increasing inequality and social injustice prevailing there.[82]

It is now well settled that human rights indicators are structured along the lines of a tripartite configuration: they are *structural*, *process* and *outcome*-based.[83] Structural indicators reflect the ratification/implementation of legal instruments and the establishment of institutional mechanisms, such as justiciability and access to justice more generally and the enactment of relevant laws. *Process*-based indicators reflect the degree to which laws are transformed into concrete policies, as is the case with national health and educational plans, universal immunisation programs, public interventions and other matters. *Outcome*-based indicators reflect attainments in the realisation of human rights. Outcome indicators may, however, be misleading because they are results which could well have arisen for other reasons. For example, an increase in life expectancy need not necessarily be the result of universal immunisation, but also that of better nutrition, access to clean water, improved health awareness, education and other things. Thus, process indicators are in a sense more important for the enjoyment of a right than

---

[78] P. Hunt, The Right of Everyone to Enjoy the Highest Attainable Standard of Physical and Mental Health, UN Doc. A/58/427 (10 October 2003), para. 10.

[79] Report on Indicators, para. 15.

[80] See, for example, CESCR General Comment 15, para. 12, referring to the right to water.

[81] Report on Indicators, para. 13.

[82] ECOSOC, Report of the OHCHR, UN Doc. E/2011/90 (26 April 2011), para. 10. The World Bank's country brief on Tunisia is specifically mentioned.

[83] Report on Indicators, paras. 16–19.

outcome indicators. It is also essential for all indicators to be disaggregated, that is to account specifically for disadvantaged and marginalised groups, women, children, minorities, to distinguish low-income people from the middle- and high-income and others so as to be able to assess disparities in the enjoyment of particular rights between various segments of the population.[84]

As has already been explained, indicators serve to confer objective attributes on the various human rights. Once these have been clearly set out their realisation must be measured against individualised benchmarks. These benchmarks will vary from country to country on the basis of available resources and technical capacity and will serve to commit each country to the particular performance standard agreed. By way of illustration, if an outcome indicator for the right to adequate housing demands that affordable and decent accommodation be made available to 80 per cent of low-income households, an appropriate and realistic benchmark for developing country X may be an increase of ten percentile points every year over a period of ten years. On the other hand, industrialised country Y, 75 per cent of whose low-income population enjoys subsidised, cheap or public accommodation, may adopt a benchmark of covering its 5 per cent shortfall within the space of a year. It is crucial to point out that benchmarks are set out in consultation with target states on the basis of their capabilities and certainly never unilaterally. This process is typically referred to as scoping. This process of consultation is also envisaged in respect of indicators, for the sole reason that because they are not expressly written into treaties, states parties may end up refusing to be bound by them. Otherwise, indicators relate to objective elements emanating from the very nature of rights. There are of course a limited number of situations where indicators are only contextually and not universally specific, as is the case with particular diseases and epidemics.[85] It is important to emphasise that the data by which the satisfaction of the benchmarks are to be assessed can be sought from government sources, intergovernmental organisations and NGOs.[86]

In practice, there is no standard set of indicators applicable to each ESC right, apart from the few indicators stipulated in the ICESCR.[87] As a result, the CESCR does not measure obligations on the basis of predefined lists of criteria, as is otherwise the case with the indicators and benchmarks elaborated

---

[84] Ibid., para. 31. CtEDAW General Recommendation 9 (1989) emphasises the need for disaggregated data in order to understand the precise situation of women.

[85] ECOSOC Report 2011, para. 14.   [86] Ibid., para. 17.

[87] Article 12 ICESCR mentions reductions to stillbirth rates and infant mortality in relation to the right to health, whereas article 10(f) CEDAW refers to reduction of female student drop-out rates in respect of the right to education.

in the context of the MDGs, which have been accepted by all participants to the process.[88] In fact, in a number of its general comments, the CESCR has called on parties to consider obtaining guidance on appropriate indicators from specialist bodies such as the WHO, the Food and Agriculture Organisation (FAO), the ILO and others.[89] As a result, although the indicators originally developed by these organisations were not geared towards the realisation of human rights, they have subsequently gone on to initiate workshops in order to formulate indicators premised on a human rights approach. Whether these are adopted as they are or undergo a process of transformation in order to bring them into line with the requirements of ESC rights, which seems more likely, is something that only time will tell.[90]

CASE STUDY 9.2
Indicators on the right to food[1]

List of illustrative indicators on the right to adequate food (UDHR, Art 25) (*MDG related indicators)

	Nutrition	Food Safety and Consumer Protection	Food Availability	Food Accessibility
	• International human right treaties, relevant to the right to adequate food ratified by the State • Date of entry into force and coverage of the right to adequate food in the Constitution or other forms of superior law • Date of entry into force and coverage of domestic laws for implementing the right to adequate food • Number of registered and/or active non-governmental organisations (per 100,000 persons) involved in the promotion and protection of the right to adequate food			
Structural	• Time frame and coverage of national policy on nutrition and nutrition adequacy norms	• Time frame and coverage of national policy on food safety and consumer protection • Number of registered and/or active civil society organisations working in the area of food safety and consumer protection	• Time frame and coverage of national policy on agricultural production and food availability • Time frame and coverage of national policy on drought, crop failure and disaster management	
	• Proportion of received complaints on the right to adequate food investigated and adjudicated by the national human rights institution, human rights ombudsperson or other mechanisms and the proportion of these responded to effectively by the government • Net official development assistance (ODA) for food security received or provided as a proportion of public expenditure on food security or Gross National Income			
Process	• Proportion of targeted population that was brought above the minimum level of dietary energy consumption* in the reporting period • Proportion of targeted population covered under public nutrition supplement programmes • Coverage of targeted population under public programmes on nutrition education and awareness • Proportion of targeted population that was extended access to an improved drinking water source* in the reporting period	• Disposal rate or average time to adjudicate a case registered in a consumer court • Share of public social sector budget spent on food safety and consumer protection advocacy, education, research and implementation of laws and regulations relevant to the right • Proportion of food producing and distributing establishments inspected for food quality standards and frequency of inspections • Proportion of cases adjudicated under food safety and consumer protection law in the reporting period	• Proportion of female headed households or targeted population with legal title to agricultural land • Arable irrigated land per person • Proportion of farmers availing extension services • Share of public budget spent on strengthening domestic agricultural production (e.g. agriculture-extension, irrigation, credit, marketing) • Proportion of per capita availability of major food items sourced through domestic production, import & food-aid • Cereal import dependency ratio in the reporting period	• Share of household consumption of major food items for targetted population group met through publicly assisted programmes • Unemployment rate or average wage rate of targeted segments of labour force • Proportion of targeted population that was brought above the poverty line in the reporting period • Work participation rates, by sex and target groups • Estimated access of women and girls to adequate food within household • Coverage of programmes to secure access to productive resources for target groups
Outcome	• Prevalence of underweight and stunting children under-five years of age* • Proportion of adults with body-mass index (BMI) < 18.5	• Number of recorded deaths and incidence of food poisoning related to adulterated food	• Per capita availability of major food items of local consumption	• Proportion of population below minimum level of dietary energy consumption* / proportion of undernourished population • Average household expenditure on food for the bottom three deciles of population or targeted population
	• Death rates, including infant and under-five mortality rates, associated with and prevalence of malnutrition (including under- overnutrition and inadequate intake of nutrients)			
24.4.08	*All indicators should be disaggregated by prohibited grounds of discrimination, as applicable and reflected in metasheets*			

[1] Report on Indicators, 24.

---

[88] See section 12.3.   [89] CESCR, General Comment 15, para. 53.

[90] See FAO, Voluntary guidelines to support the progressive realisation of the right to adequate food in the context of national food security, available at: www.fao.org/docrep/meeting/009/y9825e/y9825e00.htm, and the seventeen housing rights indicators developed by UN-HABITAT, available at: www.unhabitat.org/pmss/listItemDetails.aspx?publicationID=1749.

9.8   THE RIGHT TO HEALTH

Just like every ESC other right, health is a necessary condition for the achievement of all other civil and political as well as economic and social freedoms and entitlements. Yet, although all nations aspire to have healthy populations that are productive they are at the same time weary of investing a large part of their GDP in health-related expenditures because of the spiralling costs of healthcare and related rights. As a result, a number of countries have turned to private health provision in order to redistribute public wealth in other areas of concern. The obvious problem in such cases is that if the right to health is deemed to exist, then those who cannot afford to go private will suffer ill health or even lose their lives.

Article 12(1) of ICESCR gives rise to a 'right of everyone to the enjoyment of the highest attainable standard of physical and mental health'.[91] It is evident that the Covenant does not articulate a right to be healthy, which cannot be guaranteed even by the best possible medical attention.[92] Rather, it recognises the right to enjoy high standards of health, which represents a wholly different proposition that is largely dependent on a series of positive obligations. These obligations are of a twofold nature: on the one hand, they require the provision of adequate healthcare services, while on the other oblige the authorities to satisfy the underlying determinants of health, including basic shelter, food, water, sanitation, safe working environment, freedom from pollution, disease prevention and others.[93] This definition of the right to health with its two corresponding components is somewhat broader than the definition of 'health' found in the preamble to the Constitution of the WHO, which defines health as a 'state of complete physical, mental and social well-being and not merely the absence of disease or infirmity'.[94] Although health and well-being can never adequately be subject to quantitative computation, health indicators can paint a relatively clear picture about the availability and accessibility of healthcare. Articles 12(2) of ICESCR and 24(2) of the CRC demand at the very least: (1) the reduction of stillbirth rates and infant mortality and healthy development of the child; (2) improvement of environmental and industrial hygiene; (3) prevention, treatment and control of epidemic, endemic and other diseases; (4) provision of necessary medical assistance and healthcare to all children; (5) the combating of child disease and malnutrition; (6) ensuring appropriate pre-natal and post-natal health care for mothers.

Neither the Covenant nor the CESCR require that healthcare and its socioeconomic necessities be provided free of charge. The CESCR does, however,

---

[91] Similarly worded provisions are found also in article 5 CERD; article 12 CEDAW; article 24 CRC; article 10 San Salvador Protocol; article 16 ACHPR; article 11 European Social Charter. See generally Ssenyonjo, above note 68, 313ff.
[92] CESCR, General Comment 14, paras. 8–9.   [93] Ibid., para. 11.   [94] Ibid., para. 4.

emphasise that they must be available, affordable and offered without discrimination.[95] Affordability should not be construed narrowly. By way of illustration, a person who can purchase medicines and treatment by paying 20 per cent of his monthly salary cannot be said to afford his medicines in the same way as another who must sell his house. Affordability, therefore, must be construed by reference to a person's material capacity to live a dignified life. This means that where people are indigent or unable to pay for medical and other socio-economic necessities, lest they be deprived of a dignified life, then the state must offer these free of charge. This has certainly been the position of the South African and Argentine Constitutional and Supreme courts respectively in their dealings with HIV/AIDS sufferers who could not afford access to essential drugs. Although, as already explained, the South African Constitutional Court chooses to justify government restrictions only if they are reasonable, in the *Treatment Action Campaign* case it could find no reasonable basis for withholding a drug which prevented the transmission of HIV by indigenous mothers to their newborn.[96] Its Argentine counterpart has not demanded reasonableness in its ruling favouring unimpeded access to life-saving medicines, although this is probably implicit in its judgments. Rather, its primary consideration was the direct constitutional stipulation and the internationally recognised rights to life and health.[97]

A significant dimension in the interpretation of the right to health is that of gender. Women are routinely given no voice as regards their sexual reproductive rights and little attention is given to their particular health risks, particularly pre-natal care, child mortality and the effects of domestic violence. It is imperative, therefore, that states be obliged to integrate a gender perspective into their national health plans.[98]

Perhaps more than any other ESC right, the realisation of both strands of the right to health in developing countries is dependent significantly on international cooperation. What is striking in the modern world is that technological advances in medicine and drugs do not translate into a rise in the living standards of the billions of poor. This has given rise to a conflict between the right to health on the one hand and the right of pharmaceutical companies to protect their patented drugs from being manufactured and sold at smaller cost by generic producers. This tension is explained more fully in

---

[95] Ibid., para. 12.

[96] *South African Minister of Health* v. *Treatment Action Campaign*, 2002 (5) SA 721. This case seems to contradict *Soobramoney* v. *Minister of Health, KwaZulu-Natal*, 1998 (1) SA 765 where the Court ruled that the authorities were right in prioritising the distribution of scarce medical resources and as a result refused dialysis treatment to an elderly patient who later died. Even so, *Soobramoney* should not be read as a denial of affordable healthcare.

[97] *Asociación Benghalensis and Others* v. *Ministerio de Salud y Acción Social*, Judgment (1 June 2000).

[98] CESCR, General Comment 14, paras. 20–21.

the chapter dealing with globalisation. It suffices therefore here simply to iterate the trend whereby developing nations are now able to produce generic (cheap) drugs in order to protect their indigent populations from the spread of easily treatable or other diseases and infections.

INTERVIEW 9.1

Greek NGO implements the right to health for the socially excluded

(Tzanetos Antypas)

Tzanetos Antypas is Director of Praksis, a Greek NGO active in the creation, application and implementation of programmes related to the provision of humanitarian and medical services, particularly to socially excluded groups.[1]

According to your analyses, how many people in Greece, both immigrants and Greeks, lack access to public healthcare services and why?

On the basis of our data, it is evident that the situation is different for the two population groups. As far as third-country nationals are concerned, their legal status determines their access to public healthcare. Even so, it is possible to estimate that one-third of third-country nationals living in Athens and visit our clinic have problems accessing public healthcare services. For people without proper documentation, in particular [i.e. illegal entrants], things are quite hard indeed. They do not have access to any public healthcare service, save for emergencies which are treated with some cost to the patient and are available only during the duration of the emergency itself.

As regards Greek nationals served by our services, in the course of the past year [i.e. 2011] we observed a rather acute increase in the number of patients visiting our clinics, at a rate of 15 per cent, which accounts mainly for pharmaceutical and medical treatment.

How does your organisation substitute the absence of the state?

Through the provision of entry level medical services via our clinics in Athens and Thessaloniki, which have been working since 1996 and 1997 respectively, Praksis is able to serve indigent segments of the population that face hurdles in accessing public healthcare facilities. Such populations include the Greek indigent, homeless, uninsured persons, financial immigrants, asylum seekers, refugees and any other socially excluded and vulnerable group such as addicts, Roma, trafficking victims, those released from prison, street children, as well as any person with poor access to healthcare, psycho-social or legal support.

[1] Translation from Greek was carried out by the authors. The organisation's website is available at: www.praksis.gr/.

What are the principal medical and social needs of the increasing poor population?

Principal needs mainly consist of pharmaceutical drugs for chronic illnesses (given that these increase the cost of living in the long run), as well as the treatment of illnesses caused by poor living conditions. Moreover, dental treatment is in high demand by a large segment of the people treated in our clinics because it is a service that is costly and is not offered free of charge by the National Health System, whether for Greeks or third-country nationals living in Greece.

What measures would you recommend for the application of the right to health in respect of all those living in Greece, taking into consideration the country's financial situation?

- support and reinforcement of [private non-for-profit] organisations and groups that are active in the provision of healthcare services to vulnerable populations, since such groups and organisations are able to cover the needs of said populations with far lower cost in comparison to public entities;
- support and reinforcement of private initiative in the provision of pharmaceutical products. In other words, there needs to be support for the production of drugs by Greek pharmaceutical companies since this would decrease the cost of healthcare generally in public hospitals, as well as the cost to the patients;
- decentralisation of the health system through the support of regional healthcare institutions (e.g. support for community medical centres) since these will end up receiving the bulk of referrals and incidents that demand entry-level treatment at lower cost in comparison to a centralised institution with similar referrals and incidents;
- promulgation of a law detailing relevant procedures for the legalisation of newly arrived third-country nationals. The legalisation of their residence in Greece will culminate in the payment of national insurance premiums which ultimately will lead to increased earnings for the National Health System.

9.9   THE RIGHT TO WATER

Water is a limited natural resource that is essential for the preservation of life, in addition to its utility in cooking food, sanitation and sewerage, personal hygiene and religious rites, among other things. In 2011 it was estimated that nearly one billion people lacked access to an improved source of drinking water and 2.6 billion did not have access to improved sanitation. This is a far cry from the targets set by the MDGs and the failure is largely down to inadequate funding. Some estimates consider that if we are to halve the number of those without access to water and sanitation by 2015 an annual cost of US$16.58 billion will be required. Sadly, the total annual amount of international aid earmarked for water and sanitation is substantially less than half the above required mark.[99]

Before examining the particular contours of the right to water it is necessary to emphasise that it is a resource that is freely given (e.g. unlike agriculture, which requires cultivation of seeds). Thus, if it is to be treated as a good, or commodity, the value of water should reflect only the investment necessary to clean, purify and transport it to households. Even so, given that it constitutes an ingredient of life, by denying it to those who cannot afford to pay its additional investment cost, one is necessarily depriving the poor of their right to life. This tension is particularly reflected in those countries that possess limited water resources and those that have privatised their water distribution systems, so that the investor intends to make a profit. It is also useful to point out that domestic water consumption accounts for less than 10 per cent of total use, the rest being consumed by irrigation in agriculture and industry. This does not mean that agriculture should cease, given that it provides food that sustains life, but certain sectors that consume high levels of water, such as cotton, should not be given priority over food crops and domestic use, especially where water is scarce.

The right to water has been affirmed by the CESCR by reference to the right to an adequate standard of living in article 11(1) of ICESCR. While this provision does not specifically mention water, its list of essentials (i.e. food, clothing and housing) is merely indicative through the word 'including'.[100] Given that the right to the highest attainable standard of health requires water for drinking and sanitation,[101] it is equally implicit in this right also. Quite clearly it is also implicit in the right to life, among others, as already stated.[102] In its General Comment 15, dedicated especially to the right to water, the CESCR has elaborated the particular qualities of this entitlement. The right contemplates a degree of adequacy which, according to the CESCR,

---

[99] SR Report on the Human Right to Safe Drinking Water and Sanitation, UN Doc. A/66/255 (3 August 2011), paras. 9–12.

[100] UNGA resolution 64/292 (28 July 2010) explicitly recognised the right to water as a distinct entitlement.

[101] For the importance of sanitation as a fundamental component of the right to water, see CESCR, General Comment 15, para. 29.

[102] It is also directly recognised as a distinct right in a long list of international instruments, including article 14(2)(h) of CEDAW, article 24(2) of the CRC, article 28(2)(a) of the CRPD and in numerous provisions of IHL.

should not be measured merely according to volumetric quantities.[103] In practice, however, most institutions follow the WHO Guidelines on Domestic Water Quantity, Service Level and Health, which sets fifty litres per person daily as the minimum for basic hygienic and consumption requirements.[104]

The South African Supreme Court in *Mazibuko and Others* v. *City of Johannesburg* adopted a different approach. One of the issues in the case concerned the installation of a pre-paid meter in an impoverished Soweto neighbourhood that allocated 25 litres per person daily (10 kilolitres monthly per household being free of charge), well below the WHO's Guidelines. In keeping with earlier jurisprudence, the Court refused to determine a minimum core, adding that the City was not under a constitutional obligation to provide any particular amount of free water; rather, it was under a duty to take reasonable measures progressively to realise the achievement of the right. The Court found the policy to be reasonable because it charged excessive use, avoided waste and catered to everyone's needs, including the provision of free water for the indigent.[105]

The water must be of a specified quality, in the sense that it must be safe for consumption and as a result should be free from micro-organisms, chemical and other substances.[106] It should moreover be accessible to individual users, both physically and economically.[107] It is not always feasible to bring water into houses in shanty towns or dwellings in remote villages because of the lack of infrastructure. None the less, it is accepted that water should be within reasonable walking distance from dwelling groups, otherwise physical accessibility is essentially denied. The CESCR emphasises that water must be 'affordable for all', not necessarily free for all. This is subject to several reservations. First, there exists a 'special obligation' to provide water and sanitation to those who cannot afford them, including marginalised and vulnerable groups.[108] Secondly, the concept of affordability means that water charges may be set in such a way that higher- and middle-income people subsidise those on lower incomes, so that the latter can enjoy water free of charge or at very little cost.[109] This is the case, for example, with the Chilean Law 18,788

---

[103] CESCR, General Comment 15, para. 11.

[104] Available at: www.who.int/water_sanitation_health/diseases/WSH03.02.pdf.

[105] *Mazibuko and Others* v. *City of Johannesburg* [2009] ZACC 28, paras. 77ff., *per* O'Regan J.

[106] CESCR, General Comment 15, para. 12(b). Guaranteed also in articles 23 and 42 of the Ecuador Constitution. The Indian Supreme Court in *Subhash Kumar* v. *State of Bihar and Others* (1991) AIR 420, held that the right to life guaranteed under article 21 of the Constitution encompasses the enjoyment of pollution-free water.

[107] General Comment 15, para. 12(c).   [108] Ibid., para. 15.

[109] In fact, the Special Rapporteur on water and sanitation in her 2011 Report, para. 19, stresses that 'obtaining water at no cost may actually harm low-income households by depriving service providers of the revenue needed to expand and maintain the service and risks being unsustainable'.

where the subsidisation of water is assessed on the income of households.[110] States can additionally minimise water prices by the adaptation of low-cost techniques and technologies.[111] Finally, the price of water should not be susceptible to commodity-like fluctuations or the interventions of private water providers[112] and thus must be treated as a public good.

The obligation to provide water of a decent quality and quantity to all people is meaningless if states are not under compulsion to protect the environment where potable water is found. More so, states are responsible for preserving and augmenting their water resources so that they can be available for future generations.[113] The right to water constitutes a fine example of the extraterritorial reaches of certain ESC rights. Although country A does not have an obligation to make available water to the citizens of state B, it is none the less obliged to take all those steps on its territory that do not prejudice the enjoyment of this entitlement by the citizens of B. A likely scenario is the erection of dams or river diversions that preclude downstream consumers from enjoying water. It is for this reason that as a general rule states should not unilaterally act in this manner in the detriment of their neighbours or against 'vital human needs' of civilian populations.[114] In practice, states that share freshwater resources make an effort to enter into bilateral or multilateral agreements that regulate in detail their mutual affairs. This in no way means that conflicts over water are exceptional.

CASE STUDY 9.3
The deprivation of water rights as cruel and inhuman treatment

In *Mosetlhanyane and Others* v. *Attorney-General* (*Kalahari Bushmen* case),[1] the Botswana Court of Appeal was confronted with a claim by a group of Kalahari bushmen who had occupancy rights over an arid land but who were not permitted by the government to extract underground water. In fact, a mining company had originally dug a deep hole in the area, which once abandoned was fitted with a pump and had since then been used by the indigenous group for extracting underground water, which was their only source of water. The government recognised, albeit reluctantly, that although the indigenous

[1] *Mosetlhanyane and Others* v. *Attorney-General* (*Kalahari Bushmen* case), judgment (27 January 2011).

---

[110] Centre on Housing Rights and Evictions (COHRE), *Legal Resources for the Right to Water and Sanitation* (2008), p. 77.

[111] General Comment 15, para. 27.   [112] Ibid., para. 24.   [113] Ibid., para. 28.

[114] See articles 6(1)(b) and 10(2) of the 1997 UN Convention on the Law of the Non-Navigable Uses of International Watercourses. Irrespective of the status of the convention, the principles of equity and reasonableness upon which these provisions are based have long been considered part of customary international law.

group possessed occupancy rights in the land,[2] which by that time was a wildlife reserve, all underground streams were public property and were not subject to unilateral use, even by the land's super-adjacent occupants. In court it was shown that the lack of water had caused a number of maladies to the bushmen. The Court cited with approval General Comment 15 of the CESCR and held that it was irrational for one to possess occupancy rights but not water rights, especially if no other water is available, in which case the person was effectively denied his right of occupancy. As a result, the bushmen were entitled to water rights and a quantity that was important for their private needs.

The Court went on to invoke article 7(1) of the Constitution, which protects all persons from inhuman or degrading treatment. It held that the deprivation of water to a population lawfully occupying land which was arid amounted to such treatment and ordered the authorities to restore the applicant's pump.

[2] The group's occupancy rights were recognised a few years prior in *Sesana and Others* v. *Attorney-General* [2006] 2 BLR 633 (HC).

9.10 THE RIGHT TO EDUCATION

Education and its availability raise two practical issues. First, while the provision of quality education is expensive, no meaningful development can be achieved without it. The lack of education is a particular characteristic of those living in extreme or moderate poverty. The US Supreme Court in its landmark case of *Brown* v. *Board of Education* noted that 'it is doubtful that any child may reasonably be expected to succeed in life if he is denied the opportunity of an education'.[115] Secondly, without a quality education most civil and political rights are meaningless. Freedom of expression, assembly, democratic governance and other things can only be realised if the rights-holders are capable of understanding and pursuing their rights. Since the drafting of article 13 of ICESCR on the right to education, a number of controversies have arisen. Chief among these is the spiralling cost of public education, particularly in an era of financial constraint, which has caused many nations to partially privatise elements of their educational system or otherwise introduce direct and indirect user fees. Other controversies include discrimination in the quality of education provided to vulnerable groups, which leads to their social exclusion.

Besides the ICESCR, the right to education is enshrined, among others, in article 17(1) of the ACHPR, articles 3 and 13 of the San Salvador Protocol, article 2 of Protocol I to the ECHR, article 11(3) of the 1999 African Charter

[115] *Brown* v. *Board of Education of Topeka* 347 US 483, 493 (1954).

on the Rights and Welfare of the Child, article 5(e)(v) of ICERD, article 28 of the CRC and article 8(1) of the Declaration on the Right to Development. Moreover, the preamble to the UNESCO Constitution elevates education to a sacred duty because it leads to the achievement of dignity, understanding of peoples, development and the exchange of ideas and knowledge. All of these instruments to a large degree converge as to the projected aims and objectives of education, which by and large also determine its quality. Thus, education must be directed towards the full development of the human personality, achieving human dignity, enabling persons to effectively participate in a free society and promoting understanding between all groups and nations. In more recent years, two further elements have been recognised by the CESCR as inherent to this process: gender equality and respect for the environment.[116]

Education is distinguished on the basis of three layers, each corresponding to a more advanced level of study, namely primary, secondary and tertiary (or university) education. In between these there are several sub-categories, particularly basic education and technical or vocational education. Article 13(2)(a) of ICESCR expressly stipulates that primary education should be universal, without discrimination, and provided free of charge irrespective of a country's financial situation.[117] This is an immediate, not a progressive duty, despite the fact that public resources in the form of teachers' salaries, school buildings and books are required. Yet even if governments secure all the necessities for free education, a number of marginalised children may still be excluded through indirect costs.[118] For example, physical inaccessibility will naturally hinder children living in remote areas from travelling to school several miles away. The same is true of schools demanding specific uniforms and books, the cost of which burdens those families that cannot afford them. Finally, the universality of primary education means that states must take appropriate measures to compel *all* children to attend primary school, despite the misgivings of their parents, whether because children are considered breadwinners or because of gender discrimination, in addition to cultural practices and beliefs. Although the CESCR has explained that primary education must 'take into account the culture, needs and opportunities

---

[116] CESCR, General Comment 13, UN Doc. E/C12/1999/10 (8 December 1999), para. 5.

[117] In *SERAC* v. *Federal Republic of Nigeria and Universal Basic Education Commission*, the Nigerian government argued that because of corruption, funds destined for the realisation of basic and primary education were no longer available. As a result, it was unable to fulfil its pertinent obligations. The ECOWAS Court held that the right to primary education is universal and not subject to any resource limitations and ordered Nigeria to rectify the situation.

[118] Although the ICESCR does not impose an obligation on parties to provide day-care and pre-school access, the Brazilian Federal Supreme Court has inferred such an obligation from the country's constitutional mandate regarding the right to education: case RE 436996/SP, Judgment, 26 October 2005.

of the community',[119] this should not be used as a justificatory guise for social exclusion. Consider a situation where the children of a marginalised ethnic minority within country X are given free education only through their minority language, but not in the dominant language. Although this might seem to satisfy the cultural needs of the minority, it perpetuates the social exclusion of the group's new generation and its continued marginalisation.[120] This is why it is imperative that minority members receive a broad education equal to that of the majority,[121] unless the difference in treatment is based on objective and reasonable justification.[122]

As far as secondary and university education are concerned, article 13 of ICESCR makes some practical distinctions. Unlike primary education, which must be compulsory and universal, secondary education is to be made generally available and accessible to all, but its fee component is subject to progressive, as opposed to immediate, realisation. University education must equally be made accessible to all, but unlike the other two layers there does not exist a general right to higher education. Rather, accessibility is assessed by capacity alone, which is measured by a degree of competition between candidates. Although states are under an obligation to progressively abolish fees in public universities in accordance with article 13(2)(c) of ICESCR, this should not be given a restrictive interpretation. In countries like the UK, which have introduced significant higher education fees, prospective students are not required to pay upfront and are eligible for low-interest, subsidised, loans that also cover their accommodation and maintenance. These loans are repayable only when students start earning an average salary. The fees in this case, unfortunate as they are, link education with a guarantee of employability and should not be viewed as a denial of higher education rights.

The right to education in the ICESCR derives its philosophical foundations from a combination of socialist and liberal traditions, given that it renders the state the primary provider of education while at the same time entitling parents to direct their children's education in accordance with their religious and other beliefs.[123] This includes the right of parents to enrol their children

---

[119] CESCR, General Comment 13, para. 9. Culturally sensitive education was endorsed as far back as 1935 by the PCIJ in the case concerning *Minority Schools in Albania*, Advisory Opinion (1935) PCIJ Reports, Ser. A/B no. 64, pp. 3, 17.

[120] The HRCtee in its concluding observations on Georgia pointed out that the lack of Georgian language skills 'could lead to marginalization and under-representation of minorities in different public and private spheres'. UN Doc. CCPR/C/GEO/CO/3 (15 November 2007), para. 17.

[121] Article 4(4), 1992 UN Declaration on Minority Rights.

[122] In *D. H. and Others* v. *Czech Republic* (2008) 47 EHRR 3, para. 196, the ECtHR held that where a difference in treatment is based on race or ethnicity, 'the notion of objective and reasonable justification must be interpreted as strictly as possible'.

[123] K. D. Beiter, *The Protection of the Right to Education by International Law* (Dordrecht: Martinus Nijhoff, 2005), 24.

in private schools so long as these conform to minimum educational standards laid down or approved by the state.[124] This is part of the wider concept
of academic freedom, which on the one hand corresponds to the parents'
entitlement to educate their child according to their belief system, while on
the other hand, the right of freedom of expression allows higher education
institutions to propagate ideas freely.

9.11   THE RIGHT TO FOOD

Despite human advances in sciences close to one billion people currently suffer
from undernourishment.[125] This number is staggering if one considers that
undernourishment exists when caloric intake is below the minimum dietary
energy requirements (MDER) and is essentially a synonym for hunger; hence,
it is merely poor feeding. This situation is unjustifiable because the global food
crisis is not the result of food shortage; rather, it is the result of poor availability and accessibility on account of socio-economic factors. Food crises,
also described as famines, began to receive media attention in the late 1970s
and were originally viewed from a humanitarian perspective. Essentially, the
international community undertook an anti-hunger role through the provision
of relief shipments to the destitute. However, from the mid-1990s onwards it
became evident that a combination of sharp population increases, climatic
change, commodification of agricultural produce, unequal trade liberalisation
in the agricultural sector and poor crop management and sustainability had
led to soaring food prices beyond the reach of the poor. The problem could no
longer be handled through anti-hunger policies, but instead required a holistic
approach to the question of food accessibility and availability.

This holistic approach is encapsulated in the right to food, which is articulated in article 11 of the ICESCR.[126] There are two strands to this entitlement.
In its generic form the right to food is derived from the right to an adequate
standard of living, whereby food must be available 'in a quantity and quality
sufficient to satisfy the dietary needs of [all] individuals, free from adverse
substances and acceptable within a given culture' while at the same time its
availability must be sustainable and should not interfere with the enjoyment
of other human rights.[127] Thus, food need not necessarily be dispensed by the

---

[124] Article 13(3) ICESCR.   [125] FAO, *The State of Food Insecurity in the World* (2010), 8.

[126] The right to food is also protected in article 25 UDHR; articles 12 and 14 CEDAW; articles
25 and 27 CRC; articles 12, 15 and 17 of the San Salvador Protocol, albeit the right
to food is not directly justiciable in the Protocol. The right to food was also explicitly
recognised in principle 3 of the 2009 FAO Declaration of the World Summit on Food
Security, FAO Doc. WSFP 2009/2 (16–18 November 2009). See FAO, 'The Right to Food
and Access to Justice: Examples at the National, Regional and International Levels' (2009).

[127] CESCR, General Comment 12, paras. 6–8.

state for free but the state is under a concrete obligation to take all means at its disposal to make food affordable and available to all with a view to securing a dignified life.[128] States are certainly able to increase food production by, among other things, subsidising small-scale farming, as well as decreasing the cost of food through the elimination of all taxes and tariffs on basic foods. In addition, as already discussed, they can impose a tax on the wealthy to offset the residual cost of food production in favour of the poor. Equally, apart from its positive obligations, the state should refrain from action that removes existing access to food, particularly mass displacement, introduction of toxic substances into the food chain and other things.[129] In the *Ogoniland* case, for example, the Nigerian government had allowed foreign oil companies to take over the land occupied by the Ogoni, thus leading to widespread land and water contamination and expulsion through terror tactics. All of this resulted, as the ACHPR pointed out, in the violation of the Ogoni's right to food.[130] Strategic litigation concerned with the right to food in the developing world generally challenges the soundness of food and agricultural concessions to foreign investors in situations where local communities rely on those resources for their survival.[131]

The other component of the right to food is the right to be free from hunger, stipulated in paragraph 2 of article 11 of ICESCR. Although this provision largely describes the measures required of states unilaterally and collectively, the right to be free from hunger has been viewed by the CESCR as a minimum core obligation as follows:

> Every state is obliged to ensure for everyone under its jurisdiction access to the minimum essential food which is sufficient, nutritionally adequate and safe, to ensure their freedom from hunger.[132]

The right to be free from hunger best addresses the plight and food needs of peoples and populations. First, it requires states to plan ahead by, for example, improving methods of production or introducing appropriate food conservation on the basis of scientific knowledge.[133] Its second dimension entails the urgent distribution of food to those who are destitute and in circumstances where food is inaccessible. Such situations are typical not only

---

[128] Special Rapporteur on the Right to Food, Report on the Right to Food, UN Doc. E/CN4/2001/53 (7 February 2001), para. 14.

[129] Special Rapporteur on the Right to Food, Report on the Right to Food, UN Doc. E/CN4/2006/44 (16 March 2006), para. 22.

[130] *SERAC and Center for Economic and Social Rights* v. *Nigeria*, Case no. ACHPR/COMM/ A044/1, *AJIL* 96 (2002), 937, paras. 65–66.

[131] See, for example, *Jagannath* v. *Union of India and Others*, 1997 SCC (2) 87, where the Indian Supreme Court upheld the traditional fishing rights of a coastal community whose access to food (fish) was curtailed by the issuance of limited fishing licences to private investors.

[132] CESCR, General Comment 12, para. 14.   [133] Article 11(2)(a) ICESCR.

in the aftermath of an earthquake, tsunami or other natural disaster, but also where people have been displaced or are habitually excluded from enjoying food. This latter category is usually forgotten by governments on account of their low socio-economic status – coupled with a complete lack of basic education – which means that whatever their personal circumstances they possess little, or no, voting power.

The *Rajasthan Hunger* case[134] is instructive of a particular dimension of this approach. As an introduction to the case it should be pointed out that India and China account for 40 per cent of the world's undernourished population.[135] In terms of actual numbers, 200 million Indians fall within this category and it is not surprising that in their majority they comprise Dalits, women, poor tribal communities, children and other vulnerable populations living on the fringes of society. It is estimated that up to 2 million children die every year in India as a direct or indirect result of undernourishment.[136] By 2001 a growing number of hunger-related deaths were unfolding in Rajasthan, despite the existence of sufficient food supplies in nearby government storage. In fact, the food was left to rot and was reportedly in the process of being eaten by rodents. The underlying government indifference and poor management was found by the Indian Supreme Court to violate the constitutionally recognised right to life (article 21) as read against the directive principle on nutrition contained in article 47 of the Constitution. The government not only refused to implement the Indian Famine Code, which permitted the release of grain stocks in situations of famine, but further argued that it did not have sufficient resources as a result of the crisis. The Court naturally dismissed all these arguments and went on to issue several directives to the authorities demanding that they identify beneficiaries and make food accessible to them.[137]

A similar result was reached by the Colombian Constitutional Court in the *Abel Antonio Jaramillo* case.[138] There, thousands of internally displaced persons were left without any assistance by the Colombian authorities, including access to food. The Court held that the exposure of these people to conditions of food deprivation, among other things, was a violation of their right to food, the minimum requirements of which the state was under an obligation to provide to all in need. It went on to request the authorities to formulate an adequate plan to assist the victims. In similar fashion, the Supreme Court of

---

[134] *People's Union for Civil Liberties* v. *Union of India and Others*, Writ Petition (Civil) no. 196/2001. See also *Kishen Pattnayak and Another* v. *State of Orissa*, AIR 1989 SC 677, where the right to food as a corollary to the right to life was first expounded.

[135] FAO, Report on Food Insecurity, 10.

[136] Special Rapporteur, Right to Food Report 2006, para. 7.

[137] See FAO, Report on the Right to Food, 26, 56–7.

[138] *Abel Antonio Jaramillo and Others* v. *La Red de Solidaridad Social and Others*, T-025/2004, ibid., 25.

Nepal in a judgment issued in April 2011 examined the plight of several districts facing acute food shortages with an estimated undernourished population of 300,000. While reaffirming the constitutional right to food, it held that the state must take every available measure to protect its citizens from food scarcity caused by natural disaster.[139]

The right to food should be examined by reference to two important international efforts to boost global food supplies and prevent hunger. These consist of the 1996 Rome Declaration on World Food Security, reviewed thereafter through a series of World Food Summits (WFS) organised by FAO and the UN's MDGs. Both initiatives set out to halve the number of undernourished people by 2015, but it is highly unlikely that this will be achieved, particularly following the sharp increase in food prices between 2006 and 2008. Some countries have criticised the absence of any mention of the root causes of global food insecurity from FAO summits and declarations, particularly the impact of agricultural subsidies on poor farmers, the conversion of grains and cereals into fuel, the consequences of financial speculation on food prices and the imposition of conditionalities on developing nations. Indeed, developed nations are disinclined to discuss such issues in the context of food security alone and prefer to incorporate them in the agenda of the WTO.

A significant achievement of the 2002 WFS was the subsequent endorsement in 2004 of a set of voluntary guidelines on the Progressive Realisation of the Right to Adequate Food in the Context of National Food Security.[140] The importance of the guidelines lies in the fact that they were endorsed by all WFS not only as a matter of policy but also as a matter of pledged target. Increasingly, they are also relied on by governments and the courts. The aforementioned Nepalese Supreme Court judgment seems to have been influenced by several sections of the guidelines.

QUESTIONS

1 If a state has inadequate water resources, is it justified in rationing water to its people even slightly below the minimum threshold stipulated by the WHO?

2 Free-market economists argue that states should not intervene in the running and operation of markets because this does not allow them to reach their full potential which in turn would create numerous benefits for societies. Critically discuss, with reference to the global surge in food prices which exposes three-quarters of the world's population to acute food deprivation although there is enough food for everyone.

---

[139] Reported by www.fao.org/righttofood/news47_en.htm.
[140] Available at: www.fao.org/docrep/meeting/009/y9825e/y9825e00.htm.

3 There is an inherent tension between the values protected under intellectual property law (i.e. the property rights of the inventor) and the right of the sick and suffering to life-saving medicines in accordance with the right to health. Discuss.

4 Why is it important that benchmarks be agreed to by the target state and adapted to its particular circumstances?

5 When dealing with private actors that dispense in substance those ESC rights guaranteed by the state (e.g. water and sewerage, private social security and healthcare) are the remedies available under human rights law more effective for the victims? It may be argued that if victims were assimilated to consumers clearly enjoying the pertinent ESC rights they could turn against the providers of services on the basis of both contract and tort. In this manner they could enforce their rights directly against the 'violators'. Discuss.

9.11.1   Links between loss of the right to work, debt crisis and mental illness

The right to work, enshrined among other instruments in article 6 of ICESCR, cannot realistically be construed in such a way as to oblige states to secure employment to all their citizens. This would require a shift from capital-led economies to publicly dominated ones. Resource constraints aside, there are other ways to realise this entitlement, which is a fundamental precondition for a dignified life. According to the CESCR, states are obliged to counter unemployment by setting up employment policies that stimulate economic growth and development and raise living standards.[141] Moreover, in order to facilitate access to work they must provide appropriate vocational and technical training and establish their national economies in a manner that tends toward meaningful job creation. Significantly, the CESCR emphasises that:

States parties that are members of international financial institutions, in particular the International Monetary Fund, the World Bank and regional development banks, should pay greater attention to the protection of the right to work in influencing the lending policies, credit agreements, structural adjustment programmes and international measures of these institutions. The strategies, programmes and policies adopted by states parties under structural adjustment programmes should not interfere with their core obligations in relation to the right to work and impact negatively on the right to work of women, young persons and the disadvantaged and marginalized individuals and groups.[142]

---

[141] CESCR General Comment 18 (right to work), UN Doc. E/C12/GC/18 (6 February 2006), paras. 26–7. See also J. Sarkin and M. Koenig, 'Developing the Right to Work: Intersecting and Dialoguing Human Rights and Economic Policy', *HRQ* 33 (2011), 1.

[142] Ibid., para. 30.

This observation by the CESCR stems from the practice of the IMF of disregarding the right to meaningful employment and the associated benefits in its design of structural adjustment programmes for indebted nations (although without exception, in all its official reports and lending conditions the IMF emphasises quite the opposite). Among its lending conditions to Greece – between 2010 and 2012 – the IMF demanded the dismissal of one-third of the country's civil servants, the reduction of as much as 50 per cent of the remainder's salaries,[143] below-living-standards salaries for the bulk of private sector workers and the introduction of fees for basic and advanced healthcare. At the same time, and while the economy was shrinking, the IMF and its partners, both public and private, demanded the imposition of the highest possible taxes on all goods and services, the ultimate aim being to repay the country's debts irrespective of the suffering of the low-income and poor classes. This obviously had a detrimental effect on job creation and unemployment rose to almost 20 per cent in January 2012 – which does not take into consideration the prospective public sector dismissal demands and those not officially registered as unemployed – compared to less than 5 per cent in Austria during the same time. For a country with traditionally strong family connections, Greeks were shocked to learn that homelessness had risen by 20 per cent each year since the start of the recession,[144] whereas poverty levels had risen by 25 per cent during the same period.

No doubt, the IMF, EU member states and multilateral lending institutions are aware not only that their structural adjustment programme (SAP) for Greece stifles growth and thus hampers job creation, but that unemployment is clinically associated with high ratios of psychiatric disorders, quadrupling the odds of drug dependence, trebling the odds of phobias and functional psychosis and doubling the odds of depression-related episodes.[145] Stuckler *et al.* undertook an empirical study of twenty-six European nations for the period between 1970 and 2006 in order to assess the impact of financial volatility on death rates and the way in which governments could limit negative impacts. They found that for every percentile increase in unemployment there was an associated 0.8 per cent increase in suicides for those below sixty-five years, as well as a 0.8 per cent increase in homicides. Unemployment increases above

---

[143] Although the IMF's suggested cuts represent a decrease of 8–10 per cent in salaries and pensions, the real loss to income is closer to 40–50 per cent, if one considers elimination of salary-related benefits, introduction of fees for health and other services and sharp increases in taxes on income, property and others.

[144] P. Beaumont, 'Greek Rise in Homelessness Creates a New Poor', *The Guardian* (3 August 2011).

[145] V. Murali and F. Oyebode, 'Poverty, Social Inequality and Mental Health', *Advances in Psychiatric Treatment* 10 (2004), 216, 218–19; K. Paul and K. Moser, 'Unemployment Impairs Mental Health: Meta-analyses', *Journal of Vocational Behaviour* 74 (2009), 264, who demonstrate that the unemployed display a higher degree of psychiatric disorders than those in employment (34 against 16 per cent).

3 per cent were moreover correlated to higher suicide rates (above 4 per cent) as well as greater alcohol-related deaths. Encouragingly, they discovered that rising unemployment rates had no impact on suicides in countries where governments augmented public spending on active labour market programmes intended to sustain and create new jobs by at least US$190 annually per person.[146]

In a 1987 report, UNICEF had cautioned the World Bank institutions that SAPs had a negative impact on health and education, including job losses as a result of excessive cuts in public spending.[147] Although SAPs have in theory been replaced by new programmes requiring an impact assessment on the poor, they fail to provide social safety nets, as the case of Greece aptly demonstrates.

Following the global financial crisis of 2008 the WHO conducted a number of studies on the relationship between debt, unemployment and mental health. While acknowledging the scientific results linking unemployment, especially among men, to increased levels of mental illness and alcoholism, the reports sought ways to mitigate the effects of the debt crisis. Data shows that governments can alleviate the effects of financial crises on the unemployed through active labour market programmes that assist people to remain, or return, to employment, the enhancement of family support measures, restrictions on alcohol availability, debt relief and access to mental health-related services.[148] These findings are supported by specific case studies. During steep economic recessions in Finland and Sweden leading to high unemployment, the augmentation of social benefits and services resulted in a drop in suicide rates.[149] In the USA, on the other hand, there was a concrete link between an increase in suicide rates and a reduction in social welfare spending.[150]

This practical application aims to demonstrate that economic and social rights are interdependent, centred around the notion of a dignified life. The idea that a nation will be delivered from chaos and disaster unless it reduces public spending in all fields of social welfare has by now proved to be just a myth. A decrease in social welfare projects, including education, health and employment programmes, will not only cost more in the long run but will deprive a nation of a good part of its human capital as a result of generalised

---

[146] D. Stuckler *et al.*, 'The Public Health Effect of Economic Crises and Alternative Policy Responses in Europe: an Empirical Analysis', *Lancet* 374 (2009), 315.

[147] R. Jolly, 'Adjustment with a Human Face: a UNICEF Record and Perspective on the 1980s', *World Development* 19 (1991), 1807.

[148] WHO, Impact of Economic Crises on Mental Health (2011), 8.

[149] Ibid., 8–9.

[150] S. L. Zimmerman, 'States' Spending for Public Welfare and Their Suicide Rates, 1960 to 1995: What is the Problem?' *Journal of Nervous and Mental Disorders* 190 (2002), 349.

ill health, lack of innovation and decrease in wealth creation.[151] This does not of course mean that states should not make savings, even in sectors such as health; rather, it is the nature of the cuts and their effect on middle- and low-income populations that is important. Canada, for example, introduced significant cost containment reforms to its publicly funded health sectors in the 1990s. It did so by setting budget caps whereby the federal government adjusted funding to each province on the basis of per capita growth and inflation. Hospital budgets and medical salaries were also capped because all hospitals and physicians were publicly financed. The federal government moreover introduced price controls on pharmaceutical products by freezing their prices. Even so, the Canadian government increased public health expenditures rapidly as a share of GDP in times of recession.[152] As a result, Canada continued to enjoy one of the highest publicly funded universal health-care systems in the world. States should view the improvement of social services as an investment in their human capital and must not cave in to demands from multilateral financial institutions to demolish those services under the simplistic guise of debt reduction.

FURTHER READING

Agbakwa, S., 'Reclaiming Humanity: Economic, Social and Cultural Rights as the Cornerstone of African Human Rights', *Yale Human Rights and Development Law Journal* (*Yale Hum. Rts. & Dev. L.J.*) 5 (2000), 177.

Alfredsson, G. and Tomaševski, K. (eds.), *The Universal Declaration of Human Rights: A Common Standard of Achievement* (Dordrecht: Martinus Nijhoff, 1999).

Alston, P., 'US Ratification of the Covenant on Economic, Social and Cultural Rights: The Need for an Entirely New Strategy', *AJIL* 84 (1990), 365.

Alston, P. and Quinn, G., 'The Nature and Scope of States Parties' Obligations under the International Covenant on Economic, Social and Cultural Rights', *HRQ* 9 (1987), 156.

Baderin, M. A. and McCorquodale, R. (eds.), *Economic, Social and Cultural Rights in Action* (Oxford University Press, 2007).

Betten, L., 'The Implementation of Social and Economic Rights by the ILO', *NQHR* 6 (1998), 29.

Bilchitz, D., *Poverty and Fundamental Rights: The Justification and Enforcement of Socio-Economic Rights* (Oxford University Press, 2007).

[151] The Russian Federation, for example, at the time of writing spends 5.3 per cent of its GDP on health, well below the OECD average of 7–10 per cent. The World Bank has estimated that this has, and will continue to have, an adverse impact on labour supply because job holders with non-communicable diseases are more likely to retire early or lose their jobs and draw on state pensions. The effect is greatest among the poor. Empirical analyses moreover demonstrate that poor health affects the number of productive working hours. Men and women in good health earn about 30 and 18 per cent respectively more compared to their ill counterparts. World Bank, *Public Spending in Russia for Healthcare: Issues and Options*, (2008), 11–12.

[152] IMF, *Macro-fiscal Implications of Health Care Reform in Advanced and Emerging Economies: Case Studies* (December 2010), available at www.imf.org/external/np/pp/eng/2010/122810a.pdf, 4–6.

Boon, K., 'The Role of Courts in Enforcing Economic and Social Rights', (*Geo. Wash. Int'l L. Rev.*) (*George Washington International Law Review*) 39 (2007), 449.

Cepeda-Espinoza, M. J., 'Transcript: Social and Economic Rights and the Colombian Constitutional Court', (*Tex. L. Rev.*) (*Texas Law Review*) 89 (2010–11), 1699.

Chapman, A. A., 'Violations Approach for Monitoring the International Covenant on Economic, Social and Cultural Rights', *HRQ* 18 (1996), 23.

Chenwi, L., 'Putting Flesh on the Skeleton: South African Judicial Enforcement of the Right to Adequate Housing of those Subject to Evictions', *HRLR* 8 (2008), 105.

Coomans, F., (ed.), *Justiciability of Economic and Social Rights: Experiences from Domestic Systems* (Antwerp: Intersentia, 2006).

Courtis, C., 'The Right to Food as a Justiciable Right: Challenges and Strategies,' *MPYBUNL* 11 (2007), 317.

Davies, D. M., 'Socio-economic Rights: Do they Deliver the Goods?,' *IJCL* 6 (2008), 687.

Filmer-Wilson, E., 'Human Rights-based Approach to Development: the Right to Water', *NQHR* 23 (2005), 213.

Ghai, Y. and Cottrell, J. (eds.), *Economic, Social and Cultural Rights in Practice: The Role of Judges in Implementing Economic, Social and Cultural Rights* (London: Interights, 2004).

Henkin, L., 'Economic-social Rights as Rights: A US Perspective', *HRLJ* 2 (1981), 223.

Mowbray, J., 'The Right to Food and the International Economic System: an Assessment of the Rights-based Approach to the Problem of World Hunger', *LJIL* 20 (2007), 545.

O'Keefe., R., 'The Right to Take Part in Cultural Life under Article 15 of the ICESCR', *ICLQ* 47 (1998), 904.

10 Group rights: self-determination, minorities and indigenous peoples

CONTENTS

10.1 INTRODUCTION

Rights pertaining to groups, as opposed to individual members thereof, are also known as collective rights or solidarity rights. However, not every conceivable group possesses such rights by the mere fact that it is organised as a collectivity (e.g. political parties, activists, disabled groups and others are not endowed with collective rights). Rather, collective rights are limited to particular groupings and are typically conferred by treaty, soft law or customary international law. They are premised on the rationale that certain entitlements are meaningless outside the group and that their justiciable character is dependent on the group's continued existence and coherence. Thus, the notion of statehood is redundant without a stable population that wishes to form a nation and it is exactly in this populace, through its duly appointed representatives, that the state finds expression. As a result, the powers of the state are vested in its people and it is natural that they be endowed with entitlements that cannot be conferred on discrete individuals. By way of illustration, although the right to elect and be elected is meaningful in its personal dimension, the choice to form, secede or unite with another state cannot be exercised individually. Instead, such decisions are best taken by the affected collectivity acting as a single corpus in accordance with predefined rules. General international law informs a large part of the discussion on group rights, albeit, as will become evident, human rights considerations have increasingly been viewed as central to the rights of peoples.

This chapter will analyse the right of self-determination in respect of its external and internal dimension, the rights of minorities and the rights of indigenous peoples. Self-determination is the point of reference for any discussion of indigenous and minority rights, although it is far broader than both of these. Minority rights in turn are not considered collective entitlements in relevant international human rights instruments. None the less, as the reader will come to appreciate, they are not devoid of a collective character altogether. Indigenous rights are largely based on soft law and some of their fundamental premises (e.g. land rights) are hotly disputed by interested states. Yet it is indisputable that the international community recognises that the vulnerable status of indigenous peoples necessitates a distinctive approach based on the adoption of measures that allow the preservation of their culture and traditions, and on the other hand help them to develop, whether technologically, financially, educationally or otherwise. Group rights are controversial primarily because they give rise to questions of 'us' and 'others' in addition to challenging traditional notions of state sovereignty. The chapter is not meant to exhaust the entire range of collective rights and others, such as the right to development, are examined in subsequent chapters.

10.2   THE NATURE OF COLLECTIVE RIGHTS

The existence of collective rights is not self-evident. International law is rather hesitant to grant particular rights to groups as such, not because it refuses to acknowledge their distinct identity, but because states are weary of the effects of collective entitlements. There is also the argument in favour of the individualisation of rights in order to offer protection and remedies to the immediate victim. By way of illustration, the killing by police forces of a protestor may be perceived as a violation of the victim's right to life, as well as an attack on the protestors as a whole. Whereas human rights law would view the attack against the protestors as a violation of their freedom of expression or the right of peaceful assembly, it could not possibly render all protestors victims of the unlawful killing as this would, at the very least, hamper the family of the deceased in seeking redress. Moreover, although not impossible, it is difficult to collectivise freedom of expression and assembly in those cases where the participants do not share more or less the same ideas, beliefs and characteristics. Even so, there is no guarantee that all participants will wish to subsume their individual entitlements into a more apersonal group entitlement. This was certainly the underlying rationale in the construction of the Bill of Rights which was criticised by developing nations as a Western bias in favour of the individual, to the detriment of the person's community. The critique is that although the idea of individually justiciable rights is attractive because it is not dependent on the actions or omissions of other actors (e.g. clan leaders) in fact the removal of the individual from the group reduces the power and protection offered by the group. This Western bias, it is further argued, is evident from the fact that the Bill of Rights wholly disregarded the centrality of interdependence inherent in community life in the developing world. It is no wonder, therefore, that the ACHPR has, in addition to self-determination, included a significant list of solidarity or collective rights. These include the right to continued existence (article 20), the right to development (article 22), the right to peace and security (article 23) and the right to a generally satisfactory environment (article 24).

The debate on collective rights is far from over in international human rights discourse. Three broad types of collective entitlements may be distinguished: those stemming from the right to self-determination, those required for the protection of non-majority group members and others predicated on the collectivisation of certain individual rights. Collective rights based on self-determination presuppose the existence of a group with common characteristics centred around actual or potential forms of statehood, underpinned by the concept of peoples. The protection of peoples is achieved by means of rights, but also through international criminal justice mechanisms. The crime of genocide, for example, constitutes an indirect way of protecting the right to life of group members. Their human rights dimension is justified by the fact that the benefits accruing from the relevant entitlement produce no conflicts between individual members of the group. For example, the right to development and the right of peoples over their natural resources concern values that produce benefits for all and which are not susceptible to individual ownership to the exclusion of others.[1]

On the other hand, groups that do not qualify as peoples (i.e. non-majority groups) cannot obviously rely on entitlements stemming from the right to self-determination. Although the welfare interests of such groups, including minorities and indigenous peoples, cannot possibly conflict or harm the welfare of the majority, until recently there was strong opposition to the granting of collective entitlements. It was feared that such entitlements would ultimately lead to claims of self-determination by the non-majority group. In reality, the collective entitlements of such groups are guaranteed either by the granting of individual rights – as is the case with article 27 of the ICCPR – or through policy initiatives that do not possess collective normativity. Homosexuals, for example, can rely on the right against discrimination where their rights have been affected as a result of their sexual orientation and are

---

[1] The same is also true of the so-called right to humanitarian assistance for the victims of natural disasters or gross human rights violations. In respect of natural disasters, see UNGA resolutions 43/131 (8 December 1988) and 45/100 (14 December 1990). This right is not confined to majorities.

moreover protected in various areas of public, social and economic life by the general application of non-discrimination laws. Homosexuals do not, however, possess distinct justiciable group rights. The non-majority groups discussed in this paragraph enjoy different levels of protection under human rights law, with indigenous peoples generally deemed to possess a group entitlement, despite the absence of hard law.

The collectivisation of individual rights towards achieving the welfare of peoples is a challenging notion. As will be discussed in relevant sections of this and other chapters, it is not at all clear whether the right to peace, the right to a healthy environment or the right to be free from corruption should be framed in collective terms. By way of illustration, the Indian Supreme Court has done an excellent job of protecting the environment through public interest litigation based on the right to life and the right to information, among other things, without having to construct a collective entitlement.[2] From a practical perspective, the successful outcome of an individual suit will produce environmental effects for the entire community as a result of its trickle-down effect. As a result, a collective rights-based approach may not always constitute the optimum option for the pursuit of community objectives. Collectivised individual rights should best be viewed as policy objectives realised through mechanisms available to individual rights, rather than as collective entitlements.

In whatever manner collective rights are perceived and put into practice, care should be taken that they are not implemented in a way that prejudices the individual rights of group members. Thus, the constitutional recognition of indigenous customary law should not be employed by chief elders to impose discriminatory and derogatory treatment on vulnerable members. These members should have access to adequate relief outside the framework of customary law if they so wish. Equally, the promotion of individual rights should not be used to effectively diminish communal values or erode particular groups. This is particularly true in cases where certain privileges are afforded only to members of the majority, thus forcing non-majority groups to 'assimilate'.

10.2.1   External self-determination

Article 1(2) of the UN Charter mentions self-determination as one of its purposes, in particular as a principle whose respect ensures friendly relations between nations. The employment of self-determination in article 1 of the ICCPR and the ICESCR is of a different nature. It is not referred to merely as a principle, or a means to achieve specific targets (i.e. friendly relations), but is expressly predicated as a right of peoples. This bifurcation of the concept

---

[2] See sections 12.3.1 and 12.8.

into two distinct instruments reflects its historical evolution in the course of the twentieth century.[3] In the aftermath of World War I President Wilson of the USA included it (as point 6) in his famous 'Fourteen Points'. The idea was that since the war in Europe had to a large degree been caused by the unjust displacement of national minorities outside the borders of their homeland, which in turn led to abuses, lack of representation and ultimately revolt, it was only natural that an attempt was made to avoid a future repetition of such injustices. Wilson, without a clear understanding of the ramifications, espoused the view that any territorial settlements following the war should be 'in the interest and for the benefit' of the populations concerned.[4] Wilson had intimated therefore that the carving up of Europe should be guided not by the territorial claims of the victors but by the self-government interests of the civilian populations.[5] That this was an unrehearsed idea is evident from the fact that its implementation necessarily required a plethora of secessions and the creation of mini-states with an uncertain future. It is quintessentially for this reason that Wilsonian self-determination was soon played-down and remained a mere principle of international relations until the end of World War II.

Its elevation to the status of a right came about when the discussion on decolonisation commenced in the General Assembly of the UN in the early 1960s. There, it was agreed that peoples under colonial rule and alien domination were entitled to self-rule and to determine their own political status.[6] Naturally, these two dimensions of the entitlement cannot be exercised by some members of a group to the exclusion of others and so the right as a whole is of a collective nature and can only be exercised and enforced as such. As a result, it requires broad consensus among the constituent peoples. Of course, self-determination lends itself also to individual entitlements, such

---

[3] It should be emphasised, however, that the drafters of the UN Charter did not disregard the human rights facet of self-determination. For example, article 80(1) thereto considers that the trusteeship system established under its predecessor, the League of Nations, continues to produce rights for peoples. See *Legal Consequences for States of the Continued Presence of South Africa in Namibia* (*South West Africa* case), Advisory opinion (1971) ICJ Reports 16, paras. 58ff.

[4] A. Cassese, *Self-Determination of Peoples: A Legal Reappraisal* (Cambridge University Press, 1995), 19–23.

[5] The position on overseas colonies was, none the less, abundantly clear. A mechanism of mandates was set up which subjected peoples residing therein and 'not yet able to stand by themselves under the strenuous conditions of the modern world' to a process designed to improve their well-being and development. This process was held to constitute a 'sacred trust of civilisation' for the benefit of the pertinent populations according to article 22 of the League of Nations Covenant. See *International Status of South-West Africa*, Advisory opinion, 1950, ICJ Reports, 128, at 132, which noted that the other corollary to this process was the prohibition of annexation.

[6] UNGA resolution 1514(XV) (1960), Declaration on the granting of independence to colonial countries and peoples.

as the right to elect and be elected,[7] the right to peaceful assembly and others. However, it is the collective entitlement that is paramount in the Charter and the two Covenants and it is this which is the subject of controversy and limitations by international law. To understand why this is so, it is pertinent at this stage to distinguish between the external and internal dimension of self-determination. The external dimension dismisses any kind of colonial or racist rule and alien domination and endows victim populations with a right to dispose of such oppressive rulers.[8] It thus prohibits all types of external interference and intervention with the governance of a territory and of its peoples.[9] The internal dimension, on the other hand, refers to the right of peoples to freely determine their own political status and pursue their ESC development.[10] It also encompasses the right to freely dispose of their natural wealth and resources.[11] The internal dimension therefore informs the political organization of the state based on the wishes of its people. As will become evident in the course of this chapter it is not always easy to distinguish the internal from the external dimension in the contemporary era, particularly as a result of neo-colonialist tendencies.

The external dimension is plagued by a paradox. Peoples are allowed, on the one hand, to rid themselves of an oppressive regime, yet, on the other hand, they are prevented as far as possible from disrupting the territorial integrity of the state. In between the two ends of the paradox it is accepted that oppressed peoples are entitled to employ violence in their collective pursuit for self-government. Moreover, it is also accepted that non-oppressed peoples may demand to secede from the parent state by means of a constitutionally validated plebiscite or by other agreement, as was the case with the break up of the Soviet Union and the independence of Montenegro from Yugoslavia. The paradox is expressly stipulated in the Friendly Relations Declaration which allows peoples in their pursuit of self-determination to 'establish a sovereign and independent state, [a] free association or integration with an independent state or the emergence into any other political status',[12] as well as to seek and receive support thereof. None the less, it emphasises that none of these entitlements:

---

[7] This individual dimension has been recognised by the CERD in its General Comment 21 (23 August 1996), para. 4.

[8] Article 1(3) ICCPR; article 1(4) Protocol Additional to the 1949 Geneva Conventions and Relating to the Protection of Victims of International Armed Conflicts (1977 Protocol I).

[9] UNGA resolution 2625(XXV) (24 October 1970), Declaration on principles of international law concerning friendly relations and co-operation among states in accordance with the Charter of the UN (Friendly Relations Declaration), principles 1 and 3; HRCtee, General Comment 12 (13 March 1984), para. 6.

[10] Article 1(1) ICCPR.   [11] Article 1(2) ICCPR.

[12] These three possibilities of statehood were conceded as early as 1960 through UNGA resolution 1541(XV) (15 December 1960), entitled 'Principles which should guide members to determine whether or not an obligation exists to transmit the information called for under article 73 UN Charter'.

shall be construed as authorizing or encouraging any action which would dismember or impair, totally or in part, the territorial integrity or political unity of sovereign and independent states conducting themselves in compliance with the principle of equal rights and self-determination of peoples as described above and thus possessed of a government representing the whole people belonging to the territory without distinction as to race, creed or color.[13]

This clearly suggests that although the territorial integrity of states is a paramount principle of international relations it may give way in those cases where peoples are under an oppressive rule that stifles their right to representative government. Even so, secession is not encouraged as a means of resisting an oppressive regime because it is perceived as leading to instability and is only sparingly 'authorised' by the international community in practice.[14] One has to look at the process of decolonisation itself, which involved the least possible amount of territorial dissolution, even at the expense of national and tribal homogeneity. The colonial powers invoked the principle of *uti possidetis* in order for the new entities to inherit pre-colonial boundaries and thus avoid the ignition of territorial conflicts.[15] From the point of view of human rights, however, this artificial drawing of boundaries created a plethora of ethnic and tribal enclaves that were cut off from the public life of the state and which inhibited the development of national consciousness, ultimately igniting tribalism. Moreover, the proponents of *uti possidetis* paid little regard to the demands of peoples, minorities and the ancestral rights of indigenous peoples. Not surprisingly, most post-colonial governments represented only tribal majorities or particular elites. As a result of the ensuing oppression numerous ethnic groups in Africa waged wars of secession under the banner of self-determination, but the newly installed governments consistently argued that self-determination was only applicable against colonialism. Since colonialism had been removed, they contended that self-determination had become moot. This argument was no doubt wrongly conceived. If self-determination was destined to expire in the aftermath of decolonisation this would have been expressly stated in both the UN Charter and common article 1 of the Covenants, or would have been

---

[13] Friendly Relations Declaration, principle 5.

[14] The Badinter arbitration committee which was appointed to deal with the legal ramifications of the break up of the former Yugoslavia noted that Serbians living in Croatia did not enjoy the right to secede or join the territory of what was then the Federal Republic of Yugoslavia (now Serbia). Opinion no. 2 emphasised that 'whatever the circumstances, the right to self-determination must not involve changes to existing frontiers at the time of independence, except where the States concerned otherwise agree'. Reproduced in A. Pellet, 'The Opinions of the Badinter Arbitration Committee: a Second Breath for the Self-determination of Peoples', *EJIL* 3 (1992), 178, at 183.

[15] See M. Shaw, 'The Heritage of States: the Principle of *uti possidetis* Today', *BYIL* 67 (1996), 75.

deleted therefrom. On the contrary, self-determination is a continuing right, the protection and promotion of which is addressed to states.

For the purposes of external self-determination it should be pointed out that the beneficiaries of the right, designated under the term 'peoples', encompass majority groups. Peoples are identified by reference to race, ethnicity, language or religion, or typically by a combination thereof. Any other grouping that does not comprise a majority of the population (i.e. minorities, or indigenous groups) does not enjoy the external dimension of the right to self-determination, only its internal dimension. Simply put, minorities are not entitled to secede from the parent state. As will be analysed in the section dealing with internal self-determination, minorities are entitled to particular individualized rights pertinent to their cultural identity and representation in government, particularly as regards their affairs.[16] Defining a majority peoples is not always a simple exercise. A group may constitute a majority over the entire population of a country (e.g. peoples of Bulgarian ethnicity in Bulgaria) or in respect of a significant – not necessarily the largest part – of the national territory, especially where there is no clear majority in a given situation. By way of illustration, indigenous Africans in South Sudan, Quebecois in Quebec and Croatians inhabiting the Croatian republic in the former Yugoslavia qualify as constituent peoples entitled to external self-determination on the ground that there is no other clear numerical majority in these nations.

10.2.2 Exceptionalism in the external dimension of self-determination

We have alluded to the fact that although peoples may validly seek to violently secede from the parent state when under oppression, in practice this is effectuated only when the international community provides its blessings. It finds expression in the language and rhetoric of exceptionalism. The term denotes that even though a particular situation is treated by extraordinary standards that are not in conformity with the ordinary dictates of the law, there is no departure from the law. In the situation at hand, exceptionalism seeks to insulate and safeguard against any instance of unilateral secession, while at the same time providing a viable outlet to situations where the continuity of a state is no longer feasible or desirable. Exceptionalism is thus closer to the 'freely expressed will of peoples' dimension of self-determination than any other political or legal paradigm in history, despite its arbitrary character and absence of all sense of legal certainty. Three distinct sub-paradigms are identified in this book on the basis of exceptional state practice: (1) unilateral secession of peoples from a failed state; (2) consensual secession by means of a plebiscite or agreement; and (3) plebiscite or

---

[16] Article 27 ICCPR.

agreement imposed externally in order to end long-standing conflicts or oppressive rule.

A prime example of *de facto* exceptionalism to the *uti possidetis* rule is the unilateral secession of Somaliland. The present-day Somaliland hails its roots from the Somaliland protectorate which was governed by the British from 1884 until the beginning of decolonisation. Then, on 1 July 1960 it entered into a union with Somalia, itself recently liberated from Italian yoke, to form the Republic of Somalia. The relationship was hardly a smooth one and by the early 1980s fierce fighting broke out between the two communities which eventually led to an abrupt rift and the unilateral declaration of Somaliland independence in 1991. By the early 2000s the international legal personality of Somaliland seems to have been well entrenched, at least *de facto*. The exceptional stance of the international community towards this entity is clearly predicated on two cumulative grounds: (1) the free will of its people; and (2) the chaotic situation in which the failed state of Somalia had found itself. No doubt, foreign consent was facilitated by the introduction of democratic institutions, such as a democratically elected bicameral system[17] and multi-partyism[18] through two successful electoral campaigns in 2003 and 2010.[19]

Consensual secession is a theoretical possibility in the constitutional arrangements of federal states,[20] even though not always expressly mentioned, but is naturally discouraged in practice. Representatives of the French-speaking Québecois of Canada pursued their secessionist claim by a referendum which they ultimately lost by a slim majority. This urged the government of Canada to request its Supreme Court to offer an opinion as to whether the secession of Quebec would in any event be considered lawful under both Canadian and international law. The Court held that although the Constitution did not sanction unilateral secession, Canada would have no basis for denying it to the Québecois in the event of a positive referendum.

---

[17] Article 37 of the Somaliland Constitution.

[18] None the less, under article 9(2) of the Constitution only a maximum of three political parties can exist at any one time in the country. Although this constitutes a clear violation of the freedom of association, the drafters of the Constitution justified it on past experience whereby political affiliation was based on clanship which created political chaos and precluded any legislative or other progress.

[19] See B. Poore, 'Somaliland: Shackled to a Failed State', *Stanford Journal of International Law* (*Stan. J. Int'l L.*) 45 (2009), 117.

[20] Article 39(1) of the Ethiopian Constitution states that: 'every nation, nationality or people in Ethiopia shall have the unrestricted right to self-determination up to secession'. This is subject to a defined number of constitutional conditions, particularly a demand by a two-thirds majority of the nation's legislature and a successful referendum. Paragraph 5 defines the terms 'nation', 'nationality' and 'people' as a 'community having the following characteristics: people having a common culture reflecting considerable uniformity or similarity of custom, a common language, belief in a common bond and identity, and a common consciousness the majority of whom live within a common territory'.

The position under international law was found not to favour disintegration as long as the state in question represented the whole of the people
or peoples resident within its territory, 'on a basis of equality and without
discrimination, and respected the principles of self-determination in its own
internal arrangements'.[21] This type of consensual secession is the result of a
concession to a people in the absence of an express constitutional writ.

The third paradigm is not readily susceptible to generalisations or pre-
dictions. It is premised on the notion that certain parts of the international
community are willing to concede that under exceptional circumstances the
persistent oppression of a people justifies forcible secession if in this manner
the oppression ceases and peace is restored.[22] No doubt, this is subject to the
obvious disclaimer that the state in question does not enjoy sufficient kudos
internationally and is largely stigmatised as a 'pariah'. The exceptional element here is that this paradigm has been applied to both peoples discussed
in the previous section as well as numerical minorities. Two poignant cases
are cited in support of this concession: Kosovo and South Sudan. After many
years of conflict between the predominantly Arab Muslim Northern Sudan
against the largely Christian and Animist South, an agreement was brokered
in 2005 with the intervention of external actors whereby the peoples of the
South would decide their political status.[23] As a result, a referendum took
place in January 2011 by which the South Sudanese chose to secede from
Sudan proper with an overwhelming majority of 98 per cent.

Whereas the South Sudanese clearly constitute a people for the purposes of
article 1(1) of the ICCPR, Kosovo Albanians do not, being a minority among
ethnic Serbians. Much like the South Sudanese, the largely ethnic Albanian
population of Kosovo were the object of oppression by the post-communist
government of the Federal Republic of Yugoslavia. Following a mass exodus
of refugees and internally displaced persons in 1999 the territory of Kosovo
came under international administration and control, pending a final solution on its future political status. In 2009 Kosovo declared its unilateral secession from Serbia while still under international administration. Although at
the time of writing its status was not entirely clear, a number of countries
objected to the legitimacy of its declared statehood and made their position

---

[21] *Reference re Secession of Quebec* [1998] 2 SCR 217, para. 130.

[22] This was also the implicit position of the African Commission on Human and Peoples'
Rights in *Katangese Peoples' Congress* v. *Zaire*, 75/92 (1995), para. 6.

[23] First came a comprehensive peace agreement (CPA) which was composed of a number
of protocols on power-sharing, wealth-sharing, conflict resolution and boundary
delimitation, followed by an interim national constitution. One of these protocols, signed
in Machakos, stipulated in article 2(5) that: '[a]t the end of the six year interim period
there shall be an internationally monitored referendum, organized jointly by the GoS
[Government of Sudan] and SPLM/A [the Southern entity], for the people of South Sudan
to confirm the unity of Sudan by voting to adopt the system of government established
under the peace agreement, or to vote for secession'.

known to the ICJ, which by that time had been asked to determine whether the unilateral declaration was consonant with international law. Although the ICJ's advisory opinion lacks real legal value, given its mere iteration that the declaration itself is legitimate[24] – without however examining whether self-determination under the circumstances justifies secession – the position of intervening states demonstrates an impasse. The USA and the majority of EU member states, with the exception of Spain, Romania, Greece and Cyprus, have espoused the view that the Kosovars are entitled to secede because they qualify as peoples, have expressed their will as such and were the victims of enduring oppression. Yet they all emphasised that this was an exceptional case that was not meant to set a precedent! On the other hand, all Latin American nations,[25] as well as China,[26] Russia,[27] Belarus, Vietnam and others have argued that unilateral secession is void under international law because it violates the principle of territorial integrity and in any event is not available to minorities.

10.2.3   The essence of internal self-determination

Secession is the most extreme aspect of the right to self-determination and its occurrence is understandably rare. The satisfaction of ordinary human rights is necessarily dependent on a people's equal access to representative governance, which is the *sine qua non* requirement of self-determination. This access to the institutions of governance should be distinguished from the so-called right to democratic governance.[28] The latter is not expressly referred to as an obligation in the ICCPR or the ICESCR. Hence, a strict interpretation of common article 1 of the two Covenants dictates the right of every citizen to take part in the conduct of public affairs at all levels of government without discrimination.[29] It is presumed that if government is truly representative it will necessarily be democratic in nature and as a result the application of rights for all will be more likely than if the state were under authoritarian rule. Thus, democracy is the unspoken word in the Covenants because it was considered a dangerous device for the mostly undemocratic countries participating in the adoption of the Bill of Rights. Democracy remains none the less the natural corollary in respect of the obligation to provide peoples with equal access to governance and public affairs.

---

[24] *Accordance with International Law of the Unilateral Declaration of Independence in respect of Kosovo*, Advisory opinion (22 July 2010), paras. 78–121.

[25] See Written statement of Argentina, available at: www.icj-cij.org/docket/files/141/15666. pdf.

[26] Written statement of China, available at: www.icj-cij.org/docket/files/141/15611.pdf.

[27] Written Statement by Russia, available at: www.icj-cij.org/docket/files/141/15628.pdf.

[28] See T. M. Franck, 'The Emerging Right to Democratic Governance', *AJIL* 86 (1992), 46.

[29] CERD, General Comment 21, para. 4.

The right to free and fair elections[30] is yet another corollary, as is also the freedom of assembly, expression, association and equality before the law. Most nations in the world either fail to offer free and fair elections or are not truly representative of their people, even if they call themselves democratic. These countries are naturally opposed to democratic governance as an obligation incumbent on the state. This gives rise to the following question: is self-determination possible in the absence of democratic institutions, in the sense described? The answer to this question is obviously negative, but this has not prevented authoritarian regimes from claiming the opposite.

This state of affairs has been sustained by the political stance of so-called democratic nations in the industrialized world who scold dictatorships through national institutions such as human rights committees,[31] but are in fact content with the financial rewards and perceived stability many such regimes offer. Developed nations, for example, had consistently provided political, financial and military support to President Mubarak of Egypt since his ascent to power in 1981. His regime, although totalitarian, oppressive and quintessentially unrepresentative, remained in power for thirty years because it was perceived as a stabilising force in the Middle East and an enemy of political Islam. It was only as a result of the January–March 2011 mass civil unrest in Tunisia, Egypt, Libya and most of the Arab world that the absence of internal self-determination became apparent as a much more potent destabilising force than anything else feared in the past, which in turn forced developed nations towards a more vociferous support of widespread reform and democratisation.[32]

Free elections and equal access to governance, as inherent prerequisites of internal self-determination, constitute both procedural and substantive rights. They are procedural in the sense that they are necessary tools for the pursuit of universal representation and the protection of individual human rights. At the same time they retain their character as substantive rights *per se*, which, in the context of article 1(1) of the two Covenants, means that peoples are free to choose a political organisation that lacks typical democratic credentials. By way of illustration, an electorate may well opt for a theocratic state, a government based on communist principles, or even a severely

---

[30] Article 25 ICCPR.

[31] For example, the US Commission on International Religious Freedom in its 2010 report on Saudi Arabia found 'systematic, ongoing and egregious violations of religious' freedom. Available at: www.uscirf.gov/images/ar2010/saudiarabia2010.pdf. Yet, the US continues to sell arms to this country and considers it an important ally.

[32] See Statement by the EU High Representative on the Situation in Tunisia (17 January 2011), available at http://ec.europa.eu/delegations/egypt/press_corner/all_news/news/2011/20110117_01_en.htm. The brief US statement on the situation in Egypt (25 January 2011) essentially iterated the constituent elements of self-determination, available at www.america.gov/st/texttrans-english/2011/January/20110126133123su0.6427532.html#.

fragmented federation organised under a plethora of clans and tribes, as long as the system or government chosen by the majority does not infringe the rights of non-majorities. The freedom to determine one's political status imposes simply a limitation on the exercise of the aforementioned procedural rights, but leaves their substantive content free to the peoples concerned to decide. Moreover, it compels the state to respect and promote all other substantive human rights. In this sense, it is irrelevant if the original intended beneficiaries of self-determination in the Friendly Relations Declaration and the two Covenants were racial or religious groups.[33] Universal representation in the contemporary era suggests that the internal dimension of the right is afforded to all persons within a state regardless of racial, ethnic, religious or other affiliation. This is evident, *inter alia*, from the fact that UN treaty bodies and special rapporteurs address indigenous peoples as subjects of self-determination in respect of their right to be represented in decision-making and government institutions.[34]

CASE STUDY 10.1
Participatory budgeting in Porto Alegre, Brazil

Participatory budgeting (PB) is a mechanism through which the governed have direct access to the decision-making fora that determine where and how public finances are spent, as well as the range of taxes to be collected. There is no single model of PB and potentially it could involve participation in all fiscal and budgetary matters. Its roots lie in a social experiment implemented in the wealthy southern region of Porto Alegre in Brazil and its municipality therein in 1989 as a result of the election of the Workers' Party, whose campaign agenda was premised on democratic participation and 'the inversion of spending priorities'.[1] The implementation of PB has only occurred at the local government level and has since been adopted by over 250 municipalities in Brazil and exported to over twenty countries around the world. It is not a process that can be achieved overnight with the

---

[1] See B. Wampler, *Participatory Budgeting in Brazil: Contestation, Cooperation and Accountability* (Philadelphia: Pennsylvania University Press, 2007).

---

[33] Cassese, above note 4, 114.

[34] For example, HRCtee Report, UN Doc. A/55/40, Supp no. 40 (2000), para. 505 (referring to Australia) and the HRC Report on the situation of human rights and fundamental freedoms of indigenous peoples, UN Doc. A/HRC/12/34/Add.2 (26 August 2009), paras. 79, 81 demanding that Brazilian indigenous peoples be represented at legislative, executive and judicial institutions and that greater decision-making powers be granted to them in relation to the delivery of public services in their community.

mere promulgation of local laws in the expectation that local citizenry will demonstrate a keen and spontaneous desire to participate in the design of a public budget. In fact, it is a slow process whereby the active engagement of participants must be sought from the neighbourhood level. Moreover, it is essential that the responsibilities of local governments and participants, as well as their respective roles, be clearly delineated from the outset. These procedures must involve a significant input from the participants and not be solely dictated or designed by the authorities. When the rules of the game are put in place the participants and the authorities may discuss allocation of available resources.

PB typically involves the spending of discretionary resources, which in the case of poor municipalities could amount from zero to 15 per cent of the budget. The percentage that is allocated to discretionary purposes and which is thereafter susceptible to PB has traditionally been earmarked by participants to serve either public works or in order to address general spending policies. The participants are derived from all walks of life and possess diverse reasons for wanting to take part in this exercise; NGOs do so because of a desire to materialise their programmatic goals, private business in order to support local commerce and random individuals because of a dream of social justice, among others. In terms of actual participation, depending on how the rules of the game have been designed, voting is cast by means of neighbourhood representation, or simply by universal balloting.[2]

Participatory budgeting may be viewed as an ideal microcosmic manifestation of self-determination in a very particular sector of public affairs. Can it constitute a blueprint for broader public access in other affairs of government, or would such participation make government unnecessarily cumbersome and bureaucratic? What is the ideal level of direct public engagement in the decision-making processes of governance?

POINTS TO CONSIDER

- **Security Council resolution 713 (25 September 1991) imposed an arms embargo on the entire territory of the former Yugoslavia in order to prevent the warring parties from arming themselves and protracting the conflict. As a result, however, Bosnia and Herzegovina was unable to exercise its inherent right to self-defence, which**

[2] A. Shah, *Participatory Budgeting: Public Sector Governance and Accountability* (Washington, DC: World Bank Publications, 2007). It is worth noting that article 5(1) of Lome Convention IV, (1990) 29 ILM 783, stipulated that *man* is the 'main protagonist and beneficiary of development, which entails respect for the promotion of human rights. ... The role and potential of initiatives taken by individuals and groups shall also be recognised and fostered in order to achieve in practice real participation of the population in the development process.' This is a direct reference to participatory democracy and makes a link between the process of development and public participation in fiscal affairs.

resulted in genocide against its people. Is the survival of a people an integral part of the external dimension of self-determination? If so, may it be invoked by itself and other states as justification for defying a Security Council resolution of this nature?

- The UNGA and a specially appointed rapporteur have adopted the position that the employment of mercenaries prevents and distorts the freedom of peoples to determine their political status, thereby impairing their right to self-determination. Do you agree with this argument? Should a people whose authoritarian government employs mercenaries and flagrantly violates human rights be allowed to also employ mercenaries in order to pursue its self-determination claims?

- What are the positive and negative outcomes of a policy that provides a secessionist entitlement to all minorities and indigenous peoples?

- Many countries in the developing world subject their exploration and extraction contracts with foreign mining companies to the law of contract, rather than public/constitutional law. As a result, they claim that the terms of the agreement are confidential and not susceptible to parliamentary and public scrutiny, lest they breach their contractual obligations. Discuss with reference to the right of peoples over their natural resources.

- The right of peoples to determine their form of government means that the overwhelming majority may opt for an oppressive governance model that moreover restricts the rights of minorities. Discuss with reference to the internal dimension of self-determination.

10.3   MINORITIES AS A SUBJECT OF HUMAN RIGHTS

There is no normative definition of the term 'minority' under treaty or soft law. None the less, there is a broad consensus that it encompasses objective and subjective elements. The objective dimension suggests the existence of a group that constitutes a non-dominant minority of the entire population of a country, even if its numbers are otherwise substantial. In practical terms, a minority group amounts to at least less than half of the entire population. Moreover, members of the group must share some characteristics, such as race, religion, language, ethnicity or nationality. The subjective element is less visible, but is the cohesive substance that defines and sustains the group's identity as such: that is, the members' sense of belonging, which is reflected in cultural characteristics, ultimately giving rise to group solidarity.[35] This solidarity ensures the continuing existence of the group,

[35] F. Capotorti, Study on the rights of persons belonging to ethnic, religious and linguistic minorities, UN Doc. E/CN.4/Sub.2/384/Add 1–7 (1991), para. 568.

given that even a racial minority may in time become assimilated with the dominant racial group and implicitly renounce, or become oblivious to, its particular identity.[36] It is accepted that the existence of a minority is not dependent on the concentration of its members in specific regions; thus, they may just as well be dispersed throughout the territory of a nation.[37] A divided HRCtee has expressed the view, however, that the protection afforded under international law encompasses only minorities within a state, not otherwise majority group members living in minority regions. In the case at hand, the Committee rejected the linguistic minority status of anglophone Canadians (otherwise an overall Canadian majority) living among francophone Québecois (a minority group in Canada) in the predominantly francophone region of Quebec, Canada.[38] The objective identification of minorities necessarily means that their status as such is not inhibited by their members' lack of citizenship[39] or immigrant status. Moreover, the very fact that a country has adopted full equality laws for all persons within its jurisdiction does not extinguish the objective existence of minorities and the pertinent rights of their members.[40]

Once the essential characteristics of the minority group are established one must then ascertain who can claim membership and on what grounds, if any, such membership may be revoked. It will be demonstrated in following sections that membership thereof is a matter of personal self-identification, albeit subject to certain limitations,[41] lest any person could claim this status and genuine group members could equally be expelled arbitrarily. For

---

[36] In its concluding observations on Denmark, the HRCtee stated that the country's Supreme Court erred in failing to recognise the Thule tribe of Greenland as a separate group capable of vindicating its traditional rights, despite the tribe's perception to the contrary. It urged Denmark to consider applying the principle of self-identification in the determination of group membership: UN Doc. CCPR/C/DNK//CO/5 (16 December 2008), para. 13.

[37] HRCtee, Concluding Observations on the Fourth Periodic Report of Germany, UN Doc. A/52/40, Supp 40 (1997), para. 183.

[38] *Ballantyne, Davidson and McIntyre* v. *Canada*, UN Doc. CCPR/C/47/D/359/1989 and 385/1989/Rev.1 (31 March 1993), para. 11.2.

[39] HRCtee, Concluding Observations on the Report of Norway, UN Doc. A/49/90 (1996), para. 94; Commentary to the UN Declaration on the Rights of Persons Belonging to National, or Ethnic, Religious and Linguistic Minorities (Declaration Commentary), UN Doc. E/CN.4/Sub.2/AC.5/2005/2 (4 April 2005), para. 10.

[40] P. Thornberry, *Indigenous Peoples and Human Rights* (Manchester University Press, 2002), 154. The HRCtee chastised Gabon for denying the existence of minorities on its territory: UN Doc. CCPR/70/CO/GAB (10 November 2000), para. 17.

[41] The leading case is *Lovelace* v. *Canada*, 68 ILR 17, para. 14; see also case concerning the *Minority Schools in Albania*, Advisory opinion, (1935) PCIJ, Ser. A/B no. 64, 3, where the PCIJ stated that the existence of a minority was not subject to a legal, but a factual determination; article 3(1) of the 1994 Framework Convention for the Protection of National Minorities, ETS no. 157; article 32(6) of the 1990 CSCE Copenhagen Document on the Human Dimension (1990) 29 ILM 1305.

reasons which will be explored below the entitlement that arises from the international law of minorities is of an individual nature, as opposed to a group right, as is otherwise the case with self-determination. This individual right, modelled principally in article 27 of the ICCPR, has been reproduced, with minor modifications, in all subsequent instruments and its nature is therefore undisputed. Yet, the proper construction of this right is meaningless outside the framework of the group itself and as a result it is a legal fiction to divorce the individual from the group. It should be stressed that for reasons of cogency and stability only a closed number of minorities are recognised in international law (i.e. ethnic, religious, linguistic, national). This therefore excludes other non-dominant groups whose members share a common characteristic, such as homosexuals, communists, members of a particular gender and others. Such persons are protected under equality laws and in many cases their vulnerability may require the adoption of positive discrimination measures by the state.[42]

The current international legal framework on minority protection is based on non-discrimination and equality with members of the majority, while at the same time safeguarding and promoting through positive action the minority's distinct right to culture. The many minority rights instruments, both soft and hard law, essentially express the same principles and thus much of the analysis will be premised on the jurisprudence emanating from article 27 of the ICCPR and the 1992 UN Declaration on Minority Rights.[43]

10.3.1   The historical and political context: should minorities be treated differently from majorities?

Not much thought is put into the idea that a distinct regime on minorities must be adopted in domestic laws in order for the particular needs of minorities to be distinguished from those of the local majorities. This argument seems rational on the face of it because it suggests the obvious: that a vulnerable group whose cultural and other existence is threatened by the assimilating vigour of a majority should be protected from the threat of forced assimilation, especially where the possibility of seceding is not on the table. Yet this assumption runs counter to certain theoretical human rights foundations. Chief among these is that the ideal liberal model of rights, and

---

[42] None the less, the HRCtee in its Concluding observations on Namibia, referred to 'sexual minorities' in order to denote the absence of anti-discrimination laws applicable to homosexuals: UN Doc. CCPR/CO/81/NAM (August 2004), para. 22. A similar comment was made with reference to Poland's inability to avoid discrimination against its sexual minorities: UN Doc. CCPR/C/82/POL (2 December 2004), para. 18.

[43] UNGA resolution 47/135 (18 December 1992), Declaration on the Rights of Persons Belonging to National or Ethnic, Religious and Linguistic Minorities.

state organisation, should be grounded on the promotion of diverse multicultural societies.[44] The driving force behind this policy is that diversity enriches experiences, beliefs, ideas, cultures, technological advancement and provides a better understanding of the world.[45] Moreover, multiculturalism has the potential of contributing to the diffusion of ethnic and other differences between people and is therefore a catalyst for peace and conflict prevention.[46] At the other extreme lies the state-centric notion that national cohesion and political stability are antithetical to the preservation of ethnic diversity.

If policy-makers were to adopt the principle of multiculturalism in their effort to construct a legal regime for minorities they would be forced to reject the solution of autonomy because in most cases it is inherently divisive. Autonomy, or self-rule, would moreover signal intolerance and convey the message that nothing positive can be derived from diversity. Equally, a regime of autonomy does not guarantee the absence of discrimination by the minority against dissenting members and other minorities. In essence, therefore, one would be propagating a model based on purity of some sort, whether ethnic, racial, national, linguistic or other. This model is clearly untenable because it regresses human society back to perpetual mistrust, fracture and the likelihood of conflict. The question then beckons of whether there are alternatives to assimilation and division for minorities and if indeed the guiding principle should remain that of multiculturalism. Contemporary practice clearly disfavours assimilation[47] because it is involuntary and carries all the hallmarks of genocide where it is pursued in a forceful manner. At the same time there is an aversion to the forceful imposition of multiculturalism as a general rule of international law on the ground that it may well be opposed by the peoples of a particular nation. As a result, two broad models

---

[44] See, for example, article 151(1) of the Consolidated Treaty Establishing the European Communities, OJ C 325/33 (24 December 2002), which requires the Community to strengthen the various cultures of its member states while respecting their national and regional diversity; 2001 UNESCO Universal Declaration on Cultural Diversity, UNESCO Doc. 31C/Res25, Annex I; *Timishev* v. *Russia* (2007) 44 EHRR 37, paras. 56, 58; *Oršuš and Others* v. *Croatia*, ECtHR judgment (16 March 2010), paras. 147–8.

[45] H. Steiner, 'Ideals and Counter-ideals in the Struggle over Autonomy Regimes for Minorities', *Notre Dame Law Review* (*Notre Dame L. Rev.*) 66 (1991), 1539, at 1547.

[46] Report of the UN independent expert on minority issues, Effective Protection of the Minorities Declaration, UN Doc. A/65/287 (12 August 2010), paras. 32–8. The expert pointed to an academic study demonstrating that the risk of conflict increases if socio-economic inequalities are combined with inequality in access to political decision-making, stressing moreover that inequality in cultural status adds a further risk factor.

[47] Assimilation of minorities and indigenous peoples should be distinguished from assimilation policies in respect of migrants, which is generally viewed as a legitimate objective of the state. See the USA's UPR Report, UN Doc. A/HRC/WG.6/9/USA/1 (23 August 2010), para. 91.

have emerged depending on whether the minority is viewed collectively or from the perspective of its members:

1 autonomy, power-sharing, or other levels of self-government whether to address historic wrongs, to bring about federal devolution of power or others; and
2 minority rights to each member of the group not with a view to discriminating in their favour, but in order to preserve their distinct culture and solidarity.

Although autonomy and self-government regimes are less frequent, they are none the less entrenched in numerous constitutions[48] and have recently been imposed by the international community on post-conflict nations, as was the case with the former Yugoslavia. These regimes are tantamount to a collective minority right because the entitlement is not addressed to individual members but to the group as such. This is, however, as far as the international community wants to recognise collective entitlements – comparable to the self-determination of peoples – in respect of minorities. Irrespective of, and in conjunction with, autonomy regimes human rights law provides individual rights to minority members. This is aptly demonstrated in article 27 of the ICCPR which reads as follows:

In those states in which ethnic, religious or linguistic minorities exist, persons belonging to such minorities shall not be denied the right, in community with the other members of their group, to enjoy their own culture, to profess and practice their own religion, or to use their own language.

Although this clearly refers to an individual entitlement, it cannot exist in isolation from the group ('in community with other members of the group') and as the HRCtee has observed, the rights under article 27 'depend in turn on the ability of the minority group to maintain its culture, language or religion'.[49] This observation is no more apparent than in the case of land traditionally inhabited by minorities, particularly indigenous peoples. Such lands containing among other things ancestral burial grounds, traditional hunting and religious connotations may manifest a group's culture.[50] From an anthropological perspective this type of culture represents a group's way of life.[51] As a result, where the group's culture is under attack the focus on the purely individual entitlement is problematic and perhaps unworkable.

---

[48] Article 2 of the Spanish Constitution 'recognises and guarantees the right to autonomy of the nationalities and regions which make it up and the solidarity among all of them'.
[49] HRCtee, General Comment 23, para. 6.2.   [50] Ibid., para. 7.
[51] See R. O'Keefe, 'The Right to Take Part in Cultural Life under Article 15 of the ICESCR', *ICLQ* 47 (1998), 904.

This is exemplified by the HRCtee's approach in the *Lubicon Lake Band* case. There, the complainant argued that the provincial government of Alberta had expropriated land belonging to the Lubicon Lake indigenous group so that private companies could mine it under a concession agreement for oil and gas. The Committee merged the relevant issues under article 27, holding that the protected culture of a group encompasses its economic and social activities. Thus, if its primary source of income were to be lost on account of an oil and gas concession then the life and culture of the group would be threatened.[52]

The individualistic focus of article 27 of the ICCPR reflects a rather contemporary approach. Indeed, the post-World War I peace treaties established population exchanges along ethnic lines with a view to setting up homogenous states. Where this was not achievable the minorities in question were subjected to a regime of protection that was premised around a collective right. This was certainly considered exceptional and the expectation was that this measure would be of temporary effect as a result of the minorities' gradual assimilation. By the time the UDHR was under discussion, countries with significant minorities rejected a draft provision that would have provided a collective entitlement to minorities on the ground that it would encourage dissension.[53] The individualistic model introduced by article 27 of the ICCPR ultimately satisfied concerned states that a collective right would lead to dissent and fracture.

More importantly, the entitlement enshrined in article 27 is a *sui generis* right to a community identity and is not the byproduct of other similar rights in the ICCPR. Despite the language in article 27 denoting a negative obligation on the part of the state – 'shall not be denied the right' – the HRCtee has expressly emphasised the positive obligation of states, noting that:

Positive measures of protection are, therefore, required not only against the acts of the state party itself, whether through its legislative, judicial or administrative authorities, but also against the acts of other persons within the state party.[54]

The adoption of positive measures, in addition to ensuring the application of non-discrimination, was recognised as early as 1935 by the PCIJ in its advisory opinion on *Minority Schools in Albania*. The Court held that Albania was under an obligation to 'ensure for the minority element suitable means for the preservation of their racial peculiarities, their traditions and their national characteristics', which entailed facilitation of the right to establish

---

[52] *Lubicon Lake Band* v. *Canada*, UN Doc. CCPR/C/38/D/167/1984 (26 March 1990), paras. 32–3.

[53] J. P. Humphrey, 'The United Nations Sub-commission on the Prevention of Discrimination and Protection of Minorities', *AJIL* 62 (1968), 870.

[54] HRCtee, General Comment 23, para. 6.1.

and control 'charitable, religious and social institutions, schools and other educational establishments, with the right to use their own language and to exercise their religion freely therein'.[55]

10.3.2   Membership rights

It has already been stressed that the existence of a minority is a matter of fact and not subject to a legal or administrative determination. This leaves open two important questions. (1) Can anybody validly claim membership to a minority group? (2) Are minorities at liberty to definitively self-designate every element of their status? The first question should in general terms be answered in the negative. A person may claim membership of a minority group, with special privileges and protection thereof, only if he or she possesses the objective criteria attributable to the group and has partaken in its distinct culture since birth. This excludes persons that have acquired the distinct feature of the group, where possible, after birth but have no direct cultural link with the group. By way of illustration, a German who is fluent in the Basque language may be validly excluded from the special status offered to the Basque minority in Spain. This exclusion may come from both the group itself, as well as the state. Neither the group nor the state, however, possesses the authority to deny outright membership to persons born within the group but who for various reasons have left the communal space of the group. A person does not lose his or her lawful minority identity by reason of a conscious departure from the group for whatever reason. Rather, such departure may only affect the ability of the person to enjoy certain rights that are offered only to members living within the group's communal space.

In the *Lovelace* case, which concerned the right of indigenous women to rejoin their tribe, the applicant was a female member of the indigenous Canadian Tobique band who was born in the band's reservation. As a result of her marriage to a non-Indian she ceased to enjoy membership in accordance with article 12(1)(b) of Canada's Indian Act. Following her divorce the applicant was prevented from returning to her parents in the reserve and argued that she was effectively denied the cultural benefits of living within the community, the right to a home and the right to her minority identity. In this tug-of-war between the wishes of the group and individual self-identification the HRCtee naturally favoured the latter. It held that:

Persons who are born and brought up on a reserve, who have kept ties with their community and wish to maintain these ties must *normally* be considered as belonging to that minority within the meaning of the Covenant [emphasis added].[56]

---

[55] Case concerning *Minority Schools in Albania*, 17.   [56] *Lovelace* case, para. 14.

The Committee's use of the word 'normally' suggests that situations may arise where the severance of a former member from the communal space of the group may be justified, especially where this is 'reasonable or necessary to preserve the identity of the tribe'.[57] Thus, persons whose ancestors fled the group may reasonably be excluded where their large numbers and modern lifestyle would endanger the continued enjoyment of the group's traditional existence. The group's protected existence need not only concern the preservation of its traditional lifestyle, but also its financial well-being. The HRCtee has long maintained a distinction between the prohibition of denying group membership where objective criteria are met, and the lawful withdrawal of membership rights to those that live outside the group's communal space. In the *Kitok* case the complainant was a native Saami of Sweden whose family had herded reindeer for over one hundred years and had inherited breeding rights in the Sorkaitum village. However, under Swedish law a person loses his breeding rights if engaged in any other profession for a period of three years. The HRCtee accepted the rationale of the Swedish government in introducing this legislation, its purpose being to improve the living conditions of those Saami for whom reindeer husbandry constituted their primary income.[58] Effectively, if all Saami were allowed to occasionally engage in reindeer husbandry they would be denying those making a living from it of their future existence, bearing in mind that this activity was an 'essential element in the culture of the ethnic community'.[59] This was therefore a reasonable curtailment of the particular entitlement for the continued viability and welfare of the community as a whole.[60] The Committee emphasised, however, that such a measure did not and could not have the effect of stripping an ethnic Saami of his or her identity.[61]

Let us now discuss the other question posed at the beginning of this section. Is it open to a minority to designate its status in accordance with the wishes of the majority of its members? By way of illustration, the Treaty of Lausanne described the community living in the north-eastern region of Greece, Thrace, as a Muslim minority. The majority of this community has long desired to be designated as an ethnic Turkish minority, something which Greece had strenuously resisted, not only because of the Lausanne Treaty but also on account of the fact that this community encompassed a considerable number of Pomaks and other Muslims who did not view themselves as Turks. Given the objective identification of minorities under international law it is artificial to deny the existence of a Turkish minority to those members of the Muslim community who identify themselves as such. On the other hand, it

---

[57] Ibid., para. 17.
[58] *Kitok* v. *Sweden*, UN Doc. CCPR/C/33/D/197/1985 (27 July 1988), para. 4.2.
[59] Ibid., para. 9.2.   [60] Ibid., para. 9.8.   [61] Ibid., para. 9.7.

is not clear whether a minority may formulate its identity in a manner that prevents another group from enjoying its own culture.

A case at hand is another group in Greece whose relatively few members claim to share an ethnic Macedonian identity. This designation would otherwise be unproblematic; yet, northern Greeks have long identified themselves as Macedonians, although this is combined with an ethnic Greek identity. Quite clearly there is a conflict between the designation claimed by the two groups, one being a majority and the other a minority.[62] It is not the purpose of this section to settle this vexing question, but it is certainly emblematic of the fact that the right to self-identification of minorities was not designed to invalidate the identity and culture of other groups who enjoy long-standing usage.[63] Where no conflict exists the group may label itself according to its wishes as an extension of the self-identification principle. The CERD noted that Guyana's Amerindian Act of 2006 systematically designated this indigenous group as Amerindians, despite the group's opposition. It recommended that Guyana 'in consultation with all the indigenous communities concerned identify whether Amerindians is the preferred term'.[64]

It would be impractical to list all the range of protective measures that are affordable to minority members under human rights law as these will vary from situation to situation. The rationale of this body of law, however, is predicated on the axiom that forced assimilation is unacceptable. Minority protection itself is grounded on four requirements: protection of the existence, non-exclusion, non-discrimination and non-assimilation of minorities.[65] The necessary corollary to these requirements is the obligation to respect cultural pluralism through positive action that promotes the distinctive cultural traits of the group internally (e.g. by establishing minority-language schools) as well as more broadly within the country.[66] The extent to which a minority culture is accepted, respected and celebrated by the majority is dependent on conscious affirmative action and not hortatory legislative drafting. The non-exclusion of linguistic minorities, for example, may be achieved by recognising their language among the official languages

---

[62] The ECtHR in *Sidiropoulos and Others* v. *Greece* (1998) 27 EHRR 633, did not attempt to answer whether a distinct ethnic Macedonian minority should be recognised at a time when the Greek population of northern Greece has long been designated as Macedonian. The Court clearly suggested, however, in paras. 37–9 that the intention to dispute 'the Greek identity of Macedonia and its inhabitants and undermine Greece's territorial integrity' constituted a legitimate interference by the Greek government with the right of association (article 11 ECHR) with the aim of protecting national security and preventing disorder.

[63] For the particular, and perhaps biased, position of this author, see I. Bantekas, 'The Authority of States to Use Names in International Law and the Macedonian Affair: Unilateral Entitlements, Historic Title and Trademark Analogies', *LJIL* 22 (2009), 563.

[64] CERD, Concluding observations on Guyana, Doc. CERD/C/GUY/CO/14 (4 April 2006), para. 10; similarly in respect of Laos, Doc. CERD/C/LAO/CO/15 (18 April 2005), para. 17.

[65] Declaration Commentary, paras. 21–4.   [66] Ibid., para. 28.

of the state, or by requiring public authorities to employ it when dealing with minority members. Switzerland has granted official status to all four languages spoken by various groups on its territory.[67] Section 6(1) of the South African Constitution of 1996 has gone even further, granting official status to eleven languages and in addition promoting the languages commonly used by ethnic minorities in the country.[68] Of course, the officialisation of all minority languages is an expensive venture which stretches the resources of the state and is not viable everywhere. Hence, another model that has been pioneered in countries such as Belgium and Canada is to afford official status only to languages spoken by dominant groups, thus excluding mainly indigenous languages. This does not mean that in such countries indigenous languages are, or should be, ignored. The deficiencies of this model have been remedied elsewhere by rendering non-dominant minority languages official only at the regional level, as is the case with article 3(2) of the 1992 Spanish Constitution.

Even so, given that minority members are generally among the most vulnerable populations of all nations,[69] there is a danger that an incessant preservation of the group's distinct culture among group members may ultimately isolate the members from any sort of advancement. By way of example, if a state places minority children in separate classes because they lack command of the dominant language, something common in European nations with Roma populations, but fails to apply this policy to all children with similar language deficiencies, it is discriminating against the group.[70] Culprit states typically contend that Roma children with poor language skills are unable to attend ordinary classes and that they are privileged to be taught in their own language until they catch up. Where educational policies prevent minority children from commanding the dominant language and the country's culture alongside majority children, there is a heightened risk of grooming an estranged generation with limited skills and qualifications, thus leading it to poverty and social exclusion.[71] This is why it is imperative that minority members receive a broad education equal to that of the majority,[72] unless the

---

[67] Article 4 of the Federal Constitution of the Swiss Confederation.

[68] Constitution of South Africa 1996, section 6(5)(b). See K. Henrard, 'Language Rights and Minorities in South Africa', *International Journal on Multicultural Societies* 3 (2001), 78.

[69] There have of course existed some notable exceptions, such as the minority racist regime of South Africa and the minority Sunni leadership in Iraq during the reign of Saddam Hussein.

[70] *Oršuš and Others,* paras. 158–62. On other cases involving the educational segregation of Romani children, see *D. H. and Others* v. *Czech Republic* (2008) 47 EHRR 3; *Sampanis and Others* v. *Greece*, ECtHR judgment (5 June 2008).

[71] The HRCtee in its Concluding Observations on Georgia pointed out that the lack of Georgian language skills 'could lead to marginalization and under-representation of minorities in different public and private spheres': UN Doc. CCPR/C/GEO/CO/3 (15 November 2007), para. 17.

[72] Article 4(4), UN Minorities Declaration.

difference in treatment is based on objective and reasonable justification.[73] Preservation of a minority's culture and lifestyle does not mean that the state should allow group members to stay on the fringes of society. Culture is not a synonym for backwardness or underdevelopment. Thus, states are under an obligation to educate minority children, even if their parents are of a contrary view. Equally, the ECSR has repeatedly noted in respect of the Roma and traveller community that their particular situation must be taken into account by states. As a result they should not be allowed to live in substandard conditions without access to health or sanitary services simply because they are nomadic peoples.[74]

Finally, although some reference has been made to autonomy and self-rule, it should be emphasised that one of the key elements in the international human rights regime for minorities is the quest for their right to effective participation in decision-making at the regional level in matters that affect them.[75] The UN Minorities Commentary provides some indication of how this may be implemented in practice:

Where minorities are concentrated territorially, single-member districts may provide sufficient minority representation. Proportional representation systems, where a political party's share in the national vote is reflected in its share of the legislative seats, may assist in the representation of minorities. Some forms of preference voting, where voters rank candidates in order of choice, may also facilitate minority representation and promote inter-communal cooperation.

Much like the rationale inherent in avoiding 'over-protection' that leads to the group's isolation from the wider community, it is also wise to avoid establishing segregated institutions and public mechanisms. In the spirit of multiculturalism the Declaration warns that:

Public institutions should not be based on ethnic or religious criteria. Governments at local, regional and national levels should recognise the role of multiple identities in contributing to open communities and in establishing useful distinctions between public institutional structures and cultural identities.[76]

---

[73] In *D. H. and Others* v. *Czech Republic*, para. 196, the ECtHR held that where a difference in treatment was based on race or ethnicity, 'the notion of objective and reasonable justification must be interpreted as strictly as possible'.

[74] *Interights* v. *Greece*, Complaint no. 49/2008, ECSR decision (11 December 2009); equally by the same Committee, *Centre on Housing Rights and Evictions (COHRE)* v. *Italy*, Complaint no. 58/209, decision (25 June 2010).

[75] Article 2(2), UN Minorities Declaration; CERD, Concluding Observations on Estonia, UN Doc. CERD/C/EST/CO/8–9 (23 September 2010), para. 14; the HRCtee deplored the low representation of minorities at local level in Croatia, UN Doc. CCPR/C/HRV/CO/2 (4 November 2009), para. 18. According to the ECtHR in *Mathieu-Mohin and Clerfayt* v. *Belgium* (1987) 10 EHRR 1, this right is not violated where a linguistic minority is obliged to elect parliamentary representatives that belong to the linguistic majority in the region, as long of course as this does not impair the situation of the minority or lead to arbitrariness.

[76] Declaration Commentary, paras. 45 and 47.

This segregation may be an inevitable reality during transitional periods in post-conflict situations so as to deter the various groups from engaging in hostile acts, but it cannot remain a perpetual policy. The Dayton Peace Agreement that ended the Bosnian civil war envisaged a constitutional provision whereby membership of the House of Peoples and the Presidency was reserved solely to those who identified themselves as belonging to one of the three 'constituent people' (i.e. Bosniac, Serbs and Croats). This was certainly a welcome arrangement at the time in order to ensure peace but fifteen years later it was found by the ECtHR to be discriminatory on racial and ethnic grounds against non-constituent peoples, such as local Roma and Jews.[77]

CASE STUDY 10.2
The Malay bumiputra policy

Following the independence of Malaysia from the British in 1957 the successor government was of the opinion that indigenous Malays were financially disadvantaged in comparison to other ethnic groups, particularly the country's Chinese community. The ethnic Chinese minority had acquired some affluence as a result of commercial entrepreneurship, whereas the Malay majority lacked universal education, access to government and in rural areas people were considered 'backward'. As a result, it was decided that a degree of positive discrimination was required in order to bring the level of the indigenous majority to par with the Chinese minority. This principle was enshrined in article 153(1) of the Malaysian Constitution as an express exception to the general rule in Article 8(2) which prohibits discrimination of citizens on any ground, as follows:

It shall be the responsibility of the [Head of state] to safeguard the special position of the Malays and natives of any of the states of Sabah and Sarawak and the legitimate interests of other communities in accordance with the provisions of this Article.

Those defined as ethnic Malays (or Bumiputras) were subsequently granted privileges over and above other minority members under the pretext that by doing so inter-ethnic tensions would be diminished. This amounted to outright discrimination in all fields of public and private life. By way of illustration, companies must have a minimum *Bumiputra* equity ownership if they are to be listed on the Malaysian stock exchange. Equally, minorities are discriminated in employment opportunities in the public sector, subsidies for housing and in most other fields. Of course, the effect of these policies has culminated in discrimination against all minority groups.

---

[77] *Sejdić and Finci* v. *Bosnia and Herzegovina*, ECtHR judgment (22 December 2009), paras. 45–50.

Do you consider this policy to be sound from the point of view of advancing a relatively poor and underdeveloped ethnic group? Is this justified from an affirmative action perspective, especially given that positive discrimination is directed against members of a minority?

POINTS TO CONSIDER

- The determination of whether an ethnic minority should possess some degree of autonomy or self-rule should be made not only by members of the minority, but also by the populace of the majority. Discuss.

- Multiculturalism requires tolerance, the preservation and promotion of which is an obligation incumbent on states according to the ECtHR.[1] In a post-conflict nation where ethnic rivalry continues to ignite fierce hostilities, what type of minority regime would you recommend? How would you implement multiculturalism, if at all?

- Are minority rights tantamount to equality rights?

- The HRCtee has held that the right of minority members to profess and practise their religion does not impose an obligation on states to fund private religious schools.[2] Is this consistent with the principle of equality, particularly where the state funds religious majority schools?

- A sizeable group of German nationals claim to be an ethnic Prussian minority. There is no longer a Prussian state, its lands having been incorporated into what are today Germany and Poland. Can the group be considered an ethnic minority for the purposes of the ICCPR and the UN Minorities Declaration?

- The Roma traditional lifestyle involves constant movement within the territory of states and settlement for short periods in empty land plots. Can states restrict this movement, taking into account that this is the cornerstone of their cultural identity?[3]

---

[1] *Serif* v. *Greece* (1999) 31 EHRR 56, para. 53.

[2] *Waldman* v. *Canada*, UN Doc. CCPR/C/67/D/694/1996 (3 November 1999), para. 10.6, noting, however, that if a state chooses to fund the schools of one religious group it is discriminatory not to fund the schools of other religious communities; see also the *Belgian Linguistic case No. (2)* (1968) 1 EHRR 252, where the ECtHR held that the right to education does not provide a guarantee to the children or the parents of linguistic minorities that their overall education will be provided in their mother tongue.

[3] See *Coster* v. *UK* (2001) 33 EHRR 20.

10.4   INDIGENOUS PEOPLES: IS THERE A NEED FOR ADDITIONAL PROTECTION?

Indigenous peoples are the original inhabitants of a territory, before this was conquered or colonised, who continue to live there. From the point of view of human rights, it is important to ponder on the following issues: (1) the criteria for indigenous identity and whether any particular protection is warranted in countries primarily inhabited by indigenous peoples; (2) whether the term 'peoples' implies a right of self-determination; (3) whether there is a need for special human rights rules in addition to those that apply to all persons under general international law; and (4) whether indigenous rights are collective rights.

Indigenous claims before treaty bodies have been largely predicated on the law pertinent to minority rights in the absence of an indigenous *lex specialis*. The majority of the cases examined in the previous section by the HRCtee under article 27 of the ICCPR concerned indigenous groups. Much like the notion of terrorism, the term 'indigenous' is not defined in a comprehensive multilateral treaty with universal force. This is probably welcome because it is not susceptible to immutable definitions, particularly given that law is generally averse to concepts such as 'spiritual' or 'culture', which play a large part in the social and anthropological construction of indigenous peoples. None the less, there is significant consensus as to the essential characteristics of indigenousness. A very sketchy definition is articulated in article 1(1) of ILO Convention 169 on Indigenous and Tribal Peoples. However, the most authoritative was that offered by UN Special Rapporteur Martinez Cobo, as follows:

Indigenous communities, peoples and nations are those which, having a historical continuity with pre-invasion and pre-colonial societies that developed on their territories, consider themselves distinct from other sectors of the societies now prevailing in those territories, or parts of them. They form at present non-dominant sectors of society and are determined to preserve, develop and transmit to future generations their ancestral territories, and their ethnic identities, as the basis of their continued existence as peoples, in accordance with their own cultural patterns, social institutions and legal systems.[78]

Certain features are *sine qua non*, particularly historical continuity, occupation of ancestral lands and attachment thereto, as well as distinctiveness in culture and social institutions from the dominant groups. By way of illustration, most indigenous peoples enjoy a spiritual attachment to their land,[79] something alien to industrialised nations, as is the case with Australian aboriginals. Much like minorities the determination of indigenous status is based on self-identification and the same principles apply *mutatis mutandis*.[80]

---

[78] UN Doc. E/CN.4/Sub.2/1986/7/Add.4 (1986), para. 379.

[79] See the relevant discussion in *South Fork Band and Others* v. *USA*, 588 F 3d 718 (2009).

[80] See article 1, ILO Convention 169; articles 9 and 33(1), UNDRIP, UNGA resolution 61/295 (13 September 2007); CERD General Recommendation no VIII (22 August 1990); CERD, Concluding Observations on Indonesia, Doc. CERD/C/IDN/CO/3 (15 August 2007), para. 15, demanding that Indonesia 'respect the way in which indigenous peoples perceive and define themselves'; para. 4(a) World Bank OP 4.10, 'indigenous peoples' (July 2005).

Thus, although genetics may be useful in some clear-cut cases they have little utility for those of mixed race. In such cases it is generally agreed that cultural circumstances play a more significant role.[81]

While it is easy to identify indigenous groups in recently colonised territories, such as North and South America and Australia, it is not so in Africa or Asia where the local populations are by and large indigenous in the literal sense and dominant. It is for this reason that post-colonial governments in both Africa and Asia have refused to accept the existence of indigenous peoples therein as a distinct category warranting special protection.[82] The ACHPR has rejected this argument, claiming that in Africa 'the term indigenous population does not mean first inhabitants in reference to aboriginality as opposed to non-African communities, or those having come from elsewhere'.[83] Thus, it is legally possible for some African populations to be classified as indigenous on the basis of:

occupation and use of a specific territory; the voluntary perpetuation of cultural distinctiveness; self-identification as a distinct collectivity, as well as recognition by other groups; an experience of subjugation, marginalisation, dispossession, exclusion or discrimination.[84]

In equal measure peoples not considered indigenous in the literal sense, but who 'make up a *tribal* community whose social, cultural and economic characteristics are different from other sections of the national community, particularly because of their special relationship with their ancestral territories, and because they regulate themselves, at least partially, by their own norms, customs, and/or traditions' are protected in the same manner as indigenous peoples.[85]

The principal concern of many states with the ongoing indigenous legal discourse concerns the self-determination of indigenous groups. This preoccupation is reflected in the shift of terminology in the 1957[86] and the 1989

---

[81]   *Gibbs* v. *Capewell* (1995) 128 ALR 515, *per* Drummond J, 584.

[82]   See B. Kingsbury, 'Indigenous Peoples in International Law: A Constructivist Approach to the Asian Controversy', *AJIL* 92 (1998), 414, at 415, who juxtaposes a constructivist perspective to the positivist definition of indigenousness. He understands this as 'embodying a continuous process in which claims and practices in specific cases are abstracted in the wider institutions of international society, then made specific again at the moment of application in the political, legal and social processes of particular cases and societies'.

[83]   ACHPR, Advisory opinion on the *UN Declaration on Rights of Indigenous Peoples* (2007), para. 13.

[84]   *Centre for Minority Rights Development (Kenya) and Minority Rights Group International on behalf of Endorois Welfare Council* v. *Kenya* (*Endorois* case), Case no. 276/2003, Decision on merits (4 February 2010), para. 150.

[85]   Case of the *Saramaka People* v. *Suriname*, IACtHR judgment (28 November 2007), para. 84.

[86]   ILO Convention 107 Concerning the Protection and Integration of Indigenous and Other Tribal and Semi-Tribal Populations in Independent Countries.

ILO Conventions, from 'populations' in the former to 'peoples' in the latter. This shift in language, however, did not go as far as providing an express reference to self-determination. Yet, much like the international law pertinent to minorities, it is undisputed that indigenous peoples enjoy *mutatis mutandis* the same level of internal self-determination.[87] One could also claim that where an indigenous group constitutes a clear numerical majority it is also entitled to the external dimension of self-determination in the sense described earlier in this chapter.

The depth of international human rights law should ordinarily render claims for an indigenous *lex specialis* redundant. To some degree this is true, yet certain demands posited by indigenous peoples are not obviously covered by existing instruments and mechanisms. By way of illustration, they encompass indigenous peoples' claims to their ancestral lands, to the application of their customary/native laws and dispute mechanisms, the right to spiritual property and spiritual connection to land, the right to have agreements signed with colonisers validated and others. These claims, and many others, are reproduced as collective entitlements in the two ILO Conventions and UNDRIP and are reflective of the particular circumstances and struggles of indigenous peoples. Many of these are not, however, confirmed by the practice of states. For example, the validity of colonial treaties with natives has largely been refuted,[88] as has been the claim to exclusive indigenous land ownership. Equally, indigenous peoples have not reaped the rewards of their traditional knowledge in the pharmaceutical qualities of plants or the intellectual property of their artistic work. Increasingly, indigenous knowledge and its contribution to biodiversity is recognised in international instruments, such as the 1992 Rio Declaration of Environment and Development[89] and the 1992 Convention on Biological Diversity. Article 8(j) of the latter calls on states parties to:

Respect, preserve and maintain knowledge, innovations and practices of indigenous and local communities embodying traditional lifestyles relevant for the conservation and sustainable use of biological diversity and promote their wider application with the approval and involvement of the holders of such knowledge, innovations and practices and encourage the equitable sharing of the benefits arising from the utilisation of such knowledge, innovations and practices.

Besides the gradual erosion of their cultural heritage and the loss of their ancestral lands, indigenous communities have moreover been the target of much more repugnant violations. It is now well recorded that in many

---

[87] See articles 3–5 UNDRIP.

[88] *Lone Wolf* v. *Hitchcock* 187 US 553 (1903); *USA–UK Cayuga Indians* Arbitral Award (1926) 6 UNRIAA 173; *Netherlands* v. *USA* (*Island of Palmas* case) (1928) 2 UNRIAA 831, 858.

[89] Principle 22.

instances indigenous peoples have been unable to defend themselves against forced assimilation, physical genocide through official sterilisation policies as exemplified by Australia's policies against its Aboriginal population[90] and statistical ethnocide.[91]

10.4.1   Indigenous rights over traditional lands

Unlike capitalist societies, whose members have been schooled to view land as a commodity, the indigenous relationship to land may be described as naturalistic, religious, social and spiritual in nature, among other things.[92] The following subsections will deal with this important issue for indigenous peoples, that is, their legal relationship over land they have traditionally occupied. The aim is to demonstrate the claims themselves, as well as the legislative variations adopted by states with significant indigenous populations within the overall framework of international law and human rights advancements.

10.4.2   Indigenous land rights in contemporary international law

Indigenous rights of occupancy or communal ownership are typically reflected in domestic constitutions and, or, in land statutes. In the *Mayagna* case before the IACtHR the government of Nicaragua had granted a timber

---

[90] The Australian case against its aboriginal population is well documented and was in fact legalised through the adoption of the 1918 Aboriginals Ordinance. The Australian policy of enforced assimilation and Aboriginal child removal was initially legalised by the 1918 Aboriginals Ordinance and was subsequently defended on legalistic grounds by the Australian High Court in *Kruger* v. *The Commonwealth* (1997) 190 CLR 1. See also *Mestanza Chavez* v. *Peru*, Case 12.191, Report no. 71/03, IACHR, OEA/Ser L/V/II.118 Doc. 70 rev. 2, p. 668 (2003), where the Peruvian authorities were found to have harassed an illiterate indigenous Peruvian woman by telling her that giving birth to five children was a criminal offence and that she would have to be sterilised. See, 'Mass Sterilisation Scandal Shocks Peru', BBC News (24 July 2004), which reported 200,000 enforced sterilisations of indigenous Indians by the Fujimori regime.

[91] Thornberry, above note 40, 16–17, who cites examples of under-counting in order to deliberately marginalise particular indigenous groups.

[92] HRCtee, Indigenous Peoples and their Relationship to Land, UN Doc. E/CN.4/Sub.2/2001/21 (11 June 2001), 7–9. See also *Mayagna (Sumo) Awas Tingni Community* v. *Nicaragua*, IACtHR, Ser. C, no. 79 (31 August 2001), para. 149, which held: 'Among indigenous peoples there is a communitarian tradition regarding a communal form of collective property of the land, in the sense that ownership of the land is not centred on an individual but rather on the group and its community. Indigenous groups, by the fact of their very existence, have the right to live freely in their own territory; the close ties of indigenous people with the land must be recognized and understood as the fundamental basis of their cultures, their spiritual life, their integrity, and their economic survival. For indigenous communities, relations to the land are not merely a matter of possession and production but a material and spiritual element which they must fully enjoy, even to preserve their cultural legacy and transmit it to future generations.'

concession to a private company in respect of land occupied by an indigenous group that had not sought a title for its occupation. The Nicaraguan government argued that because the law required registration and titling, which the Mayagna had not undertaken, they possessed no valid native title. None the less, evidence furnished showed that the group had occupied the land for at least three hundred years and moreover the right of 'communal ownership of lands' was guaranteed under articles 5, 89 and 180 of the Nicaraguan Constitution. The Court and the Commission agreed that Nicaragua could not expect indigenous groups to undertake all the legal formalities associated with titling and that it had an obligation to demarcate their land, particularly since it had recognised the indigenous nature of the Mayagna. It thus affirmed their right to property under article 21 of the Inter-American Convention on Human Rights as follows:

1 The Mayagna Community has communal property rights to land and natural resources based on traditional patterns of use and occupation of ancestral territory. These rights 'exist even without state actions which specify them'. Traditional land tenure is linked to a historical continuity, but not necessarily to a single place and to a single social conformation throughout the centuries. The overall territory of the community is possessed collectively, and the individuals and families enjoy subsidiary rights of use and occupation.

2 Traditional patterns of use and occupation of territory by the indigenous communities of the Atlantic coast of Nicaragua generate customary law property systems, they are property rights created by indigenous customary law norms and practices which must be protected, and they qualify as property rights protected by article 21 of the Convention. Non-recognition of the equality of property rights based on indigenous tradition is contrary to the principle of non-discrimination set forth in article 1(1) of the Convention.

3 The Constitution of Nicaragua and the Autonomy Statute of the Regions of the Atlantic Coast of Nicaragua recognise property rights whose origin is found in the customary law system of land tenure which has traditionally existed in the indigenous communities of the Atlantic Coast. Furthermore, the rights of the community are protected by the American Convention and by provisions set forth in other international conventions to which Nicaragua is a party.

4 There is an international customary law norm which affirms the rights of indigenous peoples to their traditional lands.[93]

This IACtHR jurisprudence suggests that indigenous peoples may possess an inherent right under international law to communal ownership – subject

---

[93] *Mayagna (Sumo) Awas Tingni Community* v. *Nicaragua* judgment, para. 140.

to non-discriminatory restrictions that serve public social interests – other than through official conferral by the apparatus of the state. The essence of this observation is that native title is deemed to exist irrespective of official recognition. Such recognition serves merely to demarcate indigenous land and guarantee all the rights over it against third parties. Communal indigenous rights

encompass a broader and different concept [of territorial rights] that relates to the collective right to survival as an organized people, with control over their habitat as a necessary condition for reproduction of their culture, for their own development and to carry out their life aspirations. Property of the land ensures that the members of the indigenous communities preserve their cultural heritage.[94]

This line of thinking supports the exceptional nature of indigenous land ownership, as opposed to other forms of ownership within the same country. What this means is that although the state cannot discriminate between indigenous and other ownership, in cases of necessary expropriation for example, it should adopt measures that take into consideration the particular relationship of indigenous peoples with their land, if indeed such exists in a particular case. The IACtHR succinctly noted that:

This does not mean that every time there is a conflict between the territorial interests of private individuals or of the state and those of the members of the indigenous communities, the latter must prevail over the former. When states are unable, for concrete and justified reasons, to adopt measures to return the traditional territory and communal resources to indigenous populations, the compensation granted must be guided primarily by the meaning of the land for them.[95]

This right to communal ownership is made explicit in article 26 of the 2007 UNDRIP, which provides as follows:

1   Indigenous peoples have the right to the lands, territories and resources which they have traditionally owned, occupied or otherwise used or acquired.
2   Indigenous peoples have the right to own, use, develop and control the lands, territories and resources that they possess by reason of traditional ownership or other traditional occupation or use, as well as those which they have otherwise acquired.
3   States shall give recognition and protection to these lands, territories and resources. Such recognition shall be conducted with due respect to the customs, traditions and land tenure systems of the indigenous peoples concerned.

---

[94] Case of the *Yakye Axa Indigenous Community* v. *Paraguay*, Merits, reparations and costs, Judgment, IACtHR Ser. C, no. 125 (17 June 2005), para. 146.
[95] Ibid., para. 149.

Article 26 of UNDRIP seems to be more representative of state practice than article 14(1) of ILO Convention no. 169. The latter obliges member states to recognise the rights of ownership and possession of indigenous peoples over lands which they traditionally occupy. UNDRIP on the other hand subsumes all rights over land to 'traditional ownership or traditional occupation'.

10.4.3   Indigenous ownership as a right to property

A study of the World Bank documented the precise spectrum of land rights afforded to indigenous groups in thirty-three client countries.[96] With respect to Asia, in China,[97] Thailand and Vietnam all land is owned fully by the state. In the Philippines, in accordance with article 7 of the Indigenous Peoples Rights Act 1977, indigenous groups are entitled to claim ownership over ancestral lands as well as all natural resources. In Malaysia, some native title is recognised,[98] but in most cases indigenous peoples do not possess title and are considered 'tenants-at-will'. Similarly, in Indonesia all land belongs to the state but indigenous people enjoy some limited customary land tenure as long as there is no conflict with ordinary property law. In Cambodia, indigenous groups enjoy communal ownership rights over their lands, which is tantamount to private ownership.[99]

In South America the situation is slightly more clear and coherent. In Argentina, although community ownership of ancestral lands is recognised, it is generally hampered by bureaucratic procedural hurdles and is unavailable to indigenous peoples who have relocated to urban areas. Communal ownership rights are equally recognised in Chile, Colombia, Peru, Ecuador, Bolivia and Venezuela. In Brazil, indigenous persons retain exclusive possession and use, albeit ownership is vested in the state. In Central America the situation is more or less equally consistent. With the exception

---

[96] See IBRD Operations Evaluation Dep't, 'Implementation of Operational Directive 4.20 on Indigenous Peoples: An Independent Desk Review', pp. 5–38, available at: www.worldbank.org/oed/indigenouspeople/docs/IP1.pdf.

[97] China reserves special treatment for ethnic minorities and has set up autonomous regions, but these laws should not be viewed as also protecting indigenous peoples, despite some overlap.

[98] That indigenous land rights are tantamount to normal property rights under article 13 of the Constitution has been duly recognised by the Malaysian High Court in *Adong bin Kuwau and 51 Others* v. *The Government of Jahore* [1997] 1 MLJ 418, confirmed by the Malaysian Court of Appeal [1998] 2 MLJ 158.

[99] Cambodian Land Law 2001, articles 25–7. The Cambodian government in April 2009 proceeded to adopt legislation through which the titling of customary title could be officially concretised. See ECOSOC Permanent Forum on Indigenous Issues, Information Received from Cambodia, UN Doc. E/C.19/2010/12/Add.5 (16 February 2010). It should, however, be noted that the Cambodian government frequently flouts its indigenous laws by granting concessions on protected lands to foreign investors.

of Mexico and El Salvador, which do not recognise communal rights of ownership, Honduras, Nicaragua, Panama and Guatemala extend such rights to their indigenous peoples, subject to minor limitations. Russia, the world's largest country, does not recognise land ownership for its indigenous populations.[100]

In India and Pakistan communal ownership is possible but subject to the dictates of regional bodies and the decisions of customary councils of elders, among others. In developed nations we have already seen that land ownership is not generally afforded to indigenous peoples. In Canada, indigenous lands are held in the name of the Crown and only a right to occupy and possess is granted to indigenous persons. The Saami people in Sweden equally only enjoy usufruct rights, whereas in the USA First Nation lands are held in trust by the federal government, in which case the First Nations enjoy either beneficial interests or some limited communal ownership. Exceptionally, New Zealand recognises communal freehold in respect of the Maori. Finally, in sub-Saharan Africa the situation is somewhat confusing because post-colonial governments have recognised traditional customary tenure rights, albeit these are vested in all persons without distinction between indigenous and non-indigenous. The landmark decision in the *Endorois* case, analysed below, will most probably have an impact on African land laws in the immediate future.

In a landmark decision the ACHPR in the *Endorois* case was faced with the eviction of the Endorois people in Kenya from their ancestral lands in order to construct a game reserve and tourist facilities. The contested land was home to a lake which the Endorois believed was formed by God after sinking the particular ground as punishment against their ancestors, thus forming Lake Bogoria. All their kinsmen were buried adjacent to the lake and all their traditional ceremonies were inextricably linked to it. The Commission confirmed the Endorois' spiritual connection to the land[101] and hence found a violation of article 8 of the ACHPR relating to freedom of religion.[102] The Commission accepted that indigenous rights over traditional lands constituted 'property' and that the rights thereto were 'property rights'.[103] It went on to explain the content of these rights by reference to UNDRIP, as follows:

The jurisprudence under international law bestows the right of ownership rather than mere access. The African Commission notes that if international law were to grant access only, indigenous peoples would remain vulnerable to further violations/dispossession by the state or third parties. Ownership ensures that indigenous peoples

---

[100] See A. Shapovalov, 'Straightening out the Backward Legal Regulation of Backward Peoples' Claim to Land in the Russian North: the Concept of Indigenous Neomodernism', *Georgia International Environmental Law Review* (*Geo. Int'l Envtl. L. Rev.*) 17 (2005), 435, where the author argues that Russia adheres to the *terra nullius* doctrine.

[101] *Endorois* case, paras. 156, 166.   [102] Ibid., para. 173.   [103] Ibid., para. 187.

can engage with the state and third parties as active stakeholders than as passive beneficiaries.[104]

In the view of the African Commission, the following conclusions could be drawn: (a) traditional possession of land by indigenous people has the equivalent effect as that of a state-granted full property title; (b) traditional possession entitles indigenous people to demand official recognition and registration of property title; (c) the members of indigenous peoples who have unwillingly left their traditional lands, or lost possession thereof, maintain property rights thereto, even though they lack legal title, unless the lands have been lawfully transferred to third parties in good faith; and (d) the members of indigenous peoples who have unwillingly lost possession of their lands, when those lands have been lawfully transferred to innocent third parties, are entitled to restitution thereof or to obtain other lands of equal extension and quality.[105]

The Commission is emphatically stating that indigenous peoples possess full property rights over their ancestral lands irrespective of whether the state has registered or titled such land or whether the group has satisfied any formal property requirements.[106] The fact that they constitute property rights distinguishes them from mere access rights or privileges that can be withdrawn or sold to third parties at any time by the government. This is a development that is certainly far more progressive than the legislation applicable in many industrialised nations. The property rights of indigenous peoples involve a particular positive obligation on states. Hence, if an indigenous group enjoys the land for its hunting and fishing needs the state must preserve and sustain the relevant ecosystem. Equally, if a group believes in its spiritual attachment to a lake this must not be exploited in such a way as to deplete or pollute its waters. This is consistent with the jurisprudence of the IACtHR which has held that indigenous groups are owed special measures of protection in order to guarantee the full exercise of their rights.[107]

QUESTIONS

1 The application of native customary law in many instances, especially in Africa, is nothing more than an attempt to deny indigenous peoples universal human rights. Examples include the practice of female genital mutilation, gender-based discrimination and the permissibility of rudimentary dispute resolution mechanisms for which there is no guarantee against arbitrariness. Discuss.

---

[104] Ibid., para. 204.   [105] Ibid., para. 209.

[106] Canadian courts distinguish between title and rights and hold that a right may exist independently of a title. See *R* v. *Van der Peet* (1996) 137 DLR 289 and *R* v. *Adams* [1996] 138 DLR 657, confirmed in *Delgamuukw* v. *British Columbia* (1997) 153 DLR, para. 138.

[107] Case of the *Mayagna (Sumo) Awas Tingni Community*, paras. 148–9 and 151; case of the *Sawhoyamaxa Indigenous Community* v. *Paraguay*, Judgment on merits, reparations and costs (29 March 2006), Ser. C, no. 146, paras. 118 and 131, and case of the *Yakye Axa Indigenous Community*, paras. 124, 131, 135–7 and 154.

2 The 'treaties' entered into between the early conquerors and indigenous peoples were concluded in territories lacking a legal system and therefore the indigenous subjects were not necessarily endowed with legal personality. Do you consider that the law of contract in your, or another, country may render this agreement legally binding? If so, can the relevant private international law treaties be utilised to enforce indigenous 'treaties'?

3 Indigenous and minority women are susceptible to discrimination in two respects: for their minority or indigenous status as such, in addition to their gender. This inter-sectional discrimination does not always affect male members of the group, as is the case with the practice of rape in the context of ethnic cleansing. Do you consider that in such cases a single, unified, violation should be identified, rather than two distinct ones?

4 The original inhabitants of a particular territory are fully integrated within the dominant group that they no longer possess any distinct cultural patterns or social institutions. Can they still, none the less, claim entitlements from indigenous rights?

10.4.4 Special considerations in the design of indigenous peoples development plans within the World Bank

Since 1991 the World Bank has required borrowers to mitigate any adverse effects from their intended project on indigenous populations. To this end it has devised a layered process that is designed not only to protect indigenous peoples but also to enhance their developmental advancement. This is important because in theory the Bank is in an ideal position to implement indigenous rights since both the investor and the local government are dependent upon its approval of the loan. Thus, the Bank is well placed to influence and dictate both policy and implementation.

The Bank's Operational Policy (OP) 4.10 on indigenous peoples requires the borrower to engage in a process of 'free, prior, and informed consultation' with the affected indigenous group, which must yield 'broad community support' for the project in order for it to be financed.[108] This is subject to a five-prong process, which consists of the following:

1 screening by the Bank to identify whether indigenous peoples are present in, or have collective attachment to, the project area;[109]

2 a social assessment by the borrower;[110]

3 a process of free, prior, and informed consultation with the affected indigenous peoples' communities at each stage of the project, and particularly during project preparation, to fully identify their views and ascertain their broad community support for the project;[111]

---

[108] Para. 1, Optional Protocol 4.10.   [109] Ibid., paras. 6 and 8.
[110] Ibid., paras. 6 and 9.   [111] Ibid., paras. 6, 10–11.

4 the preparation of an Indigenous Peoples Plan (IPP) or an Indigenous Peoples Planning Framework (IPPF);[112] and

5 disclosure of the draft IPP or draft IPPF.[113]

In the screening process the Bank seeks to determine the existence of indigenous people in the project area and their attachment to it. To this end it consults qualified social scientists, particularly anthropologists with expertise in the project area. In addition, the Bank also consults the indigenous group and the borrower. Where it determines the existence of indigenous peoples it is then incumbent on the borrower to undertake a social assessment in order to evaluate the project's effects. In case potentially negative effects are detected the social impact assessment (SIA) must propose alternative measures. The SIA assesses in advance the social consequences that are likely to follow from the project, including probable impacts from environmental manipulation.[114] Although the SIA is not an exact science it may determine the impact on variables such as community structures and institutions, changes in social behaviour, local norms, customs and activities, changes in social control mechanisms, creation of employment opportunities and others.[115] It is not untypical of borrowers in general – and governments for that matter – to manipulate the SIA as a political rather than as a planning tool. This may be done in order to justify a particular policy or project rather than as a tool to mitigate the effects of the policy or the project on the affected population.

The Bank's only guarantee against manipulation is the consensus of the affected people, which itself is subject to manipulation, as will be demonstrated in the following section. Further, the borrower may well demonstrate an increase in income in respect of the group's households, which he may then interpret as a determinant in the rise of livelihood. In many cases this increase is artificial since it is the result of lump sum compensations paid to affected persons whose effects are of a limited duration. As a result, Ashley and Hussein emphasise that poverty reduction is not necessarily reflected in a sudden increase of income, but should be approached from a study of food security, vulnerability, social inferiority, access to productive means and an understanding of the objectives of each household (i.e. in the sense of what is important to them – education for their children, land security, etc.).[116]

---

[112] Ibid., paras. 6, 12–13.   [113] Ibid., paras. 6 and 15.

[114] See generally, H. A. Becker and F. Vanclay, *The International Handbook of Social Impact Assessment: Conceptual and Methodological Advances* (Cheltenham: Edward Elgar, 2006).

[115] C. J. Barrow, *Environmental and Social Impact Assessment* (London: Hodder Arnold, 1997), 234.

[116] C. Ashley and K. Hussein, *Developing Methodologies for Livelihood Impact Assessment: Experience of the African Wildlife Foundation in East Africa* (Washington DC: Overseas Development Institute Working Paper 129, 2000), 14.

Following the drafting of the social assessment the borrower must next engage in direct consultation with the indigenous peoples on the basis of three principles: (1) an appropriate gender and intergenerationally inclusive framework encompassing broad civil society representation; (2) employment of appropriate consultation methods to the cultural and social values of the affected people, with special attention to the concerns of women, youth and children and their access to development opportunities; and (3) providing full access and disclosure to the relevant reports and information. Before the Bank can go ahead and approve the loan the borrower must demonstrate that the project has received broad community support on the basis of free, prior and informed consent (FPIC).[117] It is natural, however, at this stage for the affected group and civil society organisations to barter with the borrower for further concessions, knowing full well that their agreement is necessary for the continuation of the project. This is certainly welcome, because it ensures that indigenous concerns are voiced and heard throughout the process and that indigenous social and cultural demands are met, even if the local government is opposed to them. Any special agreement must be communicated by the borrower to the Bank.[118]

On the basis of the social assessment and in consultation with the affected communities, the borrower prepares an IPP that sets out appropriate measures ensuring that the affected group will receive culturally appropriate social and economic benefits and that any adverse effects are avoided, mitigated or compensated. The role of civil society in the consultation process is critical, because indigenous peoples' access to information and their level of education may lend itself to manipulation by the borrower. By way of illustration, in the absence of civil society the borrower may paint an idyllic picture of the project without emphasising any of its social and environmental evils. Equally, the borrower may attempt to negotiate only with persons of influence and thus ignore the community's broader wishes as such.

What has not always been abundantly clear in the Bank's policies on indigenous peoples is whether its focus should be directed at preserving the group's cultural and social status quo, or whether it should also be open to the possibility that the group may wish to radically alter this traditional status. Paragraph 7 of Operational Directive 4.20 of 1991, which has now been replaced by OP 4.10, raised this issue as a dilemma for Bank management as follows:

---

[117] This is not a mere condition imposed by the Bank. Rather, it has been endorsed as a customary principle by human rights treaty bodies in relation to the taking of indigenous lands, whatever their form of land tenure. See *Angela Poma Poma* v. *Peru*, UN Doc. CCPR/C/95/D/14572006 (24 April 2009), para. 7.6; CESCR, Concluding Observations on Colombia, UN Doc. E/C.12/Add.1/74 (30 November 2001), para. 33; *Mary and Carrie Dann* (USA), IACHR Report no. 75/02, Case no. 11,140 (27 December 2002), para. 131.

[118] Optional Protocol 4.10, para. 11(e).

How to approach indigenous peoples affected by development projects is a controversial issue. Debate is often phrased as a choice between two opposed positions. One
pole is to insulate indigenous populations whose cultural and economic practices
make it difficult for them to deal with powerful outside groups. The advantages of
this approach are the special protections that are provided and the preservation of
cultural distinctiveness; the costs are the benefits forgone from development programmes. The other pole argues that indigenous people must be acculturated to dominant society values and economic activities so that they can participate in national
development. Here the benefits can include improved social and economic opportunities, but the cost is often the gradual loss of cultural differences.

OP 4.10 addresses this issue implicitly by requiring not only the informed
participation of indigenous peoples in the design of the social assessment and
the IPP, but also because all Bank-financed projects must impart culturally
appropriate social and economic benefits. The Policy goes even further by
stressing that the Bank may, *at a country's request*, support development policies that help to strengthen local laws in favour of indigenous groups, set up
poverty-reduction programmes and projects owned by indigenous peoples,
as well as addressing gender and intergenerational issues,[119] among others.

In practice, this process is expensive and cumbersome for borrowers and
to a certain degree intrusive for the target states. Moreover, vulnerable and
marginalised indigenous groups are typically exploited for their labour and
lands by local elites, including timber and natural resources corporations,
non-indigenous farmers and corrupt local government officials. Thus, there
are many actors who are averse, if not outright hostile, to the enhancement
of the status of indigenous peoples, both in terms of legal as well as financial
status. Hence, the Bank should not simply strive to accept an IPP because it
has received broad consensus from the indigenous group in the project area.
Rather, it must make every effort to eliminate any possible hostility against
the group following the completion of the project and avoid the temptation
of temporary financial benefits. The following section provides a case study
of a World Bank project that failed to satisfy these demands because both the
borrower and the Bank simply focused on the letter of the operational policy
and not its spirit.

10.4.5   The Chad–Cameroon pipeline and the Baka/Bakola: what to look for in social impact assessments

In the late 1990s the World Bank Group proceeded to provide US$115 million
towards financing the Chad–Cameroon pipeline project, which was meant
to transport Chadian oil to the Cameroonian coast. Although the Bank's
participation represented only 3 per cent of the entire amount it provided

---

[119] Optional Protocol 4.20, para. 22.

appropriate political and financial guarantees. The construction of the Cameroon portion of the pipeline was to traverse the country's Atlantic forest zone, part of which is inhabited by the Baka/Bakola indigenous peoples. These groups are also known as pygmies, but the term carries a pejorative connotation and the Bakola themselves do not accept it, despite the fact that it appears heavily in the literature. They maintain a traditional lifestyle that is distinct not only from that of the general population of Cameroon but also from neighbouring tribal and semi-tribal peoples. Unlike other groups they are principally engaged in hunting, trapping and fishing and only recently began to cultivate as an alternative to the above; yet, farming is only of secondary financial importance to them not only because of their cultural identity but also because they are not land owners.

The traversal of the pipeline through traditional Baka/Bakola lands gave rise to two interrelated issues. The first concerned the social impact of the project on this community, whereas the second involved the potential realignment of inter-ethnic relations with neighbouring groups and the state itself. The IPP foresaw that the project would bring progress to the area and proposed both individual and collective compensation which consisted in the construction of huts, the provision of tools and compensation for destroyed crops and farmland. There was also provision for a limited supply of electricity, access to healthcare and education. There is ample evidence that the borrowers did not adequately consult with all the Bakola and moreover failed to compensate all those affected in the project area.

The project was bound to disrupt the Baka/Bakola traditional lifestyle, given that the pipeline was destined to pass through forestland used for their principal activities of hunting and crop gathering. This eventuality would necessarily result in their adjustment within more confined forest space or would lead them in more rapid fashion towards agriculture as their exclusive livelihood. Both alternatives involved some social adaptation whose consequences the borrowers and the Bank failed to address. The most serious problem was that of land ownership. Under Cameroonian law customary title to land has been available since 1974 as long as the land is occupied or exploited. Land is deemed occupied where the user has constructed buildings and dwellings, whereas exploitation is demonstrated in cases of farming and grazing. The guiding principle in order for customary title to be granted is therefore 'man's clear control of the land and evident development'.[120] Given the Bakola's hunting and crop-gathering livelihood they can never expect to possess any customary law rights under the existing law. They fare no better in Cameroon's forests. The law there distinguishes between non-permanent forest domains, which may be converted for agricultural use, and permanent forest domains that are reserved for conservation. Forest

---

[120] Article 15(1) of Order no. 74–1 (6 July 1974) 'Laying down the land tenure system'.

laws have imposed severe restrictions on Bakola hunting and crop-gathering rights because forest products are limited only to personal use. Moreover, because the Bakola do not technically 'occupy' or 'exploit' converted forest land they have never been able to claim any pertinent rights. This has driven the Baka/Bakola to poverty because they traditionally barter with wild game and forest crops, this being their primary source of income. Moreover, it has forced them to become subservient to other groups that satisfy the demands of the law and which have acquired land ownership. Equally, although Cameroonian law envisages annual proceeds from a logging tax that is to be distributed to local village communities, in practice the Baka/Bakola are excluded by rival groups because they are not recognised as having resident status.[121]

As a result of the legal impediments restricting their primary (hunting and crop-gathering) and secondary financial activities (agriculture and farming) the Bakola have become subservient to neighbouring groups, namely certain Bantu tribes.[122] This situation has been exacerbated by the fact that the Bantu are farmers and therefore have come to own land. This stark inequality between the two groups has not been addressed by Cameroon, despite the obvious vulnerability of the Bakola and has led many of them to be considered Bantu serfs. This inequality has curtailed the Bakola's access to markets to sell or barter their forest products, which has in turn forced them to barter with the Bantu who naturally exploit them. Neither the borrowers nor the Bank thought it wise to alter their subservient and serf status, despite the fact that they desired to escape this cycle of exploitation, by acquiring land, educating their children and improving their standard of living, while retaining much of their traditional lifestyle. This is no doubt a misconceived policy choice that wholly misunderstands the poverty reduction and development role of the Bank. Without delaying the project the Bank should, in similar circumstances, oblige the host state to accept legislative changes that will alleviate the subservient condition of vulnerable people; in the instant case, this could have been achieved by granting the Bakola land rights and rendering them recipients of the logging tax. Although the Bank may discuss such measures after the loan agreements have been adopted, there is no guarantee that the host state will accept these legislative amendments, unless the loan is to be paid in successive tranches. Clearly, the borrower has no interest in the social re-alignment of rival indigenous groups by strengthening the position of one in order to eliminate its subservient status against another.

[121] Centre for Environment and Development (CED) *et al.*, The Situation of Indigenous Peoples in Cameroon: A Supplementary Report Submitted to CERD, Doc. CERD/C/CMR/19 (27 January 2010), paras. 13, 47ff.

[122] See G. Ngima Mawoung, *The Relationship between the Bakola and the Bantu Peoples of the Coastal Regions of Cameroon and their Perception of Commercial Forest Exploitation*, African Study Monographs 26 (2001), 209.

This case study is emblematic of the Bank's perception that the socio-economic status of indigenous peoples must remain untouched. Thus, SIA studies fail to identify the discrimination directed against them by the state and other social groups. In this manner, their cycle of poverty and underdevelopment will be perpetuated.

FURTHER READING

Anaya, S. J., *Indigenous Peoples in International Law* (Oxford University Press, 2004).

Castellino, J., 'Territoriality and Identity in International Law: the Struggle for Self-determination in the Western Sahara', *Millennium Journal of International Studies* 28 (1999), 547.

Castellino, J. and Dominguez-Redondo, E., *Minority Rights in Asia: A Comparative Legal Analysis* (Oxford University Press, 2006).

Crawford, J. (ed.), *The Rights of Peoples* (Oxford University Press, 1992).

Genugten, W. van, 'Protection of Indigenous Peoples on the African Continent: Concepts, Position Seeking and the Interaction of Legal Systems', *AJIL* 104 (2010), 29.

Keane, D., *Caste-Based Discrimination in International Human Rights Law* (Aldershot: Ashgate, 2007).

Lerner, N., *Group Rights and Discrimination in International Law* (Leiden, Boston: Martinus Nijhoff, 2003).

McHugh, P., *The Maori Magna Carta: New Zealand Law and the Treaty of Waitangi* (Oxford University Press, 1991).

Ndahinda, F. M., *Indigenousness in Africa: A Contested Legal Framework for Empowerment of Marginalised Communities* (The Hague: TMC Asser, 2011).

Pentassuglia, G., *Minorities in International Law: An Introductory Study* (Strasbourg: Council of Europe Publishing, 2002).

Ratner, S., 'Drawing a Better Line: *Uti possidetis* and the Borders of New States', *AJIL* 90 (1996), 590.

Reisman, W. M., 'Protecting Indigenous Rights in International Adjudication', *AJIL* 89 (1995), 352.

Spiliopoulou-Akermark, A., *Justifications of Minority Protection in International Law* (Leiden, Boston: Martinus Nijhoff, 1996).

Thornberry, P., *International Law and the Rights of Minorities* (Oxford: Clarendon Press, 1993).

Xanthaki, A., *Indigenous Rights and United Nations Standards: Self-Determination, Culture and Lands* (Cambridge University Press, 2007).

The human rights of women*

CONTENTS

11.1 INTRODUCTION

The disadvantages, discrimination and subordination suffered by women globally have been well documented in a variety of contexts,[1] yet the issue of women's human rights has until relatively recently been neglected in international law. The instruments composing the international Bill of Rights contain general non-discrimination clauses which include the prohibition of discrimination on the basis of sex or gender, whereby the rights within these instruments are held to be applicable to everyone, regardless of, *inter alia*, sex.[2] As this chapter will discuss, these generic discrimination clauses have, in a number of ways, proved inadequate to capture the specific nature of violations suffered by women and to provide adequate protection. Women's human rights are an overarching phenomenon touching on all aspects of the international human rights framework. The importance of addressing human rights issues as they specifically pertain to women and others suffering

---

* Chapter written by Dr Rupa Reddy, SOAS, University of London. Dr Rupa Reddy is a teaching fellow at the School of Law, SOAS, University of London. She has worked with a number of international human rights organisations, including on women's rights projects in the UK and elsewhere, and recently completed a major study on 'Approaches to Honour-Related Violence in the English Legal System'.

[1] See Chapter 1 of H. Charlesworth and C. Chinkin, *The Boundaries of International Law: A Feminist Analysis* (Manchester University Press: 2000), especially 4–14.

[2] See, for example, articles 2 UDHR, 2(1) ICCPR and 2(2) ICESCR.

disadvantage or oppression within gender-based power structures has been widely recognised.[3]

Informed, determined and vociferous campaigns by national and international women's rights movements and coalitions have brought to light, and attempted to redress, a number of inadequacies within the international human rights system. In particular, they have questioned a number of the assumptions underlying the existing framework of protection, particularly a narrow focus on non-discrimination at the expense of broader concerns reflecting the experiences of women, such as gender-based violence. The culmination of the 1976–1985 UN Decade for Women with the 1995 Beijing Fourth World Conference was instrumental in bringing key issues to the fore, followed by the Beijing Platform for Action ten years later.[4] The Platform discussed and made recommendations on a wide range of issues, including poverty, education, health, violence against women, armed conflict, political rights and the rights of the girl child, which showed the breadth of concerns relating to women's rights.

At the heart of this discussion remains the core question: why do the human rights of women still remain so contested and controversial? Conceptual and sociological approaches, such as those around cultural and social hierarchies, and the practicalities of how far to utilise existing human rights mechanisms in order to 'mainstream' women's human rights, as opposed to separate regimes specifically aimed at protecting women, have been at the centre of debates.[5] The 'generational' hierarchy created by certain approaches within the system, whereby so-called first generation civil and political rights are deemed to take priority over other rights, also forms an important part of the debates.[6] Many violations against women are committed in the private, rather than the public realm. However, international human rights law has traditionally focused on the public, 'male' sphere. An examination of the effects of this 'public/private divide' is therefore critical for the practical

---

[3] For useful introductory background perspective to these debates, see Chinkin and Charlesworth, above note 1. Also N. Burrows, 'International Law and Human Rights: the Case of Women's Rights', in T. Campbell *et al.* (eds.), *Human Rights: From Rhetoric To Reality* (London: Blackwells, 1986), pp. 80–98, and R. Cook, 'Women's International Human Rights Law: the Way Forward', *HRQ* 15 (1993), 230–61.

[4] The conference recommended the adoption of the Beijng Declaration and Platform for Action by the General Assembly. The full text of the document can be found at www. un.org/womenwatch/daw/beijing/platform/. See also R. Cook, 'Effectiveness of the Beijing Conference: Advancing International Law Regarding Women', *American Society of International Law Proceedings* 91 (1997), 310–17.

[5] See H. Charlesworth, 'Not Waving but Drowning: Gender Mainstreaming and Human Rights within the United Nations', *Harv. Hum. Rts. J.* 18 (2005), 1–18, which provides a key contribution to these debates.

[6] See C. Bunch, 'Women's Rights as Human Rights: toward a Re-Vision of Human Rights', *HRQ* 12 (1990), 486–98; and Charlesworth and Chinkin, above note 1, 206–7.

protection of women's human rights. A more recent debate has revolved around the conceptual distinction between sex and gender, and the ways in which this distinction may affect the practical application of the human rights of women. This chapter revisits these debates, and examines how they have affected the development of women's rights in international human rights law.[7] It uses the example of prosecution of 'honour crimes' in the UK to highlight the utility and limitations of international human rights law when seeking effective protection of women's rights at the domestic level.

11.2   NORMATIVE FRAMEWORK

11.2.1   Key violations of women's human rights: CEDAW

The major approach to the protection of women's human rights, from the UN Charter onwards, has been that of non-discrimination and equality. According to the HRCtee, discrimination, which is prohibited in articles 3 and 26 of the ICCPR:

> should be understood to imply any distinction, exclusion, restriction or preference which is based on any ground such as race, colour, *sex*, language, religion, political or other opinion, national or social origin, property, birth or other status, and which has the purpose or effect of nullifying or impairing the recognition, enjoyment or exercise by all persons, on an equal footing, of all rights and freedoms. (emphasis added)[8]

The prohibition forbids both direct discrimination, for example legislation stipulating that women are entitled to less inheritance than men, and indirect discrimination. The latter denotes measures that are ostensibly neutral, such as that all applicants for a particular employment position need to be of a certain height, but have a detrimental impact on one of the prohibited grounds, for example, excluding a proportionately higher number of women from gaining access. Such indirect discrimination is only justifiable where the difference in treatment is reasonable, such as where the particular work can only be satisfactorily carried out by persons of a certain height.

Earlier approaches within international human rights law to the violation of women's rights were 'protective', such as the 1948 ILO Convention Concerning Night Work of Women Employed in Industry.[9] An interim

---

[7] Related issues of women's rights including refugee law, international humanitarian law, and international criminal law will not be examined in this chapter.

[8] HRCtee, General Comment 18: Non-discrimination (Compilation of General Comments and General Recommendations Adopted by Human Rights Treaty Bodies), UN Doc. HRI/GEN/1/ Rev.1 at 26 (1994). Article 6 also refers to the definitions of non-discrimination set out in CERD and CEDAW.

[9] 81 UNTS 285. See also N. Hevener, 'An Analysis of Gender-based Treaty Law: Contemporary Developments in Historical Perspective', *HRQ* 8 (1986), 70–88.

'corrective' approach followed, which attempted to protect the rights of women, but without direct comparison to the situation of men, for example in relation to the trafficking of women. At present, the overarching approach to the protection of women's human rights is one of non-discrimination, as embodied in CEDAW.

CEDAW, or the Women's Convention, is the first major international treaty on the protection of women's rights. CEDAW marks out inequality and discrimination against women as a particular and serious form of human rights violation meriting a specific instrument. The underlying reasoning is in many senses sound, since the specificity of abuses directed towards certain vulnerable groups such as women can be most effectively addressed through particular forms of protection and remedies. However, this very specificity can also potentially result in certain important rights being inadvertently overlooked, dismissed, denigrated or marginalised, a risk that necessitates a closer assessment of CEDAW's effectiveness in protecting women's human rights.

Article 1 of CEDAW states that:

For the purposes of the present Convention, the term 'discrimination against women' shall mean any distinction, exclusion or restriction made on the basis of sex which has the effect or purpose of impairing or nullifying the recognition, enjoyment or exercise by women, irrespective of their marital status, on a basis of equality of men and women, of human rights and fundamental freedoms in the political, economic, social, cultural, civil or any other field.

The treaty elaborates on this approach in articles 2 and 3, which oblige states to promulgate policy measures to condemn discrimination against women through legislative and other means, and to take appropriate measures to guarantee the equality of women with men in all fields. However, CEDAW goes beyond traditional liberal conceptions of direct non-discrimination by setting out 'temporary special measures' ('affirmative action') to accelerate *de facto* equality between men and women. According to article 4(1), such measures are not to be considered as discrimination under the Convention, and should be discontinued 'when the objectives of equality or opportunity and treatment have been achieved'. One example of this approach could be to set quotas for the number of women given seats in schools or universities, in order to increase access for women in relation to educational opportunities.[10]

Besides a general prohibition of discrimination, CEDAW includes the right to non-discrimination against women in the fields of education,[11] health care,[12] and employment,[13] including in relation to marriage and maternity

---

[10] See CEDAW General Recommendation 25 (2004) on article 4(1), of CEDAW, on temporary special measures; especially paras. 24, 31, 32 and 37.

[11] Article 10 CEDAW.   [12] Article 12 ibid.

[13] Article 11(1) ibid.

rights in the employment context.[14] The treaty builds further on issues relating to maternity, marriage and family relations in article 16, which sets out women's rights to freely enter into marriage and to exercise equal rights and responsibilities in relation to their children.[15] CEDAW also emphasises the rights of women to equality in the administration of property and their legal capacity to administer contracts.[16] In addition, it refers to a number of other specific protections; namely, the right not to be trafficked or exploited in prostitution;[17] political and elective rights and representation in political bodies and international organisations;[18] and the right of women to attain or change nationality, including in relation to their children, regardless of their marital status.[19] As well as recognising the need for specific protections, CEDAW goes beyond the hierarchical generational paradigm established within the broader human rights treaties, by referring to the need for states to eliminate discrimination against women in any other areas of ESC rights,[20] and by addressing the particular needs of women in rural contexts.[21]

11.2.2   Critiques of CEDAW

The advent of a treaty specifically aimed at protecting the rights of women is to be welcomed. Yet a number of criticisms have been made in relation to CEDAW's content and the scope of its provisions. For example, CEDAW's provisions on ESC rights do not specifically refer to a number of important rights that have a particularly detrimental effect on the lives of women. An example of this is the right to adequate access to food. As well as acting as primary gatherers and distributers of food, where food is scarce women often deny themselves food, feeding other family members before themselves.[22] As a result, women may effectively not have the access to adequate food because of their role, but this disadvantage may not be adequately captured by more generic non-discrimination provisions that do not tackle underlying structural causes and/or impose more far-reaching positive obligations on states.

The Protocol to the ACHPR on the Rights of Women in Africa is more progressive and provides a marked contrast. Its article 15 sets out the right to food security, stating that:

States Parties shall ensure that women have the right to nutritious and adequate food. In this regard, they shall take appropriate measures to:

(a) provide women with access to clean drinking water, sources of domestic fuel, land, and the means of producing nutritious food;

---

[14] Article 11(2) ibid.   [15] Article 16 ibid.   [16] Article 15 ibid.
[17] Article 6 ibid.   [18] Articles 7 and 8 ibid.   [19] Article 9 ibid.
[20] Article 13 ibid.   [21] Article 14 ibid.
[22] See, for example, the case studies examined in C. Chinkin and S. Wright, 'The Hunger Trap: Women, Food and Self-Determination', *Mich. J. Int'l L.* 14 (1993), 262–321.

(b) establish adequate systems of supply and storage to ensure food security.

This provision recognises that the right to adequate as well as safe and nutritious food is only achievable through practical measures including access to other resources such as clean water, fuel and a source of land upon which to subsist. Another criticism concerns CEDAW's conceptual and practical application, particularly article 5 of CEDAW, which requires states parties to take all appropriate measures:

(a) To modify the social and cultural patterns of conduct of men and women, with a view to achieving the elimination of prejudices and customary and all other practices which are based on the idea of the inferiority or the superiority of either of the sexes or on stereotyped roles for men and women.

A number of states have argued that article 5 and other provisions set out in CEDAW, such as article 16, constitute an infringement of their local and personal laws. This has resulted in one of the most problematic aspects of CEDAW's application, namely, reservations.[23] CEDAW is one of the most ratified yet most reserved of the six core UN treaties, adding to questions as to its efficacy.

A number of states have entered general reservations stating that they do not consider themselves bound by provisions of the treaty which would require them to change or amend their state constitutions. Within the context of article 5, reservations have particularly related to marriage, children, divorce and inheritance. More specifically, several states have entered reservations to the effect that CEDAW is not binding in so far as it conflicts with, or is contrary to Islamic Sharia law within their domestic legal systems. Their main contention in doing so seems to be that article 5 effectively impedes their rights to determine and enforce religious and personal law norms around family law. For example, Malaysia declared that:

Malaysia's accession is subject to the understanding that the provisions of the Convention do not conflict with the provisions of the Islamic Sharia' law and the Federal Constitution of Malaysia. With regards thereto, further, the Government of Malaysia does not consider itself bound by the provisions of articles 2 (f), 5 (a), 7 (b), 9 and 16 of the aforesaid Convention.[24]

The reservation entered by Niger is even more specifically related to article 5(a), stating that it, 'expresses reservations with regard to the modification of social and cultural patterns of conduct of men and women'. It goes on to specify that this is the case due to the fact that provisions including article 5:

cannot be applied immediately, as they are contrary to existing customs and practices which, by their nature, can be modified only with the passage of time and the evolution of society and cannot, therefore, be abolished by an act of authority.[25]

---

[23] See section 2.2.1 for a more detailed discussion of the issue of reservations to treaties.
[24] See www.un.org/womenwatch/daw/cedaw/reservations-country.htm.
[25] Ibid.

However, these reservations have been objected to by several other states parties, on the basis that they conflict with the treaty's object and purpose.[26] The CtEDAW has repeatedly expressed concern as to the number of reservations, in particular in relation to issues related to culture or religion.[27] The controversies over these provisions and the practice of entering reservations in relation to them raise questions about CEDAW's efficacy. In particular, this debate highlights the limited commitment of states to the implementation of the treaty where relevant provisions are seen to conflict with alleged local norms around gender roles and equality.[28]

A further criticism of CEDAW is that its monitoring and enforcement mechanisms are weak. While this is a generic problem of the international human rights system, it has been particularly pronounced in respect of CEDAW due to the absence of a complaints procedure prior to 2000. The adoption of an Optional Protocol to CEDAW has given the Committee a more prominent role. One of its advantages is the fact that not only individual victims themselves, but also groups of victims and non-governmental organisations and others acting on the behalf of both of the latter, are able to bring communications before the Committee.[29] However, take up of the procedure has remained limited, and the implementation of decisions constitutes a major challenge in practice.[30]

One of CEDAW's major flaws is that it contains no explicit provision in relation to violence against women.[31] This is a conspicuous omission for a treaty which in other regards, has made a concerted effort to comprehensively address a number of key areas of violations of women's human rights. Unsurprisingly, the lack of insertion of a specific clause on violence against women has produced sustained criticism, which the Committee partially attempted to address in the form of the CEDAW General Recommendation 19 in 1992, which states that:

The definition of discrimination includes gender-based violence, that is, violence that is directed against a woman because she is a woman or that affects women disproportionately. It includes acts that inflict physical, mental or sexual harm or

---

[26] Examples of states which entered objections in relation to article 5 reservations by Malaysia include Finland, the Netherlands, Norway and France; in relation to Niger, by Norway, Denmark and Finland; and in the case of New Zealand, by Mexico and Sweden. See www.un.org/womenwatch/daw/cedaw/reservations-country.htm for full details of reservations, and consequent objections to this and other articles of the treaty.

[27] CEDAW General Recommendation 21 (13th session, 1994) on *Equality in Marriage and Family Relations*, paras. 41–5.

[28] See B. Clark, 'The Vienna Convention Reservations Regime and the Convention on Discrimination Against Women', *AJIL* 85 (1991), 281–321.

[29] Although see Chapter 6 of C. Mackinnon, *Are Women Human? And Other International Dialogues* (Harvard University Press, 2007), p. 65, for a brief but largely positive commentary on the aims and processes of the CEDAW Optional Protocol.

[30] See on CtEDAW, section 5.5.8. See also A. Edwards, *Violence against Women under International Human Rights Law* (Cambridge University Press, 2011), Chapter 3.

[31] Ibid.

suffering, threats of such acts, coercion and other deprivations of liberty. Gender-based violence may breach specific provisions of the Convention, regardless of whether those provisions expressly mention violence.[32]

Following this the UNGA also took up the issue of violence against women, adopting the 1994 Declaration on the Elimination of Violence Against Women (DEVAW),[33] Article 1 of DEVAW sets out the definition of violence against women as:

any act of gender-based violence that results in, or is likely to result in, physical, sexual or psychological harm or suffering to women, including threats of such acts, coercion or arbitrary deprivation of liberty, whether occurring in public or in private life.

The Special Rapporteur on violence against women, its causes and consequences (established in 1994) has also been instrumental in developing the understanding of violence against women and bringing relevant issues to the attention of a range of stakeholders. This has consisted of numerous country- and issue-based reports, such as on the intersections between culture and violence against women[34] and the due diligence standard as a tool for the elimination of violence against women, discussed in further detail below.[35]

In the Inter-American context the Inter-American Convention on the Prevention, Punishment and Eradication of Violence Against Women[36] covers several crucial aspects, including a definition which encompasses gender-based violence in both the public and private spheres. Further notable features are provisions relating to a range of civil and political and economic, social and cultural rights, specific reference to the role of cultural norms in violence against women and the need for states to employ due diligence standards in relation to violence against women. The definition of violence against women within the Protocol to the ACHPR on the Rights of Women in Africa is possibly even more progressive, given its additional reference to economic harm and situations of armed conflict and war:

'Violence against women' means all acts perpetrated against women which cause or could cause them physical, sexual, psychological, and economic harm, including the threat to take such acts; or to undertake the imposition of arbitrary restrictions on or deprivation of fundamental freedoms in private or public life in peace time and during situations of armed conflicts or of war. [37]

---

[32] CEDAW General Recommendation 19 (11th session, 1992).

[33] UNGA resolution 48/104 (20 December 1993).

[34] Report of the Special Rapporteur on violence against women, its causes and consequences: The Intersections between culture and gender, UN Doc. A/HRC/4/34 (17 January 2007).

[35] Report of the Special Rapporteur on violence against women, its Causes and Consequences: The Due Diligence Standard, E/CN.4/2006/61 (20 January 2006).

[36] Inter-American Convention on the Prevention, Punishment and Eradication of Violence against Women 'Convention Of Belem Do Para' (9 June 1994).

[37] 11 July 2003 (entry into force November 2005), article 1(j).

Notwithstanding these normative developments, responses to a number of serious and systemic acts of violence against women continue to be inadequate and unsatisfactory, in both national and international contexts. This chapter does not purport to outline the vast range of physical, emotional and other forms of violence against women which occur daily worldwide.[38] Instead, it will highlight two particular sets of issues of relevance within the international human rights context, which intersect with a number of other violations. These are the right to life and the prohibition on torture, which are frequently at issue where violence against women results in serious harm if not loss of life. As well as the omission of a provision on violence against women, CEDAW does not contain explicit provisions on the right to life or the prohibition of torture. For this reason, much of the jurisprudence in relation to these violations of women's human rights, particularly in the public sphere, has to date emerged from other UN and regional treaty bodies.[39]

With respect to the right to life,[40] until relatively recently the international human rights regime focused on state or public sphere violations, such as the death penalty, state killings and disappearances or deaths in custody, to which men have been deemed more susceptible than women.[41] Feminist scholars have argued that while women also suffer violations of their right to life in the public sphere, the majority of violations of women's right to life occur in the private or domestic sphere, and have not been adequately addressed by authorities in the majority of domestic legal systems.[42] For example, in the UK it is estimated that two women are killed each week as a result of domestic violence inflicted by partners and ex-partners.[43]

Women's right to life can raise complex questions regarding the links and overlaps between the public and private nature of violations. One such example is the ongoing and highly charged debate around abortion within the various regional systems.[44] In the European context there is no absolute prohibition on abortion, and the ECtHR has implemented the concept of the 'margin of appreciation' in order to allow individual states some degree of control over the time limit within which an abortion can legally be carried

---

[38] See K. Askin and D. Koenig (eds.), *Women and International Human Rights Law* (Hotei Publishing, 1999), I, section 3.

[39] For example, from the HRC and the CAT, as discussed below.

[40] See Chapter 6 of Edwards, above note 30, for an overview of international human rights law on the right to life and violence against women.

[41] See ibid., 263–4.

[42] See ibid., 278–9.

[43] According to statistics collated by the national domestic violence organisation Women's Aid. See www.womensaid.org.uk/domestic-violence-articles.asp?section=0001000100220041 0001&itemid=1280.

[44] See also M. K. Eriksson, 'Abortion and Reproductive Health', in Askin and Koenig, above note 38, III, 3, on the wider historical context of campaigns around reproductive rights for women.

out. Abortion laws across European states are characterised by a degree of dissonance in this regard. Under the 1967 UK Abortion Act, abortion is legal until twenty-four weeks, except in cases of substantial risk to the life of the mother or foetal abnormality. This is a comparatively high time limit in comparison to other European countries, for example France, Norway or Sweden, where the time limit is twelve weeks. At the other end of the spectrum, under Irish law, in the absence of legislation, in effect, abortion is still technically illegal except in extremely exceptional (and arbitrary) circumstances.[45] In the 2010 case of *A, B and C* a pregnant Irish cancer sufferer sought information about the risk to her life should she continue the pregnancy. She was denied this information, and was thus unable to make an informed decision as to whether to carry on with the pregnancy, at the potential risk to her own life. The ECtHR found that the denial of information about the possibility of obtaining an abortion constituted a breach of the protection of her right to life. However, despite continuing debate and controversy over this issue, the ruling has not yet been incorporated into Irish law.[46]

Since the ruling in *Vo v. France*,[47] in which the Court declined to recognise the unequivocal right to life of a foetus over that of its mother, European jurisprudence on the question of abortion has been left relatively open, and the position on the relationship between the right to life and privacy of the mother and that of the unborn foetus remains subject to the 'margin of appreciation'. In the African context, the Protocol to the ACHPR on Women's Rights also largely concerns itself with the issue of the right to abortion in therapeutic circumstances. According to its article 14 (2)(a), states parties should take all appropriate measures to:

> protect the reproductive rights of women by authorising medical abortion in cases of sexual assault, rape, incest, and where the continued pregnancy endangers the mental and physical health of the mother or the life of the mother or the foetus.

The African system equally appears to leave open the decision on balancing the right to life of the mother with that of the unborn foetus to the discretion of individual states, according to the respective status of the mother and the foetus.[48] The difficulty, as in other regions, lies in the time at which

---

[45] For example in circumstances such as those within the key 1992 *X* case where a fourteen-year-old rape victim who had been prevented from obtaining an abortion within or outside Ireland was at high risk of committing suicide. See *The Attorney General Plaintiff v. X. and Other Defendants* (1992) 1 IR (5 March 1992).

[46] *A, B and C v. Ireland*, [2010] ECHR 25579/05. This may be partly due to the ongoing debate over the need to hold a referendum on public opinion on abortion laws in Ireland. See C. Ryan, 'Irish Poised to Revisit Abortion Laws', *New York Times*, 21 February 2012 for a précis of this debate, www.nytimes.com/2012/02/22/world/europe/22iht-letter22.html?pagewanted=all.

[47] *Vo v. France* (Appl. no. 53924/00), 8 July 2004.

[48] See Edwards, above note 30, 288–9.

the right to life is interpreted as starting, and thus where the responsibility of the state begins, in deciding where this balance lies. While some states, such as Zimbabwe, allow abortion on very limited medical grounds, others such as South Africa allow the right to seek a legal abortion up to twelve weeks.[49]

More recently in the Inter-American context, there has been a religious led backlash against the use of abortion in a number of countries. Nicaragua, for example, has instituted a total ban on abortion under any circumstances, including those involving rape and incest, and a policy of prosecuting medical professionals and others who are found to be facilitating abortions, irrespective of the circumstances.[50] In Nicaragua, a political rapprochement between the incoming Sandinista leader and the country's Catholic Church leaders led to the erosion of the reproductive rights of women, many of whom had fought and campaigned for the Sandinistas to become the leaders of the country.[51] In the regional context, the very wording of article 4 of the ACHR, whereby the right to life is protected 'in general, from the moment of conception' may seem to lend support for such policies on abortion. However, jurisprudence in this region on abortion, such as the decision of the IACHR in the *Baby Boy* case,[52] demonstrates the ambiguity of the wording of article 4. In that case, an abortion performed by a doctor in the interim period between the legislation and the activation of laws rendering abortion legal in the USA, was not deemed to constitute a violation of the right to life. The abortion was performed on a foetus over the age of six months at the request of the pregnant woman and her mother. The doctor was brought to trial and later acquitted of manslaughter; however, the case was brought before the IACHR by a number of Catholic religious activists who argued that the case had not conformed to article 4. The Court's approach in this case was in fact based on the interpretation of the wording of article 4. Thus while 'in general' the right to life starts from conception, in certain circumstances, such as the potential harm to the mother, the mother's right to life should be weighed against the right to life of the foetus. The case illustrates that as in other regional systems, decisions relating to the interpretation and enforcement of the right to life in relation to controversial issues such as abortion are to a major degree left to the discretion of individual states. In many cases these choices may be based around alleged cultural or religious norms, as, for example, in Ireland and Nicaragua discussed above.

---

[49] See F. Banda, *Women, Law and Human Rights: An African Perspective* (Oxford: Hart, 2005), 184–6.

[50] See Amnesty International, *The Total Ban on Abortion in Nicaragua: Women's Lives and Health Engangered, Medical Profesionals Criminalised*, AMR 43/001/2009 (27 July 2009).

[51] As noted ibid.

[52] *Baby Boy* abortion case, Inter-American Commission on Human Rights, resolution 23/81, Case 2141 (United States of America), 6 March 1981.

Torture within the context of state institutions applies in principle to anyone regardless of sex. The UN and regional treaty bodies have made it clear that rape by state actors is deemed to constitute torture. However, in practice the jurisprudence acknowledging and affirming this principle has only emerged relatively recently. In the leading European case of *Aydin* v. *Turkey*,[53] a seventeen-year old woman suffered rape and various other forms of abuse while being held in custody. The ECtHR found that the treatment she suffered at the hands of the authorities, particularly the rape, constituted torture in violation of article 3 ECHR. This approach has also been followed in other regional jurisdictions, including the Inter-American system. In *Raquel Marti de Meja* v. *Peru*,[54] the IACHR found that the rape and intimidation of the complainant by a member of the security forces constituted a violation of article 5 ACHR. Additionally, in the *Miguel Castro-Castro Prison* v. *Peru*[55] case, the IACtHR found that female detainees who were forced to remain naked under the constant guard of armed male guards, had been subjected to a form of sexual violence constituting a violation of article 5(2) ACHR.

The majority of cases of violence against women, including rape, domestic violence and other forms of abuse, are committed within the private sphere by non-state actors, which means that such cases are seemingly not covered by CAT and other instruments which were designed to address abuses within the public domain. However, the cases discussed below demonstrate that public authorities have a duty to protect women from violence by non-state actors, including by means of repressing and adequately responding to violations against women, including domestic violence or rape. Where they fail to protect individuals despite knowing that there is a risk of torture, they may be deemed to have become acquiescent, which potentially brings these acts within the fold of the CAT definition.[56] This may for example include cases where the police do not take action following a well-founded complaint by a woman that she is at risk of an attack, and the risk later materialises.

As a practical consequence of the 'public/private divide', according to which abuses by non-state actors fall outside the remit of international human rights law, in the past states have rarely been held to be responsible for violations committed by private actors. More recently, the notion of 'positive obligation' has been developed to address this gap in protection, by imposing a series of specific duties on states to effectively address violations

[53] *Aydin* v. *Turkey* (App. nos. 28293/95, 29494/95 and 30219/96), Judgment (friendly settlement) Strasbourg (10 July 2001).

[54] IACHR, *Raquel Marti de Meja* v. *Peru*, Report no. 5/96, Case 10,970, Peru, 1 March 1996.

[55] Case of the *Miguel Castro-Castro Prison* v. *Peru*, Merits, reparations and costs, Judgment of 25 November 2006, Ser. C, no. 160.

[56] See Report of the Special Rapporteur on torture and other cruel, inhuman or degrading treatment or punishment, UN Doc. A/HRC/7/3 (15 January 2008), especially paras. 45–9 on intimate partner violence.

in the private sphere. The Honduran case of *Velásquez-Rodríguez*[57] was key in establishing the principle of 'due diligence', whereby the state can be held accountable for human rights violations committed by non-state actors if it does not take adequate steps to ensure that such crimes are adequately investigated, prosecuted and punished. This principle has found broad application in the jurisprudence of international and regional treaty bodies.

In *AT* v. *Hungary*[58] the victim claimed that the state party had failed in its duty to provide her with effective protection from serious physical and mental domestic violence from her former partner over the course of four years. She was unable to prevent him from gaining access to her residence because national legislation did not provide for restraining or protection orders, and the domestic courts did not pay sufficient attention to domestic violence. This situation was exacerbated by a lack of alternatives in the form of adequate state provision for shelters or refuges for domestic violence victims, in this case particularly so because the victim could not gain access to a shelter equipped to accommodate not only herself, but also her two children, one of whom was disabled. The CtEDAW found that the state had breached its obligations under article 2(a), (b) and (e) of CEDAW, in that it had failed to protect the complainant by adopting appropriate legislative and other measures to ensure non-discrimination. By linking this general failure of due diligence obligations with article 16 (family relations) and article 5 (cultural or traditional stereotypes perpetuating the inferiority of women in relation to men), the Committee effectively found that this form of violence against women was a violation of the treaty under due diligence principles. In this respect, the Committee specifically referred to its General Recommendation 19 on violence against women, which emphasises that:

the Convention calls on States parties to take all appropriate measures to eliminate discrimination against women by any person, organization or enterprise. Under general international law and specific human rights covenants, States may also be responsible for private acts if they fail to act with due diligence to prevent violations of rights or to investigate and punish acts of violence, and for providing compensation.[59]

In *M. C.* v. *Bulgaria*[60] a fourteen-year-old girl alleged that she had been raped by two men. She claimed that the outcome of the criminal investigation into her assault, which found that the prosecution should not proceed due to a lack of finding of force or physical resistance, constituted a lack of effective protection against rape by the Bulgarian state. The ECtHR criticised

---

[57] *Velásquez Rodríguez* v. *Honduras*, Merits, Judgment of 29 July 1988, Ser. C, no. 4.
[58] *A. T.* v. *Hungary*, UN Doc. CEDAW/C/32/D/2/2003 (26 January 2005).
[59] CEDAW General Recommendation 19, above note 32, para. 9.
[60] *M. C.* v. *Bulgaria*, (2003) 40 EHHR 20.

the state both for its failure to investigate, punish and prosecute rape and to enact effective criminal legislation in the prosecution of rape, including through its emphasis on the use of force rather than consent in defining the crime of rape. Consequently, it found that the state had failed in its due diligence obligations under article 3 ECHR.[61]

In the more recent ECtHR case of *Opuz* v. *Turkey*,[62] the applicant and her mother had suffered sustained and prolonged physical and mental domestic violence at the hands of her husband. This included severe injuries caused by the applicant's husband running them both over in his car, death threats towards them both and numerous stabbing attacks. The violence culminated in the murder of the applicant's mother. The Court stated that the escalating crimes committed by the applicant's husband:

> were sufficiently serious to warrant preventive measures and there was a continuing threat to the health and safety of the victims. When examining the history of the relationship, it was obvious that the perpetrator had a record of domestic violence and there was therefore a significant risk of further violence.[63]

The Court found that despite this, the state had failed to effectively protect the applicant and prevent further harm to herself or her family, largely through its unwillingness to pursue effective criminal proceedings against the applicant's husband. Notably, the ECtHR refuted the government's argument that state interference in the domestic violence perpetrated would have amounted to a breach of article 8 of the Convention (the right to a private and family life), because it was a 'private matter'. This stance was deemed incompatible with the positive obligation of the state to secure the victim's rights. The Court stated further that despite realising the serious and escalating nature of the violence perpetrated upon the applicant and her mother:

> it cannot be said that the local authorities displayed the required diligence to prevent the recurrence of violent attacks against the applicant, since the applicant's husband perpetrated them without hindrance and with impunity to the detriment of the rights recognised by the Convention.[64]

As a result, the Court found that the state had failed in its positive obligations and had committed a violation of article 3 ECHR. It also found a violation of the right to life of both the applicant and her mother under article 2.

Cases such as *Opuz* illustrate the interlinked nature of types of violence against women, including the link between the right to life and the prohibition

---

[61] See ibid., especially paras. 130–4, and 149–51 on violations of article 3 within the case in relation to the due diligence obligations of the state.

[62] *Opuz* v. *Turkey*, (App. no. 33401/02), Judgment (9 June 2009).

[63] Ibid., para. 134.   [64] Ibid., para. 169.

of torture. Emerging jurisprudence demonstrates that international and regional human rights regimes have begun to recognise the importance of tackling the fundamental violation of the human rights of women within the private sphere. In the case of *Gonzalez et al. (Cotton Field)* v. *Mexico*,[65] the Court confirmed that the failure of the state to adopt a 'general policy' to address the widespread and egregious violence against women in the Ciudad Juarez region of Mexico, including rapes, murders and disappearances, amounted to a breach of the due diligence principle.[66] These developments could thus be seen as an important step forward in terms of mainstreaming violations of women's rights into broader human rights frameworks.

However, as highlighted by the Special Rapporteur on Violence against Women, due diligence will need to be developed further in order to serve as effective tool in combating gender-based violence:

If we confine ourselves to the current conception of due diligence as an element of State responsibility, then obstacles relative to the capacity of the State will be determinative. If, on the other hand, we continue dare to push the boundaries of due diligence in demanding the full compliance of States with international law, including the obligation to address the root causes of violence against women and to hold non-State actors accountable for their acts, then we will move towards a conception of human rights compatible with our aspirations for a just world free of violence.[67]

QUESTIONS

1 Has the development of a specific system to protect the human rights of women, for example in the form of CEDAW, been beneficial or detrimental to women's human rights overall?

2 Should women's human rights be mainstreamed into the overarching system of international protection of human rights?

3 What has been the impact of the 'due diligence' principle in relation to the protection of the human rights of women? How effective is this principle in the protection of women's rights within the private sphere and domestic regimes?

---

[65] Case of *González et al.* (*Cotton Field*) v. *Mexico*, Preliminary objection, merits, reparations and costs, Judgment of 16 November 2009, Ser. C, no. 205.

[66] Ibid., see in particular paras. 6, 9 and 253–61.

[67] Integration of the Human Rights of Women and the Gender Perspective: Violence Against Women – The Due Diligence Standard as a Tool for the Elimination of Violence Against Women, UN Doc. E/CN.4/2006/61 (20 January 2006), para. 102.

11.3   CONCEPTUAL DEVELOPMENT

11.3.1   The development of feminist legal theory and women's human rights

The conceptual development of rights for women has a long pedigree.[68] However, the majority of discussion has been focused around authors writing within and about Western legal systems and contexts. This has been increasingly criticised, and has provided the impetus for a number of major discussions within feminist theory that reflect upon and influence concepts and practice within the current international human rights regime. Debates on the existence and nature of women's human rights predate the emergence of the international human rights system, and had, for example, already been raised by authors including Mary Wollstonecraft[69] in the eighteenth century. Early women's rights activists were also key players in the anti-slavery movement.[70] The adaptation and application of existing liberal human rights theories to rights for women in particular led to an early emphasis on gaining rights for women within the public sphere, as exemplified by feminist campaigning of the women's suffrage movement in the nineteenth and early twentieth centuries. Likewise, the emphasis during the establishment of the early international human rights regime on 'first generation' civil and political rights may also have influenced the initial focus on violations of women's human rights in the public domain.[71]

Rights frameworks based around theories of liberalism[72] focus on concepts of individual rights to non-discrimination and equality. This approach argues that women should be treated on the same footing as men in terms of their participation in public life and their treatment by public institutions, and should not be discriminated against on the basis of their sex. Liberalism rests upon the premise that certain concepts such as equal rights and opportunity, rationality and individual choice are the basis of participation in society and public life. The theory posits that all persons are free and equal, including in relation to areas such as to the right to vote, equality before the law, education, employment, as well as property rights and freedom of contract. Despite this, a number of signatory states to treaties whose provisions espouse liberal values, such as the civil and political rights contained within the ICCPR, continue to deny these rights to women. For example, while the right to

---

[68] See A. Fraser, 'Becoming Human: the Origins and Development of Women's Human Rights', *HRQ* 21 (1999), 853–906, for a historical overview of the history of campaigning around rights for women.

[69] See M. Wollstonecraft, *A Vindication of the Rights of Women* (1792).

[70] See Fraser, above note 68.

[71] See Charlesworth and Chinkin, above note 1, 14–18 and Edwards, above note 30, 39–43 for discussion of the history of feminist activism in relation to international law from the early twentieth century to present.

[72] See section 1.4.1 for discussion of liberal human rights theories.

vote was to a great extent addressed by activist and suffragist movements in the twentieth century, there still remain a number of states who have been recalcitrant in ensuring the right to vote for women, such as Saudi Arabia.[73]

11.3.2 Critiques of liberal and non-discrimination approaches to women's human rights

A liberal approach seems practical, since without representation within the public sphere, women lack a means by which to effect changes to laws and systems of government in ways which empower them and allow them to enforce these rights. Liberal feminist theorists and activists seek to gain 'insider' status to influence existing institutions in ways which uphold equality between the sexes, and to openly and legitimately attempt to promote policies and laws based on principles of non-discrimination. In this approach, the problem is not law in or of itself, but 'bad' or wrongly applied law.[74] Feminists such as Eleanor Roosevelt and the members of the Commission on the Status of Women advocated the formal equality approach during their participation in the drafting of early international human rights instruments such as the UDHR. However, later feminists, particularly in the second half of the twentieth century, began to criticise the focus on civil and political rights and the precepts of non-discrimination underlying them, for a number of reasons.[75]

One of the most important critiques of liberal feminism revolves around its failure to sufficiently recognise and respond to problems caused by the so-called 'public/private divide'. The state-centric and individualistic nature of liberal approaches to rights places the focus of reform on the public sphere rather than the private sphere of individuals' lives, which should not be interfered with unless necessary. Feminists have long argued that women's prolonged exclusion from the public sphere means that in practice a number of serious violations of their rights take place in the private sphere, such as in the family or in marriage, which are not adequately reflected in the traditional liberal paradigm of international human rights law.[76]

A second major critique of the liberal feminist approach is its acceptance, and consequent inability to adequately question, the assumption of gender neutrality or objectivity underlying systems of law, in this case the international

---

[73] Until 2011, Saudi Arabia had denied female citizens the right to vote. However, it should be noted that denial of this right has recently become increasingly untenable, with the majority of states according female citizens the right to vote. See www.guardian.co.uk/world/2011/sep/25/saudi-arabia-women-vote-elections.

[74] See Charlesworth and Chinkin, above note 1, 40.

[75] Including the debate on 'generations' of rights, as discussed above in relation to the lesser importance attached to ESC rights.

[76] See Charlesworth and Chinkin, above note 1, 56–9; and Edwards, above note 30, 64–71.

human rights law regime. Liberal feminism views gender inequality as an error within the system of law requiring rectification, rather than reflecting an in-built system of domination and hierarchy. Critics argue that underlying the outwardly neutral concept of non-discrimination is a white, male-centric, privileged 'norm' which does not encompass the experience or particular vulnerabilities of women, ethnic minorities and others who do not (and cannot) conform to this standard. International human rights laws and norms, while notionally positing that human rights are equally applicable to all, in practice enforce standards which reinforce existing power hierarchies around gender, race and other potential types of vulnerability.[77] An example is the use of masculine language and vocabulary in international human rights instruments, such as the use of the masculine pronoun in the majority of the general human rights instruments, which is seen as perpetuating the male-centredness of human rights norms, and excludes female perspectives and experiences.[78]

Building on these critiques, two major schools of feminist thought took differing approaches in order to contest assumptions of the alleged neutrality of liberal legal theory. Cultural or relational feminism builds on critiques of liberal paradigms of equality, positing that the factors that make women different from men should be celebrated and valued. It is an approach most famously argued by psychologist Carol Gilligan, who asserted that women reason in a 'different' voice based more on an ethic of care, responsibility and connection than the abstract, masculine ethic of justice propagated by the legal system and society at large.[79] She argued that this adversarial and hierarchical 'male' approach has been privileged within law, and that as a result the 'different' voice of female reasoning has been subjugated and marginalised within conceptual and practical legal frameworks. This argument has also been applied in relation to international law, for example concerning the adversarial and abstract approach of the language used within international human rights treaties.[80]

Radical feminism has deconstructed and critiqued both liberal and cultural feminism. Catherine Mackinnon in particular has argued that 'under the sameness standard, women are measured according to our correspondence with man' but 'under the difference standard, we are measured according to our lack of correspondence with him'. In either case 'masculinity, or maleness is the referent for both'[81] and a male norm poses as gender neutrality.

[77] See Edwards, ibid., 51–64, for more detailed discussion and examples of this argument in relation to international law.

[78] See Charlesworth and Chinkin, above note 1, pp. 231–32 and Edwards, above note 30, 61–4.

[79] C. Gilligan, *In a Different Voice* (Harvard University Press, 1982).

[80] See Edwards, above note 30, 62–3.

[81] C. Mackinnon, *Feminism Unmodified: Discourses on Life and Law* (Harvard University Press, 1987), 34.

It is only women's difference from men, rather than men's difference from women, that matters. In this way differences between men and women, for example such as those relating to pregnancy, can be unacknowledged by 'male-centric' legal norms, which is reflected in the length of time it took to recognise reproductive rights. Mackinnon further criticises arguments which attempt to acknowledge women's difference positively on the basis that they make certain attributes seem inherently female, rather than being attributed to women by a male system of domination for its own purposes.[82] Radical feminism therefore critiques existing male-dominated hierarchies of power from an external standpoint. Instead it advocates an approach based on how the distribution of power results in gender inequality and constructs the status of women in society; the 'dominance approach'.[83] Using this approach, once the domination of women by men is acknowledged and dealt with, it may finally be possible for the conditions of equality to exist in which women truly can see what or who women are, without the constant comparison to an unattainable male standard.

11.3.3   Critiques of 'Western' feminist approaches to women's human rights

Mackinnon's approach has left her open to a number of criticisms from other feminists. Postmodern feminists argue that it places too much emphasis on the law as a decisive and overarching mechanism in relation to the violation of women's rights, rather than on the intersection of law with other cultural or socio-political factors.[84] This critique is especially relevant in relation to the debates on cultural relativism discussed below, particularly the effective implementation of 'universal' human rights norms within local contexts using domestic legal systems.[85] In this respect, Mackinnon's 'dominance approach' has been accused of leaving little scope for resistance or strategies for change, including by actors and organisations working to protect women's human rights within the local context. This approach could therefore be seen as at odds with the long-standing and ongoing struggles of women's human rights activism. It also fails to provide an adequate account of certain violations of women's human rights, such as FGM. In Mackinnon's account, little room remains for female agency in the perpetration of FGM, since she subscribes to a theory of so-called 'false consciousness', whereby women have been passively indoctrinated into the system of male dominance. However, accounts of FGM show that women do not necessarily

---

[82] Ibid., 39.   [83] Ibid., 40.

[84] See C. Smart, *Feminism and the Power of Law* (London, New York: Routledge, 1990).

[85] See S. E. Merry, *Human Rights and Gender Violence: Translating International Law into Local Justice* (University of Chicago Press, 2009) who argues that human rights law is often only fully accepted where it is implemented in conjunction with other types of local systems and norms.

uniformly subscribe to male accounts of their well-being, and undertake actions such as FGM for wider social and cultural reasons.[86]

A major criticism of Mackinnon's work is that she 'essentialises' the voice of women by not sufficiently taking into account the diversity of their experiences, including in relation to issues of cultural, racial or other forms of diversity.[87] For example, Harris argues that Mackinnon only discusses the issue of race in a way which views the experience of oppression of black women as the same as white women, only 'more so'. However, Harris argues that the difference in discrimination is not necessarily only *quantitatively* different from that experienced by white women, but *qualitatively* so, different in its very nature, as well as in its severity.[88] One way to address this critique is through the conceptual tool of 'intersectional discrimination'. Crenshaw has analysed a number of scenarios involving violence against women of colour within the USA, and argued that where, for example, race and gender discrimination intersect black women are found to be marginalised within both feminist and anti-racist agendas, and the discrimination they suffer is either compounded or ignored.[89] More recently, she and other feminist scholars have attempted to further analyse the complexity of intersectional discrimination within the context of international human rights frameworks by using a 'traffic intersection metaphor', whereby differing forms of disempowerment are 'thoroughfares', creating intersections where multiple forms of discrimination and identity overlap and meet, resulting in compound or qualitatively different violations of women's human rights.

The latter analysis was set out in the 2001 UN OHCHR *Report on the Gender Dimensions of Racial Discrimination*, produced following an Expert Group Meeting in 2000.[90] The report details a number of practical examples of intersectional discrimination within the context of human rights violations. One example given is that of violence against women in situations of armed conflict, where women from specific ethnic or racial groups have been targeted with rape, enforced pregnancy and other forms of sexual violence as a means of 'dishonouring' or ethnically cleansing the group in question. The report argues that the intersection of gender and race in this type of violence illustrates the distinct and compound nature of intersectional discrimination, and that the response of national and international human rights regimes must take this into account if they are to effectively protect the human rights of women.

---

[86] See also section 1.5.3 for further discussion of the issue of FGM.

[87] See Charlesworth and Chinkin, note 1 above, 52–6; and Edwards, note 30 above, pp. 71–86 for further discussion of debates around essentialism.

[88] A. Harris, 'Race and Essentialism in Feminist Legal Theory', *Stan. L. Rev.* 42 (1989–1990), 581–616 at 595–6.

[89] See K. Crenshaw, 'Mapping the Margins: Intersectionality, Identity Politics and Violence Against Women of Colour', *Stan. L. Rev.* 43 (1991), 1241–99.

[90] UN OHCHR, Gender and racial discrimination: Report of the Expert Group Meeting, Zagreb, Croatia (21–4 November 2000).

These debates could be taken as reflective of more far-reaching criticisms of 'Western' feminist approaches to international human rights. These 'essentialist' approaches are perceived to have ignored the impact of intersecting forms of discrimination with gender discrimination, as well as the impact of wider historical and global contexts such as colonialism. Following from this is the ongoing conflict between cultural relativism and universal conceptions of human rights norms.[91] Related to these discourses around the power relations inherent around the formulation and application of human rights norms, non-Western feminists have criticised the lack of understanding and perceptions of cultural superiority within much Western feminist human rights discourse.[92] Yet criticism of rights discourse has often also come from Western human rights activists who do not wish to be seen as imposing culturally relativist neo-imperialistic human rights norms on other states, rather than from grassroots human rights and women's rights activists. Indeed, local women's rights activists may find rights discourse helpful in their attempts to practically implement human rights strategies. It therefore needs to be recognised that the language of rights feels 'new and empowering'[93] to many victims of human rights violations, and thus that it is neither practical, nor necessarily ethical, for others to attempt to remove this discourse from current debates around existing human rights frameworks, or to hinder it.

Criticism of Western feminists riding roughshod over local experiences are closely related to debates about 'culture', which has been used frequently on both sides, either to denigrate or to justify certain practices.[94] Such viewpoints add to the perception of culture as fixed and immutable, rather than being selected according to context by powerful members of a group in order to preserve existing power structures such as gender hierarchies.[95] They also overlook the possibility of resistance or contestation within groups as to the nature of 'culture', and that cultural practices or customs can adapt (as in the case of FGM), disappear (as in the case of Chinese foot binding), be revived (as in the case of veiling in European Muslim communities) or be imported (as in the case of the Shia practice of *mut'a*, short-term marriages used to justify

---

[91] See section 1.5; Charlesworth and Chinkin, above note 1, 222–9 on women's human rights and cultural relativism.

[92] See ibid., 46–8; J. Oloka-Oyango and S. Tamale, '"The Personal is Political", or why Women's Rights are Indeed Human Rights: an African Perspective', *HRQ* 17 (1995), 691–731, for further discussion of essentialism, the impact of colonialism on feminist discourses, and the need for Third World scholars to add their own contributions to existing feminist theories.

[93] P. Williams, *The Alchemy of Race and Rights* (Harvard University Press, 1991).

[94] See Banda, above note 49, 250–9 for a discussion on African perspectives and debates around what constitutes 'culture', particularly within the human rights industry.

[95] See Report of the Special Rapporteur on violence against women, its causes and consequences: Intersections between culture and violence against women, UN Doc. A/HRC/4/34 (17 January 2007).

the abduction of young girls by fighters in Sunni Algeria during the 1990s).[96] These examples illustrate the ways in which cultural practices or traditions are fluid, and can be exploited according to context in order to enforce gender-based human rights violations. Conversely, the fluidity of 'culture' opens up the possibility for feminists of challenging violations of women's human rights.

The debate on culture and cultural relativism has been fundamental in relation to women's rights; as has been succinctly pointed out, 'no social group has suffered greater violation of its human rights in the name of culture than women'.[97] Yet there has been a tendency in Western feminist discourse to 'orientalise' concepts around culture, and allegedly cultural forms of violence against women such as FGM. Thus 'culture' is only seen to be a relevant factor in violence against women in non-Western contexts, despite the existence of high rates of sexual and domestic violence in Western states, as well as other harmful practices such as cosmetic surgery or media portrayals of women as sexual objects.[98] A number of 'Western' feminists have argued that it is hypocritical, patronising and futile to attempt to dictate to local activists the methods by which they could or should prevent such violations. They argue that it is necessary to take a grassroots approach to such issues, so that local actors, including feminist activists, are supported and facilitated (but not dictated to or controlled) by more powerful Western feminist activists.[99] Again, ongoing conflicts around FGM provide a useful example of the necessity for feminists from a range of contexts to work together to protect the rights of female victims, but in a manner which is not perceived as Western feminist neo-imperialism.[100] As the case study below on 'honour crimes' demonstrates, these debates around culture and gender are relevant in domestic arenas, such as the multicultural context of the UK, as well as international ones.

[96] See J. Bauer and A. Helie, *Documenting Women's Rights Violations by Non-State Actors: Activist Strategies from Muslim Communities* (Montreal: International Centre for Human Rights and Democratic Development and WLUML, 2006), 67–8; and L. Volpp, 'Feminism Versus Multiculturalism', *Colum. L. Rev.* 1 (2001), 1192–3 for useful discussions around the uses and abuses of the term 'culture' in relation to the practices relating to women.

[97] A. Rao, 'The Politics of Gender and Culture in International Human Rights Discourse', in J. Peters and A. Wolper (eds.), *Women's Rights, Human Rights: International Perspectives* (London, New York: Routledge, 1995), 169.

[98] See Report of the Special Rapporteur on violence against women, above note 95, 18–19; and also R. Howard, 'Health Costs of Social Degradation and Female Self-mutilation in North America', in K. E. Mahoney and P. Mahoney (eds.), *Human Rights in the Twenty-First Century: A Global Challenge* (Dordrecht: Martinus Nijhoff, 1993).

[99] See also for example, R. Coomooraswamy, 'To Bellow like a Cow: Women, Ethnicity and the Discourse of Rights', in R. Cook (ed.), *Human Rights of Women, National and International Perspectives* (University of Pennsylvania Press, 1994), on strategies to effectively implement women's human rights within culturally diverse settings.

[100] On the particular issue of FGM, see I. Gunning, 'Arrogant Perception, World Traveling and Multicultural Feminism: The Case of Female Genital Surgeries', *Colum. Hum. Rts. L. Rev.* 23 (1991–92), 189–248. See also section 1.5.3.

11.3.4   Sex, gender and sexuality

A final conceptual point is the use of the terminology of sex or gender. Most international human rights treaties discuss discrimination on the basis of sex rather than gender, although the terms sex, gender and woman are often used interchangeably in the discourse.[101] This may reflect the liberal focus of the debate during the period in which these instruments were drafted and adopted, and assumes that there is a common standard of equality which can be reached between men and women. Use of the term 'sex' is problematic due to the assumption of male neutrality in legal norms and standards, and its focus on the biological physical attributes of 'male' and 'female'. This may be viewed as essentialist in nature, and may also be interpreted in ways which do not adequately encompass all those in need of protection, for example transgendered persons.[102]

By contrast, more recent discussions have attempted to re-examine non-discrimination norms in relation to conceptualisations around gender, as a broader social construct. A key example of a national instrument reflecting this is the 1996 South African Constitution, which specifically refers to non-discrimination on the basis of sex or gender, and sexual orientation.[103] A further example is that of violence against women. UN standard-setting documents on violence against women specifically refer to issues of gender-based violence as a form of discrimination under article 1 of CEDAW. This approach links and builds on traditional notions of equality and non-discrimination in terms of newer debates around gender, and gender-based violence, as opposed solely to the traditional approach of non-discrimination.

While the UN definitions both refer specifically to women, they also allow for a wider definition of gender which could be extended to vulnerable males, even though the majority of or a disproportionate number of victims are indeed still female. This approach takes into account social constructions of masculinity and femininity and allows for examination of broader issues of sexuality, including protection of rights in relation to freedom of sexual orientation, which are still highly underdeveloped in international human rights law.[104] The terminology around gender-based violence, as opposed to that of violence against women or sex discrimination, highlights the relevance of power hierarchies which can victimise both men and women in a variety of contexts.

---

[101] See Edwards, above note 30, 13–19 for further discussion of the debates around the terminology of sex and gender.

[102] Although see the recent report by the UN OHCHR, Discriminatory Laws and Practices and Acts of Violence against Individuals Based on their Sexual Orientation and Gender Identity, UN Doc. A/HRC/19/41 (17 November 2011).

[103] See article 9(3) Constitution of the Republic of South Africa no. 108 of 1996.

[104] See S. Fried and I. Landberg-Lewis, 'Sexual Rights: from Concept to Strategy', in Askin and Koenig, above note 38.

QUESTIONS

1　What is the relevance of feminist legal theory in relation to the human rights of women today? How can we use these theories in the current context?

2　How is 'culture' relevant to the human rights of women? How does 'cultural relativism' impact on women's human rights?

3　What is the difference between the terms 'sex' and 'gender' in terms of women's human rights?

CASE STUDY 11.1
Domestic violence

X is a young man who became the victim of domestic violence once his family realised he was gay. His family realised he was involved in a relationship with another young man, and he has consequently been subject to various forms of domestic violence, including physical and emotional abuse. He has also been informed that if he 'agrees' to a marriage to be arranged for him, all his previous actions will be forgotten, and he will no longer be subject to further abuse. Despite his attempts to alert the authorities to the abuse he is suffering, they take no steps to attempt to help him escape the situation without harm.

Does X have a case to make before the CtEDAW? What violations of international human rights standards, such as a failure of due diligence, could he claim, and what could he claim in the international context?

11.4　WOMEN'S HUMAN RIGHTS AND DOMESTIC CONTEXTS: 'HONOUR CRIMES' IN THE ENGLISH LEGAL SYSTEM

The approach of the English legal system to cases of honour-related violence provides an example of how the issues discussed above operate in practice. Honour-related violence has to date mostly been reported within ethnic minority communities in the UK. For this reason, there has been much debate as to the 'cultural' nature of such violence and the extent to which it should be treated as culturally different, in practice and strategy, to other forms of gender-based violence such as domestic violence. The following case study illustrates these issues in relation to the international human rights regime.

11.4.1 Definitions and concepts of 'honour'

A key working definition of the term 'crimes of honour' which provides a useful bridge between concepts of 'honour' and the forms of violence through which 'honour' is enforced, understands it as encompassing:

> a variety of manifestations of violence against women, including 'honour killings', assault, confinement or imprisonment, and interference with choice in marriage, where the publicly articulated 'justification' is attributed to a social order claimed to require the preservation of a concept of 'honour' vested in male (family and/ or conjugal) control over women and specifically women's sexual conduct: actual, suspected or potential.[105]

Anthropologists, feminists and other scholars argue that concepts of 'honour' are highly dependent on the twin concepts of male honour and female shame. In this conceptualisation, women are seen as the property of their male relatives, often due to reasons relating to the guarding of patriarchal control over male children, and the passing down of both the family name and inheritance. This objectification renders women disposable once they are perceived to have committed a transgression, since they are deemed to lack worth if they are no longer 'honourable'.

Honour-related violence can cover a wide spectrum of acts to control women's behaviour, ranging from emotional threats to physical violence. Three key forms of violence are especially notable, due both to their interlinked nature and their severity. These are so-called 'honour killing', forced marriage and rape. For example, refusal to enter a forced marriage, along with other attempts at sexual or other forms of autonomy on the part of women may result in 'honour killing'. Rape may be used as a form of coercion into forced marriage, and women forced into marriage may also suffer marital rape as a consequence.

Honour-related violence can therefore be seen as a form of violence against women. 'Honour' adheres differentially and unequally to men and women; women are undoubtedly the primary victims of 'crimes of honour' at the hands of largely male perpetrators,[106] and those who transgress 'honour' codes suffer harsher consequences than their male counterparts. Even where men are the victims of an 'honour killing' this usually occurs because the victim is alleged to have ruined a woman's reputation by reneging on a promise of marriage, or through an actual or suspected relationship with her.[107] Accordingly, international and European declarations have specifically

---

[105] See the introduction to their edited collection in L. Welchman and S. Hossain, *'Honour': Crimes, Paradigms and Violence Against Women* (London: Zed Books, 2005), 4.

[106] P. Sen, '"Honour" Crimes of Value and Meaning', in Welchman and Hossain, *ibid.*, 48.

[107] See H. Siddiqui, 'There is No 'Honour' in Domestic Violence, only Shame! Women's Struggles against Honour Crimes in the UK', in Welchman and Hossain, ibid., 264; and

located 'honour crimes' within the sphere of gender violence.[108] How is gender-based violence to be understood, particularly if men can also be victims of 'honour crimes'? Gender has been conceptualised as referring to the differential values historically attributed to masculinity and femininity, resulting in a 'patriarchal power legacy which manifests itself through relations of domination and subordination'.[109] The wording of CtEDAW's General Recommendation 19 provides important clues for an understanding of gender-based violence, which it defines as:

violence that is directed against a woman because she is a woman or that affects women disproportionately. It includes acts that inflict physical, mental or sexual harm or suffering, threats of such acts, coercion and other deprivations of liberty. (My emphasis)[110]

The definition does not necessitate that gender-based violence is always solely directed against women, but that this is disproportionately or primarily the case in most circumstances. This analysis also takes into account broader issues of gender and sexuality. For example, gay men and women may suffer honour-related violence if their sexual orientation becomes known and is deemed to bring shame or dishonour to their family or community.[111]

11.4.2   Practical legal approaches to 'honour crimes': culture, gender and mainstreaming

This section provides a country-specific examination of approaches to honour-related violence within the English legal system, using case examples and interviews with various actors involved with formulating and implementing relevant legal policy and practice.[112] At present within the English legal system for the most part, cases of honour-related violence are viewed through the lens of domestic violence, and therefore in practice are 'mainstreamed' into overarching frameworks addressing gender-based violence. The Association of Chief Police Officers, which is the national police body in

A. Gill, 'Reconfiguring "Honour"-Based Violence as a Form of Gender-Based Violence', in M. Idriss and T. Abbas (eds.), *Honour, Violence, Women and Islam* (New York: Taylor and Francis, 2010), 219.

[108] See the 1993 United Nations Declaration on the Elimination of Violence Against Women, UNGA resolution 48/104; and Council of Europe, So-called 'Honour Crimes', Parliamentary Assembly, resolution 1327 (4 April 2003).

[109] Y. Erturk, 'Considering the Role of Men in Gender Agenda Setting: Conceptual and Policy Issues', *Feminist Review*, 78 (2004), 3–21.

[110] See note 32 above.

[111] K. Anderson, 'Violence Against Women: State Responsibilities in International Human Rights Law to Address Harmful Masculinities', *NQHR* 26 (2008), 173–97 at 178.

[112] This data emerges from the author's unpublished thesis research, 'Approaches to Honour-related Violence in the English Legal System'.

England and Wales responsible for formulating policies to be implemented by all of the police forces under its remit, defines honour-related violence, as 'a crime or incident, which has or may have been committed to protect or defend the honour of the family and/or community'.[113] However, it simultaneously also specifically includes honour-related violence within the category of domestic abuse. The current cross-governmental definition of domestic violence is:

Any incident of threatening behaviour, violence or abuse (psychological, physical, sexual, financial or emotional) between adults, aged 18 and over, who are or have been intimate partners or family members, regardless of gender and sexuality (Family members are defined as mother, father, son, daughter, brother, sister and grandparents, whether directly related, in-laws or step-family).[114]

A number of elements of this definition of domestic violence, in particular the inclusion of a range of behaviours and perpetrators, and the specific reference to both male and female perpetrators and victims, overlap with elements found within cases of honour-related violence. However, the definition is silent on certain other, additional factors, which have been present in some cases. These include the presence of multiple perpetrators, often in conjunction with the premeditation or pre-planning of crimes, and the involvement of an even wider range of family or community members. An example of the latter which has been reported in the UK are so-called 'bounty hunters' in some communities who are enlisted to track down and at times harm potential victims who have attempted to escape honour-related violence.[115]

Interviews with key police officers and prosecutors[116] endorsed the approach of, in the majority of cases, mainstreaming honour-related violence into current domestic violence strategies. Both police and Crown Prosecution Service interviewees acknowledged that cases of honour-related violence may often overlap or coexist with domestic violence, while simultaneously retaining certain unique elements. So-called 'cultural' factors were often in practice relevant in relation to tactical policing and prosecution tactics. These include frontline officer awareness and training, victim risk and safety plans, and investigation and evidence gathering, for example through the use of 'organised crime' investigative techniques such as covert listening devices, which are not usually employed in domestic homicide cases. The

---

[113] *Honour-Based Violence Strategy*, Association of Chief Police Officers, 30 September 2008.

[114] NPIA, *Guidance on Investigating Domestic Abuse*, National Policing Improvement Agency and Association of Chief Police Officers (London, 2008).

[115] For example, see Siddiqui above in note 107, 70.

[116] Including Commander Steve Allen, the 2006–2009 Association of Chief Police Officers lead on honour-based violence; and Nazir Afzal, the Crown Prosecution Service lead prosecutor on honour-based violence.

Association of Chief Police Officers interviewee stated that honour-related violence:

does need an additional set of knowledge, awareness, and some of the tactical responses are different as well, in terms of who you share information with, in terms of the safety plans around victims ... So it's about a victim focus, it's about assessing, recognising and managing risk, it's about safety planning, it's about the quality of evidence gathering ... [but] it's also about holding perpetrators to account ... because it's got these other [aspects], you can't just say well we've got a domestic abuse response, therefore that'll do.[117]

Such strategies can be seen as the implementation of an 'intersectional discrimination' approach in order to address crimes of honour-related violence as effectively as possible, whereby the intersection of gender with race or culture is recognised in the investigation and prosecution of such crimes. NGOs working with victims of honour-related violence have also identified the need for an intersectional approach, for example in relation to the need to provide targeted and specific refuge provision for ethnic minority victims of gender-based violence, including honour-related violence.

The interviewees acknowledged potential problems arising from the stigmatisation and stereotyping of certain communities, within the multicultural context of the UK, if certain elements, such as the involvement of wider family or community members within cases of honour-related violence are seen as 'cultural'. This parallels certain aspects of the debates in international human rights law, in relation to the 'orientalisation' of certain types of women's rights violations as associated with or only practised by certain communities or cultures.

11.4.3 Non-state actors and due diligence: a human rights response?

Within the international human rights framework, actors have emphasised the patriarchal nature of honour-related violence rather than its cultural aspects. For example, the Special Rapporteur on violence against women, its causes and consequences examined 'honour killings' and forced marriage within the context of her report on cultural practices in the family that are violent towards women. However, she took care to emphasise that ideologies of masculinity and the need to regulate female sexuality are key to the perpetuation of such violence.[118] CtEDAW's General Recommendation 19 refers to forced marriage as a type of 'traditional attitude', yet at the same time firmly places it within the realm of gender-based violence. One outcome

---

[117] Association of Chief Police Officers TS1, 2008: 4 (author's transcript).

[118] R. Coomaraswamy, Report of the Special Rapporteur on Violence against Women, its Causes and Consequences: Cultural Practices in the Family that are Violent towards Women, UN Doc. E/CN.4/2002/83.

of this international recognition of honour-related violence as a form of gender-based violence are several UNGA resolutions specifically aimed at the elimination of 'crimes of honour' against women.[119]

Ensuring that violence against women is mainstreamed within a broader framework of both domestic and international human rights is an ongoing and pressing concern of feminist theory and activism. The principles and rights embodied within the European human rights system[120] which have come into force in the UK legal system through the Human Rights Act,[121] can in this context be employed to protect victims of gender violence. As well as breaching broader principles of non-discrimination (article 14), 'honour crimes' such as 'honour killing' and forced marriage connect to a number of other articles of the Human Rights Act and the ECHR, including articles 2, 3, 5, 8 and 12.

A major question which remains to be addressed in relation to the use of human rights law in cases of honour-related violence is the fact that this violence is being carried out by non-state actors. To what extent, then, in the context of the English legal system, can these crimes be addressed by human rights norms? The triggering of these protections in the international human rights regime revolves around whether or not the state authorities have exercised due diligence in preventing, investigating and punishing crimes of honour-related violence.[122] In the UK context of honour-related violence, the due diligence principle translates into the debate around the extent to which state authorities have failed in their duties to an individual, by not adequately protecting or preventing a violation of their rights by a private actor.

In this scenario, if honour-related violence is seen as primarily culturally motivated, the triggering of these obligations could revolve around the arguments raised by activists and others that public authorities have differentiated between their treatment of violence against women within minority and majority communities, due to concerns about multicultural politics. Thus the question of differentiation, and consequently due diligence, is once more focused on the issue of culture, with all the attendant problems discussed in this chapter. This approach therefore raises some tentative, but potentially

---

[119] Working Towards the Elimination of Crimes Against Women Committed in the Name of Honour, UNGA resolution 57/179 (18 December 2002) and Working Towards the Elimination of Crimes Against Women and Girls Committed in the Name of Honour, UNGA resolution 59/165 (20 December 2004). For more detailed analysis of 'honour crimes' as gender violence within the international human rights framework, see J. Connors, 'United Nations Approaches to "Crimes of Honour"', in Welchman and Hossain, above note 105.

[120] Specifically the ECHR.

[121] The Human Rights Act 1998 entered into force on 2 October 2000.

[122] See S. Farrior, 'The Due Diligence Standard and Violence Against Women', *Interights Bulletin* 14 (2004), 157; also Connors, above note 119, at 25.

controversial, questions. One is whether violence against women in ethnic minority communities is now being overemphasised, and whether this may have negative consequences for overall strategies combating violence against all women within the UK. This could be avoided if agencies responsible for preventing and punishing such abuses placed greater emphasis on treating honour-related violence as part of a wider problem of gender-based violence. There is growing support among activists and scholars for the enforcement of due diligence obligations in relation to domestic violence in general (rather than specifically honour-related violence). The basis for this is the argument that the high rates of domestic abuse of all types in the UK means that state mechanisms have failed in their obligations to adequately respond to and prevent such human rights violations by non-state actors.[123]

The discourse of human rights is undoubtedly of great symbolic and practical importance in the international strategy against gender-based violence. However, within multicultural societies such as the UK, the question is whether this discourse is of specific assistance within the context of attempts to protect potential victims of 'honour crimes'.[124] Therefore a number of questions remain as to the practical utility and implementation of human rights mechanisms within specific domestic legal systems. These are raised by the UK case study outlined below.

CASE STUDY 11.2
Banaz Mahmod

Banaz Mahmod was a twenty-year old Kurdish woman who left an abusive marriage which her family had forced her into. She was brutally raped and murdered after her family discovered that she was involved in a relationship with a young man, which they deemed would bring 'dishonour' to the family and community. Later investigations revealed that the murder was planned, premeditated and carried out by a range of private individuals, including her father, uncle and other male members of her family and wider community. Her mother was also complicit, possibly through fear for her own safety. There were a number of failures on the part of the police in this case, which led to

---

[123] For more detailed arguments as to why and how positive or horizontal obligations come into effect in relation to domestic violence in the UK, including case law, see S. Choudhry and J. Herring, 'Righting Domestic Violence', *International Journal of Law, Policy and the Family* 201(1), (2006), 95–119.

[124] See Charlesworth and Chinkin, above note 1, 211.

an investigation by the Independent Police Complaints Commission. These included a number of occasions where Banaz reported to police front desk staff that she was in fear of her life from her family because of issues of honour. On each occasion her claims were disregarded because the police officers in question did not believe that they constituted a legitimate threat, due at least in part to their lack of understanding of issues around 'honour', and the possibility of accompanying violence. On another occasion Banaz called the emergency services after breaking a window and escaping from the family residence because she feared her father was about to kill her. The attending female police officer took her to the hospital, yet dismissed her account as 'an attention-seeking ploy or a private family matter', and even considered charging her with criminal damage.[1] The Independent Police Complaints Commission found that the police response to Banaz's plight was 'at best mixed' and that she had been 'let down' by the police in London and the West Midlands in relation to 'delays in investigations, poor supervision, a lack of understanding and insensitivity'.[2] It has been argued by activists and others that the police failures in this case demonstrated an ongoing problem of poor implementation of policy, where the police are still 'merely talking the talk' rather than translating policy into practical strategies to protect victims.[3]

POINTS TO CONSIDER

- What forms of honour-related violence are present in this scenario, and what role does culture play? To what extent is it useful to view 'honour crimes' either as culturally or gender-based?

- Should such violence be 'mainstreamed' into existing or overarching domestic frameworks around gender-based violence? If so, why; and to what extent?

- Did the domestic legal system in this case adequately address the violations caused by non-state actors? Is the 'due diligence' principle worth pursuing in this and other cases of honour-related violence?

---

[1] See A. Gill, '"MPS Could Have Done More"' to Prevent the Murder of Banaz Mahmod', *The Domestic Abuse Quarterly* (2008), 24–5.

[2] See 'IPCC concludes investigation into MPS and West Midlands Police dealings with Banaz Mahmod', *Independent Police Complaints Commission* (2 April 2008).

[3] See A. Gill, 'Honor Killings and the Quest for Justice in Black and Minority Ethnic Communities in the United Kingdom', *Criminal Justice Policy Review*, 20 (2009), 475–94. See also J. Payton, 'Collective Crimes, Collective Victims: a Case Study of the Murder of Banaz Mahmod', in Idriss and Abbas (eds.), above note 107, for discussion of this case, including the police response.

FURTHER READING

Askin, K. and Koenig, D. (eds.), *Women and International Human Rights Law*, 3 vols. (Transnational Publishers: University of California, 1999).

Banda, F., *Women, Law and Human Rights: An African Perspective* (Oxford: Hart, 2005).

Charlesworth, H., 'Not Waving but Drowning: Gender Mainstreaming and Human Rights within the United Nations', *Harv. Hum. Rts. J.* 18 (2005), 1–18.

Charlesworth, H. and Chinkin, C., *The Boundaries of International Law: A Feminist Analysis* (Manchester University Press, 2000).

Chinkin, C. and Wright, S., 'The Hunger Trap: Women, Food and Self-Determination', *Mich. J. Int'l L.* 14 (1993), 262.

Coomooraswamy, R., 'To Bellow like a Cow: Women, Ethnicity and the Discourse of Rights', in R. Cook (ed.), *Human Rights of Women, National and International Perspectives* (University of Pennsylvania Press, 1994).

Crenshaw, K., 'Mapping the Margins: Intersectionality, Identity Politics and Violence Against Women of Colour', *Stan. L. Rev.* 3 (1991), 1241–99.

Edwards, A., *Violence Against Women in International Human Rights Law* (Cambridge University Press, 2011).

Erturk, Y., 'Considering the Role of Men in Gender Agenda Setting: Conceptual and Policy Issues', *Feminist Review* 78 (2004), 3–21.

Fraser, A., 'Becoming Human: the Origins and Development of Women's Human Rights', *HRQ* 21 (1999), 853–906.

Gunning, I., 'Arrogant Perception, World Traveling and Multicultural Feminism: The Case of Female Genital Surgeries', *Colum. Hum. Rts. L. Rev.* 23 (1991–92), 189–248.

Mackinnon, C., *Feminism Unmodified: Discourses on Life and Law* (Harvard University Press, 1987).

Are Women Human? And Other International Dialogues (Harvard University Press, 2007).

Merry, S. E., *Human Rights and Gender Violence: Translating International Law into Local Justice* (University of Chicago Press, 2009).

Oloka-Oyango, J. and Tamale, S., '"The Personal is Political", or Why Women's Rights are Indeed Human Rights: an African Perspective', *HRQ* 17 (1995), 691–731.

Report of the Special Rapporteur on Violence Against Women, its Causes and Consequences: Integration of the Human Rights of Women and the Gender Perspective: Violence Against Women–The Due Diligence Standard as a Tool for the Elimination of Violence Against Women, Y. Eturk, UN Doc. E/CN.4/2006/61 (20 January 2006).

Report of the Special Rapporteur on Violence Against Women, its Causes and Consequences: The Intersections between Culture and Gender, Y. Eturk, UN Doc. A/HRC/4/34 (17 January 2007).

Welchman, L. and Hossain, S., *'Honour': Crimes, Paradigms and Violence Against Women* (London: Zed Books, 2005).

Williams, P., *The Alchemy of Race and Rights* (Harvard University Press, 1991).

12 The right to development, poverty and related rights

CONTENTS

12.1 INTRODUCTION

Like self-determination and indigenous rights, the right to development is a collective entitlement. Yet, unlike its other counterparts, it was misunderstood for a long time because its very existence was erroneously associated solely with foreign aid and charity and it was not viewed through the lens of programmatic positive and negative obligations of the ailing states. As will be evident through the course of this chapter, development in its human rights context is primarily a value that translates into individual and communal well-being. This well-being may be linked to industrial or other financial development, although the correlation between the two is neither self-evident nor necessary. If this right to well-being is to make a difference in the lives of people, whether in poor or rich nations, it must be susceptible to quantifiable measurement with which one is able to assess its progress and realisation. In the last decade experts have come up with a list of detailed indicators which allow us to assess well-being more accurately. At the same time, wealthy nations have abandoned *ad hoc* unilateral efforts to assist their poorer neighbours to escape perpetual cycles of poverty by entering into institutionalised multilateral commitments to provide part of their annual earnings to developmental goals. These goals are also vigorously pursued by multilateral development banks, such as the World Bank and the African Development Bank. None the less, throughout this chapter the reader will come across a recurrent conflict between developmental goals aimed at augmenting the finances of poor nations, absent, however, a human rights approach to development based on the Bill of Rights.

First, we explore the human dimension of development as opposed to the development of nations generally. Given the inconsistency between the two we then examine the right to development from the perspective of human rights and the extent to which various private actions and activist judicial bodies have rendered it justiciable. Development aid and debt relief are central to these processes and are analysed at length with a view to determining the degree to which they contribute to well-being. The final part of the chapter is devoted to two emerging entitlements that are correlated to the right to development, namely the right to freedom from corruption and the right to a healthy environment. Although these possess a dimension other than development, they are perceived both as preconditions for development as well as strategic entry points through which the latter may be pursued.

12.2   THE HUMAN DIMENSION OF DEVELOPMENT

Development is typically associated with the collective progress of states and is often linked to indicators such as 'growth', 'per capita income' and 'balance of payments', among others. The particular indicators of this type of development are intended to measure the overall wealth of states, not the well-being of their citizens. By way of illustration, whereas a country's gross domestic product (GDP), which represents the market value of its products and services, may be high, the standard of living of its people can still remain relatively low. This is because GDP is not a measure of personal income, nor does it take into account the disparity in the distribution of wealth or the enjoyment of essential services and goods such as health care, education, water and food. The measurement of human well-being is a relatively new phenomenon in the economics and human rights literature. In 1990 the UNDP published its first *Human Development Report* with the aim of demonstrating how economic growth translates into human development. From the outset the report took the approach that:

People are the real wealth of a nation. The basic objective of development is to create an enabling environment for people to enjoy long, healthy and creative lives. This may appear to be a simple truth. But it is often forgotten in the immediate concern with the accumulation of commodities and financial wealth.[1]

---

[1] UNDP, *Human Development Report* (Oxford University Press, 1990), 9.

Human development is thus defined as enlarging peoples' choices, chief among these being the ability to lead a long and healthy life, be educated and to enjoy a decent standard of living. The report noted that although income helps formulate human choices it is merely a *means* and not an *end*. It distinguished between two sides of human development: 'the formation of human capabilities, such as improved health or knowledge...and the use that people make of their capabilities, for work or leisure'.[2] It identified three key indicators that may be used to measure human development, namely longevity, knowledge and decent living standards.[3] These three indicators are known as the Human Development Index (HDI) and offer markedly different results from the numbers reflecting the GDPs of nations. Of course, democratic governance, a solid income, the enjoyment of human rights and other dimensions are also relevant to the processes of human development.

The *2010 Human Development Report* underlined the absence of a significant correlation between economic growth and improvements in health and education in the contemporary era,[4] which unlike in past times is attributed to the fact that existing technological improvements and societal structures allow even poor countries to realise significant gains. This means that it is now cheaper to achieve good health, reduce unnecessary mortality, gain access to knowledge and enjoy decent living standards. Yet overall income remains significant because it expands people's freedoms and access to food, shelter, clothing and meaningful employment which in turn helps them spend more time with their loved ones.[5] Moreover, there is evidence that the three HDI indicators may be met to a large degree within undemocratic countries that suppress empowerment and equality, in addition to generally poorer nations.[6] China, Oman and Saudi Arabia were among the top best performers in the 2010 report. This does not mean that authoritarian rule produces well-being or that because it scores high in certain fields of human development it is necessarily sustainable in the long run.[7] The 2011 uprisings in the Arab

---

[2] Ibid., 10.   [3] Ibid., 11.

[4] By way of illustration, although Jamaica is one of the world's highest indebted nations with a financial growth that is among the weakest globally, its poverty levels have been reduced significantly (14.3 per cent in 2006) and some of its critical social indicators have increased dramatically (e.g. access to basic amenities and life expectancy). This was the result of major social initiatives in the spheres of health, housing and education, despite their numerous shortcomings. See C. Watson-Williams, *Realising Rights through Social Guarantees: The Case of Jamaica, Final Report Submitted to the World Bank* (June 2008), 5–8.

[5] UNDP, *Human Development Report: The Real Wealth of Nations* (New York: Palgrave, 2010), 6.

[6] Ibid., 8.

[7] Sen, whose influence was significant in the formulation of the HDI, has argued that only bottom-up development is sustainable, whereas development driven exclusively by governments is unsustainable because of the violation of rights and the lack of empowerment involved in the process. He measures the developmental progress of states by reference to the capabilities of their citizens (capabilities approach) and distinguishes

world clearly indicate that policies of human development can only ignore empowerment and fundamental rights at their peril.

In practice, certain international institutions and many states pay lip service to human development and clearly pursue development agendas that are inspired by the pursuit of financial growth alone. They adhere to the view that financial growth necessarily generates social benefits and is capable of producing adequate social safety nets.[8] The proponents of these views thus see poverty as entailing an absence of material goods, ownership of productive assets and financial opportunities, such as employment; as a result, they fail to consider the lack of empowerment and inclusion.[9] By way of example, the World Bank's Heavily Indebted Poor Countries (HIPC) initiative, which will be explored more fully below, was designed to provide low-interest concessional loans to heavily indebted nations in order to develop their infrastructures and capabilities, as well as allow them to augment their social spending. Although the Bank argues that the HIPC and other similar initiatives have to a large degree achieved their developmental goals[10] the UN Independent Expert on the Effects of Foreign Debt on the Enjoyment of Human Rights challenges this claim. For one thing, under the HIPC the Bank offers preferential loans only to those countries whose debts are considered unsustainable. Its assessment of debt sustainability, however, is based on the capacity of a country to service its debts, thus excluding from this category countries that pay their debts but in the process are left with no money to realise any ESC rights. On this basis the Bank has sidelined from the HIPC a number of heavily indebted and poor middle-income countries.[11]

Quite clearly, there is a deep disparity between human and financial development. This tension is exemplified in the instruments analysed in the

between positive and negative freedoms. A. Sen, 'Equality of What?' Tanner Lecture on Human Values, Stanford University (22 May 1979), 198, 218.

[8] The term generally refers to policies designed to protect persons who for whatever reason fall below the poverty line and are thus unable to help themselves.

[9] The contemporary view rejects money-centric definitions of poverty. Instead, it emphasises the link between development and freedom in which case poverty is 'understood as the deprivation of basic capabilities rather than merely as lack of income on its own': UN Doc. A/HRC/SF/2008/2 (6 August 2008), para. 12. The CESCR has defined poverty as 'a human condition characterised by the sustained or chronic deprivation of the resources, capabilities, choices, security and power necessary for the enjoyment of an adequate standard of living and other civil, cultural, economic, political and social rights': CESCR statement UN Doc. E/C.12/2001/10 (2001), para. 8. A non money-centric definition is also offered by the EU's European Consensus on Development, para. 11, OJ C46/1 (2006), which notes among other things that poverty 'includes all the areas in which people of either gender are deprived and perceived as incapacitated in different societies and local contexts'.

[10] C. A. Primo-Braga, and D. Dömeland, (eds.), *Debt Relief and Beyond: Lessons Learned and Challenges Ahead* (Washington, DC: World Bank, 2009).

[11] HRC, Report of the High-level Task Force on the Implementation of the Right to Development on its Sixth Session, UN Doc. A/HRC/15/WG.2/TF/2 (24 February 2010), para. 53.

following section. If development is to be pursued and assessed on the basis of human well-being it is imperative that it be predicated on human rights norms and considerations, rather than policies from which human rights are absent. This is not mere rhetoric, for it requires policy makers at all levels to address multidimensional poverty by reference to human rights indicators.[12] A report of the OHCHR provides the following case study to illustrate the point:

A 23-year old woman arrives at a village clinic ... complaining of pain and discharge stemming from an IUD [intra-uterine device] insertion. She tells the physician that she has already had four unwanted girl children; that her husband is a drunkard who routinely rapes her; and that she is struggling desperately just to keep her daughters and herself alive, but feels that if she could have a son he would be able to support her in later years. What is the health issue here? The treatment of an infection? The ability to freely choose a contraceptive method? The effect of societal son preferences on the woman's childbearing decisions? Or is it, most broadly, that she virtually has no control over her sexual, emotional, or physical well-being because of laws and practices that deny her basic human rights and dignity?[13]

If this case were viewed exclusively from a female health policy perspective the answers to the points raised would tend to focus on biological processes, yet, these hardly constitute the root causes of the problems faced by this woman. A human rights approach, on the other hand, would concentrate on the evident gender inequalities sustained by local laws, customs and cultural practices and would try to address them as root causes of the particular health issue.[14]

12.3   THE RIGHT TO DEVELOPMENT

Development, at least in the sense that this was conceived in the 1986 Declaration on the Right to Development (RTD),[15] is unrelated to the financial progress of nations. Moreover, because the entitlement arising from the Declaration is hard to conceptualise, developed countries wrongly perceived this to entail a perpetual obligation to finance their weaker counterparts.

---

[12] By way of illustration, all entities within the UN system involved in development projects adopted in 2003 a statement on a common understanding of a human rights-based approach (HRBA) to development cooperation. There in it is stated that all projects must be guided by the Bill of Rights and that development cooperation 'contributes to the development of the capacities of "duty-bearers" to meet their obligations and of "rights-holders" to claim their rights'. The HRBA principles are non-discrimination, empowerment, transparency, participation and accountability.

[13] OHCHR, *Claiming the Millennium Development Goals: A Human Rights Approach* (New York, Geneva: UN, 2008), 11.

[14] Ibid.

[15] UNGA resolution 41/128 (1986).

A substantial amount of academic writing in the 1980s and 1990s certainly contributed to this confusion by propagating that self-determination obliged industrialised nations to compensate developing states for their loss of earnings during colonisation, allowed them to set their own market prices for their commodities, as well as sharing the financial burden of their resurrection.[16] Such ideas naturally culminated in the downplaying of the right by wealthy nations, despite the fact that they continued to provide financial resources and assistance, making it clear, however, that such assistance was merely a unilateral undertaking that did not encompass an obligation or give rise to a legitimate expectation. Although the right to development has been subsequently clarified significantly and disengaged from foreign aid, industrialised nations have maintained this position and have persistently rejected proposals for a binding instrument.[17]

A closer reading of the Declaration reveals three fundamental building blocks which help demonstrate that the entitlement is hardly an arbitrary construction, but the natural outcome of the enforcement of the Bill of Rights. These are: 'the constant *well-being*' of all people (article 2(3)), the inextricable nexus between well-being and civil, political and ESC rights (articles 1(1) and 2(2)) and the responsibility of states internally and externally to promote such well-being through the pursuit of all human rights (articles 4–8). A structured and comprehensive definition that included all three of these elements was articulated, not without dissent, in 2010 by the UN Special Rapporteur on the RTD and it is useful to provide it at this stage as it will serve as a working definition for the purposes of this chapter:

The right to development is the right of peoples and individuals to the constant improvement of their well-being and to a national and global enabling environment conducive to just, equitable, participatory and human-centred development respectful of all human rights.[18]

This conception of development through the lens of well-being and the enjoyment of human rights are not necessarily dependent on aid or other forms of donor assistance, although these would certainly boost it. Development in this sense may be achieved even with scarce resources if they are allocated equitably, justly and with a view to alleviating human suffering.

---

[16] See M. Bedjaoui, 'The Right to Development' in M. Bedjaoui, *International Law: Achievements and Prospects* (Dordrecht: Martinus Nijhoff, 1991), 1177, at 1182ff. Others, however, took a more pragmatic view, arguing that self-determination only provides a right to pursue development, not a right to live in development. J. Donnelly, 'In search of the Unicorn: The Jurisprudence and Politics of the Right to Development', *Cal. W. Int'l L. J.* 15 (1985), 473, at 482ff.

[17] HRC, Report of the Working Group on the Right to Development on its Eleventh Session, UN Doc. A/HRC/15/23 (10 June 2010), paras. 7–12.

[18] HRC, Report of the High-level Task Force on the Implementation of the Right to Development on its Sixth Session, UN Doc. A/HRC/15/WG.2/TF/2/Add.2 (8 March 2010) (Right to Development Criteria and Sub-criteria), Annex.

The vast majority of developing nations are, however, unable to do so because they are poorly managed and are highly indebted, their administrative apparatus is enslaved to corruption and their leaderships cannot conceive of staying in power other than by abusing human rights. The link between well-being and human rights in the definition of RTD is crucial both for its legal nature as well as its enforcement and justiciability. In respect of its legal nature, although the RTD presupposes the enjoyment of the full gamut of rights encompassed in the Bill of Rights, it is not a mere compilation or synthesis of these;[19] instead, it is an independent composite right that is enjoyed both collectively and individually and which is distinguished from the discrete rights that comprise it by the fact that it obliges the duty-bearers to establish an enabling environment for the realisation of individual and collective well-being. An illustration should assist in clarifying this distinction. The right to free and universal education simply obliges states to offer this entitlement to their youth without discrimination. Education, in the context of RTD, requires not only that children attend school but that a process has been put in place through which education is linked to knowledge, technology, investment in agriculture, industry and other fields of productivity and employment, all of which will lead to job opportunities as well as social and financial development.[20] Otherwise, education becomes meaningless for both the students and the state and its pool of talent will eventually be lured abroad, thus leading to the phenomenon of braindrain.

The centrality of human rights is all the more poignant in the enforcement and implementation of the RTD and three means of implementation are recognised. (1) The first concerns states acting collectively in global and regional partnerships; (2) the second encompasses states acting individually as they adopt and implement policies that affect persons not strictly within their jurisdiction, and (3) the third mode relates to policies and programmes at the national level affecting persons within a state's jurisdiction.[21] Evidently, the implementation of RTD is not dependent on the actions of external actors in the form of aid or other assistance, but necessarily involves the active engagement of the target state. Before we go on to examine justiciability the reader will no doubt be wondering how one is able to measure and assess the quantitative and qualitative dimensions of well-being. For years the UN made strenuous efforts to identify a methodology for assessing well-being without at the same time alienating industrialised nations. Although such a methodology has not yet been endorsed universally through a binding instrument, there is broad consensus that in common with the work of other

---

[19] S. Marks, 'The Human Right to Development: between Rhetoric and Reality', *Harv. Hum. Rts. J.* 17 (2004), 137, 149.

[20] For an analysis of the objectives encompassed in education, and the right thereto, see section 9.10.

[21] Articles 2–4 of the declaration; see Right to Development Criteria and sub-criteria, paras. 16–17.

human rights treaty bodies, it is possible to distil core attributes of the right and identify indicators in three dimensions – structural, process and outcome[22] – with well-being recognised as the core norm.[23] Three attributes are structured around this, namely comprehensive and human-centred development policy, participatory human rights processes and social justice. Although the three aforementioned indicators are relevant to all three attributes of the core norm, structure more properly informs the level of commitment, process relates to rules and principles (human rights, participation, accountability and transparency), whereas outcome concerns distributional outcomes, particularly fair distribution of the benefits and burdens of development.[24] Structure, process and outcomes are roughly represented as criteria, sub-criteria and indicators in the roadmap compiled by the UN working group on the RTD, which seeks to address and assess how this right may be implemented at the national and international level. An exposition of attribute 3[25] (social justice in development see Table 12.1) will help explain how structure, process and outcomes are designed to operate.

As is the case with all three attributes, their criteria, sub-criteria and indicators not only use human rights language, but are wholly entrenched within it, thus rendering human rights the yardstick by which development policies and initiatives are to be assessed. As a result, any development policy, no matter how lofty or financially sound, that is in conflict with one or more human rights is incompatible with the RTD. Some cases are clear cut others not so. For example, aggregated results on social exclusion initiatives may fail to recognise the plight of particular groups that are routinely excluded, such as indigenous peoples and minorities. A need, therefore, arises for disaggregated policies. Equally, although the indicators may be appropriate for most circumstances, they may require realignment and adjustment in circumstances that are otherwise similar, especially if a disaggregated approach is maintained. By way of illustration, the urban poor of South Africa and the Indian rural poor face distinct health, employment and security issues arising from HIV.

12.3.1 Making the right to development justiciable

It is because of this rights-based foundation of RTD that it has the potential of becoming justiciable before national courts and international human rights bodies.[26] Individuals and groups may challenge a development policy,

---

[22] See Report on Indicators for Promoting and Monitoring the Implementation of Human Rights, UN Doc. HRI/MC/2008/3 (6 June 2008), paras. 17–26. The use of indicators and benchmarks is also discussed in relation to ESC rights in section 9.7.

[23] A more elaborate analysis of indicators and benchmarks is attempted in section 9.7.

[24] Right to Development Criteria and Sub-criteria, para. 18.

[25] Ibid., annex, paras. 14–15.

[26] On the justiciability of economic and social rights, see section 9.6.

Table 12.1 Attribute 3: social justice in development

Criteria	Sub-criteria	Indicators
3(a) To provide for fair access to and sharing of the benefits of development	3(a)(i) Equality of opportunity in education, health, housing, employment and income	Income inequality; disaggregated outcome data by population groups, for example, male–female, rural–urban, ethnic/racial and socio-economic status
	3(a)(ii) Equality of access to resources and public goods	Public expenditures benefiting poor households
	3(a)(iii) Reducing marginalisation of least developed and vulnerable countries	Global gaps in income and human well-being, mitigating differential bargaining power and adjustment costs of trade liberalisation
	3(a)(iv) Ease of immigration for education, work and revenue transfers	Flow of skilled and unskilled migrants from poor to rich countries; flow of remittances
3(b) To provide for fair sharing of the burdens of development	3(b)(i) Equitably sharing environmental burdens of development	Availability of climate change funds for developing countries; multilateral agreements to reduce negative environmental impacts; distribution of contributions to climate change
	3(b)(ii) Just compensation for negative impacts of development investments and policies	Hazardous industries, dams, natural resource concessions
	3(b)(iii) Establishing safety nets to provide for the needs of vulnerable populations in times of natural, financial or other crisis	Domestic emergency response funds; international humanitarian and reconstruction aid; countercyclical official financial flows
3(c) To eradicate social injustices through economic and social reforms	3(c)(i) Policies aimed at decent work which provide for work that is productive and delivers a fair income, security in the work place and social protection for families	Growth rate per GDP of person employed, employment to population ratio, proportion of people living on less than a dollar a day
	3(c)(ii) Elimination of sexual exploitation and human trafficking	Ratification of the protocol to prevent, suppress and punish trafficking in persons, especially women and children
	3(c)(iii) Elimination of child labour	Extent of child labour; ratification of the convention on the worst forms of child labour
	3(c)(iv) Eliminating slum housing conditions	Proportion of urban population living in slums; access to improved sanitation; and secure tenure
	3(c)(v) Land reform	Access to land; secure land rights; and remedies against land grabs

programme or legislative act on the basis that it infringes other justiciable rights. This indirect *locus standi* is subject to several limitations. For one thing, actions will generally be sustained only if brought by the citizens of the country implementing development programmes within its jurisdiction. In short, challenges cannot be directed against failure to achieve well-being, but only for violations of civil, political and ESC rights. Yet, the reader will ascertain in the examples offered that although no reference to RTD is made by the litigants and the courts the language and effects of such actions are tantamount to the right to development.

In the late 1990s Chile and South Africa pushed forward legislation aimed at curtailing social security benefits to a large part of their population. Chile did so by privatising its social security system, while South Africa by excluding all those benefiting from non-contributory schemes. In both cases the most vulnerable, such as the poor, the unemployed, part-time workers and women, were effectively denied access to health services, food stamps, micro-financing, pension entitlements and numerous other benefits. The CESCR recommended that all workers were entitled to social security benefits, which Chile was obliged to provide especially to those unable to pay private contributions.[27] In equal measure, the South African Constitutional Court ruled that all the country's residents were entitled to social security, emphasising that societal welfare indeed depends on the provision of such benefits to the least fortunate.[28]

In India and Bangladesh the concept of livelihood[29] has received much prominence from the countries' supreme courts. It was invoked in cases concerning the forceful eviction of slum dwellers or those living in informal settlements. It was held that the right to livelihood derived from the right to life, dignity of person and equal protection, all of which oblige the state to ensure that all people enjoy the basic necessities of life. The evictions amounted to a denial of the slum dwellers' right to livelihood, given that adequate housing is indispensable in order to enjoy the right to life.[30] The Bangladeshi Supreme Court emphasised that a massive eviction from an informal settlement should have been accompanied by a resettlement plan that took into consideration the ability of those evicted to secure alternative accommodation.

---

[27] CESCR, Report on Thirty-second and Thirty-third sessions, UN Doc. E/2005/22-E//C.12//2004/9 (2005), paras. 546, 569. The Committee noted that women are particularly affected, especially 'housewives' and about 40 per cent of working women who do not contribute to the social security scheme and are consequently not entitled to old-age benefits. It was stressed that working women are left with a much lower average pension than men as their retirement age is five years earlier than that of men.

[28] *Khosa and Others* v. *Minister of Social Development* [2004] 6 BCLR 569.

[29] Article 41 of the Indian Constitution expressly envisages the right to livelihood as an expansion of the right to life in the form of a directive principle of state policy.

[30] *Ain o Salish Kendra (ASK)* v. *Government of Bangladesh* (*Slum-Dwellers* case), Supreme Court of Bangladesh (1999) 19 BLD (HCD) 488; *Olga Tellis* v. *Bombay Municipality Corporation* [1985] 2 Supp. SCR 51 (India).

Finally, the obligation of a state to secure the well-being of its population encompassed within the RTD is nowhere more evident than in cases involving food shortages and primary health care. In the late 1990s an outbreak of hæmorrhagic fever swept Argentina, the government of which failed to produce and distribute the Candid 1 vaccine or otherwise tackle the spread of the fever which placed 3.5 million people at risk of contracting it. Irrespective of the reasons behind this failure, which included severe budgetary constraints and a national health system that excluded the non-insured, the Argentine Federal Court of Appeals emphasised that one of the pre-eminent objectives of the Constitution was to secure the well-being of the people on the basis of social justice.[31] This is no doubt an implicit reference to RTD.

These cases demonstrate that the debate regarding the lack of normative character of the RTD and its justiciability is without merit, at least in respect of the internal obligation of states to provide for the well-being of their people. It is inconceivable that states may argue that they would rather not spend their resources to improve the lives of their people, as though quality of life, or life itself, was unimportant compared to other political pursuits, such as defence, structural adjustment, debt servicing and other financial considerations. RTD may be invoked indirectly where a particular right is infringed in a manner that has a bearing on the well-being of vulnerable groups or entire populations.

CASE STUDY 12.1
The IMF's structural adjustment programmes (SAPs)

The IMF assists countries with balance of payments[1] problems through non-concessional and concessional facilities. Non-concessional financing allows a defaulting state to purchase a strong currency from the IMF's reserve by exchanging an equivalent amount of its own currency, with the obligation to

[1] Very crudely, a country's exports, foreign investment and loan earnings are considered as positive or surplus, whereas imports, debt servicing, exchange rate fluctuations and others count as deficit. A zero balance of payments (BOP) means that there is no surplus or deficit. Countries make up the shortfall from their annual deficits either by external borrowing or by making use of their reserve assets. However, countries with large BOP deficits are not necessarily poor, given that the USA, one of the world's richest nations, has by far the biggest deficit.

[31] *Viceconti* v. *Ministry of Health and Social Welfare*, case no 31,777/96, judgment of 2 June 1998; a similar result was reached by the Ecuadorian Constitutional Tribunal in a case concerning the withdrawal of appropriate retroviral treatment from HIV sufferers. *Mendoza and Others* v. *Minister of Public Health and the Director of the National AIDS/ HIV Program*, resolution no. 0749–2003-RA, judgment (28 January 2004).

later repurchase its own currency. This technique is of little value to low-income developing countries that are starved of cash because their poor credit rating does not allow them access to private lending. Thus, the IMF has resorted to concessional funding, which consist of preferential loans over an extended period, or grants with no, or little, expectation of repayment. In 1999 the IMF introduced an improved poverty reduction and growth facility (PRGF) with the aim of supporting the balance of payments of developing countries, sustaining growth and ultimately reducing poverty. For the purposes of the PRGF the IMF borrows funds from central banks, governments and other institutions at market interest rates and then lends them to PRGF-eligible countries that are charged an interest of only 0.5 per cent each year. The shortfall is covered by bilateral donations and the IMF's own resources.[2]

PRGF recipients must undergo severe public spending reforms for an initial period of three years, during which they must prepare a detailed plan demonstrating precisely how and where expenditure cuts are to be made and the way which additional income is to be collected from taxes and other sources. Although the borrower is responsible for preparing this plan in the form of a poverty reduction strategy paper (PRSP), given that the IMF will ultimately approve the loan on the basis of the PRSP's viability its input is clearly significant. Once the loan is approved it is subject to performance criteria and semi-annual reviews and in practice the IMF may unilaterally demand that the borrower adopt stricter spending and tax policies to meet its targets.

Structural adjustment seeks to balance payments by cutting public expenditures and increasing revenues and so raising a country's GDP. The first casualties are typically social expenditures, such as universal health, welfare, social housing, pensions, employment benefits, education and others. As a result of the loan agreement between Greece and the IMF, the Greek government proceeded in 2010 to slash by one-third all public pensions while raising the prices of necessary drugs and imposing the maximum level of VAT on all foods, thus bringing a large number of this vulnerable population below the poverty line who are unable to protest. Human rights bodies, treaty-based or other, while recognising the significance of debt relief and poverty SAPs funded by the IMF[3] have raised concerns that they negatively affect the enjoyment of economic and social rights by increasing poverty and unemployment, exacerbating income distribution and causing the collapse of

---

[2] R. M. Lastra, *Legal Foundations of International Monetary Stability* (Oxford University Press, 2006), 429–31.

[3] See e.g. Report of Independent Expert on Effects of Economic Reform Policies and Foreign Debt on the Enjoyment of Human Rights: Mission to Burkina Faso, UN Doc. A/HRC/7/9/Add.1 (11 February 2008), para. 56; Report of the Independent Expert on Technical Cooperation in Liberia, UN Doc. A/HRC/9/15 (15 August 2008), para. 51.

social services.[4] With this in mind, even where a country's GDP increases as a consequence of the measures adopted it is unlikely that the poorest of the poor will see any improvement in their lives or that the newly found wealth will increase the average level of well-being.

[4] CESCR, General Comment on plans of action for primary education (article 14), UN Doc. E/2000/22-E/C.12/1999/11, para. 324, regarding Cameroon; CtRC, Concluding Observations on Uganda, UN Doc. CRC/C/UGA/CO/2 (23 November 2005), para. 20; CtRC, Concluding Observations on Nicaragua, UN Doc. CRC/C/15/Add.265 (21 September 2005), para. 16. A divided UN CommHR has stressed that 'the exercise of the basic rights of the people of debtor countries to food, housing, clothing, employment, education, health services and a healthy environment cannot be subordinated to the implementation of structural adjustment policies and economic reforms arising from debt': resolution 2002/82 (26 April 2000), para. 6.

12.4   GLOBAL PARTNERSHIPS FOR THE FINANCING OF DEVELOPMENT

In the previous section it was explained that two of the ways by which RTD is implemented concern externally derived aid, whether unilaterally or collectively. Indeed, articles 2(1), 11(1) and 12(1) of the ICESCR suggest that states should cooperate for the realisation of human rights at the global level. None the less, the *travaux* of the Covenant do not support the contention that foreign assistance, whether material or otherwise, was ever couched in terms of an obligation.[32] This unfortunate position is consistent with the international practice in the field of donor conferences and pledges. One would have naturally thought that states going into donor conferences would be sincere about the funds they are publicly claiming to contribute and that their financial pledges would carry the same legal weight as promises and other intentional unilateral acts under international law. Yet, not only do states routinely renege on funding promises delivered at donor conferences,[33] but more disturbingly their pledges are not considered binding until such time as the pledged funds are delivered to the recipient, in which case there is no

[32] P. Alston and G. Quinn, 'The Nature and Scope of Parties' Obligations under the International Covenant on Economic, Social and Cultural Rights', *HRQ* 9 (1987), 156, at 186. As a result, this author is not convinced that the so-called right to international solidarity exerts an obligation on states to undertake joint action in response to poverty and other global crises. See, however, the Report of the UN Independent Expert on Human Rights and International Solidarity, UN Doc. A/HRC/12/27 (22 July 2009).

[33] The USA, for example, although at the 2002 Monterey Conference pledged, along with other developed nations, to offer 0.7 per cent of its annual GDP, by 2008 it had offered only a fraction of that, a mere 0.18 per cent.

right to a refund.[34] This practice exists because states are free to make up the rules in respect of donor conferences[35] and also because it was feared that if binding instruments were employed to collect voluntary contributions many states would be dissuaded from the process altogether. It is only recently that the UN has sought to streamline the process by requiring a degree of formality with regard to pledges.[36] Equally, the World Bank has introduced so-called instruments of commitment to certain human rights and environmental initiatives, which constitute binding agreements requiring parliamentary ratification.[37] These developments have only helped to decrease some empty pledges, but they have in no way reversed the negative situation.

By the end of the 1990s it became evident that the gap between the poor and the very poor had widened so much that even the slightest fluctuation in global food prices could produce waves of famine across the globe. Human development could no longer be left to the devices of poor nations or the odd donor conference set up in the aftermath of a humanitarian disaster. As a result, the Millennium Declaration was adopted by the UNGA in 2000 in the form of a political pledge by the world's leaders with the aim that it would soon be followed by concrete financial commitments under well-identified targets.[38] The Declaration was meant as a testament of solidarity against global poverty, suffering and respect for human rights. The centrality of human rights and RTD in the Declaration's aims is stark. Paragraphs 11 and 24, for example, state that:

We will spare no effort to free our fellow men, women and children from the abject and dehumanising conditions of extreme poverty, to which more than a billion of them are currently subjected. We are committed to making the right to development a reality for everyone and to freeing the entire human race from want.

We will spare no effort to promote democracy and strengthen the rule of law, as well as respect for all internationally recognised human rights and fundamental freedoms, including the right to development.

Following the Millennium Summit the UN Secretary-General finalised the text of the eight agreed MDGS. These are: (1) eradication of extreme poverty and hunger; (2) achievement of universal primary education; (3) promotion of

---

[34] J. E. Archibald, 'Pledges of Voluntary Contributions to the United Nations by Member States: Establishing and Enforcing Legal Obligations', *Geo. Wash. Int'l L. Rev.* 36 (2004), 317, at 317–18, 329. The UN does not invoke article 19 of the UN Charter in respect of unpaid voluntary contributions.

[35] R. Sabel, *Procedure at International Conferences* (Cambridge University Press, 1997), 21ff.

[36] UN Secretary-General's Bulletin on establishment and management of trust funds, UN Doc. ST/SGB/188 (1 March 1982), para. 29.

[37] See Instrument for the Revised Global Environmental Facility (GEF) of March 2008, Annex C.

[38] UNGA resolution 55/2 (18 September 2000).

gender equality and empowerment of women; (4) reduction of child mortality; (5) improvement of maternal health; (6) combating HIV/AIDS, malaria and other diseases; (7) ensuring environmental sustainability; and (8) establishment of a global partnership for development. Industrialised states thus pledged to contribute 0.7 per cent of their GDP[39] to meet these targets and in addition undertook to support exports from least developed nations, offer debt relief by cancelling all official bilateral debts in return for demonstrable commitments to poverty reduction and providing generous development assistance.[40]

The MDGs, much like the criteria and sub-criteria formulated to assess progress with RTD, are set against targets whose progress is in turn monitored by a set of indicators. For example, target 1C of goal 1 (i.e. eradication of extreme poverty and hunger) consists of halving, between 1990 and 2015, the proportion of people who suffer from hunger. This is assessed against the prevalence of underweight children under five years of age and the proportion of populations below the minimum level of dietary energy consumption. The achievement of the first seven substantive goals is predicated to a large degree on goal 8, which seeks to develop a global partnership for development through the delivery of official development assistance (ODA), debt relief, tariff and quota-free access and make available essential drugs and new technologies. Thus, ODA, which consists essentially of direct financial assistance, is complementary to other initiatives and requires that the target State is obliged to work towards implementing the targets and indicators of the MDGs. Paragraph 39 of the 2002 Monterey Consensus[41] makes it clear that ODA is reserved for countries with the least capacity of attracting foreign direct investment and its purpose is to:

[help achieve] adequate levels of domestic resource mobilisation over an appropriate time horizon, while human capital, productive and export capacities are enhanced. ODA can be critical for improving the environment for private sector activity and can thus pave the way for robust growth. ODA is also a crucial instrument for supporting education, health, public infrastructure development, agriculture and rural development and to enhance food security.

Yet, as lofty and important as the MDGs are they risk denigrating the very values they seek to exalt and protect. First and foremost the rights language entrenched in the Millennium Declaration was not iterated in the MDGs for fear that somehow the goals might be transformed into justiciable entitlements. One might naturally think that although unfortunate, lack of justiciability was a

---

[39] See para. 42 of the Monterey Consensus, below note 41.
[40] See Millennium Declaration, paras. 15–18; MDGs, goal 8, targets A-D.
[41] Monterey Consensus of the International Conference on Financing for Development, UN Doc. A/CONF.198/11 (2002). The Monterey Consensus is a political declaration of the highest calibre aimed at mobilising development assistance, international trade as an engine for development and eliminating external debt. It was followed up in 2008 by the Doha Declaration on Financing for Development.

small price to pay for securing the much needed aid to the world's poor; after all, the goals and their indicators are strikingly similar to the rights found in the Bill of Rights. Sadly, this is not the case.[42] True, there are many similarities between the goals and ESC rights. However, whereas these rights, as proclaimed in the ICESCR, are supposed to apply against all persons without any discrimination, thus reaching the poorest of the poor, the MDGs on many occasions only require states to halve certain poverty indicators. Given the absence of an obligation to disaggregate results in the MDGs it is tempting for target states to focus on the relatively well-off among the poor and make no special provision for vulnerable groups.[43] As a result, the universality element of the relevant right is lost. Moreover, some goals are clearly inconsistent with human rights. By way of illustration, goal 2 calls for universal primary education, ignoring the requirement of free and quality education as this is enshrined in article 13 of ICESCR. More worrying is the technocratic trend set in the MDGs with an emphasis on the mobilisation of financial resources over and above the transformation of power relations that play a large part in the creation of poverty and underdevelopment.[44] The MDGs therefore ignore the fundamental role of civil and political rights in the achievement of ESC rights.[45] Hence, multilateral donors seem to entertain the illusion that countries which marginalise their minorities, which provide employment to their women but provide them with menial jobs, or who allow corrupt leaders to be perpetually re-elected because other candidates do not possess the financial or other means to run for office, can eventually lead their peoples to a high standard of well-being. It is therefore imperative that any development financing possess the following characteristics: be rights sensitive and considered against human rights standards and indicators (e.g. removal of tied aid); avoid overly technocratic goals that provide good statistical reading and instead focus on transforming the lives of peoples by prioritising human rights in policy choices and resource allocation; aim to empower all people and

---

[42] In a 2006 report the OECD estimated that approximately 58 per cent of bilateral aid was tied. Tied aid refers to aid granted under condition that the recipient purchase goods and services from the donor. See OECD, '2005 Development Cooperation Report: Efforts and Policies of the Members of the Development Assistance Committee', *OECD Journal on Development* (2006), 31. There is no consensus on the ethical or legal perspectives of this practice under international law, although states are generally keen to hide so-called 'aid for trade' as was the case in the early 1990s where the UK financed the construction of the Pergau dam in Malaysia, which in turn proceeded to buy £1 billion worth of British arms. In *R* v. *Secretary of State for Foreign Affairs ex parte World Development Movement* [1995] 1 All ER 611 the High Court ruled that the project was not of any economic or humanitarian benefit to the Malaysian people. It should also be noted that the drafters of the Paris Declaration on Aid Effectiveness have pledged to minimise it and the Development Assistance Committee (DAC) of the OECD adopted in 2001 a Recommendation to Untie ODA to the Least Developed Countries.

[43] *Claiming the Millennium Development Goals*, above note 13, 4.   [44] Ibid.

[45] HRC, Consolidation of Findings of the High-level Task Force on the Implementation of the Right to Development, UN Doc. A/HRC/15/WG.2/TF/2/Add.1 (25 March 2010), paras. 65–6.

disrupt unequal power relations that thwart development for the masses; and make MDG rights justiciable, not necessarily against the donors but in respect of the institutions and mechanisms set up by target states.[46]

12.5   PRACTICAL APPLICATION

12.5.1   Microfinance: breaking the cycle of poverty by small loans to the ultra poor

Microfinance, or microcredit, involves small loans, no more than a few hundred dollars, to the poor with a view to enabling them to develop a small business and thus break free from their cycle of poverty.[47] The fundamental premise of microfinance is based on the reality that the poor and the ultra-poor have no access to commercial credit because they do not possess any collateral by which to secure the return of the capital and interest. Landless farmers, slum dwellers, the homeless, rural women and other marginalised groups are therefore excluded from credit from the day they are born. Microfinance, on the other hand, does not usually require any collateral on the part of the borrower (although certain institutions demand some form of collateral), only the regular repayment of the loan in small weekly or biweekly instalments. Although the idea is attractive it is subject to several practical limitations, especially its prohibitive transaction cost. By way of illustration, a single loan of US$10,000 requires the man-hours of one clerk, whereas one-hundred loans worth US$100 each demand one hundred times as many man-hours, in addition to as many other administrative costs. At the same time,

---

[46] Since the launch of the MDGs the question of aid effectiveness has become critical for donor states. As a result, in 2005 the Paris Declaration on Aid Effectiveness was adopted with the aim of disbursing and managing ODA more effectively. The Declaration is not binding and established a framework for bilateral partnerships between donors and creditors and individual aid-recipient countries. Aid effectiveness is linked to five mutually reinforcing principles: (1) recipient countries exercise efficient ownership over their development strategies; (2) support is based on recipient countries' strategies and institutions (alignment); (3) harmonisation and transparency of donors' actions; (4) improvement in decision-making and management; (5) mutual accountability of donors and recipients. The Paris Declaration was rigidly technocratic and is only incidentally concerned with development outcomes and hence avoids references to human rights, unlike its follow-up instrument, the 2008 Accra Agenda for Action. Moreover, the OECD DAC published its *Action-Oriented Policy Paper on Human Rights and Development* in 2007, where it identified ten principles whereby human rights play an inextricable part in donor effectiveness and harmonisation. However, in *Evaluating Development Cooperation: Summary of Key Norms and Standards* (2010), 13–14, the DAC explains its five principles for evaluating development assistance (i.e. relevance, effectiveness, efficiency, impact sustainability) without any reference to human rights indicators.

[47] The UN has shown a keen interest in microfinance as a weapon against poverty since the launch of the Secretary-General's Report on the Role of Microcredit in the Eradication of Poverty, UN Doc. A/53/223 (10 August 1998).

banks are aware that the legal expenses for the recovery of defaulted debts would exceed the capital of the loan, thus rendering microloans extremely risky. As a result, if microfinance is to become viable, and not simply an act of charity, it has to be financially self-sustainable (although this should not be an aim itself), should recoup its transaction costs and must reach all those that are deemed uncreditworthy, especially the ultra-poor.

Economics scholars are still at odds as to whether data collected from communities in receipt of microfinance demonstrate a direct correlation with a decrease of poverty. It is not the place of this book to argue either way, but most results are compelling and certainly no one is arguing that microfinance is unable to deliver development. In 2005 Khandker undertook a revised study on the matter using Bangladeshi rural poor borrowers (in their majority women) as a case study. He found that for each additional 100 Bangladeshi taka (100BDT = US$1.22 as of 2012) of credit to women borrowers there was an annual increase in household expenditures: 11.3 taka in food and 9.2 taka in non-food expenditure. Comparing poverty levels from data collected in 1991 to 1999, Khandker found that moderate poverty in all surveyed villages had declined by 17 points. Poverty rates declined 3 per cent each year, with half of this reduction being directly attributable to microfinance. Interestingly, the impact was more significant for extreme poverty rather than moderate poverty and a spill-over effect was measured in non-participating communities.[48] One of the principal benefits of microfinance is the level of empowerment it provides to impoverished women, in addition to an increase in education, health and other socio-economic levels. In fact, in certain case studies, access to low interest credit and the enhancement of women's technical skills has been found to have directly contributed to the alleviation of female trafficking, forced marriages and labour.[49]

No doubt the global microcredit architecture is far from perfect. Many micro-lenders are not reaching the poorest, principally because they are funded by external donors who expect instant results. According to a 2008 report on microfinance in India, non-poor clients (i.e. those earning more than US$1 per day) constituted 42 to 88 per cent of the clientele of five out of eight micro-lenders.[50] Thus, the ultra-poor continue to be generally excluded because most lenders are afraid of being exposed to great risks. Moreover, in order to justify the sustainability of microcredit, lenders demand immediate loan repayments at high interest rates, which forces borrowers to either

[48] S. Khandker, 'Microfinance and Poverty: Evidence using Panel Data from Bangladesh', *World Bank Economic Review* 19 (2005), 263.

[49] See Asia Foundation, *Combating Human Trafficking in Vietnam: Lessons Learned and Practical Experiences for Future Program Design and Implementation*, (August 2008), at 4–5, 12–13.

[50] K. Driscoll, 'Microcredit: not yet Panacea to End Trafficking in Women', *University of Pennsylvania Journal of Business Law (U. Pa. J. Bus. L.)* 13 (2010), 275, at 287.

take out additional loans or turn to debt bondage and prostitution, in many cases.[51] Furthermore, it is often advanced that loans given to women are frequently used by the male members of households, something not readily apparent in the statistics.[52] Finally, most micro-lenders fail to provide technical training to borrowers, therefore raising the risk that the loan will be squandered. The next section will provide a small insight into how one of the pioneering micro-lending institutions, Grameen Bank of Bangladesh, has managed to overcome many of these pitfalls.

12.5.2   Grameen micro-lending: access to credit as a human right

Muhammad Yunus, an academic, conceived the idea of microcredit in the aftermath of the Bangladeshi war of independence in the 1970s and in 1976 set up Grameen Bank.[53] Women comprise 90 per cent of Grameen's borrowers with reported loan repayment rates of 95–8 per cent. The aim of Grameen is to lift households out of poverty, and in doing so applies ten indicators: the family lives in a house with a tin roof and each member sleeps in a bed; family members drink purified water; all children above the age of six attend school; the borrower's minimum weekly loan instalment is 200 taka or more; the family uses sanitary latrine; family members have adequate clothing and mosquito nets; the family has additional sources of income, such as a vegetable garden; the borrower maintains an annual savings account of at least 5,000 taka; the family experiences no difficulty in having three square meals a day; the family can take care of all health issues.[54] Grameen loans require no collateral on the part of the borrowers and are typically disbursed on an informal basis (i.e. non-contractual), chiefly predicated on trust. Moreover, the Bank does not undertake any legal or other action in case of default, although most loans are insured in case of serious health issues or natural disasters. The Bank's stated philosophy is that credit is a human right and that all people should have access to it. To drive the point home its motto is that 'the people should not go to the bank, the bank should go to the people'. As will be explained, Grameen staff are based in rural areas and inform people individually about their micro-lending system, even those who are homeless.

---

[51] Ibid., 288–9.

[52] It has been proven by data that in cases where women take out loans but do not use them, they and their families benefit more than if the loan had gone directly to a male member of the household. See N. Goldberg, *Measuring the Impact of Microfinance: Taking Stock of What we Know* (Washington, DC: Grameen Foundation USA, 2005), 42–3.

[53] See T. Islam, *Microcredit and Poverty Alleviation* (Aldershot: Ashgate, 2007), 82–3. The author is at the same time rather critical of Grameen's role in poverty alleviation and in increasing its clients' productivity.

[54] Available at: www.grameen-info.org/index.php?option=com_content&task=view&id=23&Itemid=126.

As already stated, Grameen's aim is to provide credit to the poorest of the poor, with a special focus on women. Grameen lending is based on a group-based model. A branch is first set up covering fifteen to twenty-two villages and time is spent by the staff familiarising themselves with the local population and explaining to them what the Bank aims to achieve and offer. Once this is done, Grameen staff form a group of five prospective borrowers, only two of which are initially eligible for a loan. The group is observed for a month to see if it is conforming to the Bank's rules and it is only when the first two borrowers begin to repay the capital plus the interest that the Bank disburses loans to the other three group members. If at any point a group member defaults on her loan, all the other members of the group are excluded from further financing. Thus, despite the absence of any collateral, the Grameen model is founded on the assumption that peer pressure breeds collective responsibility, so that all members have an interest in seeing that each other's obligations are met. The interest rate on all Grameen loans is, at the time of writing, 16 per cent.[55]

Although Grameen loans are typically disbursed to help poor women develop existing skills into a viable business and livelihood, this is only conceived as a first step in the eradication of the family's poverty. The Bank sets out various non-financial conditions for the receipt of loans, namely compulsory and voluntary savings, social and physical infrastructure projects, such as housing, sanitation, drinking water, education and family planning, and extends appropriate credit for such projects. Borrowers are obliged to attend weekly meetings organised by the Bank where both financial and non-financial matters are discussed and each has to share her experience with the Bank's staff and the group. Given the Bank's interest in the enhancement of its borrowers' social capital, it closely monitors the fulfilment and improvement of its social indicators. No doubt, this is something that is of no interest to conventional banks, whose sole purpose is to make a profit. By 2007 Grameen had disbursed US$6.7 billion, served 7.4 million borrowers covering more than 80,000 villages and employed 25,283 employees in Bangladesh alone, making it the largest non-profit organisation in the world. Moreover, it has posted profits every year since 1995.[56] We have already made some references to serious criticisms of Grameen's capacity to raise its clients' productivity, provide flexibility in loan repayments or ensure that women borrowers are the actual recipients of loans. The system is far from perfect, but it is cited for present purposes as a work in progress built around an idea that has the potential to fight poverty in the developing world.

[55] Available at: www.grameen-info.org/index.php?option=com_content&task=view&id=24&Itemid=127. See also A. Bernasek, 'Banking on Social Change: Grameen Bank Lending to Women', *International Journal of Political Culture and Society* 16 (2003), 369, at 372.

[56] Available at: www.grameen-info.org/index.php?option=com_content&task=view&id=37&Itemid=86.

INTERVIEW 12.1
Microfinance NGO
(Ramanou Nassirou)

Ramanou Nassirou is the general manager of WAGES (Women and Associations for Gains both Economic and Social), a Togolese microfinance institution that began as a CARE international project in 1994 and has grown since to become the second largest MFI in Togo. As of May 2012, it has a portfolio of 13.6 billion FCFA (the Togo currency) (US$27,200,000) in active loans, 8 billion FCFA (US$16,000,000) in savings deposits, and 168,000 clients, the majority (59 per cent) of whom are women (US$1 = 500 FCFA).

How do you reach and identify your clients? In your assessment do you take into consideration the criteria for poverty set out in the Millennium Development Goals or do you employ your own?

Client outreach is achieved in several ways. As our primary service is providing loans to low-income entrepreneurs and small-to-medium enterprises (SMEs), our loan officers are in the field for 80 per cent of their working hours. In the field means visiting local markets, at small offices, boutiques, roadside stalls, hair salons, workshops, as well as farms and, in essence, any place where business can and does take place. Due to their regular presence among our targeted audience, our public profile, reputation and products are advertised on a daily basis. We furthermore advertise in the local print and radio media and rely heavily on word of mouth references from our existing clients.

As for specifically identifying our clients, we use the definition of poverty as established by the Millennium Development Goals to produce a poverty assessment tool (PAT). Though we serve the low end of the socio-economic ladder, our institution also addresses the financial needs of those outside of this zone, specifically SMEs. Our ability to be a sustainable institution depends on using profits earned from larger loans to subsidise the smaller, and higher risk, loans as the latter have far lower rates of return. The profit margin of larger loans furthermore allows us to innovate and target marginal groups with special products at lower rates of interest.

Indeed, we have specific loan and savings products tailored to reflect the variety of our clients' business interests and financial situations, most notably in terms of varying interest rates, all of which are calculated on a declining basis. For particularly vulnerable agricultural clients, we lend at an annualised 9 per cent, for all other agricultural loans, 12 per cent, while the remainder of our products are fixed at a standard 18 per cent. For clients at the low end of the socio-economic scale, we have a 'tontine' savings account, which requires a daily deposit over a three-month period before we can establish terms for a loan.

What kind of technical training do you provide to your clients?

We offer a range of specific training opportunities to our clients that serve twin purposes: on the one hand training directly increases the ability of our clients to organise their finances and run their businesses. On the other hand, the training indirectly helps our clients to manage their loans and meet their repayment schedules. We, in other words, have a vested social and self-interest in ensuring that our clients have a minimum understanding of financial and business affairs.

With this in mind our two most common training sessions relate to managing a savings account and managing a loan. Clients are taught how to read and interpret their savings and loan booklets in which all cash transactions are recorded. They are furthermore taught how to foresee financial commitments and plan accordingly; for many, financial planning is done on a day-to-day basis, but long-term planning is harder to do since their income streams can vary tremendously over the course of a year. As for our clients, we help them to build up a certain amount of capital of their own as well as extend them some ourselves.

More specific to agriculturalists and farmers, we provide training on how to transform raw products (such as drying fish for conservation, preserving jams, and so forth) into finished goods and produce them on a saleable scale. We also provide for farmers training in improved agricultural practices to increase output, in such areas as soil conservation, enrichment, fertilisation, irrigation and complementary crop selection relative to seasons and market demand.

There is also marketing training: this can be as little as having the seller be more friendly, dress better or may be as much as entirely rearranging their stall to better display their products or even relocating. Finally, we also provide functional literacy training, and training sessions to increase awareness of HIV/AIDS and malaria. In overview, the goal of our total training curriculum is to have more knowledgeable, competent and healthy clients, ultimately better able to work, provide for themselves and their families and achieve personal financial security.

Is there any evidence that micro-loans have helped to empower women or that they have assisted the very poor to raise their standard of living?

In following up with our clients after training sessions and, notably, through their loan life cycles, we have been able to establish that there is a sustained improvement of their socio-economic status.

With our female clients, we have been able to ascertain that they generally achieve greater decision-making ability within their own homes. The empowerment stems from their increased economic independence and the manner in which they utilise their increased cash flow. Instead of relying on their spouses or other family members, they are able to pay for their own expenses and needs, be it for rent, food, health care, school fees, etc. The point is that they now have their own disposable income to do with as they wish. As more active participants in the economic life of their community, they as well have a greater degree of mobility and are better able to participate within the greater community.

What results are expected by your donors and do these expectations place considerable stress on your clients?

As a microfinance institution, we have a number of international sponsors, some of who match our loans and some who provide grants to increase our lending capital. All told, such sponsorship approaches roughly 40 per cent of our total loan portfolio. We also have a few partners who provide interest-free capital, these being Babyloan (France), LendwithCARE (UK) and Kiva (USA). From each sponsor and partner, there is a basic expectation that we achieve positive financial performance tied to a direct social impact, as well as improvement in the socio-economic standing of our clients. In addition to this there is an emphasis on us maintaining our efforts on reaching the most marginalized groups.

Earlier, in the response to the first question, it was mentioned that there is a tension in our microfinance operation: to achieve sustainability, we have to work with SMEs that fall beyond our mission statement and namesake. Where we differ from larger banks is that we roll the proceeds of our more profitable loans – to be clear, the larger ones – into supporting our small loans that, without doubt, touch the poorest members of our society. If we are unable to achieve financial sustainability as a financial institution the model itself is broken. Ultimately, we rely on our sponsors to expand our operations, but in view of the long term, we need to reduce our dependence on such support.

Our mission is to provide financial services to a specific clientele in order to help expand their businesses; our bottom line is then distributed to the margins of our client base whereas the commercial banks distribute theirs to shareholders and ownership. Sponsors' and partners' pressure on us is, on the whole, manageable because we enter into relationships with a clear mutual understanding of what their expectations are and how we undertake our mission. In this way, we can operate according to our best interests as an institution for we have in advance fully communicated our intentions, methodology, and practices. By having our roadmap clearly understood by all concerned parties, we are able to maintain a consistent approach though we encounter our fair share of challenges and delays. No business is perfect and the best we can do is to continue taking risks and learn from each experience.

12.6   DEBT RELIEF AND THE ENJOYMENT OF FUNDAMENTAL RIGHTS

In 1991 Peru was forced to service its foreign debt by doubling its monthly repayment to US$150 million. During that time Latin America was hit by a cholera epidemic but most poor Peruvians were unable to purchase the necessary drugs because the government had increased the prices of all basic sanitary products in order to raise revenues for its repayment programme. In 2000 the government of Tanzania spent on debt repayment nine times more than it did on the provision of health. It may seem rational that a country must pay its debts, but at the time 1.6 million Tanzanians lived with AIDS and were hence denied access to essential medicines.[57] In both cases there is a clear link between the pressures incumbent on a country to service its foreign debt and its ability to provide basic amenities to its people. Thus, debt repayment may in certain situations constitute an impediment to the enjoyment of, at least, the most basic ESC rights. The issue is not, however, straightforward. For one thing, on what grounds can a country legitimately repudiate a debt premised on a valid contractual undertaking? Secondly, given that the ability of states to borrow money allows them to fulfil their human rights obligations by paying for necessary social services, infrastructure and education without burdening their taxpayers – especially in poor countries – what is the ideal formula at which a debt can be considered sustainable? Finally, if the human rights perspective to lending prevails over its private (commercial) dimension, how is this to be translated in practice?

Countries generally borrow from private lenders, namely banks, or public financial institutions, such as intergovernmental development banks, or a combination of the two. All lending is contractual and the lender makes his profit from the agreed interest on the capital borrowed. The contractual nature of this arrangement naturally obliges the debtor country to honour its undertaking. Yet it is not clear whether under international law the conflict between debt repayment and rights fulfilment is to be resolved in favour of the former. It is equally unclear whether a debt inherited by a despotic regime for the sake of its preservation and the persecution of its enemies should necessarily burden the people of the ruled nation and its future generations. By way of analogy, if John, a businessman, were to take out a loan which he goes on to spend on gambling, the repayment of his loan could not possibly be borne by John's employees, his family or friends, on the basis that it is a private debt. In the same manner, it is suggested by an ever-increasing number of private and public actors that certain debts incurred by states are odious or illegitimate and as such they only warrant an obligation of repayment by the same persons that contracted them. An odious debt is described

---

[57] C. Barry, 'Sovereign Debt, Human Rights and Policy Conditionality', *Journal of Political Philosophy* 19 (2011), 282, at 286.

as having been incurred by dictators and authoritarian regimes for private ends or in order to intimidate and coerce their peoples in the knowledge of the lenders. Illegitimate debts concern loans that are unfair or objectionable and debts that infringe public policy.[58] Odious debts are more or less self-explanatory and are even more repugnant where the lender was fully aware of the corruptness of the recipient and the purpose for which the money was destined.

Illegitimate debts have many faces. Banks finding themselves with a significant cash flow naturally want their cash to earn interest and so may lure developing nations to borrow under reasonable interest rates, knowing full well that these countries lack the institutional capacity to take full, or any, advantage of the loan. When these countries are later unable to service the original debt, having squandered the original capital, the banks lend more money at higher and unreasonable rates with the sole purpose of repaying the interest on the first loan. In this manner the banks are reaping a continuous and non-ending profit from interest alone, the relentless struggle for the repayment of which means that the country in question will never have the financial capacity to extinguish the capital, let alone provide essential services to its people. Illegitimate debts can be incurred not only as a result of the greed of private lenders. Multilateral institutions such as the World Bank, whether advertently or inadvertently can produce more or less similar situations. The World Bank, for example, wrongly advised developing nations in Africa to borrow money in order to privatise critical local industries while at the same time failing to warn them about exogenous shocks to their economies as a result of their exposure to open markets.[59]

Despite significant dissent, it has been convincingly argued that both odious and illegitimate debt constitute an exception to the general rule whereby government debts are binding on their successors, including the ruled peoples.[60] A recent UNCTAD study cites numerous case studies where the odious debt doctrine was sustained implicitly or explicitly in order to extinguish sovereign debt that was unconscionable.[61] Prominent among these is the *Tinoco* arbitration, where a successor Costa Rican government

---

[58] Report on Effects of Foreign Debt and other Related International Financial Obligations of States on the Full Enjoyment of all Human Rights, particularly Economic, Social and Cultural Rights (2009 Foreign Debt and Human Rights Report), UN Doc. A/64/289 (12 August 2009), paras. 8–22.

[59] K. Raffer and H. Singer, *The Foreign Aid Business: Economic Assistance and Development Cooperation* (Cheltenham, Brookfield, VT: Edward Elgar, 1996); K. Raffer, 'International Financial Institutions and Financial Accountability', *Ethics and International Affairs* 18 (2004), 61.

[60] T. H. Cheng, 'Renegotiating the Odious Debt Doctrine', *Law and Contemporary Problems* 70 (2007), 7.

[61] R. Howse, *The Concept of Odious Debt in Public International Law*, UNCTAD Discussion Paper no. 185 (2007), 10ff.

argued that the debts incurred by its predecessor, the dictator Tinoco and his entourage, could not be attributed to the state because none of the loans were in the public interest and the money was employed for private purposes. Chief Justice Taft, who sat as sole arbitrator, agreed with this position, particularly since the Royal Bank of Canada, which paid several cheques to Tinoco, was aware of the dictator's unpopularity in the country and the fact that the money was employed for illegitimate ends.[62] No doubt wealthy nations are reluctant to relieve debts under the odiousness doctrine for fear of creating a justiciable precedent and hence go on to relieve debts on other legal bases (such as debt sustainability), or as a matter of goodwill.[63] It is evident that lending entities aware of the illegitimacy of a regime and of its intentions in respect of a loan are no different from a creditor who lends to a drug dealer in order to expand his illicit activities. The debt is beyond the purview of law and justice and is not susceptible to recovery before the courts.

This position is also consistent with the customary and *jus cogens* character of fundamental human rights. If we were to separate the regime of rights from the regime of sovereign loans and argue that states have expressly excluded human rights considerations from the regime of sovereign loans, this would be tantamount to rejecting the *jus cogens* and *erga omnes* nature of fundamental rights altogether. Moreover, to suggest that present and future generations of a country whose corrupt, abusive and unrepresentative government incurred a personal debt are liable for that debt, flatly disregards the right to self-determination.[64] As a result, it is artificial and wholly illegitimate to construe loan agreements and debts outside the framework of international human rights.[65] Clearly, what is called for is the introduction of binding responsible banking rules in the field of sovereign loans, and hence the statement in the Monterey Consensus that debtors and creditors possess a 'shared responsibility' for unsustainable debt is an acknowledgement of the obvious.[66] In domestic law if a bank provided a loan to a minor without his parents' consent this would be in the knowledge that it could not retrieve any capital or interest from them. Equally, if the same bank were to lend money to a person that possessed no assets or other collateral it would risk losing its capital in case of non-payment by the debtor. As a result, domestic banking is generally a cautious business. Caution is absent in sovereign lending because of the comfort of diplomatic protection and other

---

[62] *Tinoco* arbitration (*Great Britain* v. *Costa Rica*), AJIL 18 (1923), 147, at 176.

[63] See, for example, the discussion on the post-Saddam Hussein Iraqi debt, in Howse, above note 61, pp. 15–16; 2009 Foreign Debt and Human Rights Report, above note 58, paras. 8–9.

[64] See section 10.2.

[65] See CESCR, General Comment 2, para. 9, which emphasised that 'international measures to deal with the debt crisis should take full account of the need to protect economic, social and cultural rights'.

[66] Monterey Consensus, para. 47.

assurances afforded to creditors, which typically encompass states and inter-governmental organisations in addition to private banks. Moreover, practice suggests that even solvent countries will ultimately be granted concessional funding by the World Bank, as well as bilateral and multilateral donors in order to kickstart their economies so that they can become eligible for new loans to repay their old ones.

The glaring absence of any human rights considerations is evident in the assessment of debt sustainability. This generally refers to a country's financial capacity to repay a prospective loan. Ultimately, all countries must borrow money, whether to service an existing debt or in order to undertake infrastructure or social projects. Thus, when poor countries apply for debt relief, concessional funding and regular lending the creditors will have to make an assessment of the applicant's debt sustainability. In practice, debt sustainability is narrowly defined by the ability of a country to pay its debts on the basis of its export earnings alone. By way of illustration, if the projected export earnings of country X are US$100 million in a given year and the annual repayments on interest and capital on its intended loan amount to US$95 million its debt will be considered sustainable and will be eligible for funding. This narrow method of assessment, however, fails to consider the country's expenditure for health, education, housing, infrastructure and other social projects;[67] it only caters for the interests of the lenders. Hence, in the above scenario the debtor country would be forced to meet its annual social expenditures with US$5 million, although the creditors are aware that the real costs may amount to at least US$20 million. It is no wonder that campaigners are urging multilateral creditors to redefine debt sustainability as the level of debt that allows a country to achieve its MDG targets. The Independent Expert on the Effects of Foreign Debt has suggested that:

Any concept of debt sustainability should include an assessment of what minimum expenditure is required to enable a government to meet its obligations to its citizens, including the provision of basic social services such as health and education. In particular, human rights should be used as a basis for assessing debt sustainability and for the cancellation of all unsustainable debt. Such an approach would consider all indebted countries irrespective of their income and assess the level of debt they could carry without undermining their human rights obligations.[68]

---

[67] The Paris Club, an informal gathering of nineteen creditor countries is committed to debt relief programmes for poorer nations through two general avenues: (1) longer repayment period (the maximum repayment period is now twenty-three years including six years of grace for commercial loans and forty years (including sixteen years of grace) for ODA loans); (2) debt cancellation, where for the poorest and most indebted countries the level of debt cancellation may reach 67 per cent. Despite these significant initiatives, the Paris Club's instruments and terms make no reference to HDI, the MDGs or human rights in their assessment of debt sustainability.

[68] 2009 Foreign Debt and Human Rights Report, para. 55.

CASE STUDY 12.2
Cancellation of debts incurred under Norway's 'ship export campaign'

In the late 1970s the output of Norway's ship-building industry outstripped demand. In order to avert mass redundancies and avoid crippling the sector altogether the Norwegian government devised a 'ship export campaign' on the basis of which developing countries could buy Norwegian ships under cheaper than usual credit. The deal was made even more attractive because it was tied to a 25 per cent development grant, which Norway would have had to provide according to obligations incurred under the OECD. Although this arrangement seems prima facie beneficial to both creditor and debtor, there was no serious scrutiny as to the ability of the debtors to service their loans, let alone any consideration as to whether the ships were really necessary for these developing nations. As a result, when the global price of ships was dramatically reduced in the early 1980s they no longer represented adequate security against the loans and following a sharp increase in interest rates during the same time the debtors were left with huge debts. The ships' value had fallen to almost a third of the value of their loan.

In 2006 the Norwegian government announced that it would cancel the debts of five nations arising from its ship export campaign on the ground that the scheme 'represented a development policy failure'.[1] Although this debt cancellation was declared to be complementary to Norway's other ODA, it was emphatically stressed that it represented a one-off, unilateral act and that all other bilateral debt would be handled through the processes of the Paris Club. This is despite the fact that Norway is a keen supporter of global debt relief under a binding set of rules agreed by the international community.

POINTS TO CONSIDER

- Given that the pursuit of well-being knows no borders, the right to development is incumbent also on the governments of even the richest nations.[2] Discuss.

- So-called 'vulture funds' are made up of private creditors who bought up the foreign debt of indebted poor nations at a discounted price, slightly prior to the debt relief initiatives these countries now enjoy. These funds make a profit recovering the full value of the debt, accrued interest, as well as late payment penalties. Given that these vulture funds invested money into a legitimate subrogated claim, is it just to strip them of the contractual rights entered into with

[1] Norway, Ministry of Foreign Affairs, press release no. 118/06 (2 October 2009).
[2] See Save the Children, *State of the World's Mothers 2011* (May 2011), which ranks the UK relatively low in children's well-being on account of its poor record of pre-primary enrolment (81 per cent as opposed to 100 per cent in most other European nations), which represents a significant assistance to the poor.

sovereign states? Discuss in relation to the Debt Relief (Developing Countries) Act, adopted by the UK in 2010.

• What are the obstacles preventing the World Bank from adopting an HRBA to development lending?

• A fictitious scenario. The donor community declares itself willing to give ten times more aid under condition that it is granted solely under charitable terms, rather than on the basis of the right to development or the MDGs. The money is great and so much can be done with it. It is worth sacrificing the principle? … Charity is after all benevolent and at par with the right to development. Discuss.

• The legal basis of the odious/illegitimate debt doctrine seems to be inconsistent with customary international law regarding the succession of governments – which generally posits that succeeding governments are liable for the debts incurred by their predecessors. Discuss.

12.7   THE RIGHT TO A CORRUPTION-FREE SOCIETY

Sani Abacha, the former Nigerian dictator is believed to have embezzled more than US$5.4 billion during his five-year tenure, while his generals made away with, at least, US$12 billion worth of oil revenues earned during the 1990–1 Gulf War.[69] By late 2005 the World Bank estimated that the total annual amount of bribes paid globally amounted to US$1 trillion. This is double the annual GDP of Africa as a whole and more than ten times the annual amount of development aid.[70] The obvious connection between human well-being and corruption is evident in both cases from the fact that scarce resources otherwise destined for development projects are diverted into the pockets of the few, which naturally exacerbates poverty and social injustice. Yet, there was a time during the Cold War when leading economists advocated that corruption was largely beneficial for growth in the developing world because it helped investors bypass cumbersome legal and bureaucratic hurdles, thus allowing them to amass capital, move faster and promote innovation and entrepreneurship where it was lacking.[71] The vast majority of governments in the developed world either openly endorsed the payment of bribes in order to ensure business contracts in developing

---

[69] N. Kofele-Kale, 'The Right to a Corruption-free Society as an Individual and Collective Human Right: Elevating Official Corruption to a Crime under International Law', *International Lawyer* (*Int'l Law.*) 34 (2000), 149, 162.

[70] P. Keulers, *Corruption, Poverty and Development*, ADB/OECD Regional Anti-corruption conference, Background paper (28–30 September 2005), 1.

[71] J. S. Nye, 'Corruption and Political Development: A Cost–benefit Analysis', *American Political Science Review* 61 (1967), 417, at 419.

nations or otherwise paid lip service to the enforcement of anti-corruption laws. Corruption[72] was thus utilised as a competitive advantage and is akin in nature to the illegitimate and odious debts explained in a previous section.

Spearheaded by the USA, which promulgated a Corrupt Practices Act in 1977 that made it an offence to bribe a foreign official abroad,[73] the international community finally managed to adopt its first near-universal treaty via the OECD in 1997.[74] Since then numerous regional anti-corruption treaties have been agreed, as well as a global one under the auspices of the UN, the 2003 Convention against Corruption (UNCAC).[75] The objectives of these treaty initiatives were to establish appropriate definitions, criminalise corrupt conduct under domestic or international law or both, and to facilitate cooperation between states. Although criminal justice mechanisms constitute an integral aspect of the obligation incumbent upon states to protect and fulfil human rights objectives, in the case at hand they are not necessarily aimed at alleviating human rights violations, and nor is the approach in the treaties consistent with human rights and development. None the less, there are some express or implicit linkages to rights, particularly the preamble and article 5(1) of UNCAC, which refer to the rule of law, a notion that is redundant without the protection of rights and non-discrimination. Equally, articles 5, 6(1)(b), 10 and 13 promote empowerment and participation by obliging states to disseminate, enhance public consultation and participation of civil society and provide access to information. Yet, despite these linkages one cannot plausibly entertain the suggestion that UNCAC or other regional treaties support a justiciable right to live in a corruption-free environment. Even if this were not so, such a right would be unproductive because the objectives that could be pursued by focusing on the violated underlying rights (e.g. the right to life or food) brought about by corrupt conduct are susceptible to immediate remediable measures.

By way of illustration, a law suit in favour of a corruption-free society in country X cannot produce any immediate results given that corruption is usually systemic and not attributable to any one individual. It could, of course, lead to the invalidation of public contracts and free public money. At best, a corrupt official might be prosecuted, perhaps resulting in the

---

[72] Corruption encompasses bribery, embezzlement, trading in influence, abuse of functions, illicit enrichment and obstruction of justice, although bribery and embezzlement are its most typical manifestations. The former is defined under article 15(a) UNCAC as: 'the promise, offering or giving, to a public official, directly or indirectly, of any undue advantage, for the official himself or herself or another person or entity, in order that the official act or refrain from acting in the exercise of his or her official duties'.

[73] 15 USC §§78dd-1, as amended in part by the 1988 Omnibus Trade and Competition Act and the 1998 International Anti-Bribery and Fair Competition Act.

[74] Convention on Combating Bribery of Foreign Public Officials in International Business Transactions, (1998) 37 ILM 1.

[75] 2349 UNTS 41.

confiscation of illicit assets, although in both cases a solid amount of evidence would have to be furnished, most of which would be difficult to find because illicit proceeds are usually transferred to secret locations abroad. Moreover, even if assets were seized and confiscated there is no claim, or indeed guarantee, that these would be rediverted into a development objective. If, on the other hand, one were to pursue a food shortage claim caused by governmental corruption on the basis of the right to food: (1) this would be subject to quantifiable measurement because the right requires that food is available in a quantity and quality that satisfies dietary needs;[76] (2) the action could either flag the violation, demand that the state appropriately meet the particular dietary needs of its people and/or provoke the donor community to take immediate remedial measures.[77]

We have already explained that the link between large-scale corruption and human rights, including RTD, involves the diversion of resources otherwise intended for social projects. This link is well recognised within the UN and other organisations.[78] Yet what largely goes unnoticed are the effects of needs-based (petty) corruption on the enjoyment of fundamental ESC rights, as well as RTD.[79] Low-paid public officials in poor countries, such as policemen, teachers and judges, demand payment for basic social services that are otherwise offered for free, thus ultimately providing them only to those who can afford to pay.[80] As a result, the most harmful consequence from petty corruption is the creation of inequality and discrimination between rich and poor, on the one level, and between the poor and the very poor, on the other.

---

[76] CESCR, General Comment 12, para. 8.

[77] In fact, the UN Special Rapporteur on the right to food has long identified corruption as one of seven major economic impediments that undermine and prevent the realisation of food security. UN Doc. E/CN.4/2001/53 (7 February 2001), para. 69. See also *People's Union for Civil Liberties* v. *Union of India and Others*, Petition (Civil) no. 196/2001, judgment (2 May 2003) by the Indian Supreme Court, which essentially ordered the state to feed the starving population of Rajasthan.

[78] E.g. CESCR, Concluding Observations on Moldova, UN Doc. E/C.12/1/ADD.91 (12 December 2003), para. 12; CtRC, Concluding Observations on Congo, UN Doc. CRC/C/COG/CO/1 (20 October 2006), para. 14. See also *Murungaru* v. *Kenya Anti-Corruption Commission and Another*, Nairobi High Court judgment (1 December 2006) 82 which makes a direct link between corruption and poverty, well-being and inflation. Gathii, below note 83, 179.

[79] See UNDP, *The Impact of Corruption on the Human Rights Based Approach to Development* (2004), 15, where the results of a survey demonstrated that the top three corrupt institutions identified by Indonesia's poorest quintile were the traffic police, the regular police and the judges, in that order.

[80] The UN Special Rapporteur on summary executions noted that in Nigeria: 'petty, everyday, police corruption is a constant reminder to the populace that justice can be bought, that the police cannot be relied upon for protection, and that police and criminals are all too often involved in the same enterprise'. UN Doc. E/CN.4/2006/53.Add 4 (7 January 2006), para. 106.

No doubt, therefore, given the impact of both petty and grand corruption on the enjoyment of most rights, a rights-based approach against corruption is justified, even if in rare cases it is in conflict with criminal justice,[81] national reconciliation and foreign investment policies. This proposition is not entirely straightforward even though at first glance it seems rational and practical. By way of example, the World Bank links corruption with governance and views it as an indicator of the latter's quality.[82] Governance itself is viewed as one of the benchmarks for economic growth and monetary stability which represent core objectives for the Bank. Quite clearly, the World Bank's financial and monetary considerations are at odds with an HRBA to corruption. It is no wonder, therefore, that commentators such as Gathii contend that anti-corruption reform agendas typically aim to please investors and financial institutions. As a result, a substantial amount of resources are spent, particularly by way of expensive high-profile prosecutions of grand corruption suspects, while the real problem may actually lie with systemic petty corruption which is left untreated. Ultimately, there are insufficient resources to fund access to justice mechanisms for the poor, universal education, health and others.[83] This approach clearly favours market efficiency over the provision of social services.

It is beyond the scope of this section to expand on the policies by which the HRBA to corruption can be implemented, such as through salary reforms,[84] strengthening of local integrity systems, etc. The foundation of the HRBA approach, and indeed that of UNCAC, is transparency, public participation and empowerment. These necessarily require the right of access to relevant information, not only as an obligation on the state to remove all impediments thereto but also as an actual duty to provide information.[85] Where this is coupled with a free press, freedom of expression and access to justice, empowerment and public participation in the fight against corruption are

---

[81] It is indeed rare for criminal justice mechanisms at the micro level to be incompatible with human rights objectives. The CESCR, in its Concluding Observations on Kenya, noted that despite the country's zero tolerance, corruption still affected the realisation of rights and recommended intensification of prosecutions and review of its sentencing in respect of corruption-related offences. UN Doc. E/C.12/KEN/CO/1 (1 December 2008), para. 10; CESCR, Concluding Observations on Madagascar, UN Doc. E/C.12/MDG/CO/2 (16 December 2009), para. 11, noting that impunity associated with corruption is detrimental to the enjoyment of rights.

[82] IBRD, *A Decade of Measuring the Quality of Governance: Governance Matters, Worldwide Indicators* (Washington, DC: IBRD, 2006), 9ff.

[83] J. T. Gathii, 'Defining the Relationship between Human Rights and Corruption', *U. Pa. J. Intl L.* 31 (2009–10), 125, 180, at 182–3.

[84] CESCR, Concluding Observations on Moldova, UN Doc. E/C.12/1/Add.1 (12 December 2003), para. 33, which urged Moldova to ensure better remuneration for public servants and judges.

[85] See *Claude-Reyes et al.* v. *Chile*, IACtHR judgment on merits, (19 September 2006), Ser-C, no. 1151, para. 77.

naturally guaranteed. Some countries have addressed public participation and empowerment through pilot schemes involving direct roles for the populace. Of particular interest is participatory monitoring of service delivery, which involves active citizen auditing and evaluation of public services and public contracts.[86] A recent example is the 2007 Ecuadorian Commission for the Comprehensive Auditing of the Public Credit.[87] Article 2 of the Decree establishing the commission defined comprehensive auditing as an action aimed at:

> examining and evaluating public debt contracting and/or renegotiation processes, the origin of the resources and their intended use and the implementation of programmes and projects financed by foreign and domestic loans in order to determine their legitimacy, legality, transparency, quality, efficacy and efficiency, considering legal and financial aspects, and the economic, social, regional, and ecological impacts, as well as the impact on gender, nations and communities.

The commission includes representatives from Ecuadorian civil society and international debt relief campaign organisations, among others.[88]

12.8   THE RIGHT TO A HEALTHY ENVIRONMENT

The UN Special Rapporteur on the illicit movement of toxic and dangerous wastes on the enjoyment of human rights has emphasised that 47,000 people die annually as a result of exposure to chemicals.[89] It has now become widely known that rich nations have been dumping dangerous chemicals in the developing world since at least the 1960s and that although this practice is now generally banned it persists through so-called recycling processes, which is merely a guise for the export of hazardous waste.[90] The risks to health and, ultimately, life arising from the contamination of the natural environment are self-evident. Although a number of international instruments and local

---

[86] Some commentators argue that despite its many benefits, this scheme is rather expensive and cumbersome and should be applied with caution. Keulers, above note 70, 4.

[87] Executive Decree no. 472 (9 July 2007).

[88] Report of the Independent Expert on the Effects of Foreign Debt: Mission to Norway and Ecuador, UN Doc. A/HRC/14/21/Add.1 (21 April 2010), para. 46. See also Case study 10.1 on participatory budgeting which is, however, used both as a tool to avoid corruption as well as a mechanism through which ordinary people can have a direct voice on public spending. Budget analysis is another tool, which allows a comparison of official expenditures with a view to ascertaining government priorities. See International Budget Partnerships (IBP), 'The Open Budget Survey 2010 (2011): Open Bridges, Transform Lives', available at: internationalbudget.org/files/2010_Full_Report-English.pdf.

[89] Report of the Special Rapporteur on Toxic Waste and Human Rights, UN Doc. E/CN.4/2006/42 (20 February 2006), para. 18.

[90] Report of the Special Rapporteur on Toxic Waste and Human Rights, UN Doc. E/CN.4/2004/46 (15 December 2003), para. 22.

laws articulate the right to a healthy environment it is not entirely clear whether the best policy choice is to protect the environment or peoples' rights thereto. Consider for example the argument that the financial development of nations may require deforestation or a certain degree of pollution from manufacturing facilities. Given that the protection of ecosystems *per se* lacks a human value, something otherwise inherent in the protection of people, a rights-based approach to the protection of the environment would become problematic, unless of course non-human values were to be integrated in the system and interpretation of human rights.[91] Two approaches have generally evolved in international practice. The first consists of constitutional and treaty provisions that stipulate a self-standing right to a healthy environment (RTHE), whereas the second concerns the practice of human rights treaty bodies and national courts linking the enjoyment of existing rights (particularly the right to life and that of health) to sustainable development and the protection of the natural environment.

The constitutions of several countries stipulate for a self-standing RTHE, including those of Argentina,[92] Colombia,[93] Ecuador,[94] Hungary,[95] South Korea,[96] the Philippines,[97] South Africa and others. Article 12 of the South African Constitution, for example, states that:

Everyone has the right (a) to an environment that is not harmful to their health or well-being; and (b) to have the environment protected, for the benefit of present and future generations through reasonable legislative and other measures that: (i) prevent pollution and ecological degradation; (ii) promote conservation; and (iii) secure ecologically sustainable development and use of natural resources while promoting justifiable economic and social development.

Constitutions of this nature generally impose a positive obligation on incumbent governments and promote sustainable development and intergenerational equity as fundamental corollaries to this entitlement. The right to a healthy environment is also explicitly recognised in articles 24 of the ACHPR and 11(1) of the San Salvador Protocol to the ACHR,[98] as well as article 1 of the 1998 Aarhus Convention on Access to Information, Public Participation in Decision Making and Access to Justice in Environmental Matters.[99]

Whereas the self-standing approach may be more appropriate when applied to policy-making initiatives – particularly in town planning, rural development and industrialisation – it is impractical in dealing with the effects of environmental degradation affecting the immediate health or

[91] C. Redgwell, 'Life, Universe and Everything: a Critique of Anthropocentric Rights', in A. Boyle and M. Anderson, (eds.), *Human Rights Approaches to Environmental Protection* (Oxford University Press, 1996), 71.
[92] Article 41.   [93] Articles 49 and 79.   [94] Article 14(1).   [95] Article 18.
[96] Article 35(1)–(2).   [97] Article II(16).
[98] 1988 Protocol in the Area of Economic, Social and Cultural Rights, (1989) 28 ILM 156.
[99] 2161 UNTS 447.

lives of people, particularly where this has been caused by non-state actors. The self-standing approach is also relevant in anticipating environmental security issues such as natural desertification, demographic stress, resource exploitation, unsustainable herding and agriculture that may lead to violent internal conflict or waves of environmental refugees.[100] None the less, the pursuit of environmental protection through existing rights seems to be the most prevalent approach and the one best suited to strategic litigation because of the entrenchment of these rights in domestic legal systems and the availability of access mechanisms. To a large degree this development was unavoidable because neither the ICCPR nor the ICESCR establish a self-standing RTHE and given that many constitutions require cumbersome amendment procedures the inclusion of such a right may have seemed an impossible exercise. This has resulted in an expansive construction primarily of the right to life, the right to dignity of person, the right to health and the right to food and water, among others, by national courts and human rights treaty bodies.[101] In contrast with the RTHE the rights to life and dignity consist principally of negative obligations and thus the principal aim of any litigation would aim to convince the courts of the need to set out a pertinent list of positive obligations.

The CESCR in General Comment 14 construed article 12(1) of the ICESCR (the right to the highest attainable standard of health) as encompassing all necessary socio-economic factors which lead to a healthy life, one of which is a healthy environment.[102] This necessarily requires the state to adopt pre-emptive and certainly remedial action even in cases where the harm to an entitlement caused by environmental degradation is caused by a non-state actor,[103] regardless of the latter's other personal liability. This line of

---

[100] See UNEP, *Understanding Environment, Conflict and Cooperation*, (UNEP, 2004), which links numerous conflicts in Africa to environmental degradation.

[101] The CtRC has stressed on numerous occasions that the promotion and protection of children's health and an adequate standard of living encompasses a healthy environment. Concluding Observations on Lithuania, UN Doc. CRC/C/15/Add.146 (21 February 2001), para. 36; CtRC, Concluding Observations on the DRC, UN Doc. CRC/C/COD/CO/2 (10 February 2009), para. 64; CtRC, Concluding Observations on Cameroon, UN Doc. CRC/C/CMR/CO/2 (18 February 2010), para. 63.

[102] CESCR General Comment 14, para. 4. In its General Comment 12, para. 4, the CESCR noted that the right to food 'is inseparable from social justice, requiring the adoption of appropriate economic, environmental and social policies, at both the national and international levels, oriented to the eradication of poverty and the fulfilment of all human rights for all'.

[103] See *Social and Economic Rights Action Centre (SERAC) and Center for Economic and Social Rights* v. *Nigeria* (*Ogoniland* case), Case no. ACHPR/COMM/A044/1, *AJIL* 96 (2002), 937, paras. 52–3, where the ACHPR held that the poisoning of freshwater resources through the disposal of toxic waste violated the right to life, health and property among others and imposed on the Nigerian governments strict environmental obligations.

reasoning has been adopted by other intergovernmental human rights bodies outside the UN system, such as the ECSR. In the *Marangopoulos Lignite* case, it was alleged that Greece had failed to comply with the right to health under article 11 of the European Social Charter because in the areas where lignite is mined it had taken no appropriate measures to combat public health risks.[104] The Committee upheld the jurisprudence linking the right to protection of health and the right to life with the right to a healthy environment, of which it constitutes an integral part.[105] It went on to say that although article 24(1) of the Greek Constitution renders the right to a healthy environment an individual right against the state, in the case at hand the state had failed to apply and enforce its environmental laws.[106]

The most impressive jurisprudence, however, has come from the courts of developing nations. At a time when India lacked a constitutional provision guaranteeing the right to a healthy environment the country's Supreme Court relied on article 21 of the Constitution (right to life) contending that the right to life encompassed the enjoyment of a healthy environment, including clean air and uncontaminated potable water.[107] The Indian Supreme Court was cognisant of the fact that the country's federal states and municipalities could argue that if indeed a positive obligation existed it did not concern them but the central authorities. As a result, it found that decentralised authorities were equally obliged to prevent pollution. Central to these judgments is the perceived conflict between industrialisation and ecology.[108] Although it is clear that the Court does not understand the term 'development' from an RTD perspective, but rather in terms of its financial and industrial dimension,[109] it has gone on to claim that the merits of any project must be premised on its environmental sustainability.[110] Having therefore established that ecology

---

[104] *Marangopoulos Foundation for Human Rights* v. *Greece*, Complaint no. 30/2005, ECSR decision on merits (6 December 2006).

[105] Ibid., paras. 195, 202.   [106] Ibid., paras. 208ff.

[107] *Charan Lal Sahu* v. *Union of India*, AIR (1990) SC 1480; but especially *Subhash Kumar* v. *State of Bihar*, AIR (1991) SC 420.

[108] This conflict has also been acknowledged by the ECtHR in *Hatton and Others* v. *UK* (2002) 34 EHRR 1, which dealt with noise pollution from night flights at Heathrow airport and whether this was justified on the basis of the country's economic interests. At first instance the Court was content to apply a fair balance test, arguing that states are required to minimise as far as possible such interferences to the right to privacy and family life. The Grand Chamber, however, albeit with five strongly worded dissenting opinions, declared that 'environmental protection should be taken into consideration by governments in acting within their margin of appreciation ... but it would not be appropriate for the Court to adopt a special approach in this respect by reference to a special status of environmental human rights'. *Hatton* v. *UK* (2003) 37 EHRR 28, para. 122.

[109] See e.g. *TN Godavaraman Thirumulpad* v. *Union of India and Others* (2008) 1 *Malaysian Law Journal* (*MLJ*) 997 (SC); *Bombay Dyeing and Mfg Co. Ltd* v. *Bombay Environmental Action Group and Others*, AIR (2006) SC 1489; *Essar Oil Ltd* v. *Halar Utkarsh Samiti and Others* (2004) 2 SCC 392.

[110] *Intellectual Forum, Tirupathi* v. *State of Andhra Pradesh and Others*, (2006) 2 SC 568.

and industrial development are not incompatible,[111] the Court was able to assess under each particular case whether an industrial project was environmentally sustainable. In *MC Mehta* v. *Union of India*, which concerned the discharge of untreated effluents from a tannery into the River Ganges, the Supreme Court ordered the tannery's closure despite the inevitable job losses, emphasising that human health and a balanced natural environment were of greater importance.[112] This line of construction by which the right to life has been found to encompass the right to a healthy environment has been followed by other constitutional courts.[113]

The right to a healthy environment has in practice become justiciable, whether as a self-standing entitlement or as an inextricable corollary to other rights. The courts may well halt projects that undermine the quality of life for present and future generations. Yet, procedural environmental rights are as important as their substantive counterparts. These roughly correspond to the human rights-based approach to development, mentioned in previous sections of this chapter, albeit they are specific to the RTHE. They include the right to information, participation and justice, all of which have become recurrent entitlements in soft and hard law instruments since, at least, the early 1990s.[114] Where concerned citizens are able to impart information about an existing or prospective project, which would otherwise have been confidential, possess the authority to voice their concerns and are ultimately endowed with the *locus standi* to make a claim, whether individually or collectively, it is unlikely that private polluters or a culprit state can escape detection and liability.

CASE STUDY 12.3
The *Minors Oposa* case

By the early 1990s the Philippines' tropical forests had all but dwindled as a result of uncontrolled logging. The affected communities were not given a voice in the matter and in an unprecedented suit, forty-three children, represented by their parents, lodged a complaint asking that logging licences be revoked. The children claimed that of the 16 million hectares of rain forest twenty-five years prior to the suit, only 1.2 had remained intact. The complaint alleged that deforestation not only caused an adverse effect on the communities' lives,

[111] *Vellore Citizens Welfare Forum* v. *Union of India* (1996) 5 SCC 647.
[112] *MC Mehta* v. *Union of India* (*Ganges water pollution* case) AIR (1988) SC 1037.
[113] *Farooque* v. *Bangladesh* (1997) 17 BLD (AD) 1, adopted by the Bangladesh Supreme Court; *Shehla Zia* v. *WAPDA*, PLD (1994) SC 693, adopted by the Pakistan Supreme Court; *Presidente de la sociedad MARLENE SA* v. *Municipalidad de Tibás*, Costa Rica Constitutional Court Decision no. 6918/94; *Antonio Mauricio Monroy Cespédes* case, Colombian Constitutional Court, Decision T-92/93.
[114] See e.g. principle 10 of the 1992 Rio Declaration on Environment and Development, UN Doc. A/CONF.151/26/Rev1 (14 June 1992); article 1, Aarhus Convention.

but that it moreover affected future generations and violated their right to a healthy environment. Quite clearly, the representation of the children as plaintiffs was symbolic of the rights of future generations, including the unborn.

Whereas the lower court that initially entertained the case ruled that the matter was a political one and was thus outside the ambit of the judiciary, the Supreme Court held that not only did the minors have *locus standi*, but they could moreover represent generations that were yet unborn. To the Court, the right to a healthy and balanced environment was no less important than other civil and political rights, since 'these basic rights need not even be written in the Constitution for they are assumed to exist from the inception of humankind'.[1] In this manner, it underlined the inter-dependence and indivisibility of rights.

[1] *Minors Oposa* v. *Secretary of the Dept of Environmental and Natural Resources*, Philippines Supreme Court judgment (1994) 33 ILM 173.

FURTHER READING

Alston, P. and Robinson, M. (eds.), *Human Rights and Development: Towards Mutual Reinforcement* (Oxford University Press, 2005).

Blanco, E. and Razzaque, J., 'Ecosystem Services and Human Wellbeing in a Globalised World: Assessing the Role of Law', *HRQ* 31 (2009), 692.

Bunn, I. D., The Right to Development: Implications for International Economic Law', *American University International Law Review* (*Am. U. Intl L. Rev.*) 15 (2000), 1425.

La Chimia, A. and Arrowsmith, S., 'Addressing Tied Aid: towards a More Development-oriented WTO', *Journal of International Economic Law* (*J. Int' L. Econ. L.*) 12 (2009), 707.

Fitzmaurice, M. and Marshall, J., 'The Human Right to a Clean Environment: Phantom or Reality? The European Court of Human Rights and English Courts Perspective on Balancing Rights in Environmental Matters', *NJIL* 76 (2007), 103.

Fukuda-Parr, S., 'Millennium Development Goal 8: Indicators for International Human Rights Obligations?' *HRQ* 28(2006), 966.

Ibhawoh, B., 'The Right to Development: the Politics and Polemics of Power and Resistance', *HRQ* 33 (2011), 76.

Manji, A., 'Eliminating Poverty? Financial Inclusion, Access to Land and Gender Equality in International Development', *Modern Law Review* (*MLR*) 73 (2010), 985.

Marks, S. P., *Implementing the Right to Development: The Role of International Law* (Geneva: Friedrich-Ebert-Stiftung, 2008).

Marks, S. P. and Andreassen, B. A. (eds.), *Development as a Human Right: Legal, Political and Economic Dimensions*, new edn (Antwerp: Intersentia, 2010).

Mazur, R. E., 'Realization or Deprivation of the Right to Development under Globalization? Debt, Structural Adjustment and Poverty Reduction Programs', *GeoJournal* 60 (2004), 61.

McInerney-Lankford, S. and Sano, H. O., *Human Rights Indicators in Development: An Introduction* (Washington, DC: World Bank Publications, 2010).

Meier, B. M., 'Advancing Health Rights in a Globalized World: Responding to Globalization through a Collective Human Right to Public Health', *Journal of Law, Medicine and Ethics* 35(2007), 545.

Mitlin, D. and Hickey, S., *Rights-Based Approaches to Development: Exploring the Potential and Pitfalls* (Sterling, VA: Kumarian Press, 2009).

Paulus, C. G., 'Odious Debts v. Debt Trap: a Realistic Help'?, *Brooklyn Journal of International Law* (*Brook. J. Int'l L.*) 31 (2005), 83.

Sengupta, A., 'On the Theory and Practice of the Right to Development', *HRQ* 24 (2002), 837.

Udombana, N. J., 'The Third World and the Right to Development: Agenda for a New Millennium', *HRQ* 22 (2000), 753.

13 Victims' rights and reparation

CONTENTS

13.1 INTRODUCTION

International human rights law has for a long time focused primarily on standard-setting and the establishment of institutions tasked with promoting human rights and monitoring states' compliance with their obligations. Limited attention was paid to victims as rights-holders and to the availability of effective remedies for the vindication of rights. Yet, slowly, conceptual shifts and practices, beginning at the national level, changed prevailing perceptions of victims as largely passive beneficiaries, resulting in growing calls for victims to play a more active role, particularly in the criminal justice process. The exclusion of victims and their lack of opportunity to participate effectively in proceedings that affect their rights were increasingly seen as an anomaly, raising the fundamental question of whose interests a justice system is supposed to serve.[1] This is reflected in the work of scholars and practitioners in the field of victimology and renewed interest in restorative justice.[2]

This change in thinking gained international currency initially with the 1984 UNGA Declaration of Basic Principles of Justice for Victims of Crime and Abuse of Power (hereinafter Victims' Declaration)[3] and more than twenty years later culminated in the Basic Principles and Guidelines on the Right to a Remedy and Reparation for Victims of Gross Violations of International Human Rights Law and Serious Violations of International Humanitarian Law (hereinafter Basic Principles).[4] The impetus for victims' rights owes a lot to the increasing availability of regional and international complaints procedures. The growing recourse to these procedures has enabled, if not compelled, regional and international human rights treaty bodies to develop their jurisprudence and, to varying degrees, strengthen victims' rights in the process. More recently, the establishment of international(ised) criminal tribunals, in particular the ICC, has led to a keener appreciation of victims' rights, including the right to protection and the right to participation. These developments are complemented by numerous attempts to take legal action in third countries, in particular on the grounds of universal jurisdiction, that assert and highlight the need for victims' rights in transnational proceedings. Taken together, these multiple efforts are testimony to how victims, supported by their representatives and advocacy organisations, have claimed their space in international human rights law and continue doing so in the face of a series of remaining obstacles to the vindication of their rights.

This emphasis on a victim-centred approach has not remained unchallenged. Critical observers argue that victims' politics lead to a 'privatisation' and individualisation of public concerns, feeding a growing 'victims' industry that serves to undermine the agency of individuals and groups to assert their rights as political actors.[5] These are valid concerns. However, it is important not to overlook the vital role that effective rights and remedies play for victims, considering in particular the realities of what it means to suffer serious human rights violations and grave injustices. These violations frequently have devastating consequences for the direct victim(s) and others.

---

[1] J. Doak, *Victims' Rights, Human Rights and Criminal Justice, Reconceiving the Role of Third Parties* (Oxford: Hart, 2008), 7–11.

[2] See for example the work done by the World Society of Victimology, www.worldsocietyofvictimology.org, and G. Johnstone, *Restorative Justice: Ideas, Values and Debates* (Uffculme, Devon: Willan, 2002).

[3] UNGA resolution 40/34 (29 November 1985).

[4] UNGA resolution 60/147 (16 December 2006).

[5] See on 'victims' politics' below at section 13.11.

Torture, for example, often results in lifelong physical and psychological impairment, being aimed at the destruction of the personality of its victims. Family members experience anxiety while their relative is in custody and often suffer from diminished income following the release or even death of the victim. They also have to bear the brunt of caring for and dealing with victims' attempts, which may be volatile and ultimately 'unsuccessful', to cope with the aftermath of torture without any acknowledgement of their own suffering in the process. Communities, for their part, may be in a state of fear as to who will be next, stifling the freedom of expression and action of their members.

Victims' rights, whether they take the form of a procedural right of access to justice and participation, or a substantive right to reparation, fulfil a number of important functions. Ideally, they allow victims to assert their rights, redress power imbalances manifest in violations, provide a measure of justice and furnish the victim(s) with the means to cope and rebuild their lives. They may also lead to a public acknowledgement of wrongdoing that recognises unlawful suffering, demonstrates society's respect for, and solidarity with the victim(s), and affirms the rule of law. In addition, victims' rights play an important role in contributing to prevention through deterrence (punishment and/or payment of damages or other forms of reparation) and systemic changes to counter violations, such as legislative and institutional reforms.

Notwithstanding the advancement of victims' rights and the strength of what may be called the victims' rights movement, a series of open questions and challenges remain. Do the rights granted in various treaties and declarations translate into a right to reparation under international law, and, if so, does this apply in relation to all or only some particularly serious human rights violations? Who are the rights-holders and what are their entitlements? Recent developments also raise questions of coherence and effectiveness in light of the proliferation of victims' rights in various bodies of international law, such as international human rights law, international humanitarian law and international criminal law and of the different approaches taken by various adjudicative bodies. Finally, and crucially, has the growing international recognition of these rights been matched by their effective implementation and enforcement?

13.2   THE DEVELOPMENT OF THE RIGHT TO REPARATION

Reparation is a deep-rooted and vital component of any legal order that is central to the notion of justice. It is traditionally based on the understanding that measures need to be taken to restore the order that has been disturbed by the violation. Where this is not (fully) feasible, the wrongdoer(s) must undo the wrong as much as possible to remedy the breach, a principle articulated by the PCIJ in the *Chorzów factory* case:

> The essential principle contained in the actual notion of an illegal act – a principle which seems to be established by international practice and in particular by the decisions of arbitral tribunals – is that reparation must, as far as possible, wipe-out all the consequences of the illegal act and re-establish the situation which would, in all probability, have existed if that act had not been committed.[6]

The notion that a remedy is a corollary to a right is inherent in legal systems around the world.[7] Accordingly, the victim of a breach has an individual right – which can be of a collective nature in the case of violations of group rights – to claim reparation for the harm, loss and/or other prejudices suffered as a result. However, in traditional, state-centred international law, reparation was primarily conceived as a secondary obligation owed by states to other states, not individuals, under the rules of state responsibility for a breach of a primary obligation. Even under the established rules of injury to aliens, according to which a state had to remedy a breach of an alien's rights (e.g. foreign investors), reparation was owed to the state of nationality, not the individual(s) whose rights had been violated.[8] This situation changed significantly after World War II with the recognition of a right to a remedy and reparation in various instruments, as well as reparation agreements, schemes and awards at the inter-state level for violations of human rights and humanitarian law. These parallel and to some degree mutually reinforcing developments have been instrumental in advancing the right to reparation. The latter has also been given fresh impetus by debates and measures taken in the context of political transitions. These are situations following the end of a dictatorship or a conflict that are frequently characterised by a large number of victims of gross violations committed over a long period of time, typically by multiple perpetrators often involving both state and non-state actors. Reparation fulfils a crucial role in these transitional processes. Besides vindicating rights, reparation can signal societal recognition that individuals or communities suffered wrongs, serve to restore civic trust and express solidarity with the victims.[9] Several states have provided at least some reparation in these situations, which contributes to state practice bolstering the right to reparation.[10]

---

[6] Case concerning the *Factory at Chorzów*, Claim for Indemnity, Jurisdiction (1927), PCIJ, Ser. A, no. 9.

[7] M. C. Bassiouni, 'International Recognition of Victims' Rights', *HRLR* 2 (2006), 203–79, at 206–8, and D. Shelton, *Remedies in International Human Rights Law*, 2nd edn (Oxford University Press, 2005), 22–30.

[8] See Shelton, ibid., 58–83.

[9] P. de Greiff, 'Justice and Reparations', in de Greiff (ed.), *The Handbook of Reparations* (Oxford University Press, 2006), 451–77.

[10] See case studies in Greiff, ibid., and C. Ferstman, M. Goetz and A. Stephens (eds.), *Reparations for Victims of Genocide, War Crimes and Crimes against Humanity* (Leiden, Boston: Martinus Nijhoff, 2009), Part VI.

13.3   THE RIGHT TO REPARATION IN INTERNATIONAL HUMAN RIGHTS LAW

13.3.1   Treaties and UN declarations

The right to an effective remedy for human rights violations was first recognised in article 8 UDHR: 'Everyone has the right to an effective remedy by the competent national tribunals for acts violating the fundamental rights granted him by the constitution or by law.' In a similar vein, article 2(3) ICCPR stipulates that 'any person whose rights ... are violated shall have an effective remedy'. The ICESCR has no comparable provision owing to reservations concerning the justiciability of the rights it protects.[11] Article 6 ICERD combines states parties' obligation to assure effective remedies against racial discrimination with 'the right to seek from such tribunals just and adequate reparation'. Other human rights treaties also recognise the right to reparation, or elements thereof.[12] At the regional level, article 13 ECHR stipulates that 'everyone ... shall have an effective remedy' whereas article 25 ACHR provides for a right to judicial protection and recourse that the states parties need to guarantee in their domestic legal order. The ACHPR does not stipulate an explicit right to a remedy. However, the African Commission has read such a right into article 7(1)(a) ACHPR, according to which individuals have the right to appeal against acts violating their fundamental rights.[13] The right to an effective remedy is considered non-derogable.[14] In addition, several treaties provide for a right to compensation for specific violations, such as unlawful arrest or detention,[15] miscarriage of justice[16] and the right to reparation for torture[17] and enforced disappearance, which includes an explicit right to truth.[18]

Some commentators have questioned whether an individual right to reparation has been recognised in international human rights law, arguing that relevant treaties primarily address procedural duties rather than stipulate substantive rights and that any such right can only be exercised within

[11] See section 9.6.

[12] See in particular articles 39 CRC and 24 CPED. See also articles 21 ACHPR (right of peoples to freely dispose of their wealth and natural resources) and 21 ACHR (right to property).

[13] Article 1 of the Resolution on the Right to Recourse and Fair Trial, adopted at the 11th Ordinary Session of the ACHPR in Tunis, Tunisia, in 1992.

[14] HRCtee, General Comment 29, States of Emergency (article 4), UN Doc. CCPR/C/21/Rev.1/Add.11 (31 August 2001), para. 14, and Judicial Guarantees in States of Emergency (Arts. 27(2), 25 and 8 American Convention on Human Rights), OC-9/87 (6 October 1981), paras. 23 and 41.

[15] Articles 9(5) ICCPR and 5(5) ECHR.

[16] Articles 14(6) ICCPR and 3 Protocol no. 7 to the ECHR.   [17] Article 14 CAT.

[18] Article 24 CPED.

existing proceedings before regional or international bodies.[19] However, there is a considerable body of regional and international jurisprudence in which treaty bodies and other courts have effectively interpreted the duty to grant an effective remedy as entailing that a state has to provide substantive reparation in the case of a breach of individual (or collective) rights. In addition, notwithstanding the discretionary powers of human rights treaty bodies, regional courts in particular have developed a consistent practice of awarding compensation particularly for serious violations and in the case of the IACtHR other forms of reparation. The HRCtee has made clear that '[w]ithout reparation to individuals whose Covenant rights have been violated, the obligation to provide an effective remedy, which is central to the efficacy of article 2, paragraph 3, is not discharged'.[20] Regional human rights treaty bodies and courts have developed the nature, scope and content of the right to an effective remedy and reparation in their jurisprudence, and the IACtHR in particular has repeatedly affirmed that a right to reparation flows from the Convention.[21] The jurisprudence of the Human Rights Chamber of Bosnia and Herzegovina, a hybrid human rights court composed of national and international staff mandated to apply ECHR law that was in operation from 1996 to 2003, is also noteworthy for its innovative and wide-ranging approach to ordering reparation measures.[22] In an important ruling, the ICJ affirmed the right to reparation for violations of human rights in its *Israeli Wall* advisory opinion.[23]

The UNGA has recognised the right to reparation in two landmark declarations, namely the Victims' Declaration and the Basic Principles. The latter is the culmination of sustained efforts by core states, such as Chile, the two Special Rapporteurs Professor Theo van Boven and Professor Cherif Bassiouni, and several NGOs to adopt an authoritative instrument that spells out and elaborates on international standards.[24] As a UNGA declaration the Basic Principles are not binding as such. Indeed, the text stresses their

---

[19] C. Tomuschat, *Human Rights: Between Idealism and Realism*, 2nd edn (Oxford University Press, 2008), 358–72.

[20] HRCtee, General Comment 31: Nature of the General Legal Obligation Imposed on States Parties to the Covenant, UN Doc. CCPR/C/21/Rev.1/Add.13 (26 May 2004), para. 16.

[21] See for a recent example, *Ibsen Cárdenas and Ibsen Peña* v. *Bolivia*, Merits, reparations and costs, Judgment of 1 September 2010, Ser. C, no. 217, particularly para. 226 and Part IX: Reparations.

[22] See M. Nowak, 'Reparation by the Human Rights Chamber for Bosnia and Herzegovina', in K. De Feyter *et al.* (eds.), *Out of the Ashes: Reparations for Gross Violations of Human Rights* (Antwerp, Oxford: Intersentia, 2006), 245–88.

[23] *Legal Consequences of the Construction of a Wall in the Occupied Palestinian Territory*, Advisory opinion of 9 July 2004, ICJ Reports 2004, 136, paras. 152–3.

[24] T. van Boven, 'Victims' Rights to a Remedy and Reparation: the New United Nations Principles and Guidelines', in Ferstman, above note 10, 19–40; Bassiouni, above note 7, 247–76; D. Shelton, 'The United Nations Principles and Guidelines on Reparations: Context and Contents', in De Feyter, above note 22, 11–33.

declaratory nature. This apparently cautious approach notwithstanding, the Basic Principles are suffused with the language of rights and their detailed exposition of relevant standards must be seen as an important piece of state practice that strengthens the right to reparation. The Basic Principles already exert a pull-factor that influences perceptions of reparation, treaty-making and jurisprudence. This is particularly evident in the increasing use of the language of the Basic Principles and reference to the forms of reparation stipulated therein. This is for example the case in article 24 CPED and the HRCtee's General Comment 31. It is also apparent in the practice of human rights treaty bodies, such as in decisions of the CtAT in *Guridi* v. *Spain*[25] and in the ICC context.[26]

The exercise of the right to reparation will in practice depend on the availability of legal avenues. However, this procedural challenge cannot obscure its recognition as an individual right in international human rights law, which is in principle not contingent on the existence of procedures for its enforcement.[27] This conclusion is supported by emerging practices at the inter-state and national level.[28] This finding applies in particular to gross violations of human rights as reflected in jurisprudence and the Basic Principles.[29]

13.3.2   Practice at the inter-state level

At the inter-state level, reparation for the most serious violations has its origins in war reparations.[30] German reparations to Israel and the victims of the

---

[25] *Guridi* v. *Spain*, UN Doc. CAT/C/34/D/212/2002 (17 May 2005), para. 6.8.

[26] See article 75 ICC Rome Statute. See also *Decision on victims' participation* (*Case of the Prosecutor* v. *Thomas Lubanga Dyilo*) ICC 01/04–0/06–1119 (18 January 2008), para. 92, and critical comments in Separate and Dissenting Opinion of Judge René Blattman, ibid., 49–50, paras. 4–5.

[27] See G. Echeverria, 'Do Victims of Torture and Other Serious Human Rights Violations have an Independent and Enforceable Right to Reparation?', *IJHR* 16(5) (2012), 717–36.

[28] Also H. Rombouts, P. Sardaro and S. Vandeginste, 'The Right to Reparation for Victims of Gross and Systematic Violations of Human Rights', in De Feyter, above note 22, 345–503, at 365–70. See, however, the more cautious assessment in van Boven, above note 24, 27: 'It should be recognised, however, that as transpired from the German position referred to above, there appears not to be general consensus as to the existence of a customary international law governing individual reparation claims.'

[29] As pointed out by Bassiouni, above note 7, 251, 'the terms "gross violations of international human rights law" ... should be understood to qualify situations with a view to establishing a set of facts that may figure as a basis for claims adjudication, rather than to imply a separate legal regime'. See for a discussion of the significance of the reference to gross violations also, van Boven, above note 24, 32–4, who highlights article 26 of the Basic Principles: 'it is understood that the present Principles and Guidelines are without prejudice to the right to a remedy and reparation for all violations of international human rights law and international humanitarian law'.

[30] Note the difference in terminology: whereas reparation is frequently used to denote the various forms of reparation, the word reparations has traditionally been used in the context of payments and other measures to compensate/repair (for) war related damages.

Holocaust must count as the most important example of inter-state reparations, both in terms of the seriousness of the violations and their scale. Until
the 1990s such inter-state reparations had been largely dealt with bilaterally,
with the understanding that individuals had no right to claim reparation
for violations covered in these agreements. However, litigation in the US
in Holocaust-related cases and in Switzerland in relation to German war
crimes during World War II have strengthened the position of individuals
and resulted in the setting up of reparation programmes for the benefit of
victims, such as in respect of slave and forced labour.[31] This development is
also evident in the setting up of compensation commissions and reparation
programmes in cases of mass violations other than the Holocaust, such as the
UN Compensation Commission (Iraq–Kuwait) and the Eritrea and Ethiopia
Claims Commission (in relation to the 1998 war). Operating at an inter-state
level through the UN or on the basis of bilateral agreements these commissions provide that the states (parties) may bring claims on their own behalf
or on behalf of their nationals.[32]

Reparation for violations of human rights and humanitarian law has
also been awarded in a growing number of inter-state cases. This includes
Cyprus v. *Turkey* before the ECtHR, the *Democratic Republic of Congo (DRC)*
v. *Burundi, Rwanda and Uganda* before the African Commission, as well as
DRC v. *Uganda* and *Republic of Guinea* v. *DRC* (*Ahmadou Sadio Diallo* case)
before the ICJ.[33] In these cases, reparation was due to the state successfully
claiming a violation of individual rights and/or of the obligations of the
adversarial party. Significantly, the ruling by the African Commission in *DRC*

---

[31] Foundation Remembrance, Responsibility and Future, www.stiftung-evz.de. See R. Bank,
'The New Programs for Payments to Victims of National Socialist Injustice', *German
Yearbook of International Law* (*GYBIL*) 44 (2001), at 307–52. See also the case study on
Holocaust and World War II reparations below at 13.12.

[32] The UN Compensation Commission, which operated from 1991 to 2007, received 'more
than 2.6 million claims seeking a total of approximately US$368 billion', submitted by
governments on behalf of nationals, corporations or themselves, and by UN agencies
on behalf of other individuals. See www.uncc.ch, and L. A. Taylor, 'The United Nations
Compensation Commission', in Ferstman, above note 10, 197–214. The Eritrea-Ethiopia
Claims Commission was based on a bilateral agreement signed in Algiers on 12 December
2000, pursuant to which the parties may bring claims on their own behalf and on behalf
of their nationals (natural and juridical persons) before the Permanent Court of Arbitration
against the government of (or entities controlled and owned by) the other party. See www.
pca-cpa.org/showpage.asp?pag_id=1151.

[33] *Cyprus* v. *Turkey*, (2002) 35 EHRR 30; case concerning *Armed Activities on the Territory
of the Congo* (*Democratic Republic of the Congo* v. *Uganda*) Judgment 2005, ICJ Reports
2008, 168 and *Ahmadou Sadio Diallo, Republic of Guinea* v. *Democratic Republic of Congo*
(Compensation owed by the Democratic Republic of the Congo to the Republic of Guinea),
ICJ Judgment of 19 June 2012. See also C. McCarthy, 'Reparation for Gross Violations
of Human Rights Law and International Humanitarian Law at the International Court of
Justice', in Ferstman, above note 10, 283–311.

v. *Burundi, Rwanda and Uganda* specified that the victims of violations of human rights and humanitarian law should be the ultimate beneficiaries of any reparation made. The emerging jurisprudence is an important development. It may indicate a greater willingness of states to claim human rights violations (even though such claims may be largely or solely politically motivated) and provide victims with an additional avenue. The 2012 ICJ judgment awarding compensation in the *Diallo* case sets an important precedent, albeit a series of open questions remain regarding the rights of victims in the course of such proceedings and at the enforcement stage.

13.3.3   State practice at the national and transitional level

Although state practice is far from uniform, most states recognise some form of constitutional or statutory right to reparation in cases amounting to violations of human rights. Individuals, and groups of victims, have been awarded compensation and other forms of reparation in various jurisdictions, for example in landmark cases such as *Nilabati Behera* v. *State of Orissa* in India for a violation of the right to life (death in custody).[34] In a more recent development a number of states have set up reparation schemes for violations of human rights (and humanitarian law) following the end of conflict or dictatorship.[35] An increasing number of suits brought by individuals in third countries, besides contributing to state practice, have raised the question of the jurisdictional reach of the right to reparation, namely whether it requires states to establish jurisdiction in such cases. The US Alien Torts Claim Act of 1789, though evidently not adopted for that purpose at the time, has become the most prominent legal basis for bringing human rights claims for wrongful acts committed in third countries.[36] This is ironic given that the USA entered a reservation to the effect that it understands article 14 CAT to 'provide a private right of action for damages only for acts of torture committed in territory under the jurisdiction of that State Party'. It is open to question, in the absence of explicit treaty provisions, whether states have an obligation to establish jurisdiction that enables victims of violations to bring claims for wrongful acts committed in third countries. Several states and commentators have opposed such an interpretation of article 14 CAT on

---

[34] *Nilabati Behera alias Lalita Behera* v. *State of Orissa and Others*, (1993) 2 SCC 746; Writ Petition (Civil) no. 488 of 1988.

[35] See for detailed case studies of reparation schemes in Argentina, Brazil, Chile and South Africa, de Greiff, above note 9, and in Colombia, East Timor, Guatemala and Sierra Leone, C. Evans, *The Right to Reparation in International Law for Victims of Armed Conflict* (Cambridge University Press, 2012).

[36] M. Swan, 'International Human Rights Tort Claims and the Experience of United States Courts: an Introduction to the US Case Law, Key Statutes and Doctrines', in C. Scott (ed.), *Torture as Tort: Comparative Perspectives on the Development of Transnational Tort Litigation* (Oxford: Hart, 2001), 65–107.

the ground that the obligations of states parties are confined to their jurisdiction unless otherwise indicated.[37] Yet the text of article 14 CAT could equally be read to apply to all torture victims and a teleological (purposive) interpretation of the Convention to this effect would be in line with its objective of combating torture worldwide. The CtAT in its draft general comment considered 'that obligations of States parties under article 14 are not limited to victims who were harmed in the territory of the State party or by or against nationals of the State party. The Committee has praised the efforts of States parties for providing civil remedies for victims who were subjected to torture or ill-treatment outside their territory.'[38] However, even where states provide for such jurisdiction, claimants frequently face immunity as an insurmountable barrier to holding states accountable.[39]

13.4   THE   RIGHT   TO   REPARATION   IN   INTERNATIONAL HUMANITARIAN LAW

The right to reparation has a less secure standing in international humanitarian law. Article 3 of the Hague Convention (IV) of 1907 stipulates that belligerents are 'liable to pay compensation' for violations of its provisions. Article 91 of the 1977 Additional Protocol I to the 1949 Conventions similarly provides that 'A Party to the conflict which violates the provisions of the Conventions or of this Protocol shall, if the case demands, be liable to pay compensation.' However, there are no provisions in humanitarian law treaties that explicitly stipulate a corresponding individual right. Nor is there any treaty body tasked with hearing complaints and recommending or awarding reparation. This turns the focus sharply to international customary law. Those sceptical of the existence of a right to reparation under international humanitarian law point to the limited jurisprudence, in particular the judgment of the German Federal Supreme Court in the *Distomo Massacre* case, which ruled out such a right.[40] The lack of explicit recognition in other sources is also mentioned.[41] Proponents of such a right argue that international humanitarian law recognises the duty to provide reparation.[42] This has

---

[37] See B. Fassbender, 'Can Victims Sue State Officials for Torture? Reflections on Rasul v. Myers from the Perspective of International Law', *JICJ* 6(2) (2008), 347–69.

[38] See CtAT, Draft General Comment on the obligation of States Parties to implement article 14, Working Document presented at its Forty-sixth session (9 May–3 June 2011), para. 20.

[39] See section 14.9.1.

[40] German Supreme Court, *Distomo Massacre* case, BGH-III ZR 245/98 (26 June 2003).

[41] According to Tomuschat, above note 19, 367–70, the right to reparation has not been recognised in international humanitarian law.

[42] See R. Bank and E. Schwager, 'Is there a Substantive Right to Compensation for Individual Victims of Armed Conflict against a State under International Law?', *GYBIL* 49 (2006), 367–412; L. Zegveld, 'Remedies for Victims of Violations of International Humanitarian Law',

been upheld in the jurisprudence of several courts, in particular in the Netherlands, Greece and Italy.[43] The ICJ in the *Israeli wall* advisory opinion and in *DRC* v. *Uganda* equally ruled that states have to provide reparation – 'to natural or legal persons' (*Wall* case) – for violations of international humanitarian law.[44] The fact that *ad hoc* claims commissions, such as the UNCC and the Eritrea and Ethiopia Claims Commission, are set up for the benefit of individual victims is referred to as further evidence of the recognition of the right by the Co-Rapporteur of the ILA's draft declaration of international law principles on compensation for victims of war.[45] The inclusion of the right to reparation for (serious) violations of international humanitarian law in the Basic Principles and the growing convergence of international human rights law and international humanitarian law in international jurisprudence constitute an important development. However, actual practice is still limited and some states continue to resist recognising the right to reparation for violations of international humanitarian law.

13.5   THE RIGHT TO REPARATION IN INTERNATIONAL CRIMINAL LAW

International criminal law has traditionally been concerned with the proscription, prosecution and punishment of crimes of international concern. Victims' rights were largely ignored until the adoption of the ICC Rome Statute. The sole provision of the ICTY (and ICTR) on reparation, rule 106(c) of the Rules of Procedure and Evidence, provides that for the purpose of a claim made in national proceedings, to which the victims were referred, 'the judgment of the Tribunal shall be final and binding as to the criminal responsibility of the convicted person for such injury'. It very soon became clear that this rule was inadequate. Voices calling for the Tribunal to play a greater role in awarding reparation were, in hindsight, prescient but premature.[46] It was only concerted efforts of international NGO coalitions and a

---

IRRC 851 (2003), 497–526; R. Hofman, 'Draft Declaration of International Law Principles on Compensation for Victims of War (Substantive Issues)', in International Law Association, *Compensation for Victims of War* (Rio de Janeiro Conference, 2008), 2–20. See also *Report of the International Commission of Inquiry on Darfur to the United Nations Secretary-General pursuant to Security Council resolution 1564 of 18 September 2004* (Geneva: United Nations, 25 January 2005), paras. 593–8.

[43] See Hofman, above note 42, 9–11.

[44] *Legal Consequences of the Construction of a wall in the occupied Palestinian Territory* (*Wall* case), Advisory opinion, ICJ Reports 2004, p. 136, paras. 149–53, and *DRC* v. *Uganda*, para. 259.

[45] Hofman, above note 42, 11–12.

[46] See suggestions to this effect by Judge Jorda, the then President of the ICTY and Judge Pillay, the then President of the ICTR, in UN Doc. S/2000/1063 (3 November 2000) and Letter of 14 December 2000 of the UN Secretary-General, addressed to the President of the Security Council, UN Doc. S/2000/1198 (15 December 2000) respectively.

greater willingness to acknowledge victims and their rights in proceedings that paved the way for the current ICC regime, which is a milestone as it anchors the right to reparation firmly in international criminal law.

The ICC's reparation regime differs from that of international human rights law in some important respects.[47] In contrast to violations of human rights, reparation is not owed by the state but the individual liable for the commission of international crimes falling within the ICC's jurisdiction. The Court may, pursuant to article 75(2) of the Rome Statute, make an order awarding reparation either directly against the convicted person or through the Trust Fund for the Victims of Crime set up in article 79. The Trust Fund, which relies on voluntary contributions and fines collected, is an important structure within the Court's system. It can provide both financial assistance to victims of crimes and reparation in respect of a specific case as set out in article 75. The reparation regime is at its early stages and is still to be developed by the Court with many questions awaiting resolution, an open-ended list of which may include who falls within the category of victims that may benefit from reparation awards? What are the modalities of claiming reparation? What notion of reparation will the Court apply in its jurisprudence? And how effective will it be in implementing measures and enforcing awards?[48]

Reparation under the ICC Rome Statute is owed by the individual and not the state or other entities even though the latter may bear responsibility under international law. This may lead to the individualisation of reparation and result in discrepancies in cases where state responsibility cannot be established in other fora. It also presents considerable practical challenges for the Court, particularly on how to provide reparation to a large number of victims of the most serious crimes with limited means available. However, the challenges also bear considerable potential for the Court and the Trust Fund to develop the right to reparation in the context of international criminal law and thereby contribute to further cross-fertilisation in the broader international law context.

13.6   THE RIGHT TO REPARATION AND VIOLATIONS BY NON-STATE ACTORS

As a general principle, a state is not responsible for violations by non-state actors unless it exercises effective control, colludes, acquiesces (in) or endorses

---

[47] See C. Ferstman, 'The Reparation Regime of the International Criminal Court: Practical Considerations', *LJIL* 15 (2002), 667–86.

[48] See C. Ferstman and M. Goetz, 'Reparations before the International Criminal Court: the Early Jurisprudence on Victim Participation and its Impact on Future Reparation Proceedings', in Ferstman, above note 10, 313–50, and REDRESS, *Justice for Victims: The ICC's Reparation Mandate* (London: REDRESS, 2012).

such violations.[49] A state will, however, be responsible for a breach of its positive obligations in respect of acts committed by non-state actors, for example failing to investigate violations such as forced disappearance where the identity of the perpetrators is unknown.[50] However, there will be situations where non-state actors, such as armed groups, have committed serious violations such as mass rape or killings but the state concerned will not incur liability and nor will the victims be able to obtain reparation from the perpetrators. It is with this constellation in mind that the Basic Principles exhort states to 'endeavour to establish national programmes for reparation and other assistance to victims in the event that the parties liable for the harm suffered are unable or unwilling to meet their obligations'.

13.7   THE RIGHT TO REPARATION FOR HISTORICAL INJUSTICES AND VIOLATIONS

The fact that international crimes and human rights, including the right to reparation, are relatively speaking latecomers to international law has thrown up particular challenges in relation to past injustices. Claims for reparation have in this context in particular been made for slavery and colonialism either as unjust practices in their own right or in relation to specific incidents. Examples of the latter are the massacres of the Herero by Germany in the first decade of the twentieth century and various violations attributed to the British forces in the context of the Mau Mau uprising in Kenya during the 1950s.[51] Although the documented facts of these cases appear to support reparation claims, there are a series of legal, policy, political and practical obstacles to be overcome. The acts committed were in many instances not recognised as international crimes or human rights violations at the time so that the law would have to be applied retroactively, unless national law provides otherwise.[52] Even where responsibility of a

---

[49] See in particular articles 4–11 ILC Draft Articles on Responsibility of States for internationally wrongful acts and the provisions of human rights treaties, such as article 1 CAT. Article 10 of the Draft Articles provides for a further exception where insurgents become the new government or succeed in establishing a new state. See Chapter 16 on the responsibility of NSAs.

[50] *Velásquez Rodríguez* v. *Honduras*, Merits, Judgment of 29 July 1988, Ser. C, no. 4, paras. 172–7.

[51] J. Sarkin, *Colonial Genocide and Reparations Claims in the 21st Century: The Socio-Legal Context of Claims under International Law by the Herero against Germany for Genocide in Namibia, 1904–1908* (Westport, CT: Greenwood, 2009), and the Mau Mau reparations claims in the UK, see I. Cobain, 'Mau Mau Veterans Launch Second Round of Legal Action', *The Guardian* (16 July 2012).

[52] See for a discussion of the legal challenges posed by retroactivity, M. Bossuyt and S. Vandeginste, 'The Issue of Reparation for Slavery and Colonialism and the Durban World Conference against Racism', *HRLJ* 22(9/12) (2001), 341–50.

particular state can be established, difficulties abound, especially identifying the rights-holders (beneficiaries). This is important if states were to be designated as recipients of any compensation so as to ensure that the descendants of victims or a people as a whole were to benefit.[53] An official recognition of the (historical) wrong and a fund may be best suited to provide adequate forms of reparation in this regard. However, the 2008 'deal' between Italy and Libya amply demonstrates the political dimension of addressing past injustices. Italy's move to pay Libya $5 billion and apologise for the damage inflicted during its colonial rule was widely seen as an opportunity for Italy to strengthen its strategic relationship with Libya and for the latter to obtain some benefits and enhance its international standing.[54] While remarkable, agreements of this kind appear to turn colonialism or slavery into a pretext that masks cruder current interests. It is indeed questionable to what degree, if at all, they address the nature and legacy of violations and provide acknowledgement and reparation to those whose ancestors suffered or who personally continue to suffer from the long-term effects of past injustices.

QUESTIONS

1   In his critique of the findings of the International Commission of Inquiry on Darfur, Professor Christian Tomuschat argued that 'there is no customary international law rule governing individual reparation claims'.[55] What evidence is there to support or counter this assertion?

2   Do victims of violations have a right under international law to bring reparation claims in countries other than where the violation occurred?

3   Does state practice support the assertion that international law recognises the right to reparation for serious violations of international humanitarian law?

4   Can there be a right to reparation against the state where the violation has been committed by non-state actors?

5   Does the current international legal framework provide an adequate basis for arguing reparation claims for slavery and colonialism?

---

[53]   See for a discussion of appropriate forms of reparations, M. Du Plessis, 'Reparations and International Law: How are Reparations to be determined (Past Wrong or Current Effects), Against Whom, and What Form should they take?', in M. Du Plessis and S. Peté (eds.), *Repairing the Past? International Perspectives on Reparations for Gross Human Rights Abuses* (Antwerp, Oxford: Intersentia, 2007), 147–77.

[54]   See Colonialism Reparation, *Italy–Libya* (undated), online, at, http://www.colonialismreparation.org/en/reparations/italy-libya.html.

[55]   C. Tomuschat, 'Darfur: Compensation for the Victims', *JICJ* 3(3) (2005), 579–89.

13.8   THE NOTION AND LEGAL SIGNIFICANCE OF THE TERM 'VICTIM'

In legal terms, the status of a 'victim' confers certain entitlements, namely the right to a remedy and reparation. It is also frequently equated with standing to bring claims and exercise procedural rights.[56] By that token it demarcates legal boundaries. The term 'victim' distinguishes between those whose suffering is recognised as giving rise to the right to reparation, for example where it results from arbitrary detention, and others whose suffering does not entail the same legal consequences, as would normally be the case with persons suffering harm due to economic misfortune, riots or natural disasters. The notion of victim is associated with suffering and sacrifice. This understanding is reflected in legal definitions of 'victim', such as that found in the Basic Principles and the ICC Rules of Procedure and Evidence, which refers to persons who suffer harm as a result of a violation or of having intervened to prevent victimisation (which is particularly important for human rights defenders).[57] Such harm may consist of 'physical or mental injury, emotional suffering, economic loss or substantial impairment of … fundamental rights' (Basic Principles), which may have been suffered in an individual or collective capacity, as well as by natural and, to some extent, legal persons.[58]

QUESTIONS

1 What is the legal significance of the term 'victim'?

2 Does the determination of 'victim' status depend on subjective or objective criteria?

---

[56] See section 7.2.1.

[57] Principle 8 of the Basic Principles: 'For purposes of the present document, victims are persons who individually or collectively suffered harm, including physical or mental injury, emotional suffering, economic loss or substantial impairment of their fundamental rights, through acts or omissions that constitute gross violations of international human rights law, or serious violations of international humanitarian law. Where appropriate, and in accordance with domestic law, the term "victim" also includes the immediate family or dependants of the direct victim and persons who have suffered harm in intervening to assist victims in distress or to prevent victimization.' Rule 85 of the 2002 ICC Rules of Procedure and Evidence: 'For the purposes of the Statute and the Rules of Procedure and Evidence: (a) 'Victims' means natural persons who have suffered harm as a result of the commission of any crime within the jurisdiction of the Court; (b) Victims may include organizations or institutions that have sustained direct harm to any of their property which is dedicated to religion, education, art or science or charitable purposes, and to their historic monuments, hospitals and other places and objects for humanitarian purposes.'

[58] Ibid. and section 7.2.1.

13.9   THE PROCEDURAL RIGHT TO AN EFFECTIVE REMEDY

13.9.1   Overview

The right to an effective remedy requires that victims, individually or collectively, are able to have recourse to avenues, be they judicial or otherwise, capable of redressing the alleged violation as a means of vindicating their rights. In cases of serious violations a remedy has to be of a judicial nature.[59] This requirement is of particular importance when designing reparation mechanisms that may restrict recourse to courts.[60]

Available remedies 'must be "effective" in practice as well as in law, in particular in the sense that [their] exercise must not be unjustifiably hindered by acts or omissions by the authorities of the respondent State'.[61] This formula opens the door for a host of measures that states need to take in order to ensure the effective exercise of the right to a remedy, a task that constitutes a challenge for any legal system. Besides granting the right to pursue claims for violations, states must guarantee and protect the administration of justice, including an independent judiciary, without which remedies will not be effective. Equally, it requires the absence of laws and/or jurisprudence that hinder the exercise of remedies, such as amnesties or immunities that bar the lodging of claims against the individual perpetrators or the state, or both.[62] In addition, statutes of limitation must not be unduly short as victims often experience displacement, financial hardship, trauma or other circumstances that prevent them from seeking timely recourse to available remedies.[63] An example of such an unduly short time limit is Nepal's Compensation of Torture Act according to which victims need to bring a claim within thirty-five days.[64] Moreover, the administration of claims relating to alleged violations must not be subject to undue delays and the legal system must ensure enforcement of any awards or decisions made.[65] Beyond this, states should take a range of additional steps, as specified in the Basic Principles. This involves disseminating information about available remedies, taking measures to minimise inconvenience and provide protection. It also encompasses the provision of assistance and making available other legal, diplomatic and

---

[59] *Bautista* v. *Colombia*, UN Doc. CCPR/C/55/D/563/1993 (27 October 1995), para. 8.2.

[60] This is of particular importance in the transitional context, *Rule-of-law Tools for Post Conflict States: Reparations Programmes* (New York, Geneva: United Nations, 2008), 34–6.

[61] *Aksoy* v. *Turkey*, (1996) 23 EHRR 553, para. 95.

[62] HRCtee, General Comment 31, UN Doc. CCPR/C/21/Rev.1/Add.13 (26 May 2004), para. 18.

[63] Ibid.   [64] Article 5(1) Compensation for Torture Act, 1996.

[65] See HRCtee, General Comment 32, UN Doc. CCPR/C/GC/32 (23 August 2007); REDRESS, *Waiting for Justice: The Politics of Delays in the Administration of Justice in Torture Cases: Practice, Standards and Responses* (London: REDRESS, 2008).

consular means so that victims can have effective access to justice.[66] These measures are particularly important in respect of marginalised groups or victims such as women in cases of sexual violence, given that they are often unaware of their rights, impoverished, stigmatised, discriminated against and/or reluctant to exercise their rights in formal settings.[67]

The right to bring criminal complaints is an integral part of the right to an effective remedy. In practice, however, victims of human rights violations frequently encounter obstacles that hamper their right to pursue complaints effectively. To counter this, states have to put in place an effective legal and institutional framework with a view to investigating violations, which includes the establishment of effective oversight bodies. Conversely, states may not take measures incompatible with their obligation to investigate serious violations effectively, such as amnesties, immunities and/or unreasonably short statutes of limitation.[68] There is often a close nexus between the two sets of remedies. The prospect of pursuing civil remedies and obtaining reparation is in many countries dependant on a criminal conviction, either by law or in practice. Where impunity is rife victims of violations are effectively deprived of any effective remedies. It is for this reason that victims should be able to pursue civil claims independently and irrespective of the outcome of criminal proceedings to ensure at least a measure of justice.

13.9.2   The nexus between civil and criminal proceedings: *Rajapakse* v. *Sri Lanka*

Mr Rajapakse,[69] who had claimed that he had suffered torture at the hands of the Sri Lankan police in April 2002 filed a fundamental rights petition before the Sri Lankan Supreme Court in May 2002. The hearings before the Supreme Court had been repeatedly postponed up to the point when the HRCtee decided the case in March 2005:

The Human Rights Committee observes that, as the delay in the author's fundamental rights application to the Supreme Court is dependant upon the determination of the High Court [criminal] case, the delay in determining the latter is relevant for its assessment of whether the author's rights under the Covenant were violated. It notes

---

[66] See in this regard in particular *LaGrand* (*Germany* v. *United States of America*) Judgment, ICJ Reports 2001, p. 466; case concerning *Avena and other Mexican Nationals* (*Mexico* v. *United States of America*), Judgment, ICJ Reports 2004, 12. See also J. R. Dugard, Special Rapporteur, First Report on Diplomatic Protection, UN Doc. A/CN.4/506 (7 March 2000), in particular comments on draft article 4, paras. 75–93. His proposal that there should be a right to diplomatic protection in cases of violations of *jus cogens* rights has not been endorsed by states to date.

[67] Report of the Special Rapporteur on torture and other cruel, inhuman or degrading treatment or punishment, UN Doc. A/HRC/7/3 (15 January 2008), paras. 61–2.

[68] HRCtee, General Comment 31, para. 18.

[69] UN Doc. CCPR/C/87/D/1250/2004 (14 July 2006).

the State party's argument that the author is currently availing himself of domestic remedies. The Committee observes that the criminal investigation was not initiated by the Attorney General until over three months after the incident, despite the fact that the author had to be hospitalised, was unconscious for 15 days, and had a medical report describing his injuries, which was presented to the Magistrates Court on 17 May 2002.

The HRCtee went on to find a violation of article 2(3) in connection with article 7 ICCPR:

Under article 2, paragraph 3, the State party has an obligation to ensure that remedies are effective. Expedition and effectiveness are particularly important in the adjudication of cases involving torture. The general information provided by the State party on the workload of the domestic courts would appear to indicate that the High Court proceedings and, thus, the author's Supreme Court fundamental rights case will not be determined for some time. The Committee considers that the State party may not avoid its responsibilities under the Covenant with the argument that the domestic courts are dealing with the matter, when it is clear that the remedies relied upon by the State party have been prolonged and would appear to be ineffective.

QUESTION

1 Why are non-judicial remedies considered inadequate in cases of serious violations of human rights?

13.10   THE SUBSTANTIVE RIGHT TO REPARATION

13.10.1   State responsibility

Under the rules of state responsibility states have a secondary duty in case of a breach to cease the illegal conduct, offer assurances of non-repetition and 'to make full reparation for the injury caused by the internationally wrongful act'.[70] Such reparation 'shall take the form of restitution, compensation and satisfaction, either singly or in combination'.[71] These rules provide the broader legal framework within which the right to reparation for violations of human rights and humanitarian law has developed.

13.10.2   Liability

In a typical case, violations are committed by individual officers acting on behalf of the state (see 13.6 above for violations committed by NSAs). This constellation gives rise to questions about the nature of liability of the offending

---

[70] Article 31 ILC Draft Articles on State Responsibility.   [71] Article 34 ibid.

individual and the state and the relationship between the two. Some legal systems provide for the primary if not sole liability of the individual officer responsible.[72] This may be justified by arguing that the state (and the taxpayer) should not be burdened with expenses incurred because of the wrongdoing of its officials. The prospect of having to pay substantial amounts of reparation personally can also act as deterrent for individual officers and thus have a preventive effect. The rationale for such individual liability is sound. However, the rule is disadvantageous to victims claiming reparation because individual officers are often not in a position to pay substantial compensation or may evade personal responsibility. The focus on individual liability also obscures the ultimate responsibility of the state on whose behalf individual officers act. A system that provides for primary state liability or vicarious liability is therefore better suited to address these concerns as it enables a victim of a violation to have recourse against the state. At the same time, the state would be entitled to claim back any reparation made from the individual officer(s) concerned.[73]

13.10.3   Standard of reparation

The Basic Principles speak of 'full and effective' reparation. However, if read in light of the qualifying clause 'as appropriate and proportional to the gravity of the violation and the circumstances of each case', it is clear that the standards provide states, adjudicative and other bodies with some latitude in determining reparation. This contextual nature of reparation is equally evident in the provisions vesting regional courts with discretionary power to award reparation.[74] The potential for arbitrariness of awards is in theory circumscribed by qualifying standards: reparation should as a general rule reflect the seriousness of the violation and be such the violation is remedied as much as possible in the circumstances. They are also key principles safeguarding against inappropriate awards. Reparation should be victim-oriented and non-discriminatory, which has important implications for gender and reparation that need to be taken into consideration by courts and other bodies.[75]

---

[72] See findings in the comparative study, REDRESS, *Reparation for Torture: A Survey of Law and Practice in Thirty Selected Countries* (London: REDRESS, 2003), 47–8.

[73] Principle 15 of the Basic Principles.

[74] See articles 41 ECHR, 63 ACHR and 27(1) of the ACHPR Protocol on the Establishment of an African Court on Human and Peoples' Rights, which stipulates that: 'If the Court finds that there has been violation of a human or peoples' rights, it shall make appropriate orders to remedy the violation, including the payment of fair compensation or reparation.'

[75] A. Saris and K. Lofts, 'Reparation Programmes: a Gendered Perspective', in Ferstman, above note 10, 79–100.

13.10.4   Forms of reparation

Reparation is often equated and confused with compensation. Such a narrow view is misleading notwithstanding the undeniable importance of compensation. It ignores the distinctive but interrelated functions that the various forms of reparation may serve. A victim of a violation will need the financial means and access to services to cope with the harm suffered. He or she will also seek to restore the dignity and integrity infringed by the violation, which typically calls for acknowledgement of the wrongdoing and sanctions against the perpetrators.[76] Furthermore, victims and society as a whole have an interest in seeking prevention of similar violations, which requires measures aimed at non-repetition. The various forms of reparation can be distinguished into material and non-material (moral), remedial and preventive measures of an individual or collective nature. These distinctions can help to conceptualise the types and functions of reparation measures but should not distract from a broader understanding of reparation as a process and outcome that is both holistic and responsive to context. These considerations are reflected in the Basic Principles that recognise five forms of reparation, namely restitution, compensation, rehabilitation, satisfaction and guarantees of non-repetition.

13.10.5   Restitution

Restitution is the classic form of reparation. Where restitution is feasible, namely where the harm inflicted by the violation can still be reversed, it may be sufficient to remedy a violation, together with an acknowledgment of wrongdoing (and/or compensation for any irreversible harm suffered). Restitution may consist of the following measures:

1   restoration of liberty (release): where individuals have been arbitrarily detained (or wrongfully convicted in which case the appropriate remedy may be either release or a retrial), such as in the ECtHR landmark case of *Assanidze* v. *Georgia*[77] and in the IACtHR case of *Loayza Tamayo* v. *Peru*.[78] As states have a primary duty to cease ongoing violations, remedial measures taken in such instances may strictly speaking not be classified as reparation. However, measures taken to end ongoing violations such as arbitrary detention serve a dual purpose, namely cessation and undoing a wrong, and are for this reason frequently included as forms of reparation;

---

[76]   See in this context, Y. Danieli, 'Massive Trauma and the Healing Role of Reparative Justice', in Ferstman, above note 10, 41–77.

[77]   *Assanidze* v. *Georgia*, (2004) 39 EHRR 653, paras. 202–3.

[78]   *Loayza Tamayo* v. *Peru*, Merits, 17 September 1997, Ser. C, no. 33, para. 84.

2 restoration of employment: where political opponents have been deprived of their employment rights, such as for example during the dictatorships in Argentina and Chile, or workers have been dismissed in violation of their rights, such as in *Baena-Ricardo* v. *Panama*;[79]

3 restoration of identity and citizenship: where citizens have been expelled and/or stripped of their citizenship, for example in *Modise* v. *Botswana*;[80]

4 return to one's place of residence: where individuals and groups of persons have been forcibly displaced, for example in Darfur, Sudan, since 2002;[81]

5 return of property: where property has been expropriated or seized, for example in *Papamichalopoulos* v. *Greece*.[82] Restitution and/or compensation – where return of property is not feasible – for violations of the right to property are particularly important in former Communist countries, as evident in the cases of *Brumărescu* v. *Romania* and *Broniowski* v. *Poland*,[83] as well as in Bosnia and Kosovo.[84]

13.10.6 Compensation

Compensation is in practice one of the most important forms of reparation. It is often seemingly taken for granted that compensation is beneficial and in the interest of victims, particularly where it provides the means to address the adverse consequences of violations. In economic terms, compensation makes violations costly for the perpetrators and may have a deterrent effect. However, victims often see compensation as an insufficient form of reparation where it is not accompanied by acknowledgment and/or accountability. Moreover, even where compensation is paid, the amount of compensation is frequently contested and perceived to be inadequate.

13.10.7 Types of damages

The components of compensation are similar to what is familiar in most domestic legal systems and can be said to constitute general principles of law. Compensation includes any economically assessable damages, comprising

---

[79] *Baena-Ricardo* v. *Panama*, Merits, reparations and costs, Judgment of 2 February 2001, Ser. C, no. 72, para. 203.

[80] See case study 6.1.

[81] Darfur Peace Agreement (5 May 2006), article 21: Urgent Programmes for Internally Displaced Persons (IDPs), Refugees and Other War-Affected Persons and Compensation for War Affected Persons, and Chapter IV of the Doha Document for Peace in Darfur (14 July 2011).

[82] *Papamichalopoulos* v. *Greece*, (1996) 21 EHRR 439.

[83] *Brumărescu* v. *Romania*, (2001) 33 EHRR 35; *Broniowski* v. *Poland*, (2006) 43 EHRR 1.

[84] See in this context, C. Ferstman and S. P. Rosenberg, 'Reparations in Dayton's Bosnia and Herzegovina', in Ferstman, above note 10, 483–514.

both material (pecuniary) and moral (non-pecuniary) damages. Material damages include, as specified in the Basic Principles: lost opportunities (including employment, education and social benefits); loss of earnings (including loss of earning potential); and costs required for legal or expert assistance, medicine and medical services, as well as psychological and social services. Non-material loss or moral damages are meant to compensate for harm, pain and suffering, including mental anguish, humiliation and a sense of injustice.

Punitive or exemplary damages known in particular in Anglo-American jurisprudence have not been expressly recognised by regional or international treaty bodies or courts as they go beyond compensating the actual damage caused.[85] Such damages are meant to express the public condemnation of the violation and to have a punitive and deterrent effect. Clearly, punitive or exemplary damages can be of symbolic and practical value as policy-oriented jurisprudence. However, the award of such damages does not neatly fit into the relationship between the violation and the harm caused as recognised in international law.[86] In addition, if bodies were to follow such practice it could be expected to meet considerable resistance from states parties.

The general principles governing the award of compensation are well developed in national, regional and international jurisprudence. However, determining the amount of compensation is still fraught with difficulties. This amount is highly charged. As the 'bottom line' it expresses the adjudicative body's valuation of the violation. It quantifies the suffering of the victim(s) and specifies the sum payable by the state. The ECtHR and the IACtHR are the only two international human rights bodies that have awarded specific amounts of compensation for both pecuniary and non-pecuniary harm.[87] They have awarded material damages on an equitable basis where the applicants provided sufficient proof that costs or losses had been, or would be, incurred as a result of the violation. Moral damages have been awarded in particular for serious violations in respect of which a presumption applies that they cause harm and suffering.[88] In determining quantum, courts have

---

[85] *Velásquez Rodrígues* v. *Honduras*, Interpretation of the compensatory damages, Judgment of 17 August 1990, Ser. C, no. 9, para. 38, and *Selçuk, and Asker* v. *Turkey*, (1998) 26 EHRR 477, para. 119.

[86] Although Rombouts, above note 28, 390, rightly point out that 'the fact that human rights courts do take into account the gravity of the violation for quantifying the damages might suggest that damages have a purpose that is not merely reparative'.

[87] In a noteworthy development, the ECOWAS Community Court of Justice has recently awarded specific amounts of compensation for human rights violations, namely in *Hadijatou Mani Koraou* v. *Niger*, Appl. no. ECW/CCJ/APP/08/08, Judgment no. ECN/CCJ/JUP/06/08 (27 October 2008), for violation of the prohibition of slavery. See also *Chief Ebrima Manneh* v. *The Republic of the Gambia*, Appl. no. ECW/CCJ/APP/04/07, ECW/CCJ/JUD/03/08 (5 June 2008), for violation of the right to liberty and security.

[88] *Caracazo* v. *Venezuela*, Reparations and costs, Judgment of 29 August 2002, Ser. C, no. 95, para. 50(e).

utilised factors such as the degree of suffering, the egregiousness of the violation(s), the number of violations as well as the characteristics (e.g. vulnerable children) and conduct of the parties concerned.[89]

It is difficult to quantify specific types of violations but the awards rendered provide an indication of the amounts commonly granted.[90] The ICJ, in its first judgment of this kind, awarded compensation for material and non-material injury for arbitrary detention and unlawful expulsion in *Ahmadou Sadio Diallo* (*Republic of Guinea* v. *Democratic Republic of the Congo*).[91] Treaty bodies such as the HRCtee and the African Commission have consistently held that respondent states parties responsible for violations should pay compensation without, however, specifying an amount. Effectively, this practice refers the claimant back to the national system or a negotiated settlement, which has hampered enforcement of 'awards'.[92] For their part, most national legal systems and jurisprudence recognise at least some right of victims to claim compensation for human rights violations. However, practice differs widely. Deficient legislation, lack of compensation for non-pecuniary harm, small amounts of compensation and the difficulty of enforcement are some of the key challenges encountered by victims.[93]

13.10.8   *Proyecto de Vida: Loayza Tamayo* v. *Peru*

The case of *Loayza Tamayo*[94] illustrates starkly the personal consequences of serious violations which led the IACtHR to develop 'loss of enjoyment of life' (*proyecto de vida* – 'life plan') as a further category of reparation:

She [Loayza Tamayo] has degrees in education and in social work. Prior to her detention, she was a law student and had taken a number of academic courses and

---

[89] See Shelton, above note 7, 343–8, and Rombouts, above note 28, 388–9.

[90] Non-pecuniary damages awarded by the IACtHR for violations such as arbitrary detention, torture, forced disappearances and extrajudicial killing may be a relatively paltry $10,000 but may also amount to $100,000 depending on circumstances. See C. Sandoval-Villalba, 'The Concepts of "Injured Party" and "Victim" of Gross Human Rights Violations in the Jurisprudence of the Inter-American Court of Human Rights: a Commentary on their Implications for Reparations', in Ferstman, above note 10, 243–82, at 258–71. The jurisprudence of the ECtHR also varies considerably. It has awarded significant amounts of non-pecuniary damages in instances of serious violations, such as torture, for example €120,000 in *Mikheyev* v. *Russian Federation*, para. 163.

[91] *Ahmadou Sadio Diallo (Republic of Guinea* v. *Democratic Republic of the Congo), (Compensation)*, ICJ Judgment of 19 June 2012, $85,000 for material injury and $10,000 for non-material injury.

[92] See for example, *Submission to the Human Rights Committee on Implementation of its Views in the Philippines* (London: REDRESS, December 2011).

[93] REDRESS, above note 72, 47–9.

[94] *Loayza Tamayo* v. *Peru*, Reparations and costs, Judgment of 27 November 1998, Ser. C, no. 42, particularly paras. 144–54.

seminars. She was 36 years old at the time of her detention. At the time of her detention on February 6, 1993, she was living with her children . . . [and] was working at José Gabriel Condorcanqui High School, where her area of specialization was history. . . She was definitively removed from her post on May 29, 1993, on the grounds that she had abandoned her post without just cause. At the time of her detention, she was working at the National School of Dramatic Arts . . . [and] at the School of Management of the Universidad de San Martín de Porres . . . At the time she was detained she was in the process of building a house . . . During her detention and up to the present, she has received a monthly pension from the Ministry of Health. During her incarceration, and as a consequence of the cruel, inhuman and degrading punishment to which she was subjected, she suffered serious health problems, treatment of which necessitated outlays of an unspecified amount, all paid by her next of kin. Her confinement brought on severe physical and psychological health disorders; some may be relieved with prolonged therapy, although others may be irreversible. [After her release] [s]he filed several of [sic] requests to be reinstated in her former posts . . . The outcome of these requests is unknown. She now resides in the city of Santiago, Chile, is not working, and is undergoing medical treatment financed by 'FASIC.' The so-called 'life plan' deals with the full self-actualisation of the person concerned and takes account of her calling in life, her particular circumstances, her potentialities, and her ambitions, thus permitting her to set for herself, in a reasonable manner, specific goals, and to attain those goals.

The Court found that the violations of Ms Loayza-Tamayo's human rights caused grave damage to her 'life plan'. However, it concluded that:

neither case law nor doctrine has evolved to the point where acknowledgment of damage to a life plan can be translated into economic terms. Hence, the Court is refraining from quantifying it. It notes, however, that the victim's recourse to international tribunals and issuance of the corresponding judgment constitute some measure of satisfaction for damages of these kinds.

The category of *proyecto de vida*, or life plan, which appears to be non-pecuniary in nature,[95] has attracted considerable interest but also reservations as it is viewed as unduly broadening the reach of compensation.[96] The *proyecto de vida* certainly bears the potential to contribute to a more holistic understanding of the need to address the intangible long-term effects of harm caused by serious violations.[97] However, the concept has not been

---

[95] According to the IACtHR, ibid., para.151: 'it [reparation for damages to the "life plan"] most closely approximates the ideal of *restitution in integrum*'.

[96] Rombouts, above note 28, 385, with further references.

[97] *Cantoral-Benavides* v. *Peru*, Reparations and costs, Judgment of 3 December 2001, Ser. C, no. 88, para. 60, funding scholarship for studies in respect of a violation of the right to liberty and security and freedom from torture which 'prevented the victim from fulfilling his vocation, aspirations and potential, particularly with regard to his preparation for his chosen career and his work as a professional'.

taken up by other bodies and even the IACtHR has not applied it consistently in its jurisprudence.[98]

POINTS TO CONSIDER

1 What role can the *proyecto de vida* play in developing the concept of reparation so as to be responsive to the nature of violations?

2 Can it be translated into something more tangible within the accepted legal framework of the elements of compensation?

13.10.9 Should previous conduct be taken into consideration when awarding compensation?

Individuals who become victims may prior to the violation have acted in a way seen as repugnant. This raises the vexing question whether such conduct justifies the denial of compensation. In *McCann* v. *United Kingdom*, for example, the ECtHR decided not to award compensation for a violation of the right to life to the relatives of three suspected IRA operatives who had planned a terrorist attack in Gibraltar but were confronted and killed by British forces.[99] National legal systems (in law, jurisprudence and compensation schemes) recognise that no one should benefit from a situation brought about by him- or herself.[100] This is reflected in article 8 of the European Convention on the Compensation of Victims of Violent Crimes, which stipulates that compensation may be reduced or refused on account of the victim's conduct, his or her involvement in violent or organised crimes or where it would be contrary to a sense of justice or to public policy.[101] However, there are no explicit provisions in any human rights treaties or instruments that rule out the award of compensation on account of previous conduct or public policy considerations. Not awarding compensation in such instances is problematic as it invokes the notion of an 'undeserving victim' and seems indirectly to validate a serious violation by not attaching pecuniary consequences to it. This is questionable from a policy perspective since the payment of compensation for human rights violations can also have a deterrent impact. Adjusting the amount of compensation may

---

[98] See note on the jurisprudence of the IACtHR on the 'life plan' by T. M. Antkowiak, 'Remedial Approaches to Human Rights Violations: the Inter-American Court of Human Rights and Beyond', *Colum. J. Transnat'l L.* 46 (2008), 351–419, at 371, fn.101.

[99] *McCann* v. *United Kingdom*, 21 (1996), EHRR 91.

[100] Critical in relation to the situation in the UK, Doak, above note 1, 228–9.

[101] Council of Europe, European Convention on the Compensation of Victims of Violent Crimes, opened for signature by Member States of the Council of Europe on 24 November 1983, (1983) 22 ILM 1021.

in exceptional circumstances be contemplated where the victim has directly contributed to a violation through his or her criminal and harmful conduct. However, this rationale should not be applicable in cases of absolute rights, such as the prohibition of torture, where no circumstances can justify a breach and policy considerations weigh generally in favour of awarding adequate compensation for harm suffered.

13.10.10   Reparation for the violation of collective rights: *Saramaka people* v. *Suriname*[102]

Providing compensation to groups of victims, be it for violations of collective rights or mass violations, presents a unique challenge for human rights treaty bodies. In cases of collective rights violations, such as the rights of indigenous peoples, the IACtHR has awarded collective damages in the form of a lump sum payable to a development fund for the benefit of the group concerned.[103] It has also ordered other collective measures of reparation, such as a housing programme and development programmes for communities whose members were massacred.[104] Where a number of individuals have suffered similar violations, international compensation commissions, mass claims adjudication and the IACtHR have used categories of victims entitled to fixed amounts for certain types of violation.[105]

In *Saramaka people* v. *Suriname*, the IACtHR found that Suriname had, by granting logging concessions to companies on Saramaka land, violated the rights of the Saramaka people, a tribal group, to judicial protection against violations of their right to property. The Court made a number of important findings on reparation: The group (Saramaka people) itself was entitled to compensation. The members of the community are the 'injured party' and 'beneficiaries of the collective forms of reparation'. Awards are for the benefit of the entire group. This includes funds to provide 'educational, housing, agricultural, and health projects, as well as to provide electricity and drinking water' for the benefit of the community. Awards are made through trust funds. Three parties, namely representatives from each party and a third

---

[102] *Saramaka People* v. *Suriname*, Preliminary objections, merits, reparations and costs, 28 November 2007, Ser. C, no. 172.

[103] *Aloeboetoe* v. *Suriname*, Reparations and costs, Judgment of 10 September 1993, Ser. C, no. 15, paras. 101–2. See also *Caracazo* v. *Venezuela*, para. 137; *Suárez-Rosero* v. *Ecuador*, Reparations and costs, Judgment of 20 January 1999, Ser. C, no. 44, para. 107; *'White Van' (Paniagua Morales et al.)* v. *Guatemala*, Reparations and costs, Judgment of 25 May 2001, Ser. C, no. 76, para. 223; Case of *Godinez-Cruz* v. *Honduras*, Interpretation of the judgment of reparations and costs, Judgment of 17 August 1990, Ser. C, no. 10, para. 32.

[104] *Plan de Sánchez Massacre* v. *Guatemala*, Reparations and costs, Judgment of 19 November 2004, Ser. C, no. 116, paras. 105–10.

[105] H. M. Holtzmann and E. Kristjánsdóttir (eds.), *International Mass Claims Processes: Legal and Practical Processes* (Oxford University Press, 2007).

party agreed upon, are to decide about the use of the trust fund. This set-up was chosen to encourage parties to agree on the mode of implementation, and, in the context of international human rights jurisprudence, constitutes an innovative means of administering funds made for the benefit of a group.

POINTS TO CONSIDER

1 What are the challenges of providing reparation for collective rights?

2 How satisfactorily has the IACtHR dealt with these challenges?

13.10.11   Rehabilitation

The right to rehabilitation, which is recognised in several human rights treaties,[106] addresses the multifaceted rehabilitative needs of victims caused by violations. According to the Basic Principles, 'rehabilitation should include medical and psychological care as well as legal and social services'. The state or others liable can provide such care and services either in kind or through money that enables victims to access rehabilitation. Rehabilitation appears to be most valuable if construed as an obligation of the state to establish and maintain a system that provides facilities and enables victims to access relevant services (on a priority basis where appropriate).[107] In national practice, provision and access to rehabilitation services are often either based on statutory schemes for victims of crimes or have been part of efforts to address the legacy of violations in transitional justice contexts. However, practice is largely *ad hoc*, which may also be attributed to the lack of attention to detail and effective implementation of the right to rehabilitation in the practice of treaty bodies and NGO advocacy. The General Comment on article 14 CAT under consideration by the CtAT in 2012 provided an important opportunity to address the multiple questions surrounding the nature, content and implementation of the right to rehabilitation.[108]

13.10.12   Satisfaction

The term satisfaction encompasses a plethora of largely symbolic measures. It also includes key components of justice, such as public acknowledgement,

---

[106] See e.g. articles 14 CAT, 39 CRC and 24 CPED.

[107] *Barrios Altos* v. *Peru*, Reparations and costs, Judgment of 30 November 2001, Ser. C, no. 87, para. 40; *19 Tradesmen* v. *Colombia*, Merits, reparations and costs, Judgment of 5 July 2004, Ser. C, no. 109, paras. 275–8; '*Juvenile Reeducation Institute*' v. *Paraguay*, Preliminary objections, merits, reparations and costs, Judgment of 2 September 2004, Ser. C, no. 112, paras. 318–20; CtAT, *Conclusions and Recommendations: Zambia*, UN Doc. A/57/44 (SUPP) (25 September 2002), paras. 59–67, particularly 66(g).

[108] CtAT Draft General Comment on article 14, 2012, paras. 10–14.

truth and accountability. Satisfaction is a recognised term of art in the draft articles on state responsibility,[109] the ECHR, which may include compensation or simply consist of a declaratory judgment finding a breach,[110] and the Basic Principles, with the latter being broadest in scope.[111]

Cessation of violations denotes measures taken to stop ongoing violations, such as refraining from exposing a detainee to inhuman detention conditions. Such measures correspond to states' primary obligations to respect rights and prevent violations, which raises the question whether they can or should be classified as reparation.[112]

Acknowledgement denotes accepting responsibility for the wrong done, which can take various forms, such as a public statement, or a declaration, including in the course of judicial proceedings, as in several cases before the IACtHR.[113] The acceptance of responsibility should also be reflected in official accounts of events, including in schoolbooks where appropriate. Acknowledgement serves an important function in 'setting the public record straight', and thereby serves to vindicate victims. It also acts as factual evidence that can be used to counter claims that certain violations never happened, for example the Holocaust.

Apologies are a related though conceptually distinct form of reparation.[114] They combine acknowledgement with an expression of remorse over someone's acts or omissions. Apologies have arguably been neglected as a form of reparation. This may be attributed to concerns over how genuine they are (although there are significant cultural differences – in Japan, for example, the inherent submission of making an apology may be considered sufficient whereas in Western countries greater emphasis is placed on the correspondence of the expression with the thinking and feelings of the person making the apology). There is also concern over whether a person can be judicially forced to apologise. However, the IACtHR has developed a jurisprudence of ordering states to apologise for violations.[115] Apologies to victims have also featured in official responses to violations in times of or following political

---

[109]   Article 37(2) ILC Draft articles on State Responsibility: 'Satisfaction may consist in an acknowledgement of the breach, an expression of regret, a formal apology or another appropriate modality.'

[110]   Article 41 ECHR.

[111]   Principle 22 of the Basic Principles.

[112]   Shelton, above note 7, 149. Also, van Boven, above note 24, 25.

[113]   See on this point in particular the critical assessment of J. Cavallaro and S. E. Brewer, 'Reevaluating Regional Human Rights Litigation in the Twenty-First Century: the Case of the Inter-American Court', *AJIL* 102 (2008), 768–827, at 808–16.

[114]   See in particular C. Jenkins, 'Taking Apology Seriously', in Du Plessis, above note 53, 53–81.

[115]   See for example *Cantoral-Benavides* v. *Peru*, para. 81; *Moiwana Village* v. *Suriname*, Preliminary objections, merits, reparations and costs, Judgment of 15 June 2005, Ser. C, no. 124, para. 216; *Gutierrez-Soler* v. *Colombia*, Merits, reparations and costs, Judgment of 12 September 2005, Ser. C, no. 132, para. 59.

transition.[116] This is a welcome development as apologies can constitute an important symbolic measure for victims and serve goals of restorative justice.

Truth is an integral part of acknowledgement but also a component of reparation in its own right. The IACtHR, as well as other international bodies and instruments, has recognised a distinctive right to truth, in particular in cases of enforced disappearances and extrajudicial killings.[117] This right entitles relatives to be informed about the fate and whereabouts of the victim(s), or their remains. It also encompasses access to factual and other relevant information concerning the violation, including archives.

Sanctions consist of 'judicial and administrative proceedings against the persons liable for the violations'. This category corresponds to the duty of states to investigate, prosecute and punish those responsible for serious violations.[118] Criminal accountability of the perpetrators is constitutive of adequate reparation, particularly in cases of gross violations.[119] Its opposite, i.e. impunity, leaves an important component of justice unaddressed and is prone to contribute to the perpetuation of violations.

Commemoration in the form of museums, plaques, naming streets after victims, ceremonies or educational materials combines elements of maintaining a public record of events with a recognition and restoration of the dignity of victims. Such symbolic measures form an integral part of the jurisprudence of the IACtHR.[120] They play an important role in affirming both the suffering and humanity of the victims and in empowering them to (re-)claim their place in society.

13.10.13   Guarantees of non-repetition

Guarantees of non-repetition include measures such as protection but largely denote a range of forward-looking measures that typically go beyond

---

[116] Speech by Romania's President Traian Basecu in the Romanian Parliament (18 December 2006), online, at, www.icarfoundation.ro/index.php?option=com_content&task=view&id=29&Itemid=44.

[117] See e.g. *Neira Alegria* v. *Peru*, Reparations and costs, Judgment of 19 September 1996, Ser. C, no. 29, para. 69; Human Rights Chamber for Bosnia and Herzegovina, *Selimovic and others* v. *Republic Srpska* (Decision of 7 March 2003), paras. 211–12; article 24(2) CPED; Principle 1 of the *Updated Set of Principles for the Protection and Promotion of Human Rights through action to combat Impunity*, UN Commission on Human Rights Resolution 2005/81 (21 April 2005); Principle 22 (b) and (c) of the Basic Principles.

[118] See section 2.3.2.

[119] See for example *Miguel Castro-Castro Prison* v. *Peru*, Merits, reparations and costs, Judgment of 25 November 2006, Ser. C, no. 160, paras. 436–41.

[120] Antkowiak, above note 98, 381–2.

the individual case at hand and seek to prevent the recurrence of certain violations, particularly by bringing about systemic changes. The measures identified in the Basic Principles draw on rule of law components aimed at strengthening the independence of the judiciary as well as legislative and institutional reforms, especially of law-enforcement agencies, with a view to ensuring observance of international standards.

13.10.14   A brief assessment and outlook

The adoption of the Basic Principles, the jurisprudence of national, regional and international bodies, particularly the IACtHR, as well as the work of individual experts, NGOs and victims movements worldwide have contributed to a better understanding of reparation and has strengthened the right of victims. However, several grey and underdeveloped areas remain. This applies in particular to adequate forms of reparation for violations of economic, social and cultural rights,[121] collective rights, as well as a greater awareness of the gender dimensions of reparation.[122] One of the most serious challenges facing national systems as well as regional and international bodies is how to provide adequate reparation in instances of mass violations involving a large number of victims.[123]

QUESTIONS

1 **Should the state be responsible for paying reparation for the criminal conduct (such as rape or torture) of its officials?**

2 **What understanding of reparation has motivated victims to reject compensation, particularly the offer of money to settle a case in return for dropping all claims and complaints?**

3 **How does reparation tackle impunity?**

---

[121] There is a dearth of jurisprudence in this respect, particularly at the supranational level. See, however, *The Social and Economic Rights Action Centre and the Centre for Social and Economic Rights* v. *Nigeria*, 155/96 (2001), in which the African Commission recommended a range of remedial measures for violations of economic, social and cultural rights. This situation is set to change if and when the Optional Protocol to the ICESCR becomes operational and develops its jurisprudence.

[122] See in particular the Nairobi Declaration on Women's and Girls' Rights to a Remedy and Reparation (2007). See also Report of the Special Rapporteur on Violence against Women: its Causes and Consequences, Rashida Manjoo, UN Doc. A/HRC/14/22 (23 April 2010), Paras. 12–85.

[123] L. Oette, 'Bringing Justice to Victims? Responses of Regional and International Human Rights Courts and Treaty Bodies to Mass Violations', in Ferstman, above note 10, 217–42.

13.11   THE DOUBLE-EDGED SWORD OF VICTIMS' POLITICS

The status of 'victim' has gained prominence in political debates where it has become a marker of identity and competing claims for public recognition and reparation.[124] The use of the term may in this context become a tactical weapon of choice, particularly to enhance the apparent legitimacy of claims. In this way, it puts the onus on governments or other entities to explain why they deny or neglect rights and/or contribute to 'victimisation'. The importance of the status of victim, both in terms of being entitled to reparation and having one's suffering recognised by society, is particularly apparent where groups of victims are excluded altogether. For example, the victims of systemic injustices of a collective nature characterstic of the pervasive regime of apartheid were not recognised in South Africa's official dealing with the past, in contrast to (individualised) victims of discrete gross violations.[125] Exploitation and poverty is often not portrayed in terms of violations, victim status, rights and remedies but characterised as economic or societal ills.[126] Such categorisation may result in charitable or humanitarian intervention that alleviates the suffering but will frequently have little effect on the status quo. Seizing victim status becomes against this background a highly politicised undertaking, with those who are able to influence the granting or denial of such status often acting as gatekeepers in the public debate.

Referring to oneself or one's group as victims can be a means of staking claims in the course of debates about who should be entitled to reparation: 'I am/We are deserving of justice and reparation (but you/others aren't).' This may give rise to competition between victims of violations where one group of victims sees itself as more deserving than others (or the only group worthy of reparation). This applies in particular to those who suffered particularly egregious violations, such as repeated torture compared to, for example, 'mere' short-term wrongful imprisonment, and groups that have been specifically targeted. In the context of post-atrocity or conflict situations, such as in Rwanda or the Democratic Republic of Congo, the public may find it difficult to understand why the legal status of victim attaches to certain 'violations' but not other forms of violence and/or hardship, as many people will have suffered and feel aggrieved in these circumstances.[127]

---

[124] See, in particular in relation to violations related to World War II, J. Torpey, 'Victims and Citizens: the Discourse of Reparation(s) at the Dawn of the New Millennium', in De Feyter, above note 22, 41–5.

[125] See M. Mamdani, 'Amnesty or Impunity? A Preliminary Critique of the Report of the Truth and Reconciliation Commission of South Africa (TRC)', in Du Plessis, above note 53, 83–118.

[126] B. Hours, 'NGOs and the victims industry', *Le Monde Diplomatique*, English edition (November 2008).

[127] N. Roht-Arriaza, 'Reparations, Decisions and Dilemmas', *Hastings Int'l & Comp. L. Rev.* 27 (2004), 157–219, at 188.

Devising reparation programmes that do justice to the myriad forms of victimisation is therefore extremely challenging following a conflict or mass violations. In practice, this has often resulted in collective forms of reparation, such as building schools that may, however, be barely distinguishable from development measures and thereby defeat the purpose of reparation.[128]

The portrayal of suffering and representation of victims have raised concerns. The word 'victim' often carries negative connotations of passivity, helplessness and suffering. Describing someone as a victim or a group of persons as victims can therefore be seen a form of labelling, confining those concerned into a bounded and static societal straitjacket, which ignores individuality and agency.[129] Notably, individuals who have suffered violations such as torture often prefer to refer to themselves as survivors. The difference in meaning and in connotation of such a term is apparent. However, there are limitations to its use in all circumstances. The term survivor implies that the violation was life threatening, either actually or symbolically (as a fundamental attack on the personality of the victim), which will not necessarily apply to all violations (such as forms of arbitrary arrest and detention). Moreover, many individuals will not survive violations, such as extrajudicial killings or enforced disappearances. As a legal category, it may therefore be preferable to retain the use of the term victim as shorthand for 'anyone who suffered harm as a result of a violation of his/her/their right(s)'. A plethora of people, in particular human rights defenders, speak about or on behalf of 'victims' and use the experience of suffering to pursue advocacy or other purposes. While this is often done with the best of intentions, the spectacle of suffering may easily be exploited. It also carries the risk of viewing and portraying victims as passive objects and of simultaneously appropriating their suffering and stifling their agency.[130] This is bound to create an unequal power relationship between those claiming to be able to alleviate and/or help to remedy the suffering and the individuals or groups portrayed as victims.[131] However, this risk can be mitigated through the involvement of victims. Many human rights organisations or movements are founded or actively supported by individuals who have themselves suffered violations, and often engage them in their work. The degree to which any individual or organisation speaking on behalf of victims actually has such direct links and mutual channels of communication is therefore an important yardstick of legitimacy.

[128] Ibid., 186–92.
[129] See for a succinct overview of the debate with further references, M. Clapham and S. Marks, *International Human Rights Lexicon* (Oxford University Press, 2005), 404–5.
[130] See in particular M. Mutua, *Human Rights: A Political and Cultural Critique* (Philadelphia: University of Pennsylvania Press, 2002), 27–39.
[131] Hours, above note 126.

A highly problematic aspect of victims' politics is its use as licence to justify violations. Such charges have been levelled against Israel and Rwanda, for example, and are by necessity highly contentious and fraught with difficulties. The perception of one's own victim status may have two consequences in this context. It may underpin a collectively shared fear, whether objectively justified or not, that a repetition or similar violations as the ones which caused the original victimisation may recur. This may result in an uncompromising outlook, militarisation and the willingness to use excessive force or legitimise human rights violations.[132] The victim status may also become the founding myth, *raison d'être* and legitimising factor of a state or a regime. This may be used to enshrine the latter's preeminence in national politics and provide justification for repression. It may also serve as tool of neutralising political opposition that is portrayed as pursuing the agenda of the erstwhile perpetrators even where it formulates legitimate demands or grievances.[133]

The brief review of the notion and broader debates surrounding the politics of victimhood demonstrate that the term 'victim' is by no means unproblematic. Using it requires awareness and caution, and its use in any given context should be subject to critical interrogation as to its appropriateness and the motives of the user(s) for doing so.

13.12 NEGOTIATING, LITIGATING AND ADMINISTERING REPARATIONS: EXPERIENCES FROM THE HOLOCAUST AND WORLD WAR II REPARATIONS

Reparation costs money. In instances of mass violations, the overall amount of compensation in question is by definition substantial. It is for this plain truth that states (and others) are frequently reluctant to provide reparation of their own will. The question of reparation becomes in these circumstances often a highly politicised process. It depends on the influence, standing and efficiency of victims, and/or their advocates, the availability of effective legal avenues or other mechanisms, and a variety of factors that may persuade the state or others concerned that providing reparation is the right thing to do and/or in their best interest.

The Holocaust and World War II reparations are arguably the most instructive example given their scope and time span. The question of payments

---

[132] See comparisons with, and charges of colonialism and apartheid, in Report of the Special Rapporteur on the situation of human rights in the Palestinian territories occupied since 1967, John Dugard, UN Doc. A/HRC/4/17 (29 January 2007).

[133] See for example S. Newton, 'Law and Power in the Shadow of the Genocide', *JCL* 2(1) (2007), 151–71.

for victims came to the fore in the late 1940s. Many Jewish organisations claimed compensation and restitution as 'a small measure of justice for Jewish victims of Nazi persecution'.[134] The Federal Republic of Germany, for its part, had a political interest in gaining legitimacy by showing its willingness to bear responsibility, which was viewed as a precondition for becoming accepted by other Western states and others. However, the proposals made led to fierce opposition in Israel. Compensation was seen as blood money that denigrates the suffering of the victims, the Holocaust being such an unimaginable crime that it could never be compensated for in monetary terms. Significantly, even those Jewish survivors in favour of compensation used the word *Shilumim*, i.e. recompense, instead of the term reparations (*Wiedergutmachung*) favoured by Germany. In the end, after intense negotiations, Israel and Germany reached an agreement in 1952 that paved the way for the payment of tens of billions of German marks over the next decades.[135] Since then, three important challenges have resurfaced frequently. Who should be covered by reparations? How should reparations be administered? And, can the forms of reparations available ever do justice to survivors and victims?

The official reparation schemes had significant omissions. One of the most glaring was the fact that many victims of slave labour and forced labour[136] had not received reparations and that some of the main beneficiaries thereof, in particular German companies, had not been held accountable. The victims of these violations and organisations working on their behalf, particularly the Conference on Jewish Material Claims Against Germany, employed a variety of strategies. They sought to negotiate terms with the German government and to persuade the relevant industries to provide compensation. This was complemented by resort to class action suits in the USA, i.e. legal action brought on behalf of a large number of victims who claim to have suffered common or similar harm, aimed at reaching a settlement for the benefit of all victims. In the Swiss settlement case,[137] '[Judge Koman] encouraged and actively participated in settlement negotiations, thereby

---

[134] G. Taylor, G. Schneider and S. Kagan, 'The Claims Conference and the Historic Jewish Efforts for Holocaust-Related Compensation and Restitution', in Ferstman, above note 10, 103–14, at 103.

[135] See for a detailed account, A. Colonomos and A. Armstrong, 'German Reparations to the Jews after World War II: a Turning Point in the History of Reparations', in de Greiff, above note 9, 390–419.

[136] Slave labour referred to concentration camp labour whereas forced labour referred to other forms of labour, in particular for the German industry. The majority of survivors of slave labour were Jewish and of forced labour Eastern European.

[137] This concerned a lawsuit in which the plaintiffs alleged that the Swiss Banks in question had retained and concealed the assets of Holocaust victims, laundered Nazi loot and transacted in the profits of slave labour. See *In re Holocaust Victim Assets Litig.*, 105 F. Supp.2d 139, 141–142 (E.D.N.Y. 2000).

facilitating the historic agreement that resolved the lawsuits and created the $1.25 billion settlement'.[138] A combination of factors, including international advocacy, political developments in Germany, the USA and Eastern Europe in the 1990s, and the threat of adverse judgments and consequences for the German companies that had benefited from slave/forced labour, provided the impetus for negotiations that resulted in the setting up of a foundation to compensate the victims of these violations.[139] Importantly, the payment of compensation was accompanied by an official note of apology from the German President, thus making acknowledgement an integral part of the reparations programme.

The setting up of reparations schemes resulting from advocacy, litigation and negotiations constituted an important victory for the individuals and organisations involved. However, legal and practical challenges in administering these reparations abound. How is an eighty-year-old woman living in an isolated part of the Ukraine to find out about the forced labour reparations programme? How can she prove that she was subjected to forced labour if she lost all documents in the aftermath of the war? How does one calculate adequate compensation for her, if she was not only forcibly made to perform factory work but was also repeatedly raped by her 'employers'? Those responsible for administering reparation programmes tend to utilise a number of techniques to address these challenges. This includes outreach, adequate time for submission of applications, relaxed standards of proof and standardised claims according to categories of violations. These techniques are used to enable as many genuine victims as possible to benefit from the scheme within a realistic time-frame. By their nature, these techniques are developed and applied to respond to the exigencies of the situation concerned. This means that there is often an experimental element to their use. Nevertheless, over time, individuals and organisations have developed considerable expertise and means to administer reparation schemes that address some if not all of the challenges.

Ultimately, a reparations scheme must go beyond efficient administration. Its success will in large part depend on its ability to provide reparation that is meaningful in a victim-oriented manner. This includes the role of the victim, the procedure applied and the form of reparation provided. All too often, victims have become disillusioned with bureaucratic schemes that are seen as insensitive to their experience. This is articulated in a lawyer's account of the administration of the German reparations laws of 1965:

---

[138] J. Gribetz and S. C. Reig, 'The Swiss Banks Holocaust Settlement', in Ferstman, above note 10, 115–42, at 118.

[139] J. Authers, 'Making Good Again: German Compensation for Forced and Slave Laborers', in De Greiff, above note 9, 420–48.

No one bothered to restore the survivor's dignity. On the contrary, the procedures inherent in some of the paragraphs of the [German] Restitution Laws, inflict indignities upon the claimants while at the same time German authorities are elevated to the status of superior beings who adjudge the claimant's veracity and honesty and classify them in accordance with the degree of their damage ... To receive payments, often sorely needed, the applicants had to subject themselves to the most humiliating and degrading, seemingly very correct legal type of reparations.[140]

13.13 REPARATION IN ACTION: LITIGATING HUMAN RIGHTS CASES

13.13.1 Litigation strategies

Human rights lawyers, victims' organisations and NGOs have been at the forefront of promoting victims' rights and pursuing claims on their behalf. Beyond seeking justice for the individuals, human rights cases frequently serve broader objectives. This instrumental approach is known as strategic litigation. It seeks to identify cases that address key obstacles which, if successful, set a precedent that will benefit a large number of victims.[141] This may concern the recognition (and/or elaboration) of rights or fundamental principles, the availability of legal avenues and types of reparation. An example is the landmark case of *Hadijat Mani* v. *Niger*, in which the ECOWAS Community Court of Justice ruled that Niger had to pay $19,000 compensation for failing to protect the applicant from slavery (which lasted over eight years).[142] This case resulted in the recognition of positive obligations on the part of the state to prevent slavery and set a regional precedent of awarding specific amounts of compensation.

Strategic litigation can be pursued before national, regional or international courts, or a combination thereof. It can take the form of representing claimants, public interest litigation or intervening as *amicus*, the so-called friend of the court where a third party is allowed to make submissions on legal issues if considered relevant to the case – this practice is increasingly utilised by NGOs, human rights law centres and others, often working in

---

[140] M. Kestenberg, 'Discriminatory Aspects of the German Restitution Law and Practice', quoted in Danieli, above note 76, 41–78, at 57.

[141] The NGO Interights, for example, is well-known for its strategic litigation programme. See European Roma Center, Interights and Migration Policy Group, 'Strategic Litigation of Race Discrimination in Europe: From principles to practice' (2004), online, at www.migpolgroup.com/public/docs/57.StrategicLitigationofRaceDiscriminationinEurope-fromPrinciplestoPractice_2004.pdf and www.interights.org.

[142] *Mani* v. *Niger*, 2008. See for further information on the case www.interights.org/niger-slavery.

collaboration, as a means of seeking to influence court decisions on legal principles and legal policy issues.[143]

Public interest litigation is a particular type of strategic litigation. It has been used effectively in several countries, such as India, South Africa, the USA and elsewhere. Initially, efforts largely focused on violations of civil and political rights. More recently, there has been an increasing emphasis on litigating cases of violations of economic, social and political rights. For example, in *People's Union for Civil Liberties* v. *Union of India and others*, the litigants successfully petitioned the Supreme Court of India to order the government of India to implement a series of food and benefit distribution schemes, as well as to provide access to information. Two of the lawyers involved in the case highlighted internal debates within the People's Union for Civil Liberties as to whether – given their policy nature – it would be worthwhile to pursue claims relating to the right to food before the Supreme Court. In the lawyers' analysis, the orders set an important precedent on the right to food and the entitlements flowing from it. They also point out the valuable lessons of how to break down broad ESC rights into specific demands so as to turn them into claims which can be litigated and adjudicated upon.[144]

13.13.2 Pursuing reparation claims, with particular reference to litigating torture cases

Individuals who suffer from serious violations such as torture frequently struggle to rebuild their lives as best as possible. As put in 2005 by a Chilean refugee who survived a sustained period of torture at the hands of the Pinochet regime in the 1970s:

Now I am 73. I have been here [in the UK] for 30 years and every part of my body has problems. But my biggest problem is that my head injuries meant that I could never learn English. My three daughters have children but [when] they speak to me I can't understand what they are saying and I feel bad. If you cut a wound and you

---

[143] See for example Specical Court of Sierra Leone in the Trial Chamber, *The Prosecutor against Morris Kallon*, Amicus Curiae Brief submitted by the Redress Trust, Lawyers Committee on Human Rights (now Human Rights First) and the International Commission of Jurists (on the legality of amnesties for international crimes) (24 October 2003), www.redress.org/case-docket/the-prosecutor-against-morris-kallon, and Brief of Amicus Curiae International Human Rights Organizations Center for Constitutional Rights, Human Rights Watch and International Federation of Human Rights in support of petitioner, in the case of *Hamdan* v. *Rumsfeld* (concerning Guantánamo Bay and right of access to courts) (6 January 2006), online, at, www.fidh.org/IMG/pdf/amicus012006a.pdf.

[144] See B. Guha-Khasnobis and S. Vivek, *Rights-based Approach to Development: Lessons from the Right to Food Movement in India*, WIDER Research Paper (January 2007), online, at www.wider.unu.edu/publications/working-papers/research-papers/2007/en_GB/rp2007–04/_files/78091827554093386/default/rp2007–04.pdf.

can't heal it, it gets bigger and bigger. That's what happened to me. Pinochet has never been put in prison so the wound gets bigger. I am not at peace. I want to go back to Chile, but it would be very difficult for me because they took everything...[145]

Seeking reparation may be part of the process of trying to rebuild one's life. It is also frequently driven by a series of other factors and objectives. Survivors may need financial and other help to cope with the consequences of violations. They may want to find answers, have a desire for acknowledgement, and/or retribution, and a deep-rooted quest for justice. Some survivors become highly motivated to bring about changes to the system and to enhance the protection of human rights, for example by calling for public inquiries into violations. However, empirical research shows that survivors perceive reparation in different ways.[146] This means that it is difficult if not impossible to generalise in this respect – worse, generalising may ignore survivors' agency and fail to duly consider their needs and wishes. Whereas some survivors pursue reparation vigorously, even to the point that the process of so doing might become an end in itself, others prefer not to seek justice. This can be due to multiple factors. Survivors often have a high degree of traumatisation and there is a (justified) fear of having to relive the trauma as part of an (alienating) legal procedure. Even where survivors decide to pursue reparation, it can be highly difficult because the process or outcome might not meet expectations or prove more strenuous than expected. These difficulties and challenges are often exacerbated where reparation is sought by a group of survivors. They have to agree on representation and strategies and will have to grapple with the inevitable group dynamics that such an undertaking entails. An example is the representation of victims of the Castro-Castro prison massacre in Peru that ended in open disagreement before the IACtHR.[147]

Lawyers and others representing survivors of violations encounter different types of challenges. In many instances, it will take a considerable time for the full story to emerge, especially in relation to acts of sexual violence. Accounts of arrest, detention, torture and other violations may be patchy, and even seemingly contradictory, which can often be attributed to the disorientation caused by events or injuries. Survivors will also in many instances not have obtained other vital evidence in time, such as medico-legal reports, either because it was not feasible or because they did not have any or adequate legal representation or assistance at the time. Dealing with survivors therefore differs markedly from an ordinary lawyer–client relationship and requires a high degree of empathy and understanding of survivors' experiences, which have often been highly traumatic, and their consequences.

---

[145] REDRESS, *Torture: Stories of Survival* (London: REDRESS, 2005).

[146] See for example REDRESS, *Torture Survivors' Perceptions of Reparation: Preliminary Survey* (London: REDRESS, 2001).

[147] *Miguel Castro-Castro Prison* v. *Peru*, para. 40.

INTERVIEW 13.1

Litigation, advocacy and social change

(Basil Fernando)

Basil Fernando is a Sri Lankan lawyer. He left Sri Lanka in 1989 when the country was in the grip of a state-sponsored campaign of enforced disappearances and extrajudicial killings. At the time, he became a target of the death squads on account of taking up cases against the police and some powerful persons and his human rights activism. Subsequently, he worked for the UN in post-genocide Cambodia as a Senior UN Human Rights Officer, before becoming the director of the Hong Kong based Asian Human Rights Commission (AHRC), one of the leading regional human rights organisations in Asia. Basil Fernando and the AHRC have championed a distinctive human rights approach with a strong focus on empowering people. They have also worked vigorously towards strengthening the rule of law at all levels of society, particularly at the institutional level.[1]

What is distinctive about your approach to litigation?

We try to establish a different type of lawyer–client relationship than what usually exists in Sri Lanka. The reason for this is that torture victims and victims of human rights abuse in general come from socially extremely weak sections of society. They do not have the social skills of litigants who will approach lawyers in their chambers, adjust to the time schedules of lawyers, do the preliminary work of preparation such as finding documents and providing the lawyers with various materials and pay their fees. We have created a combination of a solidarity group consisting of people who are close to victims.

Another aspect we have to be careful of all the time is the protection of the victim and also the lawyers who work on these cases. Dangers are very real and there are some well-known cases where the victim has been assassinated or very seriously harassed. The lawyers themselves have faced serious attacks such as grenade attacks on their houses and arson in their offices. Further there are peculiar difficulties in dealing with human-rights related cases. Often there are strong societal prejudices which need to be fought against slowly and attitude changes need to be brought about on issues such as the prevention of torture, extrajudicial killings and the like. In short each case is not only a legal case but a discourse with society on vital issues. Secondly, unless those who are involved in the litigation are

[1] See www.basilfernando.net and www.ahrchk.net.

motivated by other factors than pure economic factors, as is often involved in normal litigation, the kind of litigation that we are involved in cannot be consistently and perseveringly carried out.

What are you seeking to achieve through your case work?

This is a very interesting question. If you look at this problem from purely the standards of developed countries some may even perceive our work as an exercise in futility. When we undertake a case we are fully aware that if there is to be a positive outcome from a legal sense it will happen only many years later. The delay is so great that by the time a final outcome arrives it may have lost most of its social significance. Besides that, except in very rare instances, the actual award may be insignificant. For example, after a successful outcome in a fundamental rights case before the Supreme Court on issues such as torture the award may be a paltry sum. In cases of criminal charges on torture, extrajudicial killing and the like the likelihood of a successful outcome is very low. In a very few cases where there had been some sentencing of perpetrators the lengths of proceedings which may take ten years or more virtually deprives them of significance. The real deterrence value as it is now is low and the risks such as bodily harm, various types of long psychological harassment, demoralisation among the victims themselves and financial difficulties are all real problems.

However, introducing human rights remedies to a legal system where such remedies have not been a part this initial stage has to be faced at some point or another. In this process we have to condition the minds of lawyers, litigants, judges, prosecutors and also police investigators into a new kind of thinking and habits. The ultimate success of introducing human rights redresses lies with winning over public opinion in favour of such redress. For many reasons the old mentalities support various types of repression by the state either directly or indirectly. For example the idea that torture by the police is a necessary condition for social security is a social prejudice that is quite in built. Further, that torture victims are bad criminals is also a very hardened perception. We try to demonstrate that this kind of prejudice and perceptions are in fact contrary to reality, that law enforcement without torture can create far better community spirit and that society benefits from a legal system where there are adequate remedies for violations.

That kind of social discourse cannot be carried out without practical participation in the litigation process. For example, by merely teaching human rights and law reform, it is not possible to introduce adequate remedies. The people have to go to court to demonstrate the difficulties involved in actually achieving these remedies. In this process many sectors of society and the state come to understand and appreciate the meaning of adequate remedies for human rights in terms of article 2 of the ICCPR.

Can you describe how you practically work on cases? How do you identify cases, who is involved, what are the challenges and how do you seek to address them?

In many of our cases torture victims or their relatives who have heard about the work of our groups approach them when they have a difficulty. Over many years these groups are now trained to interview victims in detail in order to record what they say and also to quickly get further information by way of verification and of gaining greater details about the actual incidents. With such information the victims are helped to make formal complaints to authorities about this incident.

For example a person may be still undergoing torture and illegal detention at the same time when a relative or a friend narrates the story. The group then immediately writes letters to the relevant authorities giving the details of the incident and seeking urgent intervention. The same material collected at the early stage of the incident is also used by the AHRC to create urgent appeals on behalf of the victims. These urgent appeals are sent to large networks and intervention is sought. Thereafter the lawyers associated with the groups interview the victims and witnesses, prepare the necessary papers and file applications for litigation. When finally the case comes to court the lawyers appear for victims and where necessary also get the intervention of senior counsel. Such interventions go from the lower courts up to the Apex court. Meanwhile studies are conducted into the circumstances and the background of the case. A constant discourse is conducted in the media of the circumstances surrounding torture and related problems within the criminal justice system.

Where there are reasons to be dissatisfied with the local litigation process when the defects of litigation can amount to human rights violations communications are also filed with the HRCtee. There have been some successful outcomes of such communications. Submissions are also made to the HRC, the CtAT and relevant UN rapporteurs on the basis of these cases. The intervention of all these agencies is sought in order to improve an adequate remedy for human rights violations.

The challenges are related to a slow legal process with enormous defects in the constitutional and criminal law, which constantly conflict with all attempts to find justice. The conflict between the defective legal system and frustrations relating to justice creates various types of mentalities which obstruct the internal public opinion making progress to have changes. We try to counteract demoralising negative experiences by a regional organisation based outside the local context constantly being in support of the local effort. This includes publicity generation, training, legal advice, and finding some financial resources for the work to create a combination that can at least to some extent address these challenges. It is a unique process of collaboration of victims, local solidarity groups, lawyers and other local agents together with people from outside who constantly back up the work of each other.

How does human rights litigation fit in with your advocacy work?

The litigation connects everyone who is involved into a very real legal and societal process where people find themselves as they seek an adequate remedy for human rights violations. It is the real world from which there is no escape. The advocacy based on the real information is powerful. It seems to be just generalisations on the basis of some accepted norms and standards. The application of international standards to real situations generates information which has a greater power to create strong impressions. A discourse based on such impressions has a greater impact. A judge who is made to see many gruesome cases of torture may begin to challenge his own prejudices and open his mind into the validity of the advocacy that demands a more comprehensive remedy for abuse of rights. This happens to others too. This happens also to the international community. One of the great problems of international advocacy is that those who live in societies where rule of law and democratic systems are well established are unable to grasp the problems of countries with weak rule of law systems and various kinds of authoritarian political systems. When persons from such backgrounds are confronted with detailed information and analysis of this other situation they too are likely to look into the advocacy into these problems in a different manner.

What has been the impact of your work?

I think the impact has been very significant. There is a widespread acknowledgement of serious defects of the constitutional and criminal law system that frustrates the rule of law. In fact, there is a new language when talking about these matters. No one will challenge when it is said today that the policing system in Sri Lanka has completely collapsed. At the time when our work started such a statement would have been considered an exaggeration. This is also the case on issues such as torture and the abuse of police powers of arrest and detention for purely corrupt purposes. Like this a vast list of matters relating to inadequate remedies for human rights violations can be mentioned. All this is today very much accepted and often even regarded as an understatement rather than an exaggeration. There is greater appreciation of the problems at many levels. What prevents more rapid changes are political factors relating to the state which requires a greater political will to deal with. This is beyond the capacity of a human rights group or those involved in human rights litigation alone. However, as and when these political problems are addressed the issues of adequate remedies for human rights violations will not be lost in the debate. Sufficient public attention has been paid to these issues and there are more people who are deeply committed to pursuing this advocacy.

Can you think of any cases that stand out as a particular success or setback?

There are several cases which are simply unforgettable. Take the case of Gerard Mervyn Perera. He was arrested on mistaken identity and beaten up inside a police station to such an extent that he suffered renal failure. After two weeks in a coma he recovered and later with the help of our group filed a fundamental rights application at the Supreme Court. The case was heard in a relatively short time and the judgment is a strong case on torture. The three-bench court ordered the highest amount of compensation awarded up to then and also made some significant recommendations for the prevention of torture. After this award by the Supreme Court the Attorney General filed a criminal action against several police officers under the CAT Act, no. 22 of 1994. The torture victim was to give evidence before the High Court in this trial. After many warnings to alter his evidence or not to appear in court, which the victim refused, he was fatally wounded while he was travelling to work. Several years later at the High Court in the torture trial the accused were acquitted on the basis that the torture victim was not there to identify the perpetrators. This judgment has since been appealed and the Court of Appeal has given leave to proceed. This case expresses all the contradictions of litigation relating to torture and other human rights violations in Sri Lanka.

Then there is the case of Sugath Nishantha Fernando. Mr Fernando was a complainant in a bribery case and a torture case. Once the Commission for Bribery and Corruption filed a case against a police officer attached to the Negombo police station he received death threats demanding that he not give evidence in court. When he refused to comply, about twenty officers surrounded his house and attacked his wife, two children and himself. Later he filed a fundamental rights case before the Supreme Court regarding the torture and was granted leave to proceed. In that case he named twelve officers as respondents. Then he received death threats to withdraw the fundamental rights application within twenty-four hours or he would be assassinated. He made complaints to the Inspector General of Police and all other authorities for protection. However, no protection was provided. Later he was assassinated in broad daylight by two unidentified persons. One year has passed after this incident and no one has been arrested for the murder. The family suspect the police officers who are respondents in the above mentioned cases as having organised the murder. The widow and the two children have been receiving death threats ever since and are living in hiding, even having had to flee to a neighbouring country for some time. As the local system of litigation and protection has failed they filed a communication before the HRCtee, which admitted the communication and requested the Sri Lankan government to provide protection to the family. However, Sri Lanka has not complied with this recommendation.

The case generated an enormous amount of publicity and discussion. However, within a political context where the criminal justice system has been suppressed the case has manifested the enormous problems involved in the system to achieve an adequate remedy for human rights violations.

POINTS TO CONSIDER

- What are the most significant aspects of the recent phase of reparations for violations committed by Nazi Germany, and what are the strategies that have been used by claimants and Jewish organisations to seek and obtain reparation?

- Consider the following fictional press release: 'The victims of industrial operations, pollution and land degradation committed by the company x with the support of government y in country z are many. They are faceless but real. These victims need our help to obtain justice. You can support our work to advocate victims' rights by donating $10 per month.' What concerns does it raise in terms of victims' politics?

- Consider having to advise an individual claiming to have suffered prolonged arbitrary detention and ill-treatment in detention. The detention was justified by security legislation that allows detention without judicial review and access to a lawyer for 90 days. The individual is in financial difficulties and wonders whether to pursue a claim or to accept the settlement offered by the authorities on condition that he refrains from pursuing any civil claims, criminal complaints or other remedies in the matter. What is the dilemma posed, what are the criteria that should be taken into consideration, and what might be possible solutions?

FURTHER READING

Antkowiak, T., 'An Emerging Mandate for International Courts: Victim-Centered Remedies and Restorative Justice', *Stan. J. Int'l L.* 47(2) (2011), 279–332.

Bassiouni, C. M., 'International Recognition of Victims' Rights', *HRLR* 6 (2006), 203–79.

De Feyter, K. *et al.* (eds.), *Out of the Ashes: Reparations for Gross Violations of Human Rights* (Antwerp, Oxford: Intersentia, 2006).

De Greiff, P. (ed.), *The Handbook of Reparations* (Oxford University Press, 2006).

Doak, J., *Victims' Rights, Human Rights and Criminal Justice: Reconceiving the Role of Third Parties* (Oxford: Hart, 2008).

Du Plessis, M. and Peté, S. (eds.), *Repairing the Past? International Perspectives on Reparations for Gross Human Rights Abuses* (Antwerp, Oxford: Intersentia, 2007).

Evans, C., *The Right to Reparation in International Law for Victims of Armed Conflict* (Cambridge University Press, 2012).

Ferstman, C., Goetz, M. and Stephens, A. (eds.), *Reparations for Victims of Genocide, War Crimes* and *Crimes Against Humanity: Systems in Place and Systems in the Making* (Leiden, Boston: Martinus Nijhoff, 2009).

Lenzerini, F. (ed.), *Reparations for Indigenous Peoples: International and Comparative Perspectives* (Oxford University Press, 2009).

Randelzhofer, A. and Tomuschat, C. (eds.), *Reparation in Instances of Grave Violations of Human Rights* (The Hague, Boston, London: Kluwer Law International, 1999).

Shelton, D., *Remedies in International Human Rights Law*, 2nd edn (Oxford University Press, 2005).

Zegveld, L., 'Victims' reparations claims and international criminal courts: incompatible values', *JICJ* 8(1) (2010), 79–111.

14 The application of human rights in armed conflict and the international criminalisation process

CONTENTS

14.1 INTRODUCTION

This chapter discusses the development and application of two bodies of international law; namely international humanitarian law (IHL) and international criminal law and their interrelationship with human rights law. The killing of a civilian by a soldier during an armed conflict, for example, may constitute an IHL violation and a violation of the (human) right to life. This chapter examines this relationship, which is of particular importance for the protection of civilians, especially where the applicability of IHL is contested or where IHL constitutes an exception to certain rights, such as the right to life, or fails to prevent and/or provide effective remedies for violations. It seeks to identify the scope of application of the two bodies of law and demonstrate the degree to which the two can be reconciled. Moreover, a special case is made for the law applicable in situations of military occupation whereby human rights are subordinate to IHL. Despite this subordination, in practice because international human rights tribunals are not mandated to apply humanitarian law they necessarily interpret and enforce the rights of the victims on the basis of those human rights norms found in their respective statutes. As a result, the jurisprudence of human rights tribunals is not always consistent with IHL. Yet, such tribunals are hard pressed to accept jurisdiction over situations which would otherwise be resolved on the basis of IHL. This chapter therefore goes on to discuss the exercise of extraterritorial jurisdiction by human rights tribunals. This is particularly significant because European states involved in the occupation of Iraq or other territories generally argue that the ECHR is inapplicable. The ECtHR has taken a different approach. The parameters and consequences of this approach will be highlighted.

The second part of the chapter explores the place and function of criminal law in the prevention and protection of international human rights. In particular, we analyse the development of international criminal law as a means of prosecuting those that have violated fundamental human rights. This is not viewed as a substitution for the protection afforded by the rights regime, but as a supplement and a potential deterrent. One of the most important aspects of international criminal justice is its enforcement mechanisms, including the exercise of universal jurisdiction by local courts, as well as the establishment of the various international criminal courts and tribunals. We go on to show that international criminal justice is not free from political tensions and that states whose officials are prosecuted are in most cases reluctant to accept their prosecution.

14.2   THE FUNDAMENTAL PREMISES OF INTERNATIONAL HUMANITARIAN LAW

IHL is also known as *jus in bello* and laws of war (as opposed to the *jus ad bellum* which concerns the law relating to the use of armed force by states). Unlike human rights, which apply at all times, the application of IHL is dependent on the existence of an armed conflict. There are two types of armed conflict, international and non-international, to which distinct set of rules apply. In accordance with common article 2 of the 1949 Geneva Conventions,[1] international armed conflicts are triggered either by the mere occurrence of armed hostilities between two nations, irrespective of their intensity; an effective occupation of foreign territory, even if it is not met

---

[1] Convention for the Amelioration of the Condition of the Wounded and Sick in Armed Forces in the Field (no. I), 75 UNTS 31; Convention for the Amelioration of the Condition of the Wounded, Sick, and Ship-wrecked Members of Armed Forces at Sea (no. II), 75 UNTS 85; Convention Relative to the Treatment of Prisoners of War (no. III), 75 UNTS 135; Convention Relative to the Protection of Civilian Persons in Time of War (no. IV), 75 UNTS 287.

with resistance; a declaration of war; or by the existence of armed violence in otherwise internal conflicts in which peoples are fighting against colonial, alien and racist regimes in their exercise of self-determination.[2] The following subsections examine the fundamental tenets of IHL.

14.2.1   Distinction between combatants and non-combatants

International humanitarian law distinguishes between combatants and civilians and between military and civilian objects, requiring that only combatants and military objects be made the subject of attack.[3] This is known as the rule of distinction and is the cornerstone of IHL. A military objective encompasses those objects which by their nature, location, purpose or use make an effective contribution to military action and whose total or partial destruction, capture or neutralisation, in the circumstances ruling at the time, offers a definite military advantage.[4]

The distinction between combatants and non-combatants is equally important. Combatant status not only allows a person to be lawfully targeted, it moreover confers significant entitlements. It grants a licence to lawfully kill other combatants and be afforded prisoner of war status (POW) upon capture. Persons that do not satisfy the criteria for combatant status, such as civilians who randomly and treacherously kill members of the occupying force, do not enjoy the entitlements of combatants or the immunities of civilians from attack and are criminally liable for killing enemy personnel. It is important, therefore, to define the relevant concepts. Combatants are persons taking a direct part in hostilities. This in itself, however, is not enough. IHL requires that conflicts are fought between organised groups, whether set up by the state or private entities, such as militias, paramilitary groups and resistance movements. Only members of such groups are permitted to engage in actual combat operations. The group itself must satisfy the conditions that: (1) it is structured under an authority of responsible command; (2) its members distinguish themselves from the civilian population through a distinct emblem or uniform; (3) arms are carried openly; (4) the group conducts its operation in accordance with the laws and customs of war.[5] The rationale behind these

---

[2] 1977 Protocol I to the 1949 Geneva Conventions relative to the protection of victims in international armed conflicts (Protocol I), 1125 UNTS 3, article 1(4).

[3] Article 48, Protocol I; *Legality of the Threat or Use of Nuclear Weapons*, ICJ Reports 1996, p. 226, Advisory opinion, para. 78.

[4] Under article 52(2) of Protocol I, a 'military advantage' must be concrete, imminent and finite and not merely hypothetical or applicable to the general armed conflict as a whole. As a result, it is limited in time and space and concerns only a particular military operation. See Y. Dinstein, *The Conduct of Hostilities and the Law of International Armed Conflict* (Cambridge University Press, 2004), 87.

[5] Articles 4(A)(1)-(3) and (6) of Geneva Convention II and article 43, Protocol I. The same status is enjoyed also by persons falling under the category of *levée en masse*, which

requirements is to promote discipline, responsibility and compliance with the laws of war in exchange for recognition of legitimate combatant status. By way of illustration, members of terrorist groups do not generally satisfy conditions (2) and (4) and although they may take a direct part in hostilities they are not considered combatants.

There is dissension among scholars as to whether a distinction can be made between lawful and unlawful combatants. Some contend that the only possible distinction is between combatants and civilians, there being no other categories. Others, however, argue that persons taking a direct part in hostilities without satisfying the four criteria in the Geneva Conventions are unlawful combatants and hence do not enjoy the rights and privileges afforded to combatants.[6] The status of unlawful combatant was used by the Bush administration to deny relevant entitlements under IHL to members of the Taliban.[7]

14.2.2   Restricted targeting of military objects

In the previous section we explained the basic rule whereby IHL distinguishes between combatants and non-combatants on the basis of active participation in hostilities and emphasised that only combatants may be targeted. In practice, more complex situations may arise where the status of certain persons is not wholly susceptible to the aforementioned distinctions.

A civilian is any person who is not a member of the armed forces, a resistance movement or similar group. Moreover, the civilian population comprises all persons that are civilians.[8] On the basis of this definition the distinction between combatants and non-combatants should have been straightforward. Yet, it is not, because it is disputed whether certain activities entail a direct part in hostilities. By way of illustration, should civilian labourers working in a military factory be considered legitimate targets because they contribute to their country's war effort? To take things a step further, should such labourers be targeted when out shopping with their families? Clearly,

---

is described in article 4(A)(6) of Geneva Convention III and article 2 of the 1907 Hague Regulations. The concept refers to the spontaneous taking of arms by inhabitants of a non-occupied territory at the approach of the enemy. In this case, although such persons would normally fail to satisfy the conditions of responsible command and of sufficient distinction, they still enjoy combatant status where they satisfy the remaining two criteria.

[6] See K. Dörmann, 'The Legal Situation of Unlawful/Unprivileged Combatants', *IRRC* 85 (2003), 45; J. Callen, 'Unlawful combatants and the Geneva Conventions', *Virginia Journal of International Law* (*Virginia JIL*) 44 (2004), 1026.

[7] See G. H. Aldrich, 'The Taliban, Al-Qaeda and the Determination of Illegal Combatants', *AJIL* 96 (2002), 893.

[8] Article 50(2), Protocol I. In *ICTY Prosecutor* v. *Blaškić*, Trial Chamber judgment (3 March 2000), para. 180, the ICTY also defined them as 'persons who are not, or no longer are, members of the armed forces'.

the assumption of combatant status is less plausible in the second scenario. Both cases illustrate the pressing need for a boundary that avoids attributing each and every activity to the war effort, lest everyone be presumed to take a direct part in hostilities by reason of paying taxes which ultimately fuel the capacity of the state to wage war. Although there is no clear-cut answer to the question at hand, it seems fair to argue that civilian workers do not qualify as combatants, although a munitions factory is a legitimate military objective that can be attacked while it is working.[9] This necessarily means that the workers cannot be individually targeted whether inside the factory or outside.[10] Expert meetings convened by the ICRC suggest that in order for particular conduct to qualify as direct participation:

1   it must be likely to adversely affect the military operations or military capacity of a party to an armed conflict or, alternatively, to inflict death, injury, or destruction on persons or objects protected against direct attack (*threshold of harm*); and
2   there must be a direct causal link between the act and the harm likely to result either from that act, or from a coordinated military operation of which that act constitutes an integral part (*direct causation*); and
3   it must be specifically designed to directly cause the required threshold of harm in support of a party to the conflict and to the detriment of another (*belligerent nexus*).[11]

This discussion is meant to highlight the fact that distinguishing between combatants and non-combatants is not always a straightforward exercise. The situation is even more complicated in the context of non-international armed conflicts. Broadly speaking, these involve armed confrontations of some intensity and duration – thus excluding isolated and sporadic acts of violence – between dissident groups and government forces within the territory of a single state. The international regulation of such internal conflicts has unsurprisingly been resisted by states. They have traditionally viewed any external intervention or regulation as an encroachment in their domestic affairs and as a possible support for the rebels. It is for this reason that the 1949 Geneva Conventions contained only a single provision on non-international armed conflicts (article 3 common to all four conventions), as opposed to the elaborate body of law applicable to international armed conflicts. In

---

[9] D. Fleck, *The Handbook of Humanitarian Law in Armed Conflicts* (Oxford University Press, 1999), 163.

[10] Certainly, a case can be made in favour of targeting those persons that possess exceptional technical skills capable of producing sophisticated weaponry, because their activities contribute directly to the military superiority of the enemy. Yet, this remains a grey area subject to the dubious legality of targeted killings.

[11] ICRC, *Interpretive Guidance on the Notion of Direct Participation in Hostilities* (Geneva: ICRC, 2009), 46ff.

1977, Protocol II to the Geneva Conventions was adopted, which spelt out in more detail the rights and obligations of states in non-international armed conflicts and concretised the protection of civilian populations thereto.[12]

As a result of this uneven development of rules between the two types of armed conflict, IHL does not oblige states to recognise the rebels as legitimate combatants, even if they would otherwise qualify as such in the context of an international armed conflict. Thus, members of rebel entities, even if sufficiently organised and compliant with the *jus in bello*, can be considered common criminals by the state and be liable for murder, treason and other offences under domestic law. In practice, this means that, unlike their counterparts in international armed conflicts, members of rebel groups engaged in non-international armed conflicts will not be granted a licence to kill government soldiers or enjoy prisoner of war status upon capture under the laws of the country wherein they operate.[13] Thus, whereas general international law and IHL impose human rights restrictions on the treatment of rebel personnel and civilians in internal armed conflicts, they none the less allow states to classify participation in rebel activities under their domestic law. This by no means implies that domestic law overrides international law in internal armed conflicts. On the contrary, it is now well accepted that all parties to internal armed conflicts must comply with IHL and that persons who commit any infractions incur international criminal liability, as opposed to liability under domestic law alone.[14] It is true to say that the largest part of IHL is now common to both international and internal armed conflicts.

14.2.3   Means and methods of warfare are not unlimited

The means and methods of injuring the enemy are not unlimited. This fundamental rule is expressly provided in articles 22 and 23 of the 1907 Hague Regulations and article 35 of Protocol I of 1977 and is predicated on humanitarian principles and good faith. Humanitarian principles generally prohibit killing or wounding the enemy who has laid down his arms or is no longer able to defend himself (when a person is incapacitated in this manner he is referred to as *hors de combat*). Humanitarian principles moreover prohibit refusal to provide quarter and the causing of superfluous injury or unnecessary suffering. This prohibition includes all those weapons whose direct,

---

[12] Protocol Additional to the Geneva Convention of 1949 and Relating to the Protection of Victims of Non-International Armed Conflicts (Protocol II), 1125 UNTS 609.

[13] Although under article 6(5) of Protocol II 1977 governments are urged to offer the widest possible range of amnesties to rebel groups after the end of hostilities to the extent that these are related to their participation in the armed conflict (i.e. it would not cover common crimes or war crimes).

[14] See particularly *ICTY Prosecutor* v. *Tadić*, Decision on interlocutory appeal on jurisdiction (5 October 1995), paras. 116–17; ICC Statute, article 8(2)(c)–(e).

as opposed to incidental, use on the enemy would bring about this effect. Incendiary weapons would fall within this category. The rules on good faith prohibit killing or wounding the enemy treacherously, or deceiving him by the improper use of the flag of truce, of national emblems or by wearing enemy uniforms, as well as by the improper use of the Red Cross emblem.

14.3   RIGHTS AND OBLIGATIONS IN HUMANITARIAN LAW

The foundations of IHL are different from the body of law known as human rights. First, and most importantly, IHL permits the parties to an armed conflict to target and kill persons taking a direct part in hostilities, whereas under the international human rights regime the right to life is non-derogable, albeit limited restrictions exist exceptional circumstances. Clearly, therefore, while one may speak of the obligation of the state to preserve the life of its citizens as a matter of human rights, IHL is premised on the right to kill. This approach is hardly an anachronism. The international community has long recognised that although recourse to armed force is, and must be, prohibited[15] this fact alone does not necessarily guarantee the cessation of armed hostilities from the world stage. The prevalence of armed conflicts, whether large or small, short-lived or otherwise, has increased in the aftermath of the Cold War. Moreover, some conflicts are the direct result of causes unknown to past generations, such as disputes between pastoralist and farming communities in the developing world over access to valuable land and its natural resources.[16]

The seeming inevitability of violence in human relations even up to this day has necessitated the formulation of binding regulations that are both realistic and acceptable within the current state-centric order. By way of example, states would find unacceptable a prohibition to kill enemy combatants on the battlefield as this would render redundant the relevant provisions of the UN Charter relating to the use of force and self-defence, not to mention the rationale for the formation of professional armies. On the contrary, it would make sense to 'humanise' the conduct of warfare by restricting the range of persons that can be lawfully killed, particularly with a view

---

[15] Subject of course to the express exceptions permitted by the *jus ad bellum*, i.e. self defence (article 51 UN Charter) and UNSC authorisations (article 42 UN Charter).

[16] UNEP, Understanding Environment, Conflict and Cooperation, UNEP Doc. DEW/0571/NA (2004). More specifically, see UNEP, Post-Conflict Environmental Assessment, UNEP Doc. DEP/0816/GE (2007), 8–10, 83, which states that localised conflicts over land in Sudan have been prevalent since at least the 1930s, but these did not culminate in widespread hostilities until only recently. In the Darfur conflict, some of the contributing – not root – causes have been competition over oil and gas reserves, water and timber, confrontations over the use of agricultural land, with particular emphasis on rangeland and rain-fed land, which is scarce in the mostly arid Darfur region. Such traditional conflicts have turned large-scale because of the availability of weapons and the involvement of third parties.

to sparing the civilian population and those combatants who are no longer capable of threatening their adversaries. This 'humanisation' of war, although certainly influenced by human rights notions, should be distinguished from any discussion about rights. Indeed, the rationale for contemporary human rights is founded on the uneven distribution of power between the state and its citizens, thus requiring the state to limit its power against the governed and provide the necessary conditions for the exercise of a range of freedoms. IHL, on the other hand, is concerned with the reciprocal expectations and obligations of equal sovereigns in respect of international conflicts. It is not founded on rights claims by the actors engaged in armed conflict, but on the notion of reciprocal treatment and chivalry between the governments of the warring parties,[17] as well as self-interest.

Of course, this does not mean that IHL is simply contractual in nature; rather, those engulfed by armed hostilities are protected by a plethora of rules. Yet, it is not wise to compare these rules to, or conflate them with, the individual entitlements inherent in human rights law.[18] No doubt, IHL recognises a number of entitlements, such as those afforded to POWs in the Third Geneva Convention and these clearly mirror a species of human rights. At the same time, however, the prohibition against indiscriminate attacks on civilians or denial of quarter cannot neatly be described as individual rights because in practical terms they are not enforceable by the intended rights-holders in the midst of battle. It is for these reasons that IHL, instead of setting out lists of rights, emphasises the protection afforded to 'protected persons'. Thus, it is best to approach IHL not as a system of rights (despite the existence of numerous individual rights) but as a corpus of law whose primary interest is to offer protection.

Another difference between IHL and human rights relates to the notion of obligation. Whereas traditionally international human rights obligations are addressed to states, IHL obligations are incumbent on all parties to an armed conflict. This includes non-state actors, such as rebel and paramilitary groups, mercenaries and private security firms. All of these entities have an obligation to respect the laws of war and may not use their inferior military power in relation to government forces as an excuse to violate IHL, such as by employing terror tactics against the civilian population.

Finally, unlike human rights treaty bodies vested with the adjudication of individual complaints, IHL treaties are not supported by predetermined international enforcement mechanisms, or an individual complaints system. Enforcement jurisdiction is assumed either by national courts or other *ad hoc* or hybrid international tribunals. In any event, the primary responsibility of

---

[17] C. Droege, 'Elective Affinities? Human Rights and Humanitarian Law', *IRRC* 9 (2008), 501, at 503–4.

[18] Ibid., pp. 503–7; M. Sassóli and A. A. Bouvier, *How Does Law Protect in War?* (Geneva: ICRC, 1999), pp. 265–7.

the perpetrators is criminal, unlike human rights tribunals, where the liability sought is primarily of a civil, or similar, nature. Despite the obvious and conflicting differences between human rights and IHL they are far from being characterised as wholly incompatible. The following section attempts to highlight where they meet and how they interact.

14.4   HUMANITARIAN LAW AS *LEX SPECIALIS* TO HUMAN RIGHTS LAW

Despite the horizontal relationship between the actors that set up the rules of IHL (i.e. states acting for the benefit of their armies), as well as the authority granted to combatants to employ lethal force against their adversaries, it is generally agreed that human rights play a distinct part in the operation of IHL. For one thing, the essence of IHL is not to legitimise violence in situations of armed conflict; rather, it is to limit the range of persons and objects upon which armed force may be employed. It is no wonder, therefore, that the fundamental rule of IHL permits only the targeting of combatants and military objects. If this protection afforded to non-combatants were to be framed in human rights terms, it would encompass both an obligation on the state and an enforceable entitlement in favour of the targeted person. In IHL the individual entitlement is missing and the state is responsible for educating, preventing and punishing its forces for any infractions of the *jus in bello*. Moreover, the perpetrators of IHL violations are criminally liable under domestic and international law. Evidently, this is exclusively a state-centric process. It is also obvious that there is a practical dimension to the absence of rights in most fields of IHL. In the midst of combat operations it is futile to dispute one's combatant rights and all the individual entitlements that flow from this status.

Hence, the incorporation of a rights discourse in IHL must be couched in other terms. It is obvious that IHL and human rights share the same subjects and converge in at least two respects. First, human rights law permits derogations in times of emergency, including during armed conflict, in which case it would be lawful to kill an enemy combatant. This is consistent with the rationale of IHL. Secondly, both human rights law and IHL seek the minimisation of physical harm against combatants and other persons engaged in armed conflict when other means for neutralising them are available. While the ICJ in its 1996 advisory opinion on the *Legality of the Threat or Use of Nuclear Weapons* validated this convergence it expressly recognised the underlying limitations by observing that:

the protection of the ICCPR does not cease in times of war, except by operation of article 4 of the Covenant whereby certain provisions may be derogated from in a time of national emergency. Respect for the right to life is not, however, such a provision.

In principle, the right to be deprived of one's life applies also in hostilities. The test of what is an arbitrary deprivation of life, however, then falls to be determined by the applicable *lex specialis*, namely, the law applicable in armed conflict which is designed to regulate the conduct of hostilities. Thus, whether a particular loss of life, through the use of a certain weapon in warfare, is to be considered an arbitrary deprivation of life contrary to article 6 of the Covenant, can only be decided by reference to the law applicable in armed conflict and not deduced from the terms of the Covenant itself.[19]

The ICJ's characterisation of the *jus in bello* as *lex specialis* suggests that the permissibility of public or private conduct in armed conflicts cannot ultimately be determined by human rights rules but by IHL. In a subsequent advisory opinion on the *Legal Consequences of the Construction of a Wall in the Occupied Palestinian Territory* the Court elaborated that the interplay between the two bodies of law gives rise to three possible situations: that some matters may be exclusively regulated by IHL, others exclusively by human rights norms and yet others by a combination of both.[20] Although the ICJ has failed to specify in what manner the *jus in bello* operates as *lex specialis*, it is fair to argue that it is employed not as a tool of treaty interpretation but as a conflict of rules mechanism. This means that where a rule of IHL is in direct conflict with a rule of human rights law – assuming the two are truly irreconcilable in particular cases – the former takes precedence.[21] We have already alluded to some situations involving the primacy of IHL (e.g. the rights of combatants to kill other combatants), whereas in respect of others there is a clear synergy and compatibility between IHL and human rights. This is true for example in respect of fundamental guarantees afforded to civilian populations in situations of belligerent occupation. This solution offered by the Court is not without its critics, who generally argue that the ICJ artificially fragments the two bodies of law when it could just as well bring them together in harmony.[22] This position is also implicitly maintained by the HRCtee, which noted that:

The Covenant applies also in situations of armed conflict to which the rules of international humanitarian law are applicable. While, in respect of certain Covenant rights, more specific rules of international humanitarian law may be specially relevant for the purposes of the interpretation of Covenant rights, both spheres of law are complementary, not mutually exclusive.[23]

---

[19] *Legality of the Threat or Use of Nuclear Weapons* (1996) ICJ Reports, para. 25.

[20] *Legal Consequences of the Construction of a Wall in the Occupied Palestinian Territory* (*Wall* case), (2004) ICJ Reports, para. 106.

[21] See also *Coard* v. *USA*, IACHR, case 10.951, OEA Doc. OEA/Ser. L/V/II.106.doc3.rev (1999), para. 42, which iterated the ICJ's *lex specialis* argument.

[22] N. Prud'homme, 'Lex Specialis: Oversimplifying a More Complex and Multifaceted Relationship?' *Israel L. Rev.* 40 (2007), 536.

[23] HRCtee, General Comment 31, UN Doc. CCPR/C/21/Rev.1/Add.13 (2004), para. 11.

14.5   WHY HUMAN RIGHTS BODIES FIND THE APPLICATION OF HUMANITARIAN LAW PROBLEMATIC

Because the founding premises of IHL and human rights are different, the two bodies of law do not always approach their subject matter in the same way. This of course has not stopped human rights treaty bodies applying human rights to situations of armed conflict without making use of the *lex specialis* principle. This approach is not justified as a matter of legal doctrine but by practical considerations. Human rights treaty bodies are only empowered to apply their treaties, none of which makes direct references to IHL. As a result, the only way such courts could legitimately employ IHL is if they approximate and render it compatible with human rights law. Were human rights courts to follow the *lex specialis* approach of the ICJ they would be forced to admit the superiority of IHL over the provisions of their statutes in particular situations and thus find themselves incapable of passing judgment. None the less, no one can blame human rights treaty bodies for giving effect to the rights prescribed in their treaties.

One should also note the lack of expertise of human rights treaty bodies with other specialist areas of international law which, coupled with their desire to promote protection, may allow them to render erroneous results.[24] There is the 'danger' that if treaty bodies apply IHL instruments they will necessarily be drawn into the relevant jurisprudence of international criminal tribunals with which they may be unfamiliar. Moreover, the jurisprudence may turn out to produce results that clash with the case law of treaty bodies, not to mention that by applying IHL instruments they risk being accused of acting *ultra vires*.[25]

The ECtHR has had the opportunity to deal with situations of internal armed conflict where it was claimed by the victims that government forces used excessive force against the civilian population. In the *Isayeva, Yusupova* and *Bazayeva* cases Russian armed forces had launched a missile

---

[24] In *Medvedyev and Others* v. *France*, (2010) 51 EHRR 39, a French warship intercepted and arrested the crew of a Cambodian vessel transporting drugs following the consent of the Cambodian authorities. The ECtHR misconstrued the ambit of article 110 of UNCLOS, by asserting that non-flag states do not require the consent of the flag state in order to search and seize foreign vessels in cases of piracy, slave trade, unauthorised broadcasting and in respect of stateless ships (para. 54).

[25] The practice of the IACHR seems to be exceptional. In the *Tablada* case, paras. 157–64 Report no. 55/97, case no. 11.127 (18 November 1997) the Commission held that it could validly apply IHL because OAS member states were parties to the Geneva Conventions and also because since the American Convention did not provide for violations during armed conflict it would have to decline jurisdiction, which would have been absurd. See also *DRC* v. *Rwanda, Burundi, Uganda*, African Commission of Human Rights, decision (March 2003), Comm. no. 227/99.

attack against a civilian convoy in their pursuit of Chechen rebels, which culminated in the death of the children of one of the claimants. The Court accepted that because of the insurgency the employment of lethal force was justified, but this was necessarily limited to legitimate targets while at the same time the government was required to minimise any harm to civilians.[26] Upon finding that government forces had taken no such measures to make this distinction the Court upheld a violation of article 2 of the Convention that guarantees the right to life. The language is reminiscent of the obligation to take precautions in attack, which is inherent in IHL legal terminology.[27]

Although human rights courts cannot apply IHL over and above their founding instruments, they cannot lightly dismiss the reality of armed conflict and the rationale of IHL rules, to which in any event all states have subscribed by reason of treaty or customary international law. Hence, just like *Yusupova* and *Bazayeva* the ECtHR in *Ergi* v. *Turkey* considered the right to life in the context of military operations in a non-international armed conflict from the point of view of necessity and proportionality. While it did not dispute the army's entitlement to attack rebel elements it questioned its choice of 'feasible precautions' in order to 'minimise incidental loss to civilian life'.[28] Given that this is exactly what the relevant rules of IHL postulate it is easy to see that human rights courts are necessarily drawn into accepting and applying the fundamental guarantees of the *jus in bello* in situations of human rights violations in armed conflicts. The obligation to take precautions in order to avoid civilian casualties is addressed to government forces, not rebels, unlike IHL where the relevant obligations are addressed equally to all warring parties. The rationale of the Court is that if rebel forces can be apprehended with minimal, non-lethal, force, then any disproportionate lethal force and the use of indiscriminate weapons is a violation of the right to life and other rights.[29]

Human rights courts have not, however, gone as far as saying that government forces must try to first arrest a combatant or rebel before opening fire against him or using other lethal force. None the less, they have distinguished armed conflicts from other situations involving lower intensity hostilities, such as terrorist operations, in respect of which they have asserted the obligation of the state to arrest the accused, rather than kill, where this is feasible.

---

[26] *Isayeva, Yusupova* and *Bazayeva* v. *Russia*, (2005) 41 EHRR 39, paras. 175–8.

[27] Article 57(2)(a)(ii) Protocol I.

[28] *Ergi* v. *Turkey*, (2001) 32 EHRR 18, para. 79.

[29] *Hamiyet Kaplan* v. *Turkey*, ECtHR judgment (13 September 2005), paras. 51–5; *Isayeva* v. *Russia*, (2005) 41 EHRR 38, para. 191; *Akhmadov* v. *Russia*, ECtHR judgment (14 November 2008), para. 99.

14.6   HUMAN RIGHTS IN SITUATIONS OF MILITARY OCCUPATION

In recent times occupations have arisen by unilateral military action, or as a result of coalition initiatives supported by the UN Security Council, as was the case with the occupation of Iraq in 2003. Given that all types of military occupation involve the dissolution of sovereign powers, which are thereafter assumed by the occupier, it is only natural that international law imposes a set of strict obligations on the occupier, the purpose of which is to protect the rights of the occupied civilian population. Under article 42 of the 1907 Hague Regulations a territory is considered occupied when it is actually placed under the authority of the occupying state. In this manner, the existence of occupation is a matter of fact, rather than a matter of law and exists irrespective of its recognition by the occupier. Moreover, the legal effects of occupation extend only to territories over which the occupying power exercises effective control. This observation is particularly important for the application of human rights because under customary international law the occupier replaces the previous government in the territory concerned and must 'take all the measures in [its] power to restore, and ensure, as far as possible, public order and safety, while respecting, unless absolutely prevented, the laws in force in the country'.[30] This necessarily means that the occupier becomes the government responsible for the occupied territory and not merely an interim administrator stripped of responsibility.[31] If this were not so, there would exist no authority to protect the rights of civilian populations in occupied territories. IHL and general international law, simply put, does not accept that the occupying power can deny or relinquish its responsibility to protect the occupied population.

In the previous section we discussed the clash in certain instances between human rights and humanitarian law in situations of armed conflict. The particular context of a military occupation lies somewhere between war and peace and is generally characterised by the cessation of armed hostilities and the resumption of civilian life. Despite the absence of armed hostilities a military occupation is none the less chiefly regulated by IHL, not by human rights law, and thus the armoury of human rights is not automatically transplanted in the relationship between the occupier and the occupied population. There are some cogent reasons for this approach, particularly the possible existence of resistance movements and the resumption of armed confrontations by non-state actors against the occupier. However, unless

---

[30] Article 43, Hague Regulations; see also case concerning *Armed Activities on the Territory of the Congo* (*DRC* v. *Uganda*), Judgment, ICJ Reports 2005, p. 168, paras. 172–5.

[31] See O. B. Naftali and Y. Shany, 'Living in Denial: the Application of Human Rights in the Occupied Territories', *Israel L. Rev.* 37 (2003–4), 17, at 52–3, for an analysis of the objections of Israel and the USA on this matter.

civilians take up arms against the occupying forces in an organised manner or through the re-emergence of their national army, in which case the relevant entitlements of the *jus in bello* come into operation, the occupying power is not permitted to treat the civilian population as combatants or as otherwise lawful targets. Hence, if members of the occupied population are found to possess weapons in their homes it would be going too far to target them under the pretence that they are combatants, particularly if the local law prior to the occupation justified the possession of weapons. As a result, there is a need to determine the precise boundary between the obligation of the occupier to protect the civilian population from the entitlement under the laws of war to attack those civilians that take up arms against its authority.

This entitlement only arises where the renewed levels of violence reach the threshold of an armed conflict. In all other cases, the protection owed to the civilian population is very much akin to human rights in times of peace. Even so, the relevant *jus in bello* treaties (namely the 1907 Hague Regulations, Geneva Convention IV and Protocol I of 1977) treat the obligations of the occupier *vis-à-vis* the occupied population as 'guarantees', thus seemingly excluding the conferral of individual or collective rights.[32] The *lex specialis* character of the law of belligerent occupation does not exclude the application of human rights to the occupied population, so long as such rights are not detrimental to law and order or violate the occupier's rights under international law.

Moreover, IHL has not developed an elaborate enough corpus of rules and jurisprudence to deal with the guarantees it provides. For example, if the occupier is permitted to suspend those laws that are deemed abusive, discriminatory or of a similar nature, under what legal criteria is this to be assessed? Clearly, the introduction of legislation against discrimination, universal schooling, social security, freedom of thought, conscience and religion, among others, can only be premised on human rights law.[33] In this sense, human rights law is deemed *lex generalis* and applies by reason of the fact that no special rules of IHL exist. While it is clear that in theory the *lex generalis* nature of human rights should ensure their application in military occupations, most occupying powers would disfavour such a wholesale and automatic importation because it would entail the application of their human rights legislation in the occupied territory; the latter would effectively become an extension of their own territory for the purpose of individual rights. Such an eventuality brings with it a significant complication which the occupier would rather avoid. Whereas under the (IHL) law of occupation the occupier may derogate certain rights in order to restore public order

---

[32] See articles 43–51 1907 Hague Regulations.

[33] See A. Roberts, 'Transformative Military Occupation: Applying the Laws of War and Human Rights', *AJIL* 100 (2006), 589, at 594.

and safety, he would not be able to derogate fundamental rights if subject to human rights law.[34] Hence, the potential of human rights law in military occupation is beyond gap-filling, but may indeed transform the obligations of the occupier.

No doubt, many states have resisted the notion that human rights law can dictate how the restoration of law and order should be assessed and which courts are to adjudicate on any infractions. None the less, the jurisprudence of the ICJ,[35] human rights treaty bodies[36] and UN institutions is unequivocal that human rights are an integral part of the international law of occupation – provided of course that they do not clash with a *lex specialis* rule of IHL. However, in the course of occupation no such clashes exist because public order can only be restored through police action and not military operations that would necessitate the derogation of rights.[37] By way of illustration, where an occupier finds himself in a law enforcement situation and in a position to effectuate an arrest, he should comply with the requirements of human rights law and minimise his use of lethal force rather than kill the suspect. In theory, the very same result is warranted under IHL.[38]

That human rights law applies in occupied territories – and by extension the international human rights obligations of the occupier – is necessitated by practical considerations. Occupations can drag on for decades in relative peace and order and so it is inconceivable that the occupier could suspend the enjoyment of rights to the civilian population indefinitely. This practical necessity was recognised by the Security Council in Resolution 1483 which called on the Coalition Authority in occupied Iraq to cooperate with the UN

---

[34] Derogations in times of war and military occupation are expressly provided in the major international human rights instruments (save for the ICESCR), in situations involving 'a public emergency threatening the life of the nation' (article 4(1) ICCPR). The HRCtee has concluded as a result that military occupations justify only permissible derogations under the ICCPR. See Concluding observations on Cyprus, UN Doc. CCPR/C/79/Add.39 (21 September 1994), para. 3; Concluding Observations on Israel, UN Doc. CCPR/CO/78/ISR (21 August 2003), para. 11.

[35] *Armed Activities on the Territory of the Congo*, (New Application: 2002) (*Democratic Republic of the Congo* v. *Rwanda*), Jurisdiction and admissibility, judgment ICJ Reports 2006, p. 6, para. 216; *Wall* case, paras. 107–12.

[36] *Loizidou* v. *Turkey* (1997) 23 EHRR 513; *Cyprus* v. *Turkey* (2002) 35 EHRR 30.

[37] M. Sassòli, 'Legislation and maintenance of public order and civil life by occupying powers', *EJIL* 16 (2005), 661, at 665.

[38] N. Meltzer, *Targeted Killings* (Oxford University Press, 2007), pp. 224–30. The so-called Martens clause, for example, which is found in the preamble to the 1907 Hague Convention no. IV, was intended to offer additional protection to victims of armed conflict in situations where IHL was silent or underdeveloped. The same result is also confirmed by article 72 of Protocol I of 1977, which stipulates that the provisions of section III thereof supplement Geneva Convention IV (the Civilians and Occupation Convention) as well as 'other applicable rules of international law relating to the protection of fundamental human rights during international armed conflict'.

'in promoting the protection of human rights' in its process of governmental and judicial reform.[39] Furthermore, in respect of the West Bank and the Gaza strip, Israel has maintained that it is merely a temporary administrator for the former and that since 2005 it has had no authority over Gaza whatsoever, having withdrawn its troops from the area. In reality, Israel maintains a strong and effective military presence in the West Bank and an aerial, naval and land blockade in Gaza. Its denial of occupation is clearly aimed at avoiding the full gamut of obligations pertaining to occupying powers. Yet, even the Israeli Supreme Court has held that the Fourth Geneva Convention and the 1907 Hague Regulations are part of customary international law and apply to Israeli 'occupied territories'.[40] This is a logical, yet bold, decision that denies the Israeli government the right to suspend international law from those territories.

14.6.1   The extraterritorial application of human rights in occupied territories

It has been established that the occupier cannot deny the applicability of its ordinary human rights obligations to the population of the occupied territory. This obligation is subject to two distinct practical limitations. First, the territory in question must be actually occupied, thus excluding parts thereof that are controlled, or sufficiently resisted, by rebel movements. Secondly, the application of human rights by the occupier does not *ipso facto* entail access to its national courts, unless this possibility is expressly postulated.

The human rights obligations of a state are generally owed to all persons on its territory, both citizens and aliens; they are not owed to persons situated in other states. As a result, the ordinary operation of human rights is territorial, whereas the operation of humanitarian law is also extraterritorial, in the sense that it is applicable wherever a state undertakes armed hostilities, whether internally or abroad. We have already alluded to the fact that the extraterritorial application of human rights is exceptionally possible in situations of effective control of foreign territory; however, this is not always clear cut. The *Al-Skeini* case is instructive of the problems inherent in the extraterritorial application of a state's human rights obligations in situations of military occupation. There, Baha Mousa, a man in the custody of British soldiers in the Iraqi city of Basra, died as a result of injuries inflicted following his arrest and a further five civilians were randomly killed in the course of security operations. Although British forces were mandated

---

[39] UNSC resolution 1483 (22 May 2003), para. 8(c), (g) and (i). See also UNSC resolution 1546 (8 June 2004), para. 7(b)(iii), which subsequently extended this mandate to another entity.

[40] *Beit Sourik Village Council* v. *The Government of Israel*, HCJ 2056/04 (2 May 2004), paras. 23–5. For a more comprehensive review readers should consult Y. Shany, 'Binary Law meets Complex Reality: The Occupation of Gaza Debate', *Israel L. Rev.* 41 (2008), 68.

to exercise occupation in Al Basra and Maysan provinces they had not put in place any executive, judicial or legislative authority in Basra city. The families of the deceased applied to British courts with a view to extending the application of the UK Human Rights Act to Iraq, which incorporates the ECHR. The majority of the Court of Appeals accepted that the lack of effective control precluded the application of the ECHR generally in Basra.[41] The Court of Appeals based this conclusion on the fact that the British contingent in Basra, although patrolling its streets and ensuring law and order in the city, had not set up any administrative or judicial structures such that would challenge local institutions.

This result is unconvincing because the primary reason for the presence of British troops in Basra was the occupation of Iraq, not a peacekeeping mandate.[42] The Grand Chamber of the ECtHR naturally disagreed with this conclusion. It found that the UK itself declared to the Security Council that it had assumed governmental powers after the fall of the Baath regime in Iraq and exercised effective control in the south-east corner of the country. As a result, the Convention was applicable to the events in question.[43]

Whereas occupying states have traditionally relied on the international law of occupation in order to avoid the application of human rights law,[44] the recent 'erosion' of this body of law by human rights courts has forced states to increasingly refute their exercise of occupation by relying on technicalities. Human rights courts have been able to expand the obligations of states beyond their territories not by enforcing the positive obligations owed by occupiers under IHL, but rather through a logical and purposive interpretation of the jurisdictional clauses contained in their statutes. Article 2(1) of the ICCPR confines a state's human rights obligations to persons 'within its

---

[41] *R* v. *The Secretary of State for Defence, ex parte Al-Skeini and Others* [2005] EWCA Civ. 1609, para. 124; sustained by the House of Lords in [2008] AC 153.

[42] In the subsequent case of *R* (*on the application of Al-Saadoon and Mufdhi*) v. *Secretary of State for Defence* [2009] EWCA Civ. 7, paras. 32–3, the Court of Appeals held that the surrender of two Iraqis to the Iraqi authorities by British forces in Basra did not trigger the application of the Human Rights Act because from May 2006 onwards the forces were not authorised to carry out any military activities on Iraqi territory. At best, British forces were acting as an agent of the Iraqi courts when arresting persons accused of serious crimes. This line of reasoning was entrenched in the English Supreme Court, which dismissed an application by a soldier killed in Iraq. See *R* (*On the Application of Smith*) v. *Secretary of State for Defence et al.* [2010] UKSC 29. The ECtHR avoided determination as to whether an occupation was in existence, accepting implicitly that the detention of the applicants by British forces sufficed to bring the situation within the jurisdiction of the Convention. *Al-Saadoon and Mufdhi* v. *UK*, ECtHR judgment (2 March 2010).

[43] See *Al-Skeini and Others* v. *UK*, ECtHR judgment (7 July 2011), paras. 143–50.

[44] See Droege, above note 17, at 511–13, who refers to the drafting history of article 2(1) of the ICCPR, which originally read exactly like article 1 of the ECHR. The US delegate was successful in inserting an amendment, which reflects its current wording, with the purpose of excluding the application of the Covenant in situations of military occupation.

territory and subject to its jurisdiction', while article 1 of the ECHR states that parties 'shall secure to everyone within their jurisdiction' the rights stipulated in the Convention. The jurisdictional clause of the ICCPR is a lot more restrictive than its ECHR counterpart, given that it seems to imply a cumulative application of both criteria. However, the UN Human Rights Committee has refused to offer it such a narrow construction. Its rationale is that 'it would be unconscionable to so interpret the responsibility under article 2 of the Covenant as to permit a State party to perpetrate violations of the Covenant on the territory of another State, which violations it could not perpetrate on its own territory'.[45] Although this case concerned an extraterritorial kidnapping by state agents and not an armed conflict *per se*, we have already seen that the Committee has not hesitated to apply the Covenant to military occupations.[46]

14.6.2   The effective control test

Following the invasion of Cyprus in 1974 by Turkish armed forces the island was effectively cut in the middle; the northern part was occupied by the Turkish military, whereas the southern part remained in the hands of its elected and universally recognised government, that of the Republic of Cyprus. Despite the claims of the occupier that the Turkish armed forces merely assisted the Turkish Cypriot community in the exercise of its right of self-determination, which led to the self-proclamation of the so-called Turkish Republic of Northern Cyprus (TRNC), no state has extended recognition to the TRNC. The aim of the occupier was clearly to refute any claims of occupation, arguing instead that a new nation had emerged which was not only a distinct entity from Turkey itself but a full sovereign. By doing so it aimed to avoid all responsibility under general international law, IHL and human rights law. Within a few years of the separation of the island the Turkish government had resettled a significant number of persons from mainland Turkey with a view to altering the demographic status quo and proceeded to abrogate the property rights of Greek Cypriots who had fled in fear of their lives.

The *Loizidou* case was the first to challenge Turkish assumptions about the legal status of the occupation. The applicant lived and owned property in the occupied north prior to the invasion and was precluded by the authorities from peacefully enjoying her property rights. Turkey, on the other hand, argued that the territory of the TRNC, being an independent state, was outside its jurisdiction and hence outside the ambit of the ECHR. The central issue was therefore the precise meaning of 'jurisdiction' for the purposes of article

---

[45] *López Burgos* v. *Uruguay*, UN Doc. CCPR/C/13/D/52/1979 (29 July 1981), para. 12.3.
[46] HRCtee, General Comment 31.

1 of the ECHR, with particular reference to situations in which a state party exercised some degree of control in the territory of a non-party state. The ECtHR iterated that the responsibility of a party may be involved on account of: (1) acts of their authorities, whether performed within or outside national boundaries, which produce effects outside their own territory; as well as (2) 'when as a consequence of military action – whether lawful or unlawful – it exercises *effective control* of an area outside its national territory'.[47] Unlike other 'effective control' tests propounded for the determination of an agency relationship under general international law, for the purposes of the ECHR a detailed control over the policies and actions of the local authorities is not in fact required.[48] In the case at hand, the existence of large numbers of Turkish troops engaged in active duties in northern Cyprus was sufficient for a finding of effective overall control.[49]

Whereas Turkish military action best exemplifies a clear-cut case of belligerent occupation, there exist situations where armed violence is not followed by effective control, or where effective control is maintained only by instilling fear through the use of local agents. It is arguable whether in respect of any of these the ECHR may be triggered through the actions of the protagonist states. In the *Banković* case NATO air force bombed the headquarters of Serbian radio and television, killing several employees in the process. The ECtHR contended that the aerial nature of the assault alone did not entail an effective control of Yugoslav territory and hence did not fall within the juridical space of the Convention.[50] Whereas some commentators may have characterised the *Banković* judgment as a regression in comparison to *Loizidou*, it in fact maintains the logical fault lines between IHL and human rights as identified above. Quite clearly, in *Banković* one cannot speak of an occupation but of an armed conflict in progress. It would be stretching the law of occupation and the meaning of 'effective overall control' to deem otherwise.

The aforementioned situations should probably be contrasted from the Israeli control of Gaza, in respect of which Israel terminated its occupation in 2005, albeit maintaining full control over the largest part of the maritime and aerial entry point into Gaza. The Israeli Supreme Court has held that 'since 2005 Israel no longer has effective control over what happens in the Gaza strip'.[51] Although Israel's control of Gaza must certainly be distinguished from the Turkish occupation of Cyprus, it is undeniable that it exercises effective control over a strategic infrastructure directly affecting the people of Gaza. It should therefore bear responsibility for those rights which are directly affected by its maritime and naval blockade.

---

[47] *Loizidou* v. *Turkey*, Preliminary objections, judgment (23 March 1995), para. 62.

[48] *Loizidou* v. *Turkey* (1997) 23 EHRR 513, para. 56.   [49] Ibid.

[50] *Banković and Others* v. *Belgium and Others*, (2001) 11 BHRC 435, para. 75.

[51] *Jaber Al-Bassiouni* v. *The Prime Minister of Israel*, HCJ 9132/07 judgment (30 January 2008), para. 12.

14.6.3   The decisive influence test

The ECtHR has had the opportunity to deal with situations in which a third state was providing support to a separatist movement, without overtly employing armed force itself. In the *Ilaşcu* case the applicants were unlawfully arrested and detained by the breakaway authorities of the so-called Moldovan Republic of Transdniestria (MRT), which while claiming its unilateral independence, is in fact part of the Republic of Moldova. Yet, because of Russian military and political assistance to Transdniestria and the presence of elements of the Russian army therein[52] – as part of military arrangements predating the independence of Moldova – the Moldovan government has been unable to quell the insurrection or use force against the separatist forces. The Court decided to dilute its effective overall control standard, without sufficient legal justification, stating that Russian jurisdiction and responsibility was triggered because the MRT 'remain[ed] under the effective authority, or at the very least under the decisive influence, of the Russian Federation, and in any event that it survives by virtue of the military, economic, financial and political support given to it by the Russian Federation'.[53] The Court did not view this case as exceptional, but as an alternative to situations of occupation proper entailing effective control. It was perhaps mindful that the exercise of 'decisive influence' and 'effective authority' would not be tantamount to a military occupation, while at the same time Russia was well capable of preventing the violations attributable to the separatist Transdniestrian regime on account of their agency relationship.[54]

The ICJ's determination of effective control by proxy is much more rigid, although in principle it is at par with the case law of the ECtHR. In the *Bosnian Genocide* case the ICJ refuted the claim that the Bosnian Serb army was an agent of the FRY, irrespective of the fact that FRY paid the salaries of the army. Its rationale was predicated on the argument that an agency of this nature requires 'complete dependence' on the principal, which was missing in the present instance.[55] This responsibility of the principal in respect of acts of its agents is a significant feature of human rights law[56] – apart from the international law of state responsibility – because it serves to encompass the violations of the agent within the sphere of human rights obligations ordinarily applicable to the principal.

---

[52] *Ilaşcu and Others* v. *Moldova and Russia* (2005) 40 EHRR 46, para. 382.

[53] Ibid., para. 392.

[54] Ibid., para. 393.

[55] *Application of the Convention on the Prevention and Punishment of Genocide* (*Bosnia and Herzegovina* v. *Serbia and Montenegro*), Judgment, ICJ Reports 2007, 43, para. 392.

[56] *Issa and Others* v. *Turkey* (2005) 41 EHRR 27, para. 71; *Cyprus* v. *Turkey*, Judgment, para. 77.

CASE STUDY 14.1
Demopoulos and Others v. *Turkey,* ECtHR admissibility decision of
1 March 2010

In this case, a number of internally displaced Cypriots who lost their properties in the wake of the Turkish invasion were petitioning the ECtHR to assess their property claims against the occupying power. It will be recalled that the so-called TRNC set up by Turkey was not afforded international recognition and the occupation was deemed unlawful by the Security Council (UNSC resolution 541 (1983)). Moreover, as a result of the severity of the invasion and the subsequent occupation of northern Cyprus its Greek Cypriot inhabitants hurriedly fled to the south or elsewhere and abandoned their properties. By the time the present petitions were filed the TRNC authorities had set up a new compensation Law which established an Immovable Property Commission (IPC). The purported role of the IPC was to examine property applications of internally displaced and refugees with a view to a final, binding, settlement and compensation.

Although this would ordinarily have been a welcome development, the Compensation Law suffered from three deficiencies. First, it was contrary to article 159(1) of the TRNC Constitution, which deemed all 'abandoned' property following the invasion as belonging to itself. Second, restitution of property was a possible remedy, but not the only one. Hence, in most cases the owner would be forced to accept some form of compensation or an exchange arrangement with properties in the south of the island, something which was not, however, within the authority of the IPC. Third, unlike situations where the occupying force regulates matters pertaining to the occupied civilian population, in the present case the applicants were not under the authority of the occupant, having fled to save their lives. The central issue therefore is whether the occupying power may, in violation of international humanitarian law, overturn the laws in force of the occupied territory, so as to render itself capable of assessing anew the property rights of the civilian population.

Before we set out to examine the position of the Court, the applicants' point of view should be highlighted:

58. They emphasised that the IPC remedy was operated by the authorities of an entity widely resented and distrusted by Greek Cypriots and universally viewed (save in Turkey) as an unlawful occupier. Many property owners felt unable to submit to, or effectively collaborate with, an occupying power in such a way. It was important to note that Turkey had failed to acknowledge responsibility for any violations in this area, nor had it returned property in the *Loizidou* and *Xenides-Arestis* cases, or three years later, paid the latter applicant the award of just satisfaction, showing a consistent practice of failing to comply with Court judgments … Further, there was a continuing policy and practice to prevent the return of Greek Cypriots, reinforced by sale and development of their land, and visa provisions impeding permanent return.

59. The applicants submitted that, in cases of interference with property, restitution should be automatic in the absence of material impossibility. Denial of owners' rights could not be justified by the need to re-house Turkish Cypriots, and any interference with the rights of current users would be justified as necessary to protect the rights of the owners. The applicants were not interested in compensation calculated on the basis of a de facto expropriation and could not be required to surrender the property rights repeatedly confirmed by the Court. Return of property was only likely to occur under the Law in very limited circumstances, due to the numerous and widely framed exceptions. The remedy of exchanging property was also highly problematic since neither the IPC nor the TRNC authorities had any authority over properties in the south.

The ECtHR, while acknowledging the Commission's report which noted the TRNC policy of not allowing the entry of Greek Cypriots into northern Cyprus and of legislation interfering with property rights, went on to observe:

90. That situation has changed. There is now legislation which seeks to provide a mechanism of redress and which has been interpreted so as to comply with international law; and the political climate has ameliorated, with borders to the north no longer closed.

98. The argument that it would be galling to have recourse to authorities in northern Cyprus cannot be given decisive weight – against the background of conflict and hostility, similar argument might be raised in respect of any official body or authority on the Turkish mainland, or indeed by any victim of a violation who is faced with the prospect of asking for redress from a State which has been responsible for the injury suffered. The fact that applicants live outside the occupied area furnishes no reason in principle why they should not be expected to apply to a TRNC body where it can be demonstrated that a remedy is both practicable and normally functioning.

The reasoning of the Court seems to suggest that the restitution of a wrongful act by the occupying power (i.e. illegal appropriation of property) is subordinate to alternative remedies offered by him, even if these are unlikely to culminate in restitution. This rationale is contrary to article 43 of the 1907 Hague Regulations which obliges occupants to respect 'unless absolutely prevented, the laws in force in the country'. In the case at hand there is no compelling reason for the occupant to abrogate the property rights of the civilian population.

QUESTIONS

- **What role does international humanitarian law play in the thinking and judgments of international human rights treaty bodies, particularly the ECtHR, the IACtHR, the IACHR and the HRCtee?**
- **Does the *lex specialis* character of humanitarian law mean that human rights law is always subordinate?**

- What are the legal requirements for the application of humanitarian law and the law of belligerent occupation? What rights arise for the occupied civilian population as a result?
- What justifies the legitimacy of certain killings in humanitarian law which would otherwise be unacceptable in human rights law?
- Why is the application of human rights in armed conflicts important?

14.7   THE RELEVANCE OF THE LAW TO BATTLEFIELD CONDITIONS

14.7.1   Human physiology in combat situations

Whether or not the laws of war are consistent with combat exigencies naturally necessitates recourse to factors that are external to law. Legislative drafting that is aimed at exacting a certain conduct must be pitched at such a level that the conduct conforms to what may ordinarily be expected by the average person. If the required conduct were to exceed the ordinary capabilities of the average person, then the envisaged law would either fail or the authorities would be forced to punish the majority of the population; IHL is not excluded from this proposition. By way of illustration, it is reasonable to assume that the average person when faced with the threat of immediate and certain death unless he executes another person would be inclined to kill rather than be killed. If the law required that the threatened person must choose to die under such circumstances it would not only set an impossible standard for the average members of society (i.e. self-sacrifice), but it would moreover be absurd since what future penalty could be worse had the threatened person decided to succumb to the threat?

In the *Erdemović* case the accused was an unwilling low-ranking conscript in the Bosnian Serb army and in particular of a unit that had rounded up all Muslim males from the area of Srebrenica. When the prisoners were out of sight of the media and international peacekeepers, the leaders of the unit instructed the soldiers to open fire and kill everyone. A soldier who refused was himself immediately executed. As a result, the accused opined that any objection was pointless and proceeded to execute the order while all the time acting under duress. Cassese J argued at the appeals level that society 'should not set intractable standards of behaviour which require mankind to perform acts of martyrdom and brand as criminal any behaviour falling below those standards'.[57] As a result, article 31(1)(d) of the ICC Statute provides a full defence to

---

[57] *ICTY Prosecutor* v. *Erdemović*, Appeals chamber decision (7 October 1997), Dissenting Opinion of Judge Cassese, para. 47.

situations of duress where the accused did not contribute to the harm and the threat was beyond his control.

On the face of it, IHL does not seem to set intractable standards of behaviour to combatants. On the contrary, it would seem that obligations guaranteed to spare civilians, prisoners of war and wounded persons from harm, hardly place any suffering or stress on those engaged in armed conflict. Yet history shows that violations of IHL are a persistent factor in contemporary conflicts and in many instances governments make every effort to conceal these from public scrutiny. How can this be explained? Although the authors of this book are not sufficiently experts outside the realm of law to furnish specific solutions, the following discussion will set out some insights on the interplay between IHL and combat behaviour.

To begin this discussion we should first focus on the physiological strains of combat on the average combatant. The two strands of the human body's nervous system, the sympathetic (SNS) and the parasympathetic (PNS) ensure a healthy balance under ordinary circumstances. However, when stressors kick in, such as the prospect of lethal threat, conscious control is replaced by automation and in particular the SNS mobilises every atom in the human body as a reaction to the stressor. This is such an intense and automated process that the heart rate increases from 70 beats a minute to over 200 beats a minute, while it has been reported that in the heat of deadly combat many soldiers find themselves unable to control their bladders or sphincters.[58] A study carried out on the effects of heightened SNS as a result of combat stress demonstrates among others: diminished hearing (80 per cent), tunnel vision (80 per cent), slow motion time (65 per cent), intrusive destructive thoughts (26 per cent) and detachment (40 per cent).[59] These effects are induced by the secretion of hormones, such as adrenaline, epinephrine and norepinephrine that dilate and constrict the body's bronchial tubes, vascular system and muscles during combat.[60] This automated process and its effects on physical and perceptual functions must return to some normality following the cessation of the stressful event; if SNS continues at peak level unabated the person will die. As a result, it is the PNS that ensures the body's return to the condition of homeostasis. The nervous system thus automatically operates as a thermostat to avoid overheating, so to speak. However, the parasympathetic descent to a state of relative calmness following an immediate stress upon the nervous system is not without consequences. The person generally feels weary, sleepy and exhausted. Whereas in ordinary situations the recuperative function of PNS will typically be followed by a significant and more or

---

[58] B. K. Siddle, *Sharpening the Warrior's Edge: The Psychology and Science of Training* (Belleville, IL: PPCT Research Publications, 1995); see also D. Grossman and L. Christensen, *On Combat: The Psychology and Physiology of Deadly Conflict in War and in Peace* (Belleville, IL: PPCT Research Publications, 2008), 30–1.

[59] Grossman and Christensen, ibid., 51–122.   [60] Ibid., 16–18.

less permanent duration of normalcy, in the midst of combat the soldier and his superiors do not have this luxury. Hence, a weary combatant, who would otherwise need to rest in order to restore his physiological and mental faculties, will be forced to continue under arduous conditions. This is the norm in situations of continuous combat in which it is not unusual for troops to undergo numerous adrenaline surges followed by sharp PNS descents. This no doubt generates significant repercussions on the abilities of soldiers to operate not only in a combat environment but also in situations that do not trigger any significant stress, such as the handling of prisoners, interaction with civilians, conducting street patrols and others.

The general presumption, therefore, that soldiers perform better under combat pressure because their lives are in danger does not seem to be justified. On the contrary, it is probably discredited on the basis of the above.[61] In fact, in a study completed at the close of World War II on US infantry who had fought in northern Europe it was demonstrated that after a period of sixty days of continuous combat, 98 per cent of troops would suffer from a psychological condition, such as acute anxiety, combat exhaustion or depression, whereas the remaining 2 per cent developed an 'aggressive psychopathic personality' on the basis of which they could endure long periods of combat without any of the aforementioned symptoms common to the majority of their comrades.[62]

This discussion was intended to shed some light on whether the obligations imposed by IHL on combatants are realistic in relation to the effects of combat stress. It is clear that IHL rules do not demand unrealistic conduct from their addressees. Professional armies, on the other hand, push their personnel to their limits and combat-weary soldiers are made to undertake sensitive duties, such as guarding prisoners or civilians, without having undergone sufficient psychological and physiological recovery. This does not of course absolve soldiers of any criminal responsibility for violating IHL under such circumstances, unless their state is such that they did not intend to commit the wrongful conduct, or lacked knowledge of it (lack of *mens rea*). A soldier who commits a crime under immense stress but knowing full

---

[61] See S. L. A. Marshall, *The Soldier's Load and the Mobility of a Nation* (Arlington, VA: Marine Corps Association, 1980), who reached this conclusion. Some researchers have argued that front line soldiers during the war of the trenches in World War I in fact took a distinct joy in of killing because it served as an antidote to fear. The same researcher contended that the highest category of mental breakdown among troops consisted of those in combat support roles who did not have a chance to engage with the enemy. J. Bourke, *An Intimate History of Killing: Face to Face Killing in Twentieth Century Warfare* (London, New York: Basic Books, 2000), pp. 13, 249. These theories have largely been rejected. See E. Jones, 'The Psychology of Killing: the Combat Experience of British Soldiers during the First World War', *Journal of Contemporary History* 41 (2006), 229, at 239–46.

[62] R. L. Swank and W. E. Marchand, 'Combat Neuroses, Development of Combat Exhaustion', *Archives of Neurology and Psychiatry* 55 (1946), 236, at 244.

well and intending the consequence of his or her conduct is just as liable as a soldier under no stress whatsoever. It is obvious, however, that army leaders are responsible for their use of combat-weary soldiers in situations where their deployment raises alarm bells, or for failing to detect aggressive psychopathic personalities among their ranks. Thus, conformity with IHL is not only a matter of personal conduct, but more significantly it should also be a matter of adherence by army leaders to those rules of combat physiology that minimise the dangers of human frailty. It is right that the discussion on the application and enforcement of IHL should not focus on individual conduct alone, but should involve military policy more generally.

INTERVIEW 14.1

Battlefield compliance

(Charles Garraway and anon)

Two senior military legal advisors were interviewed for the purpose of this section. The first is Colonel (retired) Charles Garraway (CG) of the British Armed Forces. The second wished to remain anonymous and is a serving legal advisor in the armed forces of a European nation, with deployment experience in both Bosnia and Afghanistan (anon).

In your opinion, for the soldier that is being deployed on a dangerous battlefield, what role does IHL play in the midst of life-threatening combat operations? Is the threat of sanctions a sufficient disincentive or is the instinct for survival stronger?

Anon: Assuming that your question relates to actual combat situations (so called 'troops in contact'), a soldier will execute his drill in the midst of life-threatening combat operations. Rules of engagement (ROE)[1] and the principles of IHL are an inherent part of these drills. Soldiers are not compelled to apply IHL out of fear for the sanctions in case of non-compliance. I taught commanders and their subordinates that ROE and the principles of IHL are essential instruments at every level in the chain of command to ensure mission accomplishment. My motto is: a tactical success achieved by violating ROE and IHL will certainly create a strategic failure. If soldiers have to make decisions in a split second about defending themselves and afterwards it turns out that collateral damage has been caused, it does not necessarily follow that they will be prosecuted for violation of IHL or any other law.

    CG: On the battlefield, the law plays a small part, as law. Life is instinctive and while in headquarters missions can be planned with careful

---

[1] The concept and significance of ROE are explained more fully in the next section.

weighing up of legal factors, the soldier on the front line does not have that luxury. Everything he does must be instinctive – or he is dead. It is thus more important to build an ethos than to rely on law. The soldier will not be thinking of sanctions on the battlefield. When I taught soldiers how to handle prisoners of war, my key point was to tell them that they were looking in a mirror. The soldier in front of them was themselves in a different uniform. Act to them as you would like them to act to you. And in 1990/91 that worked. During a Scud missile alert at our POW camp before the ground campaign started we had one prisoner brought back from a behind-the-lines operation. He was in a tent with a guard. As we pulled on our NBC kit,[2] the guard realised the prisoner did not have any and he began to give him some of his own. When I asked him why, he told me that it just seemed the right thing to do. He had understood. However, times have changed in the last twenty years and I am not sure that a scared young Iraqi can be compared to an Islamic fanatic. Nevertheless, I still feel that sanctions are an ineffective disincentive. It has got to be something deeper – honour, humanity, call it what you will. The survival instinct is strong but it can be controlled.

In the knowledge that the enemy has a complete disregard for IHL and will attempt to kill or maim you in every possible and treacherous way, what is the mentality of combat-weary troops?

Anon: In general, they are aware that disregard for IHL as a result of the enemy's own disregard will negatively influence the operation. It is taken for granted that operations carried out in hostile environments raise the risk of blurring one's moral standards. Every soldier, and commanders in particular, must stay alert in anticipation of such blurring and be prepared to take firm action.

CG: A very good question. To be honest, I cannot comment from personal experience but I have noted an increased cynicism within the armed forces. I recently spoke at the Defence Medical Services Training Centre and was met with complete cynicism on the use of the emblem. I was told that whether or not the emblem is worn, the Taliban are deliberately targeting the medic on a patrol, identified by the different shape of his bergen.[3] The general view is that it is now better to rely on kinetic defence [i.e. use of active combat and force] rather than IHL and the emblem. This is worrying as one would expect medics more than any others to support IHL. This is precisely why trainers may have to change their approach to stress that this is a 'values' battle rather than a kinetic war.

---

[2] Nuclear, Biological and Chemical (NBC) first aid kits.

[3] Standard individual military backpack issued by armed forces.

In your experience, irrespective of what their officers say, do combat-weary troops think that IHL is realistic and in touch with their particular exigencies?

Anon: I instructed commanders (and sometimes also their subordinates) on ROE and IHL matters before their deployment to Afghanistan. If I would have asked them this question they probably would have said 'no, it is not'. In the deployment area I conducted ROE rehearsals with platoons and used real life examples in which IHL would play an important role. Because of the discussions and answers to my questions I honestly believe that they would have answered this question in the affirmative. It is important that you translate IHL to concrete situations which they could be confronted with and then explain the 'do's' and 'don'ts' from an IHL (ROE) perspective and discuss possible consequences of their actions.

CG: My experience is of traditional wars where I found that one could persuade soldiers that IHL was realistic and in touch with their particular exigencies. I suspect that it is much harder now in current conflicts.

It is rumoured that RoE in multinational combat operations in hot spots such as Iraq and Afghanistan are 'lighter' than current academic thinking on IHL. For example, street patrols, whether on foot or armoured vehicles, are given significant leeway in attacking persons who seem to be suicide bombers or in any way dangerous based on military briefings. In your experience, is this the case and is it perceived as a morale booster?

Anon: No, that is not my experience. There were strict ROE and clear standing operational procedures regarding such situations.

CG: No. I have not seen the ROE and so cannot comment in detail. However, I am aware that ROE for pre-planned targeting operations require an assurance of zero collateral damage. This goes far beyond anything required by the laws of armed conflict and reduces the proportionality balance to nothing. This is certainly the cause of some frustration as soldiers do not necessarily appreciate that this is not a legal constraint but a policy constraint. I would suggest that, after the ICRC DPH paper,[4] 'current academic thinking on IHL' is anything but clear!

Given that soldiers on the battlefield are asked to risk their lives in a place far from home and under strong local hostility, in what way does the army depict the enemy and the local civilian population – particularly where the latter has ties with the enemy and may assist it – to its battle troops?

---

[4] ICRC, *Direct Participation in Hostilities (DPH) Report*, (2009). Available at: www.icrc.org/eng/assets/files/other/icrc-002-0990.pdf.

Anon: Soldiers are taught the principles of counter-insurgency and the relationship between the enemy and the local population. They are being taught that local populations could pick up arms against our forces for many reasons. It is important that they are aware of this and are able to understand why this could happen. They are taught to be alert on this issue.

CG: I cannot talk about modern training. However, when I was teaching those soldiers who had to handle prisoners in 1990/1, I used to quote from Charles Kingsley and his character Mrs Doasyouwouldbedoneby. See the answer to the first question. One of the great dangers is to 'demonise' the enemy so that he is seen as 'subhuman' or 'different'. We were of course in those days 'liberators' of Kuwait and so the civilian population was not a problem.

Some of the responses referred to ROE and both interviewees were adamant that none of the ROE witnessed by them personally provided an explicit or implicit licence to violate IHL. This is certainly the case with most nations. The following section provides some examples that do not necessarily support this practice.

14.7.2   The dilution of humanitarian law and problems in ensuring compliance

While it is true that compliance is to some degree predicated on personal traits, its general enforcement is dependent on a coherent system of discipline that allows for no deviation. This type of discipline is the hallmark of all professional armies, yet there exists a very real tension between armies and the executive branch of government. This tension arises from the fact that the gruesome, daily, combat experience of the professional soldier is perceived as being inadequately communicated to the law-makers who make their decisions in the comfort of their office. At the same time, the law-maker is unable to communicate to the soldier the overarching political, military and economic aims of a military campaign, which are much broader than the calamities of the particular combat zone in which he or she is engaged. This tension surfaces even between senior military commanders and political leaders. By way of illustration, studies have shown that 'the perceived humanitarian bid by militaries may be overstated: commanders have little wish to see their forces lose basic war-fighting skills in the pursuit of other tasks, and in practical terms commitments in Afghanistan and Iraq have left major military actors overstretched'.[63]

More importantly, the military and the politicians cannot see eye to eye on the restrictions placed by the latter on the use of lethal force in combat

---

[63] Humanitarian Policy Group (HPG), *Resetting the Rules of Engagement: Trends and Issues in Military Humanitarian Relations* (HPG Report 21, March 2006), 2.

and peacekeeping operations. Ordinarily, the use of lethal force would be circumscribed by the relevant rules of IHL as well as any particular mandate incumbent on the mission by the UN Security Council. In practice, however, this is not the case. When armies are sent to the battlefield or peacekeeping operations, depending on the projected intensity of resistance or other difficulties of the mission, they are issued with specific instructions regulating the circumstances under which they are allowed to employ lethal force. These regulations are termed ROE.[64] While no nation has ever claimed that its ROE were contrary to its obligations under IHL, none the less IHL is simply one of the factors in drafting ROE; others include the treachery of the enemy, the hostility of the civilian population, the terrain, as well as national policy.[65] It is no wonder therefore that mission-specific ROE are considered top secret, under the justification that it is tactically mistaken for the enemy to know how he is to be engaged. As correct as this may be, it leaves much to be desired in respect of clandestine operations or combat-weary forces, or even with regard to armies that have a history of violating IHL.[66]

The secretive nature of ROE may moreover give rise to concerns for the conduct of private military companies whose operations fall within a grey zone of IHL. In general terms, mission-specific ROE are drafted by members of the senior military with policy input and approval by the executive. Although in their initial form they can be very elaborate, they distinguish between appropriate responses to 'hostile action' and 'hostile intent'. Hostile intent is certainly more difficult to substantiate and so troops are given some, but certainly limited, discretion in this regard.[67] ROE are not always static and they may change depending on the progress of the mission or the exigencies on the ground. Hence, a humanitarian mission, such as that of Somalia in 1991 (Operation Restore Hope), may escalate to a peace enforcement operation. Accordingly, in such circumstances, the ROE must be amended; this process is known as 'mission creep'.

---

[64] The US Department of Defence Dictionary of Military and Associated Terms (US Government Printing Office, 1987), JCS Pub 1, 317, defines ROE as directives issued by competent military authority which circumscribe the circumstances and limitations under which US forces will initiate and/or continue combat with the enemy.

[65] See J. A. Roach, 'Rules of Engagement', *Naval War College Review* 36, (1983), 46, at 49.

[66] See P. Rowe, 'The Rules of Engagement in Occupied Territory: Should they be Published?' *Melb. J. Int'l. L.* 8 (2007), 327, who argues that, at the very least, ROE in occupied territories should be published.

[67] *The San Remo Manual on Rules of Engagement* (San Remo: IHLI, 2008), 22, defines hostile intent as 'the threat of the imminent use of force. A determination of hostile intent is based on the existence of an identifiable threat recognisable on the basis of ... capability and intention ... Indicators of hostile intent [include]: (i) aiming or directing weapons; (ii) adopting an attack profile; (iii) closing within weapon release range; (iv) illuminating with radar or laser designators; (v) passing targeting information; (vi) laying or preparing to lay naval mine; (vii) failing to respond to proactive measures.'

The intended addressees of ROE are combat personnel. Therefore, it is important that ROE are clear and simple, leaving no doubt as to their content.[68] It is taken for granted that military forces deployed in combat operations or other danger zones are well versed in the fundamental principles of the *jus in bello*. Although this requirement seems self-evident for contemporary armies,[69] in fact the conduct of some professional armies has forced international human rights tribunals to demand that troops receive more stringent IHL education.[70] This is usually the case with armies that fail to invest in the development of their personnel and see little benefit in any comprehensive training that is not related to pure combat operations. It is not also uncommon for troops engaged in civil warfare, such as those that make up the Colombian army and its paramilitary affiliates, to be afforded a significant degree of impunity as an incentive to persist under difficult and extremely dangerous combat situations.[71] If this impunity or lack of IHL training is further compounded by ROE that are inclined to abusive behaviour their addressees will feel no constraints in their treatment of the adversary or the civilian population.

Truth be said, the professional armies of developed nations are fluent in their knowledge of IHL, undergo extensive training and are subject to frequent psychometric tests and evaluations. These armies and their executives claim that they make every effort to prevent the perpetration of crimes, yet the practice of courts-martial against heinous behaviour on the battlefield or in occupied territories demonstrates a degree of leniency that would be unacceptable if the particular crimes had taken place during civilian life. The victims and families of such crimes understandably find this leniency hard to stomach.[72]

---

[68] One of the deficiencies of the UN Somali (Restore Hope) ROE was the attempt by its drafters to insert a 'legislative approach', which made them indeterminate and unworkable in the life and death scenario of its intended addressees. See M. Martins, 'Rules of Engagement for Land Forces: a Matter of Training, not Lawyering', *Mil. L. Rev.* 143 (1994), 27, at 55.

[69] Article 83, Protocol I 1977.

[70] In *Massacre de Mapiripán* v. *Colombia*, Judgment (7 March 2005) the IACtHR ordered Colombia, among other things, to create educational programmes on human rights and IHL for all its armed forces as a preventative measure.

[71] For example, the UN Working Group on enforced and involuntary disappearances, Mission to Colombia, UN Doc. E/CN.4/2006/56/Add.1, 17 (2006), described in detail the culture of impunity associated with enforced disappearances by elements of the army and paramilitary groups.

[72] In *USA* v. *Steven Green*, US District Court judgment (30 June 2006), the accused was sentenced to life imprisonment for the rape and murder of a fourteen-year old Iraqi girl and the murder of her family. Military tribunals in past US wars were more generous to persons accused of serious crimes. In the context of the My Lai massacre in Vietnam, the perpetrator, responsible for the murder of more than one hundred civilians, had his life sentence commuted and was later pardoned. See *Calley* v. *Calloway*, 382 F Supp. 650 (1974), *rev'd* 519 F 2d 184 (1975), *cert denied* 425 US 911 (1976). In the *Baha Mousa/ Al-Skeini* case, it was the ceaseless efforts of the victim's family that led to the case being entertained and a subsequent inquiry launched.

Moreover, although we have generally little information about the content of ROE it is presumed that the average soldier will be disinclined to exercise discretion in respect of an order which seems *prima facie* unjust. Disobedience is extremely exceptional as the following real-life scenario exemplifies. During the invasion of Iraq Australian fighter pilots refused to comply with orders of US commanders to bomb particular targets because the intelligence given at pre-flight briefings and contained in their ROE did not match with the pilots' personal observations. Here is an extract from an interview by the squadron leader to the *Sydney Morning Herald* of 14 March 2004:

But it appears there were fundamental differences between the US dominated headquarters and Australian pilots over what constituted a valid military target. Squadron leader Putney said under Australia's rules of engagement pilots had to ask themselves on each mission whether it was right to drop their bombs.

'Each guy would have made that decision once to half a dozen times in the conflict. It was presented as being just one pilot in the incident, but it was all of us several times. We were providing an identification of targets in conjunction with ground forces and if we were not 100 per cent sure we were taking out a valid military target in accordance with our specifications we just did not drop'.

Squadron leader Putney said he could not comment on the reasons they aborted specific missions. But it seems that it was often to avoid the unnecessary killing of civilians. 'As we approached the target area we confirmed we had the right place. Then we'd run a check provided through our training that we were doing the right thing by our rules of engagement. We exercise those all the time. In Iraq it was a matter of the briefings we received prior in regards to our rules of engagement as to whether we thought this was a target we should be destroying. If it was not, then we decided not to deploy'. He said [continues the reporter] most decisions were made in the air, but some were command decisions.[73]

This passage is a good indication of the effects of good IHL training and of responsible military personnel who are allowed to think for themselves, without blindly following orders. The situation would certainly have been different if the Australian ROE allowed no personal evaluation of the situation or where its pilots would have been subject to severe sanctions had they refused to follow orders given during their pre-mission briefing.

The dilution of IHL through secretive ROE has been demonstrated through a series of leaks concerning confidential documents that have come to light since 2007 in respect of the US war effort in Iraq. One of these documents is a US ROE addressed to its military personnel, which although generally follows relevant IHL to the letter and emphasises the importance of good conduct, contains none the less an injunction that is highly problematic. It elaborates on those targets that are deemed as being of 'high collateral

---

[73] Available at: http://gc.nautilus.org/Nautilus/australia/afghanistan/rules-of-engagement-afghanistan-and-iraq.

damage' and in respect of which only the Secretary of Defence can authorise their destruction:

> 3.H(8) (S/REL). [High Collateral Damage Targets are those] that if struck, have a ten percent probability of causing collateral damage through blast debris and fragmentation and are estimated to result in significant collateral effects on non-combatant persons and structures, including: (A) Non-combatant casualties estimated at 30 or greater ... (C) In the case of dual-use facilities, effects that significantly impact the non-combatant population, including significant effects on the environment/facilities/infrastructure not related to an adversary's war making ability; or (D) Targets in close proximity to known human shields.[74]

Although as has already been stated the ROE were at pains to emphasise compliance with IHL, the risk to the civilian population from the operations described in the last section is very significant. It is difficult to justify the suggested casualty rate on the scale of military necessity, particularly given that the operations in Iraq did not involve a full-scale war, but were largely directed against insurgent attacks. It should be pointed out that the Obama administration subsequently proceeded to alter US ROE in Afghanistan and Iraq. This even led the military leadership of the campaign there to vociferously call for the 'easing of the rules of engagement', deeming the latest changes to be detrimental to the safety of troops and success of operations.[75]

14.8   FUNDAMENTALS OF INTERNATIONAL CRIMINAL JUSTICE

One of the stages in the development of a rights regime corresponds with the process of criminalisation. Hence, the promulgation of criminal legislation providing for a lengthy incarceration in respect of murder supplements the protection offered in respect of the right to life. Some types of punishment correspond to the violation of most human rights. It is evident of course that the addressees of criminal laws are not necessarily the addressees of international human rights obligations. By way of illustration, the protection of the right to life in human rights law is addressed to states, which in turn translate it into a negative obligation incumbent upon themselves as well as into a positive obligation by which they undertake to prevent and punish the relevant conduct of private actors. Unlike human rights law, therefore, which has traditionally been concerned with the conduct of states, criminal law makes no distinctions on the basis of the status of the offender. Whereas domestic criminal law is territorial and reflects to a large degree social

---

[74] The document is entitled SECRET/REL TO USA, IRQ, MCFI/20151003. It is reproduced at: http://file.wikileaks.org/file/us-iraq-rules-of-engagement.pdf, at 25.

[75] E. Bumiller, 'Petraeus Pledges Look at Strikes in Afghanistan', *The New York Times* (29 June 2010).

consensus as to what constitutes acceptable conduct in a particular country (e.g. in the Netherlands the controlled use of cannabis will not be prosecuted, whereas it is a criminal offence in other nations), the development of ICL requires the consent of the majority of nations, which may not always see eye to eye on all issues. Given the divergence of morals, social mores, technology, education and levels of affluence between the various nations of the world, a single, indivisible consensus on all international crimes seems rather illusionary.[76]

As a result, ICL is largely driven by compromise and selectivity and is seldom proactive. The reason for this is rather simple. While states have little problem accusing their adversaries of engaging in criminal activity and prosecuting them accordingly, they would be disinclined to take similar action in respect of their own armed forces, their political leaders or their allies because they would run the risk of losing allegiance and wide social support. This position may seem anachronistic if measured by contemporary perceptions of criminal justice, but one need only recall the heated refusals by all the former Yugoslav republics for surrendering nationals accused of atrocious international crimes to the UN war crimes tribunals, as indeed the promulgation by the Bush administration in the USA of the so-called Hague Invasion Law, which envisaged US military intervention in the Netherlands if a US national was surrendered to the ICC.[77] Three distinct phases in the development of ICL may be identified: (1) the pre-1939 era; (2) 1945 until the end of the Cold War in the early 1990s; and (3) the contemporary phase, starting with the creation of the *ad hoc* criminal tribunals for Yugoslavia and Rwanda by the UNSC and which is ongoing.

It was not too long ago that the notion of personal criminal liability for violating the law of nations was alien to international law. Prior to the commencement of World War II in 1939 it was generally assumed that all provisions in international treaties prescribing prohibited conduct were addressed to states, not physical persons, although such conduct could only be perpetrated by the latter. This meant that all infractions were attributable to the state under the law of state responsibility. The individual culprit was at best liable under domestic law and then only if his or her country of nationality had adopted implementing criminal legislation or proceeded to prosecute. This was clearly an artificial, political arrangement whose doctrinal basis was premised on the notion that physical persons did not possess legal personality under international law, i.e. that they had no rights or duties under this body of law, or capacity to enforce these in any national or

---

[76] This state of affairs is not exceptional to the field of international criminal justice. The debate between the universalist and relativist schools of human rights are to a large degree predicated on similar considerations.

[77] American Service Members' Protection Act (Hague Invasion Act), 116 Stat. 820 (2002).

international forum.[78] That this was a wholly unsatisfactory state of affairs was soon to be revealed in the aftermath of World War II when the victorious allies sought to prosecute members of the Axis power before the IMT at Nuremberg.

The IMT was established by the London Agreement of 8 August 1945 between the governments of Great Britain, the USA, France and the USSR,[79] to which the Tribunal's Charter was annexed. Article 6 of the Charter provided for prosecution of offenders in respect of war crimes, crimes against humanity and crimes against peace. One of the principal challenges to the jurisdiction of the IMT was that the three aforementioned crimes could not be attributable to them as physical persons, but to Germany, assuming that they constituted international crimes in the first place.[80] Moreover, they asserted that because physical persons were not directly subject to the dictates of international law the criminal law applicable to determine their liability was that of Germany. This result, although consistent with the wholly artificial lack of international criminal liability in the pre-1939 era, was morally detestable. Given that the prevailing laws during the reign of Hitler in Germany permitted atrocities against vulnerable groups none of the accused could have been prosecuted because their conduct was lawful. The IMT was not overly troubled in applying the solution that best served the interests of legitimacy – although it was itself accused of victors' justice and selectivity – rather than the interests of strict legality. It took the position that despite the absence of express treaty references to personal criminal liability the crimes encompassed within its Charter entailed such liability as a matter of customary international law.[81]

---

[78] Exceptionally, some prohibited conduct attracted universal condemnation and punishment, irrespective of the nationality of the offender. This is true in the case of piracy *jure gentium*, which was perpetrated on the high seas and where, therefore, no state possessed exclusive criminal jurisdiction. See E. Kontorovich, 'The Piracy Analogy: Modern Universal Jurisdiction's Hollow Foundation', *Harv. Int'l L. J.* 45 (2004), 183. Mention should also be made to the 1923 Peace Treaty of Lausanne, 28 LNTS 12, which provided a declaration of amnesty in respect of all offences committed by agents of the Ottoman empire between 1914 and 1922. Reading between the lines, the very granting of an amnesty in a treaty necessarily entails the recognition by the contracting parties of international offences. See C. M. Bassiouni, *Crimes Against Humanity in International Criminal Law* (Leiden, Boston: Martinus Nijhoff, 1992), 175–6.

[79] 5 UNTS 251.

[80] With the exception of war crimes which were contained in various multilateral treaties prior to 1939, crimes against peace and crimes against humanity lacked international codification and there is little evidence that they had crystallised as specific prohibitions under customary international law. The IMT's approach to this question was that if a war of aggression is illegal in international law then it necessarily follows that those who plan and wage such a war are committing a crime. IMT Judgment, reprinted in *AJIL* 41 (1947), 172, 218.

[81] Ibid., 218.

Quite clearly, the Nuremberg process and the contemporaneous emergence of universal and regional human rights regimes altered the legal landscape of international criminal law. Despite the advent of the Cold War in the relations between East and West it was never doubted that all treaties adopted after 1945 and which prescribed international crimes entailed the criminal liability of perpetrators – irrespective of the fact that prosecutions and extraditions were rare. This was a significant development because it meant that the validity of an international crime persisted globally and at all times even if the offender's country of nationality refused to implement the offence in its domestic laws. Equally, criminal jurisdiction in respect of prosecution meant that it was no longer territorial (i.e. belonging solely to the country where the office was physically committed) but that it was equally available to other states. Three distinct problems are associated with this phase of development of ICL: (1) the invocation of immunities in respect of state officials accused of international crimes, as well as the absolution of liability at the domestic level by the granting of amnesties; (2) the reluctance of the majority of states to exercise broad extraterritorial jurisdiction, including universal jurisdiction, coupled with a general disinclination to extradite or surrender; and (3) the absence of a powerful international authority that wielded enough credibility to compel states to prosecute, surrender and extradite in accordance with their international obligations.

All three of these limitations to some degree contributed to the regression of much of the progress made by the human rights movement, albeit they have not been viewed in solely negative terms. By way of illustration, although the granting of sweeping amnesties to each member of a rebel faction releases the orchestrators of heinous crimes and their accomplices from any future criminal liability, the proponents of amnesties claim that they may help put an end to hostilities, bring about peace and facilitate the integration of the rebels into civilian life.[82] Whether this is actually true in practice is highly debatable. None the less, in the context of the indictment of the incumbent Sudanese president by the ICC prosecutor over the ethnic cleansing in Darfur, alleged to have been committed by the government of Sudan through the *Janjaweed* militia, the majority of the AU certainly disagreed that an outright prosecution was the best way forward. Paragraph 5 of

---

[82] The AU *High level panel on Darfur* (Mbeki Report) noted that a criminal justice mechanism entrusted with prosecuting those responsible for the crimes in Darfur had to satisfy the demand for local ownership, be able to impose customary conciliatory mechanisms, be independent, enable victim participation and undertake thorough and systematic investigations. It pointed out that the ICC was merely a court of last resort and that an independent Sudanese justice system, as described above, should undertake the task of prosecuting each individual perpetrator. It, thus, clearly did not view peace negotiations as an alternative to justice mechanisms. AU Doc. PSC/AHG/2(CCVII), (29 October 2009), paras. 205–6, 244–5.

the AU's decision was clearly concerned about the imbalance of justice over the interests of peace, emphasising that:

The decision bears testimony to the glaring reality that the situation in Darfur is too serious and complex an issue to be resolved without recourse to a harmonised approach to justice and peace, neither of which should be pursued at the expense of the other. Furthermore, the decision was taken after due evaluation of the situation in Darfur informed by the commitment of member States to finding a lasting solution to the problem in Darfur with a view to restoring peace, security and stability in the Sudan and the whole region and prevent further displacement and killings in that country.[83]

Such statements and the argumentation about jeopardising peace efforts in favour of justice mechanisms should be approached with a pinch of salt, particularly since these sentiments were not universally shared by the AU as a whole, or, for that matter, by Muslims across the world. A World Public Opinion survey on the appropriateness of an ICC prosecution for Al-Bashir was approved in four out of seven large Muslim nations.[84] For whatever reasons, mostly geo-political, even the most fundamental premise of international criminal law, i.e. the prosecution and punishment of offenders, has not always been universally welcomed by all the states in the world.

14.9   THE ENFORCEMENT OF INTERNATIONAL CRIMINAL LAW

In the various human rights regimes, whether universal or regional, the determination of violations and the awarding of reparations are brought by the victims against the culprit states and their agents. In domestic legal systems, moreover, where the violation of a right entails in addition a criminal offence, the local prosecutor may initiate criminal proceedings against the culprits on his or her own initiative. When a crime under international law takes place, the victims and their families do not have access to criminal justice mechanisms, other than those of the territorial state or their country of nationality; even so, any 'participation' is more a plea for trial and punishment to the authorities rather than a suit or formal application. There are no guarantees, however, that the prosecutors in any of these two jurisdictions will indict the accused *proprio motu* (i.e. through their independent powers). The reasons are usually practical, rather than political, particularly where the culprits have fled to third states that have no desire to extradite, or because

---

[83] AU Commission, Decision on the meeting of African states parties to the Rome Statute of the International Criminal Court, (14 July 2009). See also the follow-up to this matter in AU Commission, Communique on the 3 February 2010 judgment of the ICC appeals chamber on Darfur, (4 February 2010).

[84] See www.worldpublicopinion.org/pipa/articles/btjusticehuman_rightsra/624. php?nid=&tid=&pnt=624.

the entire exercise is perceived as far too expensive and onerous on the tax-payer, especially if no results are visible in the horizon. If the territorial and nationality states are thus generally reluctant to prosecute persons accused of international crimes when this is considered a difficult, expensive or sen-sitive venture, then what chance is there for the enforcement of ICL?

To answer this question we must ascertain what is encompassed within the term 'enforcement' because this is not understood uniformly by all relevant actors and stakeholders. First of all, it is imperative that one identifies in advance the goals to be pursued by the operation of an international criminal justice mechanism; this is hardly self-evident. If the primary goal consists of general and special deterrence, incapacitation, rehabilitation or retribution, then the punishment of the offender is of paramount importance. Although some manifestations of punishment overlap with particular consequences of criminal trials they are certainly distinguishable. By way of illustration, in the immediate aftermath of World War II the heads of Britain and USSR, Churchill and Stalin, proposed the summary execution of Nazi leaders and their accomplices without the need for trials. They not only dismissed the utility of trials in respect of mass criminality, but viewed them as a public forum through which the culprits could justify their position and buy them-selves time. Roosevelt's rationale for trials over mere punishment was the same as that offered by Israel twenty years later following the abduction by its agents in Argentina of Adolf Eichmann. Eichmann was responsible for formulating Hitler's programme for the extermination of Jews and Israel could just as well have chosen to assassinate him clandestinely.

Of great importance to the supporters of international trials is the writing of a historical record and the provision of a voice to the victims and their families, followed, where appropriate, by the secondary goal of reconcilia-tion.[85] Indeed, for the Jews or the Tutsi in Rwanda the mere punishment or assassination of the genocidaires would not satisfy their desire to record the atrocities so that future generations could not forget or doubt their victimisa-tion;[86] this was something that the assassination of the culprits could by no means achieve. Trials also empower the victims, in the sense that they enable them to face up to their tormentors and through their personal account help convict those responsible. Both of these processes may ultimately facilitate,

---

[85] See L. Douglas, *The Memory of Judgment: Making Law and History in the Trials of the Holocaust* (New Haven: Yale University Press, 2001). In *ICTY Prosecutor* v. *Plavšić*, Sentencing judgment (27 February 2003), paras. 79–81, the ICTY was at pains to argue that the admission of guilt by the accused contributed to the establishment of truth and was a significant effort towards the advancement of reconciliation, which was stated as one of the tribunal's primary aims.

[86] As a result, the vast majority of European nations have rendered Holocaust denial a criminal offence, against which the freedom of expression is generally inapplicable. See e.g. the French Gayssot Act 1990. On the other hand, the first amendment to the US Constitution prohibits all restrictions to the freedom of speech.

to a larger or smaller degree, reconciliation between post-conflict communities. Finally, trials express and project the validity of international norms in a way that punishment alone cannot. They help to depoliticise acts of barbarity by turning them into legally enforceable criminal violations, making it clear that they do not belong outside the realm of law.[87]

Yet, although the international community does not seem to possess a coherent plan of objectives in respect of international trials, it would be wrong to hold trials simply because of their record-writing capacity, or for the benefit of the victims and any future reconciliation. As laudable as these objectives are, they presume *a priori* that events happened in a particular way and place pressure on the prosecutor and judges to make convictions based on these presumptions. This brings the independence and impartiality of international tribunals into question and by implication the right to a fair trial. As a result, the primary objective of international trials should not be perceived as being different from their domestic counterparts. Rather, they should strive to enforce the law through fair judicial proceedings, following which they can then fulfil any of the aforementioned secondary aims either directly[88] or indirectly. The fact that trials concerning mass atrocities may have a 'show trial' or meta-justice dimension, in that prosecution and punishment cannot even begin to encapsulate the horror of the conduct and the pain of the victims and their families,[89] should not lead to a broad dismissal of international trials. It is only natural that all those affected by the proceedings, from the accused to the victims, will seek to derive their own particular pursuits and objectives.

Fair trials in the manner described satisfy not only the requirement of legality in respect of the enforcement of ICL, but also that of legitimacy. The UNSC has given its blessing to international criminal trials from the moment it became unshackled from the rivalries of the Cold War. Two *ad hoc* tribunals were established by the Council in the form of subsidiary organs under article 29 of the UN Charter, one for Yugoslavia[90] and the other for Rwanda.[91] Unlike the Nuremberg Tribunal that was set up by a treaty the

---

[87] R. A. Duff, *Trials and Punishments* (Cambridge University Press, 1986), 235ff., for an account of expressive theories of punishment in the domestic setting; D. Luban, *Fairness to Rightness: Jurisdiction, Legality and the Legitimacy of International Criminal Law*, Georgetown Public Law Research Paper no. 1154117 (July 2008), 10.

[88] In recent years, states, sometimes through the assistance of international organisations, have resorted to truth commissions as a supplement to the operation of international criminal tribunals. Unlike the latter, truth commissions are best suited to directly serving truth-telling, reconciliation and victim participation.

[89] It is stated, for example, that the prosecution of Eichmann was not so much about the person but about emphasising that Nazi crimes were committed against the Jewish people, a fact that was not highlighted during the Nuremberg proceedings. See M. Koskenniemi, 'Between Impunity and Show Trials', *MPYBUNL* 6 (2002), 1, at 3.

[90] UNSC resolution 827 (25 May 1993).   [91] UNSC resolution 955 (8 November 1994).

ICTY and ICTR were based on UNSC resolutions, which are binding on all states in accordance with article 25 of the UN Charter. More importantly, the Council delegated significant powers to these tribunals, such as the authority to request and compel the surrender of evidence, witnesses and accused persons from UN member states.[92] Thus, the *ad hoc* tribunals possessed primacy of jurisdiction over and above domestic courts. The Council was cognisant of the politics surrounding the operation of the *ad hoc* tribunals by interested countries and went to pains to endow them with an appropriate degree of legitimacy. This included an express injunction to apply only universally recognised customary international law,[93] encompassing also fundamental notions of human rights.

The permanent members of the Security Council did not merely wish to substitute the ordinary courts of Rwanda and Yugoslavia with the establishment of the *ad hoc* tribunals. In the aftermath of the Rwandan genocide there was no criminal justice system to speak of, while in what remained of Yugoslavia the situation was not conducive to fair and impartial trials. The aim of the *ad hoc* tribunals was to concentrate on the leaders and protagonists of the atrocities and in time to integrate the proceedings within the domestic legal systems of Rwanda and the former Yugoslav republics. The legitimacy of criminal justice mechanisms against Serb perpetrators took more than a decade to develop in the psyche of the Serbian people, boosted particularly following the surrender of their president, Slobodan Milosevic, to the ICTY and the restoration of political stability in the country.[94] The investigative and judicial work of the ICTY and ICTR was aided by the authorities of other states which prosecuted accused persons in parallel with the *ad hoc* tribunals on the basis of the principle of universal jurisdiction.[95] This analysis is designed to demonstrate that international trials through *ad hoc* or hybrid tribunals are hardly isolated instances of Security Council decision-making; rather, they have been proven to generate a dynamic that engages the bigger part of the community of nations. This dynamic ensures that international trials are not an expression of exceptionalism, but part of a continuous, consistent and coherent corpus of ICL and human rights law.

---

[92] Article 29 ICTY Statute.

[93] Report of the Secretary General pursuant to Security Council resolution 808 (1993), UN Doc. S/25704 (1993), para. 2.

[94] In 2005 UNDP conducted a survey among the various ethnic groups in Bosnia and the people of Serbia. The survey showed that the majority of Bosnian Serbs and Serbs were in favour of criminal trials. However, for varying reasons that may no longer be relevant, 30 per cent of Serbs believed that the ICTY had not done a good job, but that its existence was none the less justified. See UNDP, 'Justice and Truth in BiH: Public perceptions' (2005), 15–16. Available at: www.undp.ba/upload/publications/Justice&Truth%20in%20 BH%20English.pdf.

[95] E.g. *Public Prosecutor* v. *Djajic*, AJIL 92 (1998), 528.

International criminal trials enjoy a much broader jurisdictional synergy on the basis of comity with human rights tribunals and national courts.[96] Such courts are also not averse to the idea of applying extensive human rights jurisprudence, primarily because their mandate does not restrict them to any particular rules, as is the case with human rights tribunals. Yet, they must be viewed as instigators of international criminal justice – or as its supreme court so to speak – and not as its ordinary forum. Take for example the situation in Rwanda, where the initial number of arrestees connected with the genocide exceeded 70,000. If each of these persons was to be given a fair and expeditious trial it is evident that hundreds of criminal chambers would be required.[97] International tribunals cannot by their very nature try every person accused in situations of mass criminality. They can and do, however, contribute through their undoubted resources and expertise to the clarification of international rules (e.g. such as the precise elements of international crimes) and the verification and liability of the protagonists, so that local courts and tribunals can be guided in their assessment of the criminality of other accused persons. This constitutes a substantial assistance because local courts and judges will never before have entertained cases of genocide, crimes against humanity and war crimes.

14.9.1   Universal jurisdiction and immunities

As has already been explained the principle of universal jurisdiction means that in respect of certain international crimes any country in the world may arrest and prosecute the alleged perpetrators, irrespective of the existence, or not, of a nationality or territoriality link. Scholars generally distinguish between 'pure' or 'absolute' and 'conditional' universal jurisdiction. While neither requires a link with the prosecuting state the former does not necessitate the presence of the accused therein, whereas its conditional counterpart does. Although the universality principle was only specifically inserted in treaties relating to grave breaches of the 1949 Geneva Conventions and piracy *jure gentium* (so-called treaty-based universal jurisdiction), its application is now widely recognised in respect of other international crimes, particularly crimes

---

[96] See Y. Shany, *The Competing Jurisdiction of International Courts and Tribunals* (Oxford University Press, 2003), 261.

[97] Ultimately, the absence of a judicial body and defence lawyers as a result of the genocide was remedied through the operation of so-called *gacaca* courts, which are transitional justice mechanisms that operate at cellule (village) level in Rwanda and which coexist in parallel with domestic Rwandan courts. Although this mechanism was traditionally established to deal with minor offences and family disputes at the community level on the basis of African customary law, the current *gacaca* courts were constituted under Rwandan law to prosecute the culprits of the lesser categories of the genocide. Rwandan Organic Law no. 40/2000 (26 January 2001), as revised by Organic Laws no. 16/2004 (19 June 2004) and 28/2006 (27 June 2006). *Gacaca* courts have been criticised for their manipulation by the government in meting out justice.

against humanity, genocide and torture. Crimes under international law have customarily attracted universal jurisdiction in two independent ways: (1) on the basis of the repugnant nature and scale of the conduct, as is the case with crimes against humanity[98] and torture;[99] or (2) as a result of the inadequacy of domestic law and enforcement in respect of unlawful conduct committed in locations not subject to the authority of any state, such as the high seas.

Given that the majority of international crimes are perpetrated by state actors, the exercise of universal jurisdiction has generally been challenged on the basis of the defence of immunity. Immunity from jurisdiction means that a court cannot entertain a particular suit, not that the defendant is discharged from criminal liability altogether or that the jurisdiction of the court is extinguished.[100] This means that once the procedural bar of immunity is removed (e.g. because the person benefiting from it is no longer an active office holder) the criminal liability of the accused re-emerges and that person becomes once again susceptible to criminal prosecution. Under customary law aliens have been granted immunity from municipal courts in respect of alleged international or transnational offences on two grounds. The first relates to the particular status of certain persons. Thus, it is recognised that individuals who hold the highest public offices enjoy absolute immunity from criminal prosecution before domestic courts. Its basis is not the nature of the action but the official status of the person concerned. This type of immunity is known as personal or *ratione personae* and is available to a limited number of individuals: serving heads of state, heads of diplomatic missions, their families and servants.[101] Immunity *ratione materiae* (otherwise known as functional immunity), on the other hand, does not serve to protect any particular person but the governmental function bestowed upon government agents. There is thus no predetermined restriction as to the range of persons entitled to functional immunity. It serves to protect governmental acts of one state from being assessed before the courts of another and therefore only incidentally confers immunity on the individual carrying out such

---

[98] *Federation Nationale de Deportes et Internes Resistants et Patriotes and Others v. Barbie* 78 ILR 125, 130; see also *Re Pinochet*, AJIL 93 (1999), 700, 702–3.

[99] *R v. Bow Street Metropolitan Stipendiary Magistrate and Others ex p Pinochet Ugarte (No. 3)* [1999] 2 All ER 97, 177, *per* Lord Millett who argued that serious international crimes attract universal jurisdiction where they violate *jus cogens*.

[100] *Dickinson v. Del Solar* [1930] 1 KB 376, 380, *per* Lord Hewart CJ; similarly, *Arrest Warrant of 11 April 2000 (Democratic Republic of the Congo v. Belgium)*, Judgment, ICJ Reports 2002, p. 3, paras. 47–55.

[101] SIA 1978, section 14(1) extends immunity *ratione personae* to: (1) the sovereign or other head of that state in his public capacity; (2) the government of that state; and (3) any department of that government (but not every executive entity). In *Propend Finance Pty Ltd and Others v. Sing and Others* (1998) 111 ILR 611, the English Court of Appeals held that the correct interpretation of the word 'government' in section 14(1) was in light of the concept of sovereign authority, thus encompassing police functions.

tasks. Subsequently, it is open to any person exercising official functions, from a former head of state to the lowest public official.

The obvious clash between the concepts of immunity and universal jurisdiction has proved difficult to reconcile in practice. Despite the euphoria brought about as a result of the adoption of pro-universal jurisdiction laws by countries such as Spain and Belgium in the early to late 1990s, the position of international courts and treaty bodies was that the immunity of certain public officials – namely those enjoying immunity *ratione personae* – could not be trumped by the need to punish perpetrators of crimes.[102] This, along with other factors, resulted in Spain toning down its law while Belgium rescinded it altogether under significant pressure from those states whose leaders were becoming targets of suits before its courts.[103] Belgium was, moreover, traumatised by its defeat before the ICJ in the *Arrest Warrant* case, in which its prosecutors had only done the decent thing by indicting the Congolese Foreign Minister who was alleged to have committed crimes against humanity. As has already been noted, the ICJ admitted that the Congolese Minister enjoyed immunity *ratione personae*. Clearly, the lack of international support killed the initiatives and momentum of proactive states. The situation was further exacerbated by the fact that African states, whose leaders were the major targets of criminal suits, perceived the exercise of universal jurisdiction by European countries as an attack against African political institutions. The AU, for example, found it unacceptable that European prosecutors had engaged in a widespread campaign to indict African state officials, even those accused of mass criminality, at a time when African nations had generally refrained from applying this principle of jurisdiction.[104] This diminishing trend does not, however, mean that universal jurisdiction is no

---

[102] See ICJ *Belgian Arrest Warrant* judgment, paras. 47–55; with a slim majority, the ECtHR in *Al-Adsani* v. *UK* (2002) 34 EHRR 11, paras. 55–66, suggested that immunity was inherent in the operation of international law and could not be regarded as imposing a disproportionate restriction on the right of access to court.

[103] On 15 October 2009 the Spanish Congress adopted an amendment to the *Ley Orgánica del Poder Judicial* (LOPJ), which constricted the exercise of jurisdiction to war crimes, crimes against humanity, genocide and terrorism to situations where the suspect was in Spain, the victim was a Spanish national or a connection was otherwise established with Spain. The UK government also recently proposed giving the director of public prosecutions the power to veto arrest warrants on the basis of universal jurisdiction, in an effort to avert indictments against high-profile politicians, mainly from Israel. N. Hanman, 'DPP may Get Veto Power over Arrest Warrants for War Crimes Suspects', *Guardian* (22 July 2010).

[104] Decision of the Report of the Commission on the Abuse of the Principle of Universal Jurisdiction of 1 July 2008, AU Doc. Assembly/AU/Dec.199 (XI). This culminated in an EU–AU ministerial meeting wherein it was agreed to set up a technical committee that would make recommendations about the principle and how best it could be used between the nations of the two continents. This led to the drafting of the AU-EU Expert Report on the Principle of Universal Jurisdiction, Doc. 8672/1/09/Rev. 1 (16 April 2009). The same reluctance with the scope of universal jurisdiction was also echoed in the framework of the UNGA's sixth committee's deliberations on the principle during 2009. There, a number of delegations expressed the urgency for elaboration in order to avoid abuse and politicisation (GA/L/33372 (21 October 2009)).

longer recognised as a legitimate entitlement or obligation incumbent on states, given that the majority of nations expressly support its application, even if they are at times unable to enforce it. Equally, the practice of international criminal tribunals, with minor exceptions, is to deny defendants of any immunity claims.

CASE STUDY 14.2
The indictment of Al-Bashir before the ICC

States parties to the ICC Statute retain primacy over the Court where an offence under the Statute takes place on their territory or by one of their nationals.[1] The Court enjoys only complementary (secondary) jurisdiction, which arises only if: (1) the territorial or nationality state consent to refer the situation to the Court;[2] or (2) or otherwise the Security Council acting under Chapter VII of the UN Charter refers the situation, effectively bypassing the competent states.[3] Exceptionally, where a state party refuses to cede jurisdiction to the Court, the latter may yet entertain the case, provided that the particular state party is either unable or unwilling to institute criminal proceedings. Unlike the ICTY and ICTR, whose jurisdiction is primary to that of national courts, the ICC's jurisdiction is always complementary to that of the courts of its member states.

The Sudan is not a party to the ICC Statute and ordinarily therefore the ICC would not be able to entertain any jurisdiction, let alone primacy, over crimes taking place on Sudanese territory. However, following the events of Darfur in which millions were displaced and hundreds of thousands killed by government troops, militia and to a lesser degree rebel forces, the Security Council referred the Darfur situation to the ICC on the basis of resolution 1593 of 31 March 2005. The Sudanese government reacted angrily to this referral, arguing that a country and its leaders could not be forced to succumb to the jurisdiction of a court to which they had not subscribed. In any event, Sudan contended that the principle of complementarity was applicable *vis-à-vis* Security Council referrals, in which case the Sudanese courts would have enjoyed primary jurisdiction over the ICC. The ICC Chambers rejected this position altogether. They argued:

16. ... Article 12 (2) [i.e. on the primacy of national courts over the ICC] does not apply where a situation is referred to the Court by the Security Council acting under chapter VII of the Charter, pursuant to article 13(b) of the Statute. Thus, the Court may, where a situation is referred to it by the Security Council, exercise jurisdiction over crimes committed in the territory of states which are not party to the Statute and by nationals of states not party to the Statute.[4]

---

[1] Articles 12(1) and 14(1), ICC Statute.   [2] Article 12(2), ibid.   [3] Article 13(b), ibid.

[4] *ICC Prosecutor* v. *Harun and Kushayb*, Decision on the prosecution application under article 58(7) of the Statute (27 April 2007), para. 16. See also *ICC Prosecutor* v. *Al-Bashir*, Decision on the prosecution's application for a warrant of arrest against Al-Bashir (4 March 2009), para. 40.

In the section dealing with enforcement of international criminal law we examined the function of domestic courts, international tribunals and inter-state cooperation. In the present instance enforcement is effected by the Security Council bypassing the requirement of complementarity.[5] Notice that the Council does not impose sanctions and does not make reference to the crimes alleged to have been committed, or to any particular person as being responsible for the events in Darfur. It leaves this role to prosecutorial discretion alone. The ICC Prosecutor went ahead and indicted senior members of the Sudanese government, including President Al-Bashir himself.

Those involved solely in the peace negotiations in Sudan claim that persons with the greatest responsibility for atrocities will not think twice about intensifying their criminal activity, and will certainly not consider laying down their arms, if they believe or know that they are going to be prosecuted.[6] What do you think about this interplay between the pursuit of justice versus the attainment of peace? Is it a real conflict or merely an artificial dilemma? Should the Security Council stay away from pursuing high level executioners so that they can negotiate an end to hostilities? What message will this impunity give to victims and the perpetrators? Do you consider that there is any viable guarantee that the leaders of government and rebel forces can actually help to restore peace following a long period of mass criminality?

QUESTIONS

- **Is it reasonable to expect that the indictment of rebel or government leaders before domestic and international criminal tribunals can weaken them both at home and abroad and culminate in their removal from power?**
- **What is the difference in the jurisdiction and powers enjoyed by the ICC, ICTY, ICTR and national courts?**
- **As a result of the piracy scourge off the coast of Somalia, the Security Council in operative paragraph 4 of resolution 1918 (27 April 2010), requested the Secretary-General to explore prosecution mechanisms, including 'options for creating special domestic chambers possibly with international components, a regional tribunal or an international tribunal and corresponding imprisonment arrangements, taking into account ... the existing practice in establishing international and mixed tribunals and the time and the resources necessary to achieve and sustain substantive results'. Why was the Council even thinking about establishing a new hybrid tribunal, rather than employ the services of the ICC, the courts of the regional states, or indeed allow the courts of the apprehending states (members of NATO missions) to try the accused on the basis of universal jurisdiction?**

---

[5] See D. Akande, 'The Legal Nature of Security Council Referrals to the ICC and its Impact on Al-Bashir's Immunities', *JICJ* 7 (2009), 333.

[6] A. Natsios, 'Beyond Darfur: Sudan's Slide toward Civil War', *Foreign Affairs* 87 (2008), 77, at 82; L. Oette, 'Peace and Justice, or Neither? The Repercussions of the Al-Bashir Case for International Criminal Justice in Africa and Beyond', *JICJ* 8 (2010), 345.

FURTHER READING

Dennis, M. J., 'Application of Human Rights Treaties Extraterritorially in Times of Armed Conflict and Military Occupation', *AJIL* 99 (2005), 119.

Doswald-Beck, L., 'The Right to Life in Armed Conflict: Does International Humanitarian Law Provide All the Answers'? *IRRC* 88 (2006), 881.

Drumbl, M. A., *Atrocity, Punishment and International Law* (Cambridge University Press, 2007).

Green, L. C., *The Contemporary Law of Armed Conflict* (Manchester, New York: Manchester University Press, 2008).

Hampson, F. J., 'The Relationship between International Humanitarian Law and Human Rights Law from the Perspective of a Human Rights Treaty Body', *IRRC* 90 (2008), 549.

Kress, C., 'Universal Jurisdiction over International Crimes and the Institut de Droit International', *JICJ* 4 (2006), 561.

Provost, R., *International Human Rights and Humanitarian Law* (Cambridge University Press, 2002).

Reydams, L., 'The rise and fall of universal jurisdiction' (2010), available at: www.ggs. kuleuven.be/nieuw/publications/working%20 papers/new_series/wp37.pdf.

Reydams, L., *Universal Jurisdiction: International and Municipal Legal Perspectives* (Oxford University Press, 2003).

Sassòli, M. and Olson, L. M., 'The Relationship between International Humanitarian Law and Human Rights Law where it Matters: Admissible Killings and Internment of Fighters in Non-international Armed Conflicts', *IRRC* 90 (2008), 599.

Solis, G. D., *The Law of Armed Conflict: International Humanitarian Law in War* (Cambridge University Press, 2010).

Watkin, K., 'Controlling the Use of Force: a Role for Human Rights Norms in Armed Conflict', *AJIL* 98 (2004), 1.

Human rights and counter-terrorism

CONTENTS

15.1 INTRODUCTION

The purpose of this chapter is not to describe the terrorist phenomenon, but rather to analyse the range of responses to it and their compliance with human rights law. This analysis necessarily takes into consideration the legal nature of terrorism under international law and its rapid transformations in the aftermath of the terrorist attacks against the USA on 11 September 2001 (9/11). It is as a direct result of this transformation that the international legal framework on terrorism gave way to a model whose chief proponents endeavoured to locate it as far as possible beyond the ambit of the rule of law and the reach of the judiciary. Although this position was essentially posited by the direct victim of the 9/11 attacks, the United States of America, it was also widely shared by other nations, democratic and otherwise. The subsequent practice of these nations has given rise to a barrage of litigation worldwide and the submission of reports by UN rapporteurs and NGOs condemning the limitation and outright violation of human rights under the guise of counter-terrorism. The essential nature of the argument between the two sides may be expressed with the following question. Does the real and imminent threat posed by terrorism justify exceptional measures the effect of which is to deny fundamental rights to suspected terrorists? The answer to this question is not a simple one. No doubt, governments, whether unilaterally or jointly, must take appropriate intelligence and law-enforcement measures in order to protect their people.[1] The clandestine nature of terrorism renders this task all the more difficult. Yet, if in the name of counter-terrorism states are allowed to violate fundamental human rights with impunity they can turn out to pose a larger risk for all peoples, especially long term, than the terrorists themselves. Although the terrorist phenomenon is a real challenge to our established perceptions of justice and rights, one has to think of the adverse consequences accruing to societies from an exceptional deviation as to the treatment of terrorists. Will an executive accustomed to power abuse give up this arbitrary authority lightly? What guarantees are there that the pursuit of terrorists and the subsequent limitation to rights will not turn out to be a perpetual affair? How can one be sure that the government will not extend this authority over its personal enemies and against innocent persons?

This chapter seeks to demonstrate, among other things, that these dangers to personal liberty far outweigh the threats to human safety posed by serious 'terrorist' threats. The reader will acquire an appreciation of the obligation of states to protect their citizens from terrorism, including the debate as to whether terrorists possess human rights obligations. We shall then proceed to examine the most pertinent human rights violations in counter-terrorist operations. This includes the application of the principle of legality to terrorist legislation, the permissibility of relevant derogations, the right to life and the practice of targeted killings, the various contours of unlawful detention against terrorist suspects, torture and ill-treatment in order to gather intelligence information and promote confessions and finally the practice of abductions, unlawful extraditions and illegal rendition. To be sure, counter-terrorist operations have been found to infringe a range of other civil and political rights, such as the freedom of expression and the right to a fair trial.[2] In some instances, such operations have been deemed as compromising

---

[1] In exceptional circumstances, nations may decide to negotiate with 'terrorist organisations' for the benefit of civilian populations. Following the failure of the Pakistan army to defeat an eighteen-month Taliban insurgency into the country's Swat valley, it signed a peace accord with the insurgents according to which the Taliban would be free to impose Islamic law in exchange for peace. *Report of the Special Rapporteur on the Promotion and Protection of Human Rights and Fundamental Freedoms while Countering Terrorism*, UN Doc. A/64/211 (3 August 2009), para. 36.

[2] In *Kadi and Al Barakaat International Foundation* v. *Council of the European Union* [2008] ECR I-6351, paras. 335–7, at 349, the ECJ held that the imposition of targeted sanctions (freezing orders in the case at hand) against a suspected terrorist by the EU without any remedy whatsoever in the form of judicial review or a hearing violated the right of effective judicial protection.

economic and social rights.[3] However, it would go beyond the purpose of this chapter to examine in detail all of these violations.

15.2   THE LEGAL NATURE OF TERRORISM

Two myths underpin the international legal framework on terrorism: the first is that as an international crime it lacks a globally agreed definition, while the second is that all counter-terrorist efforts have always been unconcerned with the underlying causes of terrorism. As to the former,[4] it is true that international efforts to suppress terrorism from the early 1960s to the present day have focused on the elaboration of discrete anti-terrorist treaties, each one dealing with a particular manifestation of this phenomenon. By way of illustration, the 1963 Tokyo Convention on Offences and Certain Other Acts Committed On board Aircraft is concerned with conduct jeopardising the safety of aircraft and persons on board. In the same manner, the 1963 Tokyo Convention on Offences and Certain Other Acts Committed On board Aircraft, the 1998 Convention for the Suppression of Terrorist Bombings, the 1999 Convention on the Financing of International Terrorism and the 2005 Convention on the Suppression of Acts of Nuclear Terrorism, among others, do not address terrorism holistically but deal with distinct thematic issues. The reason behind this thematic approach is not that states fundamentally disagree on the range of criminal conduct that amounts to terrorism. Rather, intractable differences have always arisen in ascribing the terrorist designation to national liberation movements and in describing state violence as terrorist, and therefore as criminal under international law. Although few, if any, states openly argue that national liberation movements fighting against alien domination and foreign occupation in their pursuit of self-determination are prevented from employing violence under international law, interested states generally refute the accusation that they are

---

[3] In another case, the EU had implemented a freezing order against the assets of the family of a listed terrorist, which included social security benefits intended solely for meeting the family's basic needs. The ECJ rejected the application of the freezing order to such payments simply because the spouse may have been able to use some of those payments and therefore gain some benefit: *M and Others* v. *HM Treasury*, ECJ judgment (29 April 2010). The ICJ equally confirmed in its *Palestine Wall* advisory opinion (2004) ICJ Reports at 136, para. 134, that one of the side effects of the construction of the wall, even for alleged counter-terrorism purposes, was the violation of the economic rights of the Palestinians because they had no access to work.

[4] See H. Duffy, *The War on Terror and the Framework of International Law* (Cambridge University Press, 2005), 17–45, who argues that 'it is difficult to sustain that international terrorism is, per se, a discrete and identifiable legal norm'. Yet, she agrees that despite the absence of a generic definition, this does not mean that a lacuna exists in international law.

suppressing legitimate self-determination claims and therefore have no qualms about branding any ensuing violence as generally criminal or terrorist.[5] Equally, no government has ever admitted to being a state sponsor of clandestine acts of violence against its civilian population, yet many developed nations routinely engage in illicit practices such as administrative detention, kidnappings of suspects, illegal renditions to third countries, targeted killings, torture and other violations of human rights and humanitarian law. Clearly, although all of these practices are contrary to fundamental human rights, states are understandably reluctant to admit them, let alone describe the relevant conduct as criminal.

As a result of these misgivings, the international community realised the futility of a comprehensive treaty definition of terrorism because it was already in full agreement about the constituent elements of this offence. These elements were aptly described in the General Assembly's 1994 Declaration on Measures to Eliminate International Terrorism, as follows:

> criminal acts intended or calculated to provoke a state of terror in the general public, a group of persons or particular persons for political purposes [and that such acts] are in any circumstances unjustifiable, whatever the considerations of a political, philosophical, ideological, racial, ethnic, religious or other nature that may be invoked to justify them.[6]

These three elements, that is: (1) the perpetration of serious criminal acts; (2) the intention to inflict terror on civilian populations, with the further aim of (3) compelling governments to do or abstain from doing any act, have been given universal acceptance by the UNSC in the aftermath of the 9/11 terrorist attacks against the USA.[7] This definition is consistent with relevant domestic legislation in most states and may therefore constitute a general principle of law. In this sense, terrorism is an aggravated form of the principal offence (i.e. murder, grievous bodily harm) coupled with a further specific intent (i.e. to compel governments and to terrorise civilian populations). That particular conduct is criminal does not necessarily render it terrorist. More importantly, terrorist conduct constitutes a crime not only under domestic law, but also under international treaty law and some states have employed wide extraterritorial statutes in order to prosecute suspected terrorists on the basis of universal jurisdiction.[8]

---

[5] See UN Report of the high-level panel on threats, challenges and change, UN Doc. A/59/565 (2 December 2004), paras. 159–60, which emphasises that the lack of a comprehensive definition has embarrassingly stumbled on the lack of regulation of states' use of force against civilians and on divergences as to whether the right to resistance against an occupying power should be overridden in the context of a possible definition of terrorism.

[6] UNGA resolution 49/60 (9 December 1994).

[7] UNSC resolution 1566 (8 October 2004); UNSC resolution 1624 (14 September 2005); High-Level Panel Report, para. 164.

[8] Article 23(4) of the Spanish *Ley Orgánica del Poder Judicial* (Judicial Branch Act) 1985.

15.3   THE DISCUSSION ON UNDERLYING OR ROOT CAUSES

By the early 1970s the UNGA had become dominated by former colonial entities and the Western bloc was no longer in the driving seat of developments. During this time it was natural for the Assembly to demonise the apartheid regimes of South Africa and Israel, at a time when the Palestinian cause and the Palestinian Liberation Organisation (PLO) were exerting a significant degree of influence on the so-called non-aligned movement. The Assembly decided to examine the issue of terrorism more closely and appointed an *ad hoc* committee for this purpose,[9] which met three times between 1972 and 1979. During that time, developing nations argued that terrorism should be examined from its root causes, such as racism, colonialism, occupation and apartheid, and that it should not be differentiated from action undertaken by national liberation movements. A parallel development, largely sponsored by Arab and developing states between 1972 and 1989, was initiated by the then UN Secretary-General Kurt Waldheim, whereby the issue of terrorism was discussed on an annual basis. The unduly long title of this annual meeting was 'Measures to prevent international terrorism which endangers or takes innocent human lives or jeopardises fundamental freedoms, and study of the underlying causes of those forms of terrorism and acts of violence which lie in misery, frustration, grievance and despair and which cause some people to sacrifice human lives, including their own, in an attempt to effect radical changes'.[10] Its sponsors were clearly of the opinion that terrorism did not comprise mere acts of random violence but was connected to other fundamental root causes. This, no doubt, is a divisive matter that is largely, if not flatly, rejected by nations in the developed world. As a result, all of the post-1990 anti-terrorist international instruments have denied the application of ideological justifications to any forms of terrorist violence. This development had the effect of obliterating the so-called political offence exception to terrorism – this refers to conduct which would be otherwise criminal but is committed on political grounds – which was prevalent in the 1970s and 1980s.[11]

For good reason, terrorist discourse by the states that have been targeted most since 9/11 is outright hostile to the idea that terrorism is somehow sustained by particular 'root causes' associated with the foreign policy of the target nations. Yet the majority of the members making up the UN accept that the lack of democratic governance, the absence of human rights and the rule of law are conducive to the spread of terrorism. The UN Global Counter-Terrorism

---

[9] UNGA resolution 3034 (XXVII) (18 September 1972).

[10] See I. Bantekas, *International Criminal Law* (Oxford: Hart, 2010), 263–4.

[11] See e.g. UNSC resolution 1373 (28 September 2001) para. 2(e); article 4(2) of the 2003 US–UK Extradition Treaty; article 6 of the 1999 International Convention for the Suppression of the Financing of Terrorism.

strategy produces an indicative list of these conducive causes, emphasising, however, that none of these justifies or excuses terrorism:

prolonged unresolved conflicts, dehumanisation of victims of terrorism in all its forms and manifestations, lack of the rule of law and violations of human rights, ethnic, national and religious discrimination, political exclusion, socio-economic marginalisation and lack of good governance.[12]

The need to promote good governance and human rights by the target states, as a direct corollary to their counter-terrorism strategies, was strongly highlighted in the report of the UN high-level panel, which suggested that sole reliance on military, police and intelligence measures serves to:

alienate large parts of the world's population and thereby weaken the potential for collective action against terrorism. The crucial need, in relation to the states in the regions from which terrorists originate, is to address not only their capacity but their will to fight terror. To develop that will – with states drawing support rather than opposition from their own publics – requires a broader-based approach.

A thread that runs through all such concerns is the imperative to develop a global strategy of fighting terrorism that addresses root causes and strengthens responsible states and the rule of law and fundamental human rights.[13]

There is clear consensus therefore that the most significant root cause of terrorism is the absence of the rule of law and good governance in certain parts of the world, in addition to the incompatibility of counter-terrorism strategies with the fundamental standards of human rights.[14] Providing the former is a task that is best suited to policy-makers and strategists, whereas the latter is more closely connected with the mandate of lawyers and human rights activists. It is impossible to win the hearts and minds of terrorist sympathisers by stamping on the same very rights that the terrorists have violated. What is significant from this examination is that the UN and its members have begun to view terrorism as a holistic phenomenon that should not be divorced from the causes that feed and sustain it, while at the same time recognising their own particular obligations, the violation of which may amount to contributory causes.

---

[12] UNGA resolution 60/288 (20 September 2006), Annex, 'UN global counter-terrorism strategy: Plan of action', section I. The link to poverty is made explicit by the reference to the MDGs and the reaffirmation to eradicate poverty, promote sustained economic growth, social exclusion agendas (particularly youth unemployment), reduce marginalisation and 'the subsequent sense of victimisation that propels extremism and the recruitment of terrorists'.

[13] High-Level Panel Report, paras. 147–8. The same conclusions were adopted in the 2002 OSCE Charter on Preventing and Combating Terrorism, para. 20.

[14] See UNSC resolution 1624; UN Secretary-General Report, Uniting against Terrorism: Recommendations for a Global Counter-terrorism Strategy, UN Doc. A/60/825 (2006).

15.4 THE OBLIGATION OF STATES TO PROTECT THEIR POPULATIONS FROM TERRORISM

The place of human rights in terrorist discourse is not obvious from the outset. Terrorism is a crime committed by private entities, as a result of which the culprits incur criminal liability. Consequently, the victims of terrorism are victims of crime and not the subjects of human rights violations, because violations of this nature can only be committed by state agents or persons acting in their name or on their behalf. Therefore, strictly speaking, terrorism only engages the application of criminal law. Although this conclusion is consistent with the fundamental premises of human rights, it does not sit well with certain states and UN human rights bodies. Since the latter cannot argue that non-state actors are incumbent with human rights obligations under the relevant treaties, they contend instead that terrorists are responsible for the 'destruction' of human rights, as opposed to their 'violation,' a term reserved for human rights infractions committed by state actors.[15] The practical effect of this distinction is limited. Yet it sends out the wrong message that the obligation to protect and promote human rights from terrorism is not fully within the material capability of states. Turkey, for example, has repeatedly stated before international forums that the obligations contained in human rights instruments are also addressed to individuals and that terrorists violate rights in the same way as states.[16] In practice, this 'destruction' of human rights by non-state actors is countered through the application of domestic and international criminal law, not by human rights law.[17] The remit of international criminal law suffices in order to prevent, suppress and prosecute terrorist attacks. Yet, the trend does give rise to some concern, since some UN bodies, such as the Commission on Human Rights, have gone beyond the 'destruction' terminology and are now expressing concerns 'at the gross violations of human rights committed by terrorists'.[18]

---

[15] UNGA resolution 48/122 (20 December 1993); UNGA resolution 49/185 (23 December 1994); UNGA resolution 50/186 (22 December 1995); UNGA resolution 51/210 (17 December 1996); UNGA resolution 52/133 (27 February 1997). This phraseology is justified by its authors on account of article 5(1) ICCPR and article 30 UDHR.

[16] UN Secretary-General, Report on Human Rights and Terrorism, UN Doc. A/58/533 (24 October 2003), paras. 4–5.

[17] Report of the Special Rapporteur on the Promotion and Protection of Human Rights and Fundamental Freedoms while Countering Terrorism, UN Doc. E/CN.4/2006/98 (28 December 2005), para. 69.

[18] Resolution 2004/44, preamble. It is a fallacy that the ECtHR supports this line of argument. In *A* v. *UK* (1999) 27 EHRR 611, para. 22, it did not intimate that individuals could violate the rights enshrined in the Convention. Rather, it emphasised that states are under a duty to ensure that no one within their jurisdiction is subjected to ill-treatment by private individuals.

Since the state is not accused of having committed, or assisted, in the perpetration of the terrorist act, it would ordinarily bear no responsibility in respect of it. Moreover, on the basis of the argument that terrorists violate or destroy human rights the stage may be set for some states to contend that human rights law does not impose a positive burden upon them to avert terrorist attacks or prosecute the culprits, thus admitting only a negative obligation regarding the right to life. This is clearly wrong and should never be supported. It may well lead to a claim that in order for a positive obligation of this nature to be assumed it is essential that suspected terrorists be ultimately stripped of their human rights.

This argument is flawed. The jurisprudence of international human rights treaty bodies suggests that states are under a positive obligation to protect their citizens' right to life when threatened by terrorist or other violence committed by private actors, as long as the risk is immediate and the authorities knew or ought to have known about it.[19]

This positive duty arising from the threat or infliction of serious crime, including terrorism, extends far beyond a mere obligation to protect one from a known imminent risk, encompassing moreover a duty to investigate, prosecute and provide remedies to the victims and their families.[20] It is exactly because of this positive obligation that states have been granted exceptional powers in their struggle against international terrorism,[21] including the power to employ lethal force under certain circumstances.

CASE STUDY 15.1
Finogenov and Chernetsova v. *Russia*: ECtHR admissibility decision of 18 March 2010

On 23 October 2002 a group of Chechen terrorists took hold of the Dubrovka theatre in Moscow and held more than nine hundred people captive and at gunpoint for three days. The terrorists had managed to booby trap the building and moreover positioned eighteen suicide bombers among the hostages in order to prevent the authorities from staging a counter-attack. The terrorists

---

[19] See *Osman* v. *UK* [1998] 29 EHRR 245, paras. 115–6; see also *Kiliç* v. *Turkey* (2000) 33 EHRR 58, para. 62; *Neira Alegría* case, IACtHR judgment (19 January 1995), para. 75; HRCtee, General Comment 31, UN Doc. CCPR/C/21/Rev.1/Add. 13 (26 March 2004), para. 8.

[20] See *Oliveira* v. *Brazil*, Report no. 37/10 (17 March 2010), paras. 82ff., where the IACHR held that Brazil had violated its obligation to protect the right to life by ignoring death threats against a journalist in Bahia, a region plagued by assassinations against people of that profession. This liability was further exacerbated by the lack of a thorough investigation.

[21] Council of Europe Guidelines on human rights and the fight against terrorism (11 July 2002), Guideline I.

demanded the withdrawal of Russian troops from Chechen territory and demonstrated their resolve by killing those hostages that resisted or who attempted to escape. Three days later the Russian security forces mounted an armed operation, which involved pumping an unknown gas into the building's ventilation system which resulted in the loss of consciousness of both the terrorists and the hostages. Although the terrorist threat had seemingly been eliminated it soon transpired that 129 hostages had also died as a result of the operation; 102 died on the spot because of the effects of the gas, including 3 who were shot, 21 died in the course of evacuation and transportation to hospital, while 6 people died subsequently in hospital. Two key questions arose in this connection: (1) whether Russia was responsible for not having foreseen the terrorist threat and subsequently for failing to take measures to protect the victims; and (2) whether the counter-terrorism operation in the theatre failed to respect the right to life of the hostages. The admissibility decision answered the first question in the negative, as follows:

173. The Court notes that, indeed, article 2(1) [right to life] enjoins the state not only to refrain from the intentional and unlawful taking of life, but also to take appropriate steps to safeguard the lives of those within its jurisdiction ... However, this obligation is not unqualified. Thus, the first sentence of article 2 of the Convention, states that everyone's right to life 'shall be protected by law'. The applicants did not suggest that the state had not complied with its general duty to secure the right to life by putting in place criminal-law provisions to deter the commission of terrorist acts, backed by law-enforcement machinery ... As to more concrete measures which would possibly have prevented the hostage-taking, the Court reiterates that not every presumed threat to life obliges the authorities to take concrete measures to avoid the risk. A duty to take specific preventive action ... arises only if the authorities knew or ought to have known at the time of the existence of a real and immediate risk to the life of an individual or individuals ... This element is absent in the present case. There is no evidence that the authorities had any specific information about the hostage-taking being prepared.

The second question was answered in late 2011 by the Court. It held that given the seriousness of the situation at the time, the hardened resolve of the terrorists and the need for immediate action, the Russian authorities were justified in using force even though this was likely to culminate, and indeed did culminate, in civilian casualties.[1] Thus, the storming of the building itself did not violate the right to life of the hostages. Even the use of the lethal gas was not a disproportionate measure because the authorities intended the incapacitation of the terrorists, not the killing of hostages, despite some obvious risks to those with ill health.[2] In terms of the ensuing rescue and evacuation operation,

[1] *Finogenov and Others* v. *Russia*, Merits judgment (20 December 2011), paras. 213, 221, 226.
[2] Ibid., paras. 227–36.

however, the Court held that it was inadequately prepared, 'in particular because of the inadequate information exchange between various services, belated beginning of the evacuation, limited on-the-field coordination of various services, lack of appropriate medical treatment and equipment on the spot, and inadequate logistics'. These were found to have breached Russia's obligations under the right to life.[3]

QUESTIONS

- If terrorists are capable of committing human rights violations by reason of acts that constitute terrorism, then the obligations addressed in human rights treaties are also addressed to them. Discuss.

- A terrorist group claims that it is seeking to reverse the acute and long-standing poverty of a population that has been financially exploited by a rich third nation under the corrupt acquiescence of the home state. Is violence justified in order to realise this cause? Are the 'root causes' of the violence significant in human rights and international law discourse and decision-making?

- Under what circumstances does a state violate its human rights obligations for failing to prevent or punish those responsible for terrorist attacks?

- In defusing serious terrorist threats states must sometimes accept heavy collateral civilian casualties in the course of their counter-terrorism operations. This is justified in order to save thousands of other lives. Discuss.

[3] Ibid., paras. 263–6.

15.5   HUMAN RIGHTS IN COUNTER-TERRORISM OPERATIONS

Given that states are responsible for protecting their populations from terrorist violence they must necessarily enjoy the right to respond to such violence in an effective and deterrent manner. While it is true that terrorism poses a severe threat to human safety, the unchallenged authority of the state to employ armed force and limit civil liberties against those whom it deems terrorists in the name of counter-terrorism risks eroding the rights of terrorists and non-terrorists alike. For, if the state possesses the unilateral power to abrogate the rights of alleged terrorists, this very designation of 'terrorist' will soon become an instrument of oppression against all its perceived enemies. In the recent 'War on Terror',[22] initiated by the USA following the

[22] This expression was deliberately coined in an address by US President G. W. Bush to a joint session of Congress and the American people on 20 September 2001, in which he declared that 'our war on terror begins with Al-Qaeda, but it does not end there. It will not end until every terrorist group of global reach has been found, stopped and defeated.' Available at: www.whitehouse.gov/news/releases/2001/09/20010920-8.html.

events of 9/11, there have been far too many cases of persons unconnected to terrorism being abducted and brutally tortured by security forces because of suspicions or wrong information suggesting a terrorist link.[23] It is not only the 'innocent' that warrant protection from the excesses of government. Societies claiming to be grounded in the rule of law should not distinguish between the 'innocent' and the 'guilty' in order to assess whether a person deserves to enjoy human rights. Human rights pertain to all persons irrespective of whether their conduct is reprehensible to the vast majority of society. The observance of human rights and the rule of law against all persons ensures not only the objectivity of the application of law but also diminishes any calls for the justification of terrorist violence by potential sympathisers and equally avoids the glorification of terrorists as martyrs.

During the 'War on Terror' many, if not most, participating states violated the rights of suspected terrorists in two ways: through clandestine acts, such as secret abductions and the use of secret torture locations; or by intentionally erroneous interpretation of human rights law in order to suit their purposes, as was the case with the US denial of *habeas corpus* rights to Guantánamo detainees – or other US-held detainees around the world – on the basis that they were outside the ambit of US federal laws, in addition to being unlawful combatants.[24] It is evident therefore that states are prepared to overtly violate human rights in the face of extreme terrorist violence. In the aftermath of 9/11 the Bush administration's invasion of Afghanistan and Iraq and the incommunicado detention of large numbers of suspects gave rise to fears that the 'War on Terror' would be fought outside the international human rights framework.[25] This perception was soon quashed by the adoption of Security Council resolutions 1456[26] and 1624,[27] which stressed that any measure taken to combat terrorism must comply with international human rights law.

The following sections will examine the limitations imposed by human rights law on select counter-terrorist operations.

---

[23] See *Al Rabiah* v. *USA*, 658 F Supp 2d 11 (DDC, 2009), where a Kuwaiti national was held at Guantánamo Bay by the US military under charges that he was an Al-Qaeda operative, despite the fact that the accused was quite obviously physically incapable of playing such a role. Under pressure from the weight of the evidence the US government later dropped its case.

[24] HRCtee, Concluding Observations on USA, UN Doc. CCPR/C/USA/CO/3/Rev.1 (18 December 2006), para. 10, which criticised the USA's restrictive interpretation of its obligations under the ICCPR.

[25] The principal Council resolution related specifically to counter-terrorism in the aftermath of 9/11 was 1373. Although this did not make any reference to human rights, the HRCtee emphasised that resolution 1373 in no way justified human rights violations, including *refoulement* to countries where the accused risked being ill-treated. HRCtee, Concluding Observations on Lithuania, UN Doc. CCPR/CO/80/LTU (4 May 2004), para. 7.

[26] UNSC resolution 1456 (20 January 2003).

[27] UNSC resolution 1624 (14 September 2005).

15.5.1   Anti-terrorist legislation and the principle of legality

The principle of legality is otherwise reflected in the Latin maxim *nullum crimen nulla poena sine lege scripta*. Although its original formulation was intended to prohibit retroactive criminal legislation, its contemporary meaning encompasses three other customary principles, which require: (1) the specificity of criminal rules; (2) the ban on analogy; and (3) interpretation of criminal rules in favour of the accused.[28] In the field of anti-terrorist legislation the lack of specificity is particularly acute. Specificity is generally satisfied 'where the individual can know from the wording of the relevant provision and, if need be, with the assistance of the court's interpretation of it, what acts and omissions will make him liable'.[29] This does not mean, however, that all criminal laws must explain in minute detail what conduct is expected. Legislative drafting of this nature would render criminal laws rigid and inflexible and incapable of responding to future social, economic and other developments. Moreover, if such rigid rules were construed restrictively, according to their letter alone, many forms of criminal conduct would escape liability because they would not exactly fit into the relevant definitions. At the other extreme, if the criminal law was excessively vague,[30] with a view to countering the problems of rigidity, it would allow great latitude to judges and would ultimately offend the rule against the employment of analogies. Thus, a balance between the two extremes is necessary and legitimate.[31]

The HRCtee has routinely criticised numerous states for promulgating criminal legislation in which the definition of terrorism was deliberately vague or broad.[32] The purpose of such legislation is to permit unhindered recourse to emergency procedures, increase the risk of arbitrary detention and reduce the application of ordinary guarantees. In the case of Israeli anti-terrorist legislation the Committee was concerned about the fact that it made no attempt to reduce delays before trial, lack of access to legal counsel and the possibility of judgments extending detention measures in the absence

---

[28] See Bantekas, above note 10, 21–8.

[29] *Kokkinakis* v. *Greece* (1994) 17 EHRR 397, para. 52.

[30] In *Hashman and Harrup* v. *UK* (2000) 30 EHRR 241, the applicants were activists who had disturbed a fox hunt and were subsequently handed with orders to keep the peace. The law upon which this penalty was imposed purported to criminalise behaviour that is 'wrong rather than right in the judgment of the majority of contemporary citizens'. In accepting that the applicants' freedom of expression had been violated the Court also ruled that this provision did not satisfy the standards set out by the rule of specificity.

[31] *Kokkinakis* judgment, para. 40.

[32] See Concluding Observations on Israel, UN Doc. CCPR/C/ISR/CO/3 (3 September 2010), para. 13; HRCtee, Concluding Observations on USA, para. 11, which noted that Executive Order 13224 (23 Sep 2001) – Blocking property and prohibiting transactions with persons who commit, threaten to commit, or support terrorism – extended the definition of terrorism to a broad range of conduct, including political dissent.

of the suspect. Moreover, the Committee noted that the relevant laws might allow the authorities to preclude disclosure to the accused owing to security concerns.[33]

These vague and overly broad laws result in rendering terrorism a catch-all criminal offence that is subject to impermissible derogations by the state. Their nature allows the authorities to freely limit other economic and social rights that are seemingly unrelated to terrorism. In *Holder et al.* v. *Humanitarian Law Project et al.* the plaintiffs had sought to provide human rights training, advocacy and peacemaking to the Kurdistan Workers' Party (PKK) in Turkey and the LTTE in Sri Lanka, both of which had already been designated terrorist organisations in the USA. Under a federal US statute it is a crime to 'knowingly provide material support or resources to a foreign terrorist organisation'.[34] Under the statute the term 'material support' means, among other things, 'training, expert advice or assistance'.[35] The US government construed the statute as prohibiting all types of training to designated terrorist organisations, including human rights training that is meant to promote non-violence within these organisations, the submission of an *amicus* brief in their favour by a lawyer, as well as helping a proscribed organisation to petition international bodies to end violent conflicts. The plaintiffs argued that the statute was unnecessarily vague thereby violating the fifth amendment to the US Constitution, which protects against abuse of government authority in a legal procedure. They also claimed a violation of the first amendment which protects the freedom of speech. The Supreme Court, however, with a majority six to three, declared that the provision of intangibles such as human rights training allowed a proscribed organisation to free resources for other illegal purposes, which it was in the interests of the executive to curtail. As a result, the prohibition of free speech was justified under the circumstances.[36]

This line of argumentation is certainly problematic, for it suggests that human rights are a weapon in the armoury of terrorists and that they should not be informed about its benefits or the range of remedies against infringement of civil liberties. This reasoning is consistent with the US government's understanding of the concept of 'lawfare' which allows fringe groups to employ international law through local courts to discredit particular states. Human rights NGOs are at the centre of lawfare because it is believed that they do not simply provide human rights consultancy to proscribed organisations but more significantly bring lawsuits worldwide against government officials

---

[33] Ibid., Israel observations; see also the HRCtee's Concluding Observations on the Russian Federation, UN Doc. CCPR/C/RUS/CO/6 (24 November 2009), para. 7, which criticised the 2006 Terrorism Law on the same grounds, adding also that it places no limits on derogations and does not take into account the obligations imposed by article 4 ICCPR.

[34] 18 USC § 2339B(a)(1).   [35] Ibid., § 2339(B)(b)(1).

[36] *Holder et al.* v. *Humanitarian Law Project et al.*, 130 S. Ct. 2705 (2010).

alleging the perpetration of international crimes.[37] By way of example, a campaign by a number of NGOs has taken place since 2002 to indict former US Secretary of Defence Donald Rumsfeld for torture inflicted against persons in the custody of the USA, following the revelation of the so-called torture memos in which he seems to have authorised illegal interrogation techniques. This campaign has been seeking Rumsfeld's criminal liability on the basis of universal jurisdiction through the courts of Germany, France, Spain and the USA.[38]

15.5.2   Permissible restrictions and derogations arising from terrorist threats

Every time an act of terrorism is perpetrated or a terrorist threat is revealed by the press or by a government, there is strong public demand to adopt timely and strict responses. It may be the case that a country's counter-terrorism legislation is inadequate to deal with the particularities of terrorist prosecution or that alternatively its intelligence has been poor and ineffective. Moreover, it may well transpire that certain modes of transport, such as air travel, have to be suspended in order to tighten controls over the ensuing threat, as was the situation in the USA in the aftermath of 9/11. Yet, no matter what the terrorist threat may be, the ability of the state to suspend the application of human rights is certainly not unrestricted. Whereas states are permitted under particular circumstances to restrict the scope of particular rights, they are otherwise prohibited from suspending fundamental human rights, even in the face of an imminent emergency. Rights susceptible to such restrictions (otherwise known as qualified rights) include the freedom of expression[39] and the right of assembly[40] among others. Their restriction by the state is justified in those circumstances where their free exercise would be detrimental to the enjoyment of other rights.

It may therefore make sense to prevent an organisation that supports terrorist causes from printing material that incites others to support such a cause, or exclude a political party that supports terrorism from enrolling in the political parties register, even if by doing so the right to freedom of expression and association are curtailed.[41] Equally, it is good law to restrict the wide publication of pictures depicting the corpse of an assassinated politician, because the public interest in being informed does not, in the circumstances of the case,

---

[37] See T. Yin, 'Boumediene and Lawfare', *University of Richmond Law Review* (*U. Rich. L. Rev.*) 43 (2009), 865.

[38] K. Gallagher, 'Universal Jurisdiction in Practice: Efforts to Hold Donald Rumsfeld and Other High-level United States Officials Accountable for Torture', *JICJ* 7 (2009), 1087.

[39] Article 19(2) ICCPR.   [40] Article 21 ICCPR.

[41] *Herri Batasuna and Batasuna* v. *Spain*, ECtHR judgment (30 June 2009). The Court justified this restriction on the international desire to condemn the public defence of terrorism.

outweigh the emotional turbulence caused to the family of the deceased.[42] The state's ability to restrict this limited number of qualified rights further necessitates that any restriction conforms to the tests of legality, necessity, proportionality and non-discrimination. These concepts will be elaborated later in this chapter but it suffices to say that what is necessary today may not be necessary tomorrow and that proportionality requires a delicate and objective balance of facts in any given case.

Human rights treaties further entitle states in times of emergency that threaten the life of a nation to suspend the application of certain rights altogether – and not simply to restrict them – through the process of derogations.[43] This, understandably, is an exceptional measure of last resort and is inapplicable to fundamental rights, namely the right to life, protection from torture, inhuman and degrading treatment or punishment, protection from slavery and from retrospective criminal laws.[44] It would seem therefore that derogable rights can be suspended by the executive every time it declares a state of emergency; however, this is not the case. Although it is generally agreed that terrorism strains the capacity of the state to protect the right to life of its citizens and as a result specific limits on some guarantees are warranted, including those concerning detention and fair trial, this prerogative of the state is limited and should be narrowly construed.[45] Thus, the ability of a state to suspend particular rights depends not only on whether this is specifically permitted in a human rights treaty, but also on whether other rules of international law allow, and to what degree, the suspension in question. By way of illustration, if a certain freedom is derogable under a human rights treaty, but the conduct implementing the derogation is considered an international crime it is impermissible. The Human Rights Committee, in its General Comment 29 (2001), provided the following illustrative examples:

(a) All persons deprived of their liberty shall be treated with humanity and with respect for the inherent dignity of the human person. Although this right, prescribed in article 10 ICCPR, is not separately mentioned in the list of non-derogable rights in article 4(2), the Committee believes that here the Covenant expresses a norm of general international law not subject to derogation. This is supported by the reference to the inherent dignity of the human person in the preamble to the Covenant and by the close connection between articles 7 and 10.

---

[42] *Hachette Filippachi Associés* v. *France* (2009) 49 EHRR 23.

[43] See R. Higgins, 'Derogations under Human Rights Treaties', *BYIL* 48 (1976–77), 281, who argues that states enjoy a wide margin of appreciation in respect of characterising a situation as being one of emergency, whereas this discretion is narrow in relation to the applicable measures of necessity.

[44] Article 4(2) ICCPR and article 15(2) ECHR.

[45] Report of the UN working group on arbitrary detention, UN Doc. E/CN.4/2004/3 (15 December. 2003), para. 60.

(b) The prohibitions against taking of hostages, abductions or unacknowledged detention are not subject to derogation. The absolute nature of these prohibitions, even in times of emergency, is justified by their status as norms of general international law.

...

(d) As confirmed by the Rome Statute of the International Criminal Court, deportation or forcible transfer of population without grounds permitted under international law, in the form of forced displacement by expulsion or other coercive means from the area in which the persons concerned are lawfully present, constitutes a crime against humanity. The legitimate right to derogate from article 12 of the Covenant during a state of emergency can never be accepted as justifying such measures.[46]

Much like the procedural guarantees required for the implementation of restrictions on rights, the same array of procedural safeguards must be put in place before a derogation issued by a state can take effect. The two most significant issues in counter-terrorist policies concern the verification and justification of the declared state of emergency and its adherence to general international law and human rights. In the *Lawless* case the British government had set up a commission charged with special powers of arrest and detention against members of the outlawed Irish Republican Army (IRA) that was engaging in terrorist activities against British elements in Northern Ireland. The British government had duly notified the CoE of this exceptional measure and so when the accused was arrested and detained under powers of the Commission the issue arose of whether the derogation was actually necessary. The ECtHR believed it to be necessary because in its assessment, under the circumstances at the time (i.e. late 1950s), the IRA and its splinter factions were operating throughout the country, were secretive and engaged in violent terrorist activities.[47] This public emergency justifying the imposition of a derogation need not necessarily materialise in the entirety of a country's territory; rather, as was evident in *Aksoy*, Turkey was able to substantiate the legality of restrictions against the right to liberty of alleged terrorists because of the extent and impact of PKK terrorist activity in South-east Turkey at the time of the complaint.[48]

What about the impact and duration of terrorism itself on the legitimacy of a derogation order? Unlike the parties to an armed conflict the clash between a state and a terrorist organisation does not involve a constant, continuous, all-out war. In fact, the terrorists may just as well be satisfied if they are successful in instilling fear in the civilian population without any recourse to violence whatsoever, if in this manner many of their objectives are met. It is important therefore for a state to be able to take exceptional measures

---

[46] HRCtee, General Comment 29, UN Doc. CCPR/C/21/Rev.1/Add 11 (31 August 2001), para. 13.

[47] *Lawless* v. *UK (No. 3)*, (1961) 1 EHRR 15, paras. 30–6.

[48] *Aksoy* v. *Turkey*, (1997) 23 EHRR 553, para. 70.

not only when a terrorist threat is present, but also when it is imminent.[49] Given that all the operations planned by organisations such as Al-Qaeda are part of a global network of terrorism that carries out violent activities when this is opportune, it may be said that as long as reliable intelligence is made available in this regard, a terrorist threat should be deemed to be imminent.

It has already been stated that the right to suspend particular rights should in no way be construed as providing a blank cheque to the executive. The exceptional measures taken in anticipation of a terrorist threat must be necessary, proportionate to the threat and consistent with general international law. In the *Aksoy* case the Court was asked to assess whether the otherwise valid Turkish derogation against the prompt charging of detainees was lawful where the period of detention without judicial control was fourteen or more days. In an earlier judgment the Court had already observed that detention under these terms for a period of six days and four hours was unjustified because it left the accused not only vulnerable to arbitrary interference with his right to liberty, but also exposed him to torture.[50] Naturally, therefore, it was held that such a lengthy detention without recourse to judicial remedies was incompatible with the obligation of the state to prevent the infliction of torture or the abuse of a person's right to liberty.[51] Similarly, the Court has consistently held that in cases where an alleged terrorist is undergoing a lengthy detention, this is not deemed to be indeterminate as long as a process of deportation has been put in place by the authorities; and therefore the accused has access to various remedies and the hope of ultimate release. Hence, a lengthy detention is arbitrary and therefore impermissible where its principal aim is to keep a dangerous suspect off the streets and this is also true of the derogation that gives rise to it.[52] If the state considers someone as posing a terrorist threat it must compile the necessary evidence against him or her before deciding to arrest and detain.

15.6   THE RIGHT TO LIFE IN COUNTER-TERRORISM OPERATIONS

15.6.1   Situations when lethal force is permissible

In late October 2010 confidential documents known as 'Iraq War Logs' were leaked by Wikileaks demonstrating that US military legal advisors in the Iraq campaign had advised aircrews that they were under no obligation to

---

[49] *A and Others* v. *UK*, ECtHR judgment (19 February 2009), paras. 176–7. The Court noted that the requirement 'of imminence cannot be interpreted so narrowly as to require a state to wait for disaster to strike before taking measures to deal with it'; see E. Bates, 'A Public Emergency Threatening the Life of the Nation? The United Kingdom's Derogation of 18 December 2001 from the European Convention on Human Rights', *BYIL* 76 (2005), 245.

[50] *Brannigan and McBride* v. *UK*, (1993) 17 EHRR 539, para. 47.

[51] *Aksoy*, para. 78.

[52] *Chahal* v. *UK*, (1997) 23 EHRR 413, para. 113; *A and Others* v. *UK*, paras. 131, 164ff.

accept the surrender of enemy personnel (whether they were designated terrorists or rebels). As a result, aircrews were at liberty to target and kill such persons. Despite the *lex specialis* character of international humanitarian law over human rights law,[53] there is nothing in that body of law that justifies the intentional killing of persons who are in the process of surrendering to their adversary. The rule against denial of quarter is absolute and the right to life protected in this rule cannot certainly be construed narrowly on the basis of a technicality (i.e. the impractical dimension of surrender to an aircrew).[54] The matter is even more pertinent in the course of counterterrorism, which does not involve a situation of armed conflict, and where therefore the absolute nature of the right to life should in theory be uncontested. It should be stated from the outset that it is false to assume that the positive obligation of the state to protect its citizens from the dangers of terrorism justifies in emergency situations the violation of rights, including the right to life.

If the right to life is absolute then any cases of lawful deprivation must apply to terrorists and non-terrorists alike. This suggests that irrespective of the security threat posed by suspected terrorists the authorities must first exhaust all means to arrest them before resorting to lethal force. This principle has been applied by the ECtHR since the *McCann* case[55] and also by the UN Human Rights Committee. In *Guerrero* v. *Colombia* a guerrilla organisation had kidnapped a former ambassador who, according to intelligence reports, was kept at a house. Upon raiding the house and failing to retrieve the victim the security forces remained hidden in the house in wait for the occupants. When the latter eventually arrived they were shot at point-blank range although none was armed at the time. The Committee dismissed the government's argument that the taking of life was justified arguing that:

> the police action was apparently taken without warning to the victims and without giving them any opportunity to surrender to the police patrol or to offer any explanation of their presence or intentions. There is no evidence that the action of the police was necessary in their own defence or that of others, or that it was necessary to effect the arrest or prevent the escape of the persons concerned.[56]

---

[53] See section 14.4.

[54] Article 23(d), Hague Regulations; article 40, Protocol I; article 8(2)(b)(xii), ICC Statute. In *Re Dostler*, 13 AD 281, at 290, a US military commission found that Hitler's Commando Order, which called for the extermination of all enemy commandos, was a war crime of this nature.

[55] *McCann* v. *UK*, (1996) 21 EHRR 97, para. 200. For a fuller analysis see section 8.2.4.

[56] *Camargo* v. *Colombia*, UN Doc. CCPR//C//15/D/45/1979 (31 March 1982), para. 14.3. The forensic reports showed that one of the female suspects was shot repeatedly after she had already died from a heart attack.

Hence, when the authorities are capable of making an arrest, or otherwise of incapacitating the accused, they are never justified in applying lethal force. Under such circumstances the invocation of self-defence is naturally implausible. In equal measure, when an arrest is impossible but the threat posed by the accused is not significant, the authorities are prohibited from violating the right to life because of its inherently disproportionate nature.[57]

Counter-terrorist operations may well involve situations where the suspected terrorists violently oppose their arrest. In such situations lethal force cannot be employed simply because the arrest is frustrated, otherwise an arrest as such would possess more value than other individual rights, including the right to life. Rather, suspects must be offered fair warning and ample opportunity to surrender before force can be used and even so the force will be permissible only if the failure to arrest is absolutely necessary to avert the risk of terrorist killings. This test of absolute necessity is subject to a very high-threshold proportionality test. The European Commission of Human Rights deemed the test to have been satisfied in *Kelly* v. *UK*, where suspected IRA terrorists drove through a checkpoint without stopping and were subsequently fired upon by the guards. The Commission took into account the highly volatile climate in Northern Ireland at the time, holding that lethal force was justified because 'the kind of harm to be averted (as the soldiers reasonably thought) by preventing their escape was even greater, namely the freedom of terrorists to resume their dealing in death and destruction'.[58] This line of reasoning is somewhat problematic because it suggests that it is permissible to kill anyone suspected of being involved in terrorism who does not heed to a call for stop and search, on the vague ground that the suspect may or can commit terrorist acts in the future. Rather, it is better to argue that in exceptional cases of imminent terrorist threat the death of the suspect is permissible where he or she is in the process of avoiding arrest, if: (1) there is a very high likelihood that the suspect is about to engage in terrorist violence; or (2) where the death caused was incidental to the force used, although none the less probable under the circumstances, but was justified on the basis of the danger posed by the specific suspects.[59]

---

[57] See *Alejandre and Others* v. *Cuba* (*Brothers to the Rescue* case), IACHR Report no. 86/99 (29 September 1999), paras. 37ff., which concerned the downing of a small civilian aircraft by Cuban authorities for allegedly having violated its airspace. See also *Nachova and Others* v. *Bulgaria*, (2006) 42 EHRR 43, para. 95, to the same effect.

[58] *Kelly* v. *UK*, (1993) 16 EHRR 20.

[59] See principle 9 of the UN Basic Principles on the use of force and firearms by law enforcement officials, UNGA resolution 45/166 (18 December 1999), which limits the use of force strictly to: 'self-defence or defence of others against the imminent threat of death or serious injury, to prevent the perpetration of a particularly serious crime involving grave threat to life, to arrest a person presenting such a danger and resisting their authority, or to prevent his or her escape, and only when less extreme means are insufficient to achieve these objectives'.

15.6.2   Targeted killings and 'shoot-to-kill' strategies

The intentional killing of a suspected terrorist by secret agents of a state on its territory would no doubt give rise to the liability of that state because of the possibility of prior arrest. What, however, if the suspect operates from the territory of a country that is either supportive of terrorism, or which is otherwise reluctant to arrest and prosecute? In such situations the suspect poses a threat that is not susceptible to lawful arrest. The question then arises as to whether, since arrest is impossible, the authorities of the target state can lawfully kill the suspect in order to avert planned terrorist attacks on its territory. The USA and Israel have routinely resorted to such extrajudicial killings,[60] which do not differ in substance from assassinations orchestrated by various nations against political exiles, enemies of the state, spies and others living abroad. It is exactly because of this risk of arbitrariness that the HRCtee has objected to the practice of targeted killings of suspected terrorists, where this is used as a substitute for arrest and prosecution and without first exhausting non-lethal means.[61]

One could well posit the argument that if a state is unable to arrest a terrorist suspect because of the intransigence or support of another nation then that state's need for security against an imminent terrorist threat can only be met by recourse to armed force against the supporting nation. The legality of such action, however, would be seriously contested. Therefore, the argument continues, targeted killings constitute the best possible alternative to the use of armed force by one state against another. This contention has been rejected by UN human rights bodies, largely because it undermines the essential foundations of human rights.[62] Moreover, the empirical evidence does not support the contention that targeted killings necessarily disable the resolve of terrorist organisations or decrease the loyalty of their sympathisers. The Israeli Supreme Court in the *Targeted Killings* case was charged with assessing this practice against Palestinian civilians who were members of alleged terrorist organisations. The Court dispensed the greater part of its analysis on the nature of the conflict and the status of the Palestinians therein, finding them not to be unlawful combatants and therefore enjoying

---

[60] See D. Kretzmer, 'Targeted Killing of Suspected Terrorists: Extra-judicial Executions or Legitimate Means of Defence?' *EJIL* 16 (2005), 171, who provides a general overview of the Israeli policy of targeted assassinations.

[61] HRCtee, Concluding Observations on Israel, UN Doc. CCPR/CO/78/ISR (21 August 2003), para. 15.

[62] Report of the Special Rapporteur on Extrajudicial, Summary or Arbitrary Executions, UN Doc. E/CN.4/2005/7 (22 December 2004), para. 41, who rejects the argument that targeting and eliminating known terrorists is more efficient and costs fewer lives than waging conventional war. He equally notes that this practice 'makes a mockery of whatever accountability mechanisms may have otherwise constrained or exposed such illegal action under either humanitarian or human rights law'.

the rights afforded under the *jus in bello* as long as they were taking a direct part in hostilities.[63] The Court accepted that targeted killings were possible so long as the information on the identity and activity of the suspects had been verified, no other means were available to the authorities and the risk of collateral damage to other civilians was not significant in relation to the military advantage anticipated.[64] This judgment cannot set a sound precedent for a very practical reason. The *jus in bello*, unlike human rights law, does not prevent states from killing enemy combatants if they can arrest or detain them, unless of course said combatants are *hors de combat* or have surrendered. The Supreme Court is here attempting to infuse human rights into its consideration of a situation that falls within the scope of the *jus in bello*.[65] Ordinarily, counter-terrorist operations involving targeted killings are perpetrated outside armed conflict situations and therefore the human rights rule that they are generally impermissible continues to apply.

Shoot-to-kill counter-terrorist policies are not merely an extension of the right of law-enforcement authorities to use lethal force against suspects that are in the process of committing a terrorist act; they are more general in nature and are understood by their addressees as encompassing all possible terrorist targets. In the aftermath of the 2005 London bombings it was revealed that Scotland Yard had in place a secret policy codenamed Operation Kratos which allowed its agents to employ lethal force against suicide bombers posing an immediate danger.[66] As a result, when Scotland Yard agents mistook a Brazilian national for a fugitive Islamist terrorist and chased him after he fled, believing that he was being pursued by criminal elements, they thought themselves justified in shooting him repeatedly at point blank range. Following an inquest over the handling of the case the Yard issued new guidelines in which it abandoned its shoot-to-kill policy.[67] The Special Rapporteur on Extrajudicial, Summary or Arbitrary Executions, Philip Alston, has criticised shoot-to-kill policies quite aptly as follows:

---

[63] See section 14.2.1 on the meaning of combatant status and of 'taking a direct part in hostilities'.

[64] *Public Committee against Torture in Israel et al.* v. *The Government of Israel*, Judgment (11 December 2006), HCJ 769/02, paras. 40–6.

[65] See also M. Milanovic, 'Lessons for Human Rights and Humanitarian Law in the War on Terror: Comparing Hamdan and Israeli Targeted Killings case', *IRRC* 89 (2007), 373, at 390.

[66] See Metropolitan Police Authority, 'Suicide Terrorism', available at: www.mpa.gov.uk/committees/mpa/2005/051027/13/, which describes Operation Kratos.

[67] An inquiry into the case stipulated that a shoot-to-kill policy was an extreme measure aimed at suicide bombers. 'By definition, it cannot be "fail safe" if there is an operational error. Under domestic law principles, the control of such a policy and its operational use should be subjected, in any event, to the *McCann* "most careful scrutiny" analysis.' IPCC, Stockwell one: Investigation into the Shooting of Jean Charles de Menezes at Stockwell Underground Station on 22 July 2005 (London: 8 November 2007), available at www.ipcc.gov.uk/stockwell_one.pdf, 111.

The rhetoric of shoot-to-kill serves only to displace clear legal standards with a vaguely defined license to kill, risking confusion among law enforcement officers, endangering innocent persons and rationalizing mistakes, while avoiding the genuinely difficult challenges that are posed by the relevant threat.[68]

Some readers may find it odd that law-enforcement authorities are precluded from engaging in targeted killings and shoot-to-kill policies in respect of suicide bombers who detonate their explosive devices at the last minute. However, it should not be forgotten that the law as it stands does not exclude the employment of lethal force altogether. Rather, it requires that the authorities undertake such intelligence and surveillance operations as are necessary to avoid killing a terrorist suspect. Hence, a suicide bomber could well be arrested well prior to carrying out the ultimate detonation. If, however, despite all intelligence efforts suicide bombers cannot be arrested in advance, it would make no sense to argue that anyone who somehow appeared to the authorities to be hiding explosives under his or her clothes could become a legitimate target. The criticism against shoot-to-kill policies is that they legitimise arbitrariness and subsequently result in decreasing the quality of intelligence and investigations because the target ends up dead!

15.7   ATTEMPTS TO JUSTIFY ARBITRARY DETENTION

In the aftermath of the 9/11 attacks a number of countries, chief among them the USA, called into question the relevance of the international human rights regime in the face of this new type of terrorism. The terrorism states were accustomed to until that time was organised around small groups, was secretive and sought to attract public sympathy and support for its ideology. Al-Qaeda, on the other hand, was not only unconcerned about receiving public sympathy from the Western populace, but instead made it its primary target of violence in order to force Western governments to cease their presence in the Muslim world. As a result, the US government in 2001 soon conceived the aforementioned 'War on Terror' doctrine, through which it claimed that the threat posed by Islamic terrorism was not susceptible to the ordinary criminal law-enforcement and human rights rules, but was instead governed by the law of armed conflict. The term 'war' was thus not used as a mere metaphor, but as indicative of the new US position on how suspected terrorists should be treated.

This new position soon materialised with the detention of suspected criminals at the US Army's Guantánamo Bay detention facility in Cuba. Those detained at Guantánamo had not only been transferred from Afghanistan and Iraq but also from other parts of the world; yet, the common characteristic

[68] Report of the Special Rapporteur, UN Doc. E/CN.4/2006/53 (8 March 2006), para. 45.

of the inmates was that none of them was officially charged and none had access to judicial remedies or to a lawyer. How was this possible? Even if these persons were to be classified as combatants or worse, as unlawful combatants, their detention at the very least would have to be fully documented and they ought to have been provided with due process rights. The expectation of the US government at the time was that if the detainees were not physically held on US territory there would exist no legal basis for granting them *habeas corpus* rights or any other access to judicial remedies. In the same spirit, it was presumed that the full range of human rights granted to US citizens would not apply to these suspected terrorists. Moreover, the objective of subsuming counter-terrorist operations within the legal framework of the *jus in bello* was to render the targeting of suspects legitimate – whereas otherwise they would have had to be arrested and lawfully prosecuted.[69] Finally, the designation of suspected terrorists as unlawful combatants was meant to deprive them of even the most rudimentary rights under the *jus in bello*, despite the fact that there are no circumstances under customary international law that permit the deprivation of these fundamental guarantees to any person.[70]

The Guantánamo *habeas* litigation first commenced with the petition brought in *Rasul* v. *Bush* on behalf of two British and one Australian nationals before the District Court for the District of Columbia. When the petition finally reached the US Supreme Court its first task was to determine whether US courts lacked jurisdiction 'to consider challenges to the legality of the detention of foreign nationals captured abroad in connection with hostilities and incarcerated at Guantánamo Bay'.[71] The Court intimated that the petitioners were not nationals of countries at war with the USA and had moreover 'been imprisoned in territory over which the United States exercises exclusive jurisdiction and control'.[72] Consequently, it held that the *habeas* statute[73] conferred on federal courts jurisdiction. This led to a tug-of-war between the Court and Congress, because soon afterwards the latter promulgated the Detainee Treatment Act of 2005 (DTA)[74] which attempted to strip federal courts of jurisdiction to entertain *habeas* petitions lodged by Guantánamo detainees. In response, the Supreme Court in *Hamdan* v. *Rumsfeld* held that the DTA could not apply retrospectively.[75] Congress, rather angrily, immediately retorted by passing the Military Commissions Act of

---

[69] Military Order of 13 November 2001, on detention, treatment and trial of certain non-citizens in the war against terrorism, F. Reg. 57833, vol. 66, no. 222, had the effect of subjecting the detainees to military commissions with unspecified *habeas* or other rights.

[70] Article 75, Protocol I 1977.

[71] *Rasul* v. *Bush* 542 US 466 (2004), 470; affirmed also in *Gherebi* v. *Rumsfeld*, 352 F. 3d 1278 (9th Cir., 2003).

[72] *Rasul*, ibid., 476.   [73] 28 USC §2241ff.   [74] 119 Stat. 2742.

[75] *Hamdan* v. *Rumsfeld* 548 US 557 (2006), 576ff.

2006,[76] effectively stripping federal courts of all jurisdiction over Guantánamo *habeas* claims, irrespective of when these were filed and proceeded to reinstate the DTA. It became clear that the only way this dispute was going to be resolved once and for all was by judicial determination as to whether Guantánamo detainees possessed *habeas* claims before federal courts under the US Constitution itself. The constitutional foundation of these *habeas* claims was confirmed by the Supreme Court in *Boumediene* v. *Bush*, which moreover held that the DTA review system was an inadequate substitute for *habeas* claims because it impeded the right to challenge one's charges, the right to collect and present evidence and because it did not provide sufficient review of the cause for detention, as well as the power to detain.[77] The result in *Boumediene* was subsequently ratified by the incoming administration[78] and entrenched as good law.[79]

By the time the effects of the *Boumediene* judgment were felt upon the counter-terrorist operations of the US military and its law-enforcement authorities a significant number of suspects had already spent years without recourse to judicial remedies or, in most cases, without their relatives or lawyers having been informed of their detention. This type of deprivation of liberty is known as secret detention and is wholly unjustified under international law. Its nature as such is determined by its incommunicado character (i.e. no access to a lawyer) and lack of disclosure of the place of detention or lack of information about the fate of the detainee.[80] What then of the argument that some form of arbitrary detention is necessary in order to counter the danger that terrorist suspects pose to national or international security, not to mention the need for protracted interrogations in order to secure vital intelligence that would otherwise be lost? Articles 9 and 5 of the ICCPR and the ECHR respectively concur that the right to liberty and security of person is subject solely to the following limitations: (1) detention following conviction by a competent court; (2) detention upon reasonable suspicion that the accused has committed an offence or is about to commit one; and (3) detention aiming to prevent unauthorised entry into a country or in order to enforce a deportation or extradition order.[81] Both instruments, however, make it abundantly clear that these limitations must be prescribed by law and that once detained the accused must be promptly informed of the reason for

---

[76] 28 USC §2241(e).   [77] *Boumediene* v. *Bush* 128 S Ct 2229 (2008), 2266–70.

[78] Review and disposition of individuals detained at the Guantánamo Bay naval base and closure of detention facilities, Executive Order no. 13,492, 74 Fed. Reg. 4,897 (27 January 2009).

[79] See also *Munaf* v. *Geren, Secretary of the Army et al.* 128 S Ct 2207 (2008), where the US Supreme Court acknowledged that persons detained in Iraq by US forces were entitled to *habeas corpus*, although jurisdiction for these claims lay with the Iraqi courts.

[80] See Joint Study on the Global Practices in Relation to Secret Detention in the Context of Countering Terrorism, UN Doc. A/HRC/13/42 (19 February 2010), paras. 8–35.

[81] For a fuller analysis of the relevant ECHR provisions, see section 8.4.

the arrest and charges against him or her. Moreover, detainees must be given prompt access to judicial remedies and a trial within reasonable time. Persons deprived of their liberty by arrest or detention shall in all circumstances be entitled to due process rights before a court by which the lawfulness of their detention can be promptly decided. It is evident therefore that the conditions pertinent to the Guantánamo detentions rendered them entirely unlawful.[82]

Although the law against unlawful detention seems fairly straightforward, there have been numerous attempts to bypass it under the guise of a seeming legality. Colombia's anti-terror legislation, for example, granted its armed forces the power ordinarily enjoyed by the judiciary, including the right to authorise detention and other measures without a prior order by regularly constituted courts.[83] The ECtHR has held that an otherwise lawful deprivation of liberty of a terrorist suspect had been rendered illegal by the fact that the authorities had failed to disclose that he was in the process of being extradited.[84] This element was particularly crucial under the facts of the case because of the frequency of torture and enforced disappearance inflicted on terrorist suspects by the requesting state.

By far the most common violation in European counter-terrorist operations has been the lengthy pre-trial detention of suspects under the guise of investigation or extradition/deportation proceedings, when in fact the aim of the authorities was to keep the accused detained as much as possible because of his or her perceived danger to the public. It is a matter of fact therefore to ascertain whether the government was not seriously trying to deport/extradite the suspect. In *A and Others* the ECtHR rejected the British derogation under the Convention that would have enabled it to indefinitely detain terrorist suspects under national security grounds.[85] Equally, the Court has held in a different case that a period of detention without judicial control for four days and six hours was contrary to the requirement that an accused be brought before a judge promptly.[86]

The lowest point in the recent history of unlawful pre-trial detention was the practice of secret detention centres on land as well as on board military aircraft. This practice was achieved as a result of collusion between the authorities of various nations. Initially, few believed the testimonies of those that had been held there, although not even the victims were fully aware of the countries in which they were held. The plot came to light only after

---

[82] Commission on Human Rights, Situation of Detainees at Guantánamo Bay, UN Doc. E/CN.4/2006/120 (15 February 2006).

[83] HRCtee, Concluding Observations on Colombia, UN Doc. CCPR/CO/80/COL (26 May 2004), para. 9.

[84] *Shamayev and Others* v. *Georgia and Russia*, ECtHR judgment (12 April 2005), para. 425.

[85] *A and Others* v. *UK*, paras. 164ff. The ECtHR rejected it also because it found that it discriminated between nationals and non-nationals.

[86] *Brogan and Others* v. *UK* (1988) 11 EHRR 117, para. 62; *Aksoy*, para. 66.

researchers discovered that flight plans from Iraq and Afghanistan had been falsified to avoid detection.[87] Unlawful detention has also had a negative spill-over as concerns organised criminal activity. UN special rapporteurs have reported an incident where elements of the Georgian mafia abducted an Algerian, thereafter selling him to the CIA, which then boarded him onto a plane towards Kabul.[88] The quality of the rule of law is in serious doubt where the authorities and organised crime collude and find common ground in justifying unlawful acts.

15.8 UNLAWFUL EXTRADITIONS AND ILLEGAL RENDITIONS OF SUSPECTED TERRORISTS

15.8.1 Washing one's hands and hiding every trace

We have already alluded that one aspect of the War on Terror was the war against human rights. This manifested itself in two ways: (1) as a struggle against the applicability of human rights and of the jurisdiction of ordinary courts, of which the Guantánamo paradigm is the most pertinent expression; and (2) by failing to fully implement this paradigm a number of states decided that the use of legal argumentation was inconvenient, cumbersome and ineffective. As a result, they decided to operate outside the law altogether. Thus, they resorted to kidnappings, secret detention centres and surrender of persons to countries where it was expected that they would be tortured and perhaps killed. All of these unlawful activities naturally took place outside the territory of the culprit states.

Before we go on to discuss the practice of illegal renditions *per se* it is perhaps instructive to examine those attempts to bypass the legal requirements of extradition. States are generally free to extradite or expel aliens, or even their own nationals, to other countries, subject to certain human rights safeguards. Chief among these is that the offence in question be a crime of equal or similar gravity in both nations (double criminality rule); that the accused will be prosecuted only for the offence for which extradition is agreed (speciality rule). Moreover, it is impermissible to try someone for the same conduct twice, even if under a different legal characterisation (double jeopardy rule). Finally, as a result of the prohibition of torture and ill-treatment under

---

[87] Joint Study on Secret Detention, paras. 98–164, which provides a detailed account of such secret detention sites and the countries involved; see also Council of Europe Parliamentary Assembly, Alleged Secret Detentions and Unlawful Inter-state Transfers Involving Council of Europe Member States, CoE Doc. 10977 (26 June 2006), and its follow-up, Secret Detentions and Illegal Transfers of Detainees Involving Council of Europe Member States: Second Report, CoE Doc. 11302 Rev (11 June 2007) (so-called Marty Report, after its author).

[88] Joint Study on Secret Detention, ibid., para. 134(b).

customary law, an additional rule has emerged whereby states are under an obligation not to extradite or expel aliens, including asylum seekers, to countries where they face a real risk of being subjected to torture and ill-treatment.

The ECtHR has consistently applied this rule to the extradition of alleged terrorists.[89] The determination of the government's knowledge of circumstances giving rise to said risk is a subjective one. If it is demonstrated that at the time of extradition the serious likelihood of ill-treatment was 'known or ought to have been known' to the extraditing state, then it is wholly liable and complicit in the ill-treatment of the accused.[90] The fact that the accused may be deemed dangerous and pose a serious threat to the community if not extradited in no way outweighs that person's right not to be subjected to a serious risk of ill-treatment.[91] In Europe, the courts' assessment of the risk of ill-treatment is adduced to a large degree from expert witnesses, as well as from NGO reports with expertise and field presence in the requesting states. This line of reasoning is not, however, without its detractors. The Canadian Supreme Court in *Suresh* v. *Canada*, where a Sri Lankan refugee argued that his deportation to that country risked a substantial likelihood of torture, held that although torture was strictly prohibited under international law there did exist exceptional circumstances where its infliction as a result of deportation is justified on the basis of a balancing of competing interests. In the case at hand, such interests included the combating of terrorism and Canadian safety.[92]

In order to bypass this procedural safeguard, some states have made use of so-called diplomatic assurances during the peak of the War on Terror. These are bilateral agreements, whether formal or in the form of a memorandum of understanding (MoU), whereby the requesting state undertakes to uphold the rights of the accused and inform the extraditing nation of the whereabouts and physical condition of the accused. Recent jurisprudence has unfortunately exposed the manipulation of these assurances and has demonstrated that state officials of the requested state were not only aware but implicitly consented to the infliction of torture upon the accused.[93] In its particular examination of the practice of diplomatic assurances the ECtHR held that it had found these to be wholly insufficient with respect to countries where ill-treatment was 'endemic and persistent'.[94] What is even more significant

---

[89] *Chahal* v. *UK* (1997) 23 EHRR 413, paras. 73–4; *Cruz Varas and Others* v. *Sweden* (1991) 14 EHRR 1, paras. 69–70.

[90] *Shamayev and Others*, para. 337.   [91] *Saadi* v. *Italy* (2009) 49 EHRR 30, paras. 138–9.

[92] *Suresh* v. *Canada (Minister of Citizenship and Immigration)* (2003) 1 SCR 3.

[93] See *Agiza* v. *Sweden*, CAT Doc. CAT/C/34/D/233/2003 (20 May 2005), and *Youssef* v. *Home Office* [2004] EWHC 1884, both of which concerned the abuse by Egypt of diplomatic assurances in respect of persons extradited under charges of terrorism. In the first case, the CtAT found the Swedish government to have breached its international obligations by illicitly colluding with CIA agents to surrender Agiza and another person to Egypt.

[94] *Ismoilov* v. *Russia and Others*, ECtHR judgment (24 April 2008), para. 127. See Chapter 8, which discusses the *Abu Qatada* case.

is that the Court has employed rule 39 of its Rules in order to adopt interim measures with regard to US extradition requests that would render extradited persons to US military commissions, despite any diplomatic assurances provided by the government of that country.[95]

In cases where even diplomatic assurances could be turned down by the courts or viewed as suspicious by the press and NGOs the abduction of the accused and his rendering to a third nation under secret arrangements became common practice. It in fact became so entrenched that when people disappeared in various parts of the world their relatives straightaway suspected government abductions related to counter-terrorism operations. Even though the illegality of an 'arrest' has been deemed by the US Supreme Court as not violating the accused's right to a fair trial,[96] still US prosecutors could not sit an accused before a court after having inflicted long-term ill-treatment upon that person. Equally, despite the vociferous position by the Bush administration that persons considered unlawful combatants and held outside US territory did not enjoy the protection of US law, it was evident that at some point the detainees' *habeas* claims would be entertained by federal courts. Hence, the abduction of suspects and their secret rendition to authoritarian regimes subject to few, if any, legal and moral impediments to torture was considered an optimal option.

15.8.2   From arbitrary detention and unlawful extradition the road to torture is open...

The inevitable consequence of arbitrary detention, particularly where it is incommunicado, is recourse to ill-treatment, torture and even death. Indeed, where law-enforcement authorities are ordered to kidnap and detain 'enemies of the state' at will, having received direct assurances of absolute impunity, while at the same time the state itself has distorted the boundaries of what constitutes lawful interrogation, cannot but take the next step which is to inflict torture in order to elicit information. Human nature, under such unchecked and clandestine circumstances, can show its darkest side, especially where the interrogators are expected, if not mandated, to produce vital intelligence. Empirical evidence suggests that systematic ill-treatment and torture are the direct products of impunity and encouragement, even in countries otherwise premised on the rule of law. This is exemplified by

---

[95] *Mustafa Kamal Mustafa (Abu Hamza) v. UK*, App. no. 36742/08, rule 39 Order (4 August 2008).

[96] This position, known as *male captus bene detentus* is generally reflected in *US v. Alvarez-Machain* (1992) 112 S Ct 2188. The courts in Europe have adopted a quite contrary view, holding that where the presence of the accused is secured by resort to a serious abuse of power by the prosecuting authorities the courts may refuse to sit in judgment. *Bennett v. Horseferry Road Magistrates' Court* [1993] 3 All ER 138, 150. See A. Choo, 'Halting Criminal Proceedings: the Abuse of Process Revisited', *Criminal Law Review* [1985] 846.

the case of the Guantánamo detainees, those subject to illegal renditions and secret detention centres, as well as in respect of persons incarcerated in Iraq by coalition forces under conditions of secrecy.[97] In practice, although publicly denied, most states earnestly believe that the infliction of torture is indispensable in the interrogation of terrorist suspects; no doubt, this is based on the perceived successes of this practice. It is probably also premised on the rationale that in order to counter an extreme form of criminal conduct, such as terrorism, extreme responses are required by the authorities, including torture. From the narrow point of view of the interrogators it is probably true that ill-treatment is capable of acquiring immediate and crucial intelligence from the suspects. None the less, in the long run it is certainly counterproductive in relation to ideological terrorism because it unites and strengthens its base and encourages sympathisers. Moreover, history teaches us that what starts off as a proclaimed exceptional erosion of civil liberties almost certainly ends up as a generalised practice, which is sustained either by authoritarianism or by instilling a perpetual terror in the psyche of the populace.

Following the 9/11 terror attacks the US Justice Department's Legal Counsel (OLC) was asked to provide advice on particular detention and interrogation policies and techniques against captured Al-Qaeda members. The OLC's first memo of 22 January 2002 argued that the country's treaty obligations towards Afghanistan had been effectively suspended because the latter was a failed state, thus negating the protections offered by the Geneva Conventions and the Torture Convention. This was followed by another memo of 1 August 2002 – now known as the Bybee torture memo, after its author – in which its authors attempted to redefine torture and the obligations of the USA. The redefinition of torture was arbitrarily premised on an augmentation of the permissible thresholds of physical and mental pain. Thus, interrogators were advised that physical pain 'must be equivalent in intensity to the pain accompanying serious physical injury, such as organ failure, impairment of bodily function, or even death'. Equally, the applicable threshold for mental pain was deemed to be severe and long-term psychological harm,[98] which is certainly far higher than the threshold required under the 1984 UN Torture Convention and customary international law.[99] As a result, the memo approved otherwise prohibited conduct, including hooding, water-boarding,[100] exploitation

---

[97] Human Rights Watch, Iraq: Wikileaks Documents Describe Torture of Detainees, (23 October 2010), available at: www.hrw.org/en/news/2010/10/24/iraq-wikileaks-documents-describe-torture-detainees.

[98] Memorandum from Jay Bybee to Alberto R. Gonzales, counsel to the President, 'Standards of conduct for interrogation under 18 USC §§ 2340–2340A', available at: www.washingtonpost.com/wp-srv/nation/documents/dojinterrogationmemo20020801.pdf.

[99] See section 8.3 for a discussion of the right to be free from torture.

[100] Water-boarding consists of immobilising the subject while on his back and then pouring water over his face in order to cause the sensation of drowning.

of phobias, the employment of stress positions, sleep deprivation and other treatment.[101] The Obama administration swiftly rescinded the orders approved by the Bybee torture memos.[102] Of equally doubtful legality is the alleged exception to torture on the basis of the so-called ticking bomb scenario, which envisages that in situations of extreme urgency a confirmed offender may be tortured in order to reveal the whereabouts of a time-bomb, or other operation that is in the process of execution and which poses an immediate threat to public safety. The Israeli Supreme Court, although ruling that brutal and inhuman interrogation techniques are prohibited at all times, did not rule out the defence of necessity against the ticking bomb scenario.[103]

One might assume that in the worst case scenario the evidence seized from a suspected terrorist following torture or ill-treatment would be declared inadmissible either because it was unlawful *per se* or because the victim's right to a fair trial had been violated.[104] Yet, if clandestine agencies enjoy impunity and are mandated to eliminate terrorism under any circumstances they are unlikely to have any desire to subject tortured suspects to trial. Knowing full well that any evidence will be treated as inadmissible the prospect of litigation is a disincentive. As a result, the suspect may, following ill-treatment, be eliminated, transferred to a country with an even more dire human rights record, or used as a decoy to lure other suspects. The situation is further exacerbated by the fact that in certain countries the law does not subject torturers to criminal liability because their conduct is deemed within the scope of their employment.[105] National courts are generally reluctant to compel disclosure in cases brought by abductees, the effect of which would be to stifle information-sharing between allied nations. This is also true in situations which may be deemed prejudicial to national security, even if the evidence sought was obtained by torture or other illegal means.

This conclusion has not only been reached by US courts,[106] but has reluctantly been accepted by courts in the UK in their examination of allegations

---

[101] D. A. Wallace, 'Torture v. the Basic Principles of the US Military', *JICJ* 6 (2008), 309.

[102] Executive Order 13491, Ensuring Lawful Interrogations, (22 January 2009).

[103] *Public Committee against Torture* v. *The State of Israel*, HCJ 5100/94 (1999).

[104] *Göçmen* v. *Turkey*, ECtHR judgment (17 October 2006), paras. 67–76; *A and Others* v. *Secretary of State for the Home Department* [2005] UKHL 71.

[105] *Rasul* v. *Myers*, 512 F. 3d 644, 661 (DC Cir., 2008); *In Re Iraq and Afghanistan Detainees Litigation*, 479 F. Supp. 2d 85 (DDC, 2007).

[106] *El Masri* v. *Tenet* (4th Cir., 2007) 479 F. 3d 296; *Mohamed* v. *Jeppesen Dataplan Inc.* (ND Cal., 2008) 539 F. Supp. 2d 1128, 1134. It should be mentioned that in subsequent phases of the latter case the Ninth Circuit took the view that an outright dismissal of a case on state secrets grounds should be disfavoured. See *Mohamed* v. *Jeppesen Dataplan Inc* (9th Cir., 2009) 563 F. 3d 992, 1006. Eventually, sensitive information was not admitted at trial. Upheld finally in *Binyam Mohamed and Others* v. *Jeppesen Dataplan Inc.*, Ninth Circuit judgment (6 September 2010).

of torture against British nationals held at Guantánamo Bay.[107] A necessary byproduct of this limitation has been the inability to claim compensation through the judiciary because a proper case cannot be made against the state for lack of evidence. Judges in the USA who have turned down similar applications deplore this failure of the legal system because it offers no protection to victims of illegal rendition or torture.[108] The Obama administration, shortly after taking up office, issued a memorandum through the Office of the Attorney-General, to the effect that the state secrets privilege should be invoked only to the extent necessary to protect against the risk of significant harm to national security. The privilege was inapplicable in order to:

(i) conceal violations of the law, inefficiency, or administrative error; (ii) prevent embarrassment to a person, organisation or agency of the US government; (iii) restrain competition; or (iv) prevent or delay the release of information the release of which would not reasonably be expected to cause significant harm to national security.[109]

The memo is in fact quite narrow in scope. For one thing, it is not addressed to the courts, which must still submit filings to the National Security or Civil Division of the Department of Justice in order to assess whether the standard is satisfied. Secondly, it is not clear whether information which is reasonably expected to cause significant harm to national security can be released, even if it contains serious human rights violations. Finally, the memo itself is not a law, but a mere instrument of guidance and does not serve, in any event, to lift the impunity of those that have ill-treated suspected terrorists. In practice, its utility seems to be rather limited as will be demonstrated elsewhere in this chapter on the basis of the litigation against a corporation that was alleged to have facilitated the logistics relating to illegal renditions.

---

[107] *In re Binyam Mohammed* [2008] EWHC 2048 (Admin), para. 105, the Queen's Bench Division of the Divisional Court held that the Foreign Office was under a duty to disclose classified information that was not only necessary but essential for the applicant's defence. It did however grant the government time to file a public interest immunity certificate, which it did, arguing that possible disclosure would hamper critical information-sharing with the USA and that such matters were best left to private discussions. The High Court eventually held that under the circumstances it would not compel disclosure ([2009] EWHC 152 (Admin)).

[108] In *Arar* v. *Ashcroft and Others*, Second Circuit judgment (2 November 2009), the Court of Appeals held that as unfortunate as the situation was for the plaintiff, who had been rendered to Syria and tortured on the basis of a collusion between US and Canadian secret services, the US Constitution did not offer an appropriate remedy. An exceptional remedy such as that created by the US Supreme Court in *Bivens* v. *Six Unknown Named Agents of the Federal Bureau of Narcotics* (1971) 403 US 388, in which a direct cause of action was allowed against the offending individuals (so-called *Bivens* action), was not possible under the circumstances.

[109] US Attorney-General, Memorandum for heads of executive departments or agencies (23 September 2009), section 1(C).

CASE STUDY 15.2
Al-Rabiah v. USA

Al-Rabiah,[1] a forty-three-year-old Kuwaiti, was seized by Afghan villagers in December 2001 as he was attempting to enter Pakistan unarmed, thereafter surrendering him to US forces. They, in turn, moved him to Guantánamo Bay in May 2002. Although the accused insisted that he was in Afghanistan on a private charitable mission, the US authorities argued that he was a logistics advisor for Bin Laden and Al-Qaeda. At the time of his capture, Al-Rabiah was overweight at 240 lb, had long suffered a knee injury, possessed no previous military training – apart from a two-week course in the Kuwaiti army – and was the father of four. He had worked for Kuwait Airways for twenty years, having never missed a day at work and was credited with an exemplary record. He had also a long history of charitable work with Muslim communities around the world with volunteering activities in Bosnia, Kosovo, Bangladesh and Afghanistan, all of which were widely known to friends and family. In fact, Al-Rabiah had written numerous letters to his family about his aid work in Afghanistan and was on a two-week leave from his employer.[2]

The US federal court that heard the *habeas corpus* petition recounted that all witness testimony against him was hugely inconsistent and that some of the witnesses had previously made false statements against other persons. Eventually, Al-Rabiah, partly as a result of sleep deprivation, partly because he was threatened with perpetual incarceration at Guantánamo unless he confessed, entered a 'full' confession that seemed incredible even to his interrogators. He confessed, for example, that he had undertaken a leading role under Bin Laden in the Tora Bora mountains in Afghanistan, despite the fact that he was physically incapable and in any event was never in Afghanistan prior to 2001.[3] The court observed that:

the Government's simple explanation is that Al-Rabiah made confessions that the court should accept as true. The simple response is that the court does not accept confessions that even the Government's own interrogators did not believe.[4]

This case study exemplifies that unlawful detention and lack of fair trial with all due process guarantees necessarily leads to interrogational anarchy and abuse. The authorities became obsessed with the accused although it was clear even to them that he could not possibly have done the things that even he himself had confessed.

---

[1] *Al-Rabiah* v. *USA*, 658 F. Supp. 2d 11 (DDC, 2009).   [2] Ibid., 20–34.   [3] Ibid.
[4] Ibid., 42.

QUESTIONS

- What tangible benefits do secret services hope to gain from the infliction of torture and arbitrary detention against suspected terrorists?

- Let us now examine the other side. What possible benefits for the prosecuting state and the international community can you see from the instigation of fair trial procedures against suspected terrorists? Think broadly and take into consideration the root causes of terrorism. Do these benefits outweigh those in question 1?

- Many, but not all, of the persons detained at Guantánamo Bay, freely admitted a smaller or larger connection with the activities of the Taliban and Al-Qaeda. This fact alone should serve to justify their prolonged detention on the ground that they pose a serious threat to security. Discuss.

- The criminal conduct of secret agents, particularly torture, in the course of sensitive counter-terrorist operations should never be made public before the courts because of the risk to the agents themselves and national security. Discuss.

- National security and human rights protection, even in the gravest of circumstances, are compatible. Discuss.

15.9   LEGAL AND OTHER STRATEGIES REGARDING DISAPPEARED TERRORIST SUSPECTS

15.9.1   The potency of advocacy and outreach

So far we have discussed the range of rights pertinent to suspects in counter-terrorist operations, as well as certain unlawful practices undertaken by states in order to create *legal black holes* that would deprive said suspects from their rights altogether.[110] While in the pre-9/11 era states stood to make significant political gains from publicly prosecuting alleged terrorists, this position has now drastically altered. Under this new paradigm the intelligence-gathering potential of detained suspects outweighs the benefits arising from their prosecution. Of course, this is not a novel idea, but in the age of the War on Terror its implementation has benefited from the secrecy of counter-terrorist operations in order to inflict torture and ill-treatment. However, governments are aware that in the current information era they cannot escape accusations of torture, nor can they expect to deter influential human rights NGOs from seeking judicial remedies in receptive forums. Moreover, the 'threat' from judicial activism is always far too great to ignore and was certainly a crucial factor, along with all the others, in the decision

---

[110] The term 'legal black hole' was probably first coined by Lord Steyn, in J. Steyn, 'Guantánamo Bay: the Legal Black Hole', *ICLQ* 53 (2004), 1.

of the US government and of its secret services to resort to unlawful kidnappings, renditions and torture of suspected terrorists in secret locations throughout the world. The purpose of this section is to give some idea of the strategies pursued by the legal teams representing the families of missing persons. It should be stated from the outset that, with minor exceptions, detained persons were foreign nationals. In this section we will describe the plight of British detainees.

The approach of the legal teams was predicated on a variety of strategies, which can roughly be broken down into legal arguments and outreach/advocacy policy goals. The legal arguments can further be broken down into identification/tracing of missing persons, followed by the pursuit of release remedies. The outreach dimension is simultaneous and inextricably linked to legal remedies and can only artificially be separated from these. Its various facets may be distinguished on the basis of their intended addressees, as follows: public policy-makers, public opinion and the courts.

15.9.2   Tracing strategies and release arguments

The first stage in this process is ascertaining that the missing person has been abducted and held by government agents, as opposed to having voluntarily disappeared or been kidnapped for financial gain. In practice, as was the case with British abductees who went missing while outside the UK, the families suspected that their loved ones might have been caught up in clean-up operations and approached the UK authorities. The latter initially argued that they themselves had no information as to their whereabouts and that equally no information was available from the countries in which they were last cited. It should be remembered that the practice of illegal abductions began as early as 2002, at which time even the existence of the Guantánamo Bay detention centre was unknown to the general public. It was only as a result of mounting newspaper stories, especially from the *Guardian*, the *Observer* and *The New York Times* that the plot started to unravel. Once this tentative link was established – in practice there were no doubt many others – the families could approach the UK authorities with more than a mere suspicion. But how could they be sure that their missing family member was in a secret detention centre and what avenues were open to the UK, which was not after all accused at that stage of being complicit? Feroz Abbasi and Shafiq Rasul, both British citizens, were arrested in Afghanistan in late 2001 in the aftermath of the coalition invasion of that country. They were soon after transferred to Guantánamo Bay and held in secret. It seems that the press tipped off the families of both men as to their whereabouts.[111]

---

[111] G. Peirce, *Dispatches from the Darkside* (London: Verso, 2010), 18.

With this information at hand the two respective legal teams set off on two distinct legal strategies. Abbasi's team focused on the diplomatic protection owed by Britain to its subjects, whereas the Rasul camp believed that it would stand a better chance by engaging the active protection of US courts. This required a firm finding of jurisdiction. Both strategies aimed at bringing detainees within the purview of a legal system and providing them with effective guarantees and protection. The diplomatic protection route presupposes that the incumbent government is either sympathetic to the particular claimant or his/her plight, or that it does not maintain the best of relations with the violating third state. None of these conditions prevailed under the circumstances at hand. The British government assured Parliament early on that despite the security situation all detainees were 'treated in accordance with humanitarian norms'.[112] As it later transpired, the British government was complicit in the ill-treatment – it is known at least that its agents were present and did not attempt to stop or mitigate it – and so prima facie it may seem that diplomatic protection was hardly the most appropriate strategy. The government put forward the contention that diplomatic protection does not extend to acts, even torture, undertaken exclusively in a third country since there exists no obligation to secure that third states acting within their own jurisdiction respect human rights. Of course, this was a narrow argument predicated solely on the territorial limitations of the ECHR.[113]

The *Abbasi* team did not press on with an *erga omnes* argument at this stage because given the security and political climate following 9/11 it would not have impressed English courts, which ultimately upheld the government's claims.[114] Although Abbasi himself was released a few years later on the strength of bilateral diplomacy, it was evident that the diplomatic protection strategy required a more potent and emotional legal argument. Quite clearly, the detainees' British nationality alone was insufficient to invoke the sympathy of the public and the judiciary. This sympathy was achieved by supplementing the nationality link with the horrendous treatment afforded to detainees. As will be observed in the section dealing with outreach/advocacy strategies, the combined effect of press revelations, investigations by British parliamentary committees and international organisations, as well as the acknowledgement of arbitrary detention by US courts, assisted in transforming the arbitrary detention and torture card to a tool for political pressure as well as a legal argument aimed at the release of the detainees. As such, it was later employed in the *Al-Rawi* and *Mohamed* litigations where the detainees were not British nationals but had been granted indefinite leave to stay in Britain.

---

[112] (2002) 378 Parliamentary Debates HC (6th Ser.), 623.

[113] In particular, in accordance with the judgment in *Bertrand Russell Peace Foundation* v. *UK* (1978) 14 D & R 117, 124.

[114] *R (Abbasi)* v. *Foreign Secretary and Home Secretary* [2002] EWCA (Civ) 1598, para. 79.

The *Rasul* legal battle effectively took off upon receipt of information that the accused was held at Guantánamo. His family, via his legal team, instituted proceedings in the USA with the hope of establishing that the courts of that country would accept jurisdiction over the illegality of his detention (*habeas corpus* claims). The relevant principles accepted by the US Supreme Court in that round of litigation has already been analysed in another section of this chapter. It should be pointed out that there is no evidence of coordination between the detainees' legal teams in the USA and the UK. What is striking between the strategies pursued in both sets of cases is that the legal arguments by the *Rasul* and subsequent teams operating in the USA were by no means radical and did not challenge long-standing legal notions. Instead, they claimed the obvious: that fundamental constitutional guarantees protect all persons in the custody of the state, irrespective of the location held. The *Abbasi* team could not raise this argument against the USA before English courts and even the very plausible *erga omnes* claim would have constituted a radical departure for a national court to accept because it would have required the British government to take measures against the USA in case it failed to provide fair trial guarantees. Yet, while the *Rasul* strategy managed to bring the detainees under the protection of the captor's supreme court, its *Abbasi* counterpart, while seemingly futile to start off with, ultimately culminated in diplomacy that led to the detainees' release.

With respect to the detainees who were long-term British residents, but not nationals, the failure of their direct diplomatic protection argument was only initially a setback – although of course it also served to prolong their detention. As it gradually became known that the UK had either been a passive participant in the brutal interrogation of persons with a British link, or had otherwise exchanged relevant intelligence with the USA,[115] the legal arguments necessarily changed. What was now crucial was to substantiate the complicity of the UK, at whatever level, which in itself demanded full or partial disclosure of sensitive information. In national law this boils down to a judicial determination of whether particular information should be made available to a private party.[116] It is in essence a conflict between the right to a fair trial and legitimate national security concerns, including the deterioration of a country's diplomatic relations. Given that public and judicial opinion were turning in favour of the detainees the British government persisted with its non-disclosure argument while at the same time made

---

[115] At some point a key witness from the UK security services testified under closed evidence that he was present during interrogation sessions and that the government was aware that the suspect was at times detained in Morocco and at others in the USA. *R (Mohamed)* v. *Secretary of State FCO* [2009] EWHC (Admin) 152, para. 88.

[116] In the case at hand it concerned the so-called public interest immunity (PII).

strenuous efforts to release the remaining British residents.[117] That judicial opinion had turned to now favour the detainees was evident from the judgment of the Court of Appeals in a claim lodged by Binyam Mohamed after his release. The Court held that otherwise confidential information which narrated acts of torture and which could not reveal any information of interest to terrorists was indeed susceptible to public scrutiny.[118]

It is interesting to note in this respect the nature and tactics of the opponent, the Blair government, which was in office at the time. Although a significant amount of the intelligence requested to be made public had already been exposed in the course of litigation in the USA, or had otherwise been revealed, the legal team of the British government continued to resist its publication! By contrast, the Bush administration gradually conceded the ill-treatment as well as the illegal renditions and reacted only by changing its domestic law, crudely and in violation of its international obligations in order to suit its political and military objectives. The British government up until the very end never conceded any knowledge or involvement and decided to fight its corner.[119]

15.9.3 Advocacy strategies

The powerful impact of advocacy strategies is evident in the case studies just described. Whether through *habeas corpus* litigation in the USA or feeble diplomatic protection claims against the British government, both culminated in the exertion of significant political pressure which resulted in the release of all known British detainees without even a criminal trial in the USA. We possess little, or no, evidence of the release attempts instigated by the governments of non-democratic states, but no doubt the lack of civil society mechanisms has precluded the exertion of adequate pressure. We have already emphasised that the litigation by and of itself was incapable of guaranteeing the release of the detainees. It is simply but a weapon in the greater conflict between governments and the legal teams/civil society, which is to a large degree a war for the control of information. Peirce, a prominent British lawyer involved in the Guantánamo litigation, notes that the confidence of the British government's case lay 'in the extent to which the secret state

---

[117] The then Minister of State for FCO pointed out that the government was pressing 'for the release of Mr Mohamed's return from Guantánamo as vigorously as before'. (2009) 707 *Parliamentary Debates* HL (5th Ser.), 805.

[118] *R (Mohamed)* v. *Secretary of State FCO* [2010] EWCA (Civ) 65, para. 52.

[119] The British Home Secretary defended the position that the secret services, and particularly MI5, had not been complicit in the torture of Mohamed, just days before the Court of Appeals judgment that declassified evidence showing the contrary and although in any event this was public knowledge. See *Sunday Times Online* (12 February 2010): www.timesonline.co.uk/tol/news/politics/article7024982.ece.

believes it has consolidated and can control any mechanism that might allow discovery and challenge. It can rely on its citizens never knowing properly, or often not knowing at all.'[120] As a result, the ultimate purpose of legal arguments, including legal action, is to sensitise public opinion in such a way that: (1) the main issue becomes common and embedded knowledge; (2) it is sustained and reinforced by further official inquiries by public bodies[121] and international organisations, as well as the press; (3) it places pressure on governments until their intransigence collapses, whether by judicial authority or policy concession, or a combination of both.

It is now widely accepted that the US government and its allies wished to conceal their arbitrary detention and illegal rendition programmes. The role of free press was paramount in exposing both of these at an early stage. Although details are not known, it is believed that the sources behind the revelations were of two types: the usual leaks from government agents with access to relevant information, as well as randomly from the general public, including plane spotters who noticed some very unusual air activity. The latter is particularly important, not only from the point of view of its effectiveness, but also because it demonstrates the interdependence between human rights protection and an open information society. Initially, the plane spotters simply took cognisance of what seemed to be government aircraft, or secretly operated aircraft, taking off and landing in remote airfields throughout Europe. This then caught the attention of the media and NGOs which resulted in efforts to examine the flight records of these mysterious aircraft with a view to ascertaining their operators and whether their landing and take-off locations coincided with secret detention sites.

In the case of flights originating from the US military base of Diego Garcia, which constitutes British sovereign territory, it became apparent, for example, that the private firm Jeppesen was operating an aircraft registered as N379P. Its particular flight patterns immediately ignited suspicions that it was carrying detainees to locations around the world. Although unofficial evidence suggests that the aircraft's flight logs may have been falsified, or indeed destroyed, NGOs sought to find tangible links between the particular flights and complicit nations. An examination of records available for at least four suspected rendition flights by this aircraft reveals that it operated under various 'special status designators' which constitute privileges affordable only to aircraft at the highest echelons of governments, in this case, the governments of the UK and the USA.[122] A Jeppesen-operated aircraft

---

[120] Peirce, above note 111, 8.

[121] For an account of the investigations carried out by British public bodies regarding the involvement of that country in torture and illegal rendition, see REDRESS, *The United Kingdom, Torture and Anti-terrorism: Where the Problems Lie* (December, 2008), pp. 13–24.

[122] Reprieve, 'Ghost determination on Diego Garcia', available at: www.reprieve.org.uk/static/downloads/Microsoft_Word_-_2009_05_20_FAC_Submission_DG.pdf.

most probably airlifted Binyam Mohamed to Guantánamo Bay, a fact which triggered a series of lawsuits against this company with a view to forcing it to release information about the rendition flights it had operated on behalf of the US government. With the intervention of the latter under a claim of national security privilege the action ultimately failed; yet, the expression of concern by the Ninth Circuit should not be underestimated in terms of having won broad judicial favour. The majority thus stated:

> We do not reach our decision lightly or without close and sceptical scrutiny of the record and the government's case for secrecy and dismissal. We expect our decision today to inform district courts that the [state secrets] privilege has its limits, that every effort should be made to parse claims to salvage a case like this [using the exclusion of privileged evidence rule], that the standards for peremptory dismissal are very high and it is the district court's role to use its fact-finding and other tools to full advantage before it concludes that the rare step of dismissal is justified ... We also acknowledge that this case presents a painful conflict between human rights and national security.[123]

By late 2010 the British government announced that it had come to a mediated settlement with all released detainees of British nationality and residency. Although the outcome of this process is confidential a significant amount of compensation was paid to the victims, presumably in return for desisting with future claims and law suits on the complicity of the UK.[124] The succeeding prime minister further announced the launching of a torture inquiry, although its results are unlikely to be made public.

15.9.4   Counter-terrorism: the real testing ground for *erga omnes*

It has been explained elsewhere in this book that the obligation to protect fundamental human rights applies against all nations and as a result every nation possess legal standing (*locus standi*) to make relevant claims or bring suits before international and domestic forums. The rationale behind the *erga omnes* doctrine is that where the victims are physically and legally unable to challenge their own state's violations, the international community should possess an obligation to do so itself. In some cases the *erga omnes* obligation may be dispensed with by publicly denouncing the relevant conduct or by openly refusing to give it approval, tacit or otherwise.

In the course of the *Al Rawi* and *Mohamed* litigation the legal teams of the two men managed to bring into the public domain various paragraphs from

---

[123] *Binyam Mohamed and Others* v. *Jeppesen Dataplan Inc.*, Ninth Circuit judgment (6 September 2010), 13556–7.

[124] (2010) 1116 *Parliamentary Debates* HC 753. In announcing the settlement the Justice Secretary, Kenneth Clarke, emphasised the obvious: 'No admissions of culpability have been made in settling those cases and nor have any of the claimants withdrawn their allegations.'

classified documents. One of these, introduced as Exhibit LC7, was a report by the British Intelligence and Security Committee (ISC) on the 'handling of detainees by UK intelligence personnel in Afghanistan, Guantánamo Bay and Iraq'.[125] The report reproduced a guidance to address the concerns raised by a British secret service officer who had witnessed the infliction of torture by US operatives:

With regard to the status of the prisoners, under the various Geneva Conventions and protocols, however they are described, are entitled to the same levels of protection. You have commented on their treatment. It appears from your description that they may not be treated in accordance with the appropriate standards. Given that they are not within our custody or control, the law does not require you to intervene to prevent this. That said, [the Government's] stated commitment to human rights makes it important that the Americans understand that we cannot be party to such ill-treatment nor can we be seen to condone it ... If circumstances allow, you should consider drawing this to the attention of a suitably senior US official locally.[126]

In other parts the guidance makes it clear that British personnel should under no circumstances engage in torture or other ill-treatment, lest they face criminal sanctions. It would seem therefore that on the face of it the British government is discharging its *erga omnes* obligations in arduous circumstances on the battlefield. A closer reading, however, demonstrates that the principal aim is to avoid possible complicity. As far as engaging with their US counterparts to persuade or chastise them to desist from employing torture there is only a very lukewarm instruction which, under the terms phrased, would carry no weight with its recipients. Rightly, therefore, the ISC report pointed out that:

These instructions did not go far enough. They should have required the [secret service] officer to report his concerns to the senior US official. They should also have required all officers to report any similar matters in the future to both the US authorities and to their respective headquarters in the UK. Furthermore, the Foreign Secretary should have been informed immediately that an officer had reported that a serious potential abuse by the US military had occurred [so that he can issue instructions].[127]

The *erga omnes* argument was only indirectly invoked in litigation in the UK and even then it was pegged to diplomatic protection and the legitimate expectations of Britons. The dilution of *erga omnes* in practice is manifest in the British government's admission that even its lukewarm application is conditioned by political expediency and the interests of diplomatic bargaining:

In deciding whether to make humanitarian representations in any case, the UK Government would have to take into account the extent to which it would have to expend significant political credit, and would have to risk losing a measure of credibility,

[125] Cm 6469 (1 March 2005).   [126] Ibid., para. 47.   [127] Ibid., para. 50.

with the state to whom the representations are made. This is so, irrespective of the context. It is particularly true in relation to *such high controversial* and (especially from the US Government's point of view) sensitive matters as Guantánamo Bay and the circumstances and conditions of persons detained there [my emphasis].[128]

This is a low point for it suggests that human rights are but a costly, albeit certainly expendable, bargaining chip in the armoury of international politics. It also makes us sceptical about the true intentions behind state action, whether condemnatory, legal or forceful, taken against other nations accused of systematic human rights violations.

INTERVIEW 15.1

Legal defender of Guantánamo detainees

(Clive Stafford Smith)

Clive Stafford Smith is a British lawyer specialising in human rights and civil liberties and is the Legal Director of Reprieve UK.[1] He has defended numerous Guantánamo Bay detainees, among others.

A large segment of the general public does not understand on what grounds a lawyer would represent suspected terrorists. What is your personal position?

Being a lawyer means fighting for the rights of the powerless and those who cannot fight for themselves against government abuse. The majority of those seeking legal representation have sufficient access to justice but those suspected of terrorism are denied all rights and are portrayed by the authorities in a manner that renders them undeserving of any legal protection.

Based on your litigation experience with suspected terrorists held abroad and the complicity of states in their illegal detention, what particular aspects of British law would you wish to see amended?

Although the perpetration of torture is a horrendous act, by far the worst element in the war against terror is the attempt by the authorities to shroud the entire process with secrecy and to deter the public and the justice system from knowing what is taking place. Naturally, this has led to states covering up their covert illegal activities in order to avoid embarrassment, thus creating a vicious cycle from which it is hard to escape.

---

[1] The organisation's website is available at: www.reprieve.org.uk.

---

[128] Reproduced in *R (Al-Rawi) and Others* v. *Secretary for Foreign and Commonwealth Affairs* [2006] EWHC 972 (Admin), para. 41.

Successive British governments are in favour of secret courts and inquiries that are meant to avoid public scrutiny of their actions, and those of their agents and allies. Instead of amending this state of affairs, the Green Paper[2] recently circulated by the British government continues to place an emphasis on national security, thus perpetuating the culture of secrecy which has resulted in the violation of fundamental rights. This has got to stop.

If you could re-design counter-terrorist strategies following the 9/11 attacks what type of actions would you recommend against suspected terrorists operating abroad?

I should recall that the first victim in the war against terror is human rights. The level of abuse perpetrated in Baghram airbase [in Iraq] is worse than Guantánamo Bay. It is essential therefore that fundamental rights be at the forefront of, and inform, all future anti-terrorist policies. The loss of civil liberties in the face of terrorism will inevitably lead to abuse. At present, the US government, in its attempt to circumvent relevant human rights issues, is employing unmanned drones whose aim is to kill without having to arrest and prosecute alleged terrorists. This is portrayed as a legitimate tool in the war against terror and as a way of avoiding further casualties. Yet, these types of operations are an affront to the right to life and the right to a fair trial that are inherent in the operation of all democratic legal systems.

[2] Justice and Security Green Paper, Cm 8194 (October 2011).

FURTHER READING

Ashby Wilson, R. (ed.), *Human Rights in the War on Terror* (Cambridge University Press, 2005).

Doswald-Beck, L., *Human Rights in Times of Conflict and Terrorism* (Oxford University Press, 2011).

Farer, T., 'Un-just War against Terrorism and the Struggle to Appropriate Human Rights', *HRQ* 30 (2008), 356.

Fitzpatrick, J., 'The War against Terrorism and Human Rights', *EJIL* 14 (2003), 241.

Gearty, C., *Essays on Human Rights and Terrorism: Comparative Approaches to Civil Liberties in Asia, the EU and North America* (London: Cameron May, 2008).

Joseph, S., 'Rendering Terrorists and the Convention against Torture', *HRLR* 5 (2005), 339.

Koh, H. H., 'The Case against Military Commissions', *AJIL* 96 (2002), 337.

de Londras, F., 'Can Counter-terrorist Internment ever be Legitimate?' *HRQ* 33 (2011), 593.

Meron, T., 'When do Acts of Terrorism Violate Human Rights?' *Israeli Yearbook of Human Rights* 29 (1989), 271.

Moeckli, D., *Human Rights and Non-Discrimination on the War on Terror* (Oxford University Press, 2008).

Pejic, J., 'Terrorist Acts and Groups: a Role for International Law?' *BYIL* 75 (2005), 71.

Rehman, J., 'Islam, War on Terror and the Future of Muslim Communities in the United Kingdom: Dilemmas of Multiculturalism', *HRQ* 29 (2007), 831.

Saul, B., *Defining Terrorism in International Law* (Oxford University Press, 2008).

Sottiaux, S., *Terrorism and the Limitation of Rights: The ECHR and the US Constitution* (Oxford: Hart, 2008).

Stubbins-Bates, E. (ed.), *Terrorism and International Law: Accountability, Remedies and Reform* (Oxford University Press, 2011).

Warbrick, C., 'The European Response to Terrorism in an Age of Human Rights', *EJIL* 15 (2004), 989.

16 Non-state actors and human rights

CONTENTS

16.1 INTRODUCTION

In previous chapters we had a chance to examine the effect, both negative and positive of NSAs on human rights, particularly terrorists, NGOs and private companies, the latter in the context of economic and social rights. The present chapter sets out to explore the theoretical underpinnings of a much larger debate as to whether NSAs possess, or should possess, human rights obligations, much in the same way as states. This debate, as will be demonstrated, is not merely theoretical, because if we are to confer such obligations to actors other than states, then we should rethink the entire architecture and rationale of the human rights system since it has traditionally been founded on the idea that by abusing their power governmental actors violate human rights. In any event, it is evident that NSAs have a significant impact on the enjoyment of human rights and that as a result some regulation and intervention is required.

The chapter sets off by examining the theoretical bases upon which an NSA may be deemed to possess human rights obligations and critiques the various approaches put forward by states and the scholarly community. It then goes on to examine a variety of NSAs along with their own distinct position as regards their human rights role. Some, such as international financial institutions, take a legalistic approach to the matter and are generally wary of accepting even the more fundamental obligations, whereas others are keen to achieve a broader human rights agenda and are willing to accept human rights commitments. Besides intergovernmental organisations we shall also be focusing on MNCs and the way in which their operations have a significant impact on the rights of populations worldwide. It shall be demonstrated that while their human rights 'obligations', if any, have largely arisen as a result of voluntary undertakings they are now entering a hybrid phase of limited regulation, or at least of an attempt at regulation. Finally, we shed some light on national liberation movements and rebel groups and their distinct responsibilities under international humanitarian law.

16.2   THE STATUS OF NON-STATE ACTORS IN HUMAN RIGHTS LAW

NSA is a negative definition encompassing entities that do not exercise governmental functions or whose conduct cannot be described as possessing a public nature. In the field of human rights it mainly covers NGOs, paramilitary groups (including terrorists), national liberation movements and corporations, whether MNCs or domestic, as well as intergovernmental organisations, despite the fact that the latter are established by state entities. The definition also covers private actors generally, such as gangs who commit crimes against women or other vulnerable groups.[1]

Traditionally, private persons were considered as subjects of international law, that is, they were deprived of international legal personality and as such did not enjoy rights or bear obligations under international law. Rights and duties were only available under domestic law. The very subject matter of this book suggests that this traditional view no longer holds sway. However, while the available jurisprudence and treaties aptly confirm that private persons enjoy rights in their personal capacity, as opposed to enjoying them through their country of nationality, in addition to bearing liability for particular international crimes, such as war crimes, it is not also clear that private persons possess human rights obligations in the same manner as states, or in any other form. The purpose of this chapter is to assess whether such obligations in fact exist and if so to determine their content.

Since the 1970s a debate has arisen as to whether this traditional conception should be adjusted to encompass the imposition of certain human rights obligation on NSAs and their members.[2] On the face of it this looks like an attractive proposition, especially considering that some NSAs are wealthier than many states (e.g. MNCs) or possess military capacity of equal value, as is

---

[1] See Chapter 11 on women's rights.

[2] See A. Clapham, *Human Rights Obligations of Non-State Actors* (Oxford University Press, 2006), 29–56 and Chapter 2, where he cites a number of legal arguments against the traditional dichotomy.

the case with certain paramilitary groups, private security firms and national liberation movements. If these NSAs possess the power and money to behave like states, it is argued that they should also shoulder the same obligations as states. It is not of course expected that NSAs should have a duty to provide the whole range of economic and social rights as this would result in the wholesale substitution of the state – although their contribution is certainly important in countries where basic services have been privatised.[3] Rather, the idea is that NSAs such as terrorists and private military companies may indeed violate entitlements such as the right to life by killing random civilians. If this proposition, however, is accepted as legitimate then states may well deny the existence of a positive duty to respect the right to life which is predicated on their duty to prevent terrorist attacks and punish the offenders. In the end what remains is merely a negative obligation.[4] One should not go to the other extreme and contend that if a positive duty exists at all for states then suspected terrorists should be stripped of all their rights, something which is vehemently rejected under customary human rights law.[5] It is clearly obvious that the shifting of human rights obligations to outlawed, or unregulated, NSAs risks rendering states 'irresponsible' towards their own specific human rights duties.

There are other legal avenues for addressing 'violations' committed by terrorists and paramilitary groups. The application of criminal law is certainly far more effective and lacks the risks identified above. Criminal law far better deals with such conduct through the process of criminal liability administered by an independent criminal justice system. This way, the positive obligation of the state to prevent and punish crime in order to uphold its human rights duties remains intact. In fact, international criminal law supplements the gaps in human rights law by expanding the ambit of actors subject to criminal liability. By way of illustration, international tribunals have accepted that war crimes committed in internal armed conflicts give rise to international criminal liability, rather than domestic liability,[6] and that mass offences, such as crimes against humanity, may indeed be planned and committed by NSAs, even though these offences were originally conceived as crimes requiring a state-like organisation on the part of the perpetrators.[7]

---

[3] See, for example, the discussion on the right to water and the right to health in sections 9.9 and 9.8 respectively.

[4] R. Provost, *International Human Rights and Humanitarian Law* (Cambridge University Press, 2002), 62ff.

[5] See section 15.4 for a discussion of terrorists as human rights duty-holders.

[6] Now firmly established in article 8(2)(c) and (e) ICC Statute.

[7] ILC, Draft Code of Crimes Against the Peace and Security of Mankind, UN Doc. A/51/10 (1996), Supp 10, 94. See also *ICTY Prosecutor* v. *Karadžić and Mladić*, R 61 Decision (11 July 1996), paras. 60–4, where essentially the ICTY admitted that a paramilitary group can commit crimes against humanity.

Equally, although human rights law requires that torture be committed by agents of the state, this is no longer a requirement in humanitarian and international criminal law.[8] Herein lies the difference between international criminal tribunals and human rights courts in ascribing duties to NSAs. The former, in their effort to avoid offering impunity to those NSAs that have clearly committed a heinous act ascribe criminal liability to the conduct irrespective of the legal status of the offender. Human rights courts, on the other hand, are uneasy with bending the requirements found in the relevant instruments, albeit they generally recognise that criminal conduct may be ascribed to NSAs where there exists an element of state involvement.[9] In the case of torture, for example, they have emphasised that NSAs can commit the offence where states violate their obligation of *non-refoulement*, such as by sending detainees to be tortured by *de facto* entities.[10]

This is not to say that the language of human rights obligations is inappropriate for all NSAs. Corporations, for example, are not illegal and their operations affect the lives of a large number of people, including their employees, customers and the local communities wherein they operate. Moreover, states use corporations in order to provide essential services to their people, such as water supply, health care, pensions, running of correctional facilities and many others. Although in all of these cases the state continues to remain the primary duty bearer, it is fair to argue that the private party should possess a complementary duty to fulfil these entitlements, otherwise it will be free to treat the right to water, sanitation, health care and other things from the perspective of supplying them to clients based only on financial considerations. Consider a situation where a poor country invites a foreign investor to construct a water supply system to all homes because it does not have the expertise or financial resources to do so itself. Although the country's water belongs to its people – as is generally the case in all constitutions – the investor may refuse to supply those households that cannot afford to pay their water bill, thus depriving them of their right to water, an essential element for the preservation of life. Where the state

---

[8] *ICTY Prosecutor* v. *Kunarac*, Trial chamber judgment (22 February 2001), para. 495, where it was held that 'the characteristic trait of the offence … is to be found in the nature of the act committed rather than the status of the person who committed it'. Confirmed on appeal in *ICTY Prosecutor* v. *Kunarac*, Appeals chamber judgment (12 June 2002), para. 148, noting that 'the public official requirement is not a requirement under customary international law in relation to the criminal responsibility of an individual for torture outside of the framework of the Torture Convention'. See also *ICTR Prosecutor* v. *Semanza*, Trial chamber judgment (15 May 2003), paras. 342–3.

[9] Exceptionally, as in *Kadic* v. *Karadžić* 70 F. 3d 232 (2nd Cir., 1995), the US second district court held that certain forms of conduct, particularly genocide and war crimes violate the law of nations even if undertaken by NSAs in their private capacity.

[10] *Ahmed* v. *Austria* [1997] 24 EHRR 278; *H. L. R.* v. *France* [1998] 26 EHRR 29; *H.M.H.I.* v. *Australia*, Communication no. 177/2001, UN Doc. A/57/44 (1 May 2002), 166.

does not possess the technical expertise to supply water and therefore to fulfil the right to water, the investor should be under a duty to do so as a result of legal compulsion. In the case at hand it could be argued that the water, as a public good, does not belong to the investor and so the latter cannot deprive its beneficiaries of it. The human rights duties of MNCs will be explored more fully in the following sections, but it suffices to say that, unlike criminal groups and organisations, MNCs must be deemed to possess particular human rights obligations that are always complementary to those of the state.

The increased blurring of the private sphere, where human rights were traditionally inapplicable, with the public sphere is the reason why more and more NSA conduct is perceived as falling within the purview of human rights law.[11] The distinction is not always obvious and an example is required to better illustrate the point. Following a natural disaster in country X a private charity contributes a significant monetary amount through a trust fund set up by the government of X, which is vastly authoritarian. The charity signs a liability exclusion clause when depositing the money and makes no further inquiry as to its use by the government, which then goes on to purchase arms in order to attack the victims and solidify its grip on power. Clearly, the charity directly contributed to the denial of fundamental rights, but is it fair for it to justify its negligence by reference to its benevolent intentions? Although the contribution was made in a private capacity its effect was to deny the enjoyment of rights, something relevant to the public sphere. Given the charity's admission into the public sphere it should at the very least be burdened with the duty to be diligent that it does not contribute to human rights violations committed by governmental authorities.[12]

Several theories have been advanced to explain the application of positive duties on NSAs, mainly derived from the sphere of humanitarian law with a particular focus on rebels, paramilitaries and non-governmental forces taking part in armed hostilities. It is first argued that such persons are bound by treaties to which their country is a party because treaties apply to the entirety of a country's territory and population.[13] Secondly, human rights and IHL treaties may well impose specific obligations on individuals and groups, as is the case with common article 3 to the 1949 Geneva Conventions. Thirdly, in situations where a group is exercising functions that ordinarily pertain to a state it is generally viewed as possessing *de facto* governmental powers and therefore liable in exactly the same manner as a

---

[11] Clapham, above note 2, 1–25.

[12] See I. Bantekas, *Trust Funds under International Law: Trustee Obligations of the UN and International Development Banks* (The Hague, TMC Asser, 2009), 190–6.

[13] Y. C. Sandoz *et al.* (eds.), *Commentary on the Additional Protocols of 8 June 1977 to the Geneva Conventions of 12 August 1949* (Leiden: Martinus Nijhoff, 1987), para. 4444.

state.[14] Such *de facto* governments cannot plausibly deny the administration of human rights to populations under their effective control given that the customary law of belligerent occupation – which applies *mutatis mutandis* in this case – obliges the occupier to protect and enforce the rights of the occupied population. Moreover, it is now firmly accepted under customary international law that the conduct of an insurrectional movement is considered an act of state when the movement succeeds to government,[15] thereby conferring conditional human rights obligations upon it. Alston has gone a step further and has tried to explain the applicability of human rights obligations, other than by relying on IHL or international criminal law. He argued in a report on the Tamil Tigers of Sri Lanka that human rights norms operate on three levels:

> As the rights of individuals, as obligations assumed by states and as legitimate expectations of the international community... As a non-state actor, the [Tamil Tigers] do not have legal obligations under the ICCPR, but remain subject to the demand of the international community, first expressed in the Universal Declaration of Human Rights, that every organ of society respect and promote human rights ... The Tamil Tigers and other armed groups must accept that insofar as they aspire to represent a people before the world, the international community will evaluate their conduct according to the Universal Declaration's 'common standard of achievement'.[16]

No doubt, the theoretical debate as to whether NSAs do or do not possess human rights obligations will intensify but will not be resolved quickly in favour of either camp. Rather, what this chapter aims to demonstrate is that whereas NSAs do not generally refuse to uphold human rights and humanitarian law, they do so through processes that are internal to them alone and not on the basis of accepted human rights standards.

16.3   MULTINATIONAL CORPORATIONS IN THE HUMAN RIGHTS ARCHITECTURE

There are numerous definitions of MNCs,[17] albeit none with any binding status, so for reasons of cogency one may argue that the term comprises companies or other entities established in more than one country with a capacity to coordinate their operations in various ways and levels. What,

---

[14] See *Government of Spain* v. *SS Arantazu Mendi and Others* [1939] AC 256, *per* Lord Atkin who defined them as exercising 'all the functions of a sovereign government in maintaining law and order'.

[15] See article 10 of the ILC Draft Articles on State Responsibility.

[16] UN Special Rapporteur on Extrajudicial, Summary or Arbitrary Executions, UN Doc. E/CN.4/2006/Add.5 (27 Mar 2006), paras. 25, 27.

[17] E.g. see *OECD Guidelines for Multinational Enterprises* (2011), (OECD Guidelines), 17, available at www.oecd.org/dataoecd/43/29/48004323.pdf.

however, makes the regulation of MNCs complex is the legal autonomy of their subsidiaries and other affiliates from the parent corporation. Most MNCs never spell out the exact nature of this relationship and may in fact deny it in order to avoid tax liabilities and take advantage of preferential audit regimes, although in fact they exert significant influence, if not outright control, over their affiliates or subsidiaries. This outward legal autonomy, however, means that the parent and its subsidiaries are subject to different domestic laws on the basis of their country of incorporation.

Corporate entities, whether MNCs or other, are potent international actors that no longer require the protection of their home country in respect of disputes arising with foreign government actors. The rights of corporations, particularly in inter-state investment relations, are clearly spelt out in bilateral investment treaties (BITs) and customary international law pertinent to investment. BITs, which are typically entered into between developed and developing nations, are meant to ensure that the host state will treat the investor fairly (i.e. the MNC), without hindrance and discrimination and will honour the terms of its mutual contract with the investor. That BITs confer rights under international law to investors, as opposed to rights under domestic laws, is evident from the fact that investors may sue for damages before international arbitral bodies on the basis of the BITs and general international law, as is the case with expropriation. Moreover, MNCs as investors enjoy additional rights and obligations from their contractual arrangements with host states. Arbitral tribunals assessing the breach of contract arising from an expropriation will naturally employ international law to construe the relevant contractual terms, rather than rely on domestic law. Equally, the World Bank's lending terms to investors and states clearly oblige both actors to adhere to a minimum set of human rights and environmental guarantees, lest the Bank remove its funding from the project in question.[18] In addition, the commercial practices of MNCs in various business fields, such as construction, has given rise to rules strictly enforced by local courts and acknowledged by states as binding. This rule-making capacity of corporate entities and MNCs is known as *lex mercatoria*.[19] Therefore, it is clear that MNCs enjoy a significant amount

[18] Article 12(d) of the 1985 Multilateral Investment Guarantee Agency (MIGA) Convention provides that '[I]n guaranteeing an investment, the Agency shall satisfy itself as to: (i) the economic soundness of the investment and its contribution to the development of the host country; (ii) compliance of the investment with the host country's laws and regulations.' World Bank: Convention Establishing the Multilateral Investment Guarantee Agency, (1985) 24 ILM 1598. Under paragraph 3.08 of MIGA's Operational Regulations, the Agency will not provide guarantees with regard, *inter alia*, to products or activities deemed illegal by the host state or international law, enterprises whose primary sources of income involve forced or child labour inconsistent with internationally recognised norms.

[19] According to Teubner, the ultimate validation of *lex mercatoria* rests on the fact that not all legal orders are created by the nation state and accordingly that private orders of regulation can create law: G. Teubner, 'Global Bukowina: Legal Pluralism in the World Society', in G. Teubner (ed.), *Global Law Without a State* (Aldershot: Dartmouth, 1997), 15.

of international legal personality, at least in respect of rights conferred upon them and their capacity to enforce them.

In terms of obligations a rather different picture emerges. While it is true that MNCs owe obligations to the host and home state under the terms of their mutual contract and corporate laws respectively, three issues remain outstanding: (1) international treaties do not as a rule confer obligations on MNCs, subject to our observations discussed in the next section; (2) the corporate and other laws of the home state do not as a rule apply to the operations of MNCs operating abroad through independent subsidiaries; and (3) the laws of the host state, particularly those that protect human rights and the environment, may be curtailed or stifled by the terms of the contract with the foreign MNC. This constitutes a significant lacuna in the protection of human rights given the lack of international obligations and the extraterritorial incapacitation of the home state.

It is evident, therefore, that since it is unlikely that a treaty will confer human rights obligations directly on MNCs, home and host states should at least strive to tighten their legislation in such a way as to prevent and punish abuses committed by MNCs both abroad and at home. This observation is subject to two serious practical problems, which may be exemplified as follows. X, a mining MNC whose parent company is seated in Belgium, sets up a subsidiary in Burma (Myanmar) which is incorporated exclusively under the latter's laws. In its efforts to lure X into Burma the government promises generous tax benefits and the relaxation of labour and environmental laws. In the course of events the Burmese government provides slave labour to the investor and prohibits all industrial action and the freedom of association to the workers 'employed' by X. In this situation X may argue that even though it is not comfortable with, or is otherwise opposed to the actions of the local government it is nonetheless compliant with the host state's laws. On the other hand, Belgium may well complain about X's complicity, but it is by no means straightforward that it can impose any penal or civil sanctions on X or its Belgian parent because unlike the parent which is not, however, overtly involved in the aforementioned acts, X is not subject to Belgian laws. If the Belgian authorities were seriously concerned they could try to establish the liability of the parent company by reference to its level of *control* or *influence* over the subsidiary X. None the less, this is not only difficult to prove in the absence of a direct paper trail or other documentary evidence but may turn out counterproductive in the business relationship between Belgium and the parent.

What is evident thus far is that despite the lack of direct obligations on MNCs in countries whose laws favour or turn a blind eye to human rights violations, MNCs can play a pertinent role in the protection of rights. They can do this because of their asymmetric financial relationship with the host nation. Coca Cola Co., for example, declared a net profit of US$9.5 billion in 2010, while the GDP of Liberia during the same period was US$1 billion, that of Sierra Leone US$2 billion, US$5 billion for Malawi, US$4.5 billion for Guinea and a meagre US$800 million for Gambia. No doubt, this asymmetry, coupled with a dedicated corporate commitment to human rights, has the potential of providing leverage to an MNC to force respect of human rights within the context of its operations despite domestic laws and practices to the contrary. Although under no obligation, powerful MNCs can equally exert their influence on local governments to abstain from committing human rights violations.

The exertion of influence and defiance of arbitrary laws and practices by MNCs has been found to give them a reputational advantage in the global consumer market, as the *Ogoniland* case aptly demonstrated. In 1995 the Abacha regime in Nigeria executed Ken Saro Wiwa and other activists who had fought a public campaign showing that the oil giant Shell had colluded with the authorities in oil-rich Ogoniland to expel the defiant local population. Moreover, it was demonstrated that both the government and Shell were responsible for polluting the water and other natural habitats to the detriment of the people's health.[20] Weeks prior to Wiwa's deplorable execution Shell was petitioned by NGOs worldwide to intervene and use its influence to avert the government's plan.[21] Shell adamantly refused to be dragged into local politics, but following Wiwa's execution the company's public image and finances suffered such a shock that it proceeded to change its official policy on human rights in 1997 through its General Business Principles. Consumer pressure is a significant aspect in the voluntary human rights policies and public pledges of MNCs as will be demonstrated in another section of this chapter and to a large degree has helped shape these policies.[22] Readers will readily combine these remarks with the use of advocacy as a potent human rights tool.[23]

16.3.1   Human rights obligations of multinational corporations

International treaties do not confer human rights obligations upon MNCs. Some, however, do so indirectly and this is achieved in two ways. The first comprises provisions that call on states parties to eliminate a prohibited

---

[20] *SERAC and Center for Economic and Social Rights v. Nigeria (Ogoniland* case), Case no. ACHPR/COMM/A044/1, *AJIL* 96 (2002), 937.

[21] K. Tangen *et al.*, 'Confronting the Ghost: Shell's Human Rights Strategy', in A Eide *et al.*, *Human Rights and the Oil Industry* (Oxford: Hart, 2000), 185.

[22] A study conducted in 2002 by Cone revealed that of US consumers aware of a corporation's negative CSR practice, 91 per cent would most probably prefer another firm, 85 per cent would disseminate this information to family or friends, 83 per cent would refuse to invest in that company, 80 per cent would refuse to work at that company and 76 per cent would boycott its products. Opinion Research Corporation International, *2002 Cone Corporate Citizenship Study*.

[23] See section 3.9.4.

conduct from corporate practice. Articles 2(e) of CEDAW, for example, and 2(1)(d) of ICERD require states to take all appropriate measures to eliminate discrimination by both public and private entities, thus implicitly encompassing corporations. The second type of obligation arises from corporate criminal liability provisions appearing in treaties, which suggest that corporations bear liability for the violation of particular conduct. This is true in respect of anti-corruption treaties, such as articles 2 and 3(2) of the 1997 OECD Convention on Combating Bribery of Foreign Public Officials in International Business Transactions and article 26 of the 2003 UN Convention against Corruption, among others. It is assumed that because a corporation incurs criminal liability it is under an obligation not only to prevent the conduct in question but also to respect the underlying right or freedom. The crime of corruption encompasses numerous underlying entitlements that are not immediately clear. Given that it involves a country's resources and culminates in the deprivation of social welfare services and goods, corruption denies the right to self-determination (sovereignty of resources), right to food, water, health, social security, adequate standard of living and the overarching right to be free from poverty.

In fact, both treaty bodies and domestic courts have held in unequivocal terms that although human rights obligations are addressed to states, where their implementation is undertaken through the medium of corporate entities, the rights in question are also shouldered by the corporation in addition to the state. In *Etcheverry* v. *Omint* the applicant, who was an HIV sufferer, was provided by his employer with membership of a private health plan. When he later became redundant he sought to continue his membership through private funds but the insurance company refused. The Argentine Supreme Court held that private health providers were under a duty to protect the right to health of their customers and that their special relationship was not simply of a contractual nature.[24] Given the ever-growing privatisation of otherwise public social services, such as education, sanitation, water supply, utilities, health care and pensions, the obligations of MNCs administering these services must be read in the light of duties to rights bearers.

Besides reading these human rights obligations in the relevant treaties, it is important to emphasise that in the early 1980s a movement began whose aim was to impose direct human rights obligations on MNCs. This started off as a standard-setting exercise in the form of non-binding guidelines issued by NGOs, business circles, or intergovernmental organisations with the hope that MNCs would voluntarily adhere whether by reason of commitment or reputational fear. Among the many hundreds of these instruments

---

[24] *Etcheverry* v. *Omint Sociedad Anónima y Servicios*, Judgment (13 March 2001). In *Restrepo and López* v. *Salud Colmena*, T-849/2001 the Colombian Constitutional Court ordered a private hospital to carry out free HIV testing for indigent AIDS sufferers.

one could highlight Social Accountability (SA) 8000,[25] the Caux Principles for Business,[26] the Extractive Industries Transparency Initiative,[27] the UN Global Compact and the OECD Guidelines for Multinational Enterprises. The UN Global Compact, for example, is comprised of ten principles founded on the Bill of Rights, the Rio Declaration on Environment and Development and anti-corruption treaties.[28] A large number of MNCs jumped enthusiastically on the bandwagon of these initiatives and despite their non-binding character many MNCs implemented them through the adoption of corporate policies.

This euphoria was perceived by an expert subsidiary body of the UN Commission on Human Rights as a signal that MNCs were not wholly hostile towards the move from voluntary to more binding obligations. This perception was ultimately erroneous, culminating in the rejection by the business community of the more assertive Norms on Transnational Corporations and Other Business Enterprises with Regard to Human Rights.[29] The Norms sought to impose on MNCs the same range of human rights obligations under international law as those addressed to states, namely to promote, respect and fulfil human rights. The Norms' expansive approach linked corporate liability not only to the company's control over particular conduct, but also its influence and benefit. The proposal created deep divisions between the business community and human rights advocates and was abandoned in favour of a special procedure that would undertake a realistic assessment of MNCs' existing human rights obligations.

The Special Representative, John Ruggie, introduced three core principles on the basis of a differentiated yet complementary framework of responsibilities between MNCs and states. These consist of: (1) the state duty to protect against human rights abuses by third parties, including business; (2) the corporate responsibility to respect human rights; and (3) the need for more effective access to justice.[30] In 2011 these were formalised into a set of Guiding Principles on Business and Human Rights: Implementing the UN Protect, Respect and Remedy Framework, which were endorsed by the UN Human Rights Council.[31] Because the Special Representative had worked very closely with the business community for a period of six years and the

---

[25] Available at: www.sa-intl.org/_data/n_0001/resources/live/2008StdEnglishFinal.pdf.

[26] Available at: www.cauxroundtable.org/index.cfm?menuid=8.

[27] Available at: http://eiti.org/eiti/principles.

[28] Available with commentary at: www.unglobalcompact.org/AboutTheGC/TheTenPrinciples/index.html.

[29] UN Doc. E/CN.4/Sub.2/2003/12/Rev.2 (2003).

[30] See Report of the Special Representative, Protect, Respect and Remedy: A Framework for Business and Human Rights, UN Doc. A/HRC/8/5 (7 April 2008).

[31] UN Doc. A/HRC/17/31 (21 March 2011), Annex (Guiding Principles Commentary).

Principles were realistic they have very rapidly been accepted as an authoritative statement of MNCs' human rights obligations.

At the heart of the Guiding Principles is the notion that states must protect against human rights abuses occurring on their territory by MNCs and other private entities. To this end they must undertake appropriate legislative and enforcement measures and should set out clearly the human rights obligations of MNCs and ensure among other things that laws pertinent to business enterprises, such as corporate law, *enable* business respect for human rights.[32] The dilemma about whether a state should choose to violate a treaty obligation rather than its human rights obligations should not arise in the first place proclaims principle 9, but in practice this may prove inevitable, particularly since international investment tribunals view all cases of expropriation solely from the point of view of the loss incurred by the investor rather than through a human rights lens.

The *Tecmed* case is illustrative of this attitude. It involved an investment agreement between Tecmed and Mexico with the purpose of constructing a landfill. Following the expiry of the first licence period, the Mexican government refused to renew the licence, arguing that the project caused adverse environmental and health effects on the local population. As a result, the investment was effectively terminated and the investor stood to suffer a financial loss. The arbitral tribunal to which the dispute was referred held that the 'government's intention [was] less important than the effects of the measures on the owner of the assets or on the benefits arising from such assets affected by the measure'.[33] It is clear that international investment law assesses contractual breaches without reference to human rights and other environmental impacts. Among a plethora of conflicting obligations there is a preference for upholding narrowly understood investment obligations above all other considerations.[34] States should adopt concrete measures to avoid such conflicts.[35] Their primary responsibility to regulate MNCs (and other private parties) in the discharge of their human rights duties has been highlighted manifold by treaty bodies.[36] The HRCtee emphasised in General

---

[32] Guiding Principles 1–3.

[33] *Tecnicas Medioambientales Tecmed SA* v. *Mexico*, ILM 43 (2004), 133, para. 116.

[34] See P. M. Dupuy, E. U. Petersmann and F. Francioni, *Human Rights in International Investment Law and Arbitration* (Oxford University Press, 2009).

[35] Simma proposes a 'human rights audit' whose objective is to incorporate all of the host state's human rights obligations into the applicable law of their mutual contract. In this manner, the investor's legitimate expectations would be clear and would remove arbitral discretion to ignore human rights. B. Simma, 'Foreign Investment Arbitration: A Place for Human Rights?' *ICLQ* 60 (2011), 573, at 592–5.

[36] CESCR, General Comment 18 (right to work), UN Doc. E/C.12/GC/18 (6 February 2006), para. 35; CESCR, General Comment 15 (right to water), UN Doc. E/C.12/2002/11 (20 January 2003), para. 23; CtRC, General Comment 5 (persons with disabilities), UN Doc. E/1995/22 (1995), para. 42; CtEDAW, General Recommendation 25, paras. 7, 29, 31–32; CtEDAW, General Recommendation 24, paras. 14–17; HRCtee, General Comment 28, para. 31.

Comment 31 that 'the positive obligations on states parties to ensure Covenant rights will only be fully discharged if individuals are protected by the state, not just against violations of Covenant rights by its agents, but also by acts committed by private persons or entities'.[37] In another section of this book this positive duty is explained in relation to terrorist acts endangering life and health.[38]

The corporate responsibility to respect human rights is complementary to that of states. At the very least it goes without saying that MNCs must respect domestic human rights law in their country of operation. This entails a duty to avoid infringing the rights of others as well as addressing adverse human rights effects caused by them.[39] The Principles clearly suggest that where domestic law falls below fundamental human rights standards MNCs should seek ways to honour the standards.[40] It is thus evident that although MNCs are not the direct bearers of duties under international human rights law they are none the less obliged to respect human rights to the degree that these are prejudiced by their operations and as long as they have the capacity to take appropriate action. This obligation is premised on a threefold dimension. First, MNCs should adopt policy commitments upon which all future internal and external company dealings must be predicated. For example, a policy commitment to respect the right to water should be interpreted by the company's legal team and management board as prohibiting all contracts that infringe this right, including arbitral suits which, if successful, risk depriving a local population of its right to water. Although consistent practice with respect to policy commitments does not exist it suffices to say that the public nature of these instruments is to make available all relevant company information to the company's stakeholders, including affected communities and consumers. In *Kasky* v. *Nike* an activist sued Nike Corporation arguing that it had used false advertising in a publicity campaign to defend itself against accusations of engaging in manufacturing under inhuman manufacturing conditions in Asia. The California Supreme Court argued that since a company's public statements could conceivably persuade consumers to buy its products such statements deserve only limited freedom of speech protection.[41]

The obligation of MNCs to respect international human rights law in the course of their operations, especially extraterritorially, is not a mere

---

[37] HRCtee, General Comment 31, para. 8. In *Arenz et al.* v. *Germany*, Comm. no. 1138/2001, UN Doc. CCPR/C/80/D/1138/2002 (24 March 2004), para. 8.5 and *Cabal & Pasini Bertran* v. *Australia*, Comm. 1020/2001, UN Doc. CCPR/C/78/D/1020/2001 (7 August 2003), para. 7.2, where the HRCtee discussed the admissibility of individual communications relating to abuse by private parties.

[38] See section 15.4 and *Osman* v. *UK* [1998] 29 EHRR 245, para. 115.

[39] Guiding Principle 11.   [40] Guiding Principle 23(b).

[41] *Kasky* v. *Nike*, 45 P.3d 243 (Cal. 2002), affirmed by the US Supreme Court in *Nike* v. *Kasky*, 539 US 654 (2003).

theoretical construction. This obligation has been enforced since World War II in cases where a number of senior industrialists were convicted for their role in accepting slave labour provided by the Nazis in their factories.[42] As far as the Guiding Principles are concerned the human rights obligations of MNCs and their corresponding liability is engaged in three situations: (1) by directly committing a violation; (2) by means of complicity; and (3) by failing to use leverage where the MNC has the 'ability to effect change in the wrongful practices of an entity that causes a harm'.[43] In *Doe* v. *Unocal*, a group of companies, including an American one, had undertaken the construction of a pipeline project in Myanmar. The regime of the country was notoriously brutal and autocratic so it was no surprise that the government procured local workers under conditions of enforced labour. The same people endured acts of murder and rape by the government while working on the project. When they filed a suit in the USA under the Aliens Tort Claims Act there was no contention that Unocal had orchestrated the violations, but that it accepted the workers knowing full well their predicament. The California District Court held that MNCs may be held liable for violations of treaties and customary law independently of the actions of states, as well as for state-like acts or state-related conduct.[44]

Complicity was at the heart of the suit in the *Wiwa* case, the facts of which are similar to the *Ogoniland* case explained above. The New York District Court upheld the complicity of Shell Nigeria and its parent companies, Shell UK and Royal Dutch Shell, in respect of the human rights abuses committed by the Nigerian police which were related to the operations of Shell in the country.[45] The importance of these cases, moreover, lies in the fact that the courts of the parent companies are increasingly willing to entertain suits by foreign victims, thus stripping corporations of their otherwise global impunity. In the *Trafigura* case, thirty-one Ivory Coast natives sued Trafigura, a Netherlands-based company, in London for illegally dumping hundreds of tonnes of toxic waste in an area outside Abidjan, an action which produced deleterious effects on the health of local communities.[46]

---

[42] See *USA* v. *Carl Krauch et al.* (*IG Farben* case); *USA* v. *Flick*; *USA* v. *Krupp*.

[43] Guiding Principles Commentary, above note 31, at 17.

[44] *Doe* v. *Unocal* (I) 963 F. Supp 880 (CD Cal, 1997). None the less, in the instant case the district court held that although Unocal benefited from the abuses it was not proven that the company wanted to control, or indeed controlled, the Burmese military to perpetrate these acts. On appeal, the Court of Appeals for the ninth circuit reversed this decision, holding that plaintiffs need only demonstrate Unocal's assistance to the military. *Doe* v. *Unocal* 248 F. 3d 915 (9th Cir., 2001).

[45] *Wiwa* v. *Royal Dutch Petroleum*, 2002 WL 319887 (SDNY, 2002).

[46] A settlement of approximately £30 million was reportedly reached with the claimants in 2009 and the Ivorian government reached its own settlement in 2007, reportedly worth a staggering 152 million euro.

The obligation of MNCs to employ leverage or their powers of influence to prevent or avoid an adverse effect is more controversial. The Guiding Principles rightly confirm that this obligation arises only where the MNC has contributed to the effect or where the effect is directly linked to its operations, products or services by its business relationship. Even so, its powers of influence, material or otherwise, should be sufficient to allow it to prevent an adverse human rights impact.[47] Of course, whether or not an MNC possesses any leverage at all is a complex issue that is not susceptible to generalisations and speculation. An illustration is necessary in order to highlight those situations where the institutions of the host nation are either corrupt or indifferent to the rights of the local population. In the 1970s Nigerian case of *Chinda* v. *Shell-BP* the claimants sought an injunction to prevent the oil companies from gas flaring, given its well-recognised effects on the environment and public health. The court came to the conclusion that a demand on Shell-BP to refrain from operating a gas flare five miles from the claimants' village was 'an absurdly and needlessly wide demand'.[48]

In between the obligation to adopt corporate policies and prevent human rights violations through non-complicity, including the use of adequate leverage, MNCs are under a duty to undertake human rights due diligence. Just like environmental impact assessment studies, which are now mandatory in all projects, human rights due diligence aims to identify, prevent, mitigate and account the adverse human rights effects of corporate operations. This should be an ongoing process and must consider all those factors where the MNC might cause or contribute to a negative impact through its own activities, or by a direct link to its operations, products, services or even by its business relationships.[49] By way of illustration, a garments producer setting up a production line in a developing country should be alert to the following factors, among others, that can have a negative human rights impact: whether its suppliers are employing children and if they are in conformity with international labour standards; whether the authorities are discharging waste from the plant into potable reservoirs or agricultural land; whether its own workers are prevented by government orders from striking. Due diligence of this nature essentially ensures that all of the corporation's departments and suppliers are in conformity with human rights law.

---

[47] Guiding Principle 19(b)(ii). See commentary in UN Doc. A/HRC/17/31 (21 March 2011), Annex, 18–19.

[48] *Chinda* v. *Shell-BP* (1974) 2 RSLR 1. Of course, this attitude has now been abandoned and is reflected in the landmark case of *Gbemre* v. *Shell and Others* (2005) AHRLR 151 (NgHC, 2005).

[49] Guiding Principle 17.

1 What are the reasons inhibiting states from fully regulating the extraterritorial activities of multinational corporations?

2 One of the key debates in the discussion on the human rights obligations of MNCs is whether in the absence of a concrete legal regime the next best thing is to demand that MNCs undertake voluntary initiatives. Some of these are discussed in the following section. What are the benefits arising from voluntary initiatives and what possible drawbacks can you identify?

3 Can NSAs assume human rights obligations under international law? If so, is the obligation of the state primary or residual to that of NSAs?

16.3.2   Corporate social responsibility

Corporate social responsibility may be viewed as having two broad aims. The first concerns an assessment of the range of persons to whom the company owes duties, whereas the second pertains to the assumption of voluntary obligations by the company for the promotion of social (essentially human rights and environmental) pursuits.[50] The two aims are interrelated. One strand of corporate theory contends that the principal aim of the corporation, and therefore of its directors, is the maximisation of the shareholders' profits.[51] In this manner shareholders have an incentive to further invest their proceeds and thus create more jobs and augment consumer spending which itself is a job creator. This is certainly an attractive proposition which is, none the less, challenged by the so-called stakeholder theory positing that corporations are not only responsible to their shareholders but owe, or should owe, particular duties to persons or communities directly or indirectly affected by their operations. These affected persons and communities (stakeholders) include the company's employees, customers, investors, suppliers and the local communities wherein it operates.[52] The Ogoni people, for example, are as much Shell's stakeholders as are its consumers in New York and its employees in London. While stakeholder theory is by no means opposed to the maximisation of shareholder profit it does not view this as the

---

[50] See I. Bantekas, 'Corporate Social Responsibility in International Law', *Boston U. Int'l L.J.* 22 (2004), 309.

[51] This is reflected in the shareholder value theory (or fiduciary capitalism) associated with Milton Friedman, who famously argued that 'the only social responsibility of business to society is the maximisation of profits to shareholders, within the legal framework and the ethical custom of society'. M. Friedman, *Capitalism and Freedom* (Chicago University Press, 1962), p. 133.

[52] H. Hansmann and R. Kraakman, 'Toward a Single Model of Corporate Governance?' in J. McCahery and P. Moeland *et al.* (eds.), *Corporate Governance Regimes: Convergence and Diversity* (Oxford University Press, 2002), 62–4.

only aim of the corporation. This line of thinking is in tune with the human rights obligations of MNCs as explained in previous sections and is also endorsed by the vast majority of MNCs in practice.

The nature of the duties to stakeholders varies. The duty of a garments retailer to its consumers is subject to the terms of its contract, whereas in the absence of contract between the manufacturer and the consumers the liability of the manufacturer is based on the law of torts. In every case the manufacturer's duty towards its consumers will no doubt be informed and shaped by reputational risk and any financial effects on the brand of the products under consideration or the company itself. This is exactly why MNCs were willing to undertake voluntary human rights obligations at a time when these were not considered binding upon them, hence the origin of their *social* responsibility. In an era where corporations, as already explained, are responsible alongside states for any adverse human rights effects caused directly or indirectly by their operations, the voluntary element of corporate responsibility seems moot. None the less, there are certain areas in which corporate responsibility may still play at least two important roles. First, it may induce corporations to undertake more extensive human rights obligations in the course of their official policies. Second, it can assist MNCs to design better human rights strategies and offer wider protection in countries where the local government is a persistent human rights violator. This is evident, for example, through the proliferation of agreements between corporations and local communities, the purpose of which is to set up grievance mechanisms,[53] adequate consultation and disclosure. In 2011 the mining law committee of the IBA produced a model mining agreement for use by mining companies and mining communities known as Model Mine Development Agreement (MMDA).[54] Although the MMDA recognizes that mining projects must be financially viable it asks the parties to take a broader look at the social, natural and economic environments of their operations. The Agreement imposes human rights obligations on the parties,[55] the duty to negotiate community development agreements with the local population,[56] as well as a company grievance mechanism with access rights for the community.[57]

Moreover, the advancement of corporate social responsibility has given rise to a trend of voluntary social reporting which makes public the human rights and environmental record of MNCs, which in turn induces them to

---

[53] In at least two countries there exists a statutory obligation to resolve such disputes involving a human rights element through arbitration. See Australia's Native Title Act 1993 and Canada's Yukon Oil and Gas Act, chapter 162.

[54] MMDA 1.0, available at www.mmdaproject.org/presentations/MMDA1_0_110404Bookletv3.pdf.

[55] Ibid., MMDA 1.0, section 10.3.   [56] Ibid., MMDA 1.0, section 22.1.

[57] Ibid., MMDA 1.0, section 27.1.

improve it. The reporting of financial, social, and environmental information within single or separate reports is known as 'triple bottom line'. An illustrative example is the Global Reporting Initiative (GRI). Its mission is to develop guidelines for reporting on and verification of economic, environmental and social performance. The GRI guidelines serve as a performance indicator for the corporation, as well as a measure of comparison within a particular industry.[58] Reports prepared on the basis of the GRI guidelines should be transparent, inclusive (i.e. involve the views of all stakeholders), auditable, complete, relevant, built within a sustainability context, accurate, neutral, comparable, clear and timely.

CASE STUDY 16.1
Shell's human rights policies

Following its poor handling of the *Ogoniland* case, Shell decided to introduce a rigorous human rights agenda. In addition to its General Business Principles Shell has produced a number of other human rights principles and policies in order to instruct and train its staff. One of these is entitled *Human Rights Dilemmas: A Training Supplement*[1] and its purpose is to set out difficult human rights questions to the company's senior staff in the field. For this case study we have selected the dilemma relating to forced labour.

You are the project manager for the construction of a pipeline to transport crude oil to a refinery site. Shell is the leader of a joint venture, with a 49 per cent share in the pipeline. The national government is the majority partner and is the operator of the pipeline. There is a lot of pressure to complete the pipeline quickly, to avoid financial penalties.

A consortium of construction and service firms has been engaged to bring the pipeline into operation. Thousands of labourers are needed to complete the project. Many of the workers concerned have been brought in from a neighbouring country. The government has agreed to special immigration arrangements for them. They are housed near the project. There is a large military presence around both the worksite and the workers' housing. Workers are moved from the housing area to the worksite and back under military guard. When they are not working they are not allowed to leave the housing area.

---

[1] Available at www-static.shell.com/static/environment_society/downloads/management_primers/human_rights_dilemmas.pdf.

---

[58] GRI Guidelines, available at www.globalreporting.org/ReportingFramework/ReportingFrameworkDownloads/.

There are reports that some workers had to pay recruitment fees – as much as 50 per cent of their pay – to get jobs on the project. When your assistant talks to the foreign workers he is told that all of them had to give their passports to the recruiters. He also finds out that the recruiters are closely connected with the army in their own country.

- Do you consider that the military presence at and near the worksite and the workers' housing indicates treatment that goes against Shell's business principles?[2]
- Do the arrangements regarding recruitment fees and passports suggest forced labour? Would you raise this with your local partner? What are your grounds for raising it? What will be your position in the discussion with your partner? And how hard are you willing to play this?
- How would this situation appear to the public, the international media, or other organisations concerned with human rights?
- Are there changes that could be made to answer charges – or a real situation – of forced labour?

---

[2] Shell's Business Principles are available at www-static.shell.com/static/aboutshell/ downloads/who_we_are/sgbps/sgbp_english.pdf.

16.4 HUMAN RIGHTS OBLIGATIONS OF INTERNATIONAL ORGANISATIONS

IGOs are set up by states with a view to accomplishing a variety of tasks which no single country could undertake on its own.[59] As a result, they are founded on the principles of consent, cooperation and the pursuit of common aims and objectives. Although the legal personality of IGOs is independent from that of their member states, it is none the less derived from their members. This means that the ambit of such derivative personality is limited to the rights and duties conferred on the IGO by its founders, subject no doubt to the IGO's implied powers, if any. From the point of view of obligations and liability, because IGOs possess a personality that is distinct from that of their member states, all contractual and other liabilities incurred by the IGO have

---

[59] Article 2(a) of the ILC Draft Articles on the Responsibility of International Organisations (2011) defines an IGO as: 'an organisation established by a treaty or other instrument governed by international law and possessing its own international legal personality. International organisations may include as members, in addition to states, other entities.'

no bearing on its members, which are considered third parties at all times.[60] The only exception to this rule would arise in circumstances where a group of states created an IGO for personal benefit and demonstrated negligence in the supervision of its activities. In this manner the states would incur liability as if they themselves had committed the unlawful act.[61] The distinction in personality between the IGO and its members further entails that rights and duties assumed by member states under a treaty are not conferred on the IGO. The practical significance of this observation, for the purposes of this book, is that the human rights obligations of states remain exclusively their own and are not assumed in parallel by the IGOs to which they are parties. Equally, states are not responsible for the human rights violations committed by IGOs to which they are parties.[62] Given that human rights treaties are not addressed to IGOs and the latter are not parties to such treaties[63] it is obvious that a significant legal gap arises in situations where violations may be attributable to IGOs.

It is instructive to provide an illustration of the way that IGOs can have an impact on the enjoyment of rights. A financing contract is agreed between developing country X and the World Bank for the construction of a dam. As it turns out the project is of little economic or investment value and results in the forceful eviction of a significant indigenous population and the impairment of the natural environment. Had it not been for the positive conduct of the World Bank the negative impact on the enjoyment of the relevant rights would not have materialised. If one were to follow the legalistic argument that IGOs are not incumbent directly with human rights obligations under treaty law, or indeed indirectly by reason of the pre-existing human rights obligations of their members, a nonsensical void arises. Moreover, the victims in both cases would be unable to pursue legal action against the IGO as a matter of tort.

It would be imprudent to simply provide theoretical analyses by reference to UN Charter provisions in order to substantiate why the UN and other IGOs are bound by general human rights law. Rather, what is important is to

---

[60] *J. H. Rayner (Mincing Lane) Ltd* v. *Department of Trade and Industry and Others and related appeals*; *MacLaine Watson & Co. Ltd* v. *Department of Trade and Industry*; *MacLaine Watson & Co. Ltd* v. *International Tin Council* (Judgment of 26 October 1989), 81 ILR 670, *per* Lord Templeman, 678. These are collectively known as the *Tin Council* case.

[61] See R. Sadurska and C. M. Chinkin, 'The Collapse of the International Tin Council: a Case of State Responsibility?' *Virginia JIL* 30 (1990), 845.

[62] Even so, the ECtHR held in *T. I.* v. *UK*, App no. 43844/98, Admissibility decision (7 March 2000), 'that it would be incompatible with member states' obligations under the ECHR to absolve themselves from responsibility in respect of human rights violations committed by IGOs to which they are parties'.

[63] Exceptionally, at the time of writing the EU was in the process of acceding to the ECHR.

understand in what manner IGOs employ human rights in their work and the processes that impede them from concretising rights considerations in their daily routine. Whereas the source of human rights obligations is external to states (i.e. they are derived from treaties they have ratified or customary law), for IGOs the source is internal. This means that the organisation itself, through its competent organs, decides which (treaty-based) human rights norms it will adhere to and then proceeds to dress up these norms in its own institutional language and law.

The ECJ, for example, has long postulated that fundamental rights are protected in the framework of the European Communities EC and the European Union EU but only as these are formulated and derived from the EU's internal order.[64] In order to avoid importing human rights obligations from the ECHR and the ICCPR the ECJ went on to formulate so-called general principles of EC law. As these were to some degree structured around the EC's economic entitlements (e.g. workers' freedom of movement and freedom of establishment for legal persons) as well as its member states' constitutional traditions, which in turn derived from their obligations under the ECHR, the relevant rights were not all that different from the jurisprudence of the ECtHR.[65] The EU, much like the UN, is not resistant to testing the compatibility of its actions with international human rights law. Certainly, while organs such as the Security Council display a lesser degree of compliance,[66] by and large the UN may be considered an IGO whose activities are consistent with, if not promoting, human rights. Just like the EU, however, it wants to internalise the processes by which human rights are infused into its daily operations.

On the other end of the spectrum one finds IGOs whose nature of operations is viewed by their appointed directors as inconsistent with human rights. International financial institutions, principally those comprising the World Bank Group, fall within this category. Although the aim of the Bank is to alleviate poverty (and of the IMF to ensure its members' balance-of-payments), itself a pursuit tied to human rights objectives, both institutions have traditionally resisted the notion that they are susceptible to any human rights obligations. What is more, although their operations have a direct significant impact on economic and social rights (e.g. because of austerity measures imposed on borrowing countries) they have long hidden behind article IV(3)(b) of the IMF Articles of Agreement which obliges the IMF to respect the domestic social

---

[64] Case 29/69, *Stauder* v. *City of Ulm* [1969] ECR 419, para. 7.

[65] See case C-274/99, *Connolly* v. *Commission* [2001] ECR I-1611, freedom of expression; Case 130/75, *Prais* v. *Council* [1976] ECR 1589, freedom of religion; Cases C-20/00 and C-64/00, *Booker Aquacultur Ltd and Hydro Seafood GSP Ltd* v. *The Scottish Ministers* [2003] ECR I-7411, right to property.

[66] For a human rights analysis of the sanctions imposed by the Council, see case study 7.2.

and political policies of members.[67] In recent years, both the Bank and the IMF have adopted operational policies that in theory oblige themselves and their borrowers to respect particular rights, especially those of indigenous peoples and in the event of persistent breaches to cease any further funding.[68] Moreover, successive legal opinions by the Bank's recent legal advisors admonish the Bank to recognize the relevance of human rights in its development policies and overall mission.[69]

In practice, the institutions comprising the World Bank pay very little attention to human rights considerations. The reason for this has to be sought not only in the politico-financial expectations of the Bank's wealthier member states, but more importantly in its embedded culture. Although the Bank is a specialised agency of the UN its employees are hired on the strength of their commercial background and are thus attuned to achieving purely commercial banking objectives. As a result, when considering financing a project in a developing country they will foremost be concerned with its financial viability and securing a commercial return for the Bank. The fact that the project in question may affect socio-economic rights in the short or long run will be of no relevance to a commercial banker whose employer has failed to cultivate a strong human rights culture. In this light, it is natural for the Bank and its employees to see human rights as a nasty impediment to their ordinary work. Therefore, the best approach in the opinion of this author in order to remedy the Bank's institutional failings is to force its wealthier contributors, rather than the Bank itself, to amend this culture by setting out clear development – albeit financially viable – objectives that benefit countries and peoples.

There exist situations where IGOs are none the less obliged in practice to adhere to international human rights law. For one thing, IGOs are not immune from the operation of customary international law and *jus cogens*.[70] It would be absurd to argue otherwise, given that custom and *jus cogens* are not dependent on a contractual undertaking, as is the case with treaties.[71] They are therefore wholly enforceable against IGOs. Moreover, IGOs trigger the application of IHL where they engage in armed hostilities or effectively occupy parts of a territory. Although it is true that the Geneva Conventions

---

[67] See S. Skogly, *The Human Rights Obligations of the World Bank and the International Monetary Fund* (London, Sydney: Cavendish, 2001).

[68] Especially the IBRD's Operational Policy 4.10 on Indigenous Peoples (July 2005).

[69] F. Coomans, 'Application of the International Covenant on Economic, Social and Cultural Rights in the Framework of International Organisations', *MPYBUNL* 11 (2007), 359, at 368–71.

[70] See, for example, Case C-162/96, *Racke* v. *Hauptzollant Mainz* [1998] ECR I-3655, para. 45.

[71] A. Reinisch, 'Developing Human Rights and Humanitarian Law Accountability of the Security Council for the Imposition of Economic Sanctions', *AJIL* 95 (2001), 851, at 858.

and general IHL were traditionally addressed to states, they are also applicable in situations of armed conflict wherein one of the parties comprises forces under the control of an international organisation. Given that the UN exercises command and operational control over forces committed by member states for peacekeeping and peace enforcement missions[72] it would be absurd to exclude the application of IHL to such forces. The purpose of IHL is to render war more humane and to minimise its effects on the wounded and *hors de combat* and as a result its application is triggered objectively by the existence of armed hostilities, not by the legal status of the parties to the conflict.[73] The obligation to abide with the laws of war is also acknowledged by the UN itself and the Secretary-General specifically issued a Bulletin in 1999, entitled 'Observance by United Nations Forces of International Humanitarian Law',[74] to make this point clear. The Bulletin, which is binding on all UN personnel, reflects fundamental principles of IHL, particularly protection of the civilian population, means and methods of combat, treatment of civilians, *hors de combat*, detained persons, the wounded, sick and medical personnel.

It is also indubitable that the UN and other organisations that have assumed the role of transitional administrators of territory that is not yet fully independent are under an obligation to provide the full range of fundamental human rights to the population of the territory in question.[75] Although this is generally stipulated in the mandate of the administering organization, as was the case with UNMIK in Kosovo,[76] given that IGOs supplement the authority of the state in the territory under consideration they are bound by the treaty law applicable therein as well as by customary law and *jus cogens*.

---

[72] Articles 6–9 of the Model Agreement between the UN and member states contributing personnel and equipment to the UN peace keeping operations, UN Doc. A/46/185 (23 May 1991), Annex, stipulates that contributed forces come under exclusive UN control and serve UN interests, rather than national ones. None the less, criminal and disciplinary control is retained by national authorities.

[73] For a more thorough analysis of the aims and principles of IHL, see section 14.2.

[74] UN Doc. ST/SGB/1999/13 (6 August 1999). The Security Council has relied on the Bulletin to emphasise that UN forces must always comply with the laws of war. See UNSC resolution 1327 (13 November 2000).

[75] On the legal and historical nature of such administration, see R. Wilde, *International Territorial Administration: How Trustee and the Civilizing Mission Never Went Away* (Oxford University Press, 2010).

[76] UNSC resolution 1244 (10 June 1999). This was further emphasised in the Report of the UN Secretary-General on the UN Interim Administration Mission in Kosovo, UN Doc. S/1999/779 (12 July 1999), para. 42, stating that UNMIK will 'be guided by internationally recognised standards of human rights as the basis for the exercise of its authority in Kosovo'.

CASE STUDY 16.2
Non-consideration of economic and social rights by the IMF in Tanzania

When Tanzania requested assistance from the IMF in 1985 the latter agreed to provide loans and assurances but conditioned them on the acceptance by the country of SAPs.[1] The measures imposed under the SAPs included the privatisation of Tanzania's mining industry, the adoption of trade liberalisation measures and the introduction of fees for health care and education, among other things. Within a space of fifteen years the school enrolment rate dropped from 80 per cent to 66 per cent and the country's illiteracy rate rose to slightly above 50 per cent. The introduction of health care fees saw the AIDS rate rise to 8 per cent and despite the deep austerity measures which the IMF promised would reduce poverty and bring prosperity, per capita income was reduced from US$309 to US$210.

The IMF's contribution to the deterioration of economic and social rights is clearly direct because it was aware that Tanzania would agree to the conditions of the SAP in order to secure the much needed loan. The Fund was either aware of or was grossly negligent about the failure of the programme and its consequences for the local population. What should be its responsibility under the circumstances and what advice would you provide in order to avoid similar social failures in the future?

[1] For an analysis of the objective of SAPs and their potential impact on the enjoyment of human rights, see case study 12.1 and section 12.4.

16.5 NATIONAL LIBERATION MOVEMENTS AND ARMED REBEL GROUPS

Unlike other NSAs national liberation movements (NLMs) and armed rebel groups are specifically mentioned in IHL treaties. The obligations towards civilians, the wounded and sick and those rendered *hors de combat* in common article 3 to the 1949 Geneva Conventions, for example, are addressed to 'each party to the conflict' and therefore also to armed rebel groups. Protocol II of 1977 to the 1949 Geneva Conventions and relating to the protection of victims of non-international armed conflicts is equally addressed to all parties to a conflict, albeit requiring that the rebels exercise significant control over part of the embattled territory. Moreover, article 1(4) of Protocol I of 1977 to the 1949 Geneva Conventions which regulates international armed conflicts assimilates three types of national liberation war to international armed conflicts. These are 'armed conflicts in which peoples are fighting against colonial domination and alien occupation and against racist regimes in the exercise of their right to self-determination'.

Many IHL treaties allow NLMs and rebel entities to make declarations of conformity with the relevant law.[77] This is more of a psychological inducement that gives the NLM a sense of external recognition while at the same time making it publicly accountable, given that NLMs incur specific obligations under the relevant treaties. It is also common for well-entrenched NLMs to enter into agreements with governmental forces, usually through a foreign mediator, in order to register their mutual intent to comply with human rights and IHL. Again, although these agreements may seem legally superfluous[78] they render the parties more accountable and cautious in their conduct and therefore are welcome. They are additionally welcome because they 'humanise' the members of the rebel entity, especially since incumbent governments typically deny that NLMs are entitled to any privileges, particularly combatant status[79] and are treated as common criminals.

Whereas the application of obligations stemming from IHL are not contested as regards NLMs and rebel entities involved in armed conflict as a matter of customary law, the same is not necessarily true as regards human rights. From a practical point of view this question is moot because the laws of war, being moreover *lex specialis* as against human rights law,[80] cover situations that would otherwise be regulated under the human rights regime. Even so, certain scholars contend that rebel groups do not possess any human rights obligations, or at least those they are unlikely to be able to uphold, such as the obligation to offer due process rights because of their inability to administer a legal system.[81] This is probably true to some degree but rebel entities are certainly in a position to guarantee fundamental human rights and should be held accountable for any failure in this regard. This conclusion is confirmed by reference to Security Council resolutions which consistently call directly on insurgents and rebels to comply with human rights and humanitarian law.[82]

None the less, humanitarian law is unable to cover all situations involving rebels and NLMs. This is particularly true in the absence of protracted armed conflict, in which case the laws of war are not triggered. In this type of

---

[77] Articles 96(3) of Protocol I of 1977 and 7(4) of the 1980 Convention on Prohibitions or Restrictions on the Use of Certain Conventional Weapons.

[78] See, however, C. Bell, 'Peace Agreements: Their Nature and Legal Status', *AJIL* 100 (2006) 373, who argues that they enjoy legal force.

[79] See *S* v. *Petane* [1988] 3 SARL 51; *Military Prosecutor* v. *Kassem and Others* [1971] 42 ILR 470.

[80] For an analysis of their *lex specialis* character, see section 14.4.

[81] L. Moir, *The Law of Internal Armed Conflict* (Cambridge University Press, 2002), p. 194.

[82] For example, UNSC resolution 1193 (28 August 1998); UNSC resolution 1213 (3 December 1998); UNSC resolution 1572 (15 November 2004); UNSC resolution 1672 (25 April 2006).

scenario the rebels do not possess *de facto* authority over part of the territory and are not engaged in armed hostilities against the government. It is unlikely that under such circumstances, which are very much akin to the legal regime governing terrorist groups, that the rebels are burdened with human rights obligations.

16.5.1 'To Suffer thy Comrades': Responding to human rights abuses by non-state actors in the Philippines

The following is an excerpt from an introduction to a report on NSAs[83] written by Robert (Bobby) Francis B. Garcia, Secretary General of PATH (Peace Advocates for Truth, Healing and Justice), and author of the book *To Suffer thy Comrades* (Manila: Anvil Publishing, 2001).

I used to be a 'non-state actor', having been a member of the Communist Party of the Philippines-New People's Army (CPP-NPA) during the 1980s, in the prime of my youth. I joined the guerrillas in the countryside and waged war against the state. Suffering torture, and perhaps a gruesome death, from government soldiers was something I dreaded but for which I somehow prepared. I never expected that the blows would come from my own comrades.

It was in 1988 when the anti-infiltration campaign called 'Oplan Missing Link' (OPML) happened. OPML would turn out to be just one of the numerous bloody campaigns undertaken by the CPP-NPA to ferret out suspected 'deep-penetration agents' (DPAs) within its ranks. The pattern in all these anti-DPA campaigns was frighteningly similar: suspicion, arrest, interrogation, forced confession, detention, execution – a bloody domino effect that had bodies writhing, rolling and dying en masse. It was November 1988 when they arrested and tortured me and threw me along with fifty-six other chained guerrillas in the Sierra Madre mountain ranges. At that time, sixty-six suspects had already been executed. One of the worst punishments we endured was the denial of food. The torturers also experimented with various combinations of physical and psychological terror tactics. A female detainee was beaten up, hung on a tree and forced to watch how they beat up other victims. Then she was made to listen to the recorded voices of her children. Some were left dangling in trees for days. They slit the captives' skin with a knife or shaved off their eyebrows for fun. Captives' legs were forced apart and their thighs were sat upon. Their skin was seared with a lamp.

In its wake, I suffered a broken jaw, concussions on my head, wounds where the chains rubbed on the skin and a battered psyche that proved much harder to heal. The sheer brutality of the experience itself may have been one of the reasons why most of us refused to talk about it for a very long time. It was much easier to talk about military atrocities than the cruelty of one's own comrades. Thus the truth was buried for a very long time.

---

[83] See REDRESS, *Not only the State: Torture by Non-state Actors* (London: REDRESS, 2006), pp. 4–7.

Talking about the experience was difficult enough as it were, finding legal redress was not even imagined. At least not until recently. In August 2003 we brought together a group of people who were directly or indirectly victimised by the CPP-NPA's anti-infiltration campaigns – former comrades who survived the torture, families who lost a member or two, and compatriots who believe that the thousands of comrades who fell in the wake of these anti-infiltration campaigns must find their due. We formed the Peace Advocates for Truth, Healing and Justice (PATH). All of our members are involved in various other advocacies and campaigns, but find this particular one far harder and fraught with obstacles. Many of us are human rights workers who never tire of hollering against the state's abuses – work that is by no means easy, but pretty much cut and dried. It enjoys the luxury of certitude and 'political correctness'.

The issue of non-state-perpetrated violations, however, such as the Philippine communist purges, is much more complex and uncertain. ... addressing the issue of past violations inevitably gets mired in political manoeuvrings. The government uses it as an effective propaganda ammunition against the rebels, while dispensing with counter-insurgency measures that fall way below human rights and international humanitarian law standards.

In addition to this, bringing up the issue remains a dangerous undertaking, simply because the CPP-NPA is still armed and active. They have also categorically dismissed any possibility of reopening the issue, claiming that it is already a closed book. The perpetrators, they say, have either fled the party or have been rightfully punished. The scores of victims' families who do not know what really happened and the thousands of dead and disappeared point to the contrary.

We at PATH have explored various legal options, one being the filing of individual criminal cases against identified lead perpetrators, such as those involved in the OPML in the province of Laguna. As expected, the wheels of justice grind to an almost standstill. Gathering evidence of a crime that happened more than a decade back poses a terrible challenge, including the lack of witnesses willing to testify and the blurring of memory through time.

The absence of an anti-torture law in the Philippines [note that this law has now been passed, see interview with Soliman Santos below] also poses a limitation, thus the charges filed are limited to serious physical injuries and serious illegal detention. The case of Jesse Marlow Libre is a particular case in point. In November 2005, we at PATH, with the help of forensic scientists and volunteer experts were able to exhume the remains of his parents, revolutionary couple Jesse and Nida Libre. They were falsely suspected as spies and killed by the CPP-NPA in Cebu on September 1985. The truth behind the disappearance of the young orphan's parents was withheld from him by the movement (they claimed the military killed them). It was only in 2005 that he learned the disconcerting reality upon seeing his parents' skeletons buried together in a mountain gravesite, bearing tell-tale signs of severe torture and violent death. Thus with the exhumation of truth comes the cry for justice.

What are the legal options available to him? We can barely find witnesses willing to testify. Who are responsible? A whole party organization was involved. What are the levels of accountability? It was a complex hierarchical set-up: there were onlookers, guards, interrogators, torturers, executioners, decision-makers and party directives. Truth and justice are simply lost in the labyrinth.

INTERVIEW 16.1

Judge and activist on Philippines' armed groups

(Soliman M. Santos)

Soliman 'Sol' M. Santos, JR, is presently a municipal judge covering three rural towns in his home province of Camarines Sur in the Bicol Region of the Philippines. He has been a long-time non-governmental human rights and international humanitarian lawyer; peace advocate, researcher and writer; and the author and editor of several books, including on non-state armed groups. He has been among the international civil society pioneers in the theory and practice of constructive engagement with these groups, starting with the anti-landmines campaign in 1997.

What are your comments on Bobby Garcia's statement from the perspective of a lawyer seeking justice for violations by NSAs?

I fully understand the difficulties that Bobby speaks of in seeking justice for violations by NSAs, particularly armed groups. To start with, the Philippine criminal justice system has many inadequacies in general, including inadequate witness protection and forensic evidence-gathering technology. These general inadequacies are compounded considering the especially difficult and complex nature of dealing with the campaign of purges involving the CPP-NPA rebel group in the 1980s, given also the passage of more than thirty years. This particular event may already need a different, more effective approach or measure of redress than the usual mode of filing and prosecuting individual criminal cases. As for continuing and current incidents of violations by non-state actors, these might be addressed more effectively by a purposive effort that engages the criminal justice system, including necessary law and justice reform and one that also explores and sets up alternative mechanisms outside that system, including the availing of relevant existing international mechanisms.

You were part of a campaign that actively lobbied for legislation that would criminalise torture and other violations by NSAs in the Philippines. What was the outcome, and what are your lessons from this experience?

The landmark Philippine Anti-Torture Law of 2009 emerged deliberately not covering non-state agent perpetrators of torture. The law's main sponsors in Congress (Parliament) and the main human rights groups campaigning for the law were largely responsible for this negative aspect of an otherwise positive outcome. On the other hand, our much smaller lobby for a definition of torture that is not limited to state agent perpetrators came into the picture, 'too little and too late', as they say. The first and main obstacle we encountered, both with fellow human rights advocates and with the main sponsors, was a traditionalist human rights paradigm that conceptually limits human rights violations to state/state agent violations. As they also say, 'old habits die hard'. The next arena for this engagement is the Anti-Enforced Disappearance Bill, already near passage into law as of the time of writing (July 2012), and it looks like the same scenario of not covering state agent perpetrators will emerge, with hardly even any lobby effort on the non-state actor angle. Advocates of this angle must definitely regroup for more effective legislative intervention in the coming days and engagements.

Attempts have been made to forge an international South–South network addressing violations by NSAs. Why is there a need for such a network and what challenges does it face?

The problems involving non-state armed groups and the contexts they are in, that is armed conflicts, are largely found in the Global South or what used to be referred to as the Third World of Asia, Africa and Latin America. The purposive efforts to address this special kind of non-state problem, for which the existing largely state-oriented mechanisms are generally inadequate or inappropriate, should also come from this global South, interlinked on a South–South basis. Being closer to the problem and its context allows for a perspective, a Southern perspective, that is more grounded and suited to addressing the problem. This importantly includes the perspectives of civil society and affected local communities, and situates and thus understands the armed conflicts in their respective political, economic, social, cultural, religious and ideological contexts and histories. This contrasts with the tendency of many Northern or Western approaches that tend to focus almost exclusively on the levels of violence but with inadequate understanding of the context. But an international South–South network necessarily has to relate to strategic partners, collaborators and cooperation points in the North, of course based on relations of equality and co-responsibility in the true spirit of internationalism. We envision the work as constructive engagement of non-state armed groups in a comprehensive range of fields and concerns affecting local communities, of which addressing their human rights violations is only one. The engagement is qualified as constructive, as opposed to destructive, as the latter kind of engagement is what states are mainly undertaking in their own approach to the problem.

The main need and challenge now is for an effective, viable and sustainable international South–South network for this comprehensive work. Our own particular attempt at this, the South–South Network (SSN) for Non-State Armed Group Engagement (www.southsouthnetwork. com) started in 2005, has unfortunately floundered and has not taken off mainly for lack of political, moral and funding support for what may be an unappreciated, controversial or even misunderstood area of work, as well due to certain organisational weaknesses.

From an international law perspective, what are the main changes needed to more effectively combat violations by NSAs?

The main changes required may be outlined on two levels which might be referred to broadly as internal and external. We already just mentioned the main change needed internally – breaking through on an effective, viable and sustainable international South–South network that can help comprehensively develop the work of constructive engagement of non-state armed groups, including addressing their human rights violations. Of course, the latter particular engagement can and should also be taken up by human rights groups and institutions in particular. The latter may be more disposed to criminal prosecution and other quasi-coercive or confrontational approaches, which are not mainly contemplated in constructive engagement by dialogue and persuasion to positively influence such armed groups.

But it is also with human rights groups and institutions where some external work by advocates of NSA engagement/accountability is needed for external changes. The main external change needed, as far as human rights groups and institutions are concerned, is one of attitude and/or orientation: a shift in the traditionalist human rights paradigm that conceptually limits human rights violations to state/state agent violations. For human rights groups and institutions to introduce or mainstream the non-state actor angle into their work on their particular human rights issue of concern like torture, even if still mainly addressing state/state agent violations, would already be a big step forward. The aforementioned breakthrough paradigm shift should/would be followed or accompanied by a breakthrough in another needed external change: developing at various levels what together might constitute a critical mass of appropriate and effective mechanisms, instruments, tools, frameworks, approaches, techniques and technology in seeking rebel accountability, including legal but not limited to it, for human rights violations.

QUESTIONS

- The personnel of private security firms regularly engage in armed hostilities with guerrillas, rebels and paramilitaries, very often in occupied territory, as is the case with post-2003 Iraq. Do these people assume obligations under international humanitarian law?

- The World Bank Group facilitates loans to developing countries and countries in default under condition of structural adjustments which generally require severe austerity measures by the borrowing nation. These measures are known to result in the elimination of many socio-economic rights, such as free education, welfare, pensions, health care and others. Who is, or should be, responsible for the violation of these rights, if at all?

- International organisations do not assume human rights obligations under treaty law, but there is nothing preventing them from assuming said obligations as a matter of customary international law. Discuss with regard to the practical considerations of this statement.

- There are at least two *de facto* states in the world today, Iraqi Kurdistan and Somaliland. Although they are not formally acknowledged as states they exercise functions and powers pertaining to states. Are they to be classified as NSAs for the purpose of attribution of human rights obligations, or are they to be assimilated to states?

FURTHER READING

Ahmed, T. and Butler, I. J., 'The European Union and Human Rights: an International Law Perspective', *EJIL* 17 (2006), 771.

Alston, P. (ed.), *Non-State Actors and Human Rights* (Oxford University Press, 2005).

Amao, O., *Corporate Social Responsibility, Human Rights and the Law: Multinational Corporations in Developing Countries* (London, New York: Routledge, 2011).

Aznar-Gomez, M. J., 'A Decade of Human Rights Protection by the UN Security Council: a Sketch of Deregulation?' *EJIL* 13 (2002), 223.

Clapham, A., 'Human Rights Obligations of Non-state Actors in Conflict Situations', *IRRC* 88 (2006), 491.

Greathead, S., 'The Multinational and the "New Stakeholder": Examining the Business Case for Human Rights', *Vand. J. Transnat'l L.* 35 (2002), 719.

Joseph, S., *Corporations and Transnational Human Rights Litigation* (Oxford: Hart, 2004).

Kamminga, M. and Zia-Zarifi, S. (eds.), *Liability of Multinational Corporations under International Law* (The Hague: Kluwer, 2005).

Khan, F., 'Pandora's Box: Managerial Discretion and the Problem of Corporate Philanthropy', *UCLA L. Rev.* 44 (1997), 579.

Kinley, D. and Tadaki, J., 'From Talk to Walk: the Emergence of Human Rights Responsibilities for Corporations at International Law', *Virginia JIL* 44 (2004), 931.

McCorquodale, R. and Simons, P., 'Responsibility Beyond Borders: State Responsibility for Extraterritorial Violations by Corporations of International Human Rights Law', *MLR* 70 (2007), 598.

Muchlinski, P., *Multinational Enterprises and the Law* (Oxford University Press, 2007).

Mujih, E., *Regulating Multinationals in Developing Countries: A Conceptual and Legal Framework for Corporate Social Responsibility* (Cheltenham: Edward Elgar, 2012).

Ratner, S., 'Corporations and Human Rights: a Theory of Legal Responsibility', *Yale L.J.* 111 (2001), 443.

Ruggie, J., 'Business and Human Rights: the Evolving International Agenda', *AJIL* 101 (2008), 819.

Walker, C. and Whyte, D., 'Contracting Out War? Private Military Companies, Law and Regulation in the United Kingdom', *ICLQ* 54 (2005), 651.

Zegveld, L., *Accountability of Armed Opposition Groups in International Law* (Cambridge University Press, 2002).

Zerk, J. A., *Multinationals and Corporate Social Responsibility: Limitations and Opportunities in International Law* (Cambridge University Press, 2011).

17 Globalisation and its impact on human rights

CONTENTS

17.1   INTRODUCTION

This chapter is necessarily interrelated with the one concerning the right to development but also informs all other chapters in one way or another. Globalisation is a topic that has been discussed from multiple perspectives, including the freedom offered to private actors by which to generate non-state sanctioned laws,[1] its traversal of traditional barriers through advanced technologies and communications and the fostering of better understanding among cultures. Although there are positive connotations to the term, it is generally viewed negatively because it is perceived as a process that was created by the rich and powerful and one which brings little, or no, benefit to the poor and vulnerable.

This chapter attempts very briefly to sketch the economic rationale underpinning globalisation and explain in what manner its adherents envisaged a better world. Given that the subject matter is vast, the analysis is limited

---

[1] See G. Teubner, 'Global Bukowina: Legal Pluralism in the World Society', in G. Teubner (ed.), *Global Law without a State* (Aldershot: Dartmouth, 1996), 3.

to three spheres which either drive the processes of globalisation, or upon which it produces a significant impact. We go on to explore the concept of trade liberalisation and whether its application has the potential to equitably distribute the financial benefits of a globalised marketplace. From there, we shall discuss the liberalisation of agricultural commodities with a view to ascertaining whether this is the right approach to food security in the developing world. A very particular aspect of the economic globalisation agenda is the protection of innovators and their patents. The chapter discusses the degree to which the protection of the intellectual property rights pertaining to pharmaceutical companies inhibits the right to health and in particular access to essential medicines for the impoverished. Intellectual property protection is an integral part of trade liberalisation and it is only natural that MNCs are eager to safeguard the fruits of their research as well as benefit from the competitive advantage of cheap labour offered by the plethora of poor nations vying for foreign investment.

The chapter does not advocate that globalisation is inherently destructive or in conflict with human rights. Quite the contrary, trade liberalisation has the potential to provide the much needed financial resources to fulfil states' human rights obligations. None the less, the means by which globalisation is pursued is inherently at odds with fundamental human rights. Its emphasis is on financial growth without any reference whatsoever to human well-being. Overall profits are viewed as more important than food security, equitable distribution of wealth and poverty reduction. Human rights play no part at all in the ebb and flow of international trade, or at least in the inception of this scheme, and it is for this reason that the UN and other intergovernmental organisations have begun to underline the importance of human rights linkages to trade.[2] As a result, one of the central ideas of globalisation, i.e. that governments, being ineffective actors, should not interfere in trade and services, is being discredited on the ground that privatisation of essential services (such as water, energy, education and pensions) leads in fact to the privatisation and irrelevance of human rights – an unacceptable outcome that is in stark conflict with the fundamental tenets of human rights.[3]

---

[2] See e.g. UNGA resolution 62/151 (6 March 2008), which noted that globalisation 'should be guided by the fundamental principles that underpin the corpus of human rights'.

[3] By way of illustration, in 1996 a World Bank report criticised leakage levels between 1 and 5 per cent in Germany's public sector water operators for being too low. The principal author of the report, who went on to become head of the World Bank's water policy unit, noted that water should be allowed to leak if the cost of fixing the leak was greater than the profit that could be made if the water was sold! This is a clear example of a policy driven by profit considerations, not human welfare or rights concerns (i.e. the right to water for present and future generations). Quoted in M. Kothari, 'Privatising Human Rights: the Impact of Globalisation on Adequate Housing, Water and Sanitation', available at: unpan1.un.org/intradoc/groups/public/documents/apcity/unpan010131.pdf, 20.

17.2   THE ORIGINS AND NATURE OF GLOBALISATION

Although globalisation is generally viewed as a complex, unavoidable[4] and multi-layered phenomenon, in reality it is neither complex, global nor a phenomenon. It is a wholly artificial construct that was purposely engineered by a handful of states in order to pursue a particular economic agenda.[5] Its theoretical underpinning is neo-liberal theory and particularly the so-called Washington Consensus which posits that free, unregulated, markets and trade liberalisation is the only way to spur financial growth. As a result, any governmental interference with market forces constitutes an impediment to growth and by extension to the potential for human well-being. This theory is largely discredited, not because increased trade and investment are inimical to human progress – quite the contrary; rather, it has been aptly demonstrated that financial growth does not necessarily translate into human well-being, and nor is there any direct correlation between the two.[6] Neo-liberalism assumes that because the competitive forces inherent in markets drive competition and innovation to produce better and cheaper products and services, citing as examples the progress of industrialised nations, this model should be encouraged worldwide, particularly in developing nations. No doubt inefficient and corrupt governments in the developing world have failed to make any tangible gains from the nationalisation of their natural resources and other industries and have instead accumulated significant debts. It was natural therefore for neo-liberal advocates to maintain that besides trade and financial liberalisation, states should accept deregulation, privatisation, unhindered foreign direct investment (FDI) and competitive exchange rates in order to attract foreign capital. They also maintained that since the public sector generally tends to expand and become inefficient, governments should be flexible and downsized and subject to strict fiscal discipline.[7]

There are several deficiencies to this otherwise laudable agenda, most of which will be explored in subsequent sections. It suffices to note at this stage that none of the pursuits of neo-liberalism were directly geared towards alleviating poverty, joblessness, universal health care or other social goals. Privatisation, one of the mantras of neo-liberalism, is a good example. By way of illustration, although the privatisation of the health and water sectors may

---

[4] R. Howard-Hassmann, 'The Second Great Transformation: Human Rights Leapfrogging in the Era of Globalisation', *HRQ* 27 (2005), 1.

[5] See particularly the forceful argument of P. O'Connell, 'On Reconciling Irreconcilables: Neo-liberal Globalisation and Human Rights', *HRLR* 7 (2007), 483, at 489.

[6] See section 12.2. Equally, UN Secretary-General Report, Globalisation and its Impact on the Full Enjoyment of All Human Rights, UN Doc. A/55/342 (31 August 2000), para. 13.

[7] W. K. Tabb, *Economic Governance in the Age of Globalisation* (New York: Columbia University Press, 2005), 3.

render these cost-effective and efficient, private operators naturally deny them to those unable to afford them; yet the right to health and water are fundamental rights whose provision is incumbent on the state. As a result, privatisation that is unregulated and not subject to any social controls will be inclined towards deprivation and discrimination between the vulnerable and the wealthy.[8]

Equally, many forms of FDI produce no benefit to host states, with labour unintensive industries being a prime example. The same is also true of investments in respect of which the investor is free to repatriate all profits without an obligation to invest in the host nation. Moreover, in a deregulated environment where the sole interest of businesses is the maximisation of profit and that of poor nations is the attraction of foreign capital, low salaries and weak labour rights are viewed as a competitive advantage. Thus, although foreign investors may not directly impose low wages or poor working conditions on host states, in most cases they would naturally favour those countries with the cheapest production costs for particular manufacturing activities. It is often argued that FDI of this type at least provides employment opportunities, even if poorly paid, allowing poor people to survive, albeit barely. This rationale, however, is antithetical to UNDP's assessment of human development, which is premised on the existence of longevity, knowledge and decent living standards. Furthermore, it is contrary to the pursuit of national financial growth because poorly paid work does not contribute to the development of skilled labour, innovation, introduction of new technologies and empowerment, and nor can it generate and finance other secondary sectors of the economy.

Two broad categories of globalisation are generally recognised. The first is the engineered model briefly described in the preceding paragraphs which is centred around private profit maximisation, which we shall term economic globalisation.[9] The second is predicated on the advances in information and communications technologies which have resulted in the shrinking of time and space, the disappearance of borders, increased interaction between people and the development of mutual values and norms.[10] One dimension of this second category is so-called subaltern globalisation (also known as globalisation from below) which is driven by those opposed to the social injustices of economic globalisation, namely the marginalised and the excluded with

---

[8] UN Commission on Human Rights, Report on Economic, Social and Cultural Rights: Liberalisation of Trade in Services and Human Rights, UN Doc. E/CN.4/Sub.2/2002/9 (25 June 2002), paras. 44–5.

[9] See W. T. Milner, 'Economic Globalisation and Rights: an Empirical Analysis', in A. Brysk (ed.), *Globalisation and Human Rights* (Berkeley: University of California Press, 2002), 77, who defines economic globalisation as the integration of economies in institutional, commercial and financial terms.

[10] UNDP, *Human Development Report* (Oxford University Press, 1999), 1.

an emphasis on the democratisation of decision-making and the diffusion of power.[11] This movement is sometimes, but rather simplistically, referred to as anti-globalisation.

The paradox of economic globalisation is that it constitutes a public policy by which to curtail public power and replace the state with private action under the banners of deregulation and privatisation. This is not merely a government-shrinking exercise but an affirmation that it is not only states that hinder good governance, international trade and prosperity, but that private actors are better off self-regulating their respective spheres of professional activity. Self-regulation may be achieved in the absence of formal laws (e.g. MNCs in their dealings with external stakeholders and host governments) as well as in the process of implementing hard law (e.g. implementation of anti-money laundering regulations by the banking sector). In every case, the chief aim of self-regulation is to replace the state in its public law-making function and preempt government action altogether. Although this idea is attractive because it minimises transactional costs and government bureaucracy, it also entails the privatisation of human rights since states are essentially absolved from many of their human rights obligations. It also has an impact on the payment of taxes by the wealthy which in turn affects the enjoyment of socio-economic rights by the poor and the middle classes.

A pervasive side effect of economic globalisation and trade liberalisation is the integration of capital and trading markets. This means, for example, that agricultural and other commodities, such as sugar, grain and hydrocarbons, are bought and sold around the world at prices subject to external variables, such as global output in any particular year and artificial price fluctuations by traders intended to increase their revenues. In short, they are subject to financial commodification. This is not necessarily a negative outcome because produce which would otherwise be bought cheaply can be traded at international prices, thus offering a higher income to least developed countries (LDCs) than if the same produce were traded locally. Attractive as this idea is, it is clearly not viable for small-scale farmers, or for countries with poor institutional capacities and weak trade deficits. This system does not allow individual producers or states to negotiate the price of their commodities, unless their production constitutes a significant bulk of global output. Given also that LDCs are by no means major trading players in international markets, the prices of basic foods for the sustenance of their people are dependent on the unregulated trading practices of certain banks and trading companies operating under huge profits in the developed world.[12] This not only

---

[11] O'Connell, above note 5, 493–4.

[12] Exogenous shocks to non-diversified economies are a major concern for LDCs. By way of illustration, with the urging and lending of the World Bank, Vietnam quickly rose

constitutes an elimination of economic sovereignty but an indirect denial of self-determination in respect of a country's natural resources. Consequently, if food production and trading are left to self-regulation alone it can lead to widespread poverty.

17.3 DOES THE EXISTING MODEL OF TRADE LIBERALISATION PROMOTE DEVELOPMENT AND ALLEVIATE POVERTY?

In the aftermath of World War II industrialised nations realised that if their production levels were to increase they would have to export their goods to even more countries in all continents. This ensured growth, investment in research, technological superiority and ample employment opportunities. The only problem was that although their products were competitive from a manufacturing point of view, they were rendered non-competitive or unattractive from a consumer standpoint the moment they entered the territory of the importing nation. This was because of the imposition of tariffs, which are essentially taxes on foreign goods entering a country and which are directly payable to the government of that country.[13] Quite clearly, tariffs are discriminatory taxes the purpose of which is to favour a domestic product over a foreign import. As a result, because the domestic product is not subject to a tariff it is cheaper and thus more attractive than its foreign competitor. Low income countries rely on tariffs not only to support their domestic industries but also because they generate significant income for the public purse. Yet, if every country were to impose tariffs in this manner or subsidise its domestic industries few exports would be financially viable and hence global production would significantly decrease and international trade would become extinct.

The only loser from tariff reduction/elimination seems to be the domestic industry for which the protectionist effect of tariffs was originally intended. Therefore, in order for developed countries to attract LDCs into the post-1945 world trading system, which was predicated on trade liberalisation (i.e. tariff and quota-free trade), they recognised the need for protectionism of

to become the fourth largest coffee producer. As a result, global coffee prices were dramatically reduced and countries like Uganda whose farming industry, both large and small-scale, was based on coffee production underwent a sharp incline in real income by the early 2000s. The erosion of LDCs' economic sovereignty by private banks and credit rating agencies is acknowledged by the ILO's World Commission on the Social Dimension of Globalisation Report, entitled *A Fair Globalisation: Creating Opportunities for All,* (2004), para. 163.

[13] Trade liberalisation encompasses tariff barriers and non-tariff barriers. As far as the former is concerned, the term tariff is broad and includes practices such as duties, surcharges and export subsidies. Non-tariff barriers include licensing requirements, quotas and arbitrary standards, among others.

certain LDC industries until such time as they could effectively compete with their foreign counterparts. This protectionism was hardly based on charity, but was the concerted result of an LDC coalition within UNCTAD, known as G77.[14] Article XVIII of the 1947 GATT[15] offered LDCs exemptions from their commitments in order to 'grant the tariff protection required for the establishment of a particular industry'. The rationale was to promote certain industries through import substitution policies and thus restrict imports. In 1965, part IV of GATT, entitled 'Trade and Development', went even further and focused on expanding LDC access to the export markets of developed nations. The key to this expansion was the principle of special and differential treatment, through which developed nations were urged to make non-reciprocal tariff concessions to LDCs. As laudable as this was, the largest portion of Part IV was not binding. In the 1970s developed countries were allowed to grant preferential tariffs to imports from LDCs, a system known as Generalised System of Preferences (GSP), which constituted an exception to the most favoured nation principle, itself a cornerstone of GATT and later the WTO.[16] Many developed countries went on to adopt GSP programmes that extended preferential terms of trade to LDCs.[17]

These concessions offered exceptionally to LDCs seem like an ideal way of introducing them to the globalised trading system with a view to eventually rendering them equal trading partners. The first preambular paragraph to the 1994 WTO Agreement[18] even stresses that one of the principal goals of liberalised trade is to raise living standards and secure full employment on the basis of sustainable development. Although this echoes some of the essential underpinnings of the right to development, in fact the neo-liberal globalised trading system did not envisage any real linkages between human rights and trade, let alone the right to development. The application of the GSP device is certainly illustrative of the benefits it provides in many cases to developed nations and the subsequent harm it causes LDCs. GSP laws and agreements, at least those originating from the EU and the USA, typically subject all the

---

[14] S. E. Roland, 'Developing Countries Coalition at the WTO: in Search of Legal Support', *Harv. Int'l L. J.* 48 (2007), 487, at 488.

[15] 55 UNTS 194.

[16] This was formalised in 1979 through an instrument known as the Enabling Clause, articles 1, 5 and 7. See 'Differential and more favourable treatment reciprocity and fuller participation of developing countries', Decision of 28 November 1979. This remains in force under article 1(b)(iv) of the 1994 WTO Agreement.

[17] The USA, for example, enacted the Africa Growth and Opportunity Act, 19 USC §3721, whereas the EU entered into the Cotonou Agreement with LDCs from Africa, the Caribbean and the Pacific (ACP), which in turn spurred other initiatives, such as 'Everything But Arms' (EBA), through which all duties and quotas were eliminated for all products (save for arms) originating from LDCs.

[18] 1994 Marrakesh Agreement Establishing the World Trade Organisation (WTO Agreement), 1867 UNTS 154.

concessions offered to a range of conditionalities, some of which are human rights-based.[19] This is consistent with the vociferous support by developed nations of non-trade issues in the international trade agenda, particularly human rights, labour rights and environmental protection. LDCs have remained hostile to such linkages, for good reason.

Under the theory of comparative advantage two or more countries with unequal industrial and financial development can still benefit from free trade between themselves by concentrating on the production of goods for which they enjoy the greatest comparative advantage and import those products in respect of which they do not enjoy an advantage. One of the comparative advantages of LDCs is the availability therein of relatively cheap labour, which means that certain products that do not require skilled labour, particularly agricultural and textile-based, are cheaper to produce. Although low wages and poor labour conditions are not conducive to the full realisation of the right to development, at least international trade liberalisation would allow cheaply made products to boost the economies of LDCs and improve their people's socio-economic status. Alas, this has not proven to be the case. The USA has consistently maintained that poor labour conditions, assessed on the basis of standards employed in developed nations and which include minimum wages and hours of work, justify the imposition of duties or trade sanctions against products originating from LDCs, thus denying them their only comparative advantage in US consumer markets.[20] This constitutes a clear form of protectionism in favour of domestic products and calls on LDCs to apply labour standards that are wholly unrealistic with their level of development.[21] The consequence of such unilateral measures is their

---

[19] L. Bartels, *Human Rights Conditionality in the EU's International Agreements* (Oxford University Press, 2005), p. 68. EC Council Regulation 980/2005 (27 June 2005) on Applying a Scheme of Generalised Tariff Preferences, OJ L 169/1, requires under its GSP Plus criteria that in order for a country to be eligible for preferential treatment it 'must ratify and effectively implement' several international conventions dealing with human rights, labour laws, environmental protection, drugs and anti-corruption.

[20] A related, highly-controversial and largely unresolved issue has to do with so-called social dumping. Article 2 of the WTO Agreement on Implementation of Article VI of the General Agreement on Tariffs and Trade 1994 (Agreement on Dumping) prohibits the introduction of imports at a price which is less than the normal value of the import. Where such a product is none the less found to have been imported, the importing state may impose an anti-dumping duty in order to offset the dumping margin. Many developed nations argue that the use of cheap labour in LDCs renders products imported therefrom subject to dumping regulations. See OECD, *Trade, Employment and Labour Standards: A Study of Core Workers' Rights and International Trade*, (1996), 170–1, which does not endorse this view.

[21] No doubt, certain well-entrenched labour rights, such as collective bargaining, freedom of association and prohibition of forced labour, are not dependent on a country's level of development, nor do they require any additional resources. See J. Bhagwati, 'Afterword: The Question of Linkage', *AJIL* 96 (2002), 126.

immediate impact on vulnerable populations. In Bangladesh, for example, the mere consideration by the US Congress of banning products manufactured by child labour led to the dismissal of female children in the textiles industry, many of whom were forced into prostitution by destitute parents.[22] Of course, we are not advocating the perpetuation of Dickensian child labour in the developing world. Rather, it is imperative that the issue be confronted holistically by the entirety of the international community, not by the type of shock treatment that is inherent in unilateral measures that produce such unintended consequences.

GSPs themselves appear to be discriminatory and arbitrary on many occasions, despite their intended goal of facilitating preferential LDC access into the international trading arena. It is reported, for example, that US domestic industries regularly lobby in favour of protectionist measures against LDC imports,[23] further aided by the fact that the executive's assessment of such measures is not subject to independent review.[24] Another protectionist measure is that employed by the USA whereby it denies GSP status to those LDC products that occupy a significant place in market percentage terms. Moreover, GSP status is denied in respect of those LDC products that are crucial in terms of their export capacity, such as agricultural goods, textiles and clothing, thus rendering these preferences more or less redundant.[25]

It is thus evident that LDCs have been exposed to a liberalised global trading system with little, or no, protection for the needs of their individual development, a system which allows rich nations to manipulate the few comparative advantages of LDCs while at the same time forcing them to reduce tariffs and non-tariff barriers to foreign imports. Although there is no doubt that international trade can benefit all countries, including LDCs, by providing them with the requisite resources for raising the living standards of their people and for meeting their human rights obligations, the impact of trade liberalisation on poverty is necessarily very country specific.[26] What works for one country, especially a developed one, need not benefit another, particularly given the heavy debt burden of LDCs, their exposure to international financial markets and currency fluctuations, their dependency on

---

[22] Bhagwati, *ibid.*, p. 132.

[23] P. Alston, 'Labour Rights Provisions in US Trade Law: Aggressive Unilateralism'? in L. A. Compa and S. F. Diamond, *Human Rights, Labour Rights and International Trade* (Philadelphia: University of Pennsylvania Press, 1996), 71, 84.

[24] *International Labour Rights Education and Research Fund* v. *Bush* 752 F Supp 495, 497 (DC, 1990).

[25] A. E. Cassimatis, *Human Rights Related Trade Measures under International Law* (Leiden, Boston: Martinus Nijhoff, 2007), 411.

[26] C. Lumina, 'Free Trade or Just Trade? The World Trade Organisation, Human Rights and Development (Part 1)', *Law, Democracy and Development* 12 (2008), 20, 25.

agriculture and thus lack of diversification, poor education, health and many other problems.

The principal impediment to poverty alleviation and development in the current scheme of international trade liberalisation is its focus on production volume rather than human development. Its adherents wrongly presuppose that the former guarantees the latter. The greatest empirical proof that this is a fallacy is the fact that even those few countries that have seen a rapid growth to their trade output (e.g. India), with the exception of China,[27] have made little progress in combating poverty overall. Other poor nations, especially those in Africa that relied almost exclusively on agriculture, as we shall see in the next section, have even found themselves worse off in terms of securing food for their people because their economies were not suited to trade liberalisation. In the absence of a true human rights-based approach to international trade none of the aforementioned inherent pitfalls of liberalisation can be mitigated. Neo-liberalism is clearly inconsistent with the right to development and the existing tentative human rights linkages to trade are not only inadequate but serve to mask the process of fragmentation between these two spheres, a development which is contrary to the human rights obligations of WTO member states.

17.3.1   Liberalisation of agriculture and its impact on food security

The effects of liberalised trade in agricultural products must be assessed against global food security and individual well-being and not on whether global output has in fact increased. In short, its measure of success should reflect tangible benefits to an ever increasing number of individual livelihoods. If this is not found to be the case then the current system must be deemed a failure. In India 60 per cent of the population lives off agriculture, whereas in Nepal the same activity attracts a staggering 93 per cent of the population. This should be contrasted with 2.7 per cent in the USA and 1.7 per cent in the UK.[28] Moreover, the vast majority of farmers in LDCs operate small-scale farms, whether family owned or leased, while at the same time dependent family members have usually no other employment and are expected to assist the principal bread winner. In contrast, few farms in the developed world are independent, with large farming conglomerates controlling overall production and prices. The bigger a farming company becomes the less it is reliant on subsidies and the more it becomes able to affect the

---

[27] China has, in fact, reduced its poverty levels (less than US$1 per day) from 85 per cent in 1981 to 16 per cent in 2005, although there are huge discrepancies especially between the urban rich and the rural poor. In any event, it is unknown whether overall poverty levels will resume once the country's growth ultimately reaches its peak.

[28] 3D, *Planting the Right Seed: A Human Rights Perspective on Agriculture Trade and the WTO*, (March 2005), 1.

cost of productivity globally. Even so, farming receives significant subsidies in the USA and the EU.

Small-scale farmers require subsidies not only to stay in business, but also in order to compete with their larger rivals who control the means of production and distribution and can thus outprice them. As a result, otherwise prohibited subsidies under the terms of the WTO's trade liberalisation are crucial for sustaining small-scale farming in LDCs, which remains by far the principal economic activity of the poor. Small-scale farming subsidies are not, however, only important because they provide employment, but also because the agricultural output of small-scale farming in the developing world is consumed locally, which in turn contributes to food security. If small-scale farmers could no longer afford the means to sow seeds and harvest their fields they would be forced to abandon farming altogether, thus leading to severe food shortages, which in turn would force the poor to buy their staple food from non-local markets, the prices of which are prohibitive. A similar outcome is guaranteed in situations where an LDC is eager to export its agricultural produce by reallocating land and resources from domestic food production without first securing adequate food supplies for its people.[29]

NGOs correctly maintain that agricultural trade liberalisation is injurious in respect of job and food security of poor people in LDCs. Apart from the reasons already analysed, they add that there is no guarantee that LDC exports will be accepted in developed nations because of food safety and packaging requirements, which LDC farmers cannot possibly meet. Moreover, because LDCs must admit high levels of imports given that they are not allowed to set quota restrictions, MNCs have been able to sell their surpluses to LDCs at prices below the cost of production (dumping) at no loss, having maintained artificially high prices in global markets in previous years.[30] Finally, it is argued that real profit from agricultural produce is made by a handful of MNCs which control global production and which are in receipt of generous

---

[29] The risks arising from export-oriented agriculture policies in LDCs were highlighted by the Special Rapporteur on the right to food in his report on Guatemala. He noted that this policy deepens extreme inequality in ownership of resources and must be replaced with a strategy that directly improves food security through implementation of agrarian reform and small-scale peasant agriculture. Report on Mission to Guatemala, UN Doc. E/CN.4/2006/ 44/Add.1 (18 January 2006), para. 58; equally in respect of Bolivia, UN Doc. A/HRC/7/5/Add.2 (30 January 2008), para. 59, and CESCR Concluding Observations on Paraguay, UN Doc. E/C.12/PRY/CO/3 (4 January 2008), para. 31.

[30] The Special Rapporteur on the right to food, while encouraging public investment in India's smallholder agriculture, noted that 'greater liberalization of trade in basic staple foods should not be pursued as long as subsidies in developed countries keep international prices at artificially low levels, otherwise India will suffer from competition from dumped agricultural products that will undermine its own production, especially of rice and wheat'. Report on Mission to India, UN Doc. E/CN.4/2006/44/Add.2 (20 March 2006), para. 48.

subsidies by developed nations, a fact which not only renders LDC exports uncompetitive abroad but also domestically.[31]

As a result, in the context of existing agricultural socio-economic relations, any benefits to LDCs from trade liberation – which is clearly asymmetrical and one-sided – are outweighed by their potentially detrimental effects on job and food security. The potential of even the slightest price volatility of staple commodities in LDCs as a result of the uncontrolled and profit-driven financialisation of commodity futures trading is devastating for those who live at, or below, the poverty line.[32] The right to food, as this has been elaborated by the CESCR,[33] must serve as the paramount criterion in any trading agenda concerning agricultural production and LDCs should not be encouraged to export their agricultural produce, or to dismantle small-scale farming, if they have not first achieved sufficient food security for domestic consumption. No one should be denied access to food on the basis of financial or other criteria.

CASE STUDY 17.1
Liberalisation of Zambia's maize production

Until the early 1990s African governments typically controlled the prices, distribution, processing and marketing of most staple agricultural products, which was maize in the case of Zambia. The margin of loss between state-mandated purchase prices and selling prices as a result of the intervening marketing costs was offset by government subsidies and low-interest loans to the state cooperatives that ran the maize industry. The deficit quickly escalated and whereas in 1984 maize subsidies accounted for 5.5 per cent of the country's budget, by 1990 the figure had reached 13 per cent.[1] It should be noted that 67 per cent of Zambia's workforce is employed in small-scale agriculture, with 80 per cent of the country's agricultural produce consisting of maize. As a result of a heavy debt burden the government of Zambia was effectively driven to partly liberalise its maize production in 1990 with full liberalisation taking place in 1995.

[1] A. Mwanaumo, W. A. Masters and P. V. Preckel, 'A Spatial Analysis of Maize Marketing Policy Reforms in Zambia', *American Journal of Agricultural Economics* 79 (1997), 514, at 514–15.

[31] See Lumina, above note 26, 27, who narrates that in 2000 every cow in the EU was subsidised by US$913, whereas each person in sub-Saharan Africa received US$8 in EU aid.
[32] UN Secretary-General Report, Globalisation and its Impact on the Full Enjoyment of all Human Rights, UN Doc. A/64/265 (7 August 2009), 10–11.
[33] See CESCR, General Comment 12: the right to adequate food, UN Doc. E/C.12/1999/5 (1999).

Following liberalisation the price offered to producers declined whereas the market price of maize in Zambia increased. Although maize was the country's staple food, local consumption naturally decreased among the rural, poor, population. Empirical evidence suggests that although production levels have increased, the emergence of a vibrant trading sector has been slow and small-scale farmers continue to be plagued by inadequate finance, storage and transportation facilities. At the same time those unable to cope with the changes were driven out of the sector altogether, which in conjunction with succeeding droughts, caused widespread malnutrition and severe health problems, including a surge in child mortality.[2]

[2] See V. Seshamani, 'The Impact of Market Liberalisation on Food Security in Zambia', *Food Policy* 23 (1998), 539.

INTERVIEW 17.1

The director of Food First

(Eric Holt-Giménez)

Dr Eric Holt-Giménez is Executive Director of the Institute for Food and Development Policy, otherwise known as "Food First." The mission of Food First is to end the injustices that cause hunger.

What would a fair, poverty-alleviation targeted international trade policy look like?

The main challenge to a fair international trade policy for poverty alleviation is to protect and improve the conditions of the 2 billion resource-poor, smallholder and subsistence farmers. The right to protect national markets from international dumping and to maintain local grain reserves (to protect against price volatility), needs to be a structural part of this policy. This probably implies taking agriculture out of the WTO and most of the bilateral free trade agreements. Tight regulation of foreign investment (trade in capital and capital goods) to protect rural communities from recent trends in land grabbing is also important.

What are the principal reasons, or actors, hindering developed states from adopting trade policies that ensure a dignified life for all people of the world?

For over two decades the trade policies of the USA and Europe have been driven by overproduction and cheap grain that is ultimately dumped abroad. The main winners in this strategy have been the international grain companies that bought grain at a deflated price. Now, grain prices are high and subject to extreme price swings. The oligopolies controlling the flow of grain and speculators in Commodity Investment Funds (CIFs) have a financial stake in this volatility. These actors, land speculators and the seed and input monopolies now attempting to break into the markets at the 'base of the pyramid' are the main obstacles to a dignified life for the poorest of the poor. Global, unregulated markets and monopolies are incapable of resolving these problems – on the contrary they have brought them on.

In terms of actual finances and global resources, is it feasible to expect that the entirety of the world's population can enjoy a decent standard of living and eliminate poverty altogether?

The world already produces enough food to feed ten billion people. The problem is that over 40 per cent of the grain produced is converted into fuel or meat. We have the resources to eliminate poverty and hunger, but not the political will to control the markets and monopolies that produce poverty. Most of the billion hungry people in the world are resource-poor subsistence farmers. Sustainable rural livelihoods based on a fair social wage (health education and welfare), access to basic resources (like land, water, health services and education) and support to develop sustainable forms of agriculture will lay the basis for the rural and urban elimination of poverty and hunger.

Please provide a practical illustration of the relevance of human rights in designing a trade agenda.

The right to food is a human right and should be justiciably recognized in trade policy. Any trade policies that impede a person's right to food, such as dumping, land grabbing investments, genetic contamination, or international hoarding and speculation should be heavily sanctioned.

17.4 HOW INTELLECTUAL PROPERTY RIGHTS HINDER ACCESS TO ESSENTIAL MEDICINES FOR THE POOREST

One of the neo-liberal assumptions was that the liberalisation of trade would ultimately reduce costs related to bureaucracy, transactions and production. Moreover, because this process was calculated to distribute income to even greater masses of people as a result of new employment opportunities, it was thought that health care and medicines would become cheaper by reason of user volume alone. However, equitable income distribution from the fruits of trade liberalisation failed to materialise and to make things worse LDCs were further burdened with heavy external debts which they were forced to service at the expense of ESC rights, including universal health care. An additional obstacle in realising the right to health, particularly accessibility to affordable medicines, is the commercial value afforded to pharmaceutical patents over and above their potential to save lives. No doubt, the regime of intellectual property (IP), including patents, serves to incentivise innovators investing time and money on new discoveries by protecting their work against usurpers. Were it not for the benefits of IP protection, pharmaceutical companies investing billions of dollars into drug research would be exposed to parallel production by generic drug manufacturers once the drug went into circulation. As a result, the general application of IP law in the field of pharmaceuticals is to reward innovation by providing a commercial head start to the innovator with a view to cementing his position in the market, recouping his research and manufacturing costs and making a profit. This IP regime, however, is clearly in conflict with the right of access to affordable medicines because pharmaceutical companies are naturally unwilling to slash their prices for the poor and the vulnerable, let alone allow generic manufacturers to produce and sell at low cost.[34] The CESCR has called on states to prevent unreasonably high medicine costs resulting from protecting intellectual property, emphasising that products should be denied patentability where 'commercialisation would jeopardise the full realisation' of other rights, particularly the right to health and adequate standard of living.[35]

Poor countries facing health epidemics are unable to pay the high prices demanded by pharmaceutical companies and thus desire the freedom to produce these drugs themselves.[36] The South African case study is instructive. In response to the country's HIV/AIDS epidemic a law[37] was adopted that allowed the health minister to curtail the patent rights of pharmaceutical MNCs through parallel imports and compulsory licences. The former refers to patented drugs already in circulation elsewhere and which are imported (at lower prices) without the patent-holder's consent, whereas compulsory licences allow generic manufacturers to cheaply produce a drug without the patent-holder's approval and in violation of his IP rights. Although both of

---

[34] In a recent test case the Egyptian Court of Administrative Justice dismissed a decree establishing a new pricing system for brand names and generic drugs, on the basis that it would render them far too expensive for the average Egyptian and would thus violate the right to obtain affordable medicines. *Egyptian Drug Pricing* case no. 2457/64 (27 April 2010).

[35] CESCR, General Comment 17: The right to moral and material interests from scientific, literary or artistic production, UN Doc. E/C.12/GC/17 (12 January 2006), para. 35.

[36] Empirical studies have demonstrated that once drugs are patented their price increases by at least 100 per cent. See A. Subramanian, 'The AIDS Crisis, Differential Pricing of Drugs and the TRIPS Agreement: Two Proposals', *Journal of World Intellectual Property* (*JWIP*) 4 (2001), 323.

[37] 2002 Medicines and Related Substances Act Control Amendment Act.

these exceptions to the rights of patent-holders[38] clearly offend his or her rights they are exceptionally permitted under article 8(1) of the WTO Agreement on Trade-Related Intellectual Property Rights (TRIPS Agreement)[39] in order to 'protect public health and nutrition', among other things.[40] As a result, cheap anti-retroviral drugs were produced or imported and distributed free of charge to those who could not afford them. A group of thirty-nine pharmaceutical MNCs commenced legal proceedings for the violation of their IP rights. The government responded that it was under a constitutional duty to protect the health of its citizens.[41] It should be stated that although the case was settled through the adoption of a joint understanding between the USA and South Africa, for a while the US government partially withheld its GSP treatment of South Africa.

Despite strong opposition from developed nations and part of the industry itself, it seems quite settled, as a result of the Doha Declaration and the TRIPS Agreement, that poor nations may validly substitute patented drugs with cheap generics in order to tackle acute health crises.[42] This view was further cemented in December 2005 by the General Council of the WTO.[43] Even so, some commentators point to attempts by certain countries to frustrate the Doha Declaration in practice, particularly through the proliferation of free trade agreements. These inhibit the use of TRIPS flexibilities by developing nations and impose on them high standards of IP protection, thus effectively precluding the manufacture or import of cheap generic drugs.[44] Recently, in response to Swiss trade agreements with LDCs that effectively negated

---

[38] Articles 30–2 of the TRIPS Agreement. These are technically known as TRIPS flexibilities.

[39] TRIPS Agreement, 1869 UNTS 299.

[40] These so-called flexibilities against the otherwise rights of the patent-holder were iterated in para. 5 of the 2001 Doha Ministerial Declaration on the TRIPS Agreement and Public Health, WTO Doc. WT/MIN(01)/DEC/2 (20 November 2001). Para. 4 of this Declaration very significantly emphasised that the TRIPS Agreement should not prevent countries from 'taking measures to protect public health and that the Agreement can and should be interpreted and implemented in a manner supportive of WTO members' right to protect public health and, in particular, to promote access to medicines for all'.

[41] *Pharmaceutical Manufacturers' Association of South Africa et al.* v. *President of the Republic of South Africa*, Case no. 4183/98 (RSA High Court, Transvaal provincial division).

[42] See *WTO Agreements and Public Health: A Joint Study by the WHO and WTO Secretariat*, (2002), 38–47, 97–111.

[43] Amendment of the TRIPS Agreement, Decision of 6 December 2005, Document WT/L/641 (8 December 2005).

[44] C. Lumina, 'Free Trade or Just Trade? The World Trade Organisation, Human Rights and Development (Part 2)', *Law Democracy and Development* 14 (2010), 1, at 15. See also the CESCR's Concluding observations on Costa Rica, which noted with concern the impact from the coming into force of the Central American Free Trade Agreement on traditional agriculture, labour rights, access to generic medicines and biodiversity, among others. UN Doc. E/C.12/CRI/CO/4 (4 January 2008), para. 27.

the right to generic drugs guaranteed by the Doha Declaration, the CESCR admonished Switzerland to

take into account its partner countries' obligations when negotiating and concluding trade and investment agreements [and] undertake an impact assessment to determine the possible consequences of its foreign trade policies and agreements on the enjoyment by the population of the state party's partner countries of their economic, social and cultural rights'.[45]

17.5 THE IMPACT OF GLOBALISATION ON TRANSNATIONAL LABOUR RELATIONS: THE OUTSOURCING OF LABOUR

Although improved communications, transport and technologies have contributed to the transnational movement of workers,[46] the principal impact of globalisation on labour relations has been in the outsourcing of labour from developed to developing nations. If this process leads to the creation of sustainable employment, technology transfer and raises the overall standard of living in the host nation it is certainly welcome. Yet, because the outsourcing of labour unleashes competition between rival nations eager to attract foreign investment it has the potential to undermine core labour standards in a number of ways.[47] Chief among these is the argument that host countries may decrease their labour standards either because these entail a high cost for the investor or because other nations have lowered theirs in an attempt to become more attractive. This is known as the 'race to the bottom'. Although most empirical studies suggest an absence of a systematic relationship between a competitive investment advantage and diminished labour

---

[45] CESCR, Concluding observations on Switzerland, UN Doc. E/C.12/CHE/CO/2–3 (26 November 2010), para. 24; in *Azanca Alhelí Meza García*, Case no. 2945–2003-AA/ TC (20 April 2004) the Constitutional Tribunal of Peru held that the state was under an obligation to provide drugs to an HIV sufferer who could not afford them on the ground that the realisation of social rights of this nature should be a priority in the country's budget.

[46] This is certainly a pertinent aspect of globalisation, having generated phenomena such as the brain drain, the trafficking of persons for sex or illicit labour, the hiring of cheap labour to work as domestic servants or maritime crews in industrialised states. According to a recent UN study, an estimated 214 million international migrants are dispersed around the world. See UN Economic and Social Affairs, Trends in International Migrant Stock: The 2008 Revision, UN Doc. POP/DB/MIG/Stock/Rev 2008 (July 2009), 1. A facet of migration will be explored in the following section.

[47] The core labour standards, as articulated by the ILO, include freedom of association, the right to collective bargaining, non-discrimination and prohibition of forced and child labour. See B. Chigara, 'Latecomers to the ILO and the Authorship and Ownership of the International Labour Code', *HRQ* 29 (2007), 6.

standards,[48] a crucial element in the investment priorities of multinationals in low-skilled, labour-intensive industries, such as garment and semi-conductor assembly lines, is in fact production cost. This encompasses labour fees and costs associated with the implementation of labour laws, including long and inflexible working hours, sanitation and dining, health and safety requirements and others. Often there is little effect on overall state revenues from the implementation of such policies, given that in the course of the race to the bottom governments are inclined to levy exceptionally low taxes, permit profit repatriation and are given no assurances that the investor will remain in the long term.

There are certain seeming paradoxes about this globalised system of labour relations. First, developed nations are not particularly upset to see low-skilled, low paid, manufacturing jobs outsourced to poor nations. This is because they are able to charge more in corporate and sales taxes from the finished product and also because outsourcing investments of this nature constitutes only a minuscule part of global FDI volume; in fact, the bulk of global FDI is received by the top ten wealthiest nations. As a result, there is constant employment generation therein which is increasingly concentrated in the services and high-technology sectors. The second paradox concerns the stance of developed nations by which they impose trade sanctions and refuse to offer GSP treatment to products originating from LDCs that lack labour standards equal to theirs. This is otherwise surprising given that more than 65,000 MNCs are currently operating in transnational manufacturing operations and the race to the bottom is a direct result of their operations. In practice, the imposition of unilateral trade measures under the guise of poor labour standards is arbitrary.

The role of MNCs in contributing to, or alleviating, human rights viola-tions is discussed elsewhere in this book. Here, it suffices to emphasise their capacity to indirectly dictate labour policies and wellbeing in the countries where they operate. Although they would otherwise be obliged to respect the core labour standards in their home states, host nations have either failed to implement international labour treaties into their domestic systems, or are inclined to turn a blind eye in order to attract and retain investors. MNCs have traditionally maintained that they would be interfering in the domestic affairs of host nations if they refused to comply with poor labour standards

---

[48] D. Rodrik, 'Labour Standards in International Trade: Do They Matter and What do we Know about Them?' in R. Lawrence, D. Rodrik and J. Whalley, *Emerging Agenda for Global Trade: High Stakes for Developing Countries* (Washington, DC: Overseas Development Council, 1996), p. 35; OECD, *International Trade and Core Labour Standards*, (2000), which bases its empirical observations on the fact that sharp FDI increases have been observed in the service sectors, thus affecting employees with better-than-average working conditions.

and as such are unable to defy the wishes of the local executive. Although there is some truth to this assertion, in most cases MNCs consciously benefit from weak local legislation and poor industrial relations. Non-compliance in such cases is nothing more than a convenient excuse. Two parallel developments have come to somewhat disrupt this state of affairs. The first is the acknowledgement within the UN system and other intergovernmental organisations of the duties owed by MNCs in the promotion of human rights through their operations.[49] An integral, but by no means exclusive, element of this dimension is corporate social responsibility.[50] The other development is the globalisation of suits involving the violation of core labour rights in forums that share a link with the violating MNC. Although this is still a work in progress, at the very least the courts of the home states of MNCs have not always considered themselves *forum non conveniens*,[51] thus paving the way for future legal actions. As a result, actions have successfully been introduced in the USA and the UK, among other countries, for the poor health and safety conditions maintained by subsidiaries abroad, or in respect of subsidiary plants that violated local labour standards.[52]

17.6   THE CHALLENGE OF MASS IRREGULAR MIGRATION

The forces of globalisation, both subaltern and neo-liberal, have generated waves of so-called economic migration from the Third World to industrialised nations. One would have thought that the outsourcing of cheap labour to LDCs would stem the flow of such migration, which is both dangerous and wholly uncertain for those willing to venture it. This is hardly the case. For one thing, as already explained, investors are not averse to wholesale relocation of their manufacturing activities if they can secure cheaper labour costs and so there is little job certainty in LDCs for low-cost workers. Secondly, cheap production costs necessarily translate into higher profits, the bulk of which is then used to pay executive salaries and shareholder dividends in the home state. This accumulation of wealth in developed nations which is spread to all levels of the secondary retail economy by reason of consumerism

---

[49] See Report of the S-G Special Representative on the Issue of Human Rights and Transnational Corporations and Other Business Enterprises, UN Doc. A/HRC/17/31 (21 March 2011), which consists of a set of Guiding Principles and a commentary thereto.

[50] See I. Bantekas, 'Corporate Social Responsibility in International Law', *B.U. Int'l L. J.* 22 (2004), 309.

[51] This is a jurisdictional principle in private law on the basis of which the courts of the forum may decline a tort suit with an international element if they determine that it is more suitable for adjudication before the courts of another nation.

[52] See *Connelly* v. *R.T.Z. Corp. Plc*, 3 WLR 373 (1997); *Lubbe* v. *Cape Plc*, 1 WLR 1545, 1604 (2000).

generally culminates in its distribution to all persons in the labour chain. Thus, executives and shareholders will spend their money on property, cars, food, entertainment, travel, etc., all of which employ paid workers, who in turn will use their own purchasing power to buy similar goods and services. None the less, certain labour activities in the developed world incur unsustainable labour costs in relation to the profit margin desired by the producer/investor.

This is true, at least, in the fields of agriculture, domestic servants, low-skilled construction, shipping and others. The wages offered by most employers in these sectors are unattractive for the local population because they are close to, or below, the local living standards and it is no wonder that employers expect to fill vacancies through migrant workers.[53] Low-cost migration is no doubt attracted by such opportunities and the broader prospect of a better livelihood. The paradox is that developed countries formally deny the existence of demand for cheap labour, yet they tacitly acknowledge that without it most seasonal agricultural activities would be in trouble and most mothers would be forced to abandon work because of the insurmountable cost of private child care facilities. The absurdity of this paradox is reflected in the ratification status of the 1990 Migrant Workers Convention,[54] which at the time of writing had not been ratified by any developed nation, even though its aim is merely to afford fundamental human rights to documented and undocumented (or irregular) migrant workers and their families. The UN Special Rapporteur on the Human Rights of Migrants has emphasised that the hostility towards irregular migration is expressed through the externalisation of migration control policies and criminalisation of labour migration.[55] A typical example of the latter is Streamline Operation which imposes federal prosecution and imprisonment against all unlawful border crossers along the USA–Mexico boundary, irrespective of their criminal record or the purpose of their crossing. As a result, this policy has placed a significant strain on local prosecutors and law-enforcement agencies and has distracted them from focusing on drug-trafficking, human trafficking and other real crimes.[56]

The mass migration associated with globalisation should not, however, be solely attributed to demand for cheap labour in the developing world, despite

---

[53] See International Federation for Human Rights (IFHR), *Migrant Workers in Saudi Arabia*, (March 2003), which noted that in 2003 migrant workers made up 50 per cent of the total Saudi workforce.

[54] ICRMW, 2220 UNTS 3.

[55] UN Special Rapporteur Report, UN Doc. A/HRC/7/12 (25 February 2008), paras. 13–59.

[56] In fact, because of the bulk of prosecutions, hearings are conducted en masse with as many as eighty accused pleading guilty simultaneously. This clear deprivation of due process rights has been stricken down by federal courts. See *USA* v. *Roblero-Solis* 588 F 3d 692 (9th Cir. 2009).

its significance. Irregular migration would be unfeasible without the availability of the means for its realisation. Technological advances in transport and telecommunications certainly facilitate the conditions for mass migration. Even so, the larger part of irregular migration is achieved through clandestine means, particularly unlawful border crossings, most typically organised by human smuggling that is unconcerned with the safety and well-being of its 'clients'. Human smuggling has turned into a lucrative underground industry and has given rise to several offshoots, the most odious of which is trafficking of women and children for sexual exploitation. It is no wonder that recent treaties focusing on organised crime have come to see the plight of trafficked persons in the light of victimhood, rather than through the lens of criminalisation.[57]

By all accounts, cheap labour is beneficial for the economies of developed nations as certain sectors would not otherwise be able to function. At the same time it is probably a myth that migrants 'steal' local jobs, given that the wages offered cannot attract the local workforce. Moreover, migrants generally repatriate their meagre earnings and thus contribute to LDC economies by providing much needed short-term liquidity. Although it seems that the liberalisation of migration is beneficial to both developed and non-developed nations – similar to the rationale offered for trade liberalisation – its unregulated nature is problematic in several respects.[58] For one thing, migrants from LDCs, whether documented or not, are viewed as second-class citizens, possess few rights and are forced to remain underground. Rapes, withholding of salaries and slave-like conditions are prevalent against female domestic servants.[59] Secondly, the underground status of migrants feeds organised crime and artificially removes every trace of human rights protection otherwise owed to migrants; in addition, they are excluded from the host countries' labour and social laws. Thirdly, irregular migration generates social disparities, which is often used by anti-immigrant propaganda to fuel unrest, xenophobia, hate crimes and other evils.[60]

---

[57] 2000 Protocol against the Smuggling of Migrants by Land, Sea and Air, Supplementing the UN Convention against Transnational Organised Crime, (2001) 40 ILM 335, articles 9(1)(a) and 16; 2000 Protocol to Prevent, Suppress and Punish Trafficking in Persons, Especially Women and Children, Supplementing the UN Convention against Transnational Organised Crime (2001) 40 ILM 335, articles 2, 3, 7(1) and 6.

[58] This view is proffered by Juss, who challenges the rationale for the current global restrictions on the freedom of movement. S. S. Juss, *International Migration and Global Justice* (Aldershot: Ashgate, 2007).

[59] Human Rights Watch, *Help Wanted: Abuses Against Female Migrant Domestic Workers in Indonesia and Malaysia*, (July 2004), available at www.hrw.org/en/node/11993/section/1.

[60] See J. Burke, 'Saudi Arabian Torment of Migrant Workers at Mercy of Abusive Madams', *The Guardian* (25 June 2011), who discusses the beheading of an Indonesian servant without any due process rights for the alleged killing of an abusive master who, among other things, would not allow her to terminate her employment and return home.

Domestic and international policies on the migration phenomenon are scattered, non-holistic and generally lack a human rights perspective. By way of illustration, the USA and Europe seek principally to tackle the flow of irregular migration from reaching their borders through police enforcement operations.[61] Equally, a good part of overseas development assistance aims to de-incentivise migration by offering aid that will lead to employment opportunities. A holistic approach would first determine the root causes of mass migration, as opposed to refugee flows. If we assume that poverty is the strongest determinant, then its root causes lie in the unequal distribution of wealth and resources, corruption, poor governance, absence of the rule of law and certainly the sort of unregulated foreign investment that is not conducive to human well-being. As long as these are left untreated people will always seek a better life elsewhere, even if their chances of survival are slim.[62]

17.7 THE *McLIBEL* CASE: SALES GLOBALISATION AND ITS IMPACT ON RIGHTS

For the practical application of this closing chapter we could have chosen a case study closely associated with one of the themes explored in the preceding sections. None the less, we opted for something that on the surface only tangentially deals with the issues arising in the globalisation debate and which could also feature in the chapter dealing with non-state actors. In that chapter it was demonstrated that MNCs possess the privilege to choose where they will manufacture their products, with nations, especially poor ones, offering a plethora of incentives in order to secure much needed capital investment. Whereas human rights-related globalisation is typically associated with the manufacturing and outsourcing perspective of MNCs (i.e. low wages, poor labour conditions, corruption, environmental degradation, etc.), little attention has been paid to their sales capacity. This is because of the much-hailed assumption that sales are determined by market forces and consumer choice. It is therefore considered axiomatic that no one in their right mind would purchase an inferior product at a high price, especially when better and cheaper products are on offer. This assumption is logical but not always practical, because it fails to appreciate the immense power of

---

[61] Not infrequently, in entry areas where illegal migration is rife, local law-enforcement officers have been known to abuse and even torture the immigrants. See *Zontul* v. *Greece*, App. no. 12297/07, ECtHR judgment (17 January 2012).

[62] In *Hirsi Jamaa and others* v. *Italy*, App. no. 27765/09, ECtHR judgment (23 February 2012), an Italian military vessel rescued a vessel sailing towards Italian waters containing African immigrants and proceeded to hand them over to Libya. The ECtHR held that Italy was aware of the treatment afforded by the Libyan authorities at the time and hence that its *refoulement* of the immigrants contravened fundamental rights.

advertising, the impact of media, the vastness of information and the pace of urban life which leave little, if any, time for informed consent on consumer choices.[63] In very simple terms, I would not buy a sweater in the knowledge that the seller or manufacturer had forced a five-year-old to knit it without pay or food. However, I would have few hesitations about eating a hamburger during a hungry lunch break if the seller's advertising campaign sheltered and cushioned me from information about cruelty to animals, low staff wages, the unhealthy nature of the food, the deliberate targeting of children as future consumers and the company's negative environmental impact.

The *McLibel* case is instructive of the way in which MNCs have assumed the mantle of making consumer choices for the public and globalised their products under the guise of 'culture'. In 1986 a little-known NGO, London Greenpeace, not to be confused with Greenpeace International, distributed a pamphlet entitled *What's Wrong with McDonalds: Everything They Don't Want you to Know*. Although this was a relatively small campaign, well before the Internet era, with the aim of educating the public on the methods of the company's food production, the products' health hazards and the company's poor animal welfare, environmental and labour record, it caused McDonalds some concern. The NGO was infiltrated for a period of about eighteen months by persons covertly working for the corporate giant and pretending to support the NGO's original cause. In fact, McDonalds had employed two separate teams of informants, none of which was aware of the others' existence! Once the informants had gathered ample material, some of which was outright stolen from the NGO's premises, the McDonalds legal team put together a case against five members of London Greenpeace, charging them with libel. McDonalds naturally assumed that the defendants would be an easy target, since prior to this litigation it had threatened major newspapers, broadcasting corporations and other smaller media outlets (including a student newspaper) with libel suits, all of which resulted in settlements and public apologies. In fact, under threat of action three of the original NGO defendants offered an apology but Helen Morris and David Steele refused to cave in.

During the first hearing before the High Court the trial was clearly unfair.[64] The defendants were denied legal aid even though they were relatively poor whereas McDonalds employed a large team of top lawyers.

---

[63] The issue of consumer rights has generally been ignored by human rights scholarship because of the classic assumption that the relations between consumer and seller are regulated predominantly by contract, whereas relations with the manufacturer are based on the law of tort. In this paradigm it is thought that the state plays no visible part and both seller and manufacturer owe no other obligations other than those already mentioned. This assumption is clearly problematic as the *McLibel* case illustrates. See I. Bantekas, 'Consumer Rights as Human Rights', *Cyprus Human Rights Law Review* 1 (2012), 1.

[64] It was not difficult for the ECtHR to reach the same conclusion. See *Steele and Morris* v. *UK* [2005] 41 EHRR 22. Unfortunately, the burden of proof in defamation and libel laws have remained largely the same.

Moreover, under English law the burden of proof in libel cases at the time rested on the defendants, not on the plaintiffs. If that was not enough, at trial the judge somehow managed to determine that the issues in the case were too complex for lay jury members to comprehend (David Steele was a postman and Helen Morris a gardener it should be noted) and so instructed that the case be heard by a single judge rather than a jury. Although the pair received some free legal advice from a human rights barrister, they defended themselves through the course of examinations and cross-examinations that lasted well over a year and on a daily basis. It is illustrative that at some point Morris was so worn out that her doctor prescribed some respite, which the court refused to provide! A year into proceedings McDonalds approached the pair for a settlement, having realised that Morris and Steele had nothing to lose personally and that the case had attracted serious negative media attention for the corporation. The trial and its outcome[65] ultimately turned out to be less important for the campaigners as the publicity which attracted the proceedings was a public relations disaster for the corporation and provided the general public with a new awareness about the health risks associated with fast food. It also brought to light the atrocious means of production and advertisement. Ultimately, the process dragged on for an extraordinary nine years and six months, with the trial alone lasting two and a half years.

One of the important issues that emerged from the campaign through the course of the proceedings was that mega-corporations such as McDonalds were using the power of advertising to 'exploit' children's vulnerabilities. Advertising tried to portray the company's food as being nutritious, which is completely antithetical to what it really is. In equal measure, the company sought to groom younger generations into an addictive fast food lifestyle knowing full well its hazardous health effects. This lifestyle is the product of a sales globalisation which MNCs are able to endorse worldwide with little hindrance, especially if no critical voices are raised. Defamation laws such as those of the UK are assisting them in their cause. The *McLibel* case demonstrates that negative rights-related sales globalisation may be overcome by active campaigning even against one of the biggest corporate giants. As Morris and Steele aptly put it: 'Who said ordinary people can't change the world?'[66]

---

[65] *McDonalds Corp v. Steel and Morris* [1997] EWHC QB 366. Incidentally, although the judge found that some allegations were true it held that others had not been proven and thus found the defendants liable. On appeal, the Court of Appeals sustained the defendants' basic argument, among others, that a McDonalds diet increases the risk for heart disease as well as cancer, but ruled against them on other grounds.

[66] The two set up a new NGO which also features an excellent documentary about the case, from which much information in this section was adapted. See www.mcspotlight.org/case/.

QUESTIONS

1 Is it at all possible to reconcile neo-liberal economic theories with the right to development?

2 The projected benefits to poverty alleviation promised by trade liberalisation is to a large degree predicated on the comparative advantages of even the poorest nations. What obstacles have developed nations posed to the comparative advantages of their developing counterparts?

3 It is not in the interests of developing nations to liberalise their agricultural sectors. Explain what the vulnerable and poor therein can expect to lose from this process and discuss the benefits that may accrue from public investment in small-scale farming.

4 Should trade liberalisation encompass the staple foods produced and consumed in developing countries? Explain.

5 The patent flexibilities of TRIPS have been extended by the Doha Declaration until 2016. What strategies would you recommend so that pharmaceutical companies can maintain their incentive for innovation through profit, while at the same time offering cheap drugs to those who need them most but cannot afford them?

6 Surely the proliferation of low-skilled jobs in poor nations is welcome because they spur growth, reduce unemployment and cater for large segments of the population, which is in any event un-skilled. Low salaries are better than no salaries and poor labour conditions are a small price to pay. Do you agree? Discuss.

FURTHER READING

Bantekas, I., Wealth and Growth-based Policies Augment Global Poverty and Erode Human Rights: a Return to Human-centred Thinking', *Int'l Hum. Rts. L. Rev.* 1 (2012), 30.

Benedek, W., De Feyter, K. and Marrella, F. (eds.), *Economic Globalisation and Human Rights* (Cambridge University Press, 2007).

Cottier, T., Pauwelyn, J. and Burgi, E., *Human Rights and International Trade* (Oxford: Oxford University Press, 2004).

Cullet, P., 'Human Rights and Intellectual Property Protection in the TRIPS Era', *HRQ* 29 (2007), 403.

Fenwick, C. and Novitz, T. (eds.), *Human Rights at Work: Perspectives on Law and Regulation* (Oxford: Hart, 2010).

Fox, E. M., 'Globalisation and Human Rights: Looking out for the Welfare of the Worst', *N.Y.U.J. Int'l L. & Pol.* 35 (2003), 201.

Harvey, D., *Neoliberalism: A Brief History* (Oxford University Press, 2005).

ILO, *Gender and Migration in Arab States: The Case of Domestic Workers* (June 2004), available at: www.ilo.org/public/english/region/arpro/beirut/downloads/publ/publ_26_eng.pdf.

Mechlem, K., 'Harmonizing Trade in Agriculture and Human Rights: Options for the Integration of the Right to Food into the Agreement on Agriculture', *MPYBUNL* 10 (2006), 127.

Morjin, J., *Reframing Human Rights and Trade: Potential and Limits of a Human Rights Perspective of WTO Law on Cultural and Educational Goods and Services* (Oxford: Hart, 2010).

Sibanda, O., 'A Human Rights Approach to World Trade Organisation Trade Policy: Another Medium for the Promotion of Human Rights in Africa', *Afr. Hum. Rts. L. J.* 5 (2005), 387.

INDEX